DICTIONARY OF COMPUTING
& INFORMATION TECHNOLOGY

English–French
French–English

DICTIONARY OF
COMPUTING
& INFORMATION
TECHNOLOGY

English–French
French–English

S.M.H. Collin

and

Françoise Laurendeau
Bernard Mouget
P.H. Collin
Annie Foroni

PETER COLLIN PUBLISHING

First published in 1991
by Peter Collin Publishing Ltd
8 The Causeway, Teddington, Middlesex, TW11 0HE

© S.M.H. Collin & F. Collin 1991

British Library Cataloguing-in-Publication Data

Collin, S.M.H.
Dictionary of computing:
  English-French/French-English.
  I. Title II. Laurendeau, Françoise
  III. Mouget, Bernard
  004.03

ISBN 0-948549-24-6

Text computer set by Systemset, Welwyn Garden City
Printed by MAME Imprimeurs, Tours, France

PREFACE

The aim of this dictionary is to give the user a basic vocabulary of terms relating to computers and information technology in French and English with translations into the other language.

The vocabulary covers the main areas of computer technology, including hardware, software, programming, networks, peripherals, together with many applications where computers are used; information technology in general, telecommunications, TV and radio, desk-top publishing, graphics and design. These are situations where the user may frequently require translations from one language into the other.

The dictionary covers not only international usage, but in some cases identifies words and expressions where American and British usages differ.

The dictionary gives many examples of how the words and expressions are used in context, and how they can be translated; these examples are supplemented by short quotations in both languages from magazines from both language areas to show the worldwide applications of the two languages.

PRÉFACE

Ce dictionnaire a pour but de vous offrir le vocabulaire essentiel de la langue de l'informatique en français et en anglais.

Outre les mots du langage courant employés dans le quotidien de l'informatique et de la micro-informatique, on trouvera aussi bien ce qui concerne les ordinateurs (matériels, logiciels, programmation, périphériques et réseaux), que les nombreuses et toutes dernières applications de l'informatique dans le traitement des données (télécommunications, infographie, PAO etc.)

Innovation importante : un grand nombre d'exemples s'efforce d'apporter une réponse aux problèmes de traduction posés par cette langue spécialisée qui est en plein développement. À l'appui de ces phrases, de multiples citations de la presse spécialisée du monde anglophone et francophone vous aideront à mieux saisir le sens des mots dans leur contexte.

COMMENT UTILISER
CE DICTIONNAIRE

Notre dictionnaire se veut clair et facile à utiliser.

Les **entrées** apparaissent en caractères gras.

Les **mots dérivés** figurent en sous-entrée et sont précédés d'un losange.

Les différentes catégories grammaticales sont introduites par une subdivision numérique en chiffres arabes: **1, 2,** etc.

Les lettres **(a)**, **(b)**, etc. introduisent une division sémantique, suivies éventuellement d'une explication en italiques entre parenthèses.

Les **abréviations** ont été réduites au minimum, en voici la liste:

adj	adjectif	adjective
adj num	adjectif numéral	numeral adjective
adv	adverbe	adverb
f	féminin	feminine
GB	Grande-Bretagne	Great Britain
inf	infinitif	infinitive
inv	invariable	invariable
m	masculin	masculine
n	nom	noun
nf	nom féminin	feminine noun
nm	nom masculin	masculine noun
nm&f	nom masculin ou féminin	masculine or feminine noun
npr	nom propre	proper noun
pl	pluriel	plural
®	nom déposé	registered trademark
vi	verbe intransitif	intransitive verb
vpr	verbe pronominal	reflexive verb
vtr	verbe transitif	transitive verb
US	États-Unis	United States

USING THE DICTIONARY

The dictionary aims to provide a clear layout which will help the user find the required translation as easily as possible. Each entry is formed of a headword in bold type, with clearly numbered divisions showing different parts of speech, or lettered divisions showing differences of meaning. Words which are derived from the main entry word are listed under that word, each time preceded by a ◊.

As far as is possible, abbreviations are not used in the dictionary, apart from the following:

adj	adjectif	adjective
adj num	adjectif numéral	numeral adjective
adv	adverbe	adverb
f	féminin	feminine
GB	Grande-Bretagne	Great Britain
inf	infinitif	infinitive
inv	invariable	invariable
m	masculin	masculine
n	nom	noun
nf	nom féminin	feminine noun
nm	nom masculin	masculine noun
nm&f	nom masculin ou féminin	masculine or feminine noun
npr	nom propre	proper noun
pl	pluriel	plural
®	nom déposé	registered trademark
vi	verbe intransitif	intransitive verb
vpr	verbe pronominal	reflexive verb
vtr	verbe transitif	transitive verb
US	États-Unis	United States

ENGLISH-FRENCH DICTIONARY
DICTIONNAIRE ANGLAIS-FRANÇAIS

Aa

A = AMPERE

A représentation hexadécimale du nombre 10 *or* A

A-bus *noun* bus *m* principal *or* bus A

A programming language (APL) *noun* langage *m* (de programmation) APL

A1, A2, A3, A4, A5 *noun* papier format A1, A2, A3, A4, A5; **you must photocopy the spreadsheet on A3 paper** = vous devez photocopier le tableau sur une feuille de format A3; **a standard 300 d.p.i. black and white A4 monitor** = écran monochrome standard de format A4, avec une définition de 300 points par pouce

A to D *or* **A/D** = ANALOG TO DIGITAL (conversion) analogique-numérique; **A to D converter** = convertisseur *m* analogique-numérique; **the speech signal was first passed through an A to D converter before being analysed** = le signal vocal est d'abord passé par le convertisseur analogique-numérique avant d'être analysé

abbreviation *noun* abréviation *f;* **within the text, the abbreviation 'proc' is used instead of processor** = dans le texte, on a remplacé le terme processeur par l'abréviation 'proc'; **abbreviated addressing** *or* **abb. add.** = adressage *m* abrégé *or* simplifié

abend *noun* = ABNORMAL END fin *f or* interruption *f* anormale (de traitement); **an interrupt from a faulty printer caused an abend** = une commande *or* un signal d'interruption venant d'une imprimante défectueuse a provoqué une fin anormale de traitement; **abend recovery program** = programme *m* de récupération de fichier après une interruption anormale; **if a fault occurs, data loss will be minimized due to the improved abend recovery program** = en cas de panne, la perte de données sera minimale grâce au nouveau programme de récupération des fichiers après interruption anormale

aberration *noun* **(a)** *(of light beam or image, etc.)* aberration *f* **(b)** *(of TV picture - caused by corrupt signal or incorrect adjustment)* distorsion *f*

abnormal *adjective* anormal, -e; **it's abnormal for two consecutive disk drives to break down** = il n'est pas normal que deux lecteurs de disquettes tombent en panne l'un après l'autre; **abnormal error** = erreur anormale; **abnormal end** *or* **abend** *or* **abnormal termination** = interruption anormale *or* prématurée
◊ **abnormally** *adverb* anormalement *or* singulièrement; **the signal is abnormally weak** = le signal est anormalement faible; **the error rate with this disk is abnormally high** = le taux d'erreur de cette disquette est singulièrement élevé

abort *verb* abandonner prématurément *or* interrompre (un programme) *or* arrêter l'éxécution (d'un programme); **the program was aborted by pressing the red button** = on a interrompu le programme en appuyant sur la touche rouge; **abort the program before it erases any more files** = arrêtez l'éxécution du programme, avant qu'il efface d'autres fichiers

above-the-line costs *plural noun (in making TV films)* frais *m* fixes

absolute address *or* **actual address** *or* **machine address** *noun* adresse *f* absolue; **program execution is slightly faster if you code only with absolute addresses** = l'exécution d'un programme est un peu plus rapide si on utilise uniquement des adresses absolues dans le code; **absolute addressing** = adressage absolu; **absolute assembler** = assembleur absolu; **absolute code** = code (binaire) absolu; **absolute instruction =** instruction absolue; **absolute loader =** chargeur absolu; **absolute maximum rating =** capacité théorique absolue; **absolute program =** programme absolu *or* en langage machine; **absolute value =** valeur absolue (d'un nombre algébrique); **the absolute value of -62.34 is 62.34 =** la valeur absolue de -62,34 est 62,34; **an absolute value of the input is generated =** il y a génération d'une valeur absolue des entrées

absorb *verb* absorber

◊ **absorptance** *noun* absorptance *f or* indice *m* d'absorption

◊ **absorption** *noun* absorption *f; (for colour)* **absorption filter =** filtre *m* d'absorption

abstract 1 *noun* résumé *m or* extrait *m or* analyse *f; in our library, abstracts are gathered together in separate volumes allowing an easy and rapid search for a particular subject =* dans notre bibliothèque, les résumés sont réunis en volumes distincts ce qui assure la facilité et la rapidité des recherches sur un sujet particulier **2** *verb* **(a)** extraire (de) *or* retirer (de) *or* soustraire (de) **(b)** résumer (un article)

◊ **abstracting & indexing (A&I)** *noun* résumé et indexation

AC = ALTERNATING CURRENT

ACC = ACCUMULATOR

acceleration time *noun* **(a)** *(to spin a disk at correct speed)* temps *m* de montée *or* d'accélération; **allow for acceleration time in the access time =** il faut inclure le temps de montée dans le temps d'accès **(b)** *(total time between access instruction and data transfer)* temps de réponse

◊ **accelerator** *noun* **accelerator card =** carte *f* accélératrice

accent *noun* accent *m;* **acute accent =** accent aigu; **circumflex accent =** accent circonflexe; **grave accent =** accent grave

◊ **accented** *adjective* accentué, -ée

accept *verb* **(a)** *(to agree)* accepter (de); **he accepted the quoted price for printing =** il a accepté le devis de l'imprimeur; **he did not accept the programming job he was offered =** il n'a pas accepté *or* il a refusé le poste de programmeur qu'on lui offrait **(b)** *(to take as compatible)* accepter; **the laser printer will accept a card as small as a business card =** l'imprimante (à) laser accepte même un imprimé de la taille d'une carte professionnelle; **the multi-disk reader will accept 3.5 inch disks as well as 5.25 inch formats =** ce lecteur multidisque accepte aussi bien les disquettes de 3,5 pouces que celles de 5,25 pouces; **call accepted signal =** signal *m* d'acceptation d'appel

◊ **acceptable** *adjective* acceptable; **the error rate was very low, and is acceptable =** le taux d'erreur était très bas et donc acceptable; **for the price, the scratched case is acceptable =** à ce prix-là, on peut accepter que la mallette ait une éraflure

◊ **acceptance** *noun* acceptation *f or* réception *f; (of lens or optic fibre)* **acceptance angle =** angle *m* de réception; **a light beam at an angle greater than the acceptance angle of the lens will not be transmitted =** un rayon lumineux d'incidence supérieure à l'angle de réception ne sera pas transmis; *(for quality)* **acceptance sampling =** échantillonnage *m* (de réception *or* de qualité); **acceptance test** *or* **testing =** test *m* d'homologation

access 1 *noun* accès *m;* **to have access to something =** avoir accès à quelque chose; **to have access to a file of data =** avoir accès à un fichier informatique; **he has access to numerous sensitive files =** il a accès à de nombreux fichiers confidentiels; **to bar access to a system =** interdire (à quelqu'un) l'accès à un système; **after he was discovered hacking, he was barred access to the system =** après avoir découvert qu'il faisait du piratage, on lui a interdit l'accès au système; **access arm =** bras *m* de lecture/écriture; **the access arm moves to the parking region during transport =** le bras de lecture est mis en position de parkage pendant le transport; **access charge =** frais *mpl* d'accès au système; **access code =** mot *m* de passe *or* code *m* d'accès (à un système); **access line =** ligne *f* d'accès; **access method =** méthode *f* d'accès; *(on circuit board or in software)* **access point =** point *m* d'accès *or* de contrôle; **direct access storage device (DASD) =** mémoire *f or* support *m* à accès direct; **direct memory access (DMA)** = accès direct à la mémoire; **disk access** = accès au disque; **disk access management** = gestion *f* d'accès aux disques; **instantaneous access** = accès instantané; **the instantaneous access of the RAM disk was welcome** = l'accès instantané au disque RAM a été bien accueilli; **parallel access** = accès parallèle; **public access terminal** = terminal *m* public; **random access** = accès aléatoire *or* sélectif *or* direct; **sequential access** = accès séquentiel; **serial access** = accès séquentiel **2** *verb (a file or a system)* accéder à *or* avoir accès à; **she accessed the employee's file stored on the computer** = elle a accédé au fichier (informatique) de l'employé stocké sur l'ordinateur

◊ **access control** *noun* contrôle *m* d'accès (au système)

◊ **access time** *noun* **(a)** *(time needed between request and data being shown)* temps *m* d'accès; **the access time of this dynamic RAM chip is around 200nS - we have faster versions if your system clock is running faster** = le temps d'accès de cette RAM dynamique est d'environ 200nS - il existe une version plus rapide si votre fréquence d'horloge est plus élevée **(b)** *(time needed to find a file, etc.)* temps *m* d'accès (à un fichier, etc.)

accessible *adjective* accessible; **details of customers are easily accessible from the main computer files** = les détails du fichier client de l'ordinateur principal sont facilement accessibles

accessions *plural noun (in libraries, etc.)* nouveaux titres *mpl or* acquisitions *fpl;* **accession number** = numéro *m* de référence *or* d'entrée

accessory *noun* accessoire *m;* **the printer comes with several accessories, such as a soundproof hood** = plusieurs accessoires, dont un capot d'insonorisation, sont fournis avec l'imprimante; **this popular home computer has a large range of accessories** = il existe de nombreux accessoires pour cet ordinateur individuel très populaire

accidental *adjective* accidentel, -elle; **always keep backup copies in case of accidental damage to the master file** = sauvegardez toujours vos données sur disquettes pour le cas où le fichier principal serait endommagé

accordion fold *or* **fanfold** *noun* papier (plié) en accordéon *or* en paravent

accumulate *verb* accumuler *or* rassembler; **we have gradually accumulated a large databank of names and addresses** = nous avons rassemblé progressivement un impressionnant fichier d'adresses

◊ **accumulator** *or* **ACC (register)** *noun* accumulateur *m or* registre *m* de cumul; **accumulator shift instruction** = commande *f* de décalage dans le registre

accurate *adjective* correct, -e *or* précis, -e *or* sans erreur; **the printed bar code has to be accurate to within a thousandth of a micron** = le code (à) barres doit être imprimé avec une précision de l'ordre du millième de micron

◊ **accurately** *adverb* correctement *or* avec précision; **the OCR had difficulty in reading the new font accurately** = le lecteur optique n'arrivait pas à lire correctement toutes les lettres de la nouvelle police de caractères *or* de la nouvelle fonte; **the error was caused because the data had not been accurately keyed** = l'erreur provenait d'une mauvaise saisie des données

◊ **accuracy** *noun* précision *f or* exactitude *f*

acetate *noun* transparent *m* (d'acétate); **the graphs were plotted on acetate, for use on an overhead projector** = les graphiques avaient été dessinés sur des transparents pour être montrés au rétroprojecteur

achieve *verb* réussir *or* parvenir à; **hardware designers are trying to achieve compatibility between all the components of the system** = les concepteurs de matériel informatique tentent de parvenir à une compatibilité totale entre tous les composants du système

achromatic *adjective* achromatique

ACIA = ASYNCHRONOUS COMMUNICATIONS INTERFACE ADAPTER

ACK or **ACKNLG** = ACKNOWLEDGE (caractère d') accusé *m* de réception (positif); **the printer generates an ACK signal when it has received data** = l'imprimante émet un signal pour accuser réception des données

Ackerman's function *noun* fonction *f* d'Ackerman

acknowledge 1 *noun* (signal or caractère d') accusé *m* de réception **2** *verb* accuser réception (d'un message) or envoyer un accusé de réception; **acknowledge character** = caractère *m* d'accusé de réception
◊ **acknowledgements** *noun* (*in books*) remerciements *mpl* (*in magazines*) crédits *mpl*

acoustic *adjective* acoustique; **acoustic hood** = capot *m* d'insonorisation; **an acoustic hood allows us to talk and print in the same room** = grâce au capot d'insonorisation, il est possible d'avoir une conversation dans la pièce où l'imprimante fonctionne; **acoustic delay line** = ligne *f* à retard acoustique; **acoustic store** or **acoustic memory** = mémoire *f* acoustique
◊ **acoustical feedback** *noun* retour *m* acoustique
◊ **acoustics** *noun* l'acoustique *f*

acoustic coupler *noun* coupleur *m* acoustique; **I use an acoustic coupler with my lap-top computer** = j'utilise un coupleur acoustique avec mon (ordinateur) portatif

acquisition *noun* acquisition *f;* **data acquisition** = acquisition *f* de données

ACR = AUDIO CASSETTE RECORDER magnétophone *m;* **ACR interface** = interface *f* magnétophone

acronym *noun* acronyme *m;* **the acronym FORTRAN means Formula Translator** = l'acronyme FORTRAN signifie 'Formula Translator'; **the acronym RAM means Random Access Memory** = RAM est l'abréviation de 'Random Access Memory'

actintic light *noun* lumière *f* actinique

action *noun* **(a)** action *f;* **action has been taken to repair the fault** = on a pris les mesures nécessaires pour remédier au défaut or pour rectifier or réparer ce qui n'allait pas; **to take action** = agir or prendre des mesures or intervenir; **action cycle** = cycle *m* fonctionnel; **action message** = message *m* d'intervention **(b)** (*photography*) **action field** = champ *m* (d'action); **action frame** = champ *m* or cadrage *m* d'une scène; **action shot** = (i) prise *f* de vue or tournage *m* d'une scène; (ii) image *f* d'une scène

activate *verb* activer or mettre en marche; **pressing CR activates the printer** = en appuyant sur la touche CR, on met l'imprimante en marche

active *adjective* actif, -ive; **active device** = dispositif (électronique) actif or armé; **active file** = fichier actif; **active star** = réseau en étoile actif; **active state** = activité *f;* **active window** = fenêtre active
◊ **activity** *noun* **(a)** activité *f;* **activity loading** = (mode de) chargement *m* en fonction du taux d'activité or de la fréquence d'utilisation; **activity ratio** = taux *m* d'activité **(b) activities** = tâches *fpl* (d'un ordinateur)

actual address or **absolute address** *noun* adresse absolue; **actual code** = code *m* absolu or code machine; **actual instruction** = instruction absolue

actuator *noun* (i) bras *m* de lecture; (ii) vérin *m*

ACU = AUTOMATIC CALLING UNIT

acuity *noun* (*sight*) acuité *f* visuelle; (*hearing*) acuité auditive

acutance *noun* acutance *f* or piqué *m*

acute *adjective* **(a)** (*pointed*) aigu, -uë **(b) acute accent** = accent aigu

A/D or **A to D** = ANALOG TO DIGITAL

ADA *noun* langage ADA

adapt *verb* adapter; **can this computer be adapted to take 5.25 inch disks?** = est-ce qu'il est possible d'adapter cet ordinateur pour les disquettes 5,25 pouces?

◊ **adapter** or **adaptor** noun adaptateur m; **the cable adapter allows attachment of the scanner to the SCSI interface** = l'adaptateur du câble permet de relier le scanner à une interface SCSI; **the cable to connect the scanner to the adapter is included in the package** = le câble de liaison entre le scanner et l'adaptateur est compris; (add-on interface board) **adapter card** = carte f adaptateur; **adapter plug** = adaptateur; **data adapter unit** = adaptateur de ligne or de voie de communication

◊ **adaptation** noun adaptation f; **the adaptation of the eye to respond to different levels of brightness** = l'adaptation or l'accommodation de l'oeil en réponse aux variations d'intensité de lumière

◊ **adaptive channel allocation** noun allocation f dynamique des voies de communication; **adaptive routing** = acheminement m or routage m dynamique; **adaptive system** = système m auto-adaptable or dynamique

adaptor see ADAPTER

ADC = ANALOG TO DIGITAL CONVERTER

add verb **(a)** (figures) additionner; **in the spreadsheet each column should be added to make a subtotal** = l'addition de chacune des colonnes du tableau donne un sous-total; **add time** = temps m d'addition; **add register** = registre m d'addition **(b)** (parts or text) ajouter; **the software house has added a new management package to its range of products** = les producteurs de logiciels ont ajouté un nouveau progiciel de gestion à leur gamme de produits; **adding or deleting material from the text is easy using function keys** = avec les touches de fonction, il est facile d'ajouter ou de supprimer du texte

◊ **added entry** noun entrée f secondaire

◊ **addend** noun cumulateur m

◊ **adder** noun additionneur m; **adder-subtractor** = additionneur-soustracteur m; **full adder** or **three input adder** = additionneur complet or à trois entrées; **half adder** or **two input adder** = demi-additionneur or additionneur à deux

entrées; **parallel adder** = additionneur parallèle; **serial adder** = additionneur séquentiel

add-in noun & adjective (dispositif, etc.) supplémentaire or additionnel, -elle; **add-in card** = carte additionnelle or carte d'extension; **the first method is to use a page description language, the second is to use an add-in processor card** = vous pouvez soit vous servir d'un langage de description de pages soit ajouter une carte processeur; **can you explain the add-in card method?** = pourriez-vous expliquer comment fonctionne le système de carte d'extension?; **processing is much faster with add-in cards** = le traitement s'effectue beaucoup plus rapidement avec les cartes d'extension

addition noun addition f; **addition record** = enregistrement m or fichier m de mise à jour; **addition time** = temps m d'addition; **addition without carry** = (i) addition sans retenue; (ii), (same as EXOR function) exclusion f réciproque or OU exclusif; **destructive addition** = addition destructive

◊ **additional** adjective additionnel, -elle or supplémentaire; **can we add three additional workstations to the network?** = peut-on ajouter trois postes or stations de travail supplémentaires au réseau?

◊ **additive colour mixing** noun synthèse f additive (de couleurs)

add-on noun & adjective (dispositif) supplémentaire or additionnel, -elle; **the add-on hard disk will boost the computer's storage capabilities** = un disque dur supplémentaire augmentera la capacité de stockage de l'ordinateur; **add-on board** = carte d'extension; **the new add-on board allows colour graphics to be displayed** = cette nouvelle carte d'extension permet l'affichage graphique en couleur
NOTE: opposite is **built-in**

address 1 noun **(a)** (street, town, etc.) adresse f; **address list** = répertoire m or liste f d'adresses; **we keep an address list of two thousand businesses in Europe** = notre fichier contient les adresses de deux mille sociétés en Europe **(b)** (in central processing unit) adresse; **each separate memory word has its own unique**

address = chaque mot en mémoire possède une adresse unique; **this is the address at which the data starts** = voici l'adresse de début des données; **absolute address** or **actual address** or **direct address** = adresse absolue; **address access time** = temps *m* d'adressage; **address bus** = bus *m* d'adresses; **address computation** = calcul *m* d'une adresse; **address decoder** = décodeur *m* d'adresses; **address field** = champ *m* d'adresse; **address format** = format *m* d'adresse; **address mapping** = table *f* de correspondance des adresses; **address mark** = marque *f* (de début) d'adresse; **address modification** = modification *f* d'adresse; **address register** = registre *m* d'adresse; **address space** = espace *m* adresse; **address strobe** = signal *m* de validité d'adresse; **address track** = piste *f* d'adresses; **address word** = mot *m* adresse; **base address** = adresse de base; **initial address** = adresse d'origine; **machine address** = adresse machine; **relative address** = adresse relative **2** *verb* **(a)** *(letter)* adresser; **to address a letter** or **a parcel** = adresser une lettre or un colis **(b)** *(in CPU)* créer or définir une adresse; **a larger address word increases the amount of memory a computer can address** = plus le mot adresse est long, plus la mémoire adressable de l'ordinateur augmente

◊ **addressability** *noun* *(of pixels)* capacité *f* d'adressage

◊ **addressable** *adjective* adressable; **all the 5Mb of RAM is addressable** = les 5Mo de RAM sont adressables en totalité; **addressable cursor** = curseur adressable; **addressable terminal** = terminal à adressage protégé

◊ **addressee** *noun (person)* destinataire *m&f*

◊ **addressing** *noun* *(accessing a location in memory)* adressage *m;* **absolute addressing** = adressage absolu; **abbreviated addressing** = adressage abrégé or simplifié; **bit addressing** = adressage binaire; **deferred addressing** = adressage différé or indirect; **direct addressing** = adressage direct; **immediate addressing** = adressage immédiat; **indexed addressing** = adressage indexé; **indirect addressing** = adressage indirect; **addressing capacity** = disponibilité *f* or capacité *f* d'adressage or de mémoire; **addressing level** = niveau *m* d'adressage; **addressing method** = méthode *f* d'adressage; **addressing mode** = mode *m* d'adressage

adjacent *adjective* adjacent, -e or contigu, -uë or à côté de; **the address is stored adjacent to the customer name field** = l'adresse est rangée en mémoire à côté du champ nom du client

adjust *verb* ajuster or régler or modifier; **you can adjust the brightness and contrast by turning a knob** = vous n'avez qu'à tourner un bouton pour régler la luminosité et le contraste

◊ **adjustment** *noun* ajustement *m* or réglage *m* or mise *f* au point or modification *f;* **the brightness needs adjustment** = la luminosité a besoin d'un réglage; **I think the joystick needs adjustment as it sometimes gets stuck** = il faudrait vérifier la manette de commande qui reste parfois coincée

administrator *noun* *(software)* gestionnaire *m;* **data administrator** = gestionnaire de données or de fichier; **database administrator (DBA)** = gestionnaire de base de données

ADP = AUTOMATIC DATA PROCESSING

advance *verb* (faire) avancer; *(paper or film)* entraîner; **the paper is advanced by turning this knob** = ce bouton sert à l'entraînement du papier; **advance the cursor two spaces along the line** = faites avancer le curseur de deux espaces (sur la ligne)

◊ **advanced** *adjective* avancé, -ée or évolué, -ée; **advanced version** = version avancée or évoluée

adventure game *noun* jeu *m* (électronique) d'aventure

aerial 1 *noun* antenne *f;* **aerial cable** = câble *m* d'antenne **2** *adjective (in the air)* aérien, -ienne or en l'air; **aerial image** = vue *f* plongeante or aérienne

affect *verb* influer sur; **changes in voltage will affect the way the computer functions** = les sautes or les variations de tension vont influer sur le fonctionnement de l'ordinateur

affirmative *adjective* affirmatif, -ive; **affirmative acknowledgement** = accusé *m* de réception positif (d'un message)

AFNOR Association française de normalisation (AFNOR)

afterglow *see* PERSISTENCE

aftersales service *noun* service *m* après-vente (SAV)

AGC = AUTOMATIC GAIN CONTROL

aggregate *noun* agrégat *m;* **data aggregate** = données *fpl* structurées

AI = ARTIFICIAL INTELLIGENCE

A & I = ABSTRACTING AND INDEXING

aid 1 *noun* aide *f or* assistance *f;* **the computer is a great aid to rapid processing of large amounts of information** = l'ordinateur est une aide importante pour le traitement d'une grande quantité de données; **diagnostic aid** = aide au diagnostic **2** *verb* aider *or* assister; **industrial design is aided by computers** = l'ordinateur est un outil très utile à l'esthétique industrielle; *see also* COMPUTER-AIDED

air gap *noun* entrefer *m*
◊ **air circuit breaker** *noun* disjoncteur *m* à air

alarm *noun* alarme *f or* signal *m* sonore; **all staff must leave the building if the alarm sounds** = tout le personnel doit quitter le bâtiment dès que la sonnerie d'alarme retentit; **an alarm rings when the printer has run out of paper** = un signal sonore prévient qu'il ne reste plus de papier dans l'imprimante

albumen plate *noun (photography)* plaque *f* photosensible à l'albumen

ALC = AUTOMATIC LEVEL CONTROL

algebra *noun* algèbre *f;* **Boolean algebra** = algèbre booléenne

ALGOL = ALGORITHMIC LANGUAGE langage *m* algorithmique *or* ALGOL

algorithm *noun* algorithme *m*
◊ **algorithmic** *adjective* algorithmique; **algorithmic language** *or* **ALGOL** = langage algorithmique *or* ALGOL

QUOTE image processing algorithms are stepby step procedures for performing image processing operations
Byte
QUOTE the steps are: acquiring a digitized image, developing an algorithm to process it, processing the image, modifying the algorithm until you are satisfied with the result
Byte
QUOTE the complex algorithms needed for geometrical calculations make heavy demands on the processor
PC Business World

alien *adjective* étranger, -ère; **alien disk** = disquette non compatible; **alien disk reader** = lecteur de disquettes non compatibles *or* lecteur multidisque; **when you have an alien disk select the multidisk option to allow you to turn the disk drive into an alien disk reader** = si la disquette n'est pas compatible, validez la fonction 'multidisque' qui permet au lecteur de lire une disquette non compatible

align *verb* **(a)** *(text)* aligner *or* cadrer **(b)** *(read/write head)* positionner *or* aligner
◊ **aligner** *noun (on typewriter, etc.)* dispositif *m* d'alignement *or* de cadrage *or* de positionnement
◊ **aligning edge** *noun (of optical character recognition system)* bord *m* d'alignement *or* de référence
◊ **alignment** *noun* alignement *m;* **in alignment** = aligné, -ée; **out of alignment** = désaligné, -ée; **alignment pin** = téton *m or* pige *f* d'alignement

allocate *verb* allouer *or* répartir *or* attribuer *or* affecter; **the operating system allocated most of main memory to the spreadsheet program** = le système d'exploitation a alloué *or* attribué presque toute la mémoire principale au tableur
◊ **allocation** *noun* allocation *f or* répartition *f or* attribution *f or* affectation *f;* **allocation of time** *or* **capital to a project** = allocation de temps *or* affectation de capitaux à un projet; **allocation routine** =

programme d'allocation; **dynamic allocation** = allocation dynamique; **band allocation** = attribution de bandes de fréquences *or* de longueurs d'ondes; **the new band allocation means we will have more channels** = la nouvelle attribution de bandes de fréquences permet d'avoir un plus grand nombre de voies de transmission

allophone *noun* allophone *m*

alpha beta technique *noun* technique *f* alpha bêta

◊ **alpha radiation** *noun* rayonnement *m* alpha; **alpha-particle** = particule *f* alpha; **alpha-particle sensitivity** = sensibilité *f* aux particules alpha

◊ **alpha wrap** *noun* enrouleur *m* alpha

alphabet *noun* alphabet *m*

◊ **alphabetic character (set)** *noun* lettres *fpl* de l'alphabet; **alphabetic string** = chaîne de caractères alphabétiques

◊ **alphabetical order** *noun* ordre *m* alphabétique

◊ **alphabetically** *adverb* alphabétiquement; en *or* par ordre alphabétique; **the files are arranged alphabetically under the customer's name** = les fichiers sont classés en *or* par ordre alphabétique sous le nom du client

◊ **alphabetize** *verb* classer par ordre alphabétique; **enter the bibliographical information and alphabetize it** = veuillez saisir les données bibliographiques et les mettre en ordre alphabétique

alphageometric *adjective* alphagéométrique

alphameric *US* = ALPHANUMERIC

alphamosaic *adjective* alphamosaïque

alphanumeric *adjective* alphanumérique; **alphanumeric characters** *or* **alphanumerics** = caractères *mpl* alphanumériques; **alphanumeric data** = données *fpl* alphanumériques; **alphanumeric display** = affichage *m* alphanumérique; **alphanumeric keyboard** = clavier *m* alphanumérique; **alphanumeric operand** = opérande *m* alphanumérique; **alphanumeric string** = chaîne *f* de caractères alphanumériques

QUOTE geometrical data takes up more storage space than alphanumeric data
PC Business World

alphaphotographic *adjective* alphaphotographique

◊ **alphasort** *verb* classer (des données) en *or* par ordre alphabétique

alter *verb* changer *or* modifier; **the program specifications have just been altered** = les spécifications du programme viennent d'être modifiées

◊ **alterable** *adjective* modifiable *or* qui peut être changé *or* qui peut être modifié; *see also* EAPROM, EAROM

◊ **alteration** *noun* changement *m or* modification *f*; **the new version of the software has many alterations and improvements** = la nouvelle version du logiciel comporte de nombreuses modifications et améliorations

alternate 1 *verb* (faire) alterner **2** *adjective* alterné, -ée; **alternate mode** = (en) mode alterné; **alternate route** = voie *f* de déroutement *or* déviation *f*

◊ **alternately** *adverb* tour à tour *or* alternativement *or* à l'alternat

◊ **alternation** *noun* alternance *f*

◊ **alternating current (AC)** *noun* courant *m* alternatif (CA)

◊ **alternator** *noun* alternateur *m*

alternative 1 *noun* alternative *f or* choix *m;* **what is the alternative to re-keying all the data?** = que peut-on faire sinon saisir de nouveau toutes les données?; **we have no alternative** = nous n'avons pas le choix *or* il n'y a rien d'autre à faire *or* il n'y a pas d'alternative **2** *adjective* autre; *(logical function)* **alternative denial** = fonction *f* NON-ET

ALU = ARITHMETIC LOGIC UNIT

AM = AMPLITUDE MODULATION

A-MAC *(low bandwidth variation of MAC)* basse fréquence multiplexée *or* A-MAC

ambient *adjective* ambiant, -e; **ambient noise level** = niveau *m* de bruit de fond *or* de bruit ambiant; **the ambient noise level in the office is greater than in the**

library = le bruit de fond dans ce bureau est plus élevé que dans la bibliothèque; **ambient temperature** = température ambiante

ambiguous *adjective* ambigu, -uë *or* équivoque; **ambiguous filename** = nom de fichier ambigu

◊ **ambiguity** *noun* ambiguïté *f;* **ambiguity error** = erreur *f* d'ambiguïté

ambisonics *noun* enregistrement *m* ambisonique *or* d'ambiance

AMM = ANALOG MULTIMETER

amendment record *noun* enregistrement *m* des détails *or* des mouvements *or* des modifications

American National Standards Institute (ANSI) *(American equivalent of)* Association française de normalisation (AFNOR)

American Standard Code for Information Interchange (ASCII) (code) ASCII

amount 1 *noun* quantité *f;* **what is the largest amount of data which can be processed in one hour?** = quelle est la quantité maximale de données qu'on puisse traiter en une heure? **2** *verb* **to amount to** = se monter à *or* s'élever à *or* équivaloir à; **the total keyboarded characters amount to ten million** = le total des caractères saisis (par clavier) est de dix millions

amp *or* **ampere (A)** *noun* ampère (A) *m*
NOTE: used with figures: **a 13-amp fuse**

ampersand (&) *noun* 'et' commercial *or* esperluette *f*

amplifier *noun* amplificateur *m;* **audio amplifier** = amplificateur audio *or* de basse fréquence; **low noise amplifier** = amplificateur à faible bruit; **amplifier class** = classe *f* d'amplificateur

◊ **amplification** *noun* amplification *f;* **increase the amplification of the input signal** = augmentez l'amplification *or* le gain du signal d'entrée; **the amplification is so high, the signal is distorting** = l'amplification est si grande qu'elle cause une distorsion du signal

◊ **amplify** *verb* amplifier; **the received signal needs to be amplified before it can be processed** = le signal reçu doit être amplifié avant d'être traité; **amplified telephone** = téléphone *m* amplifié *or* à écoute amplifiée

amplitude *noun* amplitude *f;* **amplitude distortion** = distorsion *f* d'amplitude; **amplitude modulation (AM)** = modulation *f* d'amplitude (MA); **amplitude quantization** = quantification *f* d'amplitude

analog *or* **analogue** *noun* analogue *m or* appareil *m* analogique; **analog channel** = voie *f* analogique; **analog computer** = calculateur analogique; **analog gate** = porte *f or* circuit *m* analogique; **analog input card** = carte d'entrée analogique; **analog multimeter (AMM)** = multimètre *m* analogique; **analog output card** = carte de sortie analogique; **analog recording** = enregistrement *m* analogique; **analog representation** = représentation *f* analogique; **analog signal** = signal *m* analogique; **analog to digital (A to D** *or* **A/D)** = (conversion) analogique-numérique; **analog to digital converter (ADC** *or* **A to D converter)** = convertisseur *m* analogique-numérique; **digital to analog converter (DAC** *or* **D to A converter)** = convertisseur numérique-analogique

analyse *or* **analyze** *verb* analyser; **to analyse a computer printout** = analyser une sortie d'imprimante *or* un listing; **to analyse the market potential for a new computer** = faire l'analyse du potentiel du marché pour un nouvel ordinateur

◊ **analysis** *noun* analyse *f;* **data analysis** = analyse de données; **systems analysis** = analyse de systèmes
NOTE: plural is **analyses**

◊ **analyst** *noun* analyste *m&f;* **analyst/programmer** *or* **programmer/analyst** = analyste-programmeur, -euse; **systems analyst** = analyste (de) système

◊ **analyzer** *noun* analyseur *m;* **frequency analyzer** = analyseur de fréquence

anamorphic image *noun*
anamorphose *f*

ANAPROP = ANOMALOUS
PROPAGATION

anastigmatic *adjective (lens)*
anastigmate

ancestral file *noun* fichier *m* ancêtre

ancillary equipment *noun*
accessoires *mpl or* matériels *mpl* annexes

AND *or* **coincidence function** *noun*
ET *or* fonction d'intersection; **AND** *or*
coincidence gate *or* **circuit** *or* **element =**
ET *or* circuit ET *or* porte ET; **AND** *or*
coincidence operation = ET *or* opération
ET *or* intersection logique *or* conjonction
logique

anechoic *adjective* (chambre) blanche
or sourde *or* sans écho

angle *noun* angle *m*

angstrom *noun* angström *m*

animate *verb* animer
◊ **animation** *noun* animation *f*

annotation *noun* annotation *f or*
commentaire *m;* **annotation symbol =**
symbole *m* de commentaire

annunciator *noun & adjective* (signal)
annonciateur *(m)*

anode *noun* anode *f*

anomalistic period *noun* période *f*
anomale *or* irrégulière
◊ **anomalous** *adj* **anomalous**
propagation (ANAPROP) = mauvaise
transmission d'images (due à des
perturbations atmosphériques)

ANSI *US* = AMERICAN NATIONAL
STANDARDS INSTITUTE

answer 1 *noun* réponse *f* **2** *verb* **(a)**
répondre (à quelqu'un *or* à une lettre *or*
au téléphone) **(b)** répondre à un appel;

the first modem originates the call and
the second answers it = le premier
modem transmet l'appel tandis que le
second y répond; **answer back =** signal
m de réponse; **answer time =** temps *m* de
réponse
◊ **answering machine** *noun* répondeur
m téléphonique
◊ **answering service** *noun* (service de)
permanence *f* téléphonique
◊ **answerphone** *noun* répondeur *m*
téléphonique

antenna *noun* antenne *f;* **antenna array**
= réseau *m* d'antennes; **antenna gain =**
gain *m* d'antenne

anti- *prefix* anti-; **anticoincidence circuit**
or **function =** porte *f or* circuit *m* OU
exclusif *or* fonction *f* OU exclusif
◊ **anti-tinkle suppression** *noun (in*
modem) (bouton de) suppression *f* de
signal d'appel parasite

APD = AVALANCHE PHOTODIODE

aperture *noun* ouverture *f* (d'un
objectif); **aperture card =** carte *f* à fenêtre
or à microfilm *or* à microfiche; *(of*
antenna) **aperture illumination =**
illumination *f* de l'ouverture; *(in colour*
TV or monitors) **aperture mask =** masque
m de séparation

APL = A PROGRAMMING LANGUAGE
langage *m* (de programmation) APL

apochromatic lens *noun* objectif *m*
apochromatique

apogee *noun (in a satellite's orbit)*
apogée *f*

apostrophe (') *noun (typography)*
apostrophe *f*

append *verb* annexer *or* joindre *or*
compléter
◊ **appendix** *noun (in a book)* appendice
m; (of a document) annexe *f;* **for further**
details see the appendices = voir
annexes pour tout renseignement
supplémentaire; **a complete list is**
printed in the appendix = vous trouverez
la liste complète dans l'appendice
NOTE: plural is **appendices**

appliance *noun* appareil *m* (électrique); **all electrical appliances should be properly earthed =** tout appareil électrique doit être mis à la terre

◊ **appliance computer** *noun* ordinateur *m*

application *noun* **(a)** *(asking for something)* demande *f;* **application for an account on the system =** demande de partition sur le système; **application form =** formulaire *m* de demande; **to fill in an application (form) for an account on the system =** remplir une demande de partition sur le système **(b)** *(task which a computer performs)* application *f; (in ISO/OSI network)* **application layer =** couche application; **application orientated language =** langage *m* d'application; **applications package =** progiciel *m* d'application; **applications software** *or* **applications program =** logiciel *m* *or* programme *m* d'application; **the multi-window editor is used to create and edit applications programs =** l'éditeur multifenêtre est utilisé pour créer et éditer les programmes d'application; **application specific integrated circuit (ASIC) =** circuit *m* intégré spécialisé *or* sur mesure *or* circuit spécifique à une application (ASIC); **applications terminal =** ordinateur *m* dédié *or* spécialisé

> QUOTE they have announced a fourth generation application development tool which allows users of PCs and PC networks to exchange data with mainframe databases
> *Minicomputer News*

apply *verb* **(a)** *(to ask for something)* faire une demande (de) **(b)** *(to affect or to touch)* s'appliquer (à) *or* convenir (à); **this formula applies only to data received after the interrupt signal =** cette formule ne convient qu'aux données reçues après le signal d'interruption

approve *verb* **(a) to approve of =** approuver *or* être d'accord avec *or* apprécier; **the new graphics monitor was approved by the safety council before being sold =** le nouveau moniteur graphique a été homologué par le conseil de sécurité avant d'être commercialisé; **I approve of the new editor - it's much easier to use =** le nouvel éditeur de texte

est tout à fait ce qu'il faut, et beaucoup plus facile à utiliser **(b)** *(to agree to something)* accepter *or* agréer; **the software has to be approved by the board =** le conseil d'administration doit ratifier le choix du logiciel; **an approved modem should carry a label with a green circle and the words 'Approved by ....' =** un modem agréé (par BABT) doit être muni de l'étiquette au cercle vert portant la mention 'Approved by...'

◊ **approval** *noun* **(a)** approbation *f or* homologation *f;* **a BABT approval is needed for modems =** les modems doivent être agréés par BABT (et porter la mention 'Approved by ...'); **certificate of approval =** certificat *m* d'homologation **(b) on approval =** à condition *or* à l'essai

approximate *adjective* approximatif, -ive; **we have made an approximate calculation of the time needed for keyboarding =** nous avons calculé de façon approximative le temps nécessaire à la saisie du texte

◊ **approximately** *adverb* environ *or* approximativement; **processing time is approximately 10% lower than during the previous quarter =** le temps de traitement est d'environ 10% inférieur à celui du trimestre précédent

◊ **approximating** *adjective* approché, -ée; **using approximating A to D =** en utilisant une valeur approchée de A à la place de D

◊ **approximation** *noun* approximation *f or* résultat *m* approximatif *or* estimation *f;* **approximation of keyboarding time =** calcul approximatif du temps de saisie; **the final figure is only an approximation =** ce résultat n'est qu'approximatif; **approximation error =** erreur *f* d'arrondi

APT = AUTOMATICALLY PROGRAMMED TOOLS

Arabic *adjective* **Arabic numbers** *or* **figures =** chiffres *mpl* arabes; **the page numbers are written in Arabic figures =** les pages sont numérotées en chiffres arabes

arbitration *noun (ensuring fair usage by several users)* **bus arbitration =** arbitrage *m or* gestion *f* de l'utilisation d'un bus

arcade game *noun* jeu *m* électronique dans une salle de jeux publique *or* jeu d'arcade

archetype *noun* archétype *m*

architecture *noun* architecture *f;* **network architecture** = architecture d'un réseau; **onion skin architecture** = architecture en pelure d'oignon; **the onion skin architecture of this computer is made up of a kernel at the centre, an operating system, a low-level language and then the user's programs** = l'architecture en pelure d'oignon de cet ordinateur consiste en un noyau central, une couche système d'exploitation, une couche langage de bas niveau et enfin une couche programmes utilisateur

archive 1 *noun* archives *fpl;* **archive file** = fichier archives **2** *verb* archiver; **archived copy** = copie archivée *or* copie d'archives
◊ **archival quality** *noun* qualité *f* d'archivage

> QUOTE on-line archiving is also used to keep down the interruption needed for archiving to seconds
> *Computer News*

area *noun* **(a)** (mesure de) surface *f or* aire *f;* **type area** = empagement *m;* **area composition** = composition *f or* mise *f* en page *or* disposition *f* de page **(b)** *(section of memory)* zone *f;* **area search** = recherche *f* de zone *or* recherche sélective; *(of monitor)* **image area** = zone d'affichage; *(section of main memory)* **input area** = zone d'entrée (de données) **(c)** *(part of a country)* région *f; (of town)* quartier *m or* secteur *m* (d'une ville); **area code** = indicatif *m* (téléphonique) de zone; *Canada* indicatif régional; **the area code for central London is 071** = l'indicatif (de zone) de Londres est 071; **area exchange** = central *m* répartiteur

argument *noun* argument *m or* mantisse *f or* opérande *f*

arithmetic *noun* arithmétique *f or* calcul *m;* **arithmetic capability** = capacité *f* de calcul arithmétique; **arithmetic check** = vérification *f* arithmétique; **arithmetic functions** = fonctions *fpl* arithmétiques; **arithmetic**

instruction = instruction *f* arithmétique; **arithmetic logic unit (ALU)** *or* **arithmetic unit** = unité *f* arithmétique et logique (UAL); **arithmetic operation** = opération *f* arithmétique; **arithmetic operator** = opérateur *m* arithmétique; **arithmetic register** = registre *m* arithmétique; **arithmetic shift** = décalage *m* arithmétique; **external arithmetic** = arithmétique externe; **internal arithmetic** = arithmétique interne

arm 1 *noun (mechanical device in a disk drive)* bras *m;* **access arm** = bras de lecture/écriture **2** *verb (to prepare)* préparer *or* armer; *(to activate)* valider *or* activer; **armed interrupt** = interruption validée *or* activée

array *noun (of figures or data)* tableau *m; (antennae or circuits)* (en) réseau *m;* **alphanumeric array** = tableau *m* alphanumérique; **array bounds** = bornes *fpl* d'un tableau; **array dimension** = dimension *f* d'un tableau; **array element** = valeur *f or* élément *m* dans un tableau; **array processor** = processeur vectoriel; **the array processor allows the array that contains the screen image to be rotated with one simple command** = le processeur vectoriel permet de faire pivoter le tableau qui contient l'image écran à l'aide d'une seule commande; **logic array** = réseau *or* circuit logique; **string array** = tableau de chaînes de caractères; **three-dimensional array** = tableau à trois dimensions; **two-dimensional array** = tableau à deux dimensions

arsenide *see* GALLIUM

article *noun* **(a)** *(of newspaper or magazine)* article *m;* **he wrote an article about the user group for the local newspaper** = il a écrit, pour le journal local, un article concernant le groupe d'utilisateurs **(b)** *(of file)* article **(c)** *(of contract)* clause *f or* article *m;* **see article 8 of the contract** = voir l'article 8 du contrat

artificial intelligence (AI) *noun* intelligence *f* artificielle (IA)

artwork *noun (graphical work or images which are to be printed)* maquette *f;* **the**

artwork has been sent for filming = la maquette a été envoyée au flashage

ASA = AMERICAN STANDARDS ASSOCIATION; **ASA exposure index** = indice ASA (de sensibilité d'un film)
NOTE: see DIN

ascender *noun (of a character)* hampe *m* (d'une lettre)

ASCII = AMERICAN STANDARD CODE FOR INFORMATION INTERCHANGE; **ASCII character** = caractère *m* ASCII; **ASCII file** = fichier *m* ASCII; **use a word processor or other program that generates a standard ASCII file** = utilisez un programme de traitement de texte ou un autre programme qui produira un fichier ASCII standard; **ASCII keyboard** = clavier *m* ASCII
NOTE: when speaking say 'ass-key'

ASIC = APPLICATION SPECIFIC INTEGRATED CIRCUIT

aspect *noun* (i) aspect *m or* apparence *f* ; (ii) descripteurs *mpl or* caractéristiques *fpl; (in an information retrieval system)* **aspect card** = carte *f* d'indentification; *(of pixel shapes)* **aspect ratio** = rapport *m* longueur/largeur (d'un pixel); **aspect system** = système *m* de recherche *or* de stockage par descripteurs

ASR = AUTOMATIC SEND/RECEIVE (appareil) émetteur-récepteur

assemble *verb* **(a)** *(to put together)* assembler *or* monter; **the parts for the disk drive are made in Japan and assembled in France** = les pièces du lecteur de disquettes sont fabriquées au Japon, mais l'assemblage se fait en France **(b)** *(to translate assembly code into machine code)* assembler; **there is a short wait during which time the program is assembled into object code** = il y a un certain délai pendant lequel s'effectue l'assemblage en code objet du programme; **syntax errors spotted whilst the source program is being assembled** = des erreurs de syntaxe repérées au cours de l'assemblage du programmme source **(c)** assembler un programme (routines, macros, paramètres)

◊ **assembler (program)** *noun (assembly program)* assembleur *m or* programme *m* d'assemblage; **absolute assembler** = assembleur absolu; **assembler error message** = message *m* d'erreur de l'assembleur; **cross-assembler** = assembleur croisé; **single-pass assembler** = assembleur une passe; **two-pass assembler** = assembleur deux passes

◊ **assembly** *noun* **(a)** *(putting together)* assemblage *m or* montage *m;* **there are no assembly instructions to show you how to put the computer together** = il n'y a pas de notice de montage pour aider à la mise en place de l'ordinateur; **assembly plant** = usine *f* de montage **(b)** *(converting a program into machine code)* assemblage; **assembly code** = code d'assemblage; **assembly language** *or* **assembler language** = langage *m* d'assemblage; **assembly listing** = *(display)* liste *f* (d'un programme) d'assemblage; *(in print)* listing *m or* impression *f* d'un programme d'assemblage; **assembly (language) program** = assembleur *m or* programme *m* d'assemblage; **assembly routine** *or* **system** = routine *f or* système *m* d'assemblage; **assembly time** = (i) durée *f* d'assemblage; (ii) temps *m or* période *f* d'assemblage

assertion *noun (program statement of a fact or rule)* assertion *f; (fact that is true or defined as being true)* affirmation *f or* assertion *f*

assign *verb* **(a)** assigner à *or* affecter à *or* allouer; **two PCs have been assigned to outputting the labels** = deux PC ont été affectés à la préparation des étiquettes **(b)** *(a variable)* définir (une variable); *(part of memory)* affecter (une zone de mémoire à une tâche); **assigned frequency** = fréquence *f* assignée *or* allouée

◊ **assignment** *noun* affectation *f or* attribution *f or* allocation *f;* **assignment statement** = instruction *f* d'affectation

assisted *see* COMPUTER-AIDED

associate 1 *adjective (linked)* associé, -ée **2** *noun (person)* associé, -ée *or* collègue *m&f*

◊ **associational editing** *noun* montage *m* associatif

◊ **associative addressing** or **content-addressable addressing** noun adressage m associatif; **associative processor** = processeur avec mémoire associative; **associative memory** or **storage** or **content-addressable storage** = mémoire f associative; **associative storage register** = registre m de mémoire associative

astable multivibrator noun multivibrateur m astable

asterisk (*) noun astérisque m

astigmatism noun astigmatisme m

async (informal) = ASYNCHRONOUS

asynchronous adjective asynchrone; **asynchronous access** = accès m asynchrone; **asynchronous communication** = communication f asynchrone; **asynchronous communications interface adapter (ACIA)** = interface f pour communication asynchrone; **asynchronous computer** = ordinateur m asynchrone; **asynchronous mode** = mode m asynchrone; **asynchronous port** = port m (d'accès) asynchrone; **when asynchronous ports are used no special hardware is required** = l'utilisation de ports asynchrones ne demande pas un matériel spécialisé; **asynchronous transmission** = transmission f asynchrone

QUOTE each channel handles two forms of communication: asynchronous communication is mainly for transferring data between computers and peripheral devices, while character communication is for data transfer between computers
Electronics & Power

ATC = AUTHORIZATION TO COPY

ATE = AUTOMATIC TEST EQUIPMENT

ATM = AUTOMATED TELLER MACHINE

atmosphere noun atmosphère f

◊ **atmospheric** adjective atmosphérique; **atmospheric absorption** = absorption f atmosphérique;

atmospheric conditions = conditions fpl atmosphériques

atom noun **(a)** (smallest particle of an element) atome m **(b)** (value or string that cannot be reduced to a simpler form) donnée absolue or atome

◊ **atomic** adjective (referring to atoms) atomique; **atomic clock** = horloge f atomique

attach verb attacher or joindre; **attached processor** = processeur m auxiliaire (indépendant) relié au processeur central

◊ **attachment** noun accessoire m; **there is a special single sheet feed attachment** = il existe un accessoire spécial pour l'alimentation du papier en feuille à feuille

attack noun (start of a sound) attaque f (d'un signal, etc.); **attack envelope** = enveloppe f d'attaque

attend verb assister à or être présent à; **attended operation** = opération f surveillée

◊ **attention** noun (i) attention f ; (ii) intervention f; **this routine requires the attention of the processor every minute** = ce programme exige l'intervention constante du processeur; **attention interruption** = interruption f d'intervention; **attention key** = touche f d'intervention

attenuate verb atténuer or affaiblir

◊ **attenuation** noun (reduction of a signal) atténuation f or affaiblissement m

attribute noun (of file) caractéristique f (d'un fichier); (of screen) attribut m (d'écran); **this attribute controls the colour of the screen** = cet attribut contrôle la couleur de l'écran; **screen attributes** = attributs de visualisation or d'écran

auctioneering device noun filtre m de sélection du signal maximal or minimal

audible adjective audible or perceptible à l'oreille or qu'on peut entendre; **the printer makes an audible signal when it**

runs out of paper = l'imprimante est munie d'un dispositif d'alarme sonore pour avertir qu'il ne reste plus de papier

audience *noun (of TV or radio programmes)* audience *f;* **audience rating** = indice *m* d'écoute

audio *adjective & noun* **audio active** = système *m* audio interactif; **audio cassette** = audiocassette *f;* **audio cassette recorder (ACR)** = magnétophone *m;* **audio compressor** = limiteur *m or* réducteur *m* de signal audio; **audio conferencing** = audioconférence *f;* **audio frequency** = fréquence *f* audio *or* fréquence audible *or* audiofréquence *f; (frequency range between 50-20 000Hz)* **audio range** = limites *fpl* de la bande des audiofréquences *or* gamme *f* des audiofréquences; **audio response unit** = répondeur *m* vocal; **audio slide** = diaposon *f*

◊ **audiovisual (AV)** *adjective* audiovisuel, -elle; **audiovisual aids** = matériel audiovisuel

audit *noun (noting tasks carried out by a computer)* audit *m* (informatique); **audit trail** = protocole *m* de traçage *or* de contrôle *or* de vérification

augend *noun (in an addition)* cumulande *m or* premier terme d'une addition

augment *verb* augmenter; **augmented addressing** = adressage *m* élargi

◊ **augmenter** *noun (value added to another)* cumulateur *m or* second terme d'une addition

aural *adjective* sonore *or* acoustique

authentic *adjective* authentique

◊ **authenticate** *verb* authentifier

◊ **authentication** *noun* authentification *f;* **authentication of messages** = authentification de messages

author *noun (person who wrote a program)* auteur *m;* **author language** = langage *m* de programmation EAO; **authoring system** = système adapté aux langages EAO

authority *noun* autorité *f;* **authority file** *or* **list** = fichier *m or* liste *f* de référence

authorize *verb* **(a)** *(to give permission)* autoriser (qch) *or* permettre (qch); **to authorize the purchase of a new computer system** = autoriser l'achat d'un nouveau système informatique **(b)** *(to give someone the authority to do something)* autoriser (quelqu'un à faire quelque chose) *or* donner (à quelqu'un) l'autorisation (de faire quelque chose)

◊ **authorization** *noun* **(a)** *(permission or power to do something)* autorisation *f or* permission *f;* **authorization to copy (ATC)** = autorisation *f* de copier *or* de dupliquer **(b)** *(permission to access a system)* autorisation; **authorization code** = mot *m* de passe *or* code *m* d'accès

◊ **authorized** *adjective* autorisé, -ée *or* permis, -e; **authorized user** = personne *f* autorisée (à utiliser un système)

auto *adjective & prefix* automatique *or* auto-; *(of paper in printer)* **auto advance** = alimentation *f* automatique du papier; *(of modem)* **auto-answer** = auto-réponse *f or* réponse *f* automatique; **auto-baud scanning** = reconnaissance *f* automatique du débit d'une ligne (en baud); **autoboot** = amorçage *m or* lancement *m* automatique (d'un système); *(telephone or modem)* **auto-dial** = (avec) système d'appel automatique (d'un correspondant) *or* numérotation *f* automatique; **auto-login** *or* **auto-logon** = ouverture *f* automatique de session; **auto-redial** = (modem *or* téléphone avec) système de rappel automatique d'un correspondant; **auto repeat** = répétition *f* automatique; **auto restart** = relance *f or* remise en route *f or* redémarrage *m* automatique; **auto start** = lancement *m or* mise *f* en route automatique *or* démarrage *m;* **auto stop** = arrêt *m* automatique; **auto verify** = vérification *f* automatique

automate *verb* automatiser; **automated office** = bureau *m* électronique *or* automatisé; *US* **automated teller machine (ATM)** = guichet *m* automatique de banque (GAB) *or* automate *m* bancaire

◊ **automation** *noun* automatisation *f*

automatic *noun* automatique; **automatic calling unit (ACU)** = système *m or* unité *f* d'appel automatique; *(of cursor)* **automatic carriage return** = retour *m* à la ligne automatique; **automatic checking** = auto-test *m;* **automatic data capture** = saisie *f* automatique de données; **automatic data processing (ADP)** = traitement *m* automatique de données; **automatic decimal adjustment** = *(lining up the decimal points in a column)* alignement *m* automatique des virgules; *(rounding to a certain number of decimals)* arrondi *m* à un nombre fixe de décimales; **automatic error correction** = correction *f* automatique d'erreurs; **automatic error detection** = détection *f* automatique d'erreurs; **automatic gain control (AGC)** *or* **automatic level control (ALC)** = contrôle *m* de gain automatique; *(word-processing)* **automatic letter writing** = composition *f* automatique de lettres types; *(short program)* **automatic loader** = chargeur *m* automatique; *(for telephone)* **automatic message accounting** = compteur *m* d'impulsions automatique (à domicile); **automatic programming** = programmation *f* automatique; *(of character)* **automatic repeat** = répétition *f* automatique; **automatic sequencing** = fonctionnement *m* itératif automatique; **automatic telephone exchange** = central *m* (téléphonique) automatique *or* autocommutateur *m* (téléphonique); **automatic telling machine** *or* US **automated teller machine (ATM)** = guichet *m* automatique de banque (GAB) *or* automate *m* bancaire; **automatic test equipment (ATE)** = équipement *m* de vérification automatique (EVA); **automatic vending machine** = distributeur *m* automatique (de cigarettes, etc.)

◊ **automatically** *adverb* automatiquement; **the compiler automatically corrected the syntax errors** = le compilateur a corrigé les fautes de syntaxe automatiquement; **a SBC automatically limits the movement of the machine** = un ordinateur à carte unique est, par le fait même, limité dans ses opérations; **the program is run automatically when the computer is switched on** = le programme est lancé automatiquement lors de la mise sous tension de l'ordinateur; **Automatically Programmed Tools (APT)** =

commandes numériques de machines-outils

automation *noun* automatisation *f;* **office automation** = bureautique *f*

autopositive *noun* procédé autopositif

auxiliary *adjective* auxiliaire *or* de secours; **the computer room has an auxiliary power supply in case there is a mains failure** = la salle des ordinateurs est équipée d'un bloc d'alimentation de secours en cas de panne de secteur; *(in case of breakdown)* **auxiliary equipment** = matériel *m* de secours; **auxiliary processor** = processeur *m* auxiliaire; **auxiliary storage** *or* **memory** *or* **store** = mémoire *f* auxiliaire; **disk drives and magnetic tapes are auxiliary storage on this machine** = cet appareil est équipé de lecteurs de disquettes et de bandes magnétiques qui servent de mémoire auxiliaire

AV = AUDIOVISUAL

available *adjective* disponible; **available to order only** = articles *mpl* vendus sur commande uniquement; **available light** = lumière ambiante; **available list** = liste *f* des ressources disponibles; **available point** = point *m or* élément *m* d'image; **available power** = puissance *f* maximale *or* réelle disponible; *(time during which a system may be used)* **available time** = temps *m* disponible *or* de disponibilité

◊ **availability** *noun* disponibilité *f;* **the availability of the latest software package is very good** = on trouve le nouveau progiciel dans presque tous les magasins

avalanche *noun (one action starting a number of other actions)* avalanche *f;* **there was an avalanche of errors after I pressed the wrong key** = les erreurs n'ont cessé de se multiplier lorsque j'ai appuyé sur la mauvaise touche; **avalanche photodiode (APD)** = photodiode *f* à avalanche

average 1 *adjective* moyen, -enne; **average access time** = temps *m* d'accès moyen; **average delay** = délai *m* moyen; **the average delay increases at nine-thirty when everyone tries to log-in** = après

9h30, le temps d'attente moyen est beaucoup plus long lorsque chacun tente de se loger ou d'entrer dans le système **2** *verb (to produce as an average figure)* atteindre une moyenne (de) ◊ **average out** *verb* atteindre une moyenne (de) *or* faire en moyenne *or* de moyenne; **it averages out at 120 dpi** = cela fait en moyenne 120 points par pouce *or* une moyenne de 120 points par pouce

axis *noun (around which something turns)* axe *m*; *(on a graph)* axe (de coordonnées); **the CAD package allows an axis to be placed anywhere** = ce progiciel de CAO permet de positionner un axe où l'on veut; **horizontal axis** = axe des abscisses; **vertical axis** = axe des ordonnées

NOTE: plural is **axes**

azerty keyboard *noun* clavier *m* AZERTY

NOTE: *compare with* QWERTY

azimuth *noun* azimut *m;* **azimuth alignment** = réglage *m* d'alignement des têtes *or* des angles d'azimut; **azimuth alignment is adjusted with this small screw** = c'est cette petite vis qui sert à régler l'alignement des têtes *or* des angles d'azimut; **azimuth alignment might not be correct for tape recorded on a different machine** = l'alignement des têtes va peut-être demander un réglage différent lorsqu'il s'agit de bandes enregistrées sur d'autres machines

Bb

B représentation hexadécimale du nombre 11 or B

babble *noun* diaphonie *f* or bruit *m* de fond

BABT = BRITISH APPROVAL BOARD FOR TELECOMMUNICATIONS; **a BABT approval is needed for modems** = les modems doivent être agréés par BABT (et porter la mention 'Approved by ...')

back 1 *noun* arrière *m* or dos *m;* **there is a wide range of connectors at the back of the main unit** = on trouve une variété de connecteurs au dos or sur le panneau arrière de l'unité centrale **2** *verb* aider; **battery-backed** = équipé, -ée d'une pile auxiliaire or de secours; **the RAM disk card has the option to be battery-backed** = la carte RAM peut être équipée, en option, d'une pile de secours; **battery-backed CMOS memory replaces a disk drive in this portable** = dans ce portable, le lecteur de disquettes est remplacé par une mémoire CMOS avec une pile auxiliaire

back-end processor *noun (special purpose auxiliary processor)* processeur *m* de fond or processeur principal

background *noun* **(a)** *(past work or experience)* expérience *f; his background is in the computer industry* = il a une bonne expérience de l'industrie informatique **(b)** *(part of a picture)* arrière-plan *m* or fond *m;* **the new graphics processor chip can handle background, foreground and sprite movement independently** = le nouveau processeur graphique permet de manipuler indépendamment les images d'arrière-plan et d'avant-plan ainsi que les plans-objets; *(of a computer screen)* **background colour** = (couleur de) fond *m;* **black text on a white background is less stressful for the eyes** = un texte en noir sur fond blanc est moins fatigant pour la vue; **background noise** = bruit *m* de fond; **the other machines around this device will produce a lot of background noise** = les autres appareils placés autour de cet équipement produiront un fort bruit de fond; **the modem is sensitive to background noise** = le modem est sensible au bruit de fond; *(cinema)* **background projection** = (procédé de) transparence *f* **(c)** *(system with low-priority)* non prioritaire or d'arrière-plan; **background job** = tâche *f* non prioritaire; **background printing** = impression *f* en arrière-plan; **background printing can be carried out whilst you are editing another document** = l'impression peut être exécutée en arrière-plan pendant que vous travaillez sur un autre document; **background program** = programme *m* non prioritaire; **background task** = tâche non prioritaire

◊ **background processing** *noun* **(a)** *(low priority job)* traitement *m* non prioritaire **(b)** *(not using the on-line capabilities)* traitement d'arrière-plan or de fond
NOTE: opposite is **foreground**

backing *noun & adjective* auxiliaire *(m&f)* **backing store** or **storage** or **memory** = mémoire *f* de masse or mémoire auxiliaire; **by adding another disk drive, I will increase the backing store capabilities** = je vais augmenter la capacité de mémoire auxiliaire en ajoutant un deuxième lecteur de disquettes; **paper tape is one of the slowest access backing stores** = la bande perforée est une des mémoires de rangement les plus lentes d'accès

backlit *adj (screen or display)* rétro-éclairé

backlog *noun* travail en retard or en attente or en souffrance; **the programmers can't deal with the backlog**

of **programming work =** les programmeurs ne réussissent pas à venir à bout de toute la programmation en retard; **the queue was too short for the backlog of tasks waiting to be processed** = la file d'attente trop courte ne suffisait pas à la série de tâches à traiter

back number *noun (of newspaper or magazine)* numéro *m* déjà paru *or* vieux numéro

back pack *noun (lightweight TV equipment)* équipement *m* de prise de vue portable sur le dos

backplane *noun* (circuits de) fond *m* de panier

back projection *noun (cinema)* (procédé de) transparence *f*

backscatter *noun (radio wave)* onde *f* (radio) réfléchie

backspace *noun (of cursor)* retour *m* arrière *or* rappel *m;* **backspace character** = caractère *m* de retour arrière *or* de rappel (du curseur); **backspace key** = touche *f* de retour arrière (du curseur); **if you make a mistake entering data, use the backspace key to correct it** = pour corriger une erreur de saisie de texte, utilisez la touche de retour arrière

backtrack *verb* aller à rebours *or* faire marche arrière

back up *verb* **(a)** *(to make a copy of a file or data or disk)* sauvegarder *or* faire une copie de sauvegarde; **the company accounts were backed up on disk as a protection against fire damage** = la comptabilité de la société avait été sauvegardée sur une disquette en cas d'incendie; **the program enables users to back up hard disk files with a single command** = ce programme permet de sauvegarder un fichier sur disque dur au moyen d'une seule commande **(b)** *(to help)* soutenir *or* supporter *or* étayer; **he brought along a file of documents to back up his claim** = il a apporté un dossier de documents pour étayer sa demande d'indemnisation; **the printout backed up his argument for a new system** = la sortie

d'imprimante lui a fourni la preuve qu'il fallait un nouveau système

◊ **backup** *adjective & noun* **(a)** *(which helps)* de secours *or* auxiliaire; **we offer a free backup service to customers =** nous offrons à nos clients un service d'assistance gratuit *or* un service après-vente gratuit; **battery backup =** pile *f or* alimentation *f* auxiliaire *or* de secours **(b)** **backup** *or* **backup copy =** (copie de) sauvegarde *f;* **backup file =** fichier *m* de sauvegarde; **the most recent backup copy is kept in the safe =** nous mettons toujours la plus récente sauvegarde dans le coffre fort; **backup procedure =** procédure *f* de sauvegarde; *(for volatile RAM chips)* **memory backup capacitor =** alimentation *f* de secours de la mémoire

QUOTE the system backs up at the rate of 2.5Mb per minute
Microcomputer News
QUOTE the previous version is retained, but its extension is changed to .BAK indicating that it's a back-up
Personal Computer World

Backus-Naur-Form (BNF)
convention *f* BNF *or* métalangage *m* BNF

backward *or* **backwards** *adjective & adverb* à rebours *or* de retour; **backward channel =** voie *f or* canal *m* de retour; **backward error correction =** correction *f* d'erreurs par retransmission; **backward mode =** mode *m* à rebours *or* marche *f* arrière; **backward recovery =** reconstitution *f* de procédure *or* récupération *f* de fichier à rebours; **backwards supervision =** contrôle *m* par le récepteur

bad break *noun* coupure *f* inappropriée

◊ **bad copy** *noun* texte *m or* manuscrit *m* inacceptable *or* illisible

◊ **bad sector** *noun* secteur *m* défectueux; **you will receive error messages when you copy files that are stored on bad sectors on a disk =** vous obtiendrez des messages d'erreur si vous essayez de copier des fichiers implantés sur des secteurs défectueux d'une disquette

badge reader *noun* lecteur *m* de badges; **a badge reader makes sure that only authorized personnel can gain**

access to a computer room = le lecteur de badges garantit que seules les personnes autorisées ont accès à la salle des ordinateurs

baffle *noun* (i) enceinte *f* acoustique; (ii) écran *m* *or* déflecteur *m* (de résonances parasites)

bag *noun (of elements)* éléments *mpl* en vrac

balance 1 *noun* **(a)** *(of text and graphics)* équilibre *m* *or* symétrie *f;* **the DTP package allows the user to see if the overall page balance is correct =** le logiciel de PAO permet à l'utilisateur de juger du bon équilibre *or* de la bonne disposition d'une page **(b)** *(stereophonic)* balance *f* **(c)** *(amplitude control in a stereo system)* balance; *(on cine film)* **balance stripe =** bande *f* d'équilibrage 2 *verb* équilibrer *or* égaliser; **balanced circuit =** circuit équilibré; **you must use a balanced circuit at the end of the line to prevent signal reflections =** il faut utiliser un circuit équilibré en fin de ligne pour éviter la réflexion des signaux; **balanced error =** erreur équilibrée *or* à valeur moyenne nulle; **balanced line =** ligne équilibrée

band *noun* **(a)** *(of frequencies)* bande *f* (de fréquences); **base band =** bande de base; **voice base band ranges from 20Hz to 15KHz =** la bande de base des fréquences vocales varie de 20Hz à 15KHz; **base band modem =** modem en bande de base; **do not use a base band modem with a normal phone line =** n'utilisez jamais un modem en bande de base sur une ligne téléphonique normale; **base band local area network =** réseau local en bande de base **(b)** *(on magnetic disk)* bande multipiste

◇ **banding** *noun (of an image)* **elastic banding =** recadrage *m* (d'une image sur l'écran); **elastic banding is much easier to control with a mouse =** le recadrage d'une image est plus facile à réaliser avec la souris

◇ **bandlimited** *adjective* (signal) filtré

◇ **bandpass filter** *noun* filtre *m* passe-bande

◇ **band printer** *noun* imprimante à bande

◇ **bandwidth** *noun* largeur *f* de bande (de fréquence); **telephone bandwidth is**

3100Hz = la largeur de bande d'un téléphone est de 3100Hz

bank *noun (collection of similar devices)* banque *f or* groupe *m or* bloc *m;* **a bank of minicomputers process all the raw data =** un groupe de mini-ordinateurs traite toutes les données brutes; **bank switching =** changement *m* de banque de mémoire *or* de bloc de mémoire; **memory bank =** banque de mémoire; **an add-on card has a 128Kb memory bank made up of 16 chips =** la carte d'extension possède une banque de mémoire de 128Ko constituée de 16 puces

banner *noun (newspapers)* **banner headlines =** gros titres *mpl* à la une *or* manchettes *fpl*

bar 1 *noun (thick line)* barre *f or* ligne *f or* trait *m; (printing rule)* filet *m* 2 *verb (to stop someone from doing something)* défendre *or* interdire; **to bar entry to a file =** interdire l'accès à un fichier

◇ **bar chart** *or* **bar graph** *noun* histogramme *m*

bar code *US* **bar graphics** *noun* code *m* (à) barres; **bar-code reader =** lecteur *m* (optique) de codes barres *or* stylo *m* optique

bar printer *noun* imprimante *f* à barres

barrel *noun* (i) (en forme de) tonneau *m or* baril *m* ; (ii) borne *f* (de raccordement)

◇ **barrel distortion** *noun (of lens)* distorsion *f* en barillet *or* en oreiller *or* médiane (des bordures)

◇ **barrel printer** *noun* imprimante *f* à cylindre *or* à tambour

barrier box *noun* boîtier *m* d'arrêt *or* d'isolation

baryta paper *noun* papier *m* baryté

base 1 *noun* **(a)** *(lowest or first position)* base *f* **(b)** *(collection of files)* base **(c)** *(initial or original position)* **base address =** adresse *f* de base; **base addressing =** adressage *m* relatif; *(frequency range)* **base band =** bande *f* de base; **base band modem =** modem *m* en bande de base;

base band local area network = réseau *m* local en bande de base; *(assembly language)* **base language** = langage *m* d'assemblage; *(printing)* **base line** = ligne *f* de base; *(in a CPU)* **base register** = registre *m* d'adresse *or* registre de base **(d)** *(number system)* **base 2** = base binaire *or* base 2; **base 8** = base octale *or* base 8; **base 10** = base décimale *or* base 10; **base 16** = base hexadécimale *or* base 16 **2** *verb (to calculate from)* (se) baser (sur); **we based our calculations on the basic keyboarding rate** = nous avons basé nos calculs *or* nos calculs sont basés sur la vitesse standard pour la saisie de texte; **based on** = basé, -ée sur; **based on last year's figures** = d'après les résultats de l'an dernier; **the price is based on estimates of keyboarding costs** = ce prix est basé sur diverses estimations des coûts de saisie; **disk-based system** = système utilisant un disque *or* des disquettes

BASIC = BEGINNER'S ALL-PURPOSE SYMBOLIC INSTRUCTION CODE langage *m* (de haut niveau) BASIC

basic *adjective* de base *or* fondamental, -e; **the basic architecture is the same for all models in this range** = l'architecture de base est la même pour tous les modèles de la gamme; **basic code** = code *m* élémentaire *or* de base; **basic control system (satellite) (BCS)** = système *m* satellite de base; **basic input/output operating system (BIOS)** = système *m* d'exploitation des entrées/sorties (adapté à chaque ordinateur) *or* système BIOS; **basic instruction** = instruction *f* de base *or* primitive; **basic mode link control** = protocole *m* standard de contrôle de liaisons; **basic operating system (BOS)** = système *m* d'exploitation de base; **basic telecommunications access method (BTAM)** = protocole *m* d'accès de télécommunications (britanniques) *or* méthode BTAM; *(for paper)* **basic weight** = poids *m* unitaire (d'une rame de papier)

◊ **basically** *adverb* en principe *or* fondamentalement; **the acoustic coupler is basically the same as a modem** = en principe, un coupleur acoustique est la même chose qu'un modem

◊ **basis** *noun* base *f*; **we calculated keyboarding costs on the basis of 5,500 keystrokes per hour** = le coût de la saisie

du texte a été établi sur une base de 5,500 frappes/heure

bass *noun & adjective (low sound)* (son) grave; **bass signal** = signal *m* de basse fréquence; *(knob)* **bass control** = contrôle *m* des (sons) graves; **bass driver** *or* **speaker** = haut-parleur *m* de basses fréquences *or* de graves; **bass response** = réponse *f* aux basses fréquences

batch 1 *noun* **(a)** *(group of items)* lot *m;* **the last batch of disk drives are faulty** = les lecteurs de disquettes du dernier lot sont défectueux **(b)** *(documents or tasks or data processed as a single unit)* paquet *m or* lot; **batch file** = fichier *m* de commandes; **this batch file is used to save time and effort when carrying out a routine task** = ce fichier de commandes est utilisé pour gagner du temps et de l'énergie lorsqu'on traite une routine; **(processing data in) batch mode** = mode de traitement par lots *or* par paquets; **batch region** = partition *f or* zone *f* de traitement par lots; **batch system** = système de traitement par lots *or* par paquets; **batch total** = total *m* par groupe *or* par lot **2** *verb* **(a)** *(to group data or tasks)* grouper; **batched communication** = communications *fpl* groupées **(b)** *(to put items together)* (re)grouper

◊ **batch number** *noun* numéro *m* de lot

◊ **batch processor** *noun* processeur *m* de traitement par lots *or* par paquets; **batch processing** = traitement *m* par lots *or* par paquets

battery *noun* pile *f or* batterie *f or* accu *m;* **battery backup** = pile *or* alimentation *f* auxiliaire *or* de secours; **battery-backed** = équipé, -ée d'une pile auxiliaire *or* de secours; **battery voltage level** = niveau *m* de tension *or* différence *f* de potentiel d'une pile

baud *noun* baud *m;* **baud rate** = débit *m or* vitesse *f* de transmission (en bauds); **the baud rate of the binary signal was 300 bits per second** = la vitesse de transmission (en bauds) du signal binaire était de 300 bits par seconde; **a modem with auto-baud scanner can automatically sense at which baud rate it should operate** = un modem équipé d'une reconnaissance de débit s'ajuste automatiquement à la vitesse à laquelle il doit fonctionner; **baud rate generator** =

adaptateur *m* de vitesse de transmission; **split baud rate modem =** modem *m* à deux vitesses (réception et émission); **the viewdata modem uses a 1200/75 split baud rate =** le modem viewdata reçoit à 1200 bauds et transmet à 75

Baudot code *noun* code *m* (télégraphique) Baudot

B box *noun* registre *m* secondaire

BBS = BULLETIN BOARD SYSTEM

BCC = BLOCK CHARACTER CHECK

BCD = BINARY CODED DECIMAL décimal codé binaire (DCB); **the BCD representation of decimal 8 is 1000 =** le code binaire du nombre décimal 8 est 1000; **BCD adder =** additionneur *m* binaire *or* additionneur DCB

BCH code = BOSE-CHANDHURI-HOCQUENGHEM CODE

BCPL *noun* langage *m* (de haut niveau) BCPL

BCS (a) = BRITISH COMPUTER SOCIETY **(b)** = BASIC CONTROL SYSTEM (SATELLITE)

bead *noun (small section of a program)* module *m or* sous-ensemble *m or* sous-programme *m or* fonction *f*

beam *noun* rayon *m or* rayonnement *m or* faisceau *m;* **the laser produces a thin beam of light =** le laser émet un mince rayon lumineux; **beam deflection =** déflexion *f* d'un rayon lumineux; **a magnetic field is used for beam deflection in a CRT =** dans un tube à rayons cathodiques, la déflexion du faisceau est effectuée par un champ magnétique; **beam diversity =** dédoublement *m* du faisceau; **beam splitter =** diviseur *m* optique; **beam width =** largeur *f* d'un faisceau *or* d'un lobe

beard *noun* talon *m* de caractère

beep 1 *noun (audible warning noise)* (tonalité) bip *m;* **the printer will make a**

beep when it runs out of paper = l'imprimante émet un bip pour avertir qu'il ne reste plus de papier **2** *verb* émettre *or* faire un bip; **the computer beeped when the wrong key was hit =** chaque fois qu'on appuyait sur la mauvaise touche, l'ordinateur émettait un bip

beginning *noun* commencement *m or* début *m;* **beginning of file (bof) =** (caractère de) début de fichier; **beginning of information mark (bim) =** marque *f* de début d'enregistrement; **beginning of tape (bot) marker =** marque de début de bande

Beginner's All-Purpose Symbolic Instruction Code (BASIC) *noun* langage *m* (de haut niveau) BASIC

bel *noun* bel *m*

bell character *noun* caractère *m* (de déclenchement) d'alarme *or* de signal sonore

below-the-line costs = *noun (TV crew & technicians)* frais *mpl* salariaux du personnel technique

benchmark *noun* **(a)** référence *f* **(b)** *(to test performance)* test *m* d'évaluation des performances *or* banc *m* d'essai *or* essai *m* comparatif; **the magazine gave the new program's benchmark test results =** la revue a publié les résultats du banc d'essai *or* du test d'évaluation des performances du nouveau programme
◊ **benchmark problem** *noun* test *m or* problème *m* d'étalonnage
◊ **benchmarking** *noun* étalonnage *m* des performances *or* évaluation *f* comparative des performances

Bernoulli box *noun* boîte *f* de Bernoulli

QUOTE I use a pair of Bernoulli boxes for back up and simply do a disk-to-disk copy
PC Business World

best fit *noun* meilleur choix *m*

bias *noun* **(a)** *(electrical reference level)* polarisation *f* **(b)** *(to minimize noise)* réducteur *m* de bruit *or* Dolby *m* **(c)** *(statistics)* écart *m*

◊ **biased** *adjective (electrical)* polarisé, -ée; *(orientated)* biaisé, -ée *or* partial, -e; **biased data** = données biaisées *or* orientées; *(in a floating point number)* **biased exponent** = exposant *m*

bibliographic *or* **bibliographical** *adjective* bibliographique; **bibliographical information** = notice *f* bibliographique

◊ **bibliography** *noun* **(a)** *(list of references)* bibliographie *f;* **he printed a bibliography at the end of each chapter** = il a placé une bibliographie à la fin de chaque chapitre **(b)** *(catalogue of books)* bibliographie *or* liste *f* bibliographique

bid *verb (of a computer)* demander (la ligne); **the terminal had to bid three times before there was a gap in transmissions on the network** = le terminal a dû demander trois fois la ligne avant d'obtenir un créneau sur le réseau

bi-directional *adjective* bidirectionnel, -elle; **bi-directional file transfer** = transfert de fichier bidirectionnel; **bi-directional bus** = bus bidirectionnel; **bi-directional printer** = imprimante bidirectionnelle

bifurcation *noun* bifurcation *f*

Big Blue *(informal)* la société IBM

billion *(one thousand million or one million million)* million *m* de millions; *US* milliard *m*

BIM = BEGINNING OF INFORMATION MARK

bin *noun (for paper)* bac *m* pour le papier (d'une imprimante); **lower bin** = bac inférieur; **upper bin** = bac supérieur

binary *adjective & noun* binaire; **binary adder** = additionneur *m* binaire; **binary arithmetic** = calcul *m* binaire; **binary bit** = bit *m;* **binary cell** = cellule *f* binaire; **binary chop** = *see* BINARY SEARCH; **binary code** = code *m* binaire; **binary coded characters** = caractères *mpl* codés binaires; **binary coded decimal (BCD)** =

décimal codé binaire (DCB); **binary counter** = compteur *m* binaire; **binary digit** *or* **bit** = bit *m* *or* chiffre *m* binaire *or* élément *m* binaire; **binary dump** = vidage *m* binaire; **binary encoding** = codage *m* binaire; **binary exponent** = exposant *m* binaire; **binary fraction** = fraction *f* binaire; **the binary fraction 0.011 is equal to one quarter plus one eighth (i.e. three eighths)** = la fraction binaire 0,011 est égale à un quart plus un huitième (ou trois huitièmes); **binary half adder** = demi-additionneur *m* binaire; **binary loader** = chargeur *m* binaire; **binary mantissa** = mantisse *f* binaire; **binary notation** *or* **representation** = notation *f* binaire; **binary number** = nombre *m* binaire; *(operation on two operands or on an operand in binary form)* **binary operation** = opération *f* binaire; **binary point** = virgule *f* binaire; **binary scale** = échelle *f* binaire; **in a four bit word, the binary scale is 1,2,4,8** = dans un mot à quatre bits, l'échelle binaire est 1,2,4,8; **binary search** *or* **chop** = recherche *f* (par coupe) binaire *or* recherche dichotomique *or* par dichotomie; **binary sequence** = séquence *f* binaire; **binary signalling** = transmission *f* de signaux en binaire; **binary synchronous communications (BSC)** = communication *f* synchrone binaire; **binary system** = système *m* binaire; **binary-to-decimal conversion** = conversion *f* binaire-décimale; **binary tree** = arbre *m* binaire; **binary variable** = variable *f* binaire

> QUOTE with this type of compression you can only retrieve words by scanning the list sequentially, rather than by faster means such as a binary search
> *Practical Computing*

binaural *adjective* biaural, -e *or* binaural, -e

bind *verb* **(a)** *(to link)* établir des liens; *(address)* associer; **binding time** = temps *m* d'association (d'une adresse) **(b)** *(book)* relier; **the book is bound in laminated paper** = c'est un livre avec couverture pelliculée; **a paperbound book** = un livre broché; **the sheets have been sent to the bindery for binding** = les feuilles ont été envoyées à la reliure NOTE: **binding - bound**

◊ **binder** *noun* relieur, -euse

◊ **bindery** *noun* (atelier de) reliure

◊ **binding** *noun* **(a)** (l'art de) la reliure **(b)** *(cover of a book)* reliure *or* couverture *f*; **the book has a soft plastic binding =** c'est un livre avec couverture plastique souple

BIOS = BASIC INPUT/OUTPUT SYSTEM

biosensor *noun* capteur *m or* électrode *f or* sonde *f*; **the nerve activity can be measured by attaching a biosensor to your arm =** l'activité nerveuse peut se mesurer en plaçant une électrode sur le bras

bipolar *adjective* bipolaire; **bipolar coding =** codage *m* bipolaire; **bipolar junction transistor (BJT) =** transistor *m* à jonction bipolaire; **bipolar signal =** signal *m* bipolaire; **bipolar transistor =** transistor bipolaire

biquinary code *noun* code *m* biquinaire

bistable *adjective* bistable; **bistable circuit** *or* **multivibrator =** circuit *m or* multivibrateur *m* bistable *or* bascule *f*

bit *noun* **(a)** = BINARY DIGIT bit *m or* élément *m or* nombre *m* binaire **(b)** *(smallest unit of data)* bit; **bit addressing =** adressage *m* binaire; **bit density =** densité *f* binaire; **bit handling =** traitement *m* du bit; **bit manipulation =** manipulation *f* binaire; **bit pattern =** arrangement *f* binaire; **bit position =** position *f* binaire; **bit rate =** débit *m* binaire; **bit slice design =** architecture de (processeur) *m* en tranches; **the bit slice design uses four 4-bit word processors to construct a 16-bit processor =** le processeur en tranches utilise quatre processeurs à 4 bits pour réaliser un processeur à 16 bits; **least significant bit (LSB) =** bit de poids faible; **most significant bit (MSB) =** bit de poids fort *or* bit significatif; **bit stream =** flot *m or* train *m* de bits; **bit stuffing =** remplissage *m or* garnissage *m* de bits; *(on a magnetic disk)* **bit track =** piste *f* (de données binaires); **bits per inch (bpi) =** (nombre de) bits par pouce; **bits per second (bps) =** (nombre de) bits par seconde (bps); **their transmission rate is 60,000 bits per second (bps) through a parallel connection =** leur débit est de 60 000 bits par seconde sur une liaison parallèle; **check bit =** bit de contrôle *or* clé *f* de contrôle; **mask bit =** masque *m* binaire; **sign bit =** bit de signe

◊ **bit-map** *verb* définir une table d'adressage binaire; **bit-mapped graphics =** infographie *f* par points *or* à adressage binaire

QUOTE it became possible to store more than one bit per pixel
Practical Computing
QUOTE the expansion cards fit into the PC's expansion slot and convert bit-mapped screen images to video signals
Publish
QUOTE it is easy to turn any page into a bit-mapped graphic
PC Business World
QUOTE microcomputers invariably use raster-scan cathode ray tube displays, and frequently use a bit-map to store graphic images
Soft

BJT = BIPOLAR JUNCTION TRANSISTOR

black *adjective* noir, -e; **black and white =** noir et blanc; *(screen)* monochrome; **black box =** boîte *f* noire; **black crush =** conversion *f* monochrome (d'une image couleur); **black level =** niveau *m* de noir

◊ **blackboard** *noun* tableau *m* noir; **electronic blackboard =** tableau noir électronique

◊ **blackout** *or* **black out** *noun (complete loss of electrical power)* coupure *f* (de courant) *or* panne *f* d'électricité *or* panne de secteur

◊ **black writer** *noun* imprimante *f* à définition des noirs; *compare* WHITE WRITER

blank 1 *adjective* blanc, blanche; **blank character =** caractère d'espace; **blank instruction =** instruction *f* de remplissage; **blank tape** *or* **blank disk =** bande *f* vierge *or* disque *m* vierge; **blank string =** (i) chaîne vide; (ii) chaîne *m* contenant des caractères d'espace **2** *noun* blanc *m or* case *f* vide; **fill in the blanks and insert the form into the OCR =** complétez le formulaire et introduisez-le dans le lecteur optique

◊ **blanking** *noun* suppression *f or* inhibition *f* du signal; **blanking interval =** délai *m* de retour du signal en fin d'écran; **blanking pulse =** impulsion *f* d'inhibition du signal; **line blanking interval** = délai *m* de retour de ligne

blanket cylinder   *noun* cylindre *m* porte-blanchet

◊ **blanketing** *noun* couverture *f* (d'une émission) *or* brouillage *m* (de la réception)

blast *verb* **(a)** brûler (une PROM) *or* programmer (une PROM) **(b)** libérer une partie de la mémoire *or* désallouer (une ressource)

◊ **blast-through alphanumerics** *noun* caractères *mpl* éclatés (sur un écran vidéotex)

bleed *noun (printing)* bavure *f*

◊ **bled off** *adjective* à fond(s) perdu(s); **the photo is bled off** = la photo est à fond perdu

bleep 1 *noun* bip *m or* signal *m* sonore; **the printer will make a bleep when it runs out of paper** = s'il n'y a plus de papier l'imprimante émet un bip **2** *verb* émettre *or* faire un bip; *see also* BEEP

◊ **bleeper** *noun* avertisseur *m* (pour recherche de personne); **he is in the factory somewhere - we'll try to find him on his bleeper** = il doit être quelque part dans l'usine, nous essaierons de le joindre par son avertisseur

blind *adjective* aveugle; **blind dialling** = transmission *f* en aveugle *or* sans décrochage; **blind keyboard** = clavier *m* aveugle

B-line counter *noun* registre *m* auxillaire de routage d'adresse

blinking *noun* clignotement *m or* papillotement *m*

blister pack *noun* blister *m or* emballage *m* bulle

block 1 *noun* **(a)** bloc *m;* **block character check (BCC)** = contrôle *m* de blocs de caractères; **block code** = code *m* de contrôle de bloc; **block compaction** = compactage *m or* compression *f* de bloc; **block copy** = copie d'un bloc (de texte); **block delete** = effacer en bloc; **block error rate** = taux *m* d'erreur par bloc;

block header = en-tête *m* de bloc; *(when corrupt data are present)* **block ignore character** = caractère *m* de rejet d'un bloc (dont les données sont mauvaises); **block input processing** = traitement *m* de contrôle de bloc à l'entrée; **block length** = longueur *f or* taille *f* d'un bloc; **block list** = fichier *m* d'enregistrement des blocs; **block mark** = marque *f* de sélection d'un bloc; **block operation** = manipulation *f* de blocs; **block parity** = (contrôle de) parité *f* d'un bloc; **block retrieval** = recherche *f or* extraction *f* de bloc; **block synchronization** = synchronisation *f* de blocs; **block transfer** = transfert *m or* insertion *f* d'un bloc *or* d'un paragraphe; **building block** = élément *m or* module *m;* **data block** = bloc de données; **end of block (EOB)** = (marque de) fin *f* de bloc; **interblock gap (IBG)** = espace *m* interbloc **(b)** *(wide printed bar)* bloc; **block diagram** = graphe *m or* ordinogramme *m* à pavés **(c)** **block capitals** *or* **block letters** = (lettres) majuscules *fpl or* (lettres) capitales *fpl;* **write your name and address in block letters** = écrivez votre nom et votre adresse en capitales *or* en majuscules **2** *verb* **(a)** *(to stop)* empêcher *or* bloquer *or* faire opposition (à); **the system manager blocked his request for more CPU time** = le directeur du système a fait opposition à sa demande de temps supplémentaire sur l'unité centrale **(b) to block in** = esquisser (un design)

◊ **blocking factor** *noun (records in a block)* facteur *m* (de) bloc

bloom *noun* tache *f* lumineuse sur l'écran

bloop *verb* démagnétiser

blow *verb* **(a)** *(fuse)* faire sauter (les plombs) **(b)** charger une PROM

blueprint *noun* (i) spécifications *fpl* ; (ii) plan *m or* épure *f*

◊ **blue-ribbon program** *noun (informal)* programme *m* canon (qui tourne sans erreur du premier coup)

blur 1 *noun* flou *m* **2** *verb* rendre flou; **the image becomes blurred when you turn the focus knob** = en tournant le bouton de mise au point l'image devient floue *or* perd de sa netteté

bn = BILLION

BNC = Bayonet Network Connector

BNF = BACKUS-NAUR-FORM

board *noun* **(a)** *(for printed circuit)* carte *f or* plaque(tte) *f* (présensibilisée) pour circuit imprimé; **bulletin board system (BBS)** = messagerie *f or* tableau *m* d'affichage électronique; **bus board** = carte bus *or* carte connecteur; **daughter board** = carte fille; **expansion board** *or* **add-on board** = carte d'extension; **motherboard** = carte mère; **printed circuit board (PCB)** = (carte de) circuit *m* imprimé **(b)** *(people who run company, etc.)* conseil *m* d'administration *or* directoire *m;* **editorial board** = la rédaction

> QUOTE both models can be expanded to the current maximum of the terminals by adding further serial interface boards
> *Micro Decision*

body *noun (of text)* corps *m;* **body size** = *(of text)* dimension *f* (en points) du corps d'un texte; *(of character)* corps *m* (d'un caractère); **body type** = caractères *m* utilisés pour le corps d'un texte

bof = BEGINNING OF FILE

boilerplate *noun* document *m* monté *or* créé (à partir de paragraphes standard) ◊ **boilerplating** *noun* montage *m* d'un document (à partir de paragraphes standard)

bold *adjective & noun* gras, grasse; **bold face** = caractère *m* gras

bomb 1 *verb (informal - of software)* (faire) sauter *or* (se) planter; **the program bombed, and we lost all the data** = le programme s'est planté et nous avons perdu toutes les données; **the system can bomb if you set up several desk accessories or memory-resident programs at the same time** = vous pouvez faire sauter le système si vous installez en même temps plusieurs accessoires de bureau ou programmes résidents **2** *noun* bombe *f;* **logic bomb** = bombe logique; **the system programmer installed a logic bomb when they made him redundant** = le programmeur système a installé une bombe logique lorsqu'il a été licencié

bond paper *noun* papier *m* à lettre commercial

book 1 *noun* livre *m; they can print books of up to 96 pages* = ils peuvent imprimer des livres qui ont jusqu'à 96 pages; **the book is available in paperback and hard cover** = ce livre existe en édition brochée et en édition cartonnée ◊ **booklet** *noun* livret *m or* prospectus *m or* brochure *f* ◊ **bookseller** *noun* libraire *m&f* ◊ **bookshop** *noun* librairie *f* ◊ **bookstall** *noun* kiosque *m* (à livres) ◊ **bookstore** *noun* US librairie ◊ **bookwork** *noun* **(a)** *(keeping of financial records)* comptabilité *f or* tenue *f* de livres **(b)** *(printing and binding of books)* imprimerie *f* et reliure

Boolean algebra *or* **Boolean logic** *noun* algèbre *f* booléenne *or* algèbre de Boole ◊ **Boolean connective** *noun* relation *f* booléenne ◊ **Boolean operation** *noun* opération booléenne; **Boolean operation table** = table *f* de Boole *or* table *f* de vérité; **monadic Boolean operation** = opération booléenne monadique *or* à un opérande; **dyadic Boolean operation** = opération booléenne dyadique *or* à deux opérandes; **Boolean operator** = opérateur *m* booléen; **Boolean value** = valeur *f* booléenne; **Boolean variable** = variable *f* booléenne

boom *noun (of microphone)* perche *f*

boost 1 *noun* encouragement *m or* augmentation *f;* **the prize was a real boost** = le prix a été un réel encouragement; **the new model gave a boost to the sales figures** = le nouveau modèle a fait monter les chiffres de vente **2** *verb* augmenter *or* gonfler; **the extra hard disk will boost our storage capacity by 25Mb** = le disque dur supplémentaire va augmenter *or* gonfler la capacité de mémoire de 25Mo

boot *verb* exécuter des commandes (à la mise sous tension) *or* amorcer un système ◊ **bootup** *or* **booting** *noun (of system)* amorçage *m or* lancement *m*

bootleg *noun* copie *f* illégale *or* piratée

bootstrap (loader) *noun* amorce *nf or* programme *m* d'amorçage *or* de lancement (d'un système)

QUOTE the digital signal processor includes special on-chip bootstrap hardware to allow easy loading of user programs into the program RAM
Electronics & Wireless World

booth *noun* cabine *f;* **telephone booth =** cabine téléphonique

border *noun* bordure *f or* cadre *m or* encadrement *m*

borrow *verb* **(a)** emprunter (de l'argent *or* un livre); **she borrowed a book on computer construction =** elle a emprunté un livre sur la fabrication des ordinateurs **(b)** *(in subtraction)* emprunter

BOS = BASIC OPERATING SYSTEM

Bose-Chandhuri-Hocquenghem code (BCH) *noun* code *m* BCH

bot *or* **BOT** = BEGINNING OF TAPE; **BOT marker =** marque *f* de début de bande

bottom *noun* bas *m; (of page)* **bottom space =** bas de page *or* blanc *m* de pied
◊ **bottom up method** *noun* conception *f* ascendante (d'un programme)

bounce *noun (of key)* rebond *m* (d'une touche de clavier); **de-bounce =** *(on keyboard)* (dispositif) antirebond *m*

boundary *noun* limites *fpl;* **boundary protection =** protection *f* des limites (de mémoire); **boundary punctuation =** marquage *m* de limites (d'un fichier); **boundary register =** registre *m* (d'adresses) de limites

bounds *noun* bornes *fpl or* limites *fpl;* **array bounds =** limites *fpl* de tableau

box *noun* **(a)** *(container)* boîte *f;* **the keyboard is packed in expanded polystyrene before being put into the box** = le clavier est emballé dans du polystyrène expansé avant d'être mis dans son carton; **black box =** boîte noire **(b) letter box =** boîte à *or* aux lettres **(c)** *(around text or illustration)* cadre *m;* **the comments and quotations are printed in boxes =** les commentaires et les citations sont dans des cadres *or* sont encadrés
◊ **box in** *verb* encadrer

BPI *or* **bpi** = BITS PER INCH

BPS *or* **bps** = BITS PER SECOND

bracket 1 *noun* **round brackets =** parenthèse(s) *f(pl);* **square bracket(s) =** crochet(s) *m(pl)* **2** *verb* **to bracket together =** (i) (re)grouper; (ii) mettre entre parenthèses *or* entre crochets
◊ **bracketed** *adjective* (caractère) avec empattements elzéviriens
◊ **bracketing** *noun* photographie *f* de la même scène avec plusieurs ouvertures

Braille *noun* (écriture) Braille; **she was reading a Braille book =** elle lisait un livre en (caractères) Braille; **the book has been published in Braille =** il existe une édition en Braille de ce livre; **Braille marks =** caractères *mpl* Braille

branch 1 *noun* **(a)** branche *f;* **branch instruction =** instruction *f* de branchement *or* de saut; **program branch =** branche *f* d'un programme **(b)** *(of network)* branchement *m;* **the faulty station is on this branch =** le poste défectueux est connecté sur ce branchement **2** *verb* brancher
◊ **branchpoint** *noun* point *m* de branchement

breadboard *noun* boîte *f* de connexion (sans soudure)

break 1 *noun (of program execution)* interruption *f* **2** *verb* **(a)** *(to decipher)* déchiffrer; **he finally broke the cipher system =** il a finalement réussi à déchiffrer le code *or* il a finalement trouvé la clé du code **(b) to break into a database =** piller une base de données
NOTE: **breaking - broke - has broken**
◊ **break down** *verb (to stop working)* tomber en panne; **the modem has broken**

down = ce modem ne fonctionne pas *or* est en dérangement *or* en panne; **what do you do when your line printer breaks down?** = que faut-il faire quand l'imprimante ligne tombe en panne?

◊ **breakdown** *noun* panne *f;* **we cannot communicate with our New York office because of the breakdown of the telex lines** = nous ne pouvons pas joindre notre bureau à New York à cause d'une panne des lignes de télex

◊ **breaker** *noun* **circuit breaker** = coupe-circuit *m or* interrupteur *m or* disjoncteur *m*

◊ **breakpoint** *noun (control point)* point *m* d'arrêt *or* d'interruption; **breakpoint instruction** *or* **halt** = instruction *f* d'arrêt (dans un programme); **breakpoint symbol** = symbole *m* d'arrêt (dynamique)

◊ **breakup** *noun* coupure *f or* perte *f or* distorsion *f* d'un signal

breezeway *noun* intervalle *m* de garde

B register *noun* registre *m* (d'adresse) indexé

bridge *or* **bridging product** *noun* **(a)** *(communications equipment)* dérivation *f or* pont *m* **(b)** *(between old and new systems)* équipement *m or* logiciel *m* de transition *or* passerelle *f;* **a bridging product is available for companies with both generations of machines** = une passerelle est fournie aux entreprises qui disposent des deux générations d'équipement

◊ **bridgeware** *noun* équipement *m or* logiciel *m* de transition *or* passerelle *f*

◊ **bridging** *noun* (i) mise en place d'une dérivation; (ii) transfert de programme avec l'aide d'une passerelle

brightness *noun* luminosité *f or* brillance *f;* **a control knob allows you to adjust brightness and contrast** = un bouton vous permet de régler la luminosité et les contrastes; **the brightness of the monitor can hurt the eyes** = une trop forte brillance peut causer une fatigue oculaire; **brightness range** = niveaux *mpl* de luminosité

QUOTE there is a brightness control on the front panel
Micro Decision

brilliant *adjective* brillant, -e; **the background colour is a brilliant red** = le fond est d'un rouge brillant; **he used brilliant white for the highlights** = il utilise un blanc brillant pour les mises en valeur

◊ **brilliance** *noun* brillance *f*

British Standards Institute (BSI) *(British equivalent of)* Association française de normalisation (AFNOR)

broadband *noun* large bande *f;* **broadband radio** = radio à large bande

broadcast **1** *noun* diffusion *f* radiophonique *or* radiodiffusion *f;* **broadcast homes** = foyers qui possèdent au moins un poste de télévision ou de radio; **broadcast network** = réseau *m* de radiodiffusion; **broadcast satellite technique** = technique *f* de diffusion par satellite **2** *verb* (radio)diffuser; **he broadcast the latest news over the radio** *or* **over the WAN** = il a diffusé les dernières informations à la radio *or* via le réseau étendu; **broadcasting station** = station *f* de radio

broadsheet *noun (printing)* placard *m*

broadside *noun* US prospectus *m* publicitaire

brochure *noun* brochure *f or* prospectus *m* (publicitaire); **we sent off for a brochure about maintenance services** = nous avons demandé une brochure sur les services de maintenance

bromide *or* **bromide print** *noun* **(a)** bromure *m;* **in 24 hours we had bromides ready to film** = 24 heures plus tard nous avions reçu les bromures et pouvions faire les films **(b)** *(lithographic plate used for proofing)* bromure

brown-out *noun* baisse *f or* chute *f* de courant

browse *verb (database material)* consulter une base de données sans autorisation

brute force method *noun* méthode *f* brutale

BSC = BINARY SYNCHRONOUS COMMUNICATIONS

BSI = BRITISH STANDARDS INSTITUTE

BTAM = BASIC TELECOMMUNICATIONS ACCESS METHOD

bubble memory *noun* mémoire *f* à bulles (magnétiques); **bubble memory cassette** = cassette *f* mémoire à bulles (magnétiques)

◊ **bubble sort** *noun* tri *m* par permutation (de paires *or* de bulles)

bucket *noun* emplacement *m* de rangement (en mémoire)

buckling *noun (of film)* gondolage *m*

buffer 1 *noun* **(a)** *(circuit)* (circuit) tampon *m* **(b)** *(temporary storage area for data)* (mémoire) tampon *m;* **buffer register** = registre *m* tampon; **buffer size** = taille *f* de mémoire tampon; **data buffer** = (mémoire) tampon de données; **dynamic** *or* **elastic buffer** = tampon dynamique *or* variable; **I/O buffer** = mémoire tampon d'entrée/sortie; **printer buffer** = tampon d'imprimante **2** *verb* utiliser une mémoire tampon; **buffered input/output** = entrée/sortie utilisant une mémoire tampon; **buffered memory** = mémoire avec tampon; **buffering** = utilisation de mémoire tampon; **double buffering** = utilisation de double mémoire tampon

> QUOTE the speed is enhanced by the 8K RAM printer buffer included
> QUOTE the software allocates a portion of cache as a print buffer to restore program control faster after sending data to the printer
> *Which PC?*

bug 1 *noun* **(a)** *(in software)* erreur *f or* bogue *m or* bug *m; (temporary correction made to a program)* **bug patches** = rustine *f or* replâtrage *m* **(b)** *(hidden microphone)* micro *m* espion *or* micro-espion *m or* dispositif *m* de surveillance **2** *verb* placer un micro espion *or* surveiller par micro espion; **the conference room was bugged** = il y avait des micros-espions dans la salle de conférence

buggy *noun (small computer-controlled vehicle)* chariot *m* piloté par ordinateur

building block *noun (self-contained unit to form a system)* élément *m or* module *m*

built-in *adjective* intégré, -ée *or* incorporé, -ée; **the built-in adapter card makes it fully IBM compatible** = la carte adaptateur intégrée rend l'appareil compatible IBM; **the computer has a built-in hard disk** = l'ordinateur est équipé d'un disque dur intégré; **built-in check** = système de contrôle intégré; **built-in function** = fonction incorporée

◊ **built into** *adjective* incorporé, -ée; **there are communications ports built into all modems** = tous les modems possèdent des ports de communication intégrés

NOTE: opposite is **add-on**

bulk *noun* grande quantité *or* masse *f;* **in bulk** = en vrac *or* en grande quantité *or* en masse; **bulk erase** = effacement *m* en masse; **bulk storage medium** = support *m* de stockage de grande capacité; **magnetic tape is a reliable bulk storage medium** = la bande magnétique constitue un support de stockage de grande capacité très sûr; *(for videotex)* **bulk update terminal** = terminal *m* de mise à jour rapide

bullet *noun* **(a)** vignette *f or* point *m* indicateur de couleur **(b)** *(placée devant chaque élément d'une liste imprimée)* puce *f*

bulletin board system (BBS) *noun* messagerie *f or* tableau *m* d'affichage électronique

bundle *noun (of optic fibres)* faisceau *m* de fibres optiques

◊ **bundled software** *noun* logiciel *m* inclus à l'achat d'un ordinateur

bureau *noun* bureau *m or* société *f* de services; **the company offers a number of bureau services, such as printing and data collection** = la société offre, entre autres, des services d'imprimerie et de saisie de données; **our data manipulation is handled by a bureau** = nous faisons faire la manipulation de données par une société de services informatiques; **computer bureau** = société de services et d'ingénierie informatique (SSII); **word-processing bureau** = société de traitement de texte; **we farm out the office typing to a local bureau** = nous confions notre correspondance à un bureau de secrétariat local

NOTE: the plural is **bureaux**

burner *noun* programmeur *m* de ROM *or* de mémoire morte

◊ **burn-in** *noun (for electronic components)* test *m* à chaud

◊ **burn in** *verb* **(a)** *(television or monitor screen)* faire un brûlage *m* d'écran **(b)** *(PROM chip)* graver *or* programmer

◊ **burn out** *noun (electronic circuit or device)* panne *f* par échauffement

burst *noun (signals)* rafale *f or* paquet *m or* burst *m;* **burst mode** = mode *m* de transmission de données par paquets *or* par rafales; *(TV)* **colour burst** = rafale de signaux couleur; *(consecutive errors in a transmission)* **error burst** = rafale *f* d'erreurs *or* série *f* d'erreurs consécutives

burster *noun (for paper)* rupteur *m or* séparateur *m or* éclateur *m* (de feuilles)

bus *noun* **(a)** bus *m;* **address bus** = bus d'adresses; **bi-directional bus** = bus bi-directionnel; **bus address lines** = voies de liaison d'un bus d'adresses; **bus arbitration** = arbitrage *m or* gestion *f* de (l'utilisation d'un) bus; **bus board** = carte *f* bus; **bus control lines** = lignes *fpl* de contrôle; **bus data lines** = lignes de transmission de données; **bus driver** = amplificateur *m* de courant (du bus); **bus master** = (émetteur de données) maître *m* d'un bus; **bus network** = réseau *m* de type bus; **bus slave** = (puits *or* collecteur de données) asservi à un bus *or* esclave *m* d'un bus; **bus structure** = structure *f* d'un bus; **control bus** = bus de contrôle; **daisy chain bus** = bus série *or* bus de chaîne; **data bus** = bus de données; **dual bus system** = système *m* à bus double *or* à bus auxiliaire; **input/output data bus (I/O bus)** = bus d'entrée/sortie; **memory bus** = bus de mémoire **(b)** carte connecteur *or* bus central

QUOTE mice can either be attached to the PC bus *or* a serial port
PC Business World
QUOTE both buses can be software controlled to operate as either a 16- or 32-bit interface
Electronics & Power

business *noun* **(a)** *(activity)* affaires *fpl;* **business computer** = ordinateur *m* de bureau; **business efficiency exhibition** = salon *m* de la bureautique; **business system** *or* **business package** = logiciel comptabilité/gestion *or* logiciel bureautique **(b)** *(company)* entreprise *f;* **he owns a small computer repair business** = il possède une petite entreprise de réparation d'ordinateurs; **he set up in business as an computer consultant** = il a ouvert son propre bureau d'ingénieur conseil en informatique

busy *adjective* **(a)** *(machine)* (appareil) en service; *(tone or signal)* (signal *or* tonalité) occupé, -ée; **when the busy line goes low, the printer will accept more data** = quand le signal 'occupé' s'éteint, l'imprimante peut de nouveau accepter des données; **the line is busy** = la ligne est occupée **(b)** *(background to a film shot)* fond *m* animé

buzz 1 *noun* vibration *f* sonore **2** *verb* émettre une vibration sonore *or* sonner

◊ **buzzer** *noun* buzzer *m or* sonnerie *f* d'avertissement *or* vibreur *m* sonore

◊ **buzzword** *noun (informal)* mot *m* à la mode *or* mot du jour

bypass *noun* dérivation *f;* **there is an automatic bypass around any faulty equipment** = il y a dérivation automatique lorsqu'une des machines tombe en panne

byte *noun* octet *m;* **byte addresses** = adresses *fpl* d'octets; *(variable word length computer)* **byte machine** = processeur *m* à mots variables; **byte manipulation** = manipulation *f* d'octets; *(familiar)* bidouillage *m* du bit; **byte serial transmission** *or* **mode** = transmission d'octets en série

QUOTE if you can find a way of packing two eight-bit values into a single byte, you save substantial amounts of RAM or disk space
Practical Computing

Cc

C langage *m* C

C représentation hexadécimale du nombre 12 *or* C

cable 1 *noun* **(a)** câble *m or* cordon *m or* fil *m* de liaison; **cable télévision** *or* **cable TV** = télévision câblée *or* le câble; **cable TV relay station** = relais *m* de télévision câblée **(b)** *(telegram)* câble *m or* télégramme *m;* **he sent a cable to his office asking for more money** = il a envoyé un télégramme au bureau pour redemander de l'argent; **cable address** = adresse *f* télégraphique **2** *verb* télégraphier *or* câbler *or* envoyer un câble *or* un télégramme; **he cabled his office to ask them to send more money** = il a envoyé un câble au bureau pour redemander de l'argent; **the office cabled him £1,000 to cover his expenses** = le bureau lui a envoyé un mandat télégraphique de 1000 livres sterling pour couvrir ses frais

◊ **cablegram** *noun* câblogramme *m*

◊ **cabling** *noun* *(cable as a material)* câblage *m or* câbles *mpl or* réseau *m* câblé; **using high-quality cabling will allow the user to achieve very high data transfer rates** = les câbles de haute qualité vont permettre à l'utilisateur d'obtenir un taux de transfert de données très élevé; **cabling costs up to £1 a foot** = le câble peut coûter jusqu'à 1 livre sterling les 30cm

cache 1 *noun* **cache memory** = antémémoire *f or* mémoire *f* cache ; **file access time is much quicker if the most frequently used data is stored in cache memory** = le temps d'accès est réduit lorsque les données les plus fréquemment utilisées sont placées dans la mémoire cache; **instruction cache** = antémémoire d'instruction **2** *verb*

stocker dans la mémoire cache; **this program can cache any size font** = ce programme peut stocker une police de caractères, quelle qu'en soit la taille, dans la mémoire cache

CAD = COMPUTER AIDED DESIGN *or* COMPUTER ASSISTED DESIGN conception *or* création assistée par ordinateur *or* CAO; **all our engineers design on CAD workstations** = tous nos ingénieurs travaillent sur des stations de CAO; **CAD/CAM** = COMPUTER AIDED DESIGN/COMPUTER AIDED MANUFACTURE *see also* COMPUTER AIDED

CAI = COMPUTER AIDED INSTRUCTION *or* COMPUTER ASSISTED INSTRUCTION

CAL = COMPUTER AIDED LEARNING *or* COMPUTER ASSISTED LEARNING

calculate *verb* **(a)** calculer; **the DP manager calculated the rate for keyboarding** = le directeur du centre de traitement a calculé le coût de saisie de texte sur clavier; **you need to calculate the remaining disk space** = vous devez calculer l'espace libre sur la disquette **(b)** *(to estimate)* calculer *or* juger *or* estimer; **I calculate that we have six months' stock left** = j'estime que nous avons du stock pour six mois encore

◊ **calculation** *noun* calcul *m;* **rough calculation** = approximation *f or* calcul approximatif; **I made some rough calculations on the back of an envelope** = j'ai fait un calcul approximatif au dos d'une enveloppe; **according to my calculations, we have six months' stock left =** d'après mes calculs, il nous reste du stock pour six mois

◊ **calculator** *noun* calculatrice *f or* calculette *f;* **my pocket calculator needs a new battery =** j'ai besoin d'une pile pour ma calculatrice de poche; **he worked out the discount on his calculator =** il a calculé la remise sur sa calculatrice

calibration *noun* calibrage *m or* étalonnage *m*

call 1 *noun* **(a)** *(telephone)* appel *m or* communication *f;* **call diverter =** dispositif de réacheminement *or* de déroutage d'appel; **call forwarding =** transfert *m* d'appel (automatique); **we are having all calls forwarded from the office to home =** nous avons demandé le transfert à la maison des appels que nous recevons au bureau; **local call =** communication urbaine; **long-distance call** *or* **trunk call =** communication interurbaine; **person-to-person call =** communication avec préavis; **transferred charge call** *US* **collect call =** appel en PCV; **to log calls =** enregistrer le nombre et la durée des appels; **to make a call =** appeler quelqu'un (au téléphone) *or* téléphoner (à quelqu'un); **to take a call =** répondre au téléphone **(b)** *(computer)* appel (d'un programme); **call accepted signal =** signal *m* d'appel accepté *or* d'acceptation d'appel; **call control signal =** signal *m* de contrôle d'appel; **call duration =** durée *f* d'un appel; **call duration depends on the complexity of the transaction =** la durée de l'appel varie suivant la complexité de la transaction; **charges are related to call duration =** le prix est fonction de la durée de l'appel; **call instruction =** instruction *f* d'appel; **the subroutine call instruction should be at this point =** c'est ici qu'il faudrait introduire l'instruction d'appel **2** *verb* **(a)** téléphoner à quelqu'un *or* appeler quelqu'un; **I'll call you at your office tomorrow =** je vous appellerai au bureau demain; **called party =** correspondant, -e **(b)** *(computer)* appeler un programme *or* un sous-programme *or* une routine

◊ **call box** *noun* cabine *f* téléphonique

◊ **caller** *noun* personne qui fait un appel téléphonique *or* demandeur *m*

◊ **call in** *verb* contacter (son bureau) par téléphone; **we ask the representatives to call in every Friday =** nous demandons aux représentants de communiquer par téléphone, chaque vendredi

◊ **calling** *noun* signal *m* d'appel; **calling sequence =** séquence *f* d'appel; **calling unit =** unité *f or* système *m* d'appel

◊ **call up** *verb* appeler *or* rappeler *or* afficher à l'écran; **all the customers addresses were called up =** on a affiché à l'écran les adresses de tous les clients; **call up the previous file =** rappelez le fichier précédent à l'écran; **after an input is received, the first function is called up =** dès réception de l'entrée, on appelle la première fonction

callier effect *noun* effet *m* Callier *or* le flare

calligraphy *noun* calligraphie *f*

CAM (a) = COMPUTER AIDED MANUFACTURE *or* COMPUTER ASSISTED MANUFACTURING **(b) =** CONTENT ADDRESSABLE MEMORY

Cambridge ring *noun* (réseau en) anneau *m* de Cambridge

camcorder *noun* Caméscope® *m*

cameo *noun* **(a)** impression inversée *or* blanc sur noir **(b)** *(on film)* contre-jour *m*

camera *noun (still photos)* appareil *m* photographique *or* appareil photo; *(film)* caméra *f; (TV)* caméra de télévision; **camera chain =** ensemble *m* caméra; **camera-ready copy (crc) =** copie *f* finalisée *or* prête à reproduire

CAN = CANCEL CHARACTER

cancel *verb* annuler; **cancel character (CAN) =** caractère *m* d'annulation; **the software automatically sends a cancel character after any error =** le logiciel envoie automatiquement un caractère d'annulation à chaque erreur; *(in book)* **cancel page =** page *m* corrigée qui en remplace une autre

◊ **cancellation** *noun* annulation *f*

candela *noun (light intensity)* candela *f*

canned *adjective* **(a)** *(computer)* **canned program** = programme *m* portable *or* transportable (d'une machine à l'autre) *or* programme d'une grande portabilité; **canned software** = logiciel *m* de série *or* progiciel *m* **(b)** *(TV)* **canned programme** = programme filmé *or* en différé

canonical schema *noun* schéma *m* de base de données standard *or* canonique

capability *noun* capacité *f or* facilité *f or* fonction *f;* **resolution capabilities** = capacité de définition; **electronic mail capabilities** = (avec) fonction courrier électronique; **capability list** = liste *f* des fonctions *or* des possibilités

◊ **capable** *adjective* capable; **that is the highest speed that this printer is capable of** = c'est la vitesse maximum que peut atteindre cette imprimante; **the software is capable of far more complex functions** = ce logiciel permet d'exécuter des fonctions beaucoup plus complexes

capacitance *noun* capacitance *f*

◊ **capacitative** *or* **capacitive** *adjective* capacitif, -ive

◊ **capacitor** *noun* condensateur *m or* capacité *f;* **capacitor microphone** = microphone *m* à condensateur; **ceramic capacitor** = condensateur céramique; **electrolytic capacitor** = condensateur électrolytique; **non-electrolytic capacitor** = condensateur non électrolytique; **variable capacitor** = condensateur variable *or* capacité variable; **capacitor storage** = mémoire capacitive *or* à condensateur; **memory backup capacitor** = condensateur pour mémoire RAM

capacity *noun* **(a)** *(production)* capacité *f; (amount produced)* **industrial** *or* **manufacturing** *or* **production capacity** = rendement *m;* **channel capacity** = capacité *f or* débit *m* d'une voie de transmission; **to work at full capacity** = travailler à plein régime *or* à plein rendement; **to use up spare** *or* **excess capacity** = utiliser la capacité en excédent **(b)** *(space)* capacité; **storage capacity** = capacité *f* de mémoire *or* taille *f* (de la) mémoire; **total storage capacity is now 3Mb** = la capacité de mémoire est maintenant de 3Mo

capital *(informal)* **cap** *noun* (lettre) majuscule *f or* capitale *f;* **the word BASIC is always written in caps** = BASIC s'écrit toujours avec des majuscules; **caps lock** = touche *f* de verrouillage des majuscules; **the LED lights up when caps lock is pressed** = le témoin s'allume quand la touche (des) capitales est verrouillée

capstan *noun (of tape player)* cabestan *m* (d'entraînement)

caption légende *f;* **the captions are printed in italics** = les légendes sont imprimées en italique

capture 1 *noun* **data capture** = saisie *f* de données; **data capture starts when an interrupt is received** = la saisie commence dès réception du signal d'interruption **2** *verb* saisir (des données); **the software allows captured images to be edited** = le logiciel permet d'éditer les images reçues; **scanners usually capture images at a resolution of 300 dots per inch (dpi)** = un scanner peut habituellement lire des images d'une définition de 300 points par pouce

QUOTE images can then be captured, stored, manipulated and displayed
Electronics & Wireless World

CAR = CURRENT ADDRESS REGISTER

carbon *noun* **(a)** (papier) carbone *m;* **you forgot to put a carbon in the typewriter** = vous avez oublié de mettre un carbone dans votre machine à écrire **(b)** double *m or* copie *f* carbone; **make a top copy and two carbons** = faites un original et deux doubles

◊ **carbon copy** *noun* copie *f* carbone *or* double *m;* **give me the original, and file the carbon copy** = passez-moi l'original et classez la copie dans le dossier

◊ **carbonless** *adjective* autocopiant, -e; **we use carbonless order pads** = nous utilisons des carnets de commandes autocopiants; **carbonless paper** = papier *m* autocopiant

◊ **carbon microphone** *noun* microphone *m* à charbon

◊ **carbon paper** *noun* (papier) carbone *m*

◊ **carbon ribbon** *noun* ruban *m* carbone

◊ **carbon set** *noun* formulaire *m* avec double carboné

◊ **carbon tissue** *noun* film *m* de transfert

card *noun* (a) carton *m;* **we have printed the instructions on thick white card =** nous avons fait imprimer les instructions sur carton blanc épais (b) carte *f;* **cash card** = carte de retrait (bancaire); **charge card** = carte de compte crédit; **credit card** = carte de crédit; **filing card** = fiche *f;* **index card =** fiche *or* carte de fichier; **punched card =** carte perforée; **smart card** = carte à puce *or* carte à mémoire *or* carte magnétique; **smart cards reduce fraud** = les cartes à puce aident à réduire le nombre de fraudes; **future smart cards could contain an image of the user's fingerprint for identification =** à l'avenir, on pourrait inclure les empreintes digitales de l'utilisateur sur ses cartes à mémoire à fin d'identification (c) *(punched card)* carte perforée; **card code** = code *m* de perforation de cartes; **card column =** colonne *f* de perforations (d'une carte perforée); **card feed** = (système d') alimentation *f or* entraînement *m* de cartes perforées; **card field** = champ *m* de carte (perforée); **card format =** format *m* de carte (perforée); **card image =** image *f* (mémoire) de carte; *(program)* **card loader** = chargeur *m* de cartes; **card punch (CP)** = poinçon *m* de perforation *or* perforateur *m* (pour cartes); **card reader** *or* **punched card reader =** lecteur *m* de cartes perforées; **card row =** colonne de perforations d'une carte (d) *(computer card)* carte de circuit imprimé *or* plaque *f* (présensibilisée) pour circuit imprimé; **card cage** = support *f* de cartes *or* châssis *m* avec guide-cartes *or* baie *f;* **card edge connector** = connecteur *m* de carte; **card extender** = support *m* de carte d'extension; **expansion card** *or* **expansion board** = carte d'extension; **hard card** = carte de disque dur; **card frame** *or* **card chassis** = support *m* de cartes (de circuits imprimés) *or* chassis *m* avec guide-cartes *or* baie *f*

◊ **cardboard** *noun* carton *m;* **cardboard box** = carton *or* boîte *f* en carton

◊ **card index** *noun* fichier *m;*

◊ **card-index** *verb* mettre sur fiches

◊ **card-indexing** *noun* mise *f* sur fiches; **no one can understand her card-indexing system** = personne ne comprend sa méthode de classement du fichier

cardioid response *noun* (réponse) cardioïde *f*

caret mark *or* **sign** *noun* *(used in proofreading)* signe *m* d'omission

carriage *noun* *(of typewriter or printer)* chariot *m;* **carriage control** = commande *f* de chariot; **carriage control codes can be used to move the paper forward two lines between each line of text** = les codes de commande de chariot peuvent être utilisés pour faire avancer le papier de deux interlignes; **carriage return (CR)** = touche *f or* signal *m* de retour (du chariot); **the carriage return key is badly placed for touch-typists** = les clavistes trouvent que la touche de retour est mal placée; **carriage return/line feed (CR/LF)** = retour *m* (de) chariot/retour à la ligne

carrier *noun* (a) *(photocopying or printing processes)* support *m* (d'encrage) (b) *(microfilm)* support (c) *(high frequency waveform)* (onde) porteuse *f or* (signal) porteur *m;* **carrier sense multiple access - collision detection (CSMA-CD)** = écoute *f* de signal à accès multiple avec détection de collision *or* protocole de transmission CSMA-CD; **carrier signalling** = transmission *f* par onde porteuse; **he's not using a modem - there's no carrier signal on the line** = il n'utilise pas de modem: il n'existe aucun signal porteur sur la ligne; **carrier system** = *(analog)* système *m* à courants porteurs; *(analog or digital)* système multiplex; **carrier telegraphy** = télégraphie *f* par onde porteuse; **carrier wave** = onde porteuse; **data carrier** = (i) support de données; (ii) onde porteuse de données; **data carrier detect (DCD)** = (signal) détecteur *m* d'onde porteuse *or* signal *m* de détection de porteuse; **the call is stopped if the software does not receive a DCD signal from the modem** = l'appel est bloqué si le logiciel ne reçoit pas de signal de détection de porteuse

carry 1 *noun* *(maths)* retenue *f or* report *m;* **when 5 and 7 are added, there is an answer of 2 and a carry which is put in the next column, giving 12** = lorsqu'on additionne 5 et 7, on pose 2 et on retient 1 sur la colonne des dizaines, ce qui fait 12; **carry bit** *or* **flag** = (signe de *or* bit de) report; **carry complete signal** = signal *m* de fin de report; **carry look ahead** = additionneur *m* à retenue automatique (très rapide); **carry time** = temps *m* de report; **cascade carry** = report en cascade; **end-around carry** = report circulaire *or* en boucle; **high speed carry** = report rapide; **partial carry** = report partiel; **ripple-through carry** = report rapide *or* simultané **2** *verb* transporter *or* transmettre *or* véhiculer; **the fibre optic link carried all the data** = toutes les données ont été transmises par fibres optiques; **the information-carrying abilities of this link are very good** = la capacité de transmission *or* de portage de cette liaison est excellente

cartesian coordinates *noun* coordonnées *fpl* cartésiennes
◊ **cartesian structure** *noun* structure cartésienne *f*

cartridge *noun* cartouche *f;* **data cartridge** = cartouche de données; **disk cartridge** = cartouche (de) disque *or* disque dur amovible *or* chargeur *m;* **ROM cartridge** = cartouche ROM *or* ROM amovible; **the portable computer has no disk drives, but has a slot for ROM cartridges** = cet ordinateur portatif n'est pas équipé de lecteur de disquettes mais possède un connecteur pour cartouches ROM; **tape cartridge** = cartouche (de) bande; **cartridge drive** = lecteur de cartouches; **cartridge fonts** = cartouche de police de caractères; *(for printers)* **cartridge ribbon** = ruban en cartouche
◊ **cartridge paper** *noun* papier *m* à dessin (de type 'cartridge')

cascade carry *noun* report *m* en cascade
◊ **cascade connection** *noun* connexion *f* (montée) en cascade
◊ **cascade control** *noun* contrôle *m* en cascade

case 1 *noun* **(a)** *(container)* boîtier *m* **(b)** *(typography)* casse *f;* **lower case** = minuscule *f or* bas *m* de casse; **upper case** = majuscule *f or* haut *m* de casse; **he corrected the word 'coMputer', replacing the upper case M with a lower case letter** = il a remplacé le M majuscule de 'coMputer' par une minuscule; **case change** = touche *f* des majuscules **(c)** *(cardboard cover for a book)* cartonnage *m;* **the library edition has a case and jacket** = l'édition pour bibliothèques est cartonnée avec jaquette; **case binding** = couverture *f* cartonnée **(d)** *(box)* carton *m or* boîte *f* en carton; **packing case** = caisse *f* **2** *verb* **(a)** *(to bind)* cartonner *or* relier avec couverture cartonnée; **cased book** = livre cartonné **(b)** *(to pack)* emballer *or* mettre dans une caisse
◊ **case-making machine** *noun* *(for books)* machine *f* à cartonner

casing *noun* boîtier *m or* coffret *m*

cassette *noun* cassette *f;* **you must back up the information from the computer onto a cassette** = il faut faire une cassette de sauvegarde pour vos données; **audio cassette** = audiocassette *f;* **data cassette** = cassette informatique; **video cassette** = vidéocassette *f;* **cassette recorder** = magnétophone à cassette *m;* **cassette tape** = bande *f* magnétique *or* cassette

caster machine *noun* fondeuse *f*
◊ **cast off 1** *noun* calibrage *m* d'un texte **2** *verb* calibrer un texte
◊ **casting off** *noun* calibrage d'un texte

CAT (a) = COMPUTER-AIDED *or* ASSISTED TRAINING **(b)** = COMPUTER-AIDED *or* ASSISTED TESTING

catalogue 1 *noun* catalogue *m; (directory)* **disk catalogue** = répertoire *m* des fichiers d'un disque *or* d'une disquette; **the entry in the disk catalogue is removed when the file is deleted** = le nom d'un fichier qui est effacé disparaît aussi du répertoire du disque **2** *verb* cataloguer *or* répertorier; **all the terminals were catalogued, with their location, call sign and attribute table** = tous les terminaux ont été répertoriés avec indication de leur emplacement, de leur code d'appel et de leur table d'attributs
◊ **cataloguer** *noun* archiviste *m&f*

catastrophe *noun* catastrophe *f*
◊ **catastrophic error** *noun* erreur *f* qui cause une catastrophe *or* erreur fatale; **catastrophic failure** = panne *f* fatale

catena *noun* (i) (nombre de) caractères *mpl* dans une chaîne; (ii) chaîne *f* de caractères

◊ **catenate** *verb* (en)chaîner *or* lier *or* concaténer *or* faire une concaténation

◊ **catenation** *noun* (i) chaîne *f or* concaténation *f*; (ii) enchaînement *m or* concaténation

cathode *noun* cathode *f*
NOTE: opposite is **anode**

◊ **cathode ray tube (CRT)** *noun* (i) tube *m* à rayons cathodiques *or* tube cathodique; (ii) écran (à tube cathodique); **cathode ray tube (storage)** = moniteur *m or* écran *m* (d'ordinateur)

CATV = COMMUNITY ANTENNA TELEVISION antenne *f* collective de télévision câblée *or* système de télévision (câblée) CATV; **CATV cable** = câble *m* de télévision (câblée) *or* câble CATV

CB = CITIZENS BAND RADIO

C band *noun* (fréquence de) bande *f* C

CBL = COMPUTER-BASED LEARNING

CBMS = COMPUTER-BASED MESSAGE SYSTEM

CBT = COMPUTER-BASED TRAINING

CBX = COMPUTERIZED BRANCH EXCHANGE

CCD = CHARGE COUPLED DEVICE dispositif *m* à couplage de charge; **CCD memory** = mémoire *f* CCD *or* à couplage de charge

CCITT = COMITE CONSULTATIF INTERNATIONAL DES TELEGRAPHES ET DES TELEPHONES

CCP = COMMAND CONSOLE PROCESSOR

CCTV = CLOSED CIRCUIT TELEVISION

CCU = COMMUNICATIONS CONTROL UNIT

CD = COMPACT DISK disque *m* compact *or* audio-numérique *or* disque CD

◊ **CD player** *noun* lecteur *m* de disques compacts *or* audionumériques *or* de disques CD

◊ **CD-ROM** = COMPACT DISK-READ ONLY MEMORY

cedilla *noun* *(typography)* cédille *f*

cell *noun* **(a)** *(single function in a spreadsheet)* cellule *f*; **cell reference variable** = variable *f* de référence d'une cellule **(b)** *(single memory location)* cellule; **cell phone** = téléphone *m* cellulaire

◊ **cellular** *adjective* cellulaire; **cellular phone** = téléphone cellulaire; **cellular radio** = radiotéléphone (de type) cellulaire; **cellular service** = réseau *m* radiotéléphonique

cellar *noun* pile *f* (de données en mémoire)

centi- *prefix* centi-; **centimetre** = centimètre *m*

central *adjective* central, -e *or* principal, -e; *(host computer)* **central computer** = ordinateur central *or* ordinateur hôte; **central memory (CM)** = mémoire centrale *or* principale; **central processing element (CPE)** = unité centrale de calcul (processeur en tranches); **central processing unit (CPU)** *or* **central processor** = unité centrale (de traitement) *or* processeur central; **central terminal** = terminal principal *or* central

◊ **centralized** *adjective* centralisé, -ée; **centralized data processing** = traitement centralisé de l'information; **centralized computer network** = réseau informatique centralisé

centre *US* **center 1** *noun* centre *m; (of punched tape)* **centre holes** = perforations *fpl* centrales; **centre operator** = opérateur *m* central; *(on punched tape)* **centre sprocket feed** = canal *m* d'entraînement (avec perforations centrales) **2** *verb* **(a)** *(to align read/write head)* centrer *or* aligner *or* ajuster (les têtes) **(b)** *(in text or on screen)* centrer; **which key do you press to**

centre the heading? = sur quelle touche faut-il appuyer pour centrer l'en-tête?

◊ **centering** *noun (text)* centrage *m* (d'un texte); **centering of headings is easily done, using this function key** = il est plutôt facile de centrer les en-têtes en utilisant cette touche (de fonction)

Centronics® **interface** *noun* interface parallèle (de type) Centronics

CEPT standard *noun (character standard defined by the Conference of European Post Telephone and Telegraph)* norme *f* CEPT

ceramic *noun & adjective* céramique *f*

CGA = COLOUR GRAPHICS ADAPTER

chad *noun* confetti *m;* **chadded** *or* **chadless tape** = bande semi-perforée *or* à confettis non détachés

chain 1 *noun* chaîne *f;* **chain code** = code *m* en chaîne *or* code chaîné; *(for paper)* **chain delivery mechanism** = convoyeur *m* (d'alimentation du papier); **chain list** = liste *f* en chaîne *or* liste d'articles chaînés; **chain printer** = imprimante à chaîne; **command chain** = chaîne de commandes; **daisy chain** = chaîne *f;* **daisy chain bus** = bus *m* de chaîne *or* bus série **2** *verb (files or data items)* (s')enchaîner; **more than 1,000 articles or chapters can be chained together when printing** = plus de 1000 articles ou chapitres peuvent être enchaînés à l'impression; **chained list** = fichier *m* chaîné; **chained list** = liste *f* chaînée *or* concaténée; **chained record** = enregistrement *m or* article *m* chaîné; **to daisy-chain** = relier en série *or* en cascade *or* en chaîne; **daisy-chaining saves a lot of cable** = la connexion en chaîne *or* en cascade réduit le câblage

◊ **chaining** *noun* (i) enchaînement *m* ; (ii) chaînage *m;* **chaining search** = recherche en chaîne; **data chaining** = liaison *f* de données en chaîne *or* chaînage de données

change 1 *verb (to modify)* changer *or* modifier; *(to transfer)* changer (de place *or* d'appareil) *or* transférer **2** *noun* changement *m or* modification *f;* **change**

dump = vidage *m* de mouvements (sur imprimante); **change file** = fichier *m* (de) mouvements *or* de mise à jour; **change record** = enregistrement *m* de mouvements *or* de modifications; **change tape** = bande *f* (de) mouvements

◊ **change over** *verb* passer d'un système à un autre

◊ **change-over** *noun* transfert *m or* permutation *f;* **direct change-over** = transfert direct

◊ **changer** *noun* changeur *m; (of connectors)* **gender changer** = changeur de genre; **you can interconnect all these peripherals with just two cables and a gender changer** = il est possible de relier tous ces périphériques en utilisant seulement deux câbles et un changeur de genre; **record changer** = changeur (de disques) automatique

channel 1 *noun* **(a)** canal *m or* voie *f;* **channel adapter** = interface *f or* adaptateur *m* de canal de transmission; **channel bank** = banque *f* de canaux; **channel capacity** = débit *m* d'un canal *or* d'une voie; **channel command** = commande *f* de canal; **channel group** = groupement *m* de voies; **channel isolation** = isolation *f* de canaux; **channel overload** = surcharge *f or* saturation *f* d'un canal *or* d'une voie; **channel queue** = file *f* d'attente (de demandes de service *or* de données à transmettre); **channel synchronizer** = synchroniseur *m* de canaux *or* de voies; **channel-to-channel connection** = liaison directe entre canaux; **data channel** = canal de transmission de données; **dedicated channel** = voie spécialisée *or* canal dédié; **I/O channel** = canal *or* voie d'entrée/sortie **(b)** voie (de communication); **to open up new channels of communication** = créer de nouveaux circuits de communication **2** *verb (signals or data)* acheminer *or* transmettre *or* véhiculer

◊ **channelling** *noun (protective pipes)* conduite *f or* canalisation *f*

chapter *noun* **(a)** *(of program)* module *m* **(b)** *(on a video disk)* module; **chapter stop** = (code) fin *f* de module **(c)** *(of book, etc.)* chapitre *m;* **chapter heading** = tête *f* de chapitre; **chapter headings are in 12 point bold** = les têtes de chapitre sont en caractères gras de 12 points

character *noun* caractère *m;* **alphanumeric characters** = caractères alphanumériques; **cancel character** = caractère d'annulation; **character assembly** = assemblage *m or* groupage *m* de caractères; **character blink** = caractère clignotant; **character block** = bloc *m* (de) caractères; **character byte** = octet *m* (de caractères); **character check** = contrôle *m* de caractère(s); **character code** = code *m* de caractères; **the ASCII code is the most frequently used character coding system** = le code ASCII est le code de caractères le plus fréquemment utilisé; **character density** = densité *f* de caractère; **character display** = affichage *m* de caractères *or* de texte; **character fill** = (i) remplissage *m* (avec caractères blancs); (ii) insertion *f* de caractères de remplissage (en mémoire); **character generator** = générateur *m* de caractères; **the ROM used as a character generator can be changed to provide different fonts** = on peut utiliser une ROM comme générateur de caractères pour obtenir les différentes polices; **character key** = touche *f* de caractère; **character machine** = processeur *m* en mode caractère *or* à mots variables; **character orientated (computer)** = (ordinateur) à mode caractère; **character printer** = imprimante *f* caractère (par caractère); **a daisy-wheel printer is a character printer** = l'imprimante à marguerite imprime un caractère à la fois; **character recognition** = reconnaissance *f* optique de caractères; **character repertoire** = répertoire *m* de caractères *or* répertoire typographique; **character representation** = expression *f* binaire d'un caractère; **character set** = *(codes)* jeu *m* de caractères; *(printing)* police *f* de caractères; **character skew** = angle *m or* oblique *f* (d'un caractère); **character string** = chaîne *f* de caractères; **characters per inch (cpi)** = (nombre de) caractères par pouce; **you can select 10 or 12 cpi with the green button** = le bouton vert vous permet de sélectionner 10 ou 12 caractères par pouce; **characters per second (cps)** = (nombre de) caractères par seconde (cps); **character stuffing** = (i) remplissage *m* (avec caractères blancs); (ii) insertion *f* de caractères blancs *or* de caractères de remplissage; **check character** = caractère de contrôle; **device control character** = caractère de contrôle de périphérique

◊ **characteristic 1** *noun* **(a)** *(maths)* exposant *m or* caractéristique *f;* **the floating point number 1.345 x 10³ , has a characteristic of 3** = la valeur de l'exposant du nombre 1,345 x 10³ (en virgule flottante) est de 3; **characteristic overflow** = dépassement *m* de capacité de la caractéristique **(b)** *(properties of component)* caractéristique **2** *adjective (typical or special)* caractéristique; **this fault is characteristic of this make and model of personal computer** = c'est un défaut caractéristique de cette marque et de ce modèle d'ordinateur individuel en particulier; **characteristic curve** = courbe *f* caractéristique

QUOTE the screen displays very sharp and stable characters, each cell occupying an 8 by 11 dot matrix

Computing Today

charge *noun (of electricity or of electrons)* charge *f;* **charge-coupled device (CCD)** = dispositif *m* CCD *or* à couplage de charge; **charge-coupled device memory** = mémoire *f* CCD *or* à couplage de charge; **electric charge** = charge électrique **2** *verb* charger; **battery charging** = (temps de) charge d'une pile

◊ **chargeable** *adjective* chargeable; **re-chargeable battery** = pile *f or* batterie *f* rechargeable; **a re-chargeable battery is used for RAM back-up when the system is switched off** = on utilise une pile rechargeable comme alimentation auxiliaire pour la mémoire RAM quand le système est éteint

chart *noun* diagramme *m or* graphique *m;* **bar chart** = graphique à barres *or* en tuyaux d'orgue *or* histogramme *m;* **logical chart** = diagramme logique; **pie chart** = diagramme à secteurs *or* (diagramme en) camembert *m;* **the memory allocation is shown on this pie chart** = l'attribution de mémoire est indiquée sur ce camembert; **chart recorder** = enregistreur *m* graphique; *see also* FLOWCHART

chassis *noun* châssis *m*

check 1 *noun* **(a)** vérification *f or* test *m or* contrôle *m;* **character check** = contrôle de caractère(s); **check bit** = bit *m* de contrôle; **check character** = caractère *m* de contrôle; **check digit** *or* **number** = chiffre *m or* clé *f* (numérique) de contrôle; **check indicator** = indicateur *m* de contrôle; **check key** = clé de contrôle; **check point** = point *m* de contrôle *or* de reprise; **check point dump** = vidage *m* de contrôle (sur imprimante); **check register** = registre *m* de contrôle; **check total** = CHECKSUM *(dry run of a program)* **desk check** = essai *m* à blanc *or* contrôle sur papier *m* (d'un programme) **(b)** arrêt *m* de courte durée (causé par un défaut du support magnétique); **data check** = brève interruption *f* de transmission de données (due à un défaut du support magnétique) **2** *verb* vérifier *or* tester *or* contrôler; **the separate parts of the system were all checked for faults before being packaged** = les différentes parties du système ont été contrôlées avant l'emballage; **he checked the computer printout against the invoices** = il a vérifié la sortie d'imprimante avec les factures

◊ **checker** *see* SPELL

◊ **checkerboarding** *noun* caviardage *m* (de la mémoire)

◊ **checking** *noun* examen *m* *or* vérification *f* *or* contrôle *m;* **the maintenance engineer found some defects whilst checking the equipment** = l'ingénieur de maintenance a découvert des défauts en contrôlant le matériel; **checking program** = programme *m* de contrôle; **self-checking code** = code détecteur d'erreur

◊ **checksum** *or* **check total** *noun* total *m* de vérification *or* de contrôle; **the data must be corrupted if the checksum is different** = les données sont sûrement erronées si le total de contrôle est faux

chemical **1** *adjective* chimique; **chemical reaction** = réaction *f* chimique **2** *noun* produit *m* chimique

chip *noun* puce *f* *or* circuit *m* intégré ; **chip architecture** = architecture *f* d'un circuit intégré; **chip card** = carte *f* à puce *or* carte à mémoire; **chip count** = nombre de puces (sur une carte, etc.); **it's no good, the chip count is still too high** = le nombre de puces est malheureusement encore trop élevé; **chip select line** = ligne *f* de sélection *or* de validation d'un circuit intégré; **the data strobe line is connected to the latch chip select line** = la ligne de validation de données est reliée à la ligne de sélection de la bascule; **chip set** = ensemble *m* de

circuits intégrés; **diagnostic chip** = puce de diagnostic; **they are carrying out research on diagnostic chips to test computers that contain processors** = ils font des recherches sur les puces de diagnostic destinées au contrôle des ordinateurs équipés de processeurs; **single chip computer** = ordinateur *m* monopuce *or* à puce unique; **sound chip** = (circuit intégré) générateur *m* de son

chop *see* BINARY

chord keying *noun* action *f* sur deux touches en même temps

chroma *noun* chrominance *f* *or* chroma *f; (TV)* **chroma control** = contrôle *m* chromatique; **chroma detector** = détecteur *m* chromatique

◊ **chromatic** *adjective* chromatique; **chromatic aberration** = aberration *f* chromatique; **chromatic dispersion** = dispersion *f* chromatique

◊ **chromaticity** *noun* chromaticité *f*

◊ **chrominance signal** *noun* signal *m* de chrominance

chronological order *noun* ordre *m* chronologique

CIM (a) = COMPUTER INPUT FROM MICROFILM **(b)** = COMPUTER-INTEGRATED MANUFACTURE

cine- *prefix* ciné-; **cine-camera** = caméra *f* *or* appareil *m* cinématographique; **cine-orientated image** = image orientée en film

◊ **cinema** *noun* **(a)** *(as an art)* **the cinema** = le cinéma *m* *or* l'art *m* cinématographique **(b)** *(building)* cinéma

◊ **cinematography** *noun* cinématographie *f*

cipher *noun* code *m* (chiffré) *or* écriture *f* chiffrée; **always use a secure cipher when sending data over a telephone line** = il faut toujours utiliser un code (chiffré) sûr quand vous transmettez des données par téléphone; **cipher key** = clé *f* de chiffrage *or* de cryptage; **cipher system** = code chiffré; **public key cipher** = code chiffré *m* à clé publique; **ciphertext** = message *m* chiffré *or* crypté

NOTE: opposite is **plaintext**

CIR = CURRENT INSTRUCTION REGISTER

circuit *noun* circuit *m;* **circuit board** *or* **card** = carte *f* de circuit imprimé *or* plaque *f* (présensibilisée) pour circuit imprimé; *(with circuit printed)* **printed circuit board (PCB)** = (carte de) circuit imprimé (CI); **circuit breaker** = disjoncteur *m or* interrupteur *m* (de courant); **circuit capacity** = capacité *f* d'un circuit; **circuit diagram** = diagramme *m* d'un circuit; **the CAD program will plot the circuit diagram rapidly** = le programme de CAO peut tracer le circuit très rapidement; **circuit grade** = qualité *f or* caractéristique *f* d'un circuit; **circuit noise level** = niveau *m* de bruit d'un circuit; **circuit switched digital circuitry** = circuiterie numérique commutée; **circuit switched network** = réseau *m* commuté; **circuit switching** = commutation *f* de circuit; **data circuit** = circuit de transmission *or* d'échange de données; **decision circuit** = circuit de décision; **digital circuit** = circuit numérique; **logic circuit** = circuit logique

◊ **circuitry** *noun* (ensemble de) circuits *mpl or* circuiterie *f;* **the circuitry is still too complex** = la circuiterie demeure trop complexe

circular *adjective* circulaire *or* en boucle; **circular buffer** = tampon *m* circulaire; **circular file** = fichier *m* en boucle; **circular list** = liste *f* en boucle; **circular orbit** = orbite *f* circulaire; **circular shift** = décalage *m* circulaire; **circular waveguide** = guide *m* d'ondes circulaire

◊ **circulate** *verb* **(a)** *(to go in circle)* décrire un cercle **(b)** *(to send information to)* (faire) circuler *or* distribuer

◊ **circulating** *adjective* circulant, -e; **circulating register** = registre *m* à décalage circulaire *or* à bits circulants; **circulating storage** = mémoire circulante *or* mémoire dynamique

circulation *noun* **(a)** *(of information)* circulation *f;* **the company is trying to improve the circulation of information between departments** = la société essaie d'améliorer la circulation de l'information dans les services **(b)** *(of a*

newspaper) tirage *m;* **what is the circulation of this computer magazine? =** quel est le tirage de cette revue d'informatique? *or* à combien d'exemplaires tire cette revue d'informatique?; **a specialized paper with a circulation of over 10,000 =** un journal spécialisé qui tire à plus de 10 000 exemplaires

circumflex *noun* accent *m* circonflexe

CISC = COMPLEX INSTRUCTION SET COMPUTER

citizens band radio (CB) *noun* radio *m* CB *or* radio à bande CB

cladding *noun* *(surrounding a conducting core)* gaine *f;* **if the cladding is chipped, the fibre-optic cable will not function well =** la fibre optique sera moins performante si sa gaine est endommagée

clamp *verb* verrouiller le voltage (d'un signal)

clapper *noun* *(on printer)* presseur *m*

clarity *noun* clarté *f;* **the atmospheric conditions affect the clarity of the signal =** les conditions atmosphériques influencent la clarté du signal *or* le signal est plus ou moins clair suivant les conditions atmosphériques

classify *verb* classer; **the diagnostic printouts have been classified under T for test results =** on a classé les sorties d'imprimantes avec diagnostics sous la rubrique 'Test', sous la lettre 'T'; **classified directory** = annuaire *m* téléphonique par professions

◊ **classification** *noun* classification *f*

clean 1 *adjective* *(not dirty)* propre; *(text)* (texte) sans erreur *or* sans correction; *(disk)* (disquette) vierge; **I'll have to start again - I just erased the only clean file =** il me faut tout recommencer; je viens d'effacer le seul fichier qui ne contenait aucune erreur; **clean copy =** copie *f* finale; **clean machine =** machine *f* nue; *(of memory)* **clean page =** page mémoire sans modification; **clean proof**

= épreuve *f* sans correction **2** *verb (to make clean)* nettoyer; **data cleaning** = nettoyage *m* de données *or* correction *f* d'erreurs; **head cleaning disk** = disquette *f* de nettoyage (des têtes); **use a head cleaning disk every week** = il faut utiliser la disquette de nettoyage une fois par semaine; **write errors occur if you do not use a head cleaning kit regularly** = vous aurez des erreurs d'écriture si vous ne vous servez pas régulièrement de votre disquette de nettoyage; **screen cleaning kit** = kit *m* de nettoyage pour écran

clear 1 *adjective* **(a)** *(easily understood)* clair, -e; **the program manual is not clear on copying files** = le manuel d'utilisation n'explique pas clairement la marche à suivre pour copier un fichier; **the booklet gives clear instructions how to connect the different parts of the system** = la notice indique clairement comment relier les différents modules du système; **he made it clear that the system will only work on IBM-compatible hardware** = il a bien expliqué que le système ne fonctionne qu'avec les appareils IBM et les compatibles **(b)** *(free)* libre; **clear to send (CTS)** = (signal) CTS *or* (signal de) prêt à transmettre **2** *verb* **(a)** *(to wipe out)* effacer *or* vider; **type CLS to clear the screen** = tapez CLS pour effacer *or* faire disparaître ce qu'il y a sur l'écran; **all arrays are cleared each time the program is run** = tous les tableaux sont vidés chaque fois que le programme est lancé; **to clear an area of memory** = vider une zone de mémoire; **to clear the data register** = vider le registre de données **(b)** libérer la ligne (lorsque la transmission est terminée)

◊ **clearance** *noun* autorisation *f* (d'accès à un fichier); **you do not have the required clearance for this processor** = vous n'avez pas l'autorisation d'accéder à ce processeur

click 1 *noun* **(a)** *(short sound)* clic *m* **(b)** *(pressing a key or button)* clic; **you move through text and graphics with a click of the button** = un clic vous permet de vous déplacer dans les textes et graphiques **2** *verb (to press a key or button or mouse)* cliquer; **use the mouse to enlarge a frame by clicking inside its border** = vous pouvez agrandir le cadre en cliquant (la souris) à l'intérieur de ses limites

clip 1 *noun (short piece of live film)* extrait *m* de film *or* clip *m;* **there was a clip of the disaster on the news** = un clip de l'accident a été passé aux informations **2** *verb* **(a)** attacher (avec un trombone, etc.); **the corrections are clipped to the computer printout** = les corrections sont attachées à la sortie d'imprimante **(b)** *(cut out)* couper *or* découper; **clipping service** = service *m* de coupures de presse **(c)** *(waveform)* écrêter; **the voltage signal was clipped to prevent excess signal level** = le signal a été écrêté pour éviter une amplitude excessive

◊ **clip art** *or* **clipart** *noun* image *f* clip art

◊ **clipboard** *noun* Presse-papier® *m*

clock *noun* **(a)** horloge *f;* **the micro has a built-in clock** = le micro possède une horloge incorporée; **the time is shown by the clock in the corner of the screen** = l'heure est affichée à l'horloge placée dans un coin de l'écran; **digital clock** = horloge numérique **(b)** *(used to synchronize equipment)* horloge; **clock cycle** = cycle *m* d'horloge; **clock pulse** = impulsion *f* d'horloge *or* rythme *m;* **clock rate** = vitesse *f* d'horloge; **clock track** = piste *f* d'horloge; **main clock** = horloge centrale; **programmable clock** = horloge programmable **2** *verb* synchroniser; **clocked signals** = signaux synchrones aux impulsions d'horloge

clone *noun* clone *m;* **they have copied our new personal computer and brought out a cheaper clone** = ils ont copié notre nouveau modèle d'ordinateur pour commercialiser un clone qui se vend beaucoup moins cher; **higher performance clones are available for all the models in our range** = il existe des clones de tous nos modèles et tous sont plus performants

close *verb* arrêter *or* fermer *or* terminer; **close file** = fermer un fichier *or* (opération de) fermeture *f* de fichier; **closed circuit television (CCTV)** = télévision *f* en circuit fermé; **closed loop** = boucle fermée; **closed subroutine** = sous-programme fermé; **closed user group (CUG)** = groupe *m* fermé d'utilisateurs

◊ **close-down** *noun* **(a)** *(end of braodcasting for the day)* fin *f* des émissions **(b)** *(stoppage)* **disorderly close-down** = panne *f* désordonnée

◇ **close up** *verb (typesetting)* refermer *or* rapprocher *or* resserrer; **if we close up the lines, we should save a page** = en resserrant les lignes, nous gagnerons une page

◇ **close-up** *noun (photography)* gros plan *m*

cluster *noun (of terminals)* grappe *f* (de périphériques, etc.); **cluster controller** = unité de contrôle de périphériques disposés en grappe

◇ **clustering** *noun* liaison *f* en grappe de plusieurs périphériques

QUOTE cluster controllers are available with 8 or 16 channels
Microcomputer News
QUOTE these include IBM networking and clustering hardware and software
Personal Computer World

CM = CENTRAL MEMORY

C-MAC multiplexeur *m* C-MAC

CMI = COMPUTER-MANAGED INSTRUCTION

CML = COMPUTER-MANAGED LEARNING

CMOS = COMPLEMENTARY METAL OXIDE SEMICONDUCTOR

CNC = COMPUTER NUMERIC CONTROL

coalesce *verb (to merge files)* combiner *or* fusionner *or* fondre

coat *verb* recouvrir (de) *or* revêtir (de) *or* enduire (de); **coated paper** = papier *m* couché

◇ **coating** *noun* couche *f*; **paper which has a coating of clay** = papier enduit d'une fine couche de kaolin

co-axial cable *noun* câble *m* coaxial

COBOL = COMMON ORDINARY BUSINESS ORIENTED LANGUAGE langage *m* COBOL

code 1 *noun* **(a)** code *m;* **code conversion** = conversion *f* de code **(b)** *(sequence of computer instructions)* code; **chain code** = code en chaîne *or* code chaîné; *(of main memory)* **code area** = zone *f* de code; *(of program)* **code line** = ligne *f* de code (d'un programme); **computer** *or* **machine code** = code d'instruction *or* code (en langage) machine; **direct** *or* **one-level** *or* **specific code** = code direct *or* à un niveau *or* code spécifique; **macro code** = macrocode *m;* **object code** = code objet; **optimum code** = code optimum *or* amélioré *or* accéléré; **source code** = code source; **symbolic code** = code symbolique **(c)** *(telephone)* **(dialling) code** = indicatif *m* (téléphonique); **area code** = indicatif de zone; *Canada* indicatif régional; **what is the code for Edinburgh?** quel est l'indicatif d'Edimbourg?; **country code followed by area code followed by customer's number** = indicatif du pays suivi de l'indicatif de zone suivi du numéro de votre correspondant; **international dialling code** = indicatif (téléphonique) international **(d)** **bar code** = code (à) barres; **bar-code reader** = lecteur *m* de codes (à) barres; **code element** = élément *m* d'un code; **cyclic code** = code binaire réfléchi *or* code de Gray; *(for a peripheral)* **device code** = code d'identification (de périphérique); **error code** = code (indicateur) d'erreur; **error correcting code** = code correcteur (d'erreur); **error detecting code** = code détecteur d'erreur; **escape code** = code échappement *or* code 'escape'; **machine-readable codes** = codes en langage machine; **post code** *US* **zip code** = code postal; **punched code** = code de perforation; **self-checking code** = code détecteur d'erreur; **stock code** = numéro *m* de stock 2 *verb* **(a)** *(cryptography)* coder *or* chiffrer *or* crypter **(b)** *(write in a programming language)* programmer *or* coder

◇ **coder** *noun* codeur *m; coder/decoder* **(CODEC)** = codeur/décodeur *m*

◇ **coding** *noun* codage *m or* programmation *f*; **coding sheet** *or* **coding form** = feuille *f or* formulaire *m* de programmation

CODEC = CODER/DECODER

coercivity *noun* coercibilité *f*

coherent *adjective (of waveforms)* cohérent, -e; **a laser produces coherent light =** le laser produit une lumière cohérente; *(of optical fibres)* **coherent bundle =** faisceau *m* cohérent

coil *noun* bobine *f;* **an inductor is made from a coil of (copper) wire =** un inducteur consiste en une bobine de fil (de cuivre)

coincidence circuit *or* **element** *noun* circuit *m* à coïncidence

cold *adjective* **(a)** froid, -e; **the machines work badly in cold weather =** les appareils fonctionnent mal par temps froid **(b)** *(without being prepared)* à froid *or* au démarrage; **cold fault =** erreur au démarrage; **cold standby =** système de secours lancé manuellement; **cold start =** démarrage *m* à froid *or* reprise *f* totale

collate *verb (documents)* (r)assembler *or* fusionner *or* interclasser; *(book signatures)* collationner

◊ **collating** *noun (documents)* fusionnement *m or* interclassement *m;* *(books)* collationnement *m;* **collating marks =** indices *mpl* de collationnement; **collating sequence =** séquence *f* de fusionnement *or* de classement; *(books)* ordre *m* des cahiers

◊ **collator** *noun* programme de fusionnement de données; *(machine for punched cards)* interclasseuse *f;* *(for signatures of books)* assembleuse *f*

collect *verb (data)* rassembler; **data collection =** collecte *f* de données; **data collection platform =** plate-forme *f* de collecte de données

◊ **collect transfer** *verb* récupérer des données et les transférer dans un registre

collision detection *noun* détection *f* de collision

colon (:) *noun (typography)* deux points; **semi-colon (;) =** point-virgule *m*

colophon *noun* colophon *m or* achevé *m* d'imprimer *or* marque *f* de l'éditeur *or* de l'imprimeur

colour *noun* couleur *f;* **colour balance =** équilibre *m* des couleurs; *(TV)* **colour burst =** rafale *f* de signaux couleurs; **colour cell =** cellule *f* de contrôle des couleurs; **colour decoder =** décodeur *m* de couleurs; **colour display =** affichage *m* couleur; **colour encoder =** encodeur *m* de couleurs; **colour graphics adapter (CGA) =** adaptateur *m* graphique couleur CGA *or* carte *f* CGA; **colour monitor =** moniteur *m* couleur *or* écran *m* couleur; **the colour monitor is great for games =** le moniteur couleur est excellent pour les jeux électroniques; **colour saturation =** saturation *f* de couleur; **colour separation =** séparation *f or* sélection *f* des couleurs; *(unwanted change in colour)* **colour shift =** variation *m* chromatique; **colour temperature =** température *f* chromatique; **colour transparency =** diapositive *f* couleur

QUOTE as a minimum, a colour graphics adapter (CGA) is necessary, but for best quality of graphic presentation an enhanced graphics adapter (EGA) should be considered
Micro Decision

column *noun* **(a)** colonne *f;* **to add up a column of figures =** additionner une colonne de chiffres; **put the total at the bottom of the column =** écrivez le total au bas de la colonne; **card column =** colonne de perforations (de carte perforée); **column parity =** parité *f* de colonnes; **80-column printer =** imprimante *f* 80 colonnes; **an 80-column printer is included in the price =** le prix comprend une imprimante 80 colonnes **(b)** *(in newspaper or magazine)* colonne; **column-centimetre =** centimètre-colonne *m*

◊ **columnar** *adjective* en colonne(s); **columnar graph =** diagramme *m or* graphique *m* en colonnes *or* en tuyaux d'orgue *or* histogramme *m;* **columnar working =** présentation *f* (graphique) sous forme de colonne(s) *or* sous forme d'histogramme(s)

COM = COMPUTER OUTPUT ON MICROFILM

coma *noun (lens aberration)* coma *f*

COMAL = COMMON ALGORITHMIC LANGUAGE langage (de programmation structurée) COMAL

combine *verb* combiner *or* joindre *or* fusionner; **combined head** = tête *f* de lecture/écriture; **combined station** = poste de contrôle mixte; **combined symbol matching (CSM)** = système de reconnaissance de caractères CSM (par identification des caractéristiques combinées)

◊ **combination** *noun* combinaison *f*

◊ **combinational** *adjective* combinatoire; **combinational circuit** = circuit *m* combinatoire; **combinational logic** = logique *f* combinatoire

comma (,) *noun (typography)* virgule *f;* **inverted commas** (' ' *or* " ") = guillemets *mpl*

command *noun* **(a)** *(electrical pulse or signal)* commande *f or* instruction *f or* signal *m* **(b)** *(word recognized by a computer)* commande *or* instruction *f;* **the command to execute the program is RUN** = RUN est la commande d'exécution du programme; **channel command** = commande de canal; **command code** = code *m* d'opération; **command console processor (CCP)** = processeur *m* de commande de console; **command control language** = langage *m* de contrôle *or* de pilotage (de périphériques); **command-driven program** = programme *m* activé par commande; **command file** = fichier *m* de commandes; **command file processor** = processeur *m* de fichier de commandes; **command interface** = interface *f* de commande *or* de contrôle; **command language** = langage *m* de commande; **command line** = ligne *f* de commande *or* d'instruction (d'un programme); **command prompt** = message *m* d'attente de commande; **command register** = registre *m* de commande *or* d'instruction; **command window** = fenêtre *f* de commande; **the user can define the size of the command window** = l'utilisateur peut définir la taille de la fenêtre de commande; **dot command** = commande (précédée d'un) point; **embedded command** = commande imbriquée; **interrupt command** = commande d'interruption (de programme)

comment *noun* note *f or* explication *f or* commentaire *m;* **BASIC allows comments to be written after a REM**

instruction = en BASIC il est possible d'inclure des commentaires à la suite de l'instruction REM; **comment field** = champ *m* bloc-notes

◊ **commentary** *noun* commentaire *m*

commercial *noun (TV)* pub *f or* message *m* publicitaire; **commercials** = la publicité

common *adjective* **(a)** *(which happens very often)* commun, -e *or* habituel, -elle *or* courant, -e; **this is a common fault with this printer model** = c'est un défaut courant de ce modèle d'imprimante **(b)** *(belonging to several people or programs)* commun; **common carrier** = *(transport)* entreprise *f* de transport en commun; *(information)* entreprise de diffusion d'informations grand public; *(network)* ligne banalisée *or* canal banal *or* courant porteur commun; **common channel signalling** = signalisation *f* par canal banal *or* par voie commune; **common business orientated language (COBOL)** = langage (de programmation) COBOL; **common hardware** = matériel *m* courant *or* banal *or* partagé; **common language** = langage commun *or* banal *or* partagé; **common mode noise** = (bruit) parasite courant; **common software** = logiciel commun *or* de réseau *or* partagé; **common storage area** = zone *f* commune de la mémoire; **the file server memory is mainly common storage area, with a section reserved for the operating system** = la mémoire centrale du serveur est en général banalisée en dehors de la partie réservée au système d'exploitation

communicate *verb* **(a)** communiquer; **he finds it impossible to communicate with his staff** = il n'arrive pas à communiquer avec son personnel; **communicating with head office has been quicker since we installed the fax machine** = les communications avec le siège social sont plus rapides depuis que nous avons le fax **(b)** *(computers)* communiquer *or* dialoguer; **communicating word processor (CWP)** = système de traitement de texte doté d'une interface de communication

communication *noun* **(a)** communication *f;* **communication with the head office has been made easier by the telex** = les communications avec le siège social ont été facilitées par le télex **(b) communications** = transmission *f or* (télé)communication(s) *f(pl);* **communications buffer** = (mémoire) tampon de transmission de données; **communications channel** = canal *f* de transmission; **communications computer** = ordinateur *f* de contrôle des transmissions; **communications control unit (CCU)** = contrôleur *m* de transmission *or* de communication; **communications executive** = gestionnaire *m* de télécommunication; **communications interface adapter** = adaptateur *m* d'interface de communication; **communications link** = ligne *f* de communication *or* de transmission; **communications link control** = contrôle *m* de ligne de communication *or* de transmission; **communications network** = réseau *m* de communication; **communications network processor** = processeur *m* de réseau (de communication); **communications port** = port *m or* connecteur *m* de communication; **communications satellite** = satellite *m* de télécommunication; **communications scanner** = scanner *m* de contrôle d'appel *or* de demande de communication; **data communications** = téléinformatique *f or* télématique *f or* transmission *f* de données; **data communications buffer** = mémoire tampon de transmission de données; **data communications equipment (DCE)** = appareils *mpl or* matériel *m* téléinformatique

QUOTE it requires no additional hardware, other than a communications board in the PC
Electronics & Power

community *noun* groupe *m or* communauté *f or* milieu *m;* **the local business community** = le milieu d'affaires local

◊ **community antenna television (CATV)** *noun* antenne *f* collective de télévision (câblée) *or* système de télévision câblée CATV

compact 1 *adjective* compact, -e *or* dense *or* serré, -e; **compact cassette** = cassette compacte; **compact code** = code compacté; **compact disk (CD)** = disque *m* compact *or* audionumérique *or* disque CD; **compact disk player** = lecteur *m* de disques compacts *or* de disques audionumériques *or* de disques CD; **compact disk ROM** *or* **compact disk-read**

only memory (CD-ROM) = (disque) CD-ROM; **the compact disk ROM can store as much data as a dozen hard disks** = on peut stocker autant de données sur un (disque) CD-ROM que sur une douzaine de disques durs; **compacting algorithm** = algorithme *m* de compactage **2** *verb* compacter; **data compacting** = compactage *m* de données

companding = COMPRESSING AND EXPANDING
◊ **compandor** = COMPRESSOR/EXPANDER

compare *verb* comparer
◊ **compare with** *verb* comparer à *or* avec
◊ **comparable** *adjective* comparable; **the two sets of figures are not comparable** = les deux séries de chiffres ne sont pas comparables
◊ **comparator** *noun* comparateur *m*
◊ **comparison** *noun* comparaison *f;* **there is no comparison between the speeds of the two word processors** = les vitesses de traitement de texte de ces deux logiciels ne sont pas comparables

compatible 1 *adjective* compatible; **is the hardware IBM-compatible?** = est-ce que cet appareil est compatible IBM? **2** *noun* un compatible (IBM); **this computer is much cheaper than the other compatibles** = cet ordinateur est beaucoup moins cher que les autres compatibles (IBM)
◊ **compatibility** *noun (of two hardware or software devices)* compatibilité *f*

QUOTE the compatibles bring computing to the masses
PC Business World
QUOTE low-cost compatibles have begun to find homes as terminals on LANS
Minicomputer News
QUOTE it is a fairly standard feature on most low-cost PC compatibles
Which PC?
QUOTE check for software compatibility before choosing a display or graphics adapter
PC Business World
QUOTE this was the only piece of software I found that wouldn't work, but it does show that there is no such thing as a totally compatible PC clone
Personal Computer World

compile *verb* compiler; **compiling takes a long time with this old version** = il faut beaucoup de temps pour faire la compilation avec cette ancienne version du programme; **debug your program, then compile it** = déboguez votre programme avant de le compiler; **compiled BASIC programs run much faster than the interpretor version** = les programmes en BASIC qui sont compilés sont plus rapides que les versions interprétées; *(program)* **compile and go** = (instruction de) compilation et exécution; **compile phase** = phase f de compilation

◊ **compilation** *noun* compilation f; **compilation error** = erreur f de compilation; **compilation errors result in the job being aborted** = les erreurs de compilation provoquent l'interruption inopinée de la tâche; **compilation time** = temps m de compilation *or* durée f de compilation

◊ **compiler (program)** *noun* compilateur m; **the new compiler has an in-built editor** = le nouveau compilateur possède un éditeur intégré; **this compiler produces a more efficient program** = ce compilateur génère un programme plus performant; **compiler diagnostics** = outils de diagnostic du compilateur; **compiler language** = langage m de compilation; **cross-compiler** = compilateur croisé; **we can use the cross-compiler to develop the software before the new system arrives** = nous pouvons utiliser un compilateur croisé pour développer le logiciel avant l'arrivée du nouveau système; **language compiler** = compilateur (d'un langage évolué)

complement 1 *noun* complément m; **the complement is found by changing the 1s to 0s and 0s to 1s** = on trouve les compléments en remplaçant les 1 par des 0 et les 0 par des 1; **one's complement** = complément à 1; **two's complement** = complément à 2; **nine's complement** = complément à 9; **ten's complement** = complément à 10 **2** *verb (to invert a binary digit)* calculer un complément; **complemented** = (nombre binaire, etc.) complémenté, -ée

◊ **complementary** *adjective* complémentaire; **complementary colours** = couleurs *fpl* complémentaires; **complementary operation** = opération f complémentaire

◊ **complementary metal oxide semiconductor (CMOS)** *noun* semi-conducteur m CMOS

complementation *noun* (ensemble des) nombres *mpl* complets

complete 1 *adjective* **(a)** *(finished)* complet, -ète *or* terminé, -ée; **the spelling check is complete** = la vérification orthographique est terminée; **when this job is complete, the next in the queue is processed** = une fois cette tâche exécutée, ce sera le tour de la suivante dans la file d'attente **(b)** *(total)* complet; **complete operation** = opération complète **2** *verb* terminer *or* achever; **when you have completed the keyboarding, pass the text through the spelling checker** = une fois la saisie du texte terminée, servez-vous du correcteur orthographique pour corriger les fautes

◊ **completion** *noun* fin f *or* achèvement m; **completion date for the new software package is November 15th** = le nouveau progiciel sera achevé le 15 novembre

complex *adjective* complexe; **the complex mathematical formula was difficult to solve** = cette formule mathématique complexe était difficile à résoudre; **complex instruction set computer (CISC)** = ordinateur m à jeu d'instructions complexe (CISC)

◊ **complexity** *noun* complexité f; **complexity measure** = niveau m de complexité

complicated *adjective* compliqué, -ée; **this program is very complicated** = il s'agit d'un programme très compliqué; **the computer design is more complicated than necessary** = cet ordinateur est d'une conception plus compliquée que nécessaire

component *noun (piece of machinery)* pièce f (mécanique); *(electronic device)* composant m; *(of an array or of a matrix)* composant (d'un tableau *or* d'une matrice); **component density** = densité f des composants; **component density increases with production expertise** = la densité des composants augmente avec l'expertise du fabricant; **component density is so high on this motherboard, that no expansion connectors could be fitted** = il y a une telle densité de composants sur la carte-mère qu'il sera impossible d'inclure un connecteur; **component error** = erreur f imputable à un composant défectueux; **component list** = nomenclature *f* des composants

compose *verb (typesetting)* composer; **composing room** = atelier *m* de composition *or* la composition

◊ **composition** *noun* composition *f;* **composition size** = taille *f* des caractères utilisés dans la composition

◊ **compositor** *noun* *(person)* compositeur *m or* typo(graphe) *m;* *(machine)* **electronic compositor** = compositeur électronique

composite circuit *noun* circuit *m* composite

◊ **composite video signal** *noun* signal *m* vidéo composite

compound *adjective* composé, -ée; **compound logical element** = élément *m* logique composé *or* élément logique multiple; **compound statement** = instruction composée; **the debugger cannot handle compound statements** = le débogueur ne peut agir sur les instructions composées

compress *verb* comprimer; **use the archiving program to compress the file** = utilisez un programme d'archivage pour comprimer le fichier

◊ **compressing and expanding (companding)** *noun* compression et expansion (de données)

◊ **compression** *noun* compression *f;* **data compression** = compression de données

◊ **compressor** *noun (circuit or program)* compresseur *m;* **audio compressor** = limiteur *m or* réducteur *m* de signal audio; **compressor/expander (compandor)** = dispositif *m* de compression/expansion *or* concentrateur/déconcentrateur *m* (de données vidéo)

comptometer *noun* compteur *m*

compute *verb* calculer; **connect charges were computed on an hourly rate** = les frais de connection ont été calculés sur une base horaire

◊ **computable** *adjective* calculable

◊ **computation** *noun* calcul *m*

◊ **computational** *adjective* (de) calcul; **computational error** = erreur *f* de calcul

computer *noun* **(a)** ordinateur *m;* *(calculating machine)* calculateur *m;* **analog computer** = ordinateur analogique; **business computer** = ordinateur de gestion *or* de bureau; **digital computer** = ordinateur numérique; **home computer** = ordinateur domestique; **mainframe computer** = gros ordinateur *or* ordinateur central *or* mainframe *m;* **microcomputer** *or* **micro** = micro-ordinateur *or* micro *m;* **minicomputer** *or* **mini** = mini-ordinateur *or* mini *m;* **personal computer (PC)** = ordinateur individuel *or* personnel *or* PC; **single board computer (sbc)** = ordinateur monocarte *or* à carte unique; **single chip computer** = calculateur *or* ordinateur monopuce *or* à puce unique; **supercomputer** = ordinateur géant *or* de grande puissance **(b) computer animation** = animation *f* (d'images) sur ordinateur; **computer applications** = applications *fpl* informatiques; **computer architecture** = architecture *f* d'un système; **computer bureau** = société de services et d'ingénierie informatique (SSII); **computer centre** = centre *m* de calcul; **computer code** = code *m* d'instruction *or* code (en langage) machine; **computer conferencing** = téléconférence *f* (sur réseau informatique) *or* connexion *f* (d'ordinateurs) en mode conversationnel *or* communication *f or* dialogue *m* entre ordinateurs; **computer crime** *or* **computer fraud** = fraude *f* informatique (passible du tribunal correctionnel); **computer dating** = rencontre *f* matrimoniale assistée par ordinateur; **computer department** = service *m* informatique; **computer engineer** = ingénieur *m* informaticien; **computer error** = erreur *f* due à l'ordinateur; **computer file** = fichier *m* informatique *or* d'ordinateur; **computer graphics** = infographie *f;* **computer image processing** = traitement *m* informatique de l'image; **computer independent language** = langage *m* informatique indépendant; **computer input from microfilm (CIM)** = entrée *f* (à partir de *or* par lecture de) microfilm; **computer language** = langage *m* informatique; **computer listing** = sortie *f* d'imprimante *or* listing *m; computer* **literacy** = (le fait d'avoir des) connaissances *fpl* en informatique; **computer-literate** = (personne) qui a des connaissances en informatique; **the managing director is simply not computer-literate** = le directeur général n'a aucune notion d'informatique; **computer logic** = logique *f* des ordinateurs *or* logique informatique; **computer mail** *or* **electronic mail** = messagerie *f* électronique; **computer manager** = directeur, -trice (du service) informatique; **computer network** = réseau *m* informatique *or* réseau d'ordinateurs; **computer numeric control (CNC)** = commande *m* numérique par ordinateur (pour machine-outil); **computer office system** = système bureautique *or* système informatique pour bureau; **computer operator** = opérateur, -trice d'ordinateur; *(computer architecture)* **computer organization** = architecture *f* d'un système; **computer output** = données *fpl* de sortie; **computer output on microfilm (COM)** = sortie *f* (sur) microfilm; **computer power** = puissance *f* d'un ordinateur; **computer program** = programme *m* (informatique); **the user cannot write a computer program with this system** = l'utilisateur ne peut écrire de programme avec ce système; **computer programmer** = programmeur, -euse; **computer run** = exécution *f* d'un programme; **computer science** = l'informatique *f*; **computer services** = services *mpl* informatiques; **computer stationery** = papier *m* listing; **computer system** = système informatique; **computer time** = temps *m* d'ordinateur; **running all those sales reports costs a lot in computer time** = tous ces rapports de vente coûtent cher en temps d'ordinateur; **computer word** = mot *m or* unité *f* d'information

◇ **computer generation** *noun* génération *f* d'ordinateurs

computer- *prefix*

◇ **computer-aided** *or* **computer-assisted** *adjective* assisté, -ée par ordinateur; **computer aided** *or* **assisted design (CAD)** = conception *f or* création assistée par ordinateur (CAO); **computer aided** *or* **assisted design/computer aided** *or* **assisted manufacture (CAD/CAM)** = création et fabrication assistées par ordinateur (CFAO); **computer-aided drafting** = dessin *m* assisté par ordinateur (DAO); **computer aided** *or*

assisted engineering (CAE) = ingénierie *f* assistée par ordinateur (IAO); **computer aided** *or* **assisted instruction (CAI)** = enseignement *m* assisté par ordinateur (EAO); **computer aided** *or* **assisted learning (CAL)** = formation *f* assistée par ordinateur (FAO); **computer aided** *or* **assisted manufacture (CAM)** = fabrication *f* assistée par ordinateur (FAO); **computer aided** *or* **assisted testing (CAT)** = test *m* assisté par ordinateur (TAO); **computer aided** *or* **assisted training (CAT)** = entraînement *m* assisté par ordinateur

◇ **computer-based** *adjective* = COMPUTER-AIDED; **computer-based learning (CBL)** = formation informatisée; **computer-based message system (CBMS)** = (système de) messagerie *f* électronique; **computer-based training (CBT)** = entraînement informatisé

◇ **computer-generated** *adjective* conçu, -e *or* généré, -ée par ordinateur; **computer-generated graphics** = représentations *fpl* graphiques sur ordinateur *or* infographie *f*

◇ **computer-integrated** *adjective* **computer-integrated manufacturing (CIM)** = productique intégrée; **computer-integrated systems** = systèmes (d'exploitation) intégrés; **this firm is a very well-known supplier of computer-integrated systems which allow both batch pagination of very long documents with alteration of individual pages** = cette entreprise est un fournisseur réputé de systèmes informatiques intégrés qui permettent à la fois la pagination de très longs documents et le traitement personnalisé de chaque page

◇ **computer-managed** *adjective* informatisé, -ée *or* géré, -ée par ordinateur; **computer-managed instruction (CMI)** = enseignement interactif géré par ordinateur; **computer-managed learning (CML)** = formation *m* informatisée

◇ **computer-readable** *adjective* **computer-readable codes** = codes *mpl* (en langage) machine

computerize *verb* informatiser; **our stock control has been completely computerized** = notre gestion des stocks est totalement informatisée; **they operate a computerized invoicing system** = leur facturation est informatisée; **computerized branch exchange (CBX)** =

autocommutateur *m* électronique (privé) *or* PBX électronique

◇ **computerization** *noun* informatisation *f;* computerization of the financial sector is proceeding very fast = l'informatisation du secteur financier progresse très rapidement

computing *adjective & noun* (i) informatique *f;* (ii) calcul *m* (fait par un ordinateur); **computing power** = puissance *f* de calcul; **computing speed** = vitesse *f* de calcul (par ordinateur)

concatenate *verb* enchaîner *or* concaténer; **concatenated data set** = concaténation *f* (de données) *or* données reliés en chaîne *or* données chaînées

◇ **concatenation** *noun* concaténation *f*

conceal *verb* cacher *or* dissimuler *or* masquer; **the hidden lines are concealed from view with this algorithm** = les lignes qu'on ne veut pas montrer sont masquées par cet algorithme

concentrate *verb* *(light ray)* concentrer; *(line or circuit or data)* condenser *or* compresser *or* compacter; **to concentrate a beam of light on a lens** = concentrer un rayon lumineux sur une lentille; **the concentrated data was transmitted cheaply** = les données compressées ont pu être transmises à peu de frais

◇ **concentrator** *noun (of lines or data)* concentrateur *m*

concertina fold *noun* (papier) plié en paravent *or* en accordéon

concurrent *adjective* simultané, -ée; **each concurrent process has its own window** = chacune des applications exécutées simultanément possède sa propre fenêtre; **concurrent processing** = multitraitement *m;* **three transputers provide concurrent processing capabilities for the entire department** = trois transordinateurs procurent une capacité de multitraitement suffisante pour tout le département; **concurrent operating system** = système d'exploitation multiprogramme; **concurrent programming** = multiprogrammation *f*

◇ **concurrently** *adverb* simultanément

condenser lens *noun* condensateur *m* optique

condition 1 *noun* condition *f;* **condition code register** = registre *m* des codes condition; **error condition** = condition *f* d'erreur **2** *verb* adapter *or* conditionner; **condition the raw data to a standard format** = adaptez les données brutes à un format standard

◇ **conditional** *adjective* conditionnel, -elle; **conditional breakpoint** = arrêt conditionnel; **conditional jump** *or* **branch** *or* **transfer** = branchement *or* saut conditionnel; **the conditional branch will select routine one if the response is yes and routine two if no** = le branchement conditionnel choisira le programme n° 1 ou 2 suivant que la réponse est oui ou non; **conditional statement** = commande *or* instruction conditionnelle

conduct *verb* conduire *or* transmettre; **to conduct electricity** = conduire l'électricité; **copper conducts well** = le cuivre est bon conducteur (d'électricité)

◇ **conduction** *noun* conductibilité *f or* conduction *f;* **the conduction of electricity by gold contacts** = conduction (d'électricité) par broches de contact (en) *or*

◇ **conductive** *adjective* conductible

◇ **conductor** *noun* conducteur *m;* **copper is a good conductor of electricity** = le cuivre est un bon conducteur

conduit *noun* conduite *f or* tube *m or* tuyau *m or* canalisation *f;* **the cables from each terminal are channelled to the computer centre by metal conduit** = les câbles de liaison de tous les terminaux sont acheminés par conduite métallique *or* par canalisation métallique *or* sous gaine métallique jusqu'au centre informatique

cone *noun (of loudspeaker)* cône *m or* membrane *f* conique

conference *noun (meeting)* réunion *f or* conférence *f; (large)* congrès *m;* **to be in conference** = être en conférence; **conference phone** = téléphone *m* de conférence; **conference room** = salle *f* de conférence(s); **conference call** = téléconférence; **press conference** = conférence de presse

◊ **conferencing** *noun* téléconférence *f;* **computer conferencing** = téléconférence (sur réseau informatique) *or* connexion *f* (d'ordinateurs) en mode conversationnel *or* communication *f or* dialogue *m* entre ordinateurs; **the multi-user BBS has a computer conferencing facility** = l'affichage électronique du réseau permet aux systèmes reliés de communiquer entre eux

confidence level *noun (statistics)* niveau *m* de confiance

configure *verb* configurer; **this terminal has been configured to display graphics** = ce terminal est configuré pour l'affichage de graphiques; **you only have to configure the PC once - when you first buy it** = il suffit de configurer l'ordinateur individuel une seule fois, à l'achat

◊ **configuration** *noun* configuration *f;* **configuration state** = (état de) configuration (d'un système)

◊ **configured-in** *adjective* (avec) configuration validée *or* prête à l'usage *or* disponible

◊ **configured-off** *or* **configured out** *adjective* (avec) configuration invalidée *or* indisponible

---

QUOTE the machine uses RAM to store system configuration information
PC Business World
QUOTE several configuration files are provided to assign memory to the program, depending on the available RAM on your system
PC Business World
QUOTE users can configure four of the eight ports to handle links at speeds of 64K bit/sec
Computer News
QUOTE if you modify a program with the editor, or with a wordprocessor specified in the configuration file, it will know that the program has changed and will execute the new one accordingly
PC Business World

---

conform *verb* obéir à *or* se conformer à *or* être conforme à; **the software will not run if it does not conform to the operating system standards** = le logiciel ne fonctionnera pas s'il ne répond pas aux normes du système d'exploitation

congestion *noun (of system)* encombrement *m*

conjunct *noun (in an logical function)* opérande *m* d'une opération ET *or* d'une conjonction

◊ **conjunction** *noun (logical function)* conjonction *f or* opération *f* ET *or* intersection *f*

connect *verb* connecter (à) *or* relier (à) *or* brancher (sur); **connect time** = temps *m* de connexion

◊ **connection** *noun* connexion *f;* **parallel connection** = connexion parallèle; **their transmission rate is 60,000 bps through parallel connection** = leur débit est de 60 000 bps sur connexion parallèle

connective *noun (symbol between two operands)* connectif *m*

connector *noun* connecteur *m;* **the connector at the end of the cable will fit any standard serial port** = le connecteur relié au câble s'adapte sur tout port série standard; **card edge connector** = connecteur de carte; **connector engineering** *or* **connector technology** = connectique *f*

conscious error *noun* erreur *f* consciente

consecutive *adjective* consécutif, -ive; **the computer ran three consecutive files** = l'ordinateur a exploité trois fichiers consécutifs

◊ **consecutively** *adverb* de façon consécutive *or* consécutivement *or* l'un(e) à la suite de l'autre; **the sections of the program run consecutively** = les différentes sections du programme s'éxécutent l'une à la suite de l'autre

console *noun* console *f or* poste *m* de travail; *(mainframe)* pupitre *m or* console (de commande); **the console consists of input device such as a keyboard, and an output device such as a printer or CRT** = la console comporte un périphérique d'entrée: par exemple un clavier, et un périphérique de sortie: soit une imprimante ou un écran

constant **1** *noun (as opposed to a variable)* constante *f* **2** *adjective (which does not change)* constant, -e *or* fixe; **the disk drive motor spins at a constant**

velocity = le moteur du lecteur de disquettes tourne à une vitesse constante; **constant length field** = champ de taille fixe; **constant ratio code** = code *m* à rapport (de bits) constant *or* fixe

construct *verb* construire *or* fabriquer

◊ **construction** *noun* construction *f or* fabrication *f;* **construction of the prototype is advancing rapidly** = la construction du prototype progresse rapidement; **construction techniques have changed over the past few years** = les techniques de fabrication ont évolué au cours des dernières années

consult *verb* consulter *or* demander l'avis de quelqu'un; **he consulted the maintenance manager about the disk fault** = il a demandé l'avis du responsable de (la) maintenance sur le mauvais fonctionnement du disque

◊ **consultancy** *noun* assistance *f or* conseil *f;* **a consultancy firm** = cabinet-conseil *m or* société d'assistance technique *m;* **he offers a consultancy service** = il offre une assistance technique

◊ **consultant** *noun* expert *m or* spécialiste *m&f or* ingénieur-conseil *m;* **they called in a computer consultant to advise them on the system design** = ils ont fait venir un expert en informatique pour les conseiller sur la conception du système

◊ **consulting** *adjective* **a consulting engineer** = ingénieur-conseil *m*

consumables *plural noun* consommables *mpl;* **put all the printer leads and paper under the heading 'consumables'** = il faut inclure les câbles pour imprimantes et le papier sous la rubrique 'consommables'

contact 1 *noun* **(a)** *(section of a switch or connector)* contact *m or* connexion *f;* **gold contacts** = contacts or; **the circuit is not working because the contact is dirty** = le circuit ne fonctionne pas parce que la connexion est encrassée; *(keyboard)* **contact bounce** = rebond *m* (de contact *or* de touche) **(b)** *(photography)* **contact negative** = (film) négatif *m* contact; **contact print** = épreuve *f* de contact **2** *verb* contacter *or* joindre

contain *verb* contenir; **each carton contains two computers and their peripherals** = chaque caisse contient deux ordinateurs et leurs périphériques; **we have lost a file containing important documents** = nous avons égaré un dossier contenant des documents importants

content *noun (ideas)* contenu *m* (d'une lettre)

◊ **contents** *plural noun* **(a)** *(things contained)* contenu (d'une boîte, etc.); **the contents of the bottle poured out onto the computer keyboard** = le contenu de la bouteille s'est répandu sur le clavier de l'ordinateur; **the customs officials inspected the contents of the box** = les douaniers ont examiné le contenu de la caisse; *(the words written in the letter)* **the contents of the letter** = le contenu *or* le texte de la lettre **(b)** *(list of items in a file)* répertoire *m or* liste *f*

◊ **content-addressable** *adjective* adressable par le contenu; **content-addressable file** *or* **location** = fichier *m or* location *f* adressable par le contenu; **content-addressable memory (CAM)** = mémoire *f* adressable par le contenu *or* mémoire associative

contention *noun* contention *f;* **contention bus** = bus *m* d'arbitrage *or* de régulation; **contention delay** = délai *m or* retard *m* de contention

context *noun* contexte *m;* **the example shows how the word is used in context** = l'exemple démontre l'emploi du mot dans son contexte

contiguous *adjective* contigu, -ë; **contiguous file** = fichier contigu; **contiguous graphics** = graphiques contigus; **most display units do not provide contiguous graphics: the characters have a small space on each side to improve legibility** = la plupart des écrans ne permettent pas l'affichage de graphiques contigus; chaque caractère (graphique) est bordé de chaque côté par un espace qui améliore sa lisibilité

contingency plan *noun* plan *m* d'urgence

continue *verb* continuer

◊ **continual** *adjective* continuel, -elle; **the continual system breakdowns have slowed down the processing** = les pannes continuelles du système ont ralenti le traitement

◊ **continually** *adverb* continuellement *or* sans cesse

◊ **continuation** *noun* continuation *f; (page or screen of text that follows)* **continuation page** = suite *f*

◊ **continuity** *noun* **(a)** *(conduction path)* continuité *f* **(b)** *(of scenes in film)* continuité

◊ **continuous** *adjective* continu, -e *or* en continu; **continuous data stream** = flux *m* continu *or* ininterrompu de données; **continuous feed** = alimentation (du papier) en continu; **continuous loop** = boucle *f* sans fin; **continuous signal** = signal *m* continu; **continuous stationery** = papier *m* en continu; **continuous wave** = onde *f* continue *or* entretenue

◊ **continuously** *adverb* continuellement *or* sans interruption; **the printer overheated after working continuously for five hours** = l'imprimante s'est mise à chauffer après cinq heures de marche sans interruption

contrast 1 *noun* **(a)** contraste *m; the* **control allows you to adjust brightness and contrast** = ce bouton vous permet de régler la luminosité et le contraste; **contrast enhancement filter** = filtre *m* d'amélioration du contraste **(b)** bouton *m or* touche *f* (de) contraste **2** *verb* comparer (à *or* avec); **the old data was contrasted with the latest information** = on a comparé les anciennes données aux informations les plus récentes

◊ **contrasting** *adjective* contrastant, -e *or* contrasté, -ée; **a cover design in contrasting colours** = un dessin de couverture aux couleurs contrastées

control 1 *verb (to manage)* contrôler *or* piloter; *(to monitor)* contrôler *or* surveiller *or* vérifier; **controlled vocabulary** = vocabulaire contrôlé NOTE: **controlling - controlled 2** *noun* **(a)** contrôle *m or* surveillance *f or* vérification *f;* **control total** = total *m* de vérification *or* de contrôle; **out of control** = hors de contrôle **(b)** *(section of computer)* contrôle *or* pilote *m;* **control computer** = ordinateur de contrôle; **control unit (CU)** = unité de contrôle (de processus); **control word** = mot *m* de contrôle *or* de

commande; **device control character** = caractère *m* de contrôle *or* de commande de périphérique; **line control** = commandes *fpl or* protocole *m* de transmission **(c)** *(key or data)* (i) touche *f* de commande; (ii) données *fpl or* touche de contrôle; **control block** = bloc *m* (de données) de contrôle; **control bus** = bus *m* de contrôle; **control card** = carte *f* de contrôle; **control character** = caractère *m* de contrôle; **control cycle** = cycle *m* de contrôle; **control data** = données *fpl* de commande *or* de contrôle; **control driven** = commandé par les codes CTRL *or* asservi aux codes CTRL (générés par la touche contrôle); **control field** = champ *m* de contrôle; **control instruction** = instruction *f* de contrôle; **the next control instruction will switch to italics** = la prochaine instruction de contrôle vous donnera les italiques; **control language** = langage *m* de commande; **control memory** *or* **ROM** = mémoire fixe *or* ROM; **control mode** = mode *m* (de) contrôle *or* mode CTRL; **control panel** = tableau *m* de commande; **control program/monitor** *or* **control program for microcomputers (CP/M)** = système *m* d'exploitation CP/M; **control register** = registre *m* de commande de contrôle; **control sequence** = séquence *f* de commande (d'exécution); **control signal** = signal *m* de contrôle *or* de commande; *(to the CPU)* **control statement** = instruction *f or* commande *f* de contrôle; **control token** = jeton *m* de contrôle (de réseau); *(to the CPU)* **control transfer** = transfert *m* de contrôle **(d)** **control group** = groupe *m* témoin *or* de contrôle; *(for benchmark)* **control systems** = systèmes de contrôle

◊ **controllable** *adjective* contrôlable *or* qui peut être contrôlé, -ée

◊ **controller** *noun* contrôleur *m or* pilote *m* de périphérique(s); **display controller** = contrôleur *or* pilote d'écran *or* d'affichage; **printer's controller** = contrôleur *or* pilote d'imprimante

QUOTE a printer's controller is the brains of the machine. It translates the signals coming from your computer into printing instructions that result in a hard copy of your electronic document

Publish

QUOTE there are seven print control characters which can be placed in a document

Personal Computer World

convention *noun* convention *f*

conversational *adjective* conversationnel, -elle *or* interactif, -ive; **conversational mode** mode *m* conversationnel *or* mode dialogué *or* mode interactif; **conversational terminal** = terminal conversationnel *or* interactif

◊ **conversion** *noun* conversion *f;* **conversion equipment** = convertisseur *m;* **conversion tables** *or* **translation tables** = tables *fpl* d'équivalence *or* de conversion; **conversion tables may be created and used in conjunction with the customer's data to convert it to our systems codes** = on peut établir des tables d'équivalence qui serviront à convertir les données clients aux codes utilisés par notre système; **conversion program** = (programme) convertisseur *m or* programme *m* de conversion

◊ **convert** *verb* convertir *or* adapter

◊ **convertibility** *noun* convertibilité *f*

◊ **convertible** *adjective* convertible

◊ **converter** *or* **convertor** *noun* convertisseur *m;* **the convertor allowed the old data to be used on the new system** = grâce au convertisseur les anciennes données sont acceptées par le nouveau système; **analog to digital converter (ADC)** = convertisseur analogique-numérique; **digital to analog converter (DAC)** = convertisseur numérique-analogique

◊ **convey** *verb* transmettre *or* transporter

◊ **conveyor** *noun* convoyeur *m or* bande *f* transporteuse

coordinate 1 *noun (on a graph)* **coordinates** = coordonnées; **coordinate graph** = graphe *m* (exprimé en coordonnées); **polar coordinates** = coordonnées polaires; **rectangular coordinates** = coordonnées rectangulaires 2 *verb* coordonner; **she has to coordinate the keyboarding of several parts of a file in six different locations** = elle doit coordonner la saisie des diverses parties d'un fichier qui se fait dans six centres différents

◊ **coordination** *noun* coordination *f*

copier = COPYING MACHINE, PHOTOCOPIER

copper *noun* cuivre *m*

◊ **copperplate printing** *noun* impression *f* en taille douce

coprocessor *noun* co-processeur *m;* **graphics coprocessor** = coprocesseur graphique; **maths coprocessor** = coprocesseur mathématique

copy 1 *noun* **(a)** copie *f or* double *m;* **file copy** = copie pour archivage **(b)** document *m;* **clean copy** = texte *m* sans erreur *or* sans modification; **fair copy** *or* **final copy** = texte *m* définitif; **hard copy** = sortie *f* d'imprimante *or* imprimé *m;* **rough copy** = brouillon *m or* ébauche *f;* **top copy** = original *m* **(c)** texte *m;* **Tuesday is the last date for copy for the advertisement** = le texte publicitaire doit nous arriver mardi, dernier délai; **copy reader** = lecteur, -trice **(d)** *(book or magazine or newspaper)* exemplaire *m; (issue of magazine or newspaper)* numéro *m;* **I kept yesterday's copy of 'The Times'** = j'ai toujours le 'Times' d'hier; **I read it in the office copy of 'Fortune'** = je l'ai lu dans l'exemplaire de 'Fortune' que nous avons au bureau 2 *verb* copier *or* faire une copie *or* reproduire (un document); **there is a memory resident utility which copies the latest files onto backing store every 40 minutes** = il existe un utilitaire résident qui copie les fichiers les plus récents sur un support de sauvegarde toutes les 40 minutes

◊ **copying machine** *or* **copier** *noun* photocopieur *m or* copieur *m*

◊ **copy protect** 1 *noun* dispositif *m* de protection (contre la copie) *or* dispositif anticopie 2 *verb* protéger (contre la copie); **the program is not copy protected** = le programme n'est pas protégé (contre la copie); **all disks are copy protected** = toutes les disquettes sont munies d'un dispositif anticopie *or* tous les disques sont protégés contre la copie

◊ **copy protection** *noun* (système *or* dispositif *or* codage) anticopie *or* de protection contre la copie; **a hard disk may crash because of faulty copy protection** = il arrive qu'une protection anticopie défectueuse entraîne la détérioration du disque dur; **the new program will come without copy protection** = le nouveau programme ne sera pas protégé contre la copie

copyright 1 *noun* droit *m* d'auteur *or* copyright *m or* propriété *f* littéraire;

Copyright Act = Convention *f* sur le droit d'auteur; **work which is out of copyright** = oeuvre qui est dans le domaine public; **work still in copyright** = oeuvre protégée par un copyright *or* dont les droits de reproduction sont réservés *or* oeuvre sous copyright; **infringement of copyright** *or* **copyright infringement** = contrefaçon *f or* reproduction *f* illégale *or* violation *f* du droit d'auteur; **copyright notice** = mention *f* de copyright (dans un livre); **copyright owner** = titulaire *m&f* d'un droit d'auteur *or* d'un copyright **2** *verb* déposer un copyright **3** *adjective* protégé, -ée (par un copyright); **it is illegal to take copies of a copyright work** = photocopier une oeuvre sous copyright est illégal

◊ **copyrighted** *adjective* (oeuvre) sous copyright *or* protégé -ée par un copyright

CORAL = COMMON REAL-TIME APPLICATIONS LANGUAGE langage *m* (d'application temps réel) CORAL

cord *noun* fil *m* de liaison *or* cordon *m or* câble *m*

◊ **cordless telephone** *noun* téléphone *m* sans cordon *or* sans fil

core *noun* **(a)** *(of cable)* âme *f or* coeur *m* **(b) core memory** *or* **store** = mémoire *f* centrale; **core program** = programme en mémoire centrale

coresident *adjective* *(program)* co-résident, -e

coroutine *noun* module *m* d'accompagnement *or* coroutine *f*

correct 1 *adjective* correct, -e *or* exact, -e **2** *verb* corriger; **error correcting code** = code *m* correcteur d'erreur

◊ **correction** *noun* correction *f*

◊ **corrective maintenance** *noun* maintenance *f* corrective *or* dépannage *m or* réparation *f*

correspond *verb* **(a)** *(to write letters)* correspondre *or* écrire; **to correspond with someone** = correspondre avec quelqu'un *or* être en correspondance avec quelqu'un **(b)** *(to fit or agree)* **to correspond with something** = correspondre à quelque chose

◊ **correspondence** *noun* **(a)** *(letter-writing)* correspondance *f;* **business correspondence** = correspondance commerciale *or* d'affaires; **to be in correspondence with someone** = être en correspondance avec quelqu'un **(b)** *(fitting or agreeing)* correspondance

◊ **correspondent** *noun* **(a)** *(person who writes letters)* correspondant, -e **(b)** *(journalist)* correspondant, -e *or* journaliste *m&f;* **the computer correspondent** = le correspondant (de la section) informatique; **the 'Times' business correspondent** = le correspondant économique du 'Times'

corrupt 1 *adjective* corrompu, -e *or* erroné, -ée **2** *verb* corrompre *or* détériorer *or* faire perdre l'intégrité; *(informal)* véroler; **power loss during disk access can corrupt the data** = un problème de tension pendant l'accès au disque peut détériorer *or* véroler les données *or* faire perdre l'intégrité des données

◊ **corruption** *noun* corruption *f or* détérioration *f;* **data corruption** = corruption *or* détérioration de données; **acoustic couplers suffer from data corruption more than the direct connect form of modem** = les coupleurs acoustiques sont plus susceptibles aux détériorations de données que les modems branchés directement sur la ligne; **data corruption on the disk has made one file unreadable** = la corruption de données sur la disquette a rendu le fichier impossible à lire

coulomb *noun* coulomb *m*

count *verb* compter

◊ **counting perforator** *noun* perforateur-compteur *m* (de composition)

counter *noun* compteur *m;* **the loop will repeat itself until the counter reaches 100** = la boucle se répètera jusqu'à ce que le compteur atteigne 100; **the number of items changed are recorded by the counter** = le nombre de changements est enregistré sur le compteur; **instruction** *or* **program counter** = compteur d'instruction *or* registre *m* compteur

counter- *prefix* contre-

◇ **counterprogramming** *noun* contreprogrammation *f or* mise en place d'un programme concurrent

couple *verb* joindre *or* coupler; **the two systems are coupled together** = les deux systèmes sont couplés *or* connectés l'un à l'autre

◇ **coupler** *noun* coupleur *m;* **acoustic coupler** = coupleur acoustique

courseware *noun* didacticiel *m*

coverage *noun* *(of newspaper)* couverture *f; (of broadcast)* potentiel *m* d'écoute; **press coverage** *or* **media coverage** = couverture (médiatique) *or* reportage *m;* **the company had good media coverage for the launch of its new model** = la société a eu une excellente couverture (médiatique) pour le lancement de son nouveau modèle *or* le lancement du nouveau modèle a été bien couvert par les médias

CP = CARD PUNCH

CPE = CENTRAL PROCESSING ELEMENT

cpi = CHARACTERS PER INCH

CP/M = CONTROL PROGRAM/MONITOR

cps = CHARACTERS PER SECOND

CPU = CENTRAL PROCESSING UNIT unité *f* centrale (de traitement) *or* processeur *m* central; **CPU cycle** = (temps de) cycle *m* de l'unité centrale *or* cycle d'horloge *or* cycle CPU; **CPU elements** = éléments de l'unité centrale *or* éléments CPU; **CPU handshaking** = protocole *m* d'échange d'informations entre CPU et périphérique *or* handshaking *m;* **CPU time** = temps d'utilisation de l'unité centrale *or* du processeur *or* temps CPU

CR (a) = CARRIAGE RETURN **(b)** = CARD READER

crash 1 *noun* défaillance *f or* panne *f or* crash *m;* **disk crash** = détérioration *f or*

destruction *f* (accidentelle) *or* crash du disque (dur) **2** *verb (of a computer)* tomber en panne complète (nécessitant une réparation); **the disk head has crashed and the data may have been lost** = la tête de lecture du disque est tombée en panne et il se peut que les données aient été perdues; *(of disk)* être détruit *or* détérioré

◇ **crash-protected** *adjective* protégé contre toute détérioration *or* destruction (accidentelle); **if the disk is crash-protected, you will never lose your data** = si vous vous servez d'un disque protégé contre la destruction accidentelle, vous ne perdrez jamais vos données

crawl *noun* défilement *m* ascendant du générique *or* crawl *m*

CRC (a) = CAMERA-READY COPY **(b)** = CYCLIC REDUNDANCY CHECK

create *verb* créer *or* produire; **a new file was created on disk to store the document** = on a créé un nouveau fichier sur la disquette pour archiver le document; **move to the CREATE NEW FILE instruction on the menu** = allez à CRÉATION D'UN DOSSIER sur le menu

credit *noun* **(a)** *(finance)* crédit *m;* **credit card** = carte *f* de crédit **(b) credits** = *(film)* générique *m; (magazine, etc.)* crédits *mpl*

crew *noun* équipe *f;* **camera crew** = équipe cinématographique *or* de cinéastes; **the camera crew had to film all day in the snow** = l'équipe de cinéastes a dû tourner toute la journée dans la neige

crippled leapfrog test *noun* test *m* sélectif limité *or* restreint

criterion *noun* critère *m*
NOTE: plural is **criteria**

critical *adjective* critique; **critical fusion frequency** = fréquence *f* critique de fusion; **critical resource** = ressource *f* critique

CR/LF = CARRIAGE RETURN/LINE FEED

cropping *noun* cropping *m or* découpage *m;* **the photographs can be edited by cropping, sizing, touching up, etc.** = les photos peuvent être éditées par découpage, dimensionnement, retouche etc.

cross- *prefix* contre- *or* croisé, -ée; **cross fade** = fondu *m* enchaîné; **cross modulation** = intermodulation *f*

◊ **cross-assembler** *noun* assembleur *m* croisé

◊ **cross-check** *noun* contrôle *m* croisé *or* double contrôle *or* contre-épreuve *f*

◊ **cross-compiler** compilateur *m* croisé

crossfire *noun* diaphonie *f or* interférence *f* induite

◊ **crossover** *noun* changement *m or* passage *m;* **the crossover to computerized file indexing was difficult** = il a été difficile de passer à un système d'index informatisé

◊ **cross-reference 1** *noun (in book)* renvoi *m or* référence *f; (to find a file)* référence croisée **2** *verb* faire un renvoi *or* référer (à une autre section d'un document); **the SI units are cross-referenced to the appendix** = les unités SI font l'objet d'un renvoi à l'appendice

◊ **cross-reference generator** *noun* générateur *m* de renvois

◊ **cross-section** *noun* coupe *f;* **the cross-section of the optical fibre showed the problem** = une coupe de la fibre optique a révélé la source du problème

◊ **crosstalk** *noun* diaphonie *f or* parasites *mpl;* **the crosstalk was so bad, the signal was unreadable** = il y avait une telle diaphonie que le signal était illisible *or* le signal était rendu illisible par les parasites

CRT = CATHODE RAY TUBE

cruncher, crunching *see* NUMBER

crushing *noun (TV)* écrasement *m* (de l'image)

cryogenic memory *noun* mémoire *f* cryogénique

cryptanalysis *noun* analyse *f* cryptographique

cryptography *noun* cryptographie *f*

◊ **cryptographic** *adjective* cryptographique; **cryptographic algorithm** = algorithme *m* cryptographique *or* de cryptage; **cryptographic key** = clé *f* de cryptage *or* de chiffrage

crystal *noun* cristal *m;* **liquid crystal display (LCD)** = affichage *m* à cristaux liquides; **crystal microphone** = microphone *m* à quartz; **crystal oscillator** = oscillateur *m* à quartz

CSDC = CIRCUIT SWITCHED DIGITAL CIRCUITRY

CSM = COMBINED SYMBOL MATCHING

CSMA-CD = CARRIER SENSE MULTIPLE ACCESS-COLLISION DETECTION

CTR *or* **CTRL** = CONTROL touche *f* de contrôle *or* CTR(L)

CTS = CLEAR TO SEND

CU = CONTROL UNIT

cue *noun* (message d') invitation *f* à taper une instruction

CUG = CLOSED USER GROUP

cumulative index *noun* index *m* cumulatif

current 1 *adjective* courant, -e; **current address** = adresse *f* courante; **current address register (CAR)** = registre *m* d'adresse courante; **current instruction register (CIR)** = registre d'instruction courante **2** *noun (electric)* courant *m;* **direct current (DC)** = courant continu; **alternating current (AC)** = courant alternatif (CA)

cursor *noun* curseur *m or* marqueur *m;* **cursor control keys** = touches *fpl* de contrôle du curseur; **cursor home** = coin *m* gauche supérieur (de l'écran) *or* début *m* de l'écran; **cursor pad** = touches de contrôle du curseur; **addressable cursor**

= curseur adressable; **destructive cursor** = curseur effaceur

> QUOTE above the cursor pad are the insert and delete keys, which when shifted produce clear and home respectively
> *Computing Today*
> QUOTE further quick cursor movements are available for editing by combining one of the arrow keys with the control function
> *Personal Computer World*

curve *noun* courbe *f;* **to plot a curve** = tracer une courbe; **characteristic curve** = courbe caractéristique

customer *noun* client, -e; **customer engineering** = maintenance *f* du parc clients; **customer service department** = service *m* après-vente *or* service clients

◊ **custom-built** *adjective* personnalisé, -ée *or* (fait) sur mesure *or* sur commande

◊ **custom ROM (PROM)** *noun* ROM personnalisée

◊ **customize** *verb* fabriquer sur commande *or* personnaliser; **we use customized software** = nous utilisons des logiciels personnalisés *or* écrits sur commande

cut 1 *noun* coupure *f;* **the editors have asked for cuts in the first chapter** = les éditeurs ont demandé de faire des coupures au premier chapitre *or* de réduire le premier chapitre **2** *verb* **(a)** couper; **cut-in notes** = notes *fpl* marginales; *(for paper)* **cut sheet feeder** = (système d') alimentation *f* feuille à feuille **(b)** couper *or* réduire (un texte); **the author was asked to cut his manuscript to 250 pages** = on a demandé à l'auteur de réduire son manuscrit à 250 pages NOTE: **cuts - cutting - has cut**

◊ **cut and paste** *noun* coupage/collage *m*

◊ **cut off** *verb* **(a)** couper; **six metres of paper were cut off the reel** = on a coupé six mètres du rouleau de papier **(b)** couper *or* arrêter; **the electricity supply was cut off** = il y a eu une coupure de courant *or* une panne de secteur

◊ **cutoff** *noun & adjective* point *m* d'arrêt *or* coupure *f;* **cutoff frequency** = fréquence *f* de coupure

◊ **cutting** *noun* coupure *f; (in film studio)* **cutting room** = salle *f* de montage; **press cuttings** = coupures de journal

CWP = COMMUNICATING WORD PROCESSOR

cybernetics *noun* la cybernétique

cycle *noun* cycle *m;* **action cycle** = cycle fonctionnel; **clock cycle** = cycle d'horloge; **cycle availability** = (période de) disponibilité *f* dans le cycle; **cycle count** = nombre *m* de cycles; **cycle index** = index *m* de cycle; **cycle shift** = permutation *f* circulaire; **cycle stealing** = (exploitation par) vol *m* de cycle; **cycle time** = temps *m* de cycle

◊ **cyclic** *adjective* cyclique *or* circulaire; **cyclic access** = accès *m* cyclique; **cyclic check** = contrôle *m* cyclique; **cyclic code** = code *m* binaire réfléchi *or* code de Gray; **cyclic decimal code** = code décimal réfléchi; **cyclic redundancy check (CRC)** = contrôle par redondance cyclique; **cyclic shift** = permutation *f or* décalage *m* circulaire

cylinder *noun (in multi-disks)* cylindre *m*

cypher = CIPHER

Dd

D représentation hexadécimale du nombre 13 *or* D

3D = THREE-DIMENSIONAL à trois dimensions *or* tridimensionnel, -elle

> QUOTE the software can create 3D images using data from a scanner or photographs from an electronic microscope
> *PC Business World*

DAC *or* **d/a converter** = DIGITAL TO ANALOG CONVERTER convertisseur *m* numérique-analogique; **speech is output from the computer via a D/A converter =** l'ordinateur émet un signal vocal via un convertisseur numérique-analogique; **the D/A converter on the output port controls the analog machine =** le convertisseur numérique-analogique du port de sortie contrôle la machine analogique

DAD = DIGITAL AUDIO DISK

dagger *noun (printing sign)* croix *f* (†); **double dagger =** croix double (‡)

daisy chain *noun* chaîne *f;* **daisy chain bus =** bus *m* de chaîne *or* bus série *or* en cascade; **daisy chain interrupt =** interruption en série *or* en chaîne; **daisy chain recursion =** boucle *f* de récurrence ◊ **daisy-chain** *verb* relier en chaîne *or* en série *or* en cascade

> QUOTE you can often daisy-chain cards or plug them into expansion boxes
> *Byte*

daisy-wheel *noun* marguerite *f* (d'imprimante); **daisy-wheel printer** *or* **daisy-wheel typewriter =** imprimante *f* à marguerite; **a daisy-wheel printer produces much better quality text than a dot-matrix, but is slower =** l'imprimante à marguerite donne un bien meilleur résultat que l'imprimante matricielle mais elle est plus lente

DAMA = DEMAND ASSIGNED MULTIPLE ACCESS

damage 1 *noun* dommage *m or* avarie *f;* **to suffer damage =** subir des dommages; **to cause damage =** endommager; **the breakdown of the electricity supply caused damage estimated at £100,000 =** les dommages causés par la panne d'électricité s'élèvent à environ 100 000 livres sterling **2** *verb* endommager *or* abîmer; **the faulty read/write head appears to have damaged the disks =** il semble que la tête de lecture défectueuse ait endommagé les disques; **the hard disk was damaged when it was dropped =** le disque dur a été endommagé quand on l'a laissé tomber
◊ **damaged** *adjective* endommagé, -ée *or* abîmé, -ée; *(file or data)* détérioré, -ée *or* corrompu,-e; **is it possible to repair the damaged files? =** est-il possible de récupérer les fichiers détériorés?

D to A converter = DIGITAL TO ANALOG CONVERTER

dark current *noun* courant *m* noir
◊ **dark trace tube** *noun* tube *m* ombré

darkroom *noun (photography)* chambre *f* noire

DASD = DIRECT ACCESS STORAGE DEVICE

dash *noun (short line in printing)* tiret *m; (typography)* **em dash** *or* **em rule =** tiret cadratin; **en dash** *or* **en rule =** tiret demi-cadratin *or* tiret de césure *or* tiret court

DAT = DIGITAL AUDIO TAPE bande *f* (magnétique) audionumérique; **DAT produces a very high quality sound =** une bande audionumérique produit un son de très haute qualité

data *noun* donnée(s) *f(pl)*; **data is input at one of several workstations** = les données sont saisies sur l'un des nombreux postes de travail; **the company stores data on customers in its main computer file** = les coordonnées des clients de la société sont entrées sur l'ordinateur principal; **a user needs a password to access data** = l'utilisateur doit utiliser un mot de passe pour accéder aux données; **raw data** = données brutes; **data above voice (DAV)** = (transmission de) données *fpl* supravocales; **data access management** = gestion *f* d'accès aux données; **data acquisition** = acquisition *f* de données; **data adapter unit** = adaptateur *m* de canal de transmission de données; **data administrator** = gestionnaire *m* de données; **data aggregate** = agrégat *m or* données structurées *or* agrégées; **data analysis** = analyse *f* de données; **data area** = zone *f* de données; **data block** = bloc *m* de données; **data break** = arrêt *m* de transmission de données; **data buffer** = (mémoire) tampon *m* de données; **data bus** = bus *m* de données; **data capture** = saisie *f* de données; **data carrier** = *(medium)* support *m* de données *or* d'information; *(waveform)* (onde) porteuse *f* de données; *(RS232C signal)* **data carrier detect (DCD)** = détecteur *m* d'onde porteuse *or* signal *m* de détection de porteuse; **the call is stopped if the software does not receive a DCD signal from the modem** = l'appel est bloqué si le logiciel ne reçoit pas de signal de détection de porteuse du modem; **data cartridge** = cartouche *f* de données; **data chaining** = liaison *f* (de données) en chaîne *or* chaînage de données; **data channel** = canal *m* de transmission de données; *(error in reading data)* **data check** = brève interruption de transmission de données (causée par un défaut du support magnétique); **data circuit** = circuit *m* d'échange (bi-directionnel) de données; **data cleaning** = nettoyage *m* des données *or* correction *f* d'erreurs; **data collection** = collecte *f* de données; **data collection platform** = plate-forme *f* de collecte de données; **data communications** = télématique *f or* téléinformatique *f or* transmission *f* de données; **data communications buffer** = (mémoire) tampon *m* de transmission de données; **data communications equipment (DCE)** = appareils *mpl or* matériel *m* (de) téléinformatique; **data**

communications network = réseau *m* téléinformatique *or* de transmission de données; **data compacting** = compactage *m* de données; **all the files were stored on one disk with this new data compacting routine** = tous les fichiers ont pu être stockés sur une seule disquette grâce au nouveau programme de compactage; **data compression** = compression *f* de données; **scanners use a technique called data compression which manages to reduce, even by a third, the storage required** = les scanners utilisent la technique dite de compression de données qui peut réduire du tiers la mémoire nécessaire; **data concentrator** = concentrateur *m* de données; **data connection** = connexion *f* (pour transmission de données); **data control** = contrôle *m* des données; **data corruption** = corruption *f or* détérioration *f* de données; **data corruption occurs each time the motor is switched on** = chaque fois qu'on met le système sous tension, il y a corruption de données; **data delimiter** = (symbole) délimiteur *m* de données; **data description language (DDL)** = langage *m* de description de données; **data dictionary/directory (DD/D)** = dictionnaire/répertoire *m* de données; *(part of a COBOL progam)* **data division** = rubrique *f* de déclaration des données; **data-driven** = activé, -ée par reconnaissance des données; **data element** = élément *m* de données; **data element chain** = chaîne *f* d'éléments de données; **data encryption** = chiffrage *m or* chiffrement *m or* cryptage *m* de données; **data encryption standard (DES)** = norme *f or* standard *m* de cryptage de données; **data entry** = (mode d') entrée *f or* introduction *f or* (méthode de) saisie *f* de données; **data error** = erreur *f* de données;

data field = champ *m* de données; **data file** = fichier *m* de données; **the data file has to be analysed** = il faut analyser le fichier de données; **data flow** = flux *m* de données; **data flowchart** = ordinogramme *m* de données; **the data flowchart allowed us to improve throughput, by using a better structure** = l'ordinogramme des données nous a permis d'améliorer nos résultats à l'aide d'une meilleure structure; **data flow diagram (DFD)** = diagramme *m* de flux de données; **data format** = format *m* de données; **data hierarchy** = hiérarchie *f* des données; *(between a CPU and peripherals)* **data highway** = bus *m* de transfert de données; **data independence** = autonomie *f* des données; **data input** = saisie *f or* entrée *f* de données; **data input bus (DIB)** = bus *m* d'entrée; **data integrity** = intégrité *f* des données; **data in voice (DIV)** = transmission *f* de données vocales; **data item** = élément *m* de données; **data level** = niveau *m* de données; **data link** = liaison *f* de données; **data link control** = contrôle *m* de liaison de données; **data link layer** = couche *f* (de) liaison de données; **data logging** = enregistrement *f* (automatique et chronologique) de données; **data management** = gestion *f* de données; **data manipulation language (DML)** = langage *m* de manipulation de données; **data medium** = support *m* de données; **data migration** = migration *f* de données *or* transfert *m* de données (sur dispositif hors ligne); **data name** = nom *m* de donnée; **problems occur if an ambiguous data name is chosen** = il y a des difficultés lorsque le nom de la donnée est ambigu; **data network** = réseau *m* téléinformatique *or* de transmission de données; **data origination** = génération *f or* création *f* de données;

data path = chemin *m or* trajet *m* (des données) *or* voie de transmission de données; **data pointer** = pointeur *m* (de position) de données; **data preparation** = préparation *f* des données; **data processing (DP** *or* **dp)** = traitement *m* de données *or* traitement de l'information; **data processing manager (DPM)** = responsable *m&f* du service informatique; **data protection** = protection *f* sécurité *f* des données; **Data Protection Act** = loi Informatique et Libertés; **data rate** = vitesse *f* de traitement *or* de transmission de données;

data record = enregistrement *m* de données; **data reduction** = réduction *m* de données; **data register** = registre *m* de données; **data reliability** = qualité *f or* fiabilité *f* des données; **data retrieval** = (i) recherche *f* documentaire; (ii) extraction *f* de données; **data routing** = acheminement *m or* routage *m* des données; **data security** = sécurité *f* des données *or* de l'information; **data services** = service *m* de téléinformatique *or* de transmission de données; **data set ready (DSR)** = (signal de) prêt à recevoir; **data signals** = signaux *mpl* (de transmission) de données; **data signalling rate** = débit *m or* vitesse *f* de transmission de données; **data sink** =

collecteur *m* de données *or* puits *m or* terminal *m* récepteur (de données); **data source** = source *f or* émetteur *m* de données; **data station** = poste *m* informatique de télétransmission; **data storage** = *(medium)* mémoire *f* de données; *(storing)* stockage *m or* mise *f* en mémoire (de données);

data stream = flot de données *m;* **data strobe** = (signal de) validation *f* de données transmises; **data structure** = structure *f* des données; **data switching exchange** = centre *m* de commutation des données; **data tablet** = tablette *f* à numériser *or* tablette graphique; **data terminal** = terminal *m or* poste *m* informatique; **a printer is a data terminal for computer output** = l'imprimante est un terminal de sortie d'ordinateur; **data terminal equipment (DTE)** = terminal *m* d'ordinateur; **data terminal ready (DTR)** = (signal de) prêt à transmettre; **data transaction** = transaction *f* de données; **data transfer rate** = débit *m or* vitesse *f* de transfert de données;

data translation = traduction *f or* conversion *f* de données; **data transmission** = transmission *f* de données; **data type** = type *m* de données; **data under voice (DUV)** = transmission de données subvocales; **data validation** = validation *f* de données; **data vetting** = validation *or* vérification *f* de données; **data word** = mot *m;* **data word length** = longueur *f* d'un mot

databank *noun* banque *f* de données

database *noun* base *f* de données; *(person)* **database administrator (DBA)** = responsable *m&f* de base de données; **database language** = langage *m* de base de données; **database machine** = machine *f* dédiée au traitement de bases de données; **database management system (DBMS)** *or* **database manager** = système *m* de gestion de base de données; **database mapping** = implantation *f or* configuration *f or* topologie *f* d'une base de données; **database schema** = schéma *m* de base de données; **database system** = système *m* de base de données; **on-line database** = base de données en ligne

◊ **datagram** *noun* datagramme *m*

◊ **dataline** *noun* ligne *f* de communication de données

◊ **dataplex** *noun* multiplexage *m*

◊ **dataset** *noun US* modem *m; (RS232C signal)* **dataset ready (DSR)** = (signal de modem) prêt à transmettre/recevoir

---

QUOTE data compression is the art of squeezing data more and more information into fewer and fewer bytes
Practical Computing
QUOTE a database is a file of individual records of information which are stored in some kind of sequential order
Which PC?

---

date 1 *noun* date *f;* **I have received your message of yesterday's date** = j'ai bien reçu votre message en date d'hier; **the date of creation for the file was the 10th of June** = la date de création de ce fichier est le 10 juin **2** *verb* dater (un document)

◊ **out of date** *adjective & adverb* démodé, -ée *or* dépassé, -ée; **their computer system is years out of date** = leur système informatique est totalement dépassé; **they are still using out-of-date equipment** = ils utilisent toujours du matériel dépassé

◊ **up to date** *adjective & adverb* récent, -e *or* à jour *or* moderne *or* à la page; **an up-to-date computer system** = un système informatique de modèle récent; **to bring something up to date** = mettre à jour (un fichier, etc.); **to keep something up to date** = garder *or* maintenir (un fichier) à jour; **we spend a lot of time keeping our files up to date** = nous passons beaucoup de temps à maintenir nos fichiers à jour
NOTE: when used as adjective before a noun, **out-of-date** and **up-to-date** are hyphenated

daughter board *noun* carte fille *f*

DAV = DATA ABOVE VOICE

db *or* **dB** *see* DECIBEL

DBA = DATABASE ADMINISTRATOR

DBMS = DATABASE MANAGEMENT SYSTEM

DBV = DATA BELOW VOICE

DC = DIRECT CURRENT courant *m* continu; **DC signalling** = transmission *f* directe de signaux

DCD = DATA CARRIER DETECT

DCE = DATA COMMUNICATIONS EQUIPMENT

DD = DOUBLE DENSITY

DDC = DIRECT DIGITAL CONTROL

DD/D = DATA DICTIONARY /DIRECTORY

DDE = DIRECT DATA ENTRY

DDL = DATA DESCRIPTION LANGUAGE langage *m* de description de données; **many of DDL's advantages come from the fact that it is a second generation language** = plusieurs des avantages d'un langage de description de données vient du fait qu'il s'agit d'un langage de deuxième génération

DDP = DISTRIBUTED DATA PROCESSING

dead *adjective* **(a)** *(not working)* hors service *or* inutilisable *or* mort, -e; **dead halt** *or* **drop dead halt** = arrêt *m* total; **the manual does not say what to do if a dead halt occurs** = le manuel n'explique pas la marche à suivre en cas d'arrêt total de la machine; **dead keys** = *(on computer)* touches *fpl* de fonction *or* d'intervention (qui ne produisent pas de caractères); *(on typewriter)* touches d'accents, etc. (qui ne font pas avancer le chariot); **dead matter** = sujet abandonné *or* affaire enterrée; **dead time** = temps *m* mort **(b)** *(room or space that has no acoustical reverberation)* (chambre, etc.) sourd, -e

◊ **deaden** *verb (sound)* assourdir *or* étouffer *or* amortir *or* atténuer (un son *or* bruit); *(colour)* adoucir *or* atténuer (une couleur); *(shape)* estomper (une silhouette); **acoustic hoods are used to deaden the noise of printers** = les capots d'insonorisation servent à amortir *or* atténuer le bruit des imprimantes

deadline *noun* date *f* limite *or* délai *m* (impératif); **to meet a deadline** = respecter un délai; **we've missed our October 15th deadline** = nous avons dépassé notre date limite du 15 octobre

◊ **deadlock** *noun* impasse *f*

◊ **deadly embrace** *noun* = DEADLOCK

deal 1 *noun* accord *m or* marché *m or* contrat *m;* **package deal** = contrat global *or* forfait *m;* **they agreed a package deal, which involves the development of software, customizing hardware and training of staff** = il se sont mis d'accord sur un contrat global comprenant le développement d'un logiciel, la personnalisation du matériel et la formation du personnel **2** *verb* **to deal with** = prendre quelque chose en main(s) *or* s'occuper de quelque chose; **leave it to the DTP manager - he'll deal with it** = le responsable de la PAO s'en occupera!

◊ **dealer** *noun* marchand, -e *or* revendeur, -euse; **always buy hardware from a recognized dealer** = n'achetez votre matériel informatique que chez un revendeur agréé

deallocate *verb* libérer *or* désaffecter *or* désallouer; **when a reset button is pressed all resources are deallocated** = lorsque vous appuyez sur la touche *or* le bouton de ré-initialisation, toutes les ressources sont désallouées

debit *noun* débit *m* binaire

deblock *verb* éclater *or* dégrouper (les éléments d') un bloc

de-bounce *noun* (dispositif) antirebond *m;* **de-bounce circuit** = circuit antirebond

debug *verb* déboguer *or* déverminer *or* mettre au point; **they spent weeks debugging the system** = ils ont mis des semaines à déboguer le système; **debugging takes up more time than construction** = il faut plus de temps pour déboguer un programme que pour en créer un; **debugged program** = programme débogué *or* déverminé

◊ **debugger** *noun* logiciel *m* de débogage *or* de mise au point

> QUOTE the debug monitor makes development and testing very easy
> *Electronics & Wireless World*

decade *noun* dizaine *f or* décade *f;* **decade counter** = compteur *m* décadaire

decay 1 *noun* affaiblissement *m; (of signal)* **decay time** = temps *m* d'extinction *or* délai *m* de détérioration d'un signal **2** *verb* s'affaiblir *or* s'atténuer; **the signal decayed rapidly** = le signal s'est affaibli *or* s'est éteint rapidement

decentralized computer network *noun* réseau *m* décentralisé
◊ **decentralized data processing** *noun* traitement *m* décentralisé des données

deci- *prefix* déci-

decibel (dB) *noun* décibel (dB) *m;* **decibel meter** = décibelmètre *m or* analyseur *m* de bruit

decile *noun* décile *m*

decimal (notation) *noun* (numération) décimale *f;* **correct to three places of decimals** = correct à la troisième décimale; **decimal point** = virgule *f* (décimale); **decimal system** = système *m* décimal *or* à base dix; **decimal tabbing** = tabulation *f* décimale *or* sur la virgule; **decimal tab key** = touche *f* de tabulation décimale; **decimal-to-binary conversion** = conversion *f* décimale-binaire
◊ **decimalization** *noun* décimalisation *f*
◊ **decimalize** *verb* décimaliser

decimonic ringing *noun* sonnerie *f* décimonique *or* sonnerie à résonance de fréquence *or* bip *m* d'appel

decipher *verb* déchiffrer

decision *noun* décision *f;* **to come to a decision** *or* **to reach a decision** = prendre une décision *or* se décider (à); **decision box** = symbole *m* de décision *or* de branchement *or* de condition; **decision circuit** *or* **element** = circuit *m or* élément *m* de décision; **decision instruction** = instruction *f* (d'opération) conditionnelle; **decision support system (DSS)** = système *m* d'aide à la décision (SAID); **decision table** = table *f* de décision; **decision tree** = arbre *m* de décision

deck *noun* **(a) tape deck** = (i) platine *f* magnétophone; (ii) platine magnétocassette **(b)** jeu *m* *or* paquet *m* de cartes perforées

deckle edge *noun (rough edge of paper)* bord *m* déchiqueté *or* non rogné

declare *verb* déclarer *or* faire une déclaration; **he declared at the start of the program that X was equal to nine =** au début du programme X a été déclaré égal à 9
◊ **declaration** *or* **declarative statement** *noun* déclaration *f;* **procedure declaration =** déclaration de procédure

decode *verb* décoder *or* désembrouiller
◊ **decoder** *noun* décodeur *m;* **instruction decoder =** décodeur *m* d'instruction
◊ **decoding** *noun* décodage *m*

decollate *verb (continuous stationery)* déliasser
◊ **decollator** *noun* déliasseuse *f*

decompilation *noun* décompilation *f;* **incremental compilation and decompilation =** compilation et décompilation incrémentielles

decrement *verb* décrémenter; **the register contents were decremented until they reached zero =** le contenu du registre a été décrémenté à zéro

decrypt *verb* déchiffrer *or* décrypter
◊ **decryption** *noun* déchiffrage *m or* décryptage *m;* **decryption is done using hardware to increase speed =** le déchiffrage se fait avec l'ordinateur pour aller plus vite

QUOTE typically a file is encrypted using a password key and decrypted using the same key. A design fault of many systems means the use of the wrong password for decryption results in double and often irretrievable encryption
PC Business World

dedicated *adjective (reserved for a particular use)* spécialisé, -ée *or* dédié, -ée; **there's only one dedicated graphics workstation in this network =** il n'y a qu'un seul poste réservé aux graphiques sur ce réseau; **dedicated channel =** canal spécialisé *or* voie spécialisée; **dedicated computer =** ordinateur dédié; **dedicated line =** ligne téléphonique spécialisée *or* dédiée; **dedicated logic =** fonction logique spécialisée; **the person appointed should have a knowledge of micro-based hardware and dedicated logic =** la personne nommée devra connaître le matériel micro-informatique et la logique qui s'y rapporte; **dedicated logic cuts down the chip count =** la logique dédiée réduit le nombre de puces; **dedicated word processor =** appareil de traitement de texte spécialisé

QUOTE the server should reduce networking costs by using standard networking cable instead of dedicated links
PC Business World

deduct *verb* déduire *or* soustraire

default *noun* **default drive =** lecteur *m* par défaut *or* implicite; **the operating system allows the user to select the default drive =** ce système d'exploitation permet à l'utilisateur de choisir le lecteur par défaut; **default option =** option *f* implicite *or* par défaut *or* intrinsèque; **default rate =** débit *m* par défaut *or* prédéterminé *or* implicite d'un modem; **default response =** réponse *f* intrinsèque *or* par défaut; **default value =** valeur *f* par défaut *or* intrinsèque *or* prédéterminée; **screen width has a default value of 80 =** la largeur implicite *or* par défaut de cet écran est de 80

defect *noun* faute *f or* défaut *m;* **a computer defect *or* a defect in the computer =** un défaut de l'ordinateur
◊ **defective** *adjective* défectueux, -euse; **the machine broke down because of a defective cooling system =** l'appareil est tombé en panne parce que le système de refroidissement était défectueux

defensive computing *noun* informatique *f or* programmation *f* défensive

deferred addressing *noun* adressage *m* indirect

define *verb* définir; **all the variables were defined at initialization =** toutes les variables ont été définies lors de l'initialisation

◊ **definition** *noun (of screen, value)* définition *f;* **macro definition** = macrodéfinition *f*

deflect *verb (object or beam)* (faire) dévier

◊ **deflection** *noun* déviation *f or* déflexion *f;* **deflection yokes** = déflecteurs *mpl or* armature *f* de déflexion

defocus *verb* dérégler la mise au point

degauss *verb* démagnétiser; **the R/W heads have to be degaussed each week to ensure optimum performance** = il faut démagnétiser les têtes de lecture/écriture une fois par semaine pour obtenir une performance optimale

◊ **degausser** *noun* effaceur *m* magnétique

degradation *noun (a) (loss of picture quality)* dégradation *f;* **image degradation** = dégradation de l'image **(b)** *(of computers)* dégradation *or* réduction *f* des performances; **graceful degradation** = dégradation limitée *or* douce *or* progressive

delay 1 *noun* délai *m or* retard *m;* **there was a delay of thirty seconds before the printer started printing** = l'imprimante a commencé à imprimer après un délai de trente secondes; **delay distortion** = distorsion due au retard du signal; **delay equalizer** = égaliseur *m or* compensateur *m* de phase; **delay line** = ligne *f* à *or* de retard; **delay line store** = mémoire *m* à ligne de retard; **delay vector** = vecteur *m* de retard **2** *verb* retarder

delete *verb* **(a)** *(word in text)* rayer *or* effacer *or* supprimer **(b)** *(text or data from a storage device)* effacer *or* détruire *or* supprimer; **the word-processor allows us to delete the whole file by pressing this key** = le traitement de texte permet de supprimer un fichier complet en appuyant sur cette touche; **delete character** = caractère *m* de suppression *or* d'effacement

◊ **deletion** *noun (cutting)* coupure *f or* suppression *f; (erasing)* effacement *m;* **the editors asked the author to make several deletions in the last chapter** = les

éditeurs ont demandé à l'auteur de faire plusieurs coupures dans le dernier chapitre; **deletion record** = fichier *m* de coupures *or* de corrections

delimit *verb* délimiter

◊ **delimiter** *noun (symbol or code)* délimiteur *m or* séparateur *m* (d'information)

delta *noun* connexion *f* (en) triangle *or* (en) delta; **delta clock** = horloge *f* delta *or* à relance automatique; **delta-delta** = (connexion) delta-delta; **delta modulation** = modulation *f* (en) delta; **delta routing** = acheminement *m* (en) delta

demagnetize *verb* démagnétiser

◊ **demagnetizer** *noun* effaceur *m* magnétique; **he used the demagnetizer to degauss the tape heads** = il s'est servi d'un effaceur magnétique pour démagnétiser les têtes de lecture

demand 1 *noun* **(a)** demande *f* (impérative) *or* réclamation *f;* **demand assigned multiple access (DAMA)** = accès multiple asservi à la demande; **demand multiplexing** = multiplexage asservi à la demande; **demand paging** = appel *f* de page sur demande; **demand processing** = traitement *m* (de données) sur demande *or* immédiat; **demand reading/writing** = lecture-écriture sur demande *or* directe; *(moving data from a secondary storage)* **demand staging** = transfert *m* sur demande (d'une mémoire à une autre) **2** *verb* demander *or* réclamer *or* exiger; **she demanded her money back** = elle a exigé *or* réclamé un remboursement

demarcation *noun* (ligne de) démarcation *f;* **demarcation strip** = (mise à nu de) protection *f*

democratic network *noun* réseau *m* démocratique

demodulation *noun* démodulation *f*

◊ **demodulator** *noun* démodulateur *m; see also* MODEM

demonstrate *verb* expliquer (le fonctionnement de quelque chose) *or* faire une démonstration *or* démontrer; **he demonstrated the file management program** = il a fait une démonstration du programme de gestion de fichiers

◊ **demonstration** *noun* démonstration *f;* **demonstration model** = modèle *m* de démonstration

demultiplex *verb* démultiplexer

◊ **demultiplexor** *noun* démultiplexeur *m*

denary notation *noun* numérotation *f* décimale *or* dénaire

denial *noun* déni *m or* négation *f;* **alternative denial** = opération *f* NON-ET; **joint denial** = négation *f* connexe *or* opération NON-OU *or* NI

dense index *noun* index *m* complet; **dense list** = liste *f* complète

◊ **densitometer** *noun* densitomètre *m*

◊ **density** *noun* **(a)** *(amount of light that a negative blocks)* densité *f* **(b)** *(of printed image or text)* densité; **density dial** = (bouton de) réglage *m* de densité d'impression; **when fading occurs, turn the density dial on the printer to full black** = si l'impression est trop pâle, réglez le bouton de densité (d'impression) sur le noir **(c)** *(amount of data that can be packed into a space)* densité; **double density disk (DD)** = disquette *f* double densité (DD); **high density disk (HD)** = disquette haute densité (HD); **quad density disk (QD)** = disquette quadruple densité (QD); **single density disk (SD)** = disquette simple densité (SD); **packing** *or* **recording density** = densité d'enregistrement

QUOTE diode lasers with shorter wavelengths will make doubling of the bit and track densities possible
Byte

deny access (to) *verb* interdire l'accès (à un circuit *or* à un système)

dependent *adjective* dépendant, -e; **a process which is dependent on the result of another process** = procédé dépendant des résultats *or* relié aux résultats d'un autre procédé; **the output is dependent on the physical state of the link** = le résultat de sortie est fonction de l'état (physique)

des liaisons; **machine dependent** = (logiciel) non standard *or* qui ne fonctionne que sur un type d'appareil

deposit 1 *noun (thin layer)* dépôt *m* **2** *verb* **(a)** *(to print out the content of memory)* vider sur l'imprimante (le contenu d'une mémoire) **(b)** *(to coat a surface)* enduire *or* recouvrir d'une couche **(c)** *(to write data)* enregistrer *or* mettre en registre *or* en mémoire auxilliaire

◊ **deposition** *noun (on semiconductor)* enduction *f or* dépôt *m or* pose *f* d'un enduit

depth of field *noun* profondeur *f* de champ; **depth of focus** = profondeur *f* de foyer

deque *noun* = DOUBLE-ENDED QUEUE

derive *verb* provenir (de) *or* dériver (de); **derived indexing** = indexage dérivé; **derived sound** = son dérivé

◊ **derivation graph** *noun* graphe *m* de relation

DES = DATA ENCRYPTION STANDARD

descender *noun (of 'q' or 'p')* jambage *m* (descendant)

de-scramble *verb (coded message)* déchiffrer *or* désembrouiller

◊ **de-scrambler** *noun* désembrouilleur *m or* décodeur *m*

describe *verb* décrire; **the leaflet describes the services the company can offer** = le prospectus contient une description des services offerts par la société; **the specifications are described in greater detail at the back of the manual** = on trouve une description plus détaillée des spécifications à la fin du manuel

◊ **description** *noun* description *f;* **description list** = liste *f* descriptive; **data description language (DDL)** = langage *m* de description de données; **page description language (PDL)** = langage de description de pages

◊ **descriptor** *noun* descripteur *m or* mot-clé *m*

design 1 *noun (planning)* conception *f* *or* design *m; (drawing)* esquisse *f;* **circuit design** = tracé *m* d'un circuit; **industrial design** = esthétique *f* industrielle; **product design** = conception *f* de produits; **design department** = bureau *m* d'études; **design parameters** = spécifications *fpl or* contraintes *fpl or* paramètres *mpl* de conception *or* de création; **design studio** = studio *m* de création *or* de design **2** *verb* dessiner *or* concevoir; **he designed a new chip factory** = il a fait les plans *or* l'étude de la nouvelle usine de composants

◊ **designer** *noun* dessinateur, -trice *or* concepteur, -trice *or* styliste *m&f or* projeteur *m;* **she is the designer of the new computer** = c'est elle qui a réalisé le nouvel ordinateur

desk *noun* bureau *m;* **desk diary** = agenda *m* de bureau; **desk light** = lampe *f* de bureau; **desk check** = contrôle *m* (d'un programme) sur papier

◊ **desktop** *adjective* **desktop computer (system)** = ordinateur *m* de table *or* de bureau; **desktop publishing (DTP)** = publication *f* assistée par ordinateur (PAO) *or* édition *f* électronique

QUOTE desktop publishing or the ability to produce high-quality publications using a minicomputer, essentially boils down to combining words and images on pages
Byte

desolder *verb* dessouder
◊ **desoldering tool** *noun* dessoudeur *m*

despool *verb* imprimer la file d'attente

despotic network *noun* réseau *m* (avec synchronisation) despotique

de-spun antenna *noun* antenne *f* contrarotative

destination *noun* destination *f*

destructive addition *noun* addition *f* destructive

◊ **destructive cursor** *noun* curseur *m or* marqueur *m* destructif *or* effaceur; **reading the screen becomes difficult without a destructive cursor** = l'écran devient presqu'illisible sans le curseur destructif; **destructive read** = lecture *f* destructive; **destructive readout (DRO)** = lecture destructive

detail 1 *noun* détail *m;* **detail file** = fichier *m* (de) mouvements; **in detail** = en détail; **the catalogue lists all the products in detail** = le catalogue présente une liste détaillée de tous les produits; **detail paper** = papier-calque *m* **2** *verb* énumérer *or* détailler *or* expliquer en détail

detect *verb* détecter *or* trouver; **the equipment can detect faint signals from the transducer** = l'appareil peut détecter les signaux faibles émis par le transducteur; **detected error** = erreur notifiée *or* détectée; **error detecting codes** = codes *mpl* de détection d'erreurs

◊ **detection** *noun* détection *f;* **the detection of the cause of the fault is proving difficult** = il est difficile de trouver la source du problème

◊ **detector** *noun* détecteur *m;* **metal detector** = détecteur de métal

deterministic *adjective* déterministe

develop *verb* **(a)** développer *or* mettre au point; **to develop a new product** = développer un nouveau produit **(b)** *(film)* développer

◊ **developer** *noun* **(a)** *(person)* **software developer** = créateur, -trice *or* concepteur, -trice *or* développeur *m* de logiciel *or* expert en création de logiciel **(b)** *(photography)* révélateur *m*

◊ **development** *noun* développement *m or* mise *f* au point; **research and development** = recherche *f* et développement; **development software** = logiciel *m* de développement; **development time** = temps de développement *or* de mise au point d'un nouveau produit

device *noun* dispositif *m or* (petit) appareil *m or* périphérique *m;* **device character control** = (système de) contrôle *m* de périphérique utilisant des caractères; **device code** = code *m* d'identification de périphérique; **device control character** = caractère de contrôle *or* de commande de périphérique; **device driver** = routine *f* de gestion de périphérique; **device flag** = marqueur *m or* témoin *m or* (bit) indicateur *m* d'utilisation *or* d'état; *(program)* **device independent** = (programme) indépendant *or* non tributaire *or* non spécialisé; **device priority** = priorité *f* d'un périphérique *or* d'un appareil; **the master console has a higher device priority than the printers and other terminals** = la console de commande a priorité sur l'imprimante et les autres terminaux; **device queue** = file *f* d'attente (de périphériques); **device status word (DSW)** = mot indicateur d'état; **this routine checks the device status word and will not transmit data if the busy bit is set** = cette routine vérifie l'indicateur d'état et ne transmet pas le signal si le bit occupé est présent; **I/O device** = appareil *or* périphérique *or* dispositif d'entrée/sortie; **output device** = appareil *or* périphérique *or* dispositif de sortie

Dewey decimal classification *noun* *(library)* classification *f* (suivant la méthode de) Dewey

DFD = DATA FLOW DIAGRAM

D-type flip-flop *noun* dispositif *m or* commutateur *m* à bascule de type D *or* commutateur à deux sorties

diacritic *noun* signe *m* diacritique

diagnose *verb* diagnostiquer *or* trouver

◊ **diagnosis** *noun* diagnostic *m*

diagnostic *noun* diagnostic *m;* **diagnostic aid** = aide *f* au diagnostic; **diagnostic chip** = circuit *m* intégré *or* puce *f* de diagnostic; **diagnostic message** = message *m* de diagnostic; **diagnostic program** = logiciel *m* de diagnostic; **diagnostic routine** = routine *f* de diagnostic; **diagnostic test** = test *m* de diagnostic; **self-diagnostic** = auto-diagnostic *m*

◊ **diagnostics** *noun* outils *mpl* de diagnostic; **compiler diagnostics** = outils de diagnostic du compilateur; **thorough compiler diagnostics make debugging easy** = les outils de diagnostic de compilation bien conçus facilitent le débogage; **error diagnostics** = outils de diagnostic d'erreurs

> QUOTE the implementation of on-line diagnostic devices that measure key observable parameters
> *Byte*
> QUOTE to check for any hardware problems, a diagnostic disk is provided
> *Personal Computer World*

diagonal cut *noun* coupe *f* (en) diagonale *or* en biseau

diagram *noun* diagramme *m or* graphique *m; (of data)* **flow diagram** = ordinogramme *m*

◊ **diagrammatic** *adjective* **in diagrammatic form** = sous forme de schéma; **the chart showed the sales pattern in diagrammatic form** = le tableau présentait la courbe des ventes sous forme de diagramme *or* de façon schématique

◊ **diagramatically** *adverb* sous forme de diagramme *or* de schéma; **the chart shows the sales pattern diagramatically** = le tableau présente la courbe des ventes sous forme de diagramme

dial 1 *verb (telephone)* **to dial a number** = composer *or* faire un numéro (de téléphone); **to dial the operator** = appeler la standardiste; **he dialled the code for the USA** = il a composé l'indicatif des Etats-Unis; **to dial direct** = appeler en direct; **you can dial New York direct from London** = vous pouvez appeler New York en direct depuis Londres; *(modem or telephone)* **auto-dial** = système d'appel *m* automatique (d'un correspondant) *or* système de numérotation automatique; **to dial into** = se connecter *or* entrer dans; **with the right access code it is possible to dial into a customer's computer to extract the files needed for the report** = avec un code d'accès valide, il est possible d'entrer dans le système du client et d'extraire les fichiers utiles pour établir le rapport NOTE: GB English is **dialling - dialled**, but US spelling is **dialing - dialed 2** *noun (to select)* bouton *m or* réglage *m; (on telephone or clock)* cadran m; **to tune into the radio station, turn the dial** = pour obtenir la station de radio, tournez ce bouton; **dial conference** = (facilité de) téléconférence *f* par sélection *or* par composition; **dial pulse** = impulsion *f* de cadran; **dial tone** = tonalité *f* (d'appel); **dial-in modem** = modem *m* à appel automatique; **density dial** = bouton de densité; **if the text fades, turn the density**

dial on the printer to full black = si l'impression est trop pâle, réglez le bouton de densité (d'impression) sur le noir
◇ **dialling** *noun* composition *f or* appel *f* (d'un numéro de téléphone) *or* numérotation *f;* **dialling code** = indicatif *m* téléphonique; **dialling tone** = tonalité *f* (d'appel); **direct dialling** = système d'acheminement direct des appels *or* l'automatique *m;* **international direct dialling (IDD)** = système *m* téléphonique automatique international

dialect *noun* dialecte *m;* **this manufacturer's dialect of BASIC is a little different to the one I'm used to** = cette version du BASIC offerte par le fabricant est un peu différente de celle que j'utilise

dialogue *noun* dialogue *m;* **dialogue box** = fenêtre *f* de dialogue

diameter *noun* diamètre *m*

DIANE = DIRECT INFORMATION ACCESS NETWORK FOR EUROPE

diaphragm *noun* **(a)** *(photography)* diaphragme *m* **(b)** *(loudspeaker or microphone)* diaphragme; **the diaphragm in the microphone picks up sound waves** = le diaphragme d'un microphone capte les ondes sonores

diapositive *noun* diapositive *f or* diapo *f*

diary *noun* agenda *m or* journal *m;* **diary management** = (programme) agenda

diascope *noun* projecteur *m* de diapositives

diazo (process) *noun* diazocopie *f*

DIB = DATA INPUT BUS

dibit *noun* dibit *m or* groupe de 2 chiffres binaires

dichotomizing search *noun* (méthode de) recherche *f* dichotomique *or* par dichotomie

dichroic *adjective* dichroïque

dictate *verb* dicter; **to dictate a letter to a secretary** = dicter une lettre à une secrétaire; **he was dictating orders into his pocket dictating machine** = il enregistrait ses instructions sur son Dictaphone de poche; **dictating machine** = machine *f* à dicter *or* Dictaphone® *m*
◇ **dictation** *noun* dictée *f;* **to take dictation** = prendre en dictée; **dictation speed** = vitesse *f* en sténographie

dictionary *noun* *(reference book or spelling checker or data)* dictionnaire *m;* **exception dictionary** = liste *f or* répertoire *m* d'exceptions

dielectric *noun* diélectrique *m*

differ *verb* différer *or* être différent (de); **the two products differ considerably - one has an external hard disk, the other has internal hard disk and external magnetic tape drive** = il existe une grande différence entre les deux produits: l'un d'eux possède un disque dur externe, tandis que l'autre est équipé d'un disque dur interne et d'un dérouleur de bande (magnétique) externe
◇ **difference** *noun* différence *f;* **symmetric difference** = exclusion réciproque *or* OU exclusif *or* non-équivalence
◇ **different** *adjective* différent, -e; **our product range is quite different in design from the Japanese models** = notre gamme de produits est d'une conception entièrement différente de celle des modèles japonais
◇ **differential** *adjective* différentiel, -elle; **differential PCM** = DIFFERENTIAL PULSE CODED MODULATION modulation d'impulsion codée différentielle (MIC)

diffuse *verb* (se) diffuser *or* (se) répandre; **the smoke from the faulty machine rapidly diffused through the building** = la fumée produite par la machine défectueuse s'est répandue rapidement dans tout l'immeuble; **the chemical was diffused into the substrate** = il y a eu diffusion du produit chimique dans le substrat
◇ **diffusion** *noun* diffusion *f or* dopage *m* par diffusion

Digipulse® **telephone** *noun* téléphone *m* (à impulsion numérique) Digipulse

digit *noun* chiffre *m*; **a phone number with eight digits** *or* **an eight-digit phone number** = un numéro de téléphone de huit chiffres; **the decimal digit 8** = le chiffre décimal 8 *or* la décimale 8; **the decimal number system uses the digits 0123456789** = la base de numération décimale utilise les chiffres 0123456789; **check digit** = chiffre *or* clé *f* (numérique) de contrôle; **digit place** *or* **position** = place *f* d'un chiffre

◊ **digital** *adjective* numérique; **digital audio disk (DAD)** = disque *m* audionumérique; **digital audio tape (DAT)** = bande *f* (magnétique) audionumérique; **digital cassette** = cassette *f* audionumérique; **digital circuit** = circuit *m* numérique; **digital clock** = horloge *f* numérique; **digital computer** = ordinateur *m* numérique; **digital data** = données *fpl* numériques *or* numérisées; **digital logic** = logique *f* numérique; **digital multimeter (DMM)** = multimètre *m* numérique; **digital optical reading (DOR)** = lecture *f* optique de données numériques; **digital output** = sortie *f* numérique; **digital plotter** = traceur *m* numérique; **digital readout** = affichage *m* numérique; **digital recording** = enregistrement *m* numérique; **digital representation** = représentation *f* numérique; **digital resolution** = résolution *f* d'un nombre; **digital signal** = signal *m* numérique; **digital signalling** = transmission *f* de signaux numériques; **digital signature** = signature numérique; **digital speech** = voix numérisée *or* de synthèse; **digital system** = système *m* numérique; **digital switching** = (système de) commutation *f* numérique; **digital to analog converter** *or* **D to A converter (DAC)** = convertisseur *m* numérique-analogique; **digital transmission system** = système de transmission numérique

◊ **digitally** *adverb* numériquement *or* sous forme numérique; **the machine takes digitally recorded data and generates an image** = l'appareil produit une image à partir de données enregistrées sous forme numérique

digitize *verb* numériser; **we can digitize your signature to allow it to be printed with any laser printer** = il nous est possible de numériser votre signature pour qu'elle puisse être imprimée par n'importe quelle imprimante (à) laser; **digitized photograph** = photographie *f* numérisée; **digitizing pad** = tablette *f* graphique *or* tablette à numériser

◊ **digitizer** *noun* convertisseur *m* analogique-numérique *or* numériseur *m*

DIL = DUAL-IN-LINE PACKAGE

dimension *noun* dimension *f;* **the dimensions of the computer are small enough for it to fit into a case** = l'ordinateur est assez petit pour tenir dans un porte-documents

◊ **dimensioning** *noun* calcul *m* des dimensions; **array dimensioning occurs at this line** = le calcul des dimensions du tableau se fait à cette ligne-ci

diminished radix complement *noun* complément *m* restreint

DIN = DEUTSCHE INDUSTRIENORM *(German industry standards organisation)* DIN

diode *noun* diode *f;* **light-emitting diode (LED)** = diode électroluminescente; *(indicator light)* lampe *f* témoin *or* voyant *m* (lumineux)

dioptre *US* **diopter** *noun* dioptrie *f;* **diopter lens** = lentille *f* dioptrique

DIP = DUAL-IN-LINE PACKAGE

diplex *noun* duplex *m*

dipole *noun* (i) dipôle *m* ; (ii) doublet *m*

DIP switch *noun* commutateur *m* DIP *or* à bascule

direct 1 *verb* diriger; **directed scan** = balayage dirigé **2** *adjective* direct, -e; **direct access** = accès direct; **direct (access) address** = adresse absolue *or* directe; **direct access storage device (DASD)** = mémoire *f or* support *m* à accès direct; *(TV or radio)* **direct addressing** = adressage direct; **direct broadcast satellite (DBS)** = satellite *m* de diffusion directe; **direct change-over** =

transfert direct; **direct code** = code direct *or* à un niveau; **direct coding** = codage direct; **direct connect** = connexion directe; **direct current (DC)** = courant *m* continu; **direct data entry (DDE)** = saisie *f* directe de données (au clavier) *or* entrée directe de données; *(telephone)* **direct dialling** = système d'acheminement direct des appels *or* l'automatique *m;* **direct digital control (DDC)** = commande numérique directe; **direct image film** = film *m* positif; **direct impression** = impression directe; **direct information access network for Europe (DIANE)** = DIANE; **direct-insert routine** *or* **subroutine** = programme *or* sous-programme d'insertion directe; **direct instruction** = instruction directe; *(in a private exchange) (within a private exchange)* **direct inward dialling** = accès direct au système; **direct memory access (DMA)** = accès direct à la mémoire (DMA); **direct memory access transfer between the main memory and the second processor** = transfert des données par accès direct (à la mémoire) entre la mémoire principale et le second processeur; **direct memory access channel** = voie d'accès direct à la mémoire; **direct mode** = mode direct; *(from a private exchange)* **direct outward dialling** = accès direct au réseau; **direct page register** = registre *m* de pagination à accès direct; **direct reference address** = adresse de référence directe; **direct transfer** = transfert direct **3** *adverb* directement *or* en direct; **to dial direct** = appeler *or* téléphoner en direct; **you can dial New York direct from London if you want** = vous pouvez appeler New York en direct depuis Londres

◊ **direction** *noun* **(a)** direction *f or* gestion *f;* **he took over the direction of a software distribution group** = c'est lui qui est maintenant à la tête du groupe de diffusion de logiciels **(b)** **directions for use** = mode *m* d'emploi

◊ **directional** *adjective* directionnel, -elle; **directional antenna** = antenne (uni)directionnelle; **directional pattern** = empreinte directionnelle

◊ **directive 1** *noun* directive *f adjective* **directive statement** = instruction directive

◊ **directly** *adverb* **(a)** *(immediately)* immédiatement **(b)** *(straight)* directement

◊ **director** *noun* **(a)** *(of company)* directeur, -trice; **managing director** =

directeur général; **board of directors** = conseil *m* d'administration **(b)** *(of project)* directeur, -trice *or* responsable *m&f;* **the director of the government computer research institute** = le directeur de l'institut de recherche informatique gouvernemental; **she was appointed director of the organization** = elle a été nommée directrice de l'organisation **(c)** *(of film or TV program)* réalisateur, -trice; **casting director** = responsable *m* de la distribution; **lighting director** = chef *m* éclairagiste; **technical director** = directeur technique

> QUOTE directives are very useful for selecting parts of the code for particular purposes
> *Personal Computer World*

directory *noun* **(a)** annuaire *m or* répertoire *m* d'adresses; **classified directory** = annuaire par professions; **commercial directory** *or* **trade directory** = répertoire d'entreprises; **street directory** = annuaire par rues *or* répertoire d'adresses par rues; **telephone directory** = annuaire du téléphone **(b)** **disk directory** = répertoire; **the disk directory shows file name, date and time of creation** = on trouve les titres des fichiers, la date et l'heure de leur création dans le répertoire; **directory routing** = routage *m* par répertoire

dirty bit *noun* bit *m* marqué

disable *verb* invalider *or* mettre hors service; **he disabled the keyboard to prevent anyone changing the data** = il a mis le clavier hors service pour éviter qu'on change les données; **disable interrupt** = commande *f* d'invalidation d'interruption

disarm *verb* invalider *or* désactiver; **disarmed state** = état désactivé

disassemble *verb* désassembler

◊ **disassembler** *noun* désassembleur *m*

disaster dump *noun* vidage *m* irréversible

disc = DISK
NOTE: disc is the more usual spelling in the USA

discard *verb* jeter *or* se défaire de (quelque chose) *or* rebuter

disclose *verb* révéler
◊ **disclosure** *noun* révélation *f*

disconnect *verb* débrancher *or* déconnecter; **do not forget to disconnect the cable before moving the printer =** n'oubliez pas de débrancher (le câble de) l'imprimante avant de la changer de place

discrete *adjective* discret, -ète; **a data word is made up of discrete bits =** le mot (de l'information) est formé de bits discrets

discretionary *adjective* discrétionnaire *or* au choix; **discretionary hyphen** *or* **soft hyphen =** trait d'union qui ne s'imprime pas *or* qui n'apparaît que sur l'écran

discrimination instruction *noun* instruction *f* (d'opération) conditionnelle

dish aerial *noun* antenne *f* parabolique; **we use a dish aerial to receive signals from the satellite =** nous utilisons une antenne parabolique pour capter les signaux transmis par satellite

disjointed *adjective* disjoint, -e *or* (données) qui n'ont aucune relation *or* aucun rapport (entre elles)

disjunction *noun* *(logical function)* disjonction *f* *or* opération *f* OU *or* opération de réunion *or* d'union
◊ **disjunctive search** *noun* recherche *f* par mots-clés

disk *noun* *(record* or *computer hard disk)* disque *m;* *(floppy)* disquette *f;* **backup disk =** disque(tte) de sauvegarde; **disk access =** accès *m* au disque; **disk-based (operating system) =** système d'exploitation utilisant un disque dur *or* des disquettes; **disk cartridge =** cartouche *f* disque *or* disque dur amovible *or* chargeur *m;* **disk controller =** contrôleur *m* de disque *or* de disquette; **disk-controller card =** carte *f* contrôleur de disque(tte); **disk crash =** crash *m or*

panne *f* totale d'un disque *or* d'une disquette; **disk drive =** lecteur *m* de disque *or* de disquettes; **disk file =** fichier sur disque *or* sur disquette; **disk formatting =** formatage de disque *or* de disquette; **disk index holes =** perforations *fpl* de marquage (du bord) d'un disque; **disk map =** table *f* (de classement des fichiers) du disque; **disk operating system (DOS) =** système *m* d'exploitation de disque *or* (système) DOS; **MS disk operating system** *or* **Microsoft DOS (MS-DOS)® =** (système d'exploitation) MS-DOS®; **disk pack =** chargeur *m* (de disques); **disk sector =** secteur *m* de disque *or* disquette; **disk storage =** mémoire *f* à disque; *(capacity)* capacité *f* de mémoire (de disque *or* disquette); **disk track =** piste *f* d'un disque *or* d'une disquette; **disk unit =** unité *f* de disque *or* lecteur *m* de disquettes; **fixed disk =** disque (dur) fixe *or* non amovible; **compact disk =** disque compact *or* disque audionumérique *or* disque CD; **floppy disk =** disquette *f;* **hard disk =** disque dur; **optical disk =** disque optique; **Winchester disk =** disque (dur de type) Winchester
◊ **diskette** *noun* disquette *f*
◊ **diskless** *adjective* sans disque; **diskless system =** système qui n'utilise pas de disque *or* de disquette; **they want to create a diskless workstation =** ils veulent créer un poste de travail qui n'utilise pas de disque *or* de disquette

disorderly close-down *noun* panne désordonnée *or* arrêt désordonné

dispatch *or* **despatch** *noun* envoi *m*

dispenser *noun* distributeur *m;* **cash dispenser =** distributeur de billets de banque *or* billetterie *f*

dispersion *noun* **(a)** *(of beam)* dispersion *f* **(b)** *(logical function)* fonction *f* NON-ET

displacement *noun* déplacement *m*

display 1 *noun* affichage *m or* visualisation *f;* **character display =** affichage de caractères *or* de texte; **display adapter =** adaptateur *m* d'écran; **display attribute =** attribut *m* d'écran;

display character = caractère *m* d'écran; **display character generator** = générateur *m* de caractères d'écran; **display colour** = couleur *f* d'affichage; **display controller** = contrôleur *m* d'écran; **display format** = format *m* d'affichage *or* format d'écran; **display highlights** = mots *mpl or* caractères *mpl* mis en évidence par affichage plus lumineux ou couleur contrastée; *(on screen)* mot *or* caractères en surbrillance; **display line** = ligne *f* d'écran; **display mode** = mode *m* affichage *or* visualisation; **display processor** = processeur *m* d'écran; **display register** = registre *m* d'affichage; **display resolution** = définition *f* de l'écran; **display screen** = écran *m* de visualisation; **display scrolling** = défilement *m* (du texte sur l'écran); **display size** = dimension *f* d'affichage; **display space** = espace *m* d'affichage; **display unit** = unité *f* de visualisation *or* de visu *or* écran (de visualisation); **backlit display** = écran *m* rétroéclairé; **gas discharge** *or* **gas plasma** *or* **electroluminescent display** = affichage *or* écran plasma; affichage *or* écran électroluminescent; **liquid crystal display (LCD)** = affichage à cristaux liquides **2** *verb* afficher; **the customer's details were displayed on the screen** = les coordonnées du client étaient affichées sur l'écran; **by keying HELP, the screen will display the options available to the user** = la touche HELP fera apparaître sur l'écran une description des différentes options

QUOTE the review machine also came with a monochrome display card plugged into one of the expansion slots
Personal Computer World

distance *noun* distance *f;* **signal distance** *or* **Hamming distance** = distance entre signaux *or* distance de Hamming

◊ **distant** *adjective* éloigné, -ée *or* distant, -e *or* à distance; **the distant printers are connected with cables** = les imprimantes à distance sont reliées par câbles

distinguish *verb* faire la distinction (entre une chose et une autre) *or* reconnaître (une chose); **an OCR has difficulty in distinguishing certain characters** = le lecteur optique reconnaît difficilement certains caractères

distort *verb* déformer

◊ **distortion** *noun* distorsion *f or* aberration *f or* altération *f;* **distortion optics** = lentille *f* déformante; **image distortion** = déformation *or* distorsion *or* aberration de l'image

distribute *verb* **(a)** distribuer *or* faire circuler; **distributed adaptive routing** = routage *m* adaptatif *or* flexible; **distributed database system** = système de base de données réparti *or* en réseau; **distributed data processing (DDP)** = informatique répartie; **distributed file system** = système de fichiers partagés *or* répartis; **distributed intelligence** = intelligence répartie; **distributed processing** = DISTRIBUTED DATA PROCESSING; **distributed system** = système *m* décentralisé *or* réparti

◊ **distribution** *noun* distribution *f;* **distribution network** = réseau *m* de distribution; **distribution point** = point *m or* centre *m* de distribution

dittogram *noun (printing error)* doublet *m*

DIV = DATA IN VOICE

divergence *noun (of beam)* divergence *f*

diversity *noun* diversité *f;* **beam diversity** = dédoublement *m* de faisceau

diverter *noun* dispositif *m* de transfert *or* de déroutage; **call diverter** = dispositif de transfert d'appel

divide *verb* **(a)** diviser; **to divide a number by four** = diviser un nombre par quatre; **twenty-one divided by three gives seven** = vingt-et-un divisé par trois égale sept **(b)** diviser *or* partager *or* couper (un mot); **in the hyphenation program, long words are automatically divided at the end of lines** = la coupure des mots trop longs se fait automatiquement en fin de ligne grâce au programme de césure

◊ **dividend** *noun* dividende *m*

◊ **divider** *noun* diviseur *m;* **frequency divider** = diviseur de fréquence

◊ **division** *noun* division *f or* partage *m; (of word)* coupure *f*

◊ **divisor** *noun* diviseur *m*

DMA = DIRECT MEMORY ACCESS mémoire *f* à accès direct *or* mémoire DMA; **DMA controller** = contrôleur *m* de mémoire à accès direct; **DMA cycle stealing** = vol *m* de temps de cycle de la mémoire à accès direct *or* de mémoire DMA

DML = DATA MANIPULATION LANGUAGE

DMM = DIGITAL MULTIMETER

do-nothing (instruction) *noun* instruction *f* sans effet *or* ineffective

document 1 *noun* document *m;* **document assembly** *or* **document merge** = fusion *f or* assemblage *m* de documents; **document processing** = traitement *m* de texte *or* de document; **document reader** = lecteur *m* de documents; **document recovery** = récupération *f or* régénération *f* de document; **document retrieval system** = système de recherche documentaire *or* de documents **2** *verb* documenter *or* donner les renseignements appropriés *or* renseigner

◇ **documentation** *noun* **(a)** *(all documents)* documentation *f or* dossier *m* **(b)** *(information, notes, etc.)* documentation *or* renseignements *mpl*

dollar sign ($) *noun* signe *m* du dollar

domain *noun* domaine *m;* **public domain** = domaine public; **program which is in the public domain** = programme du domaine public *or* qui n'est plus protégé par un copyright

domestic *adjective* domestique *or* national; **domestic satellite** = satellite *m* domestique

dongle *noun* circuit *m* crypté (de protection de logiciel) *or* clé *f* électronique

dope *verb* doper

◇ **dopant** *noun* dopant *m*

◇ **doped** *adjective* dopé, -ée *or* enduit, -e d'un dopant

◇ **doping** *noun* dopage *m*

DOR = DIGITAL OPTICAL RECORDING

DOS = DISK OPERATING SYSTEM système d'exploitation de disque *or* (système) DOS; **boot up the DOS after you switch on the PC** = lancez le (système) DOS après la mise en route de l'ordinateur; **Microsoft DOS** *or* **MS-DOS®** = (système d'exploitation) MS-DOS®

dot *noun* point *m; * **dot command** = commande (précédée d'un) point; **dot matrix** = matrice *f* de points; **dots per inch** *or* **d.p.i.** *or* **dpi** = (nombre de) points par pouce; **some laser printers offer high resolution printing: 400 dpi** = certaines imprimantes (à) laser sont dotées d'une haute définition de 400 points par pouce

◇ **dotted** *adjective* pointillé, -ée; **dotted line** = ligne pointillée *or* pointillé *m*

◇ **dot-matrix printer** *noun* imprimante *f* matricielle *or* à aiguilles

QUOTE the characters are formed from an array of dots like in a dot-matrix printer, except that much higher resolution is used
Practical Computing

double *adjective* double; **double buffering** = utilisation *f* de double mémoire tampon; *(typography)* **double dagger** = croix *f* double (‡); **double density** = double densité; **double-density disk** = disquette *f* double densité; **double document** = doublon *m; * **double-ended queue (deque)** = file *f* d'attente à deux entrées *or* à deux extrémités; **double exposure** = double exposition; **double-length precision** *or* **double precision** = double précision; **double precision arithmetic** = arithmétique *f* en double précision; **double sideband** = double bande latérale; **double sideband suppressed carrier (DSBSC)** = (modulation d'amplitude à) double bande latérale sans porteuse *or* à porteuse inhibée; **double-sided disk** = disquette (à) double face; **double-sided disk drive** = lecteur *m* de disquettes (à) double face; **double-sided printed circuit board** = plaque (présensibilisée) double face pour circuit imprimé; **double word** = mot *m* double *or* long

doublet *or* **diad** *noun* doublet *m or* dyade *f*

down *adverb* **(a)** *(not working)* en panne; **the computer system went down twice during the afternoon** = l'ordinateur est tombé en panne deux fois cet aprèsmidi; **down time** = temps *m* mort **(b)** *(of character)* **down stroke** = jambage *m* (descendant) (NOTE: opposite is **up**)

download *verb* télécharger; **there is no charge for downloading public domain software from the BBS** = il n'en coûte rien de télécharger, depuis le tableau d'affichage, un logiciel qui n'est pas protégé par un copyright
◊ **downloadable** *adjective* téléchargeable; **downloadable fonts** = police *f* de caractères téléchargeable
◊ **downloading** *noun* téléchargement *m*

downward *adjective* vers le bas; **downward compatibility** = compatibilité *f* avec un système de niveau inférieur; **the mainframe is downward compatible with the micro** l'unité centrale de traitement est compatible avec un micro *or* peut piloter un micro

dp *or* **DP** = DATA PROCESSING traitement *f* de l'information *or* traitement de données

d.p.i. *or* **dpi** = DOTS PER INCH (nombre de) points *mpl* par pouce; **a 300 d.p.i. black and white A4 monitor** = un moniteur monochrome format A4 avec une définition de 300 points par pouce; **a 300 dpi image scanner** = un scanner d'image avec définition de 300 points par pouce

DPM = DATA PROCESSING MANAGER

draft 1 *noun* brouillon *m or* première mouture *f;* **draft printing** = (sortie d'imprimante) qualité *f* brouillon *or* qualité listing **2** *verb* faire un brouillon *or* ébaucher *or* esquisser; **he drafted out the details of the program on a piece of paper** = il a esquissé un projet de programme sur une feuille de papier

drag *verb* (se) déplacer *or* tirer; **you can enlarge a frame by clicking inside its border and dragging to the position wanted** = pour agrandir un cadre, vous cliquez à l'intérieur de ses limites et vous déplacez la bordure à la position voulue

QUOTE press the mouse button and drag the mouse: this produces a dotted rectangle on the screen
QUOTE you can easily enlarge the frame by dragging from any of the eight black rectangles round the border, showing that it is selected

Desktop Publishing

drain 1 *noun* courant *m* de décharge **2** *verb* épuiser *or* affaiblir *or* décharger

DRAM = DYNAMIC RANDOM ACCESS MEMORY RAM dynamique *or* mémoire vive dynamique

QUOTE cheap bulk memory systems are always built from DRAMs

Electronics & Power

D-region *noun (ionosphere)* région *f* D; **the D-region is the main cause of attenuation in transmitted radio signals** = la région D est la principale cause d'affaiblissement des ondes radioélectriques

drift *noun (zone or resistance)* dérive *f*

drive 1 *noun* **disk drive** = lecteur *m* de disquettes; **tape drive** = lecteur *m or* dérouleur *m* de bandes magnétiques **2** *verb* faire marcher *or* faire fonctionner *or* entraîner; **the disk is driven by a motor** = un moteur entraîne le disque
◊ **driven** *adjective* (appareil) qui fonctionne (à l'électricité, etc.); **control driven** = commandé par les codes CTRL (générés par la touche contrôle) *or* asservi aux codes contrôle
◊ **driver** *noun* **(a)** logiciel *m* de commande de périphérique *or* gestionnaire *m* de périphérique; **printer driver** = pilote *m* d'imprimante **(b)** **line driver** = amplificateur *m* de signal

DRO = DESTRUCTIVE READOUT

drop cap *noun* lettrine *f;* **drop dead halt** *or* **dead halt** = arrêt *m* total; **drop line** = dérivation *f or* raccordement *m or* branchement *m*
◊ **drop in** *noun (on disk or tape)* parasite *m or* crasse *f*
◊ **drop out** *noun* **(a)** perte *f or* défaut *m* (de magnétisation) **(b)** *(of signal)* perte *f* de niveau

drum *noun* cylindre *m or* tambour *m;* **magnetic drum** = tambour magnétique; **drum plotter** = traceur *m or* enregistreur *m* à tambour

dry cell *noun* pile *f* sèche *or* alcaline; **dry circuit** = circuit *m* vocal; **dry contact** = contact *m* sec *or* intermittent; **dry joint** = connexion *f* bricolée; **dry run** = essai *m* à blanc *or* contrôle *m* avec un jeu d'essais

DSBSC = DOUBLE SIDEBAND SUPPRESSED CARRIER

DSE = DATA SWITCHING EXCHANGE

DSR = DATA SET READY

DSS = DECISION SUPPORT SYSTEM

DSW = DEVICE STATUS WORD

DTE = DATA TERMINAL EQUIPMENT

DTMF = DUAL TONE, MULTIFREQUENCY

DTP *or* **dtp** = DESKTOP PUBLISHING publication *f* assistée par ordinateur (PAO)

DTR = DATA TERMINAL READY

dual *adjective* double; **dual channel** = voie *f* double; **dual clocking** = (à) double chronométrie *or* (à) décalage de fréquence; **dual column** = colonne *f* double; **dual-in-line package (DIL** *or* **DIP)** = système *m* à double rang de broches (parallèles); **dual port memory** = mémoire *f* à double accès; **dual processor** = processeur *m* double; **dual system** = système *m* double; **dual tone, multifrequency (DTMF)** = signalisation *f* multifréquence

dub *verb* doubler (un film); **dubbed sound** = effets *mpl* sonores postsynchronisés
◇ **dubbing** *noun* doublage *m or* postsynchronisation *f*

duct *noun* conduit *m*

dumb terminal *noun* terminal *m* non intelligent

dummy *noun* maquette *f;* **dummy instruction** = instruction *f* de remplissage; **dummy variable** = variable *f* factice

dump 1 *noun (data)* analyse *f* (de) mémoire; *(transferring of data)* vidage *m* de transfert sur disque *or* sur support magnétique; *(copy)* vidage sur imprimante; **binary dump** = vidage binaire; **change dump** = vidage de mouvements (sur imprimante); **dump and restart** = (instruction de) vidage et reprise; **dump point** = point *m* de vidage; **memory dump** = listage *m* de mémoire *or* vidage de mémoire sur imprimante; **screen dump** = vidage d'écran sur imprimante **2** *verb* copier *or* transférer *or* vider; **the account results were dumped to the backup disk** = les résultats comptables ont été transférés sur le disque de sauvegarde

duodecimal number system *noun* système *m* duodécimal

duplex *noun* **(a)** *(photographic paper)* papier *m* photosensible double face **(b)** *(transmission of two signals)* (transmission) duplex *m;* **duplex circuit** = circuit *m* duplex; **duplex computer** = système duplex *or* ordinateurs jumelés; **duplex operation** = opération *f or* transmission *f* en duplex

duplicate 1 *noun (copy)* copie *f or* double *m;* **in duplicate** = en double exemplaire *or* en deux exemplaires; **receipt in duplicate** = reçu *m* en double exemplaire; **to print an invoice in duplicate** = établir une facture en deux exemplaires **2** *verb* copier *or* dupliquer; **to duplicate a letter** = faire une copie d'une lettre
◇ **duplicating** *noun* duplication *f;* **duplicating machine** = duplicateur *m or* copieur *m or* photocopieur *m;* **duplicating paper** = papier *m* pour duplicateur *or* copieur
◇ **duplication** *noun* reproduction *f or* duplication *f or* copie *f;* **duplication of work** = travail qui fait double emploi
◇ **duplicator** *noun* duplicateur *m or* copieur *m or* photocopieur *m;* **duplicator**

paper = papier pour duplicateur *or* copieur *or* photocopieur

durable *adjective* durable; **durable cartridge** = cartouche *f* longue durée

duration *noun* durée *f;* **pulse duration modulation (PDM)** = modulation *f* d'impulsions en durée

dustcover *noun (for a machine)* housse *f*

duty-rated *adjective* (système) évalué en cycles possibles par unité de temps *or* capacité de travail (d'un système)

QUOTE the laser printer can provide letter-quality print on ordinary cut-sheet paper and is duty-rated at up to 3,000 pages per month
Minicomputer News

DUV = DATA UNDER VOICE

dyad *noun* dyade *f*

◊ **dyadic operation** *noun* opération *f* dyadique *or* à deux opérandes

dynamic *adjective* dynamique; **dynamic allocation** = allocation *f* dymamique; **dynamic buffer** = mémoire *f* tampon dynamique; **dynamic data structure** = structure *f* de données dynamique; **dynamic dump** = vidage *m* dynamique; **dynamic memory** = mémoire dynamique; **dynamic RAM** *or* **dynamic random access memory (DRAM)** = RAM dynamique *or* mémoire vive dynamique; **dynamic microphone** = micro *m* à impulsion; **dynamic multiplexing** = multiplexage *m* dynamique; **dynamic range** = gamme *f or* amplitude *f* dynamique; **dynamic relocation (program)** = déplacement *m* dynamique; **dynamic stop** = arrêt *m* dynamique; **dynamic storage allocation** = allocation *f* dynamique de la mémoire; **dynamically redefinable character set** = police *f* de caractères vectorielle; **dynamic subroutine** = sous-programme *m* paramétrable; *compare* STATIC

Ee

E représentation hexadécimale du nombre 14 *or* E

EAN = EUROPEAN ARTICLE NUMBER

EAPROM = ELECTRICALLY ALTERABLE PROGRAMMABLE READ-ONLY MEMORY

EAROM = ELECTRICALLY ALTERABLE READ-ONLY MEMORY

earth 1 *noun* **(a)** terre *f; (for satellite transmissions)* **earth coverage =** zone *f* terrestre de couverture *or* couverture *f* terrestre; **earth station =** station *f* terrestre **(b)** *(connection representing zero potential)* prise *f* de terre; **all loose wires should be tied to earth =** tous les fils non rattachés doivent être mis à la terre *or* à la masse; **earth wire =** fil *m* de terre *or* de mise à la masse **2** *verb (to connect an electrical device to earth)* mettre à la terre *or* à la masse; **all appliances must be earthed =** tous les appareils doivent être mis à la terre NOTE: US English is **ground**

easy-to-use *adjective* facile à utiliser *or* d'utilisation facile

EAX = ELECTRONIC AUTOMATIC EXCHANGE

EBCDIC = EXTENDED BINARY CODED DECIMAL INTERCHANGE CODE

EBNF = EXTENDED BACKUS-NAUR FORM métalangage *m* BNF étendu *or* BNF étendu

EBR = ELECTRON BEAM RECORDING

echo 1 *noun* écho *m;* **echo chamber =** chambre *f* à écho; **echo check =** contrôle *m* par écho; **echo suppressor =** éliminateur *m* d'écho *or* dispositif *m* anti-écho **2** *verb* faire écho

ECL = EMITTER COUPLED LOGIC

ECMA = EUROPEAN COMPUTER MANUFACTURERS ASSOCIATION syndicat *m* européen des constructeurs d'ordinateurs; *(used to draw flowcharts)* **ECMA symbols =** symboles *mpl* ECMA

EDAC = ERROR DETECTION AND CORRECTION

edge *noun (of flat object or signal or clock pulse)* bordure *f or* bord *m or* limite *f;* **edge board** *or* **card =** carte *f* à connexion; **edge connector =** connecteur *m* de carte; **edge detection =** détection *f* de limites *or* de bordures; *(paper card)* **edge notched card =** carte *f* à encoches marginales; **edge-triggered =** déclenché par bascule de front d'impulsion

edit *verb (to format)* éditer; *(to correct text)* corriger *or* réviser (un texte avant l'impression);* **edit commands =** commandes *f* d'édition; **edit key =** touche *f* (de fonction) d'édition; **there are several special edit keys - this one will re-format the text =** il y a plusieurs touches d'édition - celle-ci permet de reformater le texte; **edit window =** fenêtre *f* d'édition; *(film or TV program)* **editing plan =** maquette *f* d'édition; **editing run =** exécution *f* d'un programme d'édition (pour contrôle); *(on microfilm)* **editing symbol =** marque *f or* symbole *m or* repère *m* de positionnement (sur microfilm); **editing terms =** commandes et instructions d'édition; **linkage editing =** mise *f* en place de liens (à l'aide d'un éditeur de liens)

◊ **edition** *noun (books or newspapers printed at one time)* édition *f;* **the second edition has had some changes to the text** = le texte de la seconde édition a été modifié; **did you see the last edition of the evening paper?** = avez-vous lu la dernière édition du journal du soir?

◊ **editor** *noun* **(a)** *(person who edits films or books)* éditeur, -trice **(b)** **editor program** = (programme) éditeur; **line editor** = éditeur ligne à ligne; **linkage editor** = éditeur de liens; **text editor** = éditeur de texte *or* programme d'édition de texte **(c)** *(of a newspaper or magazine)* rédacteur, -trice; **the editor of 'The Times'** = le rédacteur en chef du 'Times'; **the paper's computer editor** = le rédacteur de la rubrique informatique du journal

◊ **editorial 1** *adjective* éditorial, -e; **editorial processing centre** = centre *m* de traitement de texte **2** *noun (article written by the editor)* éditorial *m*

QUOTE an object orientated graphics editor enables you to add text to graphics
Byte
QUOTE while it has many formatting facilities, it does not include an editor with which to create the template for the report
Personal Computer World

EDP = ELECTRONIC DATA PROCESSING traitement *m* électronique de données *or* de l'information; **EDP capability** = capacité *f* de traitement (électronique) de données NOTE: **EDP** is more common in US English

EDS = EXCHANGEABLE DISK STORAGE

educational *adjective* éducatif, -ive; **educational TV** *or* **ETV** **programme** = programme *m* de télévision (de caractère) éducatif

EEPROM = ELECTRICALLY ERASABLE PROGRAMMABLE READ-ONLY MEMORY

EEROM = ELECTRICALLY ERASABLE READ-ONLY MEMORY

effective *adjective* effectif, -ive; **effective address** = adresse effective;

effective bandwidth = largeur de bande effective; **effective instruction** = instruction effective; **effective search speed** = vitesse de recherche effective; **effective throughput** = rendement effectif

◊ **effective aperture** *noun* **(a)** *(of aerial)* puissance *f* d'ouverture effective **(b)** *(of camera)* ouverture *f* utile

efficient *adjective* efficace *or* performant, -e *or* efficient, -e; **the program is highly efficient at sorting files** = ce programme est excellent pour le tri des fichiers

◊ **efficiently** *adverb* efficacement; **the word-processing package has produced a series of addressed letters very efficiently** = ce progiciel de traitement de texte a produit, de façon très performante, une série de lettres personnalisées

◊ **efficiency** *noun* efficacité *f or* bonne performance *or* efficience *f;* **he is doubtful about the efficiency of the new networking system** = il n'est pas vraiment sûr que le nouveau système multiposte fonctionne bien

EFT = ELECTRONIC FUNDS TRANSFER (SYSTEM)

◊ **EFTPOS** = ELECTRONIC FUNDS TRANSFER POINT-OF-SALE

EGA = ENHANCED GRAPHICS ADAPTER (carte) adaptateur *m* graphique couleur *or* carte EGA; **EGA screen** = écran EGA

QUOTE although the video BIOS services are enhanced by adding an EGA card, the DOS functions are not
.EXE

EHF = EXTREMELY HIGH FREQUENCY

EIA = ELECTRONIC INDUSTRY ASSOCIATION; **EIA interface** = interface *f* aux normes EIA

eight-bit (system) *noun* (système) huit bits; **eight-bit byte** *or* **octet** = octet *m*

◊ **eight-inch disk** *noun* disquette *f* de huit pouces; **eight-inch drive** = lecteur *m* de disquettes de huit pouces

◊ **eighty-column screen** = *noun* écran *m* (de) quatre-vingts colonnes

◇ **eighty-track disk** *noun* disque de quatre-vingts pistes

either-or operation *noun (logical function)* opération *f* OU inclusif *or* opération d'union *or* de réunion

◇ **either-way operation** *noun* mode de transmission bidirectionnelle à l'alternat

elapsed time *noun* temps *m* passé à une tâche *or* temps d'exécution d'une tâche

elastic banding *noun (defining the limits of an image on a screen)* recadrage *m* (d'une image sur l'écran)

◇ **elastic buffer** *noun* (mémoire) tampon *m* de capacité *or* de taille variable

electret *noun* électret *m;* **electret microphone** = microphone *m* à électret

electric *adjective* électrique; **electric current** = courant *m* électrique; **electric charge** = charge *f* électrique; **electric typewriter** = machine *f* à écrire électrique

◇ **electrical** *adjective* électrique; **the engineers are trying to repair an electrical fault** = les ingénieurs essaient de réparer une panne électrique

◇ **electrically** *adverb* à l'électricité *or* électriquement; **an electrically-powered motor** = un moteur électrique *or* un moteur qui marche *or* qui fonctionne à l'électricité; **electrically alterable, programmable read-only memory (EAPROM)** = mémoire *f* EAPROM *or* mémoire ROM programmable, modifiable électriquement; **electrically alterable read-only memory (EAROM)** = mémoire EAROM *or* mémoire ROM modifiable électriquement; **electrically erasable programmable read-only memory (EEPROM)** = mémoire EEPROM *or* mémoire ROM programmable et effaçable électriquement; **electrically erasable read-only memory (EEROM)** = mémoire EEROM *or* mémoire ROM effaçable électriquement

QUOTE conventional EEPROM requires two transistors to store each bit of data
Electronics & Power

electricity *noun* électricité *f;* **the electricity was cut off, and the computer crashed** = il y a eu une coupure de courant qui a été fatale à l'ordinateur; **electricity prices are an important factor in the production costs** = les frais d'électricité constituent un élément important des coûts de production

electrode *noun* électrode *f*

electrographic printer *noun see* ELECTROSTATIC PRINTER

electroluminescence *noun* électroluminescence *f*

◇ **electroluminescing** *adjective* électroluminescent, -e

◇ **electroluminescent** *adjective* électroluminescent, -e; **the screen coating is electroluminescent** = l'écran est recouvert d'une couche électroluminescente; **electroluminescent display** = affichage *or* écran électroluminescent

electrolytic capacitor *noun* condensateur *m* électrolytique; **non-electrolytic capacitor** = condensateur non électrolytique

electromagnet *noun* électro-aimant *m*

◇ **electromagnetic** *adjective* électromagnétique; **electromagnetic interference (EMI)** = interférence *f* électromagnétique; **electromagnetic radiation** = rayonnement *m* électromagnétique; **electromagnetic spectrum** = spectre *m* électromagnétique

◇ **electromagnetically** *adverb* (qui fonctionne) grâce à un électro-aimant

electromechanical switching *noun* commutation *f* électromécanique

electromotive force (EMF) *noun* force *f* électromotrice

electron *noun* électron *m;* **electron beam** = faisceau *m* électronique *or* d'électrons; *(onto microfilm)* **electron beam recording (EBR)** = enregistrement *m* par faisceau électronique (sur microfilm); **electron gun** = canon *m* à électrons

electronic *adjective* électronique; **electronic automatic exchange** = central *m* automatique électronique *or* autocommutateur *m* électronique; **electronic banking** = la bancatique; **electronic blackboard** = tableau *m* noir électronique; **electronic composition** = composition *f* électronique; **electronic data processing (EDP)** = (i) traitement *m* électronique de données; (ii) l'informatique *f*; **electronic data processing capability** = facilité *f* de traitement électronique de données; **electronic digital computer** = calculateur *m or* ordinateur *m* numérique; *(of video film)* **electronic editing** = montage *m* électronique; **electronic engineer** = ingénieur *m* électronicien; **electronic industry association interface (EIA)** = interface *f* aux normes EIA; **electronic filing** = archivage *m* sur ordinateur; **electronic funds transfer (system) (EFT)** = transfert *m* électronique de fonds; **electronic funds transfer point of sale (EFTPOS)** = terminal *m* de transfert électronique de fonds; **electronic keyboard** = clavier *m* électronique; **electronic lock** = verrou *m* (de sécurité) électronique; **electronic mail** *or* **email** *or* **e-mail** = messagerie *f or* courrier *m* électronique; **electronic mailbox** = boîte *f* aux lettres électronique; **electronic money** = monnaie *f* électronique *or* cartes *fpl* (de crédit) magnétiques; **electronic news gathering (ENG)** = journalisme *m or* reportage *m* électronique; **electronic office** = bureau *m* informatisé; **electronic office system** = (système) bureautique *f*; **electronic pen** *or* **stylus** *or* **wand** = stylo *m* optique; **electronic point-of-sale (EPOS)** = point *m* de vente électronique; **electronic publishing** = édition *f* électronique *or* publication *f* assistée par ordinateur (PAO); **electronic pulse** = impulsion *f* électronique; **electronic shopping** = achats *mpl* sur *or* par ordinateur; **electronic signature** = signature *f* électronique; **electronic smog** = pollution *f* (par rayonnement) électronique; **electronic stylus** *or* **wand** = stylo *m* électronique; **electronic switching system** = système *m* de commutation électronique *or* commutateur *m* électronique; **electronic traffic** = transmission électronique;

electronic typewriter = machine *f* à écrire électronique; *(in TV or video camera)* **electronic viewfinder** = viseur *m* électronique; **electronic wand** = stylo *m* électronique

◊ **electronically** *adverb* électroniquement *or* par système électronique; **the text is electronically transmitted to an outside typesetter** = le texte est transmis au compositeur externe par système électronique

◊ **electronics** *noun* *(science)* l'électronique *f*; **the electronics industry** = l'industrie *f* électronique; **electronics specialist** expert *m* en électronique; *(technician)* électronicien, -ienne

QUOTE electronic mail is a system which allows computer users to send information to each other via a central computer
Which PC?
QUOTE electronic publishing will be used for printing on paper, but it can be applied equally to data storage on a database, transmission via telecommunications or for use with visual presentation media such as AV slides or television
Electronic Publishing & Print Show

electro-optic effect *noun* effet *m* optronique

◊ **electrophotography** *noun* électrophotographie *f*

◊ **electrosensitive** *adjective* **electrosensitive paper** = papier *m* électrosensible *or* à transfert thermique; **electrosensitive printing** = impression *f* thermique

◊ **electrostatic** *adjective* électrostatique; **electrostatic printer** = imprimante *f* électrostatique; **electrostatic screen** = écran *m* électrostatique; **electrostatic speaker** = haut-parleur *m* électrostatique; **electrostatic storage** = mémoire *f* électrostatique

◊ **electrostatically** *adverb* par charge électrostatique

◊ **electrothermal printer** *noun* imprimante *f* thermique

elegant *adjective* **elegant programming** = programmation élégante *or* bien conçue

element *noun* **(a)** élément *m or* composant *m*; **logic element** = élément logique; **picture element** *or* **pixel** = pixel *m*; **signal element** = élément d'un signal

(b) *(cell)* élément *or* cellule *f;* **array element** = élément d'un tableau **(c)** *(coil of resistive wire)* élément **(d)** *(substance)* élément

◊ **elementary** *adjective (made of many similar small sections or objects)* élémentaire; **elementary cable section** = section *f* élémentaire de câble

ELF = EXTREMELY LOW FREQUENCY

eliminate *verb (to remove)* éliminer; **using a computer should eliminate all possibility of error in the address system** = l'ordinateur devrait servir à éliminer toute possibilité d'erreur dans le système d'adresses; **a spelling checker does not eliminate all spelling mistakes** = un correcteur orthographique n'élimine pas toutes les fautes d'orthographe

◊ **elimination** *noun* élimination *f;* **elimination factor** = facteur *m* d'élimination

QUOTE pointing with the cursor and pressing the joystick button eliminates use of the keyboard almost entirely
Soft

elite *noun (typeface)* caractères *mpl* Elite

ellipse *noun* ellipse *f*

◊ **elliptical orbit** *noun* orbite *f or* trajectoire *f* elliptique

else rule *noun* instruction ELSE (sinon); **IF X=20 THEN PRINT 'X is 20' ELSE PRINT 'X not 20'** = si X=20 imprimer 'X égale 20' sinon imprimer 'X différent de 20'

ELT = ELECTRONIC TYPEWRITER

em *noun* **em dash** *or* **em rule** = tiret *m* long *or* tiret cadratin (dont la longueur équivaut à un 'm'); *(space)* **em quad** = cadratin *m;* **ems per hour** = débit *m* d'une imprimante (mesuré en 'ems')

EM = END OF MEDIUM

email *or* **e-mail** = ELECTRONIC MAIL messagerie *f or* courrier *m* électronique

QUOTE to collect telex messages from an e-mail system, you have to remember to dial the system and check whether there are any telex messages in your mailbox
Which PC?

embedded code *noun* code *m* (d'instruction) imbriqué (dans un programme); **embedded command** = commande imbriquée (dans le texte); **embedded computer** *or* **system** = ordinateur *or* système imbriqué (dans un autre)

embolden *verb (to make a word print in bold type)* (donner une instruction d') imprimer en caractères gras

embrace *see* DEADLY

emf = ELECTROMOTIVE FORCE

EMI = ELECTROMAGNETIC INTERFERENCE

emission *noun (of a signal or radiation, etc.)* émission *f;* **the emission of the electron beam** = l'émission du faisceau électronique; **the receiver picked up the radio emission** = le récepteur a capté l'émission radiophonique

◊ **emit** *verb* émettre

◊ **emitter** *noun* émetteur *m;* **emitter-coupled logic (ECL)** = logique *f* ECL

empty *adjective* vide; **empty** *or* **null list** = liste *f* vide; **empty medium** = support *m* magnétique vierge; **empty** *or* **null set** = jeu *m or* ensemble *m* de caractères nuls; **empty slot** = (i) case *f* vide; (ii) connecteur *m or* créneau *m* (pour carte additionnelle) inutilisé; **empty** *or* **null string** = chaîne *f* vide

emulate *verb* émuler; **laser printer which emulates a wide range of office printers** = une imprimante (à) laser qui peut émuler une série d'autres imprimantes de bureau

◊ **emulation** *noun* émulation *f;* **emulation facility** = capacité *f* d'émulation

◊ **emulator** *noun* émulateur *m*

QUOTE full communications error checking built into the software ensures reliable file transfers and a terminal emulation facility enables a user's terminal to be used as if it were a terminal to the remote computer
Byte

QUOTE some application programs do not have the right drivers for a laser printer, so look out for laser printers which are able to emulate the more popular office printers
Publish

emulsion *noun (on photographic film or paper)* émulsion *f;* **emulsion laser storage** = mémoire *f* laser sur couche haute définition

en *noun (half the width of an em)* **en dash** *or* **en rule** = tiret *m* de césure *or* tiret court *or* tiret demi-cadratin (dont la longueur équivaut à un 'n'); *(space)* **en quad** = demi-cadratin *m*

enable *verb* **(a)** *(to allow to happen)* permettre *or* rendre possible; **a spooling program enables editing work to be carried out while printing is going on** = un programme de 'spooling' permet d'éditer un texte tout en imprimant **(b)** *(to use an electronic signal to start a process)* sélectionner *or* activer *or* valider; **enabling signal** = signal *m* de sélection *or* de validation *or* d'activation

encipher *verb* chiffrer *or* crypter; **our competitors cannot understand our files - they have all been enciphered** = nos concurrents ne peuvent lire nos fichiers qui sont en langage chiffré

enclose *verb (to surround)* enfermer; *(to contain)* inclure *or* contenir
◊ **enclosure** *noun (protective casing for equipment)* boîtier *m* (protecteur)

encode *verb* encoder
◊ **encoder** *noun* encodeur *m;* **colour encoder** = encodeur de couleurs; **magnetic tape encoder** = encodeur pour bandes magnétiques
◊ **encoding** *noun* encodage *m;* **binary encoding** = encodage binaire; **encoding format** = format *m* d'encodage; **magnetic encoding** = encodage magnétique

encrypt *verb* chiffrer *or* crypter; **the encrypted text can be sent along ordinary telephone lines, and no one will be able to understand it** = le message chiffré *or* crypté peut être transmis par téléphone sans que personne ne puisse le lire
◊ **encryption** *noun* chiffrage *m or* chiffrement *m or* cryptage *m;* **data encryption standard (DES)** = norme *f or* standard *m* de cryptage de données

end 1 *noun* **(a)** *(final point or last part)* fin *f;* **at the end of the data transmission** = à la fin de la transmission des données; **end product** = produit *m* fini; **far end** *or* **receiving end** = (point d') arrivée *f or* (point de) réception *f;* **in the end** = finalement *or* à la fin **(b)** (caractère) fin (de fichier); **end-around carry** = report *m* circulaire *or* en boucle; **end about shift** = décalage *m* circulaire; **end of address (EOA)** = (code de) fin d'adresse; **end of block (EOB)** = (code de) fin de bloc; **end of data (EOD)** = (code de) fin de données; **end of document** *or* **end of file (EOF)** = (code de) fin de document; **end of job (EOJ)** = (code de) fin de tâche; **end of medium (EM)** = (code de) fin de support (de données); **end of message (EOM)** = (code de) fin de message; *(on typewriter)* **end of page indicator** = signal *m* de fin de page; **end of record (EOR)** = (code de) fin d'enregistrement; **end of run routines** = routines *fpl* de clôture (d'exécution); **end of tape (EOT)** = (code de) fin de la bande (magnétique); **end of text (EOT** *or* **ETX)** = (code de) fin de texte; **end of transmission (EOT)** = (code *or* signal de) fin de la transmission **2** *verb* finir *or* arrêter
◊ **ending** *noun* **(a)** *(action)* fin *f or* arrêt *m* **(b)** *(end part)* fin *or* bout *m;* **line endings** = bouts *or* fins de lignes
◊ **endless** *adjective* sans fin *or* continu, -e; **endless loop** = boucle sans fin *or* continue *or* infinie
◊ **end user** *noun* utilisateur, -trice (final); **the company is creating a computer with a specific end user in mind** = la société cherche à créer un ordinateur adapté aux besoins de l'utilisateur

energy *noun* **(a)** *(force)* énergie *f* **(b)** *(power from electricity, etc.)* énergie; **we try to save energy by switching off the lights when the rooms are empty** = nous essayons d'économiser de l'énergie *or* du courant en éteignant les lumières lorsque les pièces sont vides; **if you**

reduce the room temperature to eighteen degrees, you will save energy = vous économiserez de l'énergie en limitant la température de la pièce à 18 degrés

◇ **energy-saving** *adjective* qui économise l'énergie; **our company is introducing energy-saving measures =** notre société met en place des mesures d'économie d'énergie

ENG = ELECTRONIC NEWS GATHERING

enhance *verb* optimiser *or* améliorer *or* relever; **enhanced dot matrix =** matrice *f* d'impression à haute définition; **enhanced graphics adapter (EGA) =** (carte) adaptateur *m* graphique couleur *or* carte EGA; **enhanced graphics adapter screen** *or* **EGA screen =** écran *m* EGA; **enhanced small device interface (ESDI) =** interface *f* ESDI

◇ **enhancement** *noun* optimisation *f or* amélioration *f*

◇ **enhancer** *noun* optimiseur *m*

QUOTE the typefaces are fairly rudimentary, especially if you are not using an enhanced graphics adapter screen
Desktop Publishing

enlarge *verb* agrandir *or* grossir

◇ **enlargement** *noun* agrandissement *m or* grossissement *m;* **an enlargement of the photograph was used to provide better detail =** on a utilisé un agrandissement de la photo pour voir les détails plus clairement

ENQ = ENQUIRY

enquiry (ENQ) *noun* (i) demande *f ;* (ii) interrogation *f or* requête *f;* **enquiry character =** caractère *m* de requête

ensure *verb* assurer; **pushing the write-protect tab will ensure that the data on the disk cannot be erased =** mettre en place le dispositif de protection d'écriture pour vous assurer de ne pas perdre vos données

enter *verb (data or code)* entrer *or* saisir *or* introduire *(des données) or* taper (un code); **to enter a name on a list =** entrer *or* inscrire un nom sur une liste; **the data has been entered =** les données ont été saisies; **enter key =** touche *f* de validation d'entrée

◇ **entering** *noun (action)* entrée *f or* saisie *f or* introduction *f* (de données)

entity *noun* entité *f*

entry *noun* **(a)** *(single record)* entrée *f* **(b)** *(place where you can enter)* entrée; *(before a routine can be entered)* **entry condition =** condition *f* d'entrée; *(in a called subroutine)* **entry instruction =** instruction *f* d'entrée; **entry point =** point *m or* adresse d'entrée; **entry time =** heure *f* d'entrée

enumerated type *noun* classement *m* énumératif

envelope *noun* **(a)** *(for sending letters)* enveloppe *f;* **air mail envelope =** enveloppe avion; **window envelope =** enveloppe à fenêtre; **sealed envelope =** enveloppe fermée *or* cachetée; **unsealed envelope =** enveloppe ouverte *or* non cachetée **(b)** *(of amplitude)* enveloppe; **attack envelope =** enveloppe d'attaque (d'un signal); **envelope delay =** (temps de) propagation *f* d'une enveloppe; **envelope detection =** détection *f* d'enveloppe **(c)** *(transmitted byte of data)* (octet) enveloppe

environment *noun* **(a)** *(condition in a computer system)* environnement *m* **(b)** *(surroundings)* environnement

QUOTE one of the advantages of working in a PC-based environment is the enormous range of software which can run on the same computer
ESL Newsletter

EOA = END OF ADDRESS

EOB = END OF BLOCK

EOD = END OF DATA

EOF = END OF FILE

EOJ = END OF JOB

EOM = END OF MESSAGE

EOR = END OF RECORD

EOT = END OF TEXT *or* END OF TRANSMISSION

episcope *or* **epidiascope** *noun* épidiascope *m or* projecteur *m* de documents opaques

epitaxy *noun* épitaxie *f*
◊ **epitaxial layer** *noun* couche *f* épitaxiale

EPOS = ELECTRONIC POINT-OF-SALE

EPROM *noun* **(a)** = ELECTRICALLY PROGRAMMABLE READ-ONLY MEMORY mémoire *f* EPROM *or* mémoire ROM programmable électriquement **(b)** = ERASABLE PROGRAMMABLE READ-ONLY MEMORY mémoire EPROM *or* mémoire ROM programmable et effaçable

QUOTE the densest EPROMs commercially available today are at the 1Mbit level
Electronics & Power

equal 1 *adjective* égal, -e **2** *verb* être égal à NOTE: **equalling - equalled** but US: **equaling - equaled**
◊ **equality** *noun* égalité *f*
◊ **equalize** *verb* égaliser *or* corriger (à l'aide d'un filtre); **the received signal was equalized to an optimum shape** = le signal d'entrée a été filtré pour obtenir une forme optimale
◊ **equalization** *noun* égalisation *f*
◊ **equalizer** *noun* égaliseur *m;* **frequency equalizer** = égaliseur de fréquence *or* filtre *m* de bande de fréquence
◊ **equally** *adverb* également

equate *verb* égaler; **the variable was equated to the input data** = la variable a pris la valeur de la donnée saisie
◊ **equation** *noun* équation *f;* **machine equation** = équation machine

equator *noun* équateur *m*
◊ **equatorial orbit** *noun* orbite *f* équatoriale

equip *verb* (s') équiper
◊ **equipment** *noun* équipement *m or* matériel *m;* **computer equipment supplier** = fournisseur *m or* revendeur *m*

d'équipements informatiques; **equipment failure** = défaillance *f* du matériel *or* de l'ordinateur

equivalence *noun* **(a)** *(being equivalent)* équivalence *f* **(b)** *(logical operation)* equivalence; **equivalence function** *or* **operation** = (i) fonction *f or* opération *f* d'équivalence; (ii) équivalence logique; **equivalence gate** = porte *f or* circuit *m* d'équivalence; **non-equivalence function (NEQ)** = fonction de disjonction *or* OU exclusif; **non-equivalence gate** = porte *f or* circuit OU exclusif
◊ **equivalent** *adjective* équivalent, -e; **to be equivalent to** = être équivalent (à) *or* équivaloir (à); **the total number of characters keyboarded so far is equivalent to one day's printing time** = le nombre de caractères saisis jusqu'ici équivaut à une journée d'impression

erase *verb* **(a)** (i) effacer; (ii) remettre à zéro **(b)** *(data)* effacer *or* détruire; **erase character** = caractère *m* d'effacement; **erase head** = tête *f* d'effacement
◊ **erasable** *adjective* effaçable *or* qui peut être effacé, -ée; **erasable storage** *or* **erasable memory** = (i) support (magnétique) effaçable *or* réutilisable; (ii) mémoire temporaire; **erasable programmable read-only memory (EPROM)** = mémoire EPROM *or* mémoire ROM programmable et effaçable
◊ **eraser** *noun* dispositif *m* d'effacement

ERCC = ERROR CHECKING AND CORRECTING

E-region *or* **Heaviside-Kennelly layer** *noun* *(section of the ionosphere)* couche *f* E

ergonomics *noun* l'ergonomie *f*
◊ **ergonomist** *noun* ergonome *m&f or* ergonomiste *m&f*

EROM = ERASABLE READ-ONLY MEMORY

erratum *noun* erratum *m*
NOTE: plural is **errata**

error *noun* erreur *f or* faute *f or* anomalie *f;* **he made an error in calculating the total** = il a fait une erreur de total; **the secretary must have made a typing error** = la secrétaire doit avoir fait une faute de frappe; **in error** *or* **by error** = par erreur; **margin of error** = marge *f* d'erreur; **error ambiguity** = erreur d'ambiguïté; **error burst** = rafale *f* d'erreurs *or* série *f* d'erreurs consécutives; **error checking and correcting code (ECCC)** = code *m* de vérification et correction d'erreurs; **error code** = code d'erreur; **error condition** = condition *f* d'erreur; **error control** = contrôle *m* d'erreurs; **error correcting codes** = codes de correction d'erreurs; *see also* GRAY CODE; **error correction** = correction *f* d'erreurs; **error detecting codes** = codes *mpl* de détection d'erreurs; **error detection** = détection d'erreurs; **error detection and correction (EDAC)** = détection et correction d'erreurs; **error diagnosis** = diagnostic *m* d'erreurs; **error diagnostics** = outils *m* de diagnostic d'erreurs; **error handling** *or* **management** = procédure *f* de traitement des erreurs *or* gestion *f* des erreurs; **error interrupt** = (signal d') interruption *f* sur (une) erreur *or* sur (un) incident; **error logging** = enregistrement *m* automatique des erreurs; **features of the program include error logging** = ce programme permet l'enregistrement (automatique) des erreurs; **error message** = message *m* d'erreur; **error propagation** = propagation *f* d'erreur; **error rate** = taux *m* d'erreur; **the error rate is less than 1%** = le taux d'erreur est inférieur à 1%; **error recovery** = reprise *f* après erreur *or* incident (sans repartir à zéro); **error routine** = routine *f* (de traitement) d'erreur; **error trapping** = détection *or* recherche *or* prévention *f* d'erreurs; **compilation error** = erreur de compilation; **diagnostic (error) message** = message *m* de diagnostic d'erreur; **execution error** = erreur d'exécution; **logical error** = erreur logique; **permanent error** = erreur permanente; **quantization error** = erreur de quantification; **recoverable error** = erreur qui peut être corrigée *or* redressée; **rejection error** = erreur de rejet *or* de refus; **scanning error** = erreur de balayage; **a wrinkled or torn page may be the cause of scanning errors** = un pli ou une déchirure dans une page peut être la cause d'une erreur de balayage *or* d'un balayage incorrect; **substitution error** = erreur de substitution; **syntax error** = faute de syntaxe; **transient error** = erreur passagère *or* momentanée; **undetected error** = erreur non détectée

QUOTE syntax errors, like omitting a bracket, will produce an error message from the compiler
Personal Computer World

ESC échappement *m or* code *m* ESC

escape character *noun* caractère *m* d'échappement; **escape codes** = codes *mpl* d'échappement; **escape key** = touche *f* d'échappement *or* touche ECHAPPEMENT *or* touche ESC
◊ **escapement** *noun (of paper in a printer)* échappement *m*

ESDI = ENHANCED SMALL DEVICE INTERFACE

ESS = ELECTRONIC SWITCHING SYSTEM

establish *verb* établir; **they established which component was faulty** = ils ont repéré le composant défectueux

etch *verb* graver; **etched type** = caractère gravé (gravure ionique *or* chimique)

ETV = EDUCATIONAL TELEVISION

ETX = END OF TEXT

Euronet *noun (telephone connected network)* Euronet *m*

European Article Number (EAN) *noun* numérotation *f* européenne des articles (NEA)

evaluate *verb* évaluer
◊ **evaluation** *noun* évaluation *f*
◊ **evaluative abstract** *noun* extrait *m or* résumé *m* critique

even *adjective (number)* pair, -e; **the first three even numbers are 2, 4, 6** = les trois premiers nombres pairs: 2,4 et 6; **even parity (check)** = contrôle *m* de parité paire; **even working** = pliage *m* en cahiers de 16, 32 ou 64 pages

event *noun* événement *m*

◊ **event-driven** *adjective* activé, -ée *or* actionné, -ée par événement

except *preposition & conjunction* sauf *or* excepté; **all the text has been keyboarded, except the last ten pages** = le texte a été saisi, sauf les dix dernières pages; *(logical function)* **except gate** = porte *f or* circuit *m* OU exclusif

◊ **exception** *noun* exception *f;* **exception dictionary** = liste *f or* répertoire *m* d'exceptions; **exception report** = rapport *m* d'exceptions *or* d'anomalies

excess *noun* excès *m;* **excess-3 code** = code *m* (binaire) plus 3; **the excess-3 code representation of 6 is 1001** = pour 6, le code (binaire) plus 3 est 1001

◊ **excessive** *adjective* excessif, -ive; **the program used an excessive amount of memory to accomplish the job** = ce programme a utilisé une quantité excessive de mémoire pour exécuter la tâche en question

exchange 1 *noun* **(a)** *(giving of one thing for another)* échange *m;* **part exchange** = reprise *f* **(b)** *(telephone equipment)* central *m* téléphonique; *(local loop)* **electronic automatic exchange** = central automatique *or* autocommutateur *m* électronique; **exchange line** = ligne *f* de jonction d'abonné (au centre téléphonique); *see also* PABX **2** *verb* **(a)** faire un échange *or* échanger (une chose contre une autre); **exchange selection** = tri *m* par échange **(b)** *(to swap data between two locations)* échanger *or* permuter *or* basculer (des données)

◊ **exchangeable** *adjective (returnable)* échangeable; *(moveable)* amovible; **exchangeable disk storage (EDS)** = disque *m* dur amovible

exclamation mark (!) *noun* point *m* d'exclamation

exclude *verb* exclure; **the interest charges have been excluded from the document** = les frais financiers n'ont pas été inclus dans le document; **the password is supposed to exclude hackers from the database** = le mot de passe est censé protéger la base de données contre le piratage

◊ **excluding** *preposition* à l'exception de

◊ **exclusion** *noun* **(a)** *(action)* exclusion *f* **(b)** *(restriction of access to a telephone line)* exclusion

◊ **exclusive** *adjective* exclusif, -ive; *(logical function)* **exclusive NOR (EXNOR)** = NI exclusif; **exclusive NOR gate** = porte *f or* circuit *m* NI exclusif; **exclusive OR (EXOR)** = OU exclusif; **exclusive OR gate** = porte *f or* circuit *m* OU exclusif

executable form *noun* programme *m* prêt à être exécuté

execute *verb (computer program)* exécuter; **execute cycle** = cycle *m* d'exécution; **execute mode** = mode *m* d'exécution; **execute phase** = phase *f* d'exécution; **execute signal** = signal *m* d'exécution; **execute statement** = déclaration *f or* message *m* d'exécution; **execute time** durée *f or* temps *m* d'exécution; **fetch-execute cycle** = EXECUTE CYCLE

◊ **execution** *noun (carrying out of a computer program)* exécution *f;* **execution address** = adresse *f* d'exécution; **execution cycle** = cycle *m* d'exécution; **execution error** = erreur *f* d'exécution; **execution phase** = phase *f* d'exécution; **execution time** = temps *f* d'exécution

QUOTE fast execution speed is the single most important feature of a C compiler
.EXE

executive 1 *adjective* **executive program** *or* **supervisor program** = programme *m* superviseur; **executive control program** = OPERATING SYSTEM; **executive instruction** = instruction *f* de superviseur **2** *noun (director)* cadre *m* de direction *or* cadre supérieur

◊ **executive terminal** *noun (business terminal)* terminal *m* de gestion *or* à usage professionnel; *(control terminal)* terminal directeur *or* exécutif *or* superviseur

exerciser *noun* testeur *m or* programme *m* de test

exhaustive search *noun* recherche *f* exhaustive *or* très poussée

exit *verb (to stop program execution)* abandonner; *(to leave a program or a loop)* quitter *or* sortir (de); **exit point =** point *m* de sortie; **you have to exit to another editing system to add headlines =** pour mettre des en-têtes, il faut quitter ce programme et entrer dans un autre

exjunction *noun (logical function)* disjonction *f*

EXNOR = EXCLUSIVE NOR *(logical function)* NI exclusif; **EXNOR gate =** porte *f or* circuit *m* NI exclusif

EXOR = EXCLUSIVE OR *(logical function)* OU exclusif; **EXOR gate =** porte *f or* circuit *m* OU exclusif

expand *verb* augmenter *or* élargir *or* agrandir; **if you want to hold so much data, you will have to expand the disk capacity =** pour conserver une telle quantité de données, il vous faudra une extension de votre disque

◇ **expandable** *adjective* extensible *or* qui peut être augmenté, -ée; **expandable system =** système *m* extensible

◇ **expander** *noun* **video expander =** déconcentrateur *m* pour transmission vidéo

◇ **expansion** *noun* expansion *f or* extension *f;* **expansion card** *or* **expansion board =** carte *f* d'extension; **expansion slot =** créneau *m or* connecteur *m* pour carte d'extension; **insert the board in the free expansion slot =** enfichez la carte d'extension dans le créneau libre; **macro expansion =** macro-expansion *f or* désassemblage *m* de macro

> QUOTE it can be attached to mast kinds of printer, and, if that is not enough, an expansion box can be fitted to the bus connector
> *Personal Computer World*

expert *noun* expert *m or* spécialiste *m&f;* **he is a computer expert =** c'est un spécialiste en informatique; **she is an expert in programming languages =** c'est une spécialiste des langages de programmation; **expert system =** système expert

expire *verb* expirer

◇ **expiration** *noun* expiration *f;* **expiration date =** *(sell-by date)* date *f* de péremption; *(time limit)* date limite *or* date d'expiration d'un délai

explicit address *noun* adresse *f* explicite

exponent *noun (maths)* exposant *m;* **binary exponent =** exposant binaire

◇ **exponential** *adjective* exponentiel, -elle

◇ **exponentiate** *verb* élever un nombre à la puissance x

◇ **exponentiation** *noun* élévation *f* (d'un nombre) à la puissance x

express *verb* exprimer *or* formuler; **express the formula in its simplest form =** réduire la formule à sa plus simple expression; **the computer structure was expressed graphically =** l'architecture *or* la structure de l'ordinateur était représentée graphiquement

◇ **expression** *noun* **(a)** *(mathematical formula)* expression *f or* formule *f* **(b)** *(definition of a variable in a program)* expression

extend *verb (to make longer)* étendre *or* allonger; **extended arithmetic element =** élément arithmétique étendu; **extended binary coded decimal interchange code (EBCDIC) =** code EBCDIC *or* code binaire à 8 bits; **extended BNF (EBNF) =** métalangage BNF étendu *or* BNF étendu; **extending serial file =** fichier *m* série extensible

◇ **extender** *noun* **card extender =** support *m* de carte d'extension; **line extender =** unité *f* d'extension d'une ligne

◇ **extensible** *adjective* extensible; **extensible language =** langage *m* extensible *or* adaptable

◇ **extension** *noun* extension *f;* **extension cable =** câble *m* d'extension; **extension memory =** extension de mémoire; *(of photographic lens)* **extension tube =** bague *m* d'extension; **filename extension =** extension *or* spécification *f* du nom du fichier

◇ **extent** *noun* longueur *f* (d'un document) *or* nombre *m* total de pages (d'un document); **by adding the appendix, we will increase the page extent to 256 =** en ajoutant l'appendice, nous ferons 256 pages au total

external *adjective* externe *or* extérieur, -e; **external clock** = horloge *f* externe *or* extérieure; **external data file** = fichier *m* de données externe; **external device** = (i) dispositif *m* externe; (ii) périphérique *m;* **external disk drive** = lecteur *m* de disquettes externe; **external interrupt** = signal *m* d'interruption externe *or* émis par un périphérique; **external label** = étiquette *f* extérieure; **external memory** = mémoire *f* externe; **external register** = registre *m* externe; *(of system)* **external schema** = schéma *m* (du point de vue) de l'utilisateur *or* vision *f* d'utilisateur; **external sort** = tri *m* sur disque *or* sur support externe; **external storage** *or* **external store** = mémoire externe

extra 1 *adjective* supplémentaire 2 *noun* **(a)** *(additionnal item)* article *m* en sus *or* en option; **the mouse and cabling are sold as extras** = la souris et le câble sont en option **(b)** *(mark at the end of a telegraphic transmission)* traînée *f* de transmission **(c) extra-terrestrial noise** = bruit *m* extra-terrestre

◊ **extracode** *noun* extracode *m*

extract *verb* extraire; **we can extract the files required for typesetting** = nous pouvons extraire les dossiers qui doivent aller à la composition; **extract instruction** = instruction d'extraction

◊ **extractor** *noun* extracteur *m*

extrapolation *noun* extrapolation *f*

extremely *adverb* extrêmement; *(from 30-300GHz)* **extremely high frequency (EHF)** = onde *f* millimétrique; *(of less than 100Hz)* **extremely low frequency (ELF)** = onde myriamétrique

eyepiece *noun (camera viewfinder)* viseur *m or* oculaire *m*

◊ **eye-strain** *noun* fatigue *f* oculaire

QUOTE to minimize eye-strain, it is vital to have good lighting conditions with this LCD system
Personal Computer World

Ff

F = FARAD

F représentation hexadécimale du nombre 15 or F

f = FEMTO- *prefix (equal to one thousandth of a million millionth or 10⁻¹⁵)* f *or* femto-

face *see* TYPEFACE

facet *noun* facette *f*
◊ **faceted code** *noun* code *m* à facettes

facility *noun* **(a)** *(being able to do something easily)* facilité *f; (service)* service *m;* **we offer facilities for processing a customer's own disks** = nous offrons à nos clients un service de traitement de leurs propres disquettes **(b)** *(communications path)* chemin *m or* voie *f or* dispositif *m* d'accès **(c)** *US* centre *m or* bureau *m;* **we have opened our new data processing facility** = nous avons ouvert un nouveau centre *or* bureau de traitement de l'information **(d) facilities** = *(equipment)* équipement *m; (buildings)* locaux *mpl;* **storage facilities** = entrepôt *m*

facsimile *noun* fac-similé *m;* **facsimile character generator** = générateur *m* de caractères fac-similés; **facsimile copy** = fac-similé; *(fax)* télécopie *f or* fax *m;* **facsimile transmission (fax** *or* **FAX) =** (système de) télécopie *or* fax *m; see also* FAX

factor *noun* **(a)** facteur *m;* **deciding factor** = facteur *or* argument *m* décisif; **the deciding factor was the superb graphics** = l'excellence des graphiques a constitué l'argument décisif; **elimination factor** = facteur *m* d'élimination **(b)** *(number)* facteur; **by a factor of ten** = dix fois *or* multiplié par dix

◊ **factorial** *noun* factorielle *f;* **4 factorial (written 4!) or 1x2x3x4 equals 24** = la factorielle de 4 (qui s'écrit 4!) ou 1x2x3x4 est 24

◊ **factorize** *verb* factoriser *or* mettre en facteur; **when factorized, 15 gives the factors 1, 15 or 3, 5** = la mise en facteur de 15 nous donne les facteurs suivants: 1, 15 ou 3, 5

factory *noun* usine *f;* **computer factory** = usine de construction d'ordinateurs; **they have opened a new components factory** = ils ont ouvert une nouvelle usine de composants électroniques; **factory price** *or* **price ex factory** = prix *m* départ usine

fade *verb (radio or electrical signal)* faiblir *or* baisser *or* perdre de l'intensité *or* s'atténuer *or* s'évanouir; *(colour or photograph)* (se) faner *or* pâlir *or* s'atténuer; **to fade out** = faire disparaître progressivement *or* faire un fondu

◊ **fading** *noun (of radio or TV signal)* affaiblissement *or* évanouissement (du signal); *(of photograph or colour)* atténuation *f;* **when fading occurs turn the density dial on the printer to full black** = si l'impression est trop pâle, réglez le bouton de densité (d'impression) sur le noir

fail *verb* (i) ne pas faire quelque chose; (ii) rater *or* ne pas réussir quelque chose; **the company failed to carry out routine maintenance of its equipment** = la société ne s'est pas souciée d'effectuer la maintenance de routine de son matériel; **the prototype disk drive failed its first test** = le premier essai du prototype de lecteur de disquettes a été un échec; **a computer has failed if you turn on the power supply and nothing happens** = on peut dire que l'ordinateur est en panne si rien ne se produit à la mise sous tension; **fail safe system** = système *m* de sécurité (en cas de défaillance *or* de coupure de courant); **fail soft system** = système *m* disjoncteur progressif

◊ **failure** *noun (of equipment)* défaillance *f or* panne *f or* arrêt *m or* incident *m or* dérangement *m; (not doing something)* manquement *m; (lack of success)* insuccès *m or* échec *m;* **failure logging** = enregistrement *m* (automatique) des états d'incidents; **failure rate** = taux *m* de défaillance; *(resuming a process or program after a failure)* **failure recovery** = reprise *f* sur incident; **induced failure** = défaillance provoquée par une cause externe *or* défaillance induite; **mean time between failures (MTBF)** = moyenne de temps de bon fonctionnement (entre les défaillances) (MTBF) *or* durée moyenne de bon fonctionnement; **power failure** = coupure *f* (de courant) *or* panne *f* d'électricité *or* de courant *or* de secteur

QUOTE if one processor system fails, the other takes recovery action on the database, before taking on the workload of the failed system
Computer News

fall back *noun* (procédure, etc. de) secours *m; (resuming a program after a fault has been fixed)* **fall back recovery** = reprise *f* au point d'appel *or* remise *f* en marche au point de reprise *or* au point d'arrêt; **fall back routines** = routines *fpl or* procédures *fpl* de secours (à utiliser en cas de panne)

false *adjective (not true or wrong)* faux, fausse *or* incorrect, -e; *(logic)* faux, fausse; **false code** = code erroné *or* erreur de code; **false drop** *or* **retrieval** = résultat *m* erroné (d'une recherche); *(error warning when no error has occurred)* **false error** = fausse erreur

FAM = FAST ACCESS MEMORY

family *noun* **(a)** *(range of typefaces)* famille *f* **(b)** *(range of machines)* famille *or* gamme *f or* série *f* (de produits)

fan 1 *noun (machine)* ventilateur *m; (spread)* éventail *m;* **if the fan fails, the system will rapidly overheat** = si le ventilateur tombe en panne, le système va rapidement (sur)chauffer **2** *verb (to cool or to spread)* ventiler; **fan antenna** = antenne *f* (en) éventail *or* semi-circulaire; **fan-in** = entrance *f or* facteur *m*

pyramidal d'entrée; **fan-out** = sortance *f or* facteur *m* pyramidal de sortie; **fanning strip** = tresse *f* de mise à la masse

◊ **fanfold** *or* **accordion paper** *noun* papier (plié) en paravent *or* en accordéon

QUOTE a filtered fan maintains positive air pressure within the cabinet, to keep dust and dirt from entering
Personal Computer World

farad (F) *noun* farad *m*

Faraday cage *noun* cage *f* de Faraday

far *adjective* lointain, -e *or* distant, -e; *(receiving end)* **far end** = (point d') arrivée *f or* (point de) réception *f*

fascia plate *noun* panneau *m* avant *or* antérieur; **the fascia plate on the disk drive of this model is smaller than those on other models** = le panneau avant du lecteur de disquettes de ce modèle est plus petit que celui des autres modèles

fast *adjective* **(a)** rapide; **fast program execution** = exécution *f* rapide d'un programme; **this hard disk is fast, it has an access time of 28ms** = c'est un disque dur très rapide avec un temps d'accès de 28ms; **fast access memory (FAM)** = mémoire *f* à accès rapide; **fast core** = mémoire centrale rapide; **the fast core is used as a scratchpad for all calculations in this system** = dans ce système, la mémoire centrale rapide sert de bloc-notes pour tous les calculs; *(for 48 or 96 baud rates)* **fast line** = ligne *f* de transmission rapide; **fast peripheral** = périphérique *m* rapide; **fast time-scale** = base *f* de temps réduite **(b)** *(lens or film)* rapide *or* sensible

fatal error *noun* erreur *f* fatale

father file *noun* fichier *m* père

fault *noun (defect)* défaut *m; (mistake)* faute *f or* erreur *f; (stoppage)* panne *f or* incident *m;* **the technical staff are trying to correct a programming fault** = les techniciens essayent de corriger une erreur de programmation; **we think there is a basic fault in the product design** = nous estimons qu'il y a une erreur fondamentale dans la conception du produit; *(in a circuit)* **fault detection** = localisation *f* (automatique) de panne; **fault diagnosis** = diagnostic *m* de localisation de panne *or* de défaillance; **fault location program** = programme *m* de localisation de panne; **fault time** = durée *f* d'une panne; **fault trace** = enregistrement *m or* traçage *m* de panne

◊ **fault tolerance** *noun* (marge de) tolérance *f* aux dérangements *or* tolérance de pannes

◊ **fault-tolerant** *adjective* (système) tolérant *or* peu sensible aux dérangements; **they market a highly successful range of fault-tolerant minis** = ils ont commercialisé, avec beaucoup de succès, une gamme de minis très tolérants *or* peu sensibles aux dérangements

◊ **faulty** *adjective* défectueux, -euse; **there must be a faulty piece of equipment in the system** = il doit sûrement y avoir un composant défectueux dans le système; **they traced the fault to a faulty cable** = ils ont découvert que la défaillance était due à un câble défecteux; **faulty sector** = secteur *m* défectueux

QUOTE before fault-tolerant systems, users had to rely on cold standby
QUOTE fault tolerance is usually associated with a system's reliability
Computer News

fax *or* **FAX 1** *noun* télécopie *f or* fax *m;* **we will send a fax of the design plan** = nous enverrons les plans par télécopie; **fax machine** = télécopieur *m or* fax *m;* **the fax machine is next to the telephone switchboard** = notre fax est tout à côté du standard téléphonique; **fax paper** = papier pour télécopieur **2** *verb* envoyer par télécopie *or* envoyer par fax *or* faxer; **I've faxed the documents to our New York office** = j'ai faxé les documents *or* j'ai envoyé les documents par télécopie à notre bureau de New York

QUOTE investment in a good modem and communications system could reduce your costs considerably on both courier and fax services
Which PC?

fd *or* **FD (a)** = FULL DUPLEX **(b)** = FLOPPY DISK

fdc = FLOPPY DISK CONTROLLER

FDM = FREQUENCY DIVISION MULTIPLEXING

fdx *or* **FDX** = FULL DUPLEX

feature *noun* caractéristique *f;* **key feature** = caractéristique principale *or* la plus importante; **the key features of this system are: 20Mb of formatted storage with an access time of 60ms** = les principales caractéristiques de ce système sont les suivantes: 20Mo de mémoire formatée avec temps d'accès de 60ms

FEDS = FIXED AND EXCHANGEABLE DISK STORAGE

feed 1 *noun (printer or photocopier)* (dispositif d') entraînement *m or* alimentation *f;* **continuous feed** = (système d') alimentation en continu; *(command)* **feed form** = (instruction de) saut *m* de page; **feed holes** = perforations *fpl* d'entraînement *or* perforations marginales; **feed horn** = (dispositif de) guidage *m* directionnel; **feed reel** = bobine *f* d'alimentation; **friction feed** = entraînement par friction *or* par rouleaux; **front feed** = alimentation par l'avant; **paper feed** = (dispositif d') alimentation *or* entraînement du papier; **sheet feed** = alimentation feuille à feuille; **sheet feed attachment** = bac d'alimentation feuille à feuille; **tractor feed** = entraînement par picots **2** *verb* alimenter *or* introduire; **the paper should be manually fed into the printer** = le papier doit être chargé manuellement dans l'imprimante; **data is fed into the computer** = les données sont introduites dans l'ordinateur NOTE: **feeding - fed**

◊ **feedback** *noun* **(a)** feedback *m or* rétroaction *f or* (action en) retour *m or* réaction *f;* **feedback control** = contrôle *m* par retour; **feedback loop** = boucle *f* de feedback *or* de réaction *or* de rétroaction; **negative feedback** = rétroaction négative; **positive feedback** = rétroaction positive *or* feedback positif *or* boucle d'amplification **(b)** réaction; **we are getting customer feedback on the new system** = nous commençons à connaître les réactions des clients face au nouveau système

feeder *noun* **(a)** *(channel)* voie *f* d'acheminement *or* de transmission de signaux; **feeder cable** = câble *m* d'acheminement des signaux *or* câble antenne-circuit **(b)** *(for paper)* système d'alimentation *or* d'entraînement (du papier)

feevee *noun US (informal)* télévision *f* câblée (payante)

feint *noun* (papier à) lignes *fpl* très pâles

female *adjective* femelle; **female connector** = connecteur *m* femelle; **female socket** = prise *f* femelle

femto- **(f)** *prefix* femto- (f); **femtosecond** = femtoseconde *f*

FEP = FRONT-END PROCESSOR

ferric oxide *noun* oxyde *m* de fer

ferrite *noun* ferrite *f;* **ferrite core** *noun* noyau *m* de ferrite

ferromagnetic material *noun* matériau *m* ferromagnétique

FET = FIELD EFFECT TRANSISTOR

fetch *verb (command)* aller chercher et lire (une instruction); **demand fetching** = accès *m* sur demande à la mémoire paginée; **fetch cycle** = cycle *m* de lecture d'une instruction; **fetch-execute cycle** *or* **execute cycle** = cycle de lecture/exécution *or* cycle d'exécution (d'une instruction); **fetch instruction** = instruction de lecture d'une instruction; **fetch phase** = phase *f* de lecture d'une instruction; **fetch protect** = protection *f* des accès mémoire; **fetch signal** = signal *m* de lecture d'instruction

FF (a) = FORM FEED **(b)** = FLIP-FLOP

fibre *noun* fibre *f;* **fibre ribbon** = ruban *m* (en) tissu (pour machine à écrire)

◊ **fibre optic cable** *or* **connection** = *noun* câble *m or* liaison *f* à fibres optiques *or* câble optique; **fibre optic connections enabling nodes up to one kilometre apart to be used** = les câbles à fibres optiques permettent de placer les noeuds jusqu'à un kilomètre l'un de l'autre

◊ **fibre optics** *noun* technologie *f* de la fibre optique *or* de la transmission *f* par fibre optique

fiche *see* MICROFICHE

fidelity *noun* fidélité *f;* **high fidelity system (hi-fi)** = système haute-fidélité *or* chaîne *f* hi-fi

field *noun* **(a)** *(area of force)* champ *m;* **field effect transistor (FET)** = transistor *m* à effet de champ (TEC); **field programmable device** = dispositif à champ programmable; **field programming** = programmation *f* de champ; **field strength** = intensité *f* de champ **(b)** *(in a record)* champ; **the employee record has a field for age** = le dossier 'employés' possède un champ 'âge'; **address** *or* **operand field** = champ d'adresse *or* d'opérande; **card field** = champ d'une carte magnétique; **data field** = zone *f* de données; **field label** = label *m or* étiquette *f* d'un champ; **field length** = taille *f* d'un champ; **field marker** *or* **separator** = séparateur *m* de champs; **protected field** = champ protégé **(c)** *(of picture on a television screen)* trame *f* d'image; **field blanking (interval)** = intervalle *m* de trame *or* suppression *f* verticale de la trame; **field frequency** = fréquence *f* de trame; **field flyback** = retour *m* de trame; **field sweep** = balayage *m* vertical; **field sync pulse** = impulsion *f* de contrôle *or* de synchronisation du balayage vertical **(d)** *(photography)* champ (d'image) **(e)** **field engineer** = ingénieur *m* d'entretien *or* d'après-vente *or* de maintenance (sur le site)

◊ **fielding** *noun* zonage *m*

FIFO = FIRST IN FIRST OUT (méthode du) premier entré premier sorti (FIFO); **FIFO memory** = mémoire *f* FIFO *or* mémoire qui fonctionne sur le principe du premier entré premier sorti; **the two computers operate at different rates, but can transmit data using a FIFO memory** = les deux ordinateurs fonctionnent à des vitesses différentes mais peuvent transmettre des données en utilisant une mémoire tampon fonctionnant sur le système 'premier entré premier sorti'; **FIFO queue** = file *f* d'attente qui fonctionne sur le principe 'premier entré premier sorti'

fifth generation computer *noun* ordinateur *m* de cinquième génération

figure *noun* **(a)** *(line illustration)* figure *f;* **see figure 10 for a chart of ASCII codes** = voir figure 10: tableau des codes ASCII **(b)** *(number)* chiffre *m;* **figures case** = chiffres et signes en code télégraphique; **in round figures** = en chiffres ronds; **they have a workforce of 2,500 in round figures** = leur personnel tourne autour de 2500 employés

file 1 *noun* **(a)** *(cardboard holder)* chemise *f or* classeur *m or* dossier *m;* **put these letters in the customer file** = classez ces lettres dans le dossier 'clients' **(b)** *(documents)* dossier; **to place something on file** = insérer au dossier *or* mettre sur fiche **(c)** *(section of data on a computer)* fichier *m;* **data file** = fichier de données; **disk file** = fichier *m* sur disque(tte); **distributed file system** = système à fichiers répartis *or* partagés; **file activity ratio** = ratio *m or* taux *m* d'activité d'un fichier; **file cleanup** = nettoyage *m or* vidage *m* de fichier; **file collating** = fusion *f or* interclassement *m* de fichier(s); **file control block** = bloc *m* de contrôle de fichier; **file conversion** = conversion *f* de fichier; **file creation** = création *f* de fichier; **file deletion** = annulation *f or* destruction *f* de fichier; **file descriptor** = descripteur *m* de fichier; **file directory** = répertoire *m* de fichiers; **file extent** = taille *f* d'un fichier; **file gap** = espace *m* neutre (séparant deux fichiers); **file handling routine** = routine *f* de manipulation de fichier; **file identification** = identification *f* de fichier; **file index** = index *m* des fichiers; **file label** = label *m or* étiquette *f or* descripteur *m* de fichier; **file layout** = structure *f* d'un fichier; **file maintenance** = mise *f* à jour *or* maintenance *f* de fichier; **file management** = gestion *f* de fichier; **file manager** = gestionnaire *m* de fichier; **file merger** = fusion *f* de fichiers; **file name** = nom *m* d'un fichier; **file organization** = *see* FILE LAYOUT; **file processing** = traitement *m* de fichier; **file protection** = (logiciel *or* dispositif de) protection *f or* sécurisation *f* de fichiers; **file protect tab** = dispositif *m* de protection d'écriture (de fichier); **file purge** = vidage *m* de fichier; **file-**

recovery utility = logiciel *m* de récupération de fichiers (après incident); **a lost file cannot be found without a file-recovery utility** = il est impossible de retrouver un fichier perdu sans l'aide d'un logiciel de récupération de fichiers; **file security** = protection *f or* sécurisation *f* de fichiers; **file server** = serveur *m;* **file set** = groupe *m* de fichiers (connexes); **file sort** = tri *m* de fichiers; **file storage** = *(action)* mise *f* en mémoire *or* stockage *m* de fichier; *(storage medium)* support *m* de données (d'un fichier); *(memory)* mémoire *f* (contenant des fichiers); **file store** = (ensemble des) fichiers en mémoire; **file structure** = structure *f* d'un fichier; **file transfer** = transfert *m* de fichier; **file update** = (i) mise à jour d'un fichier; (ii) nouvelle version d'un fichier; **file validation** = validation *f* de fichier; **change** *or* **movement file** = fichier de mouvements *or* de modifications *or* de mise à jour; **indexed file** = fichier indexé; **inverted file** = fichier inversé; **output file** = fichier de sortie; **program file** = fichier programme; **text file** = fichier texte; **threaded file** = fichier avec articles chaînés; **transaction file** = fichier de transactions 2 *verb* **to file documents** = classer des documents

◊ **filename** *noun* nom *m* d'un fichier; **filename extension** = extension du nom d'un fichier; **the filename extension SYS indicates that this is a system file** = l'extension SYS ajoutée au nom du fichier indique qu'il s'agit d'un fichier système

> QUOTE it allows users to back up or restore read-only security files and hidden system files independently
> *Minicomputer News*
> QUOTE the lost file, while inaccessible without a file-recovery utility, remains on disk until new information writes over it
> *Publish*
> QUOTE when the filename is entered at the prompt, the operating system looks in the file and executes any instructions stored there
> *PC User*

filing *noun* classement *m;* **filing cabinet** = classeur *m;* **filing card** = fiche *f* ◊ **filing system** *noun* **(a)** *(way of putting documents in order)* méthode *f* de classement *or* d'archivage **(b)** *(software)* logiciel *m* d'archivage

fill *verb* **(a)** *(to make something full)* remplir **(b)** *(to put characters into gaps)* remplir; **fill character** = caractère *m* de remplissage; **filled cable** = câble _m_ étanche **(c)** _(to draw)_ combler

◊ **fill up** _verb_ remplir; **the disk was quickly filled up** = la disquette a été très vite pleine

film 1 _noun_ **(a)** _(for photographs)_ pellicule _f_ photographique _or_ film _m;_ **film advance** = _(of film roll)_ entraînement _m_ d'un film; _(of phototypesetting machine)_ avance _f or_ pas _m or_ espacement _m;_ **film assembly** = montage _m_ d'un film; **film base** = pellicule _f;_ **film chain** = l'équipement de prise de vue et de projection de films; **film optical scanning device for input into computers (FOSDIC)** = lecteur optique de microfilms pour entrée de données sur ordinateur; **film pickup** = repiquage _m_ vidéo d'un film; _(teaching device)_ **film strip** = film fixe; **photographic film** = pellicule photographique **(b)** _(cinema)_ film; **film camera** = caméra _f_ **2** _verb_ **(a)** _(cinema)_ filmer _or_ tourner un film **(b)** _(printing)_ filmer (un texte)

◊ **filming** _noun_ **(a)** _(cinema)_ tournage _m;_ **filming will start next week if the weather is fine** = le tournage commencera la semaine prochaine s'il fait beau **(b)** _(printing)_ flashage _m_ (d'un texte)

◊ **filmsetting** _noun_ photocomposition _f_

filter 1 _noun_ **(a)** _(electronic circuit)_ filtre _m;_ **bandpass filter** = filtre passe-bande; **high pass filter** = filtre passe-haut; **low pass filter** = filtre passe-bas **(b)** _(coloured glass)_ filtre chromatique; **absorption filter** = filtre d'absorption; _(placed over a monitor)_ **character enhancement filter** = filtre d'optimisation de caractères et de protection de la vue; **filter factor** = facteur _m_ de filtre **(c)** _(pattern of binary digits)_ masque _m_ **2** _verb_ **(a)** _(to remove unwanted elements)_ filtrer **(b)** _(to select various bits)_ séparer _or_ éliminer par filtrage _or_ sélectionner

final _adjective_ dernier, -ière _or_ final, -e; **to keyboard the final data files** = saisir les derniers fichiers de données; **to make the final changes to a document** = apporter les dernières corrections à un document

find 1 _verb_ trouver _or_ retrouver _or_ repérer; **it took a lot of time to find the faulty chip** = il a fallu beaucoup de temps pour trouver la puce défectueuse;

the debugger found the error very quickly = le débogueur a repéré la faute très rapidement NOTE: **finding - found 2** _noun_ **find and replace** = (instruction de) recherche et remplacement _or_ cherche et remplace

fine _adjective_ **(a)** _(very thin)_ fin, fine _or_ mince; **the engraving has some very fine lines** = on trouve quelques lignes très fines dans cette gravure **(b)** _(excellent)_ très bon, bonne _or_ excellent, -e

◊ **fine tune** _verb_ mettre au point _or_ régler (avec grande précision); **fine-tuning improved the speed by ten per cent** = une mise au point très précise améliore la vitesse de dix pour cent

finish 1 _noun_ **(a)** _(final appearance)_ fini _m or_ finition _f;_ **the product has an attractive finish** = ce produit a un très beau fini _or_ présente une belle finition **(b)** _(end)_ fin _f_ **2** _verb_ **(a)** terminer _or_ finir; **she finished all the keyboarding before lunch** = elle a terminé la saisie avant le déjeuner **(b)** se terminer _or_ prendre fin

◊ **finished** _adjective_ fini, -e _or_ final, -e _or_ définitif, -ive; **finished document** = document définitif

finite-precision numbers _noun_ nombres _mpl_ à précision finie

firmware _noun_ logiciel _m_ intégré

first _adjective_ premier, -ière; **first fit** = algorithme de sélection de la première place suffisante; **first generation computer** = ordinateur _m_ de première génération; **first generation image** = image _f_ originale _or_ de première génération; **first in first out (FIFO)** = premier entré premier sorti; **first-level address** = adresse _f_ de premier niveau _or_ adresse réelle; **first party release** = coupure _f_ au premier raccroché

fisheye lens _noun_ fisheye _m_

fix _verb_ **(a)** _(to attach something permanently)_ fixer _or_ attacher; **the computer is fixed to the workstation** = l'ordinateur est fixé au poste de travail; **fixed and exchangeable disk storage (FEDS)** = unité comprenant des disques fixes et des disques amovibles; **fixed cycle operation** = opération _f_ en cycle fixe *or* opération synchronisée; **fixed data** = données constantes *or* permanentes; **fixed disk** = disque dur fixe *or* non amovible; **fixed field** = champ de taille constante *or* fixe; **fixed head (disk) drive** = lecteur (de disque) à tête de lecture fixe; **fixed-length record** = enregistrement *m* de longueur fixe *or* déterminée; **fixed-length word** = mot de longueur fixe *or* déterminée; **fixed program computer** = ordinateur à logique câblée; **fixed routing** = acheminement *m* pré-sélectionné; **fixed word length** = (ordinateur) à longueur de mots fixe **(b)** *(to mend)* réparer; **the technicians are trying to fix the switchboard** = les techniciens essayent de réparer le standard téléphonique; **can you fix the photocopier?** = pouvez-vous réparer le photocopieur?

◇ **fixed-point notation** *noun* notation à virgule fixe; **storage of fixed point numbers has two bytes allocated for the whole number and one byte for the fraction part** = la mise en mémoire de nombres à virgule fixe utilise deux octets pour le nombre entier et un octet pour la partie décimale; **fixed-point arithmetic** = arithmétique *f* à virgule fixe

◇ **fixing** *noun (photography)* fixage *m or* fixation *f*

flag 1 *noun (for block or field)* marqueur *m or* drapeau *m or* balise *f; (for status)* indicateur *m or* témoin *m or* drapeau *m;* **if the result is zero, the zero flag is set** = si le résultat est zéro, l'indicateur zéro est activé; **carry flag** = témoin *or* indicateur de retenue; **device flag** = (bit) indicateur *or* témoin (d'utilisation); **overflow bit** *or* **flag** = bit *m or* indicateur binaire de dépassement de capacité; **zero flag** = indicateur (binaire) zéro; **flag bit** = bit indicateur *or* indicateur binaire; **flag code** = code *m* drapeau; **flag event** = fonction *f or* condition *f* de balisage *or* de mise en place d'un drapeau; **flag register** = registre *m* des témoins *or* des drapeaux; **flag sequence** = séquence *f* de marqueurs *or* d'indicateurs *or* de drapeaux **2** *verb* marquer *or* baliser

◇ **flagging** *noun* **(a)** *(putting an indicator)* balisage *m or* marquage *m or* mise *f* en place d'un drapeau **(b)** *(picture distortion)* battement *m*

flare *noun* reflet *m or* tache *f* lumineuse *or* interférence *f* (lumineuse)

◇ **flared** *adjective* marqué, -e d'un reflet *or* taché, -e

flash *verb* (faire) clignoter; **flash A/D** = convertisseur analogique-numérique parallèle; **flash card** = carte 'flash'; **flashing character** = caractère *m* clignotant

flat *adjective* **(a)** *(in an image or photograph)* sans contraste *or* plat, -e **(b)** *(surface)* plane; **flat file** = fichier plat *or* bidimensionnel; **flat pack** = boîtier *m* plat **(c)** *(fixed)* uniforme *or* unique *or* déterminé, -ée d'avance; **flat rate** = forfait *m or* tarif *m* unique

◇ **flatbed** *noun (printer or scanner)* à plat *or* de type 'flatbed'; **scanners are either flatbed models or platen type, paper-fed models** = les scanners sont de type 'flatbed', ou possèdent un système d'entraînement du papier par rouleaux; **paper cannot be rolled through flatbed scanners** = le papier n'est pas entraîné par rouleaux dans un scanner à plat; **flatbed plotter** = table *f* traçante; **flatbed press** = presse *f* à platine (horizontale); **flatbed transmitter** = lecteur *m* de transmission à plat *or* de type 'flatbed'

◇ **flatplan** *noun* maquette *f* d'édition *or* chemin de fer

flex *noun* câble *m or* fil *m* (de liaison) *or* cordon *m* (souple)
NOTE: no plural: **pieces of flex**

flexible *adjective* flexible *or* souple; **flexible array** = tableau *m* à dimensions variables; **flexible disk** = disque *m* souple *or* disquette *f;* **flexible disk cartridge** = cartouche *f* de disquette; **flexible machining system (FMS)** = système de commandes numériques de machines-outils; **flexible manufacturing system (FMS)** = atelier *m* flexible

◇ **flexibility** *noun* flexibilité *f or* souplesse *f*

flicker 1 *noun* **(a)** *(variation of brightness)* scintillement *m or* vacillement *m* **(b)** *(video disk)* scintillement *m* **(c)** *(computer graphic image)* vacillement *or* tremblement *m* **2** *verb* clignoter *or* vaciller *or* trembler; **the image flickers when the printer is switched on** = l'image sur l'écran vacille à la mise sous tension de l'imprimante

◊ **flicker-free** *adjective* (image *or* affichage) sans vacillement *or* sans clignotement *or* sans papillotement *or* sans reflet

> QUOTE the new 640 by 480 pixel standard, coupled with the flicker- free displays on the four new monitors and a maximum of 256 colours from a palette of more than quarter of a million
>
> *PC User*

flip-flop (FF) *noun* commutateur *m* à bascule; **JK-flip-flop** = commutateur à bascule de type JK; **D-flip-flop** = commutateur à bascule de type D

flippy *noun* disquette *f* réversible

float *noun* décalage *m or* déplacement *m;* **float factor** = facteur *m* de déplacement (d'une adresse relative); **float relocate** = ré-adressage *m* par déplacement (en ajoutant une adresse origine à une adresse relative)

◊ **floating** *adjective* flottant, -e; **floating accent** = accent flottant; **floating address** = adresse relative; **floating head** = FLYING HEAD; **floating point arithmetic** = arithmétique *m* en virgule flottante; **floating point (notation)** = (notation en) virgule flottante; **the fixed number 56.47 in floating-point arithmetic would be 0.5647 and a power of 2** = en virgule flottante, le nombre 56,47 serait écrit 0,5647 puissance 2; **floating point number** = nombre en virgule flottante; **floating point operation (FLOP)** = opération en virgule flottante; **floating point processor** = processeur en virgule flottante; **the floating point processor speeds up the processing of the graphics software** = le processeur en virgule flottante accélère la vitesse de traitement de ce logiciel graphique; **this model includes a built-in floating point processor** = ce modèle est équipé d'un processeur en virgule flottante intégré; **floating symbolic address** = adresse symbolique *or* relative; **floating voltage** = courant *m* flottant

flooding *noun* routage *m* par dispersion *or* par redistribution

FLOP = FLOATING POINT OPERATION opération *f* en virgule flottante; **FLOPs per second** = (nombre d') opérations en virgule flottante par seconde

floppy disk *or* **floppy** *or* **FD** *or* **fd** *noun* disquette *f or* disque *m* souple; **floppy disk controller (FDC)** = contrôleur *m* de disquettes; **floppy disk sector** = secteur *m* de disquette; **floppy disk drive** *or* **unit** = lecteur *m* de disquettes; **floppy tape** *or* **tape streamer** = streamer *m*

flow 1 *noun* flux *m or* flot *m;* **automatic text flow across pages** = texte au kilomètre avec changement de page automatique; **the device controls the copy flow** = ce dispositif contrôle le mouvement des feuilles *or* l'alimentation du papier (en) feuille à feuille; **current flow is regulated by a resistor** = le débit d'électricité est régularisé par une résistance; **data flow** = flux des données; **flow control** = contrôle *m* du flux (de données); **flow direction** = direction *f* du flux **2** *verb* couler *or* circuler; **work is flowing normally again after the breakdown of the printer** = le travail reprend normalement après la panne de l'imprimante

◊ **flowchart** *or* **flow diagram** *noun* ordinogramme *m;* **a flowchart is the first step to a well designed program** = l'ordinogramme est à la base d'un programme bien conçu; **data flowchart** = ordinogramme de données; **flowchart symbols** = symboles d'un ordinogramme; **flowchart template** = grille *f or* modèle *m* pour ordinogramme; **logical flowchart** = ordinogramme logique

◊ **flowline** *noun* ligne *f* de jonction des symboles d'un ordinogramme

fluctuate *verb* fluctuer *or* varier; **the electric current fluctuates between 1Amp and 1.3Amp** = le courant fluctue entre 1Amp et 1,3Amp

◊ **fluctuating** *adjective* variable *or* qui fluctue *or* qui varie; **fluctuating signal strength** = intensité *f* variable du signal

◊ **fluctuation** *noun* fluctuation *f or* variation *f or* saute *f* (de courant); **voltage fluctuations can affect the functioning of the computer system** = les sautes de courant peuvent nuire au bon fonctionnement de l'ordinateur

flush 1 *verb* vider; **flush buffers** = vider la mémoire tampon **2** *adjective* **(a)** au même niveau *or* de niveau; **the covers are trimmed flush with the pages** = la couverture est rognée de niveau avec les pages **(b)** *(of text)* **flush left** = justifier à gauche *or* (au) fer à gauche; **flush right** = justifier à droite *or* (au) fer à droite

flutter *noun* variation *f* de vitesse *or* scintillement *m;* **wow and flutter are common faults on cheap tape recorders** = le pleurage et les variations de vitesse *or* le scintillement sont des défauts courants des magnétophones bon marché

flux *noun* **magnetic flux** = flux *m* magnétique

fly *verb* voler; **flying spot scan** = balayage *m* par faisceau mobile

◊ **flyback** *noun* retour *m* (d'un balayage); **field flyback** = retour de trame; **line flyback** = retour de ligne

flying head *noun (floating head)* tête *f* flottante

FM = FREQUENCY MODULATION

FMS (a) = FLEXIBLE MACHINING SYSTEM **(b)** = FLEXIBLE MANUFACTURING SYSTEM

FNP = FRONT END NETWORK PROCESSOR

f-number *noun* ouverture *f* de diaphragme *or* diaph *m*

focal length *noun* distance *f* focale

focus 1 *noun* foyer *m;* **the picture is out of focus** *or* **is not in focus** = l'image est floue *or* n'est pas au point **2** *verb* mettre au point; **the camera is focused on the foreground** = la camera est réglée pour le premier plan *or* est dirigée sur le premier plan; **they adjusted the lens position so that the beam focused correctly** = la position de la lentille a été ajustée de façon à bien mettre au point le rayon lumineux

◊ **focusing** *noun* **magnetic focusing** = concentration *f* *or* mise *f* au point magnétique

fog *noun (photography)* voile *m*

fold 1 *verb* plier *or* replier **2** *noun* pli *m* *or* pliage *m; (listing paper)* **accordion fold** *or* **fanfold** = papier (plié) en paravent *or* en accordéon

◊ **-fold** *suffix (times)* **four-fold** = quatre fois

◊ **folder** *noun* chemise *f* *or* classeur *m*

◊ **folding (a)** *noun (hashing method)* folding *m* *or* réassemblage *m* **(b)** pliage *m* *or* pliure *f*

◊ **folding machine** *noun* plieuse *f*

folio 1 *noun* **(a)** feuillet *m* *or* folio *m; (book)* in-folio *m* **(b)** numéro *m* de page **2** *verb* folioter *or* paginer

font *or* **fount** *noun* police *f* de caractères *or* fonte *f;* **font change** = changement de police de caractères; **font disk** = disquette de fontes *or* de polices de caractères; **downloadable fonts** = polices (de caractères) téléchargeables; **resident font** = police résidente

QUOTE laser printers store fonts in several ways: as resident, cartridge and downloadable fonts
Desktop Publishing Today

foolscap *noun (paper)* (papier) format *m* ministre; **the letter was on six sheets of foolscap** = la lettre était écrite sur six feuilles format ministre; **a foolscap envelope** = enveloppe longue (pour papier ministre)

foot *noun* **(a)** *(bottom part)* bas *m;* **he signed his name at the foot of the letter** = il a signé au bas de la lettre **(b)** *(measurement = 0.3048m)* pied *m*

◊ **foot candle** *noun (amount of light)* candela *f* par pied carré

◊ **footer** *or* **footing** *noun (message at the bottom of pages)* pied *m* de page

◊ **footnote** *noun* note *f* *or* renvoi *m* en bas de page

◊ **footprint** *noun* **(a)** empreinte *f* (d'un faisceau, etc.) **(b)** encombrement *m* (d'un ordinateur)

for-next loop *noun* boucle *f* conditionnelle FOR...NEXT; **for X=1 to 5: print X: next X - this will print out 1 2 3 4 5** = pour X=1 à 5: imprimer X: calculer la valeur suivante de X - le résultat imprimé sera 1 2 3 4 5

forbid *verb* interdire (quelque chose *or* de faire quelque chose); **forbidden character** *or* **combination** = caractère interdit *or* chaîne (de caractères) interdite
NOTE: **forbidding - forbade - forbidden**

force 1 *noun* force *f;* **to come into force** = entrer en vigueur; **the new regulations will come into force on January 1st** = les nouveaux règlements entreront en vigueur le 1er janvier **2** *verb* forcer (quelqu'un à faire quelque chose); **forced page break** = saut *f* de page obligatoire *or* programmé

foreground *noun* **(a)** *(front part)* premier plan; **foreground colour** = couleur *f* de premier plan **(b)** *(high priority task)* (tâche) de premier plan *or* prioritaire; **foreground/background modes** = mode d'exécution frontal/masqué; **foreground processing** *or* **foregrounding** = traitement *m* frontal; **foreground program** = programme prioritaire
◊ **foregrounding** *noun* traitement frontal

forest *noun* arborescence *f*

form 1 *noun* **(a)** *(preprinted document)* bordereau *m; (preset computer layout for addresses, etc.)* masque *m* de saisie *or* grille *f* d'écran **(b)** *(plate or block of type)* forme *f* d'impression **(c)** *(page of computer stationery)* feuillet *m* *or* page *f;* **form feed (FF)** = (instruction de) changement *m* de page; **form flash** = en-tête *m* préétabli (gardé en mémoire); **form handling equipment** = équipement de traitement de formulaires *or* de papier listing (en sortie d'imprimante); **form letter** = lettre *f* cadre *or* lettre standard; **form mode** = mode *m* masque (de saisie); **form overlay** = texte *m* *or* graphique *m* préétabli (gardé en mémoire); **form stop** = (i) arrêt *m* pour manque de papier; (ii) indicateur *m* de fin de papier **2** *verb* constituer *or* former *or* construire; **the system is formed of five separate modules** = le système est constitué de cinq modules indépendants

format 1 *noun* **(a)** *(of book)* format *m;* **the printer can deal with all formats up to quarto** = l'imprimante peut accommoder tous les formats jusqu'au quarto **(b)** *(of text)* format; *(in memory)* **address format** = format d'adresse; *(rows and columns of punched card)* **card format** = format de carte perforée; **data format** = format de données; **display format** = format d'affichage *or* format d'écran; **instruction format** = format d'instruction; **local format storage** = (mise en) mémoire *f* du format courant; **variable format** = format variable **(c)** *(syntax of instructions)* format; **symbolic-coding format** = format de langage symbolique **(d)** *(TV programme)* grille *f* d'émission; **magazine format** = format magazine **2** *verb* **(a)** *(to arrange text)* formater *or* mettre en forme; **style sheets are used to format documents** = on utilise des feuilles de style pour mettre en forme les documents; **formatted dump** = vidage *m* au format **(b)** **to format a disk** = formater un disque *or* une disquette; **disk formatting** = formatage *m* de disque *or* de disquette; **disk formatting has to be done before you can use a new floppy disk** = il faut formater toutes les nouvelles disquettes avant de les utiliser
◊ **formatter** *noun* matériel *m* *or* logiciel *m* de formatage; **print formatter** = logiciel *m* de formatage d'impression; **text formatter** = logiciel de formatage de texte

QUOTE there are three models, offering 53, 80 and 160 Mb of formatted capacity
Minicomputer News

formula *noun* formule *f;* **formula portability** = portabilité *f* d'une formule; **formula translator (FORTRAN)** = traducteur *m* de formule *or* langage *m* FORTRAN
NOTE: plural is **formulae**

FORTH langage *m* FORTH

QUOTE the main attraction of FORTH over other computer languages is that it is not simply a language, rather it is a programming tool in which it is possible to write other application specific languages
Electronics & Power

FORTRAN = FORMULA TRANSLATOR langage *m* FORTRAN

forty-track disk *noun* disquette *f* (de) quarante pistes

forward 1 *adjective* avant *or* en avant *or* en avance *or* d'avance; **forward channel** = canal (de transmission) aller; **forward clearing** = remise à l'état initial commandée par l'émetteur; **forward error correction** = correction d'erreur en cours de transmission; **forward reference** = référence par anticipation; **forward scatter** = onde éclatée progressante **2** *verb* transmettre

◊ **forward mode** *noun* (tri, etc.) en ordre croissant

FOSDIC = FILM OPTICAL SCANNING DEVICE FOR INPUT INTO COMPUTERS

fount = FONT

four-address instruction *noun* instruction *f* à quatre adresses; **four-plus-one address** = quatre adresses plus une

◊ **four-part** *adjective* **four-part invoices** = factures *fpl* en quatre exemplaires *or* en quatre épaisseurs

Fourier series *noun* série *f* de Fourier

fourth generation computers *noun* ordinateurs de quatrième génération; **fourth generation languages** = langages de quatrième génération

four-track recorder *noun* magnétophone *m* à quatre pistes

fps = FRAMES PER SECOND

fraction *noun* fraction *f*

◊ **fractional** *adjective* fractionnaire; **the root is the fractional power of a number** = la racine est la puissance fractionnaire d'un nombre; **fractional part** = partie *f* fractionnaire *or* mantisse *f*

fragmentation *noun* fragmentation *f*

frame *noun* **(a)** *(on magnetic tape)* trame *f*; *(of transmitted data)* bloc *m*; *(on magnetic tape)* **frame error** = erreur *f* de trame **(b)** *(for printed circuit boards)* support *m* de cartes (de circuits imprimés) *or* châssis *m* avec guide-cartes *or* baie *f* (pour cartes) **(c)** *(one image)* image *f* complète; **video frame** = image vidéo; **with the image processor you can**

freeze a video frame = le processeur d'images permet de figer une image *or* de faire un arrêt sur image; **frame flyback** = saut *m* d'image; **frame frequency** = fréquence *f* de l'image; **in the UK the frame frequency is 25 fps** = la télévision britannique utilise une fréquence de 25 images par seconde *or* 25 images/seconde; **frame grabber** = capteur *m* d'image vidéo; **frame store** = mémoire *f* image; **the image processor allows you to store a video frame in a built-in 8-bit frame store** = le processeur d'images permet le stockage d'une image vidéo dans une mémoire intégrée de 8 bits; **the frame store can be used to display weather satellite pictures** = la mémoire image peut servir à l'affichage des images météorologiques transmises par satellite

◊ **frames per second (fps)** *noun* *(motion or TV picture)* (nombre d') images *f* par seconde *or* images/seconde

◊ **framework** *noun* cadre *m or* structure *f*; **the program framework was designed first** = on a d'abord établi le cadre *or* la structure du programme

◊ **framing** *noun* **(a)** cadrage *m* **(b)** *(of data on tape)* synchronisation *f* de trames; **framing bit** = bit *m* de synchronisation; **framing code** = code *m* de synchronisation

fraud *noun* fraude *f*; **computer fraud** = fraude *f* informatique

QUOTE the offences led to the arrest of nine teenagers who were all charged with computer fraud
Computer News

free 1 *adjective* libre; **free indexing** = indexage *m* libre; **free line** = ligne *f* libre; **free running mode** = mode *m* multi-utilisateur; **free space loss** = perte *f* dans l'espace; **free space media** = l'espace *f*; **free wheeling** = transmission *f* sans contrôle de retour **2** *verb* libérer (de l'espace dans la mémoire)

◊ **freedom** *noun* liberté *f*; **freedom of information** = liberté d'accès à l'information; **freedom of the press** = liberté de la presse; **freedom of speech** = liberté d'expression

◊ **freely** *adverb* librement

freeze *verb* figer; **to freeze (frame)** = figer une image *or* faire un arrêt sur image; **the image processor will freeze a**

single TV frame = le processeur d'image peut figer une image de télévision isolée

F-region *(astronomy)* région *f* F

frequency *noun* fréquence *f;* **frequency changer** = convertisseur *m* de fréquence; **frequency divider** = réducteur *m* de fréquence; **frequency division multiplexing (FDM)** = multiplexage *m* par répartition en fréquence; **frequency domain** = domaine *m* de fréquence; **frequency modulation (FM)** = modulation *f* de fréquence; **frequency range** = gamme *f* de fréquences; **frequency response** = réponse *f* en fréquence; **frequency shift keying (FSK)** = (système) de modulation *f* par déplacement *or* décalage de fréquence; **frequency variation** = variation *f* de fréquence; **clock frequency** = fréquence d'horloge; **the main clock frequency is 10MHz** = la principale fréquence d'horloge est de 10MHz; *(from 30 - 300 GHz)* **extremely high frequency EHF** = onde *f* millimétrique; *(of less than 100 Hz)* **extremely low frequency (ELF)** = onde myriamétrique; *see also* LOW, HIGH, VERY, INFRA, MEDIUM

◊ **frequent** *adjective* fréquent, -e; **we send frequent telexes to New York** = nous envoyons fréquemment des télex à New York

◊ **frequently** *adverb* souvent *or* fréquemment; **the photocopier is frequently out of use** = il n'est pas rare de voir le photocopieur en dérangement

friction feed *noun* entraînement *m* par friction *or* par rouleaux

FROM = FUSIBLE READ ONLY MEMORY

front 1 *noun* avant *m or* face *f or* panneau *m* avant; **the disks are inserted in slots in the front of the terminal** = on insère les disquettes dans les fentes du panneau avant du terminal **2** *adjective* avant; **front panel** = panneau avant *or* antérieur *or* de commande; **front porch** = palier *m* avant; **front projection** = rétroprojection *f*

◊ **front-end** *adjective* frontal, -e; **front-end computer** = ordinateur frontal; **front-end processor (FEP)** = processeur

frontal; **front-end system** = système frontal

FSK = FREQUENCY SHIFT KEYING

full *adjective* **(a)** plein, -e *or* complet, -ète; **the disk is full, so the material will have to be stored on another disk** = cette disquette est pleine, il faudra donc saisir les données sur une autre disquette **(b)** *(complete)* exhaustif, -ive; **full adder** = additionneur complet *or* à trois entrées; **full duplex (FDX** *or* **fdx)** = full duplex; **full-frame time code** = comptage *m* d'images (complètes); **full-size display** = écran *m* pleine page; **full subtractor** = soustracteur complet *or* à trois entrées

◊ **fully** *adverb* complètement; **fully connected network** = réseau totalement maillé; **fully formed character** = caractère complet; **a daisy wheel printer produces fully formed characters** = la marguerite imprime des caractères complets

QUOTE transmitter and receiver can be operated independently, making full duplex communication possible
Electronics & Power

function 1 *noun* **(a)** *(mathematical formula)* fonction *f* **(b)** *(computer program instructions)* fonction; **function digit** = code *m or* caractère *m* de fonction; **function table** = table *f* de fonctions **(c)** *(special feature on a computer)* fonction; **the word-processor had a spelling-checker function but no built-in text-editing function** = cette machine de traitement de texte possédait une fonction correction orthographique *or* possédait un correcteur orthographique mais n'était pas équipée d'éditeur intégré; **function code** = code *m* de fonction **2** *verb* fonctionner *or* marcher; **the new system has not functioned properly since it was installed** = le nouvel ordinateur n'a jamais bien fonctionné depuis qu'on l'a installé

◊ **functional** *adjective* fonctionnel, -elle; **functional diagram** = schéma *or* diagramme fonctionnel; **functional specification** = spécification *f or* analyse *f* fonctionnelle; **functional unit** = appareil *m* en bon état de marche

◊ **function key** *or* **programmable function key** *noun* touche *f* de fonction; **tags can be allocated to function keys** =

on peut allouer des étiquettes aux touches de fonction; **hitting F5 will put you into insert mode =** en appuyant sur la touche de fonction F5 on se met en mode entrée

QUOTE they made it clear that the PC was to take its place as part of a much larger computing function that comprised of local area networks, wide area networks, small systems, distributed systems and mainframes
Minicomputer News
QUOTE if your computer has a MOD function, you will not need the function defined in line 3010
Computing Today
QUOTE the final set of keys are to be found above the main keyboard and comprise 5 function keys, which together with shift, give 10 user-defined keys
Computing Today

fundamental frequency *noun* fréquence *f* fondamentale

fuse 1 *noun* fusible *m;* **to blow a fuse =** faire sauter un plomb **2** *verb* faire sauter une fusible *or* un plomb; **when the air-conditioning was switched on, it fused the whole system =** on a fait sauter les plombs en branchant le climatiseur

◊ **fusible link** *noun* élément *m* fusible

◊ **fusible read only memory (FROM)** *noun* ROM *or* mémoire *f* morte à fusibles

◊ **fusion** *noun* *(combining programs, etc.)* fusion *f*

fuzzy *noun* flou, -e; **top quality paper will eliminate fuzzy characters =** un papier de qualité supérieure donnera des caractères plus nets; **fuzzy logic** *or* **fuzzy theory =** logique floue

Gg

G = GIGA *prefix* giga; **GHz** = gigahertz *m or* GHz

GaAs = GALLIUM ARSENIDE

gaffer *noun (in a studio or office)* homme à tout faire *or* gaffeur *m US* chef-électricien *m; (US - black adhesive tape)* **gaffer tape** = bande *f* adhésive noire (qui sert à tout dans un studio) *or* outil favori du gaffeur

gain 1 *noun* gain *m;* **gain control** = contrôle *m* de gain; **automatic gain control** = contrôle de gain automatique **2** *verb* **to gain access to a file** = avoir accès à *or* accéder à un fichier; **the user cannot gain access to the confidential information in the file without a password** = il est impossible d'accéder aux renseignements confidentiels du fichier sans utiliser le mot de passe

galactic noise *noun* bruits *mpl* cosmiques

galley proof *noun* épreuve *f* en placard *or* en première

gallium arsenide (GaAs) *noun* arséniure *m* de gallium (AsGa)

game *noun* jeu *m;* **computer game** = jeu électronique; **game paddle** = manette *f* (de jeu); **games software** = ludiciel *m*

gamma *noun (measure of light on photographic or TV image)* gamma *m*

ganged *adjective (mechanically linked)* (re)groupé, -ée *or* monté, -ée (en série); **ganged switch** = (re)groupement *m* de commutateurs *or* commutateurs montés en série; **a ganged switch is used to select which data bus a printer will respond to** = avec des commutateurs montés en série,

il est possible de choisir le bus de données qui va activer l'imprimante

gap *noun* **(a)** *(between recorded data)* espace *m or* intervalle *m;* **block gap** *or* **interblock gap (IBG)** = espace interbloc *or* entre blocs; **gap character** = caractère *m* de remplissage; **gap digit** = chiffre *m* de remplissage; **record gap** = intervalle blanc entre deux enregistrements **(b)** *(between read head and medium)* **air gap** *or* **head gap** = entrefer *m;* **gap loss** = perte *f* d'alignement **(c)** *(radio communications)* créneau *m or* intervalle *m*

garbage *noun* **(a)** *(radio interference)* signaux *mpl* parasites **(b)** *(information no longer required)* informations *fpl* sans intérêt *or* de rebut; *(from memory)* **garbage collection** = nettoyage *m* de mémoire; **garbage in garbage out (GIGO)** = à données erronées, résultats erronés *or* des données douteuses produisent des résultats douteux

gas discharge display *or* **gas plasma display** *noun* affichage *m or* écran *m* plasma

gate *noun* **(a)** *(logical electronic switch)* porte *f;* **AND gate** = porte *or* circuit *m* ET; **coincidence gate** = porte *or* circuit ET; **EXNOR gate** = porte *or* circuit NI exclusif; **EXOR gate** = porte *or* circuit OU exclusif; **NAND gate** = porte *or* circuit NON-ET; **negation** *or* **NOT gate** = porte *or* circuit NON; **NOR gate** = porte *or* circuit NON-OU *or* NI; **OR gate** = porte *or* circuit OU; **gate array** = circuit *m* logique complexe *or* en réseau; **gate circuit** = circuit *m* logique; **gate delay** = délai *m or* temps *m* de réponse *or* de propagation **(b)** *(connection pin of a FET device)* connecteur *m* (d'un transistor à effet de champ) **(c)** *(for film or slide)* couloir *m*

◊ **gateway** *noun* connecteur *m* *or* passerelle *f* (d'accès entre réseaux)

gather *verb* regrouper *or* rassembler; *(data)* **gather write** = grouper *or* agglomérer (des données)

gauge 1 *noun (for measuring thickness)* calibre *m; (for petrol)* jauge *f; (for air pressure)* manomètre *m* **2** *verb (thickness)* calibrer; *(petrol)* jauger *or* vérifier le niveau; *(air)* mesurer *or* vérifier la pression

gender changer *noun* changeur *m* de genre

general *adjective* **(a)** *(not special)* ordinaire *or* commun, -e **(b)** *(dealing with everything)* général, -e; **general purpose computer** = ordinateur *m* polyvalent *or* non spécialisé; **general purpose interface bus (GPIB)** = bus *m* d'interface universel *or* banalisé; **general purpose program** = programme *m* à usage multiple *or* multifonction; **general register** *or* **general purpose register (gpr)** = registre banalisé *or* général *or* polyvalent

generate *verb* produire *or* générer *or* créer; **to generate an image from digitally recorded data** = créer une image à partir de données numériques; **the graphics tablet generates a pair of co-ordinates each time the pen is moved** = une tablette graphique permet de générer deux coordonnées à chaque position du stylo; **computer-generated** = créé, -ée *or* produit, -e à l'aide d'un ordinateur; **computer-generated graphics** = représentations *fpl* graphiques sur ordinateur *or* infographie *f;* **they analyzed the computer-generated image** = ils ont fait l'analyse de l'image créée par l'ordinateur; **generated address** = adresse générée *or* calculée; **generated error** = erreur générée (par des arrondis) ◊ **generation** *noun* **(a)** *(producing data)* production *f or* création *f;* **the computer is used in the generation of graphic images** = on utilise l'ordinateur pour produire des images graphiques; **code generation is automatic** = le code est produit *or* généré automatiquement; **program generation** = création d'un programme **(b)** *(age of the technology)* génération *f; (earliest type of technology)* **first**

generation = première génération; **first generation computers** = ordinateurs de première génération; *(master copy)* **first generation image** = image originale; *(computers with transistors)* **second generation computers** = ordinateurs de deuxième génération; *(computers with integrated circuits)* **third generation computers** = ordinateurs de troisième génération; *(computers using LSI circuits from around 1970)* **fourth generation computers** = ordinateurs de quatrième génération; **fourth generation languages** = langages de quatrième génération; *(computers using fast VLSI circuits)* **fifth generation computers** = ordinateurs de cinquième génération **(c)** *(of file)* génération; **the father file is a first generation backup** = le fichier père est un fichier de sauvegarde de première génération
◊ **generator** *noun* **(a)** *(program)* générateur *m* de programmes; **character generator** = générateur de caractères **(b)** *(device generating electricity)* (appareil) générateur *m or* génératrice *f* (d'électricité); **the computer centre has its own independent generator, in case of mains power failure** = en cas de panne de courant, le centre informatique possède sa propre génératrice (d'électricité)

> QUOTE vector and character generation are executed in hardware by a graphics display processor
> *Computing Today*

generic *adjective* générique

genuine *adjective* vrai, -e *or* véritable; **authentication allows the system to recognize that a sender's message is genuine** = la procédure d'authentification permet au système de reconnaître si un message est émis par un utilisateur autorisé

geometric distortion *noun (of television picture)* distorsion *f* géométrique

geostationary satellite *noun* satellite *m* géostationnaire

germanium *noun* germanium *m*

get *noun* instruction *f* 'GET' *or* instruction 'chercher'

GHz = GIGAHERTZ

ghost *noun* image *f* fantôme; *(second cursor)* **ghost cursor** = curseur *m* secondaire

gibberish *noun* caractères *mpl* parasites

giga- *or* **G** *prefix (meaning one thousand million)* giga- *or* G; *(10⁹ bytes)* **gigabyte** = giga-octet (Go) *m; (frequency of 10⁹ Hertz)* **gigahertz** = gigahertz *m*

GIGO = GARBAGE IN GARBAGE OUT

GINO = GRAPHICAL INPUT OUTPUT

GKS = GRAPHICS KERNEL SYSTEM

glare *noun* réflexion *f;* **the glare from the screen makes my eyes hurt** = la réflexion sur l'écran me fait mal aux yeux

glitch *noun (informal)* pépin *m*

global *adjective* global, -e *or* total, -e; **global replace** = remplacement global; **global knowledge** = connaissance *f* globale *or* exhaustive; **global search and replace** = recherche *f* globale et remplace; **global variable** = variable *f* globale *or* commune *or* générale

glossy 1 *adjective* (papier couché) satiné *or* brillant; **the illustrations are printed on glossy art paper** = les illustrations sont imprimées sur papier brillant **2** *noun (informal - expensive magazines)* **the glossies** = les revues de luxe

GND = GROUND

go ahead *noun* (signal d') invitation *f* à transmettre

goal *noun* but *m* (visé *or* atteint)

gofer *noun US (informal)* homme à tout faire *or* gaffeur *m*

gold contacts *noun* contacts *mpl* or

golf-ball *noun (which produces printed characters)* boule *f* d'impression; **golf-ball printer** = imprimante *f* à boule

GOTO *(command)* instruction *f* 'GOTO' *or* instruction de saut; **GOTO 105 instructs a jump to line 105** = GOTO 105 indique un saut à la ligne 105

GPIB = GENERAL PURPOSE INTERFACE BUS

gpr = GENERAL PURPOSE REGISTER

grab *verb* saisir
◊ **grabber** *noun (of video images)* **frame grabber** = capteur *m* d'images vidéo

QUOTE sometimes a program can grab all the available memory, even if it is not going to use it
Byte
QUOTE the frame grabber is distinguished by its ability to acquire a TV image in a single frame interval
Electronics & Wireless World

graceful degradation *noun* dégradation *f* limitée *or* douce *or* progressive

grade *noun* classe *f or* qualité *f;* **a top-grade computer expert** = un expert-informaticien de première classe; **grade of service** = niveau *m* (de qualité) d'un service téléphonique
◊ **graduated** *adjective* gradué, -ée

grain *noun (on fast photographic films)* grain *m*

gram *or* **gramme** *noun* gramme *m;* **the book is printed on 70 gram paper** = ce livre est imprimé sur du papier de 70g
◊ **grammage** *noun (weight of paper)* grammage *m*
NOTE: often written as **gsm : 80 gsm paper**

grammatical error *noun* faute *f* de syntaxe
◊ **grammar** *noun* grammaire *f*

grandfather file *noun* fichier *m* grand-père; *(when followed by two other files)* fichier de première génération; **grandfather cycle** = cycle *m* de rotation des fichiers de sauvegarde

granularity *noun (size of memory segments)* segmentation *f or* modularité *f* de la mémoire

graph *noun* graphique *m or* graphe *m or* courbe *f;* **graph paper** = papier *m* quadrillé *or* millimétré; **graph plotter** = traceur *m or* grapheur *m*

◊ **graphic** *adjective* graphique; **graphic data** = données *fpl* graphiques; **graphic display** = représentation *f or* affichage *m* graphique; **graphic display resolution** = définition *f* de l'affichage graphique; **graphic language** = langage *m* graphique; **this graphic language can plot lines, circles and graphs with a single command** = avec ce langage graphique, on peut tracer des lignes, cercles et graphes avec une seule commande

◊ **graphical** *adjective* graphique; **graphical input/output (GINO)** = entrée/sortie *f* graphique

◊ **graphically** *adverb* graphiquement *or* à l'aide d'un graphique; **the sales figures are graphically represented as a pie chart** = les chiffres de vente sont reproduits graphiquement sous forme de camembert

◊ **graphics** *noun* représentations *f* graphiques; **graphics output such as bar charts, pie charts, etc.** = les représentations graphiques telles que histogrammes, camemberts, etc; **graphics art terminal** = terminal *m* graphique *or* avec écran (à affichage) graphique; **graphics character** = caractère *m* graphique; **graphics interface** = interface *f* graphique; **graphics kernel system (GKS)** = fonctions *fpl* graphiques GKS; **graphics library** = bibliothèque *f* graphique; **graphics light pen** = stylo *m* optique graphique; **graphics mode** = mode *m* graphique; **graphics pad** *or* **tablet** = tablette *f* graphique *or* à numériser; **graphics processor** = processeur *m* graphique; **graphics software** = logiciel *m* graphique; **graphics terminal** = terminal graphique *or* terminal de CAO; **graphics VDU** = écran (à affichage) graphique; **computer graphics** = représentations *fpl* graphiques sur ordinateur *or* infographie *f;* **high resolution graphics** = graphiques haute définition; **interactive graphics** graphiques interactifs *or* infographie interactive

QUOTE one interesting feature of this model is graphics amplification, which permits graphic or text enlargement of up to 800 per cent

QUOTE the custom graphics chips can display an image that has 640 columns by 400 rows of 4-bit pixel

QUOTE several tools exist for manipulating image and graphical data: some were designed for graphics manipulation

Byte

gravure *see* PHOTOGRAVURE

Gray code *noun* code *m* (de) Gray
◊ **gray scale** *US* = GREY SCALE

green phosphor *noun* phosphore *m* vert

gremlin *noun (unexplained fault in a system)* schmilblic *m or* erreur *f* inexplicable; **line gremlin** = schmilblic sur la ligne *or* perte de transmission inexplicable

grey scale *noun* **(a)** *(used to measure the correct exposure when filming)* échelle *f* de gris **(b)** *(shades of grey on a monochrome monitor)* niveaux *mpl* de gris (NOTE: US spelling is usually **gray scale**)

grid *noun* grille *f*

grip 1 *noun (person)* machiniste *m* **2** *verb* saisir *or* retenir; **in friction feed, the paper is gripped by the rollers** = dans l'entraînement par friction le papier est saisi par les rouleaux

ground 1 *noun* **(a)** *(electrical connection to earth or GND)* prise *f* de terre **(b)** *(earth)* sol *m;* **ground absorption** = perte *f* de terre; **ground station** = station *f* au sol **2** *verb US (to connect electrical device to ground)* mettre à la terre *or* à la masse NOTE: **ground** is more common in US English; the UK English is **earth**

group 1 *noun* **(a)** *(set of computer records)* groupe *m;* **group mark** *or* **marker** = marqueur *m* (de début *or* de fin) de groupe; *(of devices)* **group poll** = appel *m* sélectif de groupe **(b)** *(in telegraphic communications)* groupe (de caractères *or* de mots) **(c)** *(12 voice channel)* groupe primaire **2** *verb* (re)grouper

gsm *or* **g/m²** = GRAMS PER SQUARE METRE (PER SHEET) *(weight of paper used in printing)* gramme *m* au mètre carré; **the book is printed on 70 gsm coated paper =** ce livre est imprimé sur papier couché de 70g

guarantee *noun* garantie *f*; **the system is still under guarantee and will be repaired free of charge =** le système est toujours sous garantie et la réparation sera faite gratuitement

guard band *noun* **(a)** bande *f* de fréquence intercalaire *or* bande de protection **(b)** *(on a tape)* bande intermédiaire

◊ **guard bit** *noun* bit *m* de protection

◊ **guarding** *noun (joining a single sheet to a book or magazine)* montage *m* (d'une feuille isolée *or* d'une illustration) sur onglet

guide bars *noun (in a bar code)* lignes *fpl* guides *or* lignes de référence; **the standard guide bars are two thin lines that are a little longer than the coding lines =** les lignes guides standard se présentent sous la forme de deux lignes fines un peu plus longues que les lignes codes

guillotine *noun* massicot *m*

gulp *noun* multiplet *m* *or* groupe *m* d'octets

gun *or* **electron gun** *noun* canon *m* à électrons

gutter *noun (of pages of book)* marge *f* intérieure

Hh

H & J = HYPHENATION AND JUSTIFICATION

hack *verb (for criminal purposes)* s'introduire sans autorisation dans un système *or* faire du piratage informatique *or* pirater un système

◊ **hacker** *noun (person who breaks into computer systems)* pirate *m* (de système) informatique

> QUOTE software manufacturers try more and more sophisticated methods to protect their programs and the hackers use equally clever methods to break into them
> *Electronics & Wireless World*
> QUOTE the hackers used their own software to break into the credit card centre
> *Computer News*
> QUOTE any computer linked to the system will be alerted if a hacker uses its code number
> *Practical Computing*

halation *noun (photography)* (effet de) halo *m*

half *noun* moitié *f or* demie *f or* demi *m;* **half the data was lost in transmission** = la moitié des données ont été perdues au cours de la transmission; **the second half of the program contains some errors** la seconde partie du programme contient des erreurs; **half adder** = additionneur *m* à deux entrées *or* demi-additionneur *m;* **half duplex** = semi-duplex *m;* **half-duplex modem** = modem *m* semi-duplex; **some modems can operate in half-duplex mode if required** = certains modems peuvent fonctionner en mode semi-duplex si nécessaire; **half-height drive** = unité *f* de disquettes de demi-hauteur; **half-intensity** = demi-intensité *f; (printing)* **half space** = demi-espace *m; (first page of book)* **half title** = faux-titre *m;* **half wave rectifier** = redresseur *m* (de) simple alternance; **half word** = demi-mot *m*

◊ **halftone** *or* **half-tone** *noun* **(a)** demi-teinte *f;* **halftone process** *or* **half-toning** = *(printing)* (procédé de) similigravure *f or* simili *f* **(b)** *(illustration)* similigravure *or* simili *or* gravure *f* en demi-teinte; **the book is illustrated with twenty halftones** ce livre est contient vingt planches en demi-teinte *or* vingt similigravures

halide *noun* halogénure *m* (d'argent)

Hall effect *noun* effet *m* (de champ) Hall; **Hall effect switch** = commutateur *m* à effet (de champ) Hall

halo *noun (photography)* halo *m*

halt 1 *noun* arrêt *m;* **dead halt** *or* **drop-dead halt** = arrêt total; **halt instruction** = instruction *f* d'arrêt; **programmed halt** = arrêt programmé; **halt condition** = condition *f* d'arrêt **2** *verb* arrêter *or* interrompre; **hitting CTRL S will halt the program** = taper CTRL S pour interrompre le programme

ham *noun* **radio ham** = radio-amateur *m*

Hamming code *noun* code *m or* codage *m* de Hamming; **Hamming distance** = distance *f* de Hamming

hand *noun* main *f;* **hands off** = *(automatic)* (système) automatique *or* sans intervention manuelle; *(training)* (formation) théorique *or* sans accès à l'ordinateur; **hands on** = *(manual)* (système) manuel; *(training)* (formation) pratique *or* mise *f* en main; **the sales representatives have received hands-on experience of the new computer** = une mise en main du nouvel ordinateur a été organisée pour les délégués commerciaux; **the computer firm gives a two day hands-on training course** = la société informatique offre une formation pratique de deux jours; **hand portable set** = radiotéléphone *m*

portatif; **hand receiver** = récepteur *m*
portatif; **hand viewer** = petite
visionneuse *f* (qu'on tient à la main)

◇ **hand-held** (petit appareil) qu'on tient
à la main *or* de poche; **hand-held
computer** = petit ordinateur portatif *or*
qui tient dans une serviette *or* ordinateur
de poche

◇ **handler** *noun (driver)* logiciel *m* de
commande de périphérique *or*
gestionnaire *m* de périphérique

◇ **hand off** *verb* basculer *or* transférer la
communication d'un émetteur à l'autre

◇ **handset** *noun* combiné *m*

◇ **handy talkies** *or* **HTs** *noun*
radiotéléphones *mpl* portatifs

handshake *or* **handshaking** *noun
(between transmitter and receptor)*
protocole *m* de validation de transfert
de données *or* d'échange d'informations;
full handshaking = protocole de mise en
communication (de deux postes);
*(between computer and slower
peripheral)* **handshake I/O control** =
contrôle *m* de mise en communication

handwriting *noun* écriture *f*; **the
keyboarders are having difficulty in
reading the author's handwriting** = les
clavistes trouvent que l'écriture de
l'auteur est difficile à lire

◇ **handwritten** *adjective* écrit, -e à la
main *or* manuscrit, -e; **the author sent in
two hundred pages of handwritten
manuscript** = l'auteur a envoyé un
manuscrit de deux cents pages
entièrement écrit à la main

QUOTE all acquisition, data reduction,
processing, and memory circuitry is
contained in the single hand-held unit
Byte
QUOTE if a line is free, the device waits
another 400ms before reserving the line with
a quick handshake process
Practical Computing

---

hang *verb* se perdre *or* être accroché
dans une boucle

◇ **hangover** *noun* **(a)** *(on a TV screen)*
traînée *f or* rémanence *f* d'image **(b)** *(of
fax machine)* déréglage *m* de la qualité
d'impression

◇ **hang up** *verb (communications line)*
raccrocher; **after she had finished talking
on the telephone, she hung up** = à la fin
de la conversation téléphonique, elle a
raccroché

◇ **hangup** *noun* arrêt *m* inattendu

hard *adjective* **(a)** *(solid)* dur, -e; *(not
programmable)* fermé, -e; **hard card** =
carte *f* de disque dur; **hard copy** = copie *f*
d'écran *f or* sortie *f* d'imprimante *or* texte
imprimé; **hard copy interface** = interface
f d'imprimante; **hard disk** = disque dur;
hard disk drive = unité *f or* lecteur *m* de
disque dur; **hard disk model** = modèle
d'ordinateur avec disque dur; **hard error**
= erreur *f or* anomalie *f* persistante; **hard
failure** = panne sérieuse (d'équipement);
**the hard failure was due to a burnt-out
chip** = la panne était due à la défaillance
d'un composant; **hard hyphen** = trait *m*
d'union obligatoire **(b)** *(contrast)* fort, -e

◇ **hardback** *noun & adjective* édition *f*
cartonnée *or* reliée

◇ **hardbound** *adjective (book)* (livre)
avec couverture cartonnée

◇ **hardcover** *noun & adjective* édition *f*
cartonnée *or* reliée; **we printed 4,000
copies of the hardcover edition, and
10,000 of the paperback** = nous avons
imprimé 4000 exemplaires cartonnés et
10 000 brochés

◇ **hard-sectored** *adjective* (disque) avec
formatage physique; **hard-sectoring**
formatage *m* physique de secteurs *or*
formatage par perforations

hardware *noun* matériel *m*
informatique; **hardware compatibility** =
compatibilité *f* du matériel; **hardware
configuration** = configuration *f* du
matériel; **hardware interrupt** = (signal
d') interruption *f* provenant d'une
machine; **hardware reliability** = fiabilité
f or bonne qualité du matériel; **hardware
security** = sécurité *f* du matériel
NOTE: *compare* SOFTWARE

hardwired connection *noun* câblage
m permanent *or* connexion *f* fixe

◇ **hardwired logic** *noun* logique *f* câblée

◇ **hardwired program** *noun* programme
en logique câblée

harmonic *noun* harmonique *f*;
harmonic distortion = distorsion *f*
d'harmoniques; **harmonic telephone
ringer** = sonnerie *f* d'appel à
harmoniques

hartley *noun (unit of information equal
to 3.32 bits)* hartley *m*

hash 1 *verb* générer un hash code; **hashing function** = algorithme *m or* fonction *f* hash **2** *noun* **(a)** *see* HASHMARK **(b) hash code** = hash code *m;* **hash-code system** = système de hash code; **hash index** = index hash code; **hash table** = table *f* des adresses hash codées; **hash total** = total *m* de vérification (pour hash code); **hash value** = valeur *f* d'un hash code

◊ **hashmark** *or* **hash mark** *noun (printed sign #)* signe typographique:
NOTE: in US usage (#) means number; #32 = number 32 (apartment number in an address, paragraph number in a text, etc.). In computer usage, the pound sign (£) is often used in the US instead of the hash to avoid confusion

hazard *noun* erreur *f or* défaut *m* d'horloge; **hazard-free implementation** = application *f* qui tolère toutes les erreurs possibles

HD = HALF DUPLEX

HDLC = HIGH LEVEL DATA LINK CONTROL

HDVS = HIGH DEFINITION VIDEO SYSTEM

HDX = HALF DUPLEX

head 1 *noun* **(a) combined head** *or* **read/write head** = tête *f* de lecture/écriture *or* tête de lecture; **head alignment** = alignement *m or* positionnement *m* de la tête de lecture; **head cleaning disk** = disquette *f* de nettoyage; **head crash** = crash *m* (du disque dur) causé par la tête de lecture *or* atterrissage *m* de la tête de lecture; **head demagnetizer** = démagnétiseur *m* de tête; **head park** = mise en position de transport de la tête *or* parcage *m* de la tête; **head wheel** = molette *f* de pressage *or* galet *m* presseur; **disk head** = tête de lecture *or* de lecture/écriture de disquettes; **fixed head** = tête fixe; **floating head** *or* **flying head** = tête flottante; **playback head** = tête de lecture; **read head** = tête de lecture; **tape head** = tête de lecture *or* d'écriture de bande magnétique; **write head** = tête d'écriture **(b)** (données de) début *m* de fichier **(c)** *(of book or page)* tête; **head of form (HOF)** = tête *or* début *m* d'une page (de papier listing) **(d)** tête de bobine

or amorce *f* **(e)** *(of film or tape)* tête; **head end** = tête de réseau **2** *verb* être en tête de liste; **the queue was headed by my file** = mon fichier était en tête de la file d'attente

◊ **header** *noun* **(a)** *(in a local area network)* bloc *m* d'identification **(b)** *(at top of a list of data)* en-tête *m* de fichier; **header block** = bloc *m* d'identification; **header card** = carte *f* en-tête; **header label** = label *m* d'identification *or* de reconnaisance de bande; **tape header** = en-tête *m or* début *m* de bande **(c)** *(at top of page)* en-tête *or* titre courant

◊ **heading** *noun* **(a)** *(title)* (i) en-tête *or* titre *m* ; (ii) rubrique *f* **(b)** en-tête *or* titre *m* courant

◊ **headlife** *noun* durée *f* de vie de la tête

◊ **headline** *noun* = HEADING

◊ **headset** *or* **headphones** *noun* casque *m* (d'écoute)

◊ **headword** *noun* *(in a printed dictionary)* entrée *f*

heap *noun* **(a)** *(temporary storage area)* pile *f* **(b)** *(binary tree)* pile binaire

heat sensitive paper *noun* papier *m* thermique

heat sink *noun* dissipateur *m* thermique *or* évacuateur *m* de chaleur

Heaviside-Kennelly layer *see* E-REGION

helical scan *noun* lecture *f* hélicoïdale

helios noise *noun* bruit *m* atmosphérique causé par le soleil

help *noun* **(a)** *(which makes things easy)* aide *f;* **he finds his word-processor a great help in the office** = il trouve la machine de traitement de texte très utile pour le travail de bureau; **they need some help with their programming** = ils ont besoin d'aide pour la programmation **(b)** *(function)* aide; **hit the HELP key if you want information about what to do next** = tapez la touche HELP pour connaître la marche à suivre

Hertz *noun* hertz *m*

heterodyne *noun* hétérodyne *f*

heterogeneous network *noun* réseau *m* informatique hétérogène; **heterogeneous multiplexing** = multiplexage *m* hétérogène

heuristic *adjective* heuristique; **a heuristic program learns from its previous actions and decisions** = un programme heuristique exploite ses actions et décisions antérieures

hex *or* **hexadecimal notation** *noun* notation *f* hexadécimale; **hex dump** = vidage hexadécimal; **hex pad** = clavier hexadécimal

HF = HIGH FREQUENCY

hidden *adjective* caché, -ée; **hidden defect in a program** = vice *or* défaut caché; **hidden files** = fichiers cachés; **it allows users to backup or restore hidden system files independently** = cela permet aux utilisateurs de sauvegarder ou de restaurer un par un les fichiers cachés; *(on 2-D images)* **hidden lines** = lignes cachées; **hidden line algorithm** = algorithme *m* d'effacement de lignes cachées; **hidden line removal** = effacement *m* des lignes cachées

hierarchy *noun* hiérarchie *f*; **data hierarchy** = structure *f* hiérarchique de données

◊ **hierarchical** *adjective* hiérarchique *or* hiérarchisé, -ée; **hierarchical classification** = classification *f* hiérarchique; **hierarchical communications system** = système de communication hiérarchisé; **hierarchical computer network** = réseau d'ordinateurs hiérarchisé; **hierarchical database** = base de données hiérarchisée; **hierarchical directory** = répertoire *m* hiérarchique

hi fi *or* **hi-fi** *or* **hifi** = HIGH FIDELITY haute fidélité *or* hi-fi; **a hi fi system** *or* **a hi fi** = une chaîne haute fidélité *or* une chaîne hi-fi

high 1 *adjective* haut, -e; **high definition** = haute définition; **high definition video system (HDVS)** = système vidéo haute définition; **high density storage** = mémoire *f* *or* support *m* magnétique haute densité; **a hard disk is a high density storage medium compared to paper tape** = un disque dur est un support de haute densité par rapport à une bande perforée; **high fidelity** *or* **hifi** *or* **hi fi** = haute fidélité *or* hi-fi; **high frequency (HF)** = haute fréquence *f*; *(allows several computers to be linked)* **high-level data link control (HDLC)** = contrôle de liaison de données de haut niveau *or* protocole d'interfaçage HDLC; **high-level data link control station** = équipement interfacé HDLC; **high-level (programming) language (HLL)** = langage *m* de programmation évolué *or* de haut niveau; **programmers should have a knowledge of high-level languages, particularly PASCAL** = on demande aux programmeurs une connaissance des langages de haut niveau, dont PASCAL; **high order** = (chiffre) de poids fort; **high-order language** = HIGH-LEVEL LANGUAGE; **high pass filter** = filtre *m* passe-haut; **high performance equipment** = matériel *m* (de) haute performance; **high priority program** = programme *m* prioritaire; **high reduction** = forte réduction; **high specification** *or* **high spec** = (de) haute précision *or* (de) haute technologie; **high spec cabling needs to be very carefully handled** = les câbles (de) haute technologie doivent être manipulés avec soin; **high speed carry** = report *m* en cascade; **high usage trunk** = ligne *f* de grand débit **2** *noun* **logical high** = état *m* logique haut *or* vrai *or* 1

◊ **highlight 1** *noun* **highlights** = mots *mpl* *or* caractères *mpl* (mis) en évidence; *(on screen)* mots *or* caractères en surbrillance; *(main characteristics)* caractéristiques *fpl* principales **2** *verb* mettre en évidence *or* faire ressortir; *(on screen)* mettre en surbrillance; **the headings are highlighted in bold** = les titres sont en caractères gras pour les faire ressortir

◊ **high-resolution** *or* **hi-res** *noun* haute définition *f*; **high-resolution graphics** = graphiques *mpl* haute définition; **this high-resolution monitor can display 640 x 320 pixels** = ce moniteur haute définition permet un affichage de 640 x 320 pixels

◊ **high-speed** *adjective* ultra-rapide *or* grande vitesse; *(film)* ultrasensible; **high-speed duplicator** = duplicateur *m* grande vitesse; *(of printer)* **high-speed skip** = saut *m* rapide

highway *noun (bus)* bus *m;* **address highway** = bus d'adresses; **data highway** = bus de transfert de données

QUOTE they have proposed a standardized high-level language for importing image data into desktop publishing and other applications programs
QUOTE the computer is uniquely suited to image processing because of its high-resolution graphics
Byte

hill climbing *noun (in an expert system)* escalade *f or* méthode ascendante *f*

hi-res = HIGH RESOLUTION haute définition *f;* **hi-res graphics** = graphiques *mpl* haute définition; **this hi-res monitor can display 640 x 320 pixels** = ce moniteur haute définition permet un affichage de 640 x 320 pixels; **the new hi-res optical scanner can detect 300 dots per inch** = le nouveau scanner optique haute définition peut lire 300 points par pouce

hiss *noun* sifflement *f*

histogram *noun* histogramme *m*

hit 1 *noun* **(a)** *(successful search)* réussite *f or* trouvaille *f or* coup au but *f;* **there was a hit after just a few seconds** = on a trouvé au bout de quelques secondes à peine; **there are three hits for this search key** = cette clé produit trois réponses **(b)** *(noise)* **hit on the line** = courte perturbation sur la ligne **2** *verb (to press a key)* appuyer (sur une touche) *or* taper; **to save the text, hit ESCAPE S** = pour effectuer la sauvegarde, tapez ESCAPE S

QUOTE the cause of the data disaster is usually due to your finger hitting the wrong key
PC Business World

HLL = HIGH-LEVEL LANGUAGE

HMI = HUMAN-MACHINE INTERFACE

HOF = HEAD OF FORM

hold 1 *noun (TV)* signal *m* de synchronisation; *(oscilloscope)* commande *f* de stabilisation du signal

(après échantillonnage) **2** *verb (in memory)* garder; *(value)* garder; *(telephone)* mettre en attente; **hold current** = courant *m* de maintien *or* de veille; *(artwork)* **holding line** = ligne *f* de délimitation *or* d'arrêt; **holding loop** = boucle *f* de maintien; **holding time** = temps *m* d'occupation de la ligne

◇ **holdup** *noun* (i) temps *m* de débit d'un onduleur *or* d'un dispositif de secours; (ii) pause *f* accidentelle *or* décrochage *m*

hole *noun* **(a)** *(in punched tape or card)* perforation *f or* trou *m; (of hard-sectored disk)* **index hole** = perforation de marquage (du bord d'un disque) **(b)** *(absence of an electron)* trou

Hollerith code *noun* code *m* (de) Hollerith

hologram *noun* hologramme *m*

◇ **holographic image** *noun* hologramme; **holographic storage** = stockage *m or* mémoire *f* holographique *or* d'hologramme

◇ **holography** *noun* holographie *f*

home *noun* **(a)** *(of person)* domicile *m;* **home banking** = télébanque *f or* consultation *f* des comptes à domicile; **home computer** = ordinateur *m* domestique **(b)** *(starting point)* position *f* initiale *or* de départ; **home record** = début *m* d'enregistrement

◇ **homing** *noun* retour *m* à la source *or* à l'origine

homogeneous computer network *noun* réseau *m* informatique homogène; **homogeneous multiplexing** = multiplexage *m* homogène

hood *noun* capot *m;* **acoustic hood** = capot *m* d'insonorisation

hooking *noun (distortion of video image)* décrochage *m*

hop *noun (transmission)* bond *m*

hopper *noun* chargeur *m* de cartes perforées

horizontal *adjective* horizontal, -e; **horizontal blanking** = inhibition *or* suppression horizontale (du signal); **horizontal check** = contrôle horizontal; **horizontal synchronization pulse** = impulsion *f* de synchronisation horizontale; **horizontal wraparound** = enroulement *m or* retour *m* à la ligne (automatique)

horn *noun (radio device)* capteur *m* directionnel; *(for microwaves)* **feed horn** = dispositif *m* de guidage directionnel

host *noun & adjective* hôte *m;* **host adapter** = adaptateur *m* de l'ordinateur hôte; **the cable to connect the scanner to the host adapter is included** = le câble de liaison entre le scanner et l'ordinateur hôte est fourni
◇ **host computer** *noun* **(a)** *(main controlling computer)* ordinateur *m* principal *or* ordinateur hôte **(b)** *(used to write and debug software)* ordinateur hôte *or* serveur *m* **(c)** *(in a network)* serveur

QUOTE you select fonts manually or through commands sent from the host computer along with the text
Byte

hot chassis *noun* châssis *m* sous tension
◇ **hot frame** *noun* image *f* surexposée
◇ **hotline** *noun* service *m* d'assistance (par téléphone)
◇ **hot metal composition** *noun* composition *f* au plomb
◇ **hot spot** *noun* point chaud
◇ **hot standby** *noun* système *m* de secours prêt à fonctionner
◇ **hot type** *noun* caractère *m or* ligne-bloc *f* (fondu(e) au moment de la composition)
◇ **hot zone** *noun* zone *f* de texte

house 1 *noun (especially a printing or publishing company)* société *f or* maison *f* (d'édition, etc.); **one of the biggest software houses in the US** = une des plus grandes maisons de logiciel aux Etats-Unis; **house corrections** = corrections *fpl* de l'imprimeur; **house style** = style *m* (de la) maison **2** *verb* loger *or* placer *or* insérer; **the magnetic tape is housed in a solid plastic case** = la bande magnétique

est contenue dans un boîtier en plastique solide
◇ **housekeeping** *noun* maintenance *f* courante; **housekeeping routine** = programme *m* de maintenance *or* (programme) utilitaire *m*
◇ **housing** *noun* boîtier *m;* **the computer housing was damaged when it fell on the floor** = quand on a laissé tomber l'ordinateur, son boîtier s'est abîmé

howler *noun* **(a)** avertisseur *m* (sonore) **(b)** *(mistake)* erreur *f* monstre

HRG = HIGH RESOLUTION GRAPHICS graphiques *mpl* haute définition; **the HRG board can control up to 300 pixels per inch** = la carte graphique haute définition contrôle jusqu'à 300 pixels par pouce

HT = HANDY TALKIES

HTTP = Hyper Text Transfer Protocol
hub *noun (of disk)* moyeu *m*

Huffman code *noun* code *m* de Huffman

hum *noun* bourdonnement *m or* ronflement *m*

human-computer *or* **human-machine interface (HMI)** *noun* interface *f* utilisateur/machine *or* interface homme/machine

hunting *noun* recherche *f*

hybrid circuit *noun* circuit *m* hybride *or* mixte *or* composite; **hybrid computer** = ordinateur *m* hybride; **hybrid interface** = interface *f* hybride; **hybrid system** = système *m* hybride

hyphen *noun* trait *m* d'union; **hard hyphen** = trait d'union obligatoire; **soft** *or* **discretionary hyphen** = césure *f* d'écran
◇ **hyphenated** *adjective* (mot) qui s'écrit avec un trait d'union; **the word 'high-level' is usually hyphenated** = le mot 'high-level' s'écrit habituellement avec un trait d'union
◇ **hyphenation** *noun* césure *f or* coupure *f;* **hyphenation and justification** *or* **H & J**

= césure et justification; **an American hyphenation and justification program will not work with British English spellings** = un programme de césure et justification établi aux Etats-Unis ne peut être utilisé pour un texte en anglais britannique

QUOTE the hyphenation program is useful for giving a professional appearance to documents and for getting as many words onto the page as possible

Micro Decision

hypo *abbreviation (photographic fixing solution)* hyposulfite *m or* thiosulfate *m* de sodium

Hz = HERTZ

Ii

IAM = INTERMEDIATE ACCESS MEMORY

IAR = INSTRUCTION ADDRESS REGISTER

IAS = IMMEDIATE ACCESS STORE

IBG = INTERBLOCK GAP

IC = INTEGRATED CIRCUIT
NOTE: plural is **ICs**

icand = MULTIPLICAND

icon *or* **ikon** *noun* icône *m;* **the icon for the graphics program is a small picture of a palette =** l'icône du programme graphique ressemble à une petite palette; **click twice over the wordprocessor icon - the picture of the typewriter =** cliquer deux fois quand vous rencontrez l'icône du traitement de texte qui représente une machine à écrire

QUOTE the system has on-screen icons and pop-up menus and is easy to control using the mouse
Electronics & Power =
QUOTE an icon-based system allows easy use of a computer without the need to memorize the complicated command structure of the native operating system
Micro Decision

ID = IDENTIFICATION; **ID card =** carte *f* d'identité; **ID code =** code *m* personnel; **after you wake up the system, you have to input your ID code then your password =** après la mise en route du système, il faut tapez votre code personnel et votre mot de passe

IDA = INTEGRATED DIGITAL ACCESS

IDD = INTERNATIONAL DIRECT DIALLING

ideal *adjective* idéal, -e; *(for negatives)* **ideal format =** format professionnel

identical *adjective* identique *or* semblable; **the two systems use identical software =** les deux systèmes utilisent des logiciels identiques; **the performance of the two clones is identical =** du point de vue performance, les deux clones se valent

identify *verb* identifier; **the user has to identify himself to the system by using a password before access is allowed =** l'utilisateur doit s'identifier par un mot de passe qui lui permet d'avoir accès au système; **the maintenance engineers have identified the cause of the system failure =** les ingénieurs de maintenance ont repéré la source de la panne du système
◊ **identification** *noun* identification *f;* **identification character =** caractère *m* d'identification; *(in COBOL)* **identification division =** division *f* avec paramètres d'identification (d'un programme en COBOL)
◊ **identifier** *noun* identificateur *m or* caractère *m* d'identification; **identifier word =** identificateur *or* mot *m* d'identification
◊ **identity** *noun* identité *f;* **identity burst =** séquence *f* d'identification; **identity card =** carte *f* d'identité; **identity gate** *or* **element =** porte *f* d'identité; **identity number =** numéro *m* de code personnel; **don't forget to log in your identity number =** n'oublie pas d'entrer ton numéro de code personnel; **identity operation =** opération *f* d'identité

idiot tape *noun (tape containing unformatted text)* bande *f* idiote *or* bande de texte non formaté *or* sans paramètres d'impression

idle *adjective (machine)* au repos; *(code that means 'do nothing')* **idle character =** caractère nul; **idle time =** temps *m* mort *or* temps d'attente (entre deux opérations)

IDP = INTEGRATED DATA PROCESSING

IEE *UK* = INSTITUTION OF ELECTRICAL ENGINEERS

IEEE *USA* = INSTITUTE OF ELECTRICAL AND ELECTRONIC ENGINEERS; **IEEE bus** = bus *m* (conforme aux normes du) IEEE; **IEEE-488** = (norme d'interface parallèle standard) IEEE-488

ier *noun* = MULTIPLIER

if *or* **IF** = INTERMEDIATE FREQUENCY

IF statement *noun* instruction *f* IF (si); **IF-THEN-ELSE** = instructions IF-THEN-ELSE (branchement conditionnel)

ignore *verb* ne pas reconnaître *or* ne pas tenir compte de *or* ignorer *or* rejeter; **this command instructs the computer to ignore all punctuation** = cette commande donne ordre à l'ordinateur de ne pas tenir compte de la ponctuation; **ignore character** = caractère *m* de remplissage

IH = INTERRUPT HANDLER

IIL = INTEGRATED INJECTION LOGIC

IKBS = INTELLIGENT KNOWLEDGE-BASED SYSTEM

ikon *or* **icon** *noun* icône *m see also* ICON

ILF = INFRA LOW FREQUENCY

ILL = INTER-LIBRARY LOAN

illegal *adjective (against the law)* illégal, -e; *(against the rules)* invalide *or* qui va contre les règles de la syntaxe; **illegal character** = caractère *m* invalide; **illegal instruction** = instruction *f* invalide; **illegal operation** = opération *f* invalide

◊ **illegally** *adverb (against the law)* illégalement; *(against the rules)* de façon invalide *or* contre les règles de la syntaxe; **the company has been illegally copying copyright software** = depuis quelque temps déjà, la société fait des copies frauduleuses de logiciels protégés par le copyright

illegible *adjective* illisible; **if the manuscript is illegible, send it back to the author to have it typed** = si le manuscrit est illisible, il faut le renvoyer à l'auteur et lui demander de le faire taper à la machine

illiterate *adjective* analphabète *or* illéttré, -ée; **computer illiterate** = (personne) qui ne possède aucune connaissance informatique *or* qui ne comprend pas le jargon informatique

QUOTE three years ago the number of people who were computer illiterate was much higher than today
Minicomputer News

illuminate *verb* éclairer *or* illuminer; **the screen is illuminated by a low-power light** = l'écran est éclairé par une lampe de très faible puissance

◊ **illumination** *noun* illumination *f or* éclairage *m; (of antenna)* **aperture illumination** = illumination *f* de l'ouverture

◊ **illuminance** *noun (amount of light)* éclairement *m*

illustrate *verb* illustrer; **the book is illustrated in colour** = ce livre comporte des illustrations en couleur; **the manual is illustrated with charts and pictures of the networking connections** = le manuel contient des graphiques et des illustrations de configurations de réseaux

◊ **illustration** *noun (in a book)* illustration *f;* **the book has twenty-five pages of full-colour illustrations** = on trouve dans le livre 25 pages d'illustrations en couleur

image *noun* **(a)** *(of an area of memory)* image *f* **(b)** *(picture)* image; **image area** = zone *f* d'image; **image carrier** = support *m* de polices de caractères; *(video)* porteuse *f* d'image *or* de signal vidéo; **image degradation** = dégradation *f* de l'image; **image distortion** = distorsion *f* de l'image; **image enhancer** =

amplificateur *m* *or* intensificateur *m* d'image; **image master** = feuille *f* de style; **image plane** = plan *m* focal; **image processing** = traitement *m* de l'image; **image processor** = (i) système *m* de traitement de l'image *or* analyseur *m* d'image; (ii) processeur *m* d'image; **image retention** = rémanence *f* de l'image; **image scanner** = scanner *m* d'image; **image sensor** = capteur *m* d'images; **image stability** = stabilité *f* de l'image; **image storage space** = espace *m* mémoire de l'image *or* zone de stockage de l'image; **image table** = table *f* d'attributs

◊ **imaging** *noun* imagerie *f* médicale *or* de synthèse; **magnetic resonance imaging** = imagerie *f* par résonance magnétique (IRM); **X-ray imaging** = radioscopie *f*

immediate *adjective* immédiat, -e; **immediate access store (IAS)** = mémoire *f* interne (à accès immédiat); **immediate addressing** = adressage immédiat; **immediate instruction** = instruction immédiate; **immediate mode** = mode immédiat; **immediate operand** = opérande immédiat; **immediate processing** = traitement *m* immédiat

immunity *see* INTERFERENCE

impact *noun* (striking) impact *m*; **impact printer** = imprimante *f* à impact

impedance *noun* impédance *f*; **impedance matching** = accord *m* d'impédance; **impedance matching a transmitter and receiver minimizes power losses to transmitted signals** = l'accord d'impédance entre un émetteur et un récepteur réduit la perte de puissance des signaux transmis; **impedance mismatch** = désaccord *m* d'impédance

implant *verb* implanter; **the dopant is implanted into the substrate** = le dopant est implanté dans le substrat

implement *verb* implémenter *or* réaliser *or* exécuter
◊ **implementation** *noun* implémentation *f* *or* réalisation *f* *or* version *f*; **the latest implementation of the software runs much faster** = la dernière version du logiciel est beaucoup plus rapide

implication *noun* (logical operation) implication *f*

implied addressing *noun* adressage *m* implicite; **implied addressing for the accumulator is used in the instruction LDA,16** = l'adressage implicite pour l'accumulateur est inclus dans l'instruction LDA,16

import *verb* (a) (goods) importer (b) (data) importer; **you can import images from the CAD package into the DTP program** = il est possible d'importer des images d'un logiciel CAO dans un programme de PAO; **imported signal** = signal *m* importé
◊ **importation** *noun* (into a system) importation *f*

QUOTE text and graphics importation from other systems is possible
Publish

impression *noun* (printrun) tirage *m*; (printing) impression *f*; **impression cylinder** = cylindre *m* *or* tambour *m* d'impression

imprint *noun* (publisher's or printer's name) nom *f* de l'éditeur *or* de l'imprimeur

impulse *noun* impulsion *f* *or* excitation *f*
◊ **impulsive** *adjective* de courte durée; **impulsive noise** = bruit *m* *or* interférence *f* de courte durée

inaccurate *adjective* incorrect, -e *or* inexact, -e; **he entered an inaccurate password** = il a tapé le mauvais mot de passe
◊ **inaccuracy** *noun* erreur *f* *or* inexactitude *f*; **the bibliography is full of inaccuracies** = on trouve des tas d'erreurs dans la bibliographie

inactive *adjective* inactif, -ive *or* au repos *or* à l'arrêt

in-band signalling *noun* transmission *f* de signaux sur la bande vocale

inbuilt *adjective* intégré, -ée; **this software has inbuilt error correction** = ce logiciel possède un système de correction d'erreurs intégré

in camera process *noun* traitement *m* instantané d'un film

incandescence *noun* incandescence *f*
◊ **incandescent** *adjective* incandescent, -e; **current passing through gas and heating a filament in a light bulb causes it to produce incandescent light** = le passage du courant qui chauffe le filament dans une ampoule contenant un gaz, produit une lumière incandescente

inches-per-second (ips) (nombre de) pouces *mpl* par seconde *or* pouce(s)/seconde

in-circuit emulator *noun* émulateur *m* intégré au circuit; **this in-circuit emulator is used to test the floppy disk controller by emulating a disk drive** = cet émulateur intégré au circuit sert à tester le contrôleur de la disquette, en simulant le fonctionnement d'un lecteur de disquettes

inclined orbit *noun* orbite *f* inclinée

inclusion *noun* inclusion *f*
◊ **inclusive** *adjective* inclusif, -ive; *(logical function)* **inclusive OR** = OU inclusif

incoming *adjective* qui vient de l'extérieur; **incoming message** = message *m* reçu; **incoming traffic** = (nombre de) messages reçus *or* données reçues

incompatible *adjective* incompatible *or* non compatible; **they tried to link the two systems, but found they were incompatible** = en essayant de relier les deux systèmes, ils les ont trouvés incompatibles

incorrect *adjective* incorrect, -e *or* inexact, -e *or* erroné, -ée; **the input data was incorrect, so the output was also incorrect** = les données saisies étant incorrectes, les résultats à la sortie étaient par le fait même erronés
◊ **incorrectly** *adverb* incorrectement *or* mal; **the data was incorrectly keyboarded** = les données ont été incorrectement saisies

increment 1 *noun* **(a)** *(addition of a number)* incrémentation *f or* augmentation *f;* **an increment is added to the counter each time a pulse is detected** = le compteur est incrémenté à chaque impulsion **(b)** *(number added)* incrément *m;* **increase the increment to three** = augmentez l'incrément à trois **2** *verb* **(a)** *(to increase a number)* augmenter *or* incrémenter; **the counter is incremented each time an instruction is executed** = le compteur est incrémenté à chaque instruction exécutée **(b)** *(to move forward)* avancer d'un pas *or* d'une instruction **(c)** *(to move a document forward)* faire avancer d'un pas
◊ **incremental computer** *noun* ordinateur incrémentiel *or* à valeurs variables; **incremental data** = donnée(s) incrémentielle(s); **incremental plotter** = traceur incrémentiel

indent 1 *noun* alinéa *m* **2** *verb* faire un alinéa; **the first line of the paragraph is indented two spaces** = comptez deux espaces pour l'alinéa du premier paragraphe
◊ **indentation** *noun* alinéa *m*

independent *adjective* indépendant, -e; **machine-independent language** = langage *m* standard *or* universel
◊ **independently** *adverb* indépendamment *or* séparément; **in spooling, the printer is acting independently of the keyboard** = avec un spool, l'imprimante fonctionne indépendamment du clavier; **each item is indexed independently** = ces articles sont indexés séparément

indeterminate system *noun* système *m* indéterminé

index 1 *noun* **(a)** *(in a computer memory)* index *m;* **index build** = indexation *m; (of videotext)* **index page** = page *f* index **(b)** *(of book)* index **(c)** *(list)* index *or* répertoire *m;* **index card** = fiche *f;* **index letter** = indicatif *m* littéral; **index number** = indicatif numérique **(d)** *(computer address)* adresse indexée; **index register (IR)** = registre *m* d'index; **index value word** = mot *m* d'index **(e)**

(guide mark on film or microfilm) indice *m* de position; *(in the edge of a disk)* **index hole** = perforation *f* de marquage (du bord d'un disque) **2** *verb* **(a)** *(a book)* préparer un index *or* indexer; **the book was sent out for indexing** = le livre a été envoyé à l'extérieur pour la préparation de l'index; **the book has been badly indexed** = l'index de ce livre est très mal fait **(b)** *(to mark with an index)* indexer; **indexed address** = adresse *f* indexée; **indexed addressing** = adressage indexé; **indexed file** = fichier *m* indexé; **indexed instruction** = instruction *f* indexée; **indexed sequential access method (ISAM)** = méthode *f* d'accès séquentiel indexé (ISAM); **indexed sequential storage** = mémoire *f* séquentielle indexée

◊ **indexer** *noun (of a book)* personne qui prépare un index *or* auteur *m* d'un index

◊ **indexing** *noun* **(a)** *(in a computer)* indexation *f* **(b)** *(list of records)* classement *m* *or* indexation *f*; **indexing language** = langage *m* d'indexation **(c)** *(book)* préparation de l'index d'un livre; **computer indexing** = indexation sur ordinateur *or* préparation d'un index à l'aide d'un ordinateur

QUOTE in microcomputer implementations of COBOL, indexed files are usually based on some type of B-tree structure which allows rapid data retrieval based on the value of the key being used

PC-User

indicate *verb* indiquer *or* montrer

◊ **indication** *noun* indication *f*

◊ **indicator** *noun* indicateur *m;* **indicator chart** = tableau *m* des indicateurs; **indicator flag** = indicateur *or* témoin *m or* marqueur *m or* drapeau *m or* balise *f;* **indicator light** = voyant *m* (lumineux)

indirect *adjective* indirect, -e; **indirect addressing** = adressage *m* indirect; **indirect ray** = rayonnement *m* indirect

individual **1** *noun* individu *m* *or* personne *f;* **each individual has his own password to access the system** = chaque personne possède son propre mot de passe pour accéder au système **2** *adjective* individuel, -elle *or* personnel, -elle; **the individual workstations are all linked to the mainframe** = les divers

postes de travail indépendants sont tous reliés à l'ordinateur principal

induce *verb (electricity)* induire *or* produire un courant induit *or* produire une induction; *(mathematics)* induire; **induced failure** = défaillance *f* induite *or* ayant une cause externe; **induced interference** = interférence *f* induite *or* causée par une autre machine

◊ **inductance** *noun* inductance *f*

◊ **induction** *noun* *(electricity or mathematics)* induction *f;* **induction coil** = bobine *f* d'induction

◊ **inductive coordination** *noun* coordination *f* inductive

◊ **inductor** *noun* inducteur *m or* bobine d'induction

inert gas *adjective* gaz *m* inerte

inequivalence *noun (logical function)* exclusion *f* réciproque

inference *noun* **(a)** *(operation)* inférence *f* *or* déduction *f;* **inference engine** *or* **machine** = moteur *m* d'inférence **(b)** *(result)* déduction *f* *or* inférence; **inference control** = contrôle *m* d'inférence

inferior figures *noun* indices *mpl*

infinite *adjective* infini, -e; **infinite loop** = boucle *f* sans fin *or* infinie

◊ **infinity** *noun (quantity or distance)* infini *m*

infix notation *noun* notation *f* infixée

informatics *noun* (science de) l'informatique *f*

information *noun* **(a)** *(knowledge)* information *f* **(b)** *(data)* information *or* données *fpl;* **information bearer channel** = voie *f* de transmission d'informations; **information content** = quantité *f* d'information; **information flow control** = contrôle *m* de flux d'informations; **information input** = saisie *f* de données; *(on screen)* **information line** = ligne *f* d'état *or* d'information; **information management system** = système *m* de gestion de l'information; **information networks** = réseaux *mpl* d'information *or* réseaux informatiques; **information output =** *(on screen)* affichage *m* de données; *(on printer)* sortie *f* d'imprimante; **information processing =** traitement *m* de données *or* de l'information; **information processor =** ordinateur *m* (utilisé pour le traitement de l'information); **information provider (IP) =** source *f* d'information *or* service *m* (fournisseur) d'information *or* service de base de données spécialisée (pour vidéotex); **information rate =** vitesse *f* de sortie de l'information; **information retrieval (IR) =** (i) recherche *f* documentaire; (ii) extraction *f or* restitution *f* de données; **information retrieval centre =** centre de recherche documentaire *or* centre serveur *or* banque de données; **information storage =** stockage *m* de données *or* de l'information; **information storage and retrieval (ISR) =** stockage et restitution de données; **information structure =** structure *f* de données; **information system =** système *m* informatique; **information technology (IT) =** informatique *f or* techniques *f* de l'information; **information theory =** théorie *f* de l'information; **information transfer channel =** canal *m or* voie de transmission de l'information

QUOTE Information Technology is still too young to be an established discipline. However, the national and international IT research programmes are reasonably agreed that it comprises electronics, computing and telecommunications
Electronics and Power

infra- *prefix* infra-; *(between 300Hz-3KHz)* **infra-low frequency (ILF) =** ondes *fpl* kilométriques; *see also* FREQUENCY

infrared *adjective* infrarouge; **infrared camera =** caméra *f* de vision nocturne; **infrared communications =** communication *f* par infrarouge; **infrared detector =** détecteur *m* d'infrarouge; *(process)* **infrared photography =** photo *f* avec film sensible aux infrarouges; **infrared sights =** instruments *mpl* de vision aux infrarouges

◊ **infrasonic frequency** *noun* fréquence *f* infrasonique

◊ **infrastructure** *noun* infrastructure *f*

infringement *noun (breaking the law)* violation *f or* transgression *f;* **copyright infringement =** contrefaçon *f or* copie *f* illégale (d'une oeuvre) *or* violation *f* du droit d'auteur

inherent addressing *noun* adressage *m* inhérent *or* particulier

inherited error *noun* erreur *f* transmise *or* héritée

inhibit *verb* inhiber *or* arrêter *or* stopper; **inhibiting input =** signal *m* d'invalidation *or* d'interdiction de transmission

in-house *adverb & adjective* (i) sur place *or* dans l'entreprise; (ii) interne *or* de la maison; **all the data processing is done in-house =** tout le travail informatique se fait dans l'entreprise; **the in-house maintenance staff deal with all our equipment =** tous nos équipements sont suivis par l'équipe de maintenance de la maison

initial 1 *adjective (at the beginning)* initial, -e *or* au départ; **initial address =** adresse initiale *or* de lancement; **initial condition =** condition initiale; **initial error =** erreur *f* au départ; **initial instructions =** instructions *f* de lancement *or* instructions initiales; **initial program header =** lanceur *m* de programme de chargement; **initial program loader (IPL) =** chargeur *m* de programme de lancement; **initial value =** valeur initiale **2** *noun (first letter)* initiale *f;* **(set of) initials =** sigle *m; what do the initials IBM stand for? =** que signifie le sigle IBM?
◊ **initialization** *noun (process)* initialisation *f;* **initialization is often carried out without the user knowing =** l'initialisation peut souvent s'effectuer à l'insu de l'utilisateur
◊ **initialize** *verb (a system)* initialiser

injection laser *noun* laser *m* de portance
◊ **injection logic** *see* INTEGRATED

ink 1 *noun* encre *f;* **ink-jet printer =** imprimante *f* à jet d'encre; **colour ink-jet technology and thermal transfer technology compete with each other =** les techniques du jet d'encre couleur et du transfert thermique sont concurrentielles; **magnetic ink** = encre magnétique; **magnetic ink character recognition (MICR)** = reconnaissance *f* de caractères magnétiques **2** *verb* imprégner *or* couvrir d'encre

> QUOTE ink-jet printers work by squirting a fine stream of ink onto the paper
> *Personal Computer World*

inlay card *noun (inside tape or disk box)* étiquette *f* interne

inline 1 *noun* circuit *m* linéaire **2** *adverb* en ligne; *(that contains no loops)* **in-line program** = programme *m* linéaire; **in-line processing** = traitement *m* en ligne

inner loop *noun* boucle *f* intérieure

in phase *adverb* **(a)** *(signal)* en phase *or* synchronisé, -ée **(b)** *(film)* synchronisé, -ée

input (i/p *or* **I/P) 1** *verb* entrer *or* saisir *or* introduire (des données); **the data was input via a modem** = les données ont été introduites par l'intermédiaire d'un modem NOTE: **inputs - inputting - input 2** *noun* **(a)** *(action)* entrée *f or* saisie *f or* introduction *f* (de données) **(b)** *(data)* données *fpl* d'entrée *or* données saisies; **input area** = zone *f* d'entrée; **input block** = bloc *m* d'entrée; **input buffer register** = registre *m* tampon des entrées; **input device** = périphérique *m* d'entrée; **input lead** = câble *m* d'entrée *or* (câble de) liaison *f* d'un périphérique d'entrée; *(program)* **input mode** = mode *m* (d') entrée; **input port** = port *m* (d') entrée; **input register** = registre *m* d'entrée; **input routine** = routine *f* d'entrée *or* d'introduction de données; *(routine or area)* **input section** = section *f* d'entrée; **input statement** = déclaration *f or* message *m* d'entrée; **input storage** = mémoire *f* d'entrée; **input unit** = périphérique *m* d'entrée; **input work queue** = file *f* d'attente des données d'entrée **(c)** *(electrical signal)* signal *m* d'entrée

◊ **input-bound** *or* **input-limited** *adjective (program)* (programme) limité par la vitesse d'entrée *or* avec contrainte de vitesse d'entrée

◊ **input/output (I/O)** *noun* entrée/sortie *f;* **input/output buffer** = tampon *m* (d') entrée/sortie; **input/output bus** = bus *m* (d') entrée/sortie; **input/output channel** = canal *m or* voie *f* d'entrée/sortie; **input/output control program** = programme de contrôle d'entrée/sortie; **input/output controller** = contrôleur *m* d'entrée/sortie; **input/output device** *or* **unit** = périphérique *m* d'entrée/sortie; **input/output executive** = superviseur *m* d'entrée/sortie; **input/output instruction** = instruction *f* d'entrée/sortie; **input/output interface** = interface *f* d'entrée/sortie; *(signal)* **input/output interrupt** = (signal d') interruption *f* d'entrée/sortie; **input/output library** = bibliothèque *f* de programmes d'entrée/sortie; **input/output mapping** = configuration *f* d'entrée/sortie; **input/output port** = port *m* (d') entrée/sortie; **the joystick can be connected to the input/output port** = le manche à balai peut être connecté sur le port entrée/sortie; **input/output processor (IOP)** = processeur *m* d'entrée/sortie; **input/output referencing** = référençage *m* d'entrée/sortie; **input/output register** = registre *m* d'entrée/sortie; **input/output request (IORQ)** = requête *f* d'entrée/sortie; **input/output status word** = mot *m* d'état d'entrée/sortie; **parallel input/output (PIO)** = entrée/sortie *f* parallèle

> QUOTE inputs include raster scan files and ASCII files
> *Byte*

inquiry *noun* demande *f or* requête *f or* interrogation *f;* **inquiry character (ENQ)** = caractère *m* de requête *or* d'interrogation; **inquiry station** = poste *m* d'interrogation; **inquiry/response (function)** = (fonction) demande/ réponse *or* interrogation/réponse

insert *verb* **(a)** introduire; **first insert the system disk in the left slot** = introduire d'abord la disquette système dans le lecteur gauche **(b)** *(to add new text)* ajouter; **inserted subroutine** = sous-programme *m* additionnel

◊ **insertion loss** *noun (attenuation to a signal)* perte *f or* affaiblissement *m* d'insertion

◊ **insert mode** *noun* mode *m* insertion

install *verb* mettre en place *or* installer; **the system is easy to install and simple to use** = ce système est facile à mettre en place et à utiliser

◊ **installation** *noun* **(a)** *(equipment)* matériel *m* *or* équipement *m* informatique; **the engineers are still testing the new installation** = les ingénieurs n'ont pas terminé l'essai du nouveau système **(b)** *(setting up)* mise *f* en place *or* installation *f;* **the installation of the equipment took only a few hours** = il n'a fallu que quelques heures pour mettre l'équipement en place

instantaneous access *noun* accès *m* instantané

instant replay *noun (of video film)* visionnage *m* immédiat

instruct *verb* donner des instructions à quelqu'un *or* à un ordinateur

◊ **instruction** *noun* instruction *f;* **the instruction PRINT is used in this BASIC dialect as an operand to display the following data** = l'instruction PRINT est un opérande employé en langage BASIC pour l'affichage des données suivantes; **absolute instruction** = instruction *f* absolue; **arithmetic instruction** = instruction arithmétique; **blank** *or* **dummy** *or* **null instruction** = instruction nulle *or* de remplissage; **breakpoint instruction** = instruction d'arrêt; **decision** *or* **discrimination instruction** = instruction (d'opération) conditionnelle; **dummy instruction** = *see* BLANK INSTRUCTION; **executive instruction** = instruction de superviseur; **four-address instruction** = instruction à quatre adresses; **indexed instruction** = instruction indexée; **input/output instruction** = instruction d'entrée/sortie; **jump instruction** = instruction de branchement *or* de saut; **macro instruction** = macro-instruction *f;* **no-op instruction** = instruction vide *or* factice *or* de remplissage; **n-plus-one instruction** = instruction à n adresse(s) plus une; **supervisory instruction** = instruction de contrôle *or* de surveillance; **three-address-instruction** = instruction à trois adresses; **two-address-instruction** = instruction à deux adresses; **two-plus-one-address instruction** = instruction à deux adresses plus une; **instruction address** = adresse *f* d'instruction;

instruction address register (IAR) registre *m* d'adresse d'instruction; **instruction area** = zone *f* d'instruction (dans une mémoire); **instruction cache** = antémémoire *f* d'instruction; **instruction character** = caractère *m* d'instruction; **instruction codes** = codes d'instruction; *(IAR* or *program counter)* **instruction counter** = compteur *m* d'instruction *or* registre d'adresse d'instruction; **instruction cycle** = cycle *m* d'instruction; **instruction cycle time** = temps *m* de cycle d'instruction; **instruction decoder** = décodeur *m* d'instructions; **instruction execution time** = temps *m* d'exécution d'une instruction; **instruction format** = format *m* d'instruction; **instruction modification** = modification *f* d'une instruction; **instruction pipelining** = mode d'exécution d'instructions en pipeline *or* enchaînement d'instructions avec recouvrement; **instruction processor** = processeur *m* d'instruction; **instruction register (IR)** = registre d'instruction; **instruction repertoire** *or* **set** = jeu *m* d'instructions; **instruction storage** = *(area)* mémoire *f* d'instruction; *(storing)* mise *f* en mémoire *or* stockage *m* d'instruction; **instruction time** = temps *m* d'exécution d'une instruction *or* temps d'instruction; **instruction word** = (mot) instruction; **the manufacturers of this CPU have decided that JMP will be the instruction word to call the jump function** = les fabricants du CPU ont décidé que l'instruction JMP servirait à faire un branchement

instrumentation *noun (set of tools)* instruments *mpl; (electronic devices)* instrumentation *f;* **we've improved the instrumentation on this model to keep you better informed of the machine's position** = nous avons amélioré l'instrumentation se rapportant à ce modèle pour que vous puissiez mieux suivre l'état de la machine

insufficient *adjective* insuffisant, -e; **there is insufficient time to train the keyboarders properly** = il est impossible de former convenablement un opérateur dans un délai aussi court

insulate *verb* isoler

◊ **insulation material** *noun* isolant *m* *or* matériau *m* isolant

◇ **insulator** *noun* matériau isolant

integer *noun* (nombre) entier *m;* **double-precision integer** = nombre entier en double précision; **integer BASIC** = BASIC pour nombres entiers

◇ **integral** *noun (device)* intégré, -ée; **the integral disk drives and modem reduce desk space** = puisque les lecteurs de disquettes et le modem sont intégrés, l'encombrement est réduit

QUOTE an integral 7 inch amber display screen, two half-height disk drives and terminal emulation for easy interfacing with mainframes
Computing Today

integrated *adjective* intégré -ée; **integrated database** = base *f* de données intégrée; **integrated data processing (IDP)** = (système de) traitement de données intégré; **integrated device** = dispositif intégré; **our competitor's computer doesn't have an integrated disk drive like this model** = l'ordinateur concurrent ne possède pas de lecteur de disquettes intégré comme ce modèle-ci; **integrated digital access (IDA)** = accès au réseau numérique intégré; **integrated digital network** = réseau numérique intégré (RNI); **integrated emulator** = émulateur intégré; **integrated injection logic (IIL)** = logique *f* intégrée à injection; **integrated modem** = modem intégré; **integrated office** = (système de) bureautique intégrée; **integrated optical circuit** = circuit optique intégré; **integrated program** = programme *m* intégré; **integrated services digital network (ISDN)** = réseau *m* numérique à intégration de services (RNIS); **integrated software** = logiciel intégré

◇ **integrated circuit (IC)** *noun* circuit intégré

◇ **integration** *noun* intégration *f;* **small scale integration (SSI)** = intégration à petite échelle; **medium scale integration (MSI)** = intégration à moyenne échelle; **large scale integration (LSI)** = intégration à grande échelle; **super large scale integration (SLSI)** = intégration à super grande échelle; **very large scale integration (VLSI)** = intégration à très grande échelle; **wafer scale integration** = intégration sur tranche de silicium

integrity *noun* intégrité *f;* **integrity of a file** = intégrité d'un fichier; **the data in file has integrity** = les données de ce fichier n'ont pas été corrompues

QUOTE it is intended for use in applications demanding high data integrity, such as archival storage or permanent databases
Minicomputer News

intelligence *noun (of person or machine)* intelligence *f;* **artificial intelligence (AI)** = intelligence artificielle (IA)

◇ **intelligent** *noun (person or program or machine)* intelligent, -e; **intelligent device** = machine intelligente; **intelligent knowledge-based system (IKBS)** *or* **expert system** = système intelligent à base de connaissances *or* système expert; **intelligent spacer** = fonction césure intelligente; **intelligent tutoring system** = formation assistée par système expert; **intelligent terminal** = terminal intelligent NOTE: the opposite is **dumb terminal**

INTELSAT = INTERNATIONAL TELECOMMUNICATIONS SATELLITE ORGANIZATION INTELSAT

intensity *noun (of signal or light or sound)* intensité *f*

inter- *prefix (between)* inter-; **interblock** = entre blocs *or* interbloc

interact *verb (of two things)* interagir

◇ **interaction** *noun* interaction *f*

◇ **interactive** *adjective (system or software)* interactif, -ive; *(mode)* dialogué, -ée *or* conversationnel, -elle; **interactive cable television** = télévision câblée interactive; **interactive debugging system** = système de déverminage *or* de débogage interactif; **interactive graphics** = représentations graphiques interactives *or* infographie interactive; **the space invaders machine has great interactive graphics, the player controls the position of his spaceship with the joystick** = le jeu (électronique) 'les envahisseurs de l'espace' présente d'excellents graphiques interactifs; le joueur contrôle la position de son vaisseau spatial avec la manette (de jeu); **interactive media** = moyens de communication interactifs; **interactive mode** *or* **processing** = mode interactif *or* mode dialogué *or* mode conversationnel;

interactive routine = routine interactive; **interactive system** = système interactif; **interactive terminal** = terminal interactif *or* conversationnel; **interactive video** = vidéo *or* vidéographie interactive; **interactive videotext** = dialogue *m* vidéotex *or* vidéographie interactive

QUOTE soon pupils will be able to go shopping in a French town from the comfort of their classroom -carried to their destination by interactive video, a medium which combines the power of the computer with the audiovisual impact of video

Electronics & Power

QUOTE interactivity is a buzzword you've been hearing a lot lately. Resign yourself to it because you're going to be hearing a lot more of it

Music Technology

interblock gap (IBG) *noun* espace *m* interbloc

intercarrier noise *noun* interférence *f* entre porteuses; **television intercarrier noise is noticed when the picture and the sound signal carriers clash** = on note des interférences de porteuses sur une télévision lorsque la porteuse son et la porteuse image se rencontrent

interchange 1 *noun* échange *m or* transfert *m or* permutation *f;* **the machine allows document interchange between it and other machines without reformatting** = avec cette machine, on peut transférer des documents d'une machine à l'autre sans qu'il soit nécessaire de reformater **2** *verb* échanger (une chose contre une autre) *or* mettre une chose à la place d'une autre

◊ **interchangeable** *adjective* interchangeable

intercharacter spacing *noun* *(wordprocessing)* espacement *m* (proportionnel) de caractères

intercom *noun* Interphone® *m*

interconnect *verb* *(of several things)* interconnecter *or* relier les un(e)s aux autres; **a series of interconnected terminals** = une série de postes reliés les uns aux autres

◊ **interconnection** *noun* **(a)** *(connecting material)* interconnexion *f or* liaison *f* (entre plusieurs machines *or* dispositifs)

(b) *(connection)* raccordement *m* (au réseau téléphonique)

interface 1 *noun* interface *f;* **EIA interface** = interface EIA; **general purpose interface adapter (GPIA)** = interface universelle GPIA; **general purpose interface bus (GPIB)** = bus universel GPIB; **input/output interface** = interface d'entrée/sortie; **interface card** = carte *f* (d') interface; **interface message processor** = serveur *m* de message; **interface processor** = processeur *m* d'interface; **interface routines** = routines *fpl* d'interface; **parallel interface** = interface parallèle (NOTE: parallel interfaces are usually used to drive printers) **serial interface** = interface série (NOTE: the most common serial interface is RS232C) **2** *verb* **to interface with** = relier à (utilisant une interface) *or* interfacer avec

◊ **interfacing** *noun* *(hardware or software)* (d') interface *f*

interfere *verb* **to interfere with something** = interférer *or* nuire (à)

◊ **interference** *noun* interférence *f;* **interference fading** = affaiblissement *m or* évanouissement *m* (du signal) dû au brouillage; **interference immunity** = insensibilité *f or* tolérance *f* aux interférences; **interference pattern** = empreinte *f* d'interférence; **constructive interference** = interférence constructive; **destructive interference** = interférence destructive; **electromagnetic interference** = interférence électromagnétique; **induced interference** = interférence causée par des machines *or* interférence induite

interior label *noun* label *m* d'identification (sur le support magnétique)

interlace *verb* entrelacer

interleaved *adjective* **(a)** *(sheets of paper)* interfolié -ée *or* placé, -ée entre deux feuilles; **blank paper was interleaved with the newly printed text to prevent the ink running** = on avait placé des feuilles blanches entre les pages nouvellement imprimées pour éviter les coulures d'encre **(b)** *(sections of programs)* imbriqué,-ée *or* entrelacé, -ée

◊ **interleaving** *noun* **(a)** *(putting blank paper between printed sheets)* interfoliage *m* **(b)** *(dealing with processes alternately)* entrelacement *m or* emboîtement *m;* **multiprocessor interleaving** = multiprogrammation *f* **(c)** *(dividing data into sections)* entrelacement

> QUOTE there are two separate 40-bit arrays on each card to allow interleaved operation, achieving data access every 170ns machine cycle
> *Minicomputer News*

inter-library loan (ILL) *noun* prêt *m* interbibliothèque

interlinear spacing *noun (on a phototypesetter)* interligne *m*

interlock 1 *noun* **(a)** *(security device)* verrouillage *m or* protection *f* (par mot de passe) **(b)** *(synchronizing)* synchronisation *f;* **interlock projector** = projecteur *m* synchronisé **2** *verb* verrouiller

interlude *noun (routine)* interlude *m*

intermediate *adjective* intermédiaire; **intermediate access memory (IAM)** = mémoire *f* à accès intermédiaire; **intermediate code** = code *m* intermédiaire; **intermediate file** = fichier *m* intermédiaire; **intermediate materials** = support *m* intermédiaire; **those slides and photographs are the intermediate materials to be mastered onto the video disk** = ces diapositives et ces photos sont les supports intermédiaires qui doivent être recopiés sur le vidéodisque; **intermediate storage** = mémoire intermédiaire; **intermediate user** = utilisateur *m* intermédiaire

◊ **intermediate frequency (if** *or* **IF)** *noun* fréquence intermédiaire

intermittent error *noun* erreur *f* intermittente

internal *adjective* interne *or* intérieur, -e; **internal arithmetic** = arithmétique *f* interne; **internal character code** = code *m* de caractères interne; **internal format** = format *m* interne; **internal language** = langage *m* interne *or* langage machine

◊ **internal memory** *or* **store** *noun* mémoire *f* interne

◊ **internal sort** *noun* tri *m* en mémoire interne

◊ **internally stored program** *noun* programme *m* résident

international *adjective* international, -e; **international direct dialling (IDD)** = système téléphonique automatique international; **international dialling code** = indicatif *m* (téléphonique) international; **international number** = indicatif (téléphonique) du pays; **international prefix code** = INTERNATIONAL DIALLING CODE *(ten-digit identifying number allocated to every new book published)* **international standard book number (ISBN)** = ISBN *m; (identifying number for journals or magazines)* **international standard serial number (ISSN)** = ISSN *m*

◊ **International Standards Organization (ISO)** *noun* organisme international de normalisation ISO; **International Standards Organization Open System Interconnection (ISO/OSI)** = système ISO/OSI

interpolation *noun* interpolation *f*

interpret *verb* interpréter *or* traduire; *(programming language)* **interpreted language** = langage interprété

◊ **interpreter** *noun (software)* (programme) interpréteur *m*

◊ **interpretative** *adjective* interprétatif, -ive; **interpretative code** = code interprétatif; **interpretative program** = programme interprétatif

interrecord gap = INTERBLOCK GAP

interrogation *noun* interrogation *f;* **file interrogation** = interrogation de fichier

interrupt 1 *verb* interrompre *or* arrêter *or* stopper **2** *noun* **(a)** *(stopping of a transmission)* interruption *f* **(b)** *(signal)* interruption; **this printer port design uses an interrupt line to let the CPU know it is ready to receive data** = ce modèle de connecteur d'imprimante utilise une ligne d'interruption pour avertir l'unité centrale qu'il est prêt à recevoir des données; **armed interrupt** = interruption validée *or* activée; **interrupt**

disable = invalider or interdire une interruption; **interrupt enable** = valider une interruption; **interrupt handler (IH)** = gestionnaire m d'interruptions; **interrupt level** = niveau m d'interruption; **interrupt line** = ligne f d'interruption; **interrupt mask** = masque m d'interruption; **interrupt priorities** = priorités fpl d'interruption; see also NON-MASKABLE INTERRUPT; **interrupt request** = demande f d'interruption; **interrupt servicing** = (opérations de) contrôle et exécution d'interruption; **interrupt signal** = signal m d'interruption; **interrupt stacking** = constitution de pile d'interruptions; **maskable interrupt** = interruption qui peut être invalidée or masquée; **non-maskable interrupt (NMI)** = interruption obligatoire or qui ne peut être invalidée or qui ne peut être masquée; **polled interrupt** = interruption d'appel; **transparent interrupt** = interruption transparente or contrôlée; **vectored interrupt** = interruption vectorisée

intersection noun intersection f

interstation muting noun réduction f du bruit d'interférence interstation

interval noun intervalle m or délai m; **there was an interval between pressing the key and the starting of the printout** = il y a eu un intervalle entre le moment où on a appuyé sur la touche et la mise en marche de l'imprimante

intervention noun intervention f

interword spacing noun espacement m entre les mots

intimate adjective (software) (logiciel) sur mesure or de constructeur or adapté à un ordinateur

intrinsic adjective intrinsèque; **the base material for ICs is an intrinsic semiconductor which is then doped** = le matériau de base utilisé dans la fabrication des circuits intégrés est un semi-conducteur intrinsèque auquel on ajoute un dopant

introduce verb introduire or insérer or glisser; **errors were introduced into the text at keyboarding** = il s'est glissé des erreurs au cours de la saisie du texte

intrusion noun intrusion f

invalid adjective invalide; **he tried to use an invalid password** = il a tenté d'utiliser un mot de passe qui n'était pas valide; **the message was that the instruction was invalid** = d'après le message, l'instruction était invalide

inverse noun contraire m or inverse m or opposé m; **the inverse of true is false** = le contraire de vrai est faux; **the inverse of 1 is 0** = l'opposé de 1 est 0; **inverse video** = vidéo inversée

◊ **inversion** noun inversion f; **the inversion of a binary digit takes place in one's complement** = il y a inversion du chiffre binaire dans le complément à un

◊ **invert** verb inverser; **inverted commas (" ")** = guillemets mpl; **inverted file** = fichier inversé

◊ **inverter** noun (a) (logical gate) inverseur m (b) (circuit) **inverter (AC/DC)** = inverseur m de courant

invitation noun invitation f; **invitation to send (ITS)** = (signal d') invitation à transmettre

◊ **invite** verb inviter (quelqu'un à faire quelque chose)

invoke verb (a program) appeler

> QUOTE when an error is detected, the editor may be invoked and positioned at the statement in error
> *Personal Computer World*

involve verb comprendre or inclure; **backing up involves copying current working files onto a separate storage disk** = sauvegarder signifie faire la copie du fichier de travail actuel sur une deuxième disquette

I/O = INPUT/OUTPUT entrée/sortie f; **I/O bound** = (programme) limité par la vitesse d'entrée/sortie *or* avec contrainte de vitesse d'entrée/sortie; **I/O buffer =** tampon *m* (d') entrée/sortie; **I/O bus =** bus *m* (d') entrée/sortie; **I/O channel =** voie *f or* canal *m* (d') entrée/sortie; **I/O device =** périphérique *m* (d') entrée/sortie; **I/O file =** fichier (d') entrée/sortie; **I/O instruction =** instruction *f* (d') entrée/sortie; **I/O mapping =** adressage *m* des entrées/sorties; *compare with* MEMORY MAPPING; **I/O port =** port *m* (d') entrée/sortie; **I/O request =** requête *f* d'entrée/sortie; **I/O processor =** processeur *m* (d') entrée/sortie

ion *noun* ion *m*
◇ **ionosphere** *noun* ionosphère *f*

IOP = INPUT/OUTPUT PROCESSOR

IORQ = INPUT/OUTPUT REQUEST

i/p *or* **I/P** = INPUT

ip = INFORMATION PROVIDER *(company or user providing information for use in videotext system)* source *f* d'information *or* service (fournisseur) d'information *or* service de base de données spécialisée (pour vidéotex); **ip terminal =** terminal *m* d'entrée (de données) vidéotex

IPL = INITIAL PROGRAM LOADER

ips = INCHES PER SECOND

IR (a) = INFORMATION RETRIEVAL **(b)** = INDEX REGISTER **(c)** = INSTRUCTION REGISTER

IRC = INFORMATION RETRIEVAL CENTRE

irretrievable *adjective* qui ne peut être restitué, -ée *or* extrait, -e; **the files are irretrievable since the computer crashed =** il est impossible de restituer *or* d'extraire les fichiers depuis la panne

irreversible process *noun* processus *m* irréversible

ISAM = INDEXED SEQUENTIAL ACCESS METHOD

ISBN = INTERNATIONAL STANDARD BOOK NUMBER

ISDN = INTEGRATED SERVICES DIGITAL NETWORK

ISO = INTERNATIONAL STANDARDS ORGANIZATION
◇ **ISO/OSI** = INTERNATIONAL STANDARDS ORGANIZATION OPEN SYSTEM INTERCONNECTION

isolate *verb (to separate or to insulate)* isoler; **isolated adaptive routing =** routage *m* adaptatif protégé; **isolated location =** zone *f* protégée
◇ **isolation** *noun* isolation *f;* **isolation transformer =** transformateur *m* d'isolement *or* de protection
◇ **isolator** *noun (device or material which isolates)* isolateur *m*

isotropic *adjective* isotrope; **isotropic radiator =** émetteur *m or* antenne *f* isotrope

ISR = INFORMATION STORAGE AND RETRIEVAL

ISSN = INTERNATIONAL STANDARD SERIAL NUMBER

IT = INFORMATION TECHNOLOGY

italic *adjective & noun* italique *(m)* **the headline is printed in italic and underlined =** le titre est en italique souligné; **italics =** lettres italiques *or* italiques; **all the footnotes are printed in italics =** les notes de bas de page sont toutes en italiques; **hit CTRL I to print the text in italics =** tapez CTRL I pour imprimer les italiques

item *noun* item *m or* unité *f;* **a data item can be a word or a series of figures or a record in a file =** une unité d'information peut être soit un mot, une série de chiffres ou une entrée dans un fichier; **item size =** dimension *f* d'une unité d'information *or* d'un item

iterate *or* **iterative routine** *noun*
routine *f* itérative
◇ **iteration** *noun* itération *f*
◇ **iterative process** *noun* processus *m*
itératif

ITS = INVITATION TO SEND

Jj

jack *noun* fiche *f or* jack *m; (for modem)* **data jack** = fiche *f* TELECOM (pour modem)

jacket *noun (of book)* jaquette *f; (of record)* pochette *f;* **the book jacket has the author's name on it** = on trouve le nom de l'auteur sur la jaquette du livre

jam 1 *noun (of mechanism)* coincement *m;* **jam in the paper feed** = bourrage *m* (de l'entraînement de l'imprimante) **2** *verb* **(a)** *(to block)* (se) coincer *or* bloquer; **the recorder's not working because the tape is jammed in the motor** = le magnétophone ne fonctionne pas parce que la bande est coincée dans le moteur; **lightweight copier paper will feed without jamming** = l'emploi de papier plus mince évite le bourrage **(b)** *(to prevent transmission)* brouiller; **the TV signals are being jammed from that tower** = cette tour brouille la transmission des émissions de télévision

jar *verb* déplacer brusquement *or* secouer; **you can cause trouble by turning off or jarring the PC while the disk read head is moving** = éteindre l'ordinateur ou lui donner un coup quand la tête de lecture est en marche peut causer des ennuis; **hard disks are very sensitive to jarring** = les disques durs sont très sensibles aux secousses *or* aux chocs

JCL = JOB CONTROL LANGUAGE

jet *see* INK-JET

jitter 1 *noun* tremblotement *m or* sautillement *m* (de l'image); **looking at this screen jitter is giving me a headache** = j'ai mal à la tête à force de regarder cet écran qui tremblote **2** *verb (image or screen)* trembloter

JK-flip-flop *noun* (commutateur à) bascule *f* de type JK

job *noun* tâche *f or* travail *m;* **the next job to be processed is to sort all the records** = la tâche suivante consistera à trier tous les enregistrements; **job control file** = fichier *m* de contrôle de tâche; **job control language (JCL)** = langage *m* de commande de tâche; **job control program** = programme *m* de contrôle de tâche; **job file** = fichier de travaux *or* de tâches (à exécuter); **job mix** = ensemble des travaux *or* des tâches en cours d'exécution; **job number** = numéro *m* de suite d'une tâche dans la file d'attente; **job-orientated language** = langage d'application; **job-orientated terminal** = terminal d'application *or* terminal spécialisé; **job priority** = priorité *f* d'une tâche; **job processing** = traitement *m* de tâche; **job queue** *or* **job stream** = file *f* d'attente (des tâches *or* des travaux à exécuter); **job scheduling** = planification *f* de la séquence d'exécution des tâches *or* répartition *f* des tâches; **job statement control** = contrôle *m* d'exécution des tâches; **job step** = étape *f* d'un travail; **job stream** = suite *f* de tâches; **remote job entry (RJE)** = lancement *m or* commande *f* de tâches à distance; **stacked job control** = contrôle de travaux groupés (en pile)

◇ **jobbing printer** *noun* imprimeur *m* à façon

jog *verb* (faire) avancer image par image *or* pas à pas

joggle *verb (punched cards)* taquer

join 1 *verb* **(a)** *(to put together)* joindre *or* relier **(b)** *(to combine pieces of information)* assembler *or* fusionner; **join files** = (instruction de) fusion *f* de fichiers **2** *noun (logical function)* fonction *f* d'union *or* opération *f* OU

joint denial *noun (logical function)* négation *f* connexe *or* opération *f* NON-OU *or* NI

journal *noun* **(a)** *(record of communications)* journal *m;* **journal file** = fichier *m* chronologique *or* fichier-journal **(b)** *(list of changes to a file)* journal *m or* liste *f* des modifications; **the modified records were added to the master file and noted in the journal** = les enregistrements modifiés ont été ajoutés au fichier maître et inscrits au journal des modifications **(c)** **learned journal** = revue *f* spécialisée *or* revue savante

◊ **journalist** *noun* journaliste *m&f*

joystick *noun* manche *m* à balai *or* joystick *m or* manette *f* (de jeu); **joystick port** = connecteur *m or* port *m* (pour) manche à balai; **a joystick port is provided with the home computer** = l'ordinateur personnel possède un port pour manche à balai

judder *noun* vibration *f*

jumbo chip *noun* puce *f* géante *or* circuit *m* à très haut niveau d'intégration

jump (instruction) 1 *noun* (instruction de) branchement *m or* saut *m;* **conditional jump** = branchement *m* conditionnel; **jump operation** = opération *f* de branchement; **unconditional jump** = branchement inconditionnel **2** *verb* **(a)** effectuer un branchement *or* sauter; **jump on zero** = effectuer un branchement (conditionel) à zéro **(b)** *(to miss)* sauter; **the typewriter jumped two lines** = la machine à écrire a sauté deux lignes; **the paging system has jumped two folio numbers** = le système de pagination a sauté deux numéros de pages

◊ **jumper** *noun* *(on circuit board)* cavalier *m or* connecteur *m* mâle à deux broches *or* pont *m;* **jumper-selectable** = (circuit *or* dispositif) qui peut être sélectionné *or* validé par cavalier; **the printer's typeface was jumper-selectable** = sur cette imprimante, la police de caractères peut être sélectionnée par cavalier

junction *noun* **(a)** *(connection)* jonction *f;* **junction box** = boîte *f* de jonction *or* de raccordement **(b)** *(on semiconductor)* jonction; **bipolar junction transistor (BJT)** = transistor à jonction bipolaire

junk 1 *noun* camelote *f or* rebut *m;* **junk mail** = prospectus *mpl* publicitaires sans intérêt; **space junk** = satellites *mpl* hors d'usage *or* de rebut (qui tournent dans l'espace) **2** *verb* virer *or* éjecter *or* mettre à la poubelle; **to junk a file** = virer *or* effacer un fichier

◊ **junky** *see* TERMINAL JUNKY

justify *verb* **(a)** justifier; **justify inhibit** = (instruction d') invalider la justification; **justify margin** = *see* LEFT JUSTIFY, RIGHT JUSTIFY; **hyphenate and justify** = (fonction de) césure et justification; **left justify** = (instruction de) justifier à gauche; **right justify** = (instruction de) justifier à droite **(b)** *(computer register)* justifier (la pile)

◊ **justification** *noun* justification *f;* **hyphenation and justification** *or* **H & J** = césure *f* et justification; **an American hyphenation and justification program will not work with British English spellings** = un programme de césure et de justification établi aux Etats-Unis ne peut être utilisé pour un texte en anglais britannique; *see also* LEFT JUSTIFICATION, RIGHT JUSTIFICATION

juxtaposition *noun* juxtaposition *f*

Kk

K *prefix* **(a)** = KILO *(thousand)* k *or* kilo *m*
(b) *(represents 1,024 or 2¹⁰)* k *or* kilo
◊ **Kb** *or* **Kbyte** = KILOBYTE *(1,024 bytes)*
ko *or* Ko *or* Koctet *or* kilo-octet *m;* **the new
disk drive has a 100Kb capacity** = le
nouveau lecteur de disquettes a une
capacité de 100Ko; **the original PC
cannot access more than 640Kbytes of
RAM** = le premier ordinateur
individuel de la série ne peut accéder à
plus de 640Ko de RAM

Karnaugh map *noun* table *f* de
Karnaugh; **the prototype was checked for
hazards with a Karnaugh map** = le
prototype a fait l'objet d'un contrôle de
fiabilité statistique sur la base des tables
de Karnaugh

kernel *noun* noyau *m* (du système
d'exploitation); **graphics kernel system
(GKS)** = fonctions *fpl* graphiques GKS

kerning *noun (printing)* crénage *m or*
kerning *m*

key 1 *noun* **(a)** *(on a keyboard)* touche *f;*
there are 84 keys on the keyboard = le
clavier comporte 84 touches; **key click** =
clic *m* témoin (de fonctionnement) de
touche; **key force** = pression *f* nécessaire
pour actionner une touche; **key matrix** =
implantation *f* des touches sur un
clavier; **key number** = code *m*
numérique d'une touche; **key overlay** =
grille *f* d'aide *or* mémento *m* de fonction
des touches (de clavier); **without the key
overlay, I would never remember which
function key does what** = sans la grille
d'aide, je ne saurais jamais quelle touche
de fonction je dois utiliser; **key punch** =
perforatrice (à clavier) *f;* **key rollover** =
clavier à mémoire tampon *or* clavier
rapide; **key strip** = marquage *m*
(mnémotechnique) *or* pense-bête *m*
(indiquant la fonction d'une touche);
key travel = jeu vertical *or* course *f* d'une
touche **(b) alphanumeric key** = touche

alphanumérique; **character key** =
touche de caractère; **carriage return key**
= touche de retour du chariot; **function
key** = touche de fonction; **tags can be
allocated to function keys** = on peut
allouer une étiquette aux touches de
fonction; **shift key** = touche des
majuscules **(c)** *(important)* clé *or* clef *f;*
(printing) **key plate** = cliché *f* de base;
key terminal = terminal *m* principal **(d)**
(numbers to encrypt or decrypt a message)
clé (de cryptage et décryptage) d'un
code; **type this key into the machine, that
will decode the last message** = tapez la
clé et vous pourrez décoder le dernier
message; **key management** = gestion *f* de
clé **(e)** *(identification code)* clé
d'identification *or* clé de recherche *or*
mot-clé *m;* **we selected all the records
with the word DISK in their keys** = nous
avons sélectionné les enregistrements en
utilisant le mot DISK comme clé de
recherche; **index key** = clé d'index; **key
field** = champ *m* clé; **keyed sequential
access method (KSAM)** = méthode
d'accès séquentiel par clé **2** *verb*
actionner une touche; **to key in** = saisir
(un texte *or* des données) sur clavier *or*
taper (une commande); **they keyed in
the latest data** = ils ont saisi les toutes
dernières données (sur clavier)
◊ **keyboard 1** *noun* clavier *m; keyboard*
to disk entry = saisie *f* directe sur
disque(tte), par clavier; **ANSI keyboard**
= clavier ANSI; **ASCII keyboard** =
clavier ASCII; **ASR keyboard** = clavier
émetteur/récepteur *or* de téléscripteur;
AZERTY keyboard = clavier AZERTY
(utilisé surtout dans les pays
francophones) *or* clavier français
accentué; **interactive keyboard** = clavier
interactif; **keyboard contact bounce** =
rebond *m* d'une touche de clavier;
keyboard encoder = encodeur *m* des
touches; **keyboard layout** = disposition *f*
or implantation *f* des touches d'un
clavier; **keyboard overlay** = grille *f* d'aide
or mémento *m* (de fonction des touches)
de clavier; *(method of control)* **keyboard
scan** = contrôle *m* de clavier *or*

d'utilisation de touches; **keyboard send/receive (KSR)** = terminal *m* entrée/sortie *or* émetteur/récepteur à clavier; **QWERTY keyboard** = clavier QWERTY *or* clavier international (utilisé surtout dans les pays anglo-saxons); **touch sensitive keyboard** = clavier sensitif *or* tactile *or* à effleurement **2** *verb* saisir (des données) au clavier *or* sur clavier; **it was cheaper to have the manuscript keyboarded by another company** = il était plus économique de faire saisir le manuscrit par une société de service informatique

◊ **keyboarder** *noun* claviste *m&f or* pupitreur, -euse

◊ **keyboarding** *noun* saisie *f* (au *or* sur *or* par clavier); **the cost of keyboarding is calculated in keystrokes per hour** = le coût de saisie est calculé sur une base de frappes/heure

◊ **keypad** *noun* clavier auxiliaire *or* pavé *m;* **hex keypad** = clavier hexadécimal; **numeric keypad** = pavé numérique; **you can use the numeric keypad to enter the figures** = utilisez le pavé numérique pour saisir les chiffres

◊ **keystroke** *noun* frappe *f; he keyboards at a rate of 3500 keystrokes per hour* = il peut saisir un texte au rythme de 3500 frappes/heure; **keystroke count** = nombre *m* de frappes; **keystrokes per hour** = (nombre de) frappes par heure *or* frappes/heure; **keystroke rate** = vitesse *f* de frappe; **keystroke verification** = contrôle *m* des touches

◊ **key-to-disk** *noun* saisie *f* directe sur disque(tte)

◊ **keyword** *noun* **(a)** *(command word)* (mot de) commande *f; (important word in a title or text or subject)* mot-clé *m or* mot principal; **the BASIC keyword PRINT will display text on the screen** = en langage BASIC, la commande PRINT fera apparaître le texte sur l'écran; **computer is a keyword in IT** = le mot computer est un mot-clé en informatique **(b)** *(library system)* **keyword and context (KWAC)** = (système de) thésaurus *m or* mot-clé et contexte; **keyword in context (KWIC)** = mot-clé en contexte; **keyword out of context (KWOC)** = mot-clé hors contexte

kHz = KILOHERTZ

kill *verb* détruire *or* effacer; **kill file** = (instruction de) détruire un fichier; **kill job** = (instruction d') arrêter *or* (de) virer une tâche

kilo *prefix* **(a)** *(one thousand)* kilo *m;* **kilobaud** = kilobaud *m;* **kilohertz (kHz)** = kilohertz *m* (kHz); **kilo instructions per second (KIPS)** = millier d'instructions par seconde (KIPS); **kilo-ohm** = kilo-ohm *m;* **kiloVolt-Ampere output rating (KVA)** = mesure *f* du travail en kva; **kilowatt (kW)** = kilowatt *m* (kW) **(b)** *(1,024 units, equal to 2¹⁰)* kilo *m; (1,024 bits of data)* **kilobit** *or* **Kbit** = kilobit (kb) *m; (1,024 bytes of data)* **kilobyte** *or* **Kbyte (Kb)** = kilo-octet *m* (ko); **kiloword (KW)** = kilo-mot *m*

kilogram *or* **kilogramme (kg)** *noun* kilogramme (kg) *m*

kimball tag *noun* étiquette *f* Kimball

KIPS = KILO INSTRUCTIONS PER SECOND

kit *noun* trousse *f or* kit *m;* **screen cleaning kit** = kit de nettoyage d'écran

kludge *noun (software or hardware)* programme *or* système retapé *or* hâtivement bricolé
◊ **kludged** *adjective* retapé, -ée *or* bricolé, -ée

knob *noun* bouton *m* (de réglage, etc.); **turn the on/off knob** = tourner le bouton marche/arrêt; **the brightness can be regulated by turning a knob at the back**

of the monitor = pour ajuster la luminosité de l'écran, tourner le bouton placé à l'arrière du moniteur

knowledge *noun* connaissance *f;* **intelligent knowledge-based system (IKBS) =** système intelligent à base de connaissances *or* intelligence *f* artificielle; **knowledge-based system =** système à base de connaissances *or* système expert; **knowledge engineer =** cogniticien, -ienne; **knowledge engineering =** ingénierie *f* de la connaissance

KSR = KEYBOARD SEND/RECEIVE

KVA = KILOVOLT-AMPERE OUTPUT RATING

kW = KILOWATT

KW = KILOWORD

KWAC = KEYWORD AND CONTEXT
◇ **KWIC** = KEYWORD IN CONTEXT
◇ **KWOC** = KEYWORD OUT OF CONTEXT

LI

label 1 (a) noun *(in a computer program)* étiquette *f* or label *m* or identificateur *m;* **BASIC uses many program labels such as line numbers** = les programmes en langage BASIC contiennent plusieurs labels dont la numérotation des lignes; **label field** = champ label or champ d'identification; **label record** = enregistrement de labels or d'étiquettes or d'identificateurs; **internal label** = label d'identification (sur le support magnétique) **(b)** *(piece of paper)* étiquette *f* or label; *(for quality)* label de qualité; **external label** = étiquette externe or étiquette extérieure or apposée à l'extérieur (d'une bande, etc.) **2** verb *(to put a label on a product)* étiqueter; *(to put a label on a program)* produire un label or une étiquette (pour un programme)
NOTE: **labelling - labelled** but US **labeling - labeled**

◇ **labelling** noun *(a product)* étiquetage *m; (a program)* production *f* d'étiquettes (pour un programme); **the word-processor has a special utility allowing simple and rapid labelling** = le traitement de texte possède un utilitaire qui permet d'imprimer des étiquettes facilement et rapidement

laboratory noun laboratoire *m;* **the new chip is being developed in the university laboratories** = le travail de recherche et développement sur la nouvelle puce se fait dans les laboratoires de l'université

lag noun **(a)** *(of signal)* retard *m* or décalage *m;* **time lag is noticeable on international phone calls** = le décalage est perceptible sur les lignes téléphoniques internationales **(b)** *(of image on a CRT screen)* rémanence *f* or persistance *f* or retard d'effacement *m*

laminate verb pelliculer; **the book has a laminated cover** = c'est un livre avec couverture pelliculée

LAN or **lan** = LOCAL AREA NETWORK réseau *m* local d'entreprise; **LAN server** = serveur *m* de réseau local

QUOTE since most of the LAN hardware is already present, the installation costs are only $50 per connection
Practical Computing

landline noun câble(s) *m(pl)* souterrain(s)

language noun **(a)** *(spoken or written)* langue *f;* **he speaks several European languages** = il parle plusieurs langues européennes; **foreign language** = langue étrangère **(b)** *(for computers)* langage *m;* **assembly language** or **assembler language** = langage d'assemblage; **command language** = langage de commande or d'instruction; **compiler language** = langage de compilation; **control language** = langage de commande or de contrôle; **graphic language** = langage graphique; **high-level language (HLL)** = langage de haut niveau or langage évolué; **low-level language (LLL)** = langage de bas niveau or langage peu évolué; **machine language** = langage machine; **programming language** = langage de programmation; **query language** = langage de requête or d'interrogation; **source language** = langage source; **language assembler** = (programme) assembleur *m* (de langage); **language compiler** = (programme) compilateur *m;* **language interpreter** = (programme) interpréteur *m;* **language processor** = processeur *m* de langage; **language rules** = syntaxe *f* or règles *fpl* propres à un langage; **language support environment** = aides *mpl* à la programmation (dans un langage déterminé); *(of programming language)* **language translation** = traduction *f* d'un langage (en un autre langage); **language translator** = (programme) traducteur *m* (de langage)

lap *noun* **(a)** *(of person)* genoux *mpl;* **he placed the computer on his lap and keyboarded some orders while sitting in his car** = il a posé l'ordinateur sur ses genoux et saisi quelques commandes alors qu'il était assis dans sa voiture **(b)** *(overlap)* chevauchement *m*

◊ **laptop computer** *or* **lapheld computer** *noun* petit (ordinateur) portatif *m* (autonome)

QUOTE in our summary of seven laphelds we found features to admire in every machine
QUOTE the idea of a hard disk in a lapheld machine which runs on batteries is not brand new
PC Business World

lapel microphone *noun* micro-cravate *m*

large-scale computer *noun* gros ordinateur *m*

◊ **large-scale integration (LSI)** *noun* intégration *f* à grande échelle

laser *noun* = LIGHT AMPLIFICATION BY STIMULATED EMISSION OF RADIATION laser *m;* **laser beam recording** = enregistrement *m* par rayon laser; **laser beam communications** = communication *f* par rayon laser; **laser disk** = disque *m* optique; **emulsion laser storage** = mémoire (à) laser sur couche haute définition; **laser printer** = imprimante *f* (à) laser; *(in optical fibre)* **injection laser** = laser d'injection (dans une fibre optique)

last in first out (LIFO) *noun* (méthode du) dernier entré premier sorti; **this computer stack uses a last in first out data retrieval method** = cet ordinateur gère la pile suivant la méthode du dernier entré premier sorti *or* suivant la méthode LIFO

latch 1 *noun* (i) verrou *m or* clapet *m* ; (ii) bascule *f or* dispositif *m* de verrouillage **2** *verb* verrouiller; **the output latched high until we reset the computer** = la sortie est restée verrouillée *or* bloquée au plus haut niveau jusqu'à la ré-initialisation du système

QUOTE other features of the device include a programmable latch bypass which allows any number of latches from 0 to 8 so that this device may be used as latched or combinatorial
Electronics & Power

latency *noun* période *f or* temps *m* de latence

◊ **latent image** *noun* image *f* latente

lateral reversal *noun* inversion *f* latérale *or* effet *m* miroir

launch 1 *noun (new product)* lancement *m; (satellite)* mise *f* en orbite; **the launch of the new PC has been put back six months** = le lancement du nouvel ordinateur individuel se fera avec six mois de retard; **the launch date for the network will be September** = le lancement du réseau aura lieu en septembre **2** *verb (new product)* lancer; *(satellite)* mettre en orbite; **the new PC was launched at the Personal Computer Show** = on a lancé le nouvel ordinateur personnel au Salon de l'Informatique

◊ **launch amplifier** *noun* amplificateur *m* de signal

◊ **launch vehicle** *noun* fusée *f* porteuse *or* de lancement

layer *noun* **(a)** *(division of space)* couche *f* **(b)** *(ISO/OSI standards)* couche (de protocole); **application layer** = couche application; **data link layer** = couche liaison de données; **network layer** = couche réseau; **physical layer** = couche physique; **presentation layer** = couche présentation; **session layer** = couche session; **transport layer** = couche transport

◊ **layered** *adjective* disposé, -ée en couches; **the kernel has a layered structure according to user priority** = le noyau possède une structure en couches adaptée aux besoins de l'utilisateur

lay in *verb (to synchronize film and sound tracks)* synchroniser

◊ **layout** *noun* **(a)** mise *f* en page; **the design team is working on the layouts for the new magazine** = les concepteurs travaillent à la mise en page de la nouvelle revue **(b)** spécifications *fpl* de présentation des données **(c)** **keyboard layout** = disposition *f or* implantation *f* des touches d'un clavier

◊ **lay out** *verb* mettre en page; **the designers have laid out the pages in A4 format** = les concepteurs ont décidé de mettre en page sur format A4

LBR = LASER BEAM RECORDING

LC circuit *noun* circuit *m* LC

LCD = LIQUID CRYSTAL DISPLAY affichage *m* à cristaux liquides

QUOTE LCD screens can run for long periods on ordinary or rechargeable batteries
Micro Decision

LCP = LINK CONTROL PROCEDURE

LDS = LOCAL DISTRIBUTION SERVICE

lead[1] *noun (wire)* conducteur *m or* câble *m or* fil *m* (conducteur)

◊ **lead-in page** *noun (videotext page)* sommaire *m or* page *f* guide

◊ **leader** *noun* **(a)** *(beginning of the reel)* amorce *f;* **leader record** = enregistrement *m* de tête **(b)** *(row of dots)* pointillé *m*

◊ **leading edge** *noun (of punched card)* bord *m* d'introduction *or* bord avant

◊ **leading zero** *noun* zéro *m* de tête

lead[2] *noun (metal rod)* interligne *f*

◊ **leading** *noun (space in printing)* interligne *m; (action)* interlignage *m*

leaf *noun* **(a)** feuille *f* (de papier); *(of book)* page *f* **(b)** *(in a data tree)* élément *m* final d'une arborescence

◊ **leaflet** *noun* feuillet *m* (publicitaire)

leak 1 *noun* **(a)** *(of secret)* fuite *f;* **a leak informed the press of our new designs** = c'est grâce à une fuite que la presse a eu vent de notre nouveau modèle **(b)** *(of charge, etc.)* fuite *or* perte *f* **2** *verb* **(a)** *(information)* dévoiler *or* divulguer **(b)** *(charge, etc.)* fuir *or* perdre (sa charge); **in this circuit, the capacitor charge leaks out at 10% per second** = dans ce circuit, le condensateur perd 10% de sa charge par seconde

◊ **leakage** *noun (of signal)* fuite *f or* perte *f; (of signal)* affaiblissement *m*

QUOTE signal leakages in both directions can be a major problem in co-axial cable systems
Electronics & Wireless World

leapfrog test *noun* test *m* sélectif; **crippled leapfrog test** = test sélectif limité *or* restreint

learning curve *noun* courbe *f* d'apprentissage

lease 1 *noun* bail *m* **2** *verb* louer; **the company leases all its computers** = la société loue tous ses ordinateurs; **the company has a policy of only using leased equipment** = la société a pour politique de louer son matériel; **leased circuit** = circuit loué *or* de location; **leased line** = ligne louée *or* de location

least cost design *noun* conception *f or* design *m* économique; **the budget is only £1,000, we need the least cost design for the new circuit** = le budget n'étant que de 1000 livres, il nous faut une conception économique pour ce nouveau circuit

◊ **least recently used algorithm** *noun* algorithme *m* utilisé le moins récemment

◊ **least significant digit (LSD)** *noun* chiffre *m* le moins significatif *or* de poids faible; **least significant bit (LSB)** = bit *m* le moins significatif *or* de poids faible

leaving files open *phrase* laisse le fichier ouvert

LED = LIGHT-EMITTING DIODE diode *f* électroluminescente

left justification *noun (printing)* justification *f* à gauche

◊ **left justify** *verb (printing or binary number)* justifier à gauche

◊ **left shift 1** *noun (of bits)* décalage *m or* glissement *m* à gauche **2** *verb* effectuer un décalage à gauche

leg *noun* branchement *m*

legal *adjective* légal, -e *or* valide *or* permis, -e *or* autorisé, -ée

legible *adjective* lisible; **the manuscript is written in pencil and is hardly legible** =

le manuscrit est écrit au crayon et est à peine lisible

◊ **legibility** *noun* lisibilité *f;* **the keyboarders find the manuscript lacks legibility** = les clavistes trouvent ce manuscrit difficile à lire *or* que la lisibilité du manuscrit laisse à désirer

length *noun* longueur *f;* **block length** = longueur d'un bloc; **buffer length** = taille *f* de la mémoire tampon; **field length** = dimension *f or* taille d'un champ; **file length** = longueur *or* dimension d'un fichier; **length of filename** = longueur du nom d'un fichier; **line length** = longueur d'une ligne; **record length** = longueur *or* taille d'un enregistrement; **register length** = dimension d'un registre

lens *noun* lentille *f;* **concave lens** = lentille concave; **convex lens** = lentille convexe; **lens speed** = vitesse *f* d'ouverture d'un objectif; **lens stop** = ouverture *f* d'objectif

letter *noun* **(a)** *(piece of writing)* lettre *f;* **form letter** *or* **standard letter** = lettre type *or* lettre standard *or* lettre cadre **(b)** *(A, B, C, etc.)* lettre; **capital letter** = (lettre) majuscule *f;* **his name was written in capital letters** = son nom était écrit en majuscules

◊ **letterhead** *noun* en-tête *m* de lettre; **business forms and letterheads can now be designed on a PC** = formulaires et en-têtes peuvent être conçus sur ordinateur

◊ **near-letter-quality (NLQ) printing** *noun (of dot-matrix printer)* qualité *f* courrier

QUOTE the printer offers reasonable speeds of printing in both draft and letter-quality modes
Which PC?

level *noun* **(a)** *(of electrical signal)* niveau *m;* *(of sound)* volume *m;* **turn the sound level down, it's far too loud** = baissez le volume (du son) qui est vraiment trop fort; **sound pressure level (SPL)** = niveau de pression acoustique **(b)** *(quantity of bits)* niveau d'un signal

lexical analysis *noun* analyse *f* lexicale

lexicographical order *noun* ordre *m* lexicographique

LF (a) = LOW FREQUENCY **(b)** = LINE FEED

library *noun* **(a)** bibliothèque *f;* **the editors have checked all the references in the local library** = les éditeurs ont vérifié toutes les références à la bibliothèque locale; **a copy of each new book has to be deposited in the British Library** = il faut déposer un exemplaire de toute nouvelle publication à la British Library; **look up the bibliographical details in the library catalogue** = consultez le catalogue de la bibliothèque pour obtenir les renseignements bibliographiques **(b)** *(of programs)* bibliothèque; **he has a large library of computer games** = il possède une grande bibliothèque de jeux électroniques; **program library** = bibliothèque de programmes *or* programmathèque *f;* **software library** = logithèque *f* **(c)** *(of software)* **library function** = fonction *f* bibliothèque; **library program** = programme *m* de bibliothèque; **the square root function is already in the library program** = la fonction racine carrée se trouve déjà dans le programme de bibliothèque; **library routine** = routine de bibliothèque; **library subroutine** = sous-programme *m* de bibliothèque; *(on disk)* **library track** = piste *f* de référence; **graphics library** = bibliothèque graphique; **macro library** = bibliothèque de macros

◊ **librarian** *noun* bibliothécaire *m&f*

QUOTE a library of popular shapes and images is supplied
Practical Computing

licence *noun* permis *m or* licence *f;* **this software is manufactured under licence** = ce logiciel est fabriqué sous licence

LIFO = LAST IN FIRST OUT

lifter *noun* écarteur *m* de bande

ligature *noun* ligature *f*

light 1 *noun* lumière *f;* **the VDU should not be placed under a bright light** = il faut éviter de placer l'écran sous une lumière trop forte; **light conduit** = conducteur *m* de lumière; **light-emitting diode (LED)** = diode *f* électroluminescente; **light guide** = guide *m* optique; **light pen** = stylo *m* optique; **light pipe** = LIGHT GUIDE; **coherent light** = lumière cohérente *or* monochrome; **visible light** = lumière visible; **ultraviolet light (UV light)** = lumière ultraviolette *or* rayonnement ultra-violet; **infrared light (IR light)** = rayonnement infrarouge **2** *adjective (not dark)* clair, -e; *(typeface)* **light face** = caractères *mpl* maigres

◊ **light-sensitive** *adjective* photosensible *or* sensible à la lumière; **the photograph is printed on light-sensitive paper** = la photo est imprimée sur papier photosensible; **light-sensitive device** = dispositif *m* photosensible

lightweight *adjective* léger, -ère; **a lightweight computer which can easily fit into a suitcase** = un ordinateur léger qui tient facilement dans une valise

limits *noun (for numbers in a computer)* limites *fpl*

◊ **limited distance modem** *noun* modem *m* pour réseau local *or* à distance de transmission limitée

◊ **limiter** *noun* limitateur *m*

◊ **limiting resolution** *noun* définition *f* maximum

line *noun* **(a)** *(connection)* ligne *f or* liaison *f;* **access line** = ligne d'accès; **fast line** = ligne rapide; **line busy tone** = tonalité *f* 'occupé'; **line communications** = communication *f* par câble; **line control** = commandes *fpl or* protocole *m* de communication; **line driver** = amplificateur *m* de signal; *(in cable TV)* **line extender** = unité *f* d'extension d'une ligne; **line impedance** = impédance *f* de ligne; **line level** = niveau *m* de transmission (d'une ligne); **line load** = trafic *m or* charge *f* d'une ligne; **line speed** = débit *m* d'une ligne; **line switching** = commutation *f* de ligne; **line terminator** = dispositif *m* de fin de ligne; **line transient** = courant *m* transitoire d'une ligne **(b)** *(thin mark)* ligne *or* trait *m;* *(printing)* filet *m;* **the printer has difficulty in reproducing very fine lines** = l'imprimante ne réussit pas très bien à imprimer les lignes trop fines; **line art** = graphisme *m;* **line drawing** = dessin *m* au trait; **the book is illustrated with line drawings and halftones** = on trouve dans ce livre des dessins (au trait) et des illustrations en demi-teinte **(c)** *(on*

screen) trace *f;* **line blanking interval** = délai *m* de retour de ligne; **line drive signal** = signal (de début) de balayage; **line flyback** = retour de ligne; **line frequency** = fréquence *f* (de balayage) de ligne **(d)** *(of text)* ligne (de texte); **each page has 52 lines of text** = on compte 52 lignes de texte par page; **several lines of the manuscript have been missed by the keyboarder** = le claviste a sauté plusieurs lignes du manuscrit; **can we insert an extra line of spacing between the paragraphs?** = est-il possible d'ajouter un interligne supplémentaire entre les paragraphs?; *(of program)* **command line** = ligne de commande; *(of program)* **information line** *or* **status line** = ligne d'état; **line editor** = éditeur *m* de ligne; **line ending** = caractère *m or* symbole *m* de fin de ligne; **line feed (LF)** = saut *m* de ligne *or* interlignage *m;* **line folding** = enroulement *m* d'une ligne; *(between two lines of type)* **line increment** = incrément *m* de ligne; **line length** = longueur *f* d'une ligne *or* nombre de caractères par ligne; *(space between lines)* **line spacing** = interligne *m;* *(printing)* **lines per minute (LPM)** = (nombre de) lignes par minute *or* débit *m* **(e)** *(characters received as a single input)* ligne; **line input** = (commande de) validation *f* de ligne **(f)** *(row of commands)* ligne de programme; **line number** = numéro *f* d'une ligne (de programme)

> QUOTE straight lines are drawn by clicking the points on the screen where you would like the line to start and finish
> *Personal Computer World*
> QUOTE while pixel editing is handy for line art, most desktop scanners have trouble producing the shades of grey or half-tones found in black and white photography
> *Publish*

line of sight *noun* ligne *f* optique *or* directe

line printer *noun* imprimante *f* ligne à ligne

linear *adjective* linéaire *or* séquentiel, -elle; *(antenna)* **linear array** = antenne *f* linéaire; **linear function** = fonction *f* linéaire; **the expression Y = 10 + 5X - 3W is a linear function** = l'expression Y = 10 + 5X - 3W est une fonction linéaire; **the expression Y = (10 + 5X^2) is not a linear function** = l'expression Y = (10 + 5X^2)

n'est pas une fonction linéaire; **linear integrated circuit =** circuit *m* intégré linéaire; **linear list =** liste séquentielle; **linear program =** programme *m* linéaire; **linear programming =** programmation *f* linéaire; **linear search =** recherche séquentielle

link 1 *noun* **(a)** *(communication path)* liaison *f;* **to transmit faster, you can use the direct link with the mainframe =** pour une transmission plus rapide, vous pouvez utiliser la liaison directe avec le gros ordinateur; *(ISO/OSI layer)* **data link layer =** couche *f* liaison de données; **link control procedure (LCP) =** protocole *m* de communication; **link loss =** perte *f* de transmission; **satellite link =** liaison *or* transmission *f* par satellite **(b)** *(software routine)* lien *m;* **link trials =** tests *mpl* de contrôle de liens **2** *verb* relier *or* connecter *or* interfacer; **the two computers are linked =** les deux ordinateurs sont reliés; **link files =** (instruction d') assemblage *m or* (instruction de) concaténation *f* de fichiers; **linked list =** liste chaînée *or* concaténée; **linked subroutine =** sous-programme chaîné
◊ **linkage** *noun (of devices)* couplage *m; (for program)* création *f* de liens; **linkage editing =** mise *f* en place de liens (à l'aide d'un éditeur de liens); **linkage software =** (programme) générateur *m* de liens; **graphics and text are joined without linkage software =** les graphiques et le texte sont réunis sans l'aide d'un générateur de liens
◊ **linking** *noun* liaison *f or* enchaînement *m or* assemblage *m;* **linking loader =** chargeur/éditeur *m* de liens

LIPS = LOGICAL INFERENCES PER SECOND (nombre d') inférences *fpl* logiques par seconde

liquid crystal display (LCD) *noun* affichage *m* à cristaux liquides

LISP = LIST PROCESSING langage *m* LISP

list 1 *noun* liste *f;* **chained list =** liste chaînée *or* concaténée; **linear list =** liste séquentielle; **linked list =** liste chaînée *or* concaténée; **pushdown list =** liste inversée *or* en mode LIFO; **reference list =** liste de référence; **stop list =** liste

d'interdictions; **list processing =** (i) traitement *m* de liste; (ii) langage *m* LISP **2** *verb* lister *or* éditer sous forme de liste; **to list a program =** lister (les lignes d'instruction d') un programme
◊ **listing** *noun* **(a)** listage *m or* listing *m;* **computer listing =** listing *or* sortie *f* d'imprimante; **a program listing =** listage *or* listing d'un programme; **listing paper =** papier *m* listing *or* papier en continu **(b)** *(of cinema times, etc.)* **listings =** liste *f or* répertoire *m* (des films *or* pièces à l'affiche)

literal *noun* **(a)** *(operand)* (symbole) littéral *m* **(b)** *(printing error)* coquille *f*

literate *adjective (person who can read)* (personne) qui sait lire *or* lettré, -ée; **computer-literate =** (personne) qui a des connaissances en informatique
◊ **literacy** *noun* (le fait de) savoir lire; **computer literacy =** (le fait d'avoir des) connaissances *fpl* en informatique

lith film *noun* film *m* lith
◊ **lithography** *or* **litho** *noun* lithographie *f or* litho *f;* **offset lithography =** (lithographie) offset *m*
◊ **lithographic** *adjective* lithographique; **lithographic film =** LITH FILM

liveware *noun* personnel *m* informatique

LLL = LOW-LEVEL LANGUAGE

load 1 *noun* **(a)** *(job)* tâche *f or* charge *f;* **load sharing =** partage *m* des tâches; **line load =** trafic *m or* charge d'une ligne; **work load =** charge de travail *or* (nombre de) tâches *fpl* **(b)** *(impedance)* charge *or* facteur de charge; **load impedance =** impédance *f* de charge; **load life =** temps *m* de décharge; **matched load =** charge équilibrée **2** *verb* **(a)** *(file or program)* charger; **scatter load =** faire un chargement dispersé des données; **load and run** *or* **load and go =** (programme de) chargement-lancement *m or* charger-lancer **(b)** *(disk or cartridge, etc.)* mettre en place *or* insérer *or* introduire *or* charger; **load lower bin =** introduire le bac inférieur **(c)** *(to place an impedance)* charger une ligne
◊ **loading** *noun (of file)* chargement *m;* **loading can be a long process =** le

chargement (d'un programme) peut être assez long à effectuer

◊ **loader** *noun (program)* chargeur *m;* **absolute loader** = chargeur absolu; **binary loader** = chargeur binaire; *(program)* **card loader** = chargeur de cartes; **initial program loader (IPL)** = chargeur de programme de lancement

◊ **loadpoint** *noun (start of a recording section)* point *m* de début d'enregistrement

> QUOTE this windowing system is particularly handy when you want to load or save a file or change directories
> *Byte*

lobe *noun (of response curve)* lobe *m*

local *adjective* **(a)** *(used in a certain section of a computer program)* local, -e; **local declaration** = déclaration *f* d'une variable locale; **local memory** = mémoire locale; **local variable** = variable *f* locale **(b)** *(system with limited access)* local, -e *or* localisé, -ée; *(of terminal)* **on local** = (terminal) autonome; **local mode** = mode *m* local

◊ **local area network (LAN *or* lan)** *noun* réseau *m* local d'entreprise; **local area network server** = serveur *m* de réseau local d'entreprise

local distribution service (LDS) = *noun* station *f* relais

locate *verb* (i) se trouver; (ii) trouver *or* repérer *or* localiser *or* situer; **the computer is located in the main office building** = l'ordinateur se trouve dans l'édifice principal; **have you managed to locate the programming fault?** = avez-vous réussi à localiser l'erreur de programmation?

◊ **location** *noun* **(a)** *(absolute address)* emplacement *m* (de mémoire) **(b)** *(filming)* **on location** = (prise de vue) en extérieur; **location shots** = les extérieurs *mpl* (d'un film); **the programme was shot on location in Spain** = les extérieurs pour ce programme ont été tournés en Espagne

lock *verb* verrouiller; **locking a file** = verrouiller (l'accès à) un fichier; **to lock onto** = coupler *or* synchroniser

◊ **lockout** *noun (over a network)* lockout *m*

◊ **lock up** *noun (of computer)* blocage *m or* accrochage *m or* plantage *m*

log 1 *noun* **(a)** enregistrement *m or* entrée *f* (dans un journal *or* livre de bord) **(b)** journal *m* de bord; **system log** = journal de bord d'un système **2** *verb* **(a)** enregistrer (chronologiquement) dans un journal de bord **(b)** *(telephone)* **to log calls** = enregistrer le nombre et la durée des appels **(c)** *(computer)* **to log in** *or* **log on** = ouvrir *or* débuter une session; **automatic log on** = ouverture *f* automatique d'une session; **to log off** *or* **log out** = clore *or* fermer *or* terminer une session NOTE: the verbs can be spelled **log on, log-on,** or **logon; log off, log-off** or **logoff**

◊ **logger** *noun* enregistreur *m* (chronologique); **call logger** = enregistreur d'appels

◊ **logging** *noun (input of data)* acquisition *f or* saisie *f* de données; *(recording)* enregistrement *m;* **logging on** *or* **logging off** = ouverture *f or* clôture *f* de session; **call logging** = enregistrement d'appels; **error logging** = enregistrement automatique des erreurs; **features of the program include error logging** = ce programme permet l'enregistrement (automatique) des erreurs

> QUOTE logging on and off from terminals is simple, requiring only a user name and password
> QUOTE once the server is up and running it is possible for users to log-on
> *Micro Decision*
> QUOTE facilities for protection against hardware failure and software malfunction include log files
> *Computer News*

logarithm *noun* logarithme *m;* **decimal logarithm of 1,000 is 3 (= 10 x 10 x 10)** = le logarithme décimal de 1000 est 3 (= 10 x 10 x 10)

◊ **logarithmic** *adjective* logarithmique; **bel is a unit in the logarithmic scale** = le 'bel' est mesuré sur une échelle logarithmique; **logarithmic graph** = graphe *m* logarithmique

logic *noun* **(a)** *(thought and reasoning)* logique *f;* **formal logic** = logique formelle **(b)** *(mathematical treatment)* logique; **logic map** = configuration *m* logique; **logic state** = état *m* logique; **logic state analyzer** = analyseur *m* d'état logique; **logic symbol** = symbole *m* logique **(c)** *(for deducing results from binary data)* logique binaire; **logic bomb** = bombe *f* logique; **logic level** = niveau *m* logique; **logic operation** = opération *f* logique **(d)** *(components of a computer system)* la logique (d'un système); **sequential logic** = logique séquentielle; **logic array** = réseau *m* or circuit *m* logique; **programmable logic array (PLA)** = circuit logique programmable; **uncommitted logic array (ULA)** = circuit logique non connecté; **logic card** or **logic board** = carte *f* logique; **logic circuit** = circuit *m* logique; **logic element** = élément *m* logique; **logic flowchart** = diagramme *m* logique; **logic gate** = porte *f* or circuit *m* logique

◊ **logical** *adjective* logique; **logical reasoning can be simulated by an artificial intelligence machine** = le raisonnement logique peut être simulé par une machine intelligente *or* un système expert; **logical channel** = voie *f* logique; **logical chart** = diagramme logique; **logical comparison** = comparaison *f* logique; **logical decision** = décision *f* logique; **logical error** = erreur *f* logique; **logical expression** = expression *f* logique; **logical high** = état logique haut *or* binon 1 *or* tension haute; **logical low** = état logique bas *or* binon 0 *or* tension faible; **logical inference per second (LIPS)** = (nombre d') inférences *f* logiques par seconde; **logical operator** = opérateur *m* logique; **logical record** = enregistrement *m* or article *m* logique; **logical shift** = décalage *m* logique

◊ **logic-seeking** *adjective* (imprimante à) recherche *f* logique

QUOTE a reduction in the number of logic gates leads to faster operation and lower silicon costs
QUOTE the removal of complex but infrequently used logic makes the core of the processor simpler and faster, so simple operations execute faster
Electronics & Power

login = LOGGING IN

LOGO *noun (high level programming language)* langage *m* LOGO

logo *noun* logotype *m* or logo *m*

logoff = LOG OFF, LOGGING OFF
◊ **logon** = LOG ON, LOGGING ON
◊ **logout** = LOGGING OUT

long haul network *noun* réseau *m* très étendu

longitudinal *adjective* **longitudinal redundancy check** = clé *f* longitudinale

long persistence phosphor *noun* phosphore *m* or couche *f* phosphorée à grande persistance

look ahead *noun* lecture *f* anticipée; **carry look ahead** = retenue *f* anticipée
◊ **binary look-up** *noun* recherche *f* binaire
◊ **look-up table (LUT)** *noun* table d'équivalence *or* de référence; **look-up tables are preprogrammed then used in processing so saving calculations for each result required** = les tables d'équivalence sont préprogrammées et permettent de gagner du temps de traitement en évitant de recalculer les mêmes valeurs

QUOTE a lookup table changes a pixel's value based on the values in a table
Byte

loop 1 *noun* **(a)** *(instruction in a computer program)* boucle *f;* **closed loop** = boucle fermée; **endless loop** *or* **infinite loop** = boucle sans fin *or* infinie; **holding loop** = boucle de maintien; **modification loop** = boucle de modification; **nested loop** = boucle imbriquée *or* emboîtée; **loop body** = corps *m* de la boucle; **loop check** = vérification *f* or contrôle *m* de boucle; **loop counter** = compteur *m* de boucles; **loop program** = boucle d'itération *or* boucle de programme *or* boucle de fond *or* programme *m* itératif **(b) loop film** = film *m* en boucle; **loop network** = réseau *m* en anneau *or* en boucle **(c)** *(coiled in circle)* boucle *or* tour *m;* **loop antenna** = antenne en boucle **2** *verb* créer une boucle *or* boucler; **looping program** = boucle d'itération *or* boucle de programme *or* boucle de fond *or* programme itératif

lose *verb* perdre; **we have lost the signal in the noise** = le signal a été masqué par le bruit; **all the current files were lost when the system crashed and we had no backup copies** = tous les fichiers courants ont été perdus lors de la panne d'ordinateur parce que nous n'avions pas de copie de sauvegarde; **lost call** =

demande *f* de communication qui ne peut être établie *or* qui ne passe pas; **lost time** = temps *m* mort

loss *noun (of signal)* perte *f or* atténuation *f or* affaiblissement *m* (d'un signal)

loudness *noun* volume *m*

◊ **loudspeaker** *noun* haut-parleur *m;* *(system)* enceinte *f* acoustique

low frequency (LF) *noun (radio: 30 - 300kHz)* onde *f* kilométrique *or* basse fréquence; *(audio: 5 - 300 Hz)* audiofréquence *f or* basse fréquence; *see also* VERY; **low pass filter** = filtre *m* passe-bas; **low-priority work** = tâche *f* non prioritaire *or* d'arrière-plan; **low-resolution graphics** *or* **low-res graphics** = graphiques *mpl* de faible définition; **low speed communications** = communication *f* à faible débit

◊ **lower case** *noun* (lettre) minuscule *f or* bas *m* de casse

◊ **low-level language (LLL)** *noun* langage *m* de bas niveau *or* peu évolué

◊ **low-order digit** *noun* chiffre *m* de poids faible *or* chiffre le moins significatif; **the number 234156 has a low-order digit of 6** = 6 est le chiffre le moins significatif du nombre 234156

◊ **low-res** *see* LOW-RESOLUTION

LPM = LINES PER MINUTE

LQ = LETTER QUALITY

LSB = LEAST SIGNIFICANT BIT

LSD = LEAST SIGNIFICANT DIGIT

LSI = LARGE SCALE INTEGRATION

luggable *noun & adjective* ordinateur *m* déplaçable *or* à peu près portable

lumen *noun (SI unit of illumination)* lumen *m*

luminance *noun* luminance *f;* **luminance signal** = signal *m* de luminance

LUT LOOK-UP TABLE table *f* d'équivalence *or* de référence

QUOTE an image processing system can have three LUTs that map the image memory to the display device
Byte

lux *noun (SI unit of measurement of one lumen per square metre)* lux *m*

Mm

m *prefix* = MILLI *(one thousandth)* m *or* milli-

M *prefix* = MEGA **(a)** *(one million)* M *or* méga-; **Mbps** = MEGA BITS PER SECOND *(number of million bits transmitted every second)* Mbps *or* (nombre de) mégabits *mpl* par seconde; **MFLOPS** = MEGA FLOATING POINT OPERATIONS PER SECOND *(one million floating point operations per second)* mégaflops *mpl or* (nombre de) millions d'opérations en virgule flottante par seconde **(b)** *(equal to 1,048,576 or 2²⁰)* M; **Mbyte (Mb)** = Moctet *or* Mo; **the latest model has a 30Mbyte hard disk** = le modèle le plus récent possède un disque dur d'une capacité de 30Mo

MAC (a) = MULTIPLEXED ANALOG COMPONENTS **(b)** = MESSAGE AUTHENTICATION CODE

machine *noun* **(a)** machine *f;* **copying machine** *or* **duplicating machine** = photocopieur *m or* copieur *m; **dictating machine** = Dictaphone®*m;* **machine proof** = épreuve *f* de machine **(b)** ordinateur *m or* processeur *m or* machine; **clean machine** = processeur *m* nu; **source machine** = processeur *m* de programme source; **virtual machine** = machine virtuelle; **machine address** = adresse *f* absolue; *(fault)* **machine check** = arrêt *m* dû à une défaillance de l'appareil; **machine code** *or* **machine language** = code *m or* langage *m* machine; **machine code format** = format de code machine; **machine code instruction** = instruction *f* en code *or* en langage machine; **machine cycle** = cycle *m* de machine; *(software)* **machine-dependent** = (logiciel) non standard *or* qui ne fonctionne que sur un type d'ordinateur; **machine equation** = équation *f or* logique *f* machine; *(software)* **machine-independent** = standard *or* universel, -elle *or* qui

fonctionne sur la plupart des ordinateurs; **machine-independent language** = langage *m* standard *or* universel; **machine instruction** = instruction en langage machine; **machine intelligence** = intelligence artificielle *f;* **machine-intimate** = (logiciel) propre à la machine *or* sur mesure *or* de constructeur *or* adapté à l'ordinateur; **machine language** *or* **machine code** = langage *m or* code *m* machine; **machine language compile** = compiler en langage machine; **machine language programming** = programmation *f* en langage machine; *(command or data)* **machine-readable** = (instruction *or* donnée) en langage machine *or* exploitable par l'ordinateur; **the disk stores data in machine-readable form** = le disque garde en mémoire des données sous une forme exploitable par l'ordinateur; **machine run** = exécution *f* d'un programme; *(of foreign language)* **machine translation** = traduction *f* assistée par ordinateur; **machine word** = mot *m* machine

◊ **machinery** *noun* (l'ensemble des) machines *fpl*

◊ **machining** *noun* **(a)** *(making a product)* usinage *m* **(b)** *(books)* impression *f*

◊ **machinist** *noun* machiniste *m&f*

macro- *prefix* macro(-)

◊ **macro** *noun* macro-instruction *f or* macro *f;* **macro assembler** *or* **assembly program** = macro-assembleur *m or* programme *m* assembleur pour macrolangage; **macro call** = macro-instruction *f;* **macro code** = macrocode *m;* **macro command** = macrocommande *f;* **macro instruction** = macro-instruction *f;* **macro definition** = macrodéfinition *f;* **macro expansion** = macro-expansion *f or* désassemblage *m* de macro; **macro flowchart** = macro-ordinogramme *m;* **macro language** = macrolangage *m;* **macro library** = bibliothèque *f* de macros; **macro programming** = macroprogrammation *f*

◊ **macroelement** *noun* macro-élément *m*

◊ **macroinstruction** *noun* macro-instruction *f or* macro *f*

magazine *noun* **(a)** *(review)* revue *f or* magazine *m or* périodique *m;* **a weekly magazine** = une revue hebdomadaire; **he edits a computer magazine** = il travaille à la rédaction d'une revue de micro-informatique **(b)** *(pages of videotext system)* (nombre de) pages d'un système vidéotex **(c)** *(containing photographic film)* magasin *m*

magnet *noun* aimant *m*

◊ **magnetic** *adjective* magnétique *or* aimanté, -ée; **magnetic bubble memory** = mémoire *f* à bulles magnétiques; **magnetic card** = carte *f* magnétique; **magnetic card reader** lecteur *m* de cartes magnétiques; **magnetic cartridge** = cartouche *f* (de bande magnétique); **magnetic cassette** = cassette *f* (de bande magnétique); **magnetic cell** = cellule *f* magnétique; **magnetic core** = tore *m* magnétique; **magnetic disk** = disque *m* magnétique; **magnetic disk unit** = unité *f* de disque *or* de disquette; **magnetic drum** = tambour *m* magnétique; **magnetic encoding** = encodage *m* magnétique *or* sur support magnétique; **magnetic field** = champ *m* magnétique; **magnetic flux** = flux *m* magnétique; *(of beam of electrons)* **magnetic focusing** = concentration *f or* mise *f* au point magnétique; **magnetic head** = tête *f* magnétique; **magnetic ink** = encre *f* magnétique; **magnetic ink character recognition (MICR)** = reconnaissance *f* de caractères magnétiques; **magnetic master** = support *m* magnétique original *or* bande originale *or* disque original; **magnetic material** *or* **medium** = support *m* magnétique; **magnetic media** = les supports magnétiques; **magnetic memory** *or* **store** = mémoire *m* magnétique; **magnetic recording** = enregistrement *m* sur support magnétique; **magnetic screen** = écran *m* magnétique; **magnetic storm** = orage *m* magnétique; **magnetic strip** = piste *f* magnétique; **magnetic strip reader** = lecteur *m* de pistes magnétiques; **magnetic thin film storage** = mémoire à couches minces (magnétiques); **magnetic transfer** = transfert *m* d'un support magnétique à un autre *or* transfert magnétique

◊ **magnetic tape** *or* **mag tape** *noun* bande *f* magnétique; **magnetic tape cartridge** *or* **cassette** = cartouche *f or* cassette *f* de bande magnétique; **magnetic tape encoder** = encodeur *m* pour bandes magnétiques; **magnetic tape reader** = lecteur *m* de bandes magnétiques; **magnetic tape recorder** = magnétophone *m;* **magnetic tape transport** = dérouleur *m or* dispositif d'entraînement de bandes magnétiques

◊ **magnetize** *verb* magnétiser

magnify *verb (image)* agrandir *or* grossir *or* amplifier; **the photograph has been magnified 200 times** = cette photo a été agrandie 200 fois

◊ **magnification** *noun* agrandissement *m or* grossissement *m or* amplification *f;* **the lens gives a magnification of 10 times** = cette lentille grossit 10 fois

magnitude *noun (of a signal)* amplitude *f or* grandeur *f;* **signal magnitude** = amplitude d'un signal

mag tape *noun (informal)* = MAGNETIC TAPE

mail 1 *noun* **(a)** *(postal system)* poste *f* **(b)** *(letters sent or received)* courrier *m* arrivée *or* courrier départ **(c)** *(electronic messages)* **electronic mail** *or* **email** *or* **e-mail** = messagerie *f or* courrier *m* électronique **2** *verb* mettre à la poste; **to mail a letter** = poster une lettre

◊ **mailbox** *or* **mail box** *noun (electronic)* · boîte *f* aux lettres (électronique)

◊ **mailing** *noun* envoi *m* par la poste *or* mailing *m;* **the mailing of publicity material** = l'envoi (par la poste) de prospectus publicitaires; **direct mailing** = publipostage *m or* publicité *f* directe *or* mailing *m;* **mailing list** = fichier *m* d'adresses (destiné aux mailings); **his name is on our mailing list** = son nom figure sur votre fichier d'adresses; **to build up a mailing list** = établir un fichier d'adresses; **to buy a mailing list** = acheter un fichier d'adresses; **mailing piece** = prospectus *m* envoyé par la poste; **mailing shot** = envoi *m* de prospectus publicitaires

◊ **mail-merge** *noun* (programme d') édition *f* de lettres types

main *adjective* principal, -e; *(of antenna transmission)* **main beam** = porteuse principale; **main clock** = horloge *f* maîtresse; **main distributing frame** = tableau de distribution principal; *(in a catalogue)* **main entry** = entrée principale; **main index** = index général *or* principal; **main memory** *or* **main storage** = mémoire principale *or* centrale; **the 16-bit system includes up to 3Mb of main memory** = le système de 16 bits contient une mémoire principale d'une capacité allant jusqu'à 3Mo; **main routine** = routine principale

◇ **mainframe (computer)** *noun* gros ordinateur *or* ordinateur central *or* ordinateur principal; **mainframe access** = accès à l'ordinateur principal (par l'intermédiaire d'un micro)

mains electricity *noun* le secteur

maintain *verb* entretenir; **well maintained** = bien entretenu, -e

◇ **maintainability** *noun* maintenabilité *f*

◇ **maintenance** *noun* (i) maintenance *f or* entretien *m* ; (ii) service *m* de maintenance *or* service après-vente; **file maintenance** = mise *f* à jour de fichier *or* maintenance de fichier; **on-site maintenance** = service *m* d'assistance technique (sur le lieu de travail); **preventive maintenance** = maintenance préventive *or* entretien régulier; **remedial maintenance** = maintenance curative *or* réparation *f* **maintenance contract** = contrat *m* de maintenance; **maintenance routine** = programme de diagnostic *or* de maintenance; **remote maintenance** = télémaintenance *f*

major cycle *noun* cycle *m* principal

majuscule *noun* (lettre) majuscule *f or* capitale *f* (d'imprimerie)

make-ready time *noun* temps *m* de préparation

◇ **make up** *verb (book)* mettre en page; *(on computer)* formater

◇ **make up** *or* **makeup** *noun (of book)* mise *f* en page; *(of text, on computer)* formatage *m;* **corrections after the page makeup are very expensive** = les corrections faites après la mise en page coûtent très cher

male connector *noun* connecteur *m* mâle

malfunction 1 *noun (of hardware or software)* défaillance *f or* dysfonction *f or* dysfonctionnement *m;* **the data was lost due to a software malfunction** = les données ont été perdues par suite d'une défaillance du logiciel; **malfunction routine** = (programme) diagnostic *m* de dysfonctionnement **2** *verb* mal fonctionner *or* être en dérangement; **some of the keys on the keyboard have started to malfunction** = quelques-unes des touches du clavier ne fonctionnent déjà plus très bien

◇ **malfunctioning** *noun* mauvais fonctionnement *or* dysfonction *f or* dysfonctionnement *m*

man/machine interface (MMI) *noun* interface *f* homme/machine *or* interface utilisateur/machine

◇ **man-made** *adjective* artificiel, -elle; **man-made noise** = bruit parasite causé par une machine

manage *verb* gérer *or* diriger

◇ **manageable** *adjective* qui peut être maîtrisé, -ée *or* résolu, -e; **processing problems which are still manageable** = problèmes de traitement qui peuvent être résolus; **data should be split into manageable files** = les données devraient être réparties en fichiers plus courts et plus faciles à utiliser

◇ **management** *noun* gestion *f;* **network management** = gestion de réseau; **management information system (MIS)** = système de gestion informatisé

◇ **manager** *noun* **(a)** *(software)* gestionnaire *m;* **file manager** = gestionnaire de fichiers; **queue manager** = gestionnaire de file d'attente; **records manager** = gestionnaire d'enregistrements; **text manager** = gestionnaire de texte **(b)** *(person)* manager *m or* chef *m or* responsable *m* (de département); **data processing manager** = responsable *or* chef du service informatique

manipulate *verb* manipuler; **an image processor that captures, displays and manipulates video images** = un processeur d'images qui peut lire, afficher et manipuler les images vidéo

◇ **manipulation** *noun* manipulation *f* (de données *or* d'images); **a high-speed database management program allows the manipulation of very large amounts of data** = un gestionnaire de base de données ultra-rapide permet la manipulation d'une très grande quantité de données

mantissa *noun* mantisse *f;* **the mantissa of the number 45.897 is 0.897** = la mantisse du nombre 45,897 est 0,897

manual **1** *noun* manuel *m* (d'utilisation); **the manual is included with the system** = un manuel d'utilisation est fourni avec le système; **installation manual** = manuel d'installation *or* manual technique; **instruction manual** = manuel d'utilisation; **technical manual** = manuel technique *or* manuel d'installation; **user's manual** = manuel d'utilisation **2** *adjective* manuel, -elle; **manual data processing** = traitement de l'information sans l'aide d'un ordinateur; **manual entry** *or* **manual input** = saisie *f* de données par *or* au *or* sur clavier
◇ **manually** *adverb* manuellement *or* à la main; **the paper has to be fed into the printer manually** = l'alimentation en papier de l'imprimante se fait manuellement

manufacture *verb* fabriquer *or* manufacturer; **the company manufactures diskettes and magnetic tape** = cette société fabrique des disquettes et des bandes magnétiques
◇ **manufacturer** *noun* fabricant *m;* **if the system develops a fault it should be returned to the manufacturer for checking** = en cas de mauvais fonctionnement, renvoyer le système au fabricant; **the manufacturer guarantees the system for 12 months** = le fabricant garantit le système pendant an

manuscript *or* **MS** *noun* manuscrit *m;* **this manuscript was all written on computer** = ce manuscrit a été écrit directement sur ordinateur

map **1** *noun* carte *f or* configuration *f or* représentation *f;* **logic map** = configuration logique; **memory map** = configuration de la mémoire **2** *verb*

représenter; **to map out** = organiser *or* configurer *or* planifier; **database mapping** = configuration de base de données; **I/O mapping** = configuration d'entrée/sortie; **memory-mapped input/output** = entrée/sortie configurée en mémoire; **a memory-mapped screen has an address allocated to each pixel allowing direct access to the screen by the CPU** = un écran configuré en mémoire possède une adresse pour chaque pixel, permettant ainsi au processeur d'accéder directement à l'écran

MAR = MEMORY ADDRESS REGISTER

marching display *noun* visualisation *f* de contrôle d'entrée

margin *noun* **(a)** *(blank space)* marge *f;* **when typing the contract leave wide margins** = en tapant le contrat à la machine, n'oubliez pas de laisser des marges très larges; **the left margin and right margin are the two sections of blank paper on either side of the page** = les marges de droite et de gauche sont les blancs de chaque côté d'une page; **foot margin** = blanc *m* de pied; **top margin** = blanc de tête; **to set a margin** = fixer *or* paramétrer une marge **(b)** *(extra time or space)* marge; **safety margin** = marge de sécurité; **margin of error** = marge d'erreur
◇ **margination** *noun* paramétrage *m* de marges

mark **1** *noun* **(a)** *(sign)* marque *f or* signe *m;* **proof correction marks** = signes *mpl* de correction (d'épreuves d'imprimerie) **(b)** *(signal)* marque logique; **mark hold** = marque attente; **mark space** = marque espace **2** *verb* marquer *or* indiquer; **mark block** = (instruction de) marquer un bloc; **marking interval** = intervalle de marquage; **mark sense** = graphiter (une marque); **mark sense device** *or* **reader** = lecteur de marques magnétiques; **mark sensing card** = carte graphitée
◇ **marker** *noun* **(a)** **marker pen** = marqueur *m or* surligneur *m* **(b)** *(code)* marqueur *m or* indicateur *m or* marque; **block markers** = délimiteurs *mpl or* marques *fpl* de bloc; **field marker** = marqueur *m* de champ; **word marker** = marque *f* de début de mot
◇ **mark up** *verb* annoter une copie (en spécifiant la typographie)

◊ **marking up** *noun* annotation *f* typographique

MASER = MICROWAVE AMPLIFICATION BY STIMULATED EMISSION OF RADIATION amplificateur *m* MASER

mask 1 *noun* **(a)** *(circuit layout stencil)* masque *m;* **a mask or stencil is used to transfer the transistor design onto silicon** = on se sert d'un masque ou d'un stencil pour reproduire le tracé du circuit du transistor sur le silicium **(b)** *(photographic)* masque **(c)** *(pattern of binary digits)* masque; **mask bit** = bit masque; **mask register** = registre de masque; **interrupt mask** = masque d'interruption **2** *verb* masquer; **masked ROM** = mémoire morte masquée

◊ **maskable** *adjective* qui peut être masqué, -ée; **maskable interrupt** = interruption *f* qui peut être masquée *or* invalidée; **non-maskable interrupt (NMI)** = interruption obligatoire *or* qui ne peut être invalidée *or* qui ne peut être masquée

◊ **masking** *noun* masquage *m*

> QUOTE the device features a maskable interrupt feature which reduces CPU overheads
> *Electronics & Power*

mass media *noun* les médias *mpl or* les mass-medias *mpl*

◊ **mass storage** *noun* mémoire *f* de masse; **mass storage device** = support *m* de stockage de grande capacité; **a hard disk is definitely a mass storage device** = un disque dur constitue un véritable support de stockage de grande capacité; **mass storage system** = mémoire de masse

mast *noun* **radio mast** *or* **TV mast** = pylône *m* de radio *or* de télévision

master 1 *noun* maître *m;* **master antenna television system (MATV)** = antenne *f* de relais régional; **master card** = carte *f* maîtresse; **master clock** *or* **timing master** = horloge *f* maîtresse *or* horloge principale; **master computer** = ordinateur *m* maître *or* principal; **the master computer controls everything else** = l'ordinateur maître contrôle tout; **master control program (MCP)** = programme *m* de commande; **master data** = données permanentes *or* de base; **master disk** = disque *m* original; **master file** = fichier *m* principal *or* fichier maître *or* fichier permanent; **master/master computer system** = système maître/maître; **master program file** = fichier de programme maître; **master proof** = épreuve *f* finale; **master/slave computer system** = système *m* informatique maître/esclave; **master tape** = bande *f* originale; **master terminal** = terminal *m* principal *or* maître; **image master** = feuille *f* de style **2** *verb* **(a)** réussir (à faire quelque chose) *or* apprendre (quelque chose); **we mastered the new word-processor quite quickly** = nous avons appris à utiliser le nouveau système de traitement de texte assez rapidement **(b)** reporter *or* copier *or* recopier; **those slides and photographs are the intermediate materials to be mastered onto the video disk** = ces diapos et photos sont les supports intermédiaires qui doivent être recopiés sur le vidéodisque

◊ **mastergroup** *noun* *(600 voice channels)* groupe *m* tertiaire

match *verb* **(a)** assortir **(b)** *(to set a register)* accorder *or* équilibrer; **matched load** = charge accordée *or* équilibrée; **matching transformer** = transformateur *m* de couplage; **impedance matching** = accord *m* d'impédance

material *noun* **(a)** *(substance to make a finished product)* matériau *m;* **gold is the ideal material for electrical connections** = l'or est le matériau idéal pour la fabrication des connecteurs électriques; **synthetic materials** = matériaux synthétiques; **materials control** = contrôle d'approvisionnement en matériaux; **materials handling** = manutention *f* **(b)** matériel *m;* **display material** = matériel publicitaire

mathematics *noun* mathématiques *fpl*
◊ **mathematical** *adjective* mathématique; **mathematical model** = modèle mathématique; **mathematical subroutine** = sous-programme mathématique

◊ **maths** *or* US **math** *(informal)* = MATHEMATICS math *or* maths; **maths chip** *or* **coprocessor** = coprocesseur *m* mathématique

matrix *noun* **(a)** *(array of numbers)* matrice *f;* **matrix rotation** = rotation *f* de matrice **(b)** *(array of connections)* matrice de relation; **key matrix** = implantation *f* or matrice des touches sur un clavier **(c)** *(printing)* matrice graphique; **matrix printer** *or* **dot-matrix printer** = imprimante matricielle; **character matrix** = matrice de caractères

matt *or* **matte** **1** *noun (mask for film)* cache *m* or gobo *m* **2** *adjective (which is not shiny)* mat, matte

matter *noun* **(a)** question *f* or point *m* **(b)** *(main section of text)* corps *m* du texte; **printed matter** = imprimé *m;* **publicity matter** = imprimé *or* matériel *m* publicitaire

MATV = MASTER ANTENNA TELEVISION SYSTEM

maximum **1** *noun* maximum *m* **2** *adjective* maximum *or* maximal, -e; **maximum capacity** = capacité *f* maximale; *(of signal)* **maximum reading** = amplitude maximum enregistrée; **maximum transmission rate** = vitesse *f* maximale *or* débit *m* maximal de transmission; **maximum usable frequency** = fréquence *f* maximale utilisable; **maximum users** = nombre *m* maximum d'utilisateurs

Mb *or* **Mbyte** = MEGABYTE Mo *or* méga-octet *m*
◊ **Mb** = MEGABIT Mb *or* mégabit *m*
◊ **Mbps** = MEGABITS PER SECOND (nombre de) mégabits par seconde

QUOTE the maximum storage capacity is restricted to 8 Mbytes
Micro Decision

MBR = MEMORY BUFFER REGISTER

mC = MILLICOULOMB

MCP = MASTER CONTROL PROGRAM

MDR = MEMORY DATA REGISTER

mean **1** *noun* moyenne *f* **2** *adjective* moyen, -enne; **mean time between failures (MTBF)** = durée *f* moyenne de

bon fonctionnement *or* moyenne de temps de bon fonctionnement entre les défaillances (MTBF); **mean time to failure (MTF)** = durée moyenne de bon fonctionnement; **mean time to repair** = moyenne de temps requis pour réparation **2** *verb* signifier *or* vouloir dire; **the message DISK FULL means that there is no more room on the disk for further data** = le message DISK FULL signifie que le disque n'a plus l'espace voulu pour enregistrer de nouvelles données

measure **1** *noun* **(a)** *(way of calculating size)* mesure *f;* **square measure** = mesure de surface **(b)** **tape measure** = mètre *m* (à ruban) **(c)** *(width of a printed line)* largeur *f* d'une ligne *or* justification *f* **(d)** *(action)* mesure; **to take measures to prevent something happening** = prendre des mesures pour éviter quelque chose; **safety measures** = mesures de sécurité **2** *verb* mesurer
◊ **measurement** *noun* **(a)** **measurements** = dimensions *fpl or* encombrement *m;* **to write down the measurements of a package** = noter les dimensions d'un paquet **(b)** évaluation *f;* **performance measurement** *or* **measurement of performance is carried out by running a benchmark program** = la performance est mesurée à l'aide d'un programme test

mechanical *adjective* mécanique; **mechanical paper** = papier *m* journal
◊ **mechanism** *noun* mécanisme *m;* **the printer mechanism is very simple** = l'imprimante possède un mécanisme très simple; **the drive mechanism appears to be faulty** = il semble que le mécanisme du lecteur ne fonctionne pas très bien

media **(a)** media *or* média *m;* **the media** = les médias; **the product attracted a lot of interest in the media** *or* **a lot of media interest** = le produit a beaucoup fait parler de lui dans les medias *or* a suscité un grand intérêt médiatique; **media analysis** *or* **media research** = analyse *f* des médias; **media coverage** = couverture *f* médiatique; **we got good media coverage for the launch of the new model** = nous avons eu une bonne couverture médiatique pour le lancement du nouveau modèle NOTE:

media is followed by a singular or plural verb **(b)** *see* MEDIUM; **magnetic media =** supports *mpl* magnétiques

medium 1 *adjective (middle or average)* moyen, -enne; **a medium-sized computer system =** un système informatique de taille moyenne **(a)** moyen *m or* support *m;* **advertising medium =** support *m* publicitaire; **the product was advertised through the medium of the trade press =** la publicité pour le produit s'est faite par voie de presse spécialisée **(b) storage medium =** support *m* de stockage; **data storage mediums such as paper tape, magnetic disk, magnetic tape, card and microfiche are available =** il existe différents types de supports de stockage dont les bandes papier, les disques et bandes magnétiques, les cartes et microfiches; **data medium =** support de données *or* d'information; **empty medium =** support vierge; **magnetic medium** *or* **material =** support magnétique NOTE: plural is **mediums** or **media**

◇ **medium frequency** *noun (300-3000kHz)* onde *f* hectométrique

◇ **medium lens** *noun* objectif *m* standard *or* de focale moyenne

◇ **medium scale integration (MSI)** *noun* intégration *f* à moyenne échelle

◇ **medium speed** *noun* vitesse moyenne *or* débit moyen (de transmission)

◇ **medium wave (MW) =** MEDIUM FREQUENCY

meet *noun (logical function)* conjonction *f*

mega- *prefix* **(a)** *(one million)* méga; **megabits per second (Mbps) =** (nombre de) mégabits *mpl* par seconde; **megaflops (MFLOPS) =** million(s) d'opérations en virgule flottante par seconde *or* mégaflops *mpl* (Mflops); **megahertz (MHz) =** mégahertz *m* MHz **(b)** *(1,048,576 or 2^{20})* méga; **megabit (Mb) =** mégabit *m* (Mb); **megabyte (Mb) =** méga-octet *m* (Mo)

> QUOTE adding multiple megabytes of memory is a simple matter of plugging memory cards into the internal bus
> *Byte*

member *noun* élément *m* (d'un champ)

memomotion *noun* prise *f* de vue à cadence lente *or* décomposition *f* de mouvements

memory *noun* mémoire *f;* **associative memory =** mémoire associative; **backing memory =** mémoire auxiliaire; **bootstrap memory =** mémoire de lancement; **bubble memory =** mémoire à bulles; **cache memory =** mémoire cache *or* antémémoire *f;* **charge coupled device (CCD) memory =** (dispositif) mémoire à couplage de charge; **content-addressable memory =** mémoire adressable par son contenu; **control memory =** mémoire fixe; **core memory** *or* **primary memory =** mémoire centrale *or* à accès direct; **disk memory =** mémoire sur disque(tte); **dynamic memory =** mémoire dynamique; **external memory =** mémoire externe *or* auxiliaire; **fast access memory (FAM) =** mémoire à accès rapide; **FIFO memory** *or* **first in first out memory =** mémoire basée sur le principe 'premier entré premier sorti' *or* mémoire FIFO; **internal memory =** mémoire interne; **magnetic memory =** mémoire magnétique; **main memory =** mémoire principale *or* centrale; **non-volatile memory =** mémoire non-volatile; **random access memory (RAM) =** mémoire vive *or* mémoire RAM; **read only memory (ROM) =** mémoire morte *or* mémoire ROM; **scratchpad memory =** mémoire 'bloc-notes' *or* mémoire banale; **serial memory =** mémoire séquentielle; **magnetic tape is a high capacity serial memory =** la bande magnétique constitue une mémoire séquentielle d'une grande capacité; **static memory =** mémoire statique; **virtual memory =** mémoire virtuelle; **volatile memory =** mémoire volatile; **memory access time =** temps d'accès à la mémoire; **memory address register (MAR) =** registre *m* d'adresse en mémoire; **memory bank =** bloc *m or* banque *f* de mémoire; **memory board =** carte *f* mémoire; **memory buffer register (MBR) =** registre de mémoire tampon; **memory capacity =** capacité *f* de mémoire; **memory cell =** cellule *f* de mémoire; **memory chip =** puce *f* mémoire; **memory cycle =** cycle *m* de mémoire; **memory data register (MDR) =** registre des données en mémoire; **memory diagnostic =** diagnostic *m* de la mémoire; **memory dump =** listage *m* de mémoire *or* vidage *m* de mémoire (sur imprimante); **memory edit =**

changement *m* d'adresse en mémoire; **memory hierarchy** = hiérarchie *f* des mémoires; **memory-intensive (software)** = (logiciel) qui requiert beaucoup de mémoire; **memory location** = emplacement *m* de mémoire; **memory management** = gestion *f* de mémoire; **memory map** = configuration *f* de mémoire; **memory-mapped** = configuré, -ée en mémoire; **a memory-mapped screen has an address allocated to each pixel, allowing direct access to the screen by the CPU** = un écran configuré en mémoire possède une adresse pour chaque pixel, permettant ainsi au processeur d'accéder directement à l'écran; **memory-mapped I/O** = entrée/sortie configurée en mémoire; **memory page** = page *f* mémoire; **memory protect** = (dispositif de) protection *f* de la mémoire; **memory-resident** = résident, -e; **the system can bomb if you set up too many memory-resident programs at the same time** = le système peut planter si vous introduisez un trop grand nombre de programmes résidents; **memory switching system** = système à transfert de mémoire; **memory workspace** = zone *f* de travail (en mémoire)

◊ **memorize** *verb* mémoriser *or* mettre en mémoire

QUOTE when a program is loaded into memory, some is used for the code, some for the permanent data, and some is reserved for the stack which grows and shrinks for function calls and local data
Personal Computer World

menu *noun* menu *m;* **menu-driven software** = logiciel *m* avec menu *or* à base de menu; **menu selection** = sélection *f* par menu; **main menu** = menu principal; **pop-up menu** *or* **pull-down menu** = menu déroulant; **the pull-down menu is viewed by clicking over the icon at the top of the screen** = pour afficher le menu déroulant cliquer l'icône sur le haut de l'écran

QUOTE when the operator is required to make a choice a menu is displayed
Micro Decision

mercury delay line *noun (old method of storing data)* ligne *f* à *or* de retard au mercure

merge *verb* fusionner *or* intégrer *or* combiner; **the system automatically merges text and illustrations into the document** = ce système assure l'intégration automatique du texte et des illustrations dans le document; **merge sort** = (application de) tri *m* et fusion; *see also* MAIL-MERGE

mesh *noun* maille *f;* **mesh network** = réseau maillé *m*

message *noun* message *m;* **error message** = message d'erreur; **message authentication code (MAC)** = code d'identification de message; **message format** = format *m* de message; **message heading** = en-tête *f* de message; **message numbering** = numérotation *m* des messages; **message routing** = acheminement *m* des messages; *(number of bits)* **message slot** = créneau *m* pour message; **message switching** = commutation *f* de message; **message text** = texte *m* d'un message

metabit *noun* métabit *m*
◊ **metacompilation** *noun* métacompilation *f*
◊ **metalanguage** *noun* métalangage *m*

metal oxide semiconductor (MOS) *noun* semi-conducteur *m* MOS; **metal oxide semiconductor field effect transistor (MOSFET)** = semi-conducteur à effet de champ MOSFET; **complementary metal oxide semiconductor (CMOS)** = semi-conducteur CMOS

meter 1 *noun* compteur *m;* **electricity meter** = compteur d'électricité; **a meter attached to the photocopier records the number of copies made** = un compteur relié au photocopieur enregistre le nombre de photocopies **2** *verb* enregistrer (le nombre et la durée); **the calls from each office are metered by the call logger** = le nombre et la durée des appels effectués dans chacun des bureaux sont enregistrés sur l'enregistreur d'appels

metre *US* **meter** *noun (measure)* mètre *m;* **metre kilogram second (Ampere) (MKS(A))** = mètre kilogramme seconde (ampère) *or* mks(A)

MF = MEDIUM FREQUENCY

MFLOPS = MEGA FLOATING POINT OPERATIONS PER SECOND

MHz = MEGAHERTZ

MICR = MAGNETIC INK CHARACTER RECOGNITION

micro *noun* = MICROCOMPUTER

micro- *prefix* **(a)** *(one millionth)* micro-; **micrometre** = micromètre *m or* micron *m;* **microsecond (ms)** = microseconde *f* **(b)** *(very small)* **microcassette** = microcassette *f;* **microchip** = puce *f;* **microcircuit** = microcircuit *m;* **microcode** = microcode *m or* micro-instruction *f*

microcomputer *or* **micro** *noun* micro-ordinateur *m or* micro *m;* **microcomputer architecture** = architecture *f* de micro-ordinateur; **microcomputer backplane** = fond *m* de panier *or* carte *f* mère d'un micro-ordinateur; **microcomputer bus** = bus *m* d'un micro-ordinateur; **microcomputer development kit** = kit *m* d'extension de micro-ordinateur; **single board microcomputer** = micro-ordinateur monocarte *or* à carte unique
◊ **microcomputing** *noun* micro-informatique *f;* **the microcomputing industry** = l'industrie *f* des micro-ordinateurs

microcontroller *noun* micro-ordinateur *m* de contrôle *or* de commande; **single-chip microcontroller** = micro-ordinateur de contrôle à puce unique
◊ **microcycle** *noun* microcycle *m*
◊ **microdevice** *noun* dispositif *m or* composant *m* de très petites dimensions *or* microprocesseur *m*
◊ **microelectronics** *noun* la micro-électronique
◊ **microfiche** *noun* microfiche *f*
◊ **microfilm 1** *noun* microfilm *m;* **we hold all our records on microfilm** = toutes nos archives sont sur microfilms **2** *verb* microfilmer; **the 1989 records have been sent away for microfilming** = nous avons envoyé les archives de 1989

pour les faire microfilmer *or* pour les faire mettre sur microfilm(s)
◊ **microfloppy** *noun (usually refers to 3.5 inch disks)* (micro)disquette *f*
◊ **microform** *noun* microfiche *f*
◊ **micrographics** *noun* la micrographie
◊ **microimage** *noun* micro-image *f*
◊ **microinstruction** *noun* micro-instruction *f*
◊ **microphone** *noun* microphone *m or* micro *m;* **dynamic microphone** = micro(phone) dynamique; **lapel microphone** = micro-cravate *m;* **moving coil microphone** = micro(phone) à aimant mobile
◊ **microphotography** *noun* microphotographie *f*
◊ **microprocessor** *noun* microprocesseur *m;* **bit-slice microprocessor** = microprocesseur en tranches; **the bit-slice microprocessor uses four 4-bit processors to make a 16-bit word processor** = le microprocesseur en tranches utilise quatre processeurs à 4 bits pour réaliser un microprocesseur à 16 bits; **microprocessor addressing capabilities** = capacité *f* d'adressage mémoire d'un microprocesseur; **microprocessor architecture** = architecture *f* d'un microprocesseur; **microprocessor chip** = puce *f* microprocesseur; **microprocessor system** = microprocesseur; **microprocessor unit (MPU)** = microprocesseur
◊ **microprogram** *noun* microprogramme *m;* **microprogram assembly language** = langage *m* d'assemblage pour microprogramme; **microprogram counter** = registre *m or* compteur *m* de microprogramme; **microprogram instruction set** = ensemble des instructions *or* jeu *m* d'instructions d'un microprogramme; **microprogram store** = mémoire *f* qui contient un microprogramme
◊ **microprogramming** *noun* microprogrammation *f*
◊ **microsequence** *noun* séquence *f* de micro-instructions *or* d'instructions d'un microprogramme
◊ **microwave** *noun* micro-onde *f; (frequency)* hyperfréquence *f;* **microwave communications link** = liaison *f* hertzienne *or* liaison de transmission par hyperfréquence; **microwave relay** = relais *m* hertzien; **microwave transmission** = transmission *f* hertzienne *or* par hyperfréquence

mid-user *noun* utilisateur *m* intermédiaire

middleware *noun* progiciel *m* adapté aux besoins de l'utilisateur *or* progiciel personnalisé *or* sur mesure

migration *noun* migration *f;* **data migration** = transfert *m or* migration de données

mike *noun (familiar)* microphone *m or* micro *m*

milk disk *noun* disque *m* à traiter *or* disque relais
◊ **milking machine** *noun* concentrateur *m* de données *or* capteur *m* de données (à traiter)

milli- *prefix (one thousandth)* milli-; **milliampere (mA)** = milliampère (mA) *m;* **millicoulomb (mC)** = millicoulomb (mC) *m;* **millisecond (ms)** = milliseconde (ms) *f*

million *number (1,000,000)* million *m*

MIMD = MULTIPLE INSTRUCTION STREAM - MULTIPLE DATA STREAM

mini- *prefix (small)* mini; *(usually 3.5 inch)* **minidisk** = (mini)disquette *f; (slang)* **miniwinny** = minidisque dur (de type Winchester)
◊ **miniaturization** *noun* miniaturisation *f*

minicomputer *or* **mini** *noun* mini-ordinateur *m or* mini *m*

minimal latency coding *see* MINIMUM ACCESS CODE
◊ **minimal tree** *noun* arborescence *f* optimale

minimum *noun* minimum *m;* **minimum access code** *or* **minimum delay code** *or* **minimum latency coding** = code *m* à temps d'accès optimisé; **minimum weight routing** = routage *m* optimisé
◊ **minimize** *verb* minimiser *or* réduire; **we minimized costs by cutting down the number of components** = nous avons

réduit les frais en diminuant le nombre des composants

minmax *noun* méthode *f* mini/maxi

minuend *noun* nombre *m* duquel on soustrait

minus *or* **minus sign (-)** *noun* signe de la soustraction *or* (le signe) moins *m*

minuscule *noun* (lettre) minuscule *f*

MIPS = MILLION INSTRUCTIONS PER SECOND

mirror 1 *noun* miroir *m or* glace *f;* **mirror disk** = disque *m* miroir; **mirror image** = image *f* inversée **2** *verb* faire une sauvegarde sur deux disques

QUOTE they also offer mirror-disk protection against disk failure, providing automatic backup of a database
QUOTE disks are also mirrored so that the system can continue to run in the event of a disk crash
QUOTE mirroring of the database is handled automatically by systems software
Computer News

MIS = MANAGEMENT INFORMATION SYSTEM

MISD = MULTIPLE INSTRUCTION STREAM - SINGLE DATA STREAM

mismatch *noun* non accord *m or* désaccord *m or* discordance *f;* **impedance mismatch** = désaccord d'impédance

mix 1 *noun* mélange *m* (sonore) *or* mixage *m* **2** *verb (signals)* mélanger *or* faire un mixage; **to mix down** = mélanger *or* mixer
◊ **mixer** *noun* mélangeur *m or* mixeur *m*
◊ **mixing** *noun* **(a)** *(signals)* mixage *m;* **mixing studio** = studio de mixage **(b)** *(different typefaces)* (composition d'une ligne avec) mixage de polices de caractères *or* utilisant plusieurs polices de caractères

MKS(A) = METRE KILOGRAM SECOND (AMPERE)

MMI = MAN MACHINE INTERFACE

mnemonic *noun* (procédé) mnémonique *m;* **assembler mnemonics** *or* **mnemonic operation codes** = code *m* mnémonique d'assemblage

mobile *adjective* mobile; **mobile earth terminal** = station *f* terrestre mobile; **mobile unit** = unité *f* mobile; **mobile radiophone** = radiotéléphone *m* mobile *or* téléphone *m* cellulaire

mock-up *noun* maquette *f*

mode *noun* **(a)** *(way of doing something)* mode *m;* **when you want to type in text, press this function key which will put the terminal in its alphanumeric mode** = pour saisir un texte, appuyer d'abord sur cette touche de fonction qui met le terminal en mode alphanumérique; **burst mode** = mode (de transfert par) paquets; **byte mode** = mode octet; **control mode** = mode de contrôle; **deferred mode** = mode différé *or* en (mode) différé; **direct mode** = mode direct *or* en (mode) direct; **execute mode** = mode d'exécution; **form mode** = mode masque; **input mode** = mode entrée; **insert mode** = mode insertion; **interactive mode** = mode interactif; **replace mode** = mode remplacement; **sequential mode** = mode séquentiel **(b)** *(number of paths taken by light)* mode; **mode dispersion** = dispersion *f* modale **(c)** *(number that occurs most frequently)* mode (de la distribution)

◊ **modal** *adjective* modal, -e

QUOTE the printer gives print quality in three modes: high speed, data processing and letter-quality
Minicomputer News

model 1 *noun* **(a)** *(small-size copy)* maquette *f or* modèle *m* réduit; **he showed us a model of the new computer centre building** = il nous a fait voir la maquette du nouveau centre informatique **(b)** *(version)* modèle; **the new model B has taken the place of model A** = le nouveau modèle B remplace le modèle A; **this is the latest model** = voici notre dernier modèle; **demonstration model** = modèle de démonstration **2** *verb* modéliser NOTE: **modelling - modelled** but US **modeling - modeled**

◊ **modelling** *noun* création *f* de modèles de programmes

modem *or* **MODEM** *noun* = MODULATOR/DEMODULATOR modem *m;* **dial-in modem** = modem à appel automatique

modify *verb* modifier *or* adapter; **the keyboard was modified for European users** = le clavier a été adapté pour la vente en Europe; **we are running a modified version of the mail-merge system** = nous utilisons une version modifiée du programme d'édition de lettres types; **the software will have to be modified to run on a small PC** = il faudra modifier le logiciel pour pouvoir l'utiliser sur un PC

◊ **modification** *noun* modification *f or* changement *m;* **the modifications to the system allow it to be run as part of a LAN** = les modifications apportées au système permettent de l'utiliser sur un réseau local d'entreprise; **modification loop** = boucle *f* de modification

◊ **modified frequency modulation** *noun* modulation *f* de fréquence modifiée

◊ **modifier** *noun* modificateur *m*

modular *adjective* modulaire; **modular programming** = programmation *f* modulaire

◊ **modularity** *noun* modularité *f;* **the modularity of the software or hardware allows the system to be changed** = la modularité du logiciel ou du matériel permet de modifier le système

◊ **modularization** *noun* programmation *f* modulaire

modulate *verb* moduler; **modulated signal** = signal *m* modulé; **modulating signal** = signal *m* de modulation

◊ **modulation** *noun* modulation *f;* **amplitude modulation (AM)** = modulation d'amplitude (MA); **frequency modulation (FM)** = modulation de fréquence (MF); **pulse modulation** = modulation d'impulsion

◊ **modulator** *noun* modulateur *m;* **modulator/demodulator (modem)** = modulateur-démodulateur *or* modem *m*

module *noun* **(a)** *(section of program)* module *m* **(b)** *(piece of hardware)*

module; **a multifunction analog interface
module includes analog to digital and
digital to analog converters** = un module
d'interface analogique multifonction
comprend un convertisseur analogique-
numérique et un numérique-analogique

modulo arithmetic *noun* arithmétique
à modulo; **modulo-N** = modulo-n;
modulo-N check = contrôle *m* par
modulo-n

modulus *or* **MOD** *or* **mod** *noun*
modulo; **7 mod 3 = 1** = 7 modulo-3 = 1

momentary switch *noun* interrupteur
m temporaire

monadic (Boolean) operator *noun*
opérateur *m* monadique *or* à un
opérande; **the monadic operator NOT
can be used here** = l'opérateur
monadique NOT peut être utilisé ici;
monadic operation = opération *f*
monadique

monitor 1 *noun* **(a)** moniteur *m or* écran
m (de visualisation); **multi-scan** *or* **multi-
sync monitor** = écran multistandard;
monitor unit = moniteur **(b)**
(loudspeaker) moniteur (retour de son);
(TV control screen) moniteur (de
contrôle d'image) **(c)** *(software)* **monitor
program** = programme *m* de contrôle *or*
programme moniteur; **firmware monitor**
= moniteur intégré **(d)** *(system that
watches for faults)* (dispositif de)
contrôle *m;* **power monitor** = (dispositif
de) contrôle de l'alimentation **2** *verb* (i)
vérifier; (ii) contrôler *or* surveiller *or*
suivre; **he is monitoring the progress of
the trainee programmers** = il contrôle *or*
suit le progrès des programmeurs
débutants; **the machine monitors each
signal as it is sent out** = l'appareil
contrôle chaque signal de sortie

mono- *prefix* mono
◇ **monoaural** *adjective* monaural, -e
◇ **monochrome** *adjective & noun*
monochrome *or* noir et blanc;
monochrome monitor = écran *m*
monochrome *or* écran noir et blanc
◇ **monolithic** *adjective* (circuit intégré)
monolithique
◇ **monomode fibre** *noun* fibre *f* optique
monomode

◇ **monophonic** *adjective*
monophonique
◇ **monoprogramming system** *noun*
système *m* de monoprogrammation
◇ **monospacing** *noun* espacement *m*
uniforme
◇ **monostable** *noun* (circuit)
monostable *m*

Monte Carlo method *noun* méthode *f*
de Monte Carlo

Morse code *noun* morse *m or* alphabet
m morse; **morse key** = télégraphe *m or*
manipulateur *m* morse

MOS = METAL OXIDE
SEMICONDUCTOR semi-conducteur *m*
MOS; *see also* MOSFET; **MOS memory** =
mémoire *f* MOS; **CMOS** =
COMPLEMENTARY METAL OXIDE
SEMICONDUCTOR semi-conducteur
CMOS

QUOTE integrated circuits fall into one of two
distinct classes, based either on bipolar or
metal oxide semiconductor (MOS) transistors
Electronics & Power

mosaic *noun* mosaïque *f*

MOSFET = METAL OXIDE
SEMICONDUCTOR FIELD EFFECT
TRANSISTOR

most significant bit *or* **msb** *or* **MSB**
noun bit de poids fort *or* le bit le plus
significatif; **the most significant bit in an
eight bit binary word represents 128 in
decimal notation** = le bit le plus
significatif dans un mot de huit bits
représente 128 en notation décimale
◇ **most significant character** *or* **most
significant digit (MSD)** *noun* chiffre de
poids fort *or* le chiffre le plus significatif
NOTE: the opposite is **LSB, LSD**

motherboard *noun* carte *f* mère

motion picture *noun* film *m*
(cinématographique)

motor *noun* moteur *m*

mount *verb* monter; **the chips are
mounted in sockets on the PCB** = les

puces sont montées sur des supports implantés sur la carte de circuit imprimé

mouse *noun* souris *f;* **mouse-driven (software)** = (logiciel) contrôlé *or* piloté par une souris; *(program)* **mouse driver** = (programme) pilote *m* de souris NOTE: the plural is **mice**

> QUOTE a powerful new mouse-based editor:- you can cut, paste and copy with the mouse
> *Personal Computer World*
> QUOTE you can use a mouse to access pop-up menus and a keyboard for a word-processor
> *Byte*

mouth *noun* ouverture *f or* bouche *f*

M out of N code *noun* code *m* N dont M

move *verb* déplacer *or* changer de place; **move block** = (instruction de) déplacer un bloc; **moving coil microphone** = microphone *m* à bobine *or* à aimant mobile

◊ **movable** *adjective (which can be moved)* mobile; *(which can be removed)* amovible

◊ **movement** *noun* mouvement *m;* **movement file** = fichier *m* (de) mouvements

MPS = MICROPROCESSOR SYSTEM

MPU = MICROPROCESSOR UNIT

ms = MILLISECOND

MS = MANUSCRIPT
NOTE: plural is **MSS**

msb *or* **MSB** = MOST SIGNIFICANT BIT

MSD = MOST SIGNIFICANT DIGIT

MS-DOS® = MICROSOFT DOS MS-DOS

MSI = MEDIUM SCALE INTEGRATION

M signal *noun* signal *m* groupé

MSX *noun* norme *f or* standard *m* MSX

MTBF = MEAN TIME BETWEEN FAILURES

MTF = MEAN TIME TO FAILURE

multi- *prefix (many or more than one)* multi-; **multimegabyte memory card** = carte mémoire de plusieurs méga-octets; **a multistandard unit** = unité *f* multinorme *or* unité multistandard; **multi-access system** = système *m* à accès multiple *or* système multi-accès; **multi-address** *or* **multi-address instruction** = instruction *f* multi-adresse

◊ **multi-board computer** *noun* ordinateur *m* multicarte

◊ **multiburst signal** *noun* signal *m* multipaquet

◊ **multi-bus system** *noun* système *m* multibus *or* à bus multiples

◊ **multicasting** *noun* transmission *f* multicible

◊ **multichannel** *adjective* (système) multivoie

◊ **multicolour** *adjective* multicolore

◊ **multidimensional** *adjective* multidimensionnel, -elle; **multidimensional array** = tableau multidimensionnel; **multidimensional language** = langage multidimensionnel *or* multiniveau

◊ **multi-disk** *adjective* multidisque; **multi-disk option** = option *f* multidisque; **multi-disk reader** = lecteur *m* multidisque

◊ **multidrop circuit** *noun* circuit multipoint

◊ **multifrequency** *noun* multifréquence *f;* **dual tone, multifrequency (DTMF)** = signalisation *f* multifréquence DTMF

◊ **multifunction** *adjective* multifonction *f;* **a multifunction analog interface module includes analog to digital and digital to analog converters** = un module d'interface analogique multifonction comprend un convertisseur analogique-numérique et un convertisseur numérique-analogique; **multifunction card** = carte *f* d'extension multifonction; **multifunction workstation** = poste *m* de travail multifonction

◊ **multifunctional** *adjective* multifonction; **a multifunctional scanner** = scanner *m* multifonction

◊ **multilayer** *noun* multicouche *or* à couches multiples

◊ **multilevel** *noun* multiniveau *or* à plusieurs niveaux

◊ **multilink system** *noun* système multiligne *or* à multiples connexions *or* système maillé

◊ **multimedia** *adjective* multimédia; **multimedia mail** = message multimédia

◊ **multimeter** *noun* multimètre *m;* **analog multimeter (AMM)** = multimètre analogique; **digital multimeter (DMM)** = multimètre numérique

◊ **multimode fibre** *noun* fibre *f* optique multimode

◊ **multi-part stationery** *noun* papier *m* (listing) en plusieurs épaisseurs

◊ **multipass overlap** *noun* impression *f* à passages multiples

◊ **multiphase program** *noun* programme *m* multiphase

multiple *adjective* multiple; **multiple access** = (à) accès *m* multiple; *see* MULTI-ACCESS; **multiple address code** = code *m* multi-adresse; **multiple bus architecture** = architecture *f* à bus multiples; **multiple instruction stream - multiple data stream (MIMD)** = architecture *f* MIMD *or* architecture multiflux d'instruction-multiflux de données; **multiple instruction stream - single data stream (MISD)** = architecture *f* MISD *or* architecture multiflux d'instruction-monoflux de données; **multiple precision** = (en) multiple précision

multiplex *verb* multiplexer; **multiplexed analog components (MAC)** = format *m* MAC; **multiplexed bus** = bus *m* multiplexé

◊ **multiplexing** *noun* multiplexage *m;* **dynamic multiplexing** = multiplexage dynamique; **homogeneous multiplexing** = multiplexage homogène; **optical multiplexing** = multiplexage optique; *see also* TIME

◊ **multiplexor (MUX)** *noun* multiplexeur *m;* **a 4 to 1 multiplexor combines four inputs into a single output** = un multiplexeur 4/1 reçoit sur 4 canaux et émet sur un seul

QUOTE the displays use BCD input signals and can be multiplexed to provide up to six digits
Electronics & Power

multiply *verb* multiplier

◊ **multiplicand** *noun* multiplicande *m*

◊ **multiplication** *noun* multiplication *f;* **the multiplication of 5 and 3 equals 15** = le résultat de la multiplication de 5 par 3 est 15; **multiplication sign (x)** = signe *m* de la multiplication

◊ **multiplier** *noun* multiplicateur *m*

multipoint *adjective* multipoint

◊ **multiprecision** *noun* (en) multiple précision

◊ **multiprocessing system** *noun* système *m* multiprocesseur

◊ **multiprocessor** *noun* multiprocesseur *m;* **multiprocessor interleaving** = multiprogrammation *f*

◊ **multi-programming** *noun* multiprogrammation *f*

◊ **multi-scan** *or* **multi-sync monitor** *noun* moniteur *m* multistandard

◊ **multi-statement line** *noun* ligne *f* multi-instruction

◊ **multi-strike printer ribbon** *noun* ruban *m* multifrappe

multitasking *or* **multi-tasking** *noun* multitâche *f;* **the system is multi-user and multi-tasking** = c'est un système multi-utilisateur et multitâche; **real-time multitasking** = multitâche en temps réel

QUOTE this is a true multi-tasking system, meaning that several computer applications can be running at the same time
Which PC?
QUOTE page management programs are so greedy for memory that it is not a good idea to ask them to share RAM space with anythingelse, so the question of multi-tasking does not arise here
Desktop Publishing

multi-terminal system *noun* système *m* à plusieurs terminaux *or* système multiposte

◊ **multithread** *noun* programme *m* à plusieurs branches

◊ **multi-user system** *noun* système multi-utilisateur *or* système multiposte; **the program runs on a standalone machine or a multi-user system** = on peut exécuter le programme sur un ordinateur indépendant ou sur un système multiposte

◊ **multivibrator** *noun* multivibrateur *m;* **astable multivibrator** = multivibrateur astable

◇ **multi-window editor** *noun* logiciel *m* (de traitement de texte) multifenêtre

◇ **multi-windowing** *noun* multifenêtrage *m*

mung up *verb (informal)* bouffer *or* altérer *or* ruiner (des données *or* un fichier)

mush *noun (informal)* purée *f or* brouillard *m;* **mush area** = zone *f* de brouillage *or* de purée

music chip *noun* circuit *m* intégré générateur de son; **music synthesizer** = synthétiseur *m* de son

muting *noun* assourdissement *m or* réduction *f* de bruit ; **interstation muting** = réduction du bruit d'interférence interstation

MUX = MULTIPLEXOR multiplexeur *m*

MW = MEDIUM WAVE

Nn

n *prefix (nano-)* n *or* nano-

n-channel metal oxide semiconductor *noun* semi-conducteur *m* MOS à canal (de type) N

N-key rollover *noun* clavier *m* à mémoire sur n touches *or* clavier rapide

NAK *or* **NACK** = NEGATIVE ACKNOWLEDGEMENT

name *noun* **(a)** nom *m;* **brand name** = (nom de) marque *f* **(b)** *(to identify an address)* nom; **file name** = nom de fichier; **program name** = nom de programme; *(symbol table)* **name table** = table de noms *or* de symboles; **variable name** = nom de variable

NAND function *noun* fonction *f* NON-ET *or* NAND; **NAND gate** = porte *f or* circuit *m* NON-ET *or* NAND

nano- *or* **n** *prefix (one thousand millionth or one billionth)* nano- (n); **nanocircuit** *or* **nanosecond circuit** = circuit *m* (électronique *or* logique) à délai de réponse de l'ordre de la nanoseconde; **nanometre** *or* **nm** nanomètre *m;* **nanosecond** *or* **ns** = nanoseconde (ns) *f*
NOTE: US billion is the same as UK one thousand million (10 to the power of nine); UK billion is one million million (10 to the power of 10)

QUOTE the cache's internal RAM is accessed in under 70ns from address strobe to ready signal
Electronics & Power

narrative *noun (explanatory notes)* commentaire *m*
◊ **narrative statement** *noun* déclaration *f* (de procédure)

narrow band *noun* bande *f* étroite; **narrow band FM (NBFM)** = (système de) modulation *f* de fréquence à bande étroite

National Television Standards Committee (NTSC) *noun (used mainly in the USA and in Japan)* Comité National de Normalisation de la Télévision; **NTSC standards** = normes *fpl* NTSC; *see also* VIDEO STANDARDS

native *adjective* natif, -ive; *(first or basic format)* **native format** = format *m* initial *or* de base

natural *adjective* naturel, -elle; **natural binary coded decimal (NBCD)** = (codage) décimal codé binaire naturel; **natural language** = langage *m* naturel; **the expert system can be programmed in a natural language** = le système expert peut être programmé en langage naturel

QUOTE there are two main types of natural-language interface: those based on menus, and those where the user has to discover what questions the computer will respond to by trial and error
Electronics & Power

NBCD = NATURAL BINARY CODED DECIMAL

NBFM = NARROW BAND FREQUENCY MODULATION

NC = NUMERICAL CONTROL

NCR paper = NO CARBON REQUIRED paper *see* CARBONLESS PAPER

NDR = NON DESTRUCTIVE READOUT

near-letter-quality (NLQ) *noun (of dot-matrix printer)* qualité *f* courrier; **switch the printer to NLQ for these form letters** = mettez l'imprimante en mode courrier pour imprimer ces lettres types

needle *noun (on dot matrix printer)* aiguille *f*

negate *verb (to reverse the sign of a number)* inverser *or* affecter d'un signe négatif *or* qualifier négativement; **if you negate 23.4 the result is -23.4** = la valeur négative *or* l'opposé de 23,4 est -23,4

◊ **negation** *noun (reversing the sign of a number)* négation *f or* inversion *f*

◊ **negative 1** *adjective (meaning 'no')* négatif, -ive; *(indicates signal incorrectly or incompletely received)* **negative acknowledgement (NAK** *or* **NACK)** = accusé *m* de réception négatif (NACK); **negative feedback** = rétroaction négative; **negative number** = nombre négatif; **negative-true logic** = logique *f* négative **2** *noun (film)* négatif *m or* épreuve *f* négative; **contact negative** = (film) négatif contact

neither-nor function *noun (logical function)* fonction *f* NON-OU *or* NI

NEQ = NON-EQUIVALENCE; **NEQ function** = *(logical function)* fonction *f* de disjonction *or* OU exclusif; **NEQ gate** = porte *f or* circuit *m* OU-exclusif

nest *verb (loop or subroutine)* imbriquer *or* emboîter; **nested loop** = boucle *f* imbriquée *or* emboîtée; **nested macrocall** = macro-instruction *m* imbriquée; *(of loops)* **nesting level** = niveau *m* d'imbrication (de boucles); **nesting store** = mémoire *f* à liste permutée

network 1 *noun* réseau *m*; **communications network** = réseau de communication *or* de télécommunications; **computer network** = réseau d'ordinateurs *or* réseau informatique; **information network** = réseau informatique; **local area network (LAN)** = réseau local d'entreprise; **long haul network** = réseau à (grande) distance; **radio network** = réseau radiophonique; **television network** = réseau de télévision; **wide area network (WAN)** = réseau étendu *or* à distance; **network analysis** = analyse *f* de réseaux; **network architecture** = architecture *f* de réseau; **network control program** = programme *m* de contrôle de réseau; **network controller** = contrôleur *m* de réseau; **network database** = base *f* de données en réseau; **network diagram** = diagramme *m* (de configuration *or* de topologie) de réseau; **network hardware** = matériel *m or* équipements *mpl* de réseau (informatique); *(ISO/OSI standard layer)* **network layer** = couche *f* réseau; *see also* LAYER; **network management** = gestion *f* de réseau; **network processor** = processeur *m* de réseau; *(extra links)* **network redundancy** = liaisons *fpl* redondantes *or* auxiliaires d'un réseau; **network software** = logiciel *m* de réseau; **network structure** = structure *f* en réseau; **network timing** = synchronisation *f* de réseau **2** *verb* disposer *or* configurer en réseau; **they run a system of networked micros** = ils exploitent un réseau de micros; **the workstations have been networked together rather than used as standalone systems** = les postes de travail ont été reliés en réseau plutôt que d'être utilisés indépendamment; **networked TV programme** = programme *m* transmis sur (tout) un réseau de télévision

◊ **networking** *noun* **(a)** *(TV or radio)* transmission *f or* diffusion *f* sur (tout) un réseau **(b)** *(organization of a computer network)* architecture *f or* configuration *f* de réseau; *(interconnecting computers)* mise *f* en réseau (d'ordinateurs); **networking hardware** *or* **network hardware** = matériel *m or* équipements *mpl* de réseau *or* en réseau; **networking software** *or* **network software** = logiciel *m* de *or* pour réseau; **networking specialist** = expert *m or* spécialiste *m&f* en réseaux informatiques; **this computer firm is a UK networking specialist** = cette société informatique est une société britannique spécialisée en réseaux

---

QUOTE the traditional way of operating networks involves having a network manager and training network users to familiarize themselves with a special set of new commands

Which PC?

QUOTE workstations are cheaper the more you buy, because they are usually networked and share resources

PC Business World

---

neutral *adjective* neutre; **neutral transmission** = transmission *f* neutre

new *adjective (recent)* nouveau, nouvelle *or* récent, -e; **they have installed a new computer system** = ils ont installé un nouveau système informatique *or* un nouvel ordinateur; *(command)* **new (command)** = (commande de lancement d'une) nouvelle tâche; **new line character** = caractère *m* indiquant d'aller à la ligne; *see also* CARRIAGE RETURN (CR); LINEFEED (LF); **new technology** = nouvelle technologie *or* techniques nouvelles

◊ **news** *noun (radio or TV)* informations *fpl or* nouvelles *fpl; (in newpapers)* **business news** = chronique *f* économique; **financial news** = chronique financière; **news agency** = agence *f* de presse; **news release** = communiqué *m* de presse; **the company sent out a news release about the new laser printer** = la société a diffusé un communiqué au sujet de la nouvelle imprimante (à) laser

◊ **newsletter** *noun* **company newsletter** = bulletin *m* (d'informations) de la société

◊ **newsprint** *noun* papier *m* journal

next instruction register *noun* registre *m* d'instruction à exécuter *or* de la prochaine instruction

nexus *noun* connexion *f*

nibble *or* **nybble** *noun (half the length of a standard byte)* demi-octet *m*
NOTE: a nibble is normally 4 bits, but can vary according to different micros or people

nil pointer *noun* marqueur *m* de fin de liste

nine's complement *noun* complément *m* à neuf

n-level logic *noun* logique *f* à n niveau(x)

NLQ = NEAR-LETTER-QUALITY

nm = NANOMETRE

NMI = NON-MASKABLE INTERRUPT

NMOS = N-CHANNEL METAL OXIDE SEMICONDUCTOR

no-address operation *noun* opération *f* sans adresse *or* non adressable

node *noun* noeud *m*; **a tree is made of branches that connect together at nodes** = une arborescence est formée de branches reliées les unes aux autres par des points de liaison ou noeuds; **this network has fibre optic connection with nodes up to one kilometre apart** = ce réseau est relié par fibres optiques avec des noeuds pouvant être espacés d'un kilomètre les uns des autres

noise *noun* bruit *m or* (bruits) parasites *(mpl) or* brouillage *m;* **noise immunity** = insensibilité *f or* tolérance *f* aux bruits; **noise margin** = marge *f* de bruit *or* limite *f* de tolérance au bruit; **noise temperature** = température *f* de bruit; **galactic noise** = bruits cosmiques; **impulsive noise** = bruit intermittent; **thermal noise** = bruit thermique

> QUOTE the photographs were grainy, out of focus, and distorted by signal noise
>
> *Byte*

nomenclature *noun* nomenclature *f*

nomogram *or* **nomograph** *noun* nomographe *m or* abaque *m*

non- *prefix* non-
◊ **nonaligned** *adjective* désaligné, -ée *or* non-aligné, -ée; **nonaligned read head** = tête de lecture désalignée
◊ **non-arithmetic shift** décalage *m* logique; *also* LOGICAL SHIFT
◊ **noncompatibility** *noun* incompatibilité *f or* non compatibilité
◊ **noncounting keyboard** *noun* clavier *m* aveugle produisant une bande non justifiée
◊ **non-destructive cursor** *noun* curseur *m* non destructif; **the screen quickly becomes unreadable when using a non-destructive cursor** = l'écran devient rapidement illisible lorsqu'on utilise le curseur non destructif; **non-destructive readout (NDR)** = lecture *f* non destructive; **non-destructive test** = essai *m* non destructif; **I will carry out a number of non-destructive tests on your computer: if it passes, you can start using it again** = je vais effectuer une série de tests non destructifs sur votre machine;

si tout se passe bien, vous pourrez vous en servir de nouveau

◊ **non-equivalence function (NEQ)** *noun* fonction *f* de disjonction *or* OU exclusif; **non-equivalence gate** = porte *f or* circuit *m* OU exclusif

◊ **nonerasable storage** *noun* mémoire *f* permanente *or* qui ne peut être effacée *or* ineffaçable; **paper tape is a nonerasable storage** = une bande papier perforée est une mémoire qui ne peut être effacée

◊ **non-impact printer** *noun* imprimante *f* sans impact

◊ **nonlinear** *adjective* non-linéaire

◊ **non-maskable interrupt (NMI)** *noun* interruption *f* obligatoire *or* qui ne peut être invalidée *or* qui ne peut être masquée

◊ **non-operable instruction** *noun* instruction *f* factice *or* nulle *or* de remplissage

◊ **non-printing codes** *noun* code *m* paramétrique *or* de paramétrage de l'imprimante; **the line width can be set using one of the non-printing codes, .LW, then a number** = la largeur des lignes peut être définie par le code paramétrique .LW suivi d'un chiffre

◊ **non return to zero (NRZ)** *noun* non-retour *m or* non-remise *f* à zéro

◊ **non-scrollable** *adjective* qu'on ne peut pas faire défiler (sur l'écran)

◊ **non-volatile** *adjective* (retains data even when the power has been switched off) non-volatile; **non-volatile memory** *or* **non-volatile store** *or* **storage** = mémoire *f* non-volatile; **bubble memory is a non-volatile storage** = la mémoire à bulles est une mémoire non-volatile; **using magnetic tape provides non-volatile memory** = une bande magnétique constitue une mémoire non-volatile
NOTE: opposite is **volatile**

no-op = NO-OPERATION

no-operation *or* **no-op instruction** *noun* instruction *f* vide *or* factice *or* de remplissage

NOR function *noun* (logical function) fonction *f* NON-OU *or* NI; **NOR gate** = porte *f or* circuit *m* NON-OU *or* NI

normal *adjective* normal, -e; **the normal procedure is for backup copies to be made at the end of each day's work** = la procédure normale préconise une sauvegarde de tout le travail en fin de journée; **normal format** = format normal *or* standard; **normal range** = gamme *or* fourchette *or* plage normale

◊ **normalize** *verb* (a) *(to convert data)* normaliser (b) *(to convert characters)* uniformiser (en majuscules *or* en minuscules) *or* mettre en mode majuscule *or* minuscule (c) *(to store and represent numbers)* normaliser *or* formater (un nombre, une donnée); **all the new data has been normalized to 10 decimal places** = toutes les nouvelles données sont normalisées à dix positions décimales; *(floating point number)* **normalized form** = forme normalisée

◊ **normalization** *noun* normalisation *f or* formatage *m*; *(normalizes a floating point number)* **normalization routine** = routine *f* de normalisation

NOT function *noun* (logical inverse function) fonction *f* NON *or* fonction complément; **NOT gate** = porte *f or* circuit *m* NON *or* circuit inverseur; **NOT-AND (NAND)** = fonction NON-ET *or* NAND

notation *noun* notation *f*; **binary notation** = notation binaire; **decimal notation** = notation décimale; **hexadecimal notation** = notation hexadécimale; **infix notation** = notation infixée; **octal notation** = notation octale; **postfix notation** = notation suffixée *or* notation polonaise inversée; **normal notation: (x-y) + z, but using postfix notation: xy - z + =** en notation normale on écrit: (x-y) + z, en notation polonaise inversée on écrit: xy- z+; **prefix notation** = notation préfixée

notched *see* EDGE NOTCHED CARD

notepad *noun* bloc-notes *m*; **screen notepad** = fenêtre *f* bloc-notes

notice board *noun* tableau *m* d'affichage

n-plus-one address instruction *noun* instruction à n adresse(s) plus une

npn transistor *noun* transistor *m* (de type) npn

NRZ = NON RETURN TO ZERO

ns *abbreviation (nanosecond)* ns *or* nanoseconde *f*

NTSC = NATIONAL TELEVISION STANDARDS COMMITTEE *(used mainly in the USA and in Japan)* Comité National de Normalisation de la Télévision (NTSC); **NTSC standard** = norme *f* NTSC; *see also* VIDEO STANDARDS

QUOTE the system has a composite video output port that conforms to the NTSC video specification

Byte

n-type material *or* **N-type material** *or* **n-type semiconductor** *noun* matériau *m* semi-conducteur de type N; *see also* NPN TRANSISTOR

null *noun (nothing)* nul, nulle; **null character** = caractère nul *or* de remplissage; **null instruction** = instruction nulle *or* factice *or* de remplissage; **null list** = liste vide; **null modem** = sans modem; **this cable is configured as a null modem, which will allow me to connect these two computers together easily** = ce câble est configuré sans modem ce qui permet de connecter les deux ordinateurs sans difficulté; *(that only contains zeros)* **null set** = jeu *m* *or* ensemble *m* de caractères nuls; *(that contains no characters)* **null string** = chaîne *f* vide

QUOTE you have to connect the two RS232 ports together using a crossed cable, or null modem

PC Business World

number 1 *noun* **(a)** nombre *m;* **number cruncher** = processeur *m* mathématique pour calcul (en masse) ultra-rapide; **number crunching** = opérations numériques (en masse) ultra-rapides; **a very powerful processor is needed for graphics applications which require extensive number crunching capabilities** = il faut un processeur très puissant pour les applications graphiques qui exigent une forte capacité de traitement des nombres en masse; **number range** = gamme *f* de valeurs **(b)** *(written figure)* chiffre *m* *or* numéro *m;* **each piece of hardware has a production number** = chacune des pièces de l'ordinateur possède un numéro de fabrication; *(for parity or error detection)* **check number** = chiffre *m* *or* clé *f* (numérique) de contrôle **2** *verb* **(a)** *(a document)* numéroter; **the pages of the manual are numbered 1 to 395** = les pages de ce manuel sont numérotées de 1 à 395 **(b)** *(items on a list)* numéroter

◊ **numeral** *noun* chiffre *m; (written 1, 2, 3, 4, etc.)* **Arabic numerals** = chiffres arabes; *(written I, II, III, IV, etc.)* **Roman numerals** = chiffres romains

◊ **numeric** *adjective* numérique *or* numéral, -e; **numeric array** = tableau *m* numérique *or* de chiffres; **numeric character** = lettre *f* numérale *or* caractère *m* (à valeur) numérique; **numeric keypad** = pavé *m* *or* clavier *m* numérique; **numeric operand** = opérande *m* numérique; **numeric pad** = pavé *or* clavier numérique; **numeric punch** = perforation *f* numérique

◊ **numerical** *adjective (referring to numbers)* numérique; **numerical analysis** = analyse *f* numérique; **numerical control (NC)** *or* **computer numerical control (CNC)** = commande *f* *or* contrôle *m* numérique

nybble *or* **nibble** *noun (informal) (half the length of a standard byte)* demi-octet *m*
NOTE: a nybble is normally 4 bits, but can vary according to different micros

Oo

OA = OFFICE AUTOMATION

object *noun* **(a)** *(variable in expert system)* objet *m* **(b)** *(data in a statement)* objet; **object architecture** *or* **object-orientated architecture** = architecture orientée vers l'objet *or* adaptée à l'ojet; **object code** = code *m* objet; **object computer** = ordinateur *m* d'exécution (de programme objet); *(punched cards that contain a program)* **object deck** = jeu *m* (de cartes) objet; **object language** = langage *m* objet; *compare with* SOURCE LANGUAGE; **object program** = programme *m* objet
◇ **objective** *noun* **(a)** *(aim)* but *m or* objectif *m* **(b)** *(lens)* objectif

obtain *verb* obtenir *or* recevoir; **to obtain data from a storage device** = extraire des données rangées en mémoire; **a clear signal is obtained after filtering** = le filtrage permet d'obtenir un signal très clair

OCCAM langage *m* (de programmation) OCCAM

occur *verb* se produire *or* avoir lieu *or* survenir; **data loss can occur because of power supply variations** = les fluctuations de courant peuvent entraîner la perte de données

OCP = ORDER CODE PROCESSOR *(in a multiprocessor system)*

OCR **(a)** = OPTICAL CHARACTER READER lecteur *m* optique de caractères **(b)** = OPTICAL CHARACTER RECOGNITION reconnaissance *f* optique de caractères; **OCR font** = police *f* de caractères reconnaissable par lecteur optique

octal (notation) *adjective (notation)* octal, -e *or* en base huit; *(digit 0 to 7 in the octal system)* **octal digit** = nombre *m* en base octale; **octal scale** = base huit

octave *noun (series of eight musical notes)* octave *f*

octet *noun (group of eight bits)* octet *m*

odd *adjective (number)* impair, -e; **odd-even check** = contrôle *m* de parité paire-impaire; **odd parity (check)** = (contrôle de) parité *f* impaire *or* (contrôle d') imparité *f*

OEM = ORIGINAL EQUIPMENT MANUFACTURER

off-cut *noun (paper)* tombée *f*

off hook *adverb (telephone)* (combiné) décroché

office *noun (room or building)* bureau *m;* **office automation (OA)** = bureautique *f;* **office computer** = ordinateur *m* de bureau *or* à usage professionnel; **office copier** = copieur *m* de bureau *or* copieur professionnel; **office equipment** = équipement(s) *m(pl)* de bureau; **office of the future** = le bureau du futur; *see also* PAPERLESS OFFICE

off-line *adverb & adjective (peripheral or processing, etc.)* hors ligne *or* off-line; *(peripheral)* non-connecté, -ée *or* autonome; *(processing, etc.)* en différé; **before changing the paper in the printer, switch it off-line** = avant de remplacer le papier de l'imprimante, assurez-vous que l'imprimante est hors ligne *or* off-line; **off-line printing** = impression *f* hors ligne *or* en différé *or* par imprimante autonome; **off-line processing** traitement *m* hors ligne *or* off-line *or* en différé
NOTE: opposite is **on-line**

offprint *noun* tiré *m* à part *or* copie *f*

off screen *adverb (TV action)* (action) hors champ

offset 1 *noun* **(a)** *(printing)* offset *m;* **offset lithography** = lithographie *f* offset; **offset printing** = impression *f* (en) offset **(b)** *(quantity added to a number)* valeur *f* complémentaire; *(value to be added to a base address)* **offset value** *or* **offset word** = valeur *or* adresse *f* relative

ohm *noun* ohm *m;* **this resistance has a value of 100 ohms** = la valeur de cette résistance est de 100 ohms; *(one thousand ohms)* **kilo-ohm** = kilo-ohm
◊ **Ohm's Law** *noun* loi *f* d'Ohm

O.K. *(prompt meaning 'ready')* OK

omega wrap *noun (for threading video tape)* enrouleur-presseur *m* (de bande)

omission factor *noun* facteur *m* d'omission *or* de silence

omnidirectional *adjective* omnidirectionnel, -elle; **omnidirectional aerial** = antenne omnidirectionnelle; **omnidirectional microphone** = microphone omnidirectionnel

OMR (a) = OPTICAL MARK READER **(b)** = OPTICAL MARK RECOGNITION

on-board *adjective (on main PCB)* encarté, -ée *or* intégré, -ée

> QUOTE the electronic page is converted to a printer-readable video image by the on-board raster image processor
> QUOTE the key intelligence features of these laser printers are emulation modes and on-board memory
>
> *Byte*

on chip *noun (circuit)* circuit *m* intégré à une puce
◊ **on-chip** *adjective* intégré, -ée à une puce; **the processor uses on-chip bootstrap software to allow programs to be loaded rapidly** = le processeur utilise un logiciel de lancement intégré à la puce, pour permettre le chargement rapide des programmes

one address computer *noun* ordinateur *m* à adresse unique; **one address instruction** = instruction *f* à adresse unique *or* à adresse directe
◊ **one element** *noun (logical function)* (opération) constante *f*
◊ **one for one** *noun (programming language)* (langage de programmation) un pour un
◊ **one-level address** *noun* adresse *f* directe *or* à un niveau; **one-level code** = code direct *or* à un niveau; **one-level store** = mémoire *f* à un niveau; **one-level subroutine** = sous-programme direct

one's complement *noun* complément *m* à 1; **the one's complement of 10011 is 01100** = le complément à 1 de 10011 est 01100

one-pass assembler *noun* assembleur *m* une passe; **this new one-pass assembler is very quick in operation** = ce nouvel assembleur une passe travaille très vite
◊ **one-plus-one address** *noun* une adresse plus une

one-time pad *noun (for coding system)* clé *f* (à usage) unique

one to zero ratio *noun* rapport *m* de discrimination *or* rapport un à zéro

on hook *adverb (telephone)* (combiné) (r)accroché

onion skin architecture *noun (computer design)* architecture *f* en pelure d'oignon; **the onion skin architecture of this computer is made up of a kernel at the centre, an operating system, a low-level language and then the user's program** = cet ordinateur possède une architecture en pelure d'oignon comprenant un noyau central, un système d'exploitation, un langage de bas niveau et le programme utilisateur
◊ **onion skin language** *noun* langage *m* en pelure d'oignon

on-line *adverb & adjective (processing or peripheral, etc.)* en ligne *or* on-line; *(peripheral)* relié, -ée *or* connecté, -ée; **the terminal is on-line to the mainframe** = le terminal est en ligne avec l'ordinateur principal *or* connecté à l'ordinateur principal; **on-line database** = base *f* de données en ligne; **on-line information retrieval** = recherche *f* documentaire en ligne; **on-line processing** = traitement *m* en ligne *or* on-line; **on-line storage** = stockage *m* de données en ligne; **on-line system** = système *m* en ligne *or* relié à l'ordinateur principal; **on-line transaction processing** = traitement transactionnel en ligne

on-screen *adjective (displayed on a screen)* (affiché, -ée) à l'écran *or* visualisé, -ée

on-site *adjective* sur place; **on-site maintainance** = service *m* d'assistance technique sur le lieu de travail; **the new model has an on-site upgrade facility** = le nouveau modèle peut être optimisé sans renvoi chez le fournisseur

on the fly *adverb (without stopping the run)* à la volée

O/P *or* **o/p** = OUTPUT

opacity *noun (of optical lens)* opacité *f*
NOTE: opposite is **transmittance**

op amp = OPERATIONAL AMPLIFIER

op code = OPERATION CODE code *m* d'opération

> QUOTE the subroutine at 3300 is used to find the op code corresponding to the byte whose hex value is in B
>
> *Computing Today*

opaque *adjective* opaque; **the screen is opaque - you cannot see through it** = l'écran étant opaque, il est impossible de voir au travers; **opaque projector** = épidiascope *m or* projecteur *m* de documents opaques

open 1 *adjective* **(a)** *(file)* ouvert, -e; **you cannot access the data unless the file is open** = vous ne pouvez pas accéder aux données que si le fichier est ouvert **(b)** *(not closed)* ouvert, -e; **open access** = (poste de travail) ouvert *or* à accès illimité *or* banalisé; **open code** = code ouvert; **open-ended program** = programme extensible *or* ouvert; **open loop** = boucle ouverte; **open reel tape** = bande *f* sur bobine ouverte; **open routine** = routine ouverte; **open subroutine** = sous-programme ouvert; *(which can work with other systems)* **open system** = système ouvert; **Open System Interconnection (OSI)** = interconnexion *f* de systèmes ouverts (ISO) *or* normes ISO (pour systèmes ouverts); *see also* ISO/OSI LAYERS, INTERNATIONAL **2** *verb* **(a)** *(door or cover)* ouvrir; **first, open the disk drive door** = ouvrez d'abord la porte du lecteur de disquettes; **open the top of the computer by lifting** = soulevez le couvercle de l'ordinateur pour l'ouvrir **(b)** *(file)* ouvrir (un fichier); **you cannot access the data unless the file has been opened** = vous ne pouvez accéder aux données avant d'avoir ouvert le fichier

operand *noun* opérande *m; in the instruction ADD 74, the operator ADD will add the operand 74 to the accumulator* = par effet de l'instruction ADD 74, l'opérateur ADD va ajouter l'opérande 74 à l'accumulateur; **immediate operand** = opérande immédiat; **literal operand** = opérande littéral; **numeric operand** = opérande numérique; **operand field** = champ *m* d'opérande

operate *verb* faire marcher *or* faire fonctionner *or* mettre en marche; **do you know how to operate the telephone switchboard?** = êtes-vous capable de faire marcher le standard téléphonique?; **disk operating system (DOS)** = système *m* d'exploitation DOS; **operating code (op code)** = code *m* d'opération *or* de commande; **operating console** = poste *m or* station *f* de travail; **operating instructions** = commandes *fpl;* **operating system (OS)** = système *m* d'exploitation; **operating time** = temps *m* d'exécution (d'une tâche)

◊ **operation** *noun* opération *f;* **arithmetic operation** = opération arithmétique; **binary operation** = opération binaire; **block operation** = manipulation *f* de bloc; **Boolean operation** = opération booléenne; **complete operation** = cycle *m* complet d'exécution d'une opération; **dyadic Boolean operation** = opération booléenne dyadique *or* à deux opérandes; **no-address operation** = opération non adressable; **no-operation** instruction (**no-op**) = instruction *f* vide *or* factice *or* de remplissage; **operation code (op code)** = code *m* d'opération; **operation cycle** = cycle d'opération; *see also* FETCH-EXECUTE CYCLE, MACHINE CYCLE; **operation decoder** = décodeur *m* d'instruction; **operation field** = champ *m* d'opération; **operation priority** = ordre *m* de priorité des opérations; **operation register** = registre *m* d'opération; **operation time** = temps *m* d'exécution d'une opération; **operation trial** = essai *m* *or* test *m* opérationnel; **operations manual** = manuel *m* d'utilisation

◊ **operational** *adjective* opérationnel, -elle; **operational information** = notice *f* d'utilisation

◊ **operational amplifier (op amp)** *noun* amplificateur *m* operationnel

operator *noun* (**a**) *(person)* opérateur, -trice; **the operator was sitting at his console** = l'opérateur était assis devant l'écran de son ordinateur *or* à son pupitre; **computer operator** = opérateur *m*; **operator's console** = console *f* *or* pupitre *m* de commande *or* poste *m* de travail d'un opérateur; *(mathematical)* **operator precedence** = ordre *m* d'enchaînement des opérations *or* de mise en oeuvre des opérateurs (mathématiques); *(to work a machine)* **operator procedure** = procédure *f* de commande (**b**) *(symbol)* opérateur; **x is the multiplication operator** = x est l'opérateur de la multiplication; **arithmetic operator** = opérateur *or* symbole *m* (d'une opération) arithmétique

op register *noun* registre *m* de code d'opération

optic fibres = OPTICAL FIBRES; **fibre optics** = technologie *f* de la fibre optique *or* de la transmission par fibre optique

optical *adjective (referring to or making use of light)* optique; **an optical reader uses a light beam to scan characters, patterns or lines** = un lecteur optique utilise un rayon lumineux qui balaye les caractères, les symboles ou les lignes; **optical bar reader** *or* **bar code reader** *or* **optical wand** = lecteur (optique) de codes barres *or* stylo *m* optique; **optical character reader (OCR)** = lecteur optique de caractères; **optical character**

recognition (**OCR**) = reconnaissance *f* optique de caractères; **optical communications system** = système de communication optoélectronique; **optical data link** = liaison *f* optique pour transmission de données; **optical disk** = disque *m* optique; **optical fibre** = fibre *f* optique; **optical font** *or* **OCR font** = police *f* de caractères reconnaissable par lecture optique; **optical mark reader (OMR)** = lecteur optique de marques; **optical mark recognition (OMR)** = reconnaissance *f* optique de marques *or* de signes *or* de symboles; **optical memory** = mémoire *f* optique; **optical scanner** = scanner *m;* **optical storage** = *(action)* stockage *m* de données sur support optique; *(place)* mémoire *f* optique; **optical transmission** = transmission *f* par système optoélectronique; **optical wand** *or* **optical bar reader** = stylo *m* optique

optimization *noun* optimisation *f*

◊ **optimize** *verb* optimiser; **optimized code** = code accéléré *or* amélioré *or* optimisé

◊ **optimizer** *noun* (programme) optimiseur *m*

optimum *noun & adjective (best possible)* optimum *(m)* **optimum code** = code *m* optimal *or* code à temps d'accès minimum

option *noun* option *f;* **there are usually four options along the top of the screen** = on trouve habituellement quatre options affichées en haut de l'écran; **the options available are described in the main menu** = les options disponibles sont décrites dans le menu principal

◊ **optional** *adjective* optionnel, -elle; **the system comes with optional 3.5 or 5.25 disk drives** = le système est équipé d'un lecteur de disquettes 3,5 ou 5,25 pouces au choix

> QUOTE with the colour palette option, remarkable colour effects can be achieved on an RGB colour monitor
> *Electronics & Wireless World*

optoelectrical *adjective (which converts light to electrical signals or electrical signals into light)* optoélectrique

◊ **optoelectronic** *adjective* optoélectronique *or* optronique

◊ **optoelectronics** *noun*
l'optoélectronique *f or* l'optronique *f*

OR function *noun (logical function)*
fonction *f* OU *or* OR; **OR gate** = porte *f or*
circuit *m* OU *or* OR

orbit 1 *noun* orbite *f;* **the satellite's orbit
is 100km from the earth's surface** = le
satellite se déplace sur une orbite à
100km de la terre; **elliptical orbit** =
orbite elliptique; **geostationary orbit** =
orbite géostationnaire; **polar orbit** =
orbite polaire **2** *verb* orbiter *or* parcourir
une orbite *or* décrire une orbite; **this
weather satellite orbits the earth every
four hours** = ce satellite météorologique
décrit une orbite autour de la terre
toutes les quatre heures

order *noun* **(a)** *(instruction)* commande
f or instruction *f;* **order code** = code *m* de
commande *or* d'opération; *(in a
multiprocessor system)* **order code
processor (OCP)** = processeur *m* de
codes de commande **(b)** *(disposition)*
ordre *m;* **in alphabetical order** = en *or* par
ordre alphabétique; **ordered list** = liste
triée *or* classée en ordre (alphabétique,
etc.) **2** *verb* **(a)** *(to instruct)* donner une
commande *or* une instruction **(b)** *(to put
in order)* ordonner *or* classer *or* trier

organize *verb* organiser

◊ **organization** *noun* **(a)** *(way of
arranging)* organisation *f;* **organization
chart** = organigramme *m* **(b)** *(group of
people)* organisation

◊ **organizational** *adjective*
organisationnel, -elle

orientated *adjective* orienté, -ée;
problem-orientated language (POL) =
langage *m* de résolution de problèmes *or*
langage adapté aux problèmes *or* langage
d'application

◊ **orientation** *noun* orientation *f*

origin *noun* **(a)** *(position on a screen)*
origine *f* **(b)** *(location in memory)*
adresse *f* origine

original 1 *adjective* original, -e **2** *noun*
(a) *(document)* original *m;* **the original is
too faint to photocopy well** = l'original
n'est pas assez contrasté pour être

photocopié **(b)** *(first disk or film or
recording)* disque *or* film original *or*
bande originale

◊ **original equipment manufacturer
(OEM)** *noun* (i) constructeur *m* de
matériel informatique en pièces
détachées *or* OEM *m* ; (ii) ensemblier *m*
or revendeur *m* de systèmes agencés sur
mesure *or* utilisateur *m* intermédiaire *or*
OEM; **one OEM supplies the disk drive,
another the monitor** = un constructeur
de matériel en pièces détachées fournit
l'unité de disques, un autre le moniteur;
**he started in business as a manufacturer
of PCs for the OEM market** = il a
commencé sa carrière comme
constructeur de PC pour le marché
OEM

◊ **originate** *verb (to start)* produire *or*
créer; *(to come from)* venir de *or* sortir de;
**the data originated from the new
computer** = les données viennent *or*
sortent du nouvel ordinateur

◊ **origination** *noun* création *f or*
production *f;* **the origination of the
artwork will take several weeks** = la
création de la maquette demandera
plusieurs semaines; **data origination** =
création de données

orphan *noun* **orphan (line)** =
(première) ligne *f* (d'un paragraphe)
isolée en bas de page; *see also* WIDOW

ortho film *or* **orthochromatic film**
noun film *m* orthochromatique

orthogonal *adjective* orthogonal, -e

OS = OPERATING SYSTEM système *m*
d'exploitation

oscillator *noun* oscillateur *m*

oscilloscope *noun* oscilloscope *m*

OSI = OPEN SYSTEM
INTERCONNECTION *see also* ISO/OSI

out of band signalling *noun*
signalisation *f* hors bande (vocale)

◊ **out of phase** *adverb* déphasé, -ée

◊ **out of range** *adjective* hors de portée
or inaccessible *or* qui dépasse la capacité
(d'un ordinateur, etc.)

outage noun (of machine) (temps de) non disponibilité or interruption f de service (d'un appareil)

outdent verb faire ressortir or faire déborder une ligne (dans la marge gauche)
NOTE: opposite is **indent**

outlet noun (point de) sortie f; (electrical) prise f de courant

outline noun profil m or esquisse f; **outline flowchart** = schéma m directeur

output (o/p or **O/P) 1** noun (a) (data) sortie f; **computer output** = données fpl de sortie or sortie d'ordinateur (NOTE: opposite is **input**) (b) (action) sortie; **output area** or **block** = zone f sortie (de la mémoire); **output bound** or **limited** = limité, -ée or contraint, -e par la (vitesse de) sortie; **output buffer register** = registre m tampon de sortie; **output device** = périphérique m (de sortie); **output file** = fichier de sortie; **output formatter** = formateur m de données de sortie; **output mode** = mode m sortie; **output register** = registre m (de sortie); **output stream** = flux m (de données) de sortie; **output port** = port m or connecteur m (de) sortie; **input/output (I/O)** = entrée/sortie f see also INPUT **2** verb transmettre or transférer; **finished documents can be output to the laser printer** = les documents qui sont prêts peuvent être transmis à l'imprimante laser
NOTE: **outputting - output**

QUOTE most CAD users output to a colour plotter
PC Business World

OV = OVERFLOW

overflow or **OV** noun (a) (of storage system) dépassement m de capacité; **overflow bit** or **flag** or **indicator** = bit m or indicateur m or drapeau m or marque f de dépassement de capacité; **overflow check** = contrôle m de dépassement de capacité (b) (of line capacity) débordement m de capacité (d'une ligne)

overhead noun (a) (extra code) code m or élément m de structure; **the line numbers in a BASIC program are an overhead** = les numéros de lignes sont des éléments de structure en BASIC; **overhead bit** = bit m supplémentaire; **polling overhead** = temps m d'appels sélectifs (b) **overhead projector** = rétroprojecteur m (c) **routing overheads** = procédure f de contrôle d'acheminement or protocole m de routage (un message)

overheat verb chauffer or surchauffer; **the system may overheat if the room is not air-conditioned** = il se peut que le système chauffe si la pièce n'est pas climatisée

overink verb mettre trop d'encre or encrer de façon excessive

◊ **overinking** noun excès m d'encre; **two signatures were spoilt by overinking** = deux cahiers ont été gâchés par excès d'encre

overlap 1 noun chevauchement m or recouvrement m or superposition f; (printing) **multipass overlap** = impression f à plusieurs passages légèrement décalés or surimpression f **2** verb (se) chevaucher or (se) recouvrir or (se) superposer

overlay noun (a) (strip of paper placed over keys) **keyboard overlay** = grille f d'aide or mémento m de fonction des touches de clavier (b) (small section of a program) segment m de programme; **form overlay** = texte m or graphique m préétabli (gardé en mémoire); (software) **overlay manager** = gestionnaire m de segments de recouvrement; (area of main memory) **overlay region** = zone f de segment de recouvrement; **overlay segment** = segment de recouvrement

◊ **overlay network** noun réseau m à zone de recouvrement

◊ **overlaying** noun utilisation f d'une technique de recouvrement

overload 1 verb surcharger; **the computer is overloaded with that amount of processing** = l'ordinateur est vraiment surchargé par tout ce travail **2** noun surcharge f; **channel overload** = surcharge de la voie

overmodulation *noun* surmodulation *f*

overpunching *noun* surperforation *f*

overrun 1 *noun* engorgement *m* **2** *verb* faire une erreur de synchronisation (en transmettant trop vite)

overscan *noun* balayage *m* hors champ *or* en dehors des limites

overstrike *verb (to print on top of an existing character)* faire une surcharge *or* faire une surimpression *or* superposer des caractères (pour créer un nouveau caractère)

overtones *noun see* HARMONICS

over-voltage protection *noun* (dispositif de) protection *f* contre le survoltage *or* la surtension

overwrite *verb (data)* (i) superposer des données *or* faire une superposition d'écriture (et détruire les données en mémoire); (ii) remplacer *or* effacer *or* détruire des données par superposition d'écriture; **the latest data input has overwritten the old information =** les nouvelles données ont remplacé les anciennes (par superposition d'écriture)

oxide *noun* oxyde *m;* **ferric oxide =** oxyde ferrique; **metal oxide semiconductors (MOS) =** semi-conducteurs *m* MOS; *see also* MOSFET, CMOS, NMOS

Pp

p = PICO-

PA = PUBLIC ADDRESS

p-channel *noun* canal (de type) P; **p-channel MOS** = semi-conducteur *m* MOS à canal (de type) P; *see also* P-TYPE SEMICONDUCTOR

P-code *noun* pseudocode *m or* pseudo-instruction *f*

PABX = PRIVATE AUTOMATIC BRANCH EXCHANGE

pack 1 *noun* **(a)** *(punched cards)* paquet *m;* **disk pack** = chargeur *m* **(b)** kit *m or* trousse *f* (d'outils *or* de nettoyage, etc.); **power pack** = bloc *m* d'alimentation **2** *verb* **(a)** *(goods)* emballer *or* conditionner; **the diskettes are packed in plastic wrappers** = les disquettes sont présentées sous emballage plastique **(b)** *(to store data in a reduced form)* condenser *or* comprimer *or* compacter; **packed decimal** = décimale condensée; **packed format** = format *m* condensé

package *noun* **(a)** **package deal** = contrat *m* global *or* forfait *m;* **we are offering a package deal which includes the whole office computer system, staff training and hardware maintenance** = nous offrons un contrat global comprenant un système informatique complet pour le bureau, la formation du personnel et l'entretien du matériel **(b)** **applications package** = programme *m* d'application *or* progiciel *m;* **packaged** *or* **canned software** *or* **software package** = progiciel en coffret *or* progiciel plus manuel d'utilisation; **the computer is sold with accounting and word-processing packages** = l'ordinateur se vend avec un progiciel de comptabilité et traitement de texte

◊ **packaging** *noun* **(a)** *(material)* emballage *m or* conditionnement *m;* **airtight packaging** = emballage hermétique **(b)** *(creating books for publishers)* création *f* de livres (par des maisons spécialisés) *or* packaging *m*

◊ **packager** *noun (of books)* packager *m or* packageur *m*

packet *noun (group of bits)* paquet *m;* **packet assembler/disassembler (PAD)** = assembleur/désassembleur *m* (de paquets); **the remote terminal is connected to a PAD device through which it accesses the host computer** = le terminal éloigné est relié à un assembleur/désassembleur de paquets qui lui permet d'accéder à l'ordinateur hôte; **packet switched data service** *or* **packet switched network (PSN)** = réseau *m* de commutation de données par paquets; **packet switching** = commutation *f* (de messages) par paquets

packing *noun* **(a)** *(of goods)* emballage *m or* conditionnement *m* **(b)** *(data)* compression *f or* condensation *m or* compactage *m;* **packing density** = densité *f* d'enregistrement; **packing routine** = routine *f* de compression *or* routine de compactage **(c)** *(material to protect goods)* emballage *m*

PAD = PACKET ASSEMBLER/DISASSEMBLER

pad 1 *noun* **(a)** *(of keys)* clavier *m or* pavé *m;* **cursor pad** = touches *fpl* fléchées *or* touches de contrôle (du curseur); **keypad** = pavé *or* clavier (numérique, etc.); **hex keypad** = clavier hexadécimal; **numerical keypad** = pavé *or* clavier numérique **(b)** **digitizing pad** = tablette *f* à numériser *or* tablette graphique; **graphics pad** = tablette graphique **2** *verb* remplir; **pad character** = caractère *m* de remplissage

◊ **padding** *noun* remplissage *m*

paddle *noun* manette *f*; **games paddle** = manette de jeu

page *noun* **(a)** *(sheet of paper)* page *f* **(b)** *(side of a printed sheet or text held on a computer screen)* page; **page break** = *(point at which a page ends)* fin *f* de page; *(marker)* caractère *m* de fin de page; **page description language (PDL)** = langage *m* de description de page; **page display** = affichage *m* d'une page; *(in wordprocessing)* **page length** = longueur *f* de page *or* nombre de lignes par page; *(speed of printer)* **pages per minute (ppm)** = (nombre de) pages par minute (ppm); **page printer** = imprimante *f* (en mode) page **(c)** *(section of main store)* page (de) mémoire; **multiple base page** = système *m* multipage; **page addressing** = adressage *m* de page; **page boundary** = limite *f* de page; **page protection** = protection *f* de page; **page table** = table *f* de pages **(d)** *(section of a main program)* page 2 *verb* **(a)** *(to use a radio-pager)* **to page someone** = appeler *or* chercher à joindre quelqu'un par système d'appel (de personne) *or* par signaleur d'appel *or* par bip **(b)** *(to make a text into page)* mettre en page; *(to put numbers onto pages)* paginer **(c)** *(to divide computer store into sections)* paginer

◊ **pager** *noun* récepteur *m* de poche *or* signaleur *m* d'appel (pour système d'appel de personne) *or* bip *m*

◊ **pagination** *noun* pagination *f*

◊ **paging** *noun* **(a)** *(calling someone on his pager)* (système d') appel *m* de personne *or* radiorecherche *f* de personne; *see also* RADIO PAGING **(b)** *(of text)* mise *f* en page; *(numbering pages)* pagination **(c)** *(technique that splits main memory)* pagination *f*; **paging algorithm** = algorithme *m* de pagination

Paintbox® *noun* palette *f* graphique

paired registers *noun* registres *mpl* appariés *or* associés; **the 8-bit CPU uses a paired register to provide a 16-bit address register** = pour obtenir un registre d'adresse de 16 bits avec un processeur de 8 bits, on lui associe un deuxième registre (de 8 bits)

PAL = PHASE ALTERNATING LINE norme *f* de télévision couleur PAL

palette *noun* palette *f*

PAM = PULSE AMPLITUDE MODULATION

panel *noun* *(flat section of a casing)* panneau *m*; **the socket is on the back panel** = la prise est située sur le panneau arrière; **control panel** = panneau de contrôle; **front panel** = panneau avant

paper *noun* papier *m*; **the book is printed on 80gsm paper** = le livre est imprimé sur du papier 80 grammes; **glossy paper is used for printing half-tones** = on utilise du papier glacé pour l'impression de similigravures; **bad quality paper gives too much show-through** = un papier de mauvaise qualité est beaucoup trop transparent; **paper feed** = (dispositif d') entraînement *m or* alimentation *f* du papier; *US* **paper slew** = PAPER THROW; **paper tape** = bande *f* papier; **paper tape punch** = poinçon *m* de perforation (pour bandes papier); **paper tape reader** = lecteur *m* de bandes perforées; **paper tape feed** = (dispositif d') entraînement de la bande papier; **paper throw** = saut *m* du papier; **paper bin** *or* **paper tray** = bac *m* à papier (pour l'alimentation en feuille à feuille); *(used in printing)* **paper weight** = grammage *m*

◊ **paperback** *noun* livre *m* broché *or* livre de poche; **we are publishing the book as a hardback and as a paperback** = ce livre paraîtra en édition cartonnée et en livre de poche

◊ **paperbound** *adjective* (livre) broché *or* (édition) brochée

◊ **paper-fed** *adjective* a **paper-fed scanner** = scanner *m* avec alimentation automatique du papier

◊ **paperless** *adjective* **paperless office** = bureau *m* sans papier *or* le bureau électronique

parallel *adjective* parallèle; **parallel access** = accès *m* parallèle; **parallel adder** = additionneur *m* parallèle;

parallel computer = ordinateur _m_ parallèle; **parallel connection** = connexion _f_ (en) parallèle; **their average transmission rate is 60,000 bps through parallel connection** = leur débit de transmission est de 60 000 bits par seconde en connexion parallèle; **parallel data transmission** = transmission _f_ de données en parallèle; **parallel input/output (PIO)** = entrée/sortie _f_ (en) parallèle; **parallel input/output chip** = circuit intégré d'entrée/sortie en parallèle; **parallel input/parallel output (PIPO)** = entrée parallèle/sortie parallèle; **parallel input/serial output (PISO)** = entrée parallèle/sortie série; **parallel interface** _or_ **port** = interface _f or_ port _m_ parallèle; **parallel operation** = opération _f_ (en) parallèle; **parallel port** _see_ PARALLEL INTERFACE; **parallel priority system** = système de gestion des priorités en (fonctionnement) parallèle; **parallel printer** = imprimante _f_ parallèle _or_ imprimante ligne à ligne; **parallel processing** = traitement _m_ (en) parallèle; _(running an old and a new computer together)_ **parallel running** = exploitation _f_ en parallèle _or_ en double; **parallel search storage** = mémoire _f_ associative; **parallel transfer** = transfert _m_ (en) parallèle; **parallel transmission** = transmission _f_ (en) parallèle

parameter _noun_ paramètre _m; **the X parameter defines the number of characters displayed across a screen** = le paramètre X définit le nombre de caractères contenus dans une ligne d'écran; **the size of the array is set with this parameter** = la taille du tableau est fixée par ce paramètre; **parameter-driven software** = _(with values not yet fixed)_ logiciel _m_ paramétrable; _(with values fixed)_ logiciel paramétré _or_ paramétrique; **parameter testing** = test _m_ paramétrique; **parameter word** = mot-paramètre _m;_ **physical parameter** = paramètre physique _or_ donnée descriptive

◊ **parametric (subroutine)** _noun_ sous-programme _m_ paramétré _or_ paramétrique

◊ **parameterization** _noun_ paramétrage _m_

parity _noun_ parité _f;_ **block parity** = parité de bloc; **column parity** = parité de colonne; **even parity (check)** = (contrôle de) parité paire; **odd parity (check)** =

(contrôle de) parité impaire _or_ (d') imparité _f;_ **parity bit** = bit _m_ de parité; **parity check** = contrôle _m_ de parité; **parity flag** = indicateur _m_ de contrôle de parité; **parity interrupt** = interruption _f_ (de contrôle) de parité; **parity track** = piste _f_ de parité

parsing _noun (of high-level language)_ analyse _f_ syntaxique _or_ lexicale

part _noun_ **(a)** section _f or_ partie _f;_ **part page display** = affichage _m_ réduit _or_ d'une partie de page **(b)** spare part = pièce _f_ détachée; **the printer won't work - we need to get a spare part** = l'imprimante est en panne, il faut remplacer une pièce **(c)** _(listing paper)_ **two part stationery** = (papier listing) en double épaisseur; _see also_ MULTIPART

partial carry _noun_ report _m_ partiel

◊ **partial RAM** _noun_ (mémoire) RAM partielle _or_ incomplète

particle _noun_ particule _f_

partition **1** _noun_ division _f_ **2** _verb_ subdiviser _or_ diviser _or_ découper; **partitioned file** = fichier _m_ subdivisé _or_ fichier divisé en plusieurs parties

party line _or_ **shared line** _noun_ _(telephone line)_ ligne _f_ partagée

PASCAL _(programming language)_ langage _m_ PASCAL

pass **1** _noun_ passe _f or_ passage _m;_ **single-pass assembler** = assembleur _m_ une passe; **sorting pass** = passage de tri **2** _verb (magnetic tape)_ (faire) défiler

password _noun_ mot _m_ de passe; **the user has to key in the password before he can access the database** = l'utilisateur doit d'abord taper le mot de passe pour avoir accès à la base de données

QUOTE the system's security features let you divide the disk into up to 256 password-protected sections
Byte

patch _noun_ modification _f or_ correction _f_ provisoire

◊ **patchboard** *noun* panneau *m* de raccordement *or* tableau *m* de distribution

◊ **patchcord** *noun* cordon *m* de liaison *or* de raccordement d'un tableau de distribution

path *noun (of program)* chemin *m or* filière *f*

pattern *noun (shapes or lines)* motif *m or* forme *f or* dessin *f*; **pattern recognition** = reconnaissance *f* de formes; *(TV)* **test pattern** = mire *f* de contrôle

◊ **patterned** *adjective* avec motifs *or* avec dessins

pay TV *noun* télévision *f* câblée (payante)

◊ **paycable** *noun US* télévision câblée (payante)

PAX = PRIVATE AUTOMATIC EXCHANGE

PBX = PRIVATE BRANCH EXCHANGE

PC (a) = PERSONAL COMPUTER ordinateur *m* personnel *or* ordinateur individuel *or* PC; **PC compatible** = compatible *or* compatible PC **(b)** = PRINTED CIRCUIT (BOARD) **(c)** = PROGRAM COUNTER

QUOTE in the UK, the company is known not for PCs but for PC printers
Which PC?

PCB = PRINTED CIRCUIT BOARD

PCM (a) = PULSE CODE MODULATION **(b)** = PLUG-COMPATIBLE MANUFACTURER

PCU = PERIPHERAL CONTROL UNIT

PDL = PAGE DESCRIPTION LANGUAGE, PROGRAM DESIGN LANGUAGE

PDM = PULSE DURATION MODULATION

PDN = PUBLIC DATA NETWORK

peak 1 *noun* pic *m or* crête *f or* pointe *f*; **keep the peak power below 60 watts or the amplifier will overheat** = veillez à ce que la tension de crête ne dépasse pas 60 watts sinon l'amplificateur surchauffera; **the marker on the thermometer shows the peak temperature for today** = le marqueur du thermomètre indique la température maximum d'aujourd'hui; *(of waveform)* **peaks and troughs** = les pointes et les creux; **peak period** = heure(s) *f(pl)* de pointe; **time of peak demand** = période *f* de demande maximum; **peak output** = niveau *m* maximum de production *or* production *f* record **2** *verb* atteindre un niveau maximum; **the power peaked at 1,200 volts** = la tension a atteint le niveau maximum de 1200 volts

peek *noun* instruction *f* PEEK (de lecture directe de la mémoire); **you need the instruction PEEK 1452 here to examine the contents of memory location 1452** = vous devez utliser l'instruction PEEK 1452 pour regarder le contenu de la mémoire à l'emplacement 1452; *compare* POKE

peg *verb* **(a)** bloquer *or* verrouiller **(b)** marquer *or* atteindre (un niveau); **after he turned up the input level, the signal level meter was pegging on its maximum stop** = lorsqu'il a augmenté le niveau d'entrée, l'aiguille du mesureur de niveau a bondi en butée *or* a atteint son maximum

pel *see* PIXEL

pen *noun* stylo *m*; **pen recorder** = traceur *m or* enregistreur *m* graphique; *see also* ELECTRONIC PEN, LIGHT PEN

per *preposition* **(a) as per** = suivant *or* selon; **as per sample** = selon échantillon; **as per specification** = selon les spécifications **(b)** *(at a rate of)* par; **per day** = par jour; **per hour** = (à *or* de) l'heure; **per week** = par semaine; **per year** = par année **(c)** *(out of)* pour; **the rate is twenty-five per thousand** = le taux s'élève à vingt-cinq pour mille; **the error rate has fallen to twelve per hundred** = le taux d'erreur est tombé à douze pour cent

◊ **per cent** *adjective & adverb* pour cent; **10 per cent** = dix pour cent; **what is the** increase **per cent?** = quel est le pourcentage d'augmentation?; **fifty per cent of nothing is still nothing** = cinquante pour cent de rien est toujours rien

◊ **percentage** noun pourcentage m; **percentage increase** = pourcentage d'augmentation; **percentage point** = un pour cent

◊ **percentile** noun centile m

perfect 1 adjective parfait, -e or impeccable; **we check each batch to make sure it is perfect** = nous vérifions chaque lot pour nous assurer de la qualité **2** verb mettre au point; **he perfected the process for making high grade steel** = il a mis au point le procédé de fabrication d'un acier de haute qualité

◊ **perfect binding** noun (of books which are trimmed and glued to the cover) reliure f sans couture or perfect binding

◊ **perfect bound** adjective (livre) relié sans couture or avec perfect binding

◊ **perfectly** adverb parfaitement or impeccablement

◊ **perfector** noun presse f qui imprime recto/verso

perforations noun ligne f or colonne f de perforations or ligne perforée

◊ **perforated tape** noun bande perforée or ruban perforé

◊ **perforator** noun poinçon m de perforation; (machine) perforatrice f

perform verb (machine) marcher or fonctionner (bien or mal)

◊ **performance** noun performance f; **as a measure of the system's performance** = pour juger de la performance du système; **in benchmarking, the performances of several systems or devices are tested against a standard benchmark** = les bancs d'essais consistent à évaluer la performance de plusieurs systèmes ou périphériques en utilisant le même test standard; **high performance** = (de) haute performance

perigee noun périgée m

period noun **(a)** période f; **for a period of time** = pendant quelque temps or pendant un certain temps; **for a period of months** = pendant quelques mois; **for a six-year period** = pendant six ans or sur

une période de six ans **(b)** US (typography) point m

◊ **periodic** or **periodical 1** adjective **(a)** (from time to time) périodique or de temps en temps **(b)** (that occurs regularly) **periodic** = périodique or à intervalles réguliers; **the clock signal is periodic** = l'horloge émet un signal à intervalles réguliers **2** noun (magazine) **periodical** = périodique m

◊ **periodically** adverb périodiquement or de temps en temps

peripheral 1 adjective périphérique **2** noun périphérique m; **peripherals such as disk drives or printers allow data transfer and are controlled by a system, but contain independent circuits for their operation** = les périphériques, tels que les lecteurs de disquettes et imprimantes, qui permettent le transfert de données sont asservis à un système (central) mais fonctionnent grâce à des circuits indépendants; **fast peripheral** = périphérique rapide; **slow peripheral** = périphérique lent; **peripheral control unit (PCU)** = unité f de commande or unité de contrôle de périphérique or contrôleur m de périphérique; (program or routine) **peripheral driver** = gestionnaire m or pilote m de périphérique; **peripheral equipment** = (piece of equipment) un périphérique; (all equipment) les périphériques; **peripheral interface adapter (PIA)** = interface f or connecteur m de périphérique; **peripheral limited** = limité par (la vitesse d') un périphérique or avec contrainte de vitesse de périphérique; **peripheral memory** = mémoire f (de) périphérique; **peripheral processing unit (PPU)** = processeur m périphérique; (device driver) **peripheral software driver** = routine f de gestion de périphérique; **peripheral transfer** = échange m d'informations or de données entre unité centrale et périphérique; **peripheral unit** = périphérique

permanent adjective permanent, -e; **permanent dynamic memory** = mémoire f dynamique permanente; **permanent error** = erreur f permanente; **permanent file** = fichier m permanent; **permanent memory** = mémoire f permanente

◊ **permanently** adverb de façon permanente or en permanence or définitivement; **the production number is permanently engraved on the back of the**

computer casing = le numéro de fabrication est gravé définitivement sur le panneau arrière du boîtier de l'ordinateur

permeability *noun* perméabilité *f*

permutation *noun* permutation *f;* **this cipher system is very secure since there are so many possible permutations for the key** = ce code chiffré est très sûr puisqu'il comporte une clé avec un très grand nombre de permutations possibles

persistence *noun* persistance *f;* **slow scan rate monitors need long persistence phosphor to prevent the image flickering** = les écrans à faible fréquence de balayage ont besoin de phosphore à longue persistance pour éviter l'instabilité de l'image

person *noun* personne *f;* **person-to-person call** = appel *m* (téléphonique) avec préavis
◊ **personal** *adjective* personnel, -elle; **personal computer (PC)** = ordinateur *m* individuel *or* personnel *or* PC *m;* **personal identification device (PID)** = dispositif *m* électronique d'identification *or* carte *f* magnétique; **personal identification number (PIN)** = numéro *m* de code confidentiel *or* personnel *or* d'identification
◊ **personalize** *verb* personnaliser

PERT = PROGRAM EVALUATION AND REVIEW TECHNIQUE

petal printer = DAISY WHEEL PRINTER

pF = PICOFARAD picofarad (PF) *m*

phantom ROM *noun* (mémoire) ROM fantôme

phase 1 *noun* **(a)** *(part of a larger process)* phase *f;* **compile phase** = phase de compilation; **run phase** *or* **target phase** = phase d'exécution *or* (en) code objet **(b)** *(delay)* phase; **in phase** = en phase; **out of phase** = déphasé, -ée; **phase alternating line (PAL)** = norme *f* de télévision couleur PAL; **phase angle** = angle *m* de phase *or* de déphasage; **phase**

clipping = écrêtage *m* de phase; **phase equalizer** = égaliseur *m* *or* compensateur *m* de phase; **phase modulation** = modulation *f* de phase **2** *verb* **to phase in** = commencer *or* démarrer *or* introduire quelque chose graduellement; **to phase out** = arrêter *or* mettre fin à quelque chose graduellement; **phased change-over** = changement *m* graduel *or* progressif

phon *noun (measure of sound)* phone *m*

phone 1 *noun* téléphone *m;* **we had a new phone system installed last week** = nous avons une nouvelle installation téléphonique depuis la semaine dernière; **house phone** *or* **internal phone** = téléphone interne; **by phone** = par téléphone *or* téléphonique; **to be on the phone** = parler au téléphone; **she has been on the phone all morning** = elle a passé la matinée (à parler) au téléphone; **he spoke to the manager on the phone** = il a eu le directeur au téléphone; **card phone** = téléphone à carte; **phone book** = annuaire *m* téléphonique *or* du téléphone; **look up his address in the phone book** = cherche son adresse dans l'annuaire; **phone call** = appel *m* (téléphonique); **to make a phone call** = téléphoner *or* appeler *or* faire un appel *or* passer un coup de fil; **to answer the phone** *or* **to take a phone call** = répondre au téléphone; **phonecard** = Télécarte®*f;* **phone number** = numéro *m* de téléphone; **he keeps a list of phone numbers in a little black book** = il a une liste de numéros de téléphone dans un petit carnet noir; **the phone number is on the company notepaper** = le numéro de téléphone figure sur le papier à en-tête de la société; **can you give me your phone number?** = pouvez-vous me donner votre numéro de téléphone? **2** *verb* **to phone someone** = appeler quelqu'un *or* téléphoner à quelqu'un; **don't phone me, I'll phone you** = ne me téléphonez pas, c'est moi qui vous appellerai; **his secretary phoned to say he would be late** = sa secrétaire a téléphoné pour prévenir de son retard; **he phoned the order through to the warehouse** = il a passé la commande directement à l'entrepôt par téléphone; **to phone for something** = demander quelque chose par téléphone *or* appeler pour faire venir quelque chose; **he phoned for a taxi** = il a appelé un taxi; **to phone about something**

= téléphoner au sujet de quelque chose; **he phoned about the order for computer stationery** = il a appelé à propos de la commande de papier listing

◊ **phone back** *verb* rappeler; **the chairman is in a meeting, can you phone back in about half an hour?** = le président est en conférence, pourriez-vous rappeler dans une demi-heure environ?; **Mr Smith called while you were out and asked if you would phone him back** = M. Smith a téléphoné en votre absence et a demandé que vous le rappeliez

phoneme *noun* phonème *m;* **the phoneme 'oo' is present in the words too and zoo** = les mots 'too' et 'zoo' contiennent le phonème 'oo'

◊ **phonetic** *adjective* phonétique; **the pronunciation is indicated in phonetic script** = il y a une transcription phonétique de la prononciation

◊ **phonetics** *noun* la phonétique

phosphor *noun* phosphore; *m* **phosphor coating** = couche *f* de phosphore *or* phosphorescente; **phosphor dots** = points *mpl* de phosphore *or* de phosphorescence; **phosphor efficiency** = rendement *m* de phosphorescence; **long persistence phosphor** = phosphore à longue persistance

phosphorescence *noun* phosphorescence *f*

photo 1 *prefix (referring to light)* photo-**2** *abbreviation of* PHOTOGRAPH photo *f*
◊ **photocell** *noun* cellule *f* photoélectrique *or* photocellule *f*
◊ **photocomposition** *noun* photocomposition *f*
◊ **photoconductivity** *noun* photoconductivité *f*
◊ **photoconductor** *noun* cellule *f* photoconductrice
◊ **photocopier** *noun* photocopieur *m or* copieur *m*
◊ **photocopy 1** *noun* photocopie *f;* **make six photocopies of the contract** = faites six photocopies du contrat **2** *verb* photocopier; **she photocopied the contract** = elle a photocopié le contrat
◊ **photocopying** *noun (making photocopies)* photocopie *f;* **photocopying costs are rising each year** = les frais de

photocopie augmentent d'année en année; **photocopying bureau** = bureau *m* de photocopie; **there is a mass of photocopying to be done** = il y a une grande quantité de photocopies à faire
◊ **photodigital memory** *noun* mémoire *f* optonumérique
◊ **photodiode** *noun* photodiode *f*
◊ **photoelectric** *adjective* photoélectrique; **photoelectric cell** = cellule *f* photoélectrique *or* photocellule *f;* **the photoelectric cell detects the amount of light passing through the liquid** = la cellule photoélectrique décèle la quantité de lumière qui traverse le liquide
◊ **photoelectricity** *noun* photo-électricité *f*
◊ **photoemission** *noun* photoémission *f*

photograph *noun* photographie *f or* photo *f;* **colour photograph** = photographie en couleur *or* photo couleur; **black and white photograph** = photo en noir et blanc; **it's a photograph of the author** = c'est une photo de l'auteur; **he took six photographs of the new machine** = il a fait six photos du nouvel appareil; **we will be using a colour photograph of the author on the back of the jacket** = il y aura une photographie en couleur de l'auteur au dos de la jaquette
◊ **photographic** *adjective* photographique; **the copier makes a photographic reproduction of the printed page** = le copieur photographie le texte imprimé pour le reproduire
◊ **photographically** *adverb* photographiquement; **the text film can be reproduced photographically** = le film du texte peut être reproduit par photographie
◊ **photography** *noun* la photographie

photogravure *noun* photogravure *f*
◊ **photolithography** *noun* photolithographie *f or* photo-litho *f*
◊ **photomechanical transfer (PMT)** *noun* transfert *m* photomécanique
◊ **photometry** *noun* photométrie *f*
◊ **photon** *noun* photon *m*
◊ **photoprint** *noun (in typesetting)* épreuve *f* positive
◊ **photoresist** *noun* résine *f* photosensible; **to make the PCB, coat the board with photoresist, place the opaque**

pattern above, expose, then develop and etch, leaving the conducting tracks = pour faire un circuit imprimé il faut d'abord recouvrir la carte d'une résine photosensible puis appliquer le masque du circuit, exposer, développer et graver pour finalement obtenir le tracé; **positive photoresist =** (méthode de la) résine photosensible en positif

◊ **photosensor** *noun* détecteur *m* photoélectrique *or* photosensible

◊ **photostat 1** *noun* photostat *m or* photocopie *f* **2** *verb* faire un photostat (d'un document) *or* photocopier

◊ **phototelegraphy** *noun* transmission *f* de fac-similé

◊ **phototext** *noun* texte *m* photocomposé

◊ **phototransistor** *noun* phototransistor *m*

phototypesetter *noun* photocomposeuse *f*

◊ **phototypesetting** *noun* photocomposition *f*

photovoltaic *adjective* photovoltaïque

physical *adjective* physique; **physical database =** support *m* physique d'une base de données; **physical layer =** couche *f* physique

◊ **physical record** *noun* **(a)** *(unit of data that can be transmitted)* unité *f* physique **(b)** *(all the information for one record)* enregistrement *m* physique

PIA = PERIPHERAL INTERFACE ADAPTER

pica *noun* **(a)** *(printing measurement)* pica *or* 12 points anglais (environ 11 points Didot) **(b)** *(on a printer - ten characters to the inch)* caractère *m* pica (de 12 points anglais, environ 11 points Didot)

pickup *noun (arm and cartridge to playback music)* pick-up *m*

◊ **pickup reel** *noun* bobine *f* réceptrice *or* d'enroulement

pico- (p) *prefix (one million millionth)* pico-; **picofarad (pF) =** picofarad (PF) *m;* **picosecond (ps) =** picoseconde (Ps) *f*

picture 1 *noun* (i) dessin *m; (book)* illustration *f; (TV or book)* image *f* ; (ii) photo *f;* **this picture shows the new design =** vous pouvez voir le nouveau modèle sur cette représentation *or* cette photo *or* ce dessin; **picture beam =** spot *m* de balayage *or* faisceau *m* d'image *m;* **picture element** *or* **pixel =** élément *m* d'image *or* pixel *m see also* PIXEL; **picture phone =** visiophone *m;* **picture processing =** traitement *m* de l'image; **picture transmission =** transmission *f* d'images **2** *verb* imaginer *or* visualiser; **try to picture the layout before starting to draw it in =** essayer de visualiser l'implantation avant de commencer à dessiner

PID = PERSONAL IDENTIFICATION DEVICE

piece accent *noun* accent *m* mobile *or* caractère *m* accent

◊ **piece fraction** *noun* caractère *m* de fraction

pie chart *noun* diagramme *m* en camembert *or* camembert *m*

piezoelectric *adjective* piézo-électrique

piggyback *verb* superposer *or* monter *or* mettre en piggyback *or* monter en surface; **piggyback those two memory chips to boost the memory capacity =** superposez ces deux puces pour augmenter la capacité de la mémoire; **piggyback entry =** entrée *f* sur un système avec un mot de passe piraté *or* sur un terminal mal verrouillé

◊ **piggybacking** *noun (messages)* mise *f* en piggyback *or* superposition *f* d'un accusé de réception au message suivant

PILOT *(programming language)* langage *m* PILOT

pilot 1 *noun (used as a test)* pilote *m;* **the company set up a pilot project to see if the proposed manufacturing system was efficient =** la société a mis sur pied un projet-pilote pour évaluer le procédé de fabrication proposé; **the pilot factory has been built to test the new production process =** l'usine-pilote a été construite pour tester le nouveau procédé de fabrication; **pilot system** = système-pilote *m* **2** *verb* faire l'essai (d'un système); **they are piloting the new system** = ils font l'essai du nouveau système

PIN = PERSONAL IDENTIFICATION NUMBER numéro *m* de code confidentiel *or* personnel

pin *noun* **(a)** *(short piece of wire attached to an IC)* contact *m or* broche *f* **(b)** *(part of a plug)* broche; **use a three-pin plug to connect the printer to the mains** = il faut une fiche à trois broches pour connecter *or* brancher le système sur le secteur; **three-pin mains plug** = fiche secteur à trois broches; **two-pin mains plug** = fiche secteur à deux broches
◊ **pin cushion distortion** *noun* distorsion *f* en oreiller *or* en coussinet *or* en barillet
◊ **pinfeed** *noun* entraînement *m* (du papier) par picots; *see* TRACTOR FEED
◊ **pin photodiode** *noun* photodiode *f* (de type) PIN

pinchwheel *noun* molette *f* de serrage

PIO = PARALLEL INPUT/OUTPUT *see also* PIPO, PISO

pipeline (computer) 1 *noun* *(architecture)* en pipeline *or* en pipe-line **2** *verb* **(a)** *(to schedule inputs)* organiser en pipeline **(b)** *(to begin processing of a second instruction while still processing the first)* traiter *or* exécuter (des instructions) en pipeline
◊ **pipelining** *noun* **(a)** *(scheduling inputs)* organisation *f* en pipeline **(b)** *(processing a third instruction while still processing the second)* mode *m* de traitement *or* d'exécution en pipeline

PIPO = PARALLEL INPUT/PARALLEL OUTPUT

pirate 1 *noun* pirate *m;* **the company is trying to take the software pirates to court** = la société tente d'amener les pirates de logiciel devant les tribunaux; **pirate copy of a computer program** = exemplaire *m* d'un logiciel piraté **2** *verb* pirater; **a pirated tape** = une bande piratée; **the designs for the new system were pirated in the Far East** = les

schémas du nouveau système ont été piratés en Extrême-Orient; **he used a cheap pirated disk and found the program had bugs in it** = il a utilisé une disquette piratée bon marché et a découvert que le programme contenait des bogues
◊ **piracy** *noun* piratage *m*

PISO = PARALLEL INPUT/SERIAL OUTPUT

pitch *noun* **(a)** *(horizontal spacing)* espacement *m or* pas *m;* *(of characters)* densité *f* (de caractères) **(b)** *(of sound)* hauteur *f* d'un son; **pitch envelope** = enveloppe *f* tonale **(c)** *(movement about an axis)* tangage *m*

pix *noun* images *fpl or* illustrations *fpl or* photos *fpl*
◊ **pix lock** *noun* *(in video recording)* synchronisation *f or* topage *m*
◊ **pixel** *or* **picture element** *noun* pixel *m or* élément *m* d'image

> QUOTE an EGA display and driver give a resolution of 640 x 350 pixels and support sixteen colours
> *PC Business World*
> QUOTE adding 40 to each pixel brightens the image and can improve the display's appearance
> *Byte*

PL/1 = PROGRAMMING LANGUAGE/1 langage *m* de programmation PL/1

PLA = PROGRAMMABLE LOGIC ARRAY circuit *m* logique *or* logique *f* câblée programmable

place *noun* place *f or* position *f*

plaintext *noun* texte *m* en clair *or* non chiffré; **the messages were sent as plaintext by telephone** = le texte du message a été transmis en clair par téléphone; **enter the plaintext message into the cipher machine** = introduire le texte non chiffré dans la machine à chiffrer
NOTE: opposite is **ciphertext**

PLAN langage *m* PLAN

plan 1 *noun* **(a)** plan *m or* projet *m* **(b)** *(drawing)* plan; **plans** = jeu *m* de plans *or* les plans; **floor plan** = plan d'ensemble (d'un étage); **street plan** *or* **town plan** = plan des rues *or* plan de la ville **2** *verb* planifier *or* projeter NOTE: **planning - planned**

◊ **planchest** *noun* armoire *f or* meuble *m* à plans (d'architecte)

◊ **planner** *noun* **(a)** *(software)* agenda *m* **(b) wall planner** = planning *m* mural

◊ **planning** *noun* planification *f or* planning *m;* **long-term planning** *or* **short-term planning** = planning à longue échéance *or* à courte échéance

planet *noun* planète *f*
◊ **planetary camera** *noun* caméra *f* de poursuite

plant *verb* *(in memory)* ranger *or* implanter *or* stocker (dans la *or* en mémoire)

plasma display *or* **gas plasma display** *noun* affichage *m* (au) plasma

> QUOTE the disadvantage of using plasma technology is that it really needs mains power to work for any length of time
> QUOTE the plasma panel came out of the extended use test well
> *Micro Decision*

plate *noun* **(a)** *(in book)* planche *f* **(b)** *(printing)* cliché *m* **(c)** *(photograph)* plaque *f* photographique *or* plaque photosensible; **plate camera** = appareil (photo) *m* à plaques

platen *noun* **(a)** *(roller for paper)* rouleau *m or* cylindre *m;* **platen press** = presse *f* à platine *f* **(b)** *(for film in camera)* presseur *m*

platform *noun* plate-forme *f;* **data collection platform** = plate-forme de collecte de données

play back *verb* *(music)* (re)jouer; *(film, etc.)* passer *or* visionner; **after you have recorded the music, press this button to play back the tape and hear what it sounds like** = après avoir enregistré la musique, appuyez sur ce bouton-ci pour faire jouer la bande et vous assurer de la bonne qualité du son enregistré

◊ **playback head** *noun* tête *f* de lecture; **disk playback head** = tête de lecture de

disques; **tape playback head** = tête de lecture de bandes

player *noun* **CD player** = lecteur *m* de disques CD *or* de disques audionumériques

◊ **player missile graphics** *see* SPRITES

PLD = PROGRAMMABLE LOGIC DEVICE

plex database *noun* base *f* de données relationnelle

◊ **plex structure** *noun* structure *f* à maillage intégral *or* réseau *m* intégralement interconnecté

PL/M = PROGRAMMING LANGUAGE FOR MICROPROCESSORS langage *m* PL/M (pour microprocesseur)

plot 1 *noun (graph or map)* graphe *m or* courbe *f or* tracé *m* **2** *verb* tracer une courbe *or* un graphe (par points numérisés); **plotting mode** = mode *m* graphe

◊ **plotter** *noun* traceur *m* (de courbes); **plotter driver** = pilote *m* de traceur (de courbes); **plotter pen** = stylet *m* (de traceur); **digital plotter** = traceur numérique; **drum plotter** = traceur à tambour; **flatbed plotter** = table *f* traçante; **incremental plotter** = traceur à incrémentation; **printer-plotter** = imprimante *f* graphique; **X-Y plotter** *or* **graph plotter** = traceur de courbes *or* de graphiques

plug 1 *noun* fiche *f;* **the printer is supplied with a plug** = la fiche est fournie avec l'imprimante; **adapter plug** = adaptateur *m;* **plug-compatible** = à connecteur compatible *or* directement enfichable; **this new plug-compatible board works much faster than any of its rivals, we can install it by simply plugging it into the expansion port** = cette nouvelle carte directement enfichable travaille beaucoup plus vite que ses concurrentes, vous l'installez en l'enfichant simplement dans le connecteur d'extension; **plug-compatible manufacturer (PCM)** = fabricant *m* de produits (à connecteurs) compatibles **2** *verb* brancher; **to plug in** = *(a machine)* brancher *or* connecter; *(a board)* enficher; **no wonder the computer does**

nothing, you haven't plugged it in at the mains = ne soyez pas surpris si l'ordinateur ne fonctionne pas, vous ne l'avez pas branché sur le secteur; **plug-in unit** = extension *f* enfichable **(b)** *(to publicize)* promouvoir *or* vanter; **they ran six commercials plugging holidays in Spain** = ils ont fait un véritable matraquage publicitaire avec leurs six pubs sur les séjours en Espagne

◊ **plugboard** *or* **patchboard** *noun* panneau *m* de raccordement *or* tableau *m* de distribution

QUOTE it allows room for up to 40K of RAM via plug-in memory cartridges
Which PC?
QUOTE adding memory is simply a matter of plugging a card into an expansion bus connector
Byte

plus *or* **plus sign (+)** *noun* le signe plus *or* le signe de l'addition

PMBX = PRIVATE MANUAL BRANCH EXCHANGE

PMOS = P-channel METAL OXIDE SEMICONDUCTOR

PMR = PRIVATE MOBILE RADIO

PMT = PHOTOMECHANICAL TRANSFER

pn-junction *noun* zone *f* interface pn *or* jonction *f* pn; **diffused pn-junction** = zone interface pn *or* jonction pn à diffusion; **step pn-junction** = zone interface pn *or* jonction pn à seuil

◊ **pnp** *or* **p-n-p transistor** *noun* transistor (de type) pnp

pocket *noun* **pocket calculator** = calculatrice *f* de poche

point 1 *noun* **(a)** endroit *m* *or* point *m;* **access point** = point d'accès *or* d'entrée; **re-entry point** = point de ré-entrée *or* de rentrée; **starting point** = point de départ; *see also* BREAKPOINT **(b) binary point** = virgule *f* binaire; **decimal point** = virgule *f* (décimale); **percentage point** = un pour cent *or* point **(c)** *(British measurement in typesetting)* point (anglais) *or* un douzième de pica *or* 0,351 mm; *(French measurement)* point Didot *or* point

typographique *or* 0,324 mm; **the text of the book is set in 9 point Times** = le texte du livre est (composé) en Times 9 points; **if we increase the point size to 10, will the page extent increase?** = est-ce qu'en augmentant la taille des caractères à 10 points on augmente ainsi le nombre de pages? NOTE: usually written **pt** after figures: **10pt Times Bold 2** *verb* **to point out** = montrer

◊ **point-of-sale (POS)** *noun* point *m* de vente; **electronic point-of-sale (EPOS)** = point de vente électronique; **point-of-sale material** = publicité *f* lieu de vente (PLV); **point-of-sale terminal** *or* **POS terminal** = terminal *m* de point de vente

◊ **pointer** *noun* **(a)** *(in a computer program)* pointeur *m;* **increment the contents of the pointer to the address of the next instruction** = incrémenter le pointeur jusqu'à l'adresse (d'instruction) suivante; **data pointer** = pointeur de position de données; **pointer file** = fichier de pointeurs **(b)** *(graphical symbol)* pointeur; **desktop publishing on a PC is greatly helped by the use of a pointer and mouse** = il est beaucoup plus facile de faire de la PAO sur un ordinateur personnel avec un pointeur et une souris

◊ **point to point** *noun* (liaison) point à point

QUOTE the arrow keys, the spacebar or the mouse are used for pointing, and the enter key or the left mouse button are to pick
PC User
QUOTE pointing with the cursor and pressing the joystick button eliminates use of the keyboard entirely
Soft

poke *noun* instruction POKE (d'insertion); **poke 1423,74 will write the data 74 into location 1423** = l'instruction POKE 1423,74 écrira 74 à l'emplacement 1423; *compare* PEEK

POL = PROBLEM-ORIENTATED LANGUAGE langage *m* de résolution de problème *or* langage adapté au problème *or* langage d'application

polar *adjective* polaire; **polar coordinates** = coordonnées *fpl* polaires; **polar diagram** = diagramme *m* en coordonnées polaires; **polar orbit** = orbite *f* polaire; **polar signal** = signal *m* polarisé; **unipolar signal** = signal *m* unipolaire

◊ **polarity** *noun* polarité *f;* **electrical polarity** = polarité électrique; **magnetic polarity** = polarité magnétique; **polarity test** = test *m* de polarité; **reverse polarity** = polarité inversée

◊ **polarization** *noun* polarisation *f*

◊ **polarized** *adjective* **(a)** polarisé, -ée; **vertically polarized** = (antenne, etc.) à polarisation verticale **(b) polarized plug** = connecteur *m* à une seule position d'enfichage; **polarized edge connector** = connecteur à enfichage dirigé *or* à un seul bord d'enfichage

polaroid filter *noun* filtre *m* polaroïde

Polish notation *see* REVERSE

poll *verb (of computer)* appeler *or* interroger *or* inviter à émettre; **polled interrupt** = interruption *f* d'appel

◊ **polling** *noun (from controlling computer to terminal)* interrogation *f or* appel *m* sélectif *or* invitation *f* à émettre; **polling characters** = caractères *mpl* d'appel sélectif; **polling interval** = intervalle *m* d'appels; **polling list** = ordre *m* d'interrogation *or* d'appel (des terminaux); **polling overhead** = temps *m* d'appels sélectifs

polynomial code *noun* code *m* polynomial (de détection d'erreur par algorithme de calcul)

POP 2 langage *m* (de traitement de listes) POP 2

pop *verb* **pop-down menu** *or* **pop-up menu** = menu *m* déroulant; **to pop off** *or* **pop on** = effacer *or* afficher (une image) à un moment déterminé; **this is the last frame of the film so pop on the titles** = c'est la dernière image du film: faites apparaître les titres

◊ **pop filter** *noun* filtre *m* de micro; **every time you say a 'p' you overload the tape recorder, so put this pop filter in to stop it** = chaque fois que vous prononcez un 'p' vous saturez l'enregistrement, placez donc ce filtre pour que cela cesse

QUOTE you can use a mouse to access pop-up menus and a keyboard for word processing
Byte

porch *see* FRONT PORCH

port *noun* port *m or* point *m* d'accès *or* d'entrée/sortie; **asynchronous port** = port asynchrone; **input port** = port (d') entrée; **joystick port** = port (de) manche à balai *or* (de) manette; **output port** = port (de) sortie; **parallel port** = port parallèle; **printer port** = port (d')imprimante; **serial port** = port série; **port selector** = sélecteur *m* de port; **port sharing** = (en) port partagé *or* partage *m* de port

QUOTE the 40 Mbyte hard disk model is provided with eight terminal ports
Micro Decision

portable 1 *noun (computer)* un portatif; *(typewriter)* une portative **2** *adjective (machine)* portatif, -ive; *(program)* **portable software** *or* **portable programs** = programme *m* portable

◊ **portability** *noun (of program)* portabilité *f*

QUOTE although portability between machines is there in theory, in practice it just isn't that simple
Personal Computer World

POS = POINT-OF-SALE; **EPOS** = ELECTRONIC POINT-OF-SALE

position 1 *noun* endroit *m or* position *f;* **this is the position of that chip on the PCB** = voici le point de connexion de cette puce sur la carte **2** *verb* positionner *or* placer *or* mettre (en place); **the VDU should not be positioned in front of a window** = il faut éviter de placer l'écran devant une fenêtre; **position this photograph at the top right-hand corner of the page** = positionnez la photo dans le coin droit du haut de la page; *(accessing data)* **positioning time** = temps *m* de mise en place *or* temps d'accès

◊ **positional** *adjective* positionnel, -elle

positive *adjective* **(a)** *(meaning 'yes')* affirmatif, -ive; **positive response** = réponse *f* affirmative *or* positive **(b)** *(photographie)* épreuve positive; **positive display** = affichage *m* noir sur fond blanc; **positive presentation** = affichage en positif **(c)** *(electrical)* positif; **positive logic** = logique *f* positive; **positive terminal** = borne *f* positive

◊ **positive feedback** *noun* rétroaction positive *or* feedback positif *or* boucle *f* d'amplification; **make sure the microphone is not too close to the loudspeaker or positive feedback will occur and you will overload the amplifier** = ne placez pas le micro trop près du haut-parleur sinon le retour va saturer l'ampli

post 1 *verb (to enter data)* enregistrer **2** *prefix* post-; **post-editing** = édition *f* après compilation *or* après calculs; *(text)* **post-formatted** = (texte) mis en forme à l'impression; **post mortem (dump)** = (vidage par) autopsie *f*
◊ **postbyte** *noun* octet *m* de placement
◊ **postfix** *noun* suffixe *m;* **postfix notation** = notation suffixée *or* notation polonaise inversée; **normal notation: (x-y) + z, but using postfix notation: xy - z +** = en notation normale on écrit: (x-y) + z, en notation inversée on écrira: xy - z + NOTE: often referred to as **reverse Polish notation**
◊ **postprocessor** *noun* **(a)** *(microporcessor)* post-processeur *m* **(b)** *(program)* programme *m* de retraitement

poster *noun* poster *m or* affiche *f*

pot = POTENTIOMETER

potential *noun* potentiel *m;* **potential difference** = différence *f* de potentiel
◊ **potentiometer** *noun* potentiomètre *m*

power *noun* **1 (a)** *(measured in Watts)* puissance *f;* **automatic power off** = (dispositif d') arrêt *m or* de mise hors tension automatique; **power dump** = coupure *m* d'alimentation de courant; **power failure** = panne *f* de courant *or* de secteur; **power loss** = chute *f* de tension; **'power off'** = 'arrêt' *or* 'hors tension'; **'power on'** = 'marche' *or* 'sous tension'; **power-on reset** = réinitialisation *f* automatique à la mise sous tension; **power pack** = bloc *m* d'alimentation; **power supply** alimentation *f;* **power supply unit (PSU)** = bloc d'alimentation; **uninterruptable power supply (UPS)** = alimentation statique sans coupure *or* onduleur *m* **(b)** *(mathematical term)* puissance *f;* **5 to the power 2 is equal to 25** = 5 à la puissance deux *or* 5 au carré égale 25 NOTE: written as

small figures in superscript: **10^5** : say: 'ten to the power five' **2** *verb* **to power up** = mettre sous tension *or* mettre en marche; **powered (by)** (appareil) qui marche *or* qui fonctionne (à l'électricité, etc.)

PPM = PULSE POSITION MODULATION

ppm = PAGES PER MINUTE

pre- *prefix (before)* pré- *or* d'avance; **pre-agreed** = accepté, -ée d'avance *or* suivant accord préalable; **pre-allocation** = préallocation *f;* **pre-fetch** = appel *m* d'instruction anticipé
◊ **pre-amplifier** *noun* préamplificateur *m or* préampli *m*

precede *verb* précéder; **instruction which cancels the instruction which precedes it** = instruction qui annule l'instruction antérieure
◊ **precedence** *noun* priorité *f; (mathematical)* **operator precedence** = ordre *m* d'enchaînement des opérations *or* ordre de priorité

precise *adjective* précis, -e *or* exact, -e; **the atomic clock will give the precise time of starting the process** = l'horloge atomique indiquera l'heure précise du début du processus
◊ **precision** *noun* précision *f or* exactitude *f;* **double precision** = double précision; **multiple precision** = multiple précision; **precision of a number** = précision d'un nombre; **single precision** = simple précision

precompiled code *noun* code *m* précompilé

precondition *verb* préconditionner

predefined *adjective* défini, -e d'avance *or* prédéfini, -e
◊ **predesigned** *adjective* établi, -e d'avance *or* préétabli, -e; **a wide selection of predesigned layouts help you automatically format typical business and technical documents** = un grand choix de modèles de mise en page préétablis vous permet de formater automatiquement vos documents d'affaires ou vos documents techniques

◊ **predetermined** *adjective* déterminé, -ée *or* établi, -e d'avance *or* prédéterminé, -ée

predicate *noun* prédicat *m*

> QUOTE we should stick to systems which we know are formally sound, such as predicate logic
> *Personal Computer World*

pre-edit *verb* prééditer

pre-emphasise *verb (to boost signal)* préamplifier

prefix *noun* **(a)** *(code)* préfixe *m* **(b)** *(word)* préfixe ◊ **prefix notation** *noun* notation *f* préfixée

preformatted *adjective* formaté, -ée d'avance *or* préformaté, -ée; **a preformatted disk** = disquette *f* préformatée

premix *noun (of signals)* prémixage *m*

preparation *noun* préparation *f; (conversion into machine-readable form)* **data preparation** = préparation *f* de données

preprinted *adjective* imprimé, -ée d'avance *or* préimprimé, -ée; **preprinted form** = formulaire *m* préimprimé; **preprinted stationery** = papeterie *f* personnalisée *or* papier *m* à en-tête *or* papier préimprimé

preprocessor *noun* **(a)** *(software)* programme *m* de prétraitement **(b)** *(small computer)* préprocesseur *m* ◊ **preprocess** *verb* prétraiter des données

> QUOTE the C preprocessor is in the first stage of converting a written program into machine instructions
> QUOTE the preprocessor can be directed to read in another file before completion, perhaps because the same information is needed in each module of the program
> *Personal Computer World*

preproduction *noun* l'avant-production *f or* la préproduction

preprogrammed *adjective* programmé, -ée d'avance *or* préprogrammé, -ée

prerecord 1 *verb* enregistrer d'avance *or* préenregistrer; **the answerphone plays a prerecorded message** = le répondeur téléphonique fait entendre un message préenregistré **2** *noun* (module de) texte *m* préenregistré

presentation layer *noun (network layer)* couche *f* présentation

preset *verb* établir *or* fixer *or* programmer d'avance; **the printer was preset with new page parameters** = on avait programmé d'avance les nouveaux paramètres de page de l'imprimante NOTE: **presetting - preset**

press 1 *noun* **(a)** *(newspapers and magazines)* la presse *or* les journaux; **the local press** = les journaux régionaux; **the national press** = les grands journaux *or* les grands quotidiens *or* les journaux à gros tirage *or* la presse nationale; **the new car has been advertised in the national press** = la publicité pour la nouvelle voiture a été faite dans la presse nationale; **we plan to give the product a lot of press publicity** = nous avons l'intention de faire beaucoup de publicité dans la presse pour le produit; **there was no mention of the new product in the press** = aucun journal n'a mentionné le nouveau produit; **press conference** = conférence *f* de presse; **press coverage** = couverture *f* médiatique; **we were very disappointed by the press coverage of the new PC** = nous avons été très déçus par ce que la presse a écrit sur le nouveau PC; **press cutting** = coupure *f* de journal *or* de presse; **we have kept a file of press cuttings about the new software package** = nous avons constitué un dossier de coupures de presse sur le nouveau progiciel; **press release** = communiqué *m* de presse; **the company sent out a press release about the launch of the new scanner** = la société a publié un communiqué de presse au sujet du lancement du nouveau scanner **(b)** **printing press** = presse *f;* **the book is on the press** = le livre est sous presse **2** *verb (to push)* appuyer; **to end the program, press ESCAPE** = appuyez sur la touche

ECHAPPEMENT pour arrêter le programme

pressure pad *noun* capteur *m* de pression; **the pressure pad under the carpet will set off the burglar alarm if anyone steps on it** = le détecteur de pression caché sous le tapis déclenche une alarme si quelqu'un marche dessus

prestore *verb* stocker (des données) avant traitement

presumptive address *noun* adresse *f* de base *or* adresse origine *or* adresse primitive

◊ **presumptive instruction** *noun* instruction *f* de base *or* primitive *or* d'origine

prevent *verb* empêcher; **we have changed the passwords to prevent hackers getting into the database** = nous avons changé les mots de passe pour empêcher le piratage de la base de données

◊ **preventive** *or* **preventative** *adjective* préventif, -ive; **preventive maintenance** = maintenance *f* préventive; **we offer a preventive maintenance contract for the system** = nous offrons un contrat de maintenance préventive qui s'applique à ce système

◊ **prevention** *noun* prévention *f*

preview *verb* visualiser; *(film)* visionner

◊ **previewer** *noun* fonction 'présentation - aperçu'; **the built-in previewer allows the user to check for mistakes** = la fonction intégrée 'présentation - aperçu' permet de visualiser le document et de vérifier s'il s'est glissé des erreurs

previous *adjective* antérieur, -e *or* précédent, -e; **copy data into the present workspace from the previous file** = copiez les données du fichier précédent dans le fichier actuel

◊ **previously** *adverb* antérieurement *or* précédemment; **the data is copied onto previously formatted disks** = ces données ont été copiées sur des disquettes préformatées

primary *adjective* primaire *or* élémentaire *or* fondamental, -e; *(red, yellow and blue)* **primary colours** = couleurs *fpl* fondamentales; *(12 voice channels)* **primary group** = groupe *m* primaire; **primary key** = clé *f* primaire *or* principale; *(main memory)* **primary memory** *or* **primary store** mémoire *f* principale; **primary station** = station *f* primaire

◊ **primarily** *adverb* principalement *or* surtout

prime 1 *adjective (very important)* très important, -e *or* essentiel, -elle; **prime attribute** = caractéristique essentielle; *(TV)* **prime time** = heures *fpl* de grande écoute *or* d'écoute maximale; **we are putting out a series of prime-time commercials** = nous commençons à diffuser des spots publicitaires aux heures de grande écoute **2** *noun (number)* nombre *m* premier; **the number seven is a prime** = sept est un nombre premier

primer *noun* guide *m* élémentaire *or* manuel *m* d'utilisation élémentaire

primitive *noun* primitive *f*

print 1 *noun* **(a)** *(etched)* gravure *f;* **he collects 18th century prints** = il fait collection de gravures du 18e siècle **(b)** *(photograph)* épreuve *f or* tirage *m;* **print contrast ratio** = rapport *m* de contraste d'un imprimé **(c)** *(characters on paper)* impression *f;* **he was very pleased to see his book in print** = il était ravi de voir son livre imprimé; **the print from the daisy-wheel printer is clearer than that from the line printer** = l'imprimante à marguerite donne un meilleur résultat que l'imprimante ligne à ligne; **print control character** = caractère de contrôle d'impression; **print format** = format *m* d'impression; **print hammer** = marteau *m* d'impression; **print life** = durée *f* de vie d'une imprimante; **the printhead has a print life of over 400 million characters** = la tête d'impression peut imprimer plus de 400 millions de caractères; **print modifiers** = modificateurs *mpl or* paramètres *mpl* d'impression; **print pause** = arrêt *m* de l'impression; **print spooling** = impression en différé *or* en arrière-plan *or* par spouling; **print style** = style *m* d'impression **2** *verb* **(a)**

imprimer; **the printer prints at 60 characters per second =** cette imprimante a un débit de 60 caractères/seconde; **printed document =** document *m* imprimé *or* un écrit; **printed regulations =** règlements *m* écrits **(b)** *(book)* imprimer; **the book was printed in Hong Kong =** ce livre a été imprimé à Hong Kong; **the book is printing at the moment, so we will have bound copies at the end of the month =** le livre est sous presse, nous recevrons donc les exemplaires reliés vers la fin du mois **(c)** *(to write in capital letters)* écrire en majuscules *or* en capitales *or* en caractères d'imprimerie; **please print your name and address at the top of the form =** écrivez votre nom et votre adresse en majuscules en haut du formulaire

◊ **printed circuit** *or* **printed circuit board (PCB)** *noun* (carte de) circuit *m* imprimé

◊ **printer** *noun* **(a) computer printer =** imprimante *f* (pour ordinateur); **barrel printer =** imprimante à tambour; **bi-directional printer =** imprimante bidirectionnelle; **bubble jet printer =** imprimante à bulle d'encre; **chain printer =** imprimante à chaîne; **daisy-wheel printer =** imprimante à marguerite; **dot-matrix printer =** imprimante matricielle; **impact printer =** imprimante à impact; **ink-jet printer =** imprimante à jet d'encre; **laser printer =** imprimante (à) laser; **line printer =** imprimante ligne (à ligne); **page printer =** imprimante (en mode) page; **thermal printer =** imprimante thermique; **printer buffer =** tampon *m* d'imprimante; **printer control characters =** caractères *mpl* de contrôle d'impression; *(software)* **printer driver =** gestionnaire *m or* pilote *m* d'imprimante; **printer-plotter =** imprimante graphique; **printer port =** port *m* (d')imprimante; **printer quality =** qualité *f* d'impression (d'une imprimante); **printer-readable =** imprimable *or* qui peut être lu, -e *or* accepté, -ée par l'imprimante; **printer ribbon =** ruban *m* d'imprimante **(b)** *(company)* imprimeur *m or* imprimerie *f;* **the book will be sent to the printer next week =** on doit envoyer le livre chez l'imprimeur la semaine prochaine; **we are using Japanese printers for some of our magazines =** nous faisons imprimer quelques-unes de nos revues au Japon

◊ **printhead** *noun* tête *f* d'impression

◊ **printing** *noun (action)* impression *f*

◊ **print out** *verb* imprimer (des données)

◊ **printout** *noun* sortie *f* d'imprimante *or* listing *m;* **computer printout =** sortie d'imprimante; **the sales director asked for a printout of the agents' commissions =** le directeur des ventes a demandé un listing des commissions d'agents

◊ **printrun** *noun* tirage *m*

◊ **print shop** *noun* imprimerie *f* à façon

◊ **printwheel** *noun* marguerite *f*

prior *adjective* antérieur, -e *or* précédent, -e; **prior to =** avant; **the password has to be keyed in prior to accessing the system =** il faut taper le mot de passe avant d'accéder au système

◊ **priority** *noun* (ordre de) priorité *f;* **the operating system has priority over the application when disk space is allocated =** le système d'exploitation a priorité sur les applications en ce qui concerne l'espace alloué sur la disquette; **the disk drive is more important than the printer, so it has a higher priority =** le lecteur de disquettes est plus important que l'imprimante, il a donc la priorité sur cette dernière; **interrupt priority =** priorité d'interruption; **job priority =** priorité d'un travail; **priority interrupt =** interruption *f* prioritaire; **priority interrupt table =** table *f* des priorités d'interruption; **priority sequence =** ordre *m* de priorité; **priority scheduler =** gestionnaire *m* de priorités

privacy *noun* confidentialité *f;* **privacy of data =** confidentialité *f* des données; **privacy of information =** confidentialité de l'information; **privacy transformation =** cryptage *m* de l'information pour en assurer la confidentialité

private *adjective* privé, -e *or* privatif, -ive; **private address space =** partition *f* privée *or* espace *m* mémoire réservé (à l'usage d'un utilisateur); **private automatic branch exchange (PABX) =** autocommutateur privé (raccordé au réseau public) (PABX); **private automatic exchange (PAX) =** central téléphonique privatif (non raccordé au réseau public); **private branch exchange (PBX) =** autocommutateur privatif (raccordé au réseau public); **private dial port =** port privatif *or* réservé; **private line =** ligne *f* privée *or* réservée *or* privative; **private manual branch**

exchange (PMBX) = central téléphonique manuel privé (raccordé au secteur public); **private mobile radio (PMR) =** radiotéléphone *m or* téléphone cellulaire *or* mobile; **private telephone system =** système *m* téléphonique privatif

privilege *noun* privilège *m*

◊ **privileged** *adjective* privilégié, -ée; **privileged account =** partition privilégiée (avec niveau d'accès prioritaire); **the system manager can access anyone else's account from his privileged account =** le gestionnaire du système peut accéder à toutes les partitions à partir de sa partition privilégiée; **privileged instructions =** instructions privilégiées; **the systems manager has a privileged status so he can access any file on the system =** le gestionnaire d'un système jouit d'une partition privilégiée qui lui permet d'accéder à tous les fichiers de ce système

problem *noun* **(a)** *(question)* problème *m;* **to solve a problem =** résoudre un problème; **problem definition =** exposé *m* d'un problème; **problem-orientated language (POL) =** langage *m* de résolution de problème *or* langage adapté au problème *or* langage d'application **(b)** *(fault)* mauvais fonctionnement *m or* dysfonctionnement *m or* défaillance *f;* **problem diagnosis =** diagnostic *m* (de cause) de défaillance

procedure *noun* **(a)** *(instruction code)* procédure *f;* **this procedure sorts all the files into alphabetic order, you can call it from the main program by the instruction SORT =** cette procédure qui sert à classer les fichiers par ordre alphabétique peut être sélectionnée depuis le programme principal par la commande SORT **(b)** *(route used)* procédure *or* méthode *f or* marche *f* à suivre; **you should use this procedure to retrieve lost files =** voici la marche à suivre pour retrouver des fichiers perdus; **the procedure is given in the manual =** la procédure est expliquée dans le manuel d'utilisation; **procedure-orientated language =** langage *m* de procédure *or* langage adapté à la procédure

◊ **procedural** *adjective* à base de procédure; **procedural language =** langage de procédure

proceed *verb* continuer *or* passer à; **after spellchecking the text, you can proceed to the printing stage =** vérifiez d'abord l'orthographe, vous pourrez ensuite imprimer votre texte

process 1 *noun* (i) procédé *m or* processus *m* ; (ii) traitement *m; the* **process of setting up the computer takes a long time =** il faut quand même un certain temps pour mettre en route l'ordinateur; **there are five stages in the process =** le processus compte cinq étapes; **process bound =** (programme) limité par le traitement *or* avec contrainte de traitement; **process camera =** caméra *f* de traitement de l'image; **process chart =** schéma *m or* diagramme *m* de procédure; **process control =** commande *f or* contrôle *m* de processus; **process control computer =** ordinateur *m* de contrôle de processus *or* ordinateur industriel; **process control system =** système *m* de contrôle *or* de conduite de processus **2** *verb* traiter (des données, etc.) *or* effectuer un traitement; **we processed the new data =** nous avons traité les données; **processing all the information will take a long time =** le traitement des données sera assez long

◊ **processing** *noun* traitement *m; page* **processing time depends on the complexity of a given page =** le temps d'ordinateur requis pour le traitement d'une page de texte varie en fonction de la complexité du document; **batch processing =** traitement par lots *or* par paquets; **data processing** *or* **information processing =** traitement (automatique) de données *or* de l'information; **distributed (data) processing (DDP) =** informatique *f* répartie; **image processing =** traitement de l'image; **immediate processing =** traitement immédiat *or* sur demande; **off-line processing =** traitement (en) différé *or* hors ligne *or* off-line; **on-line processing =** traitement en ligne *or* on-line; **query processing =** traitement de requête; **real-time processing =** traitement en temps réel; **serial processing =** traitement en série; *see also* PARALLEL PROCESSING; **word-processing** *or* **text processing =** traitement de texte

processor *noun* processeur *m;* **array processor** = processeur vectoriel; **associative processor** = processeur à mémoire associative; **attached processor** = processeur auxiliaire (indépendant) relié au processeur central; **auxiliary processor** = processeur auxiliaire; **back-end processor** = processeur de fond *or* principal; **bit-slice processor** = processeur en tranches; **central processor** = processeur central; **front-end processor (FEP)** = processeur frontal; **input/output processor** = processeur d'entrée/sortie; **language processor** = processeur de langage; **network processor** = processeur de réseau; *(in a multiprocessor system)* **order code processor** = processeur de code commande; **processor-controlled keying** = saisie *f* au clavier contrôlée par ordinateur; **processor interrupt** = (instruction d') interruption *f* du processeur *or* du traitement; **processor status word (PSW)** = mot *m* d'état d'un processeur; *(operation)* **processor-limited** = dépendant, -e du processeur *or* limité, -ée par le processeur; **dual processor** = double processeur; **image processor** = machine *f* de traitement d'image *or* processeur d'image; **word-processor** *or* **text processor** = *(hardware)* machine *f* de traitement de texte; *(software)* programme *m or* logiciel *m* de traitement de texte

QUOTE each chip will contain 128 processors and one million transistors
Computer News

producer *noun (TV or film)* réalisateur, -trice; **executive producer** = directeur *m* de production

product *noun* **(a)** *(item)* produit *m* **(b)** *(result of multiplication)* produit

◊ **production** *noun (making or manufacturing)* production *f or* fabrication *f;* **production run** = *(of product)* cycle *m* de production; *(of program)* exécution *f* d'un programme

◊ **productive** *adjective* productif, -ive; *(error-free time)* **productive time** = temps productif

program 1 *noun (software)* programme *m;* **assembly program** = assembleur *m or* programme d'assemblage; **background program** = programme non prioritaire; **blue-ribbon program** = programme canon (qui tourne sans erreur du premier coup); **control program/monitor** *or* **control program for microcomputers (CP/M)** = système *m* d'exploitation CP/M; **diagnostic program** = logiciel *m* de diagnostic; **executive program** = programme superviseur; **foreground program** = programme prioritaire; **hardwired program** = programme en logique câblée; **job control program** = programme de contrôle de tâche; **library program** = programme de bibliothèque; **linear program** = programme linéaire; **user program** = programme (d') utilisateur; **program address counter** = PROGRAM COUNTER; **program branch** = branche *f* d'un programme; **program cards** = programme sur cartes perforées; **program coding sheet** = formulaire *m* de programmation; **program compatibility** = compatibilité *f* de logiciel; **program compilation** = compilation *f* de programme; **program counter (PC)** *or* **instruction address register (IAR)** = compteur *m* d'instruction *or* registre *m* compteur; **program crash** = défaillance *f or* crash *m* d'un programme; **I forgot to insert an important instruction which caused a program to crash, erasing all the files on the disk!** = j'ai omis une instruction importante dans le programme ce qui a produit le crash du programme et détruit tous les fichiers contenus sur le disque; **program design language (PDL)** = langage *m* de conception de programme; **program development** = développement *m* d'un programme; **program development system** = environnement *m* de développement de programme; **program documentation** = documentation *f* relative à l'utilisation d'un programme; **program editor** = éditeur *m* de programme; **program evaluation and review technique (PERT)** = technique *f* d'évaluation et de révision de programme; **program execution** = exécution *f* d'un programme; **program file** = fichier *m* programme; **program flowchart** = organigramme *m* de programmation; **program generator** = générateur *m* de programme; **program instruction** = commande *f or* instruction *f* d'un programme; **program library** = bibliothèque *f* de programmes; **program line** = ligne *f* (d'instruction) d'un programme; **program line number** = numéro *m* de référence d'une ligne d'un programme; **program listing** = édition listée d'un programme sur imprimante *or* listing *m or* listage *m* d'un programme; **program maintenance** = maintenance *f* d'un programme; **program name** = nom *m* d'un programme; **program origin** = adresse origine (de la première instruction d'un programme); **program register** = registre *m* d'instruction; **program relocation** = transfert *m* d'un programme (dans une autre partie de la mémoire); *(software)* **program report generator** = (programme) générateur *m* d'application; **program run** = exécution *f* d'un programme; **program segment** = segment *m* de programme; **program specifications** = spécifications *fpl* d'un programme; **program stack** = pile *f* (d'instructions d'un programme); **program statement** = instruction *f;* **program step** = pas *m or* étape *f* de programmation; **program storage** = mémoire *f* (de) programme; **program structure** = structure *f* d'un programme; **program testing** = essai *m or* test *m* d'un programme; **program verification** = vérification *f* (du bon fonctionnement) d'un programme **2** *verb* écrire un programme *or* programmer; **programmed halt** = arrêt *m* programmé; **programmed learning** = formation *f* à l'aide de didacticiel NOTE: **programs - programming - programmed**

◊ **programmable 1** *adjective* programmable; **programmable calculator** = calculatrice *f* programmable; **programmable logic array (PLA)** *or* **programmable logic device (PLD)** = circuit *m* logique programmable *or* logique câblée programmable; **programmable interrupt controller** = contrôleur *m* d'interruption programmable; **programmable key** = touche *f* (de fonction) programmable; **programmable memory (PROM)** = mémoire *f* programmable *or* (mémoire) PROM; **programmable read only memory (PROM)** = mémoire morte programmable *or* (mémoire) PROM; *see also* EAROM, EEPROM, EPROM, ROM **2** *noun* ordinateur *m;* **hand-held programmable** = ordinateur de poche

◊ **programmer** *noun* **(a)** *(person)* programmeur, -euse; **the programmer is still working on the new software** = le programmeur n'a pas encore terminé le nouveau logiciel; **analyst/programmer** *or* **programmer/analyst** = analyste-programmeur, -euse; **applications programmer** = programmeur d'application; **systems programmer** =

programmeur (de) système **(b)** *(device)* programmateur *m* (d'EPROM)

◊ **programming** *noun* **(a)** programmation *f;* **programming in logic** *or* **PROLOG** = langage *m* PROLOG; **programming language** = langage *m* de programmation; **programming standards** = normes *fpl or* standards *mpl* de programmation **(b)** programmation d'une PROM

QUOTE we've included some useful program tools to make your job easier. Like the symbolic debugger
Personal Computer World
QUOTE the other use for the socket is to program 2, 4, 8 or 16Kbyte EPROMS
Electronics & Wireless World
QUOTE each of the 16 programmable function keys has two modes - normal and shift - giving 32 possible functions
Micro Decision

programme *or* US **program** *noun (TV or radio)* programme *m* de radio *or* de télévision; **they were filming a wild life programme** = ils tournaient un programme sur les animaux sauvages; **children's programmes are scheduled for early evening viewing** = les programmes destinés aux enfants sont présentés tôt dans la soirée

project 1 *noun* projet *m;* **his latest project is computerizing the sales team** = il projette maintenant d'informatiser le service des ventes; **the design project was entirely worked out on computer** = le design a été complètement exécuté sur ordinateur *or* la conception a été entièrement assistée par ordinateur; **CAD is essential for accurate project design** = un logiciel de CAO est indispensable à la réalisation d'une conception très précise **2** *verb (to forecast)* prévoir; **the projected sales of the new PC** = les prévisions de vente du nouvel ordinateur individuel *or* du nouveau PC

◊ **projection** *noun* **(a)** *(of sales, etc.)* prévision *f or* projection *f* **(b)** *(of film, etc.)* projection *f;* **projection room** = salle *f* de projection

◊ **projector** *noun* **film projector** = projecteur *m* de cinéma *or* de films; **slide projector** = projecteur de diapositives *or* de diapos; *see also* OVERHEAD

PROLOG = PROGRAMMING IN LOGIC langage *m* PROLOG

PROM (a) = PROGRAMMABLE READ-ONLY MEMORY mémoire *f* morte programmable PROM; **PROM burner** *or* **programmer** = programmateur *m* de PROM; *see also* EPROM **(b)** = PROGRAMMABLE MEMORY mémoire *f* programmable

prompt *noun* message *m* (d'invitation à taper une instruction, etc.); **the prompt READY indicates that the system is available to receive instructions** = le message READY signifie que le système est prêt à recevoir des instructions; **command prompt** = message d'invitation à taper une commande *or* d'attente d'une commande

proof 1 *noun (from a printer)* épreuve *f*; **galley proofs** = épreuves en placards *or* en seconde; **page proof** = dernière épreuve *or* épreuve de mise en page *or* tierce *f* **2** *verb* tirer les épreuves (d'un texte)
◇ **proofer** *noun* imprimante *f* (destinée au tirage) d'épreuves; **output devices such as laser proofers and typesetters** = des périphériques tels que les imprimantes laser destinées au tirage d'épreuves et les photocomposeuses
◇ **proofing** *noun (producing proofs)* tirage *m* d'épreuves
◇ **proofread** *verb* corriger des épreuves; **has all the text been proofread yet?** = la relecture des épreuves est-elle terminée?
◇ **proofreader** *noun* correcteur, -trice d'épreuves

propagate *verb* (se) propager *or* (s') étendre; **propagated error** = erreur propagée; **propagating error** = erreur qui se propage
◇ **propagation delay** *noun* délai *m* de propagation; **propagation delay in the transmission path causes signal distortion** = le délai de propagation dans une voie de communication crée une distorsion du signal

proportion *noun* proportion *f*
◇ **proportional spacing** *noun* espacement *m* proportionnel

protect *verb* protéger; *(memory location)* **protected location** = emplacement *m* protégé; **protected storage** = mémoire *f* protégée; **copy**

protect = dispositif *m* anticopie *or* dispositif de protection contre la copie; **all the disks are copy protected** = toutes les disquettes sont munies d'un dispositif anticopie *or* tous les disques sont protégés contre la copie; **crash protected** = protégé contre la détérioration *or* contre la destruction (accidentelle); **if the disk is crash protected, you will never lose your work** = si vous vous servez d'un disque protégé contre la détérioration, vous ne perdrez jamais vos fichiers
◇ **write protect** *verb* protéger (une disquette) contre l'écriture indésirée
◇ **protection** *noun* protection *f* or sécurité *f*; **protection key** = clé *f* de protection; **protection master** = original *m* sauvegardé *or* copie *f* d'original; **copy protection** = (système *or* dispositif *or* codage) anticopie *or* (de) protection contre la copie; **a hard disk may crash because of faulty copy protection** = il arrive qu'une protection anticopie défectueuse entraîne la détérioration du disque dur; **the new program will come without copy protection** = la nouvelle version du logiciel ne sera pas protégée contre la copie; **data protection** = protection *or* sécurité des données; **Data Protection Act** = loi *f* Informatique et Libertés
◇ **protective** *adjective* protecteur, -trice; **the disks are housed in hard protective cases** = les disquettes sont rangées dans des boîtiers de protection rigides

protocol *noun* protocole *m*; **protocol standards** = les protocoles (de transmission) normalisés

QUOTE there is a very simple protocol that would exclude hackers from computer networks using the telephone system
Practical Computing

prototype *noun* prototype *m*
◇ **prototyping** *noun* fabrication *f* de prototype *or* prototypage *m*

provider *noun* **information provider (IP)** = source *f* d'information *or* service *m* (fournisseur) d'information *or* service de base de données spécialisées (pour vidéotex)

Ps = PICOSECOND

PSA *US* = PUBLIC SERVICE ANNOUNCEMENT

pseudo- *prefix* pseudo-
◊ **pseudo-code** *noun* pseudocode *m*
◊ **pseudo-digital** *adjective* (signal) analogique modulé
◊ **pseudo-instruction** *noun* instruction *f* de remplissage *or* pseudo-instruction *f*
◊ **pseudo-operation** *noun* instruction d'assemblage
◊ **pseudo-random** *adjective* pseudo-aléatoire; **pseudo-random number generator** = générateur *m* de nombres pseudo-aléatoires

PSN = PACKET SWITCHED NETWORK

PSTN = PUBLIC SWITCHED TELEPHONE NETWORK

PSU = POWER SUPPLY UNIT bloc *m* d'alimentation

PSW = PROCESSOR STATUS WORD

PTR = PAPER TAPE READER

p-type semiconductor *noun* semi-conducteur *m* de type P

public *adjective* public, publique; **public address system (PA)** = (système de) sonorisation *f*; **public data network** = réseau *m* public (de transmission de données); **public dial port** = connexion *f* au réseau public commuté; *(that has no copyright)* **public domain (PD)** = domaine *m* public; **public key cipher system** = cryptage *m* à clé publique; **public service announcement (PSA)** = *US* publicité *f* de services publics; **public switched telephone network (PSTN)** = réseau *m* téléphonique (public) commuté

publication *noun* **(a)** publication *f or* parution *f*; **the publication of the report on data protection** = la publication du rapport sur la confidentialité de l'information; **the publication date of the book is November 15th** = la date de parution du livre est fixée au 15 novembre **(b)** *(book or leaflet, etc.)* publication; **government publications can be bought at special shops** = les

écrits officiels sont en vente dans des librairies spécialisées; **the company specializes in publications for the business reader** = la maison publie des revues destinées aux hommes/femmes d'affaires

publicity *noun* publicité *f or* réclame *f*; **publicity matter** = matériel *mpl* publicitaire

publish *verb* publier; **the institute has published a list of sales figures for different home computers** = l'institut a publié une liste des statistiques de vente d'une série d'ordinateurs personnels; **the company specializes in publishing reference books** = cette maison d'édition publie principalement des livres de référence
◊ **publisher** *noun* (i) éditeur *m* ; (ii) maison *f* d'édition
◊ **publishing** *noun* édition *f or* publication *f*; **desktop publishing (DTP)** = publication *f* assistée par ordinateur (PAO); **electronic publishing** = édition électronique *or* publication assistée par ordinateur (PAO); **professional publishing** = l'édition spécialisée *or* professionnelle

QUOTE desktop publishing or the ability to produce high-quality publications using a minicomputer, essentially boils down to combining words and images on pages
Byte

pull *verb (to remove data from a stack)* extraire *or* retirer

pull-down *or* **pull-up menu** *noun* menu *m* déroulant
◊ **pull up** *verb* **to pull up a line** = élever le potentiel d'une ligne *or* brancher une ligne sur une source d'alimentation; **pull up the input line to a logic one by connecting it to 5 volts** = élever le potentiel de la ligne de réception au niveau logique un, en la connectant sur une source de courant de 5 volts

QUOTE the gated inputs lower the standby current and also eliminate the need for input pull-up or pull-down resistors
Electronics & Power

pulse 1 *noun* impulsion *f*; **pulse amplitude modulation (PAM)** = modulation *f* d'impulsions en amplitude

(MIA); **pulse code modulation (PCM) =** modulation par impulsions et codage (MIC); **pulse duration modulation (PDM) =** modulation d'impulsions en durée (MID); **pulse generator =** générateur *m* d'impulsions; **pulse modulation =** modulation d'impulsion; **pulse position modulation (PPM) =** modulation d'impulsions en position (MIP); **pulse stream =** train *m* d'impulsions; **pulse width modulation (PWM) =** modulation d'impulsions en largeur *or* en durée (MIL *or* MID) **2** *verb* émettre des impulsions; **we pulsed the input but it still would not work =** nous avons émis le signal d'entrée mais toujours sans succès

punch 1 *noun* poinçon *m* (de perforation) **2** *verb* perforer; **punch card** *or* **punched card =** carte *f* perforée; **punched card reader =** lecteur *m* de cartes perforées; **punched tag =** étiquette *f* perforée; **punched (paper) tape =** bande (papier) perforée

punctuation mark *noun* signe *m* de ponctuation

pure *adjective* pur, -e; **pure code =** code pur *or* code binaire; **pure semiconductor =** semi-conducteur simple; **pure tone =** son pur

purge *verb (file)* vider *or* purger

push *verb (to press)* appuyer (sur quelque chose) *or* enfoncer (une touche); *(to move)* (re)pousser (quelque chose); **push-down list** *or* **stack =** pile inversée *or* en mode LIFO; *see also* LIFO; **push instruction** *or* **operation =** instruction *f* d'entrée dans la pile; **push-up list** *or* **stack** = pile en file d'attente *or* en mode FIFO; *see also* FIFO

◊ **pushbutton** touche *f* *or* bouton-poussoir *m;* **pushbutton dialling =** numérotation *f* sur clavier; **pushbutton telephone =** téléphone *m* à clavier

put *verb (to place data onto a stack)* introduire *or* mettre (des données) dans la pile

PWM = PULSE WIDTH MODULATION

Qq

QBE = QUERY BY EXAMPLE

QISAM = QUEUED INDEXED SEQUENTIAL ACCESS METHOD

QSAM = QUEUED SEQUENTIAL ACCESS METHOD

QL = QUERY LANGUAGE

quad *noun* **(a)** *(sheet of paper)* quadrat *m* **(b)** *(four times)* quadruple *nm&adj* *(four bits of data)* **quad density** = quadruple densité **(c)** *(space in printing)* **em quad** = cadratin *m;* **en quad** = demi-cadratin *m*
◇ **quadding** *noun (insertion of spaces)* insertion d'espaces

QUOTE in this case, interfacing is done by a single quad-wide adapter
Minicomputer News

quadr- *prefix (meaning four)* quadr- *or* tétra-
◇ **quadrophonic** *adjective (using four speakers)* tétraphonique *or* quadriphonique
◇ **quadruplex** *noun (four signals)* quadruplex *m*
◇ **quadruplicate** *noun* **in quadruplicate** = en quatre exemplaires; **the statements are printed in quadruplicate** = les relevés sont imprimés en quatre exemplaires

quadrature *noun (video playback error)* (erreur de) quadrature *f*

quality *noun* qualité *f;* **there is a market for good quality secondhand computers** = il existe un marché pour les ordinateurs d'occasion de bonne qualité; **high quality** *or* **top quality** = de qualité supérieure *or* de choix *or* de luxe *or* (de) haut de gamme; **printer quality** = qualité *f* d'impression d'une imprimante; *see also* NEAR-LETTER,

DRAFT; **quality assurance** = assurance *f* de qualité; **quality control** = contrôle *m* de (la) qualité; **quality controller** = responsable *m&f* du contrôle de (la) qualité

QUOTE the computer operates at 120cps in draft quality mode and 30cps in near letter-quality mode
Minicomputer News

quantify *verb* **to quantify the effect of something** = quantifier; **it is impossible to quantify the effect of the new computer system on our production** = il est impossible de quantifier l'effet du nouveau système informatique sur notre production
◇ **quantifiable** *adjective* quantifiable
◇ **quantifier** *noun* quantificateur *m*

quantity *noun* **(a)** *(amount)* quantité *f;* **a small quantity of illegal copies of the program have been imported** = un petit nombre de disquettes piratées de ce programme se sont infiltrées à l'importation; **he bought a large quantity of spare parts** = il a acheté une grande quantité de pièces détachées **(b)** *(large amount)* grande quantité; **the company offers a discount for quantity purchases** = la société fait une remise sur les achats en nombre

quantize *verb* quantifier; **quantizing noise** = bruit(s) *m(pl)* de quantification
◇ **quantization** *noun* quantification *f;* **quantization error** = erreur *f* de quantification
◇ **quantizer** *noun* quantificateur *m*

quantum *noun* quantum *m*

quartile *noun* quartile *m*

quarto *noun (paper size)* (format) in-quarto

quartz (crystal) clock *noun* horloge *f* à quartz

quasi- *prefix* quasi-; *(in an assembly program)* **quasi-instruction** = label *m or* étiquette *f or* pseudo-instruction *f*

quaternary *adjective* quaternaire; **quaternary level quantization** = quantification *f* de niveau quatre

query 1 *noun (question)* question *f or* requête *f or* interrogation *f or* demande *f*; **query by example (QBE)** = requête (définie) par l'exemple; **query facility** = utilitaire *m* de requête *or* d'interrogation; **query language (QL)** = langage *m* de requête; **query processing** = traitement *m* de requête **2** *verb* poser une question *or* se renseigner (sur) *or* interroger

question 1 *noun* **(a)** *(query)* question *f*; **she refused to answer questions about faulty keyboards** = elle a refusé de répondre aux questions concernant les claviers défectueux **(b)** *(problem)* problème *m or* sujet *m*; **the main question is that of cost** = le problème essentiel est celui du coût; **the board discussed the question of launching a new business computer** = la direction a discuté du lancement d'un nouvel ordinateur de bureau **2** *verb* **(a)** *(to ask questions)* interroger (quelqu'un) *or* poser une question (à quelqu'un) **(b)** *(to query)* mettre en doute *or* se demander; **we all question how accurate the computer printout is** = nous nous demandons tous jusqu'à quel point la sortie d'imprimante est correcte

◊ **questionnaire** *noun* questionnaire *m*; **to send out a questionnaire to test the opinions of users of the system** = envoyer un questionnaire concernant le système pour faire un sondage d'opinion auprès des utilisateurs; **to answer** *or* **to fill in a questionnaire** = remplir *or* compléter un questionnaire

queue 1 *noun* **(a)** *(of people)* file *f* d'attente; **to form a queue** *or* **to join a queue** = se joindre à la file d'attente **(b)** *(of data)* file d'attente; **channel queue** = file d'attente (du service de transmission *or* de données à transmettre); **file queue** = fichiers *mpl* dans une file d'attente *or* file d'attente de fichiers; **output devices**

such as laser printers are connected on-line with an automatic file queue** = les périphériques tels que les imprimantes laser sont reliés en ligne et les fichiers sont gérés par un système de file d'attente automatique; **job queue** = file d'attente de tâches *or* de travaux; **queue discipline** = procédure *f* de file d'attente; **queue management** *or* **queue manager** = programme *m* de gestion *or* gestionnaire *m* de file d'attente; **this is a new software spooler with built-in queue management** = ce nouveau logiciel de spouling comporte un gestionnaire de file d'attente **2** *verb* prendre la file *or* placer (des données *or* des tâches) dans la file d'attente; **queued indexed sequential access method (QISAM)** = méthode *f* d'accès séquentiel indexé en file; **queued sequential access method (QSAM)** = méthode d'accès séquentiel en file; **queuing time** = temps *m* d'attente dans la file

quick *adjective* rapide
◊ **quickly** *adverb* rapidement
◊ **quicksort** *noun* tri *m* rapide

quiescent *adjective* à l'état de repos *or* au repos

quiet *adjective* silencieux, -ieuse; **laser printers are much quieter than dot-matrix** = les imprimantes laser sont beaucoup plus silencieuses *or* moins bruyantes que les imprimantes matricielles

quintet *noun (five bits)* quintet *m*

quit *verb (system or program)* quitter *or* abandonner; **do not forget to save your text before you quit the system** = n'oubliez pas de sauvegarder votre texte avant de quitter le système
NOTE: **quitting - quit**

quote 1 *verb* **(a)** *(to repeat)* citer *or* mentionner *or* rappeler; **he quoted figures from the newspaper report** = il a cité des chiffres mentionnés dans le journal; **in reply please quote this number** = veuillez rappeler ce numéro de référence dans votre réponse; **when making a complaint please quote the batch number printed on the computer case** = en cas de réclamation, mentionnez toujours le numéro de lot qui apparaît sur le boîtier de l'ordinateur **(b)** *(to estimate)* faire un devis *or* donner des prix; **to quote a price for supplying stationery** = donner un prix pour les fournitures de bureau **2** *noun (inverted commas)* **quotes** = guillemets *m;* **single quotes** = guillemets simples; **double quotes** = guillemets doubles; **the name of the company should be put in double quotes** = il faut mettre le nom de la société entre guillemets doubles

◇ **quotation marks** *noun (inverted commas)* guillemets

quotient *noun* quotient *m*

QWERTY *noun* **QWERTY keyboard** = clavier *m* QWERTY; **the computer has a normal QWERTY keyboard** = l'ordinateur possède un clavier QWERTY ordinaire; *see also* AZERTY

QUOTE the keyboard does not have a QWERTY layout but is easy to use

Micro Decision

Rr

R & D = RESEARCH AND DEVELOPMENT; **R & D department** = service *m* R et D *or* service de recherche et développement

race *noun (error condition in digital circuit)* pompage *m*

rack *noun* **(a)** *(in shop)* présentoir *m or* étagère *f;* **a rack for holding mag tapes** = un ratelier à *or* pour bandes magnétiques **(b)** *(for electronic circuit boards and peripheral devices)* baie *f or* châssis *m or* coffret *m* avec guide-cartes; **rack mounted** = (cartes) montées sur supports *or* en rack

radar *noun* radar *m*

radial transfer *noun* transfert *m* radial (de données *or* programmes)

radiant *adjective* rayonnant, -e *or* de rayonnement; **radiant energy** = énergie rayonnante *or* de rayonnement
◊ **radiate** *verb* **(a)** *(to go in all directions from a central point)* rayonner **(b)** *(to send out rays)* irradier *or* rayonner; *(of antenna)* rayonner; *(of antenna)* **radiating element** = élément *m* rayonnant
◊ **radiator** *noun* radiateur *m; (of antenna)* élément rayonnant (d'une antenne)
◊ **radiation** *noun (waves of energy)* radiation *f or* rayonnement *m; (from antenna)* rayonnement

radio *noun* radio *m; radio* **radio frequency (RF)** = fréquence *f* radio *or* radiofréquence *f;* **the radio frequency range extends from a few hertz to hundreds of gigahertz** = la gamme des radiofréquences s'étend de quelques hertz seulement à des centaines de gigahertz; **radio microphone** = micro *m* sans fil *or* micro radio; **radio pager** *or*

radio paging device = récepteur *m* de poche *or* signaleur *m* d'appel (pour système d'appel de personne); **you could contact your salesman if he had a radio pager** = vous pourriez contacter votre vendeur s'il était équipé d'un récepteur de poche; **radio paging** = (système d') appel *m* de personne *or* radiorecherche *f* de personne; **radio phone** *or* **radio telephone** = radio-téléphone *m;* **radio receiver** = récepteur *m* radio; **radio spectrum** = spectre *m* de fréquences radio; **radio telegraphy** = radiotélégraphie *f;* **radio transmission of data** = transmission *f* de données par radio *or* radiotransmission *f;* **radio waves** = ondes *f* radioélectriques
◊ **radiocommunications** *noun* la radiocommunication

radix *noun (of a number system)* base *f;* **the hexadecimal number has a radix of 16** = le nombre hexadécimal est à base 16; **radix complement** = complément à la base; *see* TEN'S, TWO'S COMPLEMENT; **radix notation** = notation *f* à base; **radix point** = emplacement *m* de la virgule

ragged *adjective* en dents de scie *or* déchiqueté, -ée; *(book)* non rogné; *(text)* **ragged left** = (texte) non justifié à gauche; **ragged right** = (texte) non justifié à droite; **ragged text** = texte non justifié

RAM = RANDOM ACCESS MEMORY mémoire *f* vive *or* (mémoire) RAM; **partial RAM** = RAM partielle; **RAM chip** = puce *f* RAM; **RAM disk** = disque *m* RAM *or* disque mémoire; **RAM loader** = (programme) chargeur *m or* programme de chargement de la mémoire vive; **RAM refresh** = (signal de) régénération *f or* rafraîchissement *m* de la mémoire RAM; **RAM refresh rate** = fréquence *f* de régénération *or* de rafraîchissement de la mémoire RAM; **self-refreshing RAM** = RAM auto-entretenue *or* autorégénérable; **dynamic RAM =** (mémoire) RAM dynamique; **static RAM =** (mémoire) RAM statique NOTE: there is no plural for RAM, and it often has no article: **512K of RAM; the file is stored in RAM**

QUOTE in addition the board features 512K of video RAM, expandable up to a massive 1MB

PC Business World

QUOTE fast memory is RAM that does not have to share bus access with the chip that manages the video display

Byte

random *adjective* aléatoire; **pseudo-random =** pseudo-aléatoire; **random number =** nombre aléatoire *or* choisi au hasard; **random number generator =** générateur *m* de nombres aléatoires; **random process =** processus *m* aléatoire

◊ **random access** *noun* accès *m* aléatoire *or* sélectif *or* direct; **disk drives are random access, magnetic tape is sequential access memory =** les lecteurs de disquettes permettent l'accès aléatoire *or* direct des données alors qu'une bande magnétique en permet l'accès séquentiel; **random access device =** dispositif *m* mémoire à accès aléatoire; **random access files =** fichiers *mpl* à accès direct *or* sélectif; **random access storage =** mémoire à accès aléatoire *or* sélectif *or* direct; **random access memory (RAM) =** mémoire *f* vive *or* mémoire à accès aléatoire *or* (mémoire) RAM

◊ **random processing** *noun* traitement *m* aléatoire *or* direct (des données)

range 1 *noun* **(a)** *(series of items)* gamme *f;* **a wide range of products =** une gamme de produits; **the catalogue lists a wide range of computer stationery =** on trouve dans le catalogue toute une gamme de papiers listing **(b)** *(reach)* portée *f or* étendue *f* **(c)** *(set of values)* gamme *or* fourchette *f;* **number range =** gamme de valeurs; **frequency range =** gamme de fréquences; **the telephone channel can accept signals in the frequency range 300 - 3400Hz** la transmission par téléphone accepte des signaux dans la gamme de fréquences 300 à 3400 Hz; **magnetic tape is stable within a temperature range of 0° to 40°C =** la bande magnétique est stable entre 0° et 40 °C **2** *verb* **(a)** *(to vary)* varier *or* s'étendre *or* aller (de ... à); **the company's**

products range from a cheap lapheld micro to a multistation mainframe = la gamme des produits de la société va du micro portatif au gros ordinateur multiposte **(b)** *(to put text in order)* aligner *or* justifier; **range left =** (ré)aligner à gauche

rank *verb* classer par rang *or* par ordre d'importance

rapid *adjective* rapide; **rapid access =** accès *m* rapide; **rapid access memory** *or* **fast access memory (FAM) =** mémoire *f* à accès rapide

raster *noun* raster *m;* **raster graphics =** infographie *f or* graphisme *m* par balayage de trame; **raster image processor =** processeur *m* d'image matricielle; **an electronic page can be converted to a printer-readable video image by an on-board raster image processor =** une page électronique peut être convertie en image vidéo imprimable à l'aide d'un processeur d'image matricielle; **raster scan =** passe *f* de balayage; **raster scanning =** balayage *m* récurrent *or* balayage (vertical) de trame

rate 1 *noun* *(ratio)* taux *m; (speed)* vitesse *f;* **the processor's instruction execution rate is better than the older version =** la vitesse d'exécution des commandes de ce processeur est plus rapide qu'avec l'ancienne version; **error rate =** taux d'erreur; *(transmitted per second)* **information rate =** débit *m* de transmission d'informations **2** *verb (to evaluate)* évaluer; **rated throughput =** rendement *m* estimé

◊ **ratings** *noun* *(of TV programmes)* taux *m* d'écoute; **ratings battle** *or* **war =** guerre *f* de taux d'écoute *or* bataille *f* d'audimat

ratio *noun* ratio *m or* rapport *m or* taux *m;* **the ratio of 10 to 5 is 2:1 =** le rapport 10 sur 5 est égal à 2:1; **the ratio of corrupt bits per transmitted message is falling with new technology =** le taux des bits corrompus par message transmis est moins élevé grâce aux nouvelles techniques

◊ **rational number** *noun* nombre *m* rationnel; **24 over 7 is a rational number =** 24/7 est un nombre rationnel; **0.333** can be written as the rational number 1/3 = on peut écrire 0,333 sous la forme du nombre rationnel 1/3

raw *adjective (not processed)* brut, -e; **raw data** = données *fpl* brutes *or* non traitées; **this small computer collects raw data from the sensors, converts it and transmits it to the mainframe** = ce petit ordinateur recueille les données brutes venant des capteurs, les convertit et les transmet au gros ordinateur

ray *noun* rayon *m or* rayonnement *m;* **the rays of light pass down the optical fibre** = les rayons lumineux se propagent dans la fibre optique

react *verb* réagir; **to react to something** = réagir à quelque chose; *(of substance)* **to react with something** = entrer en réaction avec une autre substance

◊ **reactance** *noun* réactance *f*

◊ **reaction** *noun* réaction *f*

◊ **reactive mode** *noun* mode *m* réactif

read *verb* **(a)** lire; **conditions of sale are printed in such small characters that they are difficult to read** = les conditions de vente sont imprimées en caractères si petits qu'il est très difficile de les lire; **can the OCR read typeset characters?** = est-ce qu'un lecteur optique peut lire les caractères d'imprimerie? **(b)** *(to retrieve data)* lire *or* extraire; **this instruction reads the first record of a file** = cette instruction va lire le premier enregistrement du fichier; **access time can be the time taken to read from a record** = le temps d'accès peut être le temps requis pour la lecture de données (rangées) en mémoire; **destructive read** = lecture *f* destructive; **read back check** = contrôle *m* par relecture; **read cycle** = cycle *m* de lecture; **read head** = tête *f* de lecture; *(device)* **read only** = (mémoire) à lecture seule; **read only memory (ROM)** = mémoire *f* morte *or* (mémoire) ROM; **read rate** = vitesse *f* de lecture; **read/write channel** = voie *f* de lecture/écriture; **read/write cycle** = cycle *m* de lecture/écriture; **read/write head** = tête *f* de lecture/écriture; **read/write memory** = mémoire *f* lecture/écriture

◊ **readable** *adjective* qui peut être lu, -e; **the electronic page is converted to a printer-readable video image** = le texte électronique est converti en image vidéo

qui peut être lue par l'imprimante; *(commands or data)* **machine-readable** = (commandes *or* données) directement exploitables *or* en langage machine

◊ **reader** *noun (device)* lecteur *m;* **card reader** = lecteur de cartes (magnétiques); **tape reader** = lecteur de bandes magnétiques; *see also* BAR CODE READER, OPTICAL CHARACTER READER

◊ **read-in** *or* **read in** *verb (to transfer data from an external source to main memory)* introduire *or* entrer *or* enregistrer; **the computer automatically read-in thirty values from the A/D converter** = l'ordinateur a lu *or* enregistré automatiquement trente valeurs données par le convertisseur analogique-numérique

◊ **reading** *noun* lecture *f;* **optical reading** = lecture optique

◊ **readout** *noun* affichage *m or* lecture *f;* **the readout displayed the time** = l'heure était affichée; **the clock had a digital readout** = cette horloge avait un affichage numérique; **destructive readout** = lecture *f* destructive; **readout device** = dispositif *m or* écran *m* d'affichage

QUOTE some OCR programs can be taught to read typefaces that are not in their library
Publish
QUOTE the machine easily reads in text from typewriters and daisy-wheel printers
PC Business World

ready *adjective* prêt, -e; **the green light indicates the system is ready for another program** = le voyant vert allumé signifie que le système est prêt à accepter le programme suivant; **the programming will not be ready until next week** = la programmation ne sera pas terminée avant la semaine prochaine; **the maintenance people hope that the system will be ready for use in 24 hours** = le service de maintenance espère que le système sera de nouveau en état de fonctionner dans les 24 heures; **ready state** = état prêt

real *adjective* réel, réelle

◊ **real memory** *noun* mémoire *f* réelle; *compare with* VIRTUAL MEMORY

◊ **real number** *noun* nombre *m* réel

◊ **real time** *noun* temps *m* réel; **a navigation system needs to be able to process the position of a ship in real time and take suitable action before it hits a**

rock = un système de navigation doit pouvoir faire le point en temps réel et prendre les mesures nécessaires pour éviter de heurter un écueil; *US* **program shown in real time** = émission *f* en direct; **real-time clock** = horloge *f* en temps réel; **real time execution** = exécution *f* (d'un programme) en temps réel; **real-time input** = entrée *f* en temps réel; **real-time multi-tasking** = traitement *m* multitâche en temps réel; **real-time processing** = traitement en temps réel; **real-time simulation** = simulation *f* en temps réel

◊ **real-time system** *noun* système *m* en temps réel; **in a real-time system, as you move the joystick left, the image on the screen moves left. If there is a pause for processing it is not a true real-time system** = dans un système en temps réel, le déplacement de l'image vers la gauche est parfaitement synchronisé au mouvement du manche à balai vers la gauche; s'il se produit un délai entre l'action et le résultat, il ne s'agit pas d'un véritable système en temps réel

QUOTE a real-time process is one which interacts with a real external activity and respects deadlines imposed by that activity
.EXE
QUOTE define a real-time system as any system which is expected to interact with its environment within certain timing constraints
British Telecom Technology Journal

reboot *verb* relancer; **we rebooted and the files reappeared** = nous avons relancé le système et les fichiers ont réapparu sur l'écran

recall 1 *noun* rappel *m* **2** *verb* rappeler

QUOTE automatic recall provides the facility to recall the last twenty commands and to edit and re-use them
Practical Computing

receive *verb* recevoir; **the computer received data via the telephone line** = les données ont été transmises à l'ordinateur par l'intermédiaire de la ligne téléphonique; **receive only terminal** = terminal de réception

◊ **receiver** *noun* récepteur *m;* **radio receiver** = récepteur radio; **the radio receiver picked up your signal very strongly** = votre signal a été capté très clairement par le récepteur radio; **receiver register** = registre *m* des entrées

reception *noun (of radio or TV signal)* réception *f;* **signal reception is bad with that aerial** = cette antenne ne donne pas un bonne réception

rechargeable *adjective (battery)* rechargeable

recode *verb* modifier les codes d'un programme

recognition *noun* reconnaissance *f;* **recognition logic** = logique *f* de reconnaissance; **optical character recognition** = reconnaissance optique de caractères; **optical mark recognition** = reconnaissance optique de marques *or* de signes *or* de symboles; **voice recognition** = reconnaissance de la parole *or* reconnaissance vocale

◊ **recognize** *verb* reconnaître; **the scanner will recognize most character fonts** = le scanner reconnaît la plupart des polices de caractères

◊ **recognizable** *adjective* reconnaissable

recompile *verb* effectuer une nouvelle compilation

reconfigure *verb* reconfigurer; **I reconfigured the field structure in the file** = j'ai reconfiguré la structure des champs du fichier; **this program allows us to reconfigure the system to our own requirements** = avec ce programme, il est possible de reconfigurer le système selon nos besoins

◊ **reconfiguration** *noun* reconfiguration *f*

reconnect *verb* reconnecter *or* rétablir une liaison; **the telephone engineers are trying to reconnect the telephone** = les techniciens du téléphone essayent de rétablir la liaison téléphonique

reconstitute *verb (after crash or corruption)* reconstituer *or* restaurer (des données)

record 1 *noun* **(a)** *(items of data)* article *m or* enregistrement *m;* **your record contains several fields that have been grouped together under the one heading** = votre article *or* enregistrement contient divers champs regroupés sous une même rubrique; **this record contains all their personal details =** cet enregistrement contient toutes leurs coordonnées; **chained record =** article *or* enregistrement chaîné; **change** *or* **transaction record =** enregistrement d'une modification *or* d'une transaction; **logical record =** enregistrement logique; **physical record =** enregistrement physique; **record count =** (nombre d') enregistrements dans un fichier; **record format** *or* **layout =** format *m or* présentation *f* d'un enregistrement; **record length =** longueur *f or* dimension *f* d'un enregistrement; **records manager =** gestionnaire *m* d'enregistrements; **records management =** programme de gestion d'enregistrements *or* de fichiers **(b)** *(disk)* disque *m;* **record changer =** changeur *m* de disques automatique **2** *verb* inscrire; *(data)* enregistrer; **record the results in this column =** inscrivez les résultats dans cette colonne; **this device records signals onto magnetic tape =** ce dispositif enregistre les signaux sur bande magnétique; **digitally recorded data are used to generate images =** des données enregistrées numériquement servent à générer des images; **record button =** touche *f or* bouton *m* d'enregistrement; **record gap =** espace *m* entre deux enregistrements; **record head** *or* **write head =** tête *f* d'écriture *or* d'enregistrement

QUOTE you can echo the previous record if a lot of replication is involved
QUOTE records may be sorted before the report is created, using up to nine sort fields
Byte
QUOTE file and record-locking procedures have to be implemented to make sure that files cannot be corrupted when two users try to read or write to the same record simultaneously
Micro Decision

recorder *noun* *(equipment)* enregistreur *m;* **magnetic tape recorder =** magnétophone *m*

recording *noun* **(a)** *(process of storing signals, etc.)* enregistrement *m;* **recording density =** densité *f* d'enregistrement; *(telephone line)* **recording trunk =** (ligne de) raccordement *m* **(b)** *(on record or tape)* enregistrement *m;* **a new recording of Beethoven's quartets =** un nouvel enregistrement des quatuors de Beethoven

QUOTE file and record-locking procedures have to be implemented to make sure that files cannot be corrupted when two users try to read or write to the same record simultaneously
Micro Decision

recover *verb* retrouver *or* récupérer; **it is possible to recover the data but it can take a long time =** les données sont récupérables mais il faudra beaucoup de temps pour y arriver

◊ **recoverable error** *noun* erreur récupérable *or* réparable

◊ **recovery** *noun* **(a)** *(return to normal)* restauration *f or* remise *f* en état; **automatic recovery program =** programme de restauration *or* de remise en état automatique; **failure recovery =** remise en marche *or* remise en route *or* reprise sur incident; **fall back recovery =** reprise *f* au point d'appel *or* remise *f* en marche au point de reprise *or* au point d'arrêt; *(from read to write)* **sense recovery time =** délai *m* de conversion; **recovery procedure =** procédure *f* de restauration **(b)** *(getting back something)* récupération *f;* **the recovery of lost files can be carried out using a recovery procedure =** la récupération des fichiers perdus peut se faire par une procédure de restauration

rectangular waveguide *noun* guide *m* d'ondes rectangulaire

rectify *verb* **(a)** *(to correct)* corriger; **they had to rectify the error at the printout stage =** ils ont dû corriger l'erreur à l'impression **(b)** *(to remove the positive or negative sections of a signal)* redresser

◊ **rectifier** *noun* *(electronic circuit)* circuit *m* redresseur

recto *noun* *(of page)* endroit *m or* recto *m; (page of book)* page *f* de droite *or* belle page

recursion *or* **recursive routine** *noun* routine récursive; **daisy-chain recursion =** boucle *f* de récurrence; **recursive call =** appel récursif *or* procédure récursive

redefine *verb* redéfinir *or* définir de nouveau; **we redefined the initial parameters =** nous avons défini les premiers paramètres de nouveau; **to redefine a key =** redéfinir la fonction

d'une touche; **I have redefined this key to display the figure five when pressed** = j'ai redéfini cette touche pour obtenir un 5
◊ **redefinable** *adjective* qui peut être redéfini, -e

> QUOTE the idea of the packages is that they enable you to redefine the keyboard
> *Practical Computing*
> QUOTE one especially useful command lets you redefine the printer's character-translation table
> *Byte*

red, green, blue (RGB) *noun (the three colour picture beams used in a colour TV)* rouge, vert, bleu

redial *verb (telephone)* composer (le numéro) de nouveau; **auto-redial** = (modem *or* téléphone avec) système *m* de rappel automatique

redirect *verb* réacheminer
◊ **redirection** *noun* réacheminement *m;* **call forwarding is automatic redirection of calls** = faire suivre un appel veut dire le réacheminer automatiquement

redo *verb* refaire; **redo from start** = (à) refaire à partir du début

redraw *verb* redessiner *or* dessiner de nouveau; **can the computer redraw the graphics showing the product from the top view?** = est-ce que l'ordinateur peut refaire le graphique du produit de façon à en présenter une vue plongeante?

reduce *verb* **(a)** *(to make smaller)* réduire **(b)** *(to convert data into a more compact form)* comprimer
◊ **reduced instruction set computer (RISC)** *noun* processeur à jeu d'instructions réduit *or* à architecture RISC; *compare with* WISC
◊ **reduction** *noun* réduction *f;* **we need a 25% reduction to fit the halftone in the space** = il nous faut réduire la reproduction en simili de 25% pour pouvoir l'insérer dans l'espace fixé

redundant *adjective* **(a)** *(data)* redondant, -e *or* en trop *or* superflu, -e; **the parity bits on the received data are redundant and can be removed** = les bits de parité des données reçues sont superflus et peuvent être supprimés;

redundant character = caractère de remplissage; **redundant code** = code redondant **(b)** *(equipment kept ready)* suréquipement *m* de sécurité *or* équipement redondant
◊ **redundancy** *noun* redondance *f;* **longitudinal redundancy check** = clé *f* longitudinale; **network redundancy** = liaisons redondantes *or* auxiliaires d'un réseau; **vertical redundancy check** = clé transversale; **redundancy checking** = contrôle par redondance *or* par clé

reel *noun* bobine *f;* **he dropped the reel on the floor and the tape unwound itself** = il a laissé tomber la bobine et le ruban s'est déroulé; **pick-up reel** = bobine réceptrice *or* d'enroulement; **open reel tape** = bande *f* sur bobine ouverte
◊ **reel to reel** *adjective* (copie) de bobine à bobine; **reel to reel recorder** = magnétophone *m*

re-entrant program *or* **code** *or* **routine** *noun* programme *m* ré-entrant
◊ **re-entry** *noun* rentrée *f or* ré-entrée *f;* **re-entry point** = point *m* de rentrée

refer *verb (mentionner)* mentionner *or* faire référence (à) *or* se référer (à); **the manual refers to the serial port, but I cannot find it** = le manuel mentionne un port série, mais je n'en vois aucun
◊ **reference 1** *noun* **(a)** *(value used as a starting)* référence *f;* **reference address** = adresse *f* de référence; *(of signal)* **reference level** = niveau *m* de référence; **reference time** = période *f* de référence **(b)** *(file of data)* **reference file** = fichier *m* de référence; **reference instruction** = instruction *f* de base; *(of stored data)* **reference list** = liste *f* de référence; **reference mark** = renvoi *m;* **reference retrieval system** = système *m* de référence *or* (système d') index *m;* **reference table** = table *f or* tableau *m* de référence **2** *verb* référencer; **the access time taken to reference an item in memory is short** = le temps d'accès à une donnée (en mémoire) est très court
◊ **referencing** *noun* référençage *m*

> QUOTE a referencing function dynamically links all references throughout a document
> *Byte*

reflect *verb (light or image)* réfléchir; **in a reflex camera, the image is reflected by**

an inbuilt mirror = dans un appareil reflex, l'image est refléchie par un miroir interne

◊ **reflected code** noun code m réfléchi

◊ **reflectance** noun réflectance f NOTE: the opposite is **absorptance**

◊ **reflection** noun réflexion f; **signal reflection** = coefficient m de réflexion d'un signal or signal réfléchi

◊ **reflective disk** noun disque m laser à réflexion or disque à surface réfléchissante

reflex (camera) noun appareil m (photo) reflex

reformat verb reformater; **do not reformat your hard disk unless you can't do anything else** = évitez de reformater votre disque dur à moins qu'il n'y ait aucune autre solution

◊ **reformatting** noun reformatage m; **reformatting destroys all the data on a disk** = toutes les données contenues sur un disque sont détruites par le reformatage

refract verb (se) réfracter

◊ **refraction** noun réfraction f

◊ **refractive index** noun indice m de réfraction

refresh verb **(a)** (to update a memory) mettre à jour or rafraîchir or régénérer or entretenir; **memory refresh signal** = signal m de rafraîchissement de la mémoire; **RAM refresh rate** = fréquence f de régénération or de rafraîchissement de la mémoire vive; **self-refreshing RAM** = RAM auto-entretenue or autorafraîchie **(b)** (image) **screen refresh** = rafraîchir l'écran or régénérer l'image de l'écran; **refresh rate** = fréquence de rafraîchissement (de l'écran) or de régénération (de l'image)

regenerate verb recréer or régénérer

◊ **regeneration** noun (of signal) régénération f (du signal)

◊ **regenerative memory** noun mémoire f qui demande à être rafraîchie; **dynamic RAM is regenerative memory - it needs to be refreshed every 250ns** = une RAM dynamique a besoin d'être rafraîchie toutes les 250ns; **the CRT display can be thought of as regenerative memory, it**

requires regular refresh picture scans to prevent flicker = l'écran peut être comparé à une mémoire qui demande à être rafraîchie, il doit être balayé régulièrement pour éviter de présenter des images instables; (reading that regenerates data) **regenerative reading** = lecture f régénératrice (de données)

region noun (area of memory or program) zone f or région f or partie f

◊ **regional breakpoint** noun point m d'arrêt variable (de déroulement d'un programme)

register 1 noun **(a)** (for data) registre m; **accumulator register** = accumulateur m or registre m de cumul; **address register** = registre d'adresse; **base register** = registre de base; **buffer register** = registre tampon; **circulating register** = registre à or de décalage or registre permutable or à bits circulants; **control register** = registre de contrôle or de commande; **data register** = registre de données; **external register** = accumulateur or registre externe; **index register** = registre d'index; **input/output register** = registre d'entrée/sortie; **instruction register** = registre d'instruction; **instruction address register (IAR)** = registre d'adresse d'instruction; **memory address register (MAR)** = registre des adresses (en mémoire); **next instruction register** = registre d'instruction à exécuter or de la prochaine instruction; **program status word register (PSW register)** = registre des mots d'état; **sequence control register (SCR)** = registre d'instruction à suivre or à exécuter; **shift register** = registre à or de décalage; **register addressing** = adressage m de registre; **register file** = fichier m des registres; (size in bits) **register length** = taille f d'un registre; **register map** = (affichage du) contenu des registres or (affichage de la) configuration des registres **(b)** (superimposing two images correctly) repérage m or positionnement m sur repères; **the two colours are out of register** = les deux couleurs ne sont pas en repérage **2** verb **(a)** (to react) réagir; **light-sensitive films register light intensity** = la réaction des films photosensibles varie suivant l'intensité de la lumière **(b)** (to superimpose two images) faire coïncider or positionner sur repères; **register marks** = repères mpl

regulate *verb* contrôler *or* ajuster *or* régler *or* réguler; **regulated power supply** = courant *m* régulé *or* contrôlé

rehyphenation *noun* remplacement *m* de césures

reject *verb* rejeter; **the computer rejects all incoming data from incompatible sources** = l'ordinateur rejette toute donnée venant de sources non compatibles
◊ **rejection** *noun* rejet *m;* **rejection error** = erreur *f* de rejet

relational database *noun* base *f* de données relationnelle; **relational operator** *or* **logical operator** = opérateur *m* relationnel *or* logique; **relational query** = requête *f* relationnelle; **the relational query 'find all men under 35 years old' will not work on this system** = la requête relationnelle: 'trouver tous les individus mâles de moins de 35 ans' ne peut pas être traitée par ce système
◊ **relationship** *noun* rapport *m or* relation *f*

relative *adjective* relatif, -ive; **relative address** = adresse relative; **relative coding** = codage relatif; **relative coordinates** = coordonnées relatives; **relative data** = données relatives; **relative error** = erreur relative; **relative-time clock** = horloge relative

relay 1 *noun (switch)* relais *m;* **there is a relay in the circuit** = ce circuit comporte un relais; **it is relay-rated at 5 Amps** = il est protégé par un relais à 5A; **microwave relay** = relais d'hyperfréquence **2** *verb* retransmettre; **all messages are relayed through this small micro** = tous les messages sont retransmis par l'intermédiaire de ce petit micro

release 1 *noun* **(a)** *(version of a product)* version *f;* **the latest software is release 5** = la dernière version du logiciel porte le numéro 5 **(b)** *(putting a new product on the market)* mise *f* sur le marché *or* commercialisation *f; (records)* **new releases** = nouveaux enregistrements *or* nouveaux disques; **on general release** = *(available)* (produit) sur le marché; *(shown)* (film) à l'écran **(c) press release** = communiqué *m* de presse **2** *verb (new product)* mettre (un nouveau produit) sur le marché *or* lancer *or* commercialiser (un nouveau produit)

relevant *adjective* pertinent,-e
◊ **relevance** *noun* (i) relation pertinente *f* ; (ii) pertinence *f*

reliability *noun* fiabilité *f;* **it has an excellent reliability record** = il est reconnu pour sa fiabilité; **the product has passed its reliability tests** = ce produit a réussi tous les tests de fiabilité
◊ **reliable** *adjective* fiable *or* sur lequel on peut compter *or* auquel on peut se fier *or* qui donne satisfaction; **the early versions of the software were not completely reliable** = les premières versions du logiciel ne donnaient pas complète satisfaction

relief printing *noun* impression *f* en relief

reload *verb* recharger *or* relancer; **we reloaded the program after the crash** = nous avons rechargé le programme après la panne

relocate *verb (to move data)* replacer *or* déplacer *or* translater *or* changer d'adresse; **the data is relocated during execution** = l'adresse de cette donnée est changée au cours de l'éxécution; **self-relocating program** = programme autotranslatable
◊ **relocatable** *adjective (to another area of memory)* réadressable *or* translatable; **relocatable program** = programme réadressable *or* translatable; **the operating system can load and run a relocatable program from any area of memory** = ce système d'exploitation peut charger et exécuter un programme translatable sans distinction de la zone d'origine
◊ **relocation** *noun* translation *f or* réadressage *m or* changement *m* d'adresse (en mémoire); **dynamic relocation** = translation dynamique; **relocation constant** = constante *f* de translation; **static relocation** = translation statique

REM = REMARK *(in BASIC)* instruction *f* REM (pour introduction de commentaire)

remainder 1 *noun (in division)* reste *m*; **7 divided by 3 is equal to 2 remainder 1** = 7 divisé par 3 égale 2 reste 1 **2** *verb (to sell - mainly books - below cost price)* vendre à bas prix *or* solder; **this computer model is out of date so we have to remainder the rest of the stock** = ce modèle d'ordinateur est dépassé, il faut donc solder le stock qui nous reste

remedial maintenance *noun* maintenance *f* curative

remote *adjective* éloigné, -ée *or* à distance; **users can print reports on remote printers** = les utilisateurs peuvent imprimer leurs rapports sur des imprimantes à distance; **remote console** *or* **device** = console *f* *or* poste *m* de commande *or* périphérique éloigné *or* à distance; **remote control** = télécommande *f*; **the video recorder has a remote control facility** = le magnétoscope est équipé d'une télécommande; **remote job entry (RJE)** = (système de) lancement *m* de tâches à distance; **remote station** = poste éloigné; **remote terminal** = terminal à distance *or* éloigné

remove *verb* annuler *or* enlever *or* faire disparaître *or* supprimer; **the file entry was removed from the floppy disk directory** = le fichier a été retiré *or* radié du répertoire de la disquette
◊ **removable** *adjective* amovible; **a removable hard disk** = un disque dur amovible
◊ **removal** *noun* annulation *f* *or* suppression *f*; **the removal of this instruction could solve the problem** = l'annulation de cette instruction résoudrait le problème

rename *verb* changer le nom (d'un fichier); **save the file and rename it CLIENT** = sauvegarder le fichier mais changez-en le nom et appelez-le CLIENT

renumber *noun (line, etc.)* refaire la numérotation; *(page)* repaginer

reorganize *verb* réorganiser; **wait while the spelling checker database is being reorganized** = il faut attendre que la base de données du correcteur orthographique soit réorganisée

repaginate *verb (to change the lengths of pages)* repaginer *or* paginer de nouveau; **the dtp package allows simple repagination** = le système de PAO permet de repaginer; **the text was repaginated with a new line width** = le texte a été repaginé après modification de la longueur des lignes

repair 1 *verb* réparer **2** *noun* réparation *f*

repeat *verb* répéter *or* reprendre; **repeat counter** = compteur *m* de répétitions; **repeat key** = touche *f* répétition
◊ **repeater** *noun (of signal)* répéteur *m*; **this cheap repeater does not regenerate the signals** = ce répéteur bon marché ne régénère pas les signaux
◊ **repeating group** *noun* groupe *m* (de données) à répétition *or* qui se répètent de façon périodique

reperforator *noun* (re)perforatrice *f*

repertoire *noun* répertoire *m*; **the manual describes the full repertoire** = le répertoire entier est inclus dans le manuel; **character repertoire** = police *f* de caractères; **instruction repertoire** = répertoire d'instructions

repetitive letter *noun* lettre *f* standard *or* lettre type *or* lettre cadre

replace *verb* **(a)** remplacer; **a printer ribbon needs replacing after several thousand characters** = un ruban qui a imprimé plusieurs milliers de caractères a besoin d'être changé **(b)** *(instruction)* (instruction) remplace *or* (instruction de) remplacement *m see also* SEARCH AND REPLACE, GLOBAL

replay 1 *noun* **(a)** *(data or music)* relecture *f* **(b)** *(film or video)* visionnage *m* (d'une séquence de film, au ralenti); **the replay clearly showed the winner** = le visionnage du ralenti ne laisse aucun doute sur le vainqueur; **this video recorder has a replay feature** = ce magnétoscope possède une fonction 'visionnage'; **instant replay** = visionnage *m* immédiat *or* instantané **2** *verb (something which has been recorded)* (i) faire jouer (une bande nouvellement enregistrée); (ii) rejouer une bande; (iii) faire passer *or* projeter un film; **he replayed the tape** = il a repassé la bande *or* il a remis la bande; **she recorded the TV programme on video tape and replayed it the next evening** = elle a enregistré le programme de télévision sur une bande vidéo et l'a visionné le lendemain soir

replenish *verb (a battery)* recharger (une batterie d'accumulateurs)

replicate *verb* copier *or* dupliquer; **the routine will replicate your results with very little effort** = cette routine va copier vos résultats sans aucun problème

◊ **replication** *noun (copying a record)* duplication *f; (copy)* double *m*

report generator *noun (software)* générateur *m* de rapport *or* d'état

◊ **report program generator (RPG)** *noun* générateur *m* d'application

represent *verb* représenter *or* signifier; **the hash sign is used to represent a number in a series** = le symbole # s'utilise devant un numéro de série

◊ **representation** *noun* représentation *f;* **character representation** = expression *f* binaire d'un caractère

◊ **representative** *adjective* représentatif, -ive

reprint 1 *verb* réimprimer *or* faire une réimpression **2** *noun* réimpression *f;* **we have ordered a 10,000 copy reprint** = nous réimprimons 10 000 exemplaires

repro *noun (informal)* repro(graphie) *f;* **repro proof** = épreuve *f* de reproduction

reproduce *verb* reproduire

◊ **reproduction** *noun* reproduction *f*

reprogram *verb* reprogrammer *or* programmer de nouveau

request 1 *noun* demande *f or* requête *f;* **request to send signal (RTS)** = (signal de) demande *f* (d'invitation) à émettre **2** *verb* demander (quelque chose)

require *verb (to need something)* avoir besoin de (quelque chose); *(to demand something)* demander *or* exiger (quelque chose); **delicate computer systems require careful handling** = les systèmes informatiques sont très fragiles et demandent à être manipulés avec soin

◊ **required hyphen** *or* **hard hyphen** *noun* trait *m* d'union obligatoire; *see also* SOFT

◊ **requirements** *noun* (i) besoins *mpl* ; (ii) exigences *fpl;* **memory requirements depend on the application software in use** = la quantité de mémoire nécessaire varie suivant le logiciel utilisé

re-route *verb* réacheminer; **the call diverter re-routes a call** = le dispositif de transfert d'appel sert à réacheminer les appels

rerun *verb* recommencer *or* reprendre l'exécution; **rerun point** = point *m* de reprise

res *see* RESOLUTION; **hi-res** = HIGH RESOLUTION; **low-res** = LOW RESOLUTION

resave *verb* sauvegarder de nouveau; **it automatically resaves the text** = cela permet de sauvegarder le texte de nouveau automatiquement

rescue dump *noun* vidage *m* de sauvegarde

research *noun* recherche *f;* **research and development (R & D)** = recherche et développement; **the company has spent millions of dollars on R & D** = la société a dépensé des millions de dollars pour la recherche et le développement

reserved sector *noun (area of disk)* secteur *m* réservé; *(word or phrase used as an identifier)* **reserved word** = mot *m* réservé

reset *verb* **(a)** ré-initialiser; **reset button** *or* **key** = bouton *m* de ré-initialisation; **hard reset** = ré-initialisation (du système en) utilisant le contacteur; **soft reset** = ré-initialisation (du système) par commande **(b)** *(register or counter)* remettre à zéro; **when it reaches 999 this counter resets to zero** = le compteur revient automatiquement à zéro dès qu'il atteint 999 **(c)** *(to set data to zero)* remettre à zéro

resident *adjective (data or program)* résident, -e; **resident engineer** = ingénieur *m* salarié de l'entreprise; **resident software** *or* **memory-resident software** = logiciel *m* résident

residual *adjective* résiduel, -elle; **residual error rate** = taux d'erreur résiduel
◊ **residue check** *noun* contrôle *m* sur reste

resist **1** *verb* résister (à) **2** *noun (substance not affected by etching chemicals)* substance *f* résistante (à un produit chimique); *see also* PHOTORESIST
◊ **resistance** *noun (measure of the voltage)* résistance *f*
◊ **resistor** *noun (electronic component)* résistance *f*; **resistor transistor logic (RTL)** = logique *f* (à) transistors (et) résistances *or* logique RTL; **variable resistor** = résistance variable

resolution *noun (number of pixels)* définition *f*; **the resolution of most personal computer screens is not much more than 70 dpi (dots per inch)** = la plupart des écrans d'ordinateurs individuels ont une définition qui est à peine supérieure à 70 points par pouce; **graphic display resolution** = définition d'affichage graphique; **high resolution (hi-res)** = haute définition; **the high resolution screen can display 640 by 450 pixels** = avec un écran haute définition on obtient un affichage de 640 par 450 pixels; **limiting resolution** = définition maximum; **low resolution** *or* **low-res** = basse définition

resolving power *noun (of an optical system)* pouvoir *m* de résolution

resonance *noun* résonance *f* *or* résonnance *f*

resource *noun* ressource *f*; **resource allocation** = allocation *f* de ressources; **resource sharing** = partage *m* de ressources

respond *verb* répondre (à)
◊ **response** *noun* réponse *f or* réaction *f*; *(page in a videotext)* **response frame** = cadre-réponse *m*; **response position** = emplacement *m* *or* case *f* réservé(e) à la réponse; **response time** = (i) temps *m* d'accès; (ii) temps de réponse; **the response time of this flight simulator is very good** = le temps de réponse de ce simulateur de vol est excellent

restart 1 *noun* remise *m* en marche *or* redémarrage *m* *or* relance *f* **2** *verb* redémarrer *or* remettre en marche *or* relancer; **first try to restart your system** = essayez d'abord de relancer (votre système) *or* de remettre votre système en marche

restore *verb* restaurer *or* remettre en bon état *or* récupérer

restrict *verb* limiter l'accès *or* l'utilisation (de quelque chose) *or* imposer une contrainte (à quelque chose); **the document is restricted, and cannot be placed on open access** = ce document de diffusion restreinte ne doit pas être rendu public
◊ **restriction** *noun* restriction *f or* limite *f* *or* contrainte *f*

result *noun* résultat *m*

resume *verb (to restart)* continuer *or* repartir *or* reprendre

retain *verb* conserver *or* maintenir
◊ **retention** *noun* rétention *f;* **image retention** = rémanence *f or* persistance *f* de l'image

retouch *verb* retoucher; **I retouched the scratch mark on the last print** = j'ai arrangé les griffures du dernier tirage; **the artwork for the line drawings needs retouching in places** = il y a quelques retouches à faire au dessin

retransmit *verb* retransmettre *or* transmettre de nouveau
◊ **retransmission** *noun* retransmission *f*

retrieval *noun* (i) recherche *f* (documentaire); (ii) extraction *f* (de données); **information retrieval** = recherche *f* documentaire; **information retrieval centre** = centre *m* de recherche documentaire *or* centrale *f* d'information; **text retrieval** = recherche de texte
◊ **retrieve** *verb* extraire *or* récupérer; **these are the records retrieved in that search** = voici les informations extraites au cours de cette recherche; **this command will retrieve all names beginning with S** = on utilise cette commande pour extraire la liste de tous les noms qui commencent par S

retro- *prefix* rétro-; *(device or accessory)* **retrofit** = dispositif *m* d'actualisation (d'un système)

retrospective parallel running *noun* test rétrospectif en parallèle
◊ **retrospective search** *noun* recherche *f* rétrospective

return *noun* **(a)** (instruction de) retour *m;* **the program is not working because you missed out the return instruction at the end of the subroutine** = ce programme ne marche pas parce que vous avez oublié de placer un retour à la fin de cette routine; *(after a called routine finishes)* **return address** = adresse *f* de retour **(b)** *(key on a keyboard)* (touche) entrée; **you type in your name and code number then press return** = tapez votre nom et numéro de code, puis appuyez sur la touche 'entrée' **(c)** *(at end of line)* (symbole de) fin *f* de ligne; *(code or key)* **carriage return (CR)** =

(code *or* touche de) retour (du) chariot *or* retour à la ligne
◊ **return to zero signal** signal *m* de remise à zéro *or* de ré-initialisation NOTE: opposite is **non return to zero**

reveal *verb* révéler *or* mettre à jour *or* faire apparaître

reverse 1 *adjective* inversé, -ée *or* inverse; **reverse channel** = canal *m* de retour; **reverse index** = index *m* inversé; **reverse interrupt** = interruption *f* d'inversion; **reverse polarity** = polarité inversée; **reverse Polish notation (RPN)** = notation *f* polonaise inversée; **three plus four, minus two is written in RPN as 3 4 + 2 - = 5** = suivant la notation polonaise inversée, trois plus quatre moins deux s'écrit 3 4 + 2 - = 5; **normal notation: (x-y) + z, but using RPN: xy - z+** = alors que la notation conventionnelle s'écrit: (x-y) + z, la notation polonaise inversée s'écrit: xy - z+; **reverse video** = vidéo *f* inversée **2** *verb* inverser; *(with movement)* faire marche arrière

QUOTE the options are listed on the left side of the screen, with active options shown at the top left in reverse video
PC User

revert *verb* revenir (à) *or* reprendre; **after the rush order, we reverted back to our normal speed** = une fois le travail urgent terminé, nous avons repris notre rythme normal; **revert command** = commande *f* de retour à la situation de départ

review *verb* réviser *or* vérifier; **the program allows the user to review all wrongly spelled words** = le programme permet de vérifier l'orthographe

revise *verb* revoir *or* réviser; **the revised version has no mistakes** = la version revue et corrigée ne contient aucune erreur

rewind *verb* rembobiner; **the tape rewinds onto the spool automatically** = le film s'enroule automatiquement sur la bobine

rewrite 1 *verb* réécrire *or* écrire de nouveau **2** *noun* nouvelle version *f;* **the**

program is in its second rewrite = le programme en est à sa deuxième version *or* à sa deuxième mouture

RF = RADIO FREQUENCY; **RF modulator** *or* **radio frequency modulator =** modulateur *m* de fréquence radio

RGB = RED, GREEN, BLUE

rheostat *noun* rhéostat *m*
NOTE: also called **variable potential divider**

RI = RING INDICATOR

ribbon *noun* ruban *m*; **printer ribbon =** ruban d'imprimante; **ribbon cable =** câble *m* plat

right 1 *adjective* droit, -e; **right justification =** justification *f* à droite; **right shift =** décalage *m or* glissement *m* à droite **2** *noun* droite *f*
◊ **right justify** *verb (printing)* justifier *f* à droite
◊ **right shift** *verb (maths)* effectuer un décalage à droite; *see also* LOGICAL SHIFT, ARITHMETIC SHIFT

rigid *adjective* rigide *or* dur, -e

ring 1 *noun* anneau *m*; **ring (data) network =** réseau *m* en anneau **2** *verb* téléphoner; **ring back system =** système de rappel automatique; **ring down =** faire un appel groupé; **ring indicator (RI)** = indicateur *m* d'appel
◊ **ring counter** *noun* compteur *m* (à décalage) circulaire *or* compteur annulaire
◊ **ring shift** *noun* permutation *f or* décalage *m* circulaire

RIP = REST IN PROPORTION *(typography)* (agrandir *or* réduire) proportionnellement

ripple *noun* frisure *f or* oscillations *fpl* résiduelles (sur un courant)
◊ **ripple-through carry** *noun* report *m* simultané *or* rapide

RISC = REDUCED INSTRUCTION SET COMPUTER

rise time *noun* temps *m* de montée; **the circuit has a fast rise time =** le temps de montée du circuit est très rapide
RJ 45 = Registr Jack 45
RJE = REMOTE JOB ENTRY

RMS = ROOT MEAN SQUARE valeur *f* efficace (d'amplitude *or* d'intensité, etc.); **RMS line current =** intensité *f* efficace d'une ligne

RO = RECEIVE ONLY terminal *m* d'arrivée

robot *noun* robot *m*
◊ **robotics** *noun* la robotique

QUOTE so far no robot sensor has been devised which can operate quickly enough to halt the robot if a human being is in its path of work
IEE News

robust *adjective* solide; **this hard disk is not very robust =** ce disque dur n'est pas très solide
◊ **robustness** *noun* **(a)** *(strength of a casing)* robustesse *f or* solidité *f* **(b)** *(ability to continue functioning even with faults)* capacité *f* de tolérance à l'erreur

rogue indicator *noun* indicateur *m* de contrôle
◊ **rogue value** *noun (terminator)* marque *f or* marqueur *m* de fin de fichier

role indicator *noun* indicateur *m* de fonction

roll 1 *noun (film or tape)* rouleau *m;* **he put a new roll of film into the camera =** il a mis une nouvelle pellicule dans son appareil photo **2** *verb* **(a)** *(to rotate)* faire tourner *or* basculer; **roll in =** déplacer de mémoire auxiliaire en mémoire centrale; **roll out =** rappeler de mémoire centrale en mémoire auxiliaire **(b)** tourner
◊ **rollback** *noun* rechargement *m* d'un programme (après incident)
◊ **rolling headers** *noun* titres *mpl* et en-têtes courants
◊ **rollover** *noun* mémoire *f* tampon de clavier; **key rollover =** clavier *m* rapide *or* à mémoire
◊ **roll scroll** *verb* faire défiler ligne à ligne sur l'écran

ROM = READ ONLY MEMORY; **CD-ROM** *or* **compact disk-ROM** = (disque) CD-ROM; **ROM cartridge** = cartouche *f* ROM *or* ROM *f* enfichable; **the manufacturer provided the monitor program in two ROM chips** = le constructeur a fourni le programme de commande sur deux circuits ROM NOTE: there is no plural for ROM, and it is often used without the article: **the file is stored in ROM**

◊ **romware** *noun* programmes *mpl* sur ROM

roman *noun (typeface)* romain *m;* **the text is set in Times Roman** = le texte est imprimé en Times Romain

◊ **Roman numerals** *noun (figures written I, II, III, IV, etc.)* chiffres *m* romains

root *noun* **(a)** *(in a data tree structure)* racine *f* **(b)** *(fractional power of a number)* puissance *f* fractionnaire *or* racine *f;* **square root** = racine carrée; **the square root of 25 is 5** = la racine carrée de 25 est 5; **root mean square (RMS)** = valeur *f* efficace (d'amplitude *or* d'intensité, etc.); **the root mean square of the pure sinusoidal signal is 0.7071** = la valeur efficace d'une sinusoïde parfaite équivaut à 0,7071 de son amplitude

rotary *adjective* rotatif, -ive; **rotary camera** = caméra rotative; **rotary press** = (presse) rotative *f*

◊ **rotate** *verb* tourner (autour d'un axe)

◊ **rotation** *noun* rotation *f;* **bit rotation** *or* **rotate operation** = permutation *f* de bits; **matrix rotation** = rotation de matrice

round 1 *adjective* rond, -e *or* qui tourne en rond; **round robin** = (utilisation d'un appareil) à tour de rôle **2** *verb* **to round down** = arrondir un nombre par défaut; **we can round down 2.651 to 2.65** = on peut arrondir 2,651 à 2,65 par défaut; **to round off** = arrondir (au plus près); **round off 23.456 to 23.46** = arrondir 23,456 à 23,46; **round off error** = erreur *f* d'arrondi; **to round up** = arrondir par excès; **we can round up 2.647 to 2.65** = on peut arrondir 2,647 à 2,65 par excès

◊ **rounding** *noun* **(a)** *(of a number)* arrondi *m* (au plus près) *or* troncature *f;* **rounding error** = erreur d'arrondi *or* de troncature **(b)** *(giving a smoother look)*

arrondissement *m* (d'angles); **character rounding** = arrondissement de caractère

route *noun (of message)* chemin *m or* cheminement *m or* itinéraire *m;* **the route taken was not the most direct since a lot of nodes were busy** = le chemin choisi ne s'est pas révélé le plus direct du fait que de nombreux noeuds étaient occupés; **alternate route** = voie *f* de déroutement *or* déviation *f*

◊ **routing** *noun* acheminement *m or* routage *m;* **there is a new way of routing data to the central computer** = il existe une nouvelle façon d'acheminer les données vers l'ordinateur central; **routing overheads** = procédure *f* de contrôle d'acheminement *or* protocole *m* de routage (d'un message); **the information transfer rate is very much less once all routing overheads have been accommodated** = la vitesse de transmission d'informations est beaucoup moins grande une fois qu'on tient compte du protocole de routage; **routing page** = page *f* de routage; **routing table** = table *f* de routage

routine *noun* routine *f;* **the routine copies the screen display onto a printer** = la routine permet d'imprimer le contenu de l'écran; **the RETURN instruction at the end of the routine sends control back to the main program** = l'instruction RETOUR à la fin d'une routine permet de redonner la main au programme principal; **fall back routines** = routines de secours; **floating-point routines** = routines de traitement de la virgule flottante; **input routine** = routine d'entrée; **open routine** = routine ouverte *or* auxiliaire; **packing routine** = routine de compactage de données

row *noun* **(a)** *(of characters)* ligne *f; (of perforations)* rang *m;* **the figures are presented in rows, not in columns** = les chiffres sont alignés l'un à la suite de l'autre plutôt que d'être présentés en colonnes; **each entry is separated by a row of dots** = une ligne pointillée sépare les entrées les unes des autres **(b)** *(in an array or matrix)* ligne d'un tableau *or* d'une matrice

RPG = REPORT PROGRAM GENERATOR

RPN = REVERSE POLISH NOTATION

RS-232C *(EIA approved standard used in serial data transmission, covering voltage and control signals)* norme *f* RS-232C (pour interface série) *or* (interface série normalisée) RS-232C

RSA cipher system *(the Rivest, Shamir and Adleman public key cipher system)* code *m* de cryptage RSA

RS-flip-flop = RESET-SET FLIP-FLOP commutateur *m* bascule à deux états

RTE = REAL TIME EXECUTION

RTL = RESISTOR-TRANSISTOR LOGIC

RTS = REQUEST TO SEND SIGNAL

rubber banding *see* ELASTIC BANDING

rub out *see* ERASE

rubric *noun* rubrique *f*

rule *noun* **(a)** règlement *m;* **the rule states that you wait for the clear signal before transmitting** = en règle générale, vous devez attendre le signal CTS avant de commencer à transmettre; **rule-based system** = système *m* à base de règles **(b)** *(thin line)* réglure *f;* **em rule** = tiret *m* long (dont la longueur équivaut à un 'm'); **en rule** = tiret court (dont la longueur équivaut à un 'n')

◇ **ruler** *noun* règle *f* graduée; **ruler line** = règle de tabulation

run 1 *noun* exécution *f;* **the next invoice run will be on Friday** = nous n'imprimons pas les prochaines factures avant vendredi; **program run** = exécution d'un programme; **run**

indicator = indicateur *m* (lumineux) de marche **2** *verb* fonctionner *or* être en marche; *(a program)* exécuter (un programme); **the computer has been running ten hours a day** = l'ordinateur fonctionne jusqu'à dix heures par jour; **do not interrupt the spelling checker while it is running** = n'arrêtez pas la vérification de l'orthographe en cours de route; **the new package runs on our PC** = le nouveau progiciel peut être utilisé sur notre PC; **parallel running** = exploitation *f* en parallèle *or* en double; *(to fit text around an image)* **run around** = faire l'habillage *m* d'une illustration *or* d'une gravure; **run in** = roder

◇ **runaway** *noun* opération *f* incontrôlable

◇ **running head** *noun* titre *m* courant

◇ **run on** *verb* **(a)** *(text)* composer à la suite *or* laisser courir le texte (sans interruption *or* sans alinéa); **the line can run on to the next without any space** = le texte peut courir sans alinéa **(b)** *(to print more copies)* tirer à la suite; **we decided to run on 3,000 copies to the first printing** = nous avons décidé de faire un tirage à la suite de 3000 exemplaires; **run-on price** = prix *m* d'un tirage à la suite

◇ **run-time** *or* **run-duration 1** *noun* **(a)** *(length of time a program takes to run)* durée *f* d'exécution (d'un programme) **(b)** *(time when a computer is executing a program)* temps *m* d'exécution (d'un programme) **2** *adjective* **run-time error** = erreur *f* à l'exécution; *(software)* **run-time system** = (programme) superviseur *m*

R/W = READ/WRITE

◇ **R/W cycle** = READ/WRITE CYCLE cycle *m* de lecture/écriture

◇ **R/W head** = READ/WRITE HEAD tête *f* de lecture/écriture *or* tête de lecture

RX = RECEIVE, RECEIVER; **the RXed signal needs to be amplified** = le signal reçu devrait être amplifié

Ss

S100 bus *or* **S-100 bus** *noun (IEEE-696 standard bus)* bus *m* (de type) S-100
NOTE: say 'S one hundred bus'

SAFE = SIGNATURE ANALYSIS USING FUNCTIONAL ANALYSIS

safe area *noun* zone *f* d'image reçue
◇ **safety net** *noun* (i) mesure *f* de précaution; (ii) dispositif *m* de sécurité *or* auxiliaire *or* de secours; **if there is a power failure, we have a safety net in the form of a UPS** = en cas de panne d'électricité, nous avons un onduleur qui peut prendre la relève

SAM = SERIAL ACCESS MEMORY mémoire *f* à accès séquentiel

sample 1 *noun* échantillon *m*; **the sample at three seconds showed an increase** = la prise d'échantillon toutes les trois secondes a révélé une augmentation; **sample and hold circuit** = (circuit) échantillonneur-bloqueur *m* **2** *verb* échantillonner
◇ **sampler** *noun (electronic circuit)* échantillonneur *m*
◇ **sampling** *noun* échantillonnage *m*; **sampling interval** = pas *m* d'échantillonnage; **sampling rate** = fréquence *f* d'échantillonnage

sans serif *noun* (caractère) sans empattement *m*

sapphire *noun* saphir *m*

SAR = STORE ADDRESS REGISTER

satellite *noun* **(a)** *(device)* satellite *m*; **communications satellite** = satellite de télécommunication; **direct broadcast satellite (DBS)** = satellite de diffusion directe; **weather satellite** = satellite météorologique; **satellite broadcasting** = radiodiffusion *f* par satellite; **satellite link** = liaison *f* (par) satellite; **satellite network** = réseau *m* satellite **(b)** *(small system)* système satellite *or* système auxiliaire; **satellite computer** = ordinateur *m* satellite; **satellite terminal** = terminal satellite

saturation *noun (magnetic)* saturation *f* (magnétique); **saturation noise** = bruit *m* de saturation (magnétique); *(of data and messages)* **saturation testing** = tests *mpl* de saturation

save *verb (to store data)* sauvegarder; **this WP saves the text every 15 minutes in case of a fault** = ce système de traitement de texte fait une sauvegarde toutes les 15 minutes pour prévenir une défaillance; **don't forget to save the file before switching off** = n'oubliez pas de sauvegarder le fichier avant d'éteindre votre appareil; **save area** = zone *f* de sauvegarde

sawtooth waveform *noun* onde *f* en dents de scie

SBC = SINGLE BOARD COMPUTER

S-box *noun* schéma *m* itératif de cryptage DES

scalar *noun* grandeur *f* scalaire; **a scalar has a single magnitude value, a vector has two or more positional values** = une grandeur scalaire n'a qu'une dimension, un vecteur en possède au moins deux
◇ **scale 1** *noun* échelle *f*; **large scale** = grande échelle; **small scale** = petite *or* faible échelle; *(of circuit with 500 - 10,000 components)* **large scale integration (LSI)** = intégration *f* à grande échelle; *(10 - 500 components)* **medium scale integration (MSI)** = intégration à moyenne échelle; *(1 - 10 components)* **small scale integration**

(SSI) = intégration à faible *or* petite échelle; *(with several microprocessors)* **super large scale integration (SLSI)** = intégration à super grande échelle; *(10,000 - 100,000 components)* **very large scale integration (VLSI)** = intégration à très grande échelle; **wafer scale integration** = intégration sur tranche de silicium **2** *verb* **to scale down** = réduire en proportion; **to scale up** = augmenter en proportion

scan 1 *noun* balayage *m or* scan *m;* **the heat scan of the computer quickly showed which component was overheating** = le scanner a très vite repéré le composant qui surchauffait; **the scan revealed which records were now out of date** = un balayage a fait apparaître les données périmées; **raster scan** = passe *f* de balayage **2** *verb (electronic)* scanner *or* faire un balayage *or* un scanning *or* un scannage; *(to look closely at something)* lire *or* examiner (quelque chose) attentivement; **he scanned the map for Teddington** = il a cherché Teddington sur la carte; **a facsimile machine scans the picture and converts this to digital form before transmission** = un télécopieur fait un balayage de l'image qu'il convertit en données numériques avant transmission; **the machine scans at up to 300 dpi resolution** = cet appareil peut faire un scannage avec définition allant jusqu'à 300 points par pouce; **scan area** = zone *f* de balayage; **scan length** = étendue *f* de la zone de balayage

◊ **scanner** *noun* scanner *m or* scanneur *m;* **a scanner reads the bar-code on the product label using a laser beam and photodiode** = le scanneur peut lire les codes barres sur les étiquettes des produits grâce à un rayon laser et une photodiode; **scanner memory** = mémoire d'images optiques; **image scanner** = scanner d'images; **optical scanner** = lecteur *m* optique *or* scanner

scanning *noun* balayage *m or* lecture *f or* scanning *m or* scannage *m;* **scanning device** = scanner *m or* scanneur *m or* dispositif *m* de lecture par balayage; **scanning error** = erreur de balayage; **scanning radio receiver** = récepteur *m* à recherche de signal; **scanning line** = ligne *f* de balayage; **scanning rate** = fréquence *f* de balayage; **scanning resolution** = définition *f* de lecture *or* de

balayage; **scanning software** = logiciel *m* de saisie (par balayage); **scanning speed** = vitesse *f* de balayage; **throughput is 1.3 inches per second scanning speed** = la vitesse de lecture par balayage est de 1,3 pouces par seconde; **its scanning speed is 9.9 seconds for an 8.5 inch by 11 inch document** = il lui faut 9,9 secondes pour lire un document de 8,5 x 11 pouces; **auto-baud scanning** *or* **auto-baud sensing** = sélection *f* automatique de vitesse de transmission *or* reconnaissance *f* automatique de débit d'une ligne (en bauds)

◊ **scanning spot** *noun* **(a)** *(small area of an image)* point *m* d'image **(b)** *(on a TV screen)* spot *m* de balayage; *(of satellite)* **scanning spot beam** = faisceau *m* de balayage *or* d'exploration

QUOTE scanning time per page ranged from about 30 seconds to three minutes
PC Business World

scatter *noun* onde *f* diffusée; **scatter graph** = graphique de points; **scatter proofs** = épreuves *fpl* en vrac; *see also* BACKSCATTER

◊ **scatter load** *verb* faire un chargement éclaté; **scatter read** = faire une lecture sélective

scavenge *verb* piller (une base de données)

schedule *noun* **1** *noun* programme *m or* horaire *m or* plan *m* **2** *verb (TV or radio programmes)* établir un horaire (de programme de télévision *or* radio)

◊ **scheduled circuits** *noun* lignes *fpl* spécialisées

◊ **scheduler** *noun* **(a)** *(computer program)* (programme) superviseur *m* (de multiprogrammation) *or* gestionnaire *m* de tâches **(b)** *(person)* personne *f* qui établit l'horaire (de programme de télévision *or* radio)

◊ **scheduling** *noun* **(a)** *(share of CPU)* détermination *f* de l'ordre de priorité *or* constitution *f* de file d'attente; *(of production)* ordonnancement *m;* **job scheduling** = détermination de priorité des tâches *or* gestion *f* de tâches; *(production)* ordonnancement des travaux **(b)** **programme scheduling** = établissement *m* d'un horaire de programme de télévision *or* radio

schema *noun* graphique *m or* schéma *m or* diagramme *m*
◇ **schematic 1** *adjective* schématique *or* sous forme de schéma *or* de diagramme **2** *noun* plan *m* schématique *or* diagramme *m or* schéma *m*

scientific *adjective* scientifique; **scientific calculator** = calculatrice *f* avec fonctions scientifiques

scissor *verb (text or graphics)* couper

SCR = SEQUENCE CONTROL REGISTER

scramble *verb (message)* brouiller
◇ **scrambler** *noun* **(a)** *(device that codes a data stream)* codeur *m* **(b)** *(for speech and messages)* brouilleur *m;* **he called the President on the scrambler telephone** = il a appelé le président sur la ligne protégée par brouillage

scratch 1 *noun (mark on disk or film)* égratignure *f or* griffure *f* **2** *verb (file or data)* supprimer *or* détruire
◇ **scratch file** *or* **work file** *noun (work area)* fichier *m* de travail *or* de manoeuvre; **scratch tape** = bande *f* de travail
◇ **scratchpad** *noun* mémoire *f* temporaire *or* mémoire banale *or* (mémoire) bloc-notes *m*

screen 1 *noun* **(a)** *(display device)* écran *m;* **screen border** = bordure *f* d'écran; **screen buffer** = mémoire *f* tampon d'écran; **screen dump** = vidage *m* d'écran (sur imprimante); **screen editor** = éditeur *m* d'écran; **screen format** = format *m* d'écran; **screen grab** = capture *f* d'écran; **screen memory** = mémoire *f* écran; **on-screen display** = affichage *m;* **the dtp package offers on-screen font display** = le logiciel PAO permet l'affichage des polices de caractères; **text screen** = écran de texte; **touch screen** = écran tactile **(b)** *(which protects)* écran de protection; **magnetic screen** = blindage *m or* écran magnétique; **without the metal screen over the power supply unit, the computer just produced garbage** = lorsqu'on enlevait le blindage métallique du bloc d'alimentation, l'ordinateur ne donnait plus rien de bon

2 *verb* **(a)** *(to protect)* protéger à l'aide d'un écran; **the PSU is screened against interference** = un blindage réduit les interférences du bloc d'alimentation **(b)** *(to display) (data)* afficher; *(film)* projeter; **the film is now being screened** = la projection du film est commencée **(c)** *(to select)* sélectionner *or* trier
◇ **screenful** *noun* plein écran

> QUOTE the screen memory is, in fact a total of 4K in size, the first 2K hold the character codes, of which 1K is displayed. Scrolling brings the remaining area into view
> *Computing Today*

script *noun* scénario *m*
◇ **scriptwriter** *noun* scénariste *m&f*

scroll *verb* faire défiler (un texte) *m;* **roll scroll** = faire défiler (un texte) ligne à ligne sur l'écran; **smooth scroll** = faire défiler (un texte) point par point; **scroll mode** = mode défilement
◇ **scrolling down** *noun* défilement *m* descendant *or* vers le bas; **scrolling up** = défilement ascendant *or* vers le haut

scrub *verb* effacer *or* supprimer *or* détruire; **scrub all files with the .BAK extension** = détruisez tous les fichiers avec l'extension .BAK

SCSI = SMALL COMPUTER SYSTEM INTERFACE interface *f* pour petits ordinateurs *or* interface SCSI

> QUOTE the system uses SCSI for connecting to the host and ESDI for interconnecting among drives within a multidrive system
> *Byte*

SD = SINGLE DENSITY (DISK)

SDI = SELECTIVE DISSEMINATION OF INFORMATION

SDLC = SYNCHRONOUS DATA LINK CONTROL

SDR = STORE DATA REGISTER

seal *verb* fermer hermétiquement *or* sceller; **the hard disk is in a sealed case** = le disque dur est contenu dans un boîtier scellé

search 1 *noun* recherche *f;* **chaining search =** recherche associative *or* en chaîne; **linear search** *or* **sequential search =** recherche séquentielle; **retrospective search =** recherche rétrospective; **search key =** clé *f* de recherche; **search memory =** mémoire associative; *(on word processors)* **search and replace =** fonction de recherche et remplacement *or* (re)cherche et remplace; **global search and replace =** recherche *f* globale et remplace **2** *verb* chercher *or* faire une recherche

◇ **searching storage** *noun* mémoire associative

QUOTE a linear search of 1,000 items takes 500 comparisons to find the target, and 1,000 to report that it isn't present. A binary search of the same set of items takes roughly ten divisions either to find or not to find the target
Personal Computer World

SECAM = SEQUENTIEL A MEMOIRE

second *adjective* deuxième *or* second, -e; **we have two computers, the second one being used if the first is being repaired =** nous possédons un second ordinateur pour assurer la relève si le premier tombe en panne; **second generation computers =** ordinateurs de deuxième génération; **second-level addressing =** adressage *m* indirect; **second-sourcing =** utilisation *f* d'une seconde source de composants; **second-user** *or* **second-hand =** (équipement) d'occasion

◇ **secondary** *adjective* secondaire; **secondary channel =** canal *m or* voie *f* secondaire; *(from two primary colours)* **secondary colour =** couleur *f* secondaire; **secondary station =** station *f* secondaire; **secondary storage =** mémoire *f* auxiliaire

section *noun* *(of main program)* segment *m* (exécutable)

sector 1 *noun* *(on magnetic disk)* secteur *m* **2** *verb* *(disk)* sectoriser; **(disk) sector formatting =** formatage *m* de secteurs (d'un disque); **sectoring hole =** perforation *f* de positionnement; **hard-sectored =** (disque) avec formatage physique; **soft-sectored =** (disque) formaté *or* sectorisé par logiciel; *see also* FORMAT

secure system *noun* système *m* sécurisé *or* verrouillé

◇ **secured** *adjective (file)* sécurisé, -ée

◇ **security** *noun* sécurité *f;* **the system has been designed to assure the security of the stored data =** la conception du système assure la sécurité des données en mémoire; **security backup =** copie *f* de sauvegarde; *(of users)* **security check =** contrôle *m* de sécurité

seek *verb* chercher; *(section of memory)* **seek area =** zone *f* de recherche; **seek time =** temps *m* d'accès; **the new hard disk drive has a seek time of 35ms =** le nouveau disque a un temps d'accès de 35 ms

segment 1 *noun (section of a main program)* segment *m* **2** *verb (a long program)* segmenter *or* diviser; *see also* OVERLAY

QUOTE you can also write in smaller program segments. This simplifies debugging and testing
Personal Computer World

select *verb* (i) sélectionner *or* valider; (ii) activer; *(line or signal)* **chip select (CS) =** valider *or* activer un circuit intégré

◇ **selectable** *adjective* qui n'est pas préréglé, -ée; **jumper-selectable =** (circuit *or* dispositif) qui peut être sélectionné *or* validé par cavalier; **selectable attributes =** attributs programmables (par l'utilisateur); **user-selectable =** programmable *or* définissable *or* réglable (par l'utilisateur); qui peut être modifié *or* programmé *or* sélectionné *or* validé *or* réglé suivant les besoins de l'utilisateur; **this modem has user-selectable baud rates =** les vitesses (de réception et de transmission) de ce modem sont réglables

◇ **selection** *noun* choix *m or* sélection *f;* **selection of information from a large database may take some time =** la sélection des informations contenues dans une vaste base de données peut demander beaucoup de temps

◇ **selective** *adjective* sélectif, -ive; **selective calling =** appel sélectif; **selective dump =** vidage sélectif; **selective sort =** tri sélectif

◇ **selectivity** *noun* sélectivité *f*

◊ **selector** *noun* sélecteur *m;* **the selector knob for the amplification is located there** = c'est là que se trouve le sélecteur d'amplitude; **turn the selector control** = tournez le sélecteur; **selector channel** = canal *m* sélecteur *or* de sélection

self- *prefix (referring to oneself)* auto-; **self-adapting system** = système *m* auto-adaptatif; **self-checking system** = système avec contrôle automatique *or* avec autocontrôle; **self-checking code** = code *m* autodétecteur (d'erreurs); **self-correcting codes** = codes (auto)correcteurs; **self-diagnostic** = autodiagnostic *m;* **self-documenting program** = programme *m* avec documentation en ligne; *(expert system)* **self-learning** = système auto-enrichissant *or* à acquisition de connaissances et de régles *or* autodidacte; **self-refreshing RAM** = (mémoire) RAM auto-rafraîchie *or* auto-entretenue; **self-relocating program** = (programme) autotranslatable; **self-resetting** *or* **self-restoring loop** = boucle *f* avec retour automatique à zéro *or* avec retour aux paramètres de départ

semantics *noun* sémantique *f; (use of incorrect symbol)* **semantic error** = erreur *f* (de) sémantique

semaphore *noun* **(a)** *(flags)* (fonction) sémaphore *m* **(b)** *(signalling system)* (technique) sémaphore

semi- *prefix* semi- *or* demi-; **semi-processed data** = données partiellement prétraitées

semicolon (;) *noun* point-virgule *m*

semicompiled *adjective* (programme) semi-compilé

semiconductor *noun* semi-conducteur *m;* **semiconductor device** = (composant) semi-conducteur; **semiconductor memory** = mémoire à semi-conducteur; *(solid-state laser)* **semiconductor laser** = laser *m* transistorisé

sender *noun (person)* émetteur, -euse

◊ **send-only device** *noun* (dispositif uniquement) émetteur *m*

sense 1 *verb* détecter *or* lire; **the condition of the switch was sensed by the program** = le programme a pu détecter l'état du connecteur; **this device senses the holes punched in a paper tape** = ce dispositif lit les perforations de la bande papier; **mark sense** = graphiter 2 *noun* détection *f or* lecture *f or* reconnaissance *f;* **sense recovery time** = délai *m* de retournement *or* de conversion; **sense switch** = (commutateur) détecteur *m or* indicateur *m* d'état

◊ **auto-baud sensing** *noun* reconnaissance *f* automatique du débit d'une ligne (en bauds)

◊ **sensitive** *adjective* sensible; **the computer is sensitive even to very slight changes in current** = cet ordinateur est sensible aux moindres variations du courant; **light-sensitive films change when exposed to light** = les films photosensibles réagissent à la lumière; **touch-sensitive keyboard** = clavier *m* à effleurement *or* clavier tactile

◊ **sensitivity** *noun* sensibilité *f;* **the scanner's sensitivity to small objects** = la sensibilité du scanner aux petits objets

◊ **sensor** *noun* capteur *m;* **the sensor's output varies with temperature** = le signal de sortie du capteur varie suivant la température; **the process is monitored by a bank of sensors** = ce processus est contrôlé par une batterie de capteurs; **image sensor** = capteur d'images

sentinel *noun (marker or pointer)* drapeau *m or* marqueur *m*

separate 1 *adjective* indépendant, -e *or* différent, -e; **separate channel signalling** = émission de signaux par canaux indépendants 2 *verb* séparer; *(display option)* **separated graphics** = caractères graphiques espacés *or* séparés

◊ **separation** *noun* séparation *f;* **colour separation** = séparation *f or* sélection *f* des couleurs; **colour separations** = négatifs *mpl* de séparation des couleurs

◊ **separator** *noun (symbol or code in a program)* (symbole *or* code) séparateur *m* (d'information) *or* symbole *m* intercalaire

septet *noun (word made up of seven bits)* septet *m*

sequence *noun* séquence *f or* ordre *m;* **the sequence of names is arranged alphabetically** = les noms sont classés par ordre alphabétique; **the program instructions are arranged in sequence according to line numbers** = les instructions sont ordonnées suivant le numéro de ligne; **binary sequence** = séquence binaire; **control sequence** = séquence de commande (d'exécution); **sequence check** = contrôle *m* de séquence; **sequence control register (SCR)** *or* **sequence counter** *or* **sequence register** = registre *m* de contrôle de séquence; **the logon sequence** = séquence d'ouverture de session *or* d'identification

◊ **sequencer** *noun* séquenceur *m*

◊ **sequential** *adjective* séquentiel, -elle; **sequential batch processing** = traitement *m* par lots en mode séquentiel; **sequential computer** = ordinateur *m* série; **sequential file** *or* **serial file** = fichier *m* à accès séquentiel; **sequential logic** = logique séquentielle; **if the input sequence to the sequential logic circuit is 1101 the output will always be zero (0)** = si l'entrée dans le circuit séquentiel logique est 1101, la sortie sera toujours zéro (0); **sequential mode** = mode séquentiel; **sequential operation** = opération séquentielle; **sequential processing** = traitement séquentiel (de données); **sequential search** = recherche séquentielle

◊ **sequentially** *adverb* (exécuté) en série *or* suivant un ordre séquentiel

◊ **sequential access** *noun* accès séquentiel; **sequential access storage** = mémoire *f* à accès séquentiel; **queued indexed sequential access method (QISAM)** = méthode d'accès séquentiel indexé en file; **queued sequential access method (QSAM)** = méthode d'accès séquentiel en file

Séquentiel à Mémoire (SECAM) standard de télévision SECAM

serial *adjective* (en) série *or* séquentiel, -elle; **serial access** = accès *m* séquentiel *or* accès série; **serial-access memory (SAM)** = mémoire *f* à accès séquentiel; **serial adder** = additionneur *m* (en) série; **serial computer** = ordinateur *m* série;

serial data transmission = transmission *f* de données en série; **serial file** = fichier *m* à accès séquentiel; **serial input/output (SIO)** = entrée/sortie *f* en série; *see* SERIAL TRANSMISSION; **serial input/parallel output (SIPO)** = entrée série/sortie parallèle; **serial to parallel converter** = convertisseur *m* série/parallèle; **serial input/serial output (SISO)** = entrée série/sortie série; **serial interface** *or* **port** = interface *f or* port *m* série; **parallel connections are usually less trouble to set up and use than serial interfaces, but are usually limited to 20 feet in length** = de façon générale, les connexions parallèles sont moins difficiles à mettre en place et à utiliser que les interfaces série, mais leur longueur est limitée à environ 6 mètres; **serial memory** = mémoire *f* séquentielle; **serial operation** = opération séquentielle; **serial printer** = imprimante *f* série; **serial processing** = traitement séquentiel; **serial storage** = *(action)* stockage *m* séquentiel; *(place)* mémoire *f* à accès séquentiel; **serial to parallel converter** = convertisseur *m* série/parallèle; **serial transmission** *or* **serial input/output** = transmission (en) série *or* entrée/sortie (en) série; **word serial** = transfert *m* en série (de mots binaires)

◊ **serially** *adverb* (disposé *or* monté) en série; **their transmission rate is 64,000 bits per second through a parallel connection or 19,200 serially** = leur vitesse de transmission est de 64 000 bits par seconde en connexion parallèle ou 19 200 en connexion série

◊ **series** *noun* série *f;* **series circuit** = circuit *m* (disposé en) série *or* montage *m* en série

serif *noun* empattement *m* (d'un caractère); **sans serif** = (caractère) sans empattement

server *noun (dedicated computer or peripheral)* serveur *m;* **file server** = serveur de fichier; **LAN server** = serveur de réseau local

service 1 *verb (system)* réviser *or* réparer; **the disk drives were serviced yesterday and are working well** = nous avons fait réviser *or* réparer les lecteurs de disquettes hier et tout fonctionne très bien **2** *noun* **(a)** contrôle *m;* **service bit** =

bit *m* de contrôle **(b)** maintenance *f;* **service contract** = contrat *m* de maintenance; **service program** = programme *m* de maintenance *or* (programme) utilitaire *m*

servo *or* **servomechanism** *noun* servomécanisme *m*

session *noun* session *f or* période *f* de travail; **session key** = clé d'ouverture d'une session; **session layer** = couche *f* session

set 1 *noun* **(a)** ensemble *m or* jeu *m or* série *f;* **character set** = *(code)* jeu *or* ensemble de caractères; *(typeface)* fonte *f or* police *f* de caractères; *(maths)* **set theory** = théorie *f* des ensembles **(b)** *(typeface)* corps *m* d'un caractère; **set size** = taille *f* d'un caractère (mesuré en points); **set width** = chasse *f* **(c)** *(radio or TV receiver)* poste *m* (de télévision *or* radio); **set-top converter** = convertisseur *m* de signal *or* de fréquence **(d)** *(of play or film or TV)* décors *mpl* **2** *verb* **(a)** *(to define a value)* fixer *or* programmer *or* paramétrer *or* régler; **we set the right-hand margin at 80 characters** = nous avons programmé *or* fixé la marge de droite à 80 caractères; **to set breakpoints** = programmer les points d'arrêt **(b)** *(to give a bit the value of 1)* charger un bit *or* attribuer 1 à la valeur du bit **(c)** *(to compose a text into typeset characters)* composer; **the text is set in 12 point Times Roman** = le texte est (composé) en Times romain corps 12

◊ **setting** *noun* **(a)** réglage *m; (adjusting)* **brightness setting** = réglage de la luminosité; **contrast setting** = réglage des contrastes **(b)** *(typesetting of text)* composition *f;* **the MS has been sent to the typesetter for setting** = le manuscrit a été envoyé à l'atelier pour être composé; **setting charges have increased since last year** = les frais de composition ont augmenté depuis l'an dernier; **computer setting** = composition informatisée *or* assistée par ordinateur

◊ **set up** *verb (to install)* installer; *(to initialize or start)* initialiser *or* mettre en route; **the new computer worked well as soon as the engineer had set it up** = l'ingénieur a initialisé le nouvel ordinateur qui a tout de suite bien fonctionné; *(choices)* **set-up options** = paramètres *mpl* programmables à

l'installation; *(between signal and start)* **set-up time** = temps *m* de commutation *or* de connexion

sextet *noun (byte made up of six bits)* sextet *m*

sf signalling = SINGLE FREQUENCY SIGNALLING

shade *noun (of colour)* ton *m or* nuance *f;* **shades of grey** = niveaux *mpl* de gris

◊ **shading** *noun (of drawing)* ombre *f or* ombrage *m; (lines)* hachures *fpl; (of colour)* dégradé *m*

shadow *noun (area where signals cannot be received)* ombre *f;* **the mountain casts a shadow over those houses, so they cannot receive any radio broadcasts** = la montagne fait écran à ces habitations qui ne reçoivent aucune émission radio

◊ **shadowmask** *noun (to separate three-colour picture beams)* masque *m* filtre

◊ **shadow memory** *or* **shadow page** *noun* mémoire *f* fantôme *or* mémoire paginée; **shadow page table** = table *f* de mémoire paginée

◊ **shadow ROM** *noun* mémoire morte paginée

shannon *noun* shannon *m*

◊ **Shannon's Law** *noun* loi *f* de Shannon

share *verb* partager; **the system is shared by several independent companies** = plusieurs sociétés indépendantes se partagent le système; **shared access** = accès *m* partagé; *see also* TIME-SHARING SYSTEM, MULTI-USER; **shared bus** = bus *m* partagé; **shared file** = fichier *m* commun *or* partagé; **shared line** *or* **party line** = ligne *f* partagée; **shared logic system** = système logique partagé; **shared logic text processor** = processeur *m* de traitement de texte à logique partagée; **shared memory** = mémoire partagée; **shared resources system** = système à ressources partagées *or* système multi-utilisateur; **resource sharing** = partage *m* de ressources; **time-sharing** = partage de temps *or* (système) en temps partagé

◇ **shareware** *noun* logiciel *m* pour lequel une contribution volontaire est demandée

sheet *noun* feuille *f* (de papier); **sheet feed** = alimentation *f* (en) feuille à feuille; **sheet feed attachment** = bac *m* d'alimentation automatique (en) feuille à feuille

shelf life *noun* durée *f* de vie (à l'étalage) *or* date *f* de péremption (d'un produit en magasin); **the developer has a shelf life of one year** = le révélateur doit être utilisé dans un délai d'un an

shell sort *noun* (algorithme de) tri *m* enveloppe

SHF = SUPER HIGH FREQUENCY

shield 1 *noun* écran *m or* blindage *m* de protection **2** *verb* protéger; **shielded cable** = câble *m* blindé

shift 1 *verb* **(a)** *(to move)* déplacer *or* décaler *or* permuter; **shift instruction** = instruction *f* de décalage; **shift left** = faire un décalage à gauche; **0110 left shifted once is 1100** = 0110 décalé à gauche d'un pas, devient 1100; **shift right** = faire un décalage à droite **(b)** *(typewriter, etc.)* passer en majuscule **2** *noun* **(a)** décalage *m or* permutation *f;* **arithmetic shift** = décalage arithmétique; **cyclic shift** = permutation *or* décalage circulaire; **logical shift** = décalage logique *or* non arithmétique; **shift character** = caractère *m* de déplacement; **shift code** = code *m* de déplacement; **shift register** = registre *m* à *or* de décalage **(b)** *(on typewriter, etc.)* **shift key** = touche *f* majuscule

shoot *verb* *(to film)* tourner (un film) *or* filmer; **they shot hundreds of feet of film, but none of it was any good** = ils ont pris des centaines de mètres de pellicule sans rien obtenir d'intéressant; **the programme was shot on location in Spain** = les extérieurs pour ce programme ont été tournés en Espagne
NOTE: **shooting - shot**

short *adjective* court, -e; *(expansion board)* **short card** = carte *f* (de taille)

réduite; **short haul modem** = modem *m* de courte portée

short circuit 1 *noun* court-circuit *m* **2** *verb* créer un court-circuit *or* court-circuiter; **short-circuited** = (qui a été) mis en court-circuit

shorten *verb* raccourcir *or* couper *or* réduire; **we had to shorten the file to be able to save it on one floppy** = nous avons dû raccourcir *or* couper le fichier pour réussir à le sauvegarder sur une seule disquette

short-run *adjective* tirage *m* réduit *or* limité; **a printer specializing in short-run printing** = un imprimeur qui se spécialise dans les petits tirages; **the laser printer is good for short-run leaflets** = l'imprimante (à) laser est très utile pour les tirages limités

short wave (SW) *noun* *(frequency below 60 metres)* ondes *fpl* courtes; **short-wave receiver** = récepteur *m* (d') ondes courtes

shotgun microphone *noun* microphone *m* 'canon'

show-through *noun* transparence *f;* **bad quality paper gives too much show-through** = un papier de mauvaise qualité est beaucoup trop transparent

shrink *verb* réduire *or* condenser *or* comprimer; **the drawing was shrunk to fit the space** = on a réduit le dessin pour le faire entrer dans l'emplacement prévu
NOTE: **shrinks - shrank - has shrunk**

shut down *verb* arrêter *or* fermer *or* éteindre
◇ **shut-off mechanism** *noun* mécanisme *m* d'arrêt

shutter *noun* *(of camera)* obturateur *m*

SI units = SYSTEME INTERNATIONAL UNITS unités *fpl* (de mesures) SI

sibilance *noun* sibilance *f or* sifflement *m*

sideband *noun* bande *f* latérale; **upper sideband** = bande latérale supérieure; **lower sideband** = bande latérale inférieure; **double sideband** = double bande latérale; **double sideband suppressed carrier (DSBSC)** = (modulation d'amplitude à) double bande latérale sans porteuse *or* à porteuse inhibée; **single sideband** = bande latérale unique

side lobe *noun (of aerial's response pattern)* lobe *m* latéral

sideways ROM *noun* ROM auxiliaire *or* mémoire *f* morte auxiliaire

sign 1 *noun* signe *m* (de polarité); **sign and modulus** = signe et modulo; **sign bit** *or* **sign indicator** = bit *m* de signe *or* indicateur *m* de signe; **sign digit** = binaire *m* de signe *or* chiffre (indicateur) de signe; **sign and magnitude** *or* **signed magnitude** = chiffre (de) signe; **sign position** = position *f* du signe **2** *verb* **(a)** signer; *(to logoff)* **to sign off** = terminer une session; *(to logon)* **to sign on** = débuter *or* ouvrir une session (en s'identifiant) **(b)** **signed field** = champ (de) signe; **signed magnitude** = *see* SIGN AND MAGNITUDE

signal 1 *noun* signal *m;* **the signal received from the computer contained the answer** = le signal émis par l'ordinateur contenait la réponse; **interrupt signal** = signal (d') interruption; **signal conditioning** = mise *f* en forme *or* conversion *f* de signaux; **signal conversion** = conversion de signaux; **signal converter** = convertisseur *m* de signaux; **signal distance** = distance de Hamming; **signal element** = élément (d'un) signal; **the signal element in this system is a short voltage pulse, indicating a binary one** = l'élément signal de ce système est une courte impulsion de tension qui représente un 1 binaire; **the signal elements for the radio transmission system are 10ms of 40KHz and 10ms of 60KHz for binary 0 and 1 respectively** = les signaux élémentaires de ce système de radiotransmission sont 10 ms à 40 kHz, pour le bit nul et 10 ms à 60 kHz, pour le bit chargé; **signal generator** = générateur *m* de signaux; **signal to noise ratio (S/N)** = rapport *m* signal/bruit; **signal processing** =

traitement *m* du signal; **the system is used by students doing research on signal processing techniques** = ce système est à la disposition des étudiants qui se spécialisent dans la recherche sur les techniques de traitement du signal; **the message was recovered by carrier signal processing** = le message a été récupéré en traitant *or* analysant le signal porteur **2** *verb* émettre *or* transmettre un signal; **signal to the network that we are busy** = signale au réseau que nous sommes occupés *or* envoie un signal au réseau pour prévenir que nous sommes occupés

◊ **signalling** *noun* signalisation *f;* **in band signalling** = transmission *f* de signaux sur la bande vocale

signature *noun* **(a)** *(name)* signature *f;* **do you recognize the signature on the cheque?** = reconnaissez-vous la signature sur le chèque? **(b)** *(of book)* cahier *m;* **signature (mark)** = signature **(c)** *(authentication code)* signature *or* code *m* personnel *or* confidentiel; **safe signature analysis using functional analysis (SAFE)** = technique *f* de validation de signature SAFE

signify *verb (to mean)* signifier *or* vouloir dire; **a carriage return code signifies the end of an input line** = l'envoi du code CR signifie que la ligne saisie est terminée

◊ **significance** *noun* signification *f*

◊ **significant** *adjective* significatif, -ive *or* important, -e; **significant digit codes** *or* **faceted codes** = codes *mpl* significatifs

silicon *noun* silicium *m;* **silicon chip** = puce *f or* pastille *f* de silicium; **silicon disk** *or* **RAM disk** = disque *m* RAM *or* virtuel; **silicon foundry** = fonderie *f* de silicium; **silicon gate** = semi-conducteur *m* au silicium; **silicon on sapphire (SOS)** = silicium sur saphir; **silicon transistor** = transistor *m* silicium; *(area of California)* **Silicon Valley** = Silicon Valley, région de la Californie où l'on trouve une forte concentration de sociétés productrices de semi-conducteurs; **silicon wafer** = tranche *f* de silicium

SIMD = SINGLE INSTRUCTION STREAM MULTIPLE DATA STREAM

simple *adjective (not complicated)* simple; *(hardware or software)* **simple to use =** (machine *or* logiciel) d'utilisation facile

simplex *noun (transmission in one direction)* simplex *m or* transmission *f* unidirectionnelle

simplify *verb* simplifier *or* rendre plus facile; **function keys simplify program operation =** les touches de fonction simplifient l'exploitation d'un programme

simulate *verb* simuler; **this software simulates the action of an aeroplane =** ce logiciel simule les manoeuvres aériennes *or* est un simulateur de vol
◊ **simulator** *noun* simulateur *m;* **flight simulator =** simulateur de vol
◊ **simulation** *noun* simulation *f;* **simulation software =** logiciel *m* de simulation; **simulation techniques have reached a high degree of sophistication =** les techniques de simulation sont devenues très sophistiquées

simultaneity *adjective* simultanéité *f*

simultaneous *adjective* simultané, -ée; **simultaneous processing =** traitement *m* simultané; **simultaneous transmission =** transmission *f* simultanée NOTE: same as duplex
◊ **simultaneously** *adverb* de façon simultanée *or* simultanément

sin *or* **sine** *noun (geometry)* sinus *m*
◊ **sine wave** *noun* sinusoïde *f or* onde *f* sinusoïdale

single *adjective (only one)* unique *or* simple; **single address code =** code *m* d'instruction à adresse directe *or* unique; **single address message =** message *m* à une seule adresse; **single address instruction =** instruction *f* à adresse directe *or* unique; **single board computer (SBC) =** ordinateur *m* à carte unique *or* ordinateur monocarte; **single chip computer =** ordinateur *m* à puce unique *or* ordinateur monopuce; **single density disk (SD) =** disquette *f* à simple densité; **single frequency signalling** *or* **sf signalling =** signalisation *f*

monofréquence; **single function software =** logiciel *m* d'application spécialisée; **single instruction stream multiple data stream (SIMD) =** flux *m* simple d'instruction, flux multiple de données; **single instruction stream single data stream (SISD) =** flux simple d'instruction, flux simple de données; **single key response =** (logiciel) activé par une seule touche; *(by one computer word)* **single length precision =** (en) simple précision; **single length working =** opération *f* en simple mot; **single line display =** écran *m* d'une ligne *or* (écran avec) affichage d'une ligne (à la fois); **single operand instruction =** instruction à un opérande; *(transmission in one direction)* **single operation =** transmission *f* unidirectionnelle *or* simplex *m;* **single pass operation =** opération (en) une passe *or* opération monopasse; **single pole (switch) =** (commutateur) unipolaire; **single precision =** (en) simple précision; **single scan non segmented =** balayage *m* une passe sans segmentation d'image *or* balayage d'image complète en une passe; **single sheet feed =** alimentation *f or* entraînement *m* feuille à feuille; **single sideband =** bande *f* latérale unique; **single-sided disk (SSD) =** disquette *f* simple face; *(one instruction at a time)* **single step =** (exécution) pas à pas; **single strike ribbon =** ruban *m* à un seul passage *or* non réutilisable; **single tasking =** monotâche *f;* **single user system =** système *m* mono-utilisateur *or* ordinateur *m* individuel

sink *noun (end of line)* puits *m or* collecteur *m* de données; *(conducts heat away from component)* **heat sink =** dissipateur *m* thermique; *(paths in a network)* **sink tree =** arborescence *f* en puits

sinusoidal *adjective* sinusoïdal, -e; **the carrier has a sinusoidal waveform =** le signal porteur est une sinusoïde

SIO = SERIAL INPUT/OUTPUT

siphoning *noun* siphonage *m*

SIPO = SERIAL INPUT/PARALLEL OUTPUT

SISD = SINGLE INSTRUCTION STREAM SINGLE DATA STREAM

SISO = SERIAL INPUT/SERIAL OUTPUT

site *noun* emplacement *m*
◊ **site poll** *verb* appel *m* (à émettre) à tous les terminaux d'un site; *see also* POLLING

sixteen-bit *or* **16-bit** *adjective* (système à) seize bits

sixteenmo *or* **16mo** *noun* in-16 *or* in seize *or* (à) quatre plis

size 1 *noun* dimension *f or* taille *f or* grandeur *f;* **the size of the print has been increased to make it easier to read** = la taille des caractères a été augmentée pour rendre la lecture plus facile; **page size** = taille *or* grandeur *or* format *m* de la page; **our page sizes vary from 220 x 110 to 360 x 220** = nos formats de pages varient de 220 x 110mm à 360 x 220mm; **screen size** = dimension de l'écran **2** *verb* dimensionner
◊ **sizing** *noun* modification *f* des dimensions *or* mise *f* à la taille; **photographs can be edited by cropping, sizing, touching up, etc.** = les photos peuvent être éditées par découpage, dimensionnement, retouche, etc.

skeletal code *noun* code *m* incomplet *or* code de base *or* code support *or* code paramétrable

sketch 1 *noun* esquisse *f* **2** *verb* esquisser *or* faire une esquisse

skew *noun* inclinaison *f or* obliquité *f or* biais *m*

skip *verb* **(a)** *(to transmit over an abnormally long distance)* réfléchir **(b)** sauter *or* passer *or* omettre; **the printer skipped the next three lines of text** = l'imprimante a sauté les trois lignes suivantes; **skip capability** = capacité *f* de saut; **skip instruction** = instruction *f* de saut; *(of paper in a printer)* **high-speed skip** = avance *f* rapide du papier

slash *or* **oblique stroke (/)** *noun* trait *m* oblique

◊ **slashed zero** *noun (sign Ø used to distinguish a zero from the letter O)* zéro *m* barré d'un trait oblique

slave *noun* esclave *m;* **bus slave** = (puits de données) asservi à un bus *or* esclave d'un bus; **slave cache** *or* **store** = mémoire *f* auxiliaire; **slave processor** = processeur *m* asservi; **slave terminal** = terminal *m* asservi; *(second CRT showing the same image)* **slave tube** = écran *m* asservi *or* second écran

sleep *noun* (système) en attente; *see also* WAKE-UP

sleeve *noun* pochette *f*

slew *noun (of paper in a printer)* avance *f* rapide de papier

slice *noun* tranche *f;* **bit-slice architecture** = architecture *f* en tranches; **the bit-slice design uses four four-bit word processors to make a sixteen-bit processor** = le principe du processeur en tranches est de prendre quatre processeurs quatre bits pour en faire un processeur seize bits; **time slice** = tranche de temps
◊ **slicing** *noun (from a bar of silicon crystal)* découpe *f* en pastille

slide 1 *noun* diapositive *f;* **slide projector** = projecteur *m* de diapositives; **slide/sync recorder** = magnétophone *m* avec interface synchro pour projecteur de diapos **2** *verb* glisser; **the disk cover slides on and off easily** = la disquette se glisse dans sa pochette et s'en retire tout aussi facilement

slip pages *or* **slip proofs** *noun* épreuves *fpl* en placard

slot 1 *noun* **(a)** *(long thin hole)* ouverture *f or* fente *f; (for expansion card)* *or* créneau *m;* **the system disk should be inserted into the left-hand slot on the front of the computer** = la disquette système s'insère dans la fente gauche du panneau avant de l'ordinateur; **expansion slot** = créneau pour carte d'extension; **there are two free slots in the micro, you only need one for the add-on board** = cet ordinateur possède deux créneaux libres et votre carte d'extension n'en utilisera qu'un **(b)** *(in a ring network)* **message slot =** trame *f;* **time slot =** créneau (de temps) **2** *verb* insérer dans une fente *or* une ouverture; **the disk slots into one of the floppy drive apertures =** la disquette s'insère dans l'une des deux fentes du lecteur de disquettes

slow motion *noun* ralenti *m;* **the film switched to slow motion =** le film enchaîne sur un ralenti; **play the film again in slow motion =** repassez ce film au ralenti
◊ **slow scan television** *noun* télévision *f* à balayage lent

SLSI = SUPER LARGE SCALE INTEGRATION

slug *noun (printing)* ligne-bloc *f*

slur *noun (blur of image)* bavure *f or* macule *f; (distortion of voice)* bredouillage *m*

small *adjective* petit, -e; **small caps =** petites capitales; **small computer system interface (SCSI) =** interface *f* pour petits ordinateurs; **small scale integration (SSI) =** intégration *f* à petite échelle

smart *adjective (intelligent)* intelligent, -e *or* astucieux, -euse; **smart card =** carte *f* magnétique *or* à mémoire; *(intelligent terminal)* **smart terminal =** terminal intelligent

smog *noun* **electronic smog =** pollution *f* électronique (par rayonnement)

smoke test *noun (informal)* test *m* de la fumée

smooth *verb (signal)* lisser

SNA = SYSTEMS NETWORK ARCHITECTURE

snapshot *noun* instantané *m;* **snapshot dump =** vidage *m* instantané

SNOBOL = STRING ORIENTATED SYMBOLIC LANGUAGE langage *m* (de

traitement et de manipulation de chaînes) SNOBOL

snow *noun (TV image distortion)* neige *f*

s/n ratio = SIGNAL TO NOISE RATIO rapport *m* signal/bruit

soak *verb* tester en continu sur une longue période *or* torturer; **the device was soak-tested prior to delivery =** l'appareil a été testé sous tous les angles avant la livraison

socket *noun* prise *f or* douille *f;* **female socket =** prise femelle

> QUOTE the mouse and keyboard sockets are the same, and could lead to the kind of confusion that arose with the early PCs when the keyboard could be connected to the tape socket
>
> *PC User*

soft *adjective* **(a)** *(material that loses magnetic effects)* doux, douce **(b)** *(data not permanently stored)* (données) sur support magnétique *or* effaçables; **soft copy =** texte *m* (d') écran; **soft error =** erreur *f* de logiciel; *compare with* HARD ERROR; **soft-fail =** panne douce; **soft hyphen =** césure *f* d'écran; **soft keys =** touches *fpl* programmables; **soft keyboard =** clavier *m* à touches programmables; *(instruction)* **soft-reset =** ré-initialisation *f* par logiciel; *compare with* HARD RESET; **soft-sectored disk =** disque formaté *or* sectorisé par logiciel; *(wordporcessing)* **soft zone =** zone *f* de texte

software *noun* logiciel *m;* **applications software =** logiciel d'application *or* progiciel *m;* **bundled software =** logiciel inclus *or* fourni (à l'achat d'un ordinateur); **common software =** logiciel commun; **graphics software =** logiciel graphique; **network software =** logiciel de réseau; **pirate software =** logiciel (qui a été) piraté; **system software =** logiciel système; **unbundled software =** logiciel non inclus *or* non fourni (à l'achat d'un ordinateur); **user-friendly software =** logiciel convivial; **software compatible =** (système) compatible avec des logiciels écrits pour d'autres systèmes; **software developer =** développeur *m* de logiciel; **software development =** développement

m d'un logiciel; **software documentation** = document *m* utile (se rapportant à un logiciel) *or* notice *f* d'utilisation d'un logiciel; **software engineer** = ingénieur *m* logiciel *or* ingénieur programmeur; **software engineering** = génie *m* logiciel; **software house** = société *f* spécialisée en logiciels; **software interrupt** = interruption *f* programmée *or* générée par logiciel; **software library** = bibliothèque *f* de logiciels *or* logithèque *f*; **software licence** = autorisation *m* de copie (d'un logiciel); **software life cycle** = cycle *m* de vie d'un logiciel; **software maintenance** = maintenance *f* de logiciel; **software package** = progiciel *m*; **software piracy** = piratage *m* de logiciel; **software quality assurance (SQA)** = assurance *f* qualité dans le domaine du génie logiciel; **software reliability** = fiabilité *f* d'un logiciel; **software specification** = spécifications *fpl* d'un logiciel *or* définition *f* et standards de qualité d'un logiciel; **software system** = progiciel *m*; **software tool** = outil *m* de programmation
NOTE: no plural for **software**; for the plural say **pieces of software**

solar *adjective* solaire; **solar cell** = pile *f* solaire; **solar power** = énergie *f* solaire; **solar-powered calculator** = calculatrice *f* à batteries photovoltaïques *or* à pile(s) solaire(s)

solder 1 *noun (soft lead used to join wires)* soudure *f* **2** *verb* souder

◊ **solderless** *adjective (board)* sans soudure; *(component, etc.)* enfichable

solenoid *noun* solénoïde *m*

solid *adjective (printed text)* (texte) sans interligne; **solid error** = erreur *f* certaine; **solid font printer** = imprimante *f* à caractères pleins

◊ **solid-state** *adjective* transistorisé, ée *or* à base de semi-conducteurs; **solid-state device** = dispositif transistorisé *or* à semi-conducteurs; **solid-state laser** = laser *m* à composant solide; **solid-state memory device** = mémoire transistorisée

solve *verb* résoudre (un problème)

◊ **solution** *noun* **(a)** solution *f* (à un problème) **(b)** *(liquid)* solution

son file *noun* fichier *m* fils *or* fichier de troisième génération; *compare with* FATHER FILE, GRANDFATHER FILE

sonar *noun* sonar *m*

◊ **sonic** *adjective (within the human hearing range or 20 - 20,000Hz)* sonique; *(above 20kHz)* **ultrasonic** = ultrasonique

sophisticated *adjective* sophistiqué, -ée *or* évolué, -ée *or* recherché, -ée *or* avancé, -ée; **a sophisticated desktop publishing program** = un programme de PAO évolué *or* avancé

◊ **sophistication** *noun* sophistication *f or* avance *f* technologique; **the sophistication of the new package is remarkable** = le nouveau progiciel est tout à fait sophistiqué

sort 1 *noun* tri *m*; **backward sort** = tri par ordre décroissant; **forward sort** = tri par ordre croissant **2** *verb* classer *or* trier; **to sort addresses into alphabetical order** = classer les adresses en ordre alphabétique; **bubble sort** = effectuer un tri bulle *or* un tri par permutation de paires *or* de bulles; **shell sort** = effectuer un tri 'enveloppe' *or* un tri 'bloc par bloc'; **sort/merge** = (fonction de) trier/fusionner; **tree selection sort** = tri en arborescence

◊ **sortkey** *or* **sort field** *noun* clé *f or* champ *m* de tri; **the orders were sorted according to dates by assigning the date field as the sortkey** = les commandes ont été triées sur le champ date

SOS = SILICON ON SAPPHIRE

sound *noun* son *m or* bruit *m*; **sound advance** = décalage *m* en avance de la bande son; **sound chip** = circuit *m* intégré générateur de son; **sound effects** = effets *m* sonores; **all the sound effects for the film are produced electronically** = tous les effets sonores du le film sont produits électroniquement; **sound head** = tête *f* de lecture; **sound pressure level (SPL)** = niveau *m* de pression acoustique; **sound synthesizer** = synthétiseur *m* de son; **sound track** = piste *f* sonore

◊ **soundproof** *adjective* insonorisé, -ée; **the telephone is installed in a soundproof booth** = le téléphone est dans une cabine insonorisée

source *noun* **(a)** *(point where a signal enters a network)* source *f* NOTE: opposite is **sink (b)** *(terminal on an FET device)* borne *f* d'entrée **(c)** *(initial point)* source *or* origine *f*; **source code** = code *m* source; *(set of punched cards)* **source deck** *or* **pack** = jeu *m* original; **source document** = document original *or* d'origine; *(software)* **source editor** = éditeur *m* de programme source; **source file** = fichier *m* source; **source language** = *(computer)* langage *m* source *or* d'origine; *(translation)* langue *f* de départ; **source listing** = *(text in its original form)* listing *m* (du texte) d'origine; *(of source program)* listing de programme source; **source machine** = compilateur *m* de programme source; **source program** = programme *m* source *or* d'origine

SP = STACK POINTER

space 1 *noun* **(a)** *(in text)* espace *m or* espacement *m;* **space character** = caractère *m* d'espacement *or* caractère espace *or* caractère blanc; **space bar** = barre *f* d'espacement **(b)** *(in communications)* (signal d') espace NOTE: opposite is **mark (c)** *(atmosphere)* espace; **space craft** = véhicule *m or* engin *m* spatial; **space station** *or* station *f* spatiale **2** *verb* espacer; **the line of characters was evenly spaced out across the page** = les caractères régulièrement espacés s'alignaient sur la page

◊ **spacer** *noun* gestionnaire *m* d'espaces; **intelligent spacer** = gestionnaire d'espaces intelligent

◊ **spacing** *noun* espaces *mpl;* **the spacing on some lines is very uneven** = il y a quelques lignes où les espaces sont très inégaux

span *noun* fourchette *f*

spark printer *noun* imprimante *f* thermique (à étincelle)

sparse array *noun* tableau réduit *or* matrice réduite

speaker *see* LOUDSPEAKER

spec *(informal)* = SPECIFICATION; **high-spec** = de haute précision *or* de haute technologie

special *adjective* spécial, -e; **special character** = caractère spécial; **special effects** = effets spéciaux; **special purpose** = système spécial *or* dédié; **special sort** = fonte spéciale

◊ **specialize** *verb* se spécialiser *or* être spécialiste *or* être expert; **he specializes in the design of CAD systems** = c'est un spécialiste *or* un expert en CAO

◊ **specialist** *noun* expert *m or* spécialiste *m&f;* **you need a specialist programmer to help devise a new word-processing program** = demandez l'aide d'un bon programmeur qui vous aidera à créer un nouveau (programme de) traitement de texte

specify *verb* spécifier *or* indiquer *or* préciser *or* préconiser

◊ **specification** *noun* spécification *f;* **to work to standard specifications** = travailler suivant des normes établies; **the work is not up to specification** *or* **does not meet the customer's specifications** = le travail ne répond pas au cahier des charges *or* aux spécifications du client; **high specification** *or* **high spec** = (de) haute technologie *or* (de) haute précision *or* (de) technologie avancée; **high spec cabling needs to be very carefully handled** = les câbles de haute technologie doivent être manipulés avec grand soin; **program specification** = spécifications relatives à un programme

specific address *noun* adresse *f* spécifique

◊ **specific code** *noun* code (binaire) absolu *or* code spécifique; **specific coding** = codage (binaire) à adresse absolue *or* codage spécifique

◊ **specificity** *noun* spécificité *f*

spectrum *noun* spectre *m;* **electromagnetic spectrum** = spectre électromagnétique; **spectrum analyzer** = analyseur *m* de spectre

speech *noun* parole *f or* voix *f;* **speech chip** = puce *f* de synthèse vocale; **speech plus** = transmission *f* vocale étendue; **speech processor** = processeur *m* de la parole *or* du signal vocal; **speech recognition** = reconnaissance *f* vocale *or* de la parole; **speech signal** = signal *m* vocal; **speech synthesis** = synthèse *f* vocale *or* de la parole; **speech synthesizer** = synthétiseur *m* vocal *or* de la parole

QUOTE speech conveys information, and the primary task of computer speech processing is the transmission and reception of that information

Personal Computer World

speed *noun* **(a)** *(of film)* rapidité *f or* sensibilité *f;* **high speed film is very sensitive to light** = un film ultra-sensible est extrêmement sensible à la lumière **(b)** *(time taken for a movement)* vitesse *or* rapidité *f;* **speed of loop** = fréquence *f* de boucle *or* de bouclage; **playback speed** = vitesse de défilement (d'une bande magnétique)

spellcheck *verb* faire une vérification orthographique

◊ **spellchecker** *or* **spelling checker** *noun* vérificateur *m* d'orthographe *or* programme de vérification orthographique; **the program will be upgraded with a word-processor and a spelling checker** = on va optimiser le programme en ajoutant un traitement de texte et un vérificateur d'orthographe

spherical aberration *noun* aberration *f* sphérique

spike *noun (of voltage pulse)* pointe *f*

spillage *noun* débordement *m or* excès *m*

spin *verb* (faire) tourner; **the disk was spun by the drive** = le lecteur faisait tourner la disquette; **the disk drive motor spins at a constant velocity** = le moteur du lecteur de disquettes tourne à vitesse constante
NOTE: **spinning - span - spun**

spindle *noun (for disk)* axe *m*

◊ **spindling** *noun (turning a disk by hand)* mouvement *m* de rotation (transmis manuellement)

spine *noun (of book)* dos *m;* **the author's name and the title usually are shown on the spine as well as on the title page** = de façon générale, le nom de l'auteur et le titre apparaissent au dos du livre et sur la page de titre

spirit duplicator *noun (short-run printing machine)* duplicateur *m* à alcool

SPL = SOUND PRESSURE LEVEL

splice *verb (to join ends of tape or film)* coller *or* faire un raccord; **you can use glue or splicing tape to splice the ends** = utilisez de la colle ou du ruban gommé pour raccorder les extrémités (du film); **splicing block** = colleuse *f* de film *or* de bande; **splicing tape** = ruban *m* de raccord

split screen *noun* écran *m* partagé *or* divisé

◊ **splitter** *noun* répartiteur *m;* **beam splitter** = diviseur *m* optique

spool 1 *noun (for tape or ribbon)* bobine *f* **2** *verb* faire un spooling *or* faire un spouling *or* transférer des données en mémoire tampon auxiliaire (entre périphérique lent et processeur rapide)

◊ **spooler** *or* **spooling device** *noun* spoule *m or* dispositif *m* de stockage temporaire

◊ **spooling** *noun* spouling *m or* spooling *m or* utilisation de mémoire tampon auxiliaire (entre périphérique lent et processeur rapide)

sporadic fault *noun* erreur *f* sporadique

spot *noun* point *m*

◊ **spot beam** *noun (of satellite antenna)* (antenne à) faisceau *m* étroit

spreadsheet *noun (program)* tableur *m; (printout)* tableau *m*

sprite *noun (in computer graphics)* esprit *m or* sprite *m*

sprocket *or* **sprocket wheel** *noun* roue *f* à picots

◊ **sprocket feed** *noun* entraînement *m* par picots; *see also* TRACTOR FEED

◊ **sprocket holes** *noun* perforations *fpl* d'entraînement *or* perforations marginales

spur *noun* jonction *f or* noeud *m*

SPX = SIMPLEX

SQA = SOFTWARE QUALITY ASSURANCE

square wave *noun* onde *f* carrée

SS = SINGLE-SIDED

SSBSC = SINGLE SIDEBAND SUPPRESSED CARRIER

SSD = SINGLE-SIDED DISK

SSI = SMALL SCALE INTEGRATION

stable *adjective* stable; **stable state =** état *m* stable
◊ **stability** *noun* stabilité *f;* **image stability =** stabilité de l'image

stack *noun* pile *f* (de données en mémoire); **push-down stack =** pile inversée (utilisée suivant la méthode LIFO); **virtual memory stack =** pile de mémoire virtuelle; **stack address =** adresse *f* de pile; **stack base =** (adresse de) base *f* de la pile; **stack job processor =** processeur *m* de pile de tâches; **stack pointer (SP) =** pointeur *m* de pile

stage *noun* étape *f or* phase *f or* stade *m;* **the text is ready for the printing stage =** le texte est prêt pour l'impression *or* le texte en est au stade de l'impression; **we are in the first stage of running in the new computer system =** nous n'en sommes qu'à la phase de rodage du système d'exploitation
◊ **staged** *adjective* graduel, -elle *or* effectué, -ée par étapes *or* par paliers; **staged change-over =** passage *m* graduel (à un nouveau système)

stand-alone *or* **standalone** *noun & adjective* poste *m* autonome *or* individuel; **stand-alone system =** système *m* autonome; **stand-alone terminal =** terminal *m* autonome; **the workstations have been networked together rather than used as stand-alone systems =** les postes ont été reliés en réseau plutôt que d'être utilisés comme postes autonomes *or* comme postes individuels

standard *adjective (normal or usual)* standard *or* courant, -e *or* normal, -e; **standard document** *or* **standard form** *or* **standard paragraph** *or* **standard text =** document *m or* formulaire *m or* paragraphe *m or* texte *m* standard; **standard function =** fonction *f* standard; **standard interface =** interface *f* standard *or* universelle; **standard letter =** lettre *f* type *or* lettre standard *or* lettre cadre; **standard subroutine =** sous-programme *m* standard
◊ **standardize** *verb* standardiser *or* normaliser; **the standardized control of transmission links =** le contrôle standardisé *or* normalisé des voies de transmission
◊ **standards** *noun* normes *fpl or* standards *mpl;* **production standards =** normes de qualité *or* standards de fabrication; **up to standard =** (qui est) conforme aux normes; **this batch of disks is not up to standard =** ce lot de disquettes ne répond pas aux normes; **standards converter =** convertisseur *m* de normes; **the standards converter allows us to watch US television =** c'est grâce à un convertisseur (de normes) que nous pouvons regarder des programmes de télévision américains; **video standards =** normes vidéo; *see* VIDEO; **modem standards =** normes pour modems

standby *noun* (appareil *or* dispositif) de secours *or* de réserve *or* auxiliaire; **standby equipment =** équipement *m or* système *m* auxiliaire *or* de secours; **cold standby =** système de secours lancé manuellement; **hot standby =** système de secours prêt à fonctionner; **warm standby =** équipement de secours à démarrage semi-automatique

QUOTE before fault-tolerant systems, users had to rely on the cold standby, that is switching on a second machine when the first developed a fault; the alternative was the hot standby, where a second computer was kept running continuously
Computer News

star network *noun* réseau *m* en étoile
◊ **star program** *noun* programme *m* vedette

start *noun (of file)* début *m; (of machine)* démarrage *m or* mise *f* en route; **cold start** = démarrage à froid *or* reprise *f* totale; **start bit** *or* **start element** = bit *m or* élément *m* de début; **start of header** = (code de) début d'en-tête; **start of text (SOT** *or* **STX)** = (code de) début de texte; *(of program)* **warm start** = reprise *f* sur l'instruction d'arrêt *or* reprise au point d'arrêt

stat *(informal)* = PHOTOSTAT

state *noun* état *m;* **active state** = mode *m* actif; **steady state** = état stationnaire

statement *noun* déclaration *f or* instruction *f;* **conditional statement** = instruction conditionnelle; **control statement** = *(to another branch)* instruction de branchement; *(for the CPU)* (instruction de) commande *f;* **directive statement** = directive *f;* **input statement** = instruction *or* déclaration d'entrée; **multi-statement line** = ligne multi-instruction; **narrative statement** = instruction déclarative; **statement number** = numéro *m* d'instruction

state-of-the-art *adjective (technology, etc.)* de pointe *or* avancé, -ée

QUOTE the main PCB is decidedly non-state-of-the-art
Personal Computer World

static 1 *noun* **(a)** *(TV or radio)* (bruits) parasites *mpl;* *(in recorded signal)* interférence *f or* bruit(s) *m(pl)* **(b)** *(charge)* électricité *f* statique **2** *adjective (not dynamic)* statique *or* qui n'évolue pas; **static dump** = vidage *m* statique; **static memory** = mémoire *f* statique; **static RAM** = mémoire *f* vive statique *or* RAM *f* statique; **static subroutine** = sous-programme statique

station *noun* **(a)** station *f or* poste *m or* terminal *m;* **secondary station** = station auxiliaire; **workstation** = poste de travail **(b)** **earth station** = station *f* terrestre; **radio station** = station radio; **the signal from this radio station is very weak** = le signal de cette station émettrice *or* de cet émetteur radio est très faible; **we are trying to jam the signals from that station** = nous

essayons de brouiller les signaux émis par cette station

stationary *adjective* stationnaire; **geostationary orbit** = orbite *f* (de satellite) géostationnaire

stationery *noun* papeterie *f;* **computer stationery** = papier *m* listing (pour imprimante); **continuous stationery** = papier listing *or* papier en continu; **preprinted stationery** = formulaires *mpl* préimprimés *or* papier à en-tête

statistics *noun* la statistique *f*
◊ **statistical** *adjective* statistique; **statistical time division multiplexing (STDM)** = multiplexage temporel statistique *or* en fonction des appels
◊ **statistician** *noun* statisticien, -ienne

status *noun* statut *m or* état *m;* **status bit** = bit *m* d'état; **status line** = ligne *f* d'état; **status poll** = (appel de) contrôle *m* d'état; **status register** = registre *m* d'état; **processor status word (PSW)** = mot *m* d'état (d'un processeur)

STD = SUBSCRIBER TRUNK DIALLING

STDM = STATISTICAL TIME DIVISION MULTIPLEXING

steady state *noun* état *m* stationnaire

stencil *noun* *(pre-shaped pattern)* pochoir *m* de traçage; *(for duplicating)* stencil *m;* **the stencil has all the electronic components on it** = ce pochoir contient toutes les formes pour composants électroniques; **flowchart stencil** = grille *f or* modèle *m* pour ordinogramme

step 1 *noun* étape *f or* pas *m;* **single step** = (opération) pas à pas **2** *verb (to move forwards)* faire un pas *or* avancer d'un pas; *(to move backwards)* reculer d'un pas; **we stepped forward through the file one record at a time** = nous avons repris le fichier, entrée par entrée; **we stepped forward the film one frame at a time** = nous avons projeté le film image par image
◊ **stepper motor** *or* **stepping motor** *noun* moteur *m* à pas

steradian *noun* stéradian *m*

stereo *informal* = STEREOPHONIC

stereophonic *adjective* stéréophonique *or* stéréo; **stereophonic microphone** = microphone *m* stéréophonique; **stereophonic recorder** = magnétophone *m* stéréophonique

still frame *noun* image fixe *f*

stochastic model *noun* modèle *m* stochastique

stop 1 *verb* (s') arrêter; *(in communications)* **stop and wait protocol** = protocole *m* de contrôle par signal d'arrêt **2** *noun* arrêt *m;* **tab stop** = arrêt de tabulation

◊ **stop bit** *or* **stop element** *noun* bit *m or* élément *m* d'arrêt; **stop code** = code *m* d'arrêt; **stop instruction** = instruction *f* d'arrêt; **stop list** = liste *f* des mots interdits (dans une indexation); **stop time** = temps *m* d'arrêt *or* de décélération

storage *noun (place)* mémoire *f; (action)* stockage ; **archive storage** = mémoire d'archivage; **auxiliary storage** = mémoire auxiliaire; **dynamic storage** *or* **memory** = mémoire dynamique; **external storage** = mémoire externe; **information storage** = mise *f* en mémoire *or* stockage de données; **instruction storage** = mémoire d'instruction; **intermediate storage** = mémoire intermédiaire; **mass storage system** = mémoire de masse; **nonerasable storage** = mémoire ineffaçable *or* permanente; **primary storage** = mémoire principale; **secondary storage** = mémoire secondaire *or* intermédiaire; **static storage** = mémoire statique; **temporary storage** = mémoire temporaire; **volatile storage** = mémoire volatile; **storage allocation** = allocation *f* de mémoire; **storage capacity** = capacité *f* de la mémoire *or* taille *f* de la mémoire; **storage density** = densité *f* de mémoire; **storage device** = dispositif de stockage; **storage disk** = disquette *m or* disque *m* (de) mémoire; **storage dump** = vidage *m or* listage *m* de mémoire (sur imprimante); **storage media** = supports *mpl* de stockage; **storage size** = taille *f* de

la mémoire; **storage tube** = écran *m or* tube *m* à mémoire

store 1 *noun* mémoire *f;* **store address register (SAR)** = registre *m* d'adresse en mémoire; **store data register (SDR)** = registre des données en mémoire; **store cell** = cellule *f* de mémoire; **store location** = emplacement *m* de mémoire **2** *verb (to save data)* mettre en mémoire *or* ranger en mémoire *or* mémoriser; **storing a page of high resolution graphics can require 3Mb** = il faudra jusqu'à 3Mo pour mémoriser une page de données graphiques haute-définition; *(communications)* **store and forward (system)** = (système avec facilité de) stockage *m* et retransmission *or* transmission *f* en différé; **stored program** = programme *m* mis en mémoire *or* mémorisé *or* enregistré; **stored program signalling** = signalisation *f* à contrôle programmé (en mémoire)

straight-line coding *noun* codage *m* en ligne directe

stray *adjective* égaré, -ée *or* perdu, -e; **the metal screen protects the CPU against stray electromagnetic effects from the PSU** = le blindage protège l'unité centrale des pertes *or* fuites electromagnétiques du bloc d'alimentation

streaking *noun* rayures *fpl or* zébrures *fpl or* traînage *m*

stream *noun* flux *m* (continu) *or* flot *m;* **job stream** = flux des tâches

◊ **streamer** *noun* **tape streamer** *or* **streaming tape drive** = unité *f* de sauvegarde rapide (sur bande magnétique) *or* dévideur *m or* streamer *m*

string *noun* chaîne *f or* séquence *f;* **alphanumeric string** = chaîne de caractères alphanumériques; **character string** = chaîne de caractères; **numeric string** = chaîne de caractères numériques; **null** *or* **blank string** = chaîne vide; **string area** = zone *f* mémoire *or* zone de stockage des variables; **string concatenation** = concaténation *f* de (plusieurs) chaînes; **string function** = fonction *f* (de) chaîne; **string length** = taille *f* d'une chaîne; **string matching** = comparaison *f* de chaînes; **string name** = nom *m* de chaîne; **string orientated symbolic language (SNOBOL)** = langage *m* de programmation SNOBOL; **string scanning** = balayage *m* de chaînes; **string variable** = variable *f* de chaîne

◊ **stringy floppy** *or* **tape streamer** *noun* unité *f* de sauvegarde rapide sur bande magnétique *or* streamer *m*

strip 1 *noun* bande *f or* ruban *m;* **strip window** = fenêtre *f* d'une ligne; *(on plastic cards)* **magnetic strip** = piste *f* magnétique **2** *verb* dépouiller (un message)

stripe *noun* bande *f or* raie *f* (de couleur); **balance stripe** = bande d'équilibrage (de tension)

strobe 1 *verb* émettre une impulsion *or* un signal (d'échantillonnage *or* de validation); échantillonner *or* valider **2** *noun* **address strobe** = signal de validation d'adresse; **data strobe** = signal de validation de données (transmises)

◊ **stroboscope** *or* **strobe** *noun* stroboscope *m*

stroke *noun* frappe *f*

strowger exchange *noun* central *m* téléphonique électromécanique *or* central Strowger

structure 1 *noun* structure *f;* **network structure** = structure en réseau **2** *verb* structurer *or* organiser; **you first structure a document to meet your requirements and then fill in the blanks** = vous organisez d'abord le document pour répondre à vos besoins, puis vous remplissez les blancs; **structured design** = modèle *m* structuré; **structured programming** = programmation *f* structurée

studio *noun* studio *m* (de création, d'enregistrement, de prise de vues)

STX = START OF TEXT

style sheet *noun* feuille *f* de style

stylus *noun* **(a)** *(for audio record)* aiguille *f or* pointe *f or* diamant *m* de lecture; *(for video disk)* lecteur *m* **(b)** *(pen-like device)* crayon *m* optique *or* stylet *m;* **use the stylus on the graphics tablet to draw** = pour dessiner, utilisez un crayon optique et une tablette graphique **(c)** **stylus printer** = imprimante *f* matricielle *or* à aiguilles

sub- *prefix* sous- *or* secondaire; **subaddress** = adresse *f* secondaire; **subaudio frequencies** = fréquences *fpl* inaudibles *or* infrasonores; **subclass** = sous-classe *f*

◊ **sub-edit** *or* **sub** *verb (text)* réviser; **subbing** *or* **sub-editing** = vérification *f or* révision *f*

subdirectory *noun* sous-répertoire *m*

> QUOTE if you delete a file and then delete the subdirectorywhere it was located, you cannot restore the file because thedirectory does not exist
> *Personal Computer World*

subprogram *noun* sous-programme *m*

subroutine *noun* sous-programme *m;* **closed** *or* **linked subroutine** = sous-programme fermé *or* ré-entrant; **open subroutine** = sous-programme ouvert; **static subroutine** = sous-programme statique; **two-level subroutine** = sous-programme à deux niveaux; **subrroutine call** = appel *m* d'un sous-programme

subscriber *noun (telephone or service)* abonné, -ée; **subscriber trunk dialling (STD)** = l'automatique *m*

subscript *noun* indice *m see also* SUPERSCRIPT (NOTE: used in chemical formulae: CO_2) **subscripted variable** = variable indicée *or* caractérisée par un indice

◊ **subset** *noun* sous-ensemble *m*

◊ **subsegment** *noun* sous-segment *m*

substance *noun* substance *f*

substitute *verb* substituer; **substitute character** = caractère *m* de substitution
NOTE: you substitute one thing **for** another

◊ **substitution** *noun* substitution *f;* **substitution error** = erreur *f* de substitution; **substitution table** = table *f* de substitution *or* d'équivalence

substrate *noun* substrat *m*

subsystem *noun* sous-système *m*

subtotal *noun* sous-total *m*

subtract *verb* soustraire
◊ **subtraction** *noun* soustraction *f*
◊ **subtrahend** *noun* nombre *m* à soustraire d'un autre *or* diminuteur *m*

subvoice grade channel *noun* canal *m* de fréquences subvocales

successive *adjective* successif, -ive *or* qui suit; **each successive operation adds further characters to the string** = chacune des opérations successives ajoute de nouveaux caractères à la chaîne

suffix notation *noun (postfix notation)* notation *f* suffixée *or* notation polonaise inversée

suite of programs *noun* suite *f* de programmes *or* série *f* de programmes l'un à la suite de l'autre; **the word-processing system uses a suite of three programs, editor, spelling checker and printing controller** = le système de traitement de texte utilise une série de trois programmes reliés: un éditeur de texte, un correcteur d'orthographe et un contrôleur d'impression

sum *noun* somme *f or* addition *f*
◊ **summation check** *noun* contrôle *m* par totalisation

sun outage *noun* durée *f* de non ensoleillement *or* d'ombre

super- *prefix* super- *or* sur-; **supercomputer** = ordinateur *m* géant; *(60 voice channels)* **supergroup** = groupe

m secondaire; *(900 voice channels)* **super mastergroup** = groupe quaternaire
◊ **super high frequency (SHF)** *noun* ultra-haute fréquence
◊ **super large scale integration (SLSI)** *noun* intégration *f* à super grande échelle

superheterodyne radio *noun* radio *m* superhétérodyne

superimpose *verb* surimposer

superior number *noun* chiffre *m* en exposant *or* exposant *m*

superscript *noun* exposant *m*
NOTE: used often in mathematics: **10^5** (say: ten to the power five)

supersede *verb* remplacer; **the new program supersedes the earlier one, and is much faster** = le nouveau programme, qui remplace le précédent, est beaucoup plus rapide

superstation *noun US* superstation *f*

supervise *verb* superviser *or* surveiller *or* contrôler; **the manufacture of circuit boards is very carefully supervised** = la confection des cartes de circuits imprimés est très soigneusement surveillée
◊ **supervision** *noun* supervision *f or* surveillance *f or* contrôle *m*
◊ **supervisor** *noun (person)* surveillant, -e *or* contrôleur, -euse *or* superviseur *m; (program)* programme *m* superviseur
◊ **supervisory** *adjective* de supervision *or* de surveillance *or* de contrôle; **supervisory program** *or* **executive program** = programme *m* superviseur; **supervisory sequence** = séquence *f* de contrôle; **supervisory signal** = signal *m* de contrôle *or* de supervision

supply **1** *noun* fourniture *f or* approvisionnement *m;* **the electricity supply has failed** = il y a une panne de courant; **they signed a contract for the supply of computer stationery** = ils ont signé un contrat pour la fourniture de papier listing **2** *verb* fournir *or* approvisionner; **the computer was supplied by a recognized dealer** = l'ordinateur vient de chez un fournisseur connu; **they have signed a contract to supply on-line information** = ils ont signé un contrat pour fournir des informations en ligne

◊ **supplier** *noun* fournisseur *m;* **a supplier of computer parts** = un fournisseur de composants pour ordinateurs; **a supplier of disk drives** *or* **a disk drive supplier** = un fournisseur de lecteurs de disquettes; **our Japanese suppliers have set up a warehouse in England** = nos fournisseurs japonais ont ouvert un entrepôt en Angleterre

support 1 *verb* supporter; **the main computer supports six workstations** = l'ordinateur principal accepte jusqu'à six postes de travail *or* contrôle six postes de travail 2 *noun* **(a)** support *m;* **support chip** = processeur *m* auxiliaire; **the maths support chip can be plugged in here** = le processeur arithmétique auxiliaire peut être enfiché à cet endroit; **systems support** = groupe *m* de support (d'un système informatique) **(b)** assistance *f;* **support hotline** = service *m* d'assistance technique par téléphone; **support service** = service d'assistance technique

suppress *verb (to remove)* supprimer; **the filter is used to suppress the noise due to static interference** = ce filtre sert à supprimer les bruits parasites; **suppressed carrier modulation** = modulation d'amplitude sans porteuse *or* à porteuse inhibée; **double sideband suppressed carrier (DSBSC)** = double bande latérale sans porteuse *or* à porteuse inhibée; **single sideband suppressed carrier (SSBSC)** = bande latérale unique sans porteuse *or* à porteuse inhibée

◊ **suppression** *noun* suppression *f*

◊ **suppressor** *noun* dispositif *m* antiparasite; **echo suppressor** = dispositif *m* anti-écho *or* éliminateur *m* d'écho

surge *noun (electrical)* surintensité *f or* surtension *f;* **surge protector** = limiteur *m* de tension

sustain *verb* maintenir

SW = SHORT WAVE

swap 1 *noun* = SWAPPING 2 *verb* permuter *or* basculer

◊ **swapping** *or* **swap** *noun* permutation *f or* basculement *m* (de programme)

sweep *noun* balayage *m*

swim *noun* flottement *m*

switch 1 *noun* **(a)** *(point in a computer program)* bifurcation *f* **(b)** *(device)* commutateur *m;* **switch train** = série *f* de commutateurs *or* commutateurs en série **(c)** aiguillage *m* 2 *verb (system, etc.)* **to switch on** = mettre en marche *or* mettre sous tension; **to switch off** = éteindre; *(to use something else)* **to switch over to** = changer (de); **switched network backup** = commutation *f* de secours; **switched star** = réseau *m* commuté en étoile; **switched virtual call** = communication *f* virtuelle commutée

◊ **switchboard** *noun* standard *m* téléphonique; **switchboard operator** = standardiste *m&f*

◊ **switching** *noun* commutation *f or* connexion *f;* **switching centre** = centre *m* de commutation; **switching circuit** = circuit *m* de commutation; **line switching** = commutation de ligne *or* de circuit

symbol *noun* symbole *m;* **this language uses the symbol ? to represent the print command** = ce langage utilise le symbole ? pour la commande d'impression; **graphic symbol** = symbole graphique; **logic symbol** = symbole logique; **symbol table** *or* **library** = table *f or* bibliothèque *f* de symboles

◊ **symbolic** *adjective* symbolique; **symbolic address** = adresse *f* symbolique; **symbolic code** *or* **instruction** = code *m or* instruction *f* symbolique; **symbolic debugging** = (programme de) débogage *m* symbolique; **symbolic language** = langage *m* symbolique; **symbolic logic** = logique *f* symbolique; **symbolic name** = nom *m* symbolique; **symbolic programming** = programmation *f* symbolique

symmetric difference *noun (logical function)* exclusion *f* réciproque

sync *noun (informal)* = SYNCHRONIZATION synchro *or*

synchronisation *f;* **sync bit** = bit *m* de synchro; **sync character** = caractère *m* de synchro; **sync pulses** = impulsions *fpl* de synchro; **in sync** = synchronisé, -ée *or* en synchronisme; **the two devices are out of sync** = ces deux dispositifs ne sont pas parfaitement synchronisés

◊ **synchronization** *noun* synchronisation *f;* **synchronization pulses** = impulsions *fpl* de synchronisation

◊ **synchronize** *verb* synchroniser

◊ **synchronizer** *noun* synchroniseur *m or* unité *f* de synchronisation

◊ **synchronous** *adjective* synchrone; **synchronous computer** = ordinateur *m* synchrone; **synchronous data link control (SDLC)** = procédure *f* SDLC *or* procédure de contrôle de liaison de données; **synchronous data network** = réseau *m* de données synchrone; **synchronous detection** = repérage *m* synchrone; **synchronous idle character** = caractère *m* de synchronisation; **synchronous mode** = mode *m* synchrone; **synchronous network** = réseau *m* synchrone; **synchronous system** = système *m* synchrone; **synchronous transmission** = transmission *f* synchrone

synonym *noun* synonyme *m*

◊ **synonymous** *adjective* synonyme; **the words 'error' and 'mistake' are synonymous** = 'erreur' et 'faute' sont des synonymes

syntactic error *noun* faute *f* de syntaxe

◊ **syntactical** *adjective* syntaxique *or* syntactique

syntax *noun* syntaxe *f;* **syntax analysis** = analyse *f* syntaxique *or* syntactique; **syntax error** = faute *f* de syntaxe

synthesis *noun* synthèse *f*

◊ **synthesize** *verb* synthétiser

◊ **synthesizer** *noun* synthétiseur *m;* **music synthesizer** = synthétiseur de son; **speech synthesizer** = synthétiseur vocal *or* de la parole

◊ **synthetic address** *noun* adresse calculée; **synthetic language** = langage de synthèse

sysgen = SYSTEM GENERATION

system *noun* système *m;* **adaptive system** = système auto-adaptable *or* dynamique; **computer system** = système informatique *or* ordinateur *m;* **information system** = système informatique; **interactive system** = système interactif; **operating system (op sys)** = système d'exploitation; **secure system** = système sécurisé; **system check** = diagnostic *m* de système; **system control panel** = panneau *m* de commandes d'un système; **system crash** = panne *f* de système *or* crash *m;* **system design** = conception *f or* modèle *m or* design *m* d'un système; **system diagnostics** = outils *mpl* de diagnostic d'un système; **system disk** = disquette *f* (de programme) système; **system firmware** = logiciel *m* (de) système *or* microprogrammé *m;* **system flowchart** = ordinogramme *m* d'un système; **system generation** *or* **sysgen** = génération *f* d'un système *or* à laquelle appartient un système; **system library** = bibliothèque *f* d'un système; **system life cycle** = durée *f* de vie d'un système; **system log** = journal *m* d'un système; **system security** = sécurisation *f* d'un système; **system software** = logiciel *m* d'exploitation; **system specifications** = spécifications *fpl* d'un système; **system support** = assistance *f* technique pour un système

◊ **Système international** *see* SI

◊ **systems analysis** *noun* analyse *f* de système; **systems analyst** = analyste *m&f* (de) système; **systems engineer** = ingénieur *m* système; **systems network architecture (SNA)** = architecture *f* de réseau; **systems program** = programme *m* système; **systems programmer** = programmeur *m* système

Tt

T junction = *noun* jonction *f* en T
◊ **T network** *noun* réseau *m* en T

TAB = TABULATE

tab 1 *verb* tabuler (des données) *or*
disposer (des données) en tableau *or* en
table *or* en colonne(s); **the list was neatly
lined up by tabbing to column 10 at the
start of each new line** = en appuyant sur
la touche de tabulation en début de
ligne, pour se placer à la colonne 10, la
liste avait été parfaitement alignée; **tab
memory** = mémoire *f* de tabulation; **tab
rack** *or* **ruler line** = règle *f* de tabulation; **a
tab rack shows you the left and right
margins** = la règle de tabulation indique
les marges de gauche et de droite; **tab
stops** = arrêts *mpl* de tabulation **2** *noun
(on disks)* **write-protect tab** = volet *m* de
protection d'écriture
◊ **tabbing** *noun* tabulation *f;* **tabbing can
be done from inside the program** = la
tabulation peut être incorporée au
programme; **decimal tabbing** =
tabulation décimale

table *noun* table *f or* tableau *m; decision*
table = table de décision; **lookup table
(LUT)** = table de référence *or*
d'équivalence; **this is the value of the key
pressed, use a lookup table to find its
ASCII value** = voici la fonction de cette
touche, pour la traduire en ASCII
consultez la table d'équivalence; **table
lookup** = consultation *f* d'une table de
référence; **reference program table** =
table de référence des programmes;
symbol table = table de symboles; **table
of contents** = table *f* des matières

tablet *noun* **graphics tablet** = tablette *f*
graphique *or* à numériser; **it is much
easier to draw accurately with a tablet
than with a mouse** = un dessin précis
s'obtient beaucoup plus facilement avec
une tablette à numériser qu'avec une
souris

tabulate *verb* tabuler (des données) *or*
disposer (des données) en tableau *or* en
table *or* en colonne(s)
◊ **tabular** *adjective* **in tabular form** =
tabulaire *or* disposé, -ée en tableau *or* en
table *or* en colonne(s)
◊ **tabulating** *noun (punched cards)*
traitement *m* de données (sur cartes
perforées) par tabulatrice
◊ **tabulation** *noun* tabulation *f;*
tabulation markers = repères *mpl* de
tabulation; **tabulation stops** = arrêts *mpl*
de tabulation
◊ **tabulator** *noun (on typewriters, etc.)*
tabulateur *m*

TACS = TOTAL ACCESS
COMMUNICATION SYSTEM

tactile *adjective* tactile; **tactile feedback**
= information *f* tactile; **tactile keyboard**
= clavier *m* tactile *or* sensitif *or* à
effleurement

tag *noun* **(a)** *(section of computer
instruction)* étiquette *f; (in machine
language)* adresse *f* symbolique **(b)** *(of
file or item of data)* étiquette; **each file
has a three letter tag for rapid
identification** = chaque fichier est
identifié rapidement par son étiquette
de trois lettres

tail *noun* **(a)** *(data which is the end of a
list)* fin *f* de liste **(b)** *(code which signals
the end of a message)* (code de) fin de
message

takedown *verb* déséquipement *m or*
démontage *m* (entre deux tâches);
takedown time = temps *m* de
préparation entre deux tâches

take-up reel *noun* bobine *f* réceptrice
or de réception *or* d'enroulement; **put the
full reel on this spindle, and feed the tape
into the take-up reel on the other spindle**

= placez la bobine pleine sur cet axe-ci et la bobine de réception sur celui-là

talk verb (computers) dialoguer
◊ **talkback** noun conversation f or dialogue m

> QUOTE a variety of technologies exist which allow computers to talk to one another
> *Which PC?*

tandem noun **working in tandem** = fonctionnement m en tandem; **tandem switching** = commutation f (en) tandem

tap 1 verb brancher une ligne sur une table d'écoute **2** noun **wiretap** = table f d'écoute

tape noun bande f; **cassette tape** = cassette f; **cassette tape is mainly used with home computers** = c'est en général avec les ordinateurs domestiques qu'on utilise les cassettes; **(magnetic) tape** = bande magnétique; **master tape** = bande originale; **paper tape** or **punched tape** = bande perforée or bande papier; **(video cassette) tape** = bande vidéo; **open reel tape** = bande sur bobine ouverte; **streaming tape drive** = unité f de sauvegarde (rapide) sur bande or streamer m; **tape backup** = sauvegarde f sur bande; **tape cable** or **ribbon cable** = câble m plat; **tape cartridge** = cartouche f; **tape cassette** = cassette f; **tape code** = code m de perforation or de marquage (de bande papier); **tape counter** = compteur m de déroulement; **tape deck** = (i) platine f magnétophone; (ii) platine magnétocassette m; **tape drive** = lecteur m de bandes (magnétiques) or dérouleur m de bandes; **our new product has a 96Mb streaming tape drive** = notre nouveau modèle est équipé d'un streamer de 96 Mo; **tape format** = format m de bande; **tape guide** = guide-bande m; **the tape is out of alignment because one of the tape guides has broken** = la bande est désalignée parce qu'un guide-bande est cassé; **tape head** = tête f de lecture (pour bandes magnétiques); **tape header** = en-tête m de bande; **tape label** = label m or étiquette f en-tête de bande; **tape library** = bibliothèque f de bandes or bandothèque f; **tape loadpoint** = point m de début d'enregistrement (d'une bande magnétique); **tape punch** = poinçon m (de perforation) pour bandes papier;

tape reader = lecteur m de bandes perforées; **tape recorder** = magnétophone m; **tape streamer** = streamer m; **tape timer** = compteur m de défilement; **tape to card converter** = convertisseur m bande magnétique/carte perforée; **tape transmitter** = émetteur m à bande; **tape trailer** = label m de fin de bande; **tape transport** = dérouleur m or dispositif m d'entraînement de bandes; **tape unit** = magnétophone m or magnétocassette m

target noun cible f or objectif m or but m; **target computer** = ordinateur m cible or ordinateur d'exécution; **target language** = (translation) langue f d'arrivée; (computing) langage m objet; **the target language for this PASCAL program is machine code** = pour ce qui est de ce programme en PASCAL, le langage machine constitue le langage objet
◊ **target level** = niveau m cible; **target phase** or **run phase** = phase f exécution or (en) code objet; **target program** = programme m objet

> QUOTE the target board is connected to the machine through the incircuit emulator cable
> *Electronics & Wireless World*

tariff noun (charge) tarif m; **there is a set tariff for logging on, then a rate for every minute of computer time used** = il existe un tarif forfaitaire d'utilisation plus un taux/minute de temps d'ordinateur

TASI = TIME ASSIGNED SPEECH INTERPOLATION

task noun tâche f; **task management** = gestion f de tâches; **task queue** = file f d'attente des travaux à exécuter; see also MULTITASKING

TAT = TURNAROUND TIME

TDM = TIME DIVISION MULTIPLEXING

TDS = TRANSACTION-DRIVEN SYSTEM

tearing noun (distortion of image) déchirure f

technical adjective technique; **the document gives all the technical details**

on the new computer = ce document contient tous les renseignements d'ordre technique concernant le nouvel ordinateur

◊ **technician** *noun* technicien, -ienne; **the computer technicians installed the new system** = le nouveau système a été mis en place par les techniciens; **laboratory technician** = technicien de laboratoire

◊ **technique** *noun* technique *f or* méthode *f;* **the company has developed a new technique for processing customers' disks** = la société a mis au point une nouvelle technique de traitement des disquettes clients

technology *noun* technologie *f or* technique(s) *f(pl);* **information technology (IT)** = informatique *f or* techniques *fpl* de l'information; **new technology** = techniques nouvelles *or* techniques de pointe *or* nouvelle technologie; **the introduction of new technology** = l'introduction *f* de techniques nouvelles

◊ **technological** *adjective* technologique *or* technique; **the technological revolution** = la révolution technologique

tel = TELEPHONE

tele- *prefix (referring to TV or long distance)* télé-; **telebanking** = bancatique *f;* **telecine** = télécinéma *m;* **telecommunications** = télécommunications *fpl;* **teleconference** *or* **teleconferencing** = téléconférence *f;* **telecontrol** = télécommande *f*

◊ **telegram** = *noun* télégramme *m;* **to send a telegram** = envoyer un télégramme

telegraph 1 *noun* télégraphe *m;* **telegraph office** = bureau *m* de poste (d'où on envoie un télégramme) 2 *verb* télégraphier *or* envoyer un télégramme; **they telegraphed their agreement** = ils ont envoyé un télégramme confirmant leur accord; **the photographs were telegraphed to New York** = on a télégraphié les photos à New York

◊ **telegraphic** *adjective* télégraphique; **telegraphic address** = adresse *f* télégraphique

◊ **telegraphy** *noun* télégraphie *f;* **carrier telegraphy** = radiotélégraphie *f*

teleinformatic services *noun* service *m* (de) téléinformatique

telematics *noun* télématique *f*

telemessage *noun GB* télégramme *m or* message *m* télégraphié

telemetry *noun* télémétrie *f*

teleordering *noun (book ordering system)* système de réapprovisionnement informatisé *or* géré par ordinateur

telephone 1 *noun* téléphone *m;* **we had a new telephone system installed last week** = nous avons une nouvelle installation téléphonique depuis la semaine dernière; **to be on the telephone** = parler au téléphone *or* être en ligne; **she is on the telephone to Hong Kong** = elle est en train de téléphoner à Hong Kong; **by telephone** = par téléphone; **to place an order by telephone** = faire une commmande par téléphone; **cellular telephone** = téléphone cellulaire; **conference telephone** = téléphone de *or* pour conférence; **house telephone** *or* **internal telephone** = téléphone interne; **telephone answering machine** = répondeur *m* téléphonique; **telephone book** *or* **telephone directory** = annuaire *m* des téléphones *or* annuaire téléphonique; **telephone call** = appel *m* (téléphonique); **to make a telephone call** = faire un appel *or* téléphoner *or* appeler; **to answer the telephone** *or* **to take a telephone call** = répondre au téléphone *or* prendre un appel; **telephone as a data carrier** = l'utilisation du téléphone pour la transmission de données; **telephone exchange** = central *m* téléphonique; **telephone number** = numéro *m* de téléphone; **can you give me your telephone number?** = pouvez-vous me donner votre numéro de téléphone?; **telephone operator** = standardiste *m&f;* **telephone repeater** = amplificateur *m* de téléphone; **telephone subscriber** = abonné, -ée du téléphone; **telephone switchboard** = standard *m* téléphonique 2 *verb* appeler (quelqu'un) *or* téléphoner (à quelqu'un); **he telephoned about the**

order for computer stationery = il a téléphoné au sujet de la commande de papier listing

◊ **telephonist** *noun* téléphoniste *m&f or* standardiste *m&f*

◊ **telephony** *noun* téléphonie *f*

teleprinter *noun* téléimprimeur *m or* téléscripteur *m or* télétype *m;* **you can drive a teleprinter from this modified serial port** = vous pouvez connecter un téléimprimeur sur ce port série modifié; **teleprinter interface** = interface *f* (pour) téléimprimeur; **teleprinter operator** = opérateur, -trice de téléimprimeur *or* télétypiste *m&f;* **teleprinter roll** = rouleau *m* de papier de *or* pour téléimprimeur

teleprocessing (TP) *noun* télétraitement *m*

telesales *noun (sales made by telephone)* ventes *fpl* par téléphone

◊ **teleshopping** *noun* achats *mpl* par téléphone

telesoftware (TSW) *noun* logiciel *m* téléchargé; **the telesoftware was downloaded yesterday** = on a téléchargé le logiciel hier

Teletext® *noun (over television)* Télétexte® *m*

teletype (TTY) *noun* téléscripteur *m*

◊ **teletypewriter** *noun* téléimprimeur *m*

◊ **teletypsetting** *noun* télécomposition *f*

television (TV) *noun (system)* la télévision; *(device or set)* téléviseur *m or* poste *m* (de) télévision; **television camera** = caméra *f* de télévision; **television monitor** = moniteur *m* (de) télévision; **television projector** = projecteur *m* (de) télévision; **television receiver** = téléviseur *m or* poste *m* (de) télévision; **television receiver/monitor** = moniteur/téléviseur *m;* **television scan** = balayage *m* d'écran; **television tube** = tube *m* cathodique (pour téléviseur)

telex 1 *noun* **(a)** *(system)* télex *m;* **to send information by telex** = envoyer des renseignements par télex *or* télexer des

renseignements; **the order came by telex** = la commande nous a été télexée; **telex line** = ligne *f* (de) télex; **we cannot communicate with our Nigerian office because of the breakdown of the telex lines** = il nous est impossible de joindre nos bureaux au Nigéria parce que le télex est en panne; **telex operator** = opérateur, -trice de télex *or* télexiste *m&f;* **telex subscriber** = abonné, -ée du télex **(b)** *(machine or message)* **a telex** = télex *m;* **we don't have a telex** = nous n'avons pas le télex; **he sent a telex to his office** = il a envoyé un télex à son bureau; **we received his telex this morning** = nous avons reçu son télex ce matin **2** *verb* télexer *or* envoyer un télex; **can you telex the Canadian office before they open ?** = pouvez-vous envoyer un télex au bureau canadien avant son ouverture?

template *noun* **(a)** *(cut-out shape)* gabarit *m* (de traçage) **(b)** *(standard text)* lettre *f* type *or* paragraphe *m* standard; **template command** = commande *f* de formatage (de paragraphe, etc.); **a template paragraph command enables the user to specify the number of spaces each paragraph should be indented** = une commande de formatage permet à l'utilisateur de préciser l'alinéa de chaque paragraphe **(c)** *(blank form for addresses, etc.)* masque *m* (de saisie)

temporary storage *noun (place)* mémoire *f* temporaire; *(action)* stockage *m* temporaire; **temporary register** = registre *m* temporaire

◊ **temporarily** *adverb* temporairement

ten's complement *noun* complément *m* à dix

tera- *prefix (ten to the power 12)* téra-; **terahertz** = térahertz *m*

terminal 1 *noun* **(a)** terminal *m or* poste *m* de travail; **addressable terminal** = terminal à adressage protégé; **all the messages go to all the terminals since none are addressable terminals** = tous les messages sont transmis à tous les terminaux puisqu'aucun d'eux ne possède un adressage protégé; **applications terminal** = terminal dédié *or* spécialisé; **central terminal** = terminal principal *or* central; **dumb terminal** = terminal non intelligent; **intelligent**

terminal = terminal intelligent; **the new intelligent terminal has a built-in text editor** = le nouveau terminal intelligent comporte un éditeur de texte; **master terminal** = terminal maître *or* terminal principal; **the system manager uses the master terminal to restart the system** = le gestionnaire de système utilise le terminal principal pour relancer le système; **remote terminal** = terminal à distance; **slave terminal** = terminal asservi; **terminal character set** = police *f* de caractères utilisable par un terminal; *(hardware device or IC)* **terminal controller** = contrôleur *m* de terminal; **terminal identity** = (code d') identification *f* d'un terminal; **terminal interface** = interface *f* de *or* pour terminal; **the network controller has 16 terminal interfaces** = le contrôleur de réseau possède 16 interfaces pour terminaux; **terminal junky (TJ)** = fou *m&f or* fana *m&f* d'informatique *or* infomaniaque *mf* **my son has turned into a real terminal junky** = mon fils est devenu un véritable infomaniaque; **terminal keyboard** = clavier *m* relié à un terminal **(b)** *(electrical connection point)* borne *f or* point *m* de connexion *or* de raccordement; **terminal area** = zone *f* de connexions; **terminal block** = bloc *m* de raccordement **(c)** *(point in a network terminal)* (de réseau) **2** *adjective* fatal, -e; **the computer has a terminal fault** = l'ordinateur ne peut être réparé *or* souffre d'une panne irréparable

terminate *verb* terminer

◊ **termination** *noun (stopping)* arrêt *m; (ending)* terminaison *f; (caused by a fault or power failure)* **abnormal termination** = arrêt *m* anormal

◊ **terminator** *noun* marqueur *m or* marque *f* de fin de fichier; *(connection)* **line terminator** = dispositif *m* de fin de ligne

ternary *adjective* ternaire

test 1 *noun* test *m or* essai *m; (for software)* **test bed** = banc *m* d'essai; **test data** = données *f* de contrôle; **test equipment** = testeur *m or* équipement *m* pour tests; **the engineer has special test equipment for this model** = l'ingénieur possède un équipement spécialisé pour effectuer les tests sur ce modèle; **test pattern** = mire *f* de contrôle; *see also*

BENCHMARK *(of software)* **test run** = essai (de programme) *or* test d'évaluation de performance; **a test run will soon show up any errors** = un essai fera tout de suite apparaître les erreurs **2** *verb* tester *or* contrôler *or* faire un test *or* faire un essai; **saturation testing** = tests de saturation

text *noun* texte *m;* **ragged text** = texte non justifié (à droite); **start-of-text (SOT** *or* **STX)** = (code de) début *m* de texte; **text compression** = compression *f* de texte; **text-editing facilities** = (système de) traitement de texte; **text-editing function** = fonction *f* (de) traitement de texte; **the program includes a built-in text-editing function** = une fonction traitement de texte est intégrée au programme; *(software)* **text editor** = éditeur *m* de texte; **the text editor will only read files smaller than 64Kbytes long** = cet éditeur de texte ne peut lire que les fichiers de moins de 64Ko; **text file** = fichier *m* texte; **text formatter** = programme *m* de formatage pour texte; **people use the text formatter as a basic desk-top publishing program** = on utilise le formatage de texte comme programme de base de PAO; **text management** = gestion *f* de texte; **text manipulation** = manipulation *f* de texte; **text processing** = traitement *m* de texte; **text processor** = *(hardware)* machine *f* de traitement de texte; *(software)* logiciel *m* de traitement de texte; **text register** = registre *m* de texte; **text retrieval** = recherche *f* (et extraction) de texte; **text screen** = zone *f* d'affichage de texte *or* écran *m* texte; **text-to-speech converter** = convertisseur *m* texte/signal vocal

◊ **textual** *adjective* textuel, -elle; **the editors made several textual changes before the proofs were sent back for correction** = les éditeurs ont généreusement annoté le texte avant le renvoi des épreuves pour correction

thermal *adjective* thermique; **thermal paper** = papier *m* thermique; **thermal printer** = imprimante *f* thermique

◊ **thermal transfer** *noun* transfert *m* thermique; **a thermal transfer printer** = imprimante à transfert thermique; **colour ink-jet technology and thermal transfer technology compete with each other** = les techniques du jet d'encre couleur et du transfert thermique se font concurrence

thermistor *noun* thermistor *m*

thermo-sensitive *adjective* thermosensible

thesaurus *noun* thésaurus *m*

thick *adjective* épais, épaisse; *(for circuit design)* **thick film** = couche *f* épaisse

thimble printer *noun* imprimante *f* à tulipe

thin *adjective* mince; *(for ICs)* **thin film** = couche *f* mince; **thin film memory** = mémoire *f* à couches minces; **thin window** = fenêtre *f* étroite *or* fenêtre d'une ligne

third *adjective* troisième; **third generation computer** = ordinateur *m* de troisième génération; **third party** = tiers *m*

QUOTE they expect third party developers to enhance the operating systems by adding their own libraries
PC Business World

thirty-two bit system *noun* système *m* (informatique) de 32 bits

thousand *noun* mille *m or* millier *m*

thrashing *noun* battement *m*

thread *noun* programme *m* à fonctions (en)chaînées
◇ **threaded** *adjective* **threaded file** = fichier *m* chaîné; **threaded language** = langage chaîné; **threaded tree** = arborescence chaînée

three-address instruction *noun* instruction *f* à trois adresses
◇ **three-dimensional** *or* **3D** *adjective* tridimensionnel, -elle *or* à trois dimensions *or* 3D
◇ **three input adder** *see* FULL ADDER

three-pin plug *noun* fiche *f or* connecteur *m* à trois broches

three state logic *noun* circuit *m* logique à trois états

threshold *noun* seuil *m;* **threshold gate** = circuit *m* à seuil; **threshold value** = valeur *f* de seuil

throughput *noun* rendement *m or* débit *m;* **for this machine throughput is 1.3 inches per second (ips) scanning speed** = la vitesse de balayage de cette machine est de 1,3 pouce par seconde; **rated throughput** = débit *m* théorique *or* nominal

thyristor *noun* thyristor *m*

tie line *or* **tie trunk** *noun* ligne *f* de jonction privée

tilde *noun (sign over a letter, as over ñ)* tilde *m*

tilt and swivel *adjective* (écran) orientable

time 1 *noun* temps *m;* **addition time** = temps *m* d'addition; **cycle time** = temps de cycle; **queuing time** = temps d'attente; **real time** = temps réel; **response time** = temps de réponse; **stop time** = temps d'arrêt *or* d'immobilisation; **time address code** = signal de contrôle du temps écoulé; **time assigned speech interpolation (TASI)** = interpolation *f* de signaux sur bande vocale; **time base** = base *f* de temps; **time coded page** = page *f* (vidéotex) à enchaînement programmé; **time derived channel** = voie *f* dérivée en temps; **time display** = horloge *f* numérique (qui affiche l'heure sur l'écran); **time division multiple access** = accès temporel multiplexé *or* accès multiple par division dans le temps; **time division multiplexing (TDM)** = multiplexage *m* temporel *or* multiplexage par répartition dans le temps (MRT); **time division switching** = commutation *f* temporelle; **time domain analysis** = analyse *f* du signal dans le temps; **time shift viewing** = visionnage *m* en temps différé; **time slice** = tranche *f* de temps *or* tranche horaire; **time slot** = créneau *m* (de temps) **2** *verb* minuter; **microprocessor timing** = fréquence *f* d'horloge du processeur; **network timing** = synchronisation *f* de réseau; **timing loop** = boucle *f* de temporisation *or* de synchronisation; **timing master** = horloge *f* maîtresse

◊ **timeout** *noun* sortie *f* de session

◊ **timer** *noun* chronomètre *m*

◊ **time-sharing** *noun (system)* partage *m* de temps *or* (système en) temps partagé

title *noun* titre *m or* nom *m; title of disk* = nom *or* titre d'une disquette; *(first main page)* **title page** = page *f* de titre

TJ = TERMINAL JUNKY

toggle *verb (to switch)* basculer *or* valider (à l'aide d'un commutateur à bascule); **toggle switch** = commutateur *m* à bascule

> QUOTE the symbols can be toggled on or off the display
> *Micro Decision*

token *noun (internal code)* jeton *m;* **token ring network** = réseau *m* à jeton (circulant) *or* réseau token ring; **control token** = jeton de contrôle

tomo- *prefix* tomo-

◊ **tomogram** *noun* image *f* tomographique

◊ **tomography** *noun* tomographie *f;* **computerized axial tomography (CAT)** = tomodensitométrie *f*

tone *noun* **(a)** *(sound)* tonalité *f;* **dialling tone** = tonalité d'appel; **engaged tone** = tonalité 'occupé'; **tone dialling** = numérotation *f* sur clavier tonal; **tone signalling** = signalisation tonale **(b)** *(shade)* ton *m or* nuance *f;* **the graphics package can give several tones of blue** = le progiciel graphique offre plusieurs nuances de bleu

◊ **toner** *noun (for photocopier or printer)* encre *f or* toner *m;* **toner cartridge** = cartouche *f* d'encre or de toner; **change toner and toner cartridge according to the manual** = pour remettre de l'encre ou changer la cartouche, voir la marche à suivre dans le manuel d'utilisation; **the toner cartridge and the imaging drum can be replaced as one unit when the toner runs out** = lorsque l'encre est épuisée, on remplace la cartouche et le tambour en une seule opération *or* ensemble

toolbox *noun (box of instruments)* boîte *f* à outils

◊ **toolkit** *noun (for programs)* (boîte à) outils *or* (programmes) utilitaires *mpl*

◊ **tools** *noun (for programs)* outils (de programmation)

top *noun* haut *m or* partie *f* supérieure; *(structured programming)* **top-down programming** = programmation *f* structurée suivant un ordre décroissant; **top of stack** = dessus *m* de la pile; **top space** = blanc *m* de tête *or* marge *f* supérieure

topology *noun* topologie *f;* **network topology** = topologie de réseau

torn tape *noun (communication switching method)* bande *f* perforée (pour télex hors ligne)

total *noun* total *m;* **hash total** = total de vérification (pour hash codes); **total access communication system (TACS)** = norme TACS (pour système de radio-téléphone cellulaire)

touch *verb* toucher *or* appuyer (sur); **touch pad** = pavé *m* tactile *or* à effleurement; **touch screen** = écran *m* tactile; **touch-sensitive keyboard** = clavier *m* à effleurement *or* clavier tactile

◊ **touch up** *verb* retoucher

TP = TELEPROCESSING, TRANSACTION PROCESSING

TPI = TRACKS PER INCH

trace *noun* traçage *m* d'un programme *or* d'un procédé; **trace program** = programme de traçage; **trace trap** = point *m* de contrôle (du registre) dans un programme de traçage

track 1 *noun* piste *f;* **address track** = piste adresse; **track address** = adresse de piste; **tracks per inch (TPI)** = (nombre de) pistes par pouce **2** *verb* localiser; **the read head is not tracking the recorded track correctly** = la tête de lecture fait une erreur de piste

trackball *noun* boule *m* (de pointeur)

tractor feed *noun* entraînement *m* (du papier) par picots

> QUOTE the printer is fairly standard with both tractor and cut sheet feed system
> *Which PC?*

traffic *noun* trafic *m* *or* mouvements *mpl;* **traffic analysis** = analyse *f* du trafic (sur une ligne); **traffic density** = densité *f* du trafic; **traffic intensity** = intensité *f* de trafic; **incoming traffic** = trafic *m* d'entrée *or* d'arrivée

trail *noun* trace *f;* **audit trail** = protocole *m* de traçage *or* de contrôle *or* de vérification
◊ **trailer** *noun (final byte of file)* label *m* de fin de fichier; **trailer record** = dernier enregistrement *or* enregistrement *m* de fin de fichier; **tape trailer** = label de fin de bande

transaction *noun* transaction *f* *or* mouvement *m;* **transaction-driven system (TDS)** = système *m* transactionnel; *(movement file)* **transaction file** = fichier *m* de transactions *or* fichier mouvements *or* fichier de mise à jour; **transaction processing (TP)** = traitement de mouvements; *(change record)* **transaction record** = enregistrement de mouvements *or* de transactions

transborder data flow *noun* flux *m* de données passant les frontières *or* flux transfrontière

transceiver *noun* émetteur/récepteur *m;* **radio transceiver** = émetteur/récepteur radio

transcoder *noun* transcodeur *m;* **use the transcoder to convert PAL to SECAM** = utilisez le transcodeur pour la conversion de PAL en SECAM

transcribe *verb* transcrire
◊ **transcription** *noun* transcription *f*

transducer *noun* transducteur *m;* **a pressure transducer converts physical pressure signals into electrical signals** = un transducteur de pression transforme un signal physique de pression en signal électrique

transfer **1** *verb* **(a)** *(to change command)* transférer; **all processing activities have been transferred to the mainframe** = toutes les opérations de traitement ont été transférées sur l'ordinateur principal **(b)** *(to copy a section of memory)* transférer **2** *noun* **(a)** *(between devices or memory)* transfert *m;* **radial transfer** = *(between peripherals)* transfert radial; *(between layers)* transfert intercouche *or* radial; **transfer check** = contrôle *m* de transfert; *(between devices and locations)* **transfer rate** = vitesse *f* de transfert; **transfer time** = temps *m* de transfert **(b)** *(within program)* **conditional transfer** = transfert *or* branchement *m* conditionnel; **transfer command** = instruction *f* de transfert *or* de branchement; **transfer control** = contrôle de transfert *or* de branchement

transform *verb* transformer
◊ **transformation** *noun* transformation *f*
◊ **transformational rules** *noun* régles *fpl* de transformation
◊ **transformer** *noun* transformateur *m*

transient 1 *adjective* passager, -ère *or* de courte durée *or* éphémère; **transient area** = zone (de mémoire) *f* des programmes non résidents; **transient error** = erreur *f* passagère *or* momentanée **2** *noun* **line transient** *or* **voltage transient** = courant *m* de transit *or* transitoire; **power transient** = pointe *f* de courant; **transient suppressor** = limiteur *m* *or* éliminateur *m* de courant transitoire

transistor *noun* transistor *m;* **bipolar (junction) transistor (BJT)** = transistor bipolaire *or* à jonction pnp *or* à jonction npn; **field effect transistor (FET)** = transistor à effet de champ (TEC); **transistor-resistor logic (TRL)** = logique *f* transistor résistance (LTR); **transistor-transistor logic (TTL)** = logique transistor transistor (LTT); **unipolar transistor** = transistor unipolaire

transition *noun* transition *f;* **transition point** = point *m* de transition

translate *verb (to convert data) from one form into another* traduire *or* convertir

◊ **translation tables** or **conversion tables** noun tables f de conversion or d'équivalence or de référence

◊ **translator (program)** noun programme m de traduction or d'interprétation or programme compilateur or traducteur

transmit verb transmettre

◊ **transmission** noun transmission f; **neutral transmission** = transmission neutre; **parallel transmission** = transmission (en) parallèle; **serial transmission** = transmission (en) série; **synchronous transmission** = transmission synchrone; **transmission channel** = voie f or canal m de transmission; **transmission error** = erreur f de transmission; **transmission media** = moyens mpl or supports mpl de transmission; **transmission rate** = vitesse f de transmission or débit m; their average transmission is 64,000 bits per second (bps) through a parallel connection or 19,200 bps through a serial connection = la vitesse moyenne de transmission est de 64 000 bits par seconde en connexion parallèle et 19 200 bits par seconde en connexion série; **transmission window** = fenêtre f de transmission

◊ **transmissive disk** noun disque m optique transitif

◊ **transmittance** noun transmittance f

◊ **transmitter (TX)** noun transmetteur m

transparent adjective **(a)** transparent, -e; **transparent interrupts** = interruptions transparentes; **transparent paging** = pagination f tranparente **(b)** (device or network) transparent,-e

◊ **transparency** noun (for overhead projector) transparent m; (positive film) diapositive f

transphasor noun transphaseur m

transponder noun transpondeur m or transmetteur/répondeur m

transport 1 verb transporter **2** noun **(a)** (device) **(magnetic) tape transport** = dérouleur m or dispositif m d'entraînement de bandes (magnétiques) **(b)** (ISO/OSI standard) **transport layer** = couche f transport

◊ **transportable** adjective portable; **a transportable computer is not as small as a portable** = un ordinateur portable n'est pas aussi petit or aussi léger qu'un portatif

transposition noun transposition f or inversion f or interversion f; **a series of transposition errors caused faulty results** = une série d'interversions a donné de faux résultats

Transputer® noun transordinateur m or Transputer m

transverse mode noise noun interférence f interligne

◊ **transverse scan** noun balayage transversal or lecture transversale

trap noun piège m or trappe f; **trace trap** = point m de contrôle (du registre) dans un programme de traçage

◊ **trapdoor** noun point d'entrée dans un système

tray noun bac m à papier (pour alimentation en feuille à feuille)

tree noun **tree (structure)** = (structure en) arbre m or arborescence f; **tree and branch network system** = système m arborescent; **tree selection sort** = tri m en arborescence; **binary tree** = arbre binaire

tremendously high frequency (THF) noun (between 300GHz and 3000GHz) hyper haute fréquence

triad noun triade f

trial noun essai m or test m; **trials engineer** = ingénieur m d'essai

tributary station noun station f secondaire

trim *verb* couper (très peu) *or* régulariser la coupe; *(pages of a book)* rogner; **the printed pages are trimmed to 198 x 129mm =** après l'impression, on rogne pour obtenir des pages de 198 x 129mm; **you will need to trim the top part of the photograph to make it fit =** il vous faudra couper légèrement le bord supérieur de la photo pour qu'elle ait les dimensions désirées

TRL = TRANSISTOR-RESISTOR LOGIC

Trojan Horse *noun (program)* cheval *m* de Troie

troposphere *noun* troposphère *f see also* IONOSPHERE

troubleshoot *verb (to debug)* déboguer (un logiciel); *(to locate and repair faults)* déceler et réparer une panne
◊ **troubleshooter** *noun (for debugging)* spécialiste *m&f* en débogage; *(technician)* technicien/réparateur *m* informatique

trough *noun (in a waveform)* creux *m*

TRUE *noun (logical condition)* VRAI

truncate *verb* **(a)** *(to cut short)* tronquer **(b)** *(to give an approximate value)* arrondir par défaut *or* tronquer; **3.5678 truncated to 3.56 =** 3,5678 tronqué *or* arrondi par défaut à 3,56
◊ **truncation** *noun (of value)* troncature *f;* **truncation error =** erreur *f* de troncature *or* d'arrondi

trunk *noun* circuit *m or* faisceau *m* de jonction
◊ **trunk call** *noun GB (long-distance call)* appel *m* interurbain *or* communication interurbaine
◊ **trunk exchange** *noun GB (telephone exchange)* central *m* téléphonique pour réseau interurbain

truth table *noun* table *f* de vérité; **truth value =** valeur *f* binaire *or* booléenne

TSW = TELESOFTWARE

TTL = TRANSISTOR-TRANSISTOR LOGIC logique *f* transistor-transistor (LTT); **TTL compatible =** compatible (avec) LTT; **TTL logic =** logique transistor-transistor *or* logique LTT

TTY = TELETYPE

tube *noun (TV)* tube *m*

tune *verb* **(a)** *(a system)* ajuster *or* régler *or* mettre au point; **to fine tune =** régler avec grande précision **(b)** *(radio frequency)* régler

Turing machine *noun* machine *f* de Turing *or* simulateur *m* (de) Turing
◊ **Turing test** *noun* test *m* de Turing

turn off *verb (to switch off)* éteindre; **turn off the power before unplugging the monitor =** il faut éteindre l'appareil avant de déconnecter le moniteur
◊ **turn on** *verb (to switch on)* mettre sous tension *or* mettre en marche

turnaround document *noun* document *m* circulant
◊ **turnaround time (TAT)** *noun* **(a)** *(time to switch data flow direction)* délai *m* d'inversion *or* de retournement **(b)** *US (time to activate a program and get results)* temps *m* d'exécution
◊ **turnkey system** *noun* système *m* clé en main

turtle *noun* tortue *f;* **turtle graphics =** graphisme généré à l'aide d'une tortue; **the charts were prepared using turtle graphics =** la présentation graphique a été préparée avec une tortue

tutorial *noun* tutoriel *m*

TV = TELEVISION; **TV camera =** caméra *f* de télévision

tweeter *noun (informal)* haut-parleur *m* d'aigus *or* de hautes fréquences

twisted pair cable *noun* câble *m* à paire torsadée

two-address instruction *noun* instruction *f* à deux adresses; **two-plus-**

one instruction = instruction à deux adresses plus une

◊ **two-dimensional** *adjective* à deux dimensions *or* bidimensionnel, -elle; **two-dimensional array** = tableau *m* à deux dimensions *or* bidimensionnel

◊ **two input adder** *noun* additionneur *m* à deux entrées

◊ **two-level subroutine** *noun* sous-programme à deux niveaux

◊ **two-part** *noun (paper)* (papier) double *or* en double épaisseur; **two-part stationery** = papier commercial avec double (autocopiant) *or* en double épaisseur

◊ **two-pass assembler** *noun* assembleur *m* (en) deux passes

two's complement *noun* complément *m* à deux

two way cable *noun US* câble *m* bidirectionnel

two way radio *noun* poste *m* émetteur-récepteur

two wire circuit *noun* circuit *m* à deux fils *or* bifilaire *or* bidirectionnel

TX = TRANSMITTER

type 1 *noun* **(a)** *(metal)* caractères *mpl* **(b)** *(shape)* caractères (d'imprimerie); **they switched to italic type for the heading** = ils ont changé de police de caractères et composé l'en-tête en italiques **(c)** *(variety)* type *m;* **variable data type** = variable *f* (de type non précisé); **string type** = variable chaînée *or* de type chaîne de caractères **2** *verb* taper *or* écrire à la machine; **he can type quite fast** = il a une vitesse de frappe assez rapide; **all his reports are typed on his portable typewriter** = il tape tous ses rapports sur sa (machine) portative

typeface *or* **typestyle** *or* **font** *noun* fonte *f or* police *f* de caractères

typescript *noun* texte *m or* manuscrit *m* dactylographié *or* tapuscrit *m*

typeset *verb* composer *or* faire la composition (d'un texte); **in desktop publishing, the finished work should look almost as if it had been typeset** = la PAO devrait produire un texte dont la qualité est à peu près égale à celle d'un texte photocomposé

◊ **typesetter** *noun* compositeur *m or* typographe *m;* **the text is ready to be sent to the typesetter** = le texte est prêt à être envoyé en composition

◊ **typesetting** *noun* composition *f;* **typesetting costs can be reduced by supplying the typesetter with prekeyed disks** = les frais de composition sont moins élevés si le texte est saisi sur disquette avant d'être envoyé au compositeur

typesize *noun* corps *m or* taille *f* de caractères (en points)

typewriter *noun* machine *f* à écrire; **she wrote the letter on her portable typewriter** = elle a écrit la lettre sur sa petite portative; **he makes fewer mistakes now he is using an electronic typewriter** = il fait moins d'erreurs depuis qu'il utilise une machine à écrire électronique; **typewriter faces** = caractères *mpl* de machine à écrire

◊ **typewritten** *adjective* dactylographié, -ée *or* écrit, -e à la machine

◊ **typing** *noun* dactylographie *f;* **typing error** = faute *f* de frappe; **she must have made a typing error** = elle doit avoir fait une faute de frappe; **typing pool** = pool *m* de dactylos; **copy typing** = dactylographie *f*

◊ **typist** *noun* **copy typist** = dactylo *f;* **shorthand typist** = sténo-dactylo *f*

typo *noun (typographical error)* coquille *f*

◊ **typographer** *noun* typographe *m&f*

◊ **typographic** *or* **typographical** *adjective* typographique; **no typographical skills are required for this job** = ce travail ne demande aucune expérience en typographie; **a typographical error made while typesetting is called a 'typo'** = une erreur typographique à la composition donne ce qu'on appelle une 'coquille'; **typographical error** = coquille *f*

◊ **typography** *noun* typographie *f*

Uu

UART = UNIVERSAL ASYNCHRONOUS RECEIVER/TRANSMITTER
émetteur/récepteur *m* asynchrone universel; **UART controller** = contrôleur *m* d'émetteur/récepteur asynchrone universel

UBC = UNIVERSAL BLOCK CHANNEL

UHF = ULTRA HIGH FREQUENCY

ULA = UNCOMMITTED LOGIC ARRAY

ultra- *prefix* très *or* hyper; **ultra high frequency (UHF)** = hyperfréquence *f or* ultra-haute fréquence *or* ondes décimétriques *or* ultracourtes *or* ultra-courtes; *(reduced by more than 90X)* **ultrafiche** = microfiche *f* (avec réduction de plus de 90X); *(above 20KHz)* **ultrasonic** = ultrasonore *or* ultrasonique; **ultrasound** = ultrason *m or* ultra-son *m*; **ultraviolet (UV) light** = lumière *f* ultraviolette *or* ultra-violette *or* rayonnement *m* ultraviolet *or* ultra-violet *or* (l') ultraviolet *m*; **ultraviolet erasable PROM** = mémoire morte programmable (PROM) effaçable par ultraviolet

umlaut *noun (typography)* tréma *m*

un- *prefix (meaning not)* non *or* in-; **unallowable digit** = code *m or* chiffre *m* interdit; **unauthorized** = *(person)* non autorisé, -ée; *(access)* interdit, -e; **the use of a password is to prevent unauthorized access to the data** = le mot de passe interdit aux personnes non autorisées d'avoir accès aux données; *(pages of book)* **uncut** = (livre) dont les pages ne sont pas rognées

unary operation *noun* opération *f* monadique *or* à un opérande

unattended operation *noun* tâche qui peut être exécutée automatiquement *or* fonctionnement automatique (d'un système)

◊ **unbundled software** *noun* logiciel *m* non compris *or* non inclus (dans l'offre d'achat)

◊ **unclocked** *adjective (circuit)* asynchrone *or* non asservi,-e à l'horloge

◊ **uncommitted logic array (ULA)** *noun* circuit *m* logique non connecté; **uncommitted storage list** = liste *f* des emplacements disponibles *or* non alloués

◊ **unconditional** *adjective* sans réserve *or* systématique *or* inconditionnel, -elle; **unconditional branch** *or* **jump** = branchement *m or* saut *m* inconditionnel; **unconditional transfer** = transfert *m* systématique *or* automatique
NOTE: opposite is **conditional**

underexposed *adjective (photograph)* sous-exposé, -ée

underflow *noun* dépassement *m or* débordement *m* négatif

underline *or* **underscore 1** *noun* soulignement *m or* soulignage *m or* trait *m* (sous un mot ou une ligne de texte); **the chapter headings are given a double underline and the paragraphs a single underline** = on souligne deux fois l'en-tête d'un chapitre et une seule fois celui d'un paragraphe **2** *verb* souligner; **underlining** = soulignement *m or* soulignage *m*

undertake *verb* entreprendre; **he has undertaken to reprogram the whole system** = il a entrepris de reprogrammer tout le système
NOTE: **undertaking - undertaken - undertook**

undetected *adjective* non décelé, -ée *or* non détecté, -ée; **the programming error was undetected for some time** = l'erreur de programmation n'a été détectée qu'après un certain temps

◊ **unedited** *adjective (text)* non édité, -ée *or* non corrigé, -ée

◊ **unformatted** *adjective (disk)* non formaté, -ée; **it is impossible to copy to an unformatted disk** = il est impossible de copier quoi que ce soit sur une disquette non formatée; **the cartridge drive provides 12.7Mbyte of unformatted storage** = le lecteur de cartouche donne une capacité de mémoire non formatée de 12.7Mo

uni- *prefix (meaning one or single)* uni-

◊ **unidirectional microphone** *noun* microphone *m* unidirectionnel; *compare with* OMNIDIRECTIONAL

union *noun (logical function)* union *f or* opération *f* OU

◊ **unipolar** *adjective* **(a)** *(transistor)* unipolaire **(b)** *(transmission system)* unipolaire; **unipolar signal** = signal unipolaire

uninterruptable power supply (UPS) *noun* onduleur *m*

unique *adjective* unique; **each separate memory byte has its own unique address** = chaque octet de mémoire a une adresse unique

unit *noun* **(a)** *(smallest element)* unité *f or* élément *m;* **unit buffer** = tampon *m* élémentaire; **unit record** = enregistrement *m* unique **(b)** *(single machine)* unité *or* organe *m* **arithmetic and logic unit (ALU)** = unité arithmétique et logique; **central processing unit (CPU)** = unité centrale (de traitement) *or* processeur central; **control unit** = unité de contrôle; **desk top unit** = ordinateur *m* de bureau; **input/output unit** *or* **device** = périphérique *m or* organe d'entrée/sortie

universal *adjective* universel, -elle *or* standard; **universal asynchronous receiver/transmitter (UART)** = émetteur/récepteur *m* asynchrone universel; **universal block channel (UBC)** = canal universel de transmission par blocs; **universal device (UART, USRT, USART)** = dispositif

universel; **universal product code (UPC)** = code *m* (à) barres; **universal programming** = programmation *f* en langage universel; **universal set** = ensemble *m* référentiel; **the universal set of prime numbers less than ten and greater than two is 3,5,7** = l'ensemble référentiel des nombres premiers inférieurs à dix et plus grands que deux est 3,5,7; **universal synchronous asynchronous receiver-transmitter (USART)** = émetteur/récepteur *m* synchrone asynchrone universel; **universal synchronous receiver/transmitter (USRT)** = émetteur/récepteur synchrone universel

Unix® *noun (popular operating system)* (système d'exploitation) UNIX

unmodified instruction *noun* instruction *f* dans sa forme initiale

unmodulated *adjective (signal)* non modulé, -ée; *see also* BASE BAND

unpack *verb* dégrouper *or* décondenser *or* décomprimer; **this routine unpacks the archived file** = cette routine permet de décomprimer les fichiers archivés

unplug *verb* débrancher *or* déconnecter; **do not move the system without unplugging it** = ne déplacez pas le système sans l'avoir d'abord débranché; **simply unplug the old drive and plug-in a new one** = vous n'avez qu'à déconnecter le lecteur et en connecter un nouveau à sa place

unprotected *adjective (data that can be modified)* non protégé, -ée; **unprotected field** = champ non protégé

unrecoverable error *noun* erreur *f* irrécupérable *or* impossible à corriger

unsigned *adjective (number system)* sans signe *or* en valeur absolue

unsorted *adjective (data)* non classé, -ée *or* non trié, -ée; **it took four times as long to search the unsorted file** = il a fallu quatre fois plus de temps pour chercher dans les fichiers non classés

unwanted *adjective* non requis, -e; **use the global delete command to remove large areas of unwanted text =** lorsqu'il s'agit de supprimer un texte assez long, servez-vous de la commande qui permet d'effacer en bloc

up *adverb (working or running)* en (bon) état de marche; **they must have found the fault - the computer is finally up and running =** ils ont sûrement trouvé la source du problème puisque l'ordinateur fonctionne à merveille; **up time** *or* **uptime =** temps *m* productif *or* de bon fonctionnement
NOTE: opposite is **down**

◊ **up and down propagation time** *noun* temps *m* de propagation aller (et) retour

UPC = UNIVERSAL PRODUCT CODE

update 1 *noun (file)* fichier *m* mis à jour *or* corrigé; *(action)* mise *f* à jour *or* correction (d'un texte); *(system)* nouvelle version (d'un progiciel); **update file** *or* **transaction file =** fichier *m* mouvements **2** *verb* mettre à jour *or* corriger; **we have the original and updated documents on disks =** le document original et le document corrigé se trouvent tous les deux sur disquettes

> QUOTE it means that any item of data stored in the system need be updated only once
> *Which PC?*

up/down counter *noun* compteur *m* incrémenteur/décrémenteur

upgrade *verb* optimiser *or* améliorer *or* rendre plus efficace; **they can upgrade the printer =** ils peuvent optimiser l'imprimante; **the single processor with 2Mbytes of memory can be upgraded to 4Mbytes =** il est possible d'augmenter la mémoire du processeur unique de 2Mo jusqu'à 4Mo *or* le processeur unique possède une mémoire de 2Mo extensible jusqu'à 4Mo; **all three models have an on-site upgrade facility =** les trois modèles offrent des possibilités d'extension sur site

> QUOTE the cost of upgrading a PC to support CAD clearly depends on the peripheral devices added
> *PC Business World*

upkeep *noun (software)* mise *f* à jour; *(hardware)* entretien *m or* maintenance *f;* **the upkeep of the files means reviewing them every six months =** la mise à jour des fichiers doit se faire tous les six mois

upload *verb* télécharger *or* transférer des données (d'un petit ordinateur à un plus gros); **the user can upload PC data to update mainframe applications =** l'utilisateur peut transférer les données d'un micro sur un gros ordinateur, pour mettre les applications à jour NOTE: the opposite is **download**

◊ **uploading** *noun* téléchargement *m;* **the image can be manipulated before uploading to the host computer =** on peut manipuler l'image avant son téléchargement sur l'ordinateur hôte

upper case *noun* (lettre) majuscule *f or* haut *m* de casse; **upper case M =** M majuscule

UPS = UNINTERRUPTABLE POWER SUPPLY

uptime *noun (time when a computer is functioning correctly)* temps *m* productif *or* de bon fonctionnement
NOTE: opposite is **downtime**

upwards compatible *or* US **upward compatible** *adjective (hardware or software)* compatible avec système de niveau supérieur

usable *adjective* utilisable; **the PC has 512K of usable memory =** cet ordinateur individuel possède 512K de mémoire utilisable; **maximum usable frequency =** maximum *m* de fréquence utilisable

USART = UNIVERSAL SYNCHRONOUS ASYNCHRONOUS RECEIVER-TRANSMITTER

USASCII *US* = USA STANDARD CODE FOR INFORMATION INTERCHANGE *see* ASCII

use 1 *noun* **(a)** *(way in which something can be used)* usage *m;* **the use of that file is restricted =** l'accès à ce fichier est limité; **to make use of something =** faire usage de *or* utiliser *or* employer quelque chose; **in use =** en service *or* utilisé, -ée; **sorry, the printer is already in use =** je regrette, mais il y a déjà quelqu'un qui se sert de l'imprimante; **the printer has been in use for the last two hours =** l'imprimante fonctionne depuis deux heures **(b)** *(being useful)* utilité *f;* **what use is an extra disk drive?** je ne vois pas l'utilité d'un deuxième lecteur; **it's no use, I cannot find the error =** à quoi bon, je ne réussis pas à trouver l'erreur **2** *verb* **(a)** *(to operate something)* utiliser *or* employer *or* se servir de (quelque chose); **if you use the computer for processing the labels, it will be much quicker =** la préparation de ces étiquettes se fera beaucoup plus rapidement avec l'ordinateur; **the computer is used too often by the sales staff =** les commerciaux utilisent l'ordinateur trop souvent **(b)** *(to consume power)* consommer; **it's using too much electricity =** la consommation d'électricité de cette machine est beaucoup trop forte

◊ **used** *adjective (not new)* d'occasion; **special offer on used terminals =** prix spécial pour des terminaux d'occasion

user *noun* utilisateur, -trice; **user area =** zone *f* utilisateur *or* pour programme utilisateur; **user-definable =** programmable par l'utilisateur *or* selon les besoins de l'utilisateur; **the style sheet contains 125 user-definable symbols =** la feuille de style comporte 125 symboles programmables (selon les besoins de l'utilisateur); **user-defined characters =** caractères programmés par l'utilisateur; **user documentation =** notice *f* d'utilisation destinée à l'utilisateur; **using the package was easy with the excellent user documentation =** l'excellente notice facilitait l'utilisation du progiciel; **user group =** groupe *m* d'utilisateurs; **I found how to solve the problem by asking people at the user group meeting =** j'ai trouvé la solution au problème en me renseignant auprès des autres utilisateurs rencontrés à la réunion; **user guide =** manuel *m* d'utilisation; **user ID =** mot *m* de passe *or* code *m* personnel d'un utilisateur; **if you forget your user ID, you will not be** able **to logon =** il faut vous rappeler votre mot de passe sinon vous ne pourrez pas avoir accès au système; **user interface =** interface *m* système/utilisateur; **user-operated language =** langage *m* (d')utilisateur; **user port =** port *m* pour périphériques; **user's program =** programme *m* écrit par l'utilisateur *or* programme utilisateur; **user-selectable =** programmable *or* définissable *or* réglable par l'utilisateur; qui peut être modifié, programmé, sélectionné, validé, réglé suivant les besoins de l'utilisateur; **the video resolution of 640 by 300, 240 or 200 pixels is user-selectable =** l'utilisateur peut sélectionner une résolution d'écran de 640 x 300, 240 ou 200 pixels

◊ **user-friendly** *adjective (language or system or program)* convivial, -e *or* d'utilisation facile *or* facile à utiliser; **it's such a user-friendly machine =** c'est un appareil extrêmement facile à utiliser; **compared with the previous version this one is very user- friendly =** comparée à la version précédente, celle-ci est très facile à utiliser *or* très conviviale

USRT = UNIVERSAL SYNCHRONOUS RECEIVER/TRANSMITTER

utility (program) *noun* (programme) utilitaire *m;* **a lost file cannot be found without a file-recovery utility =** il est impossible de récupérer un fichier perdu sans l'aide d'un (programme) utilitaire *or* d'un programme de récupération de fichier; **on the disk is a utility for backing up a hard disk =** la disquette comporte un utilitaire qui permet la sauvegarde de fichiers sur disque dur

UV light = ULTRAVIOLET LIGHT

Vv

V = VOLTAGE

V & V = VERIFICATION AND VALIDATION

vacuum *noun* vide *m or* vacuum *m;* **there is a vacuum in the sealed CRT** = on a fait le vide dans le tube cathodique scellé; **vacuum tube** = tube *m* à vide

V format *noun* format *m* variable

V series *noun (CCITT (UK-European) standards for data transmission using a modem)* normes *fpl or* protocoles *mpl* de transmission série V (pour modems)
NOTE: **V.21** = 300 baud transmit and receive, full duplex **V.22** = 1200 baud transmit and receive, half duplex **V.22 BIS** = 1200 baud transmit and receive full duplex **V.23** = 75 baud transmit, 1200 baud receive, half duplex

valid *adjective* valide; **valid memory address** = adresse *f* valide
◊ **validate** *verb* valider
◊ **validation** *noun* validation *f*
◊ **validity** *noun* validité *f;* **validity check** = (test de) vérification *f* de validité des données

value *noun* valeur *f;* **absolute value** = valeur absolue; **the absolute value of -62.34 is 62.34** = la valeur absolue de -62,34 est 62,34; **initial value** = valeur initiale
◊ **value added network (VAN)** *noun* réseau *m* à valeur ajoutée
◊ **value added reseller (VAR)** *noun* revendeur *m* de systèmes à valeur ajoutée

valve *noun (vacuum tube)* tube *m* (à vide) *or* valve *f or* lampe *f*

VAN = VALUE ADDED NETWORK

vapourware *noun (informal) (products which exist in name only)* produits *mpl* fictifs

VAR = VALUE ADDED RESELLER

variable 1 *adjective* variable; **variable data** = donnée(s) *f(pl)* variable(s); **variable length record** = enregistrement *m* à longueur variable; **variable word length computer** = ordinateur *m* à mots de longueur variable **2** *noun* variable *f;* **global variable** = variable globale; **local variable** = variable locale
◊ **vary** *verb* varier *or* modifier *or* changer; **the clarity of the signal can vary with the power supply** = la clarté du signal peut varier avec la tension du courant d'alimentation

VCR = VIDEO CASSETTE RECORDER

VDT *or* **VDU** = VISUAL DISPLAY TERMINAL, VISUAL DISPLAY UNIT écran *m* de visualisation *or* visuel *m*

> QUOTE it normally consists of a keyboard to input information and either a printing terminal or a VDU screen to display messages and results
> *Practical Computing*
> QUOTE a VDU is a device used with a computer that displays information in the form of characters and drawings on a screen
> *Electronics & Power*

vector *noun* **(a)** *(address to a new memory location)* vecteur *m* **(b)** *(coordinate)* vecteur; **vector graphics** *or* **vector image** *or* **vector scan** = infographie *f or* image *f* vectorisée; **vector processor** = processeur *m* vectoriel
◊ **vectored interrupt** *noun* interruption *f* vectorielle

> QUOTE the great advantage of the vector-scan display is that it requires little memory to store a picture
> *Electronics & Power*

Veitch diagram *noun* diagramme *m* de Veitch

velocity *noun* vitesse *f;* **the disk drive motor spins at a constant velocity =** le moteur du lecteur de disquettes tourne à vitesse constante

Venn diagram *noun* diagramme *m* de Venn

verify *verb* vérifier *or* contrôler
◇ **verification** *noun* vérification *f or* contrôle *m;* **keystroke verification =** contrôle *m* de la frappe; **verification and validation (V & V) =** vérification et validation *or* contrôle et validation
◇ **verifier** *noun (device)* vérificatrice *f*

version *noun* version *f;* **the latest version of the software includes an improved graphics routine =** la dernière version du logiciel comprend une routine graphique améliorée

verso *noun* verso *m; (of page)* verso *or* page *f* de gauche

vertical *adjective* vertical, -e; **vertical blanking interval =** délai *m* de retour vertical; **vertical format unit (VFU) =** unité *f* de formatage vertical; **vertical justification =** justification *f* verticale; **vertical parity check =** clé *f* de parité transversale; **vertical redundancy check (VRC) =** clé *f* transversale; **vertical scrolling =** défilement *m* vertical; **vertical tab =** tabulation *f* verticale
◇ **vertically** *adverb* verticalement; **the page has been justified vertically =** on a fait une justification verticale de la page; **vertically polarized signal =** signal *m* avec polarisation verticale *or* signal polarisé verticalement

very high frequency (VHF) *noun (between 30 - 300MHz)* onde *f* métrique *or* très haute fréquence

very large scale integration (VLSI) *noun* intégration *f* à très grande échelle

very low frequency (VLF) *noun (between 3 - 30KHz)* onde *f* myriamétrique *or* très basse fréquence

vestigial sideband *noun* bande *f* latérale résiduelle

vf band = VOICE FREQUENCY BAND

VFU = VERTICAL FORMAT UNIT

VHD = VERY HIGH DENSITY *(of disk)* très haute densité

VHF = VERY HIGH FREQUENCY

via *preposition* via *or* par *or* par l'intermédiaire de *or* en passant par; **the signals have reached us via satellite =** les signaux nous ont été transmis par satellite; **you can download the data to the CPU via a modem =** le téléchargement des données dans l'unité centrale peut se faire par l'intermédiaire d'un modem

video *noun* vidéo *f;* **video bandwidth =** largeur *f* de bande vidéo; **video camera =** vidéocaméra *f;* **infrared video camera =** vidéocamera à infrarouge; **some instructors monitor their trainees with infrared video cameras =** certains instructeurs utilisent une vidéocaméra à infrarouge pour suivre leurs élèves; **video cassette =** vidéocassette *f;* **video cassette recorder (VCR) =** magnétoscope *m;* **video compressor =** concentrateur *m or* réducteur *m* (de largeur de bande) vidéo; **video conference =** vidéoconférence *f or* visioconférence *f;* **videodisk =** disque *m* vidéo *or* vidéodisque *m;* **video display =** écran *m or* moniteur *m* vidéo; **video expander =** déconcentrateur *m* pour transmission vidéo; **video frame =** image *f* vidéo; **with an image processor you can freeze a video frame =** le processeur d'images permet de figer une image *or* de faire un arrêt sur image; **video game =** jeu *m* vidéo; **video image =** image *f* vidéo *or* image d'écran; **a printer-readable video image can be sent to a basic laser printer through a video port =** une image vidéo imprimable peut être envoyée sur une imprimante laser classique par le port vidéo; **video interface chip =** circuit intégré de carte vidéo; **video library =** vidéothèque *f;* **video memory** *or* **video RAM (VRAM) =** RAM *f* vidéo *or* mémoire *f* vidéo *or* mémoire image; **video monitor =** moniteur *m or* écran *m* vidéo; *(informal)* **video nasties =** films *mpl* d'épouvante *or* d'horreur sur vidéocassettes *or* sur bandes vidéo; **video phone** = vidéophone *m or* visiophone *m;* **video player** = lecteur *m* vidéo; **video port** = port *m* vidéo; **video random access memory (VRAM)** = mémoire vidéo à accès aléatoire (VRAM); **video recorder** = magnétoscope *m;* **video signal** = signal *m* vidéo; **video scanner** = scanner *m* d'images vidéo *or* vidéoscanner *m;* **new video scanners are designed to scan three-dimensional objects** = les nouveaux vidéoscanners ont été conçus pour le balayage d'objets à trois dimensions; **video standards** = standards *mpl or* normes *fpl* vidéo; **videotape** = bande *f* vidéo; **videotape recorder** = magnétoscope *m;* **video terminal** = terminal *m* vidéo *or* écran vidéo avec clavier

◊ **videotext** *or* **videotex** *noun* vidéotex *m or* vidéographie *f* interactive

view *verb (film, etc.)* visionner; *(display)* visualiser; **the user has to pay a charge for viewing pages on a bulletin board** = l'utilisateur paie un droit pour visualiser le tableau d'affichage

◊ **Viewdata**® *noun* système britannique équivalent au Minitel®

◊ **viewer** *noun* **(a)** *(person)* téléspectateur, -trice **(b)** *(device)* visionneuse *f*

◊ **viewfinder** *noun (eyepiece)* viseur *m;* **electronic viewfinder** = viseur électronique

◊ **viewing** *noun (film)* visionnage *m; (display)* visualisation *f*

virgin *adjective (tape or disk)* (disquette *or* bande) vierge

virtual *adjective* virtuel, -elle; **virtual address** = adresse virtuelle; **virtual circuit** = circuit virtuel; **virtual disk** = disque virtuel; **virtual machine** = machine virtuelle; **virtual memory** *or* **virtual storage (VS)** = mémoire virtuelle; **virtual terminal** = terminal virtuel

virus *noun* virus *m*

visible *adjective* visible; **visible light** = lumière *f* visible

visual 1 *adjective* visuel, -elle; **visual programming** = programmation *f*

visuelle **2** *noun* visuel *m;* **visuals** = illustrations *fpl or* iconographie *f*

◊ **visual display terminal (VDT)** *or* **visual display unit (VDU)** *noun* écran *m* de visualisation *or* visuel *m*

◊ **visualize** *verb* visualiser

VLF = VERY LOW FREQUENCY

VLSI = VERY LARGE SCALE INTEGRATION

voice *noun* voix *f;* **voice answer back** = répondeur *m* avec message vocal de synthèse; *(usually 300 - 3400 Hz)* **voice band** = bande *f* (de fréquences) vocale *or* bande de basses fréquences *or* bande téléphonique; **voice data entry** *or* **input** = saisie *f* vocale; **voice grade channel** = canal de basses fréquences; **voice messaging (system)** = répondeur *m* téléphonique; **voice output** = sortie *f* vocale; **voice print** = empreinte *f* vocale; **voice recognition** = reconnaissance *f* vocale *or* de la parole; **voice response** = VOICE OUTPUT; **voice synthesis** = synthèse *f* vocale; **voice synthesizer** = synthétiseur *m* vocal

◊ **voice-over** *noun* voix *f* hors champ *or* voix off

◊ **voice unit** *noun* unité *f* de puissance vocale

> QUOTE the technology of voice output is reasonably difficult, but the technology of voice recognition is much more complex
> *Personal Computer World*

volatile memory *or* **volatile store** *or* **volatile dynamic storage** *noun* mémoire *f* volatile NOTE: opposite is **non-volatile memory**

◊ **volatility** *noun* volatilité *f*

volt *noun* volt *m*

◊ **voltage** *noun* voltage *m or* tension *f;* **voltage dip** *or* **dip in voltage** = chute *f or* baisse *f* de tension; **voltage regulator** = régulateur *m* de tension; **voltage transient** = courant *m* de transit *or* transitoire

volume *noun* **(a)** *(total space)* volume *m* **(b)** *(sound)* volume; **volume control** = réglage *m or* contrôle *m or* bouton *m* du volume

VRAM = VIDEO RANDOM ACCESS MEMORY

VRC = VERTICAL REDUNDANCY CHECK

VS = VIRTUAL STORAGE

VTR = VIDEO TAPE RECORDER

VU = VOICE UNIT

Ww

wafer *noun (slice of silicon)* tranche *f* (de silicium)

◊ **wafer scale integration** *noun* intégration *f* sur tranche de silicium

wait condition *or* **state** *noun* *(processor not active)* état *m* d'attente *or* de latence

◊ **wait loop** *noun* boucle *f* d'attente

◊ **wait time** *noun* délai *m* d'attente *or* latence *f*

◊ **waiting list** *noun* file *f* d'attente

◊ **waiting state** *noun (computer state)* attente *f*

wake up *verb (to start or initiate)* activer *or* alerter; *(from a remote terminal)* **wake up a system =** alerter un système

walk through *verb (to examine each step of a piece of software)* réviser

WAN = WIDE AREA NETWORK

wand *noun (bar code reader or optical device)* stylo *m* optique

warm standby *noun (secondary backup device)* équipement *m* de secours à démarrage semi-automatique

◊ **warm start** *noun (of programme)* reprise *f* sur l'instruction d'arrêt *or* reprise au point d'arrêt

◊ **warm up** *verb (machine)* amorcer

QUOTE warm-up time measures how long each printer takes to get ready to begin printing
Byte

warn *verb* avertir; **he warned the keyboarders that the system might become overloaded =** il a averti les pupitreurs d'une surcharge possible du système NOTE: you warn someone **of** something, or **that** something may happen

◊ **warning** *noun* avertissement *m;* **to issue a warning =** donner un avertissement; **warning notices were put up around the high powered laser =** on a placé des panneaux d'avertissement autour du laser de puissance; **warning light =** voyant *m* d'alarme; **when the warning light on the front panel comes on, switch off the system =** lorsque le voyant placé sur le panneau avant s'allume, il faut éteindre le système

wash PROM *verb* effacer une PROM

waste instruction *noun* instruction *f* de remplissage

Watt *noun* watt *m*

wave *noun* onde *f;* **microwave =** micro-onde *f;* **sound wave =** onde sonore

◊ **waveform** *noun* (forme d') onde; **waveform digitization =** conversion *f* d'une onde en numérique *or* numérisation *f* d'une onde

◊ **waveguide** *noun* guide *m* d'onde

◊ **wavelength** *noun* longueur *f* d'onde

WBFM = WIDEBAND FREQUENCY MODULATION

weigh *verb* peser *or* pondérer

◊ **weight** *noun* poids *m;* **gross weight =** poids brut; **net weight =** poids net; **paper weight =** grammage *m;* **our paper weight is 70 - 90 gsm =** nous avons du papier de 70 - 90 grammes

◊ **weighted** *adjective* pondéré, -ée; **weighted average =** moyenne *f* pondérée; **weighted bit =** bit *m* de poids fort *or* bit lourd

◊ **weighting** *noun* pondération *f*

well-behaved *adjective (program)* (programme) policé; *(informal)* non bidouillé

wetware *noun US (informal)* le cerveau humain *or* la matière grise

What-You-See-Is-All-You-Get (WYSIAYG) *noun* ce que vous voyez est tout ce que vous obtenez

What-You-See-Is-What-You-Get (WYSIWYG) *noun* ce que vous voyez est ce que vous obtenez

while-loop *noun* boucle *f* conditionnelle 'WHILE'

white *adjective & noun* blanc, blanche; *(on video disk)* **white flag** = signal *m* blanc; *(on monitor)* **white level** = niveau *m* de blanc; **white noise** = bruit *m* blanc; **white writer** = imprimante *f* à définition des blancs NOTE: the opposite is **black writer**

wide angle lens *noun* grand-angle *m* *or* objectif *m* grand-angle *or* grand-angulaire

◊ **wide area network (WAN)** *noun* réseau *m* étendu; *compare with* LAN

wideband *noun* large bande *f;* **wideband frequency modulation (WBFM)** = modulation *f* de fréquence à large bande

widow *noun (single line)* (dernière) ligne *f* (d'un paragraphe) isolée en tête de page; *compare* ORPHAN

width *noun* largeur *f;* **line width** = longueur *f* de ligne (en caractères); **page width** = largeur de page (en caractères)

wild card *noun* joker *m;* **a wild card can be used to find all files names beginning DIC =** on peut utiliser un joker pour chercher tous les fichiers commençant par DIC

WIMP = WINDOW, ICON, MOUSE, POINTERS

Winchester disk *noun* disque *m* (dur) Winchester; **Winchester drive** = lecteur *m* de disque Winchester; **removable Winchester =** disque Winchester *or* disque dur amovible

window 1 *noun* fenêtre *f;* **several remote stations are connected to the network and each has its own window onto the hard disk =** plusieurs stations de travail distantes sont connectées au réseau, chacune disposant d'une fenêtre sur le disque dur; **the operating system will allow other programs to be displayed on-screen at the same time in different windows =** le système d'exploitation permet d'afficher d'autres programmes simultanément, chacun dans une fenêtre différente; **active window =** fenêtre active; **command window =** fenêtre de commande; **the command window is a single line at the bottom of the screen =** la fenêtre de commande est une simple ligne en bas de l'écran; **edit window =** fenêtre d'édition; **text window =** fenêtre de texte; **window, icon, mouse, pointer (WIMP) =** intégrateur *m* graphique (à fenêtre, icône, souris, pointeur) *or* WIMP **2** *verb* fenêtrer

◊ **windowing** *noun* fenêtrage *m*

QUOTE when an output window overlaps another, the interpreter does not save the contents of the obscured window

Personal Computer World

QUOTE windowing facilities make use of virtual screens as well as physical screens

Byte

QUOTE you can connect more satellites to the network, each having its own window onto the hard disk

PC Plus

QUOTE the network system uses the latest windowing techniques

Desktop Publishing

QUOTE the functions are integrated via a windowing system with pull-down menus used to select different operations

Byte

wipe *verb (to clean data from a disk)* effacer *or* détruire (des données) *or* blanchir (un disque); **by reformatting you will wipe the disk clean =** si vous reformatez, vous détruirez toutes les données du disque *or* vous blanchirez le disque

◊ **wiper** *noun (of potentiometer, etc.)* curseur *m or* variateur *m*

wire 1 *noun* fil *m* (métallique *or* électrique *or* de liaison); **telephone wires =** fils téléphoniques; *(dot-matrix printer)* **wire printer =** imprimante *f* matricielle; **wire wrap =** connexion *f* enroulée **2** *verb (to install wiring)* câbler; **the studio is wired for sound =** le studio est câblé pour la sonorisation; **wired** or **hardwired program computer** = ordinateur à logique câblée

◇ **wireless 1** noun (old use) poste m (de) radio or (de) T.S.F. **2** adjective sans fil; **wireless microphone** = microphone m sans fil pour transmission or micro-cravate m

◇ **wiretap** noun table f d'écoute

◇ **wiring** noun câblage m; **the wiring in the system had to be replaced** = il a fallu remplacer le câblage du système

WISC = WRITABLE INSTRUCTION SET COMPUTER

woofer noun (informal) haut-parleur m de graves or de basses fréquences

word noun **(a)** mot m; **words per minute (wpm** or **WPM)** = (nombre de) mots par minute; **word break** = coupure f or césure f; **word count** = nombre de mots contenus dans un fichier or un texte; (wordprocessing) **word wrap** or **wraparound** = retour m à la ligne automatique **(b)** (separate item of data) mot; **word length** = longueur f d'un mot; **word marker** = marque f de début de mot; **word serial** = série f de mots (l'un à la suite de l'autre); **word time** = temps m de transfert d'un mot

◇ **word-process** verb éditer or traiter or composer un texte sur ordinateur; **it is quite easy to read word-processed files** = on lit facilement les fichiers de texte composés sur ordinateur

◇ **word-processing (WP)** noun traitement m de texte; **load the word-processing program before you start keyboarding** = chargez le programme de traitement de texte avant de commencer à saisir le texte; **word-processing bureau** = bureau m de traitement de texte

◇ **word-processor** noun **(a)** (machine) machine f de traitement de texte **(b)** (software) logiciel m de traitement de texte

work 1 noun travail m; **work area** = espace m de travail or zone f de travail; **work disk** = disque m de travail or de manoeuvre or d'enregistrement; (scratch file) **work file** = fichier m de travail or de manoeuvre **2** verb fonctionner; **the computer system has never worked properly since it was installed** = depuis

que nous l'avons, l'ordinateur n'a jamais très bien fonctionné

◇ **working** adjective **(a)** (appareil) en état de marche **(b) working store** or **scratchpad** = mémoire f temporaire or mémoire banale or (mémoire) bloc-notes m

◇ **workload** noun charge f de travail

◇ **workspace** noun (space in memory) espace m de manoeuvre or de travail

◇ **workstation** noun (PC) poste (PC) m de travail or station f de travail; **the system includes five workstations linked together in a ring network** = le système comprend cinq postes de travail reliés en anneau; **the archive storage has a total capacity of 1200 Mb between seven workstations** = la mémoire d'archivage a une capacité de 1200 Mo pour sept stations de travail

QUOTE an image processing workstation must provide three basic facilities: the means to digitize, display and manipulate the image data

Byte

WORM = WRITE ONCE READ MANY times memory

wow noun pleurage m

WP = WORD-PROCESSING

WPM or **wpm** = WORDS PER MINUTE

wrap noun (system of threading video tape) **omega wrap** = enrouleur-presseur m de bande magnétique

◇ **wraparound** or **word wrap** noun (word-processing) retour m à la ligne automatique; (of cursor) **horizontal wraparound** = retour à la ligne or saut m de ligne automatique (en limite d'écran)

write verb **(a)** écrire **(b)** (data onto a disk or tape) enregistrer or ranger une donnée en mémoire; **access time is the time taken to read from or write to a location in memory** = le temps d'accès est le temps requis pour consulter une donnée en mémoire ou pour ranger une donnée en mémoire; **write head** = tête f d'enregistrement or d'écriture; **write once, read many times memory (WORM)** = disque m optique WORM (permettant une seule écriture et des lectures multiples); **writing pad** =

tablette *f* à numériser (pour saisie de l'écriture manuelle); **write time** = temps d'écriture *or* d'enregistrement NOTE: you write data **to** a file. Note also: **writing - wrote - has written**

◊ **writable instruction set computer (WISC)** *noun* microprocesseur *m* à jeu d'instructions modifiable (WISC)

◊ **write-permit ring** *noun* anneau *m or* bague *f* de protection d'écriture

◊ **write protect** *verb* protéger (une disquette contre l'écriture indésirée); **write-protect tab** = volet *m* de protection d'écriture

◊ **writer** *noun see* BLACK, WHITE

◊ **writing** *noun (handwriting)* écriture *f; (text)* écrit *m;* **in writing** = par écrit; **to put the agreement in writing** = rédiger un accord; **he has difficulty in reading my writing** = il trouve mon écriture difficile à lire

WYSIAYG = WHAT YOU SEE IS ALL YOU GET

WYSIWYG = WHAT YOU SEE IS WHAT YOU GET

NOTE: say 'WIZIWIG'

Xx

X = EXTENSION

X-axis *noun* axe *m* d'abscisse *or* axe des X

◇ **X-coordinate** *noun* abscisse *f* *or* coordonnée *f* horizontale

◇ **X direction** *noun* horizontale *f*

◇ **X distance** *noun* distance *f* sur l'axe des X

xerographic printer *noun* imprimante *f* xérographique

◇ **xerography** *noun* xérographie *f*

Xerox® **1** *noun* **(a)** *(photocopier)* photocopieur de marque Xerox; **to make a xerox copy of a letter** = photocopier une lettre (avec une machine Xerox); **we must order some more Xerox paper for the copier** = il faut commander de nouveau du papier Xerox pour le photocopieur; **we are having a new Xerox machine installed tomorrow** = on nous installera une nouvelle machine *or* un nouveau photocopieur Xerox demain **(b)** *(photocopy made with a xerox machine)* photocopie *f* (faite avec une machine Xerox); **to send the other party a xerox of the contract** = envoyer une photocopie du contrat à l'autre partie; **we have sent xeroxes to each of the agents** = nous avons envoyé des photocopies à chacun des agents **2** *verb* *(to make a photocopy with a xerox machine)* photocopier; **to xerox a document** = photocopier un document; **she xeroxed all the file** = elle a photocopié tout le dossier

x punch *noun* perforation *f* (de la ligne) 11 *or* perforation X

X-ray 1 *noun* **(a)** *(ray)* rayon *m* X; **X-ray imaging** = radioscopie *f* **(b)** *(photograph)* radiographie *f* *or* radio *f* **2** *verb* radiographier

X-series *noun* protocoles *mpl* de télétransmission de la série X

X-Y *noun* coordonnées *fpl;* **X-Y plotter** = traceur *m* de courbes *or* de graphiques

Yy

yaw noun *(of a satellite)* (mouvement de) lacet *m*

Y-axis noun axe *m* de l'ordonnée *or* axe des Y

◇ **Y-coordinate** noun ordonnée *f or* coordonnée *f* verticale

◇ **Y-direction** noun verticale *f*

◇ **Y-distance** noun distance *f* sur l'axe des Y

yoke noun *(coils around a TV tube)* **deflection yoke** = déflecteur *m* à enroulement

y punch noun perforation *f* (de ligne) 12 *or* perforation Y

Zz

Z = IMPEDANCE

zap *verb* faire disparaître de l'écran *or* nettoyer *or* vider l'écran; **he pressed CONTROL Z and zapped all the text** = il a tapé CONTROL Z pour vider l'écran

Z-axis *noun* axe *m* des Z

zero 1 *noun* zéro *m; **the code for international calls is zero one zero (010)** = (en Grande-Bretagne) le code téléphonique international est zéro un zéro (010); **jump on zero** = effectuer un branchement (conditionnel) à zéro; **zero compression** *or* **zero suppression** = élimination *f* des zéros (non significatifs); **zero flag** = indicateur *m* zéro; **the jump on zero instruction tests the zero flag** = l'instruction de branchement conditionnel à zéro teste l'indicateur zéro; **zero-level address** *or* **immediate address** = adresse *f* immédiate *or* directe **2** *verb* remettre à zéro *or* effacer un fichier; **to zero a device** = remettre à zéro *or* nettoyer un

dispositif programmable; **to zero fill** = garnir de zéros

◇ **zero insertion force (ZIF)** *noun (of connector)* insertion *f* sans friction *or* force *f* d'insertion zéro

ZIF = ZERO INSERTION FORCE

ZIP code *noun US (US postal delivery areas)* code *m* postal (aux E.-U.)
NOTE: the GB equivalent for this is **post code**

zone *noun (part of a screen)* zone *f; (in wordprocessing)* **hot zone** = zone de texte

zoom *verb* faire un zoom

◇ **zooming** *noun* zoom *m*

◇ **zoom lens** *noun* zoom *m or* objectif *m* à focale variable

QUOTE there are many options to allow you to zoom into an area for precision work
Electronics & Wireless World
QUOTE any window can be zoomed to full-screen size by pressing the F-5 function key
Byte

DICTIONNAIRE FRANÇAIS-ANGLAIS
FRENCH-ENGLISH DICTIONARY

Aa

A = AMPERE

A *(représentation hexadécimale du nombre 10)* A

abandonné, -ée *adj* abandoned; **affaire abandonnée** *ou* **sujet abandonné** = dead matter
◊ **abandonner** *vtr (un programme)* to abandon *ou* to exit *ou* to quit (a program); **abandonner prématurément** = to abort

abaque *nm* nomogram *ou* nomograph

aberration *nf* aberration *ou* distortion; **aberration chromatique** = chromatic aberration; **aberration de l'image** = image distortion; **aberration sphérique** = spherical aberration

abîmé, -ée *adj* damaged
◊ **abîmer** *vtr* to damage

abonné, -ée *n* subscriber; **les abonnés du téléphone** = telephone subscribers; **abonné du télex** = telex subscriber; **ligne de jonction d'abonné (au centre téléphonique)** = exchange line

abrégé, -ée *adj* abridged *ou* abbreviated; **adressage abrégé** = abbreviated addressing *ou* abb. add.
◊ **abréviation** *nf* abbreviation; **RAM est l'abréviation de 'Random Access Memory'** = the acronym RAM means Random Access Memory; **dans le texte, on a remplacé le terme 'processeur' par l'abréviation 'proc'** = within the text, the abbreviation 'proc' is used instead of 'processor'

abscisse *nf* X-coordinate; **axe d'abscisse** = X-axis *ou* horizontal axis

absolu,-e *adj* absolute; **adressage absolu** = absolute addressing; **adresse absolue** = absolute address *ou* actual address *ou* machine address *ou* direct (access) address; **l'exécution d'un programme est un peu plus rapide si on utilise uniquement des adresses absolues dans le code** = program execution is slightly faster if you code only with absolute addresses; **assembleur absolu** = absolute assembler; **capacité théorique absolue** = absolute maximum rating; **chargeur absolu** = absolute loader; **codage (binaire) absolu** = absolute coding *ou* specific coding; **code (binaire) absolu** = absolute code *ou* specific code *ou* actual code; **instruction absolue** = absolute instruction *ou* actual instruction; **programme absolu** = absolute program; **valeur absolue** = absolute value; **la valeur absolue de -62,34 est 62,34** = the absolute value of -62.34 is 62.34; **il y a génération d'une valeur absolue des entrées** = an absolute value of the input is generated; *(sans signe négatif)* **en valeur absolue** = unsigned

absorber *vtr* to absorb
◊ **absorptance** *nf* absorptance
◊ **absorption** *nf* absorption; **absorption atmosphérique** = atmospheric absorption; **filtre d'absorption** = absorption filter; **indice d'absorption** = absorptance

accéder (à) *vi* to access *ou* to gain access to; **accéder à un fichier** = to access *ou* to gain access to a file; **elle a accédé au fichier de l'employé stocké sur l'ordinateur** = she accessed the employee's file stored on the computer; **vous ne pouvez accéder aux données que si le fichier est ouvert** = you cannot access the data unless the file is open; **il est impossible d'accéder aux renseignements confidentiels du fichier sans utiliser le mot de passe** = the user cannot gain access to the confidential information in the file without a password; **le gestionnaire du système peut accéder à toutes les partitions à partir de sa partition privilégiée** = the system manager can access anyone else's account from his privileged account; **le premier ordinateur individuel de la série**

ne peut accéder à plus de **640Ko de RAM** = the original PC cannot access more than 640Kbytes of RAM

accélérateur *nm* accelerator
◇ **accélérateur, -trice** *adj* **carte accélératrice** = accelerator card
◇ **accélération** *nf* accélération; **temps d'accélération** = acceleration time
◇ **accéléré, -ée** *adj* **code accéléré** = optimized code *ou* optimum code

accent *nm* accent; **accent aigu** = acute accent; **accent circonflexe** = circumflex accent; **accent flottant** = floating accent; **accent grave** = grave accent; **accent mobile** *ou* **caractère accent** = piece accent
◇ **accentué, -ée** *adj* accented

acceptable *adj* acceptable; **le taux d'erreur était très bas et donc acceptable** = the error rate was very low, and is acceptable
◇ **acceptation** *nf* acceptance; **signal d'acceptation d'appel** = call accepted signal
◇ **accepté, -ée** *adj* **(a)** accepted; **signal d'appel accepté** = call accepted signal **(b)** agreed; **accepté d'avance** = pre-agreed
◇ **accepter** *vtr* **(a)** to accept; **il a accepté le devis de l'imprimeur** = he accepted the quoted price for printing; **il n'a pas accepté le poste de programmeur qu'on lui offrait** = he did not accept the programming job he was offered; **à ce prix-là, on peut accepter que la mallette ait une éraflure** = for the price, the scratched case is acceptable **(b)** to accept *ou* to read; **qui peut être accepté par l'imprimante** = printer-readable; **l'imprimante (à) laser accepte même un imprimé de la taille d'une carte professionnelle** = the laser printer will accept a card as small as a business card; **ce lecteur multidisque accepte aussi bien les disquettes de format 3,5 pouces que 5,25 pouces** = the multi-disk reader will accept 3.5 inch disks as well as 5.25 inch formats; **l'ordinateur principal accepte jusqu'à six postes de travail** = the main computer supports six workstations **(c)** *(être d'accord)* to agree **(d)** to approve

accès *nm* access; **accès aléatoire** = random access; **mémoire vidéo à accès aléatoire (VRAM)** = video random access memory (VRAM); **les lecteurs de** disquettes permettent l'accès aléatoire *ou* direct des données alors qu'une bande magnétique en permet l'accès séquentiel = disk drives are random access, magnetic tape is sequential access memory; **accès asynchrone** = asynchronous access; **accès cyclique** = cyclic access; **accès sur demande (à la mémoire paginée)** = demand fetching; **accès direct** = direct access *ou* random access; **mémoire** *ou* **support à accès direct** = (i) direct access storage device (DASD); (ii) core memory *ou* primary memory; **contrôleur de mémoire à accès direct** = DMA controller; **vol de temps de cycle de la mémoire à accès direct** = DMA cycle stealing; **accès direct à la mémoire** = direct memory access (DMA); **transfert des données par accès direct à la mémoire entre la mémoire principale et le second processeur** = direct memory access transfer between the main memory and the second processor; **voie d'accès direct à la mémoire** = direct memory access channel; *(téléphone)* **accès direct au réseau** = direct outward dialling; **accès direct au système** = direct inward dialling; **accès au disque** = disk access; **(poste de travail) à accès illimité** = open access (workstation); **accès instantané** = instantaneous access; **mémoire à accès intermédiaire** = intermediate access memory (IAM); **accès multiple** = multiple access; **système à accès multiple** *ou* **système multi-accès** = multi-access system; *(circuit)* **accès multiple asservi à la demande** = demand assigned multiple access (DAMA); **accès multiple par division dans le temps** = time division multiple access; **(formation) sans accès à l'ordinateur** = hands off (training); **accès parallèle** = parallel access; **accès rapide** = rapid access; **mémoire à accès rapide** = rapid access memory *ou* fast access memory (FAM); **accès au réseau numérique intégré** = integrated digital access (IDA); **accès sélectif** = random access; **accès séquentiel** *ou* **accès série** = serial access *ou* sequential access; **mémoire à accès séquentiel** = sequential access storage *ou* serial access memory; **méthode d'accès séquentiel indexé (ISAM)** = indexed sequential access method (ISAM); **méthode d'accès séquentiel par clé** = keyed sequential access method (KSAM); *(communication)* **accès temporel multiplexé** = time division multiple access; **avoir accès à** = to access; **avoir**

accès à quelque chose = to have access to something; **avoir accès à un fichier (informatique)** = to have access *ou* to gain access to a file of data; **il a accès à de nombreux fichiers confidentiels** = he has access to numerous sensitive files; **il faut vous rappeler votre mot de passe sinon vous ne pourrez pas avoir accès au système** = if you forget your user ID, you will not be able to log on; **code d'accès (à un système)** = access code; **contrôle d'accès (au système)** = access control; *(communication)* **mémoire à double accès** = dual port memory; **frais d'accès au système** = access charge; **gestion d'accès aux données** = data access management; **gestion d'accès aux disques** = disk access management; **interdire (à quelqu'un) l'accès à un système** = to bar access to a system *ou* to deny access to a system; **après avoir découvert qu'il faisait du piratage, on lui a interdit l'accès au système** = after he was discovered hacking, he was barred access to the system; **liberté d'accès à l'information** = freedom of information; *(communication)* **ligne d'accès** = access line; **méthode d'accès** = access method; **point d'accès** = *(connexion)* port; *(de matériel ou logiciel)* access point; **protection des accès mémoire** = fetch protect; **temps d'accès** = *(aux données)* access time *ou* response time; *(de tête de lecture à une piste ou à une donnée)* seek time *ou* positioning time; **le nouveau disque a un temps d'accès de 35 ms** = the new hard disk drive has a seek time of 35ms; **le temps d'accès de cette RAM dynamique est d'environ 200ns - il existe une version plus rapide si votre fréquence d'horloge est plus élevée** = the access time of this dynamic RAM chip is around 200ns - we have faster versions if your system clock is running faster; **temps d'accès à la mémoire** = memory access time; **code à temps d'accès minimum** = optimum code; **temps d'accès moyen** = average access time; **code à temps d'accès optimisé** = minimum access code *ou* minimum delay code *ou* minimum latency coding *ou* optimum code

◊ **accessible** *adj* accessible; **les détails du fichier client de l'ordinateur principal sont facilement accessibles** = details of customers are easily accessible from the main computer files

accessoire *nm* accessory *ou* attachment; **accessoires** = accessories *ou* ancillary equipment; **plusieurs accessoires, dont un capot d'insonorisation, sont fournis avec l'imprimante** = the printer comes with several accessories, such as a soundproof hood; **il existe de nombreux accessoires pour cet ordinateur populaire** = this popular computer has a large range of accessories; **il existe un accessoire spécial pour l'alimentation du papier en feuille à feuille** = there is a special single sheet feed attachment

accidentel, -elle *adj* accidental; **si vous vous servez d'un disque protégé contre la destruction accidentelle, vous ne perdrez jamais vos données** = if the disk is crash-protected, you will never lose your data

accommodation *nf (de l'oeil)* adaptation; **l'accommodation de l'oeil en réponse aux variations d'intensité de lumière** = the adaptation of the eye in response to different levels of brightness

accompagnement *nm* **module d'accompagnement** = coroutine

accord *nm* **(a)** *(compatibilité)* match; **non accord** = mismatch; **accord d'impédance** = impedance matching; **l'accord d'impédance entre un émetteur et un récepteur réduit la perte de puissance des signaux transmis** = impedance matching between a transmitter and a receiver minimizes power losses to transmitted signals **(b)** **être d'accord avec** = (i) to agree with; (ii) to approve of **(c)** *(contrat)* deal

accordéon *nm* **papier (plié) en accordéon** = accordion fold *ou* fanfold *ou* concertina fold paper

accordé, -ée *adj* matched; **charge accordée** = matched load

◊ **accorder** *vtr* to match

◊ **s'accorder** *vpr* to match *ou* to agree

accrochage *nm (erreur avec arrêt de programme)* lock up

accroché, -ée *adj* hooked; *(combiné)* (receiver) on hook
◊ **accrocher** *vtr* être accroché (dans une boucle) = to hang (in a loop)

accu = ACCUMULATEUR

accumulateur *ou* **accu** *nm* (a) battery (b) *(d'une unité centrale de traitement)* accumulator (register) *ou* ACC (register); **accumulateur externe** = external register
◊ **accumuler** *vtr* to accumulate

accusé *nm* accusé de réception = acknowledgement; *(d'un message)* accusé de réception négatif = negative acknowledge (NAK *ou* NACK); **accusé de réception positif** = affirmative acknowledge (ACK *ou* ACKNLG *ou* ACKNOWLEDGE); **caractère d'accusé de réception** = acknowledge character; **envoyer un accusé de réception** = to acknowledge
◊ **accuser** *vtr* accuser réception = to acknowledge; **accuser réception d'un message** = to acknowledge a message; **l'imprimante émet un signal pour accuser réception des données** = the printer generates an ACK signal when it has received data

achat *nm* *(article)* purchase; **faire des achats** = (i) to buy *ou* to purchase; (ii) to shop *ou* to go shopping; **achats par téléphone** = teleshopping; **achats sur** *ou* **par ordinateur** = computer shopping *ou* electronic shopping

acheminement *nm* routing; **acheminement (en) delta** = delta routing; **acheminement de données** = data routing; **acheminement adaptatif** *ou* **dynamique** = adaptive routing; **acheminement de messages** = message routing; **acheminement fixe** *ou* **présélectionné** = fixed routing; **câble d'acheminement des signaux** = feeder cable; **procédure de contrôle d'acheminement** = routing overheads; **voie d'acheminement** = feeder; *(téléphone)* **système d'acheminement direct des appels** = direct dialling
◊ **acheminer** *vtr* to route *ou* to channel; **il existe une nouvelle façon d'acheminer les données vers l'ordinateur central** = there is a new way of routing data to the central computer

acheter *vtr* to buy *ou* to purchase; **acheter un fichier d'adresses** = to buy a mailing list

achèvement *nm* completion
◊ **achevé d'imprimer** *nm* colophon
◊ **achever** *vtr* to complete

achromatique *adj* achromatic

Ackerman *npr* fonction d'Ackerman = Ackerman's function

acoustique **1** *nf* acoustics **2** *adj* acoustic; **coupleur acoustique** = acoustic coupler; **j'utilise un coupleur acoustique avec mon (ordinateur) portatif** = I use an acoustic coupler with my lap-top computer; **enceinte acoustique** = set of loudspeakers; **ligne à retard acoustique** = acoustic delay line; **mémoire acoustique** = acoustic store *ou* acoustic memory; **niveau de pression acoustique** = sound pressure level (SPL)

acquisition *nf* (a) acquisition; **acquisition de données** = data acquisition *ou* data logging; **système à acquisition de connaissances et de règles** = self-learning (expert) system (b) *(dans une bibliothèque)* accession

acronyme *nm* acronym; **l'acronyme FORTRAN signifie 'Formula Translator'** = the acronym FORTRAN means 'Formula Translator'

actif, -ive *adj* active; **dispositif (électronique) actif** = active device; **fenêtre active** = active window; **fichier actif** = active file; **mode actif** = active state; **réseau en étoile actif** = active star

actinique *adj* actintic; **lumière actinique** = actintic light

action *nf* action; *(photographie)* **champ d'action** = action field
◊ **actionné, -ée** *adj* moved by *ou* driven by; *(logiciel ou procédure)* **actionné par évènement** = event-driven
◊ **actionner** *vtr* to move *ou* to drive; **actionner une touche** = to hit a key

activation *nf* signal d'activation = enabling signal

◊ **activé, -ée** *adj (logiciel ou procédure)* driven; *(commutateur)* enabled *ou* selected *ou* armed; **programme activé par commande** = command-driven program; **activé par événement** = event-driven; **activé par reconnaissance des données** = data-driven; **interruption activée** = armed interrupt

◊ **activer** *vtr* to enable *ou* to select *ou* to arm *ou* to wake up *ou* to activate; **activer un circuit intégré** = to chip select (CS)

activité *nf* active state *ou* activity; **taux d'activité** = activity ratio; **(mode de) chargement en fonction du taux d'activité** = activity loading; **ratio *ou* taux d'activité d'un fichier** = file activity ratio

actualisation *nf* dispositif d'actualisation (d'un système) = retrofit

actuel, -elle *adj* present *ou* current; **copiez les données du fichier précédent dans le fichier actuel** = copy data into the present workspace from the previous file

acuité *nf* acuity; **acuité visuelle** = visual acuity

acutance *nf* acutance

ADA = AUTOMATIC DATA ACQUISITION; **langage ADA** = ADA

adaptable *adj* adaptable; **langage adaptable** = extensible language

adaptateur *nm* adapter *ou* adaptor; *(pour connexion)* adapter plug; **l'adaptateur du câble permet de relier le scanner à une interface SCSI** = the cable adapter allows attachment of the scanner to SCSI interface; **le câble de liaison entre le scanner et l'adaptateur est compris** = the cable to connect the scanner to the adapter is included in the package; **adaptateur de canal de transmission** = channel adapter; **adaptateur de canal de transmission de données** = data adapter unit; **adaptateur d'écran** = display adapter; **adaptateur graphique couleur CGA** = colour graphics adapter (CGA); **adaptateur**

graphique couleur EGA = enhanced graphics adapter (EGA); **adaptateur d'interface de communication** = communications interface adapter; **adaptateur de ligne *ou* de voie de communication** = data adapter unit; **adaptateur de l'ordinateur hôte** = host adapter; **adaptateur de vitesse de transmission** = baud rate generator; **carte adaptateur** = adapter card

◊ **adaptatif, -ive** *adj* adaptive; **routage adaptatif** = distributed adaptive routing; **routage adaptatif protégé** = isolated adaptive routing

◊ **adaptation** *nf* adaptation

◊ **adapté, -ée** adapted *ou* conditioned *ou* modified; **(logiciel) adapté à l'ordinateur** = machine-intimate (software); **langage adapté aux problèmes** = problem-orientated language (POL)

◊ **adapter** *vtr* to adapt *ou* to condition *ou* to modify; **est-ce qu'il est possible d'adapter cet ordinateur pour les disquettes 5,25 pouces?** = can this computer be adapted to take 5.25 inch disks?; **le clavier a été adapté pour la vente en Europe** = the keyboard was modified for European users; **adaptez les données brutes à un format standard** = condition the raw data to a standard format

addition *nf (supplément)* addition; *(opération mathématique)* addition *ou* sum; **l'addition de chacune des colonnes du tableau donne un sous-total** = in the spreadsheet each column is added to make a subtotal; **addition destructive** = destructive addition; **addition sans retenue** = addition without carry; **registre d'addition** = add register; **le signe de l'addition (+)** = plus *ou* plus sign; **temps d'addition** = add time *ou* addition time; **premier terme d'une addition** = augend; **second terme d'une addition** = augmenter

◊ **additionnel, -elle** *adj (dispositif)* additional *ou* add-on *ou* add-in; **carte additionnelle** = add-in card; **sous-programme additionnel** = inserted subroutine; **un disque dur additionnel augmentera la capacité de mémoire de l'ordinateur** = the add-on hard disk will boost the computer's storage capabilities

◊ **additionner** *vtr* to add (up)

◇ **additionneur** *nm* adder; **additionneur binaire** *ou* **additionneur DCB** = BCD adder; **additionneur à deux entrées** = half adder *ou* two input adder; **additionneur complet** *ou* **à trois entrées** = full adder *ou* three input adder; **additionneur parallèle** = parallel adder; **additionneur à retenue automatique (très rapide)** = carry look ahead; **additionneur séquentiel** = serial adder

◇ **additionneur-soustracteur** *nm* adder-subtractor

additif, -ive *adj* additive; **synthèse additive (de couleurs)** = additive colour mixing

adhésif *nm* adhesive *ou* glue

◇ **adhésif, -ive** *adj* adhesive *ou* sticky; **bande adhésive** = sticky tape; *(qui sert à tout dans un studio ou l'outil favori du gaffeur)* **bande adhésive noire** = gaffer tape

adjacent, -e *adj* adjacent

adoucir *vtr (une couleur)* to deaden (a colour)

adressable *adj* addressable; **adressable par le contenu** = content-addressable; **fichier** *ou* **location adressable par le contenu** = content-addressable file *ou* location; **mémoire adressable par le contenu** = content-addressable memory (CAM); **les 5Mo de RAM sont adressables en totalité** = all the 5Mb of RAM is addressable; **curseur adressable** = addressable cursor; **opération non adressable** = no-address operation

◇ **adressage** *nm* addressing; **adressage abrégé** *ou* **simplifié** = abbreviated addressing *ou* abb. add.; **adressage absolu** = absolute addressing; **adressage associatif** = associative addressing *ou* content-addressable addressing; **adressage binaire** = bit addressing; **infographie à adressage binaire** = bit-mapped graphics; **adressage direct** = direct addressing; **adressage élargi** = augmented addressing; **adressage des entrées/sorties** = I/O mapping; **adressage immédiat** = immediate addressing; **adressage implicite** = implied addressing; **l'adressage implicite pour l'accumulateur est inclus dans**

l'instruction **LDA,16** = implied addressing for the accumulator is used in the instruction LDA,16; **adressage indexé** = indexed addressing; **adressage indirect** = deferred addressing *ou* indirect addressing *ou* second-level addressing; **adressage inhérent** *ou* **particulier** = inherent addressing; **adressage de page** = page addressing; **terminal à adressage protégé** = addressable terminal; **adressage de registre** = register addressing; **adressage relatif** = base addressing; **capacité** *ou* **disponibilité d'adressage** = addressability *ou* addressing capacity; **méthode d'adressage** = addressing method; **mode d'adressage** = addressing mode; **niveau d'adressage** = addressing level; **définir une table d'adressage binaire** = to bit-map; **temps d'adressage** = address access time

adresse *nf* **(a)** *(en mémoire)* address; **adresse absolue** = absolute address *ou* actual address *ou* direct (access) address; **adresse de base** = base address *ou* presumptive address; **adresse calculée** = generated address; **adresse courante** = current address; **registre d'adresse courante** = current address register (CAR); **voici l'adresse de début des données** = this is the address at which the data starts; **adresse directe** *ou* **à un niveau** = direct address *ou* one-level address; **adresse effective** = effective address; **adresse d'entrée** = entry point; **adresse d'exécution** = execution address; **adresse explicite** = explicit address; **adresse générée** = generated address; **adresse immédiate** = zero-level address *ou* immediate address; **adresse indexée** = indexed address; **adresse initiale** *ou* **de lancement** = initial address; **adresse d'instruction** = instruction address; **registre d'adresse d'instruction** = instruction address register (IAR) *ou* instruction counter; **adresse machine** = machine address; **adresses d'octets** = byte addresses; **adresse origine (de la première instruction d'un programme)** = (program) origin *ou* initial address *ou* base address *ou* presumptive address; **adresse de premier niveau** = first-level address; **adresse de piste** = track address; **adresse primitive** = base address *ou* presumptive address; **adresse réelle** = first-level address; **adresse de référence** = reference address; **adresse de référence directe** = direct reference address;

adresse relative = floating address *ou* relative address; **adresse symbolique** = tag *ou* floating address *ou* symbolic address; **chaque mot en mémoire possède une adresse unique** = each separate memory word has its own unique address; **instruction à adresse unique** = one address instruction; **code d'instruction à adresse unique** = single address code; **ordinateur à adresse unique** = one address computer; **adresse virtuelle** = virtual address; **bus d'adresses** = address bus *ou* address highway; **voies de liaison d'un bus d'adresses** = bus address lines; **calcul d'une adresse** = address computation; **champ d'adresse** = address *ou* operand field; **changement d'adresse en mémoire** = relocation *ou* memory edit; **changer d'adresse** = to relocate (data); **l'adresse de cette donnée est changée au cours de l'éxécution** = the data is relocated during execution; **créer** *ou* **définir une adresse** = to address (data); **marque de début d'adresse** = address mark; **décodeur d'adresse** = address decoder; **espace adresse** = address space; **(code de) fin d'adresse** = end of address (EOA); **format d'adresse** = address format; **modification d'adresse** = address modification; **mot adresse** = address word; **plus le mot adresse est long, plus la mémoire adressable de l'ordinateur augmente** = a larger address word increases the amount of memory a computer can address; **piste d'adresses** = address track; **registre d'adresse** = address register *ou* base register; **registre des adresses en mémoire** = memory address register (MAR); **opération sans adresse** = no-address operation; **table de correspondance des adresses** = address mapping; **signal de validité d'adresse** = address strobe; **message à une seule adresse** = single address message; **une adresse plus une** = one-plus-one address; **instruction à deux adresses** = two-address instruction; **instruction à deux adresses plus une** = two-plus-one-address instruction; **instruction à trois adresses** = three-address-instruction; **instruction à quatre adresses** = four-address instruction; **quatre adresses plus une** = four-plus-one address; **instruction à n adresse(s) plus une** = n-plus-one address instruction *ou (domicile, etc.)* address; **adresse télégraphique** = cable address; **fichier d'adresses (destiné aux mailings)** = mailing list; **acheter un fichier d'adresses** = to buy a mailing list;

établir un fichier d'adresses = to build up a mailing list; **son nom figure sur notre fichier d'adresses** = his name is on our mailing list; **notre fichier contient les adresses de deux mille sociétés en Europe** = we keep an address list of two thousand businesses in Europe; **répertoire d'adresses par rues** = street directory

◊ **adresser** *vtr* **(a)** *(informatique)* to address **(b)** *(courrier)* to address; **adresser une lettre** *ou* **un colis** = to address a letter *ou* a parcel

aérien, -ienne *adj* aerial; *(photo ou film)* **vue aérienne** = aerial image

affaiblir *vtr (signal)* to attenuate; *(batterie)* to drain
◊ **s'affaiblir** *vpr* to fade *ou* to decay; **le signal s'est affaibli rapidement** = the signal decayed rapidly
◊ **affaiblissement** *nm (d'un signal)* attenuation *ou* loss *ou* fading *ou* decay *ou* leakage; **affaiblissement dû au brouillage** = interference fading; **affaiblissement d'insertion** = insertion loss

affectation *nf (d'une tâche)* assignment; *(d'une somme)* allocation; **instruction d'affectation** = assignment statement; **affectation de capitaux à un projet** = allocation of capital to a project
◊ **affecter** *vtr* **(a)** *(une zone de mémoire ou une tâche)* to assign; **deux PC ont été affectés à la préparation des étiquettes** = two PCs have been assigned to outputting the labels **(b)** *(une somme à un projet)* to allocate

affichage *nm (sur écran)* display *ou* on-screen display *ou* readout; **le logiciel de PAO permet l'affichage des polices de caractères** = the dtp package offers on-screen font display; **affichage alphanumérique** = alphanumeric display; **affichage de caractères** *ou* **de texte** = character display; **affichage du contenu des registres** *ou* **affichage de la configuration des registres** = register map; **affichage couleur** = colour display; **affichage à cristaux liquides** = liquid crystal display (LCD); **affichage de données** = information output; **affichage destructif** = destructive readout (DRO); **affichage électroluminescent** = electroluminescent display; **affichage graphique** = graphic display; **définition**

d'affichage graphique = graphic display resolution; **affichage noir sur blanc** = positive display; **affichage numérique** = digital readout; **cette horloge avait un affichage numérique** = the clock had a digital readout; **affichage d'une page** = page display; **affichage réduit** *ou* **d'une partie de page** = part page display; **affichage plasma** = gas discharge display *ou* gas plasma display *ou* plasma display; **affichage en positif** = positive presentation; **contrôleur** *ou* **pilote d'affichage** = display controller; **couleur d'affichage** = display colour; **dimension d'affichage** = display size; **dispositif** *ou* **écran d'affichage** = readout device; **espace d'affichage** = display space; **format d'affichage** = display format; **mode affichage** = display mode; **registre d'affichage** = display register; **tableau d'affichage** = notice board; **zone d'affichage de texte** = text screen

◊ **affiche** *nf* poster

◊ **afficher** *vtr (à l'écran)* to display *ou* to call up; *(faire apparaître à un moment précis)* to pop on; **l'heure était affichée** = the readout displayed the time; **les coordonnées du client étaient affichées sur l'écran** = the customer's details were displayed on the screen; **le système d'exploitation permet d'afficher d'autres programmes simultanément, chacun dans une fenêtre différente** = the operating system will allow other programs to be displayed on-screen at the same time in different windows; **un processeur d'images qui peut lire, afficher et manipuler les images vidéo** = an image processor that captures, displays and manipulates video images; **on a affiché à l'écran les adresses de tous les clients** = all the customers addresses were called up; **on trouve habituellement quatre options affichées en haut de l'écran** = there are usually four options along the top of the screen; **pour afficher le menu déroulant cliquer l'icône sur le haut de l'écran** = the pull-down menu is viewed by clicking over the icon at the top of the screen

affirmatif, -ive *adj* affirmative *ou* positive; **réponse affirmative** = positive response

◊ **affirmation** *nf* assertion

AFNOR = ASSOCIATION FRANCAISE DE NORMALISATION

agence *nf* agency; **agence de presse** = news agency

agenda *nm (carnet)* diary; *(grande feuille)* planner; **agenda de bureau** = desk diary; **(programme) agenda** = diary management (program)

agglomérer *vtr (des données)* to gather write

agrandir *vtr* to enlarge *ou* to expand; *(photo)* to enlarge *ou* to magnify; **cette photo a été agrandie 200 fois** = the photograph has been magnified 200 times

◊ **agrandissement** *nm* enlargement *ou* expansion; *(photo)* enlargement *ou* magnification; *(avec un zoom)* zooming; **on a utilisé un agrandissement de la photo pour voir les détails plus clairement** = an enlargement of the photograph was used to provide better detail

agréer *vtr* to approve *ou* to accept

agrégat *nm* aggregate

agrégé, -ée *adj* aggregate; **données agrégées** = data aggregate

aide *nf (assistance)* help *ou* aid; **ils ont besoin d'aide pour la programmation** = they need some help with their programming; **aide au diagnostic** = diagnostic aid; **l'ordinateur est une aide importante pour le traitement d'une grande quantité de données** = the computer is a great aid to rapid processing of large amounts of information; **aides à la programmation dans un langage déterminé** = language support environment; **système d'aide à la décision (SAID)** = decision support system (DSS); *(pour clavier)* **grille d'aide** = key *ou* keyboard overlay; **sans la grille d'aide, je ne saurais jamais quelle touche de fonction je dois utiliser** = without the key overlay, I would never remember which function key does what

◊ **aider** *vtr (assister)* to help *ou* to aid; *(soutenir)* to back

aigu, -uë 1 *adj* acute; **accent aigu** = acute accent; **sons aigus** = high notes **2**

nm (sons aigus) **haut-parleur d'aigus =** tweeter

aiguillage *nm* switch
◊ **aiguille** *nf* needle; **imprimante à aiguilles =** dot-matrix printer

aimant *nm* magnet; **micro(phone) à aimant mobile =** moving coil microphone
◊ **aimanté, -ée** *adj* magnetic

aire *nf (surface)* area

ajouté, -ée *adj* added; **réseau à valeur ajoutée =** value added network (VAN); **revendeur de systèmes à valeur ajoutée =** value added reseller (VAR)
◊ **ajouter** *vtr* to add; *(introduire)* to insert; **avec les touches de fonction, il est facile d'ajouter au texte ou de le couper =** adding or deleting material from the text is easy using function keys; **les producteurs de logiciels ont ajouté un nouveau progiciel de gestion à leur gamme de produits =** the software house has added a new management package to its range of products

ajustement *nm* adjustment *ou* tuning
◊ **ajuster** *vtr* to adjust *ou* to tune *ou* to regulate; **pour ajuster la luminosité de l'écran, tourner le bouton placé à l'arrière du moniteur =** the brightness can be regulated by turning a knob at the back of the monitor; **ajuster avec grande précision =** to fine tune; **ajuster la tête de lecture =** to align a read/write head

alarme *nf* alarm; **caractère (de déclenchement) d'alarme =** bell character; **tout le personnel doit quitter le bâtiment dès que la sonnerie d'alarme retentit =** all staff must leave the building if the alarm sounds; **voyant d'alarme =** warning light

albumen *nm* albumen; *(photo)* **plaque photosensible à l'albumen =** albumen plate

alcalin, -e *adj* **pile alcaline =** dry cell

alcool *nm* alcohol *ou* spirit; **duplicateur à alcool =** spirit duplicator

aléatoire *adj* random; **accès aléatoire =** random access; **les lecteurs de disquettes permettent l'accès aléatoire des données alors qu'une bande magnétique en permet l'accès séquentiel =** disk drives are random access, magnetic tape is sequential access memory; **mémoire à accès aléatoire =** random access memory (RAM) *ou* random access storage; **mémoire vidéo à accès aléatoire (VRAM) =** video random access memory (VRAM); **dispositif mémoire à accès aléatoire =** random access device; **nombre aléatoire =** random number; **générateur de nombres aléatoires =** random number generator; **processus aléatoire =** random process; **traitement aléatoire (des données) =** random processing; **pseudo-aléatoire =** pseudo-random

alerter *vtr* to alert; **alerter un système =** to wake up a system

algèbre *nf* algebra; **algèbre booléenne** *ou* **algèbre de Boole =** Boolean algebra *ou* Boolean logic

ALGOL *voir* ALGORITHMIQUE

algorithme *nm* algorithm; **algorithme de compactage =** compacting algorithm; **algorithme cryptographique** *ou* **de cryptage =** cryptographic algorithm; **algorithme d'effacement de lignes cachées =** hidden line algorithm; **algorithme hash =** hashing function; **algorithme de pagination =** paging algorithm; **algorithme utilisé le moins récemment =** least recently used algorithm
◊ **algorithmique** *adj* algorithmic; **langage algorithmique =** algorithmic language (ALGOL)

aligné, -ée *adj* aligned *ou* in alignment
◊ **alignement** *nm* alignment; **alignement automatique des virgules =** automatic decimal adjustment; **alignement de la tête de lecture =** head alignment; **réglage d'alignement des têtes** *ou* **des angles d'azimut =** azimuth alignment; **c'est cette petite vis qui sert à régler l'alignement des têtes** *ou* **des angles d'azimut =** azimuth alignment is adjusted with this small screw; **bord d'alignement =** aligning edge; **dispositif**

d'alignement = aligner; **perte d'alignement** = gap loss; **téton** *ou* **pige d'alignement** = alignment pin

◇ **aligner** *vtr (tête de lecture)* to align *ou* to line up; *(texte ou colonne)* to align *ou* to range *ou* to line up; **les chiffres sont alignés l'un à la suite de l'autre plutôt que d'être présentés en colonnes** = the figures are presented in rows, not in columns; **en appuyant sur la touche de tabulation en début de ligne, pour se placer à la colonne 10, la liste avait été parfaitement alignée** = the list was neatly lined up by tabbing to column 10 at the start of each new line; *(justifier)* **aligner à gauche** = to range left

alimentation *nf* **(a)** *(papier)* feed *ou* paper feed; *(cartes perforées)* card feed; **alimentation automatique du papier** = auto advance; **alimentation par l'avant** = front feed; **alimentation du papier en continu** = continuous feed; **alimentation du papier (en) feuille à feuille** = (single) sheet feed; **ce dispositif contrôle l'alimentation du papier (en) feuille à feuille** = the device controls the copy flow; **système d'alimentation feuille à feuille** = cut sheet feeder; **système d'alimentation du papier** = feeder; **bac d'alimentation feuille à feuille** = sheet feed attachment; *(pour film)* **bobine d'alimentation** = feed reel; **scanner avec alimentation automatique du papier** = paper-fed scanner **(b)** *(électricité)* power supply; **bloc d'alimentation** = power pack *ou* power supply unit (PSU); **alimentation auxiliaire** *ou* **de secours** = battery backup; **alimentation de secours de la mémoire** = memory backup capacitor; **alimentation statique sans coupure** = uninterruptable power supply (UPS); **brancher une ligne sur une source d'alimentation** = to pull up a line; **(dispositif de) contrôle de l'alimentation** = power monitor; **coupure d'alimentation de courant** = power dump

◇ **alimenter** *vtr* to feed

l'alimentation est assurée par une pile au lithium de 6V ou 4 piles au manganèse de 1,5V
Science et Vie

alinéa *nm* indent *ou* indentation; **faire un alinéa** = to indent (a paragraph); **comptez deux espaces pour l'alinéa du premier paragraphe** = indent the first paragraph two spaces

aller *nm* outward direction *ou* journey; **canal (de transmission) aller** = forward channel; **temps de propagation aller (et) retour** = up and down propagation time

◇ **aller** *vi* to go; *(varier)* **aller (de ... à)** = to range (from ... to); **la gamme des produits de la société va du micro portable au gros ordinateur multiposte** = the company's products range from a cheap lapheld micro to a multistation mainframe; *(dans un texte)* **aller à la ligne** = to start a new line *ou* a new paragraph; **caractère indiquant d'aller à la ligne** = new line character

allocation *nf* allocation *ou* assignment; **allocation dynamique** = dynamic allocation; **allocation dynamique des voies de communication** = adaptive channel allocation; **allocation de mémoire** = storage allocation; **allocation de temps a un projet** = allocation of time to a project; **programme d'allocation** = allocation routine

allonger *vtr* to extend

allophone *adj* allophone

alloué, -ée *adj* **fréquence allouée** = assigned frequency; **liste des emplacements non alloués** = uncommitted storage list

◇ **allouer** *vtr* to allocate *ou* to assign; **on peut allouer une étiquette aux touches de fonction** = tags can be allocated to function keys; **le système d'exploitation a alloué presque toute la mémoire principale au tableur** = the operating system allocated most of main memory to the spreadsheet program

alpha *nm (lettre de l'alphabet grec)* alpha; **enrouleur alpha** = alpha wrap; **particule alpha** = alpha-particle; **sensibilité aux particules alpha** = alpha-particle sensitivity; **rayonnement alpha** = alpha radiation; **technique alpha bêta** = alpha beta technique

alphabet *nm* alphabet; **lettres de l'alphabet** = alphabetic character set

◇ **alphabétique** *adj* alphabetical; **chaîne de caractères alphabétiques** = alphabetic string; **ordre alphabétique** = alphabetical order; **en** *ou* **par ordre alphabétique** = in alphabetical order *ou* alphabetically; **classer (des données) en** _ou_ **par ordre alphabétique** = to alphasort _ou_ to alphabetize; **les noms sont classés par ordre alphabétique** = the sequence of names is arranged alphabetically; **les fichiers sont classés en** _ou_ **par ordre alphabétique sous le nom du client** = the files are arranged alphabetically under the customer's name; **veuillez saisir les données bibliographiques et les mettre en ordre alphabétique** = enter the bibliographical information and alphabetize it

◊ **alphabétiquement** _adv_ alphabetically _ou_ in alphabetical order

alphagéométrique _adj_ alphageometric

alphamosaïque _adj_ alphamosaic

alphanumérique _adj_ alphanumeric; **affichage alphanumérique** = alphanumeric display; **caractères alphanumériques** = alphanumeric characters _ou_ alphanumerics; **chaîne de caractères alphanumériques** = alphanumeric string; **clavier alphanumérique** = alphanumeric keyboard; **données alphanumériques** = alphanumeric data; **opérande alphanumérique** = alphanumeric operand; **touche alphanumérique** = alphanumeric key

alphaphotographique _adj_ alphaphotographic

altération _nf (du signal)_ distortion

◊ **altérer** _vtr (signal)_ to distort; _(données ou fichier)_ to mung up

alternance _nf_ alternation; **redresseur (de) simple alternance** = half wave rectifier

◊ **alternat** _nm_ **à l'alternat** = alternately; **mode de transmission bidirectionnelle à l'alternat** = either-way operation

◊ **alternateur** _nm_ alternator

◊ **alternatif, -ive** _adj_ alternating; **courant alternatif (CA)** = alternating current (AC)

◊ **alterné, -ée** _adj_ alternate; **mode alterné** = alternate mode

◊ **alterner** _vtr_ to alternate; **faire alterner** = to alternate

A-MAC _(basse fréquence multiplexée)_ A-MAC

ambiant, -e _adj_ ambient; **lumière ambiante** = available light; **niveau de bruit ambiant** = ambient noise level; **température ambiante** = ambient temperature

ambigu, -uë _adj_ ambiguous; **nom de fichier ambigu** = ambiguous filename

◊ **ambiguïté** _nf_ ambiguity; **erreur d'ambiguïté** = error ambiguity

ambisonique _adj_ **enregistrement ambisonique** = ambisonics

âme _nf (d'un câble)_ core

amélioration _nf_ improvement _ou_ enhancement; **filtre d'amélioration du contraste** = contrast enhancement filter

◊ **amélioré, -ée** _adj_ improved _ou_ upgraded _ou_ enhanced _ou_ optimized; **code amélioré** = optimum code _ou_ optimized code

◊ **améliorer** _vtr_ to improve _ou_ to upgrade _ou_ to enhance _ou_ to optimize; **le nouveau modèle peut être amélioré sans renvoi chez le fournisseur** = the new model has an on-site upgrade facility

amont _nm_ **en amont** = above _ou_ upstream

amorçage _nm (de système)_ booting _ou_ boot-up; _(automatique)_ auto-boot; **programme d'amorçage** = bootstrap; **chargeur de programme d'amorçage** = bootstrap loader

◊ **amorce** _nf_ **(a)** _(d'une bande ou d'un film)_ head _ou_ leader **(b)** _(programme)_ bootstrap

◊ **amorcer** _vtr_ **(a)** _(système)_ to boot up _ou_ to bootstrap; _(automatiquement)_ to auto boot **(b)** to warm up

amortir _vtr (un son ou bruit)_ to deaden; **les capots d'insonorisation servent à amortir le bruit des imprimantes** = acoustic hoods are used to deaden the noise of printers

amovible _adj_ exchangeable _ou_ removable _ou_ movable; **disque dur amovible** = exchangeable disk storage

(EDS) *ou* removable hard disk *ou* disk cartridge; **disque (dur) non amovible** = fixed disk; **disque Winchester amovible** = removable Winchester; **ROM amovible** = ROM cartridge

ampère (A) *nm* ampere *ou* amp (A)

ampli *nm* amplifier; **ne placez pas le micro trop près du haut-parleur sinon le retour va saturer l'ampli** = make sure the microphone is not too close to the loudspeaker or positive feedback will occur and you will overload the amplifier

amplificateur *ou* **ampli** *nm* amplifier; **amplificateur audio** = audio amplifier; **amplificateur de basse fréquence** = audio amplifier; **amplificateur de courant (du bus)** = bus driver; **amplificateur à faible bruit** = low noise amplifier; **amplificateur d'image** = image enhancer; **amplificateur MASER** = microwave amplification by stimulated emission of radiation (MASER); **amplificateur operationnel** = operational amplifier *ou* op amp; **amplificateur de signal** = (i) launch amplifier; (ii) line driver; **amplificateur de téléphone** = telephone repeater; **classe d'amplificateur** = amplifier class

◊ **amplification** *nf (du son ou du signal)* amplification; *(de l'image)* magnification; **augmentez l'amplification** = increase the amplification (of the input signal); **l'amplification est si grande qu'elle cause une distorsion du signal** = the amplification is so high that it distorts the signal; **boucle d'amplification** = positive feedback

◊ **amplifié, -ée** *adj (son ou signal)* amplified; *(image)* magnified; **téléphone amplifié** *ou* **à écoute amplifiée** = amplified telephone

◊ **amplifier** *vtr (son ou signal)* to amplify; *(image)* to magnify; **le signal reçu doit être amplifié avant d'être traité** = the received signal needs to be amplified before it can be processed

◊ **amplitude** *nf (d'un signal)* amplitude *ou* magnitude; *(du son)* **amplitude dynamique** = dynamic range; **amplitude maximum enregistrée** = maximum reading; **distorsion d'amplitude** = amplitude distortion; **modulation d'amplitude (MA)** = amplitude

modulation (AM); **modulation d'impulsions en amplitude (MIA)** = pulse amplitude modulation (PAM); **quantification d'amplitude** = amplitude quantization

> l'amplitude des échos renvoyés renseigne sur la nature des tissus traversés et l'axe X, sur leur position
> *Techniques hospitalières*

analogique *adj* analog; **appareil analogique** = analog *ou* analogue; **calculateur analogique** = analog computer; **carte d'entrée analogique** = analog input card; **carte de sortie analogique** = analog output card; **circuit analogique** = analog circuit *ou* gate; **enregistrement analogique** = analog recording; **multimètre analogique** = analog multimeter (AMM); **ordinateur analogique** = analog computer; **porte** *ou* **circuit analogique** = analog gate; **représentation analogique** = analog representation; **signal analogique** = analog signal; **signal analogique modulé** = pseudo-digital signal; **voie analogique** = analog channel

◊ **analogique-numérique** *adj* analog to digital (A to D *ou* A/D); **convertisseur analogique-numérique (CAN)** = analog to digital converter *ou* A to D converter (ADC); *(numérisateur)* digitizer; **le signal vocal est d'abord passé par le convertisseur analogique-numérique avant d'être analysé** = the speech signal was first passed through an A to D converter before being analysed; **convertisseur analogique-numérique parallèle** = flash A/D; *voir aussi* NUMERIQUE-ANALOGIQUE

◊ **analogue** *nm&adj* analog *ou* analogue

> les mémoires analogiques enregistrent l'image telle qu'elle est vue sur l'écran
> *Techniques hospitalières*

analyse *nf* **(a)** analysis; **analyse cryptographique** = cryptanalysis; **analyse de données** = data analysis; *(d'un programme)* **analyse fonctionnelle** = functional specification; **analyse des médias** = media analysis *ou* media research; **analyse mémoire** = dump; **analyse numérique** = numerical analysis; **analyse de réseaux** = network analysis; **analyse du signal dans le temps** = time domain analysis; **analyse de systèmes** = systems analysis **(b)** *(d'un langage informatique)* **analyse lexicale** = lexical analysis *ou* parsing; **analyse syntaxique** = syntactical analysis **(c)** *(résumé)* abstract

◊ **analyser** *vtr* to analyse *ou* to analyze; **analyser un listing** = to analyse a computer printout

◊ **analyseur** *nm* analyzer; **analyseur de bruit** = decibel meter; **analyseur d'état logique** = logic state analyzer; **analyseur de fréquence** = frequency analyzer; **analyseur d'image** = image processor; **analyseur de spectre** = spectrum analyzer

◊ **analyste** *nm&f* analyst; **analyste (de) système** = systems analyst

◊ **analyste-programmeur, -euse** *n* analyst/programmer *ou* programmer/analyst

anamorphose *nf* anamorphic image

anastigmate *adj* anastigmatic

ancêtre *nm* ancestor; **fichier ancêtre** = ancestral file

angle *nm* angle; *(inclinaison)* **angle d'un caractère** = character skew; *(entre deux signaux)* **angle de phase** *ou* **de déphasage** = phase angle; *(d'une lentille)* **angle de réception** = acceptance angle

angström *nm* angstrom

animation *nf* animation; **animation (d'images) sur ordinateur** = computer animation

◊ **animé, -ée** *adj* busy *ou* animated; **dessin animé** = cartoon; *(d'un film)* **fond animé** = busy background

◊ **animer** *vtr* to animate

anneau *nm* **(a)** *(dispositif)* ring; **anneau de protection d'écriture** = write-permit ring **(b)** **réseau en anneau** = ring (data) network *ou* loop network; **(réseau en) anneau de Cambridge** = Cambridge ring; **le système comprend cinq postes de travail reliés en anneau** = the system includes five workstations linked together in a ring network

annexe *nf* appendix; **voir annexes pour tout renseignement supplémentaire** = for further details see the appendices

◊ **annexer** *vtr* to append

annonciateur, -trice *adj* (signal) **annonciateur** = annunciator

annotation *nf* annotation; **annotation typo(graphique)** = marking up

◊ **annoter** *vtr* to annotate; *(en spécifiant la typographie)* to mark up

annuaire *nm* directory; **annuaire des téléphones** *ou* **annuaire téléphonique** = telephone book *ou* phone book *ou* telephone directory; **cherche son adresse dans l'annuaire (téléphonique)** = look up his address in the directory *ou* in the phone book; **annuaire téléphonique par professions** = classified directory; **annuaire par rues** = street directory

annulaire *adj* ring; **compteur annulaire** = ring counter

annulation *nf* cancellation; *(effacement)* deletion *ou* removal; **l'annulation de cette instruction résoudrait le problème** = the removal of this instruction could solve the problem; **annulation de fichier** = file deletion; **caractère d'annulation** = cancel character (CAN); **le logiciel envoie automatiquement un caractère d'annulation à chaque erreur** = the software automatically sends a cancel character after any error

◊ **annuler** *vtr* to cancel; *(effacer)* to delete *ou* to remove

anode *nf* anode

anomale *adj* anomalistic; **période anomale** = anomalistic period

◊ **anomalie** *nf* fault *ou* error; **anomalie persistante** = hard error; **rapport d'anomalies** = exception report

anormal, -e *adj* abnormal; **arrêt anormal** = abnormal termination; **erreur anormale** = abnormal error; **fin anormale** = abnormal end *ou* abend; **une commande d'interruption venant d'une imprimante défectueuse a provoqué une fin anormale de traitement** = an interrupt from a faulty printer caused an abend; **interruption anormale** = abnormal end *ou* abend *ou* abnormal termination; **programme de récupération de fichier après une interruption anormale** = abend recovery program; **en cas de panne, la**

perte de données sera minimale grâce au nouveau programme de récupération des fichiers après interruption anormale = if a fault occurs, data loss will be minimized due to the improved abend recovery program

◊ **anormalement** *adv* abnormally; **le signal est anormalement faible** = the signal is abnormally weak

ANSI = AMERICAN NATIONAL STANDARDS INSTITUTE; **clavier ANSI** = ANSI keyboard

antémémoire *nf* cache memory *ou* cache storage; **antémémoire d'instruction** = instruction cache

antenne *nf* antenna *ou* aerial; **antenne en boucle** = loop antenna; **antenne collective de télévision (câblée)** = community antenna television (CATV); **antenne contrarotative** = de-spun antenna; **antenne (uni)directionnelle** = directional antenna; **antenne (en) éventail** *ou* **semi-circulaire** = fan antenna; **antenne isotrope** = isotropic radiator; **antenne linéaire** = linear array; **antenne parabolique** = dish aerial; **nous utilisons une antenne parabolique pour capter les signaux transmis par satellite** = we use a dish aerial to receive signals from the satellite; **antenne de relais régional** = master antenna television system (MATV); **câble d'antenne** = aerial cable; **câble antenne-circuit** = feeder cable; **gain d'antenne** = antenna gain; **réseau d'antennes** = antenna array

pour qu'une antenne parabolique capte correctement les émissions renvoyées par les satellites géostationnaires, son axe doit être parallèle aux ondes acheminant ces émissions
Science et Vie

antérieur, -e *adj* **(a)** prior *ou* previous; **instruction qui annule l'instruction antérieure** = instruction which cancels the instruction which precedes it **(b)** anterior *ou* front; **panneau antérieur** = fascia plate *ou* front panel

◊ **antérieurement** *adv* previously

anti- *préfixe* anti-

◊ **anti-écho** *adj inv* **dispositif anti-écho** = echo suppressor

anticipation *nf* anticipation; **référence par anticipation** = forward reference

◊ **anticipé, -ée** *adj* anticipated; **appel d'instruction anticipé** = pre-fetch(ing); **lecture anticipée** = look ahead; **retenue anticipée** = carry look ahead

anticopie *adj* **système** *ou* **dispositif anticopie** = copy protection *ou* copy protect device; **toutes les disquettes sont munies d'un dispositif anticopie** = all disks are copy protected; **il arrive qu'une protection anticopie défectueuse entraîne la détérioration du disque dur** = a hard disk may crash because of faulty copy protection

antiparasite *adj* **dispositif antiparasite** = interference suppressor

antirebond *nm&adj* de-bounce

aperçu *nm* viewing; **fonction 'présentation - aperçu'** = previewer; **la fonction intégrée 'présentation - aperçu' permet de visualiser le document et de vérifier s'il s'est glissé des erreurs** = the built-in previewer allows the user to check for mistakes

APL langage (de programmation) APL = A Programming Language (APL)

apochromatique *adj* apochromatic; **objectif apochromatique** = apochromatic lens

apogée *nf* apogee

apostrophe (') *nf* apostrophe

apparaître *vi* to appear; **faire apparaître** = to reveal; *(sur l'écran)* to display; **la touche HELP fera apparaître sur l'écran une description des différentes options** = by keying HELP, the screen will display the options available to the user; **c'est la dernière image du film: faites apparaître les titres** = this is the last frame of the film so show the titles

appareil *nm* machine; *(électrique)* appliance; *(de petite taille)* device; **appareil en bon état de marche** = functional unit; **appareil cinématographique** = cine camera; **tout**

appareil électrique doit être mis à la terre = all electrical appliances should be properly earthed; **appareil d'entrée/sortie** = I/O device; **appareil photographique** *ou* **appareil photo** = camera; **appareil (photo) à plaques** = plate camera; **appareil de sortie** = output device; **appareils (de) téléinformatique** = data communications equipment (DCE); **appareil de traitement de texte** = word processor; **appareil de traitement de texte spécialisé** = dedicated word processor; **arrêt dû à une défaillance de l'appareil** = machine check; **(logiciel) qui ne fonctionne que sur un type d'appareil** = machine-dependent (software); **priorité d'un appareil** = device priority

apparence *nf* aspect *ou* appearance

apparié, -ée *adj* paired; **registres appariés** = paired registers

appel *nm* **(a)** *(d'un programme ou d'une instruction)* call; **appel d'instruction anticipé** = pre-fetch; **appel de page sur demande** = demand paging; **appel récursif** = recursive call; **instruction d'appel** = call instruction; **c'est ici qu'il faudrait introduire l'instruction d'appel** = the subroutine call instruction should be at this point; **reprise au point d'appel** = fall back recovery; **séquence d'appel** = calling sequence **(b)** *(entre stations)* call; **durée d'un appel** = call duration; **la durée de l'appel varie suivant la complexité de la transaction** = call duration depends on the complexity of the transaction; **les frais sont fonction de la durée de l'appel** = charges are related to call duration; **scanner de contrôle d'appel** = communications scanner; **signal d'appel accepté** *ou* **signal d'acceptation d'appel** = call accepted signal; **signal de contrôle d'appel** = call control signal; **unité** *ou* **système d'appel** = calling unit **(c)** *(de l'ordinateur principal aux terminaux ou périphériques)* **appel sélectif** = polling; **appel sélectif de groupe** = group poll; **temps d'appels sélectifs** = polling overhead; **caractères d'appel sélectif** = polling characters; **interruption d'appel sélectif** = polled interrupt; **intervalle d'appels sélectifs** = polling interval; **ordre d'appel (des terminaux)** = polling list **(d)** *(téléphonique)* (phone *ou* telephone) call; *(numérotation)* dialling; **(système d')** **appel automatique d'un**

correspondant = auto-dial (system); *(relie l'ordinateur au téléphone)* **système** *ou* **unité d'appel automatique** = automatic calling unit (ACU); **modem à appel automatique** = dial-in modem; **appel en PCV** = collect call; *US* transferred charge call; **(système d') acheminement direct des appels** = direct dialling; **enregistrer le nombre et la durée des appels** = to log calls; **faire un appel** = to make a (phone *ou* telephone) call; **personne qui fait un appel (téléphonique)** = caller; **faire un appel groupé** = to ring down; *(d'un système d'appel ACU)* **indicateur d'appel** = ring indicator (RI); **prendre un appel** = to answer the telephone *ou* to take a telephone call; **tonalité (d'appel)** = dialling tone *ou* dial tone; **transfert d'appel (automatique)** = call forwarding; **dispositif de transfert** *ou* **de réacheminement** *ou* **de déroutage d'appel** = call diverter; **nous avons demandé le transfert à la maison des appels que nous recevons au bureau** = we are having all calls forwarded from the office to home **(e)** **(système d')** **appel de personne** = (radio) paging; **appeler** *ou* **chercher à joindre quelqu'un par système d'appel** *ou* **par signaleur d'appel** = to page someone

◊ **appeler** *vtr* **(a)** *(un programme ou une routine)* to call *ou* to invoke; **dès réception de l'entrée, on appelle la première fonction** = after an input is received, the first function is called up **(b)** *(un périphérique ou une station)* to call **(c)** *(afficher)* **appeler à l'écran** = to call up **(d)** *(au téléphone)* to telephone *ou* to phone *ou* to call (someone) *ou* to make a (telephone) call; **ne me téléphonez pas, c'est moi qui vous appellerai** = don't phone me, I'll phone you; **je vous appellerai au bureau demain** = I'll call you at your office tomorrow; **appeler en direct** = to dial direct; **vous pouvez appeler New York en direct depuis Londres** = you can dial New York direct from London; **appeler la standardiste** = to dial the operator; **appeler pour faire venir quelque chose** = to phone for something; **il a appelé un taxi** = he phoned for a taxi; **il a appelé à propos de la commande de papier listing** = he phoned about the order for computer stationery **(e)** **appeler quelqu'un par système d'appel (de personne)** *ou* **par signaleur d'appel** *ou* **par bip** = to page someone

appendice *nm* appendix; **vous trouverez la liste complète dans l'appendice =** a complete list is printed in the appendix

application *nf* application; **applications informatiques =** computer applications; **circuit intégré spécifique à une application (ASIC) =** application specific integrated circuit (ASIC); *(dans un réseau ISO/OSI)* **couche application =** application layer; **générateur d'application =** report program generator (RPG); **langage d'application =** job-orientated language *ou* problem-orientated language (POL); **logiciel** *ou* **programme d'application =** applications software *ou* applications program; **l'éditeur multifenêtre est utilisé pour créer et éditer les programmes d'application =** the multi-window editor is used to create and edit applications programs; **progiciel d'application =** applications package; **programmeur d'application =** applications programmer; **terminal d'application =** job-orientated terminal

appliquer *vtr* to apply; **pour faire un circuit imprimé il faut d'abord recouvrir la carte d'une résine photosensible puis appliquer le masque du circuit, exposer, développer et graver pour finalement obtenir le tracé =** to make the PCB, coat the board with photoresist, place the opaque pattern above, expose, then develop and etch, leaving the conducting tracks

◊ **s'appliquer (à)** *vpr* to apply (to something)

apprécier *vtr* to appreciate *ou* to approve of (something)

apprendre *vtr* to learn *ou* to master (a subject *ou* a technique); **nous avons appris assez rapidement à utiliser le nouveau système de traitement de texte =** we mastered the new word-processor quite quickly

apprentissage *nm* training *ou* learning; **courbe d'apprentissage =** learning curve

approbation *nf* approval

approché, -ée *adj* approximate *ou* approximating; **en utilisant une valeur approchée de A à la place de D =** using approximating A to D

approuver *vtr&i* to approve something *ou* of something; **le conseil d'administration doit approuver le choix du logiciel =** the software has to be approved by the board

approvisionnement *nm* supply
◊ **approvisionner** *vtr* to supply

approximatif, -ive *adj* approximate *ou* rough; **calcul approximatif =** rough calculation; **j'ai fait un calcul approximatif sur le dos d'une enveloppe =** I made some rough calculations on the back of an envelope; **calcul approximatif du temps de saisie =** approximation of keyboarding time; **nous avons calculé de façon approximative le temps nécessaire à la saisie du texte =** we have made an approximate calculation of the time needed for keyboarding; **résultat approximatif =** approximation; **ce résultat n'est qu'approximatif =** the final figure is only an approximation
◊ **approximation** *nf* *(résultat approximatif)* approximation; *(calcul approximatif)* rough calculation
◊ **approximativement** *adv* approximately

appuyer *vi* to press (on) *ou* to touch *ou* to push (something); **appuyer sur une touche =** to press *ou* to hit a key; **appuyez sur la touche ECHAPPEMENT pour arrêter le programme =** to end the program, press ESCAPE

après *prép* **(a)** after; **édition après compilation** *ou* **après calculs =** post-editing **(b)** **d'après =** according to; **d'après les résultats de l'an dernier =** based on last year's figures
◊ **après-vente** *adj inv* **service après-vente (SAV) =** *(bureau)* customer service department; *(service offert)* maintenance service *ou* aftersales service *ou* backup service; **nous offrons à nos clients un service après-vente gratuit =** we offer a free backup service to customers

arabe *adj* Arabic; **chiffres arabes =** Arabic numbers *ou* figures *ou* numerals;

les pages sont numérotées en chiffres arabes = the page numbers are written in Arabic figures

arbitrage *nm* arbitration; **arbitrage de bus** = bus arbitration; **bus d'arbitrage** = contention bus

arborescence *nf (structure en arbre)* tree *ou* forest (structure); **une arborescence est formée de branches reliées les unes aux autres par des points de liaison ou noeuds** = a tree is made of branches that connect together at nodes; **arborescence optimale** = minimal tree; **arborescence en puits** = sink tree; **élément final d'une arborescence** = leaf; **tri en arborescence** = tree selection sort

◊ **arborescent, -e** *adj* **système arborescent** = tree and branch network system

arbre *nm (structure)* tree (structure); **arbre binaire** = binary tree; **arbre de décision** = decision tree

archétype *nm* archetype

architecture *nf* architecture; **architecture à bus multiples** = multiple bus architecture; **architecture d'un circuit intégré** = chip architecture; **architecture de micro-ordinateur** = microcomputer architecture; **architecture MIMD** *ou* **architecture multiflux d'instruction-multiflux de données** = multiple instruction stream - multiple data stream (MIMD); **architecture MISD** *ou* **architecture multiflux d'instruction-monoflux de données** = multiple instruction stream - single data stream (MISD); **architecture orientée vers l'objet** *ou* **adaptée à l'objet** = object architecture *ou* object-orientated architecture; **architecture en pelure d'oignon** = onion skin architecture; **cet ordinateur possède une architecture en pelure d'oignon comprenant un noyau central, un système d'exploitation, un langage de bas niveau et le programme utilisateur** = the onion skin architecture of this computer is made up of a kernel at the centre, an operating system, a low-level language and then the user's program; **architecture de réseau** = networking *ou* network architecture *ou* systems network architecture (SNA); **architecture d'un**

système = computer architecture *ou* computer organization; **architecture en tranches** = bit-slice architecture *ou* design

archivage *nm* archiving; **copie pour archivage** = archive copy *ou* file copy; **mémoire d'archivage** = archive storage; **la mémoire d'archivage a une capacité de 1200Mo pour sept stations de travail** = the archive storage has a total capacity of 1200Mb between seven workstations; **méthode d'archivage** = filing system; **qualité d'archivage** = archival quality

◊ **archivé, -ée** *adj* archived; **copie archivée** = archived copy

◊ **archiver** *vtr* to archive; **archiver des documents** = to file documents

◊ **archives** *fpl* archive(s); **copie d'archives** = archived copy; **fichier archives** = archive file

◊ **archiviste** *nm&f* archivist

argument *nm* argument; **argument décisif** = deciding factor; **l'excellence des graphiques a constitué l'argument décisif** = the deciding factor was the superb graphics

arithmétique **1** *nf* arithmetic; **arithmétique en double précision** = double precision arithmetic; **arithmétique externe** = external arithmetic; **arithmétique interne** = internal arithmetic; **arithmétique à virgule fixe** = fixed-point arithmetic; **arithmétique en virgule flottante** = floating point arithmetic **2** *adj* arithmetic; **capacité de calcul arithmétique** = arithmetic capability; **décalage arithmétique** = arithmetic shift; **élément arithmétique étendu** = extended arithmetic element; **fonctions arithmétiques** = arithmetic functions; **instruction arithmétique** = arithmetic instruction; **opérateur** *ou* **symbole (d'une opération) arithmétique** = arithmetic operator; **opération arithmétique** = arithmetic operation; **registre arithmétique** = arithmetic register; **unité arithmétique et logique (UAL)** = arithmetic logic unit (ALU) *ou* arithmetic unit; **vérification arithmétique** = arithmetic check

armature *nf* **armature de déflexion** = deflection yokes

armé, -ée *adj* armed *ou* enabled; **dispositif armé** = armed *ou* active device ◊ **armer** *vtr* to arm *ou* to enable *ou* to activate

arrangement *nm* order *ou* pattern *ou* layout; **arrangement binaire** = bit pattern

arrêt *nm* (a) *(d'un appareil)* stop *ou* halt *ou* pause; *(fin d'une opération)* ending *ou* termination; *(défaillance)* failure *ou* check; *(position d'un commutateur)* 'power off' *ou* 'off'; **arrêt anormal** = abnormal termination; **arrêt automatique** = auto stop *ou* automatic power off; *(d'un programme)* **arrêt conditionnel** = conditional breakpoint; *(causé par un défaut du support magnétique)* **arrêt de courte durée** = check; **arrêt dû à une défaillance de l'appareil** = machine check; **arrêt désordonné** = disorderly close-down; **arrêt dynamique** = dynamic stop; **arrêt de l'impression** = print pause; *(d'un programme)* **arrêt inattendu** = hangup; **arrêt pour manque de papier** = form stop; **arrêt programmé** = programmed halt; **arrêt de tabulation** = tab stop *ou* tabulation stop; *(panne)* **arrêt total** = dead halt *ou* drop dead halt; **le manuel n'explique pas la marche à suivre en cas d'arrêt total de la machine** = the manual does not say what to do if a dead halt occurs; **arrêt de transmission de données** = data break; *(appareil)* **à l'arrêt** = inactive (machine); **bit** *ou* **élément d'arrêt** = stop bit *ou* stop element; *(pour téléphone)* **boîtier d'arrêt** = barrier box; **code d'arrêt** = stop code; *(d'un programme)* **condition d'arrêt** = halt condition; **instruction d'arrêt** = halt instruction *ou* stop instruction *ou* breakpoint instruction; *(imprimerie)* **ligne d'arrêt** = holding line; **mécanisme d'arrêt** = shut-off mechanism; *(d'un programme)* **point d'arrêt** = breakpoint *ou* cutoff; **remise en marche** *ou* **reprise au point d'arrêt** = fall back recovery; **reprise sur l'instruction d'arrêt** *ou* **reprise au point d'arrêt** = warm start; **protocole de contrôle par signal d'arrêt** = stop and wait protocol; **symbole d'arrêt (dynamique)** = breakpoint symbol; **temps d'arrêt** = stop time (b) **faire un arrêt sur image** = to freeze (frame); **le processeur d'images permet de faire un arrêt sur image** = with an image processor you can freeze a video frame

arrêter *vtr* to stop *ou* to halt *ou* to shut down; *(terminer)* to close *ou* to end; *(interrompre)* to interrupt; *(empêcher)* to inhibit; **arrêtez l'éxécution du programme, avant qu'il efface d'autres fichiers** = abort the program before it erases any more files; **arrêter (quelque chose) graduellement** = to phase out; **(instruction d')** **arrêter une tâche** = kill job ◊ **s'arrêter** *vpr* to stop

arrière 1 *nm* back; **pour ajuster la luminosité de l'écran, tourner le bouton placé à l'arrière du moniteur** = the brightness can be regulated by turning a knob at the back of the monitor **2** *adj* back; **la prise est située sur le panneau arrière** = the socket is on the back panel; **on trouve une variété de connecteurs sur le panneau arrière de l'unité centrale** = there is a wide range of connectors at the back of the main unit **3** *adv* **marche arrière** = backward mode; **faire marche arrière** = to reverse ◊ **arrière-plan** *nm* background; **ce nouveau processeur graphique permet de manipuler indépendamment les images d'arrière-plan et d'avant-plan ainsi que les plans-objets** = the new graphics processor chip can handle background, foreground and sprite movement independently; **impression en arrière-plan** = print spooling; **l'impression peut être exécutée en arrière-plan pendant que vous travaillez sur un autre document** = background printing can be carried out whilst you are editing another document; **tâche d'arrière-plan** = low-priority work; **traitement d'arrière-plan** = background processing

arrivée *nf* (a) arrival *ou* end; **(point d')** **arrivée** = far end *ou* receiving end; *(transmission)* **terminal d'arrivée** = receive only (RO) (b) **langue d'arrivée** = target language

arrondi *nm* *(au plus près)* rounding; *(par défaut)* truncation; **arrondi à un nombre fixe de décimales** = automatic decimal adjustment; **erreur d'arrondi** = approximation error *ou* round off error *ou* rounding error; *(par défaut)* truncation error ◊ **arrondir** *vtr* *(au plus près)* to round off; *(par défaut)* to truncate *ou* to round down; *(par excès)* to round up; **arrondir**

23,456 à 23,46 = to round off 23.456 to 23.46; **3,5678 arrondi par défaut à 3,56 =** 3.5678 truncated to 3.56; **on peut arrondir 2,651 à 2,65 par défaut =** we can round down 2.651 to 2.65; **on peut arrondir 2,647 à 2,65 par excès =** we can round up 2.647 to 2.65

◊ **arrondissement** *nm* rounding

arséniure *nm* arsenide; **arséniure de gallium (GaAs) =** gallium arsenide

article *nm* **(a)** *(d'un fichier)* article *ou* record; **votre article contient divers champs regroupés sous une même rubrique =** your record contains several fields that have been grouped together under the one heading; **article chaîné =** chained record; **fichier avec articles chaînés =** threaded file; **article logique =** logical record **(b)** *(de journal ou de revue)* article; **il a écrit, pour le journal local, un article concernant le groupe d'utilisateurs =** he wrote an article about the user group for the local newspaper **(c)** *(item de production)* article; **article en sus** *ou* **en option =** extra; **numérotation européenne des articles (NEA) =** European Article Number (EAN) **(d)** *(d'un contrat)* clause *ou* article; **voir l'article 8 du contrat =** see clause 8 of the contract

artificiel, -elle *adj* man-made; **intelligence artificielle (IA) =** artificial intelligence (AI) *ou* machine intelligence

l'intelligence artificielle n'est plus un domaine réservé: tous les utilisateurs peuvent y avoir accès
L'Evénement

ASA = AMERICAN STANDARDS ASSOCIATION *(sensibilité d'un film)* **indice ASA =** ASA exposure index

ascendant, -e *adj* upward; **analyse ascendante =** bottom up analysis; **conception ascendante (d'un programme) =** bottom up method; *(sur l'écran)* **défilement ascendant du générique =** crawl; *(dans un système expert)* **méthode ascendante =** hill climbing

ASCII = AMERICAN STANDARD CODE FOR INFORMATION INTERCHANGE; **caractère ASCII =** ASCII character; **clavier ASCII =** ASCII keyboard; **code ASCII =** ASCII code; **le code ASCII est**
le code de caractères le plus fréquemment utilisé = the ASCII code is the most frequently used character coding system; **fichier ASCII =** ASCII file; **utilisez un programme de traitement de texte ou un autre programme qui produira un fichier ASCII standard =** use a word processor or other program that generates a standard ASCII file

aspect *nm* aspect

assemblage *nm* **(a)** *(conversion d'un programme en code machine)* assembly; **assemblage de caractères =** character assembly; **il y a un certain délai pendant lequel s'effectue l'assemblage du programme en code objet =** there is a short wait during which time the program is assembled into object code; **assemblage de documents =** document assembly *ou* document merge; **des erreurs de syntaxe repérées au cours de l'assemblage du programmme source =** syntax errors spotted whilst the source program is being assembled; **code d'assemblage =** assembly code; **codes mnémoniques d'assemblage =** assembler mnemonics *ou* mnemonic operation codes; **durée d'assemblage =** assembly time; **instruction d'assemblage =** pseudo-operation; **langage d'assemblage =** assembly language *ou* assembler language *ou* base language; **langage d'assemblage pour microprogramme =** microprogram assembly language; **liste** *ou* **listing** *ou* **impression d'un programme d'assemblage =** assembly listing; **période** *ou* **temps d'assemblage =** assembly time; **programme d'assemblage =** assembler (program) *ou* assembly (language) program *ou* assembly routine; **système d'assemblage =** assembly system **(b)** *(liaison de différents programmes ou fichiers)* linking *ou* merging; **(instruction d') assemblage de fichiers =** link files **(c)** *(montage d'un appareil)* assembly; **les pièces du lecteur de disquettes sont fabriquées au Japon, mais l'assemblage se fait en France =** the parts for the disk drive are made in Japan and assembled in France

assembler *vtr* **(a)** *(convertir un programme)* to assemble (a program) **(b)** *(relier différents programmes)* to link *ou* to join *ou* to merge **(c)** *(réunir les cahiers d'un livre)* to collate **(d)** *(monter un appareil)* to assemble

◊ **assembleur** *nm (programme)* assembler (program) *ou* assembly (language) program; **assembleur absolu =** absolute assembler; **assembleur croisé =** cross-assembler; **assembleur de langage =** language assembler; **programme assembleur pour macrolangage =** macro assembler *ou* assembly program; **assembleur une passe =** one-pass assembler *ou* single-pass assembler; **ce nouvel assembleur une passe travaille très vite =** this new one-pass assembler is very quick in operation; **assembleur (en) deux passes =** two-pass assembler; **message d'erreur de l'assembleur =** assembler error message

◊ **assembleur/désassembleur** *nm* assembler/disassembler; **assembleur/désassembleur de paquets =** packet assembler/disassembler (PAD); **le terminal éloigné est relié à un assembleur/désassembleur de paquets qui lui permet d'accéder à l'ordinateur hôte =** the remote terminal is connected to a PAD device through which it accesses the host computer

◊ **assembleuse** *nf (machine pour assembler les cahiers d'un livres)* collator

assertion *nf* assertion

asservi, -e *adj* slave; *(puits ou collecteur de données)* **asservi à un bus =** bus slave; **asservi aux codes contrôle =** control driven; **accès mutiple asservi à la demande =** demand assigned multiple access (DAMA); **multiplexage asservi à la demande =** demand multiplexing; **non asservi à l'horloge =** unclocked; **écran asservi =** slave tube; **processeur asservi =** slave processor; **terminal asservi =** slave terminal

comme dans tout système asservi, des problèmes de stabilité interviennent lors de la conception, imposant telle ou telle architecture
Electronique Radio Plans

assigné, -ée *adj* assigned; **fréquence assignée =** assigned frequency

◊ **assigner** *vtr* to assign

assistance *nf* **(a)** backup *ou* support (service); **nous offrons à nos clients un service d'assistance gratuit =** we offer a free backup service to customers; **assistance technique =** *(par téléphone)* support hotline; *(sur le lieu de travail)* on-site maintenance **(b)** consultancy; **il offre une assistance technique =** he offers a consultancy service; **société d'assistance technique =** a consultancy firm

◊ **assisté, -ée** *adj* assisted; **assisté par ordinateur =** computer-aided *ou* computer-assisted; **conception** *ou* **création assistée par ordinateur (CAO) =** computer-aided *ou* assisted design (CAD); **création et fabrication assistées par ordinateur (CFAO) =** computer-aided *ou* assisted design/computer aided *ou* assisted manufacture (CAD/CAM); **dessin assisté par ordinateur (DAO) =** computer-aided drafting; **enseignement assisté par ordinateur (EAO) =** computer-aided *ou* assisted instruction (CAI); **entraînement assisté par ordinateur (ENAO) =** computer-aided *ou* assisted training (CAT); **fabrication assistée par ordinateur (FAO) =** computer-aided *ou* assisted manufacture (CAM); **formation assistée par ordinateur (FAO) =** computer-aided *ou* assisted learning (CAL); **ingénierie assistée par ordinateur (IAO) =** computer-aided *ou* assisted engineering (CAE); **publication assistée par ordinateur (PAO) =** desktop publishing (DTP) *ou* electronic publishing; **rencontres matrimoniales assistées par ordinateur =** computer dating; **test assisté par ordinateur (TAO) =** computer-aided *ou* assisted testing (CAT); **traduction assistée par ordinateur =** machine translation

◊ **assister 1** *vtr (aider)* to help *ou* to aid **2** *vi (participer à)* to attend

associatif, -ive *adj* associative; **adressage associatif =** associative addressing *ou* content-addressable addressing; **mémoire associative =** parallel search storage *ou* associative memory *ou* content-addressable memory (CAM) *ou* search memory *ou* searching storage; **montage associatif =** associational editing; **processeur à mémoire associative =** associative processor; **recherche associative =** chaining search; **registre de mémoire associative =** associative storage register

association *nf* **(a)** association; **Association française de normalisation (AFNOR) =** *(équivalent de)* British Standards Institute (BSI) **(b)** *(adresse)* **temps d'association =** binding time

◊ **associé, -ée 1** *n* associate **2** *adj* associate *ou* joined; *(par deux)* paired; **registres associés** = paired registers

◊ **associer** *vtr* to associate; *(adresse)* to bind

assortir *vtr* to match

assourdir *vtr (un son)* to deaden

◊ **assourdissement** *nm (d'un son)* muting *ou* deadening

assurance *nf* assurance; **assurance de qualité** = quality assurance; **assurance qualité dans le domaine du génie logiciel** = software quality assurance (SQA)

◊ **assurer** *vtr (confirmer)* to ensure; **mettre en place le dispositif de protection d'écriture pour vous assurer de ne pas perdre vos données** = pushing the write-protect tab will ensure that the data on the disk cannot be erased

astable *adj* astable; **multivibrateur astable** = astable multivibrator

astérisque (*) *nm* asterisk

astigmatisme *nm* astigmatism

astucieux, -euse *adj* smart

asynchrone *adj* (i) asynchronous; (ii) unclocked; **accès asynchrone** = asynchronous access; **communication asynchrone** = asynchronous communication; **émetteur/récepteur asynchrone universel** = universal asynchronous receiver/transmitter (UART); **contrôleur d'émetteur/récepteur asynchrone universel** = UART controller; **interface pour communications asynchrones** = asynchronous communications interface adapter (ACIA); **mode asynchrone** = asynchronous mode; **ordinateur asynchrone** = asynchronous computer; **port (d'accès) asynchrone** = asynchronous port; **l'utilisation de ports asynchrones ne demande pas un matériel spécialisé** = when asynchronous ports are used no special hardware is required; **transmission asynchrone** = asynchronous transmission

atelier *nm (d'usine)* shop *ou* workshop; **atelier de composition** = composing room; **atelier flexible** = flexible manufacturing system (FMS)

atmosphère *nf* atmosphere

◊ **atmosphérique** *adj* atmospheric; **absorption atmosphérique** = atmospheric absorption; **bruit atmosphérique causé par le soleil** = helios noise; **conditions atmosphériques** = atmospheric conditions

atome *nm* atom

◊ **atomique** *adj* atomic; **horloge atomique** = atomic clock

> dans un atome, la plupart des électrons tournent autour du noyau et leur mouvement de rotation suffit encore à engendrer un champ magnétique
> *Science et Vie*

attacher *vtr* to attach *ou* to fix; *(avec un trombone, etc.)* to clip; **les corrections sont attachées à la sortie d'imprimante** = the corrections are clipped to the computer printout

attaque *nf (d'une note)* attack; *(d'un signal)* **enveloppe d'attaque** = attack envelope

atteindre *vtr* to reach; **atteindre un niveau maximum** = to peak; **la tension a atteint le niveau maximum de 1200 volts** = the power peaked at 1,200 volts

attente *nf* (a) wait *ou* waiting state; **boucle d'attente** = wait loop; **délai d'attente** = wait time; **état d'attente** = sleep *ou* wait condition; **file d'attente** = queue *ou* waiting list; **file d'attente des données d'entrée** = input work queue; **file d'attente de demandes de service** *ou* **de données à transmettre** = channel queue; **file d'attente à deux entrées** *ou* **à deux extrémités** = double-ended queue *ou* deque; **file d'attente de fichiers** = file queue; **file d'attente de périphériques** = device queue; **file d'attente des tâches** *ou* **des travaux à exécuter** = job queue *ou* job stream; **la file d'attente trop courte ne suffisait pas à la série de tâches à traiter** = the queue was too short for the backlog of tasks waiting to be processed; **file d'attente qui fonctionne sur le principe 'premier entré premier sorti'** =

FIFO queue; **constitution de file d'attente = ** scheduling; **gestionnaire de file d'attente = ** queue manager *ou* queue management program; **ce nouveau logiciel de stockage des fichiers d'impression comporte un gestionnaire de file d'attente =** this is a new software spooler with a built-in queue management; **imprimer la file d'attente =** to despool; **se joindre à la file d'attente =** to form a queue *ou* to join a queue; **pile en file d'attente =** push-up list *ou* stack; **procédure de file d'attente =** queue discipline; **temps d'attente dans une file d'attente =** queuing time; **message d'attente de commande =** command prompt; **temps d'attente (entre deux opérations) =** idle time; **travail en attente =** backlog **(b)** *(communication)* **marque (d') attente =** mark hold; **mettre en attente =** to hold

attention *nf* attention

atténuation *nf (d'un signal)* attenuation *ou* loss *ou* fading *ou* decay
◊ **atténuer** *vtr (un signal)* to attenuate; *(un son ou un bruit ou une couleur)* to deaden; **les capots d'insonorisation servent à atténuer le bruit des imprimantes =** acoustic hoods are used to deaden the noise of printers
◊ **s'atténuer** *vpr (signal)* to decay *ou* to fade

le taux d'atténuation des signaux, compris entre 50 et 200 décibels par kilomètre, est encore trop élevé
Informatique et bureautique

atterrissage *nm* **atterrissage de la tête de lecture =** head crash

attribuer *vtr* to allocate; *(une valeur)* to set; **le système d'exploitation a attribué presque toute la mémoire principale au tableur =** the operating system allocated most of main memory to the spreadsheet program
◊ **attribut** *nm* attribute; **attributs de visualisation** *ou* **d'écran =** display attributes *ou* screen attributes; **cet attribut contrôle la couleur de l'écran =** this attribute controls the colour of the screen; **table d'attributs =** image table
◊ **attribution** *nf* allocation *ou* assignment; **attribution de bandes de fréquences =** band allocation; **la nouvelle attribution de bandes de fréquences**

permet d'avoir un plus grand nombre de voies de transmission = the new band allocation means we will have more channels

audible *adj* audible; **fréquence audible =** audio frequency

audience *nf* audience

audimat *nm (télévision)* **bataille d'audimat =** ratings battle *ou* war

audio- *préfixe* audio-
◊ **audio** *adj (audible)* audio; **fréquence audio =** audio frequency; **limiteur** *ou* **réducteur de signal audio =** audio compressor; **système audio interactif =** audio active system
◊ **audiocassette** *nf* audio cassette
◊ **audioconférence** *nf* audio conferencing
◊ **audiofréquence** *nf* audio frequency; **gamme des audiofréquences** *ou* **limites de la bande des audiofréquences =** audio range
◊ **audionumérique** *adj* **bande (magnétique) audionumérique =** digital audio tape (DAT); **une bande audionumérique produit un son de très haute qualité =** DAT produces a very high quality sound; **cassette audionumérique =** digital cassette; **disque audionumérique =** digital audio disk (DAD) *ou* compact disk (CD) *ou* CD; **lecteur de disques audionumériques =** compact disk player *ou* CD player
◊ **audiovisuel, -elle** *adj* audiovisual (AV); **matériel audiovisuel =** audiovisual aids

audit *nm (informatique)* audit

augmentation *nf* increase *ou* boost; *(valeur)* increment; **pourcentage d'augmentation =** percentage increase; **quel est le pourcentage d'augmentation? =** what is the increase per cent?
◊ **augmenté, -ée** *adj* increased *ou* boosted; *(en valeur)* incremented *ou* increased; *(en qualité ou en puissance)* upgraded; **code augmenté =** shift code; **dont la dimension peut être augmentée =** expandable
◊ **augmenter** *vtr* to increase *ou* to boost; *(en valeur)* to increment *ou* to increase;

(en qualité ou en puissance) to scale up *ou* to upgrade; *(la dimension)* to expand; **le disque dur supplémentaire va augmenter la capacité de mémoire de 25Mo** = the extra hard disk will boost our storage capacity by 25Mb; **il est possible d'augmenter la mémoire du processeur unique de 2Mo jusqu'à 4Mo** = the single processor with 2Mbytes of memory can be upgraded to 4Mbytes

auteur *nm* author; **droit d'auteur** = copyright; **Convention sur le droit d'auteur** = Copyright Act; **titulaire d'un droit d'auteur** = copyright owner; **violation du droit d'auteur** = infringement of copyright *ou* copyright infringement

authentification *nf* authentication; **authentification de messages** = authentication of messages

◊ **authentifier** *vtr* to authenticate

◊ **authentique** *adj* authentic

auto- *préfixe* self-

◊ **auto-adaptable** *adj* adaptive; **système auto-adaptable** = adaptive *ou* dynamic system

◊ **auto-adaptatif, -ive** *adj* self-adapting; **système auto-adaptatif** = self-adapting system

◊ **autocommutateur** *nm* automatic exchange; **autocommutateur électronique** = electronic automatic exchange; **autocommutateur électronique privé** = computerized branch exchange (CBX); **autocommutateur privatif (raccordé au réseau public)** = private branch exchange (PBX); **autocommutateur privé (raccordé au réseau public) (PABX)** = private automatic branch exchange (PABX)

◊ **autocontrôle** *nm* **système avec autocontrôle** = self-checking system

◊ **autocopiant, -e** *adj* carbonless; **papier autocopiant** = carbonless paper; **papier commercial avec double autocopiant** = two-part stationery; **nous utilisons des carnets de commandes autocopiants** = we use carbonless order pads

◊ **autocorrecteur, -trice** *adj* self-correcting; **code autocorrecteur** = self-correcting code

◊ **autodétecteur, -trice** *adj* self-checking; **code autodétecteur (d'erreur)** = self-checking code

◊ **autodiagnostic** *nm* self-diagnostic

◊ **autodidacte** *adj (système)* self-learning (system)

◊ **auto-enrichissant, -e** *adj* **système auto-enrichissant** = self-learning system

◊ **auto-entretenu, -e** *adj* **mémoire vive (RAM) auto-entretenue** = self-refreshing RAM

automate *nm* robot; **automate bancaire** = automated teller machine (ATM); *US* automatic telling machine

automatique **1** *nm (téléphone)* **l'automatique** = direct dialling system *ou* subscriber trunk dialling (STD) **2** *adj* automatic; **alignement automatique des virgules** = automatic decimal adjustment; **alimentation automatique (du papier)** = auto advance; **(système d') appel automatique d'un correspondant** *ou* **numérotation automatique** = auto-dial (system); *(relie l'ordinateur au téléphone)* **système** *ou* **unité d'appel automatique** = automatic calling unit (ACU); **modem à appel automatique** = dial-in modem; **arrêt automatique** = auto stop; **(dispositif d') arrêt** *ou* **de mise hors tension automatique** = automatic power off; **central téléphonique automatique** = automatic telephone exchange; **changeur (de disques) automatique** = record changer; **chargeur automatique** = automatic loader; **composition automatique de lettres standard** = automatic letter writing; **compteur d'impulsions automatique (à domicile)** = automatic message accounting; **système avec contrôle automatique** = self-checking system; **correction automatique d'erreurs** = automatic error correction; **(système de) démarrage** *ou* **lancement automatique** = auto boot; **détection automatique d'erreurs** = automatic error detection; **distributeur automatique (de cigarettes, etc.)** = automatic vending machine; **distributeur automatique de billets** = *(de banque - DAB)* cash dispenser; *(de parking)* ticket machine; **enregistrement automatique des erreurs** = error logging; **ce programme comprend un enregistrement automatique d'erreurs** = features of the program include error logging; **fonctionnement automatique**

(d'un système) = unattended operation; **fonctionnement itératif automatique** = automatic sequencing; **contrôle de gain automatique** = automatic gain control (AGC) *ou* automatic level control (ALC); **guichet automatique de banque (GAB)** = automated teller machine (ATM); *US* automatic telling machine; **lancement automatique (d'un programme)** = auto start; **numérotation automatique** = auto-dial; **ouverture automatique de session** = auto-login *ou* auto-logon; **programmation automatique** = automatic programming; *(modem ou téléphone)* **système de rappel automatique d'un correspondant** = auto-redial; **reconnaissance automatique du débit d'une ligne (en baud)** = auto-baud scanning; **relance** *ou* **remise en marche** *ou* **redémarrage automatique** = auto restart; **horloge à relance automatique** = delta clock; **répétition automatique** = auto repeat *ou* automatic repeat; **réponse automatique** = auto-answer; **retour à la ligne automatique** = automatic carriage return; **saisie automatique de données** = automatic data capture; **système automatique** = hands off system; **système téléphonique automatique international** = international direct dialling (IDD); **traitement automatique de données** = automatic data processing (ADP); **transfert automatique** = automatic *ou* unconditional transfer; **vérification automatique** = auto verify; **equipement de vérification automatique (EVA)** = automatic test equipment (ATE)

◊ **automatiquement** *adv* automatically; **le compilateur a corrigé les fautes de syntaxe automatiquement** = the compiler automatically corrected the syntax errors; **le programme est lancé automatiquement lors de la mise sous tension de l'ordinateur** = the program is run automatically when the computer is switched on; **tâche qui peut être exécutée automatiquement** = unattended operation

automatisation *nf* automation
◊ **automatisé, -ée** *adj* automated; **bureau automatisé** = automated office
◊ **automatiser** *vtr* to automate

autonome *adj* **(a)** *(indépendant)* autonomous **(b)** *(indépendant de l'ordinateur principal)* off-line; **impression par imprimante autonome** = off-line printing **(c)** *(poste non relié en*

réseau) **poste autonome** = stand-alone *ou* standalone; **les postes ont été reliés en réseau plutôt que d'être utilisés comme postes autonomes** = the workstations have been networked together rather than used as stand-alone systems; **système autonome** = stand-alone system; **terminal autonome** = stand-alone terminal

◊ **autonomie** *nf* independence; **autonomie des données** = data independence

autopositif, -ive *adj (procédé)* autopositive

autopsie *nf* post mortem; **vidage par autopsie** = post mortem dump

autorafraîchi, -e *adj* self-refreshing; **mémoire vive (RAM) autorafraîchie** = self-refreshing RAM

autorégénérable *adj* **mémoire vive** *ou* **RAM autorégénérable** = self-refreshing RAM

autoréponse *nf* auto-answer

autorisation *nf* authorization; *(à un fichier ou à une machine)* **autorisation d'accès** = clearance; **vous n'avez pas l'autorisation d'accéder à ce processeur** = you do not have the required clearance for this processor; **autorisation de copie d'un logiciel** = software licence; **autorisation de copier** *ou* **de dupliquer** = authorization to copy (ATC); **donner (à quelqu'un) l'autorisation (de faire quelque chose)** = to authorize (someone to do something)

◊ **autorisé, -ée** *adj* authorized; *(permis par la syntaxe du langage)* legal; **personne autorisée (à utiliser un système)** = authorized user; **la procédure d'authentification permet au système de reconnaître si un message est émis par un utilisateur autorisé** = authentication allows the system to recognize that a sender's message is genuine; **non autorisé** = unauthorized; **le mot de passe interdit aux personnes non autorisées d'avoir accès aux donnés** = the use of a password is to prevent unauthorized access to the data

◊ **autoriser** *vtr* to authorize; **autoriser quelque chose** *ou* **quelqu'un à faire**

quelque chose = to authorize something
ou someone to do something; **autoriser
l'achat d'un nouveau système
informatique** = to authorize the
purchase of a new computer system

◊ **autorité** *nf* authority

autotest *nm* automatic checking

autotranslatable *adj (programme)*
self-relocating (program)

auxiliaire *adj* auxiliary *ou* secondary;
(appareil ou dispositif de secours)
standby *ou* backing (device) *ou* safety net;
alimentation auxiliaire = battery
backup; **clavier auxiliaire** = keypad;
équipement *ou* **système auxiliaire** =
standby equipment; **liaisons auxiliaires
d'un réseau** = network redundancy;
mémoire auxiliaire = secondary storage;
backing memory *ou* storage *ou* store;
auxiliary memory *ou* storage *ou* store;
external memory; slave cache *ou* store;
**cet appareil est équipé de lecteurs de
disquettes et de bandes magnétiques qui
servent de mémoire auxiliaire** = disk
drives and magnetic tape are auxiliary
storage on this machine; **je vais
augmenter la capacité de mémoire
auxiliaire en ajoutant un deuxième
lecteur de disquettes** = by adding another
disk drive, I will increase the backing
store capabilities; **mémoire morte** *ou*
ROM auxiliaire = sideways ROM;
mettre en mémoire auxiliaire = to
deposit; **pile auxiliaire** = battery backup;
processeur auxiliaire = auxiliary
processor *ou* support chip; **le processeur
arithmétique auxiliaire peut être enfiché
à cet endroit** = the maths support chip
can be plugged in here; **registre
auxiliaire de routage d'adresse** = B-line
counter; **routine auxiliaire** = open
routine; **station auxiliaire** = secondary
station; **système auxiliaire** = satellite
(system); **système à bus auxiliaire** = dual
bus system

avalanche *nf* avalanche; **photodiode à
avalanche** = avalanche photodiode
(APD)

avance *nf* **(a)** *(du papier ou d'un film)*
advance; **avance rapide du papier** = high-
speed skip *ou* slew **(b)** *(progrès)* advance;
avance technologique = sophistication

◊ **d'avance** *ou* **à l'avance** *loc adv* in
advance *ou* pre- *ou* forward; **accepté
d'avance** = pre-agreed; **définir d'avance** =
to predefine; **déterminer d'avance** = to
predetermine *ou* to preset; **enregistrer
d'avance** = to prerecord; *(plan)* **établir
d'avance** = to predesign; **un grand choix
de modèles de mise en page établis
d'avance vous permet de formater
automatiquement vos documents
d'affaires ou vos documents techniques** =
a wide selection of predesigned layouts
help you automatically format typical
business and technical documents; **fixer
d'avance** = to preset; **formaté d'avance** =
preformatted; **imprimé d'avance** =
preprinted; **programmer d'avance** = to
preprogram *ou* to preset; **on avait
programmé d'avance les nouveaux
paramètres de page de l'imprimante** =
the printer was preset with new page
parameters

◊ **avancé, -ée** *adj* advanced; *(de pointe)*
sophisticated *ou* state-of-the-art; **un
programme de PAO avancé** = a
sophisticated desktop publishing
program

avancer *vtr&i* to advance; **faire
avancer** = to advance; **faites avancer le
curseur de deux espaces (sur la ligne)** =
advance the cursor two spaces along the
line; *(incrémenter)* **faire avancer d'un pas**
= to increment; **faire avancer image par
image** *ou* **pas à pas** = to jog

avant 1 *nm* front; **alimentation par
l'avant** = front feed **2** *adj inv* front; **bord
avant** = leading edge; **palier avant** =
front porch; **panneau avant** = front *ou*
front panel *ou* fascia plate; **le panneau
avant du lecteur de disquettes de ce
modèle est plus petit que celui des autres
modèles** = the fascia plate on the disk
drive of this model is smaller than those
on other models; **on insère les disquettes
dans les fentes du panneau avant du
terminal** = the disks are inserted in slots
in the front of the terminal **3** *prep & adv*
before *ou* prior to; **il faut taper le mot de
passe avant d'accéder au système** = the
password has to be keyed in prior to
accessing the system

avarie *nf* damage

avertir *vtr* to warn; **il a averti les
pupitreurs d'une surcharge possible du**

système = he warned the keyboarders that the system might become overloaded

◇ **avertissement** *nm* warning; **donner un avertissement** = to issue a warning; **on a placé des panneaux d'avertissement autour du laser de puissance** = warning notices were put up around the high powered laser

◇ **avertisseur** *nm* **(a)** *(sonore)* buzzer **(b)** *(pour recherche de personne)* bleeper; **il doit être quelque part dans l'usine, nous essaierons de le joindre par son avertisseur** = he is in the factory somewhere - we'll try to find him on his bleeper

aveugle *adj* blind; **clavier aveugle** = blind keyboard; **transmission en aveugle** = blind dialling

avion *nm* aicraft *ou* plane; **enveloppe avion** = air mail envelope; **papier avion** = air mail paper

avis *nm* advice; **demander l'avis de quelqu'un** = to consult someone; **il a demandé l'avis du responsable de (la) maintenance sur le mauvais fonctionnement du disque** = he consulted the maintenance manager about the disk fault

axe *nm* **(a)** axis; **ce progiciel de CAO permet de positionner un axe où l'on veut** = the CAD package allows an axis to be placed anywhere; **axe d'abscisse** *ou* **axe des X** = X-axis *ou* horizontal axis; **axe de l'ordonnée** *ou* **axe des Y** = Y-axis *ou* vertical axis; **axe des Z** = Z-axis **(b)** *(qui fait tourner un disque)* spindle

AZERTY *(premières lettres du rang supérieur gauche de certains claviers utilisés dans les pays francophones)* **clavier AZERTY** = AZERTY keyboard

azimut *nm* azimuth; **réglage d'alignement des angles d'azimut** = azimuth alignment; **c'est cette petite vis qui sert à régler l'alignement des angles d'azimut** = azimuth alignment is adjusted with this small screw

Bb

B *(représentation hexadécimale du nombre 11)* B

bac *nm (pour alimentation automatique du papier en feuille à feuille)* (paper) bin *ou* (paper) tray *ou* sheet feed attachment; **bac du dessous** *ou* **bac inférieur** = lower bin; **introduire le bac inférieur** = load lower bin; **bac du dessus** *ou* **bac supérieur** = upper bin

badge *nm* badge; **lecteur de badges** = badge reader; **le lecteur de badges garantit que seules les personnes autorisées ont accès à la salle des ordinateurs** = a badge reader makes sure that only authorized personnel can gain access to a computer room

bague *nf* **(a)** ring; **bague de protection d'écriture** = write-permit ring **(b)** *(pour lentille photographique)* **bague d'extension** *ou* **bague macro** = extension tube

baie *nf* card cage *ou* card frame *ou* card chassis; **baie avec guide-cartes** = rack

baisse *nf (de signal)* fading; **baisse de courant** = brown-out
◊ **baisser** *vi (signal)* to fade

balai *nm* **manche à balai** = joystick; **connecteur** *ou* **port pour manche à balai** *ou* **de manche à balai** = joystick port; **ce modèle d'ordinateur personnel possède un connecteur pour manche à balai** = a joystick port is provided with the home computer

balance *nf (d'un ensemble stéréophonique)* balance

balayage *nm* scan *ou* sweep; *(action)* scanning; **le balayage a fait apparaître les données périmées** = the scan revealed which records were out of date; **balayage de chaînes** = string scanning; **balayage dirigé** = directed scan; **balayage d'écran** = television scan; **balayage par faisceau mobile** = flying spot scan; **balayage hors champ** *ou* **en dehors des limites** = overscan; **télévision à balayage lent** = slow scan television; **balayage récurrent** *ou* **balayage de trame** = raster scanning; **graphisme par balayage de trame** = raster graphics; **balayage vertical** = field sweep; **impulsion de contrôle** *ou* **de synchronisation du balayage vertical** = field sync pulse; **définition de balayage** = scanning resolution; **dispositif de lecture par balayage** = scanning device; **erreur de balayage** = scanning error; **un pli ou une déchirure dans une page peut être la cause d'une erreur de balayage** *ou* **d'un balayage incorrect** = a wrinkled or torn page may be the cause of scanning errors; **faire un balayage** = to scan; **un télécopieur fait un balayage de l'image qu'il convertit en données numériques avant transmission** = a facsimile machine scans the picture and converts this to digital form before transmission; **faisceau de balayage** = scanning spot beam; **fréquence de balayage** = scanning rate; **les écrans à faible fréquence de balayage ont besoin de phosphore à longue persistance pour éviter l'instabilité de l'image** = slow scan rate monitors need long persistence phosphor to prevent the image flickering; **ligne de balayage** = scanning line; **logiciel de saisie par balayage** = scanning software; **passe de balayage** = raster scan; **retour d'un balayage** = flyback; **signal (de début) de balayage** = line drive signal; **spot de balayage** = picture beam *ou* scanning spot; **vitesse de balayage** = scanning speed; **la vitesse de lecture par balayage est de 1,3 pouces par seconde** = throughput is 1.3 inches per second scanning speed; **zone de balayage** = scan area; **étendue de la zone de balayage** = scan length
◊ **balayer** *vtr* to scan *ou* to sweep; **le lecteur optique utilise un rayon lumineux**

qui balaye les caractères, les symboles ou les lignes = an optical reader uses a light beam to scan characters, patterns or lines

> il faut un moniteur spécialisé ayant une fréquence de balayage compatible avec les performances et bien souvent un écran aux dimensions généreuses
> *L'Ordinateur Individuel*

balisage *nm* flagging

◇ **balise** *nf* (indicator) flag

◇ **baliser** *vtr* to flag

banal *adj* common; **canal banal** = common carrier; **signalisation par canal banal** = common channel signalling; **langage banal** = common language; **matériel banal** = common hardware; **mémoire banale** = working store *ou* scratch pad (memory)

◇ **banalisé, -ée** *adj* common *ou* general purpose; **bus d'interface banalisé** = general purpose interface bus (GPIB); **ligne banalisée** = common carrier; **poste de travail banalisé** = general purpose computer *ou* open access workstation; **registre banalisé** = general register *ou* general purpose register (gpr)

◇ **banaliser** *vtr (une mémoire ou un ordinateur)* to use as common storage *ou* to use as general purpose computer; **la mémoire centrale du serveur est en général banalisée en dehors de la partie réservée au système d'exploitation** = the file server memory is mainly common storage area, with a section reserved for the operating system

banc d'essai *nm* benchmark *ou* test bed; **les bancs d'essais consistent à évaluer la performance de plusieurs systèmes ou périphériques en utilisant le même test standard** = in benchmarking, the performances of several systems or devices are tested against a standard benchmark; **la revue a publié les résultats du banc d'essai du nouveau programme** = the magazine gave the new program's benchmark test results

bancatique *nf* electronic banking *ou* telebanking

bande *nf* (a) stripe; **bande de couleur** = colour stripe; **bande d'équilibrage (de tension)** = balance stripe **(b)** bande transporteuse = conveyor (for paper); **imprimante à bande** = band printer **(c)** strip *ou* band; *(sur une bande magnétique)* **bande intermédiaire** = guard band **(d)** *(ruban)* tape; **bande (magnétique) audionumérique** = digital audio tape (DAT); **une bande audionumérique produit un son de très haute qualité** = DAT produces a very high quality sound; **bande sur bobine ouverte** = open reel tape; **bande magnétique** = magnetic tape *ou* mag tape; **bande magnétique en cassette** = cassette tape; **bande idiote** *ou* **bande de texte non formaté** *ou* **sans paramètres d'impression** = idiot tape; **bande (de) mouvements** = change tape; **bande originale** = master tape *ou* magnetic master; **bande papier** = paper tape *ou* punched tape; **bande papier perforée** = punched (paper) tape *ou* perforated tape; **bande semi-perforée** *ou* **à confettis non détachés** = chadded *ou* chadless tape; **bande vidéo** = videotape *ou* video cassette tape; **largeur de bande vidéo** = video bandwidth; **bande vierge** = blank tape; **cartouche bande** *ou* **cartouche de bande magnétique** = (magnetic) tape cartridge; **cassette de bande magnétique** = (magnetic) tape cassette; **convertisseur bande magnétique/carte perforée** = tape to card converter; **début de bande** = tape header; **marque de début de bande** = beginning of tape (bot) marker; **dérouleur de bande(s) magnétique(s)** = tape drive *ou* magnetic tape transport; **écarteur de bande** = lifter; **encodeur pour bande magnétique** = magnetic tape encoder; **en-tête de bande** = tape header; **entraînement de bande** = tape transport; **(code de) fin de la bande (magnétique)** = end of tape (EOT); **label de fin de bande** = tape trailer; **format de bande** = tape format; **lecteur de bande (magnétiques)** = tape drive *ou* magnetic tape reader; **lecteur de bandes perforées** = paper tape reader; **tête de lecture** *ou* **d'écriture de bandes magnétiques** = tape head; **tête de lecture de bandes** = tape playback head **(e)** *(de fréquences)* (frequency) band; **bande de base** = base band; **modem en bande de base** = base band modem; **n'utilisez jamais un modem en bande de base sur une ligne téléphonique normale** = do not use a base band modem with a normal phone line; **la bande de base des fréquences vocales varie de 20Hz à 15KHz** = voice base band ranges from 20Hz to 15KHz; **réseau local en bande de base** = base band local area network;

bande C = C band; **bande étroite** = narrow band; **(système de) modulation de fréquence à bande étroite** = narrow band FM (NBFM); **bande de fréquences** = frequency band; **bande (de fréquences) intercalaire** *ou* **bande de protection** = guard band; **bande (de fréquences) vocale** *ou* **bande de basses fréquences** *ou* **bande téléphonique** = voice band; **filtre de bande de fréquences** = frequency equalizer; **large bande** = broadband *ou* wideband; **modulation de fréquence à large bande** = wideband frequency modulation (WBFM); **radio à large bande** = broadband radio; **largeur de bande (de fréquences)** = bandwidth; **largeur de bande effective** = effective bandwidth; **la largeur de bande d'un téléphone est de 3100Hz** = telephone bandwidth is 3100Hz; **bande (de fréquences) vocale** = voice band; **transmission de signaux sur la bande vocale** = in-band signalling; **signalisation hors bande (vocale)** = out of band signalling; **bande latérale** = sideband; **double bande latérale** = double sideband; **bande latérale inférieure** = lower sideband; **bande latérale résiduelle** = vestigial sideband; **bande latérale supérieure** = upper sideband; **bande latérale unique** = single sideband; **double bande latérale sans porteuse** *ou* **à porteuse inhibée** = double sideband suppressed carrier (DSBSC)

la bande de fréquence destinée à la radiodiffusion par satellite est la bande des 12 GHz
Electronique Radio Plans

◊ **bandothèque** *nf* tape library

banque *nf (groupe)* bank; **banque de canaux** = channel bank; **banque de données** = *(sur ordinateur)* databank; *(centre ou service)* information retrieval centre; **banque de mémoire** = memory bank; **changement de banque de mémoire** = bank switching; **la carte d'extension possède une banque de mémoire de 128Ko constituée de 16 puces** = an add-on card has a 128Kb memory bank made up of 16 chips

le petit disque (CD-ROM) permet aux professionnels d'accéder à des banques de données tout en restant dans l'environnement bureautique
Micro Systèmes

barillet *nm* small barrel; **distorsion en barillet** = pin cushion distortion

barre *nf* **(a)** bar; *(d'un clavier)* **barre d'espacement** = space bar **(b)** *(trait)* **code (à) barres** = (i) bar code; *US* bar graphics; (ii) universal product code (UPC); **lecteur (optique) de code (à) barres** = optical bar reader *ou* bar code reader *ou* optical wand; **graphique à barres** = bar chart; **imprimante à barres** = bar printer

barré, -ée *adj* crossed; **zéro barré d'un trait oblique** = slashed zero

baryté, -ée *adj* **papier baryté** = baryta paper

bas *nm* bottom *ou* foot; **bas de casse** = lower case; **bas de page** = bottom space; **note** *ou* **renvoi en bas de page** = footnote; **il a signé au bas de la lettre** = he signed his name at the foot of the letter; **vers le bas** = downward

◊ **bas, basse** *adj* low; **basse définition** = low resolution *ou* low-res; **basse fréquence** = low frequency (LF); **canal de basses fréquences** = voice grade channel; **haut-parleur de basse fréquence** = woofer *ou* bass speaker *ou* bass driver; **réponse aux basses fréquences** = bass response; **signal de basse fréquence** = bass signal; **transmission de données (numérisées) sur basse fréquence** = data in voice (DIV); **basse fréquence multiplexée A-MAC** = A-MAC; **très basse fréquence** = very low frequency (VLF); **transmission de données (numérisées) sur très basse fréquence** = data under voice (DUV); **langage de bas niveau** = low-level language (LLL)

◊ **basse** *nf (note musicale)* **haut-parleur de basses** = bass driver *ou* bass speaker *ou* woofer

bascule *nf* bistable circuit *ou* multivibrator; **déclenchée par bascule de front d'impulsion** = edge-triggered; **commutateur à bascule** = DIP switch *ou* flip-flop (FF) *ou* toggle switch; **valider (à l'aide d'un commutateur à bascule)** = to toggle; **commutateur à bascule à deux états** = RS-flip-flop *ou* reset-set flip-flop; **commutateur à bascule de type D** = D-(type) flip-flop; **commutateur à bascule de type JK** = JK-flip-flop

◊ **basculement** *nm (de programme)* swapping *ou* swap

◊ **basculer** *vtr* to roll *ou* to swap *ou* to toggle; *(des données)* to exchange;

basculer la communication d'un émetteur à l'autre = to hand off

base *nf* **(a)** base *ou* basis; **base de la pile** = stack base; **base de temps** = time base; **base de temps réduite** = fast time-scale; **le coût de la saisie du texte a été établi sur une base de 5500 frappes/heure** = we calculated keyboarding costs on the basis of 5,500 keystrokes per hour **(b)** **à base de** = based on; **système à base de connaissances** = knowledge-based system; **système intelligent à base de connaissances** = intelligent knowledge-based system (IKBS); **à base de procédure** = procedural **(c)** **base de base** = basic; **l'architecture de base est la même pour tous les modèles de la gamme** = the basic architecture is the same for all models in this range; **adresse de base** = base address *ou* presumptive address; **bande de base** = base band; **modem en bande de base** = base band modem; **n'utilisez jamais un modem en bande de base sur une ligne téléphonique normale** = do not use a base band modem with a normal phone line; **réseau local en bande de base** = base band local area network; **cliché de base** = key plate; **code de base** = basic code *ou* skeletal code; **format de base** = native format; **instruction de base** = basic instruction *ou* presumptive instruction; **ligne de base** = base line; **registre de base** = base register; **système d'exploitation de base** = basic operating system (BOS); **système satellite de base** = basic control system (satellite) (BCS) **(d)** **base de données** = database; **consulter une base de données sans autorisation** = to browse; **configuration de base de données** *ou* **implantation** *ou* **topologie d'une base de données** = database mapping; **langage de base de données** = database language; **responsable de base de données** = database administrator (DBA); **schéma de base de données** = database schema; **schéma de base de données standard** *ou* **canonique** = canonical schema; **service de base de données spécialisée (pour vidéotex)** = information provider (IP); **système de base de données** = database system; **système de base de données réparti** *ou* **en réseau** = distributed database system; **système de gestion de base de données** = database management system (DBMS) *ou* database manager; **machine dédiée au traitement de bases de données** = database machine; **base de données**

hiérarchisée = hierarchical database; **base de données en ligne** = on-line database; **base de données en réseau** = network database; **base de données relationnelle** = plex database *ou* relational database **(e)** *(de numération)* radix *ou* base; **complément à la base** = radix complement; **notation en base** = radix notation; **base binaire** *ou* **base 2** = base 2; **base décimale** *ou* **base 10** = base 10; **système à base dix** = decimal system; **base hexadécimale** *ou* **base 16** = base 16; **le nombre hexadécimal est en base 16** = the hexadecimal number has a radix of 16; **base octale** *ou* **base 8** = base 8 *ou* octal scale; **(notation) en base huit** = octal (notation); **nombre en base octale** = octal digit

basé, -ée *adj* based on

◇ **baser** *vtr* to base; **nous avons basé nos calculs** *ou* **nos calculs sont basés sur la vitesse standard pour la saisie de texte** = we based our calculations on the basic keyboarding rate; **ce prix est basé sur diverses estimations des coûts de saisie** = the price is based on estimates of keyboarding costs

◇ **se baser (sur)** *vpr* to base oneself (on something)

BASIC = BEGINNER'S ALL-PURPOSE SYMBOLIC INSTRUCTION CODE; **langage BASIC** = BASIC (language); **écrire un programme en BASIC** = to write a program in BASIC

battement *nm (anomalie d'un programme)* thrashing; *(défaut de synchronisation de tête de lecture)* flagging

batterie *nf* **(a)** *(pile)* battery **(b)** *(groupe d'objets)* **ce processus est contrôlé par une batterie de capteurs** = the process is monitored by a bank of sensors

cet appareil peut fonctionner soit sur 220V, soit sur batterie 12V, avec une faible consommation

Opto électronique

baud *nm* baud; **le modem viewdata reçoit à 1200 bauds et transmet à 75** = the viewdata modem uses a 1200/75 split baud rate; **reconnaissance automatique de débit d'une ligne (en**

bauds) = auto-baud scanning *ou* auto-baud sensing

Baudot *npr* **code** **(télégraphique)** **Baudot** = Baudot code

baver *vi (imprimerie)* to bleed
◊ **bavure** *nf* bleed *ou* slur

BCH = BOSE-CHANDHURI-HOCQUENGHEM; **code BCH** = BCH code

BCPL = BASIC COMBINED PROGRAMMING LANGUAGE; **langage BCPL** = BCPL

bel *nm* bel; **le 'bel' est mesuré sur une échelle logarithmique** = bel is a unit in the logarithmic scale

Bernoulli *npr* **boîte de Bernoulli** = Bernoulli box

biais *nm (inclinaison d'un caractère)* skew
◊ **biaisé, -ée** *adj* biased; **données biaisées** = biased data

biaural, -e *adj* binaural

bibliographie *nf* bibliography; **il a placé une bibliographie à la fin de chaque chapitre** = he printed a bibliography at the end of each chapter
◊ **bibliographique** *adj* bibliographic *ou* bibliographical; **liste bibliographique** = bibliography; **notice bibliographique** = bibliographical information

bibliothécaire *nm&f* librarian
◊ **bibliothèque** *nf* library; **consultez le catalogue de la bibliothèque pour obtenir les renseignements bibliographiques** = look up the bibliographical details in the library catalogue; **les éditeurs ont vérifié toutes les références à la bibliothèque locale** = the editors have checked all the references in the local library; **bibliothèque de bandes** = tape library; **il possède une grande bibliothèque de jeux électroniques** = he has a large library of computer games; **bibliothèque graphique** = graphics library; **bibliothèque de logiciels** = software library; **bibliothèque**

de macros = macro library; **bibliothèque de programmes** = program library; **bibliothèque de programmes d'entrée/sortie** = input/output library; **bibliothèque de symboles** = symbol library; **bibliothèque du système** = system library; **fonction bibliothèque** = library function; **programme de bibliothèque** = library program *ou* library routine; **la fonction racine carrée se trouve déjà dans le programme de bibliothèque** = the square root function is already in the library program; **sous-programme de bibliothèque** = library subroutine

bidimensionnel, -elle *adj* two-dimensional; **fichier bidimensionnel** = flat file; **tableau bidimensionnel** = two-dimensional array

bidirectionnel, -elle *adj* bi-directional; **bus bidirectionnel** = bi-directional bus; **câble bidirectionnel** = two way cable; **circuit bidirectionnel** = two wire circuit; **imprimante bidirectionnelle** = bi-directional printer; **mode de transmission bidirectionnelle à l'alternat** = either-way operation; **transfert de fichier bidirectionnel** = bi-directional file transfer

> en général, dans une liaison informatique bidirectionnelle, les échanges se font à la même vitesse dans les deux sens
>
> *Action PC*

bidouillage *nm (familier)* manipulation; **bidouillage du bit** = byte manipulation
◊ **bidouillé, -ée** *adj (familier)* manipulated *ou* altered; *(programme qui fonctionne tel que prévu parce qu'il n'a pas été manipulé)* **programme non bidouillé** = well-behaved program

bifilaire *adj* **circuit bifilaire** = two-wire circuit

bifurcation *nf (d'un système)* bifurcation; *(embranchement d'un programme)* switch

billet *nm (de banque)* banknote; **distributeur de billets de banque** = cash dispenser
◊ **billetterie** *nf* cash dispenser

binaire **1** *adj* binary; **additionneur binaire** = BCD adder *ou* binary adder; **adressage binaire** = bit addressing; **infographie à adressage binaire** = bit-mapped graphics; **définir une table d'adressage binaire** = to bit-map; **arbre binaire** = binary tree; **arrangement binaire** = bit pattern; **base binaire** *ou* **base 2** = base 2; **calcul binaire** = binary arithmetic; **caractère codé binaire** = binary coded character; **cellule binaire** = binary cell; **chargeur binaire** = binary loader; **chiffre binaire** = bit *ou* binary digit; **groupe de 2 chiffres binaires** = dibit; **codage binaire** = binary encoding; **code binaire** = binary code *ou* pure code; **le code binaire du nombre décimal 8 est 1000** = the BCD representation of decimal 8 is 1000; **code binaire à 8 bits (EBCDIC)** = extended binary coded decimal interchange code (EBCDIC); **code binaire réfléchi** = cyclic code; **communication synchrone binaire** = binary synchronous communications (BSC); **compteur binaire** = binary counter; **conversion décimale-binaire** = decimal-to-binary conversion; **recherche par coupe binaire** = binary search *ou* binary chop *ou* binary look-up; **débit binaire** = bit rate *ou* debit; **décimal codé binaire (DCB)** = binary coded decimal (BCD); **demi-additionneur binaire** = binary half adder; **densité binaire** = bit density; **échelle binaire** = binary scale; **dans un mot à quatre bits, l'échelle binaire est 1,2,4,8** = in a four bit word, the binary scale is 1,2,4,8; **élément binaire** = binary digit *ou* bit; **encodage binaire** = binary encoding; **exposant binaire** = binary exponent; **expression binaire d'un caractère** = character representation; **fraction binaire** = binary fraction; **la fraction binaire 0,011 est égale à un quart plus un huitième (ou trois huitièmes)** = the binary fraction 0.011 is equal to one quarter plus one eighth (i.e. three eighths); **indicateur binaire** = flag bit; **indicateur binaire de dépassement de capacité** = overflow bit *ou* flag; **logique binaire** = logic; **manipulation binaire** = bit manipulation; **mantisse binaire** = binary mantissa; **masque binaire** = mask bit; **nombre binaire** = binary number *ou* bit; **notation binaire** = binary notation *ou* representation; **opération binaire** = binary operation; **position binaire** = bit position; **séquence binaire** = binary sequence; **système binaire** = binary system; **valeur binaire** = truth value; **variable binaire** = binary variable;

vidage binaire = binary dump; **virgule binaire** = binary point **2** *nm* **binaire de signe** = sign digit; **transmission de signaux en binaire** = binary signalling

◊ **binaire-décimale** *adj* binary-to-decimal; **conversion binaire-décimale** = binary-to-decimal conversion

ces tensions sont ensuite codées en numération binaire: 011 pour 3 volts, 101 pour 5 volts, etc.
Science et Vie

binaural, -e *adj* binaural

binding *nm (type de reliure)* **perfect binding** = perfect binding

binon *nm (élément binaire)* **binon 0** = logical low; **binon 1** = logical high

BIOS = BASIC INPUT/OUTPUT OPERATING SYSTEM *voir* EXPLOITATION

bip *nm* **(a)** *(tonalité)* beep *ou* bleep; **bip d'appel** = decimonic ringing; **émettre** *ou* **faire un bip** = to beep *ou* to bleep; **lorsqu'on appuie sur la mauvaise touche, l'ordinateur émet un bip** = the computer beeps when the wrong key is hit; **s'il n'y a plus de papier, l'imprimante émet un bip** = the printer will make a beep *ou* a bleep when it runs out of paper **(b)** *(récepteur d'appel de personne)* pager; **appeler** *ou* **chercher à joindre quelqu'un par bip** = to page someone *ou* to call someone on his pager

en effet, un avertisseur émet un bip si la résistance mesurée descend au-dessous d'une certaine valeur
Electronique pratique

bipolaire *adj* bipolar; **codage bipolaire** = bipolar coding; **signal bipolaire** = bipolar signal; **transistor bipolaire** = bipolar transistor; **transistor à jonction bipolaire** = bipolar junction transistor (BJT)

biquinaire *adj* biquinary; **code biquinaire** = biquinary code

bistable *adj* bistable; **circuit** *ou* **multivibrateur bistable** = bistable circuit *ou* multivibrator

bit *nm* bit *ou* binary digit *ou* binary bit; **(système) huit bits =** eight-bit (system); **code binaire à 8 bits (EBCDIC) =** extended binary coded decimal interchange code (EBCDIC); **registre à bits circulants =** circulating register; **bit de contrôle =** check bit *ou* service bit; **bit de dépassement de capacité =** overflow bit *ou* flag *ou* indicator; **bit indicateur =** flag bit; **bit lourd =** weighted bit; **bit marqué =** dirty bit; **bit masque =** mask bit; **bit de parité =** parity bit; **bit de poids faible =** least significant bit (LSB); **bit de poids fort** *ou* **bit lourd** *ou* **bit significatif =** weighted bit *ou* most significant bit (msb *ou* MSB); **(nombre de) bits par pouce =** bits per inch (bpi); **bit de protection =** guard bit; **(nombre de) bits par seconde (bps) =** bits per second (bps); **le débit est de 60 000 bits par seconde sur une liaison parallèle =** the transmission rate is 60,000 bits per second (bps) through a parallel connection; **bit de signe =** sign bit *ou* sign indicator; **bit significatif** *ou* **le bit le plus significatif =** most significant bit (msb *ou* MSB); **bit le moins significatif =** least significant bit (LSB); **bit supplémentaire =** overhead bit; **bit de synchronisation =** framing bit; **bidouillage de bits =** byte manipulation; **remplissage** *ou* **garnissage de bits =** bit stuffing; **train de bits =** bit stream; **traitement du bit =** bit handling

> sur une surface de 1 centimètre carré, ils savent faire tenir 100 (cent) millions de bits ou unités de base d'information, 1 ou 0 par exemple
>
> *Le Point*

blanc *nm* **(a)** *(couleur)* white (colour); **noir et blanc =** black and white; **photo en noir et blanc =** black and white photograph; **affichage noir sur blanc =** positive display; **impression blanc sur noir =** cameo; **imprimante à définition des blancs =** white writer; *(d'un affichage)* **niveau de blanc =** white level **(b)** *(typographie)* space *ou* blank; **blanc de pied =** bottom space *ou* foot margin; **blanc de tête =** top space *ou* top margin **(c)** *(d'un programme)* **essai à blanc =** desk check *ou* dry run; *voir aussi* MONOCHROME

◊ **blanc, blanche 1** *adj* **(a)** *(couleur)* white **(b)** *(sans signification)* blank; **bruit blanc =** white noise; **caractère blanc =** space character; **remplissage avec caractères blancs** *ou* **insertion de caractères blancs =** character stuffing;

chambre blanche = anechoic chamber; **signal blanc =** white flag

◊ **blanchir** *vtr (un disque)* to wipe clean; **si vous reformatez, vous blanchirez le disque =** by reformatting you will wipe the disk clean

blindage *nm (de protection)* screen *ou* shield; **un blindage réduit les interférences du bloc d'alimentation =** the PSU is screened against interference; **blindage magnétique =** magnetic screen *ou* shield; **lorsqu'on enlevait le blindage métallique du bloc d'alimentation, l'ordinateur ne donnait plus rien de bon =** without the metal screen over the power supply unit, the computer just produced garbage

blindé, -ée *adj* shielded; **câble blindé =** shielded cable

blister *nm* blister pack

bloc *nm* **(a)** *(de texte)* block; **copie d'un bloc (de texte) =** block copy; *(traitement de texte)* **(instruction de) déplacer un bloc =** move block; **(instruction de) marquer un bloc =** mark block; **(code** *ou* **marque de) fin de bloc =** end of block (EOB); **en-tête de bloc =** block header **(b)** *(groupe de caractères* **ou** *de données)* **bloc de caractères =** character block; **contrôle de blocs de caractères =** block character check (BCC); **bloc (de données) de contrôle =** control block; **bloc de contrôle de fichier =** file control block; **bloc de données =** data block; **bloc d'entrée =** input block; **bloc d'identification =** header *ou* header block; **changement de bloc de mémoire =** bank switching; **bloc de raccordement =** terminal block; **caractère de rejet d'un bloc (dont les données sont mauvaises) =** block ignore character; **(contrôle de) parité d'un bloc =** block parity; **code de contrôle de bloc =** block code; **traitement de contrôle de bloc à l'entrée =** block input processing; **compactage** *ou* **compression de bloc =** block compaction; **délimiteurs** *ou* **marques de bloc =** block markers; **entre blocs =** interblock; **espace entre blocs =** block gap *ou* interblock gap (IBG); **facteur de bloc =** blocking factor; **fichier d'enregistrement des blocs =** block list; **longueur** *ou* **taille d'un bloc =** block length; **manipulation de bloc(s) =** block operation; **marque de sélection d'un bloc**

= block mark; **transfert** *ou* **insertion d'un bloc** = block transfer; **recherche** *ou* **extraction de bloc** = block retrieval; **synchronisation de blocs** = block synchronization; **taux d'erreur par bloc** = block error rate; **effectuer un tri bloc par bloc** = to shell sort **(c) effacer en bloc** = to block delete; **lorsqu'il s'agit de supprimer un texte assez long, servez-vous de la commande qui permet d'effacer en bloc** = use the global delete command to remove large areas of unwanted text **(d)** *(groupe d'objets ou d'items)* bank; *(groupe de données transmises)* frame **(e)** *(source d'électricité)* **bloc d'alimentation** = power pack *ou* power supply unit (PSU)

blocage *nm (arrêt total de programme causé par une erreur)* lock up

bloc-notes *nm* notepad *ou* scratchpad; **champ bloc-notes** = comment field; **fenêtre bloc-notes** = screen notepad; **mémoire bloc-notes** = scratchpad memory *ou* working store

bloquer *vtr (arrêter)* to block; *(coincer)* to jam; **la sortie est restée bloquée au plus haut niveau jusqu'à la ré-initialisation du système** = the output latched high until we reset the computer

BNF = BACKUS-NAUR-FORM; **convention BNF** *ou* **métalangage BNF** = BNF; **métalangage BNF étendu** *ou* **BNF étendu** = extended BNF (EBNF)

bobine *nf* **(a)** *(de film)* reel *ou* spool; **il a laissé tomber la bobine et le ruban s'est déroulé** = he dropped the reel on the floor and the tape unwound itself; **bobine d'alimentation** = feed reel; **bobine réceptrice** *ou* **de réception** *ou* **d'enroulement** = take-up reel *ou* pickup reel *ou* pick-up reel; **(copie) de bobine à bobine** = reel to reel (copying); **bande sur bobine ouverte** = open reel tape; **tête de bobine** = head **(b)** *(de fil conducteur)* coil; **microphone à bobine** = moving coil microphone; **bobine d'induction** = induction coil *ou* inductor; **un inducteur consiste en une bobine de fil (de cuivre)** = an inductor is made from a coil of (copper) wire

bof = BEGINNING OF FILE *voir* DEBUT

bogue *nm* bug; *voir aussi* DEBOGAGE, DEBOGUER

boîte *nf* **(a)** box; **boîte en carton** = cardboard box *ou* case **(b) boîte de connexion (sans soudure)** = breadboard; **boîte de jonction** *ou* **de raccordement** = junction box; **boîte noire** = black box **(c) boîte à outils** = *(de réparation)* toolbox; *(utilitaires pour programmes)* toolkit; *(zone de mémoire)* **boîte aux lettres (BAL)** = (electronic) mailbox *ou* mail box

boîtier *nm* (i) case; (ii) casing *ou* housing; **boîtier d'arrêt** *ou* **d'isolation** = barrier box; **boîtier protecteur** = enclosure; *(de circuit intégré)* **boîtier plat** = flat pack; **le numéro de fabrication est gravé de façon permanente sur le panneau arrière du boîtier de l'ordinateur** = the production number is permanently engraved on the back of the computer casing; **les disquettes sont rangées dans des boîtiers de protection rigides** = the disks are housed in hard protective cases; **quand on a laissé tomber l'ordinateur, son boîtier s'est abîmé** = the computer casing was damaged when it fell on the floor

bombe *nf* bombe; **bombe logique** = logic bomb; **le programmeur système a installé une bombe logique lorsqu'il a été licencié** = the system programmer installed a logic bomb when they made him redundant

bond *nm (transmission)* hop

Boole *n* **algèbre de Boole** = Boolean algebra *ou* Boolean logic; **table de Boole** = Boolean operation table

◊ **booléen, -éenne** *adj* Boolean; **algèbre booléenne** = Boolean algebra *ou* Boolean logic; **opérateur booléen** = Boolean operator; **opération booléenne** = Boolean operation; **opération booléenne à un opérande** = monadic Boolean operation; **opération booléenne dyadique** *ou* **opération booléenne à deux opérandes** = dyadic Boolean operation; **relation booléenne** = Boolean connective; **valeur booléenne** = Boolean value *ou* truth value; **variable booléenne** = Boolean variable

bord   *nm* edge; *(d'un système de reconnaissance optique)* **bord d'alignement** *ou* **de référence** = aligning edge; *(d'une feuille de papier)* **bord déchiqueté** *ou* **non rogné** = deckle edge; *(d'une carte perforée)* **bord d'introduction** *ou* **bord avant** = leading edge

◊ **bordure** *nf* border *ou* edge; **bordure d'écran** = screen border; *(par système de reconnaissance optique)* **détection de bordures** = edge detection

borne *nf* **(a)** *(de raccordement)* terminal *ou* barrel; *(d'un transistor à effet de champ)* **borne d'entrée** = source; **borne positive** = positive terminal **(b)** *(limites)* bounds; **bornes d'un tableau** = array bounds

boucle *nm* loop; **boucle d'amplification** = positive feedback; **boucle d'attente** = wait loop; **boucle conditionnelle 'WHILE'** = while-loop; **boucle conditionnelle FOR...NEXT** = for-next loop; **boucle continue** *ou* **sans fin** = continuous loop *ou* infinite loop *ou* endless loop; **boucle emboîtée** = nested loop; **boucle de feedback** = feedback loop; **boucle fermée** = closed loop; **boucle de fond** = loop *ou* looping program; **boucle imbriquée** = nested loop; **boucle intérieure** = inner loop; **boucle d'itération** = loop *ou* looping program; **boucle de maintien** = holding loop; **boucle de modification** = modification loop; **boucle ouverte** = open loop; **boucle de programme** = loop *ou* looping program; **boucle de réaction** = feedback loop; **boucle de récurrence** = daisy-chain recursion; **boucle avec retour automatique à zéro** *ou* **aux paramètres de départ** = self-resetting *ou* self-restoring loop; **boucle de rétroaction** = feedback loop; **boucle de temporisation** *ou* **de synchronisation** = timing loop; **être accroché dans une boucle** = to hang (in a loop); **compteur de boucles** = loop counter; **contrôle de boucle** = loop check; **corps de la boucle** = loop body; **créer une boucle** = to loop; **fréquence de boucle** = speed of loop; **vérification de boucle** = loop check **(b) en boucle** = circular; **antenne en boucle** = loop antenna; **fichier en boucle** = circular file; **film en boucle** = loop film; **liste en boucle** = circular list; **report en boucle** = end-around carry; **réseau en boucle** = loop network

◊ **bouclage** *nm* **fréquence de bouclage** = speed of loop

◊ **boucler** *vtr* to loop

bouffer *vtr (des données* *ou* *un fichier)* to mung up

boule *nf* ball; **boule d'impression** = golf-ball; **imprimante à boule** = golf-ball printer; **boule (de pointeur)** = trackball

bourdonnement *nm* hum

bourrage *nm (de l'entraînement du papier)* jam (in the paper feed); **l'emploi de papier plus mince évite le bourrage** = lightweight copier paper will feed without jamming

bout *nm* end *ou* ending; **bouts de ligne** = line endings

bouton *nm (de réglage, etc.)* knob *ou* dial; **pour obtenir la station de radio, tournez ce bouton** = to tune into the radio station, turn the dial; **pour ajuster la luminosité de l'écran, tourner le bouton placé à l'arrière du moniteur** = the brightness can be regulated by turning a knob at the back of the monitor; **bouton (de) contraste** = contrast knob *ou* dial; **bouton de densité** = density dial; **si l'impression est trop pâle, réglez le bouton de densité (d'impression) sur le noir** = if the text fades, turn the density dial on the printer to full black; **bouton d'enregistrement** = record button; **tourner le bouton marche/arrêt** = to turn the on/off knob; **bouton du volume** = volume control

◊ **bouton-poussoir** *nm* pushbutton

bpi = BITS PAR POUCE

bps = BITS PAR SECONDE

Braille *npr (écriture pour personnes aveugles)* Braille; **caractères Braille** = Braille marks; **elle lisait un livre en (caractères) Braille** = she was reading a Braille book; **il existe une édition en Braille de ce livre** = the book has been published in Braille

branche *nf* branch; **(programme) à plusieurs branches** = multithread (program); **branche d'un programme** = program branch; **une arborescence est formée de branches reliées les unes aux autres par des points de liaison ou noeuds** = a tree is made of branches that connect together at nodes

◇ **branchement** *nm* branch; *(de télévision câblée)* drop line; *(de routine)* leg; **le poste défectueux est connecté sur ce branchement** = the faulty station is on this branch; **effectuer un branchement** = to jump; **instruction de branchement** = branch instruction *ou* jump instruction *ou* transfer command; **branchement conditionnel** = conditional jump *ou* conditional transfer; **le branchement conditionnel choisira le programme 1 ou 2 suivant que la réponse est oui ou non** = the conditional branch will select routine one if the response is yes and routine two if no; **(instruction de) branchement conditionnel à l'indicateur zéro** = jump on zero; **effectuer un branchement (conditionnel) à zéro** = to jump on zero; **point de branchement** = branchpoint; **branchement inconditionnel** = unconditional jump; **contrôle de branchement** = transfer control; **opération de branchement** = jump operation; **symbole de branchement** = decision box

brancher 1 *vi (faire un branchement)* to branch **2** *vtr* **(a)** to plug *ou* to plug in; **ne soyez pas surpris si l'ordinateur ne fonctionne pas, vous ne l'avez pas branché sur le secteur** = no wonder the computer does nothing, you haven't plugged it in at the mains **(b)** to connect; **brancher une ligne sur une table d'écoute** = to tap a line

bras *nm* arm; **bras de lecture/écriture** = access arm *ou* actuator; **le bras de lecture est mis en position de parkage pendant le transport** = the access arm moves to the parking region during transport

bredouillage *nm (distorsion de la voix lors de la transmission)* slur

bricolé, -ée *adj* kludged *ou* kluged; **connexion bricolée** = dry joint; **programme** *ou* **système hâtivement bricolé** = kludge *ou* kluge

brillance *nf* brightness *ou* brilliance; **une trop forte brillance peut causer une** fatigue oculaire = the brightness of the monitor can hurt the eyes

brillant, -e *adj* **(a)** brilliant; **le fond est d'un rouge brillant** = the background colour is a brilliant red; **il utilise un blanc brillant pour les mises en valeur** = he uses brillant white for the highlights **(b)** glossy; **papier (couché) brillant** = glossy paper; **les illustrations sont imprimées sur papier brillant** = the illustrations are printed on glossy art paper

broche *nf (de connecteur)* pin; **fiche** *ou* **connecteur à trois broches** = three-pin plug; **prise secteur à deux broches** *ou* **à trois broches** = two-pin *ou* three-pin mains socket; **il faut un fiche à trois broches pour connecter** *ou* **brancher le système sur le secteur** = use a three-pin plug to connect the printer to the mains; **système à double rang de broches (parallèles)** = dual-in-line package (DIL *ou* DIP)

◇ **broché, -ée** *adj* **livre broché** = paperbound book *ou* paperback; **édition brochée** = paperbound edition *ou* paperback edition

brochure *nf* booklet *ou* brochure; **nous avons demandé une brochure sur les services de maintenance** = we sent off for a brochure about maintenance services

bromure *nf (imprimerie)* bromide *ou* bromide print; **24 heures plus tard nous avions reçu les bromures et pouvions faire les films** = in 24 hours we had bromides ready to film

brouillage *nm* **(a)** *(codage)* **il appelé le président sur la ligne protégée par brouillage** = he called the President on the scrambler telephone **(b)** *(parasites)* noise; **brouillage (de la réception)** = blanketing; **zone de brouillage** = mush area

◇ **brouillard** *nm (de transmission)* mush

brouiller *vtr* **(a)** *(coder)* to scramble **(b)** *(par interférence)* to jam; **cette tour brouille la transmission des émissions de télévision** = the TV signals are being jammed from that tower; **nous essayons de brouiller les signaux émis par cette station** = we are trying to jam the signals from that station

◇ **brouilleur** *nm* **codeur brouilleur** = scrambler

brouillon *nm* draft *ou* rough copy; **faire un brouillon** = to draft *ou* to make a rough copy; **(sortie d'imprimante) qualité brouillon** = draft printing

bruit *nm* **(a)** noise *ou* sound; **(niveau de) bruit ambiant** *ou* **bruit de fond** = ambient noise level *ou* background noise; **le bruit de fond dans ce bureau est plus élevé que dans la bibliothèque** = the ambient noise level in the office is greater than in the library **(b)** *(interférence)* static; **bruit atmosphérique causé par le soleil** = helios noise; **bruit blanc** = white noise; **bruits cosmiques** = galactic noise; **bruit de courte durée** = impulsive noise; **bruit extra-terrestre** = extra-terrestrial noise; **bruit de fond** = background noise *ou* babble; **le modem est sensible au bruit de fond** = the modem is sensitive to background noise; **les autres appareils placés autour de cet équipement produiront un fort bruit de fond** = the other machines around this device will produce a lot of background noise; **bruit intermittent** = impulsive noise; **bruits de numérisation** = quantizing noise; **bruit parasite causé par une machine** = man-made noise; **bruit thermique** = thermal noise; **analyseur de bruit** = decibel meter; **insensibilité au bruit** = noise immunity; **marge de bruit** = noise margin; **niveau de bruit d'un circuit** = circuit noise level; **réduction de bruit** = noise muting; **réduction du bruit d'interférence interstation** = interstation muting; **température de bruit** = noise temperature; **tolérance au bruit** = noise immunity; **limite de tolérance au bruit** = noise margin

brûler *vtr (une PROM)* to blast

◇ **brûlage** *nm* **faire un brûlage d'écran** = to burn in

brut, -e *adj* **(a)** raw; **données brutes** = raw data; **ce petit ordinateur recueille les données brutes venant des capteurs, les convertit et les transmet au gros ordinateur** = this small computer collects raw data from the sensors, converts it and transmits it to the mainframe **(b)** **poids brut** = gross weight

brutal, -e *adj (pour résoudre des problèmes informatiques)* **méthode brutale** = brute force method

bruyant, -e *adj* noisy; **les imprimantes laser sont beaucoup moins bruyantes que les imprimantes matricielles** = laser printers are much quieter than dot-matrix

BTAM = BASIC TELECOMMUNICATIONS ACCESS METHOD *(protocole d'accès de télécommunications britannique)* BTAM

bug *nm (dans un programme)* bug; *voir aussi* DEBOGAGE, DEBOGUER

bulle *nf* **(a)** bubble; **emballage bulle** = blister pack **(b)** bubble; **mémoire à bulles (magnétiques)** = (magnetic) bubble memory; **cassette mémoire à bulles (magnétiques)** = bubble memory cassette; **la mémoire à bulles est une mémoire non-volatile** = bubble memory is a non-volatile storage; **effectuer un tri bulle** *ou* **un tri par permutation de bulles** = to bubble sort

bulletin *nm (d'une société)* **bulletin d'informations** = (company) newsletter

bureau *nm* **(a)** *(meuble)* desk; **agenda de bureau** = desk diary; **lampe de bureau** = desk light; **ordinateur de bureau** = desk top unit *ou* desktop computer (system) **(b)** office; **il a ouvert son propre bureau d'ingénieur conseil en informatique** = he set up in business as an computer consultant; **bureau électronique** *ou* **automatisé** = automated office; **bureau d'études** = design department; **bureau informatisé** = electronic office; **bureau sans papier** *ou* **le bureau électronique** = paperless office; **le bureau du futur** = office of the future; **copieur de bureau** = office copier; **ordinateur de bureau** = business computer *ou* office computer; **système informatique pour bureau** = computer office system **(c)** *(société de services)* bureau; *US* facility; **bureau de photocopie** = photocopying bureau; **bureau de traitement de texte** = word-processing bureau; **nous avons ouvert un nouveau bureau de traitement de**

l'information = we have opened our new data processing facility; **nous confions notre correspondance à un bureau de secrétariat local** = we farm out the office typing to a local bureau
◇ **bureautique** *nf* office automation (OA); **logiciel bureautique** = business system *ou* business package; **salon de la bureautique** = business efficiency exhibition; **système bureautique** = computer office system *ou* electronic office system; **système de bureautique intégrée** = integrated office

burst *nm (de signaux)* burst

bus *nm* bus *ou* highway; **bus A** *ou* **bus principal** = A-bus; **bus d'adresses** = address bus *ou* address highway; **voies de liaison d'un bus d'adresses** = bus address lines; **bus d'arbitrage** *ou* **de régulation** = contention bus; **système à bus auxiliaire** = dual bus system; **bus bidirectionnel** = bi-directional bus; **bus de chaîne** *ou* **bus en cascade** *ou* **bus série** = daisy chain bus; **bus de contrôle** = control bus; **bus de données** *ou* **bus de transfert de données** = data bus *ou* data highway; **système à bus double** *ou* **à bus auxiliaire** = dual bus system; **bus d'entrée** = data input bus

(DIB); **bus (d') entrée/sortie** = I/O bus *ou* input/output (data) bus; **bus (conforme aux normes du) IEEE** = IEEE bus; **bus d'interface universel** *ou* **banalisé** = general purpose interface bus (GPIB); **bus de mémoire** = memory bus; **bus de micro-ordinateur** = microcomputer bus; **bus multiplexé** = multiplexed bus; **système multibus** *ou* **à bus multiples** = multi-bus system; **bus principal** *ou* **bus A** = A-bus; **bus de régulation** = contention bus; **bus série** *ou* **bus de chaîne** = daisy chain bus; **bus universel GPIB** = general purpose interface bus (GPIB); **arbitrage** *ou* **gestion de bus** = bus arbitration; **architecture à bus multiples** = multiple bus architecture; **(puits** *ou* **collecteur de données) asservi à un bus** = bus slave; **carte bus** = bus board; **esclave d'un bus** = bus slave; **gestion de (l'utilisation d'un) bus** = bus arbitration; **(émetteur de données) maître d'un bus** = bus master; **réseau de type bus** = bus network; **structure d'un bus** = bus structure

but *nm (visé ou atteint)* goal *ou* objective *ou* target

buzzer *nm* buzzer

Cc

C *(représentation hexadécimale du nombre 12)* C

C langage C = C language

C *(fréquence)* **bande C** = C band

CA = COURANT ALTERNATIF

cabestan *nm (d'une bande)* **cabestan d'entraînement** = capstan

cabine *nf* booth; **cabine téléphonique** = call box *ou* telephone booth

cabinet-conseil *nm* consultancy firm

câblage *nm* cabling *ou* wiring; **il a fallu remplacer le câblage du système** = the wiring in the system had to be replaced; **câblage permanent** = hardwired connection

câble *nm* **(a)** *(de liaison)* cable *ou* flex *ou* lead; **câble d'acheminement des signaux** *ou* **câble antenne-circuit** = feeder cable; **câble blindé** = shielded cable; **câble CATV** *ou* **câble de télévision (câblée)** = CATV cable; **câble coaxial** = co-axial cable; **câble d'entrée** = input lead; **câble étanche** = filled cable; **câble d'extension** = extension cable; **câble à fibres optiques** *ou* **câble optique** = fibre optic cable *ou* fibre optic connection; **les câbles à fibres optiques permettent de placer les noeuds jusqu'à un kilomètre l'un de l'autre** = fibre optic connections enable nodes up to one kilometre apart to be used; **câble de liaison** *ou* **de raccordement d'un tableau de distribution** = patchcord; **câble plat** = tape cable *ou* ribbon cable; **câble(s) souterrain(s)** = landline; **communication par câble** = line communications; **section élémentaire de câble** = elementary cable section **(b)** *(câblage)* cabling; **le câble peut coûter jusqu'à 12 francs les 30cm** = cabling

costs up to 12 francs a foot; **les câbles de haute qualité vont permettre à l'utilisateur d'obtenir un taux de transfert de données très élevé** = using high-quality cabling will allow the user to achieve very high data transfer rates; **les câbles (de) haute technologie doivent être manipulés avec soin** = high spec cabling needs to be very carefully handled **(c)** *(télégramme)* cable; **envoyer un câble** = to cable; **il a envoyé un câble au bureau pour redemander de l'argent** = he cabled his office to ask them to send more money **(d)** *(télévision)* **le câble** = cable television *ou* cable TV

◊ **câblé, -ée** *adj* **(a)** **réseau câblé** = cabling **(b)** **logique câblée** = hardwired logic; **logique câblée programmable** = programmable logic array (PLA); **ordinateur à logique câblée** = wired *ou* hardwired program computer *ou* fixed program computer; **programme en logique câblée** = hardwired program **(c)** **télévision câblée** = cable télévision *ou* cable TV; *(payante)* pay TV; *US* paycable; **télévision câblée interactive** = interactive cable television; **relai de télévision câblée** = cable TV relay station; **système de télévision câblée CATV** = community antenna television (CATV)

◊ **câbler** *vtr* **(a)** *(poser des câbles)* to wire *ou* to cable; **le studio est câblé pour la sonorisation** = the studio is wired for sound **(b)** *(envoyer un télégramme)* to wire *ou* to cable

◊ **câblogramme** *nm* cablegram *ou* telegram

cache **1** *nf* **mémoire cache** = cache memory; **stocker dans la mémoire cache** = to cache; **ce programme peut stocker une police de caractères, quelle qu'en soit la taille, dans la mémoire cache** = this program can cache any size font; **le temps d'accès est réduit lorsque les données les plus fréquemment utilisées sont placées dans la mémoire cache** = file access time is much quicker if the most frequently used data is stored in cache memory **2** *nm (masque pour film)* matt *ou* matte

◊ **caché, -ée** *adj* hidden; **fichiers cachés** = hidden files; **cela permet aux utilisateurs de sauvegarder ou de restaurer un par un les fichiers cachés** = it allows users to backup or restore hidden system files independently; **lignes cachées** = hidden lines; **effacement des lignes cachées** = hidden line removal; **algorithme d'effacement de lignes cachées** = hidden line algorithm; **vice** *ou* **défaut caché** = hidden defect in a program

◊ **cacher** *vtr* to hide *ou* to conceal

cacheté, -ée *adj* **enveloppe cachetée** = sealed envelope; **enveloppe non cachetée** = unsealed envelope

cadence *nf* speed; **prise de vue à cadence lente** = memomotion

cadrage *nm (d'une image)* framing; **cadrage d'une scène** = action frame; **dispositif de cadrage** = aligner

cadran *nm* dial; *(de téléphone)* **impulsion de cadran** = dial pulse

cadratin *nm* em quad; *(tiret dont la longueur équivaut à un 'm')* **tiret cadratin** = em dash *ou* em rule; *voir aussi* DEMI-CADRATIN

cadre *nm* **(a)** *(bordure)* border *ou* box; **les citations sont dans des cadres** = the quotations are printed in boxes **(b)** chassis *ou* frame; **cadre sous tension** = hot chassis **(c)** *(structure d'un programme)* framework; **on a d'abord établi le cadre du programme** = the program framework was designed first **(d)** *(élément de base)* **lettre cadre** = form letter *ou* standard letter **(e)** *(administrateur)* **cadre de direction** *ou* **cadre supérieur** = director *ou* manager

◊ **cadre-réponse** *nm (d'une page vidéotex)* response frame

◊ **cadrer** *vtr (une image sur l'écran)* to align

cage *nf* cage; **cage de Faraday** = Faraday cage

cahier *nm* **(a)** *(section d'un livre)* signature; **ordre des cahiers** = collating sequence; **pliage en cahiers de 16, 32 ou 64 pages** = even working **(b)** **cahier des charges** = job specification; **le travail ne répond pas au cahier des charges** = the work is not up to specification *ou* does not meet the customer's specifications

caisse *nf* packing case; **mettre dans une caisse** = to pack in a case *ou* to case

calcul *nm* **(a)** calculation; *(fait par un ordinateur)* computation *ou* computing; **j'ai fait un calcul approximatif au dos d'une enveloppe** = I made some rough calculations on the back of an envelope; **d'après mes calculs, il nous reste du stock pour six mois** = according to my calculations, we have six months' stock left; **calcul approximatif** = rough calculation; **calcul des dimensions** = dimensioning; **le calcul des dimensions du tableau se fait à cette ligne-ci** = array dimensioning occurs at this line; **édition après calculs** = post-editing; **centre de calcul** = computer centre; **erreur de calcul** = computational error; **puissance de calcul** = computing power; **processeur mathématique pour calcul (en masse) ultra-rapide** = number cruncher; *(processeur en tranches)* **unité centrale de calcul** = central processing element (CPE); **vitesse de calcul (par ordinateur)** = computing speed **(b)** arithmetic; **calcul binaire** = binary arithmetic;

◊ **calculable** *adj (par ordinateur)* computable

◊ **calculateur** *nm* computer; **calculateur analogique** = analog computer; **calculateur numérique** = electronic digital computer

◊ **calculatrice** *nf* calculator; **il a calculé la remise sur sa calculatrice** = he worked out the discount on his calculator; **calculatrice de poche** = pocket calculator; **j'ai besoin d'une pile pour ma calculatrice de poche** = my pocket calculator needs a new battery; **calculatrice avec fonctions scientifiques** = scientific calculator

◊ **calculé, -ée** *adj* calculated; *(sur ordinateur)* computed; **adresse calculée** = generated address *ou* synthetic address

◊ **calculer** *vt* to calculate; *(ordinateur)* to compute; **il a calculé la remise sur sa calculatrice** = he calculated *ou* he worked out the discount on his calculator; **le** directeur du centre de traitement a calculé le coût de saisie de texte sur clavier = the DP manager calculated the rate for keyboarding; **vous devez calculer l'espace libre sur la disquette** = you need to calculate the remaining disk space; **les frais de connection ont été calculés sur une base horaire** = connect charges were computed on an hourly rate

◊ **calculette** *nf* pocket calculator

calendrier *nm* calendar; **calendrier de bureau** = desk planner

calibrage *nm* calibration; **calibrage d'un texte** = cast off *ou* casting off
◊ **calibrer** *vtr* **(a)** to gauge **(b) calibrer un texte** = to cast off (a text)
◊ **calibre** *nm* gauge

Callier *n* **effet Callier** = callier effect

calligraphie *nf* calligraphy

Cambridge *n* **(réseau en) anneau de Cambridge** = Cambridge ring

camembert *nm* *(diagramme)* pie chart; **l'attribution de mémoire est indiquée sur ce camembert** = the memory allocation is shown on this pie chart

caméra *nm* cine camera *ou* film camera; **caméra de télévision** = television camera *ou* TV camera; **caméra de poursuite** = planetary camera; **caméra de traitement de l'image** = process camera; **caméra de vision nocturne** = infrared camera; **ensemble caméra** = camera chain

Caméscope® *nm* camcorder

canal *nm* **(a)** *(voie de transmission)* channel; **canal (de transmission) aller** = forward channel; **canal banal** = common carrier; **signalisation par canal banal** = common channel signalling; **canal de basses fréquences** = voice grade channel; **canal dédié** = dedicated channel; **canal (d') entrée/sortie** = input/output channel *ou* I/O channel; **canal de retour** = backward channel; **canal sélecteur** *ou* **de sélection** = selector channel; **canal spécialisé** = dedicated

channel; **canal de transmission** = transmission channel *ou* communications channel; **interface** *ou* **adaptateur de canal de transmission** = channel adapter; **canal de transmission de données** = data channel; **adaptateur de canal de transmission de données** = data adapter unit; **canal de transmission de l'information** = information transfer channel; **canal (de type) P** = p-channel; **semi-conducteur MOS à canal (de type) P** = p-channel MOS; **banque de canaux** = channel bank; **commande de canal** = channel command; **débit d'un canal** *ou* **d'une voie** = channel capacity; **interface** *ou* **adaptateur de canal de transmission** = channel adapter; **isolation de canaux** = channel isolation; **liaison directe entre canaux** = channel-to-channel connection; **surcharge** *ou* **saturation d'un canal** = channel overload; **synchroniseur de canaux** = channel synchronizer **(b)** *(télévision)* channel; **Canal 5** = Channel 5 **(c)** *(sur carte perforée)* **canal d'entraînement (avec perforations centrales)** = centre sprocket feed

◊ **canalisation** *nf* channelling *ou* conduit; **les câbles de liaison de tous les terminaux sont acheminés par canalisation métallique jusqu'au centre informatique** = the cables from each terminal are channelled to the computer centre by metal conduit

candela *nm* candela; **candela par pied carré** = foot candle

canon *nm* **(a) canon à électrons** = electron gun **(b) microphone 'canon'** = shotgun microphone **(c)** *(qui tourne sans erreur du premier coup)* **programme canon** = blue-ribbon program

canonique *adj* canonical; **base de données canonique** = canonical schema

CAO = CONCEPTION ASSISTEE PAR ORDINATEUR computer-aided *ou* assisted design (CAD); **tous nos ingénieurs travaillent sur des stations de CAO** = all our engineers design on CAD workstations

> la CAO (conception assistée par ordinateur) est l'ensemble des procédés de création, de calcul, de description d'objets virtuels à l'aide d'un ordinateur
> *Science et Vie Micro*

capable *adj* capable

capacitance *nf* capacitance

capacité *nf* **(a)** *(espace)* capacity; **le modèle le plus récent possède un disque dur d'une capacité de 30Mo** = the latest model has a 30Mbyte hard disk; **le nouveau lecteur de disquettes a une capacité de 100Ko** = the new disk drive has a 100Kb capacity; **capacité d'adressage** = *(espace adressable)* addressing capacity; *(en infographie)* addressability; **capacité d'un circuit** = circuit capacity; **utiliser la capacité en excédent** = to use up spare *ou* excess capacity; **capacité maximale** = maximum capacity; **capacité de mémoire** = memory capacity *ou* storage capacity; **la capacité de mémoire est maintenant de 3Mo** = total storage capacity is now 3Mb; **(mémoire) tampon à capacité variable** = elastic buffer; *(capacité maximale d'un système)* **capacité théorique absolue** = absolute maximum rating; **capacité d'une voie de transmission** = channel capacity; **débordement de capacité (d'une ligne)** = overflow; **(nombre) qui dépasse la capacité (de mémoire) d'un ordinateur** = out of range (number); **dépassement de capacité** = overflow *ou* OV; **contrôle de dépassement de capacité** = overflow check; **bit** *ou* **indicateur** *ou* **drapeau** *ou* **marque de dépassement de capacité** = overflow bit *ou* flag *ou* indicator; **support de stockage de grande capacité** = bulk sotrage medium *ou* mass storage device **(b)** *(possibilité)* capability; **capacité de définition** = resolution capabilities; **capacité d'émulation** = emulation facility; **capacité de traitement (électronique) de données** = EDP capability; **la capacité de transmission** *ou* **de portage de cette liaison est excellente** = the information-carrying abilities of this link are very good **(c)** *(condensateur)* capacitor; **capacité variable** = variable capacitor

> la gamme propose un choix de disques durs d'une capacité de 20Mo à 660Mo
> *L'Ordinateur Individuel*

capacitif, -ive *adj* capacitative *ou* capacitive; **mémoire capacitive** = capacitor storage

capitale *nf* **(a)** *(imprimerie)* capital (letter) *ou* cap; **petites capitales** = small caps; *(d'une machine à écrire ou d'un clavier)* **touche (des) capitales** = shift key; **le voyant s'allume quand la touche (des) capitales est verrouillée** = the LED lights up when caps lock is pressed **(b)** *(écrit à la main)* **(lettres) capitales** = block capitals *ou* block letters; **écrire en capitales** = to write in block capitals *ou* to print; **écrivez votre nom et votre adresse en capitales** = write your name and address in block letters *ou* print your name and address

capot *nm* hood; **capot d'insonorisation** = acoustic hood

capteur *nm* sensor; *(médical)* biosensor; **ce processus est contrôlé par une batterie de capteurs** = the process is monitored by a bank of sensors; **le signal de sortie du capteur varie suivant la température** = the sensor's output varies with temperature; **capteur d'images** = image sensor; **capteur d'images vidéo** = frame grabber; *(pour ondes radio)* **capteur directionnel** = horn; **capteur de pression** = pressure pad

capture *nf (pour numériser une image)* **(effectuer une) capture d'écran** = screen grab

caractère *nm* **(a)** character; **caractère (de déclenchement) d'alarme** = bell character; **caractères alpha-numériques** = alphanumeric characters; **caractère d'annulation** = cancel character (CAN); **le logiciel envoie automatiquement un caractère d'annulation à chaque erreur** = the software automatically sends a cancel character after any error; **caractère blanc** = space character; **insertion de caractères blancs** = character fill; **remplissage avec caractères blancs** = character stuffing; **caractère clignotant** = (i) flashing character; (ii) character blink; **caractères codés binaires** = binary coded characters; **caractère de contrôle** = check character *ou* control character; **caractère de contrôle d'impression** = print control character; **caractère de contrôle** *ou* **de commande de périphérique** = device control character; **caractère d'échappement** = escape character; *(sur écran vidéotex)* **caractères éclatés** =

blast-through alphanumerics; **caractère d'écran** = display character; **caractère d'effacement** = delete character *ou* erase character; **caractère (d')espace** = blank character *ou* space character; **caractère d'espacement** = space character; **caractères (mis) en évidence** = highlights; **caractère de fonction** = function digit; **caractère graphique** = graphics character; **caractère d'identification** = identification character *ou* identifier; **caractère d'instruction** = instruction character; **caractère interdit** = forbidden character; **chaîne de caractères interdits** = forbidden combination; **caractère d'interrogation** = enquiry character (ENQ); **caractère invalide** = illegal character; **caractère nul** = idle character *ou* null character; **caractère (à valeur) numérique** = numeric character; **caractères parasites** = gibberish; **caractère de rejet d'un bloc (dont les données sont mauvaises)** = block ignore character; **caractère de remplissage** = fill character *ou* gap character *ou* ignore character *ou* null character *ou* redundant character; **insertion de caractères de remplissage (en mémoire)** = character fill; **caractère de requête** = enquiry character (ENQ); **(nombre de) caractères par seconde (cps)** = characters per second (cps); **caractère de signal sonore** = bell character; **caractère de suppression** = delete character; **caractères en surbrillance** = highlights **(b) ordinateur à mode caractère** = character orientated computer; **(système de) contrôle de périphérique utilisant des caractères** = device character control; **affichage de caractères** = character display; **assemblage de caractères** = character assembly; **bloc (de) caractères** = character block; **chaîne de caractères** = character string *ou* catena; **nombre de caractères dans une chaîne** = catena; **code de caractères** = character code; **le code ASCII est le code de caractères le plus fréquemment utilisé** = the ASCII code is the most frequently used character coding system; **code de caractères interne** = internal character code; **contrôle de caractère(s)** = character check; **contrôle de blocs par caractères** = block character check (BCC); **densité de caractère** = character density; **écrire en caractères d'imprimerie** = to print *ou* to write in capital letters; **ensemble de caractères** = character set; **ensemble de caractères**

nuls = empty *ou* null set; **espacement (proportionnel) de caractères** = intercharacter spacing; **expression binaire d'un caractère** = character representation; **générateur de caractères** = character generator; **on peut utiliser une ROM comme générateur de caractères pour obtenir les différentes polices** = the ROM used as a character generator can be changed to provide different fonts; **générateur de caractères fac-similés** = facsimile character generator; **groupage de caractères** = character assembly; **imprimante caractère (par caractère)** = character printer; **jeu de caractères** = character set; **jeu de caractères nuls** = empty *ou* null set; **lecteur optique de caractères** = optical character reader (OCR); **matrice de caractères** = character matrix; **police de caractères** = font *ou* fount *ou* character set *ou* character repertoire; **police de caractères reconnaissable par lecture optique** = optical font *ou* OCR font; **police de caractères téléchargeable** = downloadable font; **police de caractères vectorielle** = dynamically redefinable character set; **processeur en mode caractère** = character machine; **reconnaissance optique de caractères** = optical character recognition (OCR); **système de reconnaissance de caractères CSM (par identification des caractéristiques combinées)** = combined symbol matching (CSM); **remplissage avec caractères blancs** = character stuffing; **répertoire de caractères** = character repertoire; **support de polices de caractères** = image carrier; **touche de caractère** = character key; **vérification de caractère** = character check **(c)** *(lettre-bloc d'imprimerie)* **caractères d'imprimerie** = type *ou* font; **caractères fondus au moment de la composition** = hot metal type; **caractères utilisés pour le corps d'un texte** = body type; **caractère accent** = piece accent; **caractères Braille** = Braille marks; **caractère complet** = fully formed character; **la marguerite imprime des caractères complets** = a daisy wheel printer produces fully formed characters; **caractères Elite** = elite; **caractère gras** = bold face; **(donner une instruction d') imprimer en caractères gras** = to put in bold *ou* to embolden; **caractères de machine à écrire** = typewriter faces; **caractère spécial** = special character; **(nombre de) caractères par pouce** = characters per inch (cpi); **le bouton vert vous permet de sélectionner**

10 ou 12 caractères par pouce = you can select 10 or 12 cpi with the green button; **(nombre de) caractères par seconde (cps)** = characters per second (cps); **imprimante à caractères pleins** = solid font printer; **taille des caractères utilisés dans la composition** = composition size

caractéristique 1 *nf*(a) characteristic *ou* feature *ou* aspect; **caractéristique essentielle** *ou* **principale** *ou* **la plus importante** = prime attribute *ou* main feature *ou* key feature *ou* highlight; **les principales caractéristiques de ce système sont les suivantes: 20Mo de mémoire formatée avec temps d'accès de 60ms** = the key features of this system are: 20Mb of formatted storage with an access time of 60ms; **caractéristique d'un circuit** = circuit grade; **caractéristique d'un fichier** = attribute; **dépassement de capacité de la caractéristique** = characteristic overflow **(b)** *(math)* **en virgule flottante, la valeur de la caractéristique du nombre 1,345 x 10³ est de 3** = the floating point number 1.345 x 10³ , has a characteristic of 3 **2** *adj* characteristic; **courbe caractéristique** = characteristic curve; **c'est un défaut caractéristique de cette marque et de ce modèle d'ordinateur individuel en particulier** = this fault is characteristic of this make and model of personal computer

carbone *nm* *(papier)* carbon (paper); **vous avez oublié de mettre un carbone dans votre machine à écrire** = you forgot to put a carbon in the typewriter; **copie carbone** = carbon copy; **ruban carbone** = carbon ribbon

◊ **carboné, -ée** *adj* carbon-coated; **formulaire avec double carboné** = carbon set

cardioïde *adj&nf* (réponse) **cardioïde** = cardioid response

carré *nm* square; **5 au carré égale 25** *ou* **le carré de 5 est 25** = 5 to the power 2 is equal to 25 *ou* 5 squared equals 25

◊ **carré, -ée** *adj* **(a)** square; *(poids du papier)* **grammes au mètre carré** = grams per square metre (gsm *ou* g/m²); **racine carrée** = square root **(b) onde carrée** = square wave

carte *nf* **(a)** *(de circuit)* card *ou* board; **carte accélératrice** = accelerator card; **carte adaptateur** = adapter card; **carte adaptateur graphique couleur** = enhanced graphics adapter (EGA) *ou* EGA card; **carte bus** = bus board; **carte CGA** = colour graphics adapter (CGA) *ou* CGA card; **carte de circuit imprimé** = printed circuit board *ou* card; **carte connecteur** = bus board; **carte à connexion** = edge board *ou* card; **carte de contrôle** = control card; **carte contrôleur de disque(tte)** = disk-controller card; **carte de disque dur** = hard card; **carte EGA** = EGA card *ou* enhanced graphics adapter (EGA); **carte d'extension** = expansion card *ou* expansion board *ou* add-on board *ou* add-in card; **carte fille** = daughter board; **carte graphique** = graphics board; **la carte graphique haute définition contrôle jusqu'à 300 pixels par pouce** = the HRG board can control up to 300 pixels per inch; **carte (d') interface** = interface card; **carte logique** = logic card *ou* logic board; **carte mémoire** = memory board; **carte mère** = motherboard; **carte mère d'un micro-ordinateur** = microcomputer backplane; **carte processeur** = processor card; **vous pouvez soit vous servir d'un langage de description de pages soit ajouter une carte processeur** = you can use a page description language, or an add-in processor card; **micro-ordinateur à carte unique** = single board microcomputer; **ordinateur à carte unique** = single board computer (SBC *ou* sbc); **carte vidéo** = video card; **circuit intégré de carte vidéo** = video interface chip; **connecteur de carte** = (card) edge connector; **connecteur** *ou* **créneau pour carte d'extension** = expansion slot; **chassis avec guide cartes** = card cage *ou* card frame *ou* card chassis; **support de cartes** = card cage *ou* card frame *ou* card chassis; **support de carte d'extension** = card extender **(b) carte perforée** = punch card *ou* punched card; *(pour microfilm)* **carte à encoches marginales** = edge notched card; **carte en-tête** = header card; **carte à fenêtre** = aperture card; **carte maîtresse** = master card; **carte à microfilm** *ou* à **microfiche** = aperture card; **(système d') alimentation** *ou* **entraînement de cartes perforées** = card feed; **champ de carte** = card field; **chargeur de cartes** = card loader *ou* hopper; **code de perforation de carte** = card code; **format de carte (perforée)** = card format; **jeu** *ou* **paquet de cartes perforées** = deck of punch cards;

image (mémoire) de carte = card image; lecteur de cartes perforées = card reader ou punched card reader; programme sur cartes perforées = program cards (c) carte magnétique = (i) magnetic card; (ii) personal identification device (PID); (iii) smart card; champ de carte (magnétique) = card field; lecteur de cartes magnétiques = magnetic card reader; carte (magnétique) de crédit = credit card ou electronic money; carte magnétique à mémoire = smart card ou chip card; à l'avenir, on pourrait inclure les empreintes digitales de l'utilisateur sur ses cartes à mémoire à fin d'identification = future smart cards could contain an image of the user's fingerprint for identification; carte à puce = chip card ou smart card; les cartes à puce aident à réduire le nombre de fraudes = smart cards reduce fraud; carte de retrait (bancaire) = cash card; téléphone à carte = card phone (c) carte de fichier = index card; carte 'flash' = flash card; carte graphitée = mark sensing card; carte d'identité = identity card ou ID card (d) (géographique) map

cartésien, -ienne adj cartesian; coordonnées cartésiennes = cartesian coordinates; structure cartésienne = cartesian structure

carton nm (a) (boîte) cardboard box ou case; le clavier est emballé dans du polystyrène expansé avant d'être mis dans son carton = the keyboard is packed in expanded polystyrene before being put into the box (b) (matériel plus épais que le papier) card; (très épais et solide ou pour boîtes) cardboard; nous avons fait imprimé les instructions sur carton blanc épais = we have printed the instructions on thick white card

◊ cartonnage nm (reliure cartonnée) case

◊ cartonné, -ée adj (reliure) cased; couverture cartonnée = case binding; relier avec couverture cartonnée = to case (a book); livre avec couverture cartonnée ou livre cartonné = cased book ou hardbound book; édition cartonnée = hardback ou hardcover; ce livre paraîtra en édition cartonnée et en livre de poche = we are publishing the book as a hardback and as a paperback; l'édition pour bibliothèques est cartonnée avec jaquette = the library edition has a case and jacket; nous avons imprimé 4000 exemplaires cartonnés et 10 000 brochés = we printed 4,000 copies of the hardcover edition, and 10,000 of the paperback

◊ cartonner vtr (un livre) to case (a book); machine à cartonner = case-making machine

cartouche nf cartridge; cartouche (de) bande = tape cartridge; cartouche (de) bande magnétique = magnetic cartridge; cartouche (de) disque = disk cartridge; cartouche de disquette = flexible disk cartridge; cartouche de données = data cartridge; (d'imprimante) cartouche d'encre ou de toner = toner cartridge; cartouche longue durée = durable cartridge; cartouche de police de caractères = cartridge fonts; cartouche ROM = ROM cartridge; cet ordinateur portatif n'est pas équipé de lecteur de disquettes mais possède un connecteur pour cartouches ROM = the portable computer has no disk drives, but has a slot for ROM cartridges; ruban d'imprimante en cartouche = cartridge ribbon; lecteur de cartouches = cartridge drive

cascade nf bus en cascade = daisy chain bus; connexion (montée) en cascade = cascade connection; la connexion en cascade réduit le câblage = daisy-chaining saves a lot of cable; contrôle en cascade = cascade control; relier en cascade = to daisy-chain; report en cascade = cascade carry ou high speed carry

case nf (d'un formulaire) case vide = blank (space); (d'un formulaire graphité) case réservée à la réponse = response position

casque nm (d'écoute) headset ou headphones

casse nf (imprimerie) case; (minuscule) bas de casse = lower case; (majuscule) haut de casse = upper case

cassette nf cassette ou tape cassette ou cassette tape; c'est en général avec les ordinateurs domestiques qu'on utilise les cassettes = cassette tape is mainly used with home computers; cassette audionumérique = digital cassette;

cassette de bande magnétique = magnetic cassette; **cassette compacte** = compact cassette; **cassette informatique** = data cassette; **cassette mémoire à bulles (magnétiques)** = bubble memory cassette; **il faut faire une cassette de sauvegarde pour vos données** = you must back up the information from the computer onto a cassette; **magnétophone à cassette** = cassette recorder

catalogue *nm* catalogue; *(bibliothèque)* **responsable de catalogue** = cataloguer

◊ **cataloguer** *vtr* to catalogue

catastrophe *nf* catastrophe; **erreur qui cause une catastrophe** = catastrophic error

cathode *nf* cathode

◊ **cathodique** *adj* **tube à rayons cathodiques** *ou* **tube cathodique** = cathode ray tube (CRT); **tube cathodique pour téléviseur** = television tube

CATV *voir* ANTENNE ; **câble CATV** = CATV cable

cavalier *nm* jumper; **(circuit** *ou* **dispositif) qui peut être sélectionné** *ou* **validé par cavalier** = jumper-selectable; **sur cette imprimante, la police de caractères peut être sélectionnée par cavalier** = the printer's typeface is jumper-selectable

caviardage *nm (familier)* **caviardage de la mémoire** = checkerboarding

CB = CITIZEN BAND; **radio CB** *ou* **radio à bande CB** = citizens band radio *ou* CB radio

CC = COURANT CONTINU

CCD *voir* DISPOSITIF ; **mémoire CCD** = CCD memory

CCITT = COMITE CONSULTATIF INTERNATIONAL DES TELEGRAPHES ET DES TELEPHONES

CD = COMPACT DISK; **disque CD** *ou* **CD** = compact disk *ou* CD; **lecteur de disques CD** = compact disk player *ou* CD player

◊ **CD-ROM** = COMPACT DISK-READ ONLY MEMORY; **disque CD-ROM** = CD-ROM *ou* compact disk ROM *ou* compact disk-read only memory; **on peut stocker autant de données sur un (disque) CD-ROM que sur une douzaine de disques durs** = a CD-ROM can store as much data as a dozen hard disks

le CD-ROM est un support technologiquement stable, fiable et de moins en moins cher

Micro Systèmes

contrairement à l'idée reçue, les coûts d'une diffusion de l'information sur support CD-ROM sont globalement inférieurs à ceux d'une impression papier

Micro Systèmes

cédille *nf* cedilla

cellulaire *adj* cellular; **radiotéléphone (de type) cellulaire** = cellular radio; **téléphone cellulaire** = cell phone *ou* cellular phone *ou* mobile radiophone *ou* private mobile radio (PMR)

◊ **cellule** *nf* cell; *(d'un tableau)* element; **cellule binaire** = binary cell; **cellule de contrôle des couleurs** = colour cell; **cellule magnétique** = magnetic cell; **cellule de mémoire** = memory cell; **cellule photoconductrice** = photoconductor; **cellule photoélectrique** = photoelectric cell *ou* photocell; **la cellule photoélectrique décèle la quantité de lumière qui traverse le liquide** = the photoelectric cell detects the amount of light passing through the liquid; **variable de location** *ou* **de référence d'une cellule** = cell reference variable

cent *num* hundred; **pour cent** = per cent; **un pour cent** = one per cent *ou* one percentage point; **dix pour cent** = 10 per cent; **le taux d'erreur est tombé à douze pour cent** = the error rate has fallen to twelve per hundred

centi- *préf* centi-

centile *nm* percentile

centimètre *nm* centimetre; **centimètre-colonne** = column-centimetre

centrage *nm (d'un texte)* centering

central *nm (téléphonique)* telephone exchange; **central automatique** = automatic telephone exchange; **central automatique électronique** = electronic automatic exchange; **central répartiteur** = area exchange; **central téléphonique électromécanique** *ou* **central Strowger** = strowger exchange; **central téléphonique manuel privé (raccordé au secteur public)** = private manual branch exchange (PMBX); **central téléphonique privatif (non raccordé au réseau public)** = private automatic exchange (PAX); *voir aussi* AUTOCOMMUTATEUR

◊ **central, -e** *adj* central; **horloge centrale** = main clock; **mémoire centrale** = core memory *ou* core store *ou* main memory *ou* main storage *ou* central memory *ou* primary memory; **programme en mémoire centrale** = core program; **mémoire centrale rapide** = fast core; **dans ce système, la mémoire centrale rapide sert de bloc-notes pour tous les calculs** = the fast core is used as a scratchpad for all calculations in this system; **opérateur central** = centre operator; **ordinateur central** = mainframe (computer) *ou* central computer; *(d'une carte perforée)* **perforations centrales** = centre holes; **processeur central** = central processor *ou* central processing unit (CPU); **terminal central** = central terminal; *(processeur en tranches)* **unité centrale de calcul** = central processing element (CPE); **unité centrale (de traitement)** *ou* **processeur central** = central processing unit (CPU) *ou* central processor; **éléments de l'unité centrale** = CPU elements; **(temps de) cycle de l'unité centrale** = CPU cycle; **temps d'utilisation de l'unité centrale** = CPU time

◊ **centrale** *nf* centre; **centrale d'information** = information retrieval centre

◊ **centralisé, -ée** *adj* centralized; **réseau informatique centralisé** = centralized computer network; **traitement centralisé de l'information** = centralized data processing

centre *nm* centre; *US* center; **centre de calcul** = computer centre; **centre de commutation des données** = data switching exchange; **centre de distribution** = distribution point; **centre de recherche documentaire** *ou* **centre serveur** = information retrieval centre; **centre de traitement de texte** = editorial processing centre; **nous avons ouvert un nouveau centre de traitement de l'information** = we have opened our new data processing facility

centrer *vtr* to centre; *US* to center; **sur quelle touche faut-il appuyer pour centrer l'en-tête?** = which key do you press to centre the heading?; **il est plutôt facile de centrer les en-têtes en utilisant cette touche de fonction** = centering of headings is easily done, using this function key

Centronics **interface parallèle (de type) Centronics** = Centronics interface

CEPT = CONFERENCE OF EUROPEAN POST, TELEPHONE AND TELEGRAPH STANDARD; **norme CEPT** = CEPT standard

céramique *adj* ceramic; **condensateur céramique** = ceramic capacitor

cercle *nm* circle; **décrire un cercle** = (i) to draw a circle; (ii) to circulate

certain, -e *adj* certain; **erreur certaine** = solid error

césure *nf* **(a)** *(procédure)* hyphenation *ou* word break; **césure et justification** = hyphenation and justification *ou* H & J; **(fonction de) césure et justification** = hyphenate and justify; **fonction césure intelligente** = intelligent spacer; **programme de césure et justification** = H & J program; **un programme de césure et de justification établi aux Etats-Unis ne peut être utilisé pour un texte en anglais britannique** = an American hyphenation and justification program will not work with British English spellings; **replacement de césures** = rehyphenation **(b)** *(trait d'union)* hyphen; **césure d'écran** = soft *ou* discretionary hyphen; **tiret de césure (dont la longueur équivaut à un 'n')** = en dash *ou* en rule

CFAO = CREATION ET FABRICATION ASSISTEES PAR ORDINATEUR

la CFAO (création et fabrication assistées par ordinateur) fait intervenir l'ordinateur d'un bout à l'autre du processus de production (conception d'un objet, simulation de son comportement et fabrication à l'aide de robots commandés par ordinateur)
Science et Vie Micro

CGA *voir* ADAPTATEUR; **carte CGA** = CGA card

chaînage *nm* chaining; **chaînage de données** = data chaining

◊ **chaîne** *nf* **(a)** *(série de caractères)* chain *ou* daisy chain *ou* string *ou* catenation; **(nombre de) caractères dans une chaîne** = catena; **chaîne de caractères** = character string *ou* catena; **chaîne de caractères alphabétiques** = alphabetic string; **chaîne de caractères alphanumériques** = alphanumeric string; **chaîne contenant des caractères d'espace** = blank string; **chaîne (de caractères) interdite** = forbidden combination; **chaîne de caractères numériques** = numeric string; **chaîne de commandes** = command chain; **chaîne d'éléments de données** = data element chain; **chaîne vide** = empty string *ou* null string *ou* blank string; **balayage de chaînes** = string scanning; **bus de chaîne** = daisy chain bus; **comparaison de chaînes** = string matching; **concaténation de chaînes** = string concatenation; **fonction (de) chaîne** = string function; **nom de chaîne** = string name; **taille d'une chaîne** = string length; **variable de chaîne** = string variable; **variable de type chaîne de caractères** = string type **(b) en chaîne** = chained *ou* chaining *ou* chain; **code en chaîne** = chain code; **la connexion en chaîne réduit le câblage** = daisy-chaining saves a lot of cable; **interruption en chaîne** = daisy chain interrupt; **liaison de données en chaîne** = data chaining; **liste en chaîne** = chain list; **recherche en chaîne** = chaining search; **relier en chaîne** = to daisy-chain; **données reliés en chaîne** = concatenated data set **(c)** *(série d'appareils)* **une chaîne haute fidélité** *ou* **une chaîne hi-fi** = a hi fi system *ou* a hi fi set **(d) imprimante à chaîne** = chain printer

◊ **chaîné, -ée** *adj* chained; **arborescence chaînée** = threaded tree; **article chaîné** = chained record; **fichier avec articles chaînés** = threaded file; **liste d'articles chaînés** = chain list; **code chaîné** = chain code; **données chaînées** = concatenated data set; **enregistrement chaîné** = chained record; **fichier chaîné** = chained file *ou* threaded file; **programme à fonctions chaînées** = thread; **langage chaîné** = threaded language; **liste chaînée** = chained list *ou* linked list; **sous-programme chaîné** = linked subroutine; **variable chaînée** = string type

◊ **chaîner** *vtr* to catenate *ou* to concatenate *ou* to chain

chaleur *nf* heat; **évacuateur de chaleur** = heat sink

chambre *nf* chamber *ou* room; **chambre blanche** = anechoic chamber; **chambre à écho** = echo chamber; **chambre noire** = darkroom

champ *nm* **(a)** *(section de fichier ou de carte)* field; **le dossier 'employés' possède un champ 'âge'** = the employee record has a field for age; **les commandes ont été triées sur le champ date** = the orders were sorted according to dates by assigning the date field as the sortkey; **champ d'adresse** = address field; **champ bloc-notes** = comment field; **champ d'une carte magnétique** = magnetic card field; **champ de carte perforée** = punched card field; **champ clé** = key field; **champ de contrôle** = control field; **champ de données** = data field; **champ label** *ou* **champ d'identification** = label field; **champ d'opérande** = operand field; **champ d'opération** = operation field; **dispositif à champ programmable** = field programmable device; **champ protégé** = protected field; **champ de taille constante** *ou* **fixe** = fixed field; **champ de tri** = sortkey *ou* sort field; **dimension d'un champ** = field length; **élément** *ou* **item d'un champ** = member; **étiquette** *ou* **label d'un champ** = field label; **intensité de champ** = field strength; **marqueur de champ** = field marker; **programmation de champ** = field programming; **séparateur de champs** = field marker *ou* separator; **taille d'un champ** = field length **(b)** *(télévision)* **(action) hors champ** = off screen (action); **balayage hors champ** = overscan; **champ d'une scène** = action frame; *(photo)* **profondeur de champ** = depth of field **(c) champ magnétique** = magnetic field; **semiconducteur à effet de champ MOSFET** = metal oxide semiconductor field effect transistor (MOSFET); **transistor à effet de champ (TEC)** = field effect transistor (FET)

certains champs comportent plusieurs options non visibles dans ce menu; pour les visualiser, vous utilisez la touche de fonction F1

L'Ordinateur Individuel

le champ magnétique apparaît donc comme créé par le mouvement de particules électrisées

Science et Vie

changement *nm* **(a)** *(dans un texte ou fichier)* alteration *ou* change *ou* modification *ou* variation; **changement d'adresse en mémoire =** memory edit **(b)** *(d'un système à un autre)* change *ou* change-over *ou* crossover; **changement de banque** *ou* **de bloc de mémoire =** bank switching; **changement graduel** *ou* **progressif =** phased change-over; **(instruction de) changement de page =** form feed; **changement de police de caractères =** font change

◊ **changer** *vtr* **(a)** to alter *ou* to change *ou* to modify *ou* to vary; **sauvegarder le fichier mais changez-en le nom et appelez-le CLIENT =** save the file and rename it CLIENT; **qui peut être changé =** alterable **(b)** to change *ou* to switch over to *ou* to change over to; **changer d'appareil =** to change machines; **changer de place =** to move *ou* to change places **(c)** to replace; **un ruban qui a imprimé plusieurs milliers de caractères a besoin d'être changé =** a printer ribbon needs replacing after several thousand characters

◊ **changeur** *nm* changer; **changeur de disques (automatique) =** record changer; **changeur de genre =** gender changer; **il est possible de relier tous ces périphériques en utilisant seulement deux câbles et un changeur de genre =** you can interconnect all these peripherals with just two cables and a gender changer

chapitre *nm* chapter; **tête de chapitre =** chapter heading; **les têtes de chapitre sont composées en caractères gras de 12 points =** chapter headings are in 12 point bold

charbon *nm* **microphone à charbon =** carbon microphone

charge *nf* **(a)** charge *ou* load; **charge électrique =** electric charge; **par charge électrostatique =** electrostatically; **(temps de) charge d'une pile =** battery charging **(b)** *(d'une ligne)* line load; **charge accordée** *ou* **équilibrée =** matched load; **facteur de charge =** load **(c)** **dispositif à couplage de charge =** charge-coupled device (CCD); **mémoire à couplage de charge =** CCD memory *ou* charge-coupled device memory **(d)** **charge de travail =** workload **(e)** **cahier des charges =** job specification; **le travail ne répond pas au cahier des charges =** the work is not up to specification *ou* does not meet the customer's specifications

◊ **chargement** *nm* *(d'un programme)* loading; **le chargement (d'un programme) peut être assez long à effectuer =** loading can be a long process; **chargement dispersé des données =** scatter load; **faire un chargement dispersé** *ou* **éclaté =** to scatter load; **lanceur de programme de chargement =** initial program header; **programme de chargement-lancement =** load and run *ou* load and go; **programme de chargement de la mémoire vive =** RAM loader

◊ **charger** *vtr* **(a)** *(batterie)* to charge; **charger une ligne =** to load a line **(b)** *(programme)* to load; **charger une PROM =** to blow a PROM **(c)** *(papier ou cartes)* to feed *ou* to load (into a printer, etc.); **le papier doit être chargé manuellement dans l'imprimante =** the paper should be manually fed into the printer **(d)** **charger un bit =** to set a bit

◊ **chargeur** *nm* **(a)** disk cartridge *ou* disk pack **(b)** *(de programme)* loader *ou* bootstrap (loader); **chargeur absolu =** absolute loader; **chargeur automatique =** automatic loader; **chargeur binaire =** binary loader; **chargeur/éditeur de liens =** linking loader; **chargeur de programme de lancement =** initial program loader (IPL); **(programme) chargeur de la mémoire vive =** RAM loader **(c)** **chargeur de cartes =** card loader; **chargeur de cartes perforées =** hopper

le chargement d'une fiche en mémoire ou une impression tiendront compte automatiquement des liens avec d'autres fichiers

L'Ordinateur Individuel

pour charger plusieurs fichiers en une seule opération séparez le nom de chaque fichier par un espace

L'Ordinateur Individuel

chariot *nm* **(a)** *(machine à écrire ou traitement de texte)* carriage; **commande de chariot** = carriage control; **les codes de commande de chariot peuvent être utilisés pour faire avancer le papier de deux interlignes** = carriage control codes can be used to move the paper forward two lines between each line of text; **retour de chariot** = carriage return; **touche de retour du chariot** = carriage return key **(b) chariot piloté par ordinateur** = buggy

chasse *nf (imprimerie)* set width

châssis *nm* chassis; **châssis avec guide cartes** = card cage *ou* card frame *ou* card chassis; **châssis sous tension** = hot chassis

chaud, -e *adj* **(a)** hot; **test à chaud** = burn-in **(b) point chaud** = hot spot; **zone chaude** = hot zone

chauffer *vi* to heat *ou* to overheat; **il se peut que le système chauffe si la pièce n'est pas climatisée** = the system may overheat if the room is not air-conditioned

chef *nm* head of department *ou* manager; **chef éclairagiste** = lighting director; **chef du service informatique** = data processing manager

chemin *nm* path *ou* route; **le chemin choisi ne s'est pas révélé le plus direct du fait que de nombreux noeuds étaient occupés** = the route taken was not the most direct since a lot of nodes were busy; **chemin des données** = data path; *(maquette d'édition)* **chemin de fer** = editing plan *ou* flatplan

◇ **cheminement** *nm* route

chemise *nf (pour dossier)* cardboard file *ou* folder

chercher *vtr* **(a)** *(dans un programme ou un texte)* to search *ou* to seek; *(instruction)* **chercher** = get *(instruction)*; *(instruction)* **cherche et remplace** = find and replace; *(instruction)* **aller chercher et lire** = fetch *(instruction)* **(b)** *(examiner attentivement)* **il a cherché Saint-Victor-de-Réno sur la carte** = he scanned the map for St Victor-de-Réno

cheval de Troie *nm* *(programme pirate)* Trojan Horse

chevauchement *nm* lap *ou* overlap
◇ **(se) chevaucher** *vi* to overlap

chiffrage *nm* encryption; **chiffrage de données** = data encryption; **clé de chiffrage** = cryptographic key *ou* cipher key

◇ **chiffre** *nm* **(a)** *(informatique)* digit *ou* figure *ou* number; **chiffre binaire** = bit *ou* binary digit; **groupe de 2 chiffres binaires** = dibit; **chiffre de contrôle** = check digit *ou* check number; **chiffre de remplissage** = gap digit; **chiffre (indicateur) de signe** = sign digit **(b)** number *ou* figure *ou* digit; **chiffre en exposant** = superior number; **chiffre de poids faible** = least significant digit (LSD) *ou* low-order digit; **chiffre de poids fort** = most significant digit (MSD); **chiffre le moins significatif** = least significant digit (LSD); **chiffre le plus significatif** = most significant character *ou* most significant digit (MSD); **la base de numération décimale utilise les chiffres 0123456789** = the decimal number system uses the digits 0123456789; **en chiffres ronds** = in round figures; **place d'un chiffre** = digit place *ou* position; **tableau de chiffres** = numeric array **(b)** *(caractère d'imprimerie)* numeral *ou* figure *ou* digit; **un numéro de téléphone de huit chiffres** = a phone number with eight digits *ou* an eight-digit phone number; **chiffres arabes** = Arabic numbers *ou* figures *ou* numerals; **chiffres et signes en code télégraphique** = figures case; **chiffres romains** = Roman numbers *ou* figures *ou* numerals

◇ **chiffré, -ée** *adj* **code chiffré** *ou* **écriture chiffrée** = cipher *ou* cipher system; **code chiffré à clé publique** = public key cipher; **nos concurrents ne peuvent lire nos fichiers qui sont en langage chiffré** = our competitors cannot understand our files - they have all been enciphered; **message chiffré** = coded message; **le message chiffré peut être transmis par téléphone sans que personne ne puisse le lire** = the encrypted text can be sent along ordinary telephone lines, and no one will be able to understand it; **texte non chiffré** = plaintext

◇ **chiffrement** *nm* encryption; **chiffrement de données** = data encryption

◇ **chiffrer** *vtr* to code *ou* to encipher *ou* to encrypt

chimique *adj* chemical; **produit chimique** = chemical; **réaction chimique** = chemical reaction

choc *nm* jar *ou* jolt; **les disques durs sont très sensibles aux chocs** = hard disks are very sensitive to jarring

choix *nm* (a) choice; *(entre deux choses)* alternative; *(de plusieurs articles)* selection; **nous n'avons pas le choix** = we have no alternative; **au choix** = (i) optional; (ii) discretionary; **le système est équipé d'un lecteur de disquettes 3,5 ou 5,25 pouces au choix** = the system comes with optional 3.5 or 5.25 inch disk drives (b) **de choix** = high quality *ou* top quality; **meilleur choix** = best fit

chroma *voir* CHROMINANCE

◇ **chromatique** *adj* chromatic; **aberration chromatique** = chromatic aberration; **contrôle chromatique** = chroma control; **détecteur chromatique** = chroma detector; **dispersion chromatique** = chromatic dispersion; **séparation** *ou* **sélection chromatique** = colour separation; **température chromatique** = colour temperature; **variation chromatique** = colour shift

◇ **chromaticité** *nf* chromaticity

chrominance *ou* **chroma** *nf* chrominance *ou* chroma; **signal de chrominance** = chrominance signal

chronique *nf (d'un journal)* column; **chronique économique** = business news; **chronique financière** = financial news

chronologique *adj* chronological; **fichier chronologique** = journal file; **ordre chronologique** = chronological order

chronomètre *nm* timer

◇ **chronométrie** *nf* timing *ou* time measurement; **(à) double chronométrie** = dual clocking

chute *nf* fall; **chute de courant** = brown-out; **chute de tension** = power loss

cible *nm* target; **niveau cible** = target level; **ordinateur cible** = target computer

cinéaste *nm* **équipe de cinéastes** = camera crew; **l'équipe de cinéastes a dû tourner toute la journée dans la neige** = the camera crew had to film all day in the snow

cinéma *nm* (a) *(art cinématographique)* **le cinéma** = the cinema (b) *(bâtiment)* cinema

◇ **cinématographie** *nf* cinematography

◇ **cinématographique** *adj* (of) film *ou* (of the) cinema; **appareil cinématographique** = cine camera; **l'art cinématographique** = the cinema; **équipe cinématographique** = camera crew

cinq *adj num* five

◇ **cinquième** *num* fifth; **ordinateur de cinquième génération** = fifth generation computer

circonflexe *adj* **accent circonflexe** = circumflex

circuit *nm* (a) circuit; **circuit à deux fils** = two wire circuit; **(ensemble de) circuits** = circuitry; **le programme de CAO peut tracer le circuit très rapidement** = the CAD program will plot the circuit diagram rapidly; **circuit bifilaire** *ou* **bidirectionnel** = two wire circuit; **circuit bistable** = bistable circuit *ou* bistable multivibrator; **circuit à coïncidence** = coincidence circuit; **circuit combinatoire** = combinational circuit; **circuit composite** = composite circuit *ou* hybrid circuit; *(pour protection de logiciel)* **circuit crypté** = dongle; **circuit de décision** = decision circuit *ou* element; **circuit déparasité** = de-bounce circuit; **circuit duplex** = duplex circuit; **circuit d'échange de données** = data circuit; **circuit équilibré** = balanced circuit; **il faut utiliser un circuit équilibré en fin de ligne pour éviter la réflexion des signaux** = you must use a balanced circuit at the end of the line to prevent signal reflections; **circuit d'équivalence** = equivalence gate; **circuit ET** = AND gate *ou* coincidence gate; **circuit hybride** = hybrid circuit; **(carte de) circuit imprimé**

(CI) *ou* **plaque présensibilisée pour circuit imprimé** = printed circuit *ou* printed circuit board (PCB) *ou* circuit board *ou* card; **plaque (présensibilisée) double face pour circuit imprimé** = double-sided printed circuit board; **circuit intégré** = integrated circuit (IC) *ou* chip; **architecture d'un circuit intégré** = chip architecture; **ensemble des circuits intégrés** = chip set; **ligne de sélection** *ou* **de validation d'un circuit intégré** = chip select line; **circuit intégré de diagnostic** = diagnostic chip; **circuit intégré de carte vidéo** = video interface chip; **cet émulateur intégré au circuit sert à tester le contrôleur de la disquette, en simulant le fonctionnement d'un lecteur de disquettes** = this in-circuit emulator is used to test the floppy disk controller by emulating a disk drive; **circuit à très haut niveau d'intégration** = jumbo chip; **circuit inverseur** = NOT gate; **circuit de jonction** = trunk; **circuit LC** = LC circuit; **circuit linéaire** = in-line; **circuit logique** = gate circuit *ou* logic array *ou* logic circuit *ou* logic gate; **circuit logique complexe** *ou* **en réseau** = gate array; **circuit logique non connecté** = uncommitted logic array (ULA); **circuit logique programmable** = programmable logic array (PLA); **circuit logique à trois états** = three state logic; **circuit loué** *ou* **de location** = leased circuit; **circuit mixte** = hybrid circuit; **circuit NI** = NOR circuit *ou* gate; **circuit NI exclusif** = exclusive NOR gate *ou* EXNOR gate; **circuit NON** = NOT gate *ou* negation gate; **circuit NON-ET** *ou* **circuit NAND** = NAND circuit *ou* gate; **circuit NON-OU** = NOR circuit *ou* gate; **circuit numérique** = digital circuit; **circuit optique intégré** = integrated optical circuit; **circuit OU** = OR gate; **circuit OU exclusif** = EXOR gate *ou* exclusive OR circuit *ou* gate; **circuit de transmission de données** = data circuit; **circuit virtuel** = virtual circuit; **circuit vocal** = dry circuit **(b) câble antenne-circuit** = feeder cable; **capacité d'un circuit** = circuit capacity; **caractéristique d'un circuit** = circuit grade; **commutation de circuit** = circuit switching; **diagramme d'un circuit** = circuit diagram; **émulateur intégré au circuit** = in-circuit emulator; **niveau de bruit d'un circuit** = circuit noise level; **qualité d'un circuit** = circuit grade; **tracé d'un circuit** = circuit design **(c) télévision en circuit fermé** = closed circuit television (CCTV) **(d)** *(d'information ou communication)* **créer de nouveaux**

circuits de communication = to open up new channels of communication

◊ **circuiterie** *nf* circuitry; **la circuiterie demeure trop complexe** = the circuitry is still too complex; **circuiterie numérique commutée** = circuit-switched digital circuitry

circulaire *adj* circular *ou* cyclic; **compteur (à décalage) circulaire** = ring counter; **décalage circulaire** = circular shift *ou* end about shift *ou* cyclic shift; **guide d'ondes circulaire** = circular waveguide; **orbite circulaire** = circular orbit; **permutation circulaire** = cyclic shift *ou* ring shift; **report circulaire** = end-around carry; **tampon circulaire** = circular buffer

le circuit imprimé pourra être gravé, d'après le dessin proposé, soit par un procédé photographique, soit en recopiant ce dessin à l'aide de pastilles et de rubans
Electronique pratique
en dernier lieu, on implantera les circuits intégrés
Electronique pratique

circulant, -e *adj* circulating; **document circulant** = turnaround document; **mémoire circulante** = circulating storage; **registre à bits circulants** = circulating register

circulation *nf* circulation; **la société essaie d'améliorer la circulation de l'information dans les services** = the company is trying to improve the circulation of information between departments

circuler *vi* to flow; **faire circuler** = to circulate *ou* to distribute

citer *vtr* to quote; **il a cité des chiffres mentionnés dans le journal** = he quoted figures from the newspaper report

clair, -e *adj* **(a)** *(non encrypté)* clear; **texte en clair** = plaintext; **les messages ont été transmis en clair par téléphone** = the messages were sent as plaintext by telephone **(b)** *(sans parasites)* **le signal est plus ou moins clair suivant les conditions atmosphériques** = the atmospheric conditions affect the clarity of the signal **(c)** *(pâle)* light

◊ **clairement** *adv* clearly; **la notice indique clairement comment relier les** différents modules du système = the booklet gives clear instructions how to connect the different parts of the system; le manuel d'utilisation n'explique pas clairement la marche à suivre pour copier un fichier = the program manual is not clear on copying files

clapet *nm* latch

clarté *nf* clarity; les conditions atmosphériques influencent la clarté du signal = the atmospheric conditions affect the clarity of the signal

classe *nf* class *ou* grade; de première classe = first class *ou* top grade; un expert-informaticien de première classe = a top-grade computer expert

◊ **classement** *nm* **(a)** *(de dossiers, etc.)* filing *ou* indexing *ou* classification; *(de données)* classement énumératif (de données) = enumerated type; méthode de classement = filing system **(b)** *(des cahiers d'un livre)* séquence de classement = collating sequence

◊ **classer** *vtr* to classify *ou* to order *ou* to sort *ou* to file; classer des documents = to file documents; on a classé les sorties d'imprimantes avec diagnostics sous la rubrique 'Test' = the diagnostic printouts have been classified under T for test results; liste classée (en ordre alphabétique, etc.) = ordered list; classer en *ou* par ordre alphabétique = to alphabetize *ou* to alphasort; classer les adresses en ordre alphabétique = to sort addresses into alphabetical order; les noms sont classés par ordre alphabétique = the sequence of names is arranged alphabetically; classer par rang *ou* par ordre d'importance = to rank; non classé, -ée = unsorted; il a fallu quatre fois plus de temps pour chercher dans les fichiers non classés = it took four times as long to search the unsorted files

◊ **classeur** *nm (en carton)* file *ou* folder; *(meuble)* filing cabinet

◊ **classification** *nf* classification; classification (suivant la méthode de) Dewey = Dewey decimal classification; classification hiérarchique = hierarchical classification

clause *nf (d'un document)* article

clavier *nm* **(a)** *(de machine à écrire ou d'ordinateur)* keyboard; *(de petite dimension ou auxiliaire)* pad *ou* keypad; le clavier comporte 84 touches = there are 84 keys on the keyboard; clavier ANSI = ANSI keyboard; clavier ASCII = ASCII keyboard; clavier auxiliaire = keypad; clavier aveugle = blind keyboard; clavier aveugle produisant une bande non justifiée = noncounting keyboard; *(clavier utilisé surtout dans les pays francophones)* clavier AZERTY = AZERTY keyboard; clavier à effleurement = tactile keyboard *ou* touch-sensitive keyboard; clavier électronique = electronic keyboard; clavier émetteur-récepteur *ou* de téléscripteur = ASR keyboard; clavier français accentué = AZERTY keyboard; clavier hexadécimal = hex keypad *ou* hex pad; clavier interactif = interactive keyboard; clavier à mémoire sur n touches = N-key rollover; clavier numérique = numeric keypad *ou* numeric pad; *(clavier international utilisé surtout dans les pays anglo-saxons)* clavier QWERTY = QWERTY keyboard; clavier rapide = n-key rollover; clavier relié à un terminal = terminal keyboard; clavier tactile *ou* sensitif = tactile keyboard *ou* touch-sensitive keyboard; clavier à touches programmables = soft keyboard; contrôle de clavier = keyboard scan; disposition des touches d'un clavier = keyboard layout; écran vidéo avec clavier = video terminal; grille d'aide *ou* mémento (de fonction des touches) de clavier = keyboard overlay; implantation des touches d'un clavier = keyboard layout *ou* key matrix; rebond d'une touche de clavier = keyboard contact bounce; saisie au *ou* sur *ou* par clavier = keyboarding *ou* manual entry *ou* manual input; saisie directe sur disque(tte), par clavier = keyboard to disk entry; saisir (des données) au clavier *ou* sur clavier = to keyboard *ou* to key in; saisie au clavier contrôlée par ordinateur = processor-controlled keying **(b)** *(de téléphone)* keypad *ou* dial pad; clavier tonal = tone dialling pad; numérotation sur clavier tonal = tone dialling; numérotation sur clavier = pushbutton dialling; téléphone à clavier = pushbutton telephone; terminal entrée-sortie *ou* émetteur-récepteur à clavier = keyboard send/receive (KSR)

◇ **claviste** *nm&f* keyboarder; **le claviste a sauté plusieurs lignes du manuscrit** = several lines of manuscript have been missed by the keyboarder

> bien que la souris soit supportée, la totalité des fonctions peut être exécutée à partir du clavier
> *L'Ordinateur Individuel*

clé *ou* **clef** *nf* **(a)** key; *(de chiffrage ou de cryptage)* cipher key *ou* cryptographic key; **il a finalement trouvé la clé du code** = he finally broke the cipher system; **tapez la clé et vous pourrez décoder le dernier message** = type this key into the machine, that will decode the last message; **nous avons sélectionné les enregistrements en utilisant le mot DISK comme clé de recherche** = we selected all the records with the word DISK in their keys; **code chiffré** *ou* **cryptage à clé publique** = public key cipher (system); **clé à usage unique** = one-time pad **(b)** *(de programmation)* **clé de contrôle** = check key; **clé numérique de contrôle** = check bit *ou* check digit *ou* check number; **clé électronique** = dongle; **clé d'identification** = key; **clé d'index** = index key; **clé primaire** *ou* **principale** = primary key; **clé de protection** = protection key; **clé de recherche** = search key; **clé transversale** = vertical redundancy check (VRC); **clé de parité transversale** = vertical parity check; **clé de tri** = sortkey; **champ clé** = key field; **contrôle par clé** = redundancy checking; **gestion de clé** = key management; **méthode d'accès séquentiel par clé** = keyed sequential access method (KSAM); *voir aussi* MOT-CLE **(c)** *(de porte ou de système)* **système clé en main** = turnkey system

clef *nf* = CLE

clic *nm* click; **clic témoin (de fonctionnement) de touche** = key click; **un clic vous permet de vous déplacer dans les textes et graphiques** = you move through text and graphics with a click of the button

> par un simple clic sur un bouton, on se trouve dans la structure de la base, la procédure concernée s'affichant sur l'écran
> *L'Ordinateur Individuel*

cliché *nm (imprimerie)* plate; **cliché de base** = key plate

client, -e *n* customer; **maintenance du parc clients** = customer engineering; **service clients** = customer service department

clignotant *nm* flashing light
◇ **clignotant, -e** *adj* flashing *ou* blinking; **caractère clignotant** = flashing character *ou* character blink
◇ **clignotement** *nm (d'un caractère brillant)* blinking; *(télévision)* flicker; **sans clignotement** = flicker-free
◇ **clignoter** *vi (lumière ou voyant)* to blink *ou* to flash; *(télévision)* to flicker

clip *nm (extrait de film)* clip; **un clip de l'accident a été passé aux informations** = there was a clip of the disaster on the news; **image clip art** = clip art *ou* clipart

cliquer *vi* to click; **pour afficher le menu déroulant cliquer l'icône sur le haut de l'écran** = the pull-down menu is viewed by clicking over the icon at the top of the screen; **vous pouvez agrandir le cadre en cliquant (la souris) à l'intérieur de ses limites** = use the mouse to enlarge a frame by clicking inside its border

> avec la souris, il suffit de pointer et de cliquer
> *L'Ordinateur Individuel*

clone *nm* clone; **ils ont copié notre nouveau modèle d'ordinateur pour commercialiser un clone qui se vend beaucoup moins cher** = they have copied our new personal computer and brought out a cheaper clone; **il existe des clones de tous nos modèles et tous sont plus performants** = higher performance clones are available for all the models in our range

clore *vtr (sur ordinateur)* **clore une session** = to log off *ou* log out

clôture *nf (sur ordinateur)* **clôture de session** = logging off; **routines de clôture d'exécution (d'un programme)** = end of run routines

C-MAC *(norme de télévision)* **multiplexeur C-MAC** = C-MAC

CMOS **semi-conducteur CMOS** = complementary metal oxide semiconductor (CMOS)

coaxial, -e *adj* co-axial; **câble coaxial** = co-axial cable

COBOL = COMMON BUSINESS ORIENTATED LANGUAGE; **langage COBOL** = COBOL

> le COBOL étant le langage de programmation des applications de gestion le plus répandu au monde
> *L'Information professionnelle*

codage *nm* coding *ou* encoding; **codage à adresse absolue** = specific coding; **codage binaire** = binary encoding; **codage bipolaire** = bipolar coding; **codage direct** = direct coding; **codage de Hamming** = Hamming code; **codage en ligne directe** = straight-line code; **codage relatif** = relative coding; **codage spécifique** = specific coding; **modulation par impulsions et codage (MIC)** = pulse code modulation (PCM)

code *nm* **(a)** code; *(de chiffrage ou de cryptage)* cipher key *ou* cipher system; **code absolu** = absolute *ou* specific code; **code accéléré** = optimized code; **code d'accès (à un système)** = access code *ou* authorization code; **code amélioré** = optimized code; **code (à) barres** = (i) bar code; *US* bar graphics; (ii) universal product code (UPC); **lecteur de codes (à) barres** = bar-code reader; **lecteur optique de codes barres** = optical bar reader *ou* bar code reader *ou* optical wand; **code de base** = basic code; **code binaire** = binary code; **le code binaire du nombre décimal 8 est 1000** = the BCD representation of decimal 8 is 1000; **code binaire absolu** = absolute *ou* specific code; **code binaire plus 3** = excess-3 code; **pour 6, le code binaire plus 3 est 1001** = the excess-3 code representation of 6 is 1001; **code binaire à 8 bits** = extended binary coded decimal interchange code (EBCDIC); **code binaire réfléchi** = cyclic code; **code biquinaire** = biquinary code; **code de caractères** = character code; **code de caractères interne** = internal character code; **ASCII est le code de caractères le plus fréquemment utilisé** = the ASCII code is the most frequently used character coding system; **code en chaîne** *ou* **code chaîné** = chain code; **code chiffré** = cipher *ou* cipher system; **code chiffré à clé publique** = public key cipher; **il a finalement réussi à déchiffrer le code** *ou* **il a finalement trouvé la clé du code** = he

finally broke the cipher system; **il faut toujours utiliser un code chiffré sûr quand vous transmettez des données par téléphone** = always use a secure cipher when sending data over a telephone line; **code de commande** = operating code *ou* op code *ou* order code; **processeur de codes de commande** = order code processor (OCP); **code compacté** = compact code; *(pour accès à un système)* **code confidentiel** = signature; **numéro de code confidentiel** = personal identification number (PIN) *ou* identity number; **code de contrôle de bloc** = block code; **code décimal réfléchi** = cyclic decimal code; **code direct** = direct code *ou* one-level code; **code drapeau** = flag code; **code EBCDIC** *ou* **code binaire à 8 bits** = extended binary coded decimal interchange code (EBCDIC); **code échappement** *ou* **code 'escape'** = escape code; **code élémentaire** = basic code; **code d'erreur** = error code; **code correcteur d'erreurs** = error correcting code; **code détecteur d'erreurs** *ou* **code de détection d'erreurs** = error detecting code *ou* self-checking code; **code indicateur d'erreur** = error code; **code de vérification et correction d'erreurs** = error checking and correcting code (ECCC); **code erroné** *ou* **erreur de code** = false code; **code ESC** = ESC code; **code à facettes** = faceted code; **code de fin de document** = end of document *ou* end of file (EOF); **code de fin de données** = end of data (EOD); **code de fonction** = function code *ou* function digit; **code (de) Gray** = Gray code *ou* cyclic code; **code de Hamming** = Hamming code; **code (de) Hollerith** = Hollerith code; **code de Huffman** = Huffman code; **code d'identification** = identity number *ou* ID code; **numéro de code d'identification** = personal identification number (PIN) *ou* identity number; **code d'identification de périphérique** = device code; **code d'instruction** = computer code *ou* instruction code; **code d'instruction imbriqué (dans un programme)** = embedded code; **code intermédiaire** = intermediate code; **code interprétatif** = interpretative code; **code en langage machine** *ou* **code machine** = computer code *ou* computer-readable code *ou* machine code *ou* actual code; **format de code machine** = machine code format; **instruction en code machine** = machine code instruction; *(d'un clavier)* **code de majuscules** = figures shift; *(pour bande papier)* **code de marquage** = tape code;

code à un niveau = direct code *ou* one-level code; **code numérique d'une touche** = key number; **code objet** = object code; **code d'opération** = command code *ou* operation code *ou* operating code *ou* op code; **code optimal** = optimum code; **code optimisé** = optimized code; **code optimum** = optimum code; **code ouvert** = open code; **code de perforation de bande papier** = tape code *ou* punched code; **code de perforation de carte** = card code; **code personnel** = signature *ou* ID code; **numéro de code personnel** = personal identification number (PIN) *ou* identity number; **n'oublie pas d'entrer ton numéro de code personnel** = don't forget to log in your PIN number *ou* identity number; **après la mise en route du système, il faut tapez votre code personnel et votre mot de passe** = after you wake up the system, you have to input your ID code then your password; **code postal** = postcode; *US* ZIP code; **code pur** = pure code; **code à rapport (de bits) constant** *ou* **fixe** = constant ratio code; **code redondant** = redundant code; **code réfléchi** = reflected code; **code source** = source code; **code spécifique** = specific code; **code de structure** = overhead; **code symbolique** = symbolic code; *(de l'image)* **code de synchronisation** = framing code; **code à temps d'accès minimum** = optimum code; **code à temps d'accès optimisé** = minimum access code *ou* minimum delay code *ou* minimum latency coding **(b) commandé par les codes CTRL** *ou* **asservi aux codes CTRL (générés par la touche contrôle)** = control-driven; **conversion de code** = code conversion; **élément d'un code** = code element; **erreur de code** = false code; **ligne de code (d'un programme)** = code line; **macro code** = macro code; **modifier les codes d'un programme** = to recode a program; **zone de code** = code area **(c) hash code** = hash code; **générer un hash code** = to hash; **index hash code** = hash index; **système de hash code** = hash-code system; **total de vérification pour hash code** = hash total; **valeur de vérification pour hash code** = hash value

◇ **codé, -ée** *adj* coded; **caractères codés binaires** = binary coded characters; **décimal codé binaire (DCB)** = binary coded decimal (BCD)

◇ **coder** *vtr* to code

◇ **codeur** *nm* coder; **codeur-décodeur** = coder/decoder (CODEC)

ce code est une suite de trois nombres de 1 à 16, ce qui donne 4096 façons différentes de choisir son numéro secret
Electronique pratique

coercibilité *nf* coercivity

coffret *nm* **(a)** box *ou* casing; **progiciel en coffret** = packaged *ou* canned software *ou* software package **(b) coffret avec guide-cartes** = rack

cogniticien, -ienne *n* knowledge engineer

cohérent, -e *adj* coherent; **faisceau cohérent** = coherent bundle; **lumière cohérente** = coherent light; **le laser produit une lumière cohérente** = the laser produces coherent light

coin *nm* corner; **coin gauche supérieur de l'écran** = cursor home

coincement *nm (papier ou bande)* jam
◇ **coincer** *vtr (papier ou bande)* to jam; **le magnétophone ne fonctionne pas parce que la bande est coincée dans le moteur** = the recorder's not working because the tape is jammed in the motor
◇ **se coincer** = *vpr* to jam *ou* to become jammed

coïncidence *nf* coincidence; **circuit à coïncidence** = coincidence circuit

collationner *vtr (les cahiers d'un livre)* to collate
◇ **collationnement** *nm (des cahiers d'un livre)* collating; **indices de collationnement** = collating marks

collecte *nf* collection; **collecte de données** = data collection; **plate-forme de collecte de données** = data collection platform
◇ **collecteur** *nm* collector; **collecteur de données** = (data) sink

collectif, -ive *adj* collective; **antenne collective de télévision (câblée)** = community antenna television (CATV)

coller *vtr (film)* to splice

◊ **colleuse** *nf* **colleuse de film** *ou* **de bande** = splicing block

collision *nf* collision; **détection de collision** = collision detection; **écoute de signal à accès multiple avec détection de collision CSMA-CD** = carrier sense multiple access collision detection (CSMA-CD)

colonne *nf* column; **écrivez le total au bas de la colonne** = put the total at the bottom of the column; **additionner une colonne de chiffres** = to add up a column of figures; **écran (de) quatre-vingts colonnes** = eighty-column screen; **imprimante 80 colonnes** = 80-column printer; **le prix comprend une imprimante 80 colonnes** = an 80-column printer is included in the price; **colonne double** = dual column; **en colonne(s)** = columnar *ou* in tabular form; **disposé en colonne(s)** = in tabular form; **disposer (des données) en colonne(s)** = to tab *ou* to tabulate; **diagramme** *ou* **graphique en colonnes** = columnar graph; **présentation graphique sous forme de colonne(s)** = columnar working; **parité de colonnes** = column parity; **colonne de perforations (d'une carte)** = perforations *ou* card row *ou* card column

colophon *nm (symbole d'une société)* colophon

coma *nm (aberration de lentille)* coma

COMAL = COMMON ALGORITHMIC LANGUAGE; **langage (de programmation structurée) COMAL** = COMAL

combinaison *nf* combination

combinatoire *adj* combinational; **circuit combinatoire** = combinational circuit; **logique combinatoire** = combinational logic

combiné *nm* handset
◊ **combiner** *vtr&i (plusieurs fichiers)* to combine *ou* to merge *ou* to coalesce

commande *nf* **(a)** *(d'un produit)* order; **donner une commande** = to order; **fabriquer sur commande** = to customize; **nous utilisons des logiciels écrits sur commande** = we use customized software; **fait sur commande** = custom-built; **articles vendus sur commande uniquement** = articles available to order only **(b)** *(instruction de programme)* command *ou* instruction *ou* operating instruction *ou* control; **en langage BASIC, la commande PRINT fera apparaître le texte sur l'écran** = the BASIC keyword PRINT will display text on the screen; **commande de canal** = channel command; **commande de chariot** = carriage control; **les codes de commande de chariot peuvent être utilisés pour faire avancer le papier de deux interlignes** = carriage control codes can be used to move the paper forward two lines between each line of text; **commande conditionnelle** = conditional statement; **commandes d'édition** = edit commands; **commandes et instructions d'édition** = editing terms; **commande d'exécution** = execute command; **RUN est la commande d'exécution du programme** = the command to execute the program is RUN; **commande imbriquée (dans le texte)** = embedded command; **commande d'interruption (de programme)** = interrupt command; **commande d'invalidation d'interruption** = disable interrupt; **commande numérique** = numerical control (NC) *ou* computer numerical control (CNC); **commande numérique directe** = direct digital control (DDC); **commandes numériques de machines-outils** = Automatically Programmed Tools (APT) *ou* computer numeric control (CNC); **système de commandes numériques de machines-outils** = flexible machining system (FMS); **(caractère de) commande de périphérique** = device control character; **commande précédée d'un point** *ou* **commande point** = dot command; **commande de processus** = process control; **commande de stabilisation du signal (après échantillonnage)** = hold; **commande de tâches à distance** = remote job entry (RJE); **commandes de transmission** = line control **(c)** **chaîne de commandes** = command chain; **code de commande** = operating code *ou* op code *ou* order code; **processeur de codes de commande** = order code processor (OCP); **données de commande** = control data; **fenêtre de commande** = command window; **la fenêtre de commande est une simple ligne en bas de l'écran** = the command window is a single line at the bottom of the screen; **l'utilisateur peut définir la taille de la fenêtre de commande** = the user can define the size of the command window; **fichier de commandes** = batch file *ou* command file; **processeur de fichier de commandes** = command file processor; **instruction de commande** = control statement; **interface de commande** = command interface; **langage de commande** = command language *ou* control language; **langage de commande de tâche** = job control language (JCL); **ligne de commande** = command line; **logiciel de commande de périphérique** = driver *ou* handler; **message d'attente de commande** = command prompt; **micro-ordinateur de commande** = microcontroller; **mot de commande** = keyword *ou* control word; *(d'un appareil)* **panneau de commande** = front panel *ou* control pannel; **procédure de commande** = operator procedure; **processeur de commande de console** = command console processor (CCP); **programme de commande** = master control program (MCP); **programme activé par commande** = command-driven program; **pupitre de commande d'un opérateur** = operator's console; **registre de commande** = command register *ou* control register; **registre de commande de contrôle** = control register; **séquence de commande (d'exécution)** = control sequence; **signal de commande** = control signal; **touche de commande** = control (key)

◊ **commandé, -ée** *adj* driven; **commandé par les codes CTRL (générés par la touche contrôle)** = control-driven

commencement *nm* beginning

◊ **commencer** *vtr* to begin; **commencer quelque chose graduellement** = to phase something in

commentaire *nm* **(a)** commentary *ou* narrative **(b)** *(écrit)* annotation *ou* comment *ou* commentary *ou* narrative; **symbole de commentaire** = annotation symbol; **en BASIC il est possible d'inclure des commentaires à la suite de l'instruction REM** = BASIC allows comments to be written after a REM instruction

commercial, -e *adj* commercial *ou* business; **correspondance commerciale** =

business correspondence; **'et' commercial (&)** = ampersand

◊ **commercialisation** *nf* commercialization; *(disque ou film ou logiciel)* release

◊ **commercialiser** *vtr* to market; **commercialiser (un nouveau produit)** = to release (a new product) on the market

commun, -e *adj* common *ou* general; **courant porteur commun** = common carrier; **fichier commun** = shared file; **langage commun** = common language; **logiciel commun** = common software; **signalisation par voie commune** = common channel signalling; **variable commune** = global variable; **zone commune de mémoire** = common storage area

communauté *nf* community

communication *nf* **(a)** *(information)* communication; **créer de nouveaux circuits de communication** = to open up new channels of communication; **les communications avec le siège social ont été facilitées par le télex** = communication with the head office has been made easier by the telex; **les communications avec le siège social sont plus rapides depuis que nous avons un appareil de télécopie** = communicating with head office has become quicker since we installed a fax machine **(b)** *(télécommunication)* communications; **communication asynchrone** = asynchronous communications; **interface pour communication asynchrone** = asynchronous communications interface adapter (ACIA); **communication par câble** = line communications; **communication à faible débit** = low speed communications; **communications groupées** = batched communication; **système de communication hiérarchisé** = hierarchical communications system; **communication par infrarouge** = infrared communications; **moyens de communication interactifs** = interactive media; **communication entre ordinateurs** = computer conferencing; **communication par rayon laser** = laser beam communications; **communication synchrone binaire** = binary synchronous communications (BSC); **basculer la communication d'un émetteur à l'autre** =

to hand off; **connecteur de communication** = communications port; **contrôleur de communication** = communications control unit (CCU); **interface de communication** = communications interface; **adaptateur d'interface de communication** = communications interface adapter; **système de traitement de texte doté d'une interface de communication** = communicating word processor (CWP); **ligne de communication** = communications link; **ligne de communication de données** = dataline; **contrôle de ligne de communication** = communications link control; **contrôle de mise en communication** = handshake I/O control; **protocole de mise en communication (de deux postes)** = full handshaking; **port de communication** = communications port; **réseau de communication** = communications network; **scanner de demande de communication** = communications scanner **(c)** *(appel téléphonique)* call; **communication interurbaine** = long-distance call *ou* trunk call; **communication urbaine** = local call; **communication avec préavis** = person-to-person call

communiqué *nm* communiqué de presse = news release *ou* press release; **la société a diffusé** *ou* **a publié un communiqué au sujet de la nouvelle imprimante (à) laser** = the company sent out a news release about the new laser printer

◊ **communiquer** *vi* to communicate; **il n'arrive pas à communiquer avec son personnel** = he finds it impossible to communicate with his staff; **l'affichage électronique du réseau permet aux systèmes reliés de communiquer entre eux** = the multi-user BBS has a computer conferencing facility

commutateur *nm* switch; **commutateur électronique** = electronic switching system; **commutateur à bascule** = flip-flop (FF) *ou* toggle switch; **valider à l'aide d'un commutateur à bascule** = to toggle; **commutateur à bascule de type D** *ou* **commutateur à deux sorties** = D-type flip-flop *ou* D-flip-flop; **commutateur à bascule de type JK** = JK-flip-flop; **commutateur bascule à deux états** = RS-flip-flop *ou* reset-set flip-flop; **commutateur DIP** = DIP switch;

commutateur à effet (de champ) Hall = Hall effect switch; **commutateurs (montés) en série** *ou* **groupement de commutateurs** *ou* **commutateurs chaînés** = switch train *ou* ganged switch; **avec des commutateurs montés en série, il est possible de choisir quel bus de données va activer l'imprimante** = a ganged switch is used to select which data bus a printer will respond to

◊ **commutation** *nf* switching; **commutation de circuit** = circuit switching; **commutation électromécanique** = electromechanical switching; **système de commutation électronique** = electronic switching system; **commutation de ligne** = line switching; **commutation de message** = message switching; **commutation de messages par paquets** = packet switching; **réseau de commutation de données par paquets** = packet switched data service *ou* packet switched network (PSN); **(système de) commutation numérique** = digital switching; **commutation de secours** = switched network backup; **commutation (en) tandem** = tandem switching; **commutation temporelle** = time division switching; **centre de commutation** = switching centre; **centre de commutation des données** = data switching exchange; **circuit de commutation** = switching circuit; **temps de commutation** = set-up time

◊ **commuté, -ée** *adj* switched; **circuiterie numérique commutée** = circuit-switched digital circuitry; **communication virtuelle commutée** = switched virtual call; **réseau commuté** = circuit switched network; **réseau commuté en étoile** = switched star; **connexion au réseau public commuté** = public dial port

compact, -e *adj* compact; **cassette compacte** = compact cassette; **disque compact** = compact disk *ou* CD; **lecteur de disques compacts** = compact disk player *ou* CD player

compactage *nm* packing *ou* compacting *ou* compaction; **compactage de bloc** = block compaction; **compactage de données** = data compacting; **algorithme de compactage** = compacting algorithm; **tous les fichiers ont pu être stockés sur une seule disquette grâce au nouveau programme de compactage** = all the files were stored on one disk with this new data compacting routine; **routine de compactage (de données)** = packing routine

◊ **compacté, -ée** *adj* **code compacté** = compact code

◊ **compacter** *vtr* to compact *ou* to concentrate *ou* to pack

comparable *adj* comparable; **les deux séries de chiffres ne sont pas comparables** = the two sets of figures are not comparable; **les vitesses de traitement de texte de ces deux logiciels ne sont pas comparables** = there is no comparison between the speeds of the two word processors

comparaison *nf* comparison; **comparaison de chaînes** = string matching; **comparaison logique** = logical comparison

comparateur *nm* comparator

comparer *vtr* **comparer (à *ou* avec)** = to contrast *ou* to compare with; **on a comparé les anciennes données aux informations les plus récentes** = the old data was contrasted with the latest information; **comparée à la version précédente, celle-ci est très facile à utiliser** = compared with the previous version this one is very user-friendly

compatible 1 *adj* compatible; **l'unité centrale de traitement est compatible avec un micro** = the mainframe is downward compatible with the micro; **compatible avec un système de niveau supérieur** = upwards compatible; *US* upward compatible; **compatible avec un système de niveau inférieur** = downwards compatible; *US* downward compatible; **appareil** *ou* **machine à connecteur compatible** = plug-compatible machine; **fabricant de produits à connecteurs compatibles** = plug-compatible manufacturer (PCM); **est-ce que cet appareil est compatible IBM?** = is the hardware IBM-compatible?; **(système) compatible avec des logiciels écrits pour d'autres systèmes** = software compatible (system); **(logiciel** *ou* **appareil) compatible (avec un) PC** = PC-compatible (software *ou* computer); **compatible (avec) TTL** = TTL compatible; **non compatible** =

incompatible; **disquette non compatible** = alien disk; **si la disquette n'est pas compatible, validez la fonction 'multidisque' qui permet au lecteur de lire une disquette non compatible** = when you have an alien disk select the multi-disk reader option to allow you to turn the disk drive into an alien disk reader **2** *nm* a compatible; **un compatible IBM** = an IBM compatible; **cet ordinateur est beaucoup moins cher que les autres compatibles IBM** = this computer is much cheaper than the other compatibles

◊ **compatibilité** *nf* compatibility; **compatibilité de logiciel** = program compatibility; **compatibilité du matériel** = hardware compatibility; **compatibilité avec un système de niveau inférieur** = downwards compatibility; *US* downward compatibility; **non compatibilité** = noncompatibility

compensateur *nm* **compensateur de phase** = phase equalizer *ou* delay equalizer

compilation *nf* compilation; **faire la compilation** = to compile; **effectuer une nouvelle compilation** = to recompile; **il faut beaucoup de temps pour faire la compilation avec cette ancienne version du programme** = compiling takes a long time with this old version of the software; **(instruction de) compilation et exécution** = compile and go; **compilation et décompilation incrémentielles** = incremental compilation and decompilation; **compilation de programme** = program compilation; **un outil de diagnostic de compilation bien conçu facilite le débogage** = thorough compiler diagnostics make debugging easy; **durée de compilation** = compilation time; **erreur de compilation** = compilation error; **diagnostic d'erreurs de compilation** = compiler diagnostics; **les erreurs de compilation provoquent l'interruption inopinée de la tâche** = compilation errors result in the job being aborted; **édition après compilation** = post-editing; **langage de compilation** = compiler language; **phase (de) compilation** = compile phase; **temps de compilation** = compilation time

◊ **compilateur** *nm* compiler (program); **ce compilateur génère un programme plus performant** = this compiler produces a more efficient program; **le nouveau**

compilateur possède un éditeur intégré = the new compiler has an in-built editor; **compilateur croisé** = cross-compiler; **nous pouvons utiliser le compilateur croisé pour développer le logiciel avant l'arrivée du nouveau système** = we can use the cross-compiler to develop the software before the new system arrives; **(programme) compilateur d'un langage évolué** = language compiler *ou* translator (program); **outil de diagnostic du compilateur** = compiler diagnostics; **ordinateur compilateur** = source machine

◊ **compiler** *vtr* to compile; **déboguez votre programme avant de le compiler** = debug your program, then compile it; **les programmes en BASIC qui sont compilés sont plus rapides que les versions interprétées** = compiled BASIC programs run much faster than the interpretor version; **compiler en langage machine** = to machine language compile

complément *nm* complement; **calculer un complément** = to complement; **on trouve les compléments en remplaçant les 1 par des 0 et les 0 par des 1** = the complement is found by changing the 1s to 0s and 0s to 1s; **complément à 1** *ou* **à un** = one's complement; **le complément à 1 de 10011 est 01100** = the one's complement of 10011 is 01100; **complément à 2** *ou* **à deux** = two's complement; **complément à 9** *ou* **à neuf** = nine's complement; **complément à 10** *ou* **à dix** = ten's complement; **complément à la base** = radix complement; **complément restreint** = diminished radix complement; **fonction complément** = NOT function

◊ **complémenté, -ée** *adj* *(nombre binaire, etc.)* complemented

◊ **complémentaire** *adj* complementary; **couleurs complémentaires** = complementary colours; **opération complémentaire** = complementary operation; **valeur complémentaire** = offset

complet, -ète *adj* complete *ou* full; **additionneur complet** = full adder; **caractère complet** = fully formed character; **la marguerite imprime des caractères complets** = a daisy wheel printer produces fully formed characters; **cycle complet d'exécution d'une opération** = complete operation; **index complet** = dense index; **liste complète** = dense list; **(ensemble des) nombres complets** = complementation; **opération complète** = complete operation; **soustracteur complet** = full subtractor

◊ **complètement** *adv* fully

◊ **compléter** *vtr* **(a)** to fill in *ou* to complete; **complétez le formulaire et introduisez-le dans le lecteur optique** = fill in the blanks and insert the form into the OCR **(b)** *(ajouter des données à un fichier)* to append

complexe *adj* complex; **cette formule mathématique complexe était difficile à résoudre** = the complex mathematical formula was difficult to solve; **circuit logique complexe** = gate array; **ordinateur à jeu d'instructions complexe** = complex instruction set computer (CISC)

◊ **complexité** *nf* complexity; **niveau de complexité** = complexity measure

compliqué, -ée *adj* complicated; **il s'agit d'un programme très compliqué** = this program is very complicated; **cet ordinateur est d'une conception plus compliquée que nécessaire** = the computer design is more complicated than necessary

comporter *vtr* to include; **ce circuit comporte un relais** = there is a relay in the circuit; **la disquette comporte un utilitaire qui permet la sauvegarde de fichiers sur disque dur** = on the disk is a utility for backing up a hard disk

composant *nm* component; *(d'un tableau* *ou* *d'une matrice)* element *ou* item; **ils ont ouvert une nouvelle usine de composants électroniques** = they have opened a new components factory; **erreur imputable à un composant défectueux** = component error; **densité des composants** = component density; **il y a une telle densité de composants sur la carte-mère qu'il sera impossible d'inclure un connecteur** = component density is so high on this motherboard, that no expansion connectors could be fitted; **la densité des composants augmente avec l'expertise du fabricant** = component density increases with production expertise; **nomenclature des composants** = component list

les deux composants sont logés dans des boîtiers DIL en céramique ou plastique
Electronique

composé, -ée *adj* compound; **élément logique composé** = compound logical element; **instruction composée** = compound statement; **le débogueur ne peut agir sur les instructions composées** = the debugger cannot handle compound statements

◊ **composer** *vtr* **(a)** *(typographie)* to set *ou* to typeset; **le texte est composé en Times romain corps 12** = the text is set in 12 point Times Roman; **le manuscrit a été envoyé à l'atelier pour être composé** = the MS has been sent to the typesetter for setting; **composer un texte sur ordinateur** = to word-process; **on lit facilement les fichiers de texte composés sur ordinateur** = it is quite easy to read word-processed files; **composer à la suite** = to run on **(b)** *(téléphone)* **composer un numéro** = to dial a number; **composer de nouveau** = to redial; **il a composé l'indicatif des Etats-Unis** = he dialled the code for the USA

composite *adj* composite; **circuit composite** = composite circuit *ou* hybrid circuit; **signal vidéo composite** = composite video signal

compositeur *nm (personne ou machine)* compositor *ou* typesetter; **compositeur électronique** = electronic compositor

◊ **composition** *nf* **(a)** *(typographie)* composition *ou* setting *ou* typesetting; **faire la composition d'un texte** = to typeset a text; **le texte est prêt à être envoyé en composition** = the text is ready to be sent to the typesetter; **les frais de composition ont augmenté depuis l'an dernier** = setting charges have increased since last year; **les frais de composition sont moins élevés si le texte est saisi sur disquette avant d'être envoyé au compositeur** = typesetting costs can be reduced by supplying the typesetter with prekeyed disks; **taille des caractères utilisés dans la composition** = composition size; **atelier de composition** *ou* **la composition** = composing room; **composition informatisée** *ou* **assistée par ordinateur** = computer setting; **composition électronique** = electronic composition; **composition au plomb** = hot metal composition **(b)** *(d'un numéro de téléphone)* dialling

compresser *vtr* to concentrate *ou* to compress; **les données compressées ont pu être transmises à peu de frais** = the concentrated data was transmitted cheaply

◊ **compresseur** *nm* compressor

◊ **compression** *nf* compression *ou* compaction *ou* packing; **compression de bloc** = block compaction; **compression de données** = data compression; **les scanners utilisent la technique dite de compression de données qui peut réduire du tiers la mémoire nécessaire** = scanners use a technique called data compression which manages to reduce, even by a third, the storage required; **compression de texte** = text compression; **compression et expansion (de données)** = compressing and expanding *ou* companding; *(pour données vidéo)* **dispositif de compression-expansion** = compressor/expander *ou* compandor; **routine de compression** = packing routine

avec l'apparition de nouvelles possibilités de compression des images, il est probable que les CD-ROM de demain jongleront de plus en plus avec le multimédia
Micro Systèmes

comprimer *vtr* **(a)** *(des données)* to compress *ou* to pack; **utilisez un programme d'archivage pour comprimer le fichier** = use the archiving program to compress the file **(b)** *(une photo)* to reduce *ou* to shrink

compris, -e *adj* included; **logiciel non compris dans l'offre d'achat** = unbundled software

comptabilité *nf* accounting *ou* accountancy; **logiciel comptabilité-gestion** = business system *ou* business package

comptage *nm* counting; **comptage d'images complètes** = full-frame time code

compte *nm* **(a)** account; **carte de compte crédit** = charge card; **compte bancaire** = bank account; **consultation à domicile des comptes** = home banking

(b) tenir compte de = to take account of; **ne pas tenir compte de** = to ignore; **cette commande donne ordre à l'ordinateur de ne pas tenir compte de la ponctuation** = this command instructs the computer to ignore all punctuation

compter *vi* **(a)** to count **(b) compter sur (quelque chose)** = to count on *ou* to rely on (something); **programme sur lequel on peut compter** = reliable program

◊ **compteur** *nm* counter *ou* meter *ou* comptometer; **le nombre de changements est enregistré sur le compteur** = the number of items changed are recorded by the counter; **la boucle se répètera jusqu'à ce que le compteur atteigne 100** = the loop will repeat itself until the counter reaches 100; **un compteur relié au photocopieur enregistre le nombre de photocopies** = a meter attached to the photocopier records the number of copies made; **compteur binaire** = binary counter; **compteur de boucles** = loop counter; **compteur (à décalage) circulaire** *ou* **compteur annulaire** = ring counter; **compteur décadaire** = decade counter; **compteur de défilement** = tape timer; **compteur de déroulement** = tape counter; **compteur d'électricité** = electricity meter; *(téléphone)* **compteur d'impulsions automatique (à domicile)** = automatic message accounting; **compteur incrémenteur-décrémenteur** = up/down counter; **compteur d'instruction** *ou* **registre compteur** = instruction counter *ou* program counter (PC) *ou* instruction address register (IAR); *(de routines ou de tâches)* **compteur de répétitions** = repeat counter

concaténation *nf* catenation *ou* concatenation; **faire une concaténation** = to catenate *ou* to concatenate; **concaténation de données** = concatenated data set; **concaténation de (plusieurs) chaînes** = string concatenation; **(instruction de) concaténation de fichiers** = link files

◊ **concaténé, -ée** *adj* chained *ou* linked *ou* concatenated (data); **liste concaténée** = chained list *ou* linked list

◊ **concaténer** *vtr* to catenate *ou* to concatenate

concave *adj* concave; **lentille concave** = concave lens

concentrer *vtr* to concentrate; **concentrer un rayon lumineux sur une lentille** = to concentrate a beam of light on a lens

◊ **concentrateur** *nm* concentrator; **concentrateur de données** = data concentrator; **concentrateur (de largeur de bande) vidéo** = video compressor

◊ **concentrateur-déconcentrateur** *nm (de données vidéo)* compressor/expander *ou* compandor

◊ **concentration** *nf* concentration; **concentration au point magnétique** *ou* **concentration magnétique** = magnetic focusing

concepteur, -trice *n* designer; **concepteur de logiciel** = software developer; **les concepteurs ont décidé de mettre en page sur format A4** = the designers have laid out the pages in A4 format; **les concepteurs travaillent à la mise en page de la nouvelle revue** = the design team is working on the layouts for the new magazine

◊ **conception** *nf* design; **un logiciel de CAO est indispensable à la réalisation d'une conception très précise** = CAD is essential for accurate project design; **conception ascendante d'un programme** = bottom up method; **conception assistée par ordinateur (CAO)** = computer-aided *ou* assisted design (CAD); **conception économique** = least cost design; **conception de produits** = product design; **langage de conception de programme** = program design language (PDL); **conception d'un système** = system design; **spécifications** *ou* **contraintes** *ou* **paramètres de conception** = design parameters

concevoir *vtr* to design; **formulaires et en-têtes de lettres peuvent être conçus sur ordinateur** = business forms and letterheads can now be designed on a PC

◊ **conçu, -e** *adj* designed; **conçu par ordinateur** = computer-generated; **programmation bien conçue** = elegant programming

concurrence *nf* competition; **les techniques du jet d'encre et du transfert thermique se font concurrence** = colour ink-jet technology and thermal transfer technology compete with each other

◊ **concurrent, -e** *adj* competing; **mise en place d'un programme concurrent =** counterprogramming

condensateur *nm* capacitor; **condensateur céramique =** ceramic capacitor; **condensateur électrolytique =** electrolytic capacitor; **condensateur non électrolytique =** non-electrolytic capacitor; **condensateur optique =** condenser lens; **condensateur variable =** variable capacitor; **condensateur pour mémoire RAM =** memory backup capacitor; **mémoire à condensateur =** capacitor storage; **microphone à condensateur =** capacitor microphone

◊ **condensation** *nf (de données ou lignes)* packing *ou* concentration

◊ **condensé, -ée** *adj* concentrated *ou* packed; **décimale condensée =** packed decimal; **format condensé =** packed format

◊ **condenser** *vtr* **(a)** *(des données ou lignes)* to concentrate *ou* to pack **(b)** *(image ou photo)* to shrink

condition *nf* **(a)** condition *ou* state; **condition d'arrêt =** halt condition; **condition d'entrée =** entry condition; **condition d'erreur =** error condition; **condition initiale =** initial condition; **registre des codes condition =** condition code register; **symbole de condition =** decision box **(b)** **conditions atmosphériques =** atmospheric conditions

◊ **conditionnel, -elle** *adj* conditional; **arrêt conditionnel =** conditional breakpoint; **boucle conditionnelle 'WHILE' =** while-loop; **boucle conditionnelle FOR...NEXT =** for-next loop; **branchement conditionnel =** conditional jump *ou* branch *ou* transfer; **le branchement conditionnel choisira le programme 1 ou 2 suivant que la réponse est oui ou non =** the conditional branch will select routine one if the response is yes and routine two if no; **instruction de branchement conditionnel à l'indicateur zéro =** jump on zero; **effectuer un branchement conditionnel à zéro =** to jump on zero; **commande conditionnelle =** conditional statement; **instruction conditionnelle =** conditional statement; **instruction d'opération conditionnelle =** decision *ou* discrimination instruction; **saut conditionnel =** conditional jump *ou* branch *ou* transfer; **transfert conditionnel =** conditional transfer

◊ **conditionner** *vtr* **(a)** *(des données)* to pack **(b)** *(un produit)* to package

conducteur *nm* **(a)** *(d'électricité)* conductor; **le cuivre est bon conducteur (d'électricité) =** copper is a good conductor of electricity *ou* copper conducts well **(b)** *(fil)* lead; *(fibre optique)* **conducteur de lumière =** light conduit

◊ **conductibilité** *nf* conduction

◊ **conductible** *adj* conductive

◊ **conduction** *nf* *(d'électricité)* conduction; **conduction (d'électricité) par broches de contact en or =** the conduction of electricity by gold contacts

◊ **conduire** *vtr* to conduct; **conduire l'électricité =** to conduct electricity

conduit *nm* duct

◊ **conduite** *nf* conduit *ou* channelling

cône *nm (d'un haut-parleur)* cone

conférence *nf* conference; **être en conférence =** to be in a meeting; **salle de conférence(s) =** conference room *ou* meeting room; **conférence de presse =** press conference; **téléphone de *ou* pour conférence =** conference telephone *ou* conference phone; *voir aussi* TELECONFERENCE

confetti *nm* chad; **bande à confettis non détachés =** chadded *ou* chadless tape

confiance *nf* confidence; **niveau de confiance =** confidence level

confidentialité *nf* privacy *ou* confidentiality; **confidentialité des données =** privacy of data; **confidentialité de l'information =** privacy of information; **cryptage de l'information pour en assurer la confidentialité =** privacy transformation

◊ **confidentiel, -elle** *adj* confidential *ou* private; **numéro de code confidentiel =** personal identification number *ou* PIN number

configuration *nf* configuration *ou* mapping; *(graphique)* map; **configuration d'une base de données =**

database mapping; **configuration disponible** = configured-in; **configuration d'entrée-sortie** = I/O mapping; **configuration invalidée** *ou* **indisponible** = configured-off *ou* configured out; **configuration logique** = logic map; **configuration du matériel** = hardware configuration; **configuration de mémoire** = memory map; **configuration prête à l'usage** = configured-in; **configuration des registres** = register map; **configuration de réseau** = networking; **configuration (d'un système)** = configuration state; **configuration validée** = configured-in

◊ **configurer** *vtr* to configure *ou* to map out; **il suffit de configurer l'ordinateur individuel une seule fois, à l'achat** = you only have to configure the PC once - when you first buy it; **ce câble est configuré sans modem ce qui me permet de connecter les deux ordinateurs sans difficulté** = this cable is configured as a null modem, which will allow me to connect these two computers together easily; **ce terminal est configuré pour l'affichage de graphiques** = this terminal has been configured to display graphics; **configuré en mémoire** = memory-mapped; **entrée-sortie configurée en mémoire** = memory-mapped input/output; **un écran configuré en mémoire possède une adresse pour chaque pixel, permettant ainsi au processeur d'accéder directement à l'écran** = a memory-mapped screen has an address allocated to each pixel, allowing direct access to the screen by the CPU; **configurer en réseau** = to network

conforme *adj* **être conforme à** = to conform to; **conforme aux normes** = up to standard

◊ **se conformer** *vpr* to conform to

conique *adj* conical; *(d'un haut-parleur)* **membrane conique** = cone

conjonction *nf* **conjonction logique** = AND operation *ou* coincidence operation *ou* conjunction *ou* meet

connaissance *nf* **(a)** knowledge; **connaissance globale** *ou* **exhaustive** = global knowledge; **ingénierie de la connaissance** = knowledge engineering; **système à base de connaissances** =

knowledge-based system; **système intelligent à base de connaissances** = intelligent knowledge-based system (IKBS) *ou* expert system **(b)** **connaissances en informatique** = computer literacy; **personne qui a des connaissances en informatique** = computer-literate person; **personne qui ne possède aucune connaissance informatique** = computer illiterate person

connecté, -ée *adj* connected; **le terminal est connecté à l'ordinateur principal** = the terminal is on-line to the mainframe; **circuit logique non connecté** = uncommitted logic array (ULA)

◊ **connecter** *vtr (joindre)* to link; *(brancher)* to plug in; **les deux systèmes ont été connectés l'un à l'autre** = the two systems are coupled together; **vous n'avez qu'à déconnecter le lecteur et en connecter un nouveau à sa place** = simply unplug the old drive and plug-in a new one; **élevez le potentiel de la ligne de réception au niveau logique un, en la connectant sur une source de courant de 5 volts** = pull up the input line to a logic one by connecting it to 5 volts

◊ **connecteur** *nm (électrique)* connector *ou* plug; *(d'un transistor à effet de champ)* gate; **le connecteur relié au câble s'adapte sur tout port série standard** = the connector at the end of the cable will fit any standard serial port; **connecteur à trois broches** = three-pin plug; *(appareil)* **à connecteur compatible** = plug-compatible (machine); **fabricant de produits à connecteurs compatibles** = plug-compatible manufacturer (PCM); **connecteur de carte** = (card) edge connector; **carte connecteur** = bus board; **connecteur pour carte d'extension** = expansion slot; **connecteur à une seule position d'enfichage** = polarized plug; **connecteur à enfichage dirigé** *ou* **à un seul bord d'enfichage** = polarized edge connector; **connecteur femelle** = female connector; **connecteur (pour carte additionnelle) inutilisé** = empty slot; **connecteur mâle** = male connector; **connecteur mâle à deux broches** = jumper; **connecteur de périphérique** = peripheral interface adapter (PIA)

◊ **connectique** *nf* connector technology *ou* engineering

connectif, -ive *adj* connective

connexe *adj* **négation connexe** = joint denial

connexion *nf* connection *ou* contact *ou* nexus *ou* switching; *(pour transmission de données)* data connection; **le circuit ne fonctionne pas parce que la connexion est encrassée** = the circuit is not working because the contact is dirty; **connexion bricolée** = dry joint; **connexion (montée) en cascade** = cascade connection; **la connexion en chaîne *ou* en cascade réduit le câblage** = daisy-chaining saves a lot of cable; **connexion (en) delta** = delta; **connexion directe** = direct connect; **connexion enroulée** = wire wrap; **connexion fixe** = hardwired connection; **connexion (d'ordinateurs) en mode conversationnel** = computer conferencing; **connexion (en) parallèle** = parallel connection; **leur débit de transmission est de 60 000 bits par seconde sur connexion parallèle** = their transmission rate is 60,000 bps through parallel connection; **connexion au réseau public commuté** = public dial port; **connexion (en) triangle** = delta; *(pour prototype)* **boîte de connexion sans soudure** = breadboard; **carte à connexion** = edge board *ou* card; **point de connexion** = terminal; **temps de connexion** = connect time *ou* set-up time; **zone de connexion** = terminal area

conscient, -e *adj* **erreur consciente** = conscious error

consécutif, -ive *adj* consecutive; **l'ordinateur a exploité trois fichiers consécutifs** = the computer ran three consecutive files; **de façon consécutive** = consecutively

◊ **consécutivement** *adv* consecutively

conseil *nm* *(firme ou bureau)* consultancy

conserver *vtr* to retain

console *nf* console; **console d'un opérateur** = operator's console; **la console comporte un périphérique d'entrée: par exemple un clavier, et un périphérique de sortie: soit une imprimante ou un écran** = the console consists of input device such as a keyboard, and an output device such as

a printer or CRT; **processeur de commande de console** = command console processor (CCP)

le groupe espère bien profiter de sa position stratégique pour transformer ses consoles de jeu en terminaux de communication
L'Express

consommation *nf* consumption; **la consommation d'électricité de cette machine est beaucoup trop forte** = this machine uses too much electricity; **produits de consommation** = consumables; **il faut inclure les câbles pour imprimantes et le papier sous la rubrique 'produits de consommation'** = put all the printer leads and paper under the heading consumables'

◊ **consommer** *vtr* to use

constant, -e *adj* constant; **le moteur du lecteur de disquettes tourne à vitesse constante** = the disk drive motor spins at a constant velocity; **code à rapport (de bits) constant** = constant ratio code; **données constantes** = fixed data; **opération constante** = one element; **champ de taille constante** = fixed field

◊ **constante** *nf* constant; **constante de translation** = relocation constant

constituer *vtr* to form *ou* to make up; **le système est constitué de cinq modules indépendants** = the system is formed of five separate modules; **nous avons constitué un dossier de coupures de presse sur le nouveau progiciel** = we have made up a file of press cuttings about the new software package

constructeur *nm* manufacturer; **constructeur de matériel informatique en pièces détachées** = original equipment manufacturer (OEM); **il a commencé (sa carrière) comme constructeur de PC pour le marché de matériel en pièces détachées** = he started in business as a manufacturer of PCs for the OEM market; **(logiciel) de constructeur** = machine-intimate (software); **syndicat européen des constructeurs d'ordinateurs** = European Computer Manufacturers Association (ECMA)

constructif, -ive *adj* **interférence constructive** = constructive interference

construction *nf* construction *ou* building; **la construction du prototype progresse rapidement** = construction of the prototype is advancing rapidly

◊ **construire** *vtr* to construct *ou* to build *ou* to form

consultation *nf* consultation; **consultation d'une table de référence** = table lookup

◊ **consulter** *vtr* to consult; **consulter une base de données sans autorisation** = to browse through a database; **le temps d'accès est le temps requis pour consulter une donnée en mémoire** = access time is the time taken to read from a location in memory

contact *nm* **(a)** contact; **épreuve** *ou* **planche de contact** = contact print; **(film) négatif contact** = contact negative **(b)** *(broche)* pin; **contacts or** = gold contacts; **contact sec** *ou* **intermittent** = dry contact

◊ **contacter** *vtr* to contact (someone); **contacter par téléphone** = to call in *ou* to phone

contenir *vtr* to contain *ou* to enclose; **chaque caisse contient deux ordinateurs et leurs périphériques** = each carton contains two computers and their peripherals; **la bande magnétique est contenue dans un boîtier en plastique rigide** = the magnetic tape is housed in a solid plastic case; **nous avons égaré un dossier contenant des documents importants** = we have lost a file containing important documents

contention *nf* contention; **délai** *ou* **retard de contention** = contention delay

contenu *nm* **(a)** *(abstrait)* content; **le contenu d'une lettre** = the content of a letter; **adressable par le contenu** = content-addressable; **fichier** *ou* **location adressable par le contenu** = content-addressable file *ou* location; **mémoire adressable par son** *ou* **le contenu** = content-addressable memory (CAM) **(b)** *(physique)* contents; **le contenu de la bouteille s'est répandu sur le clavier de l'ordinateur** = the contents of the bottle poured out onto the computer keyboard; **les douaniers ont examiné le contenu de la caisse** = the customs officials inspected the contents of the box

contexte *nm* context; **l'exemple démontre l'emploi du mot dans son contexte** = the example shows how the word is used in context

contigu, -ë *adj* contiguous *ou* adjacent; **fichier contigu** = contiguous file; **graphiques contigus** = contiguous graphics; **la plupart des écrans ne permettent pas l'affichage de graphiques contigus** = most display units do not provide contiguous graphics

continu, -e *adj* continuous *ou* endless; **boucle continue** = endless loop; **courant continu (CC)** = direct current (DC); **flux continu de données** = continuous data stream; **onde continue** = continuous wave; **signal continu** = continuous signal; **en continu** = continuous; **papier en continu** = continuous stationery *ou* listing paper; **(système d') alimentation du papier en continu** = continuous feed

continuation *nf* continuation

continuel, -elle *adj* continual; **les pannes continuelles du système ont ralenti le traitement** = the continual system breakdowns have slowed down the processing

◊ **continuellement** *adv (fréquemmenet)* continually; *(sans interruption)* continuously

continuité *nf* continuity

contraint, -e *adj* limited; **contraint par la vitesse de sortie** = output-bound *ou* output-limited

◊ **contrainte** *nf* restriction; **imposer une contrainte (à quelque chose)** = to restrict (something); **contraintes de conception** *ou* **de création** = design parameters; *(programme)* **avec contrainte de traitement** = process-bound (program); **avec contrainte de vitesse d'entrée** = input-bound *ou* input-limited (program); *(transmission)* **avec contrainte de vitesse de périphérique** = peripheral-limited (transmission)

contraire *nm* inverse; **le contraire de vrai est faux** = the inverse of true is false

contrarotatif, -ive *adj* **antenne contrarotative** = de-spun antenna

contrastant, -e *adj (effet, etc.)* contrasting

◊ **contraste** *nm* contrast; **bouton de contraste** = contrast dial; **ce bouton vous permet de régler la luminosité et le contraste** = this control allows you to adjust brightness and contrast; **filtre d'amélioration du contraste** = contrast enhancement filter; **rapport de contraste d'un imprimé** = print contrast ratio; **sans contraste** = flat

◊ **contrasté, -e** *adj* contrasting; **un dessin de couverture aux couleurs contrastées** = a cover design in contrasting colours

les jeux d'ombres d'un objet en mouvement, mais restant à la même distance de la caméra, provoquant des variations de contraste que l'objectif cherche constamment à suivre
Audio Vidéo

contrat *nm* contract *ou* deal; **contrat global** = package deal; **il se sont mis d'accord sur un contrat global comprenant le développement d'un logiciel et la personnalisation du matériel** = they agreed a package deal, which involves the development of software and customizing hardware; **nous offrons un contrat global comprenant un système informatique complet pour le bureau, la formation du personnel et l'entretien du matériel** = we are offering a package deal which includes the whole office computer system, staff training and hardware maintenance; **contrat de maintenance** = maintenance contract *ou* service contract

contre- *préf* counter- *ou* cross-
◊ **contre-jour** *nm (d'un film)* cameo
◊ **contre-épreuve** *nf* cross-check
◊ **contrefaçon** *nf* infringement of copyright *ou* copyright infringement
◊ **contreprogrammation** *nf (télévision)* counterprogramming

contrôlable *adj* controllable

contrôle *nm* **(a)** check *ou* checking *ou* control *ou* supervision *ou* verification; **contrôle d'accès (au système)** = access control; *(du courant)* **contrôle de l'alimentation** = power monitor;

contrôle de boucle = loop check; **contrôle de caractère(s)** = character check; **contrôle de blocs par caractères** = block character check (BCC); **contrôle en cascade** = cascade control; **contrôle chromatique** = chroma control; **contrôle de clavier** = keyboard scan; **contrôle par clé** = redundancy checking; **contrôle croisé** = cross-check; **contrôle cyclique** = cyclic check; **contrôle de dépassement de capacité** = overflow check; **contrôle des données** = data control; **contrôle par écho** = echo check; **contrôle d'erreurs** = error control; **contrôle d'exécution des tâches** = job statement control; **contrôle du flux (de données)** = flow control; **contrôle de flux d'informations** = information flow control; **contrôle de frappe** = keystroke verification; **contrôle de gain** = gain control; **contrôle de gain automatique** = automatic gain control (AGC) *ou* automatic level control (ALC); **contrôle des (sons) graves** = bass control; **contrôle horizontal** = horizontal check; **contrôle d'imparité** = odd parity check; **contrôle d'inférence** = inference control; **(opérations de) contrôle et exécution d'interruption** = interrupt servicing; **contrôle avec un jeu d'essai** = dry run; **contrôle de liaison de données** = data link control; **contrôle de liaisons de données de haut niveau** = high-level data link control (HDLC); **contrôle de ligne de communication** *ou* **de transmission** = communications link control; **contrôle de mise en communication** = handshake I/O control; **contrôle numérique** = numerical control (NC) *ou* computer numerical control (CNC); *(d'un programme)* **contrôle sur papier** = desk check; **contrôle de parité** = parity check; **contrôle de parité impaire** *ou* **d'imparité** = odd parity check; **contrôle de parité paire** = even parity check; **contrôle de parité paire-impaire** = odd-even parity check; **contrôle de processus** = process control; **contrôle de (la) qualité** = quality control; **contrôle par le récepteur** = backwards supervision; **contrôle par redondance** = redundancy checking; **contrôle par redondance cyclique** = cyclic redundancy check (CRC); **contrôle par retour** = feedback control; **contrôle des touches** = keystroke verification; **contrôle d'utilisation de touches** = keyboard scan; **contrôle de travaux groupés en pile** = stacked job control; **contrôle et validation** = verification and validation (V & V); **contrôle du volume (du son)** = volume control; **de contrôle** =

supervisory; **bit de contrôle** = check bit *ou* service bit; **bloc (de données) de contrôle** = control block; **bloc de contrôle de fichier** = file control block; **bus de contrôle** = control bus; **caractère de contrôle** = check character *ou* control character; **caractère de contrôle de périphérique** = device control character; **caractère de contrôle d'impression** = print control character; **carte de contrôle** = control card; **cellule de contrôle des couleurs** = colour cell; **code de contrôle de bloc** = block code; **champ de contrôle** = control field; **chiffre de contrôle** = check digit; **clé de contrôle** = check number *ou* check key *ou* check bit; **clé numérique de contrôle** = check digit; **cycle de contrôle** = control cycle; *(en cas d'erreur ou de panne)* **dispositif de contrôle** = monitor; **données de contrôle** = test data *ou* control data; **fichier de contrôle de tâche** = job control file; *(groupe témoin)* **groupe de contrôle** = control group; **hors de contrôle** = out of control; **impulsion de contrôle du balayage vertical** = field sync pulse; **indicateur de contrôle** = check indicator; **indicateur de contrôle de parité** = parity flag; **instruction de contrôle** = control statement *ou* supervisory instruction *ou* control instruction; **la prochaine instruction de contrôle vous donnera les italiques** = the next control instruction will switch to italics; **interface de contrôle** = command interface; **jeton de contrôle (de réseau)** = control token; *(de périphériques)* **langage de contrôle** = command control language; **lignes de contrôle** = bus control lines; **micro-ordinateur de contrôle** = microcontroller; **micro-ordinateur de contrôle monopuce** *ou* **à puce unique** = single-chip microcontroller; *(pour couleur d'écran de télévision)* **mire de contrôle** = test pattern; **mode (de) contrôle** = control mode; **mot de contrôle** = control word; **ordinateur de contrôle** = control computer; **ordinateur de contrôle des transmissions** = communications computer; **panneau de contrôle** = control panel; **point de contrôle** = *(de logiciel ou de matériel)* access point; *(de logiciel)* check point; **poste de contrôle mixte** = combined station; **procédure de contrôle d'acheminement** = routing overheads; **programme de contrôle** = checking program *ou* monitor program; **programme de contrôle d'entrée-sortie** = input/output control program; **programme de contrôle de réseau** =

network control program; **programme de contrôle de tâche** = job control program; *(pour contrôle d'erreurs ou d'utilisateurs)* **protocole de contrôle** = audit trail; **registre de contrôle** = check register; **registre de commande de contrôle** = control register; **responsable du contrôle de (la) qualité** = quality controller; **scanner de contrôle d'appel** = communications scanner; **séquence de contrôle** = supervisory sequence; **signal de contrôle** = control signal *ou* supervisory signal; **signal de contrôle d'appel** = call control signal; **systèmes de contrôle** = control systems; **système avec contrôle automatique** *ou* **avec autocontrôle** = self-checking system; **système de contrôle intégré** = built-in check; **tests de contrôle de liens** = link trials; **total de contrôle** = checksum *ou* check total *ou* control total; **les données sont sûrement erronées si le total de contrôle est faux** = the data must be corrupted if the checksum is different; **touche de contrôle** = control key (CTRL); **touches de contrôle du curseur** = cursor control keys *ou* cursor pad *ou* arrowed keys; **transmission sans contrôle de retour** = free wheeling; **unité de contrôle (de processus)** = control unit (CU); **vidage de contrôle (sur imprimante)** = check point dump; *(affichage des derniers caractères saisis)* **visualisation de contrôle d'entrée** = marching display

◇ **contrôlé, -ée** *adj* controlled; **qui peut être contrôlé** = controllable; **courant contrôlé** = regulated power supply; **interruption contrôlée** = transparent interrupt; **vocabulaire contrôlé** = controlled vocabulary

◇ **contrôler** *vtr* **(a)** to check *ou* to supervise *ou* to test *ou* to monitor *ou* to verify; **ce processus est contrôlé par une batterie de capteurs** = the process is monitored by a bank of sensors; **il contrôle le progrès des programmeurs débutants** = he is monitoring the progress of the trainee programmers; **l'appareil contrôle chaque signal de sortie** = the machine monitors each signal as it is sent out; **l'ingénieur de maintenance a découvert des défauts en contrôlant le matériel** = the maintenance engineer found some defects whilst checking the hardware; **les différentes parties du système ont été contrôlées avant l'emballage** = the separate parts of the system were all checked for faults before being packaged **(b)** to control *ou* to regulate; **l'ordinateur principal contrôle six postes de travail** = the main computer supports six workstations

◊ **contrôleur, -euse** *n* supervisor *ou* controller; **contrôleur d'affichage** = display controller; **contrôleur de communication** = communications control unit (CCU); **contrôleur de disque** *ou* **de disquettes** = disk controller *ou* floppy disk controller (FDC); **carte contrôleur de disque** *ou* **de disquettes** = disk-controller card; **contrôleur d'écran** = display controller; **contrôleur d'émetteur-récepteur asynchrone universel** = UART controller; **contrôleur d'entrée-sortie** = input/output controller; **contrôleur d'imprimante** = printer controller; **contrôleur de mémoire à accès direct** = DMA controller; **contrôleur de périphérique(s)** = peripheral control unit (PCU); **contrôleur de réseau** = network controller; **contrôleur de terminal** = terminal controller; **contrôleur de transmission** *ou* **de communication** = communications control unit (CCU)

convenir (à) *vi* to apply (to); **cette formule ne convient qu'aux données reçues après le signal d'interruption** = this formula applies only to data received after the interrupt signal

convention *nf* convention; **Convention sur le droit d'auteur** = Copyright Act

conversation *nf (entre chambre de contrôle et studio)* talkback

◊ **conversationnel, -elle** *adj* interactive *ou* conversational; **mode conversationnel** = conversational mode *ou* interactive mode *ou* interactive processing; **connexion d'ordinateurs en mode conversationnel** = computer conferencing; **terminal conversationnel** = conversational *ou* interactive terminal

conversion *nf* conversion; **conversion binaire-décimale** = binary-to-decimal conversion; **conversion de code** = code conversion; **conversion décimale-binaire** = decimal-to-binary conversion; *(d'un format en un autre)* **conversion de données** = data translation; **conversion de fichier** = file conversion; *(d'une image couleur)* **conversion monochrome** = black crush; **conversion d'une onde en numérique** = waveform digitization;

conversion de signaux = signal conditioning *ou* signal conversion; **délai de conversion** = sense recovery time; **programme de conversion** = conversion program; **tables de conversion** = translation tables *ou* conversion tables

convertibilité *nf* convertibility

◊ **convertible** *adj* convertible

◊ **convertir** *vtr* to convert *ou* to translate

◊ **convertisseur** *nm* converter *ou* convertor *ou* conversion equipment; **grâce au convertisseur les anciennes données sont acceptées par le nouveau système** = the convertor has allowed the old data to be used on the new system; **convertisseur analogique-numérique** = analog to digital converter *ou* A to D converter (ADC); *(numérisateur)* digitizer; **le signal vocal est d'abord passé par le convertisseur analogique-numérique avant d'être analysé** = the speech signal was first passed through an A to D converter before being analysed; **convertisseur analogique-numérique parallèle** = flash A/D; **convertisseur de fréquence** = frequency changer *ou* set-top converter; **convertisseur de normes** = standards converter; **c'est grâce à un convertisseur de normes que nous pouvons regarder des programmes de télévision américains** = the standards converter allows us to watch US television; **convertisseur numérique-analogique** = digital to analog converter *ou* D to A converter (DAC); **le convertisseur numérique-analogique du port de sortie contrôle la machine analogique** = the D/A converter on the output port controls the analog machine; **l'ordinateur émet un signal vocal via un convertisseur numérique-analogique** = speech is output from the computer via a D/A converter; *(de télévision)* **convertisseur de signal** = set-top converter; **convertisseur texte-signal vocal** = text-to-speech converter; **programme convertisseur** = conversion program

convexe *adj* convex; **lentille convexe** = convex lens

convivial,-e *adj* user-friendly; **appareil convivial** = user-friendly machine; **comparée à la version précédente, celle-ci est très conviviale** = compared with the previous version, this one is very user-friendly

◊ **convivialité** *nf* user-friendliness *ou* being user-friendly

> toutefois, ce que le logiciel gagne en convivialité pour le débutant, il le perd en rigueur
>
> *Science et Vie Micro*

convoyeur *nm* conveyor; *(d'alimentation du papier)* chain delivery mechanism

coordination *nf* coordination; **coordination inductive** = inductive coordination

coordonnée *nf* (a) *(math)* coordinate; **coordonnées** = X-Y coordinates; **coordonnées cartésiennes** = cartesian coordinates; **coordonnée horizontale** = X-coordinate; **coordonnées polaires** = polar coordinates; **diagramme en coordonnées polaires** = polar diagram; **coordonnées rectangulaires** = rectangular coordinates; **coordonnées relatives** = relative coordinates; **coordonnée verticale** = Y-coordinate (b) *(données)* data *ou* details; **les coordonnées des clients de la société sont entrées sur l'ordinateur principal** = the company stores data on customers in its main computer file *ou* customer details are stored on the company's main computer

◊ **coordonner** *vtr* to coordinate; **elle doit coordonner la saisie des diverses parties d'un fichier qui se fait dans six centres différents** = she has to coordinate the keyboarding of several parts of a file in six different locations

copie *nf* (a) *(action)* duplication *ou* copying; *(illégal)* piracy; *(d'un logiciel)* **autorisation de copie** = software licence; *(système ou dispositif ou codage)* **protection contre la copie** = copy protection *ou* copy protect; **tous les disques sont protégés contre la copie** = all disks are copy protected; **la nouvelle version du logiciel ne sera pas protégée contre la copie** = the new program will come without copy protection (b) *(double)* copy *ou* duplicate; *(d'un article de revue scientifique)* offprint; **copie pour archivage** = file copy; **copie d'un bloc (de texte)** = block copy; *(d'une lettre)* **copie carbone** = carbon copy; **passez-moi l'original et classez la copie dans le**

dossier = give me the original, and file the carbon copy; **copie d'écran** = hard copy; *(d'un texte)* **copie finale** = clean copy; *(pour imprimerie)* **copie finalisée** = camera-ready copy (crc); **copie illégale** = pirate copy; **copie (de protection) d'original** = protection master; **copie piratée** = pirate copy *ou* bootleg copy; *(pour imprimerie)* **copie prête à reproduire** = camera-ready copy (crc); *(sur disquette)* **copie de sauvegarde** = security backup; **faire une copie** = to copy; **faire une copie d'une lettre** = to duplicate a letter

◊ **copier** *vtr* to copy *ou* to duplicate *ou* to replicate; **cette routine va copier vos résulats sans aucun problème** = the routine will replicate your results with very little effort; **il est impossible de copier quoi que ce soit sur une disquette non formatée** = it is impossible to copy to an unformatted disk; **il existe un utilitaire résident qui copie les fichiers les plus récents sur un support de sauvegarde toutes les 40 minutes** = there is a memory resident utility which copies the latest files onto backing store every 40 minutes; *(de logiciel)* **autorisation de copier** = authorization to copy (ATC)

◊ **copieur** *nm* copier *ou* copying machine *ou* duplicating machine *ou* duplicator *ou* photocopier; **copieur de bureau** *ou* **copieur professionnel** = office copier; **papier pour copieur** = duplicating paper *ou* duplicator paper

co-processeur *ou* **coprocesseur** *nm* coprocessor; **coprocesseur graphique** = graphics coprocessor; **coprocesseur mathématique** = maths chip *ou* maths coprocessor

copyright *nm* copyright; **oeuvre sous copyright** *ou* **protégée par un copyright** = copyright work *ou* copyrighted work *ou* work still in copyright; **photocopier une oeuvre sous copyright est illégal** = it is illegal to take copies of a copyright work; **(document, etc.) qui n'est plus protégé par un copyright** = (document) which is out of copyright *ou* in the public domain; **programme qui n'est plus protégé par un copyright** = program which is in the public domain; **déposer un copyright** = to copyright; **mention de copyright (dans un livre)** = copyright notice; **titulaire d'un copyright** = copyright holder *ou* owner

coquille *nf* typographical error *ou* literal *ou* typo; **une erreur typographique à la composition donne ce qu'on appelle une 'coquille'** = a typographical error made while typesetting is called a 'typo'

CORAL COMMON REAL-TIME APPLICATIONS LANGUAGE; **langage CORAL** = CORAL; *voir aussi* LANGAGE

cordon *nm (de liaison)* cord *ou* cable; **cordon souple** = flex; **téléphone sans cordon** = cordless telephone; **cordon de liaison** *ou* **de raccordement d'un tableau de distribution** = patchcord

co-résident, -e *adj* coresident

coroutine *nf* coroutine

corps *nm* body; **corps de boucle** = loop body; **corps d'un caractère** = body size *ou* set; *(en points)* typesize; **corps du texte** = matter; **caractères utilisés pour le corps d'un texte** = body type; **dimension (en points) du corps d'un texte** = body size

correct, -e *adj* accurate *ou* correct

◇ **correctement** *adv* accurately; **le lecteur optique n'arrivait pas à lire correctement toutes les lettres de la nouvelle police de caractères** *ou* **de la nouvelle fonte** = the OCR had difficulty in reading the new font accurately

correcteur, -trice **1** *n (d'épreuves)* proofreader **2** *adj* **code correcteur** = self-correcting code; **code correcteur d'erreurs** = error correcting code

correction *nf* **(a)** *(d'un texte imprimé)* correction; **corrections de l'imprimeur** = house corrections; **épreuve sans correction** = clean proof; **texte sans correction** = clean text; **signes de correction (d'épreuves d'imprimerie)** = proof correction marks **(b)** *(de données)* correction *ou* update; **correction d'erreurs** = error correction *ou* data cleaning; **correction automatique d'erreurs** = automatic error correction; **correction d'erreurs par retransmission** = backward error correction; **correction d'erreurs en cours de transmission** = forward error correction; **détection et correction d'erreurs** = error detection and

correction (EDAC); **code de vérification et correction d'erreurs** = error checking and correcting code (ECCC); **correction provisoire** = patch; **fichier des corrections** = deletion record

◇ **correctif, -ive** *adj* corrective; **maintenance corrective** = corrective maintenance

correspondance *nf* correspondence; **correspondance commerciale** *ou* **d'affaires** = business correspondence; **être en correspondance avec quelqu'un** = to correspond with someone *ou* to be in correspondence with someone

◇ **correspondant, -e** *n* **(a)** *(journaliste)* correspondent; **le correspondant (de la section) informatique** = the computer correspondent; **le correspondant économique du 'Figaro'** = the 'Figaro' business correspondent **(b)** *(d'une communication téléphonique)* called party

correspondre *vi* **(a)** *(coïncider)* to correspond; **correspondre à quelque chose** = to correspond with something **(b)** *(écrire)* **correspondre avec quelqu'un** = to correspond with someone

corriger *vtr* **(a)** to correct *ou* to rectify; *(mettre à jour)* to update; **erreur qui peut être corrigée** = recoverable error; **erreur impossible à corriger** = unrecoverable error; **fichier corrigé** = update (file); **le document original et le document corrigé se trouvent tous les deux sur disquettes** = we have the original and updated documents on disks **(b)** *(texte écrit)* to edit *ou* to correct; **corriger des épreuves** = to proofread; **ils ont dû corriger l'erreur à l'impression** = they had to rectify the error at the printout stage; **page corrigée qui en remplace une autre** = cancel page; **non corrigé** = unedited **(c)** *(un signal)* to equalize

corrompre *vtr* to corrupt; **les données de ce fichier n'ont pas été corrompues** = the data in this file has not been corrupted *ou* has integrity

◇ **corrompu, -e** *adj (fichier)* damaged; *(données* ou *fichier)* corrupt

◇ **corruption** *nf* corruption; **corruption de données** = data corruption; **la corruption de données sur la disquette a rendu le fichier impossible à lire** = data corruption on the disk has made one file unreadable; **chaque fois qu'on met le système sous tension, il y a corruption de données =** data corruption occurs each time the motor is switched on

cosmique *adj* **bruits cosmiques =** galactic noise

côté *nm* side; **à côté de =** adjacent to; **l'adresse est rangée en mémoire à côté du champ nom du client =** the address is stored adjacent to the customer name field

couche *nf* **(a)** *(zone d'une structure)* layer; **couche application =** application layer; **couche (de) liaison de données =** data link layer; **couches multiples =** multilayer; *voir aussi* MULTICOUCHE; **couche physique =** physical layer; **couche présentation =** presentation layer; **couche réseau =** network layer; **couche session =** session layer; **couche transport =** transport layer; **disposé en couches =** layered; **le noyau possède une structure en couches adaptée aux besoins de l'utilisateur =** the kernel has a layered structure according to user priority **(b)** *(enduit)* coating; **couche épitaxiale =** epitaxial layer; **couche de phosphore** *ou* **couche phosphorescente =** phosphor coating; **couche phosphorée à grande persistance =** long persistence phosphor; **mémoire laser sur couche haute définition =** emulsion laser storage; **mémoire à couches minces magnétiques =** magnetic thin film storage **(c)** *(ionosphère)* **couche E =** E-region *ou* Heaviside-Kennelly layer

◊ **couché, -ée** *adj* **papier couché =** coated paper

couler *vi* to flow

couleur *nf* colour; **couleur d'affichage =** display colour; **couleurs complémentaires =** complementary colours; **couleurs fondamentales =** primary colours; **couleur de premier plan =** foreground colour; **adaptateur graphique couleur EGA =** enhanced graphics adapter (EGA); **adaptateur graphique couleur CGA =** colour graphics adapter (CGA); **affichage couleur =** colour display; **cellule de contrôle des couleurs =** colour cell; **décodeur de couleurs =** colour decoder; **diapositive couleur =** colour

transparency; **écran couleur =** colour monitor; **encodeur de couleurs =** colour encoder; **équilibre des couleurs =** colour balance; **moniteur couleur =** colour monitor; **le moniteur couleur est excellent pour les jeux électroniques =** the colour monitor is great for games; **photographie en couleur** *ou* **photo couleur =** colour photograph; **saturation de couleur =** colour saturation; **sélection** *ou* **séparation des couleurs =** colour separation; **négatifs (de séparation des) couleurs =** colour separations

coulomb *nm* coulomb

coup *nm* **(a)** blow *ou* knock; **éteindre l'ordinateur ou lui donner un coup quand la tête de lecture est en marche peut causer des ennuis =** you can cause trouble by turning off or jarring the PC while the disk read head is moving **(b)** **passer un coup de fil =** to make a phone call

coupe *nf* cross-section; **une coupe de la fibre optique a révélé la source du problème =** the cross-section of the optical fibre showed the source of the problem; **coupe (en) diagonale** *ou* **en biseau =** diagonal cut

◊ **coupe-circuit** *nm* circuit breaker

couper *vtr* **(a)** to clip *ou* to cut *ou* to cut off *ou* to scissor; *(très peu)* to trim; **on a coupé six mètres du rouleau de papier =** six metres of paper were cut off the reel; **il vous faudra couper légèrement le bord supérieur de la photo pour qu'elle ait les dimensions désirées =** you will need to trim the top part of the photograph to make it fit **(b)** to cut; **couper un mot =** to delete a word; **couper un texte =** to cut *ou* to shorten a text; **nous avons dû couper le fichier pour réussir à le sauvegarder sur une seule disquette =** we had to shorten the file to be able to save it on one floppy

◊ **coupage-collage** *nm (traitement de texte)* cut and paste

couplage *nm* **(a)** linkage; **transformateur de couplage =** matching transformer **(b)** **dispositif à couplage de charge =** charge-coupled device (CCD); **(dispositif) mémoire à couplage de charge =** charge-coupled device memory *ou* CCD memory

◇ **coupler** *vtr* to couple *ou* to lock onto; **les deux systèmes sont couplés l'un à l'autre =** the two systems are coupled together

◇ **coupleur** *nm* coupler; **coupleur acoustique =** acoustic coupler

le magnétophone peut être couplé à un micro-ordinateur

Science et Vie

coupure *nf* **(a)** *(dans un texte)* cut *ou* deletion; **les éditeurs ont demandé de faire des coupures au premier chapitre =** the editors have asked for cuts *ou* deletions in the first chapter; **fichier des coupures =** deletion record **(b)** *(découpure)* cutting; **coupure de journal** *ou* **de presse =** press cutting; **nous avons constitué un dossier de coupures de presse sur le nouveau progiciel =** we have kept a file of press cuttings about the new software package; **service de coupures de presse =** clipping service **(c)** *(césure d'un mot)* division *ou* hyphenation *ou* word break; **coupure inappropriée =** bad break; **la coupure des mots trop longs se fait automatiquement en fin de ligne grâce au programme de césure =** in the hyphenation program, long words are automatically divided at the end of lines **(d)** *(de transmission)* **coupure au premier raccroché =** first party release; **coupure d'un signal =** breakup **(e)** *(d'électricité)* cut *ou* cutoff; **coupure de courant =** blackout *ou* black out *ou* power failure; **coupure d'alimentation de courant =** power dump; **alimentation statique sans coupure =** uninterruptable power supply (UPS); **il y a eu une coupure de courant =** the electricity supply was cut off; **il y a eu une coupure de courant qui a été fatale à l'ordinateur =** the electricity was cut off, and the computer crashed; **fréquence de coupure =** cutoff frequency

courant *nm* *(électrique)* electric current; **courant alternatif (CA) =** alternating current (AC); **courant continu (CC) =** direct current (DC); **courant de décharge =** drain; **courant flottant =** floating voltage; **produire un courant induit =** to induce a current; **courant de maintien =** hold current; **courant noir =** dark current; **courant porteur commun =** common carrier; *(d'une ligne)* **courant de transit** *ou* **transitoire =** line transient *ou* voltage transient; **limiteur** *ou* **éliminateur**

de courant transitoire = transient suppressor; **courant de veille =** hold current; **amplificateur de courant de bus =** bus driver; **baisse** *ou* **chute de courant =** brown-out; **coupure de courant =** power failure; **coupure d'alimentation de courant =** power dump; **il y a eu une coupure de courant =** the electricity supply was cut off; **il y a eu une coupure de courant qui a été fatale à l'ordinateur =** the electricity was cut off, and the computer crashed; **inverseur de courant =** inverter (AC/DC); **panne de courant =** power failure; **prise de courant =** outlet *ou* electric socket

◇ **courant, -e** *adj* **(a)** *(normal)* common *ou* current *ou* standard; **c'est un défaut courant de ce modèle d'imprimante =** this is a common fault with this printer model; **adresse courante =** current address; **registre d'adresse courante =** current address register (CAR); **(mise en) mémoire du format courant =** local format storage; **registre d'instruction courante =** current instruction register (CIR); **matériel courant =** common hardware; **maintenance courante =** housekeeping; **(bruit) parasite courant =** common mode noise **(b)** **titre courant =** running head; **titres et en-têtes courants =** rolling headers

courbe *nf* graph *ou* plot *ou* curve; **tracer une courbe (par points numérisés) =** to plot a graph *ou* a curve; **courbe d'apprentissage =** learning curve; **courbe caractéristique =** characteristic curve; **traceur de courbes =** X-Y plotter *ou* graph plotter

courir *vi* to run; *(un texte)* **laisser courir (sans interruption** *ou* **sans alinéa) =** to run on; **le texte peut courir sans alinéa =** the line can run on to the next without any space

courrier *nm* mail; **courrier 'arrivée' =** incoming mail; **courrier 'départ' =** outgoing mail; **courrier électronique =** electronic mail *ou* email *ou* e-mail; **fonction courrier électronique =** electronic mail capabilities; **qualité courrier =** near-letter-quality *ou* NLQ (printing); **mettez l'imprimante en mode courrier pour imprimer ces lettres cadres =** switch the printer to NLQ for these form letters

course *nf* course d'une touche = key travel

court, -e *adj* short; **il est impossible de former convenablement un opérateur dans un délai aussi court =** there is insufficient time to train a keyboarder properly *ou* it is impossible to train the keyboarders properly in such a short space of time; **ondes courtes =** short wave (SW); **modem de courte portée =** short haul modem; *(imprimerie)* **tiret court (dont la longueur équivaut à un 'n')** = en dash *ou* en rule

◊ **court-circuit** *nm* short circuit; **créer un court-circuit =** to short-circuit; **qui a été mis en court-circuit =** short-circuited

◊ **court-circuiter** *vtr* to short-circuit

coussinet *nm* **distorsion en coussinet** = pin cushion distortion

couture *nf* seam; *(livre)* **relié sans couture =** perfect bound; **reliure sans couture =** perfect binding

couverture *nf* **(a)** *(d'un livre)* cover *ou* binding; **couverture cartonnée =** case binding; **livre avec couverture cartonnée** = hardbound book *ou* cased book; **relier avec couverture cartonnée =** to case a book; **c'est un livre avec couverture pelliculée =** the book has a laminated cover; **c'est un livre avec couverture plastique souple =** the book has a soft plastic binding **(b)** *(suppression d'une émission)* blanketing **(c)** coverage; **couverture médiatique =** media coverage *ou* press coverage; **la société a eu une excellente couverture médiatique pour le lancement de son nouveau modèle =** the company had good media coverage for the launch of its new model; **nous avons eu une bonne couverture médiatique pour le lancement du nouveau modèle =** we got good media coverage for the launch of the new model; **zone terrestre de couverture** *ou* **couverture terrestre =** earth coverage

il faudra d'ici là qu'il se prononce sur les demandes de la chaîne d'une extension de la couverture terrestre de ce réseau
Le Figaro

CP/M = CONTROL PROGRAM/MONITOR *ou* CONTROL PROGRAM FOR MICROCOMPUTERS;

système d'exploitation CP/M = CP/M; *voir aussi* EXPLOITATION

cps = CARACTERES PAR SECONDE

CPU = CENTRAL PROCESSING UNIT; **protocole d'échange d'informations entre CPU et périphérique =** CPU handshaking; **cycle CPU =** CPU cycle; **éléments CPU =** CPU elements; **temps CPU =** CPU time; *voir aussi* UNITE

crash *nm* crash *ou* system crash; **crash du disque (dur) =** (hard) disk crash; **crash du disque dur causé par la tête de lecture =** head crash; **crash d'un programme =** program crash

crasse *nf* dirt; *(parasite sur bande)* drop in

crawl *nm (défilement de générique)* crawl

crayon *nm* pencil; **crayon optique =** stylus; **pour dessiner, utilisez un crayon optique et une tablette graphique =** use the stylus to draw on the graphics tablet

créateur, -trice *n* créateur de logiciel = software developer

◊ **création** *nf* **(a)** creation *ou* origination *ou* generation; **la création de la maquette demandera plusieurs semaines =** the origination of the artwork will take several weeks; **allez à CREATION D'UN DOSSIER sur le menu =** move to the CREATE NEW FILE instruction on the menu; **création de données =** data origination; **création de fichier =** file creation; **création de liens =** linkage; **expert en création de logiciel =** software developer; **création d'un programme =** program generation **(b)** design; **studio de création =** design studio; **spécifications** *ou* **contraintes** *ou* **paramètres de création =** design parameters; **création et fabrication assistées par ordinateur (CFAO) =** computer-aided *ou* assisted design/computer-aided *ou* assisted manufacture (CAD/CAM)

crédit *nm* **(a)** *(d'argent)* credit; **carte de crédit =** credit card **(b)** *(de film ou revue)* **crédits =** credits

créer *vtr* to create *ou* to generate *ou* to originate; **créer une adresse** = to address; **créé à l'aide d'un ordinateur** = computer-generated; **document créé à partir de paragraphes standard** = boilerplate; **on a créé un nouveau fichier sur la disquette pour archiver le document** = a new file was created on disk to store the document; **créer une image à partir de données numériques** = to generate an image from digitally recorded data; **ils ont fait l'analyse de l'image créée par l'ordinateur** = they analyzed the computer-generated image; **demandez l'aide d'un bon programmeur qui vous aidera à créer un nouveau (programme de) traitement de texte** = ask a specialist programmer to help you to devise a new word-processing program

crénage *nm (d'une photo)* kerning

créneau *nm* **(a)** *(pour carte de circuit)* slot; **créneau pour carte d'extension** = expansion slot; **créneau inutilisé** = empty slot; **cet ordinateur possède deux créneaux libres et votre carte d'extension n'en utilisera qu'un** = there are two free slots in the micro, you only need one for the add-on board; **enfichez la carte d'extension dans le créneau libre** = insert the board in the free expansion slot **(b)** *(transmission)* **créneau pour message** = message slot; **créneau de temps** = time slot

crête *nf* peak; **veillez à ce que la tension de crête ne dépasse pas 60 watts sinon l'amplificateur surchauffera** = keep the peak power below 60 watts or the amplifier will overheat

creux *nm* trough; *(d'une onde)* **les pointes et les creux** = peaks and troughs

cristal *nm* crystal; **affichage à cristaux liquides** = liquid crystal display (LCD)

le groupe électronique nippon est parvenu à réaliser un écran à cristaux liquides qui, contrairement aux écrans usuels, garantit sous tous les angles de vision une image nette et une haute définition
Electronique

critère *nm* criterion
NOTE: le pluriel est **criteria**

critique *adj* **(a)** critical; *(de l'image)* **fréquence critique de fusion** = critical fusion frequency; **ressource critique** = critical resource **(b)** **résumé critique** = evaluative abstract

crochet(s) *nm(pl)* square bracket(s); **mettre entre crochets** = to bracket together

croisé, -ée *adj* cross-; **assembleur croisé** = cross-assembler; **compilateur croisé** = cross-compiler; **nous pouvons utiliser un compilateur croisé pour développer le logiciel avant l'arrivée du nouveau système** = we can use a cross-compiler to develop the software before the new system arrives; **contrôle croisé** = cross-check; **référence croisée** = cross-reference

croissant, -e *adj* increasing; **en ordre croissant** = forward mode; **tri par ordre croissant** = forward sort

croix (†) *nf (signe typographique)* dagger; **croix double (‡)** = double dagger

cropping *nm (de photo)* cropping

cryogénique *adj* cryogenic; **mémoire cryogénique** = cryogenic memory

cryptage *nm (système)* cipher; *(procédure)* encryption; **algorithme de cryptage** = cryptographic algorithm; **clé de cryptage** = cipher key *ou* cryptographic key; **cryptage à clé publique** = public key cipher system; **cryptage de données** = data encryption; **norme** *ou* **standard de cryptage de données** = data encryption standard (DES); **cryptage de l'information pour en assurer la confidentialité** = privacy transformation
◊ **crypter** *vtr* to code *ou* to encipher *ou* to encrypt; **circuit crypté (pour protection de logiciel)** = dongle; **message crypté** = ciphertext *ou* encrypted text; **le message crypté peut être transmis par téléphone sans que personne ne puisse le lire** = the encrypted text can be sent along ordinary telephone lines, and no one will be able to understand it
◊ **cryptographie** *nf* cryptography
◊ **cryptographique** *adj* cryptographic; **algorithme cryptographique** =

cryptographic algorithm; **analyse cryptographique** = cryptanalysis

CSM = COMBINED SYMBOL MATCHING *voir* SYSTEME

CSMA-CD = CARRIER SENSE MULTIPLE ACCESS-COLLISION DETECTION *voir* COLLISION

CTR *ou* **CTRL mode CTRL** = control mode; **touche CTRL** = control key *ou* CONTROL; **commandé par les codes CTRL** *ou* **asservi aux codes CTRL** = control-driven; *voir aussi* CONTROLE

CTS = CLEAR TO SEND; **signal CTS** = CTS

cuivre *nm* copper

cumul *nm* **de cumul** = cumulative; **registre de cumul** = accumulator register

◊ **cumulande** *nm (nombre d'une addition auquel on en ajoute un autre)* augend

◊ **cumulateur** *nm (nombre ajouté au cumulande)* addend *ou* augmenter

◊ **cumulatif, -ive** *adj* cumulative; **index cumulatif** = cumulative index

curatif, -ive *adj* remedial; **maintenance curative** = remedial maintenance

curseur *nm* cursor; **curseur adressable** = addressable cursor; **curseur destructif** = destructive cursor; **l'écran devient presqu'illisible sans le curseur destructif** = reading the screen becomes difficult without a destructive cursor; **curseur non destructif** = non-destructive cursor; **curseur effaceur** = destructive cursor; **curseur secondaire** = ghost cursor; **touches de contrôle du curseur** = cursor control keys *ou* cursor pad *ou* arrowed keys

cybernétique *nf* **la cybernétique** = cybernetics

cycle *nm* cycle; **cycle de contrôle** = control cycle; **cycle CPU** = CPU cycle; *(d'une instruction)* **cycle d'exécution** = execute cycle; **opération en cycle fixe** = fixed cycle operation; **cycle fonctionnel** = action cycle; **cycle d'horloge** = clock cycle *ou* CPU cycle; **cycle d'instruction** = instruction cycle; **temps de cycle d'instruction** = instruction cycle time; **cycle de lecture** = read cycle; **cycle de lecture d'une instruction** = fetch cycle; **cycle de lecture-exécution** = fetch-execute cycle *ou* execute cycle; **cycle de machine** = machine cycle; **cycle de mémoire** = memory cycle; **cycle d'opération** = operation cycle; **cycle principal** = major cycle; **cycle de production** = production run; **cycle de rotation des fichiers de sauvegarde** = grandfather cycle; **cycle de l'unité centrale** = CPU cycle; **cycle de vie d'un logiciel** = software life cycle; **(période de) disponiblité dans le cycle** = cycle availability; **(système) évalué en cycles possibles par unité de temps** = duty-rated (system); **index de cycle** = cycle index; **nombre de cycles** = cycle count; **temps de cycle** = cycle time; **(exploitation par) vol de cycle** = cycle stealing; **vol de temps de cycle de la mémoire à accès direct** *ou* **de mémoire DMA** = DMA cycle stealing

◊ **cyclique** *adj* cyclic; **accès cyclique** = cyclic access; **contrôle cyclique** = cyclic check; **contrôle par redondance cyclique** = cyclic redundancy check (CRC)

cylindre *nm* cylinder *ou* drum *ou* platen; **cylindre d'impression** = impression cylinder; **cylindre porte-blanchet** = blanket cylinder; **imprimante à cylindre** = barrel printer

Dd

D *(représentation hexadécimale du nombre 13)* D

D dispositif *ou* **commutateur à bascule de type D =** D-type flip-flop

D *(ionosphère)* **région D =** D-region; **la région D est la principale cause d'affaiblissement des ondes radioélectriques =** the D-region is the main cause of attenuation in transmitted radio signals

dactylo *nf* copy typist; **pool de dactylos =** typing pool
◊ **dactylographie** *nf* (copy) typing
◊ **dactylographié, -ée** *adj* typewritten; **texte** *ou* **manuscrit dactylographié =** typescript

DAO = DESSIN ASSISTE PAR ORDINATEUR

datagramme *nm* datagram

date *nf* date; **la date de création de ce fichier est le 10 juin =** the date of creation for the file was the 10th of June; **j'ai bien reçu votre message en date d'hier =** I have received your message of yesterday's date; **date limite** *ou* **date d'expiration de délai =** expiration date *ou* deadline; **nous avons dépassé notre date limite du 15 octobre =** we've missed our October 15th deadline; **date de péremption =** expiration date; *(d'un produit en magasin)* shelf life
◊ **dater** *(un document)* to date

db *ou* **dB** = DECIBEL

DCB = DECIMAL CODE BINAIRE binary coded decimal; **additionneur DCB =** BCD adder

DD = DISQUETTE DOUBLE DENSITE

débit *nm* throughput *ou* transmission rate *ou* speed; *(en bauds)* baud rate; **communication à faible débit =** low speed communications; **débit binaire =** bit rate debit; **débit d'un canal** *ou* **d'une voie de transmission =** channel capacity; **débit par défaut** *ou* **pré-déterminé** *ou* **implicite d'un modem =** default rate; **débit de données =** data transfer rate; **le débit d'électricité est régularisé par une résistance =** current flow is regulated by a resistor; **débit d'une imprimante =** printer output; *(mesuré en 'ems')* ems per hour; **cette imprimante a un débit de 60 caractères/seconde =** the printer prints at 60 characters per second; **débit ligne =** *(d'une imprimante)* lines per minute (LPM); *(transmission de données)* line speed; **reconnaissance automatique de débit d'une ligne (en bauds) =** auto-baud scanning *ou* auto-baud sensing; **un modem équipé d'une reconnaissance de débit s'ajuste automatiquement à la vitesse à laquelle il doit fonctionner =** a modem with auto-baud scanner can automatically sense at which baud rate it should operate; **débit théorique** *ou* **nominal =** rated throughput; **débit de transmission de données =** data signalling rate; **débit de transmission d'informations =** information rate; **débit maximal de transmission =** maximum transmission rate; **débit moyen de transmission =** medium speed; *(transmission)* **ligne de grand débit =** high usage trunk; *(onduleur* ou *dispositif de secours)* **temps de débit =** holdup

débogage *nm* debugging; **débogage symbolique =** symbolic debugging; **logiciel de débogage =** debugger; **spécialiste en débogage =** troubleshooter; **système de débogage interactif =** interactive debugging system

◊ **débogué, -ée** *adj* debugged; **programme débogué =** debugged program

◊ **déboguer** *vtr* to debug *ou* to troubleshoot; **il faut plus de temps pour déboguer un programme que pour en créer un** = debugging takes up more time than construction; **ils ont mis des semaines à déboguer le système** = they spent weeks debugging the system

déborder *vtr&i* to overflow *ou* to go beyond; **la photo déborde le bord de la page** = the photo is bled off; *(dans la marge de gauche)* **faire déborder une ligne** = to outdent

◊ **débordement** *nm (d'une mémoire tampon)* spillage; *(de capacité d'une ligne ou d'un ordinateur)* overflow; **débordement négatif** = underflow

débrancher *vtr* to disconnect *ou* to unplug; **ne déplacez pas le système sans l'avoir d'abord débranché** = do not move the system without unplugging it; **n'oubliez pas de débrancher (le câble de) l'imprimante avant de la changer de place** = do not forget to disconnect the cable before moving the printer

début *nm* beginning *ou* start; **début de bande** = tape header; *(pour le curseur)* **début de l'écran** = cursor home; *(données)* **début d'enregistrement** = home record; *(transmisssion)* **début d'en-tête** = start of header; **(caractère de) début de fichier** = beginning of file (bof); **(données de) début de fichier** = head; *(papier listing)* **début d'une page** = head of form (HOF); **(code de) début de texte** = start-of-text (SOT *ou* STX); **bit** *ou* **élément de début** = start bit *ou* start element; **marque de début de bande** = beginning of tape (bot) marker; **marque de début d'enregistrement** = beginning of information mark (bim); **marque de début de mot** = word marker; *(d'une bande)* **point de début d'enregistrement** = (tape) loadpoint

débuter *vtr* **débuter une session (à l'ordinateur)** = to log in *ou* log on

décadaire *adj* decade; **compteur décadaire** = decade counter
◊ **décade** *nf* decade

décalage *nm* **(a)** *(glissement d'un bit)* shift; **décalage arithmétique** = arithmetic shift; **décalage circulaire** = circular shift *ou* cyclic shift *ou* end about shift; **décalage à droite** = right shift; **faire** *ou* **effectuer un décalage à droite** = to right shift *ou* to shift right; **décalage à gauche** = left shift; **faire** *ou* **effectuer un décalage à gauche** = to left shift *ou* to shift left; **décalage logique** = logical shift *ou* non-arithmetic shift; **instruction de décalage** = shift instruction; **instruction de décalage dans le registre** = accumulator shift instruction; **registre à** *ou* **de décalage** = shift register *ou* circulating register **(b)** *(de données)* **(à) décalage de fréquence** = dual clocking **(c)** *(de temps)* lag; **le décalage est perceptible sur les lignes téléphoniques internationales** = time lag is noticeable on international phone calls

◊ **décalé, -ée** *adj* shifted; **0110 décalé à gauche d'un pas, devient 1100** = 0110 left shifted once is 1100

◊ **décaler** *vtr* to shift

◊ **décelé, -ée** *adj* detected *ou* found; **non décelé** = undetected

◊ **déceler** *vtr* to detect *ou* to find; **la cellule photo-électrique décèle la quantité de lumière qui traverse le liquide** = the photoelectric cell detects the amount of light passing through the liquid

décélération *nf* deceleration; **temps de décélération** = stop time

décentralisé, -ée *adj* decentralized; **réseau décentralisé** = decentralized computer network; **système décentralisé** = distributed system; **traitement décentralisé des données** = decentralized data processing

décharge *nf (de pile)* discharge; **courant de décharge** = drain; **temps de décharge (d'un circuit d'impédance)** = load life

◊ **décharger** to discharge *ou* to drain *ou* to unload

déchiffrage *nm* decryption *ou* deciphering *ou* de-scrambling; **le déchiffrage se fait avec l'ordinateur pour aller plus vite** = decryption is done by computer to increase speed

◊ **déchiffrer** *vtr (un code)* to decipher *ou* to decrypt *ou* to break *ou* to de-scramble; **il a finalement réussi à déchiffrer le code**

= he finally deciphered the code *ou* broke the cipher system

déchiqueté, -ée *adj* ragged; *(papier)* **bord déchiqueté** = deckle edge

déchirure *nf* tear *ou* tearing

déci *préfixe* deci-

décibel *nm* decibel (dB *ou* db)
◊ **décibelmètre** *nm* decibel meter

décile *nm* decile

décimal, -e *adj* decimal; **décimal codé binaire (DCB)** = binary coded decimal (BCD); **base décimale** *ou* **base 10** = base 10; **le chiffre décimal 8** = the decimal digit 8; **code décimal réfléchi** = cyclic decimal code; **notation** *ou* **numération décimale** = decimal notation *ou* denary notation; **système décimal** = decimal system; **tabulation décimale** = decimal tabbing; **touche de tabulation décimale** = decimal tab key; **virgule décimale** = decimal point
◊ **décimal-binaire** *adj* decimal-to-binary; **conversion décimale-binaire** = decimal-to-binary conversion
◊ **décimale** *nf* decimal; **la décimale 8** = the decimal digit 8; **décimale condensée** = packed decimal; **arrondi à un nombre fixe de décimales** = automatic decimal adjustment; **correct à la troisième décimale** = correct to three places of decimals
◊ **décimalisation** *nf* decimalization
◊ **décimaliser** to decimalize

décimétrique *adj* decimetre; **ondes décimétriques** = ultra high frequency (UHF)

décimonique *adj* decimonic; **sonnerie décimonique** = decimonic ringing

décisif, -ive *adj* **l'excellence des graphiques a constitué l'argument décisif** = the deciding factor was the superb graphics
◊ **décision** *nf* decision; **décision logique** = logical decision; **arbre de décision** = decision tree; **circuit de décision** = decision circuit; **élément de décision** = decision element; **prendre une décision** = to come to a decision *ou* to reach a decision; **symbole de décision** = decision box; **système d'aide à la décision (SAID)** = decision support system (DSS); **table de décision** = decision table

déclaratif, -ive *adj* declarative *ou* narrative; **instruction déclarative** = narrative statement
◊ **déclaration** *nf* declaration *ou* statement *ou* declarative statement *ou* narrative statement; **déclaration d'entrée** = input statement; **déclaration d'exécution** = execute statement; **déclaration de procédure** = procedure declaration; **déclaration d'une variable locale** = local declaration; **faire une déclaration** = to declare *ou* to state; **rubrique de déclaration des données** = data division
◊ **déclarer** *vtr* to declare *ou* to state; **au début du programme, X a été déclaré égal à 9** = he declared at the start of the program that X was equal to nine

déclenché, -ée *adj* triggered; **déclenché par bascule de front d'impulsion** = edge-triggered
◊ **déclencher** *vtr* to trigger *ou* to set off; **le détecteur de pression caché sous le tapis déclenche un système d'alarme si quelqu'un marche dessus** = the pressure pad under the carpet will set off the burglar alarm if anyone steps on it

décodage *nm* decoding
◊ **décoder** *vtr* to decode
◊ **décodeur** *nm* decoder; *(message)* descrambler; **décodeur d'adresse** = address decoder; **décodeur de couleurs** = colour decoder; **décodeur d'instruction** = operation decoder *ou* instruction decoder

décompilation *nf* decompilation; **compilation et décompilation incrémentielles** = incremental compilation and decompilation

décomposition *nf* decomposition; **décomposition de mouvements** = memomotion

décomprimer *vtr* to decompress *ou* to unpack; **ce sous-programme permet de décomprimer les fichiers archivés** = this routine unpacks the archived files

déconcentrateur *nm* **déconcentrateur pour transmission vidéo** = video expander

décondenser *vtr (des données)* to unpack

déconnecter *vtr* to disconnect *ou* to unplug; **vous n'avez qu'à déconnecter le lecteur et en connecter un nouveau à sa place** = simply unplug the old drive and plug-in a new one

décors *nm (film ou théâtre)* set

découpage *nm* cutting; *(photo ou image)* cropping; **les photos peuvent être éditées par découpage, dimensionnement, retouche, etc.** = photographs can be edited by cropping, sizing, touching up, etc.
◊ **découpe** *nf* cutting; *(du silicium)* **découpe en pastille** = slicing (from a bar of silicon crystal)
◊ **découper** *vtr* to cut *ou* to clip; *(un fichier trop long)* to partition

décrémenter *vtr* to decrement; **le contenu du registre a été décrémenté à zéro** = the register contents were decremented until they reached zero

décrire *vtr* to describe; **décrire un cercle** = to go in a circle *ou* to circulate; **décrire une orbite** = to orbit; **ce satellite météorologique décrit une orbite autour de la terre toutes les quatre heures** = this weather satellite orbits the earth every four hours

décrochage *nm* **(a)** *(arrêt dans un programme ou dispositif)* holdup **(b)** *(distorsion d'image vidéo)* hooking **(c)** *(modem)* **transmission sans décrochage** = blind dialling
◊ **décroché, -ée** *adj (combiné du téléphone)* off hook

décroissant, -e *adj* descending; **programmation structurée suivant un ordre décroissant** = top-down programming; **tri par ordre décroissant** = backward sort

décryptage *nm* decryption
◊ **décrypter** *vtr* to decrypt

dédié, -ée *adj* dedicated; **canal dédié** = dedicated channel; **ligne téléphonique dédiée** = dedicated line; **la logique dédiée réduit le nombre de puces** = dedicated logic cuts down the chip count; **ordinateur dédié** = dedicated computer; **système dédié** = special purpose system; **terminal dédié** = applications terminal *ou* dedicated computer

dédoublement *nm* division *ou* dividing; **dédoublement de faisceau** = beam diversity

déduction *nf* deduction *ou* inference

déduire *vtr* to deduct

défaillance *nf* failure *ou* malfunction *ou* crash; **les données ont été perdues par suite d'une défaillance du logiciel** = the data was lost due to a software malfunction; **défaillance induite** *ou* ayant **une cause externe** = induced failure; **défaillance du matériel** *ou* de l'ordinateur = equipment failure; **défaillance d'un programme** = program crash; **diagnostic (de cause) de défaillance** = problem diagnosis; **diagnostic de localisation de défaillance** = fault diagnosis; **moyenne de temps de bon fonctionnement entre les défaillances (MTBF)** = mean time between failures (MTBF); **taux de défaillance** = failure rate

défaire *vtr* to undo
◊ **se défaire de** *vpr* to discard (something)

défaut *nm* **(a)** fault *ou* defect; *(de magnétisation)* drop out; **nous estimons qu'il y a un défaut dans la conception même du produit** = we think there is a basic fault in the product design; **défaut caché** = hidden defect in a program; **défaut d'horloge** = hazard; **un défaut de l'ordinateur** = a computer defect *ou* a defect in the computer **(b)** **par défaut** = by default; **débit par défaut d'un modem** = default rate; **la largeur par défaut de cet écran est de 80** = screen width has a default value of 80; **lecteur par défaut** = default drive; **ce système d'exploitation permet à l'utilisateur de choisir le lecteur par défaut** = the operating system allows the user to select the default drive; **option par défaut** = default option;

réponse par défaut = default response; valeur par défaut = default value (c) 3,5678 arrondi par défaut à 3,56 = 3.5678 truncated to 3.56

> le gestionnaire d'écran par défaut correspond aux écrans EGA (vous n'avez donc rien à faire si vous possédez un tel écran)
>
> *L'Ordinateur Individuel*

défectueux, -euse *adj* defective *ou* faulty; **il arrive qu'une protection anticopie défectueuse entraîne la détérioration du disque dur** = a hard disk may crash because of faulty copy protection; **ils ont découvert que la défaillance était due à un câble défectueux** = they traced the fault to a faulty cable; **erreur imputable à un composant défectueux** = component error; **il doit sûrement y avoir un composant défectueux dans le système** = there must be a faulty piece of equipment in the system; **secteur défectueux** = bad *ou* faulty sector; **l'appareil est tombé en panne parce que le système de refroidissement était défectueux** = the machine broke down because of a defective cooling system

défendre *vtr* (a) *(empêcher)* to forbid *ou* to bar (b) *(protéger)* to defend

◇ **défensif, -ive** *adj* defensive; **informatique** *ou* **programmation défensive** = defensive computing

défilement *nm* (a) *(du texte sur l'écran)* (display) scrolling; **défilement ascendant** *ou* **vers le haut** = scrolling up; *(d'un générique sur film)* crawl; **défilement descendant** *ou* **vers le bas** = scrolling down; **défilement vertical** = vertical scrolling; **mode défilement** = scroll mode (b) *(d'une bande magnétique)* running *ou* playing; **compteur de défilement** = tape timer; **vitesse de défilement** = playback speed

◇ **défiler** *vi* to pass; **faire défiler** = *(un texte)* to scroll; *(une bande)* to pass *ou* to play back; **faire défiler (un texte) ligne à ligne sur l'écran** = to roll scroll; **faire défiler (un texte) point par point** = to smooth scroll; **qu'on ne peut pas faire défiler (sur l'écran)** = non-scrollable

défini, -e *adj* defined; **défini d'avance** = predefined

◇ **définir** *vtr* (a) to define; *(une variable)* to define *ou* to assign; **toutes les variables ont été définies lors de l'initialisation** = all the variables were defined at initialization; **définir de nouveau** = to redefine; **nous avons défini les premiers paramètres de nouveau** = we redefined the initial parameters (b) **définir une adresse** = to address

◇ **définissable** *adj* selectable; *(par l'utilisateur)* user-selectable

définitif, -ive *adj* finished; **document définitif** = finished document; **texte définitif** = fair copy *ou* final copy

définition *nf (de l'image)* definition *ou* resolution; **définition de l'affichage graphique** = graphic display resolution; **définition de l'écran** = screen *ou* display resolution; **la plupart des écrans d'ordinateurs individuels ont une définition qui est à peine supérieure à 70 points par pouce** = the resolution of most personal computer screens is not much more than 70 dpi (dots per inch); **définition de lecture** *ou* **de balayage** = scanning resolution; **définition maximum** = limiting resolution; **basse** *ou* **faible définition** = low resolution *ou* low-res; **graphiques de faible définition** = low-resolution graphics *ou* low-res graphics; **capacité de définition** = resolution capabilities; **haute définition** = high definition *ou* high resolution *ou* hi-res; **avec un écran haute définition on obtient un affichage de 640 par 450 pixels** = a high resolution screen can display 640 by 450 pixels; **graphiques haute définition** = high-resolution graphics *ou* hi-res graphics; **la carte graphique haute définition contrôle 300 pixels par pouce** = the HRG board can control up to 300 pixels per inch; **matrice d'impression à haute définition** = enhanced dot matrix; **ce moniteur haute définition permet un affichage de 640 x 320 pixels** = this hi-res monitor can display 640 x 320 pixels; **le nouveau scanner optique haute définition peut lire 300 points par pouce** = the new hi-res optical scanner can detect 300 dots per inch; **système vidéo haute définition** = high definition video system (HDVS)

> ces super-consoles peuvent manier en un temps plus réduit davantage d'informations, et donc présenter des jeux avec une meilleure définition graphique
>
> *L'Express*

définitivement *adv* permanently; **le numéro de fabrication est gravé définitivement sur le panneau arrière du boîtier de l'ordinateur** = the production number is permanently engraved on the back of the computer casing

déflecteur *nm (de résonances parasites)* baffle; **déflecteur à enroulement** = deflection yoke
◊ **déflexion** *nf* deflection; **déflexion d'un rayon lumineux** = beam deflection; **dans un tube à rayons cathodiques, la déflexion du faisceau est effectuée par un champ magnétique** = a magnetic field is used for beam deflection in a CRT; **armature de déflexion** = deflection yokes

déformant, -e *adj* distorting; **lentille déformante** = distortion optics
◊ **déformation** *nf* distortion; **déformation de l'image** = image distortion
◊ **déformer** *vtr* to distort

dégradation *nf (des performances d'un appareil)* degradation; **dégradation de l'image** = image degradation; **dégradation limitée** *ou* **douce** *ou* **progressive** = graceful degradation
◊ **dégradé** *nm* shading

dégrouper *vtr* to unpack; **dégrouper un bloc** *ou* **les éléments d'un bloc** = to deblock

délai *nm* delay *ou* interval; *(date limite)* deadline; **l'imprimante a commencé à imprimer après un délai de trente secondes** = there was a delay of thirty seconds before the printer started printing; **le révélateur doit être utilisé dans un délai d'un an** = the developer has a shelf life of one year; **délai d'attente** = ' wait time; **délai de contention** = contention delay; *(d'une mémoire vive)* **délai de conversion** = sense recovery time; **délai de détérioration d'un signal** = decay time; **délai (de transmission) d'une enveloppe** = envelope delay; **délai d'inversion** *ou* **de retournement** = turnaround time (TAT); **délai moyen** = average delay; **délai de propagation** = propagation delay; *(d'une image)* **délai de retour de ligne** = line blanking interval; **délai de retour du signal en fin d'écran** = blanking interval; **délai de**

transfert = envelope delay; **date d'expiration de délai** = expiration date

déliasser *vtr (papier listing)* to decollate
◊ **déliasseuse** *nf* decollator

délimitation *nf* limit; *(de couleur ou d'image)* **ligne de délimitation** = holding line
◊ **délimiter** *vtr* to delimit
◊ **délimiteur** *nm (symbole)* **délimiteur de données** = data delimiter; **délimiteurs de bloc** = block markers

delta *nm (lettre de l'alphabet grec)* delta; **acheminement (en) delta** = delta routing; **horloge delta** = delta clock; **modulation (en) delta** = delta modulation
◊ **delta-delta** *nm (connexion)* delta-delta

démagnétiser *vtr* to demagnetize *ou* to bloop *ou* to degauss; **il faut démagnétiser les têtes de lecture/écriture une fois par semaine pour obtenir une excellente performance** = the R/W heads have to be degaussed each week to ensure optimum performance
◊ **démagnétiseur** *nm* demagnetizer; **démagnétiseur de tête** = head demagnetizer

demande *nf* request; *(impérative)* demand; *(de renseignement)* inquiry *ou* enquiry *ou* query; *(d'emploi, etc.)* application; **signal de demande d'invitation à émettre** = request to send signal (RTS); **demande d'interruption** = interrupt request; **demande de partition sur le système** = application for an account on the system; **(fonction) demande-réponse** = inquiry/response (function); **accès multiple asservi à la demande** = demand assigned multiple access (DAMA); **multiplexage asservi à la demande** = demand multiplexing; **faire une demande (de)** = to apply (for); **formulaire de demande** = application form; **remplir une demande de partition sur le système** = to fill in an application (form) for an account on the system; **sur demande** = on demand; **accès sur demande à la mémoire paginée** = demand fetching; **appel de page sur demande** = demand paging; **lecture-écriture sur demande** = demand reading/writing; **traitement (de données) sur demande** = demand processing *ou* immediate processing; **scanner de demande de communication** = communications scanner

◊ **demander** *vtr* **(a)** to request; *(impérativement)* to demand; **demander quelque chose par téléphone** = to phone for something; **demander la ligne** = to bid; **le terminal a dû demander trois fois la ligne avant d'obtenir un créneau sur le réseau** = the terminal had to bid three times before there was a gap in transmissions on the network **(b)** *(nécessiter)* to require; **les systèmes informatiques sont très fragiles et demandent à être manipulés avec soin** = delicate computer systems require careful handling

◊ **se demander** *vpr* to wonder; **nous nous demandons tous jusqu'à quel point la sortie d'imprimante est correcte** = we all question how accurate the computer printout is

◊ **demandeur** *nm (au téléphone)* caller

démarrage *nm* start; **(système de) démarrage automatique** = autoboot; **équipement de secours à démarrage semi-automatique** = warm standby; **démarrage à froid** = cold start; **erreur au démarrage** = cold fault

◊ **démarrer 1** *vi* to start **2** *vtr* to start (something); **démarrer quelque chose graduellement** = to phase something in

demi, -e *adj* half *ou* semi-

◊ **demi-additionneur** *nm* half adder *ou* two input adder; **demi-additionneur binaire** = binary half adder

◊ **demi-cadratin** *nm (imprimerie)* en quad; *(dont la longueur équivaut à un 'n')* **tiret demi-cadratin** = en dash *ou* en rule

◊ **demi-espace** *nm* half space

◊ **demi-hauteur** *nf* half height; **unité de disquettes de demi-hauteur** = half-height drive

◊ **demi-intensité** *nf* half intensity

◊ **demi-mot** *nm* half word

◊ **demi-octet** nibble *ou* nybble

◊ **demi-teinte** *nf* halftone *ou* half-tone; **gravure en demi-teinte** = halftone process *ou* half-toning; **ce livre contient vingt planches en demi-teinte** = the book is illustrated with twenty halftones

démocratique *adj* democratic; **réseau démocratique** = democratic network

démodé, -ée *adj* out of date

démodulateur *nm* demodulator; *voir aussi* MODULATEUR

◊ **démodulation** *nf* demodulation; *voir aussi* MODULATION

démonstration *nf* demonstration; **faire une démonstration** = to demonstrate; **il a fait une démonstration du programme de gestion de fichiers** = he demonstrated the file management program; **modèle de démonstration** = demonstration model

démontage *nm* taking down; *(entre deux tâches)* takedown

◊ **démonter** *vtr* to take down

démontrer *vtr* to demonstrate

démultiplexer *vtr* to demultiplex

◊ **démultiplexeur** *nm* demultiplexor

dénaire *adj* denary; **numérotation dénaire** = denary notation

dense *adj* dense *ou* compact

◊ **densité** *nf* density; **densité binaire** = bit density; **densité de caractère** = character density *ou* pitch; **densité des composants** = component density; **il y a une telle densité de composants sur la carte-mère qu'il sera impossible d'inclure un connecteur** = component density is so high on this motherboard, that no expansion connectors could be fitted; **la densité des composants augmente avec l'expertise du fabricant** = component density increases with production expertise; **densité d'enregistrement** = recording density *ou* packing density; **densité de mémoire** = storage density; *(sur une ligne)* **densité du trafic** = traffic density; **bouton** *ou* **réglage de densité d'impression** = density dial; **si l'impression est trop pâle, réglez le bouton de densité (d'impression) sur le noir** = if the text fades, turn the density dial on the printer to full black; **disquette double densité (DD)** = double-density disk (DD); **disquette haute densité (HD)** = high density disk (HD); **mémoire** *ou*

support magnétique haute densité = high density storage; **un disque dur est un support de haute densité par rapport à une bande perforée** = a hard disk is a high density storage medium compared to paper tape; *(vidéo disque)* **très haute densité** = very high density (VHD); **quadruple densité** = quad density; **disquette quadruple densité (QD)** = quad density disk (QD); **disquette à simple densité (SD)** = single density disk (SD)
◊ **densitomètre** *nm* densitometer

dépannage *nm* repair *ou* corrective maintenance

départ *nm* start; **au départ** = at the beginning; **erreur au départ** = initial error; **langue de départ** = source language; **boucle avec retour automatique aux paramètres de départ** = self-resetting *ou* self-restoring loop; **point de départ** = starting point; **position de départ** = home; **prix départ usine** = factory price *ou* price ex factory

dépassé, -ée *adj* out of date; **leur système informatique est totalement dépassé** = their computer system is years out of date; **ils utilisent toujours du matériel dépassé** = they are still using out-of-date equipment
◊ **dépassement** *nm (de capacité)* overflow *ou* OV; **bit** *ou* **indicateur** *ou* **drapeau** *ou* **marque de dépassement de capacité** = overflow bit *ou* flag *ou* indicator; **contrôle de dépassement de capacité** = overflow check; **dépassement négatif** = underflow

dépendant, -e *adj* dependent; **dépendant du processeur** = processor-limited; **procédé dépendant des résultats d'un autre procédé** = a process which is dependent on the result of another process

déphasage *nm* phase displacement; **angle de déphasage** = phase angle
◊ **déphasé, -ée** *adj* out of phase

déplacement *nm* displacement *ou* shift *ou* relocation; *(d'une adresse relative)* float; **déplacement dynamique** = dynamic relocation (program); **modulation par déplacement de fréquence** = frequency shift keying (FSK);

caractère de déplacement = shift character; **code de déplacement** = shift code; *(d'une adresse relative)* **facteur de déplacement** = float factor; *(en ajoutant une adresse origine à une adresse relative)* **ré-adressage par déplacement** = float relocate
◊ **déplacer** *vtr* to move *ou* to displace *ou* to relocate; **(instruction de) déplacer un bloc** = move block; **déplacer de mémoire auxiliaire en mémoire centrale** = to roll in; **déplacer une souris (sur son tapis)** = to drag (a mouse); **pour agrandir un cadre, vous cliquez à l'intérieur de ses limites et vous déplacez la bordure à la position voulue** = you can enlarge a frame by clicking inside its border and dragging to the position wanted

déposer *vtr* to deposit; **il faut déposer un exemplaire de toute nouvelle publication à la Bibliothèque Nationale** = a copy of each new book has to be deposited in the Bibliothèque Nationale; **déposer un copyright** = to copyright (a book)
◊ **dépôt** *nm* **(a)** deposit **(b)** *(d'un enduit)* deposition

dépouiller *vtr (enlever les codes de contrôle d'un message)* to strip (a message)

dérangement *nm* failure *ou* fault; **être en dérangement** = to malfunction; **ce modem est en dérangement** = the modem has broken down; **(marge de) tolérance aux dérangements** = fault tolerance; **système tolérant** *ou* **peu sensible aux dérangements** = fault-tolerant system

déréglage *nm* maladjustment; *(d'un appareil photo)* defocussing; *(d'un appareil de télécopie)* **déréglage de la qualité d'impression** = hangover
◊ **dérégler** *vtr* to adjust badly; *(d'un appareil photo, etc.)* **dérégler la mise au point** = to defocus

dérivation *nf* **(a)** *(communication)* bridge *ou* bridging product; **mise en place d'une dérivation** = bridging **(b)** *(système de secours)* bypass; **il y a dérivation automatique lorsqu'une des machines tombe en panne** = there is an automatic bypass around any faulty equipment **(c)** *(d'une télévision câblée)* drop line

dérive *nf (changement dans un circuit)* drift

dérivé, -ée *adj* derived; **indexage dérivé** = derived indexing; **son dérivé** = derived sound; **voie dérivée en temps** = time derived channel

◊ **dériver (de)** *vi (venir de)* to derive (from)

dernier, -ière *adj* final; **apporter les dernières corrections à un document** = to make the final changes to a document; **saisir les derniers fichiers de données** = to keyboard the final data files; **dernier entré premier sorti** = last in first out (LIFO); *voir aussi* LIFO

déroulant, -e *adj* **menu déroulant** = pop-up *ou* pull-up menu; pop-down *ou* pull-down menu; **pour afficher le menu déroulant cliquer l'icône sur le haut de l'écran** = the pull-down menu is viewed by clicking over the icon at the top of the screen

déroulement *nm* **compteur de déroulement** = tape counter

◊ **dérouleur** *nm* **dérouleur de bande(s) magnétique(s)** = tape drive *ou* magnetic tape transport

déroutage *nm* **dispositif de déroutage** = diverter; **dispositif de déroutage d'appel** = call diverter

◊ **déroutement** *nm (communication)* **voie de déroutement** = alternate route

DES = DATA ENCRYPTION STANDARD; **schéma itératif de cryptage DES** = S-box; *voir aussi* NORME

désaccord *nm* mismatch; **désaccord d'impédance** = impedance mismatch

désactivé *nf* disactivated *ou* disarmed; **état désactivé** = disarmed state

◊ **désactiver** to disactivate *ou* to disarm

désaffecter *vtr* to deallocate

désaligné, -ée *adj* nonaligned *ou* out of alignment; **la bande est désalignée parce qu'un guide-bande est cassé** = the tape is out of alignment because one of the tape guides has broken; **tête de lecture désalignée** = nonaligned read head

désallouer *vtr (une ressource)* to deallocate *ou* to blast; **lorsque vous appuyez sur la touche de ré-initialisation, toutes les ressources sont désallouées** = when a reset button is pressed all resources are deallocated

désassemblage *nm* disassembling; **désassemblage de macro** = macro expansion

◊ **désassembler** *vtr* to disassemble

◊ **désassembleur** *nm* disassembler

descripteur *nm* descriptor; **descripteur de fichier** = file descriptor *ou* file label; **système de recherche** *ou* **de stockage par descripteurs** = aspect system

◊ **descriptif, -ive** *adj* **donnée descriptive** = physical parameter; **liste descriptive** = description list

◊ **description** *nf* description; **le prospectus contient une description des services offerts par la société** = the leaflet describes the services the company can offer; **on trouve une description plus détaillée des spécifications à la fin du manuel** = the specifications are described in greater detail at the back of the manual; **langage de description de données** = data description language (DDL); **plusieurs des avantages d'un langage de description de données vient du fait qu'il s'agit d'un langage de deuxième génération** = many of DDL's advantages come from the fact that it is a second generation language; **langage de description de pages** = page description language (PDL)

désembrouillage *nm* de-scrambling

◊ **désembrouiller** *vtr* to de-scramble *ou* to decode

◊ **désembrouilleur** *nm* de-scrambler

déséquipement *nm (entre deux tâches)* takedown

design *nm (conception)* design; **le design a été complètement exécuté sur ordinateur** = the design project was entirely worked out on computer; **design d'un système** = system design; **design économique** = least cost design; **studio de design** = design studio

désordonné, -ée *adj* disorderly; **arrêt désordonné** *ou* **panne désordonnée** = disorderly close-down

despotique *adj* **réseau (avec synchronisation) despotique** = despotic network

dessin *nm* **(a)** *(illustration ou image)* drawing *ou* picture; **vous pouvez voir le nouveau modèle sur ce dessin** = this picture shows the new design; **dessin assisté par ordinateur (DAO)** = computer-aided drafting; **dessin au trait** = line drawing; **on trouve dans ce livre des dessins au trait et des illustrations en demi-teinte** = the book is illustrated with line drawings and halftones **(b)** *(représentation d'une forme)* pattern; **avec dessins** = patterned

◇ **dessinateur, -trice** *adj* designer

◇ **dessiner** *vtr* to draw *ou* to design; **dessiner de nouveau** = to redraw *ou* to redesign

dessouder *vtr* to desolder

◇ **dessoudeur** *nm* desoldering tool

dessous *nm* bottom; *(pour papier d'imprimante)* **bac du dessous** = lower bin

dessus *nm* top; **dessus de pile** = top of stack; *(pour papier d'imprimante)* **bac du dessus** = upper bin

destinataire *nm&f* addressee

◇ **destination** *nf* destination

destructif, -ive *adj* destructive; **addition destructive** = destructive addition; **affichage destructif** = destructive readout (DRO); **l'écran devient rapidement illisible lorsqu'on utilise le curseur non destructif** = the screen quickly becomes unreadable when using a non- destructive cursor; **interférence destructive** = destructive interference; **lecture destructive** = destructive read *ou* readout; **non destructif** = non-destructive; **curseur non destructif** = non-destructive cursor; **essai non destructif** = non-destructive test; **lecture non destructive** = non-destructive readout (NDR); **je vais effectuer une série de tests non destructifs sur votre machine; si tout se passe bien, vous pourrez vous en servir de nouveau** = I will carry out a number of non-destructive tests on your computer: if it passes, you can start using it again

◇ **destruction** *nf* destruction; **destruction accidentelle** = crash; **protégé contre toute destruction accidentelle** = crash-protected; **si vous vous servez d'un disque protégé contre la destruction accidentelle, vous ne perdrez jamais vos données** = if the disk is crash-protected, you will never lose your data; **destruction de fichier** = file deletion

détaché, -ée *adj* detatched; **pièce détachée** = spare part

détail *nm* detail; **en détail** = in detail; **expliquer en détail** = to explain in detail

◇ **détaillé, -ée** *adj* detailed; **le catalogue présente une liste détaillée de tous les composants** = the catalogue lists all the components in detail

◇ **détailler** *vtr* to detail

détecté, -ée *adj* detected; **erreur détectée** = detected error; **erreur non détectée** = undetected error

◇ **détecter** *vtr* to detect *ou* to sense; **l'appareil peut détecter les signaux faibles émis par le transducteur** = the equipment can detect faint signals from the transducer; **l'erreur de programmation n'a été détectée qu'après un certain temps** = the programming error was undetected for some time; **le programme a pu détecter l'état du connecteur** = the condition of the switch was sensed by the program

◇ **détecteur** *nm* detector; **détecteur chromatique** = chroma detector; **détecteur d'infrarouge** = infrared detector; **détecteur de métal** = metal detector; **détecteur d'onde porteuse** = data carrier detect (DCD); **détecteur photoélectrique** *ou* **photosensible** = photosensor; **le détecteur de pression caché sous le tapis déclenche un système d'alarme si quelqu'un marche dessus** =

the pressure pad under the carpet will set off the burglar alarm if anyone steps on it; **çode détecteur d'erreurs** = error detecting code *ou* self-checking code; **commutateur détecteur** = sense switch

◊ **détection** *nf* detection *ou* sense; **détection automatique d'erreurs** = automatic error detection; **détection de collision** = collision detection; **détection d'enveloppe** = envelope detection; **détection d'erreurs** = error trapping *ou* error detection; **détection et correction d'erreurs** = error detection and correction (EDAC); **détection de limites** *ou* **de bordures** = edge detection; **codes de détection d'erreurs** = error detecting codes; **signal de détection de porteuse du modem** = data carrier detect (DCD); **l'appel est bloqué si le logiciel ne reçoit pas de signal de détection de porteuse** = the call is stopped if the software does not receive a DCD signal from the modem

détérioration *nf* **(a)** corruption; **détérioration de données** = data corruption **(b)** *(disque)* crash; **protégé contre toute détérioration accidentelle** = crash-protected **(c)** *(d'un signal)* decay; **délai de détérioration d'un signal** = decay time

◊ **détérioré, -ée** *adj (fichier)* damaged; *(données)* corrupted; *(disque)* crashed

◊ **détériorer** *vtr (fichier)* to damage; *(données)* to corrupt; **un problème de tension pendant l'accès au disque peut détériorer les données** = power loss during disk access can corrupt the data; **est-il possible de récupérer les fichiers détériorés?** = is it possible to repair the damaged files?

détermination *nf* **détermination de priorité des tâches** = job scheduling

◊ **déterminé, -ée** *adj* determined; **enregistrement de longueur déterminée** = fixed-length record; **mot de longueur déterminée** = fixed-length word; **déterminé d'avance** = predetermined

◊ **déterministe** *adj* deterministic

détruire *vtr* **(a)** *(disque)* to crash **(b)** *(donnée ou fichier)* to erase *ou* to delete *ou* to wipe *ou* to kill *ou* to scrub *ou* to scratch; **(instruction de) détruire un fichier** = kill file; **détruire des données par superposition d'écriture** = to overwrite; **détruisez tous les fichiers avec**

l'extension .BAK = scrub all files with the .BAK extension; **si vous reformatez, vous détruirez toutes les données du disque** = by reformatting you will wipe the disk clean

◊ **détruit, -e** *adj* **(a)** *(disque)* crashed **(b)** *(donnée ou fichier)* erased *ou* deleted *ou* wiped *ou* killed *ou* scrubbed *ou* scratched

deux *adj num* two; **instruction à deux adresses** = two-address instruction; **instruction à deux adresses plus une** = two-plus-one-address instruction; **file d'attente à deux entrées** *ou* **à deux extrémités** = double-ended queue *ou* deque; **en deux exemplaires** = in duplicate; **établir une facture en deux exemplaires** = to print an invoice in duplicate; **complément à deux** = two's complement

◊ **deuxième** *adj num & nm* second; **ordinateurs de deuxième génération** = second generation computers

développement *nm* development; **développement d'un programme** = program development; **environnement de développement de programmes** = program development system; **logiciel de développement** = development software; **recherche et développement** = research and development; **temps de développement d'un nouveau produit** = development time

◊ **développer** *vtr* to develop; **développer un nouveau produit** = to develop a new product

◊ **développeur, -euse** *n* développeur de logiciel = software developer

déverminage *nm* debugging; **système de déverminage interactif** = interactive debugging system

◊ **déverminé, -ée** *adj* debugged; **programme déverminé** = debugged program

◊ **déverminer** *vtr* to debug

déviation *nf* **(a)** alternate route **(b)** *(de rayon)* deflection

◊ **dévier** *vtr (rayon)* to deflect

dévideur *nm* streamer

devis *nm* quote *ou* estimate; **faire un devis** = to quote *ou* to give an estimate

Dewey *npr* **classification (suivant la méthode de) Dewey** = Dewey decimal classification

diacritique *adj* **un signe diacritique** = a diacritic

diagnostic *nm* diagnosis *ou* diagnostic; **diagnostic (de cause) de défaillance** = problem diagnosis; **diagnostic d'erreurs** = error diagnosis; **diagnostic d'erreurs de compilation** = compiler diagnostics; **diagnostic de localisation de panne** *ou* **de défaillance** = fault diagnosis; **diagnostic de la mémoire** = memory diagnostic; **diagnostic de système** = system check; **aide au diagnostic** = diagnostic aid; **circuit intégré** *ou* **puce de diagnostic** = diagnostic chip; **logiciel de diagnostic** = diagnostic program; **message de diagnostic** = diagnostic message; **message de diagnostic d'erreur** = diagnostic error message; **outils de diagnostic** = diagnostics *ou* system diagnostics; **outils de diagnostic du compilateur** = compiler diagnostics; **des outils de diagnostic de compilation bien conçus facilitent le débogage** = thorough compiler diagnostics make debugging easy; **outils de diagnostic d'erreurs** = error diagnostics; **programme de diagnostic** = maintenance routine; **programme diagnostic de dysfonctionnement** = malfunction routine; **puce de diagnostic** = diagnostic chip; **ils font des recherches sur les puces de diagnostic destinées au contrôle des ordinateurs équipés de processeurs** = they are carrying out research on diagnostic chips to test computers that contain processors; **routine de diagnostic** = diagnostic routine; **test de diagnostic** = diagnostic test
◊ **diagnostique** *adj* diagnostic
◊ **diagnostiquer** *vtr* to diagnose

diagonal, -e *adj* diagonal
◊ **diagonale** *nf* **coupe en diagonale** = diagonal cut

diagramme *nm* diagram *ou* chart *ou* flowchart *ou* schema *ou* graph; **diagramme en camembert** = pie chart; **diagramme d'un circuit** = circuit diagram; **diagramme en colonnes** *ou* **en tuyaux d'orgue** = columnar graph; **diagramme de flux de données** = data flow diagram (DFD); **diagramme**

fonctionnel = functional diagram; **diagramme logique** = logical chart *ou* logical flowchart; **diagramme à secteurs** = pie chart; **diagramme de Venn** = Venn diagram; **sous forme d'un diagramme** = diagramatically *ou* in schematic form; **le tableau présente la courbe des ventes sous forme de diagramme** = the chart shows the sales pattern diagramatically

dialecte *nm* dialect

dialogue *nm* dialogue; *(entre chambre de contrôle et studio)* talkback; **fenêtre de dialogue** = dialogue box; **dialogue vidéotex** = interactive videotext
◊ **dialogué, -ée** *adj* conversational *ou* interactive; **mode dialogué** = conversational *ou* interactive mode
◊ **dialoguer** *vi* *(ordinateurs)* to communicate (with) *ou* to talk (to)

diamant *nm* diamond; **diamant de lecture** = stylus

diamètre *nm* diameter

DIANE = DIRECT INFORMATION ACCESS NETWORK FOR EUROPE *ou* DIANE

diaph *ou* **diaphragme** *nm* *(d'appareil photo)* **ouverture de diaphragme** *ou* **diaph** = f-number

diaphonie *nf* crosstalk *ou* babble; **diaphonie induite** = crossfire; **il y avait une telle diaphonie que le signal était illisible** = the crosstalk was so bad, the signal was unreadable

> sa gamme s'est grandement élargie avec, en particulier, un suppresseur de diaphonie
> *Audio Tech*

diaphragme *nm* diaphragm; **le diaphragme d'un microphone capte les ondes sonores** = the diaphragm in the microphone picks up sound waves; *(d'appareil-photo)* **ouverture de diaphragme** *ou* **diaph** = f-number

diapo *nf* = DIAPOSITIVE slide *ou* transparency; **magnétophone avec interface synchro pour projecteur de diapos** = slide/sync recorder; **diapo-son** = audio slide

diapositive *ou* **diapo** *nf* slide *ou* transparency; **diapositive couleur** = colour transparency *ou* colour slide; **projecteur pour diapositives** = slide projector *ou* diascope

diazocopie *nf* diazo (process)

dibit *nm* dibit

dichotomie *nf* dichotomy; **recherche par dichotomie** = binary search *ou* binary chop *ou* dichotomizing search
◊ **dichotomique** *adj* **recherche dichotomique** = binary search *ou* binary chop *ou* dichotomizing search

dichroïque *adj* dichroic

Dictaphone® *nm* dictating machine

dictée *nf* dictation; **prendre en dictée** = to take dictation
◊ **dicter** *vtr* to dictate; **dicter une lettre à quelqu'un** = to dictate a letter to someone; **machine à dicter** = dictating machine

dictionnaire *nm* dictionary; **dictionnaire-répertoire de données** = data dictionary/directory (DD/D)

didacticiel *nm* courseware; **formation à l'aide de didacticiel** = programmed learning

Didot *npr (imprimerie)* **11 points Didot** = pica
NOTE: un point Didot = 0,324mm; 11 points Didot = environ 12 points anglais

diélectrique *adj* dielectric

différé *nm* **en différé** = off-line; **impression en différé** = off-line printing *ou* print spooling; **mémoire auxiliaire pour impression en différé** = spooler *ou* spooling device; **programme en différé** = canned programme; **traitement en différé** = off-line processing; **(système avec facilité de) transmission en différé** = store and forward (system)
◊ **différé, -ée** *adj* deferred; **mode différé** = deferred mode; **visualisation en temps différé** = time shift viewing

différence *nf* **(a)** difference; **il existe une grande différence entre les deux produits** = the two products differ considerably **(b) différence de potentiel** = potential difference
◊ **différent, -e** *adj* different *ou* separate; **être différent (de)** = to differ (from); **notre gamme de produits est d'une conception entièrement différente de celle des modèles japonais** = our product range is quite different in design from the Japanese models
◊ **différentiel, -elle** *adj* differential; **modulation d'impulsion codée différentielle (MIC)** = differential pulse code modulation (PCM)
◊ **différer** *vi* to differ

diffusé, -ée *adj* **onde diffusée** = scatter
◊ **diffuser** *vtr* **(a)** to send out; **la société a diffusé un communiqué au sujet de la nouvelle imprimante (à) laser** = the company sent out a news release about the new laser printer **(b)** *(à la radio, etc.)* to broadcast; **il a diffusé les dernières informations à la radio** *ou* **via le réseau étendu** = he broadcast the latest news over the radio *ou* over the WAN
◊ **se diffuser** *vpr (gaz ou fumée)* to diffuse
◊ **diffusion** *nf* **(a)** diffusion; **entreprise de diffusion d'informations grand public** = common carrier **(b) diffusion radiophonique** = broadcast; **diffusion sur (tout) un réseau** = networking; **satellite de diffusion directe** = direct broadcast satellite (DBS); **technique de diffusion par satellite** = broadcast satellite technique **(c)** *(de gaz ou fumée)* **il y a eu diffusion du produit chimique dans le substrat** = the chemical was diffused into the substrate **(d) dopage par diffusion** = diffusion; **jonction pn à diffusion** = diffused pn-junction; **zone interface pn à diffusion** = diffused pn-junction

Digipulse® *nm* **téléphone Digipulse** = Digipulse telephone

dimension *nf* dimension *ou* size *ou* measurements; **noter les dimensions d'un paquet** = to write down the measurements of a package; **dispositif** *ou* **composant de très petite dimension** = microdevice; **dimension d'affichage** = display size; **dimension d'un champ** = field length; *(imprimerie)* **dimension (en**

points) du corps d'un texte = body size; dimension de l'écran = screen size; dimension d'un enregistrement = record length; dimension d'un fichier = file length; dimension d'un registre = register length; à deux dimensions = two-dimensional; tableau à deux dimensions = two-dimensional array; à trois dimensions = three-dimensional *ou* 3D; calcul des dimensions = dimensioning; le calcul des dimensions du tableau se fait à cette ligne-ci = array dimensioning occurs at this line; *(d'une image ou d'une photo)* modification des dimensions = sizing

◊ **dimensionnement** *nm (d'image ou photo)* sizing; les photos peuvent être éditées par découpage, dimensionnement, retouche, etc. = photographs can be edited by cropping, sizing, touching up, etc.

◊ **dimensionner** *vtr (image ou photo)* to size

diminuteur *nm (d'une soustraction)* subtrahend

DIN *(normes allemandes pour l'industrie)* = DEUTSCHE INDUSTRIENORM

diode *nf* diode; diode électroluminescente = light-emitting diode (LED)

petit clavier auxiliaire où chaque touche est accompagnée d'une diode
Audio Tech
des diodes électroluminescentes permettent de contrôler si l'installation s'est effectuée correctement
Electronique

dioptrie *nf* dioptre; *US* diopter

◊ **dioptrique** *adj* dioptre; *US* diopter; lentille dioptrique = dioptre lens

DIP = DUAL-IN-LINE PACKAGE; commutateur DIP = DIP switch; *voir aussi* BROCHE

dipôle *nm* dipole

direct *nm* en direct = direct; appeler *ou* téléphoner en direct = to dial direct; vous pouvez appeler New York en direct depuis Londres = you can dial New York direct from London; émission en direct =

live broadcast; *US* program shown in real time

◊ **direct, -e** *adj* direct; accès direct = direct access *ou* random access; accès direct à la mémoire (DMA) = direct memory access (DMA); transfert des données par accès direct (à la mémoire) entre la mémoire principale et le second processeur = direct memory access transfer between the main memory and the second processor; voie d'accès direct à la mémoire = direct memory access channel; accès direct au réseau = direct outward dialling; accès direct au système = direct inward dialling; fichiers à accès direct = random access files; mémoire *ou* support à accès direct = random access storage *ou* direct access storage device (DASD); contrôleur de mémoire à accès direct = DMA controller; vol de temps de cycle de la mémoire à accès direct = DMA cycle stealing; les lecteurs de disquettes permettent l'accès direct des données alors qu'une bande magnétique en permet l'accès séquentiel = disk drives are random access, magnetic tape is sequential access memory; *(téléphone)* système d'acheminement direct des appels = direct dialling; adressage direct = direct addressing; adresse directe = one-level address *ou* direct (access) address *ou* zero-level address *ou* immediate address; adresse de référence directe = direct reference address; instruction à adresse directe = one address instruction *ou* single address instruction; code d'instruction à adresse directe = single address code; codage direct = direct coding; code direct = direct code *ou* one-level code *ou* specific code *ou* single address code; commande numérique directe = direct digital control (DDC); *(d'un modem)* connexion directe = direct connect; satellite de diffusion directe = direct broadcast satellite (DBS); impression directe = direct impression; programme *ou* sous-programme d'insertion directe = direct-insert routine *ou* subroutine; instruction directe = direct instruction; lecture-écriture directe = demand reading/writing; *(transmission en ligne droite)* ligne directe = line of sight; mode direct = direct mode; publicité directe = direct mailing; saisie directe de données (par clavier) *ou* entrée directe de données = direct data entry (DDE); sous-programme direct = one-level subroutine; traitement direct (des données) = random processing; transfert

direct = direct change-over *ou* direct transfer; **transmission directe de signaux** = DC signalling

◊ **directement** *adv* directly *ou* direct

directeur, -trice 1 *n* director; **le directeur de l'institut de recherche informatique gouvernemental** = the director of the government computer research institute; **elle a été nommée directrice de l'organisation** = she was appointed director of the organization; **directeur (du service) informatique** = computer manager; *(film ou télévision)* **directeur de production** = executive producer; **directeur technique** = technical director **2** *adj* **schéma directeur** = outline flowchart; **terminal directeur** = executive terminal

◊ **direction** *nf (sens)* direction; **direction du flux** = flow direction

◊ **directionnel, -elle** *adj* directional; **antenne directionnelle** = directional antenna; **capteur directionnel** = horn; *(antenne ou microphone)* **empreinte directionnelle** = directional pattern; **(dispositif de) guidage directionnel** = feed horn

directive *nf (instruction)* directive statement

dirigé, -ée *adj* directed; **balayage dirigé** = directed scan

◊ **diriger** *vtr* **(a)** *(pointer)* to direct; **la camera est dirigée sur le premier plan** = the camera is focused on the foreground **(b)** *(gérer)* to manage

discordance *nf* mismatch

discret, -ète *adj* discrete; **le mot de l'information est formé de bits discrets** = a data word is made up of discrete bits

discrétionnaire *adj* discretionary

disjoint, -e *adj* disjointed

disjoncteur *nm (de courant)* circuit breaker; **disjoncteur à air** = air circuit breaker; **système disjoncteur progressif** = fail soft system

disjonction *nf* disjunction *ou* exjunction; *(fonction logique)* **fonction de**

disjonction = non-equivalence function *ou* NEQ function

disparaître *vi* to disappear; **faire disparaître** = to remove; **faire disparaître de l'écran** = to clear (the screen) *ou* to zap; **tapez CLS pour faire disparaître ce qu'il y a sur l'écran** = type CLS to clear the screen; **faire disparaître progressivement** = to fade out

dispersé, -ée *adj* scattered; **chargement dispersé de données** = scatter load

◊ **dispersion** *nf* dispersion; **dispersion chromatique** = chromatic dispersion; **dispersion modale** = mode dispersion; **routage par dispersion** = flooding

disponibilité *nf* **(a)** availability; **(période de) disponibilité dans le cycle** = cycle availability; *(d'un appareil)* **temps de disponibilité** = available time; **temps de non disponibilité** = outage **(b)** capacity; **disponibilité d'adressage** = addressing capacity

◊ **disponible** *adj* **(a)** available; *(en mémoire)* **liste des emplacements disponibles** = uncommitted storage list; **puissance maximale** *ou* **réelle disponible** = available power; **liste des ressources disponibles** = available list; **temps disponible** = available time **(b)** *(d'un dispositif)* **configuration disponible** = configured-in

disposé, -ée *adj* set *ou* laid out; **disposé en tableau** *ou* **en table** *ou* **en colonnes** = (set) in tabular form *ou* in columns

◊ **disposer** *vtr* to set *ou* to lay out; **disposer en réseau** = to network; **disposer en tableau** *ou* **en table** *ou* **en colonnes** = to set in tabular form *ou* in columns

dispositif *nm* device; **dispositif d'affichage** = readout device; **dispositif anticopie** = copy protect device; **toutes les disquettes sont munies d'un dispositif anticopie** = all disks are copy protected; **dispositif anti-écho** = echo suppressor; **dispositif antirebond** = de-bounce (device); **dispositif à champ programmable** = field programmable device; **dispositif de compression-expansion** *ou* **dispositif concentrateur-déconcentrateur (de données vidéo)** =

compressor/expander *ou* compandor; **dispositif à couplage de charge** = charge coupled device (CCD); **dispositif d'effacement** = eraser; **dispositif d'entrée-sortie** = input-output device *ou* I/O device; **dispositif externe** = external device; **dispositif de fin de ligne** = line terminator; **dispositif (électronique) d'identification** = personal identification device (PID); **dispositif intégré** = integrated device; **dispositif de lecture par balayage** = scanning device; **dispositif de mémoire** = storage device; **dispositif de protection (contre la copie)** = copy protect device; **dispositif de protection d'écriture (de fichier)** = file protect tab; **dispositif de réacheminement** *ou* **de déroutage d'appel** = call diverter; **dispositif de sortie** = output device; **dispositif de transfert** *ou* **de déroutage** = diverter; **dispositif de transfert d'appel** = call diverter; **dispositif transistorisé** *ou* **à semi-conducteurs** = solid-state device; **dispositif de type D** = D-type flip-flop

disposition *nf (arrangement)* layout; **disposition des touches d'un clavier** = keyboard layout; **le logiciel de PAO permet à l'utilisateur de juger de la bonne disposition d'une page** = the DTP package allows the user to see if the overall page balance is correct

disque *nm* **(a)** *(magnétique)* disk; **disque audionumérique** = digital audio disk (DAD); **disque compact** *ou* **audionumérique** *ou* **disque CD** = compact disk *ou* CD; **disque dur** = hard disk; **disque dur amovible** = exchangeable disk storage (EDS) *ou* disk cartridge; **disque dur fixe** *ou* **non amovible** = fixed disk; **carte de disque dur** = hard card; **modèle d'ordinateur avec disque dur** = hard disk model; **système d'exploitation utilisant un disque dur** = disk-based operating system; **un disque dur est un support de haute densité par rapport à une bande perforée** = a hard disk is a high density storage medium compared to paper tape; **disque magnétique** = magnetic disk; **disque de mémoire** = storage disk; **disque optique** = laser disk *ou* optical disk; **disque original** = master disk *ou* magnetic master; **disque RAM** = RAM disk *ou* silicon disk *ou* virtual disk; **les résultats comptables ont été transférés sur le disque de sauvegarde** = the account results were copied to the

backup disk; **disque souple** = flexible disk *ou* floppy disk *ou* floppy *ou* FD; **disque de travail** *ou* **de manoeuvre** *ou* **d'enregistrement** = work disk; **disque vidéo** = videodisk; **disque vierge** = blank disk; **disque virtuel** = virtual disk *ou* RAM disk *ou* silicon disk; **disque (dur) Winchester** = Winchester disk; **disque Winchester amovible** = removable Winchester; **accès au disque** = disk access; **gestion des accès aux disques** = disk access management; **contrôleur de disque** = disk controller; **carte contrôleur de disque** = disk-controller card; **cartouche disque** = disk cartridge; **changeur de disques automatique** = record changer; **crash** *ou* **panne totale d'un disque** = disk crash; **fichier sur disque** = disk file; **formatage de disque** = disk formatting; **formater un disque** = to format a disk; **lecteur de disque (dur)** = disk drive; **lecteur de disques compacts** *ou* **de disques audionumériques** *ou* **de disque CD** = compact disk player; **lecteur de disque dur** = hard disk drive; **mémoire à disque** = disk memory; **perforation de disque** = hard-sectoring; **perforations de marquage (du bord) d'un disque** = disk index holes; **piste d'un disque** = disk track; **disque de quatre-vingts pistes** = eighty-track disk; **répertoire des fichiers d'un disque** = disk catalogue; **le nom d'un fichier qui est effacé disparaît aussi du répertoire du disque** = the entry in the disk catalogue is removed when the file is deleted; **saisie directe sur disque, par clavier** = keyboard to disk entry *ou* key-to-disk; **secteur de disque** = disk sector; **système d'exploitation de disque** = disk operating system (DOS); **table (de classement) des fichiers du disque** = disk map; **tête de lecture de disques** = disk playback head; **tri sur disque** = external sort; **unité de disque** = disk unit; **qui utilise un disque** = disk-based; **système qui utilise un disque** = disk-based system; **qui n'utilise pas de disque** *ou* **sans disque** = diskless; **système qui n'utilise pas de disque** = diskless system; **ils veulent créer un poste de travail qui n'utilise pas de disque** = they want to create a diskless workstation **(b)** *(non magnétique)* record; **nouveaux disques** = new releases

---

le disque dur fait désormais partie du quotidien: il est devenu un élément indispensable, voire vital, du poste de travail

L'Ordinateur Individuel

disquette *nf* disk *ou* diskette *ou* floppy disk *ou* floppy *ou* flexible disk *ou* FD; **microdisquette** = microfloppy; **minidisquette** = minidisk; **disquette compatible** = compatible disk; **disquette non compatible** = alien disk; **disquette double densité (DD)** = double density disk (DD); **disquette haute densité (HD)** = high density disk (HD); **disquette quadruple densité (QD)** = quad density disk (QD); **disquette simple densité** = single density disk (SD); **disquette (à) double face** = double-sided disk; **disquette de 3,5 pouces** = 3.5 inch disk; **disquette de 5,25 pouces** 5.25 inch disk; **disquette de huit pouces** = eight-inch disk; **disquette (de) mémoire** = storage disk; **disquette de nettoyage** = head cleaning disk; **il faut passer la disquette de nettoyage une fois par semaine** = use a head cleaning disk every week; **vous aurez des erreurs d'écriture si vous ne vous servez pas régulièrement de votre disquette de nettoyage** = write errors occur if you do not use a head cleaning kit regularly; **disquette de polices de caractères** *ou* **de fontes** = font disk; **disquette (de) programme système** = system disk; **disquette réversible** = flippy; **disquette de sauvegarde** = backup (disk); **contrôleur de disquettes** = disk controller *ou* floppy disk controller (FDC); **carte contrôleur de disquettes** = disk-controller card; **cartouche de disquette** = flexible disk cartridge; **crash** *ou* **panne totale d'une disquette** = disk crash; **fichier sur disquette** = disk file; **formatage de disquette** = disk formatting; **formater une disquette** = to format a disk; **il faut formater toutes les nouvelles disquettes avant de les utiliser** = you have to format new disks before you can use them; **lecteur de disquettes** = disk drive *ou* disk unit *ou* floppy disk drive *ou* unit; **lecteur de disquettes (à) double face** = double-sided disk drive; **lecteur de disquettes de huit pouces** *ou* **de 5,25 pouces** *ou* **3,5 pouces** = eight-inch disk drive *ou* 5.25 inch disk drive *ou* 3.5 inch disk drive; **lecteur de disquettes externe** = external disk drive; **mémoire à disquette** = disk memory *ou* storage; **piste d'une disquette** = disk track; **disquette (de) quarante pistes** = forty-track disk; **secteur de disquette** = disk sector floppy disk sector; **système utilisant des disquettes** = disk-based system; **système d'exploitation utilisant des disquettes** = disk-based operating system; **système qui n'utilise pas de** disquette = diskless system; **tête de lecture** *ou* **de lecture-écriture de disquettes** = disk head

dissipateur *nm* **dissipateur thermique** = heat sink

distance *nf* distance; **distance entre signaux** = signal distance; **distance focale** = focal length; **distance de Hamming** = Hamming distance; **à distance** = distant *ou* remote; **console** *ou* **poste de commande** *ou* **périphérique à distance** = remote console *ou* device; **lancement de tâches à distance** = remote job entry (RJE); **les utilisateurs peuvent imprimer leurs rapports sur des imprimantes à distance** = users can print reports on remote printers; **les imprimantes à distance sont reliées par câbles** = the distant printers are connected with cables; **modem à distance de transmission limitée** = limited distance modem; **réseau à distance** = wide area network (WAN); **réseau à grande distance** = long haul network; **terminal à distance** = remote terminal
◊ **distant, -e** *adj* distant *ou* far; **plusieurs stations de travail distantes sont connectées au réseau, chacune disposant d'une fenêtre sur le disque dur** = several remote stations are connected to the network and each has its own window onto the hard disk

distorsion *nf* distortion *ou* aberration *ou* breakup; **distorsion d'amplitude** = amplitude distortion; **distorsion en barillet** *ou* **en oreiller** *ou* **en coussinet** = barrel distortion *ou* pin cushion distortion; **distorsion géométrique** = geometric distortion; **distorsion d'harmoniques** = harmonic distortion; **distorsion de l'image** = image distortion; **distorsion due au retard du signal** = delay distortion

distribuer *vtr* to distribute *ou* to circulate
◊ **distributeur** *nm (appareil)* dispenser; **distributeur automatique (de cigarettes, etc.)** = automatic vending machine; **distributeur de billets de banque** = cash dispenser
◊ **distribution** *nf* **(a)** distribution; *(télévision* *ou* *téléphone)* **centre de distribution** = distribution point; *(informatique)* **réseau de distribution** =

distribution network **(b)** *(téléphonique)* **tableau de distribution =** plugboard *ou* patchboard; **tableau de distribution principal =** main distributing frame **(c)** *(film ou théâtre)* casting; **responsable de la distribution =** casting director

divergence *nf* divergence

diversité *nf* diversity

divisé, -ée *adj* **(a)** divided *ou* split *ou* partitioned; **écran divisé =** split screen; **fichier divisé en plusieurs parties =** partitioned file **(b)** *(math)* **vingt-et-un divisé par trois égale sept =** twenty-one divided by three gives seven
◊ **diviser** *vtr* **(a)** to divide *ou* to partition *ou* to split **(b)** *(math)* **diviser un nombre par quatre =** to divide a number by four
◊ **diviseur** *nm* **(a)** divider *ou* dividor *ou* splitter; **diviseur optique =** beam splitter; **diviseur de fréquence =** frequency divider **(b)** *(math)* divisor *ou* factor
◊ **division** *nf* **(a)** division *ou* partition **(b)** *(math)* division

divulguer *vtr* to leak

dix *adj num & nm* ten; **complément à dix =** ten's complement

DMA = DIRECT MEMORY ACCESS; **vol de temps de cycle de mémoire DMA =** DMA cycle stealing; *voir aussi* ACCES

document *nm* document *ou* copy; **document définitif =** finished document; **document imprimé =** printed document; **document monté** *ou* **créé (à partir de paragraphes standard) =** boilerplate; **montage d'un document (à partir de paragraphes standard) =** boilerplating; **document original** *ou* **d'origine =** source document; **classer** *ou* **archiver des documents =** to file documents; **(code de) fin de document =** end of document *ou* end of file (EOF); **fusion** *ou* **assemblage de documents =** document assembly *ou* document merge; **lecteur de documents =** document reader; **projecteur de documents opaques =** episcope *ou* epidiascope; **récupération** *ou* **régénération de document =** document recovery; **système de recherche de documents =** document retrieval system;

traitement de document = document processing
◊ **documentaire** *adj* **recherche documentaire =** data retrieval *ou* information retrieval (IR); **recherche documentaire en ligne =** on-line information retrieval; **centre de recherche documentaire =** information retrieval centre; **système de recherche documentaire =** document retrieval system
◊ **documentation** *nf* documentation; **documentation relative à l'utilisation d'un programme =** program documentation; **programme avec documentation en ligne =** self-documenting program
◊ **documenter** *vtr* to document

dollar *nm* dollar; **signe du dollar ($) =** dollar sign

domaine *nm* domain; **domaine de fréquence =** frequency domain; **domaine public =** public domain (PD); **(document, etc.) du domaine public =** (document) in the public domain; **oeuvre qui est dans le domaine public =** work which is out of copyright; **programme du domaine public =** program which is in the public domain

domestique *adj* domestic; **ordinateur domestique =** home computer; **satellite domestique =** domestic satellite

domicile *nm* home; **consultation à domicile des comptes =** home banking

dommage *nm* damage; **les dommages causés par la panne d'électricité s'élèvent à environ 100 000 francs =** the breakdown of the electricity supply caused damage estimated at 100,000 francs; **subir des dommages =** to suffer damage

domotique *nf* integrated home system

donnée(s) *nf(pl)* **(a)** *(valeur ou chaîne non réductible)* **donnée absolue =** atom **(b)** data *ou* information; **données agrégées =** data aggregate; **données alphanumériques =** alphanumeric data; **données biaisées =** biased data; **données brutes =** raw data; **données chaînées =** concatenated data set; **données de**

commande *ou* de contrôle = control data; données constantes *ou* permanentes = fixed data; données d'entrée = input; données graphiques = graphic data; données incrémentielles = incremental data; données numériques *ou* numérisées = digital data; données orientées = biased data; données permanentes *ou* de base = master data *ou* fixed data; (nombre de) données reçues = incoming traffic; données reliées en chaîne = concatenated data set; données relatives = relative data; données saisies = (computer) input; données de sortie = computer output; données structurées = data aggregate; données supravocales = data above voice (DAV); accéder aux données = to access data; l'utilisateur doit utiliser un mot de passe pour accéder aux données = a user needs a password to access data; accès aux données = data access; gestion d'accès aux données = data access management; acheminement de données = data routing; acquisition de données = data acquisition; affichage de données = information output; analyse de données = data analysis; autonomie des données = data independence; banque de données = databank; basculer des données = to exchange data; base de données = database; base de données en ligne = on-line database; base de données hiérarchisée = hierarchical database; configuration *ou* implantation *ou* topologie d'une base de données = database mapping; langage de base de données = database language; responsable de base de données = database administrator (DBA); schéma de base de données = database schema; service de base de données spécialisée (pour vidéotex) = information provider (IP); système de base de données = database system; système de base de données réparti *ou* en réseau = distributed database system; système de gestion de base de données = database management system (DBMS) *ou* database manager; machine dédiée au traitement de bases de données = database machine; bloc de données = data block; bus de données = data bus *ou* data highway; cartouche de données = data cartridge; chaînage de données = data chaining; champ de données = data field; chemin des données = data path; chiffrage *ou* chiffrement de données = data encryption; collecte de données = data collection; plate-forme de collecte de données = data collection platform;

collecteur de données = data sink; ligne de communication de données = dataline; centre de commutation des données = data switching exchange; compactage de données = data compacting; compression de données = data compression; les scanners utilisent la technique dite de compression de données qui peut réduire du tiers la mémoire nécessaire = scanners use a technique called data compression which manages to reduce, even by a third, the storage required; contrôle des données = data control; conversion de données = data translation; corruption de données = data corruption; la corruption de données sur la disquette a rendu le fichier impossible à lire = data corruption on the disk has made one file unreadable; chaque fois qu'on met le système sous tension, il y a corruption de données = data corruption occurs each time the motor is switched on; création de données = data origination; cryptage de données = data encryption; norme *ou* standard de cryptage de données = data encryption standard (DES); *(d'un programme en COBOL)* rubrique de déclaration des données = data division; (symbole) délimiteur de données = data delimiter; langage de description de données = data description language (DDL); plusieurs des avantages d'un langage de description de données viennent du fait qu'il s'agit d'un langage de deuxième génération = many of DDL's advantages come from the fact that it is a second generation language; détérioration de données = data corruption; les coupleurs acoustiques sont plus susceptibles aux détériorations de données que les modems branchés directement sur la ligne = acoustic couplers suffer from data corruption more than the direct connect form of modem; dictionnaire-répertoire de données = data dictionary/directory (DD/D); échanger *ou* permuter des données = to exchange data; circuit d'échange de données = data circuit; élément de données = data element *ou* data item; chaîne d'éléments de données = data element chain; émetteur de données = data source; enregistrement de données = data record; enregistrement (automatique et chronologique) de données = data logging; entrée de données = data input *ou* data capture *ou* data entry; bus d'entrée de données = data input bus (DIB); **routine d'entrée** *ou* **d'introduction de données** = input routine; **erreur de données** = data error; **à données erronées, résultats erronés** *ou* **des données douteuses produisent des résultats douteux** = garbage in garbage out (GIGO); **extraction de données** = data retrieval *ou* information retrieval (IR); **fiabilité des données** = data reliability; **fichier de données** = data file; **fichier de données externe** = external data file; **il faut analyser le fichier de données** = the data file has to be analysed; **file d'attente des données d'entrée** = input work queue; **(code de) fin de données** = end of data (EOD); **flot de données** = data stream; **flux de données** = data flow; **diagramme de flux de données** = data flow diagram (DFD); **format de données** = data format; **génération de données** = data origination; **gestion de données** = data management; **gestionnaire de données** = data administrator; **hiérarchie des données** = data hierarchy; **système avec intégration de données** = firmware; **intégrité des données** = data integrity; **un problème de tension pendant l'accès au disque peut faire perdre l'intégrité des données** = power loss during disk access can corrupt the data; **introduction de données** = data entry; **lecture optique de données numériques** = digital optical reading (DOR); **liaison de données** = data link; **liaison de données en chaîne** = data chaining; **contrôle de liaison de données** = data link control; **couche de liaison de données** = data link layer; **langage de manipulation de données** = data manipulation language (DML); **mémoire de données** = data memory *ou* storage; **mise en mémoire de données** = data storage; **migration de données** *ou* **transfert de données (sur dispositif hors ligne)** = data migration; **nettoyage des données** = data cleaning; **niveau de données** = data level; **nom de donnée** = data name; **il y a des difficultés lorsque le nom de la donnée est ambigu** = problems occur if an ambiguous data name is chosen; **ordinogramme de données** = data flowchart; **l'ordinogramme des données nous a permis d'améliorer nos résultats à l'aide d'une meilleure structure** = the data flowchart allowed us to improve throughput, by using a better structure; **permuter des données** = to exchange data; **pointeur (de position) de données** = data pointer; **(onde) porteuse de données**

= data carrier; **préparation des données** = data preparation; **protection des données** = data protection; **qualité des données** = data reliability; **activé par reconnaissance des données** = data-driven; **récupérer des données (et les transférer dans un registre)** = to collect transfer; **réduction de données** = data reduction; **registre de données** = data register; **réseau de transmission de données** = data network; **routage de données** = data routing;

saisie de données = data input *ou* data capture; **saisie directe de données (au clavier)** *ou* **entrée directe de données** = direct data entry (DDE); **les données ont été saisies** = the data has been entered; **les données sont saisies sur l'un des nombreux postes de travail** = data is input at one of several workstations; **sécurité des données** = data security *ou* data protection; **source de donnés** = data source; **stockage de données** = data storage *ou* information storage; **stockage de données sur disque** *ou* **disquette** = disk storage; **stockage et restitution de données** = information storage and retrieval (ISR); **structure des données** = data structure *ou* information structure; **structure dynamique de données** = dynamic data structure; **structure hiérarchique de données** = data hierarchy; **support de données** = data medium; **support de données d'un fichier** = file storage; **(mémoire) tampon de données** = data buffer; **traduction de données** = data translation; **traitement de données** = data processing (DP *ou* dp) *ou* information processing; **traitement décentralisé des données** = decentralized data processing; **traitement électronique de données** = electronic data processing (EDP); **capacité de traitement électronique de données** = EDP capability; **facilité de traitement électronique de données** = electronic data processing capability;

vitesse de traitement de données = data rate; **trajet des données** = data path; **transaction de données** = data transaction; **transfert de données** = data transfer *ou* data migration; **transfert des données par accès direct (à la mémoire) entre la mémoire principale et le second processeur** = direct memory access transfer between the main memory and the second processor; **bus de transfert de données** = data highway; **vitesse de transfert de données** *ou* **débit de données**

= data transfer rate; **transmission de données** = data communication(s); **transmission de données vocales** = data in voice (DIV); **transmission de données subvocales** = data under voice (DUV); **arrêt de transmission de données** = data break; *(causé par un défaut du support magnétique)* data check; **canal de transmission de données** = data channel; **adaptateur de canal de transmission de données** = data adapter unit; **connexion pour transmission de données** = data connection; *(causée par un défaut du support magnétique)* **brève interruption de transmission de données** = data check; **lignes de transmission de données** = bus data lines; **réseau de transmission de données** = data communications network; **service de transmission de données** = data services; **signaux de transmission de données** = data signals; **(mémoire) tampon de transmission de données** = data communications buffer; **vitesse de transmission de données** = data rate *ou* data signalling rate; **voie de transmission de données** = data path; **type de données** = data type; **validation de données** = data validation; **validation** *ou* **vérification de données** = data vetting; **signal de validation de données transmises** = data strobe; *(en mémoire)* **zone de données** = data area *ou* data field

donner *vtr* to give; **donner un avertissement** = to issue a warning; **donner une commande** *ou* **une instruction** = to give an instruction *ou* a command *ou* an order

dopage *nm* doping; **dopage par diffusion** = diffusion
◊ **dopant** *nm* dopant; **enduit d'un dopant** = doped
◊ **dopé, -ée** *adj* doped
◊ **doper** to dope

DOS = DISK OPERATING SYSTEM; **système (d'exploitation) DOS** = DOS; **lancez le système DOS après la mise en route de l'ordinateur** = boot up the DOS after you switch on the PC; *voir aussi* DISQUE

dos *nm* back; *(d'un livre)* spine; **on trouve une variété de connecteurs au dos de l'unité centrale** = there is a wide range of connectors at the back of the main unit; **de façon générale, le nom de l'auteur**
et le titre apparaissent au dos du livre et sur la page de titre = the author's name and the title usually are shown on the spine as well as on the title page; **il y aura une photographie en couleur de l'auteur au dos de la jaquette** = we will be using a colour photograph of the author on the back of the jacket

dossier *nm* file *ou* (complete) documentation on a subject; **classez ces lettres dans le dossier 'clients'** = put these letters in the customer file; **insérer un document au dossier** = to place a document on file

doublage *nm (d'un film)* dubbing

double 1 *nm* duplicate *ou* copy; *(avec carbone)* carbon copy *ou* carbon; *(action)* replication *ou* copying; **faites un original et deux doubles** = make a top copy and two carbons; **formulaire avec double carboné** = carbon set; **papier avec double autocopiant** = two-part stationery 2 *adj* double *ou* dual; *(double épaisseur)* two-part; **mémoire à double accès** = dual port memory; **double bande latérale** = double sideband; **(modulation d'amplitude à) double bande latérale sans porteuse** *ou* **à porteuse inhibée** = double sideband suppressed carrier (DSBSC); **(à) double chronométrie** = dual clocking; **double contrôle** = cross-check; **disquette double densité (DD)** = double density disk (DD); **travail qui fait double emploi** = duplication of work; *(papier, etc.)* **en double épaisseur** = two-part; **papier listing en double épaisseur** = two part computer stationery; **en double exemplaire** = in duplicate; **reçu en double exemplaire** = receipt in duplicate; *(photo)* **double exposition** = double exposure; **disquette (à) double face** = double-sided disk; **lecteur de disquettes (à) double face** = double-sided disk drive; **papier photosensible double face** = duplex; **plaque (présensibilisée) double face pour circuit imprimé** = double-sided printed circuit board; **utilisation de double mémoire tampon** = double buffering; **double précision** = double-length precision *ou* double precision; **arithmétique en double précision** = double precision arithmetic; **double processeur** = dual processor; **système à double rang de broches (parallèles)** = dual-in-line package (DIL *ou* DIP); **système à bus double** = dual bus system; **colonne double** = dual column; *(symbole typographique)* **croix double (‡)** = double dagger; *(typographie)* **guillemets doubles** = double quotes; *(code informatique)* **mot double** = double word; **processeur double** = dual processor; **système double** = dual system; *(transmission)* **voie double** = dual channel

◊ **doubler** *vtr (un film)* to dub

◊ **doublet** *nm (mot de deux bits)* dyad *ou* doublet; *(antenne radio)* dipole; *(erreur d'imprimerie)* dittogram

◊ **doublon** *nm* double document

douille *nf* socket

doute *nm* doubt; **mettre en doute** = to doubt *ou* to question (something)

◊ **doux, douce** *adj* **(a)** soft; **dégradation douce** = graceful degradation; **panne douce** = soft-fail **(b)** impression en taille douce = copperplate printing

drapeau *nm* flag *ou* indicator flag; **drapeau de dépassement de capacité** = overflow bit *ou* flag *ou* indicator; **code drapeau** = flag code; **mise en place d'un drapeau** = flagging; **condition** *ou* **fonction de mise en place d'un drapeau** = flag event; **registre des drapeaux** = flag register; **séquence de drapeaux** = flag sequence

droit *nm* **(a)** *(ce qui est exigible ou conforme à un règlement)* right; **droit d'auteur** = copyright; **Convention sur le droit d'auteur** = Copyright Act; **titulaire d'un droit d'auteur** = copyright owner; **violation du droit d'auteur** = infringement of copyright *ou* copyright infringement; **oeuvre dont les droits de reproduction sont réservés** = work still in copyright **(b)** *(somme d'argent)* **l'utilisateur paie un droit pour visualiser les pages de la messagerie** = the user has to pay a charge for viewing pages on a bulletin board

◊ **droit, -e** *adj* right

◊ **droite** *nf* right; **décalage** *ou* **glissement à droite** = right shift; **effectuer un décalage à droite** = to right shift *ou* to shift right; **au fer à droite** = flush right; **justification à droite** = right justification; **justifié à droite** = flush right *ou* right justified; **justifier à droite** = to right justify; **(instruction de) justifier à droite** = right justify

DTMF = DUAL TONE, MULTIFREQUENCY *voir* SIGNALISATION

duodécimal, -e *adj* duodecimal; **système duodécimal** = duodecimal number system

duplex *nm&adj* duplex *ou* diplex; **circuit duplex** = duplex circuit; **opération** *ou* **transmission en duplex** = duplex operation; **système duplex** = duplex computer; **full duplex** = full duplex (FDX *ou* fdx); **semi-duplex** = half duplex; **modem semi-duplex** = half-duplex modem

duplicateur *nm* duplicator *ou* duplicating machine; **duplicateur à alcool** = spirit duplicator; **duplicateur grande vitesse** = high-speed duplicator; **papier pour duplicateur** = duplicating paper *ou* duplicator paper

◊ **duplication** *nf* duplication *ou* replication; *(action)* duplicating

◊ **dupliquer** *vtr* to duplicate *ou* to replicate

dur, -e *adj* hard *ou* rigid; **disque dur** = hard disk; **disque dur amovible** = exchangeable disk storage (EDS); *(de type Winchester)* removable Winchester; **carte de disque dur** = hard card

durable *adj* durable

◊ **durée** *nf* duration; **durée d'appel** = call duration; **la durée de l'appel varie suivant la complexité de la transaction** = call duration depends on the complexity of the transaction; **le prix est fonction de la durée de l'appel** = charges are related to call duration; **durée d'assemblage (d'un programme)** = assembly time; **durée de compilation (d'un programme)** = compilation time; **durée d'exécution (d'un programme)** = run-time *ou* run-duration *ou* execute time; **durée moyenne de bon fonctionnement entre les défaillances** = mean time between failures (MTBF); **durée d'une panne** = fault time; **durée de vie d'un système** = system life cycle; **durée de vie de la tête (de lecture)** = headlife; **de courte durée** = impulsive *ou* transient; **bruit** *ou* **interférence de courte durée** = impulsive noise; **cartouche longue durée** = durable cartridge; **modulation d'impulsions en durée (MID)** = pulse duration modulation (PDM) *ou* pulse width modulation (PWM)

dyade *nf (mot de deux bits)* doublet *ou* dyad

dyadique *adj* dyadic; **opération dyadique** = dyadic operation; **opération booléenne dyadique** = dyadic Boolean operation

dynamique *adj* dynamic; **acheminement dynamique** = adaptive routing; **allocation dynamique** = dynamic allocation; **allocation dynamique de la mémoire** = dynamic storage allocation; **arrêt dynamique** = dynamic stop; **déplacement dynamique** = dynamic relocation (program); **gamme** *ou* **amplitude dynamique** = dynamic range; **mémoire dynamique** = dynamic memory *ou* dynamic storage; **mémoire dynamique permanente** = permanent dynamic memory; **mémoire tampon dynamique** = dynamic buffer; **mémoire vive dynamique** = dynamic RAM *ou* dynamic random access memory (DRAM); **micro(phone) dynamique** = dynamic microphone; **multiplexage dynamique** = dynamic multiplexing; **(mémoire) RAM dynamique** = dynamic RAM *ou* dynamic random access memory (DRAM); **routage dynamique** = adaptive routing; **structure de données dynamique** = dynamic data structure; **système dynamique** = adaptive system; **tampon dynamique** = dynamic *ou* elastic buffer; **translation dynamique** = dynamic relocation; **vidage dynamique** = dynamic dump

dysfonction *nf* malfunction *ou* malfunctioning

◊ **dysfonctionnement** malfunction *ou* malfunctioning; **(programme) diagnostic de dysfonctionnement** = malfunction routine

la première branche du réseau dut être recâblée à la suite de dysfonctionnement
L'Information professionnelle

Ee

E *(représentation hexadécimale du nombre 14)* E

E *(ionosphère)* **couche E =** E-region *ou* Heaviside-Kennelly layer

EAO = ENSEIGNEMENT ASSISTE PAR ORDINATEUR; **langage de programmation EAO =** author language; **système adapté aux langages EAO =** authoring system

EAPROM = ELECTRICALLY ALTERABLE, PROGRAMMABLE READ-ONLY MEMORY; **mémoire EAPROM =** EAPROM; *voir aussi* MEMOIRE

EAROM = ELECTRICALLY ALTERABLE READ-ONLY MEMORY; **mémoire EAROM =** EAROM; *voir aussi* MEMOIRE

ébauche *nf* rough copy *ou* draft
◊ **ébaucher** to draft

EBCDIC = EXTENDED BINARY CODED DECIMAL INTERCHANGE CODE; **code EBCDIC =** EBCDIC; *voir aussi* CODE BINAIRE

écart *nm (statistiques)* deviation
◊ **écarteur** *nm (éloigne la bande de la tête pendant le rembobinage)* lifter

échange *nm* exchange *ou* interchange *ou* transfer; **échange d'informations** *ou* **de données =** data transfer; **protocole d'échange d'informations** *ou* **de données entre unité centrale et périphérique =** CPU handshaking; **circuit d'échange (bi-directionnel) de données =** data circuit; **faire un échange =** to exchange (one thing for another); **tri par échange =** exchange selection
◊ **échangeable** *adj* exchangeable

◊ **échanger** *(une chose contre une autre)* to exchange; *(permuter)* to interchange

échantillon *nm* sample; **selon échantillon =** as per sample; **la prise d'échantillon toutes les trois secondes a révélé une augmentation =** samples at three seconds showed an increase
◊ **échantillonnage** *nm* sampling; *(de réception de signal* ou *de qualité)* acceptance sampling; **fréquence d'échantillonnage =** sampling rate; **pas d'échantillonnage =** sampling interval
◊ **échantillonner** *vtr* to sample; *(par impulsion)* to strobe
◊ **échantillonneur** *nm* sampler
◊ **échantillonneur-bloqueur** *nm&adj* **(circuit)** échantillonneur-bloqueur **=** sample and hold circuit

le signal radio analogique qui entre dans ce magnétophone est transformé en numérique avec une fréquence d'échantillonnage de 44,1 ou 48kHz
Audio Tech

échappement *nm* **(a)** escape (ESC); **caractère d'échappement =** escape character; **code d'échappement =** escape code; **touche d'échappement =** escape key (ESC); **appuyez sur la touche ÉCHAPPEMENT pour arrêter le programme =** to end the program, press ESCAPE **(b)** *(mouvement du papier dans une machine à écrire)* escapement

échauffement *nm* (over)heating; **panne par échauffement =** burn out

échéance *nf* **planning à courte échéance =** short-term planning; **planning à longue échéance =** long-term planning

échec *nm* failure; **le premier essai du prototype de lecteur de disquettes a été un**

échec = the prototype disk drive failed its first test

échelle *nf* scale; **échelle binaire =** binary scale; **dans un mot à quatre bits, l'échelle binaire est 1,2,4,8 =** in a four bit word, the binary scale is 1,2,4,8; **échelle de gris =** grey scale; *US* gray scale; **le 'bel' est mesuré sur une échelle logarithmique =** bel is a unit in the logarithmic scale; **grande échelle =** large scale; **intégration à grande échelle =** large-scale integration (LSI); **intégration à très grande échelle =** very large scale integration (VLSI); **intégration à super grande échelle =** super large scale integration (SLSI); **intégration à moyenne échelle =** medium scale integration (MSI); **petite** *ou* **faible échelle =** small scale; **intégration à petite** *ou* **à faible échelle =** small scale integration (SSI)

écho *nm* echo; **chambre à écho =** echo chamber; **contrôle par écho =** echo check; **(dispositif) éliminateur d'écho =** echo suppressor; **faire écho =** to echo; **sans écho =** anechoic

ECL = EMITTER-COUPLED LOGIC; **logique ECL =** ECL

éclairage *nm* lighting *ou* illumination
◊ **éclairagiste** *nm&f (film ou télévision)* lighting engineer; **chef éclairagiste =** lighting director
◊ **éclairement** *nm* illuminance
◊ **éclairer** *vtr* to light *ou* to illuminate; **l'écran est éclairé par une lampe de très faible puissance =** the screen is illuminated by a low-power light

éclaté, -ée *adj* scattered; *(sur écran vidéotex en mode graphique)* **caractères éclatés =** blast-through alphanumerics; **faire un chargement éclaté =** to scatter load; **onde éclatée progressante =** forward scatter
◊ **éclater** *vtr&i* **éclater (les éléments d')** **un bloc =** to deblock
◊ **éclateur** *nm (de papier listing)* burster

ECMA = EUROPEAN COMPUTER MANUFACTURERS ASSOCIATION; **symboles ECMA =** ECMA symbols; *voir aussi* SYNDICAT

économie *nf* saving *ou* economy; **la société met en place des mesures d'économie d'énergie =** the company is introducing energy-saving measures
◊ **économique** *adj* economical; **conception** *ou* **design économique =** least cost design; **le budget n'étant que de 4000 francs, il nous faut un design économique pour ce nouveau circuit =** the budget is only 4000 francs, we need the least cost design for the new circuit
◊ **économiser** *vtr* to save; **qui économise l'énergie =** energy-saving; **vous économiserez de l'énergie en limitant la température de la pièce à 18 degrés =** if you reduce the room temperature to eighteen degrees, you will save energy

écoulé, -ée *adj (temps)* passed; **signal de contrôle du temps écoulé =** time address code

écoute *nf* **(a)** listening; *(télévision)* **heures de grande écoute** *ou* **d'écoute maximale =** prime time; **nous commençons à diffuser des spots publicitaires aux heures de grande écoute =** we are putting out a series of prime-time commercials; **indice d'écoute =** audience rating; **potentiel d'écoute =** coverage; **taux d'écoute =** ratings **(b)** **table d'écoute =** wiretap; **brancher une ligne sur une table d'écoute =** to tap (a telephone)

écran *nm* **(a)** *(d'ordinateur ou pour projections)* screen; **écran (d'affichage** *ou* **d'ordinateur) =** screen *ou* monitor *ou* cathode ray tube (CRT); **écran asservi** *ou* **second écran =** slave tube; **écran couleur =** colour monitor; **écran électroluminescent =** electroluminescent display screen; **écran électrostatique =** electrostatic screen; **écran EGA =** enhanced graphics adapter screen *ou* EGA screen; **écran (à affichage) graphique =** graphics VDU; **terminal avec écran (à affichage) graphique =** graphics art terminal; **écran magnétique =** magnetic screen; **écran à mémoire =** storage tube; **écran monochrome** *ou* **écran noir et blanc =** monochrome monitor; **écran multistandard =** multi-scan *ou* multi-sync monitor; **écran partagé** *ou* **divisé =** split screen; **écran plasma =** gas discharge display *ou* gas plasma display; **écran pleine page =** full-size display;

écran (de) quatre-vingts colonnes =
eighty-column screen; **écran rétroéclairé
=** backlit display; **écran tactile =** touch
screen; **écran texte =** text screen; **écran
vidéo =** video monitor; **écran vidéo avec
clavier =** video terminal; **écran de
visualisation =** display screen *ou* readout
device *ou* visual display terminal (VDT)
ou visual display unit (VDU); **à l'écran =**
(données) on-screen; *(film)* on general
release; **adaptateur d'écran =** display
adapter; **afficher** *ou* **appeler** *ou* **rappeler** *ou*
faire apparaître des données à l'écran =
to call up data; **rappelez le fichier
précédent à l'écran =** call up the previous
file; **la touche HELP fera apparaître sur
l'écran une description des différentes
options =** by keying HELP, the screen
will display the options available to the
user; **on a affiché à l'écran les adresses de
tous les clients =** all the customers
addresses were called up; **les
coordonnées du client étaient affichées
sur l'écran =** the customer's details were
displayed on the screen; **attributs d'écran
=** display attributes *ou* screen attributes;
bordure d'écran = screen border; **faire un
brûlage d'écran =** to burn in; **capture
d'écran =** screen grab; **caractère d'écran
=** display character; **générateur de
caractères d'écran =** display character
generator; **césure d'écran =** soft *ou*
discretionary hyphen; **coin gauche
supérieur (de l'écran)** *ou* **début de l'écran
=** cursor home; **contrôleur** *ou* **pilote
d'écran =** display controller; **copie
d'écran =** hard copy; **défilement du texte
sur l'écran =** display scrolling; **définition
de l'écran =** display resolution *ou* screen
resolution; **éditeur d'écran =** screen
editor; **format d'écran =** display format
ou screen format; **grille d'écran =** form;
kit de nettoyage pour écran = screen
cleaning kit; **ligne d'écran =** display line;
mémoire (d') écran = screen memory;
mémoire tampon d'écran = screen
buffer; **plein écran =** screenful;
processeur d'écran = display processor;
texte (d') écran = soft copy; **vidage
d'écran (sur imprimante) =** screen dump
(b) *(de protection)* screen *ou* shield; *(d'un
haut-parleur)* baffle; **écran
électromagnétique =** electromagnetic
shield; **faire écran =** to block; **la
montagne fait écran à ces habitations qui
ne reçoivent aucune émission radio =** the
mountain casts a shadow over those
houses, so they cannot receive any radio
broadcasts; **protéger à l'aide d'un écran =**
to screen *ou* to shield

il s'agit d'une machine sans clavier, de la
classe et de la puissance d'une station de
travail et équipée d'un écran qui est au moins
de la taille d'une page
Science et Vie Micro
les écrans tactiles permettent de sélectionner
la fonction désirée, sans apprentissage
préalable, par simple pointage d'un menu sur
un écran
Electronique (Suisse)

écrasement *nm (de l'image)* crushing

écrêtage *nm* clipping; **écrêtage de
phase =** phase clipping
◊ **écrêter** *vtr* to clip; **le signal a été
écrêté pour éviter une amplitude
excessive =** the voltage signal was
clipped to prevent excess signal level

écrire *vtr* to write; *(échanger des lettres)*
to correspond; **écrire à la machine =** to
type; **machine à écrire =** typewriter;
machine à écrire électrique = electric
typewriter; **machine à écrire électronique
=** electronic typewriter; **écrire en
majuscules** *ou* **en capitales** *ou* **en
caractères d'imprimerie =** to print;
**écrivez votre nom en majuscules en début
de page =** write your name in capitals *ou*
print your name at the top of the sheet of
paper; **écrire de nouveau =** to rewrite;
écrire un programme = to write a
program *ou* to program; **(mot) qui s'écrit
avec un trait d'union =** hyphenated
(word); **le mot 'arrière-plan' s'écrit
habituellement avec un trait d'union =**
the word 'arrière-plan' is usually
hyphenated *ou* is usually written with a
hyphen *ou* is usually spelled with a
hyphen
◊ **écrit** *nm* written document *ou* printed
document *ou* publication; **les écrits
officiels sont en vente dans des librairies
spécialisées =** government publications
can be bought at special shops; **par écrit
=** in writing
◊ **écrit, -e** *adj* written; **écrit à la machine
=** typewritten; **écrit à la main =**
handwritten; **règlements écrits =** printed
regulations
◊ **écriture** *nf* **(a)** writing *ou* handwriting;
il trouve mon écriture difficile à lire = he
has difficulty in reading my writing; **les
clavistes trouvent que l'écriture de
l'auteur est difficile à lire =** the
keyboarders are having difficulty in
reading the author's handwriting **(b)**
(d'une disquette) **anneau** *ou* **bague de**

protection d'écriture = write-permit ring;
**dispositif de protection d'écriture de
fichier =** file protect tab; **temps
d'écriture =** write time; **tête d'écriture =**
(d'un disque) record head *ou* write head;
(d'une bande) tape head; *(d'une
disquette)* **volet de protection d'écriture =**
write-protect tab **(c) écriture chiffrée =**
cipher

édité, -ée *adj* edited; **non édité =**
unedited
◊ **éditer** *vtr* to edit; **éditer sous forme de
liste =** to list; **éditer un texte sur
ordinateur =** to edit a text on screen
◊ **éditeur** *nm (programme)* editor
program; **éditeur d'écran =** screen
editor; **éditeur de liens =** linkage editor;
éditeur de ligne = line editor; **éditeur de
programme =** program editor; **éditeur de
texte =** text editor; **cet éditeur de texte ne
peut lire que les fichiers de moins de
64Ko =** the text editor will only read
files smaller than 64Kbytes long
◊ **éditeur, -trice** *nm (qui s'occupe de la
publication d'oeuvres littéraires)*
publisher; **nom de l'éditeur =** imprint
◊ **édition** *nf* **(a)** *(de programme ou de
texte sur ordinateur)* editing; **édition
après compilation** *ou* **après calculs =**
post-editing; **(programme d') édition de
lettres types =** mail-merge; **commandes
et instructions d'édition =** editing terms
ou edit commands; **fenêtre d'édition =**
edit window; **programme d'édition de
texte =** text editor; **exécution d'un
programme d'édition (pour contrôle) =**
editing run; **touche (de fonction)
d'édition =** edit key; **il y a plusieurs
touches d'édition - celle-ci permet de
reformater le texte =** there are several
special edit keys - this one will re-format
the text **(b)** *(fabrication de livres)*
publishing; **édition électronique =**
electronic publishing *ou* desktop
publishing (dtp); **l'édition spécialisée** *ou*
professionnelle = professional
publishing; **maison d'édition =**
publishing firm *ou* publisher **(c)** *(d'un
livre ou d'un journal ou d'une revue)*
edition; **édition cartonnée** *ou* **reliée =**
hardback *ou* hardcover (edition);
**l'édition pour bibliothèques est cartonnée
avec jaquette =** the library edition has a
case and jacket; **avez-vous lu la dernière
édition du journal du soir? =** did you see
the last edition of the evening paper?; **le
texte de la seconde édition a été modifié =**
the second edition has had some changes

to the text **(d)** *(d'un film)* editing;
maquette d'édition = editing plan
◊ **éditorial** *nm (article)* editorial *ou*
leading article

éducatif, -ive *adj* educational;
**programme de télévision de caractère
éducatif =** educational TV (ETV)

EEPROM = ELECTRICALLY
ERASABLE PROGRAMMABLE READ-
ONLY MEMORY; **mémoire EEPROM =**
EEPROM; *voir aussi* MEMOIRE

EEROM = ELECTRICALLY ERASABLE
READ-ONLY MEMORY; **mémoire
EEROM =** EEROM; *voir aussi*
MEMOIRE

effaçable *adj* erasable; *(données)* soft;
mémoire effaçable = erasable memory;
**mémoire morte programmable (PROM)
effaçable par ultraviolet =** ultraviolet
erasable PROM; **mémoire ROM
effaçable électriquement =** electrically
erasable read-only memory (EEROM);
**mémoire ROM programmable et
effaçable =** erasable programmable
read-only memory (EPROM); **mémoire
ROM programmable et effaçable
électriquement =** electrically erasable
programmable read-only memory
(EEPROM); **support (magnétique)
effaçable =** erasable storage *ou* erasable
memory
◊ **effacement** *nm* deletion; **effacement
des lignes cachées =** hidden line
removal; *(d'un disque ou d'une bande)*
effacement en masse = bulk erase;
caractère d'effacement = delete
character *ou* erase character; **dispositif
d'effacement =** eraser; **retard
d'effacement =** lag; **tête d'effacement =**
erase head
◊ **effacer** *vtr* to erase *ou* to delete *ou* to
scrub *ou* to kill *ou* to wipe *ou* to clear *ou* to
rub out; **effacer en bloc =** to block delete;
**lorsqu'il s'agit de supprimer un texte
assez long, servez-vous de la commande
qui permet d'effacer en bloc =** use the
global delete command to remove large
areas of unwanted text; **effacer les
données d'un disque =** to wipe a disk
clean; **effacer des données par
superposition d'écriture =** to overwrite;
**tapez CLS pour effacer ce qu'il y a sur
l'écran =** type CLS to clear the screen;
effacer un fichier = to delete *ou* to kill *ou*

to junk *ou* to zero a file; *(faire disparaître à un moment déterminé)* **effacer une image** = to pop off an image; **(instruction d')** **effacer une PROM** = wash PROM; **qui peut être effacé** = erasable; **qui ne peut être effacé** = nonerasable; **mémoire qui ne peut être effacée** = nonerasable storage; **une bande papier perforée est une mémoire qui ne peut être effacée** = paper tape is a nonerasable storage

◊ **effaceur** *nm* effaceur magnétique = degausser *ou* demagnetizer; **il s'est servi d'un effaceur magnétique pour démagnétiser les têtes de lecture** = he used the demagnetizer to degauss the tape heads; **curseur** *ou* **marqueur effaceur** = destructive cursor

effectif, -ive *adj* effective; **adresse effective** = effective address; **instruction effective** = effective instruction; **largeur de bande effective** = effective bandwidth; **puissance d'ouverture effective** = effective aperture; **rendement effectif** = effective throughput; **vitesse de recherche effective** = effective search speed

effectuer *vtr* to carry out; **il faut quand même un certain temps pour effectuer la mise en route de l'ordinateur** = the process of setting up the computer takes a long time; **la société ne s'est pas souciée d'effectuer la maintenance de routine de son matériel** = the company failed to carry out routine maintenance of its equipment; **je vais effectuer une série de tests non destructifs sur votre machine; si tout se passe bien, vous pourrez vous en servir de nouveau** = I will carry out a number of non-destructive tests on your computer: if it passes, you can start using it again; **effectuer un branchement** = to jump; **effectuer un traitement** = to process; **effectuer un tri bulle** *ou* **un tri par permutation de paires** *ou* **de bulles** = to bubble sort

effet *nm* effect; **effet (de champ) Hall** = Hall effect; **commutateur à effet (de champ) Hall** = Hall effect switch; **semi-conducteur à effet de champ MOSFET** = metal oxide semiconductor field effect transistor (MOSFET); **transistor à effet de champ (TEC)** = field effect transistor (FET); **effet optronique** = electro-optic effect; **effets sonores** = sound effects; **tous les effets sonores dans le film sont** produits électroniquement = all the sound effects for the film were produced electronically; **effet sonore postsynchronisé** = dubbed sound; **instruction sans effet** = do-nothing (instruction)

efficace *adj* efficient; **intensité efficace d'une ligne** = RMS line current; **rendre plus efficace** = to upgrade; *(d'amplitude ou d'intensité, etc.)* **valeur efficace** = root mean square (RMS); **la valeur efficace d'une sinusoïde parfaite équivaut à 0,7071 de son amplitude** = the root mean square of the pure sinusoidal signal is 0.7071 of its amplitude

◊ **efficacement** *adv* efficiently

◊ **efficacité** *nf* efficiency

efficience *nf* efficiency

◊ **efficient, -e** *adj* efficient

effleurement *nm* **clavier à effleurement** = tactile keyboard *ou* touch-sensitive keyboard; **pavé à effleurement** = touch pad

EGA = ENHANCED GRAPHICS ADAPTER; **carte EGA** = EGA card; **écran EGA** = EGA screen; *voir aussi* ADAPTATEUR

égal, -e *adj* equal; **être égal à** = to equal

◊ **également** *adv* equally

◊ **égaler** *vtr* to equate *ou* to equal; **5 à la puissance deux** *ou* **5 au carré égale 25** = 5 to the power 2 is equal to 25 *ou* equals 25

égalisateur *nm* equalizer; **égalisateur de phases** = delay equalizer

◊ **égalisation** *nf* equalization

◊ **égaliser** to equalize *ou* to balance; *(à l'aide d'un filtre)* to equalize

◊ **égaliseur** *nm* equalizer; **égaliseur de fréquence** = frequency equalizer; **égaliseur de phase** = phase equalizer

◊ **égalité** *nf* equality

égaré, -ée *adj* stray

égratignure *nf* scratch

EIA = ELECTRONIC INDUSTRY ASSOCIATION; **interface aux normes EIA** = EIA interface

éjecter vtr (un fichier) to junk (a file)

élargi, -e adj augmented ou expanded; **adressage élargi** = augmented addressing
◊ **élargir** vtr to expand

électret nm electret; **microphone à électret** = electret microphone

son nom s'explique par le fait que ce microphone miniature ne comporte pas moins de 3 capsules à électret
Audio Tech

électricien nm electrician; **chef-électricien** = gaffer

électricité nf electricity; **électricité statique** = static; **à l'électricité** = electrically; **conduire l'électricité** = to conduct electricity; **les frais d'électricité constituent un élément important des coûts de production** = electricity prices are an important factor in the production costs; **moteur qui marche** ou **qui fonctionne à l'électricité** = electric motor ou electrically-powered motor; **panne d'électricité** = blackout ou power failure
◊ **électrique** adj electric ou electrical; **charge électrique** = electric charge; **courant électrique** = electric current; **machine à écrire électrique** = electric typewriter; **moteur électrique** = electric motor ou electrically-powered motor; **les ingénieurs essaient de réparer une panne électrique** = the engineers are trying to repair an electrical fault; **polarité électrique** = electrical polarity
◊ **électriquement** adv electrically; **mémoire ROM effaçable électriquement** = electrically erasable read-only memory (EEROM); **mémoire ROM modifiable électriquement** = electrically alterable read-only memory (EAROM); **mémoire ROM programmable et effaçable électriquement** = electrically erasable programmable read-only memory (EEPROM); **mémoire ROM programmable, modifiable électriquement** = electrically alterable, programmable read-only memory (EAPROM)

électro-aimant nm electromagnet; **qui fonctionne grâce à un électro-aimant** = electromagnetically powered

électrode nf electrode ou biosensor; **l'activité nerveuse peut se mesurer en plaçant une électrode sur le bras** = the nerve activity can be measured by attaching a biosensor to your arm

électroluminescence nf electroluminescence
◊ **électroluminescent, -e** adj electroluminescent ou electroluminescing; **affichage** ou **écran électroluminescent** = electroluminescent display; **l'écran est recouvert d'une couche électroluminescente** = the screen coating is electroluminescent; **diode électroluminescente** = light emitting diode (LED)

électrolytique adj electrolytic; **condensateur électrolytique** = electrolytic capacitor; **condensateur non électrolytique** = non-electrolytic capacitor

électromagnétique adj electromagnetic; **écran** ou **blindage électromagnétique** = electromagnetic shield; **le blindage protège l'unité centrale des pertes** ou **fuites électromagnétiques du bloc d'alimentation** = the metal screen protects the CPU against stray electromagnetic effects from the PSU; **interférence électromagnétique** = electromagnetic interference (EMI); **rayonnement électromagnétique** = electromagnetic radiation; **spectre de fréquences électromagnétiques** = electromagnetic spectrum

électromécanique adj electromechanical; **central téléphonique électromécanique** = strowger exchange; **commutation électromécanique** = electromechanical switching

électromoteur, -trice adj electromotive; **force électromotrice** = electromotive force (EMF)

électron nm electron; **canon à électrons** = electron gun; **faisceau d'électrons** = electron beam

électronicien, -ienne n electronic specialist; **ingénieur électronicien** = electronic engineer

électronique 1 *nf* l'électronique = electronics; **un expert en électronique** = an electronics specialist 2 *adj* electronic; **autocommutateur électronique** *ou* **central automatique électronique** = electronic automatic exchange; **autocommutateur électronique privé** *ou* **PBX électronique** = computerized branch exchange (CBX); **boîte aux lettres électronique** = electronic mailbox *ou* mail box; **bureau électronique** = automated office *ou* paperless office; **clavier électronique** = electronic keyboard; **clé électronique** = dongle; **commutateur électronique** *ou* **système de commutation électronique** = electronic switching system; **compositeur électronique** = electronic compositor; **composition électronique** = electronic composition; **courrier électronique** = electronic mail *ou* email *ou* e-mail; **dispositif électronique d'identification** = personal identification device (PID); **édition électronique** = electronic publishing *ou* desktop publishing; **faisceau électronique** = electron beam; **enregistrement par faisceau électronique (sur microfilm)** = electron beam recording (EBR); **impulsion électronique** = electronic pulse; **jeu électronique** = computer game; **l'industrie électronique** = the electronics industry; **journalisme** *ou* **reportage électronique** = electronic news gathering (ENG); **machine à écrire électronique** = electronic typewriter; **messagerie électronique** *ou* **courrier électronique** = electronic mail *ou* email *ou* e-mail; *(dans une société)* computer-based message system (CBMS); **monnaie électronique** = electronic money; *(de vidéofilm)* **montage électronique** = electronic editing; **point de vente électronique** = electronic point-of-sale (EPOS); **pollution (par rayonnement) électronique** = electronic smog; **signature électronique** = electronic signature; **stylo électronique** = electronic wand *ou* stylus; **par système électronique** = electronically; **le texte est transmis au compositeur externe par système électronique** = the text is electronically transmitted to an outside typesetter; **tableau d'affichage électronique** = bulletin board system (BBS); **tableau noir électronique** = electronic blackboard; **traitement électronique de données** = electronic data processing (EDP); **facilité de traitement électronique de données** = electronic data processing capability; **transfert électronique de fonds** = electronic funds transfer (system) (EFT); **terminal de transfert électronique de fonds** = electronic funds transfer point of sale (EFTPOS); **transmission électronique** = electronic traffic; **verrou (de sécurité) électronique** = electronic lock; *(d'une caméra)* **viseur électronique** = electronic viewfinder

◊ **électroniquement** *adv* electronically; **tous les effets sonores dans le film sont produits électroniquement** = all the sound effects for the film are produced electronically

électrophotographie *nf* electrophotography

électrosensible *adj* electrosensitive; **papier électrosensible** = electrosensitive paper

électrostatique *adj* electrostatic; **par charge électrostatique** = electrostatically; **écran électrostatique** = electrostatic screen; **haut-parleur électrostatique** = electrostatic speaker; **imprimante électrostatique** = electrostatic printer; **mémoire électrostatique** = electrostatic storage

élégant, -e *adj* elegant; **programmation élégante** = elegant programming

élément *nm* element *ou* item *ou* building block *ou* unit; *(d'un champ)* member; **élément final d'une arborescence** = leaf; **élément arithmétique étendu** = extended arithmetic element; **élément binaire** = binary digit *ou* bit; **élément d'un code** = code element; **élément de décision** = decision element; **élément de données** = data element *ou* data item; **élément d'image** = picture element *ou* pixel; **élément logique** = logic element; **élément logique composé** *ou* **élément logique multiple** = compound logical element; *(code)* **élément de structure** = overhead; **élément d'un signal** = signal element; **élément dans un tableau** = array element; **éléments de l'unité centrale** *ou* **éléments CPU** = CPU elements; **chaîne d'éléments de données** = data element chain

élémentaire *adj* elementary *ou* primary; **code élémentaire** = basic code;

guide élémentaire *ou* **manuel d'utilisation élémentaire** = primer; **section élémentaire de câble** = elementary cable section; **tampon élémentaire** = unit buffer

élévation *nf (math)* **élévation (d'un nombre) à la puissance x** = exponentiation

◊ **élever** *vtr* **(a)** élever (un nombre) à la puissance x = to exponentiate **(b)** élever le potentiel d'une ligne = to pull up a line; **élever le potentiel de la ligne de réception au niveau logique un, en la connectant sur une source de courant de 5 volts** = to pull up the input line to a logic one by connecting it to 5 volts

◊ **s'élever à** *vpr* to amount to

éliminateur *nm* suppressor; **éliminateur de courant transitoire** = transient suppressor; **éliminateur d'écho** = echo suppressor

◊ **élimination** *nf* suppression *ou* elimination; **élimination des zéros (non significatifs)** = zero compression *ou* zero suppression; **facteur d'élimination** = elimination factor

◊ **éliminer** to eliminate; *(par filtrage)* to filter; **l'ordinateur devrait servir à éliminer toute possibilité d'erreur dans le système d'adresses** = using a computer should eliminate all possibility of error in the address system; **un correcteur orthographique n'élimine pas toutes les fautes d'orthographe** = a spelling checker does not eliminate all spelling mistakes

Elite *(caractères typographiques)* **caractères Elite** = elite font *ou* elite characters

ellipse *nf* ellipse

◊ **elliptique** *adj* elliptical; **orbite elliptique** = elliptical orbit

éloigné, -ée *adj* distant *ou* remote; **console éloignée** *ou* **poste de commande** *ou* **périphérique éloigné** = remote console *ou* device; *(centre de communication)* **poste éloigné** = remote station; **terminal éloigné** = remote terminal

ELSE *(sinon)* **instruction ELSE** = else rule

emballage *nm* packing *ou* packaging; **emballage bulle** = blister pack; **emballage hermétique** = airtight packaging

◊ **emballer** to pack; *(dans une caisse)* to case

emboîté, -ée *adj* nested; **boucles emboîtées** = nested loop

◊ **emboîter** *vtr* to nest

embranchement *nm* branch

émetteur *nm* emitter *ou* sender *ou* send-only device; **remise à l'état initial commandée par l'émetteur** = forward clearing; **émetteur à bande** = tape transmitter; **émetteur de données** = data source; **émetteur isotrope** = isotropic radiator; **le signal de cet émetteur radio est très faible** = the signal from this radio station is very weak

◊ **émetteur, -trice** *adj* **le signal de cette station émettrice est très faible** = the signal from this radio station is very weak

◊ **émetteur-récepteur** **1** *nm* transceiver; **émetteur-récepteur radio** = radio transceiver; **émetteur-récepteur asynchrone universel** = universal asynchronous receiver-transmitter (UART); **contrôleur d'émetteur-récepteur asynchrone universel** = UART controller; **émetteur-récepteur synchrone universel** = universal synchronous receiver-transmitter (USRT); **émetteur-récepteur synchrone asynchrone universel** = universal synchronous asynchronous receiver-transmitter (USART) **2** *adj* **appareil émetteur-récepteur** = automatic send/receive (ASR); **clavier émetteur-récepteur** = ASR keyboard; **poste émetteur-récepteur** = two way radio; **terminal émetteur-récepteur à clavier** = keyboard send/receive (KSR)

◊ **émettre** *vtr* to emit; **un multiplexeur 4/1 reçoit sur 4 canaux et émet sur un seul** = a 4 to 1 multiplexor combines four inputs into a single output; **émettre un bip** = to bleep; **émettre des impulsions** = to pulse; **émettre un signal** = to signal; **nous avons émis le signal d'entrée mais toujours sans succès** = we pulsed the input but it still would not work; **émettre un signal d'échantillonnage** *ou* **de validation** = to strobe; **signal d'interruption émis par un périphérique** =

external interrupt; **émettre une vibration sonore** = to buzz; *(de l'ordinateur aux périphériques)* **invitation à émettre** = polling; **inviter à émettre** = to poll; *(transmission)* **(signal de) demande d'invitation à émettre** = request to send signal (RTS)

émission *nf* emission; *(transmission de données)* **émission en duplex** = duplex operation; **l'émission du faisceau électronique** = the emission of the electron beam; *(radio)* **le récepteur a capté l'émission radiophonique** = the receiver picked up the radio emission; **fin des émissions** = close-down; *(télévision)* **grille d'émission** = format

empagement *nm* type area

empattement *nm* serif; **caractère avec empattements** = serif character; **avec empattements elzéviriens** = bracketed (serif); **(caractère) sans empattement** = sans serif

empêcher *vtr* to prevent *ou* to block; **nous avons changé les mots de passe pour empêcher le piratage de la base de données** = we have changed the passwords to prevent hackers getting into the database

emplacement *nm* location *ou* site; **emplacement de mémoire** = memory location; **emplacement protégé** = protected location; **emplacement de rangement (en mémoire)** = bucket; *(d'un formulaire)* **emplacement réservé à la réponse** = response position

emploi *nm* **(a)** use; **mode d'emploi** = directions for use **(b)** **travail qui fait double emploi** = duplication of work
◊ **employer** *vtr* to use something *ou* to make use of something

empreinte *nf* print *ou* pattern; *(d'un faisceau, etc.)* footprint; *(d'antenne ou de microphone)* **empreinte directionnelle** = directional pattern; **empreinte d'interférence** = interference pattern; **empreinte vocale** = voice print

emprunter *vtr* to borrow; **elle a emprunté un livre sur la fabrication des**

ordinateurs = she borrowed a book on computer construction

émulateur *nm* emulator; **émulateur intégré** = integrated emulator; **émulateur intégré au circuit** = in-circuit emulator
◊ **émulation** *nf* emulation; **capacité d'émulation** = emulation facility
◊ **émuler** *vtr* to emulate; **une imprimante (à) laser qui peut émuler une série d'autres imprimantes de bureau** = laser printer which emulates a wide range of office printers

émulsion *nf* emulsion

en-tête *nm* heading; **formulaires et en-têtes de lettres peuvent être conçus sur un PC** = business forms and letterheads can be designed on a PC; **en-tête de bande** = tape header; **en-tête de bloc** = block header; **en-tête courant** = form flash; **en-tête de fichier** = (file) header; **en-tête de lettre** = letterhead; **en-tête de message** = message heading; **en-tête préétabli** = form overlay *ou* form flash; **carte en-tête** = header card; **(code de) début d'en-tête** = start of header; **papier à en-tête** = headed paper *ou* preprinted stationery

ENAO = ENTRAINEMENT ASSISTE PAR ORDINATEUR

encadré, -ée *adj* framed *ou* boxed in; **les citations sont encadrées** = the quotations are printed in boxes
◊ **encadrement** *nm* frame *ou* box *ou* border
◊ **encadrer** *vtr* to frame *ou* to box in

encarté, -ée *adj* on-board

enceinte *nf* **enceinte acoustique** = set of loudspeakers *ou* baffle

enchaîné, -ée *adj* chained; **programme à fonctions enchaînées** = thread; *(signal)* **fondu enchaîné** = cross fade
◊ **enchaînement** *nm* chaining *ou* linking *ou* catenation; **ordre d'enchaînement des opérations** = operator precedence; **page (vidéotex) à**

enchaînement programmé = time coded page

◊ **enchaîner** *vtr* to chain *ou* to link *ou* to concatenate *ou* to catenate; **plus de 1000 articles ou chapitres peuvent être enchaînés à l'impression** = more than 1,000 articles or chapters can be chained together when printing; **le film enchaîne sur un ralenti** = the film switches to slow motion

◊ **s'enchaîner** *vpr* to be chained *ou* to be linked

encoche *nf* notch; **carte à encoches marginales** = edge notched card

encodage *nm* encoding; **encodage binaire** = binary encoding; **encodage magnétique** *ou* **sur support magnétique** = magnetic encoding; **format d'encodage** = encoding format

◊ **encoder** *vtr* to encode

◊ **encodeur** *nm* encodeur pour bandes magnétiques = magnetic tape encoder; **encodeur (de) couleurs** = colour encoder; **encodeur de touches** = keyboard encoder

encombrement *nm* **(a)** dimension(s) *ou* measurements; *(surface utilisée par un ordinateur sur un bureau)* footprint **(b)** *(d'un réseau de transmission)* congestion

encre *nf* ink; *(pour photocopieur, imprimante laser, etc.)* toner; **encre magnétique** = magnetic ink; *(d'une imprimante laser)* **cartouche d'encre** = toner cartridge; **lorsque l'encre est épuisée, on remplace la cartouche et le tambour ensemble** = the toner cartridge and the imaging drum can be replaced as one unit when the toner runs out; **pour remettre de l'encre ou changer la cartouche, voir la marche à suivre dans le manuel d'utilisation** = change toner and toner cartridge according to the manual; **excès d'encre** = overinking; **mettre un excès d'encre** *ou* **mettre trop d'encre** = to overink; **deux cahiers ont été gâchés par excès d'encre** = two signatures were spoilt by overinking; **imprégner** *ou* **couvrir d'encre** = to ink; **imprimante à jet d'encre** = ink-jet printer; **les techniques du jet d'encre couleur et du transfert thermique sont concurrentielles** = colour ink-jet technology and thermal transfer technology compete with each other

◊ **encrer** *vtr* to ink; **encrer de façon excessive** = to overink

endommagé, -ée *adj* damaged

◊ **endommager** *vtr* to damage *ou* to cause damage; **le disque dur a été endommagé quand on l'a laissé tomber** = the hard disk was damaged when it was dropped; **il semble que la tête de lecture défectueuse ait endommagé le disque** = the faulty read/write head appears to have damaged the disk

endroit *nm* **(a)** *(emplacement)* point *ou* position **(b)** *(bon côté)* recto

enduction *nf* deposition

◊ **enduire** to coat (a surface) *ou* to deposit (a substance on a surface)

◊ **enduit** *nm* coating; *(sur un semi-conducteur)* **pose** *ou* **dépôt d'un enduit** = deposition

◊ **enduit, -e** *adj* coated; **papier enduit d'une fine couche de kaolin** = paper which has a coating of clay; **enduit d'un dopant** = doped

énergie *nf* energy; **nous essayons d'économiser de l'énergie en éteignant les lumières lorsque les pièces sont vides** = we try to save energy by switching off the lights when the rooms are empty; **vous économiserez de l'énergie en limitant la température de la pièce à 18 degrés** = if you reduce the room temperature to eighteen degrees, you will save energy; **qui économise l'énergie** = energy-saving; **notre société met en place des mesures d'économie d'énergie** = our company is introducing energy-saving measures

enfermer *vtr* to enclose

enfichable *adj (qui se branche)* plug-in; *(qui ne demande pas de soudure)* solderless; **extension enfichable** = plug-in unit; **directement enfichable** = plug-compatible; **cette nouvelle carte directement enfichable travaille beaucoup plus vite que ses concurrentes, vous l'installez en l'enfichant simplement dans le connecteur d'extension** = this new plug-compatible board works much faster than any of its rivals, you can install it by simply plugging it into the expansion port; **ROM enfichable** = ROM cartridge

◊ **enfichage** *nm* plugging; **connecteur** *ou* **fiche à une seule position d'enfichage** = polarized plug; **connecteur (de carte) à**

enfichage dirigé *ou* **à un seul bord d'enfichage** = polarized edge connector

◊ **enficher** *vtr* to plug in

enfoncer *vtr* to press *ou* to push in

engorgement *nm* *(transmission)* overrun

enlever *vtr* to remove

enregistré, -ée *adj* recorded; **amplitude maximum enregistrée** = maximum reading; *(pour film)* **commentaire enregistré** = voice-over; **des données enregistrées numériquement servent à générer des images** = digitally recorded data are used to generate images; **programme enregistré** = stored program

◊ **enregistrement (a)** *(support)* record *ou* recording; *(procédure)* recording; *(entrée dans un journal ou livre de bord)* log; *(procédure)* logging; **votre enregistrement contient divers champs regroupés sous une même rubrique** = your record contains several fields that have been grouped together under one heading; **cet enregistrement contient toutes leurs coordonnées** = this record contains all their personal details; **enregistrement ambisonique** *ou* **d'ambiance** = ambisonics; **enregistrement chaîné** = chained record; **enregistrement de données** = data record; *(automatique et chronologique)* data logging; **enregistrement (automatique) des erreurs** = error logging; **ce programme permet l'enregistrement (automatique) des erreurs** = features of the program include error logging; **enregistrement d'erreur dans un système** = fault trace; **enregistrement par faisceau électronique (sur microfilm)** = electron beam recording (EBR); **(nombre d') enregistrements dans un fichier** = record count; **enregistrement de labels** *ou* **d'étiquettes** *ou* **d'identificateurs** = label record; **enregistrement logique** = logical record; **enregistrement de longueur fixe** *ou* **déterminée** = fixed-length record; **enregistrement à longueur variable** = variable length record; **enregistrement de mouvements** *ou* **de modifications** *ou* **de détails** = change record *ou* amendment record; **enregistrement numérique** = digital recording; **enregistrement physique** = physical record; **enregistrement par rayon laser** = laser beam recording; **enregistrement sur support magnétique** = magnetic recording; **enregistrement de tête** = leader record; **enregistrement de transactions** = transaction record; *(dans un fichier)* **début d'enregistrement** = home record; **point de début d'enregistrement** = loadpoint; **densité d'enregistrement** = recording density *ou* packing density; **dernier enregistrement** *ou* **enregistrement de fin de fichier** = trailer record; **disque d'enregistrement** = work disk; **espace entre deux enregistrements** = record gap; **fichier d'enregistrement des blocs** = block list; **(code de) fin d'enregistrement** = end of record (EOR); **format** *ou* **présentation d'un enregistrement** = record format *ou* layout; **programme de gestion d'enregistrements** = records management; **gestionnaire d'enregistrements** = records manager; **intervalle blanc entre deux enregistrements** = record gap; **longueur** *ou* **dimension** *ou* **taille d'un enregistrement** = record length; **temps d'enregistrement** = write time; **tête d'enregistrement** = record head *ou* write head; **touche** *ou* **bouton d'enregistrement** = record button **(b)** *(surtout musique)* **un nouvel enregistrement des quatuors de Beethoven** = a new recording of Beethoven's quartets; **nouveaux enregistrements** = new releases **(c)** *(téléphone)* **enregistrement d'appels** = call logging

◊ **enregistrer** *vtr* **(a)** *(données)* to record *ou* to read-in *ou* to read in *ou* to write *ou* to post; *(en mémoire auxiliaire)* to deposit; *(dans un journal ou livre de bord)* to log *ou* to write; *(le nombre et la durée)* to meter; **ce dispositif enregistre les signaux sur bande magnétique** = this device records signals onto magnetic tape; *(dicter)* **il enregistrait ses instructions sur son Dictaphone de poche** = he was dictating orders into his pocket dictating machine; *(musique* *ou* *effet sonore)* **enregistrer d'avance** = to prerecord **(b)** *(téléphone)* **enregistrer le nombre et la durée des appels** = to log calls

◊ **enregistreur** *nm* **(a)** recorder; *(d'une imprimante)* **enregistreur graphique** = chart recorder *ou* pen recorder; **enregistreur à tambour** = drum plotter **(b)** *(téléphone)* logger; **enregistreur d'appels** = call logger; **le nombre et la** durée des appels effectués dans chacun des bureaux sont enregistrés sur l'enregistreur d'appels = the calls from each office are metered by the call logger

enroulé, -ée *adj* wound; **connexion enroulée =** wire wrap

◊ **enroulement** *nm* **(a)** *(d'un fil ou d'un film)* winding; **bobine d'enroulement =** pickup reel *ou* pick-up reel *ou* take-up reel; *(télévision)* **déflecteur à enroulement =** deflection yoke **(b)** *(traitement de texte)* **enroulement à la ligne =** horizontal wraparound; **enroulement d'une ligne =** line folding

◊ **enrouler** *vtr* to wind

◊ **s'enrouler** *vpr* to wind *ou* to rewind; **le film s'enroule automatiquement sur la bobine =** the tape rewinds onto the spool automatically

◊ **enrouleur-presseur** *nm* **enrouleur-presseur de bande magnétique =** omega wrap

enseignement *nm* teaching *ou* instruction; **enseignement assisté par ordinateur (EAO) =** computer-aided *ou* assisted instruction (CAI); **enseignement interactif géré par ordinateur =** computer-managed instruction (CMI)

ensemble *nm* set; **ensemble de caractères =** character set; **ensemble de caractères nuls =** empty set *ou* null set; **ensemble référentiel =** universal set; **ensemble des tâches** *ou* **travaux en cours d'exécution =** job mix; *(math)* **théorie des ensembles =** set theory

ensemblier *nm* original equipment manufacturer (OEM)

ensoleillement *nm* period of sunshine; **durée de non ensoleillement =** sun outage

entendre *vtr* to hear; *(son)* **qu'on peut entendre =** audible

en-tête *nm* heading

entier, -ière *adj* full *ou* complete; **nombre entier =** integer; **BASIC pour nombres entiers =** integer BASIC; **nombre entier en double précision =** double-precision integer

entité *nf* entity

entraînement *nm* **(a)** *(pour bande ou cartes ou film ou papier)* feed *ou* advance *ou* transport; **(dispositif d') entraînement de la bande papier =** paper tape feed; **(système d') entraînement de cartes perforées =** card feed; **entraînement feuille à feuille =** single sheet feed; **entraînement d'un film =** film advance; **entraînement par friction** *ou* **par rouleaux =** friction feed; **(dispositif d') entraînement du papier =** paper feed *ou* feeder; **ce bouton sert à l'entraînement du papier =** the paper is advanced by turning this knob; **entraînement par picots =** tractor feed *ou* pinfeed *ou* sprocket feed; *(de cartes)* **canal d'entraînement (avec perforations centrales) =** centre sprocket feed; **perforations d'entraînement =** feed holes *ou* sprocket holes **(b) entraînement informatisé =** computer-based training (CBT)

◊ **entraîner** *vtr* **(a)** *(bande ou cartes ou film ou papier)* to move *ou* to advance *ou* to feed **(b)** to drive; **un moteur entraîne le disque =** the disk is driven by a motor **(c)** to produce; **les fluctuations de courant peuvent entraîner la perte de données =** data loss can occur because of power supply variations

un moteur commande l'entraînement du film
Science et Vie

entrance *nf (facteur d'entrée d'un circuit)* fan-in

entré, -ée *adj* entered *ou* input; **dernier entré premier sorti =** last in first out (LIFO); **cet ordinateur gère la pile suivant la méthode du 'dernier entré premier sorti' =** this computer stack uses a last in first out data retrieval method; **(méthode du) premier entré premier sorti (FIFO) =** first in first out (FIFO); **mémoire qui fonctionne** *ou* **qui est basée sur le principe 'premier entré premier sorti' =** FIFO memory *ou* first in first out memory; **les deux ordinateurs fonctionnent à des vitesses différentes mais peuvent transmettre des données en utilisant une mémoire tampon fonctionnant sur le système 'premier entré premier sorti' =** the two computers operate at different rates, but can transmit data using a FIFO memory

entrée *nf* **(a)** input (i/p *ou* I/P) *ou* entry; *(action)* entering; **entrée de données** = data input *ou* data entry; **entrée directe de données** = direct data entry (DDE); **entrée à partir de** *ou* **par lecture de microfilm** = computer input from microfilm (CIM); **entrée sur un système avec un mot de passe piraté** *ou* **sur un terminal mal verrouillé** = piggyback entry; **entrée en temps réel** = real-time input; **additionneur à deux entrées** = half adder *ou* two input adder; **additionneur à trois entrées** = full adder *ou* three input adder; **bloc d'entrée** = input block; **traitement de contrôle de bloc à l'entrée** = block input processing; **bus d'entrée** = data input bus (DIB); **câble d'entrée** *ou* **liaison d'un périphérique d'entrée** = input lead; **condition d'entrée** = entry condition; **visualisation de contrôle d'entrée** = marching display; **déclaration d'entrée** = input statement; **données d'entrée** = input data; *(d'un circuit)* **facteur pyramidal d'entrée** = fan-in; **file d'attente des données d'entrée** = input work queue; **file d'attente à deux entrées** = double-ended queue *ou* deque; **heure d'entrée** = entry time; **instruction d'entrée** = entry instruction; **instruction d'entrée dans la pile** = push instruction *ou* operation; **lecteur optique de microfilms pour entrée de données sur ordinateur** = film optical scanning device for input into computers (FOSDIC); **(programme) limité par la vitesse d'entrée** *ou* **avec contrainte de vitesse d'entrée** = input-bound *ou* input-limited; **mémoire d'entrée** = input storage; **mode (d') entrée** = input mode; **périphérique d'entrée** = input device *ou* unit; **point** *ou* **adresse d'entrée** = *(de logiciel)* entry point *ou* access point; *(dans un système)* access point *ou* trapdoor; **port (d') entrée** = input port; **registre d'entrée** = input register *ou* receiver register; **registre tampon des entrées** = input buffer register; **routine d'entrée** = input routine; **section d'entrée** = input section; **signal d'entrée** = input signal; **soustracteur à trois entrées** = full subtractor; **terminal d'entrée (de données) vidéotex** = i/p terminal; **zone d'entrée** = input area **(b)** **touche entrée** *ou* **de validation d'entrée** = return (key) *ou* enter (key) *ou* carriage return (CR); **tapez votre nom et numéro de code, puis appuyez sur la touche 'entrée'** = you type in your name and code number then press return **(c)** *(dans un index ou dictionnaire)* entry *ou* headword; *(dans*

un journal ou livre de bord) log; **entrée principale** = main entry; **entrée secondaire** = added entry

◊ **entrée/sortie** *nf* input/output *ou* I/O; **entrée/sortie configurée en mémoire** = memory-mapped input/output; *(en FORTRAN)* **entrée/sortie graphique** = graphical input/output (GINO); **entrée/sortie utilisant une mémoire tampon** = buffered input/output; **entrée/sortie (en) parallèle** = parallel input/output (PIO); **circuit intégré d'entrée/sortie en parallèle** = parallel input/output chip; **entrée parallèle/sortie parallèle** = parallel input/parallel output (PIPO); **entrée parallèle/sortie série** = parallel input/serial output (PISO); **entrée/sortie (en) série** = serial input/output (SIO); **entrée série/sortie parallèle** = serial input/parallel output (SIPO); **entrée série/sortie série** = serial input/serial output (SISO); **adressage des entrées/sorties** = input/output mapping; **appareil** *ou* **dispositif d'entrée/sortie** = I/O device; **bus (d') entrée/sortie** = input/output bus *ou* input/output data bus; **canal d'entrée/sortie** = input/output channel; **configuration d'entrées/sortie** = input/output mapping; **contrôleur d'entrée/sortie** = input/output controller; **fichier (d') entrée/sortie** = input/output file; **instruction d'entrée/sortie** = input/output instruction; **interface d'entrée/sortie** = input/output interface; **(signal d') interruption d'entrée/sortie** = input/output interrupt; **(programme) limité par la vitesse d'entrée/sortie** = input/output bound (program); **mot d'état d'entrée/sortie** = input/output status word; **périphérique d'entrée/sortie** = input/output device *ou* unit; **point** *ou* **port (d') entrée/sortie** = input/output port; **le manche à balai peut être connecté sur le port entrée/sortie** = the joystick can be connected to the input/output port; **processeur d'entrée/sortie** = input/output processor (IOP); **bibliothèque de programmes d'entrée/sortie** = input/output library; **programme de contrôle d'entrée/sortie** = input/output control program; **référençage d'entrée/sortie** = input/output referencing; **registre d'entrée/sortie** = input/output register; **requête d'entrée/sortie** = input/output request (IORQ); **superviseur d'entrée/sortie** = input/output executive; **tampon (d') entrée/sortie** =

input/output buffer; **terminal à clavier d'entrée/sortie** = keyboard send/receive (KSR); **voie (d') entrée/sortie** = input/output channel
NOTE: on peut utiliser la forme abréviée **I/O** dans tous les exemples ci-dessus: **I/O channel; I/O buffer; serial I/O**

entrefer *nm* air gap *ou* head gap

entrelacé, -ée *adj* interleaved
◊ **entrelacement** *nm* interleaving
◊ **entrelacer** *vtr* to interleave; *(balayage d'image)* to interlace

entrepôt *nm* warehouse *ou* storage facilities

entreprendre *vtr* to undertake; **il a entrepris de reprogrammer tout le système** = he has undertaken to reprogram the whole system
◊ **entreprise** *nf (société)* business *ou* firm *ou* company; **il possède une petite entreprise de réparation d'ordinateurs** = he owns a small computer repair business; **dans l'entreprise** = in-house; **tout le travail informatique se fait dans l'entreprise** = all the data processing is done in-house; **répertoire d'entreprises** = commercial directory *ou* trade directory

entrer 1 *vtr (des données)* to enter *ou* to input; *(par lecture)* to read in; **entrer un nom sur une liste** = to enter a name on a list **2** *vi* **(a)** to access *ou* to enter *ou* to dial into; **avec un code d'accès valide, il est possible d'entrer dans le système du client et d'extraire les fichiers utiles pour établir le rapport** = with the right access code it is possible to dial into a customer's computer to extract the files needed for the report **(b) entrer en vigueur** = to come into force; **les nouveaux règlements entreront en vigueur le 1er janvier** = the new regulations will come into force on January 1st

entretenir *vtr* **(a)** *(appareil)* to maintain **(b)** *(image ou mémoire)* to refresh
◊ **entretenu, -e** *adj* **(a)** *(appareil)* serviced *ou* maintained; **bien entretenu** = well maintained *ou* well looked after **(b)** *(continu)* continuous; **onde entretenue** = continuous wave

◊ **entretien** *nm (d'appareil)* maintenance *ou* upkeep; **entretien régulier** = preventive maintenance; **ingénieur d'entretien (sur le site)** = field engineer

énumératif, -ive *adj* enumerative; *(classement)* enumerated type
◊ **énumérer** *vtr* to detail *ou* to list

enveloppe *nf* **(a)** *(octet de données)* envelope; **effectuer un tri 'enveloppe'** = to shell sort **(b)** *(amplitude)* **enveloppe d'attaque (d'un signal)** = attack envelope; **enveloppe tonale** = pitch envelope; **délai (de transmission) d'une enveloppe** = envelope delay; **détection d'enveloppe** = envelope detection **(c)** *(pour envoyer une lettre)* envelope; **enveloppe avion** = air mail envelope; **enveloppe à fenêtre** = window envelope; **enveloppe fermée** *ou* **cachetée** = sealed envelope; **enveloppe longue (pour papier ministre)** = foolscap envelope; **enveloppe ouverte** *ou* **non cachetée** = unsealed envelope

environ *adv* approximately; **le temps de traitement est d'environ 10% inférieur à celui du trimestre précédent** = processing time is approximately 10% lower than during the previous quarter

environnement *nm* environment; **environnement de développement de programmes** = program development system *ou* environment

envoi *nm* dispatch *ou* despatch; *(par la poste)* mailing; *(prospectus envoyé par la poste)* mail shot *ou* mailing piece; **l'envoi (par la poste) de prospectus publicitaires** = *(action)* the mailing of publicity material
◊ **envoyer** *vtr* to dispatch *ou* to despatch *ou* to send; **envoyer par la poste** = to mail *ou* to post; **envoyer par télécopie** *ou* **envoyer par fax** = to fax *ou* to send by fax; **envoyer un télex** = to telex

EOF = END OF FILE *voir* FIN

EOM = END OF MESSAGE *voir* FIN

EOT = END OF TRANSMISSION *voir* FIN

épais, épaisse *adj* thick; **couche épaisse** = thick film

◇ **épaisseur** *nf* **papier listing en double épaisseur** = two-part computer stationery; **papier listing en plusieurs épaisseurs** = multi-part computer stationery

éphémère *adj* transient

épidiascope *nm* episcope *ou* epidiascope

épitaxial, -e *adj* epitaxial; **couche épitaxiale** = epitaxial layer
◇ **épitaxie** *nf* epitaxy

épreuve *nf* (a) *(imprimerie)* proof; **épreuve finale** = master proof; **épreuve de machine** = machine proof; **épreuve de mise en page** *ou* **dernière épreuve** = page proof; **épreuves en placard** *ou* **en première** = galley proofs *ou* slip pages *ou* slip proofs; **épreuve sans correction** = clean proof; **épreuve de reproduction** = repro proof; **épreuves en vrac** = scatter proofs; **correcteur, -trice d'épreuves** = proofreader; **corriger des épreuves** = to proofread; **imprimante (destinée au tirage) d'épreuves** = proofer; **des périphériques tels qu'imprimantes laser destinées au tirage d'épreuves et photocomposeuses** = output devices such as laser proofers and typesetters; **la relecture des épreuves est-elle terminée?** = has all the text been proofread yet?; **signes de correction d'épreuve** = proof correction marks; **tirage d'épreuves** = proofing; **tirer les épreuves (d'un texte)** = to proof (b) *(photo)* print; **épreuve de contact** = contact print; **épreuve positive** = photoprint

EPROM = ERASABLE PROGRAMMABLE READ-ONLY MEMORY; **mémoire EPROM** = EPROM; *voir aussi* MEMOIRE

épuiser *vtr (une pile)* to drain

épure *nf* blueprint

équateur *nm* equator

équation *nf* equation; **équation machine** = machine equation

équatorial, -e *adj* equatorial; **orbite équatoriale** = equatorial orbit

équilibrage *nm* balancing; **bande d'équilibrage (de tension)** = balance stripe

◇ **équilibré, -ée** *adj* balanced; **charge équilibrée** = matched load; **circuit équilibré** = balanced circuit; **il faut utiliser un circuit équilibré en fin de ligne pour éviter la réflexion des signaux** = you must use a balanced circuit at the end of the line to prevent signal reflections; **erreur équilibrée** = balanced error; **ligne équilibrée** = balanced line

◇ **équilibre** *nm* balance; **le logiciel de PAO permet à l'utilisateur de juger du bon équilibre d'une page** = the DTP package allows the user to see if the overall page balance is correct; **équilibre des couleurs** = colour balance

◇ **équilibrer** *vtr* to balance *ou* to match

équipe *nf* team *ou* crew; **équipe cinématographique** *ou* **de cinéastes** = camera crew; **l'équipe de cinéastes a dû tourner toute la journée dans la neige** = the camera crew had to film all day in the snow

équipé, -ée *adj* fitted with; **équipé d'une pile auxiliaire** *ou* **de secours** = battery-backed; **la carte RAM peut être équipée, en option, d'une pile de secours** = the RAM disk card has the option to be battery-backed

◇ **équipement** *nm* (a) equipment; **fournisseur** *ou* **revendeur d'équipements informatiques** = computer equipment supplier; **équipement de traitement de papier listing (en sortie d'imprimante)** = form handling equipment; **équipement de vérification automatique (EVA)** = automatic test equipment (ATE) (b) installation(s) *ou* facilities

◇ **équiper** *vtr* to equip

équivalence *nf* (a) *(fonction logique)* equivalence; **fonction** *ou* **opération d'équivalence** = equivalence function *ou* operation; **fonction non équivalence** = non-equivalence function (NEQ) *ou* symmetric difference; **porte** *ou* **circuit d'équivalence** = equivalence gate (b) **table d'équivalence** = look-up table (LUT) *ou* conversion table *ou* translation table *ou* substitution table; **les tables**

d'**équivalence sont préprogrammées et permettent de gagner du temps de traitement en évitant de recalculer les mêmes valeurs** = lookup tables are preprogrammed then used in processing so saving calculations for each result required; **on peut établir des tables d'équivalence qui serviront à convertir les données clients aux codes utilisés par notre système** = conversion tables may be created and used in conjunction with the customer's data to convert it to our system codes

◊ **équivalent, -e** *adj* equivalent; **être équivalent (à)** = to be equivalent to *ou* to amount to

◊ **équivaloir (à)** to be equivalent to *ou* to amount to; **le nombre de caractères saisis jusqu'ici équivaut à une journée de temps d'impression** = the total number of characters keyboarded so far is equivalent to one day's printing time

équivoque *adj* ambiguous

ergonome *nm&f* ergonomist
◊ **ergonomie** *nf* ergonomics
◊ **ergonomiste** *nm&f* ergonomist

erratum *nm* erratum

erreur *nf* error *ou* fault *ou* inaccuracy; **on trouve des tas d'erreurs dans la bibliographie** = the bibliography is full of inaccuracies; **il me faut tout recommencer; je viens d'effacer le seul fichier qui ne contenait aucune erreur** = I'll have to start again - I just erased the only clean file; **nous estimons qu'il y a une erreur fondamentale dans la conception du produit** = we think there is a basic fault in the product design; **par erreur** = by error; **application qui tolère toutes les erreurs possibles** = hazard-free implementation; **erreur d'ambiguïté** = ambiguity error *ou* error ambiguity; **erreur anormale** = abnormal error; **erreur d'arrondi** = approximation error; **erreur de balayage** = scanning error; **un pli ou une déchirure dans une page peut être la cause d'une erreur de balayage** = a wrinkled or torn page may be the cause of scanning errors; **erreur de calcul** = computational error; **erreur certaine** = solid error; **erreur de code** = false code; **erreur de compilation** = compilation error; **les erreurs de compilation provoquent l'interruption inopinée de la**

tâche = compilation errors result in the job being aborted; **erreur consciente** = conscious error; **erreur qui peut être corrigée** *ou* **redressée** = recoverable error; **erreur au démarrage** = cold fault; **erreur au départ** = initial error; **erreur détectée** = detected error; **erreur de données** = data error; **erreur équilibrée** = balanced error; **erreur à l'exécution** = run-time error *ou* execution error; **erreur fatale** = fatal error *ou* catastrophic error; **erreur générée (par des arrondis)** = generated error; **erreur héritée** = inherited error; **erreur d'horloge** = hazard; **erreur imputable à un composant défectueux** = component error; **erreur inexplicable** = gremlin; **erreur intermittente** = intermittent error; **erreur irrécupérable** *ou* **impossible à corriger** = unrecoverable error; **erreur de logiciel** = soft error; **erreur logique** = logical error; **erreur momentanée** = transient error; **erreur monstre** = howler; **erreur non détectée** = undetected error; **erreur notifiée** = detected error; **erreur de numérisation** = quantization error; **erreur due à l'ordinateur** = computer error; **erreur passagère** = transient error; **erreur permanente** = permanent error; **erreur persistante** = hard error; **la tête de lecture fait une erreur de piste** = the read head is not tracking the recorded track correctly; **les techniciens essayent de corriger une erreur de programmation** = the technical staff are trying to correct a programming fault; **erreur qui se propage** = propagating error; **erreur propagée** = propagated error; **erreur de quantification** = quantization error; **erreur de rejet** = rejection error; **erreur relative** = relative error; **erreur sporadique** = sporadic fault; **erreur de substitution** = substitution error; **faire une erreur de synchronisation (en transmettant trop vite)** = to overrun; **il a fait une erreur de total** = he made an error in calculating the total; **erreur de trame** = frame error; **erreur transmise** = inherited error; **erreur de transmission** = transmission error; **erreur à valeur moyenne nulle** = balanced error; **code d'erreur** *ou* **code indicateur d'erreur** = error code; **condition d'erreur** = error condition; **contrôle d'erreurs** = error control; **correction d'erreurs** = error correction *ou* data cleaning; **correction automatique d'erreurs** = automatic error correction; **code de correction d'erreurs** *ou* **code correcteur d'erreurs** = error correcting code; **code de vérification et**

correction d'erreurs = error checking and correcting code (ECCC); **correction d'erreurs en cours de transmission** = forward error correction; **correction d'erreurs par retransmission** = backward error correction; **détection d'erreurs** = error detection; **détection et correction d'erreurs** = error detection and correction (EDAC); **détection** *ou* **recherche** *ou* **prévention d'erreurs** = automatic error detection *ou* error trapping; **code de détection d'erreurs** *ou* **code détecteur d'erreurs** = error detecting code *ou* self-checking code; **diagnostic d'erreurs** = error diagnosis; **diagnostic d'erreurs de compilation** = compiler diagnostics; **outils de diagnostic d'erreurs** = error diagnostics; **enregistrement automatique des erreurs** = error logging; **ce programme permet l'enregistrement des erreurs** = features of the program include error logging; **fausse erreur** = false error; **(signal d') interruption sur erreur** = error interrupt; **marge d'erreur** = margin of error; **message d'erreur** = error message; **message de diagnostic d'erreurs** = diagnostic (error) message; **propagation d'erreurs** = error propagation; **rafale d'erreurs** *ou* **série d'erreurs consécutives** = error burst; **reprise après erreur (sans repartir à zéro) d'erreur** = error recovery; **routine (de traitement) d'erreur** = error routine; **sans erreur** = accurate; **texte sans erreur** = clean copy *ou* clean text; **taux d'erreur** = error rate; **le taux d'erreur est inférieur à 1%** = the error rate is less than 1%; **taux d'erreur par bloc** = block error rate; **procédure de traitement des erreurs** *ou* **gestion des erreurs** = error handling *ou* management

erroné, -ée *adj* incorrect *ou* false; *(corrompu)* corrupt; **code erroné** = false code; **résultat erroné (d'une recherche)** = false drop *ou* retrieval

E/S = ENTREE/SORTIE

ESC = ECHAPPEMENT; **code ESC** = escape *ou* ESC code; **touche ESC** = escape key *ou* ESC key

escalade *nf (dans un système expert)* hill climbing

esclave *nm* slave; **(puits** *ou* **collecteur de données) esclave d'un bus** = bus slave

ESDI = ENHANCED SMALL DEVICE INTERFACE; **interface ESDI** = ESDI

espace *nm* **(a)** *(blanc)* space *ou* spacing *ou* blank; **il y a quelques lignes où les espaces sont très inégaux** = the spacing on some lines is very uneven; **caractère d'espace** = blank character *ou* space character; **chaîne contenant des caractères d'espace** = blank string; **gestionnaire d'espaces** = spacer; *(imprimerie)* **insertion d'espaces** = quadding **(b)** *(étendue)* space *ou* area; **espace adresse** = address space; **espace d'affichage** = display space; **espace de manoeuvre** *ou* **de travail** = workspace *ou* work area; **espace mémoire de l'image** = image storage space **(c)** *(distance)* gap; **espace entre deux enregistrements** = record gap; **espace interbloc** = interblock gap (IBG); *(séparant deux fichiers)* **espace neutre** = file gap **(d)** **l'espace** = space *ou* free space media; **perte dans l'espace** = free space loss **(e)** *(forme de signal)* **marque espace** = mark space

◊ **espacement** *nm (d'imprimante)* space *ou* spacing; *(de film)* film advance; **espacement (proportionnel) de caractères** = intercharacter spacing; **espacement entre les mots** = interword spacing; **espacement proportionnel** = proportional spacing; **espacement uniforme** = monospacing; *(d'un clavier)* **barre d'espacement** = space bar; **caractère d'espacement** = space character

◊ **espacé, -ée** *adj* spaced; **caractères graphiques espacés** = separated graphics; **les caractères régulièrement espacés s'alignaient sur la page** = the line of characters was evenly spaced out across the page

◊ **espacer** to space out

esperluette (&) *nf* ampersand

espion *nm* spy; **micro espion** = bug; **surveiller par micro espion** *ou* **installer des micros espions** = to bug

esprit *nm (symbole mobile d'infographie)* sprite

esquisse *nf* outline *ou* sketch *ou* design; **faire une esquisse** = to sketch *ou* to outline

◊ **esquisser** *vtr* to sketch *ou* to outline *ou* to draft *ou* to block in; **il a esquissé un projet de programme sur une feuille de papier =** he drafted out the details of the program on a piece of paper

essai *nm* test *ou* trial; *(d'un programme)* test run; **un essai fera tout de suite apparaître les erreurs =** a test run will soon show up any errors; **essai à blanc** *ou* **contrôle avec un jeu d'essais =** desk check *ou* dry run; **essai comparatif =** benchmark; **essai opérationnel =** operation trial; **à l'essai =** on approval; **banc d'essai =** benchmark *ou* test bed; **les bancs d'essais consistent à évaluer la performance de plusieurs systèmes ou périphériques en utilisant le même test standard =** in benchmarking, the performances of several systems or devices are tested against a standard benchmark; **faire un essai =** to test *ou* to pilot; **ils font l'essai du nouveau système =** they are piloting the new system; **ingénieur d'essai =** trials engineer

essentiel, -elle *adj* main *ou* essential *ou* prime; **caractéristique essentielle =** prime attribute

esthétique *nf* **esthétique industrielle =** industrial design

estimation *nf* approximation *ou* estimate
◊ **estimé, -ée** *adj* estimated *ou* calculated *ou* rated; **rendement estimé =** rated throughput
◊ **estimer** *vtr* to estimate *ou* to calculate; **j'estime que nous avons du stock pour six mois encore =** I calculate that we have six months' stock left

estomper *vtr (une silhouette)* to deaden

ET (a) AND; **circuit ET** *ou* **porte ET =** AND gate *ou* coincidence gate *ou* circuit; **opération ET =** coincidence operation **(b) et commercial (&) =** ampersand

établi, -e *adj* established; **travailler suivant des normes établies =** to work to standard specifications; **établi d'avance =** predetermined *ou* predesigned
◊ **établir** *vtr* to establish; **demande de communication qui ne peut être établie =**
lost call; **établir un fichier d'adresses =** to build up a mailing list; **établir d'avance =** to preset *ou* to predetermine *ou* to predesign

étalonnage *nm* **(a)** standardization *ou* calibration **(b)** étalonnage des performances = benchmarking; **test** *ou* **problème d'étalonnage =** benchmark problem

étanche *adj* watertight; *(par remplissage)* **câble étanche =** filled cable

étape *nf* stage *ou* step; **étape de programmation =** program step; **étape d'un travail =** job step; **effectué par étapes =** staged; **le processus compte cinq étapes =** there are five stages in the process

état *nm* **(a)** *(d'un ordinateur ou périphérique)* state *ou* status; **état d'attente** *ou* **de latence =** wait condition *ou* state; **état désactivé =** disarmed state; **remise à l'état initial commandée par l'émetteur =** forward clearing; **état logique =** logic state; **état logique bas =** logical low; **état logique haut =** logical high; **analyseur d'état logique =** logic state analyzer; **(appareil) en (bon) état de marche =** in working order; **état prêt =** ready state; **état stable =** stable state; **état stationnaire =** steady state; *(d'un périphérique)* **appel de contrôle d'état =** status poll; **bit d'état** *ou* **bit indicateur d'état** *ou* **marqueur d'état =** status bit *ou* device flag; **circuit logique à trois états =** three state logic; **indicateur d'état =** status word; **cette routine vérifie l'indicateur d'état et ne transmet pas le signal si le bit occupé est présent =** this routine checks the device status word and will not transmit data if the busy bit is set; **ligne d'état =** information line *ou* status line; **mot d'état** *ou* **mot indicateur d'état =** status word *ou* device status word (DSW); **mot d'état d'entrée/sortie =** input/output status word; **mot d'état d'un processeur =** processor status word (PSW); **registre d'état =** status register; **registre des mots d'état =** program status word register (PSW register) **(b)** report; **générateur d'état =** report generator

éteindre *vtr* **(a)** to shut down *ou* to switch off *ou* to turn off; **il faut éteindre l'appareil avant de déconnecter le**

moniteur = turn off the power before unplugging the monitor; **éteindre l'ordinateur ou lui donner un coup quand la tête de lecture est en marche peut causer des ennuis =** you can cause trouble by turning off or jarring the PC while the disk read head is moving **(b)** *(s'affaiblir)* to decay *ou* to fade; **le signal s'est éteint rapidement =** the signal decayed rapidly

étendre *vtr* to extend

◊ **s'étendre** *vpr* **(a)** s'étendre (de ... à) = to range (from ... to); **la gamme des radiofréquences s'étend de seulement quelques hertz à des centaines de gigahertz =** the radio frequency range extends from a few hertz to hundreds of gigahertz **(b)** to propagate

étendu, -e *adj* extended; **élément arithmétique étendu =** extended arithmetic element; **métalangage BNF étendu** *ou* **BNF étendu =** extended Backus-Naur Form *ou* extended BNF (EBNF); **réseau étendu =** wide area network (WAN); **réseau très étendu =** long haul network

◊ **étendue** *nf* (i) extent; (ii) range

étincelle *nf* spark; **imprimante thermique à étincelle =** spark printer

étiquetage *nm* labelling

◊ **étiqueter** *vtr* to label

◊ **étiquette** *nf* **(a)** *(informatique)* label *ou* quasi-instruction; **étiquette en-tête de bande =** tape label; **étiquette d'un champ =** field label; **étiquette de fichier =** file label; **chaque fichier est identifié rapidement par son étiquette de trois lettres =** each file has a three letter tag for rapid identification; **on peut allouer une étiquette aux touches de fonction =** tags can be allocated to function keys; **enregistrement d'étiquettes =** label record; **production d'étiquettes (pour un programme) =** labelling (of a program); **produire une étiquette (pour un programme) =** to label (a program) **(b)** *(d'un produit)* label *ou* tag; **étiquette externe** *ou* **extérieure** *ou* **apposée à l'extérieur =** external label; **étiquette Kimball =** Kimball tag; **étiquette interne =** inlay card; **étiquette perforée =** punched tag

étoile *nf* star; **réseau en étoile =** star network; **réseau commuté en étoile =** switched star

étouffer *vtr (un son ou bruit)* to deaden

étranger, -ère *n&adj* alien *ou* foreign

étroit, -e *adj* narrow; **bande étroite =** narrow band; **modulation de fréquence à bande étroite =** narrow band FM (NBFM); *(d'un affichage)* **fenêtre étroite =** thin window

étude *nf* **(a)** study **(b)** design; **il a fait l'étude de la nouvelle usine de composants =** he designed a new chip factory; **bureau d'études =** design department

ETX = END OF TEXT *voir* FIN

Euronet *(réseau téléphonique)* Euronet

européen, -enne *adj* European; **numérotation européenne des articles (NEA) =** European Article Number (EAN)

EVA = EQUIPEMENT DE VERIFICATION AUTOMATIQUE

évacuateur *nm* **évacuateur de chaleur =** heat sink

évaluation *nf* evaluation *ou* measurement; **technique d'évaluation et de révision de programme =** program evaluation and review technique (PERT); **évaluation comparative des performances =** benchmarking; **test d'évaluation de performances =** benchmark; **la revue a publié les résultats du test d'évaluation des performances du nouveau programme =** the magazine gave the new program's benchmark test results

◊ **évaluer** *vtr* to evaluate *ou* to rate; **les bancs d'essais consistent à évaluer la performance de plusieurs systèmes ou périphériques en utilisant le même test standard =** in benchmarking, the performances of several systems or devices are tested against a standard benchmark

s'évanouir *vpr (signal)* to fade

◊ **évanouissement** *nm (du signal)* fading; **évanouissement (du signal) dû au brouillage** = interference fading

événement *nm* event; **activé** *ou* **actionné par événement** = event-driven

éventail *nm* fan; **antenne (en) éventail** = fan antenna

évidence *nf* evidence; **mettre en évidence** = to highlight; **mots** *ou* **caractères (mis) en évidence** = highlights; **mots** *ou* **caractères mis en évidence (par affichage plus lumineux ou couleur contrastée)** = display highlights

évolué, -ée *adj* sophisticated *ou* advanced; **langage de programmation évolué** = high-level programming language (HLL); **un programme de PAO évolué** = a sophisticated desktop publishing program; **langage peu évolué** = low-level language (LLL)

◊ **évoluer** *vi* to move *ou* to develop; **qui n'évolue pas** = static

exact, -e *adj* correct *ou* precise *ou* accurate

◊ **exactitude** *nf* accuracy *ou* precision

examen *nm* checking *ou* scanning

◊ **examiner** *vtr* **(a)** *(attentivement)* to examine *ou* to scan **(b)** *(vérifier)* to check

excellent, -e *adj* excellent *ou* fine; **ce programme est excellent pour le tri des fichiers** = the program is highly efficient at sorting files

excepté 1 *prep* except **2** *adj* excepted

◊ **exception** *nf* exception; **liste** *ou* **répertoire d'exceptions** = exception dictionary; **rapport d'exceptions** = exception report; **à l'exception de** = excluding

excès *nm* excess; *(de données dans une mémoire tampon)* spillage

◊ **excessif, -ive** *adj* excessive; **ce programme a utilisé une quantité excessive de mémoire pour exécuter la tâche en question** = the program used an excessive amount of memory to accomplish the job

excitation *nf (électrique)* impulse

exclamation *nf* exclamation; **point d'exclamation (!)** = exclamation mark

exclure *vtr* to exclude

exclusif, -ive *adj* exclusive; **(fonction) NI exclusif** = exclusive NOR (EXNOR); **porte** *ou* **circuit NI exclusif** = exclusive NOR gate *ou* EXNOR gate; **(fonction) OU exclusif** = exclusive OR (EXOR) *ou* non-equivalence function *ou* NEQ function; **porte** *ou* **circuit OU exclusif** = exclusive OR gate *ou* EXOR gate

◊ **exclusion** *nf* exclusion; **exclusion réciproque** = inequivalence *ou* symmetric difference *ou* addition without carry

exécuter *vtr* to execute *ou* to implement; *(un programme)* to run *ou* to execute (a program); **une fois cette tâche exécutée, ce sera le tour de la suivante dans la file d'attente** = when this task is complete, the next in the queue is processed; **on peut exécuter le programme sur un ordinateur indépendant ou un système multiposte** = the program runs on a standalone machine or a multi-user system; **exécuter des commandes (à la mise sous tension)** = to boot; *(programme)* **prêt à être exécuté** = executable form; **tâche qui peut être exécutée automatiquement** = unattended operation

◊ **exécutif, -ive** *adj* **terminal exécutif** = executive terminal

◊ **exécution** *nf* execution *ou* run; **(instruction de) compilation et exécution** = compile and go; **exécution d'un programme** = computer run *ou* machine run *ou* production run *ou* program execution *ou* program run; **exécution d'un programme en temps réel** = real time execution; **exécution de commandes (à la mise sous tension)** = boot up *ou* booting; **exécution d'un programme d'édition (pour contrôle)** = editing run; **adresse d'exécution** = execution address; **(opérations de) contrôle et exécution d'interruption** = interrupt servicing; **contrôle d'exécution des tâches** = job statement control; **cycle d'exécution** =

execute cycle *ou* execution cycle; **cycle de lecture/exécution** *ou* **cycle d'exécution (d'une instruction)** = fetch-execute cycle *ou* execute cycle; **déclaration** *ou* **message d'exécution** = execute statement; **durée** *ou* **temps d'exécution (d'un programme)** = execute time *ou* run-time *ou* run-duration; **erreur à l'exécution** = run-time error *ou* execution error; **mode d'exécution** = execute mode; **ordinateur d'exécution** = target computer *ou* object computer; **phase d'exécution** = execute phase *ou* run phase *ou* target phase; **routines de clôture (d'exécution)** = end of run routines; **signal d'exécution** = execute signal; **temps d'exécution** = *(d'une instruction)* instruction execution time *ou* instruction time; *(d'une opération)* operation time; *(d'un programme)* execution time *ou* run-time *ou* run-duration; *US* turnaround time (TAT); *(d'une tâche)* operating time *ou* elapsed time

exemplaire *nm* **(a)** *(d'un journal ou revue)* copy; **je l'ai lu dans l'exemplaire de 'Science et Vie' que nous avons au bureau** = I read it in the office copy of 'Science et Vie' **(b) en double exemplaire** *ou* **en deux exemplaires** = in duplicate; **établir une facture en deux exemplaires** = to print an invoice in duplicate; **reçu en double exemplaire** = receipt in duplicate; **en quatre exemplaires** = in quadruplicate; **les relevés sont imprimés en quatre exemplaires** = the statements are printed in quadruplicate

exemple *nm* example; **requête (définie) par l'exemple** = query by example (QBE)

exhaustif, -ive *adj* exhaustive *ou* global; **connaissance exhaustive** = global knowledge; **recherche exhaustive** = exhaustive search; **procédure de recherche et remplacement exhaustive** = global search and replace

exigence(s) *nf(pl)* requirement(s)

◊ **exiger** *vtr* to demand *ou* to require

expansion *nf* expansion

expérience *nf* experience *ou* background; **il a une bonne expérience de**

l'industrie informatique = his background is in the computer industry

expert *nm* expert *ou* specialist *ou* consultant; **expert en électronique** = an electronics specialist; **ils ont fait venir un expert en informatique pour les conseiller sur la conception du système** = they called in a computer consultant to advise them on the system design

◊ **expert, -e** *adj* être expert (en *ou* dans) = to specialize (in); **c'est un expert en DAO** = he specializes in the design of CAD systems **(b) système expert** = expert system *ou* knowledge-based system *ou* intelligent knowledge-based system (IKBS); **formation assistée par système expert** = intelligent tutoring system

les systèmes experts sont les premiers produits de l'intelligence artificielle
L'Ordinateur Individuel

expiration *nf* expiration; **date d'expiration (d'un délai)** = expiration date

◊ **expirer** *vi* to expire

explication *nf* explanation *ou* comment

explicite *adj* explicit; **adresse explicite** = explicit address

expliquer *vtr* to explain; *(le fonctionnement de quelque chose)* to demonstrate

exploitable *adj* exploitable par l'ordinateur = machine-readable; **le disque garde en mémoire des données sous une forme exploitable par l'ordinateur** = the disk stores data in machine-readable form; **(commandes** *ou* **données) directement exploitables** = machine-readable (instructions *ou* data)

◊ **exploitation** *nf* operation *ou* running *ou* working; **exploitation en parallèle** *ou* **en double** = parallel running; **logiciel d'exploitation** = systems software; **système d'exploitation** = operating system *ou* op sys (OS); **système d'exploitation de disque** *ou* **système d'exploitation DOS** = disk operating system (DOS); **système d'exploitation CP** = control program/monitor *ou* control program for microcomputers

(CP/M); **le système d'exploitation des entrées/sorties** = basic input/output operating system (BIOS)

exploration *nf (par balayage)* scanning; **faisceau d'exploration** = scanning spot beam

exposant *nm* exponent *ou* characteristic; *(dans un système à virgule flottante)* biased exponent; **exposant binaire** = binary exponent; **chiffre en exposant** = superior number *ou* superscript

exposé *nm* statement; **exposé d'un problème** = problem definition

exposer *vtr (photo)* to expose
◊ **exposition** *nf (photo)* exposure; **double exposition** = double exposure

expression *nf* **(a)** expression *ou* representation; **expression binaire d'un caractère** = character representation; **expression logique** = logical expression **(b) liberté d'expression** = freedom of speech
◊ **exprimer** *vtr* to express

extensible *adj* extensible *ou* expandable; **le processeur unique possède une mémoire de 2Mo extensible jusqu'à 4Mo** = the single processor with 2Mbytes of memory can be upgraded to 4Mbytes; **langage extensible** = extensible language; **programme extensible** = open-ended program; **système extensible** = expandable system
◊ **extension** *nf* **(a)** extension *ou* expansion; **les trois modèles offrent des possibilités d'extension sur site** = all three models have an on-site upgrade facility; *(circuit)* **extension enfichable** = plug-in unit; **extension du nom du fichier** = filename extension; **l'extension SYS ajoutée au nom du fichier indique qu'il s'agit d'un fichier système** = the filename extension SYS indicates that this is a system file; **pour conserver une telle quantité de données, il vous faudra une extension de votre disque** = if you want to hold so much data, you will have to expand the disk capacity; **extension de mémoire** = extension memory; *(pour lentille photographique)* **bague d'extension** *ou* **macro** = extension tube;

câble d'extension = extension cable; **kit d'extension de micro-ordinateur** = microcomputer development kit **(b)** **carte d'extension** = expansion card *ou* expansion board *ou* add-in card *ou* add-on board; **cette nouvelle carte d'extension permet l'affichage graphique en couleur** = the new add-on board allows colour graphics to be displayed; **pourriez-vous expliquer comment fonctionne le système de carte d'extension?** = can you explain the add-in card method?; **le traitement s'effectue beaucoup plus rapidement avec les cartes d'extension** = processing is much faster with add-in cards; **carte d'extension multifonction** = multifunction card; **créneau** *ou* **connecteur pour carte d'extension** = expansion slot; **support de carte d'extension** = card extender; **unité d'extension d'une ligne** = line extender

extérieur *nm* **(a) (prise de vue) en extérieur** = on location (filming); **les extérieurs (d'un film)** = location shots; **les extérieurs pour ce programme ont été tournés en Espagne** = the programme was shot on location in Spain **(b) qui vient de l'extérieur** = incoming
◊ **extérieur, -e** *adj* external; **étiquette extérieure** = external label; **horloge extérieure** = external clock

externe *adj* external; **défaillance ayant une cause externe** = induced failure; **dispositif externe** = external device; **fichier de données externe** = external data file; **horloge externe** = external clock; **lecteur de disquettes externe** = external disk drive; **mémoire externe** = external memory *ou* external storage *ou* external store; **registre externe** = external register; **signal d'appel externe** = external interrupt; **tri sur support externe** = external sort

extinction *nf* extinction *ou* decay; **temps d'extinction d'un signal** = decay time

extra-terrestre *adj* extra-terrestrial; **bruit extra-terrestre** = extra-terrestrial noise

extracode *nm (routine)* extracode

extracteur *nm (masque)* extractor

◊ **extraction** *nf* extraction; *(de données ou de fichiers)* extraction *ou* retrieval; **extraction de bloc =** block retrieval; **extraction de données =** data retrieval *ou* information retrieval (IR); **instruction d'extraction =** extract instruction

extraire *vtr* to extract; *(données ou fichiers)* to retrieve *ou* to read *ou* to extract; *(une donnée d'une pile)* to pull; **extraire des données rangées en mémoire =** to obtain data from a storage device; **il est impossible d'extraire les fichiers depuis la panne =** the files are irretrievable since the computer crashed; **nous pouvons extraire les dossiers qui doivent aller à la composition =** we can extract the files required for typesetting; **on utilise cette commande pour extraire la liste de tous les noms qui commencent par S =** this command will retrieve all names beginning with S

◊ **extrait** *nm* **(a)** *(d'un article)* abstract; **extrait critique =** evaluative abstract **(b)** **extrait de film =** clip

◊ **extrait, -e** *adj* retrieved; **qui peut être extrait =** retrievable; **qui ne peut être extrait =** irretrievable

extrapolation *nf* *(déduction)* extrapolation

extrémité *nf* end; **file d'attente à deux extrémités =** double-ended queue *ou* deque

Ff

F *(représentation hexadécimale du nombre 15)* F

F *abbrév* = FARAD

f *abbrév* = FEMTO

F *(ionosphère)* **région F** = F-region

fabricant *nm* manufacturer; **le fabricant garantit le système pendant un an** = the manufacturer guarantees the system for 12 months; **en cas de mauvais fonctionnement, renvoyer le système au fabricant** = if the system develops a fault it should be returned to the manufacturer
◊ **fabrication** *nf* construction *ou* production; **chacune des pièces de l'ordinateur possède un numéro de fabrication** = each piece of hardware has a production number; **le numéro de fabrication est gravé définitivement sur le panneau arrière du boîtier de l'ordinateur** = the production number is permanently engraved on the back of the computer casing; **les techniques de fabrication ont évolué au cours des dernières années** = construction techniques have changed over the past few years; **fabrication assistée par ordinateur (FAO)** = computer-aided *ou* assisted manufacture (CAM); *voir aussi* CFAO

fabriquer *vtr* to construct *ou* to manufacture; **cette société fabrique des disquettes et des bandes magnétiques** = the company manufactures diskettes and magnetic tape; **fabriquer sur commande** = to customize

face *nf (d'un appareil)* front; *(d'un disque)* side; **disquette simple face (SSD)** = single-sided disk (SSD); **disquette (à) double face** = double-sided disk; **lecteur de disquettes (à) double face** = double-sided disk drive; **papier photosensible double face** = duplex; **plaque présensibilisée double face pour circuit imprimé** = double-sided printed circuit board

facette *nf* facet; **code à facettes** = faceted code

facile *adj* easy; **rendre quelque chose plus facile** = to make something easy *ou* to simplify something; **facile à utiliser** *ou* **d'utilisation facile** = user-friendly *ou* easy-to-use; **c'est un appareil extrêmement facile à utiliser** = it's a very user-friendly machine; **les données devraient être réparties en fichiers plus faciles à utiliser** = data should be split into more manageable files
◊ **facilité** *nf* capacity *ou* capability; **facilité de traitement électronique de données** = electronic data processing capability

façon *nf* **imprimerie à façon** = print shop; **imprimeur à façon** = jobbing printer

fac-similé *nm* fax *ou* facsimile (copy); **générateur de caractères fac-similés** = facsimile character generator; **transmission de fac-similé** = fax transmission; *(anciennement)* phototelegraphy; *voir aussi* FAX, TELECOPIE

facteur *nm* **(a)** factor; **facteur de bloc** = blocking factor; **facteur de charge** = load; **facteur décisif** = deciding factor; *(d'une adresse relative)* **facteur de déplacement** = float factor; **facteur d'élimination** = elimination factor; *(de lumière)* **facteur de filtre** = filter factor; **facteur d'omission** *ou* **de silence** = omission factor; *(de circuit)* **facteur pyramidal d'entrée** = fan-in; **facteur pyramidal de sortie** = fan-out **(b)** *(math)* factor; **mettre en facteur** = to factorize;

la mise en facteur de 15 nous donne les facteurs suivants: **1, 15 ou 3, 5** = when factorized, 15 gives the factors 1, 15 or 3, 5

un faisceau lumineux de longueur d'onde inférieure à 950nm ne sera détecté que par la photodiode supérieure et sera entièrement absorbé par celle-ci
Opto électronique

factice *adj* false; **instruction factice** = no-operation instruction *ou* no-op instruction *ou* non-operable instruction *ou* null instruction; **variable factice** = dummy variable

factorielle *nf* factorial; **la factorielle de 4 (qui s'écrit 4!) est 1x2x3x4 ou 24** = 4 factorial (written 4!) is 1x2x3x4 or 24

◊ **factoriser** *vtr* to factorize

faible *adj* weak *ou* low; **communication à faible débit** = low speed communications; **graphique de faible définition** = low-resolution graphics *ou* low-res graphics; **bit de poids faible** = least significant bit (LSB); **chiffre de poids faible** = least significant digit (LSD) *ou* low-order digit; *(état logique)* **tension faible** = logical low

◊ **faiblir** *vi (signal)* to fade *ou* to decay

faire *vtr* **(a)** *(agir)* to do (something); **ne pas faire quelque chose** = to fail to do something; **homme à tout faire** = general assistant; *(dans un studio de cinématographie)* gaffer; *US* gofer **(b)** *(produire)* to make (something); **il a fait six photos de la nouvelle machine** = he took six photographs of the new machine

faisceau *nm* **(a)** *(rayon)* beam; **faisceau de balayage** = scanning spot beam; **faisceau électronique** *ou* **d'électrons** = electron beam; **enregistrement par faisceau électronique (sur microfilm)** = electron beam recording (EBR); **faisceau étroit** = spot beam; **faisceau d'exploration** = scanning spot beam; **faisceau d'image** = picture beam; **faisceau lumineux** = light beam; **balayage par faisceau mobile** = flying spot scan; **dédoublement de faisceau** = beam diversity; **largeur d'un faisceau** = beam width **(b)** *(groupement de fibres optiques)* bundle; **faisceau cohérent** = coherent bundle **(c)** *(de connexions)* **faisceau de jonction** = trunk

famille *nf* family *ou* group

fana *nm (familier)* **fana d'informatique** = terminal junky (TJ)

faner *vi (couleur ou photo)* to fade

fantôme *nm* ghost *ou* phantom; *(télévision)* **image fantôme** = ghost (image); **mémoire fantôme** = shadow memory *ou* shadow page; **(mémoire) ROM fantôme** = phantom ROM

FAO (a) fabrication assistée par ordinateur (FAO) = computer-aided *ou* assisted manufacture (CAM); **système adapté aux langages FAO** = authoring system **(b)** formation assistée par ordinateur (FAO) = computer-aided *ou* assisted learning (CAL); **langage de programmation FAO** = author language

farad (F) *nm* farad (F)

Faraday *n* **cage de Faraday** = Faraday cage

fatal, -e *adj* fatal *ou* terminal; **erreur fatale** = fatal error *ou* catastrophic error; **panne fatale** = catastrophic failure

fatigue *nf* tiredness; **fatigue oculaire** = eye-strain

faute *nf* **(a)** *(erreur)* error; **faute de frappe** = typing error; **elle doit avoir fait une faute de frappe** = she must have made a typing error; **faute de syntaxe** = grammatical error *ou* syntax error **(b)** *(défaut)* defect *ou* fault

faux, fausse *adj* false; **fausse erreur** = false error

◊ **faux-titre** *nm* half title

fax *nm* **(a)** *(message)* fax *ou* facsimile transmission **(b)** *(machine)* fax (machine); **notre fax est tout à côté du standard téléphonique** = the fax machine

is next to the telephone switchboard; **envoyer quelque chose par fax =** to fax something
◊ **faxer** *vtr* to fax; **j'ai faxé les documents à notre bureau de New York =** I've faxed the documents to our New York office; *voir aussi* TELECOPIE

fdx = FULL DUPLEX *voir* DUPLEX

feedback *nm* feedback; **feedback acoustique =** acoustical feedback; **feedback positif =** positive feedback; **boucle de feedback =** feedback loop

femelle *adj* female; **connecteur femelle =** female connector; **prise femelle =** female socket

femto- (f) *préf* femto- (f)
◊ **femtoseconde** *nf* femtosecond

fenêtrage *nm (d'écran)* windowing

fenêtre *nf* **(a)** window; **le système d'exploitation permet d'afficher d'autres programmes simultanément, chacun dans une fenêtre différente =** the operating system will allow other programs to be displayed on-screen at the same time in different windows; **plusieurs stations de travail distantes sont connectées au réseau, chacune disposant d'une fenêtre sur le disque dur =** several remote stations are connected to the network and each has its own window onto the hard disk; **fenêtre active =** active window; **fenêtre bloc-notes =** screen notepad; **fenêtre de commande =** command window; **la fenêtre de commande est une simple ligne en bas de l'écran =** the command window is a single line at the bottom of the screen; **l'utilisateur peut définir la taille de la fenêtre de commande =** the user can define the size of the command window; **fenêtre de dialogue =** dialogue box; **fenêtre d'édition =** edit window; **fenêtre étroite** *ou* **fenêtre d'une ligne =** strip window *ou* thin window; **fenêtre de texte =** text window; **fenêtre de transmission =** transmission window **(b) enveloppe à fenêtre =** window envelope
◊ **fenêtrer** *vi (écran)* to window

fente *nf* slot *ou* aperture; **insérer dans une fente =** to slot in(to); **la disquette s'insère dans l'une des deux fentes du lecteur de disquettes =** the disk slots into one of the floppy drive apertures; **insérer la disquette dans la fente gauche du panneau avant de l'ordinateur =** insert the disk into the left-hand slot on the front of the computer

fer *nm* **(a)** iron; **oxyde de fer =** ferric oxide **(b) au fer à droite =** flush right; **au fer à gauche =** flush left

fermé, -ée *adj* closed; **boucle fermée =** closed loop; **enveloppe fermée =** sealed envelope; **groupe fermé d'utilisateurs =** closed user group (CUG); **sous-programme fermé =** closed *ou* linked subroutine; **télévision en circuit fermé =** closed circuit television (CCTV)
◊ **fermer** *vtr* to close *ou* to shut down; **fermer hermétiquement =** to seal; **fermer un fichier =** to close a file; **fermer une session =** to log off *ou* log out
◊ **fermeture** *nf* **(opération de) fermeture de fichier =** close file

ferrique *adj* **oxyde ferrique =** ferric oxide
◊ **ferrite** *nf* ferrite; **noyau de ferrite =** ferrite core
◊ **ferromagnétique** *adj* ferromagnetic; **matériau ferromagnétique =** ferromagnetic material

feuille *nf* sheet (of paper); *(imprimerie)* leaf; **placé entre deux feuilles =** interleaved; **on avait placé des feuilles blanches entre les pages nouvellement imprimées pour éviter les coulures d'encre =** blank paper was interleaved with the newly printed text to prevent the ink running; **alimentation (en) feuille à feuille =** (single) sheet feed; **bac d'alimentation feuille à feuille =** sheet feed attachment; **système d'alimentation feuille à feuille =** cut sheet feeder; **entraînement feuille à feuille =** single sheet feed; **feuille de programmation =** coding sheet *ou* coding form; **feuille de style =** style sheet *ou* image master; **la feuille de style comporte 125 symboles programmables (par l'utilisateur) =** the style sheet contains 125 user-definable symbols
◊ **feuillet** *nm* **(a)** *(d'ancien manuscrit)* folio **(b) feuillet publicitaire =** leaflet

fiabilité *nf* reliability; **cette appareil est reconnu pour sa fiabilité** = this machine has an excellent reliability record; **ce produit a réussi tous les tests de fiabilité** = the product has passed its reliability tests; **fiabilité des données** = data reliability; **fiabilité d'un logiciel** = software reliability

◊ **fiable** *adj* reliable

fibre *nm* fibre; *US* fiber; **fibre optique** = optical fibre; **technologie de la fibre optique** *ou* **de la transmission par fibre optique** = fibre optics; **fibre optique monomode** = monomode fibre; **fibre optique multimode** = multimode fibre; **câble à fibres optiques** = fibre optic cable *ou* fibre optic connection; **les câbles à fibres optiques permettent de placer les noeuds jusqu'à un kilomètre l'un de l'autre** = fibre optic connections enable nodes up to one kilometre apart to be used; **faisceau de fibres optiques** = bundle; **liaison à fibres optiques** = fibre optic cable *ou* fibre optic connection

fiche *nf* **(a)** *(carte)* filing card *ou* index card; **faire une fiche** = to place something on file; **mettre sur fiches** = to card-index; **mise sur fiches** = card-indexing **(b)** *(pour prise de courant)* plug; *(pour téléphone)* jack; **la fiche est fournie avec l'imprimante** = the printer is supplied with a plug

◊ **fichier** *nm* **(a)** *(sur cartes)* card index; **personne ne comprend sa méthode de classement du fichier** = no one can understand her card-indexing system; **carte de fichier** = index card **(b)** **fichier d'adresses (destiné aux mailings)** = mailing list; **son nom figure sur notre fichier d'adresses** = his name is on our mailing list; **établir un fichier d'adresses** = to build up a mailing list; **acheter un fichier d'adresses** = to buy a mailing list **(c)** *(informatique)* file *ou* data file; **fichier à accès séquentiel** = serial file; **fichier bidimensionnel** = flat file; **fichier en boucle** = circular file; **fichiers cachés** = hidden files; **cela permet aux utilisateurs de sauvegarder ou de restaurer un par un les fichiers cachés** = it allows users to backup or restore hidden system files independently; **fichier chaîné** = chained file; **fichier avec articles chaînés** = threaded file; **fichier chronologique** = journal file; **fichier de commandes** = batch file *ou* command file; **ce fichier de commandes est utilisé pour gagner du temps et de l'énergie lorsqu'on traite une routine** = this batch file is used to save time and effort when carrying out a routine task; **processeur de fichier de commandes** = command file processor; **fichier contigu** = contiguous file; **fichier de contrôle de tâche** = job control file; **fichier corrigé** = corrected file *ou* update (file); **fichier des coupures** *ou* **des corrections** = deletion record; **fichier sur disque** *ou* **sur disquette** = disk file; **fichier divisé en plusieurs parties** = partitioned file; **fichier de données** = data file; **il faut analyser le fichier de données** = the data file has to be analysed; **fichier de données externe** = external data file; **fichier d'enregistrement des blocs** = block list; **fichier (d') entrée/sortie** = I/O file; **fichiers dans une file d'attente** = file queue; **fichier fils** = son file; **fichier grand-père** = grandfather file; **fichier indexé** = indexed file; **fichier informatique** = computer file; **avoir accès à un fichier informatique** = to have access to a file of data; **fichier intermédiaire** = intermediate file; **fichier inversé** = inverted file; **fichier-journal** = journal file; **fichier maître** = master file; **fichier de manoeuvre** = scratch file *ou* work file; **(ensemble des) fichiers en mémoire** = file store; **fichier mis à jour** = update (file); **fichier de mise à jour** = change file *ou* transaction file *ou* addition record; **fichier de modifications** = change *ou* movement file; **fichier (de) mouvements** = detail file *ou* movement file *ou* change file *ou* transaction file *ou* update file; **fichier d'ordinateur** = computer file; **laisser le fichier ouvert** = leave file open; **système à fichiers partagés** = distributed file system; **fichier père** = father file; **le fichier père est un fichier de sauvegarde de première génération** = the father file is a first generation backup; **fichier permanent** = permanent file *ou* master file; **fichier plat** = flat file; **fichier de pointeurs** = pointer file; **fichier principal** = master file; **fichier programme** = program file; **fichier de programme maître** = master program file; **fichier de référence** = authority file *ou* authority list *ou* reference file; **fichier des registres** = register file; **système à fichiers répartis** = distributed file system; **fichier de sauvegarde** = backup *ou* backup file; **cycle de rotation des fichiers de sauvegarde** = grandfather cycle; **fichier série extensible** = extending serial file; **fichier de sortie** = output file; **fichier** source = source file; **fichier subdivisé =** partitioned file; **fichier de tâches (à exécuter) =** job file; **fichier texte =** text file; **fichier de transactions =** transaction file; **fichier de travail =** scratch file *ou* work file; **avoir accès à** *ou* **accéder à un fichier =** to gain access to a file; **annulation de fichier =** file deletion; **archivage de fichiers =** file sort; **bloc de contrôle de fichier =** file control block; **conversion de fichier =** file conversion; **création de fichier =** file creation; **(données de) début de fichier =** head (of file); **descripteur de fichier =** file descriptor *ou* file label; **destruction de fichier =** file deletion; **dimension d'un fichier =** file length; **dispositif de protection d'écriture de fichier =** file protect tab; **en-tête de fichier =** header; **étiquette de fichier =** file label; **fermer un fichier =** to close a file; **(instruction de) fermeture de fichier =** close file; **file d'attente de fichiers =** file queue; **enregistrement en fin de fichier =** trailer record; **fusion de fichiers =** file merger *ou* file collating; **(instruction de) fusion de fichier =** join *ou* merge files; **(système de) gestion de fichier =** file management (system); **programme de gestion de fichier =** records management; **gestionnaire de fichier =** file manager; **groupe de fichiers (connexes) =** file set; **identification de fichier =** file identification; **index des fichiers =** file index; **intégrité d'un fichier =** integrity of a file; **interclassement de fichiers =** file collating; **interrogation de fichier =** file interrogation; **label de fichier =** file label; **label de fin de fichier =** trailer; **longueur d'un fichier =** file length; **maintenance de fichier =** file maintenance; **mise en mémoire d'un fichier =** file storage; **mise à jour d'un fichier =** file update *ou* file maintenance; **nettoyage de fichier =** file cleanup; **nom d'un fichier =** file name *ou* filename; **extension du nom d'un fichier =** filename extension; **l'extension SYS ajoutée au nom du fichier indique qu'il s'agit d'un fichier système =** the filename extension SYS indicates that this is a system file; **longueur du nom d'un fichier =** length of filename; **spécification du nom du fichier =** filename extension; **protection de fichiers =** file security; **(logiciel** *ou* **dispositif de) protection de fichier =** file protection; **ratio d'activité d'un fichier =** file activity ratio; **logiciel de récupération de fichiers (après incident) =** file-recovery utility; **il est impossible de** retrouver un fichier perdu sans l'aide d'un logiciel de récupération de fichiers = a lost file cannot be found without a file-recovery utility; **répertoire de fichiers =** file directory; **routine de manipulation de fichier =** file handling routine; **sécurisation de fichiers =** file security; **(logiciel** *ou* **dispositif de) sécurisation de fichier =** file protection; **serveur de fichier =** file server; **stockage de fichier =** file storage; **structure d'un fichier =** file layout *ou* file structure; **système à fichiers =** distributed file system; **taille d'un fichier =** file extent; **taux d'activité d'un fichier =** file activity ratio; **traitement de fichier =** file processing; **transfert de fichier =** file transfer; **tri de fichiers =** file sort; **validation de fichier =** file validation; **version améliorée** *ou* **nouvelle version d'un fichier =** file update; **vidage de fichier =** file purge *ou* file cleanup

> pour créer un nouveau fichier, exécutez la commande 'Nouveau document'
> *L'Ordinateur Individuel*
> en apparence, rien n'est plus simple que de copier un fichier sur disquette, puis d'utiliser cette disquette sur un second ordinateur
> *Action PC*

fidélité *nf* fidelity; **haute fidélité =** high fidelity *ou* hifi *ou* hi fi *ou* hi-fi; **chaîne haute fidélité** *ou* **système haute fidélité =** high fidelity system *ou* hi fi system *ou* hifi *ou* hi-fi

se fier *vpr (appareil)* **auquel on peut se fier =** reliable (machine)

FIFO = FIFO FIRST IN FIRST OUT; **méthode FIFO =** first in first out; **mémoire FIFO =** FIFO memory *ou* first in first out memory; **pile en mode FIFO =** push-up list *ou* stack; *voir aussi* PREMIER

figer *vtr* to freeze; **figer une image =** to freeze a frame; **le processeur d'images permet de figer une image =** with an image processor you can freeze a video frame

figure *nf* figure; **voir figure 10: tableau des codes ASCII =** see figure 10 for a chart of ASCII codes

◊ **figurer** *vi* to appear (on); **son nom figure sur notre fichier d'adresses =** his name is on our mailing list

fil *nm* **(a)** *(métallique ou électrique)* wire; *(de liaison)* lead *ou* flex *ou* cord *ou* cable; **circuit à deux fils** = two wire circuit; **fil de mise à la masse** = earth wire; **fils téléphoniques** = telephone wires; **fil de terre** = earth wire; **sans fil** = wireless; **micro** *ou* **microphone sans fil** = radio microphone; **téléphone sans fil** = cordless telephone **(b) passer un coup de fil** = to make a phone call

file *nf* queue; **prendre la file** = to queue; **méthode d'accès séquentiel en file** = queued sequential access method (QSAM); **méthode d'accès séquentiel indexé en file** = queued indexed sequential access method (QISAM); **file d'attente** = queue *ou* waiting list; *(de demandes de transmission ou de données à transmettre)* = channel queue; *(des données d'entrée)* input work queue; *(de fichiers)* file queue; *(de périphériques)* device queue; *(de tâches ou de travaux à exécuter)* job queue *ou* job stream *ou* task queue; **imprimer la file d'attente** = to despool; **se joindre à la file d'attente** = to form a queue *ou* to join a queue; **placer (des données** *ou* **des tâches) dans la file d'attente** = to queue; **file d'attente à deux entrées** *ou* **à deux extrémités** = double-ended queue *ou* deque; **file d'attente qui fonctionne sur le principe 'premier entré premier sorti'** = FIFO queue; **fichiers dans une file d'attente** = file queue; **programme de gestion** *ou* **gestionnaire de file d'attente** = queue management *ou* queue manager; **ce nouveau logiciel de spouling comporte un gestionnaire de file d'attente** = this is a new software spooler with built-in queue management; **pile en file d'attente** = push-up list *ou* stack; **procédure de file d'attente** = queue discipline; **les périphériques tels que les imprimantes laser sont reliés en ligne et les fichiers sont gérés par un système de file d'attente automatique** = output devices such as laser printers are connected on-line with an automatic file queue; **temps d'attente dans la file** = queuing time

filet *nm (imprimerie)* bar *ou* line

filière *nf (d'un programme)* path

fille *nf* **carte fille** = daughter board

film *nm* **(a)** *(matériau)* film; **film lith** = lith film; **film de transfert** = carbon tissue **(b)** photographic film; **film en boucle** = loop film; **photo avec film sensible aux infrarouges** = infrared photography; **traitement de film instantané** *ou* **intégré dans l'appareil** = in camera process; **entraînement d'un film** = film advance **(c)** *(cinématographique)* film *ou* motion picture; **film fixe** = film strip; **extrait de film** = clip; **l'équipement de prise de vue et de projection de films** = film chain; **image orientée en film** = cine-orientated image; **montage d'un film** = film assembly; **repiquage vidéo d'un film** = film pickup; **tourner un film** = to film *ou* to shoot

◊ **filmer** *vtr* to shoot *ou* to film; *(imprimerie)* **filmer un texte** = to film copy; *(télévision)* **programme filmé** = canned programme

fils *nm* **fichier fils** = son file

filtrage *nm* filtering; **éliminer par filtrage** = to filter

◊ **filtre** *nm* **(a)** *(de lumière ou couleur)* filter; **filtre d'absorption** = absorption filter; **filtre d'amélioration du contraste** = contrast enhancement filter; *(pour écran d'ordinateur)* **filtre d'optimisation de caractères et de protection de la vue** = character enhancement filter; **filtre polaroïde** = polaroid filter; **facteur de filtre** = filter factor **(b)** *(de fréquence, etc.)* **filtre de bande de fréquences** = frequency equalizer; **filtre passe-bande** = bandpass filter; **filtre passe-bas** = low pass filter; **filtre passe-haut** = high pass filter; **filtre de sélection du signal maximal** *ou* **minimal** = auctioneering device **(c) filtre de microphone** = pop filter; **chaque fois que vous prononcez un 'p' vous saturez l'enregistrement, placez donc ce filtre pour que cela cesse** = every time you say a 'p' you overload the tape recorder, so put this pop filter in to stop it

◊ **filtré, -ée** *adj* **(a)** filtered **(b) signal filtré** = bandlimited signal

◊ **filtrer** *vtr* to filter; **le signal d'entrée a été filtré pour obtenir une forme optimale** = the received signal was equalized to an optimum shape

fin *nf* **(a)** end *ou* completion *ou* ending *ou* finish; *(radio ou télévision)* **fin des émissions** = close-down; **mettre fin à**

quelque chose graduellement = to phase something out; **prendre fin** = to end *ou* to finish; **à la fin** = (i) in the end *ou* finally; (ii) at the end; **à la fin de la transmission des données** = at the end of the data transmission **(b) (code de) fin d'adresse** = end of address (EOA); *(de traitement informatique)* **fin anormale** = abend *ou* abnormal end; **(code de) fin de la bande (magnétique)** = end of tape (EOT); **label de fin de bande** = tape trailer; **(marque** *ou* **code de) fin de bloc** = end of block (EOB); **(code de) fin de document** = end of document *ou* end of file (EOF); **(code de) fin de données** = end of data (EOD); **(code de) fin d'enregistrement** = end of record (EOR); **enregistrement de fin de fichier** = trailer record; **(caractère) fin de fichier** = end of file (EOF); **label de fin de fichier** = trailer; **marque** *ou* **marqueur de fin de fichier** = rogue value *ou* terminator; **fin de ligne** = line ending; **caractère** *ou* **symbole de fin de ligne** = line ending *ou* return; **dispositif de fin de ligne** = line terminator; **fin de liste** = tail; **marqueur de fin de liste chaînée** = nil pointer; **(code de) fin de message** = end of message (EOM) *ou* tail; **(code) fin de module** = chapter stop; **(caractère** *ou* **instruction de) fin de page** = page break; *(sur machine à écrire)* **signal de fin de page** = end of page indicator; **signal de fin de report** = carry complete signal; **(code de) fin de support de données** = end of medium (EM); **(code de) fin de tâche** = end of job (EOJ); **(code de) fin de texte** = end of text (EOT *ou* ETX); **(code** *ou* **signal de) fin de la transmission** = end of transmission (EOT); **sans fin** = endless; **boucle sans fin** = continuous loop *ou* infinite loop *ou* endless loop

fin, -e *adj* fine; **on trouve quelques lignes très fines dans cette gravure** = the engraving has some very fine lines

final , -e *adj* final *ou* finished; **copie finale** = clean copy; **épreuve finale** = master proof

◊ **finaliser** *vtr* to finalize; **copie finalisée** = camera-ready copy (crc)

finir 1 *vtr&i* to end *ou* to finish *ou* to complete 2 *vtr* to finish

◊ **fini** *nm* finish; **ce produit a un très beau fini** = the product has an attractive finish

◊ **fini, -e** *adj* **(a)** finished; **produit fini** = end product **(b)** finite; **nombres à précision finie** = finite-precision numbers

◊ **finition** *nf* finish; **ce produit présente une très belle finition** = the product has an attractive finish

firmware *nm (données* ou *programme intégré à l'ordinateur)* firmware

fisheye *nm (lentille)* fisheye lens

fixage *nm* = FIXATION

fixation *nf (stade de développement d'un film)* fixing

fixe *adj* **(a)** fixed; **connexion fixe** = hardwired connection; **disque (dur) fixe** = fixed disk; **unité comprenant des disques fixes et des disques amovibles** = fixed and exchangeable disk storage (FEDS) **(b) film fixe** = film strip; **image fixe** = still frame **(c) cycle fixe** = fixed cycle; **opération en cycle fixe** = fixed cycle operation; **longueur fixe** = fixed length; **enregistrement de longueur fixe** = fixed-length record; **mot de longueur fixe** = fixed-length word; **ordinateur à longueur de mots fixe** = fixed word length computer; **mémoire fixe** = control memory *ou* ROM *ou* read only memory; **code à rapport de bits fixe** = constant ratio code; **taille fixe** = fixed length; **champ de taille fixe** = constant length field *ou* fixed field; **tête de lecture fixe** = fixed head disk (drive); **virgule fixe** = fixed point; **arithmétique à virgule fixe** = fixed-point arithmetic; **notation à virgule fixe** = fixed-point notation; **la mise en mémoire de nombres à virgule fixe utilise deux octets pour le nombre entier et un octet pour la partie décimale** = storage of fixed point numbers has two bytes allocated for the whole number and one byte for the fraction part

fixer *vtr* to fix *ou* to set; **l'ordinateur est fixé au poste de travail** = the computer is fixed to the workstation; **fixer d'avance** = to preset; **fixer une marge** = to set a margin; **nous avons fixé la marge de droite à 80 caractères** = we set the right-hand margin at 80 characters

flare *nm (effet Callier)* Callier effect

flash *nm* carte 'flash' = flash card
◊ **flashage** *nm (imprimerie)* **flashage d'un texte** = filming of copy

flatbed *nm* de type 'flatbed' = flatbed; **lecteur de transmission de type 'flatbed'** = flatbed transmitter; **les scanners sont de type 'flatbed', ou possèdent un système d'entraînement du papier par rouleau** = scanners are either flatbed models or platen type, paper-fed models

fléché, -ée *adj* arrowed *ou* with an arrow; *(de direction du curseur)* **touches fléchées** = cursor pad *ou* arrowed pad

flexibilité *nf* flexibility
◊ **flexible** *adj* flexible; **atelier flexible** = flexible manufacturing system (FMS); **routage flexible** = distributed adaptive routing

flot *nm* flow *ou* stream; **flot de données** = data stream

flottant, -e *adj* floating; **accent flottant** = floating accent; **courant flottant** = floating voltage; **tête flottante** = floating head *ou* flying head; **arithmétique en virgule flottante** = floating point arithmetic; **en virgule flottante, le nombre 56,47 serait écrit 0,5647 puissance 2** = the fixed number 56.47 in floating-point arithmetic would be 0.5647 and a power of 2; **nombre en virgule flottante** = floating point number; **notation en virgule flottante** = floating point notation; **opération en virgule flottante** = floating point operation (FLOP); **(nombre d') opérations en virgule flottante par seconde** = floating point operations *ou* FLOPs per second; **(nombre de) millions d'opérations en virgule flottante par seconde** = mega floating point operations per second *ou* megaflops *ou* MFLOPS; **processeur en virgule flottante** = floating point processor; **le processeur en virgule flottante accélère la vitesse de traitement de ce logiciel graphique** = the floating point processor speeds up the processing of the graphics software; **ce modèle est équipé d'un processeur en virgule flottante** = this model includes a built-in floating point processor

flottement *nm* swim

flou, -e 1 *adj* **(a)** fuzzy; **rendre flou** = to blur; **un papier de qualité supérieure donnera des caractères moins flous** = top quality paper will eliminate fuzzy characters; **l'image est floue** = the picture is out of focus *ou* is not in focus; **en tournant le bouton de mise au point l'image devient floue** = the image becomes blurred when you turn the focus knob **(b) logique floue** = fuzzy logic *ou* fuzzy theory **2** *nm* **le flou** = blur

fluctuation *nf* fluctuation; **fluctuation de l'intensité du signal** = fluctuating signal strength; **les fluctuations de courant peuvent entraîner la perte de données** = data loss can occur because of power supply variations
◊ **fluctuer** *vi* to fluctuate; **le courant fluctue entre 1Amp et 1,3Amp** = the electric current fluctuates between 1Amp and 1.3Amp; **courant qui fluctue** = fluctuating current

flux *nm* flow *ou* stream; **flux de données** = data flow; **flux (de données) de sortie** = output stream; **flux continu** *ou* **ininterrompu de données** = continuous data stream; **flux magnétique** = magnetic flux; **flux simple d'instruction, flux multiple de données** = single instruction stream multiple data stream (SIMD); **flux simple d'instruction, flux simple de données** = single instruction stream single data stream (SISD); **flux des tâches** = job stream; **contrôle du flux** = flow control; **contrôle de flux d'informations** = information flow control; **diagramme de flux de données** = data flow diagram (DFD); **direction du flux** = flow direction

focal, -e *adj* focal; **distance focale** = focal length; **plan focal** = image plane
◊ **focale** *nf (distance)* **objectif de focale moyenne** = medium lens; **objectif à focale variable** = zoom lens

folding *nm (méthode de génération d'adresses)* folding

folio *nm* folio
◊ **folioter** *vtr* to folio *ou* to number the pages of a book

fonction *nf* **(a)** function *ou* capability; **multiplexage temporel en fonction des**

appels = statistical time division multiplexing (STDM); **le temps d'ordinateur requis pour le traitement d'une page de texte varie en fonction de la complexité du document** = page processing time depends on the complexity of a given page; **le résultat de sortie est fonction de l'état (physique) des liaisons** = the output is dependent on the physical state of the link **(b)** *(informatique)* **fonction bibliothèque** = library function; **cette machine de traitement de texte possédait une fonction correction orthographique mais n'était pas équipée d'éditeur intégré** = the word-processor had a spelling-checker function but no built-in text-editing function; **fonction courrier électronique** = electronic mail capabilities; **fonctions graphiques GKS** = graphics kernel system (GKS); **fonction hash** = hashing function; **fonction incorporée** = built-in function; **fonction linéaire** = linear function; **l'expression Y (10 + 5X²) n'est pas une fonction linéaire** = the expression $Y (10 + 5X^2)$ is not a linear function; **l'expression Y 10 + 5X - 3W est une fonction linéaire** = the expression $Y 10 + 5X - 3W$ is a linear function; **code** *ou* **caractère de fonction** = function digit; **code de fonction** = function code; **indicateur de fonction** = role indicator; **liste des fonctions** = capability list; **table de fonctions** = function table; **touche de fonction** = (programmable) function key; *(qui ne produit pas de caractère)* dead key; **en appuyant sur la touche de fonction F5 on se met en mode entrée** = hitting F5 will put you into insert mode; **on peut allouer des étiquettes aux touches de fonction** = tags can be allocated to function keys; **mémento de fonction des touches** = key overlay **(c)** *(fonction logique)* function; **fonction de disjonction** = non-equivalence function *ou* NEQ function; **fonction d'équivalence** = equivalence function *ou* operation; **fonction logique spécialisée** = dedicated logic (function); **fonction NON** *ou* **fonction complément** = NOT function; **fonction NON-ET** *ou* **NAND** = NOT-AND *ou* NAND function *ou* dispersion; **fonction NON-OU** *ou* **NI** = NOR function *ou* neither-nor function; **fonction d'union** = join (function)

◇ **fonctionnel, -elle** *adj* functional; **analyse** *ou* **spécification fonctionnelle** = functional specification; **cycle fonctionnel** = action cycle; **diagramme** *ou*

schéma fonctionnel = functional diagram

◇ **fonctionnement** *nm (d'un appareil)* working *ou* operation *ou* running; **fonctionnement automatique (d'un système)** = unattended operation; **durée moyenne de bon fonctionnement** = mean time to failure (MTF); **durée moyenne de bon fonctionnement** *ou* **moyenne de temps de bon fonctionnement entre les défaillances** = mean time between failures (MTBF); **temps de bon fonctionnement** = up time *ou* uptime; **mauvais fonctionnement** = malfunctioning

◇ **fonctionner** *vi* to function *ou* to run *ou* to work; **l'imprimante fonctionne depuis deux heures** = the printer has been in use for the last two hours; **l'ordinateur fonctionne jusqu'à dix heures par jour** = the computer has been running ten hours a day; **le service de maintenance espère que le système sera de nouveau en état de fonctionner dans les 24 heures** = the maintenance people hope that the system will be ready for use *ou* up and running in 24 hours; **faire fonctionner** = to drive *ou* to operate; **ce modem ne fonctionne pas** = the modem has broken down; **fonctionner bien** *ou* **mal** = to perform well *ou* badly; **il n'est pas vraiment sûr que le nouveau système multiposte fonctionne bien** = he is doubtful about the efficiency of the new networking system; **ils ont sûrement trouvé la source du problème puisque l'ordinateur fonctionne à merveille** = they must have found the fault - the computer is finally up and running; **quelques-unes des touches du clavier ne fonctionnent déjà plus très bien** = some of the keys on the keyboard have started to malfunction; **depuis que nous l'avons, l'ordinateur n'a jamais très bien fonctionné** = the computer system has never worked properly since it was installed; **mal fonctionner** = to malfunction; **(appareil) qui fonctionne à l'électricité** = (machine) powered by electricity *ou* driven by electricity; **un moteur qui fonctionne à l'électricité** = an electrically-powered motor; **(appareil) qui fonctionne grâce à un électro-aimant** = device which works electromagnetically; **logiciel qui fonctionne sur la plupart des ordinateurs** = machine-independent software; **logiciel qui ne fonctionne que sur un type d'ordinateur** = machine-dependent software; **installation de secours prête à fonctionner** = hot standby

fond *nm* **(a)** background; **bruit de fond** = background noise; **le modem est sensible au bruit de fond** = the modem is sensitive to background noise; **les autres appareils placés autour de cet équipement produiront un fort bruit de fond** = the other machines around this device will produce a lot of background noise; **couleur de fond** = background colour; **un texte en noir sur fond blanc est moins fatigant pour la vue** = black text on a white background is less stressful for the eyes; **traitement de fond** = background processing **(b)** *(d'un film)* fond animé = busy background **(c)** *(circuits)* **fond de panier** = (microcomputer) backplane; **processeur de fond** = back-end processor; *(arts graphiques)* **la photo est à fond perdu** = the photograph is bled off

fondamental, -e *adj* basic; **couleurs fondamentales** = primary colours; **fréquence fondamentale** = fundamental frequency

◊ **fondamentalement** *adv* basically

fonderie *nf* foundry; **fonderie de silicium** = silicon foundry

fondeuse *nf (de caractères d'imprimerie)* caster machine

fondre *vi (fusionner des fichiers)* to merge *ou* to join *ou* to coalesce (files)

fonds *nm* funds; **transfert électronique de fonds** = electronic funds transfer (system) (EFT); **terminal de transfert électronique de fonds** = electronic funds transfer point of sale (EFTPOS)

fondu *nm (signal audio)* cross fade; **faire un fondu** = to fade out

◊ **fondu, -e** *adj (métal)* melted; **caractères fondus** *ou* **ligne-bloc fondue au moment de la composition** = hot metal characters *ou* hot type

fonte *nf* font *ou* fount *ou* character set *ou* typeface *ou* typestyle; **fonte spéciale** = special sort; **disquette de fontes** = font disk

force *nf* force; **force électromotrice** = electromotive force (EMF)

forfait *nm* flat rate *ou* package deal

◊ **forfaitaire** *adj* **tarif forfaitaire** = set tariff *ou* fixed rate; **il existe un tarif forfaitaire d'utilisation plus un taux/minute de temps d'ordinateur** = there is a set tariff for logging on, then a rate for every minute of computer time used

format *nm* **(a)** format; **format de carte (perforée)** = card format; **format d'écran** = display format *ou* screen format; **écran monochrome standard de format A4, avec une définition de 300 points par pouce** = a standard 300 d.p.i. black and white A4 monitor; **format d'impression** = print format; *(de papier)* **l'imprimante peut accommoder tous les formats jusqu'au quarto** = the printer can deal with all formats up to quarto; **nos formats de pages varient de 220 x 110mm à 360 x 220mm** = our page sizes vary from 220 x 110mm to 360 x 220mm; **papier format A1, A2, A3, A4, A5** = A1, A2, A3, A4, A5 paper; **vous devez photocopier le tableau sur une feuille de format A3** = you must photocopy the spreadsheet on A3 paper; **(papier) format ministre** = foolscap; **la lettre était écrite sur six feuilles format ministre** = the letter was on six sheets of foolscap; **format de la page** = page size; *(de photos)* **format professionnel** = ideal format; **format standard** = normal format *ou* standard format **(b)** *(informatique)* **format d'adresse** = address format; **format d'affichage** = display format; **format de base** = native format; **format de code machine** = machine code format; **format condensé** = packed format; **(mise en) mémoire d'un format courant** = local format storage; **format de données** = data format; **format d'encodage** = encoding format; **format d'un enregistrement** = record format *ou* layout; **format initial** = native format; **format d'instruction** = instruction format; *(de données dans l'unité centrale)* **format interne** = internal format; **format de langage symbolique** = symbolic-coding format; **format de message** = message format; **format normal** = normal format; *(de données)* **format variable** = variable format *ou* V format; **vidage au format** = formatted dump **(c)** *(de programme de télévision)* **format magazine** = magazine format

◊ **formatage** *nm (d'un texte)* make up *ou* makeup; *(de nombres ou données)* normalization; *(d'un disque ou d'une disquette)* (disk) formatting; **formatage de secteurs (d'un disque)** = (disk) sector formatting; **formatage de secteurs permanents** = hard-sectoring; **(disque) avec formatage physique** = hard-sectored (disk); **logiciel** *ou* **matériel de formatage** = formatter; **logiciel de formatage d'impression** = print formatter; **logiciel** *ou* **programme de formatage pour texte** = text formatter; **on utilise le formatage de texte comme programme de base de PAO** = people use the text formatter as a basic desk-top publishing program; **commande de formatage (de paragraphe, etc.)** = template command; **une commande de formatage permet à l'utilisateur de préciser l'alinéa de chaque paragraphe** = a template paragraph command enables the user to specify the number of spaces each paragraph should be indented; **unité de formatage vertical** = vertical format unit (VFU)

◊ **formaté, -ée** *adj (disque ou disquette)* formatted; **formaté d'avance** = preformatted; **(disque) formaté par logiciel** = soft-sectored (disk); **non formaté** = unformatted; **il est impossible de copier quoi que ce soit sur une disquette non formatée** = it is impossible to copy to an unformatted disk *ou* to a disk which has not been formatted; **bande de texte non formaté** = idiot tape; **le lecteur de cartouche a une capacité de stockage non formaté de 12,7Mo** = the cartridge drive provides 12.7Mbyte of unformatted storage

◊ **formater** *vtr (un texte)* to make up; *(un nombre, une donnée)* = to normalize; *(un disque ou une disquette)* to format; **vous devez formater toutes les nouvelles disquettes avant de les utiliser** = you have to format new disks before one can use them

◊ **formateur** *nm* formatter; **formateur de données de sortie** = output formatter

le formatage consiste donc à poser des marques sur la couche magnétique de la disquette
Science et Vie Micro
lorsqu'un disque est formaté, des codes magnétiques sont inscrits sur sa surface, la divisant en secteurs (les parts de gâteau) et en pistes (les arcs de cercles concentriques)
Science et Vie Micro

formation *nf* teaching *ou* instruction *ou* learning; **formation pratique** = hands-on instruction; **la société informatique offre une formation pratique de deux jours** = the computer firm gives a two day hands-on training course; **formation à l'aide de didacticiels** = programmed learning; **formation assistée par ordinateur (FAO)** = computer-aided *ou* assisted learning (CAL); **formation assistée par système expert** = intelligent tutoring system; **formation informatisée** = computer-managed learning (CML) *ou* computer-based learning (CBL)

forme *nf* form *ou* pattern; **sous forme de diagramme** = diagramatically *ou* in diagrammatic form; **sous forme numérique** = digitally; **mettre en forme** = to format; **(texte) mis en forme à l'impression** = post-formatted (text); **on utilise des feuilles de style pour mettre en forme les documents** = style sheets are used to format documents; **forme d'impression** = (printing) form; **forme d'onde** = waveform; **reconnaissance de formes** = pattern recognition

formel, -elle *adj* **logique formelle** = formal logic

former *vtr* to form

formulaire *nm* form; **formulaires et en-têtes de lettres peuvent être conçus sur un PC** = business forms and letterheads can now be designed on a PC; **formulaire de demande** = application form; **formulaire de programmation** = (program) coding sheet *ou* coding form; **formulaire préimprimé** = preprinted form; **formulaires préimprimés** = preprinted stationery

◊ **formule** *nf* formula *ou* expression; **portabilité d'une formule** = formula portability; **réduire une formule à sa plus simple expression** = to express a formula in its simplest form; *(langage FORTRAN)* **traducteur de formule** = formula translator (FORTRAN)

◊ **formuler** *vtr* to express

fort, -e *adj* important *ou* significant; **de poids fort** = high order; **bit de poids fort** = most significant bit (MSB); **chiffre de poids fort** = most significant character *ou* most significant digit (MSD); **forte réduction** = high reduction

FORTH langage FORTH = FORTH

FORTRAN = FORMULA TRANSLATOR; **langage FORTRAN** = FORTRAN; *voir aussi* FORMULE

FOSDIC = FILM OPTICAL SCANNING DEVICE FOR INPUT INTO COMPUTERS *voir aussi* LECTEUR

fou, folle *n* fou d'informatique = terminal junky (TJ)

fourchette *nf* range *ou* span; **fourchette normale** = normal range

Fourier *npr* **série de Fourier** = Fourier series

fournir *vtr* to supply; **ils ont signé un contrat pour fournir des informations en ligne** = they have signed a contract to supply on-line information

fournisseur *nm* supplier; **un fournisseur de composants pour ordinateurs** = a supplier of computer parts; **un fournisseur d'équipements informatiques** = a computer equipment supplier; **un fournisseur de lecteurs de disquettes** = a supplier of disk drives *ou* a disk drive supplier; **l'ordinateur vient de chez un fournisseur connu** = the computer was supplied by a recognized dealer; **service fournisseur d'information** = information provider (IP)

foyer *nm* focus; **profondeur de foyer** = depth of focus

fraction *nf* fraction; **fraction binaire** = binary fraction; **la fraction binaire 0,011 est égale à un quart plus un huitième (ou trois huitièmes)** = the binary fraction 0.011 is equal to one quarter plus one eighth (i.e. three eighths); *(d'une imprimante)* **caractère de fraction** = piece fraction

◊ **fractionnaire** *adj* fractional; **partie fractionnaire** = fractional part; **puissance fractionnaire** = root *ou* fractional power; **la racine est la puissance fractionnaire d'un nombre** = the root is the fractional power of a number

fragmentation *nf* fragmentation

frais *nmpl* costs; **frais fixes** = fixed costs *ou* above-the-line costs; *(télévision ou publicité)* **frais salariaux du personnel technique** = below-the-line-costs

français *adj* French; **clavier français accentué** = AZERTY keyboard

frappe *nf* keystroke *ou* stroke; **contrôle de la frappe** = keystroke verification; **faute de frappe** = typing error; **faire une faute de frappe** = to make a typing error; **nombre de frappes** = keystroke count; **nombre de frappes par heure** *ou* **frappes/heure** = keystrokes per hour; **elle peut saisir un texte au rythme de 3500 frappes/heure** = she keyboards at a rate of 3500 keystrokes per hour; **vitesse de frappe** = keystroke rate; **il a une vitesse de frappe assez rapide** = he can type quite fast

fraude *nf* fraud; *(passible du tribunal correctionnel)* **fraude informatique** = computer crime *ou* computer fraud

◊ **frauduleux, -euse** *adj* fraudulent; **depuis quelque temps déjà, la société fait des copies frauduleuses de logiciels protégés par le copyright** = the company has been illegally copying copyright software for some time

fréquence *nf* **(a)** frequency; *(vitesse)* rate; **fréquence de balayage** = scanning rate; **fréquence de balayage de ligne** = line frequency; **fréquence de boucle** *ou* **de bouclage** = speed of loop; **fréquence de coupure** = cutoff frequency; **fréquence de l'image** = frame frequency; **la télévision britannique utilise une fréquence de 25 images par seconde** *ou* **25 images/seconde** = in the UK the frame frequency is 25 fps; **fréquence de trame** *ou* **d'image** = field frequency; **(b)** frequency; **fréquence allouée** *ou* **assignée** = assigned frequency; **fréquence audio** *ou* **fréquence audible** = audio frequency; **fréquence fondamentale** = fundamental frequency; **fréquence critique de fusion** = critical fusion frequency; **fréquence d'horloge** = clock frequency; **la principale fréquence d'horloge est de 10MHz** = the main clock frequency is 10MHz; **fréquence inaudible** *ou* **infrasonore** = subaudio frequency; **fréquence infrasonique** = infrasonic frequency; **fréquence intermédiaire** = intermediate frequency (if *ou* IF); **fréquence maximale utilisable** = maximum usable frequency; **fréquence radio** *ou* **radiofréquence** = radio frequency (RF); **bande de fréquences** = frequency band; **bande (de fréquences) intercalaire** = guard band; **bande des fréquences vocales** *ou* **bande de basses fréquences** = voice band; **la bande de base des fréquences vocales varie de 20Hz à 15KHz** = voice base band ranges from 20Hz to 15KHz; **basse fréquence** = low frequency (LF); **basse fréquence multiplexée (A-MAC)** = A-MAC; **très basse fréquence** = very low frequency (VLF); **canal de basses fréquences** = voice grade channel; **canal de fréquences subvocales** = subvoice grade channel; **haut-parleur de basses fréquences** = woofer; **réponse aux basses fréquences** = bass response; **signal de basse fréquence** = bass signal; **convertisseur de fréquence** = frequency changer; **décalage de fréquence** = dual clocking; **(système de) modulation par décalage de fréquence** = frequency shift keying (FSK); **diviseur de fréquence** = frequency divider; **domaine de fréquence** = frequency domain; **égaliseur de fréquence** *ou* **filtre de bande de fréquences** = frequency equalizer; **gamme de fréquences** = frequency range; **haute fréquence** = high frequency (HF); **hyper haute fréquence** = tremendously high frequency (THF); **très haute fréquence** = very high frequency (VHF); **ultra-haute fréquence** = ultra high frequency (UHF); **modulation de fréquence (MF)** = frequency modulation (FM); **modulation de fréquence à large bande** = wideband frequency modulation (WBFM); **réducteur de fréquence** = frequency divider; **multiplexage par répartition en fréquence** = frequency division multiplexing (FDM); **réponse en fréquence** = frequency response; **sonnerie à résonnance de fréquence** = decimonic ringing; **variation de fréquence** = frequency variation

---

pour avoir une chance d'obtenir un filtre fonctionnant à une fréquence d'horloge assez élevée (quelques dizaines de hertz), il est nécessaire d'écrire le programme en langage machine

Electronique Applications

---

fréquent, -e *adj* frequent

friction *nf* friction; *(d'un connecteur)* **insertion sans friction** = zero insertion force (ZIF); *(du papier, etc.)* **entraînement par friction** = friction feed

frisure *nf (sur un courant)* ripple

froid, -e *adj* **(a)** cold; **les appareils fonctionnent mal par temps froid** = the machines work badly in cold weather **(b)** **démarrage à froid** = cold start

front *nm* front; **déclenché par bascule de front d'impulsion** = edge-triggered
◊ **frontal, -e** *adj* front-end; **mode d'exécution frontal/masqué** = foreground/background modes; **ordinateur frontal** = front-end computer; **processeur frontal** = front-end processor (FEP); **système frontal** = front-end system; **traitement frontal** = foreground processing *ou* foregrounding

frontière *nf (entre deux pays)* border *ou* frontier; **flux de données passant les frontières** = transborder data flow

fuir *vi (robinet, etc)* to leak
◊ **fuite** *nf (d'un robinet* ou *d'un secret)* leak *ou* leakage; **c'est grâce à une fuite que la presse a eu vent de notre nouveau modèle** = a leak informed the press of our new designs

fumée *nf* smoke; **test de la fumée** = smoke test

fusée *nf* rocket; **fusée porteuse** *ou* **de lancement** = launch vehicle

fusible 1 *nm* fuse; **mémoire ROM** *ou* **mémoire morte à fusibles** = fusible read only memory (FROM) **2** *adj* **élément fusible** = fusible link

fusion *nf* fusion *ou* merge *ou* merger *ou* merging; **fusion de documents** = document assembly *ou* document merge; **fusion de fichiers** = file collating *ou* file merger; **(instruction de) fusion de fichiers** = join *ou* merge files; **(application de) tri et fusion** = merge sort; *(de l'image)* **fréquence critique de fusion** = critical fusion frequency

◇ **fusionnement** *nm* *(données)* collating; **séquence de fusionnement =** collating sequence; **programme de fusionnement de données =** collator

◇ **fusionner** *vtr&i (fichiers)* to combine *ou* to merge *ou* to join (files); *(données ou documents)* to collate (data)

futur *nm* the future; **le bureau du futur =** the office of the future

Gg

G = GIGA giga- *ou* G

g *abbrév* = GRAMME; **ce livre est imprimé sur papier couché de 70g** = the book is printed on 70 gram *ou* 70 gsm coated paper

GAB = GUICHET AUTOMATIQUE DE BANQUE

gabarit *nm* **gabarit (de traçage)** = template

gaffeur *nm* gaffer; *US* gofer

gain *nm* gain; **augmentez le gain du signal d'entrée** = increase the amplification of the input signal; **contrôle de gain** = gain control; **contrôle de gain automatique** = automatic gain control (AGC) *ou* automatic level control (ALC)

gaine *nf* cladding; **la fibre optique sera moins performante si sa gaine est endommagée** = if the cladding is chipped, the fibre-optic cable will not function well

galet *nm* **galet presseur** = head wheel

gallium *nm* **arséniure de gallium** = gallium arsenide

gamma *nm (rayon)* gamma

gamme *nf* range *ou* family; **gamme des audiofréquences** = audio range; **gamme de fréquences** = frequency range; **la transmisison par téléphone accepte des signaux dans la gamme de fréquences 300 à 3400 Hz** = the telephone channel can accept signals in the frequency range 300 - 3400Hz; **gamme dynamique** = dynamic range; **gamme normale** = normal range; **une gamme de produits** = a wide range of products; **on trouve dans le catalogue toute une gamme de papiers listing** = the catalogue lists a wide range of computer stationery; **(de) bas de gamme** = cheap *ou* down market; **(de) haut de gamme** = up market *ou* high quality *ou* top quality *ou* top of the range; **gamme de valeurs** = number range

garantie *nf* guarantee; **le système est toujours sous garantie et la réparation sera faite gratuitement** = the system is still under guarantee and will be repaired free of charge
◇ **garantir** *vtr* **le fabricant garantit le système pendant un an** = the manufacturer guarantees the system for 12 months

garde *nf (de signal de télévision)* **intervalle de garde** = breezeway

garder *vtr* **(a)** to keep; **garder (un fichier) à jour** = to keep something up to date **(b)** *(en mémoire)* to hold

garnir *vtr (une section de la mémoire)* **garnir de zéros** = to zero fill
◇ **garnissage** *nm (pour transmission)* **garnissage de bits** = bit stuffing

gauche **1** *nm* left; **décalage** *ou* **glissement à gauche** = left shift; **effectuer un décalage à gauche** = to left shift; **(au) fer à gauche** = flush left; **justification à gauche** = left justification; **justifié à gauche** = flush left *ou* left justified; **justifier à gauche** = to left justify; **(instruction de) justifier à gauche** = left justify; **page de gauche** = left-hand page **2** *adj* left

gaz *nm* gas; **gaz inerte** = inert gas

géant, -e *adj* giant *ou* jumbo; **ordinateur géant** = supercomputer; **puce géante** = jumbo chip

général, -e *adj* general; **index général** = main index; **registre général** = general register *ou* general purpose register (gpr); *(d'un programme)* **variable générale** = global variable

générateur *nm* **(a)** *(d'électricité)* generator **(b)** *(appareil)* **générateur d'impulsions** = pulse generator; *(circuit intégré)* **générateur de son** = sound chip *ou* music chip **(c)** *(programme)* **générateur d'application** = report program generator (RPG); **générateur de caractères** = character generator; **on peut utiliser une ROM comme générateur de caractères pour obtenir les différentes polices** = the ROM used as a character generator can be changed to provide different fonts; **générateur de caractères fac-similés** = facsimile character generator; **générateur de liens** = linkage software; **les graphiques et le texte sont réunis sans l'aide d'un générateur de liens** = graphics and text are joined without linkage software; **générateur de nombres aléatoires** = random number generator; **générateur de programme** = program generator; **générateur de renvois** = cross-reference generator

◊ **génération** *nf* **(a)** *(période dans le temps)* generation; **génération d'ordinateurs** = computer generation; **génération d'un système** *ou* **à laquelle appartient un système** = system generation *ou* sysgen; **première génération** = first generation; **le fichier père est un fichier de sauvegarde de première génération** = the father file is a first generation backup; **image de première génération** = first generation image; **ordinateur de première génération** = first generation computer; **deuxième génération** = second generation; **ordinateurs de deuxième génération** = second generation computers; **troisième génération** = third generation; **ordinateurs de troisième génération** = third generation computers; **langages de quatrième génération** = fourth generation languages; **ordinateurs de quatrième génération** = fourth generation computers; **ordinateurs de cinquième génération** = fifth generation computers **(b)** *(création ou production)* origination; **génération de données** = data origination

◊ **génératrice** *nf* génératrice *(d'électricité)* = generator; **en cas de panne de courant, le centre informatique possède sa propre génératrice (d'électricité)** = the computer centre has its own independent generator, in case of mains power failure

◊ **généré, -ée** *adj* generated; **généré par ordinateur** = computer-generated; **adresse générée** = generated address; **le code est généré automatiquement** = code generation is automatic; **erreur générée (par des arrondis)** = generated error

◊ **générer** *vtr* to generate; **une tablette graphique permet de générer deux coordonnées à chaque position du stylo** = the graphics tablet generates a pair of co-ordinates each time the pen is moved

générique 1 *nm (de film)* credits; **défilement ascendant du générique** = crawl **2** *adj* generic

génie *nm* engineering; **génie logiciel** = software engineering

genre *nm* gender; **changeur de genre** = gender changer; **il est possible de relier tous ces périphériques en utilisant seulement deux câbles et un changeur de genre** = you can interconnect all these peripherals with just two cables and a gender changer

géométrie *nf* geometry

◊ **géométrique** *adj* **distorsion géométrique** = geometric distortion

géostationnaire *adj (de satellite)* **orbite géostationnaire** = geostationary orbit; **satellite géostationnaire** = geostationary satellite

la durée de vie de ces deux tubes est inférieure à celle de l'ensemble du système TDF1-TDF2, évaluée à environ huit ans à partir de sa mise en orbite géostationnaire
Le Figaro
l'ensemble des satellites géostationnaires étant situé dans le plan de l'équateur terrestre, le mât principal fixe de l'antenne aura donc une orientation telle qu'il soit perpendiculaire au plan de l'équateur
Science et Vie

géré, -ée *adj* **géré par ordinateur** = computer-managed; **enseignement interactif géré par ordinateur** = computer-managed instruction (CMI)

◊ **gérer** *vtr* to manage

germanium (Ge) *nm* germanium

gestion *nf* direction *ou* management; **gestion d'accès aux données** = data access management; **gestion des accès aux disques** = disk access management; **gestion de (l'utilisation d'un) bus** = bus arbitration; **gestion de clé** = key management; **gestion de données** = data management; **gestion des erreurs** = error handling *ou* management; **gestion de fichier** = file management; **gestion de mémoire** = memory management; **gestion de réseau** = network management; **gestion de tâches** = job scheduling *ou* task management; **gestion de texte** = text management; **ordinateur de gestion** = business computer; **programme de gestion d'enregistrements** *ou* **de fichiers** = records management; **programme de gestion de file d'attente** = queue management *ou* queue manager; **routine de gestion de périphérique** = peripheral software driver; **système de gestion de base de données** = database management system (DBMS) *ou* database manager; **système de gestion de l'information** = information management system; **système de gestion informatisé** = management information system (MIS); **terminal de gestion** = executive terminal

◇ **gestionnaire** *nm* administrator *ou* manager; **gestionnaire de base de données** = database administrator (DBA); **un gestionnaire de base de données ultra-rapide permet la manipulation d'une très grande quantité de données** = a high-speed database management program allows the manipulation of very large amounts of data; **gestionnaire de données** = data administrator; **gestionnaire d'enregistrements** = records manager; **gestionnaire d'espaces** = spacer; **gestionnaire d'espaces intelligent** = intelligent spacer; **gestionnaire de fichiers** = file manager; **gestionnaire de file d'attente** = queue management *ou* queue manager; **ce nouveau logiciel de spouling comporte un gestionnaire de file d'attente** = this is new software spooler with a built-in queue management; **gestionnaire d'imprimante** = printer driver; **gestionnaire d'interruptions** = interrupt handler (IH); **gestionnaire de périphérique** = device driver *ou* handler *ou* peripheral driver; **gestionnaire de priorités** = priority scheduler;

gestionnaire de segments de recouvrement = overlay manager; **gestionnaire de tâches** = scheduler; **gestionnaire de télécommunication** = communications executive; **gestionnaire de texte** = text manager

GHz = GIGAHERTZ

giga- (G) *(un milliard)* giga- (G)
◇ **gigahertz (GHz)** *nm* gigahertz (GHz)
◇ **giga-octet (Go)** *nm* gigabyte

> il supporte des capacités mémoire pouvant aller jusqu'à 4 giga-octets
> *L'Ordinateur Individuel*

GKS = GRAPHICS KERNEL SYSTEM; **fonctions graphiques GKS** = graphics kernel system (GKS)

glacé, -ée *adj (papier)* glossy; **on utilise du papier glacé pour l'impression de similigravures** = glossy paper is used for printing half-tones; *(papier couché)* **papier glacé** = art paper

glissement *nm* shift; **glissement à gauche** = left shift
◇ **glisser** *vtr* to slide
◇ **se glisser** *vpr* **(a)** to slide; **la disquette se glisse dans la pochette et s'en retire tout aussi facilement** = the disk cover slides on and off easily **(b)** to creep in; **il s'est glissé des erreurs au cours de la saisie du texte** = errors crept *ou* were introduced into the text at keyboarding

global, -e *adj* global; *(d'un sujet ou d'un problème)* **connaissance globale** = global knowledge; **contrat global** = package deal; **nous offrons un contrat global comprenant un système informatique complet pour le bureau, la formation du personnel et l'entretien du matériel** = we are offering a package deal which includes the whole office computer system, staff training and hardware maintenance; *(traitement de texte)* **recherche globale et remplace** = global search and replace; **variable globale** = global variable

gobo *nm (pour film)* matt *ou* matte

gondolage *nm* buckling

gonfler *vtr* **(a)** *(avec de l'air)* to blow **(b)** *(augmenter l'importance)* to boost; **le disque dur supplémentaire va gonfler la capacité de mémoire de 25Mo** = the extra hard disk will boost our storage capacity by 25Mb

GOTO instruction 'GOTO' *ou* **instruction de saut** = GOTO; **GOTO 105 indique un saut à la ligne 105** = GOTO 105 instructs a jump to line 105

GPIA = GENERAL PURPOSE INTERFACE ADAPTER; **interface universelle GPIA** = general purpose interface adapter (GPIA)

GPIB = GENERAL PURPPOSE INTERFACE BUS; **bus universel GPIB** = general purpose interface bus (GPIB)

gradué, -ée *adj* graduated

graduel, -elle *adj* gradual *ou* phased *ou* staged; **changement graduel** = phased change-over; **passage graduel (à un nouveau système)** = staged change-over

◇ **graduellement** *adv* **arrêter** *ou* **mettre fin à quelque chose graduellement** = to phase out something *ou* to phase something out; **commencer** *ou* **démarrer** *ou* **introduire quelque chose graduellement** = to phase in something *ou* to phase something in

grain *nm (du papier)* grain

grammage *nm (du papier)* grammage *ou* paper weight

en dehors des classiques papiers blancs aux divers grammages, les imprimantes à laser acceptent de nombreux autres types de support
L'Ordinateur Individuel
ne pas employer de papiers trop légers, d'un grammage inférieur à 80 grammes
L'Ordinateur Individuel

grammaire *nf* grammar

gramme (g) *nm* gram (g); *(poids du papier)* **gramme au mètre carré (g/m²)** = grams per square metre (gsm); **le livre est imprimé sur du papier 80 grammes** = the book is printed on 80gsm paper; **nous avons du papier de 70 - 90 grammes** = our paper weights are 70 - 90 gsm

grand, -e *adj (stature)* tall *ou* big; *(quantité)* large; **ligne de grand débit** = high usage trunk; **grande vitesse** = high-speed; **duplicateur grande vitesse** = high-speed duplicator

◇ **grand-angle** *ou* **grand-angulaire** *nm&adj* **(objectif) grand-angle** *ou* **grand-angulaire** = wide angle lens

◇ **grandeur** *nf* size; *(d'un signal, etc.)* magnitude; **grandeur de page** = page size

◇ **grand-père** *nm* **fichier grand-père** = grandfather file

graphe *nm* graph *ou* plot; *(exprimé en coordonnées)* coordinate graph; **graphe logarithmique** = logarithmic graph; **graphe à pavés** = block diagram; **graphe de relation** = derivation graph; **mode graphe** = plotting mode; **tracer un graphe (par points numérisés)** = to plot a graph

◇ **grapheur** *nm* graph plotter

◇ **graphique 1** *nm* **(a)** chart *ou* diagram *ou* graph *ou* schema; **graphique à barres** *ou* **en colonnes** *ou* **en tuyaux d'orgue** = bar chart *ou* columnar graph; **à l'aide d'un graphique** = graphically; **traceur de graphiques** = X-Y plotter *ou* graph plotter; **graphique de points** = scatter graph **(b)** *(représentations graphiques)* graphics; **graphiques contigus** = contiguous graphics; **la plupart des écrans ne permettent pas l'affichage de graphiques contigus; chaque caractère (graphique) est bordé de chaque côté par un espace qui améliore sa lisibilité** = most display units do not provide contiguous graphics: their characters have a small space on each side to improve legibility; **graphiques de faible définition** = low-resolution graphics *ou* low-res graphics; **graphiques haute définition** = high resolution graphics *ou* hi-res graphics; **graphiques interactifs** = interactive graphics; **le jeu (électronique) 'les envahisseurs de l'espace' présente d'excellents graphiques interactifs; le joueur contrôle la position de son vaisseau spatial avec la manette (de jeu)** = the space invaders machine has great interactive graphics, the player controls the position of his spaceship on the screen with the joystick **2** *adj* graphic *ou* graphical; **(carte) adaptateur graphique couleur EGA** = enhanced graphics adapter (EGA); **affichage graphique =** graphic display; **définition de l'affichage graphique =** graphic display resolution; **caractère graphique =** graphics character; **la carte graphique haute définition contrôle jusqu'à 300 pixels par pouce =** the HRG board can control up to 300 pixels per inch; **coprocesseur graphique =** graphics coprocessor; **données graphiques =** graphic data; **écran (à affichage) graphique =** graphics VDU; **enregistreur graphique =** chart recorder; **entrée-sortie graphique =** graphical input/output (GINO); **fonctions graphiques GKS =** graphics kernel system (GKS); **imprimante graphique =** printer-plotter; **intégrateur graphique (à fenêtre, icône, souris, pointeur) =** window, icon, mouse, pointer (WIMP); **langage graphique =** graphic language; **avec ce langage graphique, on peut tracer des lignes, cercles et graphes avec une seule commande =** this graphic language can plot lines, circles and graphs with a single command; **logiciel graphique =** graphics software; **mode graphique =** graphics mode; **palette graphique =** Paint Box®; **processeur graphique =** graphics processor; **représentation graphique =** graphic display *ou* graphics; **les représentations graphiques telles que histogrammes, camemberts, etc =** graphics output such as bar charts, pie charts, etc.; **représentations graphiques sur ordinateur =** computer-generated graphics; **stylo optique graphique =** graphics light pen; **symbole graphique =** graphic symbol; **bibliothèque de symboles graphiques =** graphics library; **tablette graphique =** graphics pad *ou* graphics tablet *ou* digitizing pad; **terminal graphique** *ou* **terminal avec écran à affichage graphique =** graphics terminal *ou* graphics art terminal; **traceur** *ou* **enregistreur graphique =** pen recorder

◇ **graphiquement** *adv* graphically; **les chiffres de vente sont reproduits graphiquement sous forme de camembert =** the sales figures are graphically represented as a pie chart

◇ **graphisme** *nm* line art; **graphisme par balayage de trame =** raster graphics

les langages graphiques permettent la présentation de résultats sous forme de graphiques plus ou moins riches

L'Information professionnelle

graphité, -ée *adj* **carte graphitée =** mark sensing card

◇ **graphiter** *vtr (une marque)* to mark sense

grappe *nf (de périphériques, etc.)* cluster; **unité de contrôle de périphériques disposés en grappe =** cluster controller; **liaison en grappe de plusieurs périphériques =** clustering

gras, grasse *adj (caractère)* bold; **caractère gras =** bold face; **(instruction d') imprimer en caractères gras =** bold *ou* embolden

grave *adj&nm (son)* bass; **contrôle des (sons) graves =** bass control; **haut-parleur de graves =** bass driver *ou* bass speaker *ou* woofer

gravé, -ée *adj* **caractère gravé =** etched type

◇ **graver** *vtr* to etch; **pour faire un circuit imprimé il faut d'abord recouvrir la carte d'une résine photosensible puis appliquer le masque du circuit, exposer, développer et graver pour finalement obtenir le tracé =** to make the PCB, coat the board with photoresist, place the opaque pattern above, expose, then develop and etch, leaving the conducting tracks

◇ **gravure** *nf* **(a)** *(oeuvre)* print; **il fait collection de gravures du 18ᵉ siècle =** he collects 18th century prints **(b)** *(procédé)* engraving; **gravure en demi-teinte =** halftone process *ou* half-toning

Gray *n* **code (de) Gray =** Gray code *ou* cyclic code

grille *nf* **(a)** grid; **grille d'aide (de fonction des touches) de clavier =** key overlay *ou* keyboard overlay; **sans la grille d'aide, je ne saurais jamais quelle touche de fonction je dois utiliser =** without the key overlay, I would never remember which function key does what **(b)** *(format pré-établi)* **grille d'écran =** form; *(de programme de télévision)* **grille d'émission =** format; **grille pour ordinogramme =** flowchart template *ou* flowchart stencil

gris *nm* grey; *US* gray; **échelle de gris =** grey scale; *US* gray scale; **niveaux de gris**

= (i) shades of grey; *US* shades of gray; (ii) grey scale; *US* gray scale

◊ **gris, -e** *adj* grey; *US* gray

l'image est recueillie en échelle de gris sur l'enregistreur à fibres optiques utilisant un papier sensible aux ultraviolets et à développement immédiat
Techniques hospitalières

gros, grosse *adj* large *ou* big; **gros ordinateur** = mainframe computer; *(photographie)* **gros plan** = close-up

◊ **grossir** *vtr* to enlarge *ou* to magnify; **cette lentille grossit 10 fois** = the lens gives a magnification of 10 times

◊ **grossissement** *nm* enlargement *ou* magnification

groupage *nm* assembly; **groupage de caractères** = character assembly

◊ **groupe** *nm* **(a)** group; *(de caractères ou de mots)* group *ou* batch *ou* set; *(collection de données ou d'objets semblables)* bank; **un groupe de mini-ordinateurs traite toutes les données brutes** = a bank of minicomputers process all the raw data; **groupe de contrôle** = control group; **groupe de fichiers (connexes)** = file set; **groupe témoin** = control group; *(de périphériques)* **appel sélectif de groupe** = group poll; **marqueur (de début ou de fin) de groupe** = group mark *ou* marker; *(pour vérification d'erreurs)* **total par groupe** = batch total **(b)** *(voies de communication)* **groupe primaire** = primary group; **groupe tertiaire** = mastergroup **(c)** **groupe d'utilisateurs** = user group; **groupe fermé d'utilisateurs** = closed user group (CUG)

◊ **groupé, -e** *adj* batched; **communications groupées** = batched communication; **signal groupé** = M signal; *(commutateurs)* **groupés en série** = ganged

◊ **groupement** *nm* group; **groupement de commutateurs (en série)** = ganged switch; **groupement de voies** = channel group

◊ **grouper** *vtr* **(a)** to group *ou* to bracket together; **grouper des données** = to gather write **(b)** *(dispositifs)* to group

guichet *nm* **guichet automatique de banque (GAB)** = automated teller machine (ATM); *US* automatic telling machine

guidage *nm* *(de signaux)* **dispositif de guidage directionnel** = feed horn

◊ **guide** *nm* **(a)** *(livre ou manuel)* guide; **guide élémentaire** = primer **(b)** *(dispositif)* **guide d'ondes** = waveguide; **guide d'ondes circulaire** = circular waveguide; **guide d'ondes rectangulaire** = rectangular waveguide; **guide optique** = light guide **(c)** *(d'un code (à) barres)* **lignes guides** = guide bars; **les lignes guides standard se présentent sous la forme de deux lignes fines un peu plus longues que les lignes codes** = the standard guide bars are two thin lines that are a little longer than the coding lines **(d)** *(de vidéotex)* **page guide** = lead in page

◊ **guide-bande** *nm* tape guide; **la bande est désalignée parce qu'un guide-bande est cassé** = the tape is out of alignment because one of the tape guides has broken

guillemets *nm* quotation marks *ou* quotes *ou* inverted commas; **guillemets doubles (" ")** = double quotes; **il faut mettre le nom de la société entre guillemets** = the name of the company should be put in double quotes; **guillemets simples (' ')** = single quotes

Hh

habillage *nm (d'une gravure ou d'une image)* **faire l'habillage** = to run around

hachures *nf (d'un dessin)* shading

Hall *npr* **effet (de champ) Hall** = Hall effect; **commutateur à effet (de champ) Hall** = Hall effect switch

halo *nm (photographie)* halo; **effet de halo** = halation

halogénure *nf* **halogénure (d'argent)** = halide

Hamming *npr* **code** *ou* **codage de Hamming** = Hamming code; **distance de Hamming** = signal distance *ou* Hamming distance

hampe *nf (d'une lettre)* ascender

handshaking *nm* handshaking; *voir aussi* ECHANGE

harmonique *nf* harmonic; **distorsion d'harmoniques** = harmonic distortion; **sonnerie d'appel à harmoniques** = harmonic telephone ringer

hartley *nm (mesure d'information)* hartley

hasard *nm* chance; **au hazard** = at random; **nombre choisi au hasard** = random number

hash *nm* hash; **table des adresses hash codées** = hash table; **algorithme** *ou* **fonction hash** = hashing function; **hash code** = hash code; **générer un hash code** = to hash; **index hash code** = hash index; **système de hash code** = hash-code system; **total de vérification pour hash code** = hash total; **valeur d'un code hash** = hash value

haut *nm* **(a)** top; *(caractère d'imprimerie)* **haut de casse** = upper case **(b) (de) haut de gamme** = high quality *ou* top quality *ou* up market

◊ **haut, -e** *adj* **(a)** high; **haute définition** = high resolution *ou* hi-res *ou* high definition; **graphiques haute définition** = hi-res graphics *ou* high-resolution graphics; **carte graphique haute définition** = HRG board; **matrice d'impression à haute définition** = enhanced dot matrix; **ce moniteur haute définition permet un affichage de 640 x 320 pixels** = this high-resolution monitor can display 640 x 320 pixels; **système vidéo haute définition** = high definition video system (HDVS); **haute densité** = high density; **disquette haute densité (HD)** = high density disk (HD); **très haute densité** = very high density (VHD); **haute fréquence** = high frequency (HF); **haut-parleur de hautes fréquences** = tweeter; **hyper haute fréquence** = tremendously high frequency (THF); **très haute fréquence** = very high frequency (VHF); **ultra-haute fréquence** = ultra high frequency (UHF); **on demande aux programmeurs une connaissance des langages de haut niveau, dont PASCAL** = programmers should have a knowledge of high-level languages, particularly PASCAL; **(de) haute performance** = high performance; **matériel (de) haute performance** = high performance equipment; **(de) haute précision** *ou* **(de) haute technologie** = high specification *ou* high spec; **les câbles (de) haute technologie doivent être manipulés avec soin** = high spec cabling needs to be handled very carefully **(b) état logique haut** *ou* **1** = logical high **(c) filtre passe haut** = high pass filter

◊ **haute-fidélité** *nf* high fidelity *ou* hifi *ou* hi-fi *ou* hi fi; **chaîne haute-fidélité** = high fidelity system *ou* hi-fi

> le système comprend, dans une mallette, un boîtier, un casque haute-fidélité, un cordon de raccordement pour chaîne hi-fi, magnétophone ou téléviseur
>
> *L'Evénement*

hauteur *nf* height; **hauteur d'un son =** pitch

haut-parleur *nm* loudspeaker; **ne placez surtout pas le micro trop près du haut-parleur sinon le retour va saturer l'ampli =** make sure the microphone is not too close to the loudspeaker or positive feedback will occur and you will overload the amplifier; **haut-parleur d'aigus** *ou* **de hautes fréquences =** tweeter; **haut-parleur de graves** *ou* **de basses fréquences =** bass driver *ou* bass speaker *ou* woofer; **haut-parleur électrostatique =** electrostatic speaker

HD = HAUTE DENSITE; **disquette HD =** high density disk

HDLC = HIGH-LEVEL LINK CONTROL (HDLC); **protocole d'interfaçage HDLC =** HDLC; **équipement interfacé HDLC =** high-level data link control station

hebdomadaire *adj* weekly; **une revue hebdomadaire =** a weekly magazine

hectométrique *adj* hectometric; **ondes hectométriques =** medium frequency

hélicoïdal, -e *adj* **balayage** *ou* **lecture hélicoïdale =** helical scan

HELP *(touche de clavier d'aide à l'utilisateur)* **tapez la touche HELP pour connaître la marche à suivre =** hit the HELP key if you want information about what to do next

hermétique *adj* airtight; **emballage hermétique =** airtight packaging
◊ **hermétiquement** *adv* **fermer hermétiquement =** to seal

hertz *nm* Hertz
◊ **hertzien, -ienne** *adj* hertzian; **liaison hertzienne =** microwave communications link; **relais hertzien =**

microwave relay; **transmission hertzienne =** microwave transmission

hétérodyne *adj* heterodyne

hétérogène *adj* heteregeneous; **multiplexage hétérogène =** heterogeneous multiplexing; **réseau informatique hétérogène =** heterogeneous network

heure *nf* **(a)** hour; **à** *ou* **de l'heure =** per hour; **(nombre de) frappes/heure =** keystrokes per hour **(b)** time; **heure d'entrée =** entry time; *(télévision)* **heures de grande écoute** *ou* **d'écoute maximale =** prime time

heuristique *adj* heuristic; **un programme heuristique exploite ses actions et décisions antérieures =** a heuristic program learns from its previous actions and decisions

hexadécimal, -e *adj* **base hexadécimale =** base 16; **clavier hexadécimal =** hexadecimal *ou* hex (key)pad; **notation hexadécimale =** hexadecimal *ou* hex notation; **vidage hexadécimal =** hex dump; *voir aussi* A, B, C, D, E, F

hiérarchie *nf* hierarchy; **hiérarchie des données =** data hierarchy; **hiérarchie des mémoires =** memory hierarchy
◊ **hiérarchique** *adj* hierarchical; **classification hiérarchique =** hierarchical classification; **répertoire hiérarchique =** hierarchical directory; **structure hiérarchique de données =** data hierarchy
◊ **hiérarchisé, -ée** *adj* hierarchical; **base de données hiérarchisée =** hierarchical database; **réseau d'ordinateurs hiérarchisé =** hierarchical computer network; **système de communication hiérarchisé =** hierarchical communications system

hi-fi *nf&adj* high fidelity *ou* hifi *ou* hi-fi; **système hi-fi =** high fidelity system *ou* hi-fi; **une chaîne hi-fi =** a hi fi system *ou* a hi-fi; *voir aussi* HAUTE-FIDELITE

histogramme *nm* bar chart *ou* bar graph *ou* histogram *ou* columnar graph;

présentation (graphique) sous forme d'histogramme = columnar working

Hollerith *npr* code (de) Hollerith = Hollerith code

hologramme *nm* hologram *ou* holographic image; **stockage** *ou* **mémoire d'hologramme** = holographic storage
◊ **holographie** *nf* holography
◊ **holographique** *adj* **stockage** *ou* **mémoire holographique** = holographic storage

homme *nm* **(a)** man; **homme à tout faire** = general assistant; *(dans un studio de cinématographie)* gaffer; *US* gofer **(b)** **interface homme-machine** = man machine interface (MMI) *ou* human-computer *ou* human-machine interface (HMI)

homogène *adj* homogeneous; **multiplexage homogène** = homogeneous multiplexing; **réseau informatique homogène** = homogeneous computer network

homologation *nf* (official) approval; **certificat d'homologation** = certificate of approval; **test d'homologation** = acceptance test *ou* testing
◊ **homologuer** *vtr* to approve officially; **le nouveau moniteur graphique a été homologué par le conseil de sécurité avant d'être commercialisé** = the new graphics monitor was approved by the safety council before being sold

horaire *nm* schedule; **établir un horaire de programmes (de télévision** *ou* **radio)** = to schedule programmes; **établissement d'un horaire de programmes (de télévision** *ou* **radio)** = programme scheduling; **personne qui établit un horaire de programmes (de télévision** *ou* **radio)** = scheduler; **tranche horaire** = time slice

horizontal, -e *adj* horizontal; **abscisse** *ou* **coordonnée horizontale** = X-coordinate; *(pour détection d'erreurs de transmission)* **contrôle horizontal** = horizontal check; **impulsion de synchronisation horizontale** = horizontal synchronization pulse;

inhibition *ou* **suppression horizontale (du signal)** = horizontal blanking
◊ **horizontale** *nf* **(a)** horizontal line **(b)** *(coordonnées)* X direction
◊ **horizontalement** *adv* horizontally

horloge *nf* **(a)** *(qui marque l'heure)* clock; *(qui affiche l'heure sur l'écran)* time display; **l'heure est affichée à l'horloge placée dans un coin de l'écran** = the time is shown by the clock in the corner of the screen; **le micro possède une horloge incorporée** = the micro has a built-in clock; **horloge atomique** = atomic clock; **horloge numérique** = digital clock **(b)** *(de synchronisation)* clock; **cycle d'horloge** = clock cycle *ou* CPU cycle; **erreur** *ou* **défaut d'horloge** = hazard; **fréquence d'horloge** = clock frequency; **fréquence d'horloge du processeur** = microprocessor timing; **la principale fréquence d'horloge est de 10MHz** = the main clock frequency is 10MHz; **impulsion d'horloge** = clock pulse; **signaux synchrones aux impulsions d'horloge** = clocked signals; **piste d'horloge** = clock track; **vitesse d'horloge** = clock rate; **horloge centrale** = main clock; **horloge delta** *ou* **à relance automatique** = delta clock; **horloge en temps réel** = real-time clock; **horloge externe** *ou* **extérieure** = external clock; **horloge maîtresse** *ou* **horloge principale** = main clock *ou* master clock *ou* timing master; **horloge programmable** = programmable clock; **horloge relative** = relative-time clock

hors *prép* out of; **hors service** = out of service *ou* dead

hôte *nm* host; **ordinateur hôte** = central computer *ou* host computer; **on peut manipuler l'image avant son téléchargement sur l'ordinateur hôte** = the image can be manipulated before uploading to the host computer; **le câble de liaison entre le scanner et l'ordinateur hôte est fourni** = the cable to connect the scanner to the host adapter is included in the package; **adaptateur de l'ordinateur hôte** = host adapter

housse *nf (de protection d'un appareil)* dustcover

Huffman *npr* code de Huffman = Huffman code

huit 1 *nm* **base huit** = octal scale *ou* octal notation **2** *adj num* eight; **(système) huit bits** = eight-bit (system); **disquette de huit pouces** = eight-inch disk; **lecteur de disquettes de huit pouces** = eight-inch drive

hybride *adj* hybrid; **circuit hybride** = hybrid circuit; **interface hybride** = hybrid interface; **ordinateur hybride** = hybrid computer; **système hybride** = hybrid system

hyper *préfixe* ultra; **hyper haute fréquence** = tremendously high frequency (THF)

◊ **hyperfréquence** *nf* ultra high frequency (UHF) *ou* microwave; **relais d'hyperfréquence** = microwave relay; **transmission par hyperfréquence** = microwave transmission; **liaison de transmission par hyperfréquence** = microwave communications link

hyposulfite *nm (pour fixage en photographie)* **hyposulfite de sodium** = sodium thiosulfate; *(familier)* hypo; *voir aussi* THIOSULFATE

Hz = HERTZ

Ii

IA = INTELLIGENCE ARTIFICIELLE

IAO = INGENIERIE ASSISTEE PAR ORDINATEUR

IBM **la société IBM** = IBM; *(familier)* Big Blue

icône *nm* icon *ou* ikon; **l'icône du programme graphique ressemble à une petite palette** = the icon for the graphics program is a small picture of a palette; **cliquer deux fois quand vous rencontrez l'icône du traitement de texte** = click twice over the wordprocessor icon; **pour afficher le menu déroulant cliquer l'icône sur le haut de l'écran** = the pull-down menu is viewed by clicking over the icon at the top of the screen
◊ **iconographie** *nf (ensemble des illustrations d'un livre ou d'une revue)* visuals *ou* illustrations

idéal,-e *adj* ideal

identificateur *nm* identifier (word) *ou* label; **enregistrement d'identificateurs** = label record
◊ **identification** *nf* identification; *(de message)* authentication; **identification de fichier** = file identification; **bloc d'identification** = header (block); **caractère d'identification** = identification character *ou* identifier; **champ d'identification** = label field; **code d'identification de périphérique** = device code; **(code d') identification d'un terminal** = terminal identity; *(d'une personne)* **numéro de code d'identification** = personal identification number (PIN); **dispositif électronique d'identification** = personal identification device (PID); **label d'identification (sur le support magnétique)** = interior label; **label d'identification de bande** = header label; **mot d'identification** = identifier word;

division avec paramètres d'identification (d'un programme en COBOL) = identification division; *(qui définit le format d'une bande magnétique)* **séquence d'identification** = identity burst
◊ **identifier** *vtr* to identify; **l'utilisateur doit s'identifier par un mot de passe qui lui permet d'avoir accès au système** = the user has to identify himself to the system by using a password before access is allowed

identique *adj* identical; **les deux systèmes utilisent des logiciels identiques** = the two systems use identical software

identité *nf* **(a)** identity; **carte d'identité** = identity card *ou* ID card **(b)** *(fonction logique)* **opération d'identité** = identity operation; **porte d'identité** = identity gate *ou* element

idiot, -e *adj (non formaté)* **bande idiote** = idiot tape

IEEE *USA* = INSTITUTE OF ELECTRICAL AND ELECTRONIC ENGINEERS (IEEE); **bus (conforme aux normes du) IEEE** = IEEE bus; *(pour interface parallèle standard)* **norme IEEE-488** = IEEE-488

IF *(si)* **instruction IF** = IF statement
◊ **IF-THEN-ELSE** *(branchement conditionnel)* **instruction IF-THEN-ELSE** = IF-THEN-ELSE

ignorer *vtr* to ignore

illégal, -e *adj* **(a)** *(document)* illegal; **copie illégale** = *(d'un programme)* bootleg (copy); *(d'un livre ou d'un programme)* pirated copy **(b)** *(action)* **copie illégale** *ou* **reproduction illégale (d'une oeuvre)** = infringement of copyright *ou* copyright infringement

◊ **illégalement** *adv* illegally

illimité, -ée *adj* (poste de travail) à accès illimité = open access (station)

illisible *adj* illegible; si le manuscrit est illisible, il faut le renvoyer à l'auteur et lui demander de le faire taper à la machine = if the manuscript is illegible, send it back to the author to have it typed; texte illisible = bad copy

illumination *nf* illumination; *(d'une antenne)* illumination de l'ouverture = aperture illumination
◊ **illuminer** *vtr* to illuminate

illustration *nf* *(de livre ou revue)* illustration *ou* picture; *(l'ensemble des illustrations)* **illustrations** = pix *ou* visuals; **ce livre comporte des illustrations en couleur** = the book is illustrated in colour; **on trouve dans le livre 25 pages d'illustrations en couleur** = the book has twenty-five pages of full-colour illustrations; **le manuel contient des graphiques et des illustrations de configurations de réseaux** = the manual is illustrated with charts and pictures of the networking connections
◊ **illustrer** *vtr* to illustrate

image *nm* picture; *(vidéo ou télévision)* **image complète** = frame; **image d'écran** = video frame *ou* image; **image fantôme** = ghost image; **image inversée** = mirror image; **image latente** = latent image; **image mémoire de carte** = card image; **image orientée en film** = cine-orientated image; **image originale** *ou* **de première génération** = first generation image; **(nombre d') images par seconde** *ou* **images/seconde** = frames per second (fps); **image vidéo** *ou* **image d'écran** = video image *ou* video frame; **capteur d'images vidéo** = frame grabber; **le processeur d'images permet le stockage d'une image vidéo dans une mémoire intégrée de 8 bits** = the image processor allows you to store a video frame in a built-in 8-bit frame store; **amplificateur** *ou* **intensificateur d'image** = image enhancer; **analyseur d'image** = image processor; **(faire un) arrêt sur image** = (to) freeze (frame); **le processeur d'image permet de faire un arrêt sur image** = with an image processor you can freeze a video frame; **capteur d'image** = image

sensor; **comptage d'images (complètes)** = full-frame time code; **déformation** *ou* **distorsion** *ou* **aberration de l'image** *ou* image distortion; **dégradation de l'image** = image degradation; **distorsion de l'image** = image distortion; **élément d'image** = picture element *ou* pixel; **faisceau d'image** = picture beam; **figer une image** = to freeze a frame; **fréquence d'image** = frame frequency; **la télévision britannique utilise une fréquence de 25 images par seconde** *ou* **25 images/seconde** = in the UK the frame frequency is 25 frames per second *ou* 25 fps; **mémoire image** = *(télévision)* frame store; *(vidéo)* video memory *ou* video RAM (VRAM); **espace mémoire de l'image** = image storage space; **la mémoire image peut servir à l'affichage des images météorologiques transmises par satellite** = the frame store can be used to display weather satellite pictures; **mémoire d'images optiques** = scanner memory; *(onde)* **porteuse d'image** = image carrier; **processeur d'image** = image processor; **le processeur d'image peut figer une image de télévision isolée** = the image processor will freeze a single TV frame; **rémanence de l'image** = image retention *ou* hangover; **saut d'image** = frame flyback; **scanner d'images** = image scanner; **stabilité de l'image** = image stability; **traînée d'image** = hangover; **traitement de l'image** = image processing *ou* picture processing; **traitement informatique de l'image** = computer image processing; **machine** *ou* **système de traitement de l'image** = image processor; **transmission d'images** = picture transmission; **zone d'image** = image area; **zone d'image reçue** = safe area; **zone de stockage de l'image** = image storage space

◊ **imagerie** *nf* **imagerie médicale** *ou* **de synthèse** = imaging; **imagerie par résonance magnétique (IRM)** = magnetic resonance imaging

des affections non décelables par examens classiques sont maintenant détectées précocement grâce à l'imagerie médicale, augmentant ainsi considérablement les chances de guérison

01 Informatique

imbrication *nf* interleaving; *(de boucles ou instructions)* nesting; *(code, etc.)* embedding; **niveau d'imbrication (de boucles)** = nesting level

◊ **imbriqué, -ée** *adj* interleaved; *(boucle ou instruction)* nested; *(code, etc.)* embedded; **boucle imbriquée** = nested loop; **code imbriqué (dans un programme)** = embedded code; **commande imbriquée (dans le texte)** = embedded command; **ordinateur** *ou* **système imbriqué (dans un autre)** = embedded computer *ou* system

◊ **imbriquer** *vtr (une boucle ou une instruction)* to nest; **macro-instruction imbriquée** = nested macrocall

immédiat, -e *adj* immediate; **adressage immédiat** = immediate addressing; **adresse immédiate** = zero-level address *ou* immediate address; **instruction immédiate** = immediate instruction; **mode immédiat** = immediate mode; **opérande immédiat** = immediate operand; *(de données, de musique enregistrées)* **relecture immédiate** = instant replay; **traitement (de données) immédiat** = demand processing *ou* immediate processing; *(d'un film)* **visionnage immédiat** = instant replay

◊ **immédiatement** *adv* immediately *ou* directly

immobilisation *nf* immobilisation; **temps d'immobilisation** = stop time

impact *nm* impact; **imprimante à impact** = impact printer; **imprimante sans impact** = non-impact printer

la compétition entre les imprimantes à 'impact' (marguerite et aiguilles) et les 'non impact' (jet d'encre, laser, thermique) est de plus en plus vive

L'Ordinateur Individuel

impair, -e *adj* odd; **(contrôle de) parité impaire** = odd parity (check)

◊ **imparité** *nf* **(contrôle d') imparité** = odd parity (check)

impasse *nf* deadlock

impeccable *adj* perfect

◊ **impeccablement** *adv* perfectly

impédance *nf* impedance *ou* load; **impédance de charge** = load impedance; **impédance de ligne** = line impedance; **accord d'impédance** = impedance matching; **l'accord d'impédance entre un émetteur et un récepteur réduit la perte de puissance des signaux transmis** = impedance matching a transmitter and receiver minimizes power losses to transmitted signals; **charge d'impédance** = load; **temps de décharge d'un circuit d'impédance** = load life; **désaccord d'impédance** = impedance mismatch

implantation *nf* implantation d'une **base de données** = database mapping; **implantation des touches d'un clavier** = keyboard layout *ou* key matrix

◊ **implanter** *vtr* **(a)** *(ranger dans la mémoire)* to plant **(b)** to implant; **le dopant est implanté dans le substrat** = the dopant is implanted into the substrate

implémentation *nf* implementation

◊ **implémenter** *vtr* to implement

implication *nf* implication

implicite *adj* implied *ou* (by) default; **adressage implicite** = implied addressing; **l'adressage implicite pour l'accumulateur est inclus dans l'instruction LDA,16** = implied addressing for the accumulator is used in the instruction LDA,16; **débit implicite d'un modem** = default rate; **la largeur implicite de cet écran est de 80** = screen width has a default value of 80; **lecteur implicite** = default drive; **option implicite** = default option

important, -e *adj* important *ou* significant; **très important** = most important *ou* prime; **caractéristique la plus importante** = key feature

importation *nf* importation

◊ **importé, -e** *adj* **signal importé** = imported signal

◊ **importer** *vtr* to import; **il est possible d'importer des images d'un logiciel CAO dans un programme de PAO** = you can import images from the CAD package into the DTP program

impression *nf* impression *ou* printing *ou* print; **si l'impression est trop pâle, réglez le bouton de densité (d'impression) sur le noir** = when fading occurs, turn the density dial on the printer to full black; **impression en arrière-plan** = background printing; **l'impression peut**

être exécutée en arrière-plan pendant que vous travaillez sur un autre document = background printing can be carried out whilst you are editing another document; **impression en différé** = print spooling *ou* off-line printing; **impression directe** = direct impression; **impression d'étiquettes** = labelling; **impression hors ligne** *ou* **par imprimante autonome** = off-line printing; *(blanc sur noir)* **impression inversée** = cameo; **impression à passages multiples** = multipass overlap; **impression d'un programme d'assemblage** = assembly listing; **impression (en) offset** = offset printing; **impression par spouling** = print spooling; **impression en taille douce** = copperplate printing; **impression thermique** = electrosensitive printing; **arrêt de l'impression** = print pause; **bande sans paramètres d'impression** = idiot tape; **boule d'impression** = golf-ball; **caractères de contrôle d'impression** = print *ou* printer control characters; **cylindre** *ou* **tambour d'impression** = impression cylinder; *(télévision ou télécopie)* **déréglage de la qualité d'impression** = hangover; *(copieur ou imprimante)* **réglage de densité d'impression** = density dial; **format d'impression** = print format; **logiciel de formatage d'impression** = print formatter; *(plaque ou bloc)* **marteau d'impression** = print hammer; **matrice d'impression à haute définition** = enhanced dot matrix; **modificateurs** *ou* **paramètres d'impression** = print modifiers; **qualité d'impression (d'une imprimante)** = printer quality; **style d'impression** = print style; **tête d'impression** = printhead; **la tête d'impression peut imprimer plus de 400 millions de caractères** = the printhead has a print life of over 400 million characters

◊ **imprimable** *adj* printer-readable; **une image vidéo imprimable peut être envoyée sur une imprimante laser classique par le port vidéo** = a printer-readable video image can be sent to a basic laser printer through a video port

◊ **imprimante** *nf* (computer) printer; **imprimante à aiguilles** = stylus printer *ou* dot-matrix printer; **imprimante à bande** = band printer; **imprimante à barres** = bar printer; **imprimante bidirectionnelle** = bi-directional printer; **imprimante à boule** = golf-ball printer; **imprimante à bulle d'encre** = bubble jet printer;

imprimante caractère (par caractère) = character printer; **imprimante à caractères pleins** = solid font printer; **imprimante à chaîne** = chain printer; **imprimante 80 colonnes** = 80-column printer; **le prix comprend une imprimante 80 colonnes** = an 80-column printer is included in the price; **imprimante à cylindre** *ou* **à tambour** = barrel printer; **imprimante à définition des blancs** = white writer; **imprimante à définition des noirs** = black writer; **imprimante électrostatique** = electrostatic printer; **imprimante graphique** = printer-plotter; **imprimante à impact** = impact printer; **imprimante sans impact** = non-impact printer; **imprimante à jet d'encre** = ink-jet printer; **imprimante (à) laser** = laser printer; **imprimante ligne à ligne** = line printer; **imprimante à marguerite** = daisy-wheel printer; **l'imprimante à marguerite donne un bien meilleur résultat que l'imprimante matricielle mais elle est plus lente** = a daisy-wheel printer produces much better quality text than a dot-matrix, but is slower; **l'imprimante à marguerite imprime un caractère à la fois** = a daisy-wheel printer is a character printer *ou* prints one character at a time; **imprimante matricielle** = dot-matrix printer *ou* stylus printer *ou* wire printer; **imprimante (en mode) page** = page printer; **imprimante parallèle** = parallel printer; **imprimante à tambour** = barrel printer; **imprimante thermique** = thermal *ou* electrothermal printer; **imprimante thermique (à étincelle)** = spark printer; **imprimante à transfert thermique** = thermal transfer printer; **imprimante à tulipe** = thimble printer; **contrôleur** *ou* **pilote d'imprimante** = printer controller; **débit d'une imprimante (mesuré en 'ems')** = printer output *ou* ems per hour; **durée de vie d'une imprimante** = print life; **gestionnaire d'imprimante** = printer driver; **interface d'imprimante** = hard copy interface; **pilote d'imprimante** = printer driver; **port (d')imprimante** = printer port; **ruban d'imprimante** = printer ribbon; **sortie d'imprimante** = computer listing *ou* hard copy *ou* information output *ou* computer printout; **tampon d'imprimante** = printer buffer; **vidage sur imprimante** = dump; **vidage d'écran sur imprimante** = screen dump; **vidage de mouvements (sur imprimante)** = change dump; **vider sur l'imprimante (le contenu d'une mémoire)** = to deposit

◊ **imprimé** *nm* **(a)** *(document)* printed matter; **imprimé publicitaire =** publicity matter; **rapport de contraste d'un imprimé =** print contrast ratio **(b)** *(sortie d'imprimante ou texte d'écran)* hard copy

> imprimantes à aiguilles, à jet d'encre, à laser, thermiques: les technologies d'impression progressent et les choix de matériels se diversifient
> *L'Ordinateur Individuel*

◊ **imprimé, -e** *adj* **(a)** *(document)* printed; **document imprimé =** printed document; **texte imprimé =** hard copy; **imprimé d'avance =** preprinted **(b)** **circuit imprimé (CI) =** printed circuit *ou* printed circuit board (PCB); **carte de circuit imprimé** *ou* **plaque (présensibilisée) pour circuit imprimé =** printed circuit card *ou* printed circuit board *ou* PCB; **plaque (présensibilisée) double face pour circuit imprimé =** double-sided printed circuit board

◊ **imprimer** *vtr* to print; **le livre est imprimé sur du papier 80 grammes =** the book is printed on 80gsm paper; **nous faisons imprimer quelques-unes de nos revues au Japon =** we are using Japanese printers for some of our magazines; **nous n'imprimons pas les prochaines factures avant vendredi =** the next invoice run will be on Friday; **il était ravi de voir son livre imprimé =** he was very pleased to see his book in print; **ce livre a été imprimé à Hong Kong =** the book was printed in Hong Kong; **imprimer (des données) =** to print out (data); **(instruction d') imprimer en caractères gras =** bold *ou* embolden; **imprimer la file d'attente =** to despool; **trait d'union qui ne s'imprime pas =** discretionary hyphen *ou* soft hyphen

◊ **imprimerie** *nf (l'art)* printing; *(atelier)* printing house *ou* printing press *ou* printer's; **le texte a été envoyé à l'imprimerie la semaine dernière =** the text was sent to the printer's last week; **imprimerie à façon =** print shop; **imprimerie et reliure =** bookwork; **écrire en caractères d'imprimerie =** to print

◊ **imprimeur** *nm* printer; **on doit envoyer le livre chez l'imprimeur la semaine prochaine =** the book will be sent to the printer next week; **corrections de l'imprimeur =** house corrections; **imprimeur à façon =** jobbing printer; **nom de l'imprimeur =** imprint

impulsion *nf* impulse *ou* pulse; **impulsion de cadran =** dial pulse;

impulsion électronique = electronic pulse; **impulsion d'horloge =** clock pulse; **signaux synchrones aux impulsions d'horloge =** clocked signals; **impulsion d'inhibition du signal =** blanking pulse; **impulsion de synchronisation horizontale =** horizontal synchronization pulse; **impulsion de synchronisation du balayage vertical =** field sync pulse; **émettre des impulsions =** to pulse; *(d'échantillonnage ou de validation)* to strobe; **déclenché par bascule de front d'impulsion =** edge-triggered; **générateur d'impulsions =** pulse generator; **micro à impulsion =** dynamic microphone; **modulation d'impulsions =** pulse modulation; **modulation d'impulsions en amplitude (MIA) =** pulse amplitude modulation (PAM); **modulation d'impulsions en durée (MID) =** pulse duration modulation (PDM); **modulation d'impulsions en largeur ou en durée (MIL ou MID) =** pulse width modulation (PWM); **modulation d'impulsions en position (MIP) =** pulse position modulation (PPM); **modulation par impulsions et codage (MIC) =** pulse code modulation (PCM); **train d'impulsions =** pulse stream

> d'un point de vue pratique, ce codage qui ne fait appel qu'aux chiffres 1 et 0 est traduit en impulsions électriques (les 1) séparées par l'absence de signal (les 0)
> *Science et Vie*

imputable *adj* attributable; **erreur imputable à un composant défectueux =** component error

in-folio *nm&adj* folio

in-quarto (format) **in-quarto =** quarto

in-seize *ou* **in-16** *nm&adj* sixteenmo *ou* 16mo

inacceptable *adj* unacceptable *ou* not acceptable; **texte inacceptable =** bad copy

inaccessible *adj* out of range

inactif, -ive *adj* inactive; **instruction inactive =** no-op instruction

inapproprié, -ée *adj* improper; **coupure inappropriée =** bad break

inattendu, -e *adj* unexpected; *(d'un programme)* **arrêt inattendu** = hangup

inaudible *adj* inaudible; **fréquences inaudibles** = subaudio frequencies

incandescence *nf* incandescence

◊ **incandescent, -e** *adj* incandescent; **le passage du courant qui chauffe le filament dans une ampoule contenant un gaz, produit une lumière incandescente** = current passing through gas and heating a filament in a light bulb causes it to produce incandescent light

incident *nm (d'un ordinateur ou d'un programme)* failure *ou* fault; **enregistrement (automatique) des états d'incidents** = failure logging; **(signal d') interruption sur incident** = error interrupt; *(sans repartir à zéro)* **reprise sur incident** = failure recovery *ou* error recovery

inclinaison *nf (d'un caractère)* skew

◊ **incliné, -ée** *adj* inclined *ou* tilted; **orbite inclinée** = inclined orbit

inclure *vtr* **(a)** *(contenir)* to enclose; **les frais financiers n'ont pas été inclus dans le document** = the interest charges have been excluded from the document **(b)** *(comprendre)* to involve

◊ **inclus, -use** *adj* enclosed; **logiciel inclus à l'achat d'un ordinateur** = bundled software; **logiciel non inclus (dans l'offre d'achat)** = unbundled software

◊ **inclusif, -ive** *adj* inclusive; *(fonction logique)* **OU inclusif** = inclusive OR; **opération OU inclusif** = either-or operation

◊ **inclusion** *nf* inclusion

incompatibilité *nf* noncompatibility

◊ **incompatible** *adj* incompatible; **en essayant de relier les deux systèmes, ils les ont trouvés incompatibles** = they tried to link the two systems, but found they were incompatible

incomplet, -ète *adj* incomplete; **code incomplet** = skeletal code; **(mémoire) RAM incomplète** = partial RAM

inconditionnel, -elle *adj* unconditional; **branchement** *ou* **saut inconditionnel** = unconditional branch *ou* jump

incontrôlable *adj* uncontrollable; *(d'un dispositif ou d'un ordinateur)* **opération incontrôlable** = runaway

incorporé, -ée *adj* built-in; **fonction incorporée** = built-in function

incorrect, -e *adj* false *ou* inaccurate *ou* incorrect; **les données saisies étant incorrectes, les résultats à la sortie étaient par le fait même erronés** = the input data was incorrect, so the output was also incorrect

◊ **incorrectement** *adv* incorrectly; **les données ont été incorrectement saisies** = the data was incorrectly keyboarded

incrément *nm* increment; **incrément de ligne** = line increment; **augmentez l'incrément à trois** = increase the increment to three

◊ **incrémentation** *nf* increment; **traceur à incrémentation** = incremental plotter

◊ **incrémenter** *vtr* to increment; **le compteur est incrémenté à chaque instruction exécutée** = the counter is incremented each time an instruction is executed

◊ **incrémenteur-décrémenteur** *nm* **compteur incrémenteur-décrémenteur** = up/down counter

◊ **incrémentiel, -elle** *adj* incremental; **compilation et décompilation incrémentielles** = incremental compilation and decompilation; **donnée(s) incrémentielle(s)** = incremental data; **ordinateur incrémentiel** = incremental computer; **traceur incrémentiel** = incremental plotter

indépendamment *adv* independently; **avec un spoul, l'imprimante fonctionne indépendamment du clavier** = in spooling, the printer is acting independently of the keyboard

◊ **indépendant, -e** *adj* independent *ou* separate; **émission de signaux par canaux indépendants** = separate channel signalling; **langage informatique indépendant** = computer independent language; **on peut exécuter le programme sur un ordinateur indépendant ou un système multiposte =** the program runs on a standalone machine or a multi-user system; **programme indépendant =** device-independent program

indéterminé, -ée *adj* indeterminate; **système indéterminé =** indeterminate system

index *nm (d'un livre ou d'un programme)* index; *(système de recherche)* reference retrieval system; **l'index de ce livre est très mal fait =** the book has been badly indexed; **index complet =** dense index; **index cumulatif =** cumulative index; **index de cycle =** cycle index; **index des fichiers =** file index; **index général ou principal =** main index; **index hash code =** hash index; **préparation de l'index d'un livre =** indexing; **préparation d'un index à l'aide d'un ordinateur =** computer indexing; **le livre a été envoyé à l'extérieur pour la préparation de l'index =** the book was sent out for indexing; **personne qui prépare un index ou auteur d'un index =** indexer; **clé d'index =** index key; **mot d'index =** index value word; **page index =** index page; *(informatique)* **registre d'index =** index register (IR)
◊ **indexage** *nm* indexing; **indexage libre =** free indexing; **indexage dérivé =** derived indexing
◊ **indexation** *nf* indexing; **indexation sur ordinateur =** computer indexing; **langage d'indexation =** indexing language; **résumé et indexation =** abstracting & indexing (A&I)
◊ **indexé, -ée** *adj* indexed; **adressage indexé =** indexed addressing; **adresse indexée =** indexed address; **fichier indexé =** indexed file; **instruction indexée =** indexed instruction; **mémoire séquentielle indexée =** indexed sequential storage; **méthode d'accès séquentiel indexé (ISAM) =** indexed sequential access method (ISAM); **méthode d'accès séquentiel indexé en file =** queued indexed sequential access method (QISAM); **registre (d'adresse) indexé =** B register
◊ **indexer** *vtr* to index

indicateur *nm* **(a)** *(symbole ou code)* indicator *ou* (indicator) flag *ou* marker; **indicateur binaire =** flag bit; **indicateur**

binaire de dépassement de capacité = overflow bit *ou* flag; **indicateur de contrôle =** check indicator *ou* rogue indicator; **indicateur de contrôle de parité =** parity flag; **(bit) indicateur d'état ou d'utilisation =** device flag; **cette routine vérifie l'indicateur d'état et ne transmet pas le signal si le bit occupé est présent =** this routine checks the device status word and will not transmit data if the busy bit is set; **indicateur de mot =** word marker; **indicateur de retenue =** carry flag; **indicateur de signe =** sign bit *ou* sign indicator; **indicateur (binaire) zéro =** zero flag; **si le résultat est zéro, l'indicateur zéro est activé =** if the result is zero, the zero flag is set; **bit indicateur =** flag bit; **mise en place d'un indicateur =** flag event; **mot indicateur d'état =** device status word (DSW); **séquence d'indicateurs =** flag sequence; **tableau des indicateurs =** indicator chart **(b)** *(dispositif)* **(commutateur) indicateur d'état =** sense switch; **indicateur de fin de papier =** form stop

indicatif *nm* **(a)** *(téléphonique)* (dialling) code; **quel est l'indicatif de Bruxelles? =** what is the code for Brussels?; **indicatif international =** international dialling code; **indicatif du pays =** country code *ou* international number; *(Canada)* **indicatif régional =** area code; **indicatif de zone =** area code; **l'indicatif (de zone) de Londres est 071 =** the area code for central London is 071; **indicatif du pays suivi de l'indicatif de zone suivi du numéro de votre correspondant =** country code followed by area code followed by customer's number **(b) indicatif littéral =** index letter; **indicatif numérique =** index number

indice *nm* **(a)** subscript *ou* inferior figure; **variable caractérisée par un indice =** subscripted variable **(b)** *(des cahiers d'un livre)* **indices de collationnement =** collating marks; *(sur film)* **indice de position =** index **(c)** *(télévision)* **indice d'écoute =** audience rating **(d)** *(de la lumière)* **indice de réfraction =** refractive index
◊ **indicé, -ée** *adj* **variable indicée =** subscripted variable

indiquer *vtr* to mark *ou* specify *ou* to indicate

indirect, -e *adj* indirect; **adressage indirect** = deferred *ou* indirect *ou* second-level addressing; **rayonnement indirect** = indirect ray

indisponible *adj (non-activé)* **configuration indisponible** = configured off *ou* configured out

individuel, -elle *adj* **(a)** individual; **ordinateur individuel** = personal computer *ou* PC **(b) poste individuel** = stand-alone *ou* standalone; **les postes ont été reliés en réseau plutôt que d'être utilisés comme postes individuels** = the workstations have been networked together rather than used as stand-alone systems

inductance *nf* inductance
◊ **inducteur** *nm* inductor
◊ **inductif, -ive** *adj* **coordination inductive** = inductive coordination
◊ **induction** *nf (électricité)* induction; **bobine d'induction** = induction coil *ou* inductor; **produire une induction** = to induce (a current)
◊ **induire** *vtr (un courant)* to induce (a current)
◊ **induit, -e** *adj* **(a)** *(électricité)* **produire un courant induit** = to induce a current **(b)** *(produite par une cause externe)* **défaillance induite** = induced failure **(c)** *(produite par d'autres machines)* **diaphonie** *ou* **interférence induite** = crossfire *ou* induced interference

industrie *nf* industry; **l'industrie électronique** = the electronics industry
◊ **industriel, -elle** *adj* industrial; **esthétique industrielle** = industrial design; **ordinateur industriel** = process control computer

ineffaçable *adj* **mémoire ineffaçable** = nonerasable memory

ineffectif, -ive *adj* ineffective; **instruction ineffective** = do-nothing (instruction)

inerte *adj* inert; **gaz inerte** = inert gas

inexact, -e *adj* inaccurate *ou* incorrect
◊ **inexactitude** *nf* inaccuracy

inexplicable *adj* inexplicable *ou* strange; **erreur inexplicable** = gremlin; **perte de transmission inexplicable** = line gremlin

inférence *nf* inference; **(nombre d') inférences logiques par seconde** = logical inference per second (LIPS); **contrôle d'inférence** = inference control; **moteur d'inférence** = inference engine *ou* machine

inférieur, -e *adj* lower; *(pour papier d'une imprimante)* **bac inférieur** = lower bin; **introduire le bac inférieur** = load lower bin

infini *nm* infinity
◊ **infini, -e** *adj* infinite

infixé, -ée *adj* **notation infixée** = infix notation

influer *vi* to affect; **les sautes** *ou* **les variations de tension vont influer sur le fonctionnement de l'ordinateur** = changes in voltage will affect the way the computer functions

infographie *nf* computer graphics *ou* computer-generated graphics *ou* raster graphics; **infographie interactive** = interactive graphics; **infographie par points** *ou* **à adressage binaire** = bit-mapped graphics

infomaniaque *nm&f* terminal junky (TJ); **mon fils est devenu un véritable infomaniaque** = my son has turned into a real terminal junky

informaticien, -ienne *n&adj* **ingénieur informaticien** = computer engineer

information *nf* **(a)** *(ensemble de données)* information; **information sans intérêt** *ou* **de rebut** = garbage; **canal** *ou* **voie de transmission de l'information** = information transfer channel; **contrôle de flux d'information** = information flow control; **liberté d'accès à l'information** = freedom of information; **ligne d'information** = information line; **ordinateur utilisé pour le traitement de l'information** = information processor;

quantité d'information = information content; **réseaux d'information** = information networks; **sécurité de l'information** = data security; **source d'information** *ou* **service (fournisseur) d'information** = information provider (IP); **stockage de l'information** = information storage; **support d'information** = information *ou* data medium; **système de gestion de l'information** = information management system; **techniques de l'information** = information technology (IT); **théorie de l'information** = information theory; **traitement de l'information** = data processing (DP *ou* dp) *ou* information processing; **traitement centralisé de l'information** = centralized data processing; **traitement électronique de l'information** = electronic data processing (EDP); **unité d'information** = computer word; **vitesse de sortie de l'information** = information rate; **voie de transmission d'information** = information bearer channel **(b)** *(nouvelles)* **informations** = news; **bulletin d'informations de la société** = company newsletter

informatique 1 *nf* computing *ou* electronic data processing (EDP) *ou* information technology (IT); **(science de) l'informatique** = computer science *ou* informatics; **informatique défensive** = defensive computing; *(loi)* **loi Informatique et Libertés** = Data Protection Act; **informatique répartie** = distributed (data) processing (DDP); **connaissances en informatique** = computer literacy; **(personne) qui a des connaissances en informatique** = computer-literate (person); **le directeur général n'a aucune notion de l'informatique** = the managing director is simply not computer-literate *ou* is computer-illiterate **2** *adj* computer; **applications informatiques** = computer applications; **cassette informatique** = data cassette; **(personne) qui ne possède aucune connaissance informatique** *ou* **qui ne comprend pas le jargon informatique** = computer-illiterate; **fournisseur** *ou* **revendeur d'équipements informatiques** = computer equipment supplier; **fichier informatique** = computer file; *(passible du tribunal correctionnel)* **fraude informatique** = computer crime *ou* computer fraud; **langage informatique** = computer language; **langage**

informatique indépendant = computer independent language; **logique informatique** = computer logic; **matériel informatique** = hardware; *(ensemble du matériel et de l'équipement)* installation; **personnel informatique** = liveware; **pirate (de système) informatique** = hacker; **poste informatique de télétransmission** = data station; **réseau informatique** = computer network *ou* information network; **réseau informatique centralisé** = centralized computer network; **réseau informatique homogène** = homogeneous computer network; **l'éditeur de la rubrique informatique du journal** = the paper's computer editor; **service informatique** = computer department; **directeur, -trice (du service) informatique** = computer manager; **responsable** *ou* **chef du service informatique** = data processing manager (DPM); **système informatique** = information system *ou* computer system; **système informatique pour bureau** = computer office system; **cette entreprise est un fournisseur réputé de systèmes informatiques intégrés qui permettent à la fois la pagination de très longs documents et le traitement personnalisé de chaque page** = this firm is a very well-known supplier of computer-integrated systems which allow batch pagination of very long documents with alteration of individual pages; **terminal** *ou* **poste informatique** = data terminal; **traitement informatique de l'image** = computer image processing; **société de services et d'ingénierie informatique (SSII)** = computer bureau

◊ **informatisation** *nf* computerization; **l'informatisation du secteur financier progresse très rapidement** = computerization of the financial sector is proceeding very fast

◊ **informatisé, -ée** *adj* computer-managed; **bureau informatisé** = electronic office; **entraînement informatisé** = computer-based training (CBT); **formation informatisée** = computer-based learning (CBL) *ou* computer-managed learning (CML); **leur facturation est informatisée** = they operate a computerized invoicing system; **système de gestion informatisé** = management information system (MIS); **notre gestion des stocks est totalement informatisée** = our stock control has been completely computerized; **système** de réapprovisionnement informatisé = computerized stock system

◇ **informatiser** *vtr* to computerize

infra- *préfixe* infra-

◇ **infrarouge** **1** *nm* infrared; **communication par infrarouge** = infrared communications; **détecteur d'infrarouge** = infrared detector; **instruments de vision aux infrarouges** = infrared sights; **photo avec film sensible aux infrarouges** = infrared photography; **vidéocamera à infrarouge** = infrared video camera **2** *adj* **rayons infrarouges** *ou* **rayonnement infrarouge** = infrared light (IR light)

◇ **infrasonique** *adj* infrasonic; **fréquence infrasonique** = infrasonic frequency

◇ **infrasonore** *adj* **fréquences infrasonores** = subaudio frequencies

◇ **infrastructure** *nf* infrastructure

ingénierie *nf* engineering; **ingénierie assistée par ordinateur (IAO)** = computer-aided *ou* assisted engineering (CAE); **ingénierie de la connaissance** = knowledge engineering; **société de services et d'ingénierie informatique (SSII)** = computer bureau

◇ **ingénieur** *nm* engineer; **ingénieur électronicien** = electronic engineer; **ingénieur d'entretien** *ou* **d'après-vente** *ou* **de maintenance (sur le site)** = field engineer; **ingénieur d'essai** = trials engineer; **ingénieur informaticien** = computer engineer; **ingénieur logiciel** *ou* **ingénieur programmeur** = software engineer; **ingénieur système** = systems engineer

◇ **ingénieur-conseil** *nm* consulting engineer *ou* engineering consultant

inhérent, -e *adj* inherent; **adressage inhérent** = inherent addressing

inhibé, -ée *adj* inhibited *ou* suppressed; **modulation d'amplitude à porteuse inhibée** = suppressed carrier modulation; *(de modulation d'amplitude)* **bande latérale unique à porteuse inhibée** = single sideband suppressed carrier (SSBSC); **double bande latérale à porteuse inhibée** = double sideband suppressed carrier (DSBSC)

◇ **inhiber** *vtr* to inhibit *ou* to suppress

◇ **inhibition** *nf* inhibition *ou* suppression; **inhibition du signal** = blanking; **impulsion d'inhibition du signal** = blanking pulse; **inhibition horizontale (du signal)** = horizontal blanking

ininterrompu, -e *adj* continuous; **flux ininterrompu de données** = continuous data stream

initiale *nf (lettre)* initial

◇ **initial, -e** *adj* **(a)** initial; **adresse initiale** = initial address; **condition initiale** = initial condition; **format initial** = native format; **instruction initiale** = initial instruction; **instruction dans sa forme initiale** = unmodified instruction; *(du curseur)* **position initiale** = home; **valeur initiale** = initial value **(b)** **lettre initiale** = initial; **signer de ses initiales** = to initial (a document)

◇ **initialisation** *nf (d'un système)* initialization; **l'initialisation peut souvent s'effectuer à l'insu de l'utilisateur** = initialization is often carried out without the user knowing

◇ **initialiser** *vtr (un système)* to set up *ou* to initialize; **l'ingénieur a initialisé le nouvel ordinateur qui a tout de suite bien fonctionné** = the new computer worked well as soon as the engineer had set it up

injection *nf* injection; *(par fibre optique)* **laser d'injection** = injection laser; **logique intégrée à injection** = integrated injection logic (IIL)

inscrire *vtr* to enter *ou* to record; **inscrire un nom sur une liste** = to enter a name on a list; **inscrivez les résultats dans cette colonne** = record the results in this column

insensibilité *nf* **insensibilité au bruit** = noise immunity; **insensibilité aux interférences** = interference immunity

insérer *vtr* to introduce *ou* to load; **insérer au dossier** = to place something on file; **insérer dans une fente** *ou* **une ouverture** = to slot; **la disquette s'insère dans l'une des deux fentes du lecteur de disquettes** = the disk slots into one of the floppy drive apertures

◇ **insertion** *nf* **(a)** *(dans un texte)* **insertion d'un bloc** *ou* **d'un paragraphe** =

block transfer; **mode insertion** = insert mode; **programme** *ou* **sous-programme d'insertion directe** = direct-insert routine *ou* subroutine **(b)** *(connecteur)* **insertion sans friction** *ou* **à force d'insertion zéro** = zero insertion force (ZIF); *(de signal)* **perte** *ou* **affaiblissement d'insertion** = insertion loss

insonorisation *nf* soundproofing; **capot d'insonorisation** = acoustic hood; **grâce au capot d'insonorisation, il est possible d'avoir une conversation lorsque l'imprimante fonctionne** = an acoustic hood allows us to talk while the printer is working

◊ **insonorisé, -ée** *adj* soundproof; **le téléphone est dans une cabine insonorisée** = the telephone is installed in a soundproof booth

instabilité *nf* instabilité; *(de l'image)* flickering

installation *nf* installation; **installation de secours prête à fonctionner** = hot standby

◊ **installer** *vtr* to install *ou* to set up; **on nous installera une nouvelle machine** *ou* **un nouveau photocopieur Xerox demain** = we are having a new xerox machine installed tomorrow

instantané *nm* snapshot

◊ **instantané, -ée** *adj* instantaneous *ou* instant; **accès instantané** = instantaneous access; **l'accès instantané au disque RAM a été bien accueilli** = the instantaneous access of the RAM disk was welcome; **traitement instantané d'un film** = in camera process; *(de mémoire ou de registre)* **vidage instantané** = snapshot dump

instruction *nf* instruction *ou* command *ou* order *ou* (program) statement; *(mot)* instruction word; **l'instruction PRINT est un opérande employé en langage BASIC pour l'affichage des données suivantes** = the instruction PRINT is used in this BASIC dialect as an operand to display the following data; **instruction absolue** = absolute instruction; **instruction à adresse unique** *ou* **à adresse directe** = one-address instruction; **instruction à deux adresses** = two-address instruction; **instruction à deux**

adresses plus une = two-plus-one-address instruction; **instruction à n adresse(s) plus une** = n-plus-one address instruction; **instruction à trois adresses** = three-address instruction; **instruction à quatre adresses** = four-address instruction; **instruction quatre adresses plus une** = four-plus-one address instruction; **instruction d'affectation** = assignment statement; **instruction d'appel** = call instruction; **c'est ici qu'il faudrait introduire l'instruction d'appel** = the subroutine call instruction should be at this point; **instruction arithmétique** = arithmetic instruction; **instruction d'arrêt (dans un programme)** = breakpoint instruction *ou* halt instruction; **instruction d'assemblage** = pseudo-operation; **instruction de base** = basic instruction *ou* reference instruction; **instruction de branchement** *ou* **de saut** = branch instruction *ou* jump instruction; **les fabricants du CPU ont décidé que l'instruction JMP servirait à faire un branchement** = the manufacturers of this CPU have decided that JMP will be the instruction word to call the jump function; **instruction en code** *ou* **en langage machine** = machine code instruction; **instruction composée** = compound statement; **le débogueur ne peut agir sur les instructions composées** = the debugger cannot handle compound statements; **instruction conditionnelle** = conditional statement; **instruction d'opération conditionnelle** = discrimination instruction *ou* decision instruction; **instruction de contrôle** = control statement *ou* control instruction; *(de surveillance)* supervisory instruction; **la prochaine instruction de contrôle vous donnera les italiques** = the next control instruction will switch to italics; **instruction déclarative** = narrative statement; **instruction directe** = direct instruction; **instruction directive** = directive statement; **commandes et instructions d'édition** = editing terms; **instruction effective** = effective instruction; **instruction d'entrée** = entry instruction; **instruction d'entrée dans la pile** = push instruction *ou* operation; **instruction (d') entrée/sortie** = I/O instruction *ou* input/output instruction; **instruction d'extraction** = extract instruction; **instruction factice** = no-operation instruction *ou* no-op instruction *ou* null instruction; **instruction dans sa forme initiale** =

unmodified instruction; **instruction 'GET'** *ou* **instruction 'chercher'** = get instruction; **instruction 'GOTO'** *ou* **instruction de saut** = GOTO instruction; **instruction IF (si)** = IF statement; **instructions IF-THEN-ELSE (branchement conditionnel)** = IF-THEN-ELSE; **instruction immédiate** = immediate instruction; **instruction inactive** *ou* **de remplissage** = no-op instruction; **instruction indexée** = indexed instruction; **instruction ineffective** *ou* **sans effet** = do-nothing (instruction); **instruction invalide** = illegal instruction; **instructions de lancement** *ou* **instructions initiales** = initial instructions; **instruction en langage machine** = machine instruction; **instruction de lecture d'une instruction** = fetch instruction; **instruction multi-adresse** = multi-address *ou* multi-address instruction; **instruction nulle** = blank *ou* dummy *ou* null instruction; **instruction d'origine** *ou* **primitive** = presumptive instruction; **instructions privilégiées** = privileged instructions; **instruction de remplissage** = blank instruction *ou* dummy instruction *ou* pseudo-instruction *ou* null instruction; **instruction de superviseur** = executive instruction; **instruction de vidage et reprise** = dump and restart instruction; **instruction vide** = no-operation instruction *ou* no-op instruction; **adresse d'instruction** = instruction address; **antémémoire d'instruction** = instruction cache; **avancer le registre d'une instruction** = to increment (the register); **caractère d'instruction** = instruction character; **code d'instruction** = computer code *ou* instruction code *ou* machine code; **compteur d'instruction** = instruction counter *ou* program counter (PC) *ou* instruction address register (IAR); **cycle d'instruction** = instruction cycle; **cycle de lecture d'une instruction** = fetch cycle; **décodeur d'instruction** = instruction decoder *ou* operation decoder; *(à quelqu'un *ou* à un ordinateur)* **donner une instruction** = to order *ou* to instruct; **format d'instruction** = instruction format; **jeu d'instructions** = instruction repertoire *ou* set; **langage d'instruction** = command language; **phase de lecture d'une instruction** = fetch phase; **signal de lecture d'instruction** = fetch signal; **ligne d'instruction (d'un programme)** = command line; **mémoire d'instruction** = instruction storage; **mise en mémoire** *ou* **stockage d'instruction** =

instruction storage; **mode d'exécution d'instructions en pipeline** *ou* **enchaînement d'instructions avec recouvrement** = instruction pipelining; **modification d'une instruction** = instruction modification; **mot instruction** = instruction word; **processeur d'instruction** = instruction processor; **processeur à jeu d'instructions réduit** = reduced instruction set computer (RISC); **registre d'instruction** = command register *ou* instruction register (IR); **registre d'adresse d'instruction** = instruction address register (IAR); **registre d'instruction courante** = current instruction register (CIR); **registre d'instruction à exécuter** *ou* **de la prochaine instruction** = next instruction register; **registre d'instruction à suivre** = sequence control register (SCR); **répertoire d'instructions** = instruction repertoire; **temps de cycle d'instruction** = instruction cycle time; **temps d'exécution d'une instruction** *ou* **temps d'instruction** = instruction (execution) time; **zone d'instruction (dans une mémoire)** = instruction area

instrument *nm* tool; **instruments (de précision)** = instrumentation; **instruments de vision aux infrarouges** = infrared sights

◊ **instrumentation** *nf* instrumentation; **nous avons amélioré l'instrumentation se rapportant à ce modèle pour que vous puissiez mieux suivre l'état de la machine** = we've improved the instrumentation on this model to keep you better informed of the machine's position

insuffisant, -e *adj* insufficient

intégral, -e *adj* integral; **structure à maillage intégral** = plex structure

intégrateur *nm* intégrateur graphique **(à fenêtre, icône, souris, pointeur)** = window, icon, mouse, pointer (WIMP)

◊ **intégration** *nf* **(a)** integration; **ce système assure l'intégration automatique du texte et des illustrations dans le document** = the system automatically merges text and illustrations into the document **(b)** *(de composants)* **intégration à grande échelle** = large-scale integration (LSI); **intégration à très grande échelle** = very large scale integration (VLSI); **intégration à super**

grande échelle = super large scale integration (SLSI); **intégration à moyenne échelle** = medium scale integration (MSI); **intégration à faible** *ou* **petite échelle** = small scale integration (SSI); **intégration sur tranche de silicium** = wafer scale integration **(c) réseau numérique à intégration de services (RNIS)** = integrated services digital network (ISDN); **système avec intégration de données** = system firmware

l'intégration de textes, tables et graphiques au sein d'un document est dynamique
Informatique & Bureautique

intégré, -ée *adj* integrated *ou* integral *ou* built-in *ou* inbuilt *ou* on-board; **(logiciel) intégré à une puce** = on-chip (software); **base de données intégrée** = integrated database; **(système de) bureautique intégrée** = integrated office; **la carte adaptateur intégrée rend l'appareil compatible IBM** = the built-in adapter card makes it fully IBM compatible; **circuit intégré** = integrated circuit (IC); **circuit intégré de diagnostic** = diagnostic chip; **circuit intégré d'entrée/sortie en parallèle** = parallel input/output chip; **circuit intégré linéaire** = linear integrated circuit; **architecture d'un circuit intégré** = chip architecture; **ensemble des circuits intégrés** = chip set; **circuit optique intégré** = integrated optical circuit; **ligne de sélection** *ou* **de validation d'un circuit intégré** = chip select line; **système de contrôle intégré** = built-in check; **ce logiciel possède un système de correction d'erreurs intégré** = this software has inbuilt error correction; **dispositif intégré** = integrated device; **l'ordinateur est équipé d'un disque dur intégré** = the computer has a built-in hard disk; **émulateur intégré au circuit** = in-circuit emulator; **cet émulateur intégré au circuit sert à tester le contrôleur de la disquette, en simulant le fonctionnement d'un lecteur de disquettes** = this in-circuit emulator is used to test the floppy disk controller by emulating a disk drive; **puisque les lecteurs de disquettes et le modem sont intégrés l'encombrement est réduit** = the integral disk drives and modem reduce desk space; **l'ordinateur concurrent ne possède pas de lecteur de disquettes intégré comme ce modèle-ci** = our competitor's computer doesn't have an integrated disk drive like this model;

logiciel intégré = integrated software; **le processeur utilise un logiciel de lancement intégré à la puce, pour permettre le chargement rapide des programmes** = the processor uses on-chip bootstrap software to allow programs to be loaded rapidly; **logique intégrée à injection** = integrated injection logic (IIL); **modem intégré** = integrated modem; **moniteur intégré** = firmware monitor; **tous les modems possèdent des ports de communication intégrés** = there are communications ports built into all modems; **productique intégrée** = computer-integrated manufacturing (CIM); **programme intégré** = integrated program *ou* integrated software; **réseau numérique intégré (RNI)** = integrated digital network; **accès au réseau numérique intégré** = integrated digital access (IDA); **systèmes d'exploitation intégrés** = computer-integrated systems; **cette entreprise est un fournisseur réputé de systèmes informatiques intégrés qui permettent à la fois la pagination de très longs documents et le traitement personnalisé de chaque page** = this firm is a very well-known supplier of computer-integrated systems which allow batch pagination of very long documents with alteration of individual pages; **(système de) traitement de données intégré** = integrated data processing (IDP); **traitement de film intégré dans l'appareil** = in camera process

◊ **intégrer** *vtr* **(a)** to build (a disk drive, etc.) into **(b)** *(des fichiers)* to merge

le circuit intégré se présente sous forme d'un boîtier comportant 16 broches 'dual in line' (2 rangées de 8). La broche no 16 est affectée au 'plus' alimentation tandis que la broche no 8 est à relier au 'moins'
Electronique pratique

intégrité *nf* integrity; **intégrité des données** = data integrity; **faire perdre l'intégrité des données** = to corrupt data; **un problème de tension pendant l'accès au disque peut faire perdre l'intégrité des données** = power loss during disk access can corrupt the data; **intégrité d'un fichier** = integrity of a file

intelligence *nf* intelligence; **intelligence artificielle (IA)** = artificial intelligence (AI) *ou* machine intelligence;

intelligence répartie = distributed intelligence

◊ **intelligent, -e** adj intelligent ou smart; **fonction césure intelligente** = intelligent spacer; **gestionnaire d'espaces intelligent** = intelligent spacer; **machine intelligente** = intelligent device; **terminal intelligent** = intelligent terminal ou smart terminal; **le nouveau terminal intelligent comporte un éditeur de texte** = the new intelligent terminal has a built-in text editor; **terminal non intelligent** = dumb terminal

intensificateur nm **intensificateur d'image** = image enhancer

◊ **intensité** nf intensity; **intensité de champ** = field strength; **intensité de trafic** = traffic intensity; **fluctuation de l'intensité du signal** = fluctuating signal strength; **perdre de l'intensité** = to fade

interactif, -ive adj interactive; **clavier interactif** = interactive keyboard; **enseignement interactif géré par ordinateur** = computer-managed instruction (CMI); **graphiques interactifs** ou **infographie interactive** = interactive graphics; **le jeu (électronique) 'les envahisseurs de l'espace' présente d'excellents graphiques interactifs; le joueur contrôle la position de son vaisseau spatial avec la manette (de jeu)** = the space invaders machine has great interactive graphics, the player controls the position of his spaceship with the joystick; **mode interactif** = conversational mode ou interactive mode ou interactive processing; **moyens de communication interactifs** = interactive media; **routine interactive** = interactive routine; **système interactif** = interactive system; **système audio interactif** = audio active system; **système de déverminage** ou **de débogage interactif** = interactive debugging system; **télévision câblée interactive** = interactive cable television; **terminal interactif** = interactive terminal; **vidéo** ou **vidéographie interactive** = interactive video

◊ **interaction** nf interaction

◊ **interagir** vi to interact

interbloc adj interblock; **espace interbloc** = interblock gap (IBG) ou block gap

intercalaire adj (entre deux bandes de communication) **bande (de fréquences) intercalaire** = guard band; (d'un programme) **symbole intercalaire** = separator

interchangeable adj interchangeable

interclassement nm (cartes perforées) collating; **interclassement de fichier(s)** = file collating

◊ **interclasser** vtr (des cartes perforées ou des fichiers) to collate

◊ **interclasseuse** nf (de cartes perforées) collator

interconnecté, -ée adj interconnected; **réseau intégralement interconnecté** = plex structure

◊ **interconnecter** vtr to interconnect

◊ **interconnexion** nf interconnection; **interconnexion de systèmes ouverts (ISO)** ou **normes ISO (pour systèmes ouverts)** = Open System Interconnection (OSI)

intercouche adj **transfert intercouche** = radial transfer

interdiction nf interdiction; **liste d'interdictions** = stop list; **signal d'interdiction de transmission** = inhibiting input

◊ **interdire** vtr (quelque chose ou de faire quelque chose) to forbid (something); (l'accès à un circuit ou à un système) to deny ou to bar access (to a circuit ou to a system); **le mot de passe interdit aux personnes non autorisées d'avoir accès aux données** = the use of a password is to prevent unauthorized access to the data; **interdire l'accès à un fichier** ou **à un dossier** = to bar entry to a file; **interdire une interruption** = to interrupt disable

◊ **interdit, -e** adj unauthorized; **caractère interdit** = forbidden character; **chaîne (de caractères) interdite** = forbidden combination; **code** ou **chiffre interdit** = unallowable digit; (dans une indexation) **liste des mots interdits** = stop list

interfaçage nm interfacing; **protocole d'interfaçage HDLC** = high-level data link control (HDLC)

◊ **interface** *nf* interface; **interface de canal de transmission** = channel adapter; **interface de commande** *ou* **de contrôle** = command interface; **interface pour communication asynchrone** = asynchronous communications interface adapter (ACIA); **adaptateur d'interface de communication** = communications interface adapter; **interface d'entrée/sortie** = input/output interface; **interface EIA** = electronic industry association interface *ou* EIA interface; **interface ESDI** = enhanced small device interface (ESDI); **interface graphique** = graphics interface; **interface homme/machine** = man/machine interface (MMI); **interface hybride** = hybrid interface; **interface d'imprimante** = hard copy interface; **interface magnétophone** = ACR interface; **interface parallèle** = parallel interface; **interface parallèle (de type) Centronics** = Centronics interface; **interface de périphérique** = peripheral interface adapter (PIA); **interface SCSI pour petit ordinateur** = small computer system interface (SCSI); **interface série** = serial interface; **interface standard** = standard interface; **interface système/utilisateur** = user interface; **interface (pour) téléimprimeur** = teleprinter interface; **interface de** *ou* **pour terminal** = terminal interface; **le contrôleur de réseau possède 16 interfaces pour terminaux** = the network controller has 16 terminal interfaces; **interface universelle** = standard interface; **interface universelle GPIA** = general purpose interface adapter (GPIA); **interface utilisateur-machine** = human-computer *ou* human-machine interface (HMI); **carte (d') interface** = interface card; **processeur d'interface** = interface processor; **relier avec une interface** = to interface with; **routines d'interface** = interface routines

◊ **interfacé, -ée** *adj* interfaced; **équipement interfacé HDLC** = high-level data link control station

◊ **interfacer** *vtr* to interface (with) *ou* to link

ce produit est une interface qui, placée entre le lecteur de disquettes et son contrôleur, interdit physiquement l'écriture sur la disquette mais en autorise la lecture
Le Monde informatique

interférence *nf* interference *ou* static; **interférence constructive** = constructive interference; **interférence de courte durée** = impulsive noise; **interférence destructive** = destructive interference; **interférence électromagnétique** = electromagnetic interference (EMI); **interférence induite** = *(par une autre voie de transmission)* crossfire *ou* crosstalk; *(par une autre machine)* induced interference; **interférence interligne** = transverse mode noise; **interférence lumineuse** = flare; **réduction du bruit d'interférence interstation** = interstation muting; **interférence entre porteuses** = intercarrier noise; **on note des interférences de porteuses sur une télévision lorsque la porteuse son et la porteuse image se rencontrent** = television intercarrier noise is noticed when the picture and the sound signal carriers clash; **empreinte d'interférence** = interference pattern; **insensibilité** *ou* **tolérance aux interférences** = interference immunity

◊ **interférer** *vi* to interfere with something

interfoliage *nm* interleaving
◊ **interfolié, -ée** *adj* interleaved

intérieur, -e *adj* internal *ou* inner; **boucle intérieure** = inner loop; *(d'un livre)* **marge intérieure** = gutter

interlignage *nm (imprimerie)* leading; *(imprimante d'ordinateur)* line feed (LF)
◊ **interligne 1** *nf (lame de métal)* lead **2** *nm* **(a)** *(espace entre les lignes d'imprimerie)* leading *ou* line spacing *ou* interlinear spacing; **est-il possible d'ajouter un interligne supplémentaire entre les paragraphes?** = can we insert an extra line of spacing between the paragraphs?; **texte sans interligne** = solid text **(b)** *(entre deux lignes de communication)* **interférence interligne** = transverse mode noise

interlude *nm* interlude

intermédiaire *adj* intermediate; **bande intermédiaire** = guard band; **code intermédaire** = intermediate code; **fichier intermédiaire** = intermediate file; **fréquence intermédiaire** = intermediate frequency (if *ou* IF); **mémoire intermédiaire** = intermediate storage *ou* secondary storage; **mémoire à accès intermédiaire** = intermediate access memory (IAM); **support intermédiaire =** intermediate materials; **ces diapositives et photos sont les supports intermédiaires qui doivent être recopiés sur le vidéodisque =** those slides and photographs are the intermediate materials to be mastered onto the video disk; **utilisateur intermédiaire =** mid-user **(b) par l'intermédiaire de =** via; **les données ont été transmises à l'ordinateur par l'intermédiaire du téléphone =** the computer received data via the telephone line; **le téléchargement des données dans l'unité centrale peut se faire par l'intermédiaire d'un modem =** you can download the data to the CPU via a modem

intermittent, -e *adj* intermittent; **bruit intermittent =** impulsive noise; **contact intermittent =** dry contact; **erreur intermittente =** intermittent error

intermodulation *nf* cross modulation

international, -e *adj* **(a)** international; **indicatif (téléphonique) international =** international dialling code; **système téléphonique automatique international =** international direct dialling (IDD) **(b)** *(utilisé surtout dans les pays anglo-saxons)* **clavier international =** QWERTY keyboard

interne *adj* **(a)** internal; **arithmétique interne =** internal arithmetic; **code de caractères interne =** internal character code; **étiquette interne =** inlay card; **format interne =** internal format; **langage interne =** internal language; **mémoire interne =** internal memory *ou* store; **tri en mémoire interne =** internal sort; **mémoire interne à accès immédiat =** immediate access store (IAS) **(b)** in-house; **téléphone interne =** house phone *ou* house telephone *ou* internal telephone

Interphone® *nm* intercom

interpolation *nf* interpolation; **interpolation de signaux sur bande vocale =** time assigned speech interpolation (TASI)

interprétatif, -ive *adj* interpretative; **code interprétatif =** interpretative code;

programme interprétatif = interpretative program
◊ **interprétation** *nf* interpretation; **programme d'interprétation =** translator (program)
◊ **interprété, -ée** *adj* interpreted; **langage interprété =** interpreted language
◊ **interpréter** *vtr* to interpret
◊ **interpréteur** *nm* (language) interpreter

interrogation *nf* enquiry (ENQ) *ou* inquiry *ou* query *ou* interrogation; *(de plusieurs postes de travail)* polling; **interrogation de fichier =** file interrogation; **(fonction) interrogation-réponse =** inquiry/response (function); **caractère d'interrogation =** inquiry character (ENQ); **langage d'interrogation =** query language; **ordre d'interrogation (des terminaux) =** polling list; **poste d'interrogation =** inquiry station; **utilitaire d'interrogation =** query facility

interroger *vtr* to query; *(une série de postes de travail)* to poll; **interroger quelqu'un =** to question someone

interrompre *vtr* to halt *ou* to interrupt; **taper CTRL S pour interrompre le programme =** hitting CTRL S will halt the program; **on a interrompu le programme en appuyant sur la touche rouge =** the program was aborted by pressing the red button

interrupteur *nm (de courant)* circuit breaker *ou* switch; **interrupteur temporaire =** momentary switch
◊ **interruption** *nf* **(a)** break *ou* interrupt; **interruption anormale =** abnormal end *ou* abend *ou* abnormal termination; **programme de récupération de fichier après une interruption anormale =** abend recovery program; **en cas de panne, la perte de données sera minimale grâce au nouveau programme de récupération des fichiers après interruption anormale =** if a fault occurs, data loss will be minimized due to the improved abend recovery program; **interruption d'appel =** polled interrupt; **interruption d'entrée/sortie =** input/output interrupt; **interruption sur (une) erreur** *ou* **sur (un) incident =** error interrupt; **interruption d'intervention =** attention interruption;

interruption qui peut être masquée *ou* **invalidée** = maskable interrupt; **interruption obligatoire** *ou* **qui ne peut être invalidée** *ou* **qui ne peut être masquée** = non-maskable interrupt (NMI); **interruption (de contrôle) de parité** = parity interrupt; **interruption prioritaire** = priority interrupt; **interruption provenant d'une machine** = hardware interrupt; *(instruction)* **interruption du processeur** *ou* **du traitement** = processor interrupt; **interruption en série** *ou* **en chaîne** = daisy chain interrupt; **interruption transparente** *ou* **contrôlée** = transparent interrupt; **interruption vectorisée** = vectored interrupt; **commande d'interruption (de programme)** = interrupt command; **contrôle et exécution d'interruption** = interrupt servicing; **brève interruption de transmission de données (causée par un défaut du support magnétique)** = data check; **commande d'invalidation d'interruption** = disable interrupt; **demande d'interruption** = interrupt request; **gestionnaire d'interruptions** = interrupt handler (IH); **invalider** *ou* **interdire une interruption** = to interrupt disable; **ligne d'interruption** = interrupt line; **masque d'interruption** = interrupt mask; **niveau d'interruption** = interrupt level; **constitution de pile d'interruptions** = interrupt stacking; **point d'interruption** = breakpoint; **priorité d'interruption** = interrupt priority; **signal d'interruption** = interrupt signal; **valider une interruption** = to interrupt enable **(b)** *(d'un appareil)* **interruption de service** = outage; **sans interruption** = continuously; **l'imprimante se mettait à chauffer après cinq heures de marche sans interruption** = the printer overheated after working continuously for five hours

intersection *nf (logique)* intersection *ou* conjunction; *(fonction logique)* **fonction d'intersection** = coincidence function

interstation *adj* between stations; **réduction du bruit d'interférence interstation** = interstation muting

interurbain, -e *adj* appel interurbain = long-distance call; *GB* trunk call; **central téléphonique pour réseau interurbain** = *GB* trunk exchange; **communication**

interurbaine = long-distance call; *GB* trunk call

intervalle *nm* gap *ou* interval; **il y a eu un intervalle entre le moment où on a appuyé sur la touche et la mise en marche de l'imprimante** = there was an interval between pressing the key and the starting of the printout; **intervalle d'appels** = polling interval; **intervalle blanc entre deux enregistrements** = record gap; *(de signal de télévision)* **intervalle de garde** = breezeway; **intervalle de marquage** = marking interval; **l'horloge émet un signal à intervalles réguliers** = the clock signal is periodic

intervenir *vi* to take action
◊ **intervention** *nf* attention *ou* intervention; **ce programme exige l'intervention constante du processeur** = this routine requires the attention of the processor every minute; **interruption d'intervention** = attention interrupt; **message d'intervention** = action message; **touche d'intervention** = attention key

interversion *nf* transposition; **une série d'interversions a donné de faux résultats** = a series of transposition errors caused faulty results

intrinsèque *adj* **(a)** intrinsic; **le matériau de base utilisé dans la fabrication des circuits intégrés est un semi-conducteur intrinsèque auquel on ajoute un dopant** = the base material for ICs is an intrinsic semiconductor which is then doped **(b)** default; **réponse intrinsèque** = default response; **option intrinsèque** = default option; **valeur intrinsèque** = default value

introduction *nf* **(a)** entry; **introduction de données** = data entry *ou* input; **routine d'introduction de données** = input routine **(b)** *(d'une carte)* **bord d'introduction** = leading edge
◊ **introduire** *vtr* **(a)** *(dans un ordinateur)* to enter *ou* to input; *(par lecture)* to read in; **introduire des données** = to input *ou* to enter data; **les données ont été introduites par l'intermédiaire d'un modem** = the data was input via a modem; **les données sont introduites dans l'ordinateur** = data is fed into the

computer; **introduire des données dans la pile (de mémoire)** = to put data onto a stack **(b)** *(dispositif, etc.)* to insert *ou* to introduce *ou* to load; **introduire ensuite le bac inférieur** = then load lower bin; **introduire d'abord la disquette système dans le lecteur gauche** = first insert the system disk in the left slot **(c)** *(un système, etc.)* to introduce; **introduire quelque chose graduellement** = to phase something in

◊ **s'introduire** *vpr* to get into; **s'introduire sans autorisation dans un système** = to hack into a system

intrusion *nf* intrusion

inutilisé, -ée *adj* (i) unused; (ii) empty; **connecteur** *ou* **créneau inutilisé** = empty slot

invalidation *nf* **commande d'invalidation d'interruption** = disable interrupt; **signal d'invalidation de transmission** = inhibiting input

◊ **invalide** *adj* invalid *ou* illegal; **caractère invalide** = illegal character; **de façon invalide** = illegally; **instruction invalide** = illegal instruction; **d'après le message, l'instruction était invalide** = the message was that the instruction was invalid; **opération invalide** = illegal operation

◊ **invalidé, -ée** *adj* **(a)** *(dispositif)* disarmed *ou* disabled; **configuration invalidée** = configured off *ou* configured out **(b) interruption invalidée** = masked interrupt

◊ **invalider** *vtr* **(a)** *(un dispositif)* to disable *ou* to disarm **(b)** to mask *ou* to inhibit; **(instruction d') invalider une interruption** = interrupt disable; **interruption qui peut être invalidée** = maskable interrupt; **interruption qui ne peut être invalidée** = non-maskable interrupt (NMI); **(instruction d') invalider la justification** = justify inhibit

inversé, -ée *adj* reverse; **fichier inversé** = inverted file; **image inversée** = mirror image; **impression inversée** *ou* **caractère inversé** = cameo; **index inversé** = reverse index; **liste inversée** = pushdown list; **notation polonaise inversée** = reverse Polish notation (RPN) *ou* postfix notation *ou* suffix notation; **en notation normale on écrit: (x-y) + z, en notation polonaise inversée on écrira: xy - z + =** normal notation: (x-y) + z, but using postfix notation: xy - z +; **pile inversée (utilisée suivant la méthode LIFO)** = push-down list *ou* stack; **polarité inversée** = reverse polarity; **vidéo inversée** = inverse *ou* reverse video

◊ **inverser** *vtr* to reverse *ou* to invert; *(une valeur)* to negate

◊ **inverseur** *nm* inverter; **inverseur de courant** = inverter (AC/DC); **circuit inverseur** = NOT gate

◊ **inversion** *nf* inversion *ou* transposition; *(d'une valeur)* negation; **il y a inversion du chiffre binaire dans le complément à un** = the inversion of a binary digit takes place in one's complement; *(d'une image)* **inversion latérale** = lateral reversal; *(de la direction du flux de données)* **délai d'inversion** = turnaround time (TAT); *(pour terminaison de transmission)* **interruption d'inversion** = reverse interrupt

investiguer *vtr* **investiguer un système (sans autorisation)** = to hack

invitation *nf* **(a) (message d') invitation à taper une instruction** = prompt *ou* cue **(b)** *(à un terminal)* **invitation à émettre** = polling; **(signal d') invitation à transmettre** = go ahead *ou* invitation to send (ITS)

ion *nm* ion

◊ **ionosphère** *nf* ionosphere

IRM = IMAGERIE PAR RESONNANCE MAGNETIQUE

irradier *vtr* to radiate

irrécupérable *adj* **erreur irrécupérable** = unrecoverable error

irrégulier, -ière *adj* irregular; *(d'un satellite)* **période irrégulière** = anomalistic period

irréparable *adj* **l'ordinateur souffre d'une panne irréparable** = the computer has a terminal fault

irréversible *adj* irreversible; **processus irréversible** = irreversible process; **vidage irréversible** = disaster dump

ISBN = INTERNATIONAL STANDARD BOOK NUMBER

ISO = INTERCONNEXION DE SYSTEMES OUVERTS *voir aussi* INTERCONNEXION

ISO = INTERNATIONAL STANDARDS ORGANIZATION *voir aussi* ORGANISME

ISO/OSI = INTERNATIONAL STANDARDS ORGANIZATION - OPEN SYSTEM INTERCONNECTION; **système ISO/OSI** = ISO/OSI system

isolant *nm* insulation material *ou* insulator

◇ **isolant, -e** *adj* **matériau isolant** = insulation material *ou* insulator

◇ **isolateur** *nm* **(a)** insulator **(b)** isolator

◇ **isolation** *nf* **(a)** insulation **(b)** isolation; **isolation de canaux** = channel isolation; **boîtier d'isolation** = barrier box

◇ **isolement** *nm* **(a)** insulation **(b)** isolation; **transformateur d'isolement** = isolation transformer

◇ **isoler** *vtr* **(a)** to insulate **(b)** to isolate

isotrope *adj* isotropic; **émetteur** *ou* **antenne isotrope** = isotropic radiator

ISSN = INTERNATIONAL STANDARD SERIAL NUMBER

italique 1 *nm* italic; **tapez CTRL I pour imprimer les italiques** = hit CTRL I to print the text in italics; **les notes de bas de page sont toutes en italique** = all the footnotes are printed in italics; **le titre est en italique souligné** = the headline is printed in italic and underlined; **ils ont changé de police de caractères et imprimé l'en-tête en italiques** = they switched to italic type for the heading **2** *adj* italic; **lettres italiques** = italics

item *nm* item; **dimension d'un item** = item size

itératif, -ive *adj* **fonctionnement itératif automatique** = automatic sequencing; **processus itératif** = iterative process; **programme itératif** = loop program *ou* looping program; **routine itérative** = iterate *ou* iterative routine

◇ **itération** *nf* **boucle d'itération** = iteration *ou* loop program *ou* looping program

Jj

jack *nm* jack

jambage *nm (d'un caractère)* descender *ou* down stroke

jaquette *nf* jacket; **on trouve le nom de l'auteur sur la jaquette du livre =** the book jacket has the author's name on it

jauge *nf* gauge

◊ **jauger** *vtr* to gauge

jet *nm* jet; **imprimante à jet d'encre =** ink-jet printer; **les techniques du jet d'encre couleur et du transfert thermique sont concurrentielles =** colour ink-jet technology and thermal transfer technology compete with each other

jeton *nm* token; **jeton de contrôle (de réseau) =** control token; **réseau à jeton (circulant) =** token ring network

jeu *nm* **(a)** set; **jeu de caractères =** character set; **jeu de caractères nuls =** empty *ou* null set; **jeu de cartes perforées =** (card) deck; *(qui contient un programme)* **jeu (de cartes) objet =** object deck; **jeu d'instructions =** instruction repertoire *ou* instruction set; **jeu d'instructions réduit =** reduced instruction set; **contrôle avec un jeu d'essai =** dry run **(b)** game; **jeu d'arcade =** arcade game; **jeu électronique** *ou* **jeu ordinateur =** computer game; **jeu (électronique) d'aventure =** adventure game; **jeu vidéo =** video game; **manette de jeu =** games paddle **(c)** **jeu vertical d'une touche =** key travel

une station de travail portable achitecturée autour d'un processeur à jeu d'instructions réduit Mips
Le Monde informatique
même si un nombre croissant de boutiques spécilisées dans le jeu ordinateur se convertissent, sur le tard, au jeu vidéo
L'Express
deux ans auparavant, le marché des jeux vidéo à domicile était encore l'un des plus florissants de l'industrie du jouet
L'Express

JK **(commutateur à) bascule (de type) JK** = JK-flip-flop

joindre *vtr* **(a)** *(réunir)* to join *ou* to couple *ou* to combine *ou* to link **(b)** *(attacher)* to attach *ou* to append **(c)** *(contacter)* to contact; **chercher à joindre quelqu'un par système d'appel (de personne)** *ou* **par signaleur d'appel** *ou* **par bip =** to call someone on a bleeper *ou* to page someone

joker *nm* wild card; **on peut utiliser un joker pour chercher tous les fichiers commençant par DIC =** a wild card can be used to find all files names beginning DIC

jonction *nf* junction; *(dans un réseau)* spur; **jonction pn=** pn-junction; **jonction pn à diffusion =** diffused pn-junction; **jonction pn à seuil =** step pn-junction; **boîte de jonction =** junction box; **circuit** *ou* **faisceau de jonction =** trunk; **ligne de jonction d'abonné (au centre téléphonique) =** exchange line; **ligne de jonction privée =** tie line *ou* tie trunk; **transistor à jonction bipolaire =** bipolar junction transistor (BJT); **transistor à jonction pnp** *ou* **npn =** bipolar (junction) transistor (BJT) *ou* pnp transistor

jouer *vtr (un enregistrement)* to play (back); **après avoir enregistré la musique, appuyez sur ce bouton-ci pour faire jouer la bande et vous assurer de la bonne**

qualité du son enregistré = after you have recorded the music, press this button to play back the tape and hear what it sounds like; **faire jouer une bande nouvellement enregistrée** = to replay a new recording

jour *nm* **(a)** day; **à jour** = up to date; **garder** *ou* **maintenir (un fichier) à jour** = to keep (a file) up to date; **nous passons beaucoup de temps à maintenir nos fichiers à jour** = we spend a lot of time keeping our files up to date; **mettre à jour** = *(un fichier)* to update *ou* to bring up to date; *(mémoire)* to refresh; **mise à jour** = (file) update *ou* upkeep *ou* maintenance; **la mise à jour des fichiers doit se faire tous les six mois** = the upkeep of the files means reviewing them every six months; **enregistrement** *ou* **fichier de mise a jour** = addition record *ou* change file *ou* movement file *ou* update; **terminal de mise à jour rapide** = bulk update terminal **(b)** *(faire apparaître)* **mettre à jour** = to reveal **(c) mot du jour** = buzzword

journal *nm* **(a)** diary *ou* journal; **les enregistrements modifiés ont été ajoutés au fichier maître et inscrits au journal des modifications** = the modified records were added to the master file and noted in the journal; **journal de bord** = log; **journal de bord d'un système** = system log; **enregistrer dans un jounal de bord** = to log; **entrée dans un journal de bord** = log **(b)** newspaper; **coupure de journal** = press cutting; **papier journal** = mechanical paper *ou* newsprint; **les journaux** = the press; **aucun journal n'a mentionné le nouveau produit** = there was no mention of the new product in the press; **les grands journaux** *ou* **les journaux à gros tirage** = the national press; **les journaux régionaux** = regional newspaper *ou* the local press

◊ **journalisme** *nm* journalism; **journalisme électronique** = electronic news gathering (ENG)

◊ **journaliste** *nm&f* correspondent *ou* journalist

joystick *nm* joystick

juger *vi* to calculate *ou* to evaluate *ou* to measure; **pour juger de la performance du système** = to measure the system's performance *ou* as a measure of the system's performance

jumelé, -ée *adj* ordinateurs jumelés = duplex computer

justification *nf* justification; **justification à droite** = right justification; **justification à gauche** = left justification; **justification verticale** = vertical justification; **césure et justification** = hyphenation and justification *ou* H & J; *(fonction)* hyphenate and justify; **un programme de césure et de justification établi aux Etats-Unis ne peut être utilisé pour un texte en anglais britannique** = an American hyphenation and justification program will not work with British English spellings; **(instruction d') invalider la justification** = justify inhibit

◊ **justifié, -ée** *adj (texte)* justified; **justifié à droite** = right justified; **justifié à gauche** = left justified; **texte non justifié à droite** = ragged text; **non justifié à droite** = ragged right; **non justifié à gauche** = ragged left

◊ **justifier** *vtr* **(a)** *(un texte)* to justify *ou* to range; **justifier à droite** = to right justify *ou* to flush right; *(instruction)* right justify *ou* to flush right; **justifier à gauche** = to left justify *ou* to flush left; *(instruction)* left justify *ou* flush left **(b)** *(registre)* to justify

juxtaposition *nf* juxtaposition

Kk

k = KILO

K = KILO

Karnaugh *npr* **table de Karnaugh =** Karnaugh map; **le prototype a fait l'objet d'un contrôle de fiabilité statistique sur la base des tables de Karnaugh =** the prototype was checked for hazards with a Karnaugh map

Kbit = KILOBIT

kerning *nm (une image ou photo)* kerning

kg = KILOGRAMME

kHz = KILOHERTZ

kilo 1 *nm (abréviation)* = KILOGRAMME (k) **2** *(abréviation)* = 1000 (k) **3** *(quantité d'information)* = 1024 (K)

◇ **kilobaud** *nm* kilobaud

◇ **kilobit (Kbit)** *nm* kilobit (Kbit)

◇ **kilogramme (kg)** *nm* kilogram; **mètre kilogramme seconde (ampère)** *ou* **mks(A) =** metre kilogram second (Ampere) *ou* MKS(A)

◇ **kilohertz (kHz)** *nm* kilohertz (kHz)

◇ **kilométrique** *adj* **ondes kilométriques =** infra-low frequency (ILF)

◇ **kilo-mot** *nm* kiloword (KW)

◇ **kilo-octet (Ko)** *nm* kilobyte *ou* Kbyte (Kb)

◇ **kilo-ohm** *nm* kilo-ohm

◇ **kilowatt (kW)** *nm* kilowatt (kW)

Kimball *npr* **étiquette Kimball® =** Kimball tag

kiosque *nm* **kiosque (à livres) =** bookstall

KIPS = KILO INSTRUCTIONS PER SECOND *voir* MILLIER

kit *nm* kit *ou* pack; **kit d'extension de micro-ordinateur =** microcomputer development kit; **kit de nettoyage pour écran =** screen cleaning kit

Ko = KILO-OCTET kilobyte *ou* Kbyte (Kb); **le nouveau lecteur de disquettes a une capacité de 100Ko =** the new disk drive has a 100Kb capacity; **le premier ordinateur individuel de la série ne peut accéder à plus de 640Ko de RAM =** the original PC cannot access more than 640Kbytes of RAM

Koctet = KILO-OCTET

kva = KILOVOLT-AMPERE OUTPUT; **mesure du travail en kva =** kiloVolt-Ampere output rating (KVA)

kW = KILOWATT

LI

label *nm* **(a)** *(étiquette)* label; *(sur support magnétique)* **label d'identification interne** = interior *ou* internal label; **label de qualité** = quality label **(b)** *(d'un programme)* label *ou* quasi-instruction; **les programmes en langage BASIC contiennent plusieurs labels dont la numérotation des lignes** = BASIC uses many program labels such as line numbers; **label d'un champ** = field label; **champ label** = label field; **enregistrement de labels** = label record

laboratoire *nm* laboratory; **le travail de recherche et développement sur la nouvelle puce se fait dans les laboratoires de l'université** = the new chip is being developed in the university laboratories; **technicien de laboratoire** = laboratory technician

lacet *nm (mouvement de satellite)* yaw

lampe *nf* **(a)** lampe de bureau = desk light **(b)** lampe témoin = (i) light emitting diode; (ii) warning light **(c)** *(dans un ordinateur)* valve

lancement *nm* **(a)** *(d'un programme)* start; **lancement automatique** = auto-start; **adresse de lancement** = initial address; **chargeur de programme de lancement** = initial program loader (IPL); **instructions de lancement** = initial instructions **(b)** *(d'un système)* boot-up *ou* booting; *(automatique)* auto-boot; **mémoire de lancement** = bootstrap memory; **programme de lancement** = bootstrap **(c)** lancement de tâches à distance = remote job entry (RJE) **(b)** launch; **fusée de lancement** = launch vehicle **(d)** *(un nouveau produit)* launch; **le lancement du nouvel ordinateur individuel se fera avec six mois de retard** = the launch of the new PC has been put back six months; **le lancement du réseau aura lieu en septembre** = the launch date for the network will be September

◊ **lancer** *vtr* **(a)** *(un programme)* to start **(b)** *(un système)* to boot (up) **(c)** *(une fusée)* to launch **(d)** *(un nouveau produit)* to launch *ou* to release; **on a lancé le nouvel ordinateur personnel au Salon de l'Informatique** = the new PC was launched at the Personal Computer Show

◊ **lanceur** *nm* lanceur de programme de chargement = initial program header

langage *nm* **(a)** language; **langage algorithmique** *ou* **ALGOL** = algorithmic language *ou* ALGOL; **langage (de programmation) APL** = A programming language (APL); **langage (de haut niveau) BASIC** = Beginner's All-Purpose Symbolic Instruction Code (BASIC); **langage (de haut niveau) BCPL** = BCPL; **(langage) C** = C (language); **langage (de programmation) COBOL** = common business-orientated language (COBOL); **langage (de programmation structurée) COMAL** = common algorithmic language (COMAL); **langage (d'application temps réel) CORAL** = common real-time applications language (CORAL); **système adapté aux langages EAO** *ou* **FAO** = authoring system; **langage FORTH** = FORTH; **langage FORTRAN** = formula translator (FORTRAN); **langage LISP** = list processing (LISP); **langage LOGO** = LOGO; **on demande aux programmeurs une connaissance des langages de haut niveau, plus spécialement PASCAL** = programmers should have a knowledge of high-level languages, particularly PASCAL; **langage (de traitement et de manipulation de chaînes) SNOBOL** = string-orientated symbolic language (SNOBOL) **(b)** **langage adaptable** *ou* **extensible** = extensible language; **langage d'application** = job-orientated language *ou* problem orientated language (POL); **langage d'application temps réel** = common real-time applications language (CORAL); **langage d'assemblage** = assembly language *ou* assembler language *ou* base language; **langage d'assemblage pour microprogramme** = microprogram assembly language; **langage de base de données** = database language; **langage de commande** *ou* **d'instruction** = command language *ou* control language; **langage de commande de tâche** = job control language (JCL); **langage commun** *ou* **banal** *ou* **partagé** = common language; **langage de compilation** = compiler language; **langage de conception de programme** = program design language (PDL); **langage de contrôle** *ou* **de pilotage (de périphériques)** = command control language; **langage de description de données** = data description language (DDL); **plusieurs des avantages du langage de description de données vient du fait qu'il s'agit d'un langage de deuxième génération** = many of DDL's advantages come from the fact that it is a second generation language; **langage de description de page** = page description language (PDL); **langage évolué** = high-level language (HLL); **langage peu évolué** = low-level language (LLL); **langage graphique** = graphic language; **avec ce langage graphique, on peut tracer des lignes, cercles et graphes avec une seule commande** = this graphic language can plot lines, circles and graphs with a single command; **langage informatique** = computer language; **langage informatique indépendant** = computer independent language; **langage d'indexation** = indexing language; **langage d'instruction** = command language *ou* control language; **langage interne** *ou* **langage machine** = internal language; **langage interprété** = interpreted language; **langage d'interrogation** = query language (QL); **langage machine** = machine code *ou* machine language; *(commandes ou données)* **en langage machine** = machine-readable; **codes en langage machine** = machine-readable codes; **compiler en langage machine** = machine language compile; **instruction en langage machine** = machine (code) instruction; **programmation en langage machine** = machine language programming; **langage de manipulation de données** = data manipulation language (DML); **langage multidimensionnel** *ou* **multiniveau** = multidimensional language; **langage naturel** = natural language; **le système expert peut être programmé en langage naturel** = the

expert system can be programmed in a natural language; **langage de bas niveau** *ou* **peu évolué** = low-level language (LLL); **langage de haut niveau** *ou* **évolué** = high-level language (HLL); **langage objet** = object language *ou* target language; **pour ce qui est de ce programme en PASCAL, le langage machine constitue le langage objet** = the target language for this PASCAL program is machine code; **langage d'origine** = source language; **langage partagé** = common language; **langage en pelure d'oignon** = onion skin language; **langage de pilotage (de périphériques)** = command control language; **langage de procédure** *ou* **langage adapté à la procédure** = procedure-orientated language *ou* procedural language; **langage de programmation** = programming language; **langage de programmation EAO** = author language; **langage de programmation évolué** *ou* **de haut niveau** = high-level (programming) language (HLL); **langages de quatrième génération** = fourth generation languages; **langage de requête** *ou* **d'interrogation** = query language (QL); **langage de résolution de problème** *ou* **langage adapté au problème** = problem-orientated language (POL); **langage source** = source language; **langage standard** *ou* **universel** = machine-independent language; **langage symbolique** = symbolic language; **format de langage symbolique** = symbolic-coding format; **langage de synthèse** = synthetic language; **processeur de langage** = language processor

langue *nf* language; **il parle plusieurs langues européennes** = he speaks several European languages; *(en traduction)* **langue d'arrivée** = target language; **langue de départ** = source language; **langue étrangère** = foreign language

large *adj* broad *ou* wide **large bande** = broadband *ou* wideband; **modulation de fréquence à large bande** = wideband frequency modulation (WBFM); **radio à large bande** = broadband radio

◇ **largeur** *nf* **(a)** width; **la largeur implicite** *ou* **par défaut de cet écran est de 80** = screen width has a default value of 80; **largeur de page (en caractères)** = page width **(b)** **largeur de bande (de fréquences)** = bandwidth; **largeur de bande effective** = effective bandwidth; **largeur de bande vidéo** = video bandwidth; **concentrateur** *ou* **réducteur de largeur de bande vidéo** = video compressor; **la largeur de bande d'un téléphone est de 3100Hz** = telephone bandwidth is 3100Hz; **largeur d'un faisceau** *ou* **d'un lobe** = beam width; **modulation d'impulsions en largeur (MIL)** = pulse width modulation (PWM)

laser *nm* = LIGHT AMPLIFICATION BY STIMULATED EMISSION OF RADIATION laser; **laser à composant solide** = solid-state laser; **laser d'injection (dans une fibre optique)** = injection laser; **laser de portance** = injection laser; **laser transistorisé** = semiconductor laser; **communication par rayon laser** = laser beam communications; **enregistrement par rayon laser** = laser beam recording; **imprimante (à) laser** = laser printer; **mémoire laser sur couche haute définition** = emulsion laser storage

> grâce à un laser à semi-conducteur émettant une lumière bleue (au lieu de l'infrarouge proche), le diamètre du faisceau est réduit de moitié (0,4 micron), ce qui double la densité d'information du disque
>
> *Science et Vie Micro*

latence *nf* wait time; **état de latence** = wait condition *ou* state; **période** *ou* **temps de latence** = latency
◊ **latent, -e** *adj* latent; **image latente** = latent image

latéral, -e *adj* lateral *ou* side; **bande latérale** = sideband; **bande latérale inférieure** = lower sideband; **bande latérale résiduelle** = vestigial sideband; **bande latérale supérieure** = upper sideband; **bande latérale unique** = single sideband; **bande latérale unique sans porteuse** *ou* **à porteuse inhibée** = single sideband suppressed carrier (SSBSC); **double bande latérale** = double sideband; **double bande latérale sans porteuse** *ou* **à porteuse inhibée** = double sideband suppressed carrier (DSBSC); **inversion latérale** = lateral reversal; **lobe latéral** = side lobe

LC circuit LC = LC circuit

lecteur, -trice *n* **(a)** *(personne)* reader; *(d'épreuves)* copy reader *ou* proofreader **(b) lecteur de badges** = badge reader; **le lecteur de badges garantit que seules les** personnes autorisées ont accès à la salle des ordinateurs = a badge reader makes sure that only authorized personnel can gain access to a computer room; **lecteur de bandes (magnétiques)** = tape drive *ou* tape reader *ou* magnetic tape reader; **lecteur de bandes perforées** = (paper) tape reader; **lecteur de cartes magnétiques** = card reader *ou* magnetic card reader; **lecteur de cartes perforées** = card reader *ou* punched card reader; **lecteur de cartouche** = cartridge drive; **lecteur (optique) de code barres** = bar-code reader; **lecteur par défaut** *ou* **implicite** = default drive; **ce système d'exploitation permet à l'utilisateur de choisir le lecteur par défaut** = the operating system allows the user to select the default drive; **lecteur de disque** *ou* **de disquettes** = disk drive; **lecteur de disque dur** = hard disk drive; **lecteur de disques compacts** *ou* **de disques audionumériques** *ou* **de disques CD** = compact disk player *ou* CD player; **lecteur de disquettes** = (floppy) disk drive *ou* unit; **lecteur de disquettes (à) double face** = double-sided disk drive; **lecteurs de disquettes de 5,25 pouces et de 3,5 pouces** = 5.25 and 3.5 inch drives; **lecteur de disquettes de huit pouces** = eight-inch drive; **lecteur de disquettes externe** = external disk drive; **lecteur de documents** = document reader; **lecteur de marques magnétiques** = mark sense device *ou* reader; **lecteur multidisque** *ou* **lecteur de disquettes non compatibles** = alien disk reader *ou* multi-disk reader; **si la disquette n'est pas compatible, validez la fonction 'multidisque' qui permet au lecteur de lire une disquette non compatible** = when you have an alien disk select the multi-disk reader option to allow you to turn the disk drive into an alien disk reader; **lecteur optique** = optical scanner; **un lecteur optique utilise un rayon lumineux qui balaye les caractères, les symboles ou les lignes** = an optical reader uses a light beam to scan characters, patterns or lines; **lecteur optique de caractères** = optical character reader (OCR); **police de caractères reconnaissable par lecteur optique** = optical font *ou* OCR font; **lecteur optique de code barres** = optical bar reader *ou* bar code reader *ou* optical wand; **lecteur optique de marques** = optical mark reader (OMR); **lecteur optique de microfilms pour entrée de données sur ordinateur** = film optical scanning device for input into computers

(FOSDIC); **lecteur de pistes magnétiques** = magnetic strip reader; **lecteur vidéo** = video player

en introduisant la carte dans le lecteur, les trois chiffres sont lus par un dispositif optique approprié

Electronique pratique

lecture *nf* **(a)** reading *ou* readout; **lecture anticipée** = look ahead; **lecture par balayage** = scanning; **dispositif de lecture par balayage** = scanning device; **définition de lecture par balayage** = scanning resolution; **la vitesse de lecture par balayage est de 1,3 pouces par seconde** = throughput is 1.3 inches per second scanning speed; **lecture destructive** = destructive read *ou* destructive readout; **lecture hélicoïdale** = helical scan; **lecture optique** = optical reading; **police de caractères reconnaissable par lecture optique** = optical font *ou* OCR font; **lecture optique de données numériques** = digital optical reading (DOR); **lecture régénératrice (de données)** = regenerative reading; **le temps d'accès peut être le temps requis pour la lecture de données (mises) en mémoire** = access time can be the time taken to read from a record; **cycle de lecture** = read cycle; **cycle de lecture d'une instruction** = fetch cycle; **cycle de lecture-exécution (d'une instruction)** = fetch-execute cycle *ou* execute cycle; **instruction de lecture d'une instruction** = fetch instruction; **phase de lecture d'une instruction** = fetch phase; **signal de lecture d'instruction** = fetch signal; **tête de lecture** = playback head *ou* read head *ou* sound head; *(pour bande magnétique)* tape head *ou* tape playback head; **tête de lecture de disquettes** = disk head *ou* read head; **tête de lecture de disques** = disk playback head; **tête de lecture fixe** = fixed head; **vitesse de lecture** = read rate **(b)** *(reconnaissance ou identification automatique)* sense
◊ **lecture-écriture** *nf* (i) read/write; (ii) reading/writing; **lecture-écriture sur demande** *ou* **directe** = demand reading/writing; **bras de lecture-écriture** = access arm; **cycle de lecture-écriture** = read/write cycle *ou* R/W cycle; **mémoire lecture-écriture** = read/write memory; **tête de lecture-écriture** = combined head *ou* read/write head *ou* R/W head; **voie de lecture-écriture** = read/write channel

légal, -e *adj* legal

légende *nf* caption; **les légendes sont imprimées en italique** = the captions are printed in italics

léger, -ère *adj* lightweight; **un ordinateur léger qui tient facilement dans une valise** = a lightweight computer which can easily fit into a suitcase

lent, -e *adj* slow; **périphérique lent** = slow peripheral; **prise de vue à cadence lente** = memomotion

lentille *nf* lens; **lentille concave** = concave lens; **lentille convexe** = convex lens; **lentille déformante** = distortion optics; **lentille dioptrique** = dioptre lens; *US* diopter lens

lettre *nf* **(a)** *(message)* letter; **lettre type** *ou* **lettre standard** = form letter *ou* standard letter *ou* repetitive letter *ou* template (letter); **composition automatique de lettres standard** = automatic letter writing; **boîte à** *ou* **aux lettres** = letter box *ou* mailbox; **boîte aux lettres électronique** = electronic mailbox; **en-tête de lettre** = letterhead; **faire une copie d'une lettre** = to copy *ou* to duplicate a letter **(b)** *(caractère)* letter; **lettres italiques** = italics; **lettre majuscule** = capital letter; **lettre minuscule** = lower case; **lettre numérale** = numeric character
◊ **lettré, -ée** *adj* literate
◊ **lettrine** *nf* drop cap

lexical, -e *adj* **analyse lexicale** = lexical analysis *ou* parsing

lexicographique *adj* lexicographical; **ordre lexicographique** = lexicographical order

liaison *nf* line *ou* link; *(action)* linking; *(entre plusieurs machines ou dispositifs)* interconnection; **liaison de données** = data link; **liaison (de données) en chaîne** = data chaining; **contrôle de liaison de données** = data link control; **contrôle de liaison de données de haut niveau** = high-level data link control (HDLC); **couche (de) liaison de données** = data link layer; **liaison directe entre canaux** = channel-to-channel connection; **pour une transmission plus rapide, vous pouvez utiliser la liaison directe avec le gros**

ordinateur = to transmit faster, you can use the direct link with the mainframe; **liaison à fibres optiques** = fibre optic cable *ou* connection; **liaison optique pour transmission de données** = optical data link; **(câble de) liaison d'un périphérique d'entrée** = input lead; **liaison par satellite** = satellite link; **liaison (de transmission) hertzienne** *ou* **liaison de transmission par hyperfréquence** = microwave communications link; **cordon de liaison** = cord; **cordon de liaison d'un tableau de distribution** = patchcord; **fil de liaison** = cord; **une arborescence est formée de branches reliées les unes aux autres par des points de liaison ou noeuds** = a tree is made of branches that connect together at nodes

> le principal paramètre d'une liaison série est la vitesse de transmission qui se mesure théoriquement en bits par seconde mais aussi en bauds ou encore, ce qui est moins rigoureux, en caractères par seconde
>
> *Action PC*

libérer *vtr (de l'espace dans la mémoire)* to free *ou* to deallocate *ou* to blast; *(une ligne lorsque la transmission est terminée)* to clear

liberté *nf* freedom; **loi Informatique et Libertés** = Data Protection Act; **liberté d'accès à l'information** = freedom of information; **liberté d'expression** = freedom of speech; **liberté de la presse** = freedom of the press

libraire *nm&f* bookseller
◊ **librairie** *nf* bookshop; *US* bookstore

libre *adj* clear *ou* free; **indexage libre** = free indexing; **ligne libre** = free line
◊ **librement** *adv* freely

licence *nf* licence; **ici, ce logiciel est fabriqué sous licence** = the software is manufactured in this country under licence

lien *nm (entre programmes)* link; **création de liens** = linkage; **éditeur de liens** = linkage editor; **chargeur-éditeur de liens** = linking loader; **établir des liens** *ou* **utiliser un éditeur de liens** = to bind; **(programme) générateur de liens** = linkage software; **les graphiques et le texte sont réunis sans l'aide d'un**

générateur de liens = graphics and text are joined without linkage software; **mise en place de liens (à l'aide d'un éditeur de liens)** = linkage editing; **tests de contrôle de liens** = link trials

lier *vtr (des données)* to catenate *ou* to concatenate (data)

lieu *nm* **(a)** place; **publicité lieu de vente (PLV)** = point-of-sale material **(b)** **avoir lieu** = to occur

LIFO = LAST IN FIRST OUT; **liste en mode LIFO** = pushdown list; **pile en mode LIFO** = push-down list *ou* stack; **cet ordinateur gère la pile suivant la méthode LIFO** = this computer stack uses a last in first out data retrieval method; *voir aussi* DERNIER

ligature *nf* ligature

ligne *nf* **(a)** *(d'un texte)* line; **on compte 52 lignes de texte par page** = each page has 52 lines of text; **le claviste a sauté plusieurs lignes du manuscrit** = several lines of manuscript have been missed by the keyboarder; **ligne de base** = base line; **ligne de code (d'un programme)** = code line; **ligne de commande** *ou* **d'instruction d'un programme** = command line *ou* program line; **numéro d'une ligne (de programme)** = (program) line number; **ligne d'écran** = display line; *(sur l'écran)* **ligne d'état** *ou* **d'information** = information line; *(vitesse d'une imprimante)* **lignes par minute (LPM)** = lines per minute; **ligne multi-instruction** = multi-statement line; **caractère** *ou* **symbole de fin de ligne** = line ending; **caractère indiquant d'aller à la ligne** = new line character; *(d'une imprimante)* **débit ligne** = lines per minute (LPM); **écran d'une ligne** *ou* **(écran avec) affichage d'une seule ligne (à la fois)** = single line display; **éditeur de ligne** = line editor; **enroulement d'une ligne** = line folding; **enroulement** *ou* **retour à la ligne (automatique)** = horizontal wraparound; **fenêtre d'une ligne** = thin window; **fins de lignes** = line endings; **imprimante ligne à ligne** = line printer *ou* parallel printer; **l'imprimante à marguerite donne un meilleur résultat que l'imprimante ligne à ligne** = the print from the daisy-wheel printer is clearer than that from the line printer; **longueur d'une ligne** *ou* **nombre de caractères par ligne** = line length *ou* line width; **retour de chariot-retour à la ligne** = carriage return/line feed (CR/LF); **retour à la ligne automatique** *ou* **saut de ligne automatique (en limite d'écran)** = wraparound *ou* horizontal wraparound *ou* word wrap **(b)** *(trait)* line; **l'imprimante ne réussit pas très bien à imprimer les lignes trop fines** = the printer has difficulty in reproducing very fine lines; **(papier à) lignes très pâles** = feint; *(d'affichage 3D)* **lignes cachées** = hidden lines; **effacement des lignes cachées** = hidden line removal; **algorithme d'effacement de lignes cachées** = hidden line algorithm; *(de code barres)* **lignes guides** *ou* **lignes de référence** = guide bars; **les lignes guides standard se présentent sous la forme de deux lignes fines un peu plus longues que les lignes codes** = the standard guide bars are two thin lines that are a little longer than the coding lines; *(de dessin ou de couleur)* **ligne de délimitation** *ou* **d'arrêt** = holding line; **ligne de jonction des symboles d'un ordinogramme** = flowline **(c)** *(rang d'une série d'items)* row; *(ligne d'un tableau ou d'une matrice)* row; **ligne de perforations** *ou* **ligne perforée** = perforated line *ou* perforations; **une ligne pointillée sépare les entrées les unes des autres** = each entry is separated by a row of dots **(d)** *(d'image de télévision)* line; **délai de retour de ligne** = line blanking interval; **fréquence (de balayage) de ligne** = line frequency; **retour de ligne** = line flyback **(e)** *(de communication)* line; **ligne d'accès** = access line; **ligne banalisée** = common carrier; **ligne de communication** *ou* **de transmission** = communications link; **ligne de communication de données** = dataline; **lignes de contrôle** = bus control lines; **ligne optique** *ou* **directe** = line of sight; **ligne d'interruption** = interrupt line; **ligne (de communication) rapide** = fast line; **ligne à** *ou* **de retard** = delay line; **mémoire à ligne de retard** = delay line store; **ligne de sélection** *ou* **de validation d'un circuit intégré** = chip select line; **lignes de transmission de données** = bus data lines; **la ligne de validation de données est reliée à la ligne de sélection de la bascule** = the data strobe line is connected to the latch chip select line; **ligne équilibrée** = balanced line; **brancher une ligne sur une source d'alimentation** = to pull up a line; **charge d'une ligne** = line load; **charger une ligne**

= to load a line; **contrôle de ligne de communication** *ou* **de transmission** = communications link control; **courant transitoire d'une ligne** = line transient; **élever le potentiel d'une ligne** = to pull up a line; **élever le potentiel de la ligne de réception au niveau logique un, en la connectant sur une source de courant 5 volts** = to pull up the input line to a logic one by connecting it to 5 volts; **impédance de ligne** = line impedance; *(lorsque la transmission est terminée)* **libérer la ligne** = to clear the line; **temps d'occupation de la ligne** = holding time; **trafic** *ou* **charge d'une ligne** = line load; **unité d'extension d'une ligne** = line extender **(f) en ligne** = on-line; **le terminal est en ligne avec l'ordinateur principal** = the terminal is on-line to the mainframe; **base de données en ligne** = on-line database; **recherche documentaire en ligne** = on-line information retrieval; **stockage de données en ligne** = on-line storage; **système en ligne** = on-line system; **traitement en ligne** = in-line processing *ou* on-line processing; **traitement transactionnel en ligne** = on-line transaction processing; **hors ligne** = off-line; **avant de remplacer le papier de l'imprimante, assurez-vous que l'imprimante est hors ligne** = before changing the paper in the printer, switch it off-line; **impression hors ligne** = off-line printing; **traitement hors ligne** = off-line processing **(g)** *(téléphonique)* **ligne de grand débit** = high usage trunk; **ligne de jonction d'abonné (au centre téléphonique)** = exchange line; **ligne libre** = free line; **ligne louée** *ou* **de location** = leased line; **ligne privée** *ou* **réservée** *ou* **privative** = private line; **ligne téléphonique spécialisée** *ou* **dédiée** = dedicated line *ou* scheduled circuit; **être en ligne** = to be on the telephone **(h)** **codage en ligne directe** = straight-line coding

◊ **ligne-bloc** *nf* slug; *(fondue au moment de la composition)* hot metal type

limitateur *nm* limiter

◊ **limite** *nf* **(a)** *(d'étendue)* edge *ou* boundary *ou* bounds *ou* limit; **limite de page** = page boundary; **limites de tableau** = array bounds; **balayage en dehors des limites** = overscan; **détection de limites** = edge detection; **marquage de limites (d'un fichier)** = boundary punctuation;

protection des limites (de mémoire) = boundary protection; **registre (d'adresses) de limites** = boundary register **(b)** *(de niveau)* restriction; **limites de la bande des audiofréquences** = audio range; **limite de tolérance au bruit** = noise margin **(c)** **date limite** = deadline *ou* expiration date; **nous avons dépassé notre date limite du 15 octobre** = we've missed our October 15th deadline

◊ **limité, -ée** *adj* limited; **limité par le processeur** = processor-limited; **limité par la (vitesse de) sortie** = output bound *ou* limited; **(programme) limité par la vitesse d'entrée/sortie** = I/O bound (program); **limité par (la vitesse d') un périphérique** = peripheral limited; **dégradation limitée** = graceful degradation; **modem à distance de transmission limitée** = limited distance modem; **test sélectif limité** = crippled leapfrog test; **tirage limité** = short run; **l'imprimante (à) laser est très utile pour les tirages limités** = a laser printer is good for short-run printing

◊ **limiter** *vtr* to limit *ou* to restrict; **limiter l'accès** *ou* **l'utilisation (de quelque chose)** = to restrict access to (something)

◊ **limiteur** *nm* **limiteur de courant transitoire** = transient suppressor; **limiteur de signal audio** = audio compressor; **limiteur de tension** = surge protector

linéaire *adj* linear; **antenne linéaire** = linear array; **circuit linéaire** = in-line *ou* linear circuit; **circuit intégré linéaire** = linear integrated circuit; **fonction linéaire** = linear function; **l'expression Y 10 + 5X - 3W est une fonction linéaire** = the expression Y 10 + 5X - 3W is a linear function; **l'expression Y (10 + 5X²) n'est pas une fonction linéaire** = the expression Y (10 + 5X²) is not a linear function; **programmation linéaire** = linear programming; **programme linéaire** = in-line program *ou* linear program

liquide *adj* liquid; **affichage à cristaux liquides** = liquid crystal display (LCD)

tout se fait par l'intermédiaire d'un petit écran à cristaux liquides par simple branchement sur le réseau secteur

L'Evénement

lire *vtr* **(a)** *(personne)* to read; **les clavistes trouvent ce manuscrit difficile à lire** = the keyboarders find the

manuscript lacks legibility; **les conditions de vente sont imprimées en caractères si petits qu'il est très difficile de les lire** = conditions of sale are printed in such small characters that they are difficult to read **(b)** *(par tête de lecture, etc.)* to read; *(par détection)* to sense; **qui peut être lu** = readable; **qui peut être lu par l'imprimante** = printer-readable; **le texte électronique est converti en image vidéo qui peut être lue par l'imprimante** = the electronic page is converted to a printer-readable video image; **l'ordinateur a lu automatiquement trente valeurs données par le convertisseur analogique-numérique** = the computer automatically read-in thirty values from the A/D converter; **est-ce qu'un lecteur optique peut lire les caractères d'imprimerie?** = can an OCR read typeset characters?; **il lui faut 9,9 secondes pour lire un document de 8,5 x 11 pouces** = its scanning speed is 9.9 seconds for an 8.5 inch by 11 inch document; **un processeur d'images qui peut lire, afficher et manipuler les images vidéo** = an image processor that captures, displays and manipulates video images; **un scanner peut habituellement lire des images d'une définition de 300 points par pouce** = scanners usually capture images at a resolution of 300 dots per inch (dpi); **aller chercher et lire (une instruction)** = fetch (instruction); **cette instruction va lire le premier enregistrement du fichier** = this instruction reads the first record of a file; **ce dispositif lit les perforations de la bande papier** = this device senses the holes punched in a paper tape

◊ **lisibilité** *nf* legibility; **les clavistes trouvent que la lisibilité du manuscrit laisse à désirer** = the keyboarders find the manuscript lacks legibility

◊ **lisible** *adj* legible; **le manuscrit est écrit au crayon et est à peine lisible** = the manuscript is written in pencil and is hardly legible

LISP = LIST PROCESSING; **langage LISP** = LISP

listage *nm* listing; **listage de mémoire** = memory dump

◊ **liste** *nf* **(a)** list; **liste d'adresses** = address list; **liste (d'un programme) d'assemblage** = assembly listing; **liste en boucle** = circular list; **liste en chaîne** *ou* **liste d'articles chaînés** = chain list *ou* chained list *ou* linked list; **liste complète** = dense list; **liste concaténée** = chain list *ou* chained list *ou* linked list; **liste descriptive** = description list; **liste d'exceptions** = exception dictionary; **liste des fonctions** capability list; **liste d'interdictions** = stop list; **liste inversée** *ou* **en mode LIFO** = pushdown list; **liste des modifications** = journal; **liste des possibilités** = capability list; **liste de référence** = authority file *ou* reference list; **liste séquentielle** = linear list; **liste vide** = empty *ou* null list; **éditer sous forme de liste** = to list; **entrer** *ou* **inscrire un nom sur une liste** = to enter a name on a list; **marqueur de fin de liste** = nil pointer; **traitement de liste** = list processing **(b)** *(des films ou pièces à l'affiche)* listings

◊ **lister** *vtr* to list; **lister (les lignes d'instruction d') un programme** = to list a program; **édition listée d'un programme sur imprimante** = program listing

◊ **listing** *nm* **listing d'imprimante** = (computer) listing *ou* printout; **le directeur des ventes a demandé un listing des commissions d'agents** = the sales director asked for a printout of the agents' commissions; **listing (du texte) d'origine** = source listing; **listing d'un programme** = program listing; **listing d'un programme d'assemblage** = assembly listing; **listing de programme source** = source listing; **papier listing** = listing paper *ou* continuous stationery *ou* computer stationery; *(sortie d'imprimante)* **qualité listing** = draft printing

lith *adj* **film lith** = lith film

litho *nf* = LITHOGRAPHIE

◊ **lithographie** *ou* **litho** *nf* lithography *ou* litho; **lithographie offset** = offset lithography

◊ **lithographique** *adj* lithographic

littéraire *adj* literary; **propriété littéraire** = copyright

littéral, -e *nm&adj* **(symbole) littéral** = literal; **indicatif littéral** = index letter; **opérande littéral** = literal operand

livre *nm* book; **ils peuvent imprimer des livres qui ont jusqu'à 96 pages** = they can print books of up to 96 pages; **livre broché** *ou* **livre de poche** = paperback; **livre cartonné** = cased book; **ce livre existe en édition brochée et en édition cartonnée** = the book is available in paperback and hard cover; **création de livres (par des maisons spécialisées)** = packaging

◊ **livret** *nm* booklet

lobe *nm* lobe; **lobe latéral** = side lobe

local, -e 1 *nm* room; **locaux** = facilities **2** *adj* local; **mémoire locale** = local memory; **mode local** = local mode; **réseau local (d'entreprise)** = local area network (LAN); **modem pour réseau local** = limited distance modem; **serveur de réseau local** = local area network server *ou* LAN server; **variable locale** = local variable; **déclaration d'une variable locale** = local declaration

localisation *nf* location; **localisation (automatique) de panne** = fault detection; **diagnostic de localisation de panne** *ou* **de défaillance** = fault diagnosis; **programme de localisation de panne** = fault location program

◊ **localisé, -ée** *adj* local

◊ **localiser** *vtr* to locate *ou* to track; **avez-vous réussi à localiser l'erreur de programmation?** = have you managed to locate the programming fault?

location *nf* hiring *ou* leasing; **circuit de location** = leased circuit; **ligne de location** = leased line

lockout *nm* lockout

logarithme *nm* logarithm; **le logarithme décimal de 1000 est 3 (= 10 x 10 x 10)** = decimal logarithm of 1,000 is 3 (= 10 x 10 x 10)

◊ **logarithmique** *adj* logarithmic; **le 'bel' est mesuré sur une échelle logarithmique** = bel is a unit in the logarithmic scale; **graphe logarithmique** = logarithmic graph

loger *vtr* to house

logiciel *nm* software; *(pour lequel une contribution volontaire est demandée)* shareware; **logiciel d'application** = applications software; **logiciel**

d'archivage = filing system; **logiciel de commande de périphérique** = handler *ou* driver; **logiciel commun** *ou* **partagé** = common software; **logiciel comptabilité-gestion** *ou* **logiciel bureautique** = business system *ou* business package; **logiciel de débogage** *ou* **de mise au point** = debugger; **logiciel de développement** = development software; **logiciel de diagnostic** = diagnostic program; **logiciel d'exploitation** = systems software; **logiciel de formatage** = formatter; **logiciel de formatage d'impression** = print formatter; **logiciel de formatage de texte** = text formatter; **logiciel graphique** = graphics software; *(à l'achat d'un ordinateur)* **logiciel inclus** *ou* **fourni** = bundled software; **logiciel non inclus** *ou* **non fourni** = unbundled software; **logiciel intégré** = integrated software; **logiciel paramétrique** = parameter-driven software; **nous utilisons des logiciels personnalisés** *ou* **écrits sur commande** = we use customized software; **logiciel de récupération de fichiers (après incident)** = file-recovery utility; **il est impossible de retrouver un fichier perdu sans l'aide d'un logiciel de récupération de fichiers** = a lost file cannot be found without a file-recovery utility; **logiciel de réseau** = network software; **logiciel résident** = resident software *ou* memory-resident software; **logiciel de série** = canned software; **logiciel non standard** *ou* **qui ne fonctionne que sur un type d'appareil** = machine-dependent software; **logiciel système** = systems software; **logiciel de traitement de texte** = word-processing program *ou* word-processing software *ou* word-processor; **logiciel téléchargé** = telesoftware (TSW); **logiciel d'utilisation facile** = user-friendly software; **bibliothèque de logiciels** = software library; **(système) compatible avec des logiciels écrits pour d'autres systèmes** = software compatible (system); **compatibilité de logiciel** = program compatibility; **créateur** *ou* **concepteur de logiciel** *ou* **expert en création de logiciels** = software writer; **cycle de vie d'un logiciel** = software life cycle; **définition et standards de qualité d'un logiciel** = software specification; **développement d'un logiciel** = software development; **développeur de logiciel** = software developer; **erreur de logiciel** = soft error; **fiabilité d'un logiciel** = software reliability; **assurance qualité dans le domaine du génie logiciel** = software

quality assurance (SQA); **disque formaté** *ou* **sectorisé par logiciel** = soft-sectored disk; **génie logiciel** = software engineering; **ingénieur logiciel** = software engineer; **interruption programmée** *ou* **générée par logiciel** = software interrupt; **maintenance de logiciel** = software maintenance; **piratage de logiciel** = software piracy; **logiciel (qui a été) piraté** = pirate software; **spécifications d'un logiciel** = software specification; **société spécialisée en logiciels** = software house

logique 1 *nf* logic; **la personne nommée devra connaître le matériel micro-informatique et la logique qui s'y rapporte** = the person appointed should have a knowledge of micro-based hardware and dedicated logic; **logique binaire** = logic; **logique câblée** = hardwired logic; **ordinateur à logique câblée** = fixed program computer; **programme en logique câblée** = hardwired program; **logique câblée programmable** = programmable logic array (PLA); **logique combinatoire** = combinational logic; **la logique dédiée réduit le nombre de puces** = the dedicated logic cuts down the chip count; **logique ECL** = emitter-coupled logic (ECL); **logique floue** = fuzzy logic *ou* fuzzy theory; **logique formelle** = formal logic; **logique intégrée à injection** = integrated injection logic (IIL); **logique machine** = machine equation; **logique négative** = negative-true logic; **logique à n niveau(x)** = n-level logic; **logique numérique** = digital logic; **logique des ordinateurs** *ou* **logique informatique** = computer logic; **logique positive** = positive logic; **logique de reconnaissance** = recognition logic; **logique séquentielle** = sequential logic; **logique transistor résistance (LTR)** = transistor-resistor logic (TRL); **logique transistor transistor (LTT)** = transistor-transistor logic (TTL) **2** *adj* logical *ou* logic; **bombe logique** = logic bomb; **un programmeur système a installé une bombe logique lorsqu'il a été licencié** = a system programmer installed a logic bomb when they made him redundant; **carte logique** = logic card *ou* logic board; **circuit logique** = gate circuit *ou* logic circuit; **circuit logique complexe** *ou* **en réseau** = gate array; **circuit logique non connecté** = uncommitted logic array (ULA); **circuit logique programmable** = programmable logic array (PLA); **circuit**

logique à trois états = three state logic; **comparaison logique** = logical comparison; **configuration logique** = logic map; **décalage logique** = logical shift *ou* non-arithmetic shift; **décision logique** = logical decision; **diagramme logique** = logic flowchart *ou* logical chart; **élément logique** = logic element; **élément logique composé** *ou* **élément logique multiple** = compound logical element; **enregistrement** *ou* **article logique** = logical record; **équivalence logique** = equivalence function *ou* operation; **erreur logique** = logical error; **état logique** = logic state; **analyseur d'état logique** = logic state analyzer; **état logique bas** *ou* **0** = logical low; **état logique haut** *ou* **1** = logical high; **expression logique** = logical expression; **fonction logique spécialisée** = dedicated logic; **(nombre d') inférences logiques par seconde** = logical inference per second (LIPS); **marque logique** = logical mark; **niveau logique** = logic level; **opérateur logique** = relational operator *ou* logical operator; **opération logique** = logic operation; **ordinogramme logique** = logical flowchart; **porte** *ou* **circuit logique** = logic gate; **le raisonnement logique peut être simulé par une machine intelligente** *ou* **un système expert** = logical reasoning can be simulated by an artificial intelligence machine; **(imprimante à) recherche logique** = logic-seeking (printer); **réseau** *ou* **circuit logique** = logic array; **symbole logique** = logic symbol; **voie logique** = logical channel

◊ **logithèque** *nf* software library

LOGO **langage LOGO** = LOGO

logo *nm* = LOGOTYPE

◊ **logotype** *nm* logo

loi *nf* law; **loi d'Ohm** = Ohm's Law; *voir aussi* LIBERTE

lointain, -e *adj* far

long, longue *adj* **(a)** long; **enveloppe longue (pour papier ministre)** = foolscap envelope; **mot long** = double word; **tiret long (dont la longueur équivaut à un 'm')** = em dash *ou* em rule **(b) cartouche longue durée** = durable cartridge

longitudinal, -e *adj* longitudinal; **clé longitudinale** = longitudinal redundancy check

longueur *nf* length; *(d'un document)* extent; **longueur d'un bloc** = block length; **longueur d'un enregistrement** = record length; **longueur d'un fichier** = file length; **longueur du nom d'un fichier** = length of filename; **enregistrement de longueur fixe** *ou* **déterminée** = fixed-length record; **mot de longueur fixe** *ou* **déterminée** = fixed-length word; **longueur d'une ligne** = line length *ou* line width; **longueur d'un mot** = (data) word length; **ordinateur à mots de longueur fixe** = fixed word length computer; **ordinateur à mots de longueur variable** = variable word length computer; **longueur d'onde** = wavelength; **longueur de page** = page length; **enregistrement à longueur variable** = variable length record

lot *nm* **(a)** *(d'un produit)* batch; **les lecteurs de disquettes du dernier lot sont défectueux** = the last batch of disk drives are faulty; **numéro de lot** = batch number **(b)** *(de données)* **total par lot** = batch total; **traitement par lots** = batch processing; **mode de traitement par lots** = (processing data in) batch mode; **traitement par lots en mode séquentiel** = sequential batch processing; **partition** *ou* **zone de traitement par lots** = batch region; **processeur de traitement par lots** = batch processor; **système de traitement par lots** = batch system

loué, -ée *adj* leased; **circuit loué** = leased circuit; **ligne louée** = leased line

◊ **louer** *vtr* to lease; **la société loue tous ses ordinateurs** = the company leases all its computers; **la société a pour politique de louer son matériel** = the company has a policy of only using leased equipment

lourd, -e *adj* **bit lourd** = weighted bit

LTR = LOGIQUE TRANSISTOR RESISTANCE

LTT = LOGIQUE TRANSISTOR TRANSISTOR

ludiciel *nm* games software

lumen *nm* lumen

lumière *nf* light; **il faut éviter de placer l'écran sous une lumière trop forte =** the VDU should not be placed under a bright light; **lumière actinique =** actintic light; **lumière ambiante =** available light; **lumière cohérente** *ou* **monochrome =** coherent light; **lumière ultraviolette =** ultra-violet light *ou* UV light; **lumière visible =** visible light; **conducteur de lumière =** light conduit

luminance *nf* luminance; **signal de luminance =** luminance signal

lumineux, -euse *adj* **rayon lumineux =** (light) beam; **déflexion d'un rayon lumineux =** beam deflection; **tache lumineuse** *ou* **interférence lumineuse =** *(photographie)* flare; *(sur écran)* bloom

luminosité *nf* brightness; **un bouton vous permet de régler la luminosité et les contrastes =** a control knob allows you to adjust brightness and contrast; **niveaux de luminosité =** brightness range

lux *nm* lux

luxe *nm* **de luxe =** high quality *ou* top quality; **les revues de luxe =** glossy magazines; *(familier)* the glossies

Mm

M = MEGA

m = METRE, MILLI-

M code N dont M = M out of N code

mA = MILLIAMPERE milliampere (mA)

MA = MODULATION D'AMPLITUDE

MAC = MULTIPLEXED ANALOG COMPONENTS; **format MAC** = MAC

machine *nf* **(a)** *(appareil)* machine; *(l'ensemble des machines)* machinery; **bruit parasite causé par une machine** = man-made noise *ou* induced interference; **machine à cartonner** = case-making machine; **machine à dicter** = dictating machine; **machine à écrire** = typewriter; **caractères de machine à écrire** = typewriter faces; **machine à écrire électrique** = electric typewriter; **machine à écrire électronique** = electronic typewriter; **il fait moins d'erreurs depuis qu'il utilise une machine à écrire électronique** = he makes fewer mistakes now he is using an electronic typewriter; **écrit à la machine** = typewritten; **machine de Turing** = Turing machine; *(d'imprimante ou presse)* **épreuve de machine** = machine proof **(b)** *(ordinateur)* machine; **machine dédiée au traitement de bases de données** = database machine; **machine intelligente** = intelligent device; **machine nue** = clean machine; **machine de traitement de texte** = word-processor; **machine virtuelle** = virtual machine; **cycle de machine** = machine cycle; **équation** *ou* **logique machine** = machine equation; **langage machine** *ou* **code machine** = computer code *ou* machine code *ou* machine language *ou* internal language; **format de code machine** = machine code format; *(instruction ou donnée)* **en langage machine** = machine-readable; **codes en langage machine** = computer-readable codes *ou* machine-readable codes; **compiler en langage machine** = machine language compile; **instruction en code** *ou* **en langage machine** = machine code instruction *ou* machine instruction; **programmation en langage machine** = machine language programming; **programme en langage machine** = absolute program; **interface utilisateur-machine** *ou* **interface homme-machine** = human-computer *ou* human-machine interface (HMI); **mot machine** = machine word; **(logiciel) propre à la machine** = intimate *ou* machine-intimate (software); **(signal d') interruption provenant d'une machine** = hardware interrupt

◊ **machine-outil** *nf* machine-tool; **commandes numériques de machines-outils** = Automatically Programmed Tools (APT); **système de commandes numériques de machines-outils** = flexible machining system (FMS)

◊ **machiniste** *nm&f* *(opérateur)* machinist; *(théâtre ou film)* grip

macro¹ *nf* = MACROCOMMANDE, MACRO-INSTRUCTION macro; **bibliothèque de macros** = macro library; **désassemblage de macro** = macro expansion

macro-² *préfixe* macro-

◊ **macro-assembleur** *nm* macro assembler *ou* assembly program

◊ **macrocode** *nm* macro code

◊ **macrocommande** *ou* **macro¹** *nf* macro command *ou* macro instruction

◊ **macrodéfinition** *nf* macro definition

◊ **macro-élément** *nm* macroelement

◊ **macro-expansion** *nf* macro expansion

◊ **macro-instruction** *ou* **macro¹** *nf* macro command *ou* macro instruction *ou* macro *ou* macro call; **macro-instruction imbriquée** = nested macro call

◇ **macrolangage** *nm* macro language; **programme assembleur pour macrolangage** = macro assembler *ou* macro assembly program

◇ **macro-ordinogramme** *nm* macro flowchart

◇ **macroprogrammation** *nf* macro programming

macule *nf (d'image)* slur

magasin *nm (pour pellicule)* magazine

magazine *nf* magazine; **format magazine** = magazine format

magnétique *adj* magnetic; **bande magnétique** = magnetic tape *ou* mag tape; *(en cassette)* cassette tape; **cartouche** *ou* **cassette de bande magnétique** = magnetic tape cartridge *ou* cassette; **dérouleur de bandes magnétiques** = magnetic tape transport; **encodeur pour bandes magnétiques** = magnetic tape encoder; **lecteur de bandes magnétiques** = magnetic tape reader; **mémoire à bulles magnétiques** = magnetic bubble memory; **carte magnétique** = magnetic card *ou* smart card *ou* personal identification device (PID); **champ d'une carte magnétique** = card field; **lecteur de cartes magnétiques** = magnetic card reader; **cartes (de crédit) magnétiques** = electronic money; **cellule magnétique** = magnetic cell; **champ magnétique** = magnetic field; **disque magnétique** = magnetic disk; **écran magnétique** = magnetic screen; **effaceur magnétique** = degausser *ou* demagnetizer; **il s'est servi d'un effaceur magnétique pour démagnétiser les têtes de lecture** = he used a demagnetizer to degauss the tape heads; **encodage magnétique** *ou* **sur support magnétique** = magnetic encoding; **encre magnétique** = magnetic ink; **flux magnétique** = magnetic flux; **lecteur de marques magnétiques** = mark sense device *ou* reader; **mémoire magnétique** = magnetic memory *ou* store; **mémoire à couches minces magnétiques** = magnetic thin film storage; **mise au point magnétique** = magnetic focusing; **orage magnétique** = magnetic storm; **piste magnétique** = magnetic strip; **lecteur de pistes magnétiques** = magnetic strip reader; **polarité magnétique** = magnetic polarity; **reconnaissance de caractères**

magnétiques = magnetic ink character recognition (MICR); **imagerie par résonnance magnétique (IRM)** = magnetic resonance imaging; **support magnétique** = magnetic material *ou* medium; **les supports magnétiques** = magnetic media; **support magnétique original** = magnetic master; **support magnétique vierge** = empty medium; **données sur support magnétique** = soft data; **enregistrement sur support magnétique** = magnetic recording; **tambour magnétique** = magnetic drum; **tête magnétique** = magnetic head; **tore magnétique** = magnetic core; **transfert d'un support magnétique à un autre** *ou* **transfert magnétique** = magnetic transfer

◇ **magnétisation** *nf* magnetization; **perte** *ou* **défaut de magnétisation** = drop out

◇ **magnétiser** *vtr* to magnetize

> le champ ainsi créé magnétise les particules métalliques prisonnières de la surface du disque, forçant l'alignement de leurs pôles
> *Science et Vie Micro*

magnétocassette *nf* tape unit; **platine magnétocassette** = tape deck

magnétophone *nm* (magnetic) tape recorder *ou* audio cassette recorder (ACR) *ou* tape unit *ou* reel to reel recorder; **magnétophone à cassette** = cassette recorder; **magnétophone à quatre pistes** = four-track recorder; **magnétophone stéréophonique** = stereophonic recorder; **interface magnétophone** = ACR interface; **platine magnétophone** = tape deck

magnétoscope *nm* video recorder *ou* video cassette recorder (VCR) *ou* videotape recorder

maigre *adj (imprimerie)* **caractères maigres** = light face

mailing *nm* (direct) mailing

maillage *nm (de réseau ou de données)* **structure à maillage intégral** = plex structure

◇ **maille** *nf* mesh

◇ **maillé, -ée** *adj* **réseau maillé** = mesh network; **réseau totalement maillé** =

fully connected network; **système maillé = multilink system**

main *nf* hand; **(qui fonctionne) à la main =** (which works) manually; **écrit à la main =** handwritten; *(d'un ordinateur)* **mise en main =** hands-on training; **une mise en main du nouvel ordinateur a été organisée pour les délégués commerciaux =** the sales representatives have received hands-on experience of the new computer; **(petit appareil) qu'on tient à la main =** hand-held (device)

mainframe *nm* mainframe computer

maintenabilité *nf* maintainability

maintenance *nf (d'un appareil)* maintenance *ou* service *ou* upkeep; **contrat de maintenance =** maintenance contract *ou* service contract; **maintenance corrective =** corrective maintenance; **maintenance courante =** housekeeping; **maintenance curative =** remedial maintenance; **maintenance de fichier =** file maintenance; **maintenance de logiciel =** software maintenance; **maintenance du parc clients =** customer engineering; **maintenance préventive =** preventive maintenance; **nous offrons un contrat de maintenance préventive qui s'applique à ce système =** we offer a preventive maintenance contract for the system; **maintenance d'un programme =** program maintenance *ou* maintenance routine *ou* housekeeping routine; **ingénieur de maintenance (sur le site) =** field engineer; **programme de maintenance =** service program; **service de maintenance =** maintenance (service)

maintenir *vtr* **(a)** to retain *ou* to sustain **(b) maintenir (un fichier) à jour =** to keep (a file) up to date; **nous passons beaucoup de temps à maintenir nos fichiers à jour =** we spend a lot of time keeping our files up to date

◊ **maintien** *nm* **boucle de maintien =** holding loop; **courant de maintien =** hold current; **délai** *ou* **retard de maintien =** contention delay

maison *nf (société)* house; **maison d'édition =** publisher *ou* publishing house; **une des plus grandes maisons de logiciel aux Etats-Unis =** one of the biggest software houses in the US; **de la maison =** in-house; **tous nos équipements sont suivis par l'équipe de maintenance de la maison =** the in-house maintenance staff deal with all our equipment; **style (de la) maison =** house style

maître, maîtresse *n* master; *(émetteur de données)* **maître d'un bus =** bus master; **carte maîtresse =** master card; **fichier maître =** master file; **fichier de programme maître =** master program file; **horloge maîtresse =** main clock *ou* master clock *ou* timing master; **ordinateur maître =** master computer; **l'ordinateur maître contrôle tout =** the master computer controls everything else; **terminal maître =** master terminal

◊ **maître-esclave** *nm* **système informatique maître-esclave =** master/slave computer system

◊ **maître-maître** *nm* **système maître-maître =** master/master computer system

◊ **maîtriser** *vtr* to control *ou* to manage; **qui peut être maîtrisé =** manageable

majuscule *nf&adj* **(lettre) majuscule =** capital *ou* cap *ou* capital letter *ou* block capital; *(imprimerie)* **majuscule =** upper case; **écrire en majuscules =** to write in capital letters *ou* to print; **BASIC s'écrit toujours avec des majuscules =** the word BASIC is always written in caps; **son nom était écrit en majuscules =** his name was written in capital letters; **écrivez votre nom et votre adresse en majuscules en haut du formulaire =** please print your name and address at the top of the form; **écrivez votre nom et votre adresse en majuscules =** write your name and address in block letters; **M majuscule =** capital M *ou* upper case M; **il a remplacé le M majuscule de 'coMputer' par une minuscule =** he corrected the word 'coMputer', replacing the upper case M with a lower case letter; **passer en majuscule =** to shift; **touche des majuscules =** shift key; **touche de verrouillage des majuscules =** caps lock; **mettre en mode majuscule ou minuscule** *ou* **uniformiser (en majuscules ou minuscules) =** to normalize

mal *adv* incorrectly; **mal fonctionner =** to malfunction

mâle *adj* male; **connecteur mâle** = male connector; **connecteur mâle à deux broches** = jumper

manager *nm* manager

manche *nf* **manche à balai** = joystick; **port pour manche à balai** = joystick port; **l'ordinateur personnel possède un port pour le manche à balai** = the computer comes with a joystick port

manchettes *nf* banner headlines

manette *nf* **manette (de jeu)** = games paddle *ou* joystick; **port (de) manette** = joystick port

manipulation *nf (de données ou d'images)* manipulation; **manipulation binaire** = bit manipulation; **manipulation de bloc** = block operation; **routine de manipulation de fichier** = file handling routine; **manipulation d'octets** = byte manipulation; **manipulation de texte** = text manipulation; **un gestionnaire de base de données ultra-rapide permet la manipulation d'une très grande quantité de données** = a high-speed database management program allows the manipulation of very large amounts of data; **langage de manipulation de données** = data manipulation language (DML)
◊ **manipuler** *vtr* to manipulate; **les câbles de technologie avancée doivent être manipulés avec grand soin** = high spec cabling needs to be very carefully handled; **on peut manipuler l'image avant son téléchargement sur l'ordinateur hôte** = the image can be manipulated before uploading to the host computer; **un processeur d'images qui peut lire, afficher et manipuler les images vidéo** = an image processor that captures, displays and manipulates video images

manoeuvre *nf* **disque de manoeuvre** = work disk; **espace de manoeuvre** = workspace; **fichier de manoeuvre** = scratch file *ou* work file

manomètre *nm* gauge

manquement *nm* failure

mantisse *nf* mantissa *ou* argument *ou* fractional part; **mantisse binaire** = binary mantissa; **la mantisse du nombre 45,897 est 0,897** = the mantissa of the number 45.897 is 0.897

manuel *nm* manual; **manuel d'installation** = installation manual *ou* technical manual; **manuel d'utilisation** = user guide *ou* user's manual *ou* instruction manual; **un manuel d'utilisation est inclus avec le système** = a user's guide *ou* an instruction manual is included with the system; *(package)* **progiciel plus manuel d'utilisation** = packaged *ou* canned software *ou* software package; **manuel d'utilisation élémentaire** = primer
◊ **manuel, -elle** *adj* manual; **système manuel** = hands on system; **système sans intervention manuelle** = hands off system
◊ **manuellement** *adv* manually; **l'alimentation du papier se fait manuellement** = the paper has to be fed into the printer manually

manufacturer *vtr* to manufacture

manuscrit *nm* manuscript *ou* MS; **ce manuscrit a été écrit directement sur ordinateur** = this manuscript was all written on computer; **l'auteur a envoyé un manuscrit de deux cents pages entièrement écrit à la main** = the author sent in two hundred pages of handwritten manuscript; **manuscrit dactylographié** = typescript
◊ **manuscrit, -e** *adj* handwritten

manutention *nf* (materials) handling

maquette *nf* *(illustrations)* artwork; *(d'un livre ou d'une revue)* dummy; *(prototype de test)* mock-up; *(modèle réduit)* model; **la maquette a été envoyée au flashage** = the artwork has been sent for filming; **il nous a fait voir la maquette du nouveau centre informatique** = he showed us a model of the new computer centre building; *(chemin de fer)* **maquette d'édition** = editing plan

marche *nf* **(a)** **marche/arrêt** = on/off; **tourner le bouton marche/arrêt** = turn the on/off knob; **'marche'** = 'power on'; **indicateur (lumineux) de marche** = run indicator; **mettre en marche** = to operate *ou* to power up *ou* to switch on *ou* to turn on *ou* to activate; **en appuyant sur la touche CR, on met l'imprimante en marche** = pressing CR activates the printer; **appareil en (bon) état de marche** = functional unit *ou* machine which is up and running; **remise en marche automatique** = auto restart; **remise en marche au point de reprise** *ou* **au point d'arrêt** = failure recovery *ou* fall back recovery; **marche arrière** = backward mode; **faire marche arrière** = to backtrack **(b) marche à suivre** = procedure; **voici la marche à suivre pour retrouver des fichiers perdus** = you should use this procedure to retrieve lost files

◊ **marcher** *vi* to function *ou* to perform; **faire marcher** = to operate *ou* to drive; **êtes-vous capable de faire marcher le standard téléphonique?** = do you know how to operate the telephone switchboard?; *(appareil)* **qui marche (à l'électricité, etc.)** = powered (by electricity, etc.); **un moteur qui marche à l'électricité** = an electrically-powered motor

marge *nf* **(a)** *(espace blanc autour d'un texte)* margin; **en tapant le contrat à la machine, n'oubliez pas de laisser des marges très larges** = when typing the contract don't forget to leave wide margins; **les marges de droite et de gauche sont les blancs de chaque côté d'une page** = the left margin and right margin are the two sections of blank paper on either side of the page; **marge intérieure** = gutter; **marge supérieure** = top space; **fixer** *ou* **paramétrer une marge** = to set a margin; **paramétrage de marges** = margination **(b)** *(limite)* margin; **marge de tolérance au bruit** = noise margin; **marge d'erreur** = margin of error; **marge de sécurité** = safety margin

◊ **marginal** *adj* **carte à encoches marginales** = edge notched card; *(d'un texte)* **notes marginales** = cut-in notes; *(d'une carte perforée)* **perforations marginales** = feed holes *ou* sprocket holes

marguerite *nf* daisy-wheel *ou* printwheel; **imprimante à marguerite** = daisy-wheel printer; **l'imprimante à marguerite donne un bien meilleur** résultat que **l'imprimante matricielle mais elle est plus lente** = a daisy-wheel printer produces much better quality text than a dot-matrix, but is slower

marquage *nm* marking; *(avec drapeau ou balise)* flagging; **marquage des touches (de clavier)** = key strip; *(d'un fichier)* **marquage de limites** = boundary punctuation; *(de bande papier)* **code de marquage** = tape code; *(entre des signaux)* **intervalle de marquage** = marking interval; *(du bord d'un disque)* **perforation de marquage** = (disk) index hole

◊ **marque** *nf* **(a)** mark *ou* marker; *(logique)* mark; *(drapeau ou balise)* flag *ou* indicator; **marque (de début) d'adresse** = address mark; *(signal)* **marque attente** = mark hold; **marques de bloc** *ou* **de sélection d'un bloc** = block markers *ou* block marks; **marque de début d'enregistrement** = beginning of information mark (bim); **marque de début de mot** = word marker; **marque de dépassement de capacité** = overflow bit *ou* flag *ou* indicator; **marque de fin de fichier** = terminator; *(sur microfilm)* **marque de positionnement** = editing symbol; **lecteur de marques magnétiques** = mark sense device *ou* mark reader; **lecteur optique de marques** = optical mark reader (OMR); **reconnaissance optique de marques** = optical mark recognition (OMR) **(b)** *(d'un produit)* **nom de marque** = brand name; **marque de l'éditeur** *ou* **de l'imprimeur** = colophon

◊ **marqué, -ée** *adj* **bit marqué** = dirty bit; **image marquée d'un reflet** = flared image

◊ **marquer** *vtr* to mark; *(d'un drapeau ou d'une balise)* to flag; **(instruction de) marquer un bloc** = mark block

◊ **marqueur** *nm* **(a)** cursor; **marqueur effaceur** = destructive cursor **(b)** marker; *(drapeau ou balise)* flag *ou* indicator flag; **marqueur de champ** = field marker; **marqueur d'état** *ou* **d'utilisation** = device flag; **marqueur de fin de fichier** = terminator; **marqueur (de début** *ou* **de fin) de groupe** = group mark *ou* marker; **marqueur de fin de liste** = nil pointer; **séquence de marqueurs** = flag sequence **(c)** *(stylo feutre)* marker pen

marteau *nm* **marteau d'impression** = print hammer

MASER MICROWAVE AMPLIFICATION BY STIMULATED EMISSION OF RADIATION; **amplificateur MASER =** MASER

masquage *nm* masking

◊ **masque** *nm* **(a)** mask; **on se sert d'un masque ou d'un stencil pour reproduire le tracé du circuit du transistor sur le silicium =** a mask or stencil is used to transfer the transistor design onto silicon **(b) masque binaire** *ou* **bit masque =** mask bit; **masque d'interruption =** interrupt mask; **registre de masque =** mask register **(c)** *(de saisie)* form *ou* template; **mode masque =** form mode **(d)** *(télévision)* **masque filtre =** shadowmask; **masque de séparation =** aperture mask

◊ **masqué, -ée** *adj* masked; **mémoire morte masquée =** masked ROM; **mode d'exécution frontal-masqué =** foreground/background modes

◊ **masquer** *vtr* to mask *ou* to conceal; **le signal a été masqué par le bruit =** we have lost the signal in the noise; **les lignes qu'on ne veut pas montrer sont masquées par cet algorithme =** the hidden lines are concealed from view with this algorithm; **qui peut être masqué =** maskable; **interruption qui peut être masquée =** maskable interrupt; **interruption qui ne peut être masquée =** non-maskable interrupt (NMI)

mass-media *nm* **les mass-medias =** the mass media

masse *nf* **(a)** bulk; *(d'un disque ou d'une bande)* **effacement en masse =** bulk erase; **mémoire de masse =** bulk storage *ou* mass storage; **en masse =** in bulk; **opérations numériques en masse ultra-rapides =** number crunching; **processeur mathématique pour calcul en masse ultra-rapide =** number cruncher; **il faut un processeur très puissant pour les applications graphiques qui exigent une forte capacité de traitement des nombres en masse =** a very powerful processor is needed for graphics applications which require extensive number crunching capabilities **(b)** *(d'un appareil électrique)* **mettre à la masse =** to earth; **fil de mise à la masse =** earth wire; **tresse de mise à la masse =** fanning strip

massicot *nm* guillotine

mat, matte *adj* matt *ou* matte

matériau *nm* material; **l'or est le matériau idéal pour la fabrication des connecteurs électriques =** gold is the ideal material for electrical connections; **matériau ferromagnétique =** ferromagnetic material; **matériau isolant =** insulator *ou* insulation material; **matériau semi-conducteur (de type) n =** n-type material *ou* N-type material *ou* n-type semi-conductor; **matériaux synthétiques =** synthetic materials; **contrôle d'approvisionnement en matériaux =** materials control

matériel *nm* **(a)** *(informatique)* hardware; **matériels annexes =** ancillary equipment; **matériel courant** *ou* **banal** *ou* **partagé =** common hardware; **matériel de formatage =** formatter; **compatibilité du matériel =** hardware compatibility; **configuration du matériel =** hardware configuration; **défaillance du matériel =** equipment failure; **fiabilité** *ou* **bonne qualité du matériel =** hardware reliability; **sécurité du matériel =** hardware security **(b)** equipment; **matériel audiovisuel =** audiovisual aids; **matériel de bureau =** office equipment *ou* business equipment; **matériel (de) haute performance =** high performance equipment; **matériel publicitaire =** publicity matter *ou* display material; **matériel de secours =** auxiliary equipment; **matériel (de) téléinformatique =** data communications equipment (DCE); **manutention du matériel =** materials handling

math *nf* = MATHEMATIQUE maths; *US* math

◊ **mathématique** **1** *nf* **les mathématiques =** mathematics **2** *adj* mathematical; **coprocesseur mathématique =** maths chip *ou* maths coprocessor; **modèle mathématique =** mathematical model; **ordre de mise en oeuvre des opérateurs mathématiques =** operator precedence; **sous-programme mathématique =** mathematical subroutine

◊ **maths** *nf* = MATH

matrice *nf* **(a)** *(tableau de nombres ou données)* matrix; **matrice réduite =** sparse array; **rotation de matrice =**

matrix rotation **(b)** *(connexions)* **matrice de relation** = matrix; **matrice des touches sur un clavier** = key matrix **(c)** *(graphique)* **matrice de caractères** = character matrix; **matrice d'impression à haute définition** = enhanced dot matrix; **matrice de points** = dot matrix

◇ **matriciel, -elle** *adj* **imprimante matricielle** = matrix printer *ou* dot-matrix printer *ou* wire printer; **processeur d'image matricielle** = raster image processor; **une page électronique peut être convertie en image vidéo imprimable à l'aide d'un processeur d'image matricielle** = an electronic page can be converted to a printer-readable video image by an on-board raster image processor

◇ **matricielle** *nf (imprimante)* matrix printer *ou* dot-matrix printer *ou* wire printer

les matricielles à aiguilles sont aussi capables de travailler en couleur. De très beaux résultats mais une limitation: les teintes ne peuvent pas se mélanger
L'Ordinateur Individuel

mauvais, -e *adj* **(a)** wrong *ou* inaccurate; **il a tapé le mauvais mot de passe** = he entered an inaccurate password; **l'erreur provenait d'une mauvaise saisie des données** = the error was caused because the data had not been accurately keyed **(b)** anomalous; *(due à des perturbations atmosphériques)* **mauvaise transmission d'images** = anomalous propagation (ANAPROP)

maximal, -e *adj* maximum; **capacité maximale** = maximum capacity; **débit maximal de transmission** = maximum transmission rate; **fréquence maximale utilisable** = maximum usable frequency; **vitesse maximale** = maximum transmission rate

◇ **maximum 1** *nm* maximum **2** *adj* maximum; **amplitude maximum enregistrée** = maximum reading; **définition maximum** = limiting resolution; **période de demande maximum** = time of peak demand; **niveau maximum de production** = peak output; **atteindre un niveau maximum** = to peak; **la tension a atteint le niveau maximum de 1200 volts** = the power peaked at 1,200 volts; **nombre maximum d'utilisateurs** = maximum users; **le marqueur du thermomètre indique la température maximum d'aujourd'hui** = the marker on the thermometer shows the peak temperature for today; **c'est la vitesse maximum que peut atteindre cette imprimante** = that is the highest speed that this printer is capable of

Mb *ou* **Mbit** = MEGABIT

Mbps = MEGABITS PAR SECONDE

mC = MILLICOULOMB

mécanique *adj* mechanical

◇ **mécanisme** *nm* mechanism; **l'imprimante possède un mécanisme très simple** = the printer mechanism is very simple; **il semble que le mécanisme du lecteur ne fonctionne pas très bien** = the drive mechanism appears to be faulty

média *nm* media; **les médias** = the media; **les médias** *ou* **les mass-media** = the mass media; **analyse des médias** = media analysis *ou* media research; **le produit a beaucoup fait parler de lui dans les medias** = the product attracted a lot of interest in the media *ou* a lot of media interest

◇ **médiatique** *adj* **couverture médiatique** = media coverage *ou* press coverage; **le produit a eu un gros intérêt médiatique** = the product attracted a lot of interest in the media *ou* a lot of media interest; **nous avons eu une bonne couverture médiatique pour le lancement du nouveau modèle** = we got good media coverage for the launch of the new model

médical, -e *adj* **imagerie médicale** = imaging

méga- *préfixe* mega-

◇ **mégabit (Mb)** *nm* megabit *ou* Mbit (Mb); **(nombre de) mégabits par seconde (Mbps)** = megabits per second (Mbps)

◇ **mégaflops (Mflops)** *nm* = MILLION(S) D'OPÉRATIONS EN VIRGULE FLOTTANTE PAR SECONDE megaflops *ou* Mflops

◇ **mégahertz (MHz)** *nm* megahertz (MHz)

◇ **méga-octet** *ou* **Moctet (Mo)** *nm* megabyte *ou* Mbyte (Mb); **carte mémoire de plusieurs méga-octets** = multimegabyte memory card

mélange *nf (sonore)* mix
◊ **mélanger** *vtr (des signaux audio)* to mix *ou* to mix down
◊ **mélangeur** *nm (de signaux audio)* mixer

membrane *nf* **membrane conique =** cone

mémento *nm* **mémento de clavier =** keyboard overlay; **mémento de fonction des touches =** key overlay

mémoire *nf* memory *ou* store *ou* storage; **mémoire à accès aléatoire** *ou* **sélectif** *ou* **direct =** random access storage *ou* memory; **mémoire à accès direct =** direct access storage device (DASD); **contrôleur de mémoire à accès direct =** DMA controller; **vol de temps de cycle de la mémoire à accès direct** *ou* **de mémoire DMA =** DMA cycle stealing; **mémoire à accès intermédiaire =** intermediate access memory (IAM); **mémoire à accès rapide =** rapid access memory *ou* fast access memory (FAM); **mémoire à accès séquentiel =** serial access memory (SAM) *ou* sequential access storage; **mémoire à double accès =** dual port memory; **mémoire acoustique =** acoustic store *ou* acoustic memory; **mémoire adressable par son contenu** *ou* **mémoire associative =** content-addressable memory (CAM) *ou* associative memory; **mémoire d'archivage =** archive storage; **mémoire associative =** associative memory *ou* content-addressable storage *ou* parallel search storage *ou* search memory *ou* searching storage; **processeur à mémoire associative =** associative processor; **registre de mémoire associative =** associative storage register; **mémoire auxiliaire =** auxiliary storage *ou* memory *ou* store *ou* backing memory; **cet appareil est équipé de lecteurs de disquettes et de bandes magnétiques qui servent de mémoire auxiliaire =** disk drives and magnetic tapes are auxiliary storage on this machine; **mémoire banale** *ou* **mémoire 'bloc-notes' =** scratchpad memory *ou* working store; **mémoire à bulles (magnétiques) =** (magnetic) bubble memory; **cassette mémoire à bulles (magnétiques) =** bubble memory cassette; **mémoire cache =** cache memory; **le temps d'accès est réduit**

lorsque les données les plus fréquemment utilisées sont placées dans la mémoire cache = file access time is much quicker if the most frequently used data is stored in cache memory; **stocker dans la mémoire cache =** to cache; **mémoire capacitive** *ou* **à condensateur =** capacitor storage; **mémoire CCD** *ou* **à couplage de charge =** charge coupled device memory *ou* CCD memory; **mémoire centrale =** core memory *ou* store *ou* central memory; **dans ce système, la mémoire centrale rapide sert de bloc-notes pour tous les calculs =** the fast core is used as a scratchpad for all calculations in this system; **programme en mémoire centrale =** core program; **mémoire centrale à accès direct =** core memory *ou* primary memory; **mémoire centrale rapide =** fast core; **mémoire circulante** *ou* **mémoire dynamique =** circulating storage; **mémoire de contrôles =** control memory; **mémoire à couches minces (magnétiques) =** (magnetic) thin film storage *ou* memory; **mémoire cryogénique =** cryogenic memory; **mémoire à disque =** disk memory; **mémoire de données =** data memory *ou* storage; **mémoire dynamique =** dynamic memory *ou* dynamic storage; **mémoire dynamique permanente =** permanent dynamic memory;
mémoire EAPROM = electrically alterable, programmable read-only memory (EAPROM); **mémoire EAROM =** electrically alterable read-only memory (EAROM); **mémoire écran =** screen memory; **mémoire EEPROM =** electrically erasable programmable read-only memory (EEPROM);
mémoire EEROM = electrically erasable read-only memory (EEROM); **mémoire effaçable =** erasable memory; **mémoire électrostatique =** electrostatic storage; **mémoire d'entrée =** input storage; **mémoire EPROM =** erasable programmable read-only memory (EPROM); **mémoire externe (auxiliaire) =** external memory *ou* external storage *ou* external store; **mémoire fantôme =** shadow memory *ou* shadow page; **(mise en) mémoire de fichiers =** file storage; **(mise en) mémoire du format courant =** local format storage; **mémoire FIFO** *ou* **mémoire qui fonctionne sur le principe du premier entré premier sorti =** FIFO memory *ou* first in first out memory; **mémoire fixe =** control memory *ou* ROM; **mémoire holographique** *ou* **d'hologramme =** holographic storage;

mémoire image = frame store; **la mémoire image peut servir à l'affichage des images météorologiques transmises par satellites** = the frame store can be used to display weather satellite pictures; **le processeur d'images permet le stockage d'une image vidéo dans une mémoire intégrée de 8 bits** = the image processor allows you to store a video frame in a built-in 8-bit frame store; **espace mémoire de l'image** = image storage space; **mémoire d'images optiques** = scanner memory; **mémoire ineffaçable** = nonerasable storage; **mémoire d'instruction** = instruction storage; **mémoire intermédiaire** = intermediate storage; **mémoire interne** = internal memory *ou* store; **mémoire interne (à accès immédiat)** = immediate access store (IAS); **tri en mémoire interne** = internal sort; *(d'un système)* **mémoire de lancement** = bootstrap memory; **mémoire (à) laser sur couche haute définition** = laser emulsion storage; **mémoire à ligne de retard** = delay line store; **mémoire à liste permutée** = nesting store; **mémoire locale** = local memory;
mémoire magnétique = magnetic memory *ou* store; **mémoire magnétique haute densité** = high density storage; **mémoire de masse** = mass storage *ou* bulk storage; **mémoire morte** = read only memory (ROM); **(support de) mémoire morte** *ou* **fixe** *ou* **à lecture seule** = read only memory; **mémoire morte auxiliaire** = sideways ROM; **mémoire morte à fusibles** = fusible read only memory (FROM);
mémoire morte masquée = masked ROM; **mémoire morte programmable** = programmable memory (PROM) *ou* programmable read only memory (PROM); **mémoire morte programmable effaçable par ultraviolet** = ultraviolet erasable PROM; **programmeur de mémoire morte** = burner; **mémoire MOS** = MOS memory; **mémoire à un niveau** = one-level store; **mémoire non-volatile** = non-volatile memory; **mémoire optique** = optical storage *ou* optical memory; **mémoire optonumérique** = photodigital memory; **mémoire paginée** = shadow memory *ou* shadow page; **accès sur demande à la mémoire paginée** = demand fetching; **mémoire (de) périphérique** = peripheral memory; **mémoire permanente** = permanent memory *ou* nonerasable storage;

mémoire principale = primary memory *ou* primary store *ou* primary storage *ou* central memory (CM) *ou* main memory *ou* main storage; **le système de 16 bits contient une mémoire principale d'une capacité allant jusqu'à 3Mo** = the 16-bit system includes up to 3Mb of main memory; **mémoire (de) programme** = program storage; **mémoire PROM** = programmable memory (PROM) *ou* programmable read only memory (PROM); **PROM effaçable par ultraviolet** = ultraviolet erasable PROM; **mémoire protégée** = protected storage; *(mémoire vive)* **mémoire RAM** = random access memory; **condensateur pour mémoire RAM** = memory backup capacitor; **la bande perforée est une des mémoires de rangement les plus lentes d'accès** = paper tape is one of the slowest access backing stores; **mémoire réelle** = real memory; *(mémoire morte)* **mémoire ROM** = read only memory; **mémoire ROM effaçable électriquement** = electrically erasable read-only memory (EEROM); **mémoire ROM fantôme** = phantom ROM; **mémoire ROM à fusibles** = fusible read only memory (FROM); **mémoire ROM modifiable électriquement** = electrically alterable read-only memory (EAROM); **mémoire ROM programmable et effaçable** = erasable programmable read-only memory (EPROM); **mémoire ROM programmable et effaçable électriquement** = electrically erasable programmable read-only memory (EEPROM); **mémoire ROM programmable, modifiable électriquement** = electrically alterable, programmable read-only memory (EAPROM); **mémoire secondaire** *ou* **intermédiaire** = secondary storage; **mémoire séquentielle** = serial memory *ou* sequential storage; **la bande magnétique constitue une mémoire séquentielle d'une grande capacité** = magnetic tape is a high capacity serial memory; **mémoire séquentielle indexée** = indexed sequential storage; **mémoire statique** = static memory *ou* static storage; **mémoire tampon** = buffer (memory); **mémoire tampon d'entrée/sortie** = I/O buffer; **registre de mémoire tampon** = memory buffer register (MBR); **taille de la mémoire tampon** = buffer length *ou* buffer size; **mémoire tampon de transmission de données** = data communications buffer; **mémoire tampon dynamique** = dynamic buffer;

qui possède une mémoire tampon = buffered; **utilisation de mémoire tampon** = buffering; **entrée/sortie utilisant une mémoire tampon** = buffered input/output; **utilisation de double mémoire tampon** = double buffering; **utiliser une mémoire tampon** = to buffer; **les deux ordinateurs fonctionnent à des vitesses différentes mais peuvent transmettre des données en utilisant une mémoire tampon fonctionnant sur le système 'premier entré premier sorti'** = the two computers operate at different rates, but can transmit data using a FIFO memory; **mémoire temporaire** = temporary storage *ou* erasable storage *ou* erasable memory; *(bloc-notes)* **mémoire temporaire** = working store *ou* scratchpad; **mémoire vidéo** *ou* **mémoire image** = video memory; **mémoire vidéo à accès aléatoire** = video random access memory (VRAM); **mémoire virtuelle** = virtual memory *ou* virtual storage (VS); **mémoire vive** *ou* **mémoire RAM** = random access memory (RAM); **mémoire vive dynamique** = dynamic RAM *ou* dynamic random access memory (DRAM); **mémoire vive** *ou* **mémoire à accès aléatoire** *ou* **(mémoire) RAM** = random access memory (RAM); **(programme) chargeur** *ou* **programme de chargement de la mémoire vive** = RAM loader; **mémoire volatile** = volatile memory *ou* volatile store *ou* storage *ou* volatile dynamic storage; **accès direct à la mémoire** = direct memory access (DMA); **temps d'accès à la mémoire** = memory access time; **changement d'adresse en mémoire** = memory edit; **registre d'adresse en mémoire** = memory address register (MAR) *ou* store address register (SAR);

alimentation de secours de la mémoire = memory backup capacitor; **allocation de mémoire** = storage allocation; **allocation dynamique de la mémoire** = dynamic storage allocation; **banque de mémoire** = memory bank; **la carte d'extension possède une banque de mémoire de 128Ko constituée de 16 puces** = an add-on card has a 128Kb memory bank made up of 16 chips; **bus de mémoire** = memory bus; **capacité de mémoire** = memory capacity *ou* storage capacity; **la capacité de mémoire est de 3Mo** = total storage capacity is 3Mb; **capacité de mémoire de disque** *ou* **de disquette** = disk storage capacity; *(de circuit intégré)* **carte mémoire** = memory board; *(carte magnétique)* **carte (magnétique) à**

mémoire = chip card *ou* smart card; **cellule de mémoire** = memory cell *ou* store cell; **clavier à mémoire** = key rollover; **configuration de la mémoire** = memory map; **configuré en mémoire** = memory-mapped; **entrée/sortie configurée en mémoire** = memory-mapped I/O *ou* memory-mapped input/output; **un écran configuré en mémoire possède une adresse pour chaque pixel, permettant ainsi au processeur d'accéder directement à l'écran** = a memory-mapped screen has an address allocated to each pixel, allowing direct access to the screen by the CPU; **cycle de mémoire** = memory cycle; **densité de mémoire** = storage density; **diagnostic de la mémoire** = memory diagnostic; **dispositif mémoire** = storage device; **disquette** *ou* **disque de mémoire** = storage disk;

disque mémoire = RAM disk; **écran à mémoire** = storage tube; **emplacement de mémoire** = store location; **extension de mémoire** = extension memory; **fichiers en mémoire** = file store; **gestion de mémoire** = memory management; **hiérarchie des mémoires** = memory hierarchy; **implanter** *ou* **ranger** *ou* **stocker (dans la** *ou* **en mémoire)** = to plant *ou* to store; **listage de mémoire** = memory dump; **mettre en mémoire** = to memorize *ou* to store *ou* to deposit (data); **programme mis en mémoire** = stored program; **mise en mémoire** = storage; **mise en mémoire de données** = data storage; **mise en mémoire de fichier** = file storage; **mise en mémoire du format courant** = local format storage; **mise en mémoire d'instruction** = instruction storage;

nettoyage de mémoire = garbage collection; **page mémoire** = memory page; **protection des accès mémoire** = fetch protect; **(dispositif de) protection de la mémoire** = memory protect; **puce mémoire** = memory chip; **(signal de) régénération** *ou* **rafraîchissement de la mémoire RAM** = RAM refresh; **registre d'adresse en mémoire** = store address register (SAR) *ou* memory adress register (MAR); **registre des données en mémoire** = store data register (SDR); **(logiciel) qui requiert beaucoup de mémoire** = memory-intensive (software);

segmentation *ou* **modularité de la mémoire** = granularity; **système à transfert de mémoire** = memory switching system; **taille (de la) mémoire** = storage capacity; **tube à mémoire** =

storage tube; **vidage de mémoire (sur imprimante)** = memory dump; **voie d'accès direct à la mémoire** = direct memory access channel; **zone mémoire** = storage area; **zone mémoire de stockage de variables** = string area; **zone commune de la mémoire** = common storage area; **zone de travail en mémoire** = memory workspace

> d'autres constructeurs ont adopté des cartes de mémoire vive permanente comme mémoire de masse sur des portables légers
> *L'Ordinateur Individuel*

mémorisé, -ée *adj* memorized *ou* stored; **programme mémorisé** = stored program

◊ **mémoriser** *vtr* to memorize *ou* to store; **il faudra jusqu'à 3Mo pour mémoriser une page de données graphiques haute-définition** = storing a page of high resolution graphics can require 3Mb

mentionner *vtr* to quote *ou* to refer to; **en cas de réclamation, mentionnez toujours le numéro de lot qui apparaît sur le boîtier de l'ordinateur** = when making a complaint please quote the batch number printed on the computer case; **le manuel mentionne un port série, mais je n'en vois aucun** = the manual refers to the serial port, but I cannot find it

menu *nm* menu; **menu déroulant** = pop-down menu *ou* pop-up menu *ou* pull-down *ou* pull-up menu; **pour afficher le menu déroulant cliquer l'icône sur le haut de l'écran** = the pull-down menu is viewed by clicking over the icon at the top of the screen; **menu principal** = main menu; **logiciel avec menu** *ou* **à base de menu** = menu-driven software; **sélection par menu** = menu selection

mercure *nm* mercury; **ligne à** *ou* **de retard au mercure** = mercury delay line

mère *nf* mother; **carte mère** = motherboard; **carte mère d'un micro-ordinateur** = microcomputer backplane

message *nm* **(a)** message; *(affiché à l'écran)* **message de diagnostic** = diagnostic message; **message de diagnostic d'erreur** = diagnostic (error) message; **message d'entrée** = input

statement; **message d'erreur** = error message; **vous obtiendrez des messages d'erreur si vous essayez de copier des fichiers implantés sur des secteurs défectueux d'une disquette** = you will receive error messages when you copy files that are stored on bad sectors on a disk; **message d'exécution** = execute statement **(b)** **message d'invitation à taper une commande** *ou* **message d'attente d'une commande** = (command) prompt; **le message READY signifie que le système est prêt à recevoir des instructions** = the prompt READY indicates that the system is available to receive instructions **(c)** *(informations transmises)* **message chiffré** *ou* **crypté** = ciphertext; **message multimédia** = multimedia mail; **message reçu** = incoming message; **(nombre de) messages reçus** = incoming traffic; **acheminement des messages** = message routing; **authentification de messages** = authentication of messages; **commutation de message** = message switching; **créneau pour message** = message slot; **en-tête de message** = message heading; **(code de) fin de message (EOM)** = end of message (EOM); **format de message** = message format; **code d'identification de message** = message authentication code (MAC); **numérotation des messages** = message numbering; **serveur de message** = interface message processor; **texte d'un message** = message text

messagerie *nf* **messagerie électronique** = computer mail *ou* electronic mail *ou* email *ou* e-mail; *(dans une société)* computer-based message system (CBMS)

mesure *nf* **(a)** *(dimension)* measure *ou* measurement; **mesure de surface** = square measure **(b)** *(fait)* **sur mesure** = custom-built; **logiciel sur mesure** = customized software *ou* machine-intimate software *ou* intimate software **(c)** *(action)* measure; **mesures de sécurité** = safety measures; **prendre des mesures** = to take action; **prendre des mesures pour éviter quelque chose** = to take measures to prevent something happening; **on a pris les mesures nécessaires pour remédier au défaut** *ou* **pour rectifier** *ou* **réparer ce qui n'allait pas** = action has been taken to repair the fault

◊ **mesurer** *vtr* to measure *ou* to gauge; **la performance est mesurée à l'aide d'un programme test** = performance measurement *ou* measurement of performance is carried out by running a benchmark program

◊ **mesureur** *nm* gauge *ou* meter

métabit *nm* metabit

métacompilation *nf* metacompilation

métal *nm* metal; **détecteur de métal** = metal detector

métalangage *nm* metalanguage; **métalangage BNF** = Backus-Naur-Form (BNF); **métalangage BNF étendu** = extended BNF (EBNF)

méthode *nf* procedure *ou* technique; **méthode ascendante** = hill climbing method; **méthode brutale** = brute force method; **méthode de classement** *ou* **d'archivage** = filing system

mètre (m) *nm* metre; *US* meter; *(poids du papier, par feuille)* **gramme au mètre carré** = grams per square metre (gsm *ou* g/m²); **mètre kilogramme seconde (ampère) (mks(A))** = metre kilogram second (Ampere) (MKS(A)) **(b) mètre (à ruban)** = tape measure

◊ **métrique** *adj* metric; **ondes métriques** = very high frequency (VHF)

mettre *vtr* to put; *(une ligne)* **mettre en attente** = to hold; **mettre sur fiche** = to place something on file; **mettre en forme** = to format; **texte mis en forme à l'impression** = post-formatted text; *(un fichier, etc.)* **mettre à jour** = to update a file *ou* to bring a file up to date; **mettre en marche** = *(faire fonctionner)* to operate; *(mettre sous tension)* to switch on; **mettre à la masse** *ou* **à la terre** = to earth; **tous les appareils doivent être mis à la masse** *ou* **à la terre** = all appliances must be earthed; **mettre en mémoire** = to store; **programme mis en mémoire** = stored program; **mettre au point** = *(un produit)* to develop *ou* to perfect; *(une lentille)* to focus; *(un appareil)* to tune; **il a mis au point le procédé de fabrication d'un acier de haute qualité** = he perfected the process for making high grade steel;

mettre au point (avec grande précision) = to fine tune; **mettre en place** = to install *ou* to set up *ou* to position; **il n'a fallu que quelques heures pour mettre l'équipement en place** = the installation of the equipment took only a few hours; **mettre en page** = to put into page *ou* to set in page; **les concepteurs ont décidé de mettre en page sur format A4** = the designers have laid out the pages in A4 format; **mettre (des données) dans la pile** = to put data onto a stack; **mettre sous tension** = to power up *ou* to switch on; **mettre à la terre** *ou* **à la masse** = to earth; **tous les appareils doivent être mis à la terre** = all appliances must be earthed; **tous les fils non rattachés doivent être mis à la terre** *ou* **à la masse** = all loose wires should be earthed *ou* tied to earth; *voir aussi* MISE

MF = MODULATION DE FREQUENCE

Mflop = MEGAFLOP

MIA = MODULATION D'IMPULSION EN AMPLITUDE

MIC = MODULATION PAR IMPULSIONS ET CODAGE

micro¹ *nm* = MICRO-ORDINATEUR micro *ou* microcomputer; **l'unité centrale de traitement peut piloter un micro** = the mainframe is downward compatible with the micro

l'Institut a depuis longtemps mis en place des micros pour répondre à ses besoins de gestion mais aussi dans un but pédagogique
L'Information professionnelle

micro² *nm* = MICROPHONE mike *ou* microphone; **micro à aimant mobile** = moving coil microphone; **micro dynamique** *ou* **à impulsion** = dynamic microphone; **micro radio** = radio microphone; **micro sans fil** = wireless microphone; **filtre de micro** = pop filter

◊ **micro-cravate** *nm* lapel microphone

◊ **micro-espion** *nm* bug; **placer un micro-espion** *ou* **surveiller par micro espion** = to bug; **il y avait des micros-espions dans la salle de conférence** = the conference room was bugged

micro-³ *préfixe (petit)* micro-

◊ **microcassette** *nf* microcassette

◇ **microcircuit** *nm* microcircuit
◇ **microcode** *nm* microcode

micro-cravate *voir* MICRO²

microcycle *nm* microcycle
◇ **microdisquette** *nf* microfloppy
◇ **micro-électronique** *nf* la micro-électronique = microelectronics

micro-espion *voir* MICRO²

microfiche *nf* microfiche *ou* microform; *(avec réduction de plus de 90X)* ultrafiche
◇ **microfilm** *nm* microfilm; **toutes nos archives sont sur microfilms** = we hold all our records on microfilm; **lecteur optique de microfilms pour entrée de données sur ordinateur** = film optical scanning device for input into computers (FOSDIC); **entrée (à partir de** *ou* **par lecture de) microfilm** = computer input from microfilm (CIM); **sortie (sur) microfilm** = computer output on microfilm (COM)
◇ **microfilmer** *vtr* to microfilm; **nous avons envoyé les archives de 1989 pour les faire microfilmer** *ou* **pour les faire mettre sur microfilm(s)** = the 1989 records have been sent away for microfilming
◇ **micrographie** *nf* la micrographie = micrographics
◇ **micro-image** *nm* microimage
◇ **micro-informatique** *nf* microcomputing; **il travaille à la rédaction d'une revue de micro-informatique** = he edits a computer magazine
◇ **micro-instruction** *nf* microcode *ou* microinstruction
◇ **micromètre** *nm* micrometre

micron *nm* micrometre

micro-onde *nf* microwave

micro-ordinateur *ou* **micro¹** *nm* microcomputer *ou* micro; **micro-ordinateur à carte unique** = single board microcomputer; **micro-ordinateur de contrôle** *ou* **de commande** = microcontroller; **micro-ordinateur de contrôle à puce unique** *ou* **monopuce** = single chip microcontroller; **micro-**

ordinateur portatif = microwriter; **bus d'un micro-ordinateur** = microcomputer bus; **kit d'extension de micro-ordinateur** = microcomputer development kit; **l'industrie des micro-ordinateurs** = the microcomputing industry

microphone *ou* **micro²** *nm* microphone; *(familier)* mike; **microphone à bobine** *ou* **à aimant mobile** = moving coil microphone; **microphone à charbon** = carbon microphone; **microphone à condensateur** = capacitor microphone; **microphone dynamique** = dynamic microphone; **microphone à électret** = electret microphone; **microphone omnidirectionnel** = omnidirectional microphone; **microphone à quartz** = crystal microphone; **microphone sans fil (pour transmission)** = wireless microphone

microphotographie *nf* microphotography

microprocesseur *nm* microprocessor (system) *ou* microprocessor unit (MPU) *ou* microdevice; **microprocesseur en tranches** = bit-slice microprocessor; **le microprocesseur en tranches utilise quatre processeurs à 4 bits pour réaliser un microprocesseur à 16 bits** = the bit-slice microprocessor uses four 4-bit processors to make a 16-bit word processor; **architecture d'un microprocesseur** = microprocessor architecture; **capacité d'adressage mémoire d'un microprocesseur** = microprocessor addressing capabilities; **puce microprocesseur** = microprocessor chip

microprogrammation *nf* microprogramming
◇ **microprogramme** *nm* microprogram; **compteur de microprogramme** = microprogram counter; **ensemble des instructions** *ou* **jeu d'instructions d'un microprogramme** = microprogram instruction set; **langage d'assemblage pour microprogramme** = microprogram assembly language; **mémoire qui contient un microprogramme** = microprogram store; **registre de microprogramme** = microprogram counter; **séquence de**

micro-instructions *ou* **d'instructions d'un microprogramme** = microsequence

◇ **microprogrammé** *nm* (system) firmware

microseconde *nf* microsecond (ms)

MID = MODULATION D'IMPULSIONS EN DUREE

migration *nf* migration; **migration de données** = data migration

MIL = MODULATION D'IMPULSIONS EN LARGEUR

milli- (m) *préfixe* milli- (m)

◇ **milliampère (mA)** *nm* milliampere (mA)

◇ **millicoulomb (mC)** *nm* millicoulomb (mC)

millier *nm* thousand; *(mesure de puissance d'un ordinateur)* **milliers d'instructions par seconde** = kilo instructions per second (KIPS)

millimétré *adj* **papier millimétré** = graph paper

◇ **millimétrique** *adj* **onde millimétrique** = extremely high frequency (EHF)

million *nm* million; **million de millions** = billion; **million(s) d'instructions par seconde (Mips)** = million instructions per second; **million(s) d'opérations en virgule flottante par seconde (Mflops)** = megaflops (MFLOPS)

l'un des chiffres les plus significatifs est le coût du 'million d'instructions par seconde', unité de mesure de puissance des processeurs informatiques
L'Information professionnelle

milliseconde (ms) *nf* millisecond (ms)

MIMD = MULTIPLE INSTRUCTION STREAM - MULTIPLE DATA STREAM; **architecture MIMD** = MIMD; *voir aussi* FLUX

mince *adj* fine *ou* thin; **couche mince** = thin film; **mémoire à couches minces** =

thin film memory; **mémoire à couches minces magnétiques** = magnetic thin film storage

mini 1 *nm* = MINI-ORDINATEUR **2** *préfixe* mini-

miniaturisation *nf* miniaturization

minidisquette *nf* minidisk

mini/maxi *adj inv* **méthode mini/maxi** = minmax (method)

minimiser *vtr* to minimize

minimum 1 *nm* minimum **2** *adj* minimum; **code à temps d'accès minimum** = optimum code

mini-ordinateur *ou* **mini** *nm* minicomputer *ou* mini

ministre *nm* **(papier) format ministre** = foolscap; **la lettre était écrite sur six feuilles format ministre** = the letter was on six sheets of foolscap

Minitel® *nm* *système de télécommunication français équivalent au système britannique* Viewdata®

minuscule *nf&adj* **(lettre) minuscule** = lower case *ou* minuscule; **mettre en mode majuscule ou minuscule** *ou* **uniformiser en majuscules ou minuscules** = to normalize

minute *nf* minute; **(nombre de) lignes par minute (lpm)** = lines per minute (LPM); **(nombre de) pages par minute (ppm)** = pages per minute (ppm)

◇ **minuter** *vtr* to time

MIP = MODULATION D'IMPULSIONS EN POSITION

MIPS = MILLIONS D'INSTRUCTIONS PAR SECONDE

mire *nf (télévision)* **mire de contrôle** = test pattern

miroir *nm* mirror; **disque miroir =** mirror disk; **effet miroir =** lateral reversal

MISD = MULTIPLE INSTRUCTION STREAM - SINGLE DATA STREAM; **architecture MISD =** MISD

mise *nf* **mise sur fiches =** card-indexing; **mise à jour =** update *ou* upkeep; **mise à jour de fichier =** file maintenance; **la mise à jour des fichiers doit se faire tous les six mois =** the upkeep of the files means reviewing them every six months; **fichier de mise à jour =** change file *ou* transaction file; **mise en main =** hands-on training; **une mise en main du nouvel ordinateur a été organisée pour les délégués commerciaux =** the sales representatives have received hands-on experience of the new computer; **mise à la masse =** earthing; **fil de mise à la masse =** earth wire; **mise en mémoire de données =** information storage *ou* data storage; **mise en mémoire de fichier =** file storage; **ordre de mise en oeuvre des opérateurs (mathématiques) =** operator precedence; **mise en orbite =** launch; **mise en page =** page layout *ou* page makeup *ou* paging; **les concepteurs travaillent à la mise en page de la nouvelle revue =** the design team is working on the layouts for the new magazine; **les corrections faites après la mise en page coûtent très cher =** corrections after the page makeup are very expensive; **mise en piggyback =** piggybacking; **mise en place =** installation; **temps de mise en place =** positioning time; **mise en place de liens (à l'aide d'un éditeur de liens) =** linkage editing; **mise en place d'un programme concurrent =** counterprogramming; **mise au point =** *(d'un produit)* development; *(d'une lentille)* focusing; **mise au point magnétique =** magnetic focusing; **dérégler la mise au point =** to defocus; **logiciel de mise au point =** debugger; **temps de mise au point d'un nouveau produit =** development time; **mise en réseau (d'ordinateurs) =** networking; **mise en route =** start; *(d'une photo)* **mise à la taille =** sizing; **(dispositif de) mise hors tension automatique =** automatic power off; **réinitialisation automatique à la mise sous tension =** power-on reset; *voir aussi* METTRE

mixage *nm* **(a)** *(signaux audio)* mix *ou* mixing; **faire un mixage =** to mix; **studio de mixage =** mixing studio **(b)** *(polices de caractères)* mixing

◊ **mixer** *vtr (signaux audio)* to mix down

◊ **mixeur** *nm (circuit électronique)* mixer

mixte *adj* **circuit mixte =** hybrid circuit; **poste de contrôle mixte =** combined station

mks(A) = METRE KILOGRAMME SECONDE (AMPERE)

mnémonique *adj* mnemonic; **code mnémonique d'assemblage =** assembler mnemonics *ou* mnemonic operation codes

Mo = MEGA-OCTET megabyte *ou* Mbyte (Mb); **le modèle le plus récent possède un disque dur d'une capacité de 30Mo =** the latest model has a 30Mbyte hard disk

mobile *adj* mobile *ou* movable; **accent mobile =** piece accent; **balayage par faisceau mobile =** flying spot scan; **microphone à aimant mobile =** moving coil microphone; **radiotéléphone mobile =** mobile radiophone; **station terrestre mobile =** mobile earth terminal; **téléphone mobile =** private mobile radio (PMR); **unité mobile =** mobile unit

Moctet = MEGA-OCTET

modal, -e *adj* modal; **dispersion modale =** mode dispersion

mode *nm* mode; **mode actif =** active state; **mode d'adressage =** addressing mode; **mode affichage =** display mode; **pour saisir un texte, appuyer d'abord sur cette touche de fonction qui met le terminal en mode alphanumérique =** when you want to type in text, press this function key which will put the terminal into its alphanumeric mode; **mode asynchrone =** asynchronous mode; **(ordinateur) à mode caractère =** character orientated (computer); **mode (de) contrôle** *ou* **mode CTRL =** control mode; **mode conversationnel =** conversational mode *ou* interactive mode; **mode défilement** = scroll mode; **mode dialogué** = conversational mode; **mode différé** *ou* **en (mode) différé** = deferred mode; **mode direct** *ou* **en (mode) direct** = direct mode; **mode (d') entrée** = input mode; **mode d'exécution** = execute mode; **mode d'exécution frontal/masqué** = foreground/background modes; **mode graphe** = plotting mode; **mode graphique** = graphics mode; **mode immédiat** = immediate mode; **mode insertion** = insert mode; **mode interactif** = interactive mode; **mode local** = local mode; **mode masque (de saisie)** = form mode; **mode multi-utilisateur** = free running mode; **mode octet** = byte mode; **mode remplacement** = replace mode; **mode séquentiel** = sequential mode; **mode sortie** = output mode; **mode de traitement de données par paquets** *ou* **par lots** = batch mode; **mode (de transfert par) paquets** = burst mode **(b) mode d'emploi** = directions for use **(c)** mode *ou* fashion; **à la mode** = fashionable; **mot à la mode** = buzzword

modèle *nm* **(a)** *(d'un produit)* model; **voici notre dernier modèle** = this is the latest model; **le nouveau modèle B remplace le modèle A** = the new model B has taken the place of model A; **modèle de démonstration** = demonstration model; **modèle d'un système** = system design; **création de modèles (sur ordinateur)** = modelling **(b) modèle réduit** = (scale) model **(c) modèle pour ordinogramme** = flowchart stencil *ou* flowchart template **(d) modèle mathématique** = mathematical model

◊ **modéliser** *vtr* to model

modem *nm* = MODULATEUR-DEMODULATEUR modulator-demodulator *ou* modem; *US* dataset; **notre modem ne fonctionne pas** *ou* **est en dérangement** *ou* **en panne** = the modem has broken down; **certains modems peuvent fonctionner en mode semi-duplex si nécessaire** = some modems can operate in half-duplex mode if required; **modem à appel automatique** = dial-in modem; **modem en bande de base** = base band modem; **n'utilisez jamais un modem en bande de base sur une ligne téléphonique normale** = do not use a base band modem with a normal phone line; **modem de courte portée** = short haul modem; **modem intégré** = integrated modem; **modem pour réseau local** *ou* **modem à distance de transmission limitée** = limited distance modem; **modem semi-duplex** = half-duplex modem; **le modem viewdata reçoit à 1200 bauds et transmet à 75** = the viewdata modem uses a 1200/75 split baud rate; **modem à deux vitesses (réception et émission)** = split baud rate modem; **débit par défaut** *ou* **prédéterminé** *ou* **implicite d'un modem** = default rate; **sans modem** = null modem; **ce câble est configuré sans modem ce qui permet de connecter les deux ordinateurs sans difficulté** = this cable is configured as a null modem, which will allow me to connect these two computers together easily

le modem permet la transmission de données informatiques par l'intermédiaire d'une ligne téléphonique classique
Science et Vie Micro

modifiable *adj* alterable; **mémoire ROM modifiable électriquement** = electrically alterable read-only memory (EAROM); **mémoire ROM programmable, modifiable électriquement** = electrically alterable, programmable read-only memory (EAPROM); **processeur à jeu d'instructions modifiable (WISC)** = writable instruction set computer (WISC)

modificateur *nm* modifier; **modificateurs d'impression** = print modifiers

◊ **modification** *nf* alteration *ou* change *ou* modification *ou* adjustment; **les modifications apportées au système permettent de l'utiliser sur un réseau local d'entreprise** = the modifications to the system allow it to be run as part of a LAN; **la nouvelle version du logiciel comporte de nombreuses modifications et améliorations** = the new version of the software has many alterations and improvements; **modification d'adresse** = address modification; **modification d'une instruction** = instruction modification; **modification provisoire** = patch; **boucle de modification** = modification loop; **enregistrement de modifications** = change record *ou* amendment record; **fichier de modifications** = change *ou* movement file; **les enregistrements modifiés ont été ajoutés au fichier maître et inscrits au journal des modifications** = the modified records were added to the master file and noted in the journal; **liste des modifications** = journal; **page mémoire sans modification** = clean page; **texte sans modification** = clean copy

◊ **modifié, -ée** *adj* modified; **modulation de fréquence modifiée** = modified frequency modulation; **nous utilisons une version modifiée du programme d'édition de lettres types** = we are running a modified version of the mail-merge system

◊ **modifier** *vtr* to adjust *ou* to alter *ou* to change *ou* to modify *ou* to vary; **les spécifications du programme viennent d'être modifiées** = the program specifications have just been altered; **il faudra modifier le logiciel pour pouvoir l'utiliser sur un ordinateur individuel** = the software will have to be modified to run on a small PC; **modifier les codes d'un programme** = to recode a program; **qui peut être modifié** = alterable *ou* selectable; *(débit, vitesse, etc.)* **qui peut être modifié suivant les besoins de l'utilisateur** = user-selectable

modulaire *adj* modular; **programmation modulaire** = modular programming *ou* modularization

la quatrième version offre désormais un environnement intégré et permet la programmation modulaire
Informatique & Bureautique

modularité *nf* modularity; **la modularité du logiciel ou du matériel permet de modifier le système** = the modularity of the software or hardware allows the system to be changed; **modularité de la mémoire** = granularity

modulateur *nm* modulator; **modulateur de fréquence radio** = radio frequency modulator *ou* RF modulator

◊ **modulateur-démodulateur** *nm* modulator-demodulator *ou* modem; *US* dataset; *voir aussi* MODEM

modulation *nf* modulation; **modulation d'amplitude (MA)** = amplitude modulation (AM); **(système) de modulation par décalage de fréquence** = frequency shift keying (FSK); **modulation (en) delta** = delta modulation; **modulation de fréquence (MF)** = frequency modulation (FM); **modulation de fréquence à large bande** = wideband frequency modulation (WBFM); **modulation de fréquence modifiée** = modified frequency modulation; **modulation d'impulsions** = pulse modulation; **modulation d'impulsions en amplitude (MIA)** = pulse amplitude modulation (PAM); **modulation par impulsions et codage (MIC)** = pulse code modulation (PCM); **modulation d'impulsions en durée (MID)** = pulse duration modulation (PDM); **modulation d'impulsions en largeur** *ou* **en durée (MIL** *ou* **MID)** = pulse width modulation (PWM); **modulation d'impulsions en position (MIP)** = pulse position modulation (PPM); **modulation de phase** = phase modulation; **signal de modulation** = modulating signal

module *nm (d'un programme)* bead; *(d'un programme* *ou* *d'un système)* module; *(d'un programme* *ou* *d'un vidéodisque)* chapter; *(d'un système)* building block; **module d'accompagnement** = coroutine; **un module d'interface analogique multifonction comprend un convertisseur analogique-numérique et un convertisseur numérique-analogique** = a multifunction analog interface module includes analog to digital and digital to analog converters; **(code) fin de module** = chapter stop

ce logiciel est intégré, ce qui signifie qu'il possède différents modules (au nombre de quatre) ayant chacun une vocation propre: traitement de texte, tableur et graphiques, gestion de fichiers et rapports, communication
L'Ordinateur Individuel

modulé, -ée *adj* **signal modulé** = modulated signal; **(signal) analogique modulé** = pseudo-digital; **non modulé** = unmodulated

◊ **moduler** *vtr* to modulate

modulo *nm* **(a) modulo-n** = modulo-N; **contrôle par modulo-n** = modulo-N check **(b)** modulus *ou* mod; **7 modulo-3 égale 1** = 7 mod 3 is 1; **signe et modulo** = sign and modulus

moins *nm* **le signe moins (-)** = minus *ou* minus sign

mois *nm* month; **pendant quelques mois** = for a period of months

moitié *nf* half; **la moitié des données ont été perdues au cours de la transmission =** half the data was lost in transmission

molette *nf* serrated wheel; **molette de pressage =** head wheel; **molette de serrage =** pinchwheel

momentané, -ée *adj* temporary; **erreur momentanée =** transient error

monadique *adj* monadic; **opérateur monadique =** monadic (Boolean) operator; **l'opérateur monadique NOT peut être utilisé ici =** the monadic operator NOT can be used here; **opération monadique =** monadic operation *ou* unary operation

monaural, -e *adj* monoaural

moniteur *nm* **(a)** *(écran de visualisation)* monitor (unit); **moniteur couleur =** colour monitor; **le moniteur couleur est excellent pour les jeux électroniques =** the colour monitor is great for games; **moniteur intégré =** firmware monitor; **moniteur multistandard =** multi-scan *ou* multi-sync monitor; **moniteur (de) télévision =** television monitor; **moniteur vidéo =** video monitor **(b)** *(programme)* **programme moniteur =** monitor program **(c)** *(de contrôle d'image de télévision)* monitor **(d)** *(haut-parleur)* **moniteur (retour de son) =** monitor

◊ **moniteur/téléviseur** *nm* television receiver/monitor

monnaie *nf* money; **monnaie électronique =** electronic money

mono- *préfixe* mono-

◊ **monocarte** *n&adj* **ordinateur monocarte =** single board computer (sbc)

◊ **monochrome** *adj (moniteur ou écran)* black and white *ou* monochrome; **conversion monochrome (d'une image couleur) =** black crush; **écran monochrome =** monochrome monitor *ou* black and white screen; **lumière monochrome =** coherent light

◊ **monoflux** *n&adj* **architecture multiflux d'instruction-monoflux de**

données = multiple instruction stream - single data stream (MISD)

◊ **monofréquence** *n&adj* **signalisation monofréquence =** single frequency signalling *ou* sf signalling

◊ **monolithique** *adj (circuit intégré)* monolithic

◊ **monomode** *nm&adj* **fibre optique monomode =** monomode fibre

◊ **monopasse** *n&adj* **opération monopasse =** single pass operation

◊ **monophonique** *adj* monophonic

◊ **monoprogrammation** *nf* **système de monoprogrammation =** monoprogramming system

◊ **monopuce** *n&adj* **ordinateur monopuce =** single chip computer

◊ **monostable** *adj (circuit)* monostable

◊ **mono-utilisateur** *n&adj* **système mono-utilisateur =** single-user system

◊ **monotâche** *n&adj* single-tasking

montage *nm* **(a)** *(d'une machine ou d'un appareil)* assembly; **il n'y a pas de notice de montage pour aider à la mise en place de l'ordinateur =** there are no assembly instructions to show you how to put the computer together; **usine de montage =** assembly plant **(b)** *(d'une feuille isolée ou d'une illustration)* **montage sur onglet =** guarding **(c)** *(des parties d'un texte)* editing; *(à partir de paragraphes standard)* **montage d'un document =** boilerplating **(d)** *(d'un film)* film editing; **montage associatif =** associational editing; **montage électronique =** electronic editing; **salle de montage =** cutting room **(e)** *(imprimerie)* film assembly

Monte Carlo *npr* **méthode de Monte Carlo =** Monte Carlo method

monté, -ée *adj* **(a)** mounted; **cartes montées sur supports** *ou* **en rack =** rack mounted cards **(b)** **monté en série =** ganged; **commutateurs montés en série =** ganged switch; **avec des commutateurs montés en série, il est possible de choisir le bus de données qui va activer l'imprimante =** a ganged switch is used to select which data bus a printer will respond to **(c)** **document monté à partir de paragraphes standard =** boilerplate

◊ **montée** *nf* **temps de montée =** rise time; **le temps de montée du circuit est très rapide =** the circuit has a fast rise time; **il faut inclure le temps de montée dans le temps d'accès =** allow for acceleration time in the access time

◊ **monter** *vtr* **(a)** to mount; **les puces sont montées dans des supports implantés sur la carte de circuit imprimé =** the chips are mounted in sockets on the PCB; **monter en surface =** to piggyback **(b) le nouveau modèle a fait monter les chiffres de vente =** the new model gave a boost to the sales figures

◊ **se monter à** *vpr* to amount to

montrer *vtr* to indicate *ou* to point out

morse *nm* **morse** *ou* **alphabet morse =** Morse code; **télégraphe** *ou* **manipulateur morse =** Morse key

mort, -e *adj* **(a) mémoire morte =** read only memory (ROM); **mémoire morte masquée =** masked ROM; **mémoire morte programmable** *ou* **PROM =** programmable memory (PROM); **mémoire morte programmable effaçable par ultraviolet =** ultraviolet erasable PROM; **programmeur de mémoires mortes =** burner **(b) temps mort =** *(dû au mauvais fonctionnement)* dead time *ou* down time; *(lorsque la machine n'est pas utilisée)* idle time *ou* lost time

MOS = METAL OXIDE SEMICONDUCTOR; **mémoire MOS =** MOS memory; **semi-conducteur MOS =** MOS; **semi-conducteur MOS à canal (de type) P =** p-channel MOS

mosaïque *nf* mosaic

MOSFET = METAL OXIDE SEMICONDUCTOR FIELD EFFECT TRANSISTOR; **semi-conducteur à effet de champ MOSFET =** MOSFET

mot *nm* **(a)** *(d'un texte)* word; **mot du jour** *ou* **mot à la mode =** buzzword; **(nombre de) mots par minute =** words per minute (wpm *ou* WPM); **mot de passe =** access code *ou* authorization code *ou* password; **entrée sur un système avec un mot de passe piraté =** piggyback entry; **il faut vous rappeler votre mot de passe sinon vous ne pourrez pas avoir accès au système =** if you forget your user ID, you will not be able to logon; **l'utilisateur doit d'abord taper le mot de passe pour**

avoir accès à la base de données = the user has to key in the password before he can access the database; **mot principal =** keyword; **mots (mis) en évidence** *ou* **en surbrillance =** highlights; **nombre de mots contenus dans un fichier** *ou* **un texte =** word count **(b)** *(informatique)* word *ou* computer word *ou* data word; **mot adresse =** address word; **mot de commande =** keyword; **mot de contrôle =** control word; **mot double** *ou* **mot long =** double word; **mot d'état** *ou* **mot indicateur d'état =** processor status word (PSW) *ou* device status word (DSW); **mot d'état d'entrée/sortie =** input/output status word; **registre des mots d'état =** program status word register (PSW register); **mot d'identification =** identifier word; **mot d'index =** index value word; **mot instruction =** instruction word; **mot de longueur fixe** *ou* **déterminée =** fixed-length word; **(ordinateur) à longueur de mots fixe =** fixed word length; **mot machine =** machine word; **mot réservé =** reserved word; **processeur à mots variables =** byte machine *ou* character machine; **espacement entre les mots =** interword spacing; **indicateur de mot =** word marker; **longueur d'un mot =** data word length *ou* word length; **marque de début de mot =** word marker; **série de mots (l'un à la suite de l'autre) =** word serial; **temps de transfert d'un mot =** word time

◊ **mot-clé** *nm* key *ou* keyword *ou* descriptor; **le mot 'ordinateur' est un mot-clé en informatique =** 'computer' is a keyword in IT; **recherche par mots-clés =** disjunctive search

◊ **mot-paramètre** *nm* parameter word

en contrepartie, l'égarement de ce mot de passe interdit tout accès à la structure, ce qui signifie à plus ou moins long terme la 'mort' de la base

L'Ordinateur Individuel

développé en LISP et récrit en COBOL, ce programme fonctionne par repérage des mots-clés

L'Ordinateur Individuel

moteur *nm* motor; **un moteur électrique** *ou* **un moteur qui marche** *ou* **qui fonctionne à l'électricité =** an electrically-powered motor; **moteur d'inférence =** inference engine *ou* machine

motif *nm* pattern; **avec motifs =** patterned

mouture *nf* le programme en est à sa deuxième mouture = the program is in its second rewrite; **première mouture** = draft

mouvement *nm* **(a)** *(déplacement)* movement; *(de transmissions)* traffic; **ce dispositif contrôle le mouvement des feuilles** = the device controls the copy flow; *(sur une ligne)* **mouvements** = traffic **(b)** *(modifications)* movement *ou* transaction; **bande (de) mouvements** = change tape; **décomposition de mouvement** = memomotion; **enregistrement de mouvements** = amendment record *ou* change record *ou* transaction record; **fichier (de) mouvements** = change file *ou* detail file *ou* movement file *ou* update file; **traitement de mouvements** = transaction processing (TP); **vidage de mouvements (sur imprimante)** = change dump

moyen *nm* **(a)** mean **(b)** medium; **moyens de transmission** = transmission media; **moyens de communication interactifs** = interactive media

moyen, -enne *adj* average *ou* mean *ou* medium; **temps d'accès moyen** = average access time; **délai moyen** = average delay; **durée moyenne de bon fonctionnement** = mean time to failure (MTF); **intégration à moyenne échelle** = medium scale integration (MSI); **objectif de focale moyenne** = medium lens; **un système informatique de taille moyenne** = a medium-sized computer system; **après 9h30, le temps d'attente moyen est beaucoup plus long lorsque chacun tente de se loger sur le système pour travailler** = the average delay increases at nine-thirty when everyone tries to log-in; **vitesse moyenne** = medium speed

moyenne *nf* average *ou* mean; **moyenne pondérée** = weighted average; **atteindre une moyenne (de)** *ou* **faire en moyenne** = to average (out); **cela fait en moyenne 120 points par pouce** *ou* **une moyenne de 120 points par pouce** = it averages out at 120 dpi; **moyenne de temps de bon fonctionnement entre les défaillances (MTBF)** = mean time between failures (MTBF); **moyenne de temps requis pour réparation** = mean time to repair

moyeu *nm* hub

MRT = MULTIPLEXAGE PAR REPARTITION DANS LE TEMPS

ms = MILLISECONDE

MS-DOS® = MICROSOFT DISK OPERATING SYSTEM; **(système d'exploitation) MS-DOS** = MS-DOS® *ou* Microsoft DOS®; *voir aussi* DOS

MSX *(pour ordinateurs individuels)* **norme** *ou* **standard MSX** = MSX

MTBF = MEAN TIME BETWEEN FAILURES *voir* MOYENNE

multi- *préfixe* multi-
◇ **multi-accès** *n&adj* **système multi-accès** = multi-access system
◇ **multi-adresse** *n&adj* **code multi-adresse** = multiple address code; **instruction multi-adresse** = multi-address instruction
◇ **multibus** *n&adj* **système multibus** = multi-bus system
◇ **multicarte** *n&adj* **ordinateur multicarte** = multi-board computer
◇ **multicible** *n&adj* **transmission multicible** = multicasting
◇ **multicolore** *adj* multicolour
◇ **multicouche** *n&adj* multilayer
◇ **multidimensionnel, -elle** *adj* multidimensional; **langage multidimensionnel** = multidimensional language; **tableau multidimensionnel** = multidimensional array
◇ **multidisque** *n&adj* multi-disk; **lecteur multidisque** = multi-disk reader; **option multidisque** = multi-disk option
◇ **multifenêtrage** *nm* multi-windowing
◇ **multifenêtre** *n&adj* **logiciel (de traitement de texte) multifenêtre** = multi-window editor
◇ **multiflux** *n&adj* **architecture multiflux d'instruction-monoflux de données** = multiple instruction stream - single data stream (MISD); **architecture multiflux d'instruction-multiflux de données** = multiple instruction stream - multiple data stream (MIMD)
◇ **multifonction** *n&adj* multifunctional *ou* multifunction; **carte d'extension multifonction** = multifunction card; **un module d'interface analogique multifonction comprend un convertisseur analogique-numérique et un**

convertisseur numérique-analogique = a multifunction analog interface module includes analog to digital and digital to analog converters; **poste de travail multifonction** = multifunction workstation; **programme multifonction** = general purpose program; **scanner multifonction** = a multifunctional scanner

◊ **multifrappe** *n&adj* **ruban multifrappe** = multi-strike printer ribbon

◊ **multifréquence** *n&adj* multifrequency; **signalisation multifréquence DTMF** = dual tone, multifrequency (DTMF)

◊ **multi-instruction** *n&adj* **ligne multi-instruction** = multi-statement line

◊ **multiligne** *n&adj (système de transmission)* multi-line; **système multiligne** = multilink system

◊ **multimédia** *nm&adj* multimedia; **message multimédia** = multimedia mail

◊ **multimètre** *nm* multimeter; **multimètre analogique** = analog multimeter (AMM); **multimètre numérique** = digital multimeter (DMM)

◊ **multimode** *n&adj* multimode; **fibre optique multimode** = multimode fibre

les noeuds sont réunis 2 à 2 par deux fibres optiques multimodes. La distance maximale entre noeuds est de 2000m
Opto électronique

multiniveau *n&adj* multilevel; **langage multiniveau** = multidimensional language

◊ **multinorme** *n&adj* multistandard; **unité multinorme** = a multistandard unit

◊ **multipage** *n&adj* **système multipage** = multiple base page

◊ **multipaquet** *n&adj* **signal multipaquet** = multiburst signal

◊ **multiphase** *n&adj* **programme multiphase** = multiphase program

multiple *adj* multiple; **(à) accès multiple** = multiple access; **système à accès multiple** = multi-access system; **accès multiple asservi à la demande** = demand assigned multiple access (DAMA); **accès multiple par division dans le temps** = time division multiple access; **architecture à bus multiples** = multiple bus architecture; **système à bus multiples** = multi-bus system; **(en) multiple précision** = multiprecision *ou* multiple precision; **(à) couches multiples**

= multilayer; **élément logique multiple** = compound logical element; **programme à usage multiple** = general purpose program

multiplet *nm* n-bit byte

multiplex *nm* multiplex; **système multiplex** = carrier system

◊ **multiplexage** *nm* multiplexing *ou* dataplex; **multiplexage asservi à la demande** = demand multiplexing; **multiplexage dynamique** = dynamic multiplexing; **multiplexage hétérogène** = heterogeneous multiplexing; **multiplexage homogène** = homogeneous multiplexing; **multiplexage optique** = optical multiplexing; **multiplexage par répartition en fréquence** = frequency division multiplexing (FDM); **multiplexage par répartition dans le temps (MRT)** *ou* **multiplexage temporel** = time division multiplexing (TDM); **multiplexage temporel statistique** *ou* **en fonction des appels** = statistical time division multiplexing (STDM)

◊ **multiplexé, -ée** *adj* multiplexed; **accès temporel multiplexé** = time division multiple access; **bus multiplexé** = multiplexed bus

◊ **multiplexeur** *nm* multiplexor (MUX); **un multiplexeur 4/1 reçoit sur 4 canaux et émet sur un seul** = a 4 to 1 multiplexor combines four inputs into a single output; **multiplexeur C-MAC** = C-MAC

il est à remqrquer que le multiplexage de 12 canaux vidéo sur une seule fibre est une première avec la qualité de transmission obtenue
Opto électronique

multiplicande *nm* multiplicand

◊ **multiplicateur** *nm* multiplier

◊ **multiplication** *nf* multiplication; **le résultat de la multiplication de 5 par 3 est 15** = the multiplication of 5 and 3 equals 15; **signe de la multiplication (x)** = multiplication sign

◊ **multiplié, -ée** *adj* **multiplié par dix** = by a factor of ten

◊ **multiplier** *vtr* to multiply; **les erreurs n'ont cessé de se multiplier lorsque j'ai appuyé sur la mauvaise touche** = there was an avalanche of errors after I pressed the wrong key

multipoint *n&adj* multipoint; **circuit multipoint** = multidrop circuit

◇ **multiposte** *nm&adj* **système multiposte** = multi-terminal system *ou* multi-user system; **on peut exécuter le programme sur un ordinateur indépendant ou un système multiposte** = the program runs on a standalone machine or a multi-user system

> l'utilisation des bases de données en multiposte s'est par ailleurs considérablement améliorée grâce au regroupement des fichiers sur le disque: un fichier contenant les données et un second contenant la structure du programme
> *L'Ordinateur Individuel*

multiprocesseur *nm&adj* multiprocessor; **entrelacement (de traitement) par multiprocesseur** = multiprocessor interleaving; **système multiprocesseur** = multiprocessing system

◇ **multiprogrammation** *nf* multi-programming *ou* concurrent programming *ou* multiprocessor interleaving

◇ **multiprogramme** *nm&adj* **système d'exploitation multiprogramme** = concurrent operating system

◇ **multistandard** *n&adj inv* **écran** *ou* **moniteur multistandard** = multi-scan *ou* multi-sync monitor; **unité multistandard** = a multistandard unit

◇ **multitâche** *n&adj* multitasking *ou* multi-tasking; **multitâche en temps réel** =

real-time multitasking; **c'est un système multi-utilisateur et multitâche** = the system is multi-user and multi-tasking; **traitement multitâche en temps réel** = real-time multi-tasking

> les participants auront cinq jours pour apprendre à utiliser un ordinateur dans un environnement multitâche et multi-utilisateur
> *Informatique & Bureautique*

multitraitement *nm* concurrent processing; **trois transordinateurs procurent une capacité de multitraitement suffisante pour tout le département** = three transputers provide concurrent processing capabilities for the entire department

multi-utilisateur *n&adj* **mode multi-utilisateur** = free running mode; **système multi-utilisateur** = multi-user system *ou* shared resources system; **c'est un système multi-utilisateur et multitâche** = the system is multi-user and multi-tasking

◇ **multivibrateur** *nm* multivibrator; **multivibrateur astable** = astable multivibrator; **multivibrateur bistable** = bistable circuit *ou* multivibrator

◇ **multivoie** *nm&adj (protocole d'accès au réseau)* multichannel

myriamétrique *adj* **onde myriamétrique** = very low frequency (VLF) *ou* extremely low frequency (ELF)

Nn

N code N dont M = M out of N code

N matériau semi-conducteur de type N = n-type material *ou* N-type material *ou* n-type semiconductor; **semi-conducteur MOS à canal (de type) N =** n-channel metal oxide semiconductor

n instruction à n adresse(s) plus une = n-plus-one address instruction; **logique à n niveau(x) =** n-level logic; **clavier à mémoire sur n touche(s) =** N-key rollover

n = NANO-

NACK *ou* **NAK** = NEGATIVE ACKNOWLEDGE *ou* NEGATIVE ACKNOWLEDGEMENT *voir aussi* ACCUSE

NAND = NOT-AND; **circuit NAND =** NAND gate; **fonction NAND =** NAND function *ou* NOT-AND; **porte NAND =** NAND gate; *voir aussi* NON-ET

nano- (n) *préfixe* nano- (n)
◊ **nanomètre** *nm* nanometre (nm)
◊ **nanoseconde (ns)** *nf* nanosecond (ns); **circuit (électronique** *ou* **logique) à délai de réponse de l'ordre de la nanoseconde =** nanocircuit *ou* nanosecond circuit

le temps de base d'un cycle est passé de 18,5 nanosecondes à 17,2 et la mémoire d'arrière plan passe de 256Mo à 1Go
L'Information professionnelle

natif, -ive *adj* native

national, -e *adj* national; **la presse nationale =** the national press; **la publicité pour la nouvelle voiture a été faite dans la presse nationale =** the new car has been advertised in the national press

naturel, -elle *adj* natural; **décimal codé binaire naturel =** natural binary coded decimal (NBCD); **langage naturel =** natural language; **le système expert peut être programmé en langage naturel =** the expert system can be programmed in a natural language

NEA = NUMEROTATION EUROPEENNE DES ARTICLES

nécessaire *adj* necessary; **la quantité de mémoire nécessaire varie suivant le logiciel utilisé =** memory requirements depend on the application software in use

négatif *nm (film)* negative; **négatif contact =** contact negative; **négatifs (de séparation des) couleurs =** colour separations

négatif, -ive *adj* negative; **accusé de réception négatif (NACK) =** negative acknowledge (NAK *ou* NACK); **affecter (un nombre) d'un signe négatif =** to negate (a number); **dépassement** *ou* **débordement négatif =** underflow; **nombre négatif =** negative number; **rétroaction négative =** negative feedback; **la valeur négative de 23,4 est -23,4 =** if you negate 23.4 the result is -23.4
◊ **négation** *nf (fonction logique)* negation *ou* denial; **négation connexe =** joint denial
◊ **négativement** *adv* **qualifier négativement =** to negate

neige *nf (distorsion de l'image de télévision)* snow

net, nette *adj* **(a)** *(déductions faites)* **poids net =** net weight **(b)** *(clair)* **un papier de qualité supérieure donnera des caractères plus nets =** top quality paper will eliminate fuzzy characters

◊ **netteté** *nf* **en tournant le bouton de mise au point l'image perd de sa netteté =** the image becomes blurred when you turn the focus knob

nettoyage *nm* **(a)** cleaning; **disquette de nettoyage (des têtes) =** head cleaning disk; **il faut passer la disquette de nettoyage une fois par semaine =** use a head cleaning disk every week; **vous aurez des erreurs d'écriture si vous ne vous servez pas régulièrement de votre disquette de nettoyage =** write errors will occur if you do not use a head cleaning kit regularly; **kit de nettoyage pour écran =** screen cleaning kit **(b)** *(faire disparaître les erreurs)* cleaning *ou* cleanup; **nettoyage de données =** data cleaning; **nettoyage de fichier =** file cleanup; **nettoyage de mémoire =** garbage collection

◊ **nettoyer** *vtr* **(a)** to clean **(b)** *(faire disparaître le texte)* **nettoyer l'écran =** to zap; **nettoyer un dispositif programmable =** to zero a device

neuf *nm&adj num* nine; **complément à neuf =** nine's complement

neutre *adj* neutral; *(séparant deux fichiers)* **espace neutre =** file gap; **transmission neutre =** neutral transmission

NI *(logique)* NOR; **fonction NI =** neither-nor function *ou* NOR function; **opération NI =** joint denial; **porte** *ou* **circuit NI =** NOR gate; **NI exclusif =** exclusive NOR (EXNOR); **porte** *ou* **circuit NI exclusif =** exclusive NOR gate *ou* EXNOR gate

niveau *nm* **(a)** *(hauteur)* level; **vérifier le niveau =** to gauge (the level of something); **au même niveau** *ou* **de niveau =** flush; **la couverture est rognée de niveau avec les pages =** the covers are trimmed flush with the pages **(b) niveau de production =** production level; **niveau maximum de production =** peak output; **atteindre un niveau maximum =** to peak; **la tension a atteint le niveau maximum de 1200 volts =** the power peaked at 1,200 volts; **niveau de qualité d'un service téléphonique =** grade of service **(c) niveau d'adressage =** addressing level; **niveau de bruit d'un circuit =** circuit

noise level; **niveau cible =** target level; **niveau de complexité =** complexity measure; **niveau de confiance =** confidence level; **niveau de données =** data level; **niveau d'imbrication (de boucles) =** nesting level; **niveau d'interruption =** interrupt level; **niveau logique =** logic level; **niveaux de luminosité =** brightness range; **niveau de pression acoustique =** sound pressure level (SPL); **niveau de référence =** reference level; **niveau d'un signal =** signal level; **perte de niveau (d'un signal) =** drop out; **niveau de transmission (d'une ligne) =** line level; **adresse à un niveau =** one-level address; **adresse de premier niveau =** first-level address; **code à un niveau =** direct code *ou* one-level code *ou* specific code; **mémoire à un niveau =** one-level store; **à plusieurs niveaux** *ou* **multiniveau =** multilevel; **langage de bas niveau =** low-level language (LLL); **langage de haut niveau =** high-level language (HLL); **langage de programmation de haut niveau =** high-level (programming) language (HLL) *ou* high-order language; **on demande aux programmeurs une connaissance des langages de haut niveau, plus spécialement PASCAL =** programmers should have a knowledge of high-level languages, particularly PASCAL; **sous-programme à deux niveaux =** two-level subroutine **(d)** *(saturation)* **niveau de blanc =** white level; **niveaux de gris =** (i) grey scale; *US* gray scale; (ii) shades of grey; *US* shades of gray; **niveau de noir =** black level

tout signal de niveau compris entre +3 et +25 volts est considéré comme étant au niveau logique

Action PC

nocturne *adj* nocturnal; **caméra de vision nocturne =** infrared sights

noeud *nm* **(a)** branchpoint; **une arborescence est formée de branches reliées les unes aux autres par des points de liaison ou noeuds =** a tree is made of branches that connect together at nodes **(b)** node; **ce réseau est relié par fibres optiques avec des noeuds pouvant être espacés d'un kilomètre les uns des autres =** this network has fibre optic connection with nodes up to one kilometre apart

noir *nm* black; **noir et blanc** = black and white *ou* monochrome; **écran noir et blanc** = monochrome monitor; **photo en noir et blanc** = black and white photograph; **affichage noir sur blanc** = positive display; **imprimante à définition des noirs** = black writer; **niveau de noir** = black level

◊ **noir, -e** *adj* black; **boîte noire** = black box; **chambre noire** = darkroom; **courant noir** = dark current; **tableau noir** = blackboard; **tableau noir électronique** = electronic blackboard

nom *nm* (a) name; **nom de chaîne** = string name; **nom de donnée** = data name; **il y aura des difficultés si le nom de donnée est ambigu** = problems occur if an ambiguous data name is chosen; **nom d'un fichier** = file name *ou* filename; **l'extension SYS ajoutée au nom du fichier indique qu'il s'agit d'un fichier système** = the filename extension SYS indicates that this is a system file; **changer le nom (d'un fichier)** = to rename (a file); **extension du nom d'un fichier** = filename extension; **longueur du nom d'un fichier** = length of filename; **nom d'un programme** = program name; **nom de variable** = variable name (b) title; **nom sur une disquette** = title of disk (c) *(de l'éditeur ou de l'imprimeur)* imprint

NMOS = N-CHANNEL METAL OXIDE SEMICONDUCTOR; **semi-conducteur NMOS** = NMOS; *voir aussi* N

nombre *nm* (a) *(math)* number; **il faut un processeur très puissant pour les applications graphiques qui exigent une forte capacité de traitement des nombres en masse** = a very powerful processor is needed for graphics applications which require extensive number crunching capabilities; **nombre aléatoire** *ou* **choisi au hasard** = random number; **nombre en base octale** = octal digit; **nombre binaire** = binary number *ou* bit; **résolution d'un nombre binaire** = digital resolution; **(ensemble des) nombres complets** = complementation; **nombre entier** = integer; **nombre entier en double précision** = double-precision integer; **BASIC pour nombres entiers** = integer BASIC; **nombre négatif** = negative number; **nombres à précision finie** = finite-precision numbers; **nombre**

premier = prime; **sept est un nombre premier** = the number seven is a prime; **nombre rationnel** = rational number; **nombre réel** = real number (b) quantity *ou* number; **nombre de cycles** = cycle count; **nombre de frappes** = keystroke count; **nombre de mots (contenus dans un fichier** *ou* **un texte)** = word count; **nombre maximum d'utilisateurs** = maximum (number of) users; **nombre total de pages (d'un document)** = extent (of a document); **un petit nombre de disquettes piratées de ce programme se sont infiltrées à l'importation** = a small quantity of illegal copies of the program have been imported; **la société fait une remise sur les achats en nombre** = the company offers a discount for quantity purchases

nomenclature *nf* nomenclature *ou* list; **nomenclature des composants** = component list

nominal, -e *adj* **débit nominal** = rated throughput

nomographe *nm* nomogram *ou* nomograph

NON *(logique)* NOT; **fonction NON** = NOT function *ou* negation; **porte** *ou* **circuit NON** = NOT gate; *voir aussi* NON-ET, NON-OU

non- *préfixe* non- *ou* un-
◊ **non-aligné, -ée** *adj* nonaligned
◊ **non-connecté, -ée** *adj* (i) unconnected; (ii) off-line
◊ **non-équivalence** *nf* symmetric difference

NON-ET *(logique)* NAND; **circuit NON-ET** = NAND gate; **fonction NON-ET** *ou* **opération NON-ET** = NAND function *ou* NOT-AND *ou* alternative denial *ou* dispersion; **porte** *ou* **circuit NON-ET** = NAND gate

non-linéaire *adj* nonlinear

NON-OU *(logique)* **fonction NON-OU** = neither-nor function *ou* NOR function; **opération NON-OU** = joint denial; **porte** *ou* **circuit NON-OU** = NOR gate; *voir aussi* NI

non-remise *nf* **non-remise à zéro =** non return to zero (NRZ)

◊ **non-retour** *nm* **non-retour à zéro =** non return to zero (NRZ)

◊ **non-volatile** *adj* non-volatile; **mémoire non-volatile =** non-volatile memory *ou* non-volatile store *ou* storage; **la mémoire à bulles est une mémoire non-volatile =** bubble memory is a non-volatile storage; **une bande magnétique constitue une mémoire non-volatile =** magnetic tape provides non-volatile memory

normal, -e *adj* **(a)** normal *ou* standard; **format normal =** normal format; **fourchette** *ou* **gamme** *ou* **plage normale =** normal range; **la procédure normale préconise une sauvegarde de tout le travail en fin de journée =** the normal procedure is for backup copies to be made at the end of each day's work **(b)** **en notation normale on écrit: (x-y) + z, en notation suffixée on écrit: xy- z+ =** normal notation: (x-y) + z, but using postfix notation: xy - z + **(c)** **il n'est pas normal que deux lecteurs de disquettes tombent en panne l'un après l'autre =** it's abnormal for two consecutive disk drives to break down

◊ **normalisation** *nf* **(a)** *(de données)* normalization; **routine de normalisation =** normalization routine **(b)** standardization; **Comité National de Normalisation de la Télévision =** National Television Standards Committee (NTSC); **organisme international de normalisation ISO =** International Standards Organization (ISO)

> bénéficiant d'un numéro et d'un protocole de normalisation de l'ISO (International Standards Organization), il est déjà utilisé par les organisations internationales, certaines administrations et quelques grandes entreprises
> *Informatique & Bureautique (Suisse)*

normalisé, -ée *adj* **(a)** *(d'un nombre en virgule flottante)* **forme normalisée =** normalized form **(b)** standardized; **le contrôle normalisé des voies de transmission =** the standardized control of transmission links; **les protocoles (de transmissions) normalisés =** protocol standards

◊ **normaliser** *vtr* to normalize *ou* to standardize; **toutes les nouvelles données sont normalisées à dix positions décimales =** all the new data has been normalized to 10 decimal places

norme *nf* standard; **travailler suivant des normes établies =** to work to standard specifications; **(qui est) conforme aux normes =** up to standard; **norme CEPT =** CEPT standard; **norme de cryptage de données =** data encryption standard (DES); **interface aux normes EIA =** EIA interface *ou* electronic industry association interface (EIA); **normes pour modems =** modem standards; **normes NTSC =** NTSC standards; **normes de programmation =** programming standards; **normes de qualité =** production standards; **ce lot de disquettes ne répond pas aux normes =** this batch of disks is not up to standard; **normes vidéo =** video standards; **convertisseur de normes =** standards converter

notation *nf* notation; **notation binaire** *ou* **en base binaire =** binary notation; **notation décimale =** decimal notation; **notation hexadécimale =** hex *ou* hexadecimal notation; **notation infixée =** infix notation; **notation octale =** octal notation; **notation polonaise inversée =** reverse Polish notation (RPN); **alors que la notation conventionnelle s'écrit: (x-y) + z, la notation polonaise inversée s'écrit: xy - z+ =** normal notation: (x-y) + z, but using RPN: xy - z+; **notation préfixée =** prefix notation; *(notation polonaise inversée)* **notation suffixée =** postfix notation *ou* suffix notation; **notation à virgule fixe =** fixed-point notation

note *nf* comment *ou* note; **note en bas de page =** footnote; **notes marginales =** cut-in notes

notice *nf* **(a)** **notice bibliographique =** bibliographical information **(b)** *(d'utilisation)* direction for use; **notice d'utilisation =** operational information; **l'excellente notice d'utilisation facilitait l'emploi du progiciel =** using the package was easy with the excellent user documentation

notifié, -ée *adj* **erreur notifiée =** detected error

nouveau, nouvelle 1 *adj* new; **ils ont installé un nouveau système informatique** *ou* **un nouvel ordinateur =** they have installed a new computer system; *(commande de lancement)* **nouvelle tâche =** new; **nouvelle technologie** *ou* **techniques nouvelles =** new technology; **nouvelle version d'un fichier =** file update

◇ **nouvelle** *nf* piece of news; **nouvelles =** news

noyau *nm (du système d'exploitation)* kernel; **noyau de ferrite =** ferrite core

npn *ou* **NPN** transistor (de type) npn = npn transistor; **transistor à jonction npn =** bipolar (junction) transistor (BJT)

> le constructeur prétend avoir réalisé un circuit ECL avec des transistors bipolaires de type PNP dont le temps de communication est de 35 picosecondes, soit six fois mieux que le record précédent (qui remonte à 1986) et aussi bien que si on utilisait des transistors de type NPN
>
> *01 Informatique*

ns = NANOSECONDE

NTSC = NATIONAL TELEVISION STANDARDS COMMITTEE; **normes NTSC =** NTSC standards; *voir aussi* NORMALISATION

nu, nue *adj* **machine nue** *ou* **processeur nu =** clean machine

nuance *nf* shade *ou* nuance *ou* tone; **le progiciel graphique offre plusieurs nuances de bleu =** the graphics package can give several tones of blue

nuire (à) *vi* to interfere with something

nul, nulle *adj* null; **caractère nul =** null character *ou* idle character; **jeu** *ou* **ensemble de caractères nuls =** empty *ou* null set; **instruction nulle =** blank *ou* dummy *ou* null instruction *ou* non-operable instruction *ou* no-op instruction

numéral, -ale *adj* numeric; **lettre numérale =** numeric character

◇ **numération** *nf* number representation; **numération à base =** radix numeration

numérique *adj* **(a)** *(se rapportant à un nombre)* numeric *ou* numerical; **analyse numérique =** numerical analysis; **caractère (à valeur) numérique =** numeric character; **clavier numérique =** numeric keypad *ou* numeric pad *ou* numerical pad; **code numérique d'une touche =** key number; **commande** *ou* **contrôle numérique =** numerical control (NC) *ou* computer numerical control (CNC); **indicatif numérique =** index number; **opérande numérique =** numeric operand; **opérations numériques (en masse) ultra-rapide =** number crunching; **pavé numérique =** numeric keypad *ou* numeric pad *ou* numerical keypad; **utilisez le pavé numérique pour saisir les chiffres =** you can use the numeric keypad to enter the figures; **perforation numérique =** numeric punch; **tableau numérique =** numeric array **(b)** *(représenté par un nombre)* **affichage numérique =** digital readout; **calculateur** *ou* **ordinateur numérique =** electronic digital computer; **circuit numérique =** digital circuit; **circuiterie numérique commutée =** circuit-switched digital circuitry; **commande numérique directe =** direct digital control (DDC); **(système de) commutation numérique =** digital switching; **données numériques =** digital data; **lecture optique de données numériques =** digital optical reading (DOR); **enregistrement numérique =** digital recording; **horloge numérique =** digital clock; *(qui affiche l'heure sur l'écran)* time display; **logique numérique =** digital logic; **multimètre numérique =** digital multimeter (DMM); **ordinateur numérique =** digital computer; **représentation numérique =** digital representation; **réseau numérique à intégration de services (RNIS) =** integrated services digital network (ISDN); **réseau numérique intégré (RNI) =** integrated digital network; **accès au réseau numérique intégré =** integrated digital access (IDA); **signal numérique =** digital signal; **signature numérique =** digital signature; **sortie numérique =** digital output; **sous forme numérique =** digitally; **l'appareil produit une image à partir de données enregistrées sous forme numérique =** the machine takes digitally recorded data and generates an image;

système numérique = digital system; système de transmission numérique = digital transmission system; **traceur numérique** = digital plotter; **transmission de signaux numériques** = digital signalling

numérique-analogique *adj* **convertisseur numérique-analogique** = digital to analog converter *ou* D to A converter *ou* DAC *ou* d/a converter; **l'ordinateur émet un signal vocal via un convertisseur numérique-analogique** = speech is output from the computer via a D/A converter; **le convertisseur numérique-analogique du port de sortie contrôle l'ordinateur analogique** = the D/A converter on the output port controls the analog machine

◊ **numériquement** *adv* digitally

◊ **numérisation** *nf* digitization; **numérisation d'une onde** = waveform digitization

◊ **numérisé, -ée** *adj* digitized *ou* digital; **données numérisées** = digital data; **photographie numérisée** = digitized photograph; **voix numérisée** = digital speech

◊ **numériser** *vtr* to digitize; **tablette à numériser** = data tablet *ou* digitizing pad *ou* graphics pad *ou* tablet; *(pour saisie de l'écriture manuelle)* writing pad; **il nous est possible de numériser votre signature pour qu'elle puisse être imprimée par n'importe quelle imprimante (à) laser** = we can digitize your signature to allow it to be printed with any laser printer

◊ **numériseur** *nm* digitizer

numéro *nm* (a) number; **numéro de code confidentiel** = personal identification number (PIN); **numéro de code personnel** *ou* **de code d'identification** = identity number; **n'oublie pas d'entrer ton numéro de code personnel** = don't forget to log in your identity number; **chaque pièce d'équipement possède un numéro de fabrication** = each piece of hardware has a production number; **le numéro de fabrication est gravé de façon permanente sur le panneau arrière du boîtier de l'ordinateur** = the production number is permanently engraved on the back of the computer casing; **numéro d'instruction** = statement number; **numéro de référence d'une ligne d'un programme** = program line number; **numéro de lot** = batch number; **numéro de référence** *ou* **d'entrée** = accession number; **numéro de stock** = stock code; **numéro de suite d'une tâche dans la file d'attente** = job number; **numéro de téléphone** = phone number *ou* telephone number; **composer un numéro (de téléphone)** = to dial a number; **le numéro de téléphone figure sur le papier à en-tête de la société** = the phone number is on the company notepaper; **pouvez-vous me donner votre numéro de téléphone?** = can you give me your telephone number? (b) *(d'un journal* ou *d'une revue)* copy; **numéro déjà paru** *ou* **vieux numéro** = back number; **j'ai toujours le numéro du 'Figaro' d'hier** = I kept yesterday's copy of 'Le Figaro'

> il inscrira également le numéro du central vidéotex de son arrondissement, son numéro personnel d'identification et son mot de passe
>
> *Informatique & Bureautique (Suisse)*

numérotation *nf* (a) notation; **numérotation décimale** *ou* **dénaire** = denary notation (b) numbering; **numérotation européenne des articles (NEA)** = European Article Number (EAN); **numérotation des messages** = message numbering; **refaire la numérotation** = to renumber (c) dialling; **système de numérotation automatique** = auto-dial; **numérotation sur clavier** = pushbutton dialling; **numérotation sur clavier tonal** = tone dialling

◊ **numéroter** *vtr* to number; **les pages de ce manuel sont numérotées de 1 à 395** = the pages of the manual are numbered 1 to 395

Oo

obéir *vi* obéir à = to conform to *ou* to obey to

objectif *nm* (a) objective *ou* target (b) *(lentille)* lens; **objectif à focale variable =** zoom lens; **objectif grand-angle =** wide angle lens; **objectif standard** *ou* **de focale moyenne =** medium lens; **ouverture d'objectif =** lens stop; **vitesse d'ouverture d'un objectif =** lens speed

> des chercheurs de l'Université d'Edimbourg viennent de faire tenir une caméra vidéo sur une surface de 8 millimètres carrés, avec des objectifs de la taille d'une tête d'épingle
> *Le Point*

objet *nm* object; **code objet =** object code; **phase (en) code objet =** run phase *ou* target phase; **jeu (de cartes) objet =** object deck; **langage objet =** object language *ou* target language; **pour ce qui est de ce programme en PASCAL, le langage machine constitue le langage objet =** the target language for this PASCAL program is machine code; **programme objet =** object program *ou* target program; **architecture orientée vers l'objet** *ou* **adaptée à l'objet =** object architecture *ou* object-orientated architecture

obligatoire *adj* (a) compulsory *ou* forced; **saut de page obligatoire =** forced page break; **trait d'union obligatoire =** hard hyphen *ou* required hyphen (b) **interruption obligatoire =** non-maskable interrupt (NMI)

oblique *adj* oblique; *(d'un caractère)* character skew; **trait oblique =** slash *ou* oblique stroke; **zéro barré d'un trait oblique =** slashed zero
◊ **obliquité** *nf* skew

obtenir *vtr* to obtain; **le filtrage permet d'obtenir un signal très clair =** a clear signal is obtained after filtering; **ce que**

vous voyez est ce que vous obtenez = What-You-See-Is-What-You-Get (WYSIWYG); **ce que vous voyez est tout ce que vous obtenez =** What-You-See-Is-All-You-Get (WYSIAYG)

obturateur *nm* shutter

OCCAM langage (de programmation) **OCCAM =** OCCAM

occasion *nf* **d'occasion =** used; **(équipement) d'occasion =** second-user *ou* second-hand (equipment)

occupation *nf* **temps d'occupation de la ligne =** holding time
◊ **occupé, -ée** *adj (signal ou tonalité)* busy; **tonalité 'occupé' =** line busy tone *ou* engaged tone; **la ligne est occupée =** the line is busy; **quand le signal 'occupé' s'éteint, l'imprimante peut de nouveau accepter des données =** when the busy line goes low, the printer will accept more data

octal, -e *adj (notation)* octal; **base octale** *ou* **base 8 =** base 8; **nombre en base octale =** octal digit; **notation octale =** octal notation

octave *nf* octave

octet *nm* eight-bit byte *ou* octet; **octet (de caractères) =** character byte; **octet de placement =** postbyte; **adresses d'octets =** byte addresses; **giga-octet (Go) =** gigabyte *ou* Gbyte; **groupe d'octets =** gulp; **manipulation d'octets =** byte manipulation; **mode octet =** byte mode; **transmission d'octets en série =** byte serial transmission *ou* mode

> tout repose sur un bus 64 bits bénéficiant d'un débit de 150 millions d'octets par seconde
> *L'Information professionnelle*

oculaire 1 *nm (d'un appareil photo)* eyepiece **2** *adj* of the eye; **fatigue oculaire** = eye-strain

OEM = ORIGINAL EQUIPMENT MANUFACTURER; **un OEM fournit l'unité de disques, un autre le moniteur** = one OEM supplies the disk drive, another the monitor; *voir aussi* CONSTRUCTEUR, ENSEMBLIER

oeuvre *nf* (a) work; **oeuvre protégée par un copyright** *ou* **dont les droits de reproduction sont réservés** *ou* **oeuvre sous copyright** = work still in copyright (b) **ordre de mise en oeuvre des opérateurs (mathématiques)** = operator precedence

off *adv* **voix off** = voice over

off-line *adj* (a) off-line; **avant de remplacer le papier de l'imprimante, assurez-vous que l'imprimante est off-line** = before changing the paper in the printer, switch it off-line; **traitement off-line** = off-line processing (b) *(système)* autonome; *voir aussi* LIGNE

offset *nm* offset; **impression (en) offset** = offset printing; **lithographie offset** = offset lithography

Ohm *npr* **loi d'Ohm** = Ohm's Law

◊ **ohm** *nm* ohm; **la valeur de cette résistance est de 100 ohms** = this resistance has a value of 100 ohms

oignon *nm* onion; **architecture en pelure d'oignon** = onion skin architecture; **l'architecture en pelure d'oignon de cet ordinateur consiste en un noyau central, une couche système d'exploitation, une couche langage de bas niveau et enfin une couche programmes utilisateur** = the onion skin architecture of this computer is made up of a kernel at the centre, an operating system, a low-level language and then the user's programs; **langage en pelure d'oignon** = onion skin language

OK *adv (prêt - message d'invitation à taper une instruction)* O.K.

ombrage *nm (d'un dessin)* shading

◊ **ombre** *nf* (a) *(d'un dessin)* shading; *(créée par un corps opaque)* shadow; **durée d'ombre** = sun outage

◊ **ombré, -ée** *adj* **tube ombré** = dark trace tube

omettre *vtr* to skip

omission *nf (de correction d'épreuves)* **signe d'omission** = caret mark *ou* sign; *(d'une recherche)* **facteur d'omission** = omission factor

omnidirectionnel, -elle *adj* omnidirectional; **antenne omnidirectionnelle** = omnidirectional aerial; **microphone omnidirectionnel** = omnidirectional microphone

on-line *adj* on-line; **traitement on-line** = on-line processing; *voir aussi* LIGNE

onde *nf* wave *ou* waveform; **onde carrée** = square wave; **onde continue** *ou* **entretenue** = continuous wave; **onde courte** = short wave (SW); **récepteur (d')ondes courtes** = short-wave receiver; **ondes décimétriques** *ou* **ultracourtes** = ultra high frequency (UHF); **onde en dents de scie** = sawtooth waveform; **onde diffusée** = scatter; **onde éclatée progressante** = forward scatter; **onde hectométrique** = medium frequency; **onde kilométrique** = infra-low frequency (ILF); **onde métrique** = very high frequency (VHF); **onde millimétrique** = extremely high frequency (EHF); **onde myriamétrique** = very low frequency (VLF) *ou* extremely low frequency (ELF); **onde porteuse** = carrier wave; **onde porteuse de données** = data carrier; **détecteur d'onde porteuse** = data carrier detect (DCD); **télégraphie par onde porteuse** = carrier telegraphy; **onde (radio) réfléchie** = backscatter; **onde sinusoïdale** = sine wave; **onde sonore** = sound wave; **conversion d'une onde en numérique** = waveform digitization; **forme d'onde** = waveform; **guide d'onde** = waveguide; **guide d'ondes circulaire** = circular waveguide; **longueur d'onde** = wavelength; **numérisation d'une onde** = waveform digitization

onduleur *nm* uninterruptable power supply (UPS); **temps de débit d'un onduleur** = holdup

onglet *nm (d'une feuille isolée ou d'une illustration)* guard; **montage sur onglet =** guarding

opacité *nf* opacity

◊ **opaque** *adj* opaque; **l'écran étant opaque, il est impossible de voir au travers =** the screen is opaque - you cannot see through it; **projecteur de documents opaques =** episcope *ou* epidiascope

opérande *nm* operand *ou* argument; *(d'une opération ET ou d'une conjonction)* conjunct; **par effet de l'instruction ADD 74, l'opérateur ADD va ajouter l'opérande 74 à l'accumulateur =** in the instruction ADD 74, the operator ADD will add the operand 74 to the accumulator; **opérande alphanumérique =** alphanumeric operand; **opérande immédiat =** immediate operand; **opérande littéral =** literal operand; **opérande numérique =** numeric operand; **champ d'opérande =** address *ou* operand field; **instruction à un opérande =** single operand instruction; **opérateur à un opérande =** monadic (Boolean) operator; **opération à un opérande =** unary operation; **opération booléenne à un opérande =** monadic Boolean operation; **opération booléenne à deux opérandes =** dyadic Boolean operation

opérateur, -trice *n* **(a)** *(personne)* operator; **l'opérateur était assis devant l'écran de son ordinateur** *ou* **à son pupitre =** the operator was sitting at his console; **console** *ou* **pupitre de commande** *ou* **poste de travail d'un opérateur =** operator's console; **opérateur d'ordinateur =** computer operator; **opérateur de télex =** telex operator **(b)** *(d'une multiplication)* operator; **x est l'opérateur de la multiplication =** x is the multiplication operator; **opérateur arithmétique =** arithmetic operator; **opérateur booléen =** Boolean operator; **opérateur central =** centre operator; **opérateur logique =** logical operator; **opérateur monadique** *ou* **à un opérande =** monadic (Boolean) operator; **opérateur relationnel** *ou* **logique =** relational operator *ou* logical operator; **ordre de mise en oeuvre des opérateurs (mathématiques) =** operator precedence

◊ **opération** *nf* **(a)** *(math)* operation; **opération arithmétique =** arithmetic

operation; **opération binaire =** binary operation; **opération booléenne =** Boolean operation; **opération booléenne à deux opérandes =** dyadic Boolean operation; **opération booléenne à un opérande =** monadic Boolean operation; **opération (booléenne) dyadique =** dyadic (Boolean) operation; **opération en virgule flottante =** floating point operation (FLOP); **(nombre d') opérations en virgule flottante par seconde =** FLOPs per second **(b)** *(activité)* operation; **opération de branchement =** jump operation; **opération complémentaire =** complementary operation; **opération complète =** complete operation; **opération en cycle fixe** *ou* **opération synchronisée =** fixed cycle operation; **opération en duplex =** duplex operation; **opération d'identité =** identity operation; **opération invalide =** illegal operation; **opération logique =** logic operation; **opération monadique =** monadic operation; **opération non adressable =** no-address operation; **opération surveillée =** attended operation; **champ d'opération =** operation field; **code d'opération =** command code *ou* operating code *ou* op code *ou* order code; **cycle d'opération =** operation cycle; **cycle complet d'exécution d'une opération =** complete operation; **ordre d'enchaînement des opérations =** operator precedence; **ordre de priorité des opérations =** operation priority; **registre d'opération =** operation register; **registre de code d'opération =** op register; **temps d'exécution d'une opération =** operation time **(c)** *(logique)* opération d'équivalence = equivalence function *ou* operation; **opération ET =** AND operation *ou* conjunction; **opération NON-ET =** NAND operation *ou* **opération NON-OU** *ou* **NI =** NOR operation *ou* joint denial; **opérations numériques (en masse) ultra-rapide =** number crunching; **opération OU =** OR operation *ou* disjunction; **opération OU inclusif =** inclusive OR operation *ou* either-or operation

◊ **opérationnel, -elle** *adj* operational; **amplificateur opérationnel =** operational amplifier (op amp); **essai** *ou* **test opérationnel =** operation trial

opposé *nm* inverse; **l'opposé de 1 est 0 =** the inverse of 1 is 0; **l'opposé de 23,4 est -23,4 =** if you negate 23.4 the result is -23.4

opposition *nf* faire opposition (à) = to block; **le directeur du système a fait opposition à sa demande de temps supplémentaire sur l'unité centrale** = the system manager blocked his request for more CPU time

optimal, -e *adj* optimum; **arborescence optimale** = minimal tree; **code optimal** = optimum code

◊ **optimisation** *nf* enhancement *ou* optimization

◊ **optimisé, -ée** *adj* optimized; **code optimisé** = optimized code; **code à temps d'accès optimisé** = minimum access code *ou* minimum delay code *ou* minimum latency coding; **routage optimisé** = minimum weight routing

◊ **optimiser** *vtr* to enhance *ou* to optimize *ou* to upgrade; **ils peuvent optimiser l'imprimante** = they can upgrade the printer; **le nouveau modèle peut être optimisé sans renvoi chez le fournisseur** = the new model has an on-site upgrade facility

◊ **optimiseur** *nm* enhancer; **(programme) optimiseur** = optimizer

optimum *nm&adj* optimum; **code optimum** = optimum code

option *nf* **(a)** option; **les options disponibles sont décrites dans le menu principal** = the options available are described in the main menu; **on trouve habituellement quatre options affichées en haut de l'écran** = there are usually four options along the top of the screen; **option implicite** *ou* **par défaut** *ou* **intrinsèque** *ou* **pré-caractérisée** = default option; **option multidisque** = multi-disk option **(b)** **article en option** = extra; **la souris et le câble sont en option** = the mouse and cabling are sold as extras

◊ **optionnel, -elle** *adj* optional

optique *adj* optical *ou* optic; **câble** *ou* **liaison à fibres optiques** *ou* **câble optique** = fibre optic cable *ou* connection; **les câbles à fibres optiques permettent de placer les noeuds jusqu'à un kilomètre l'un de l'autre** = fibre optic connections enable nodes up to one kilometre apart to be used; **circuit optique intégré** = integrated optical circuit; **condensateur optique** = condenser lens; **disque optique** = laser disk *ou* optical disk; **diviseur**

optique = beam splitter; **fibre optique** = optical fibre; **technologie de la fibre optique** *ou* **de la transmission par fibre optique** = fibre optics; **fibre optique monomode** = monomode fibre; **fibre optique multimode** = multimode fibre; **guide optique** = light guide; **mémoire d'images optiques** = scanner memory; **lecteur optique** = optical scanner; **un lecteur optique utilise un rayon lumineux qui balaye les caractères, les symboles ou les lignes** = an optical reader uses a light beam to scan characters, patterns or lines; **lecteur optique de caractères** = optical character reader (OCR); **lecteur optique de code barres** = bar reader *ou* optical bar code reader *ou* optical wand; **lecteur optique de marques** = optical mark reader (OMR); **lecture optique** = optical reading; **police de caractères reconnaissable par lecture optique** = optical font *ou* OCR font; **lecture optique de données numériques** = digital optical reading (DOR); **liaison optique pour transmission de données** = optical data link; **ligne optique** = line of sight; **mémoire optique** = optical memory *ou* optical storage; **multiplexage optique** = optical multiplexing; **reconnaissance optique de caractères** = optical character recognition (OCR); **reconnaissance optique de marques** *ou* **de signes** *ou* **de symboles** = optical mark recognition (OMR); **stylo optique** = electronic pen *ou* stylus *ou* wand; light pen *ou* optical wand *ou* bar-code reader; **stylo optique graphique** = graphics light pen; **stockage de données sur support optique** = optical storage

optoélectrique *adj* optoelectrical

optoélectronique **1** *nf* **l'optoélectronique** = optoelectronics **2** *adj* optoelectronic; **système de communication optoélectronique** = optical communications system; **transmission par système optoélectronique** = optical transmission

optonumérique *adj* **mémoire optonumérique** = photodigital memory

optronique **1** *nf* **l'optronique** = optoelectronics **2** *adj* optoelectronic; **effet optronique** = electro-optic effect

on n'utilise plus uniquement radar et électronique, mais l'optronique - ce sont des systèmes de détection optique
Opto électronique

or *nm* gold; **contacts or** = gold contacts

OR porte *ou* **circuit OR** = OR gate; *voir aussi* OU

orage *nm* storm; **orage magnétique** = magnetic storm

orbite *nf* orbit; **le satellite se déplace sur une orbite à 100km de la surface de la terre** = the satellite's orbit is 100km from the earth's surface; **orbite circulaire** = circular orbit; **orbite elliptique** = elliptical orbit; **orbite équatoriale** = equatorial orbit; **orbite géostationnaire** = geostationary orbit; **orbite inclinée** = inclined orbit; **orbite polaire** = polar orbit; **décrire une orbite** = to orbit; **ce satellite météorologique décrit une orbite autour de la terre toutes les quatre heures** = this weather satellite orbits the earth every four hours; **mettre en orbite** = to launch into orbit; **mise en orbite** = launching (into orbit); **parcourir une orbite** = to orbit
◇ **orbiter** *vtr* to orbit

ordinateur *nm* computer *ou* computer system *ou* machine; *(utilisé pour le traitement de l'information)* information processor; **ordinateur à adresse unique** = one address computer; **ordinateur asynchrone** = asynchronous computer; **ordinateur de bureau** *ou* **à usage professionnel** = business computer *ou* desk top unit *ou* office computer; **ordinateur central** = *(gros ordinateur)* mainframe (computer); *(ordinateur hôte)* central computer; **ordinateur de contrôle** = control computer; **ordinateur de contrôle de processus** *ou* **ordinateur industriel** = process control computer; **ordinateur de contrôle des transmissions** = communications computer; **ordinateur dédié** = dedicated computer; **ordinateur domestique** = home computer; **ordinateur d'exécution de programme objet** = object computer; **ordinateur géant** *ou* **de grande puissance** = supercomputer; **ordinateur de gestion** *ou* **de bureau** = business computer; **ordinateur hôte** = host computer;

adaptateur de l'ordinateur hôte = host adapter; **ordinateur hybride** = hybrid computer; **ordinateur imbriqué (dans un autre)** = embedded computer *ou* system; **ordinateur incrémentiel** *ou* **à valeurs variables** = incremental computer; **ordinateur individuel** = personal computer (PC) *ou* single-user system; **ordinateurs jumelés** = duplex computer; **ordinateur à logique câblée** = fixed program computer; **ordinateur maître** *ou* **principal** = master computer; **ordinateur monocarte** *ou* **à carte unique** = single board computer (sbc); **ordinateur monopuce** *ou* **à puce unique** = single chip computer; **ordinateur à mots de longueur variable** = variable word length computer; **ordinateur multicarte** = multi-board computer; **ordinateur numérique** = digital computer; **ordinateur parallèle** = parallel computer; **ordinateur personnel** = personal computer *ou* PC; **ordinateur de poche** *ou* **portatif** *ou* **qui tient dans une serviette** = hand-held programmable *ou* hand-held computer; **ordinateur polyvalent** *ou* **non spécialisé** = general purpose computer; **ordinateur principal** = *(gros ordinateur)* mainframe (computer); *(ordinateur hôte)* host computer; **accès à l'ordinateur principal (par l'intermédiaire d'un micro)** = mainframe access; **ordinateur série** = sequential computer; **ordinateur de table** *ou* **de bureau** = desktop computer (system); **(formation) sans accès à l'ordinateur** = hands off (training); **achats sur** *ou* **par ordinateur** = electronic shopping; **(logiciel) adapté à l'ordinateur** = machine-intimate (software); **animation (d'images) sur ordinateur** = computer animation; **archivage sur ordinateur** = electronic filing; **assisté par ordinateur** = computer-aided *ou* computer-assisted; **conception assistée par ordinateur (CAO)** = computer-aided *ou* assisted design (CAD); **enseignement assisté par ordinateur (EAO)** = computer-aided *ou* assisted instruction (CAI); **entraînement assisté par ordinateur (ENAO)** = computer-aided *ou* assisted training (CAT); **fabrication assistée par ordinateur (FAO)** = computer-aided *ou* assisted manufacture (CAM); **formation assistée par ordinateur (FAO)** = computer-aided *ou* assisted learning (CAL); **ingénierie assistée par ordinateur (IAO)** = computer-aided *ou* assisted engineering (CAE); **publication assistée par**

ordinateur (PAO) = desktop publishing (DTP) *ou* electronic publishing; **rencontre matrimoniale assistée par ordinateur** = computer dating; **test assisté par ordinateur (TAO)** = computer-aided *ou* assisted testing (CAT); **traduction assistée par ordinateur** = machine translation; **commandes numériques par ordinateur (pour machine-outil)** = computer numeric control (CNC); **communication entre ordinateurs** = computer conferencing; **conçu** *ou* **généré par ordinateur** = computer-generated; **créé** *ou* **produit à l'aide d'un ordinateur** = computer-generated; **ils ont fait l'analyse de l'image créée par l'ordinateur** = they analyzed the computer-generated image; **défaillance de l'ordinateur** = equipment failure; **défaut de l'ordinateur** = computer defect *ou* defect in the computer; **erreur due à l'ordinateur** = computer error; **exploitable par l'ordinateur** = machine-readable; **fichier d'ordinateur** = computer file; **génération d'ordinateurs** = computer generation; **ordinateurs de première génération** = first generation computers; **ordinateurs de deuxième génération** = second generation computers; **ordinateurs de troisième génération** = third generation computers; **ordinateurs de quatrième génération** = fourth generation computers; **ordinateurs de cinquième génération** = fifth generation computers; **géré par ordinateur** = computer-managed; **enseignement interactif géré par ordinateur** = computer-managed instruction (CMI); **système de réapprovisionnement géré par ordinateur** = teleordering; **gros ordinateur** *ou* **ordinateur central** = mainframe (computer) *ou* large-scale computer; **indexation sur ordinateur** *ou* **préparation d'un index à l'aide d'un ordinateur** = computer indexing; **lecteur optique de microfilms pour entrée de données sur ordinateur** = film optical scanning device for input into computers (FOSDIC); **logiciel qui fonctionne sur la plupart des ordinateurs** = machine-independent software; **logiciel qui ne fonctionne que sur un type d'ordinateur** = machine-dependent software; **logique des ordinateurs** = computer logic; **modèle d'ordinateur avec disque dur** = hard disk model; **opérateur d'ordinateur** = computer operator; **chariot piloté par ordinateur** = buggy; **puissance d'un ordinateur** = computer power; **représentations graphiques sur ordinateur** = computer-generated graphics *ou* computer graphics; **réseau d'ordinateurs** = computer network; **réseau d'ordinateurs hiérarchisé** = hierarchical computer network; **saisie au clavier contrôlée par ordinateur** = processor-controlled keying; **temps d'ordinateur** = computer time; **tous ces rapports de vente coûtent cher en temps d'ordinateur** = running all those sales reports costs a lot in computer time; **terminal d'ordinateur** = data terminal equipment (DTE); **traitement de l'information sans l'aide d'un ordinateur** = manual data processing; **usine de construction d'ordinateurs** = computer factory

ordinogramme *nm* flow diagram *ou* flowchart; **l'ordinogramme est à la base d'un programme bien conçu** = a flowchart is the first step to a well designed program; **ordinogramme à pavés** = block diagram; **ordinogramme de données** = data flowchart; **l'ordinogramme des données nous a permis d'améliorer nos résultats à l'aide d'une meilleure structure** = the data flowchart allowed us to improve throughput, by using a better structure; **ordinogramme logique** = logical flowchart; **ordinogramme d'un système** = system flowchart; **grille** *ou* **modèle pour ordinogramme** = flowchart template; **ligne de jonction des symboles d'un ordinogramme** = flowline; **symboles d'un ordinogramme** = flowchart symbols

ordonnancement *nm* scheduling

ordonnée *nf* Y-coordinate; **axe de l'ordonnée** = Y-axis *ou* vertical axis

ordonner *vtr* to order; **les instructions sont ordonnées suivant le numéro de ligne** = the program instructions are arranged in sequence according to line numbers

ordre *nm* order *ou* sequence; **en** *ou* **par ordre alphabétique** = in alphabetical order; **les noms sont classés par ordre alphabétique** = the sequence of names is arranged alphabetically; **liste triée** *ou* **classée en ordre (alphabétique, etc.)** = ordered list; **ordre d'appel (des teminaux)** = polling list; *(d'un livre)* **ordre des cahiers** = collating sequence; **ordre**

chronologique = chronological order; **(tri, etc.) en ordre croissant** = forward mode; **ordre d'enchaînement des opérations** = operator precedence; **ordre d'interrogation (des terminaux)** = polling list; **ordre lexicographique** = lexicographical order; **ordre de priorité** = priority sequence; **ordre de priorité des opérations** = operation priority

oreiller *nm* pillow; **distorsion en oreiller** = pin cushion distortion

organe *nm* unit; **organe d'entrée/sortie** = input/output unit; **organe de traitement** = processing unit

organigramme *nm* organization chart; **organigramme de programmation** = program flowchart

organisation *nf* organization

◇ **organisationnel, -elle** *adj* organizational

◇ **organiser** *vtr* to organize *ou* to structure *ou* to map out; **vous organisez d'abord le document pour répondre à vos besoins, puis vous remplissez les blancs** = you first structure a document to meet your requirements and then fill in the blanks

organisme *nm* **Organisme international de normalisation ISO** = International Standards Organization (ISO)

orientable *adj (écran)* tilt and swivel (screen)

◇ **orientation** *nf* orientation

◇ **orienté, -ée** *adj* **(a)** orientated; **image orientée en film** = cine-orientated image **(b)** *(biaisé)* biased; **données orientées** = biased data

original *nm* original; *(d'une lettre ou d'un document écrit à la machine)* top copy; **l'original n'est pas assez contrasté pour être photocopié** = the original is too faint to photocopy well; *(d'une disquette)* **original sauvegardé** *ou* **copie d'original** = protection master

◇ **original, -e** *adj (bande ou disque ou film)* original; **bande originale** = master tape *ou* original tape; **disque original** = master disk *ou* original disk; **document**

original = source document; **image originale** = first generation image; *(de cartes perforées)* **jeu original** = source deck *ou* pack; *(bande ou disque)* **support magnétique original** = magnetic master; **le texte original est chez l'éditeur pour correction** = the unedited text is with the publisher for editing

origine *nm* origin *ou* source; **adresse origine** = origin *ou* presumptive address; *(de la première instruction d'un programme)* = program origin; **document d'origine** = source document; **instruction d'origine** = presumptive instruction; **listing (du texte) d'origine** = source listing; **programme d'origine** = source program; *(signal ou donnée)* **retour à l'origine** = homing

orthochromatique *adj* orthochromatic; **film orthochromatique** = orthochromatic film *ou* ortho film

orthogonal, -e *adj* orthogonal

orthographe *nm* spelling; **vérificateur d'orthographe** = spellchecker *ou* spelling checker; **on va optimiser le programme en ajoutant un traitement de texte et un vérificateur d'orthographe** = the program will be upgraded with a word-processor and a spelling checker; **vérifiez d'abord l'orthographe, vous pourrez ensuite imprimer votre texte** = after spellchecking the text, you can proceed to the printing stage

◇ **orthographique** *adj* **faire une vérification orthographique** = to spellcheck; **programme de vérification orthographique** = spellchecker *ou* spelling checker

oscillateur *nm* oscillator; **oscillateur à quartz** = crystal oscillator

◇ **oscillation** *nf* oscillation; **oscillations résiduelles (sur un courant)** = ripple

◇ **oscilloscope** *nm* oscilloscope

les deux oscilloscopes portables disposent de quatre voies, d'une bande passante de 100MHz et ont des possibilités de mesures intégrées

Electronique pratique

OU *(logique)* OR; **fonction OU** = OR function; **opération OU** = join *ou* union *ou* disjunction; **porte** *ou* **circuit OU** = OR gate; **OU exclusif** = exclusive OR (EXOR); **fonction OU exclusif** = non-equivalence function *ou* NEQ function *ou* anticoincidence function; **porte** *ou* **circuit OU exclusif** = exclusive OR gate *ou* EXOR gate *ou* anticoincidence circuit; **OU inclusif** = inclusive OR; **opération OU inclusif** = either-or operation

outil *nm* tool; **l'ordinateur est un outil très utile à l'esthétique industrielle** = industrial design is aided by computers; **outils de diagnostic** = system diagnostics *ou* diagnostics; **outils de diagnostic du compilateur** = compiler diagnostics; **un outil de diagnostic de compilation bien conçu facilite le débogage** = thorough compiler diagnostics make debugging easy; **outils de diagnostic d'erreurs** = error diagnostics; **outil de programmation** = software tool; **boîte à outils** = toolkit *ou* toolbox; *voir aussi* MACHINE-OUTIL

ouvert, -e *adj* **(a)** open; **bande sur bobine ouverte** = open reel tape; **boucle ouverte** = open loop; **code ouvert** = open code; **fichier ouvert** = open file; **le fichier demeure ouvert** = leaving files open; **vous ne pouvez accéder aux données que si le fichier est ouvert** = you cannot access the data unless the file is open; **poste de travail ouvert** = open access terminal; **programme ouvert** = open-ended program; **routine ouverte** = open routine; **sous-programme ouvert** = open subroutine; **système ouvert** = open system; **interconnexion de systèmes ouverts (ISO)** *ou* **normes ISO (pour systèmes ouverts)** = Open System Interconnection (OSI) **(b)** **enveloppe ouverte** = open *ou* unsealed envelope

ouverture *nf* **(a)** *(fente)* mouth *ou* slot; **insérer dans une ouverture** = to slot (in) **(b)** **ouverture d'objectif** = lens stop *ou* aperture; **ouverture utile** = effective aperture; **vitesse d'ouverture d'un objectif** = lens speed **(c)** *(d'antenne)* **illumination de l'ouverture** = aperture illumination **(d)** *(d'une session d'ordinateur)* **ouverture de session** = logging on; **ouverture automatique de session** = auto-login *ou* auto-logon *ou* automatic log on

ouvrir *vtr* **(a)** to open; **ouvrez d'abord la porte du lecteur de disquettes** = first, open the disk drive door; **soulevez le couvercle de l'ordinateur pour l'ouvrir** = open the top of the computer by lifting **(b)** **ouvrir un fichier** = to open a file; **vous ne pouvez accéder aux données avant d'avoir ouvert le fichier** = you cannot access the data unless the file has been opened **(c)** **ouvrir une session** = to log in *ou* to log on

oxyde *nm* oxide; **oxyde de fer** *ou* **oxyde ferrique** = ferric oxide *ou* ferrite

Pp

P canal (de type) P = p-channel; **semi-conducteur** de type **P** = p-type semiconductor; **semi-conducteur MOS à canal (de type) P** = p-channel MOS

PABX = PRIVATE AUTOMATIC BRANCH EXCHANGE *voir aussi* AUTOCOMMUTATEUR

packager *ou* **packageur** *nm (de livres)* (book) packager

page *nf* **(a)** page; *(de papier listing)* form; **en ajoutant l'appendice, nous ferons 256 pages au total** = by adding the appendix, we will increase the page extent to 256; **page corrigée (qui en remplace une autre)** = cancel page; *(d'un livre)* **page de droite** *ou* **belle page** = recto *ou* right-hand page; **page de gauche** = verso *ou* left-hand page; **page de titre** = title page; **bas de page** = bottom space; **belle page** = recto *ou* right-hand page; *(de papier listing)* **début d'une page** = head of form (HOF); **disposition de page** = area composition; **épreuve en page** = page proof; **fin de page** = page break; **format de la page** = page size; **imprimante (en mode) page** = page printer; **langage de description de page** = page description language (PDL); **largeur de page (en caractères)** = page width; **longueur de page** *ou* **nombre de lignes par page** = page length; **mettre en page** = to make up *ou* to page *ou* to lay out; **les concepteurs ont décidé de mettre en page sur format A4** = the designers have laid out the pages in A4 format; **mise en page** = layout *ou* makeup *ou* paging; **les concepteurs travaillent à la mise en page de la nouvelle revue** = the design team is working on the layouts for the new magazine; **les corrections faites après la mise en page coûtent très cher** = corrections after page makeup are very expensive; **nombre total de pages (d'un document)** = extent (of a document); *(vitesse d'une imprimante)* **(nombre de) pages par minute (ppm)** = pages per minute (ppm); **pied de page** = footer *ou* footing; *(pour imprimante)* **(instruction de) saut de page** *ou* **changement de page** = form feed; **taille de la page** = page size; **tête d'une page (de papier listing)** = head of form (HOF) **(b)** *(d'écran)* page; **affichage d'une page mémoire** = page display; **caractère d'instruction de fin de page** = page break character *ou* indicator; **écran pleine page** = full-size display; **signal de fin de page** = end of page indicator **(c)** *(de système vidéotex)* **page guide** = lead in page; **page index** = index page; **(nombre de) pages** = magazine **(d)** *(en mémoire)* **page mémoire** = memory page; **page mémoire sans modification** = clean page; **page de routage** = routing page; **adressage de page** = page addressing; **appel de page sur demande** = demand paging; **limite de page** = page boundary; **protection de page** = page protection; **table de pages** = page table

◊ **pagination** *nf* **(a)** pagination *ou* paging **(b)** *(de mémoire paginée)* **pagination transparente** = transparent paging; **algorithme de pagination** = paging algorithm; **registre de pagination à accès direct** = direct page register

◊ **paginé, -ée** *adj* **mémoire paginée** = shadow memory *ou* shadow page; **mémoire morte paginée** = shadow ROM; **table de mémoire paginée** = shadow page table

◊ **paginer** *vtr (un livre)* to folio *ou* to page *ou* to paginate; **paginer de nouveau** = to repaginate

pair, -e *adj* even; **les trois premiers nombres pairs sont 2,4 et 6** = the first three even numbers are 2, 4, 6; **(contrôle de) parité paire** = even parity (check)

◊ **pair-impair, -e** *adj* **contrôle de parité paire-impaire** = odd-even check

◊ **paire** *nf* pair; **effectuer un tri par permutation de paires** = to bubble sort

PAL = PHASE ALTERNATING LINE; **norme de télévision couleur PAL** = PAL

pâle *adj* pale; **si l'impression est trop pâle, réglez le bouton de densité (d'impression) sur le noir** = when fading occurs turn the density dial on the printer to full black

palette *nf (de couleurs)* palette; **palette graphique** = Paintbox®

palier *nm* **(a)** step *ou* stage; **effectué par paliers** = staged **(b)** *(élément du signal télévisé)* **palier avant** = front porch

pâlir *vi (couleur)* to fade

panier *nm* **(circuits de) fond de panier** = (microcomputer) backplane

panne *nf* **(a)** breakdown *ou* failure *ou* fault; *(complète)* crash; **la panne était due à la défaillance d'un composant** = the hard failure was due to a burnt-out chip; **nous ne pouvons pas joindre notre bureau à New York à cause d'une panne des lignes de télex** = we cannot communicate with our New York office because of the breakdown of the telex lines; **panne désordonnée** = disorderly close-down; **panne douce** = soft-fail; **panne par échauffement** = burn out; **panne fatale** = catastrophic failure; **panne sérieuse (d'équipement)** = hard failure; **panne totale d'un disque** *ou* **d'une disquette** = disk crash; **panne d'électricité** *ou* **de courant** *ou* **de secteur** = power failure *ou* electrical failure *ou* blackout; **il y a eu une panne de courant** *ou* **de secteur** = the electricity supply has failed *ou* the electricity supply was cut off; **les ingénieurs essaient de réparer une panne d'électricité** = the engineers are trying to repair an electrical failure; **panne de système** = system crash; **durée d'une panne** = fault time; **enregistrement** *ou* **traçage de panne** = fault trace; **localisation (automatique) de panne** = fault detection; **diagnostic de localisation de panne** = fault diagnosis; **programme de localisation de panne** = fault location program; **tolérance de pannes** = fault tolerance **(b)** **en panne** = down; **ce modem est en panne** = the modem has broken down; **l'imprimante est en panne, il faut remplacer une pièce** = the printer

won't work - we need to get a spare part; **on peut dire que l'ordinateur est en panne si rien ne se produit à la mise sous tension** = a computer has failed if you turn on the power supply and nothing happens; **tomber en panne** = to break down; **que faut-il faire quand l'imprimante ligne tombe en panne?** = what do you do when your line printer breaks down?; **l'ordinateur est tombé en panne deux fois cet après-midi** = the computer system went down twice during the afternoon; **tomber en panne complète** = to crash; **la tête de lecture du disque est tombée en panne et il se peut que les données aient été perdues** = the disk head has crashed and the data may have been lost

panneau *nm* **(a)** *(d'un appareil)* panel; **panneau avant** = front *ou* front panel *ou* fascia plate; **le panneau avant du lecteur de disquettes de ce modèle est plus petit que celui des autres modèles** = the fascia plate on the disk drive of this model is smaller than those on other models; **panneau arrière** = back panel; **la prise est située sur le panneau arrière** = the socket is on the back panel; **le numéro de fabrication est gravé de façon permanente sur le panneau arrière du boîtier de l'ordinateur** = the production number is permanently engraved on the back of the computer casing; **panneau de commande** *ou* **panneau de contrôle** = control panel; **panneau de commande d'un système** = system control panel; **panneau de raccordement** = plugboard *ou* patchboard **(b)** *(pour affiches)* **on a placé des panneaux d'avertissement autour du laser de puissance** = warning notices were put up around the high powered laser

PAO = PUBLICATION ASSISTEE PAR ORDINATEUR

papeterie *nf* stationery; **papeterie personnalisée** = preprinted stationery

papier *nm* paper; **un papier de mauvaise qualité est beaucoup trop transparent** = bad quality paper gives too much show-through; **le papier doit être chargé manuellement dans l'imprimante** = the paper should be manually fed into the printer; **nous avons du papier de 70 - 90 grammes** = our paper weight is 70 - 90 gsm; **le livre est**

imprimé sur du papier 80 grammes = the book is printed on 80gsm paper; **papier en accordéon** = fanfold *ou* accordion fold paper; **papier autocopiant** = carbonless paper; **papier baryté** = baryta paper; **papier en continu** = continuous stationery; **papier couché** = coated paper; **papier enduit d'une fine couche de kaolin** = paper which has a coating of clay; **papier à dessin (de type 'cartridge')** = cartridge paper; **papier pour duplicateur** *ou* **copieur** = duplicating paper *ou* duplicator paper; **papier électrosensible** = electrosensitive paper; **papier à en-tête** = headed paper *ou* preprinted stationery; **papier à lettre** = writing paper; **papier à lettre commercial** = bond paper; **on utilise du papier glacé pour l'impression de similigravures** = glossy paper is used for printing half-tones; **papier journal** = newsprint *ou* mechanical paper; **papier listing** = computer stationery *ou* continuous stationery *ou* listing paper; **équipement de traitement de papier listing (en sortie d'imprimante)** = form handling equipment; **papier millimétré** = graph paper; **papier (plié) en paravent** = accordion fold *ou* fanfold paper; **papier photosensible double face** = duplex; **papier préimprimé** = preprinted stationery; **papier quadrillé** = graph paper; **papier thermique** = heat sensitive paper *ou* thermal paper; **(dispositif d') alimentation** *ou* **entraînement du papier** = paper feed; **arrêt par manque de papier** = form stop; *(pour l'alimentation en feuille à feuille)* **bac à papier** = paper bin *ou* paper tray; **bande papier** = (paper) tape *ou* punched tape; **(dispositif d') entraînement de la bande papier** = paper tape feed; **poinçon de perforation pour bandes papier** = paper tape punch; **le bureau sans papier** = the paperless office; **contrôle d'un programme sur papier** = desk check of a program; **feuille de papier** = sheet (of paper); **indicateur de fin de papier** = form stop; **rouleau de papier de** *ou* **pour télécopieur** = fax roll; **saut du papier** = paper throw

◊ **papier-calque** *nm* detail paper

papillotement *nm (d'une image)* flicker *ou* blinking; **sans papillotement** = flicker-free

paquet *nm* **(a)** pack; **paquet de cartes perforées** = card deck **(b)** *(groupes de données)* batch; **traitement par paquets** = batch processing; **mode de traitement par paquets** = batch mode; **processeur de traitement par paquets** = batch processor; **système de traitement par paquets** = batch system **(c)** *(données de tailles uniformes)* packet; **commutation (de messages) par paquets** = packet switching; **réseau de commutation de données par paquets** = packet switched data service *ou* packet switched network (PSN) **(d)** *(signaux intermittents)* burst; **mode de transmission** *ou* **de transfert par paquets** = burst mode

par *prép* **(a)** per; **par année** = per year; **par heure** = per hour; **par jour** = per day; **par semaine** = per week **(b)** par *ou* par l'intermédiaire de *ou* en passant par = by *ou* via; **les signaux nous ont été transmis par satellite** = the signals have reached us via satellite

parabolique *adj* **antenne parabolique** = dish aerial; **nous utilisons une antenne parabolique pour capter les signaux transmis par satellite** = we use a dish aerial to receive signals from the satellite

paragraphe *nm* paragraph; **paragraphe standard** = template (paragraph); *(traitement de texte)* **transfert** *ou* **insertion d'un paragraphe** = block transfer

paraître *vi* to be published; **ce livre paraîtra en édition cartonnée et en livre de poche** = the book will be published as a hardback and as a paperback; *(d'une revue* ou *d'un journal)* **numéro déjà paru** = back number

parallèle *adj* parallel; **accès parallèle** = parallel access; **additionneur parallèle** = parallel adder; **connexion (en) parallèle** = parallel connection; **leur débit de transmission est de 60 000 bits par seconde en connexion parallèle** = their average transmission rate is 60,000 bps through parallel connection; **convertisseur analogique-numérique parallèle** = flash A/D; **entrée/sortie (en) parallèle** = parallel input/output (PIO); **circuit intégré d'entrée/sortie en parallèle** = parallel input/output chip; **entrée parallèle/sortie parallèle** = parallel input/parallel output (PIPO); **entrée parallèle/sortie série** = parallel input/serial output (PISO); **entrée**

série/sortie parallèle = serial input/parallel output (SIPO); **exploitation (en) parallèle** = parallel running; **système de gestion des priorités en parallèle** = parallel priority system; **imprimante parallèle** = parallel printer; **interface parallèle** = parallel interface; **opération (en) parallèle** = parallel operation; **ordinateur parallèle** = parallel computer; **port parallèle** = parallel port; **traitement (en) parallèle** = parallel processing; **transfert (en) parallèle** = parallel transfer; **transmission (en) parallèle** = parallel transmission; **transmission de données en parallèle** = parallel data transmission

paramétrable *adj* programmable *ou* dynamic; **code paramétrable** = skeletal code; **sous-programme paramétrable** = dynamic subroutine

◊ **paramétrage** *nm* parameterization; **paramétrage de marges** = margination; **code de paramétrage de l'imprimante** = non-printing codes

◊ **paramètre** *nm* parameter; **la taille du tableau est fixée par ce paramètre** = the size of the array is set with this parameter; **le paramètre X définit le nombre de caractères contenus dans une ligne d'écran** = the X parameter defines the number of characters displayed across a screen; **paramètres de conception** *ou* **de création** = design parameters; **paramètres d'impression** = print modifiers; **bande sans paramètres d'impression** = idiot tape; **paramètre physique** = physical parameter; **paramètres programmables à l'installation** = set-up options

◊ **paramétré, -ée** *adj* **sous-programme paramétré** = parametric (subroutine)

◊ **paramétrer** *vtr* to set *ou* to program; **paramétrer une marge** = to set a margin

◊ **paramétrique** *adj* **code paramétrique de l'imprimante** = non-printing codes; **la largeur des lignes peut être définie par le code paramétrique .LW suivi d'un chiffre** = the line width can be set using one of the non-printing codes, .LW, then a number; **logiciel paramétrique** = parameter-driven software; **sous-programme paramétrique** = parametric (subroutine); **test paramétrique** = parameter testing

parasite **1** *nm* **(a)** *(qui nuit à l'enregistrement sur disque)* drop in **(b)**

(bruits) **parasites** = noise *ou* static; *(causés par une autre voie de transmission)* crosstalk **2** *adj* **bruits parasites** = noise *ou* static; *(causés par une autre voie de transmission)* crosstalk; **bruits parasites courants** = common mode noise; **caractères parasites** = gibberish; **signaux parasites** = garbage

paravent *nm* **papier (plié) en paravent** = accordion fold *ou* fanfold *ou* concertina fold paper

parc *nm* total number (of computers *ou* of clients); **maintenance du parc clients** = customer engineering

parcage *nm* **parcage de la tête de lecture** = head park

parcourir *vtr* **parcourir une orbite** = to orbit

parenthèses *nfpl* (round) brackets; **mettre entre parenthèses** = to put between *ou* in brackets

parité *nf* parity; **parité de bloc** = block parity; **parité de colonne** = column parity; **bit de parité** = parity bit; **clé de parité transversale** = vertical parity check; **contrôle de parité** = parity check; **(contrôle de) parité d'un bloc** = block parity (check); **(contrôle de) parité impaire** = odd parity (check); **(contrôle de) parité paire** = even parity (check); **contrôle de parité paire-impaire** = odd-even check; **indicateur de contrôle de parité** = parity flag; **interruption (de contrôle) de parité** = parity interrupt; **piste de parité** = parity track

théoriquement, le bit de parité placé en fin des 7 ou 8 bits utiles du caractère, sert à contrôler la qualité de la transmission
Action PC

parole *nf* speech *ou* voice; **processeur de la parole** = speech processor; **reconnaissance de la parole** = speech recognition *ou* voice recognition; **synthèse de la parole** = speech synthesis; **synthétiseur de la parole** = speech synthesizer

part *nf* **tiré à part** = offprint

partage *nm* division *ou* sharing; **(en) partage de port** = port sharing; **partage de ressources** = resource sharing; **partage des tâches** = load sharing; **partage de temps** = time-sharing

◊ **partagé, -ée** *adj* divided *ou* shared *ou* split; **accès partagé** = shared access; **bus partagé** = shared bus; **écran partagé** = split screen; **fichier partagé** = shared file; **système à fichiers partagés** = distributed file system; **langage partagé** = common language; **ligne partagée** = party line *ou* shared line; **logiciel partagé** = common software; **processeur à logique partagée** = shared logic text processor; **matériel partagé** = common hardware; **mémoire partagée** = shared memory; **(en) port partagé** = port sharing; **système logique partagé** = shared logic system; **système à ressources partagées** = shared resources system; **système en temps partagé** = time-sharing system

◊ **partager** *vtr* to divide *ou* to share *ou* to split; **plusieurs sociétés indépendantes se partagent le système** = the system is shared by several independent companies

partial, -e *adj* biased

particule *nf* particle; **particule alpha** = alpha-particle; **sensibilité aux particules alpha** = alpha-particle sensitivity

particulier, -ière *adj* **adressage particulier** = inherent addressing

partie *nf* part *ou* section *ou* region; **partie fractionnaire** = fractional part; **affichage d'une partie de page** = part page display

◊ **partiel, -ielle** *adj* **(mémoire) RAM partielle** = partial RAM; **report partiel** = partial carry

◊ **partiellement** *adv* partially; **données partiellement prétraitées** = semi-processed data

partition *nf* partition *ou* area; **partition privée** = private address space; **partition privilégiée (avec niveau d'accès prioritaire)** = privileged account; **le gestionnaire d'un système jouit d'une partition privilégiée qui lui permet d'accéder à tous les fichiers de ce système** = the systems manager has a privileged status so he can access any file on the system; **partition de traitement par lots** = batch region

paru *voir* PARAITRE

parution *nf* publication; **la date de parution du livre est fixée au 15 novembre** = the publication date of the book is November 15th

parvenir *vi* **parvenir à** = to achieve; **les concepteurs de matériel informatique tentent de parvenir à une compatibilté totale entre tous les composants du système** = the hardware designers are trying to achieve compatibility between all the components of the system

pas *nm* **(a)** *(d'un programme)* step; **pas de programmation** = program step; **avancer d'un pas** *ou* **faire un pas (en avant)** = to step (forward); **faire avancer d'un pas** = to increment; **exécution** *ou* **opération pas à pas** = single step opération; **reculer d'un pas** *ou* **faire un pas en arrière** = to step backward **(b)** *(d'un moteur)* step; **moteur à pas** = stepper motor *ou* stepping motor **(c)** *(taille de caractères)* pitch **(d)** *(d'un film)* film advance

PASCAL **langage PASCAL** = PASCAL

passage *nm* **(a)** pass; **ruban à un seul passage** = single strike ribbon; **passage de tri** = sorting pass **(b)** *(d'un système à un autre)* crossover

passager, -ère *adj* transient; **erreur passagère** = transient error

◊ **passe** *nf* pass; **passe de balayage** = raster scan; **balayage une passe sans segmentation d'image** *ou* **balayage d'image complète en une passe** = single scan non segmented; **assembleur une passe** = one-pass assembler *ou* single-pass assembler; **ce nouvel assembleur une passe travaille très vite** = this new one-pass assembler is very quick in operation; **assembleur deux passes** = two-pass assembler; **impression en plusieurs passes légèrement décalées** = multipass overlap; **opération (en) une passe** = single pass operation **(b)** **mot de passe** = password; **il faut vous rappeler votre mot de passe sinon vous ne pourrez** pas avoir accès au système = if you forget your user ID, you will not be able to logon; **l'utilisateur doit d'abord taper le mot de passe pour avoir accès à la base de données** = the user has to key in the password before he can access the database

◊ **passe-bande** *adj inv* **filtre passe-bande** = bandpass filter

◊ **passe-bas** *adj inv* **filtre passe-bas** = low pass filter

◊ **passe-haut** *adj inv* **filtre passe-haut** = high pass filter

◊ **passer 1** *vtr* **passer un coup de fil** = to make a phone call; **demande de communication qui ne passe pas** = lost call **2** *vi* **passer à** = to proceed; **passer d'un système à un autre** = to change over; **il a été difficile de passer à un système d'index informatisé** = the crossover to computerized file indexing was difficult

passerelle *nf* bridge *ou* bridging product *ou* bridgeware; *(d'accès entre réseaux)* gateway; **une passerelle est fournie aux entreprises qui disposent des deux générations d'équipement** = a bridging product is available for companies with both generations of machines; **transfert de programme avec l'aide d'une passerelle** = bridging

et, surtout, il dispose de passerelles qui lui permettent d'être utilisé dans un environnement industriel
L'Evénement

pastille *nf* **pastille de silicium** = silicon chip; *(du silicium)* **découpe en pastille** = slicing

pause *nf* pause *ou* short stop; **pause accidentelle** = holdup

pavé *nm* **(a)** pad *ou* keypad; **pavé à effleurement** *ou* **pavé tactile** = touch pad; **pavé numérique** = numeric keypad; **utilisez le pavé numérique pour saisir les chiffres** = you can use the numeric keypad to enter the figures **(b)** graphe *ou* ordinogramme à pavés = block diagram

payer *vtr* to pay; **l'utilisateur paie un droit pour visualiser le tableau d'affichage** = the user has to pay a charge for viewing pages on a bulletin board

pays *nm* country; **indicatif (téléphonique) du pays** = country code

PBX = PRIVATE BRANCH EXCHANGE; **PBX électronique** = computerized branch exchange (CBX); *voir aussi* AUTOCOMMUTATEUR

PC = PERSONAL COMPUTER PC; *voir aussi* ORDINATEUR

PCV *(communication téléphonique payable par le destinataire)* **appel en PCV** = collect call; *US* transferred call

PEEK *(lecture directe de la mémoire)* **instruction PEEK** = PEEK instruction; **vous devez utliser l'instruction PEEK 1452 pour regarder le contenu de la mémoire à l'emplacement 1452** = you need the instruction PEEK 1452 here to examine the contents of memory location 1452

pellicule *nf* (i) film; (ii) film base; **pellicule photographique** = (photographic) film; **il a mis une nouvelle pellicule dans son appareil photo** = he put a new roll of film into the camera

◊ **pelliculé, -ée** *adj* **c'est un livre avec couverture pelliculée** = the book is bound in laminated paper

◊ **pelliculer** *vtr* to laminate

pelure *nf* skin; **architecture en pelure d'oignon** = onion skin architecture; **cet ordinateur possède une architecture en pelure d'oignon comprenant un noyau central, un système d'exploitation, un langage de bas niveau et le programme utilisateur** = the onion skin architecture of this computer is made up of a kernel at the centre, an operating system, a low-level language and then the user's program; **langage en pelure d'oignon** = onion skin language

pendant *prép* for *ou* during; **pendant quelque temps** *ou* **pendant un certain temps** = for a period of time; **pendant quelques mois** = for a period of months; **pendant six ans** = for a six-year period

pense-bête *nm (indiquant la fonction des touches)* key strip

pépin *nm* glitch

perceptible *adj* perceptible à l'oreille = audible

perche *nf (d'un microphone)* boom

perdre *vtr* **(a)** to lose; **tous les fichiers courants ont été perdus lors de la panne d'ordinateur et nous n'avions pas de copie de sauvegarde =** all the current files were lost when the system crashed and we had no backup copies **(b)** *(condensateur)* **perdre sa charge =** to leak; **dans ce circuit, le condensateur perd 10% de sa charge par seconde =** in this circuit, the capacitor charge leaks out at 10% per second
◊ **se perdre** *vpr* **se perdre dans une boucle =** to hang
◊ **perdu, -e** *adj (égaré)* stray

père *nm* father; **fichier père =** father file

péremption *nf* expiration; **date de péremption =** expiration date; *(d'un produit en magasin)* sell-by date

perfect binding *nm* perfect binding; **(livre) avec perfect binding =** perfect bound (book)

perforateur *nm (pour cartes)* card punch (CP)
◊ **perforateur-compteur** *nm (de bandes papier)* counting perforator
◊ **perforation** *nf* **(a)** *(de bande papier)* hole *ou* perforation; **perforations centrales =** centre holes; **perforations d'entraînement** *ou* **perforations marginales =** feed holes *ou* sprocket holes; **code de perforation =** tape code; **poinçon de perforation =** paper tape punch *ou* perforator **(b)** *(de carte perforée)* **perforation numérique =** numeric punch; **perforation (de la ligne) 11** *ou* **perforation X =** x punch; **perforation (de ligne) 12** *ou* **perforation Y =** y punch; **code de perforation de carte =** card code *ou* punched code; **colonne de perforation (d'une carte) =** card row *ou* card column; **poinçon de perforation (pour cartes) =** card punch (CP) **(c)** *(de disque)* **perforations =** hard-sectoring; **perforations de marquage (du bord) d'un**

disque = disk index holes; **perforation de positionnement =** sectoring hole
◊ **perforatrice** *nf* perforator *ou* reperforator; **perforatrice (à clavier) =** key punch
◊ **perforé, -ée** *adj* **bande (papier) perforée =** (paper) tape *ou* punched (paper) tape *ou* perforated tape; *(pour télex hors ligne)* torn tape; **lecteur de bandes perforées =** paper tape reader; **carte perforée =** punch card *ou* punched card; **(système d') alimentation** *ou* **entraînement de cartes perforées =** card feed; **chargeur de cartes perforées =** hopper; **lecteur de cartes perforées =** card reader *ou* punched card reader; **étiquette perforée =** punched tag; **ligne perforée =** perforations; *(sur carte)* card row *ou* card column; **ruban perforé =** perforated tape
◊ **perforer** *vtr* to punch

performance *nf* performance; *(d'un appareil)* **bonne performance =** efficiency; **dégradation** *ou* **réduction des performances =** degradation; **étalonnage des performances** *ou* **évaluation comparative des performances =** benchmarking; **les bancs d'essais consistent à évaluer la performance de plusieurs systèmes ou périphériques en utilisant le même test standard =** in benchmarking, the performances of several systems or devices are tested against a standard benchmark; **pour juger de la performance du système =** as a measure of the system's performance; **(de) haute performance =** high performance; **matériel (de) haute performance =** high performance equipment
◊ **performant, -e** *adj* efficient; **ce progiciel de traitement de texte a produit, de façon très performante, une série de lettres personnalisées =** the word-processing package has produced a series of addressed letters very efficiently

périgée *nm* perigee

période *nf* period *ou* time; **période d'assemblage =** assembly time; **période de latence =** latency; **période de référence =** reference time; **période de travail =** session
◊ **périodique 1** *nm (revue)* magazine *ou* periodical **2** *adj* periodic *ou* periodical

◊ **périodiquement** *adv* periodically

périphérique *nm* (external) device *ou* peripheral (unit) *ou* peripheral equipment; **les périphériques, tels que les lecteurs de disquettes et les imprimantes, qui permettent le transfert de données sont asservis à un système (central) mais fonctionnent grâce à des circuits indépendants** = peripherals such as disk drives or printers allow data transfer and are controlled by a system, but contain independent circuits for their operation; **périphérique d'entrée** = input device *ou* input unit; **(câble de) liaison d'un périphérique d'entrée** = input lead; **périphérique d'entrée/sortie** = input/output device *ou* unit *ou* I/O device *ou* unit; **périphérique lent** = slow peripheral; **périphérique rapide** = fast peripheral; **périphérique de sortie** = output device *ou* unit; **caractère de contrôle de périphérique** = device control character; **(système de) commande** *ou* **contrôle de périphérique utilisant des caractères** = device character control; **unité de commande** *ou* **unité de contrôle de périphérique** *ou* **contrôleur de périphérique** = peripheral control unit (PCU) *ou* peripheral controller; **échange d'information entre CPU et périphérique** = CPU handshaking *ou* peripheral transfer; **file d'attente de périphériques** = device queue; **gestion de périphérique** = device control; **routine de gestion de périphérique** = peripheral software driver; **gestionnaire de périphérique** = device driver *ou* device handler *ou* peripheral driver; **code d'identification de périphérique** = device code; **interface** *ou* **connecteur de périphérique** = peripheral interface adapter (PIA); **limité par (la vitesse d') un périphérique** *ou* **avec contrainte de vitesse de périphérique** = peripheral-limited; **mémoire (de) périphérique** = peripheral memory; **langage de pilotage de périphériques** = peripheral command control language; **pilote de périphérique** = device driver *ou* peripheral controller; **port pour périphériques** = user port; **priorité d'un périphérique** = device priority; **processeur périphérique** = peripheral processing unit (PPU); **signal d'appel émis par un périphérique** = external interrupt

permanence *nf* **(service de) permanence téléphonique** = answering service; **en permanence** = permanently

◊ **permanent, -e** *adj* **(a)** permanent; **câblage permanent** = hardwired connection; **données permanentes** = fixed data; **erreur permanente** = permanent error; **fichier permanent** = permanent file *ou* master file; **mémoire permanente** = permanent memory *ou* nonerasable storage; **mémoire dynamique permanente** = permanent dynamic memory **(b)** **de façon permanente** = permanently

perméabilité *nf* permeability

permettre *vtr* to enable; **permettre quelque chose** = to authorize something; **ce logiciel permet d'exécuter des fonctions beaucoup plus complexes** = the software is capable of far more complex functions; **un gestionnaire de base de données ultra-rapide permet la manipulation d'une très grande quantité de données** = a high-speed database management program allows the manipulation of very large amounts of data; **un programme de spouling permet d'éditer un texte tout en imprimant** = a spooling program enables editing work to be carried out while printing is going on

◊ **permis** *nm* licence

◊ **permis, -e** *adj* authorized *ou* legal

◊ **permission** *nf* authorization

permutable *adj* **registre permutable** = circulating register

◊ **permutation** *nf* permutation *ou* interchange *ou* change-over; *(de programmes)* swapping *ou* swap; *(de bits ou de mots de données)* shift *ou* rotation; **ce code chiffré est très sûr puisqu'il comporte une clé avec un très grand nombre de permutations possibles** = this cipher system is very secure since there are so many possible permutations for the key; **permutation de bits** = bit rotation *ou* rotate operation; **permutation circulaire** = cyclic shift *ou* cycle shift; **tri par permutation (de paires ou de bulles)** = bubble sort; **effectuer un tri par permutation de paires ou de bulles** = to bubble sort

◊ **permuté, -ée** *adj* **mémoire à liste permutée** = nesting store

◊ **permuter** *vtr* to interchange; *(programmes)* to swap; *(bits ou mots de données)* to shift *ou* to rotate; **permuter des données** = to exchange data

persistance *nf* persistence *ou* afterglow; **persistance de l'image** = image retention *ou* lag; **phosphore à longue persistance** *ou* **couche phosphorée à grande persistance** = long persistence phosphor; **les écrans à faible fréquence de balayage ont besoin de phosphore à longue persistance pour éviter l'instabilité de l'image** = slow scan rate monitors need long persistence phosphor to prevent the image flickering

◊ **persistant, -e** *adj* **anomalie** *ou* **erreur persistante** = hard error

personnalisé, -ée *adj* custom-built *ou* customized; **nous utilisons des logiciels personnalisés** = we use customized software; **papeterie personnalisée** = preprinted stationery; **ROM personnalisée** = custom ROM (PROM)

◊ **personnaliser** *vtr* to customize *ou* to personalize

personne *nf* person *ou* individual; **chaque personne possède son propre mot de passe pour accéder au système** = each individual has his own password to access the system

◊ **personnel** *nm* personnel; **personnel informatique** = liveware

◊ **personnel, -elle** *adj* personal *ou* individual; **code personnel** = ID code; **après la mise en route du système, il faut tapez votre code personnel et votre mot de passe** = after you wake up the system, you have to input your ID code then your password; **numéro de code personnel** = identity number *ou* personal identification number *ou* PIN number; **ordinateur personnel** = personal computer (PC) *ou* home computer

perte *nf* loss; *(fuite)* leakage *ou* leak; **perte d'alignement** = gap loss; **perte de charge** = leak *ou* leakage; **perte dans l'espace** = free space loss; **perte d'insertion** = insertion loss; **perte de magnétisation** = drop out; *(d'un signal)* **perte de niveau** = drop out; *(radio ou télévision)* **perte d'un signal** = breakup; **perte de terre** = ground absorption; **perte de transmission** = link loss; **perte de transmission inexplicable** = line gremlin

pertinence *nf* relevance

◊ **pertinent, -e** *adj* relevant; **relation pertinente** = relevance

perturbation *nf* disturbance; **courte perturbation sur la ligne** = hit on the line

petit, -e *adj* small; **petites capitales** = small caps; **interface pour petits ordinateurs** = small computer system interface (SCSI)

PF = PICOFARAD

phase *nf* **(a)** *(étape)* phase *ou* stage; **nous n'en sommes qu'à la phase de rodage du système d'exploitation** = we are in the first stage of running in the new computer system; **phase de compilation** = compile phase; **phase d'exécution** = execute phase *ou* execution phase; **phase exécution en code objet** = target phase *ou* run phase; **phase de lecture d'une instruction** = fetch phase **(b)** *(d'un signal)* phase; **angle de phase** = phase angle; **écrêtage de phase** = phase clipping; **égalisateur** *ou* **compensateur de phase** = delay equalizer *ou* phase equalizer; **modulation de phase** = phase modulation; **en phase** = in phase; *voir aussi* DEPHASE

phone *nm (unité de puissance sonore)* phon

◊ **phonème** *nm* phoneme; **les mots 'tout' et 'roue' contiennent le phonème 'ou'** = the phoneme 'ou' is present in the words 'tout' and 'roue'

◊ **phonétique 1** *nf* **la phonétique** = phonetics **2** *adj* phonetic; **il y a une transcription phonétique de la prononciation** = the pronunciation is indicated in phonetic script

phosphore *nm* phosphor; **phosphore à longue persistance** = long persistence phosphor; **phosphore vert** = green phosphor; **couche de phosphore** = phosphor coating; **points de phosphore** = phosphor dots

◊ **phosphoré, -ée** *adj* **couche phosphorée à longue persistance** = long persistence phosphor coating

◊ **phosphorescence** *nf* phosphorescence; **points de phosphorescence** = phosphor dots;

rendement de phosphorescence = phosphor efficiency

◊ **phosphorescent, -e** *adj* **couche phosphorescente** = phosphor coating

photo- *préf* photo

photo *nf* = PHOTOGRAPHIE **(a)** *(image)* photo *ou* photograph *ou* picture; *(l'ensemble des photos d'une revue, etc.)* pix; **c'est une photo de l'auteur** = it's a photograph of the author; **il a fait six photos du nouvel ordinateur** = he took six photographs of the new machine; **vous pouvez voir le nouveau modèle sur cette photo** = this picture shows the new design; **photo couleur** = colour photograph; **photo en noir et blanc** = black and white photograph **(b)** *(art)* photography; **photo avec film sensible aux infrarouges** = infrared photography; **appareil photo** = camera

photocellule *nf* photocell

photocomposé, -ée *adj* **texte photocomposé** = phototypeset text; **la PAO devrait produire un texte dont la qualité est à peu près égale à celle d'un texte photocomposé** = in desktop publishing, the finished work should look almost as if it had been typeset

◊ **photocomposeuse** *nf* phototypesetter

◊ **photocomposition** *nf* filmsetting *ou* photocomposition *ou* phototypesetting

photoconductivité *nf* photoconductivity

◊ **photoconducteur, -trice** *adj* **cellule photoconductrice** = photoconductor

photocopie *nf* **(a)** photocopy *ou* photostat; *(faite avec une machine de marque Xerox)* Xerox (copy); **faites six photocopies du contrat** = make six photocopies of the contract; **envoyer une photocopie du contrat à l'autre partie** = to send the other party a xerox of the contract; **nous avons envoyé des photocopies à chacun des agents** = we have sent photocopies to each of the agents **(b)** photocopying; **bureau de photocopie** = photocopying bureau; **les frais de photocopie augmentent d'année en année** = photocopying costs are rising each year

◊ **photocopier** *vtr* to photocopy *ou* to photostat; *(avec une machine de marque Xerox)* to xerox; **elle a photocopié le contrat** = she photocopied the contract; **elle a photocopié tout le dossier** = she xeroxed all the file; **photocopier un document** = to xerox a document; **photocopier une lettre** = to make a xerox copy *ou* a photocopy of a letter

◊ **photocopieur** *nm* photocopier *ou* copier *ou* copying machine *ou* duplicating machine *ou* duplicator; *(de marque Xerox)* Xerox® (machine); **on nous installera un nouveau photocopieur Xerox demain** = we are having a new Xerox machine installed tomorrow

photodiode *nf* photodiode; **photodiode à avalanche** = avalanche photodiode (APD); **photodiode (de type) PIN** = pin photodiode

ce détecteur est composé de deux photodiodes au silicium superposées, chacune ayant une réponse spectrale différente

Opto électronique

photo-électricité *nf* photoelectricity

◊ **photoélectrique** *adj* photoelectric; **cellule photoélectrique** = photocell *ou* photoelectric cell; **la cellule photoélectrique décèle la quantité de lumière qui traverse le liquide** = the photoelectric cell detects the amount of light passing through the liquid; **détecteur photoélectrique** = photosensor

photoémission *nf* photoemission

photographie *nf* **(a)** *(l'image)* photograph; **photographie en couleur** = colour photograph; **il y aura une photographie en couleur de l'auteur au dos de la jaquette** = we will be using a colour photograph of the author on the back of the jacket; **photographie numérisée** = digitized photograph **(b)** la **photographie** = photography; **le film du texte peut être reproduit par photographie** = the text film can be reproduced photographically; **photographie de la même scène avec plusieurs ouvertures** = bracketing

◊ **photographier** *vtr* to photograph; **le copieur photographie le texte imprimé pour le reproduire** = the copier makes a photographic reproduction of the printed page

◊ **photographique** *adj* photographic; **appareil photographique** *ou* **appareil photo** = camera; **pellicule photographique** = (photographic) film; **plaque photographique** = (photographic) plate

◊ **photographiquement** *adv* photographically

◊ **photogravure** *nf* photogravure

photo-litho *nf* photolithography
◊ **photolithographie** *nf* photolithography

photomécanique *adj* photomechanical; **transfert photomécanique** = photomechanical transfer (PMT)

photométrie *nf* photometry

photon *nm* photon

photosensible *adj* light-sensitive; **détecteur photosensible** = photosensor; **dispositif photosensible** = light-sensitive device; **les films photosensibles réagissent à la lumière** = light-sensitive films change when exposed to light; **papier photosensible** = light-sensitive paper; **la photo est imprimée sur papier photosensible** = the photograph is printed on light-sensitive paper; **papier photosensible double face** = duplex (paper); **plaque photosensible** = (photographic) plate; **résine photosensible** = photoresist; **(méthode de la) résine photosensible en positif** = positive photoresist

photostat *nm* photostat; **faire un photostat (d'un document)** = to photostat (a document)

phototransistor *nm* phototransistor

photovoltaïque *adj* photovoltaic; **calculatrice à batteries photovoltaïques** = solar-powered calculator

ces photodiodes sont de type photovoltaïque et ne nécessitent pas de polarisation
Opto électronique

physique *adj* physical; **couche physique** = physical layer; **enregistrement physique** = physical

record; **(disque) avec formatage physique** = hard-sectored (disk); **paramètre physique** = physical parameter; **support physique d'une base de données** = physical database; **unité physique** = physical record

pic *nm* peak

pica *nm (12 points anglais, environ 11 points Didot)* pica

pick-up *nm* pickup

pico- (P) *préf (un million de millions de fois plus petit)* pico-
◊ **picofarad (PF)** *nm* picofarad (pF)
◊ **picoseconde (Ps)** *nf* picosecond (ps)

picot *nm* **entraînement (du papier) par picots** = tractor feed *ou* sprocket feed *ou* pinfeed; **roue à picots** = sprocket wheel

pièce *nf* part *ou* component; **pièce détachée** = spare part; **l'imprimante est en panne, il faut remplacer une pièce** = the printer won't work - we need to get a spare part

pied *nm* foot; **blanc de pied** = bottom space *ou* foot margin; **pied de page** = footer *ou* footing

piézo-électrique *adj* piezoelectric

ce système piézo-électrique fonctionne même à travers les obstacles perturbants du type vitre ou eau
Hi-fi Vidéo

piggyback *nm* piggyback; **mettre en piggyback** = to piggyback; **mise en piggyback** = piggybacking

pile *nf* **(a)** *(binaire)* heap; *(de données en mémoire)* stack; *(pour stockage de données en mode LIFO)* cellar; **pile en file d'attente (en mode FIFO)** = push-up list *ou* stack; **pile d'instructions d'un programme** = program stack; **constitution de pile d'interruptions** = interrupt stacking; **pile inversée (en mode LIFO)** = push-down list *ou* stack; **pile de mémoire virtuelle** = virtual memory stack; **processeur de pile de tâches** = stack job processor; **adresse de pile** = stack address; **base de la pile** = stack base; **dessus de la pile** = top of stack; **introduire** *ou* **mettre (des données) dans la pile** = to put data onto a stack; **pointeur de pile** = stack pointer (SP) **(b)** battery; **niveau de tension** *ou* **différence de potentiel d'une pile** = battery voltage level; **pile auxiliaire** *ou* **de secours** = battery backup; **équipé d'une pile auxiliaire** *ou* **de secours** = battery-backed; **dans ce portable, le lecteur de disquettes est remplacé par une mémoire CMOS avec pile auxiliaire** = battery-backed CMOS memory replaces a disk drive in this portable; **la carte RAM peut être équipée, en option, d'une pile de secours** = the RAM disk card has the option to be battery-backed; **pile rechargeable** = re-chargeable battery; **pile sèche** *ou* **alcaline** = dry cell; **pile solaire** = solar cell

piller *vtr* **piller une base de données** = to break into a database *ou* to scavenge a database

PILOT **langage PILOT** = PILOT

pilotage *nm* control; **langage de pilotage (de périphériques)** = (peripheral) command control language

◇ **pilote** *nm* **(a)** control *ou* pilot; **pilote d'écran** *ou* **d'affichage** = display controller; **pilote d'imprimante** = printer's controller *ou* printer driver; **pilote de périphérique(s)** = controller *ou* device driver *ou* peripheral driver; **(programme) pilote de souris** = mouse driver; **pilote de traceur (de courbes)** = plotter driver **(b)** **la société a mis sur pied un projet-pilote pour évaluer le procédé de fabrication proposé** = the company set up a pilot project to see if the proposed manufacturing system was efficient; **système-pilote** = pilot system; **l'usine-pilote a été construite pour tester le nouveau procédé de fabrication** = the pilot factory has been built to test the new production process

◇ **piloté, -ée** *adj* **chariot piloté par ordinateur** = buggy

◇ **piloter** *vtr* to control

les pilotes de périphériques ou 'device drivers' sont des programmes ajoutés au système d'exploitation (DOS) pour piloter des accessoires et des périphériques
L'Ordinateur Individuel

PIN = P-TYPE, INTRINSIC AND N-TYPE; **photodiode PIN** = pin photodiode

pipe-line *ou* **pipeline** *nm* **ordinateur avec architecture en pipeline** *ou* **en pipe-line** = pipeline computer; **exécuter** *ou* **traiter (des instructions) en pipeline** = to pipeline; **mode d'exécution** *ou* **de traitement en pipeline** = pipelining; **mode d'exécution d'instructions en pipeline** = instruction pipelining; **organisation en pipeline** = pipelining; **organiser en pipeline** = to pipeline

piqué *nm (de lentille)* acutance

piratage *nm* piracy; **faire du piratage informatique** = to hack; **nous avons changé les mots de passe pour empêcher le piratage de la base de données** = we have changed the passwords to prevent hackers getting into the database; **piratage de logiciel** = software piracy

◇ **pirate** *nm (de logiciels)* pirate; *(pirate de système informatique)* hacker; **la société tente d'amener les pirates de logiciel devant les tribunaux** = the company is trying to take the software pirates to court

◇ **piraté, -ée** *adj* pirated; **une bande piratée** = a pirated tape; *(d'enregistrement)* **copie piratée** = bootleg; **exemplaire d'un logiciel piraté** = pirate copy of a computer program; **logiciel piraté** = pirate software; **entrée sur un système avec un mot de passe piraté** = piggyback entry

◇ **pirater** *vtr* to pirate; **pirater un système** = to hack; **logiciel qui a été piraté** = pirate software; **il a utilisé une disquette piratée bon marché et a découvert que le programme contenait des bogues** = he used a cheap pirated disk and found the program had bugs in it; **les différents schémas du nouveau système ont été piratés en Extrême-Orient** = the designs for the new system were pirated in the Far East

piste *nf* **(a)** *(de disque ou de bande)* track; **piste d'adresses** = address track; **piste de données binaires** = bit track; **piste d'horloge** = clock track; **piste de parité** = parity track; **(nombre de) pistes par pouce** = tracks per inch (TPI); **piste de référence** = library track; **piste sonore** = sound track; **adresse de piste** = track address; **la tête de lecture fait une erreur**

de piste = the read head is not tracking the recorded track correctly; **disquette (de) quarante pistes** = forty-track disk; **magnétophone à quatre pistes** = four-track recorder; **disque de quatre-vingts pistes** = eighty-track disk **(b)** *(de carte magnétique)* **piste magnétique** = magnetic strip; **lecteur de pistes magnétiques** = magnetic strip reader

pixel *nm* picture element *ou* pixel

le pixel correspond à la plus petite unité d'information d'une image numérique
Science et Vie Micro

PL/1 = PROGRAMMING LANGUAGE/1
voir aussi PROGRAMMATION

placard *nm* broadsheet; **épreuves en placard** = galley proof *ou* slip pages *ou* slip proofs

place *nf* place; **place d'un chiffre** = digit place *ou* position; **changer (quelque chose) de place** = to move (something); **mettre en place** = to install *ou* to position; **mise en place** = installation; **mise en place de liens** = linkage editing; **temps de mise en place** = positioning time; **mettre une chose à la place d'une autre** = to interchange; **sur place** = on-site *ou* in-house; *(ordinateur)* on local
◊ **placement** *nm* octet de placement = postbyte
◊ **placer** *vtr* to position; **il faut éviter de placer l'écran devant une fenêtre** = the VDU should not be positioned in front of a window; **on avait placé des feuilles blanches entre les pages nouvellement imprimées pour éviter les coulures d'encre** = blank paper was interleaved with the newly printed text to prevent the ink running

plage *nf* **(a)** *(écart)* gap; *(d'erreurs)* error range; **plage normale** = normal (error) range **(b)** *(d'un disque)* track

cela assure une très grande précision dans le positionnement du laser, la recherche d'une plage déterminée est du même coup facilitée et se fait dans des temps extrêmement courts
Hi-fi Vidéo

plan *nm* **(a)** *(photo)* **plan focal** = image plane; **gros plan** = close-up **(b)** *(avant)* **premier plan** = foreground; **couleur de premier plan** = foreground colour **(c)**

(prioritaire) **tâche de premier plan** = foreground job; *voir aussi* ARRIERE-PLAN **(d)** *(design)* blueprint *ou* plan; **il a fait les plans de la nouvelle usine de composants** = he designed the new chip factory; *(d'un étage)* **plan d'ensemble** = floor plan; **armoire** *ou* **meuble à plans** = planchest; **jeu de plans** = plans **(e)** *(des rues d'une ville)* street plan *ou* town plan **(f)** *(planning)* plan; *(suivant un horaire)* schedule; **plan d'urgence** = contingency plan

plan, -e *adj* flat; **surface plane** = flat *ou* plane surface

PLAN *(langage de bas niveau)* **langage PLAN** = PLAN

planche *nf* *(illustration)* plate

planète *nf* planet

planification *nf* planning; **planification de la séquence d'exécution des tâches** = job scheduling
◊ **planifier** *vtr&i* to plan *ou* to map out
◊ **planning** *nm* **(a)** *(planification)* planning; **planning à longue échéance** *ou* **à courte échéance** = long-term planning *ou* short-term planning **(b)** *(calendrier)* **planning mural** = wall planner

plantage *nm* *(familier)* lock up
◊ **planter** *vi* *(familier)* **(se) planter** = to bomb; **le programme s'est planté, nous avons perdu toutes les données** = the program bombed, and we lost all the data

plaque *nf* **(a)** board *ou* card; **plaque (présensibilisée) pour circuit imprimé** = printed circuit board (PCB); **plaque double face pour circuit imprimé** = double-sided printed circuit board **(b)** plate; **plaque photographique** *ou* **photosensible** = photographic plate; **appareil photo à plaques** = plate camera

plaquette *nf* *(pour circuit imprimé)* board

plasma *nm* plasma; **affichage** *ou* **écran (au) plasma** = (gas) plasma display *ou* gas discharge display *ou* electroluminescent display

plat, -e *adj* **(a)** flat; **boîtier plat** = flat pack; **câble plat** = tape cable *ou* ribbon cable; **fichier plat** = flat file

◊ **à plat** *adv (scanner, etc.)* flatbed; **le papier n'est pas entraîné par rouleaux dans un scanner à plat** = in flatbed scanners the paper is not fed in through rollers; **lecteur de transmission à plat** = flatbed transmitter

plate-forme *nm* platform; **plate-forme de collecte de données** = data collection platform

platine *nf* **(a)** turntable *ou* deck; **platine magnétophone** *ou* **platine magnétocassette** = tape deck **(b)** presse à **platine** = platen press *ou* flatbed press

le marché de la hi-fi est ici composé des produits suivants: platines CD, platines tourne-disques, platine K7, tuners, amplis, chaînes composées
Audio Vidéo

plein, -e *adj* full; **cette disquette est pleine, il faudra donc saisir les données sur une autre disquette** = the disk is full, so the material will have to be stored on another disk; **la disquette a été très vite pleine** = the disk was quickly filled up; **écran pleine page** = full-size display

pleurage *nm (d'une bande)* wow

pli *nm* fold; *(papier)* **(à) quatre plis** = sixteenmo *ou* 16mo

◊ **pliage** *nm (papier)* fold *ou* folding; **pliage en cahiers de 16, 32 ou 64 pages** = even working

◊ **plier** *vtr* to fold

◊ **plieuse** *nf (pour papier)* folding machine

◊ **pliure** *nf* folding

plomb *nm* **(a)** lead; **composition au plomb** = hot metal setting **(b)** fuse; **faire sauter un plomb** = to blow a fuse; **on a fait sauter les plombs en branchant le climatiseur** = when the air-conditioning was switched on, it fused the whole system

plongeant, -e *adj* **vue plongeante** = aerial image

plus 1 *conj* **code (binaire) plus 3** = excess-3 code; **pour 6, le code (binaire) plus 3 est 1001** = the excess-3 code representation of 6 is 1001; **une adresse plus une** = one-plus-one address; **instruction à n adresse(s) plus une** = n-plus-one address instruction **2** *nm (le signe de l'addition)* **le signe plus (+)** = plus *ou* plus sign

PLV = PUBLICITE LIEU DE VENTE *voir aussi* LIEU

pn jonction pn *ou* **zone interface pn** = pn-junction; **jonction pn à diffusion** *ou* **zone interface pn à diffusion** = diffused pn-junction; **jonction pn à seuil** *ou* **zone interface pn à seuil** = step pn-junction

◊ **pnp transistor (de type) pnp** = pnp transistor; **transistor bipolaire** *ou* **à jonction pnp** = bipolar (junction) transistor (BJT)

poche *nf* **(a)** pocket; **calculatrice de poche** = pocket calculator; **ordinateur de poche** = hand-held computer **(b)** **livre de poche** = paperback; **ce livre paraîtra en édition cartonnée et en livre de poche** = we are publishing the book as a hardback and as a paperback

◊ **pochette** *nf (d'un disque)* jacket *ou* sleeve

pochoir *nm* **pochoir de traçage** = stencil; **ce pochoir contient toutes les formes pour composants électroniques** = the stencil has all the electronic components on it

poids *nm* **(a)** weight; **poids brut** = gross weight; **poids net** = net weight; *(d'une rame de papier)* **poids unitaire** = basic weight **(b)** **bit de poids faible** = least significant bit (LSB); **chiffre de poids faible** = least significant digit (LSD) *ou* low-order digit; **bit de poids fort** = weighted bit *ou* most significant bit (MSB); **chiffre de poids fort** = high order digit *ou* most significant digit (MSD) *ou* most significant character

poinçon *nm (de perforation)* punch; *(de cartes)* card punch (CP); *(de bandes papier)* perforator *ou* (paper) tape punch

point *nm* **(a)** dot; **(nombre de) points par pouce** = dots per inch *ou* d.p.i. *ou* dpi;

certaines imprimantes (à) laser sont dotées d'une haute définition de 400 points par pouce = some laser printers offer high resolution printing at 400 dpi; un moniteur monochrome format A4 avec une définition de 300 points par pouce = a 300 d.p.i. black and white A4 monitor; un scanner d'image avec définition de 300 points par pouce = a 300 dpi image scanner; point de contrôle = available point; point d'image = scanning spot; *(d'un écran)* points de phosphore *ou* de phosphorescence = phosphor dots *ou* spots; matrice de points = dot matrix; commande (précédée d'un) point = dot command; graphique de points = scatter graph (b) *(typographie)* full stop; *US* period; point d'exclamation (!) = exclamation mark; point d'interrogation (?) = question mark; point et virgule (;) = semi-colon; deux points (:) = colon; *(placé devant chaque élément d'une liste)* point indicateur de couleur = (colour) bullet (c) *(mesure de taille de caractères)* point; est-ce qu'en augmentant la taille des caractères à 10 points on augmente ainsi le nombre de pages? = if we increase the point size to 10, will the page extent increase?; *(0.324 mm)* point Didot *ou* point typographique = point; *(environ 11 points Didot)* 12 points anglais = pica; le texte du livre est (composé) en Times 9 points = the text of the book is set in 9 point Times (d) *(endroit)* point d'accès = *(d'entrée/sortie)* port; *(pour contrôle d'une carte ou d'un logiciel)* access point; point d'arrêt = cutoff; *(d'exécution d'un programme)* breakpoint; point d'arrêt variable = regional breakpoint; *(après incident)* remise en marche au point d'arrêt *ou* au point de reprise *ou* reprise au point d'appel fall back recovery *ou* failure recovery; (point d') arrivée = far end *ou* receiving end; *(de film ou écran)* point chaud = hot spot; point de branchement = branchpoint; point de connexion = terminal; voici le point de connexion de cette puce sur la carte = this is the position of that chip on the PCB; point de contrôle = check point; point de début d'enregistrement = loadpoint; point de départ = starting point; point d'entrée = entry point; point d'entrée dans un système = trapdoor; (liaison) point à point = point to point (connection); point de raccordement = terminal; point de réception = receiving point; point de ré-entrée *ou* de rentrée = re-entry point; point de reprise = re-entry point *ou* check point; point de sortie =

exit point; point de vidage = dump point (e) point de vente = point-of-sale (POS); point de vente électronique = electronic point-of-sale (EPOS); terminal de point de vente = point-of-sale terminal *ou* POS terminal (f) *(sujet)* matter (g) *(valeur)* percentage point (h) au point = *(image)* in focus; *(appareil)* tuned *ou* adjusted; *(program)* debugged; l'image n'est pas au point = the picture is out of focus *ou* is not in focus; mettre au point = *(une image)* to focus; *(un appareil)* to tune *ou* to adjust; *(un programme)* to debug; *(un produit)* to develop *ou* to perfect; la position de la lentille a été ajustée de façon à bien mettre au point le rayon lumineux = they adjusted the lens position so that the beam focused correctly; mettre au point (avec grande précision) = to fine tune; il a mis au point le procédé de fabrication d'un acier de haute qualité = he perfected the process for making high grade steel; mise au point = *(d'une image)* focusing; *(d'un appareil)* tuning *ou* adjustment; *(d'un programme)* debugging; *(d'un produit)* development; mise au point magnétique = magnetic focusing; dérégler la mise au point = to defocus; une mise au point très précise améliore la vitesse de dix pour cent = fine-tuning improved the speed by ten per cent; logiciel de mise au point = debugger; temps de mise au point d'un nouveau produit = development time

◊ **point-virgule** (;) *nm* semi-colon

sur des réseaux privés point à point, le codeur-décodeur d'images fonctionne dans une plage de débit comprise entre 9600bps et 384Kbps
Informatique & Bureautique (Suisse)

pointe *nf* (a) *(de tension)* spike; pointe de courant = power transient (b) *(d'une onde)* les pointes et les creux = peaks and troughs (c) heure(s) de pointe = peak period; techniques de pointe = high technology

pointeur *nm* pointer; fichier de pointeurs = pointer file; pointeur (de position) de données = data pointer; pointeur de pile = stack pointer (SP); la PAO sur ordinateur personnel est facilitée par l'emploi d'un pointeur et d'une souris = desktop publishing on a PC is greatly helped by the use of a pointer and mouse; incrémenter le pointeur jusqu'à l'adresse (d'instruction) suivante = increment the contents of the pointer to the address of the next instruction

pointillé *nm* **(a)** dotted line **(b)** perforated line *ou* perforations
◊ **pointillé, -ée** *adj* **ligne pointillée** = dotted line

POKE *(de modification en mémoire)* **instruction POKE** = POKE instruction; **l'instruction POKE 1423,74 écrira 74 à l'emplacement 1423** = POKE 1423,74 will write the data 74 into location 1423

polaire *adj* **(a)** polar; **coordonnées polaires** = polar coordinates; **diagramme en coordonnées polaires** = polar diagram **(b) orbite polaire** = polar orbit
◊ **polarisation** *nf* polarization *ou* bias; *(antenne ou signal)* **à** *ou* **avec polarisation verticale** = vertically polarized; **signal avec polarisation verticale** = vertically polarized signal
◊ **polarisé, -ée** *adj* biased *ou* polarized; **signal polarisé** = polar signal; **signal polarisé verticalement** = vertically polarized signal
◊ **polarité** *nf* polarity; **polarité électrique** = electrical polarity; **polarité inversée** = reverse polarity; **polarité magnétique** = magnetic polarity; **test de polarité** = polarity test

polaroïde *adj* **filtre polaroïde** = polaroid filter

police *nf* **police de caractères** = font *ou* fount *ou* typeface *ou* typestyle *ou* character set; **police de caractères reconnaissable par lecture optique** = optical font *ou* OCR font; **police résidente** = resident font; **police de caractères téléchargeable** = downloadable fonts; **police de caractères utilisable par un terminal** = terminal character set; **police de caractères vectorielle** = dynamically redefinable character set; **cartouche de police de caractères** = cartridge fonts; **changement de police de caractères** = font change; **disquette de polices de caractères** = font disk; **support de polices de caractères** = image carrier; **utilisation de plusieurs polices de caractères** = font mixing

policé, -ée *adj (programme)* well-behaved

pollution *nf* **pollution (par rayonnement) électronique** = electronic smog

polonais, -e *adj* **notation polonaise inversée** = reverse Polish notation (RPN) *ou* postfix notation; **alors que la notation conventionnelle s'écrit: (x-y) + z, la notation polonaise inversée s'écrit: xy - z+** = normal notation: (x-y) + z, but using RPN: xy - z+

polynomial, -e *adj* polynomial; **code polynomial** = polynomial code

polyvalent, -e *adj* **ordinateur polyvalent** = general purpose computer; **registre polyvalent** = general register *ou* general purpose register (gpr)

pompage *nm (erreur dans un circuit numérique)* race

ponctuation *nf* punctuation; **signe de ponctuation** = punctuation mark

pondération *nf* weighting
◊ **pondéré, -ée** *adj* weighted; **moyenne pondérée** = weighted average
◊ **pondérer** *vtr* to weight

pont *nm (connecteur)* jumper

pool *nm* **pool de dactylos** = typing pool

POP **langage (de traitement de listes) POP 2** = POP 2

port *nm* port; **port asynchrone** = asynchronous port; **l'utilisation de ports asynchrones ne demande pas un matériel spécialisé** = when asynchronous ports are used no special hardware is required; **port de communication** = communications port; **port (d') entrée** = input port; **port (d') entrée/sortie** = I/O port *ou* input/output port; **le manche à balai peut être connecté sur le port entrée/sortie** = the joystick can be connected to the input/output port; **port (d')imprimante** = printer port; **port (de) manche à balai** *ou* **(de) manette** = joystick port; **port parallèle** = parallel port; **(en) port partagé** *ou* **partage de port** = port sharing; **port pour périphériques** = user port; **port privatif** *ou* **réservé** = private dial port; **port série** = serial interface *ou* port; **port (de) sortie** = output port; **port vidéo** = video port; **sélecteur de port** = port selector

portabilité *nf* portability; **portabilité d'une formule** = formula portability

◊ **portable** *adj* **(a)** portable *ou* transportable; **équipement de prise de vue portable sur le dos** = back pack; **ordinateur à peu près portable** = luggable computer; **un ordinateur portable n'est pas aussi petit qu'un portatif** = a transportable computer is not as small as a portable **(b) programmes portables** = portable software *ou* portable programs *ou* canned programs

portage *nm* **la capacité de portage de cette liaison est excellente** = the information-carrying abilities of this link are very good

portance *nf* **laser de portance** = injection laser

portatif, -ive 1 *n (ordinateur)* **un portatif** = a portable; *(machine à écrire)* **une portative** = a portable; **elle a écrit la lettre sur sa petite portative** = she wrote the letter on her portable typewriter **2** *adj* portable; **petit (ordinateur) portatif (autonome)** = laptop computer *ou* lapheld computer; **petit ordinateur portatif (qu'on tient à la main)** = handheld computer; **radiotéléphones portatifs** = portable phones; **récepteur portatif** = hand receiver *ou* hand portable set

porte *nf* gate; **porte d'équivalence** = equivalence gate; **porte ET** = AND gate *ou* coincidence gate; **porte d'identité** = identity gate *ou* element; **porte logique** = logic gate; **porte NI** = NOR gate; **porte NI exclusif** = exclusive NOR gate *ou* EXNOR gate; **porte NON** = NOT gate; **porte NON-ET** *ou* **NAND** = NAND gate; **porte NON-OU** *ou* **NI** = NOR gate; **porte OU** = OR gate; **porte OU exclusif** = except gate *ou* exclusive OR gate *ou* EXOR gate *ou* non-equivalence gate

portée *nf* range; **modem de courte portée** = short haul modem *ou* short range modem; **hors de portée** = out of range

porteur, -euse *adj* **(a) courant porteur commun** = common carrier; **système à courant porteur** = carrier system; **onde porteuse** = carrier wave; **détecteur d'onde porteuse** = data carrier detect (DCD); **télégraphie par onde porteuse** = carrier telegraphy; **transmission par onde porteuse** = carrier signalling; **elle n'utilise pas de modem: il n'existe aucun signal porteur sur la ligne** = she's not using a modem - there's no carrier signal on the line **(b) fusée porteuse** = launch vehicle

◊ **porteuse** *nf (onde)* carrier; **porteuse de données** = data carrier; **interférence entre porteuses** = intercarrier noise; **on note des interférences de porteuses sur une télévision lorsque la porteuse son et la porteuse image se rencontrent** = television intercarrier noise is noticed when the picture and the sound signal carriers clash; **modulation d'amplitude sans porteuse** *ou* **à porteuse inhibée** = suppressed carrier modulation; **bande latérale unique sans porteuse** *ou* **à porteuse inhibée** = single sideband suppressed carrier (SSBSC); **bandes latérales** *ou* **double bande latérale sans porteuse** *ou* **à porteuse inhibée** = double sideband suppressed carrier (DSBSC); **l'appel est bloqué si le logiciel ne reçoit pas de signal de détection de porteuse** = the call is stopped if the software does not receive a DCD signal from the modem; **porteuse d'image** *ou* **de signal vidéo** = image carrier; **porteuse principale** = main beam; **signal de détection de porteuse** = data carrier detect (DCD)

pose *nf (d'un enduit)* deposition

positif *nm (photo ou film)* positive; **affichage en positif** = positive presentation; **(méthode de la) résine photosensible en positif** = positive photoresist (technique)

◊ **positif, -ive** *adj* positive; **accusé de réception positif (d'un message)** = affirmative acknowledgement; **borne positive** = positive terminal; **épreuve positive** = photoprint; **feedback positif** *ou* **rétroaction positive** = positive feedback; **film positif** = positive film *ou* direct image film; **logique positive** = positive logic; **réponse positive** = positive response

position *nf* place *ou* position; **position binaire** = bit position; *(du curseur, etc.)* **position initiale** *ou* **de départ** = home; **mise en position de transport de la tête** = head park; **modulation d'impulsions en position (MIP)** = pulse position modulation (PPM)

◊ **positionnel, -elle** *adj* positional

◊ **positionnement** *nm* **positionnement de la tête de lecture** = head alignment; *(de machine à écrire)* **dispositif de positionnement** = aligner; *(sur microfilm)* **marque** *ou* **repère** *ou* **symbole de positionnement** = editing symbol; *(marque de secteur de disque)* **perforation de positionnement** = sectoring hole

◊ **positionner** *vtr* to position *ou* to align; **positionnez la photo dans le coin droit du haut de la page** = position this photograph at the top right-hand corner of the page; *(deux images)* **positionner sur repères** = to register

possibilité *nf* possibility *ou* capability; **liste des possibilités** = capability list

◊ **possible** *adj* possible; **rendre possible** = to enable

post- *préfixe* post-

postal *adj* postal; **code postal** = post code; *US* ZIP code

◊ **poste 1** *nf (courrier)* mail; **bureau de poste** = post office; **envoi par la poste** = mailing; **envoyer par la poste** *ou* **mettre à la poste** = to mail *ou* to post; **prospectus envoyé par la poste** = mailing piece **2** *nm* **(a)** *(ordinateur)* station *ou* terminal; **poste de contrôle mixte** = combined station; **poste éloigné** = remote station; **poste informatique de télétransmission** = data terminal *ou* data station; **poste d'interrogation** = inquiry station; **poste de travail** = workstation *ou* (operating) console *ou* terminal; **poste de travail multifonction** = multifunction workstation; **poste de travail d'un opérateur** = operator's console; **le système comprend cinq postes de travail reliés en anneau** = the system includes five workstations linked together in a ring network **(b) poste (de) radio** *ou* **(de) T.S.F.** = radio (set); **poste (de) télévision** = television (TV) *ou* television receiver *ou* television set; **foyers qui possèdent au moins un poste de télévision ou de radio** = broadcast homes

poster 1 *nm (affiche)* poster **2** *vtr* **poster une lettre** = to post *ou* to mail a letter

post-processeur *nm* postprocessor

postsynchronisation *nf* dubbing

◊ **postsynchronisé, -ée** *adj* dubbed; **effet sonore postsynchronisé** = dubbed sound

potentiel *nm* **(a)** *(possibilité)* potential; **potentiel d'écoute** = coverage **(b)** *(tension)* potential *ou* voltage level; **différence de potentiel** = potential difference; **différence de potentiel d'une pile** = battery voltage level; **élever le potentiel d'une ligne** = to pull up a line; **élever le potentiel de la ligne de réception au niveau logique un, en la connectant sur une source de courant de 5 volts** = pull up the input line to a logic one by connecting it to 5 volts

◊ **potentiomètre** *nm* potentiometer

poubelle *nf* **mettre à la poubelle** = to junk

pouce *nm* **(a)** *(mesure de longueur)* inch; **disquette de 3,5 pouces** *ou* **de 5,25 pouces** = three and a half inch disk *ou* five and a quarter inch disk; **disquette de huit pouces** = eight inch disk; **lecteur de disquettes de 3,5 pouces** *ou* **de 5,25 pouces** *ou* **de 8 pouces** = three and a half inch *ou* five and a quarter inch *ou* eight inch (disk) drive **(b)** *(nombre de)* **pouces par seconde** *ou* **pouces/seconde** = inches per second (ips); **la vitesse de balayage de cette machine est de 1,3 pouce par seconde** = for this machine throughput is 1.3 inches per second (ips) scanning speed; **(nombre de) bits par pouce** = bits per inch (bpi); **(nombre de) caractères par pouce** = characters per inch (cpi); **le bouton vert vous permet de sélectionner 10 ou 12 caractères par pouce** = you can select 10 or 12 cpi with the green button; **(nombre de) pistes par pouce** = tracks per inch (TPI); **(nombre de) points par pouce** = dots per inch *ou* d.p.i. *ou* dpi; **un moniteur monochrome format A4 avec une définition de 300 points par pouce** = a 300 d.p.i. black and white A4 monitor; **un scanner d'image avec définition de 300 points par pouce** = a 300 dpi image scanner; **certaines imprimantes (à) laser sont dotées d'une haute définition de 400**

points par pouce = some laser printers offer high resolution printing at 400 dpi

pourcentage *nm* percentage; **pourcentage d'augmentation** = percentage increase; **quel est le pourcentage d'augmentation?** = what is the increase per cent?

poursuite *nf* **caméra de poursuite** = planetary camera

poussé, -ée *adj* **recherche très poussée** = exhaustive search

pratique *adj (mise en main)* **formation pratique** = hands-on training; **la société informatique offre une formation pratique de deux jours** = the computer firm gives a two day hands-on training course

pré- *préfixe* pre-
◊ **préallocation** *nf* pre-allocation

préampli *nm* = PREAMPLIFICATEUR
◊ **préamplificateur** *nm* pre-amplifier
◊ **préamplifier** *vtr (fréquence)* to pre-emphasise

préavis *nm* **appel** *ou* **communication (téléphonique) avec préavis** = person-to-person call

précaution *nf* precaution; **mesure de précaution** = safety measure *ou* safety net

précédemment *adv* previously
◊ **précédent, -e** *adj* prior *ou* previous; **comparée à la version précédente, celle-ci est très facile à utiliser** = compared with the previous version this one is very user-friendly; **copiez les données du fichier précédent dans le fichier actuel** = copy data into the present workspace from the previous file
◊ **précéder** *vtr* to precede

précis, -e *adj* precise *ou* accurate; **l'horloge atomique indiquera l'heure précise du début du processus** = the atomic clock will give the precise time of starting the process
◊ **préciser** *vtr* to specify
◊ **précision** *nf* accuracy *ou* precision; **avec précision** = accurately; **le code (à)**

barres doit être imprimé avec une précision de l'ordre du millième de micron = the printed bar code has to be accurate to within a thousandth of a micron; **régler un appareil avec grande précision** = to fine tune a machine; **précision d'un nombre** = precision of a number; **nombres à précision finie** = finite-precision numbers; **double précision** = double-length precision *ou* double precision; **arithmétique en double précision** = double precision arithmetic; **(de) haute précision** = high specification *ou* high spec; **(en) multiple précision** = multiple precision *ou* multiprecision; **(en) simple précision** = single-length precision *ou* single precision

précompilé, -ée *adj* precompiled; **code précompilé** = precompiled code

préconditionner *vtr* to precondition

préconiser *vtr* to recommend *ou* to specify; **la procédure normale préconise une sauvegarde de tout le travail en fin de journée** = the normal procedure is for backup copies to be made at the end of each day's work

prédéfini, -e *adj* predefined

prédéterminé, -ée *adj* predetermined; **débit prédéterminé d'un modem** = default rate; **valeur prédéterminée** = default value

prédicat *nm* predicate

prééditer *vtr* to pre-edit

préenregistré, -ée *adj* prerecorded; **(module de) texte pré-enregistré** = prerecord; **le répondeur téléphonique fait entendre un message pré-enregistré** = the answerphone plays a prerecorded message
◊ **pré-enregistrer** *vtr* to prerecord

préétabli, -e *adj* predesigned; **en-tête préétabli** = form flash; *(gardé en mémoire)* **texte** *ou* **graphique préétabli** = form overlay; **un grand choix de modèles de mise en page préétablis vous permet de formater automatiquement vos documents techniques** = a wide selection of predesigned layouts helps you automatically format typical business and technical documents

préfixe *nm* prefix
◊ **préfixé, -ée** *adj* notation préfixée = prefix notation

préformaté, -ée *adj* preformatted; **disquette préformatée** = preformatted disk; **ces données ont été copiées sur des disquettes préformatées** = the data is copied onto previously formatted disks

préimprimé, -ée *adj* preprinted; **formulaires préimprimés** = preprinted stationery; **papier préimprimé** = preprinted stationery

prématuré, -ée *adj* unexpected; **interruption prématurée** = abormal end *ou* abend *ou* abnormal termination
◊ **prématurément** *adv* **abandonner** *ou* **interrompre (un programme) prématurément** = to abort (a program)

premier, -ière 1 *n* **(a)** first; **épreuve en première** = galley proof; **coupure au premier raccroché** = first party release; **(méthode du) premier entré premier sorti (FIFO)** = first in first out (FIFO); **file d'attente qui fonctionne sur le principe 'premier entré premier sorti'** = FIFO queue; **mémoire basée sur le principe 'premier entré premier sorti'** = FIFO memory *ou* first in first out memory; **les deux ordinateurs fonctionnent à des vitesses différentes mais peuvent transmettre des données en utilisant une mémoire tampon fonctionnant sur le système 'premier entré premier sorti'** = the two computers operate at different rates, but can transmit data using a FIFO memory **2** *adj* **(a)** **première génération** = first generation; **le fichier père est un fichier de sauvegarde de première génération** = the father file is a first generation backup; **image de première génération** = first generation image; **ordinateur de première génération** = first generation computer; **première mouture** = draft; **adresse de premier niveau** = first-level address; **algorithme de sélection de la première place suffisante** = first fit **(b)** *(avant ou prioritaire)* **premier plan** = foreground; **couleur de premier plan** = foreground colour; **tâche de premier plan** =

foreground task **(c)** **nombre premier** = prime; **sept (7) est un nombre premier** = the number seven is a prime

prémixage *nm* premix

préparation *nf* preparation; **la préparation de ces étiquettes se fera beaucoup plus rapidement avec l'ordinateur** = if you use the computer for processing the labels, it will be much quicker; **préparation de données** = data preparation; **temps de préparation** = make-ready time; **temps de préparation entre deux tâches** = takedown time

préprocesseur *nm* preprocessor

préproduction *nf* preproduction

préprogrammé, -ée *adj* preprogrammed
◊ **préprogrammer** *vtr* to preprogram; **les tables d'équivalence sont préprogrammées et permettent de gagner du temps de traitement en évitant de recalculer les mêmes valeurs** = lookup tables are preprogrammed and then used in processing to save redoing the calculations for each result required
◊ **préréglé, -ée** *adj* preset; **qui n'est pas préréglé** = selectable
◊ **pré-sélectionné, -ée** *adj* preselected; **acheminement pré-sélectionné** = fixed routing

présent, -e *adj* present; **être présent à** = to attend (something)

présentation *nf* presentation; *(format)* **présentation d'un enregistrement** = record format *ou* layout; *(d'un réseau)* **couche présentation** = presentation layer; *(traitement de texte)* **fonction 'présentation - aperçu'** = previewer; **la fonction intégrée 'présentation - aperçu' permet de visualiser le document et de vérifier s'il s'est glissé des erreurs** = the built-in previewer allows the user to check for mistakes
◊ **présenter** *vtr* to present; **les disquettes sont présentées sous emballage plastique** = the diskettes are packed in plastic wrappers
◊ **présentoir** *nm* rack

presse *nf* (a) la presse = the press; nous avons été très déçus par ce que la presse a écrit sur le nouvel ordinateur individuel = we were very disappointed by the press coverage of the new PC; nous avons l'intention de faire beaucoup de publicité dans la presse pour le produit = we plan to give the product a lot of press publicity; la presse nationale = the national press; la publicité pour la nouvelle voiture a été faite dans la presse nationale = the new car has been advertised in the national press; agence de presse = news agency; communiqué de presse = news release *ou* press release; la société a publié un communiqué de presse au sujet du lancement du nouveau scanner = the company sent out a press release about the launch of the new scanner; conférence de presse = press conference; coupure de presse = press cutting; nous avons constitué un dossier de coupures de presse sur le nouveau progiciel = we have kept a file of press cuttings about the new software package; service de coupures de presse = clipping service; liberté de la presse = freedom of the press (b) *(d'imprimerie)* printing press; le livre est sous presse = the book is on the press; le livre est sous presse, nous recevrons donc les exemplaires reliés vers la fin du mois = the book is printing at the moment, so we will have bound copies at the end of the month; presse à platine = platen press *ou* flatbed press

◊ **Presse-papier**® *nm* clipboard

◊ **presseur** *nm* clapper *ou* platen; galet presseur = head wheel

◊ **pression** *nf* pression; pression acoustique = sound pressure; niveau de pression acoustique = sound pressure level (SPL); pression nécessaire pour actionner une touche = key force; capteur *ou* détecteur de pression = pressure pad; le détecteur de pression caché sous le tapis déclenche une alarme si quelqu'un marche dessus = the pressure pad under the carpet will set off the burglar alarm if anyone steps on it; vérifier la pression = to gauge (pressure)

prêt *nm* loan; prêt interbibliothèque = inter-library loan (ILL)

prêt, -e *adj* ready; le texte est prêt pour l'impression = the text is ready for the printing stage *ou* for the printer; le voyant vert allumé signifie que le système est prêt à accepter le programme suivant = the green light indicates the system is ready for another program; (signal de) prêt à transmettre = clear to send (CTS) *ou* data terminal ready (DTR); *(signal de modem)* prêt à transmettre/recevoir = dataset ready (DSR); configuration prête à l'usage = configured-in; état prêt = ready state

prétraitement *nm* programme de prétraitement = preprocessor

◊ **prétraiter** *vtr* prétraiter des données = to preprocess data; données partiellement prétraitées = semi-processed data

préventif, -ive *adj* preventive *ou* preventative; maintenance préventive = preventive maintenance; nous offrons un contrat de maintenance préventive qui s'applique à ce système = we offer a preventive maintenance contract for the system

◊ **prévention** *nf* prevention; prévention d'erreur = error trapping

primaire *adj* primary; clé primaire = primary key; *(voies de communication)* groupe primaire = primary group; station primaire = primary station

primitif, -ive *adj* adresse primitive = presumptive address; instruction primitive = presumptive instruction

primitive *nf (unité de base)* primitive

principal, -e *adj* principal *ou* central *ou* main; caractéristique principale = key feature *ou* highlight; les principales caractéristiques de ce système sont les suivantes: 20Mo de mémoire formatée avec temps d'accès de 60ms = the key features of this system are: 20Mb of formatted storage with an access time of 60ms; clé principale = primary key; cycle principal = major cycle; entrée principale = main entry; fichier principal = master file; horloge principale = master clock *ou* timing master; index principal = main index; mémoire principale = primary memory *ou* store *ou* storage; main memory *ou* store *ou* storage; central memory (CM); ce système de 16 bits contient une mémoire principale d'une capacité allant jusqu'à

3Mo = this 16-bit system includes up to 3Mb of main memory; **menu principal** = main menu; **mot principal** = keyword; **ordinateur principal** = master computer *ou* host computer; *(gros ordinateur)* mainframe; **accès à l'ordinateur principal** = mainframe access; **porteuse principale** = main beam; **processeur principal** = back-end processor; **routine principale** = main routine; **tableau de distribution principal** = main distributing frame; **terminal principal** = key terminal *ou* central terminal *ou* master terminal; **le gestionnaire de système utilise le terminal principal pour relancer** = the system manager uses the master terminal to restart the system

◊ **principalement** *adv* primarily *ou* mainly

prioritaire *adj* priority; **interruption prioritaire** = priority interrupt; **programme prioritaire** = high priority program *ou* foreground program; **programme non prioritaire** = background program; **tâche prioritaire** = foreground task *ou* work; **tâche non prioritaire** = background *ou* low-priority task *ou* work; **traitement non prioritaire** = background processing; *(film)* **(procédé de) transparence non prioritaire** *ou* **d'arrière-plan** = background projection

◊ **priorité** *nf* precedence *ou* priority; **la console de commande a priorité sur l'imprimante et les autres terminaux** = the master console has a higher device priority than the printers and other terminals; **le lecteur de disquettes est plus important que l'imprimante, il a donc la priorité sur cette dernière** = the disk drive is more important than the printer, so it has a higher priority; **le système d'exploitation a priorité sur les applications en ce qui concerne l'espace alloué sur la disquette** = the operating system has priority over applications when disk space is allocated; **priorité d'interruption** = interrupt priority; **table des priorités d'interruption** = priority interrupt table; **priorité d'un périphérique** *ou* **d'un appareil** = device priority; **priorité d'une tâche** *ou* **d'un travail** = job priority; **détermination de priorité des tâches** = job scheduling; **(système de) gestion des priorités en (fonctionnement) parallèle** = parallel priority (system); **gestionnaire de priorités** = priority scheduler; **ordre de priorité** = order of priority; **ordre de priorité des opérations** = operation priority *ou* operator precedence *ou* priority sequence; **détermination de l'ordre de priorité** = scheduling

prise *nf* **(a)** *(électrique)* socket; **il faut une prise à trois broches pour connecter** *ou* **brancher le système sur le secteur** = a three-pin socket is needed to connect the printer to the mains; **prise de courant** = outlet *ou* socket; **prise de terre** = earth; *US* ground; **prise femelle** = female connector; **prise secteur à deux broches** = two-pin mains socket; **prise secteur à trois broches** = three-pin mains socket **(b)** taking; **prise de vue** = shooting; **prise de vue à cadence lente** = memomotion; **prise de vue en extérieur** = filming *ou* shooting on location **(c)** **prise d'échantillon** = sampling; **la prise d'échantillon toutes les trois secondes a révélé une augmentation** = the sample at three seconds showed an increase

privatif, -ive *adj* private; **autocommutateur privatif (raccordé au réseau public)** = private branch exchange (PBX); **central téléphonique privatif (non raccordé au réseau public)** = private automatic exchange (PAX); **ligne privative** = private line; **port privatif** = private dial port; **système téléphonique privatif** = private telephone system

privé, -ée *adj* **(a)** private; **autocommutateur privé (raccordé au réseau public) (PABX)** = private automatic branch exchange (PABX); **central téléphonique manuel privé (raccordé au secteur public)** = private manual branch exchange (PMBX); **ligne privée** = private line **(b)** **partition privée** = private address space

privilège *nm* privilege

◊ **privilégié, -ée** *adj* priviledged; **instructions privilégiées** = privileged instructions; *(avec niveau d'accès prioritaire)* **partition privilégiée** = privileged account; **le gestionnaire d'un système jouit d'une partition privilégiée qui lui permet d'accéder à tous les fichiers de ce système** = the systems manager has a privileged status so he can access any file on the system; **le gestionnaire du système peut accéder à toutes les partitions à partir de sa partition**

privilégiée = the systems manager can access anyone else's account from his privileged account

problème *nm* **(a)** problem *ou* question; **le problème essentiel est celui du coût** = the main question is that of cost **(b)** problem; **problème d'étalonnage** = benchmark problem; **exposé d'un problème** = problem definition; **résoudre un problème** = to solve a problem; **langage de résolution de problèmes** *ou* **langage adapté aux problèmes** = problem-orientated language (POL)

procédé *nm* process

◇ **procédure** *nf* procedure; **cette procédure qui sert à classer les fichiers par ordre alphabétique peut être sélectionnée depuis le programme principal par la commande SORT** = this procedure sorts all the files into alphabetic order, you can call it from the main program by the instruction SORT; **la procédure est expliquée dans le manuel d'utilisation** = the procedure is given in the manual; **la procédure normale préconise une sauvegarde de tout le travail en fin de journée** = the normal procedure is for backup copies to be made at the end of each day's work; **procédure de commande** = operator procedure; **procédure de contrôle d'acheminement** = routing overheads; **procédure de contrôle de liaison de données** *ou* **procédure SDLC** = synchronous data link control (SDLC); **procédure de file d'attente** = queue discipline; **procédure récursive** = recursive call; **procédure de sauvegarde** = backup procedure; **procédures de secours** = fall back routines; **procédure de traitement des erreurs** = error handling *ou* management; **à base de procédure** = procedural; **déclaration de procédure** = procedure declaration; **diagramme de procédure** = process chart; **langage de procédure** *ou* **langage adapté à la procédure** = procedure-orientated language *ou* procedural language; **schéma de procédure** = process chart

processeur *nm* processor; **il faut un processeur très puissant pour les applications graphiques qui exigent une forte capacité de traitement des nombres en masse** = a very powerful processor is needed for graphics applications which require extensive number crunching capabilities; **processeur à architecture RISC** = reduced instruction set computer (RISC); **processeur auxiliaire** = auxiliary processor; **processeur auxiliaire relié au processeur central** = attached processor; **processeur central** = central processing unit (CPU) *ou* central processor; **processeur de codes commande** = order code processor; **processeur de commande de console** = command console processor (CCP); **processeur double** = dual processor; **processeur d'écran** = display processor; **processeur d'entrée/sortie** = input/output processor (IOP); **processeur de fichier de commandes** = command file processor; **processeur de fond** *ou* **processeur principal** = back-end processor; **processeur frontal** = front-end processor (FEP); **processeur graphique** = graphics processor; **processeur d'image** = image processor; **processeur d'image matricielle** = raster image processor; **processeur d'instruction** = instruction processor; **processeur d'interface** = interface processor; **processeur de langage** = language processor; **processeur mathématique pour calcul (en masse) ultra-rapide** = number cruncher; **processeur à mémoire associative** = associative processor; **processeur en mode caractère** = character machine; **processeur à mots variables** = byte machine; **processeur nu** = clean machine; **processeur de la parole** *ou* **du signal vocal** = speech processor; **processeur périphérique** = peripheral processing unit (PPU); **processeur de programme source** = source machine; **processeur de réseau** = network processor; **processeur de réseau de communication** = communications network processor; **processeur de traitement par lots** *ou* **par paquets** = batch processor; **processeur en tranches** = bit-slice processor; **le processeur en tranches utilise quatre processeurs à 4 bits pour réaliser un processeur à 16 bits** = the bit slice design uses four 4-bit word processors to construct a 16-bit processor; **processeur vectoriel** = array processor; **le processeur vectoriel permet de faire pivoter le tableau qui contient l'image écran à l'aide d'une seule commande** = an array processor allows the array that contains the screen image to be rotated with one simple command;

processeur en virgule flottante = floating point processor; **un processeur en virgule flottante est installé sur ce modèle** = this model includes a built-in floating point processor; **le processeur en virgule flottante accélère la vitesse de traitement de ce logiciel graphique** = a floating point processor speeds up the processing of the graphics software; **dépendant du processeur** ou **limité par le processeur** = processor-limited; **double processeur** = dual processor; **post-processeur** = postprocessor; **temps d'utilisation du processeur** = CPU time

processus *nm* process; **ce processus est contrôlé par une batterie de capteurs** = the process is monitored by a bank of sensors; **le processus compte cinq étapes** = there are five stages in the process; **processus aléatoire** = random process; **processus irréversible** = irreversible process; **processus itératif** = iterative process; **commande** ou **contrôle** ou **conduite de processus** = process control; **ordinateur de contrôle de processus** = process control computer; **système de contrôle** ou **de conduite de processus** = process control system

productif, -ive *adj* productive; **temps productif** = up time ou uptime ou productive time

◊ **production** *nf* **(a)** creation ou generation ou origination **(b)** *(d'un produit)* production; **l'avant-production** = preproduction; **cycle de production** = production run; **niveau maximum de production** ou **production record** = peak output **(c)** *(d'un film)* **directeur de production** = executive producer

◊ **productique** *nf* **productique intégrée** = computer-integrated manufacturing (CIM)

◊ **produire** *vtr* to create ou to generate ou to originate; **on utilise l'ordinateur pour produire des images graphiques** = the computer is used in the generation of graphic images; **produire un label** ou **une étiquette (pour un programme)** = to label (a program); **cette clé produit trois réponses** = there are three hits for this search key

◊ **se produire** *vpr* to occur

◊ **produit** *nm* product; **produit fini** = end product; **produits fictifs** = vapourware; **conception de produits** = product design

◊ **produit, -e** *adj* created ou generated ou originated; **le code est produit automatiquement** = code generation is automatic; **produit à l'aide d'un ordinateur** = computer-generated

profession *nf* profession; **annuaire par professions** = classified directory

◊ **professionnel, -elle** *adj* **copieur professionnel** = office copier; **format professionnel** = ideal format; **ordinateur** ou **terminal à usage professionnel** = office computer ou executive terminal

profil *nm* outline

profondeur *nf* depth; **profondeur de champ** = depth of field; **profondeur de foyer** = depth of focus

progiciel *nm* applications software ou software system ou applications package; **l'ordinateur se vend avec un progiciel de comptabilité et traitement de texte** = the computer is sold with accounting and word-processing packages; **progiciel adapté aux besoins de l'utilisateur** ou **progiciel personnalisé** = customized software ou middleware; **progiciel en coffret** ou **progiciel plus manuel d'utilisation** = packaged software ou software package

programmable *adj* programmable ou selectable; **programmable par l'utilisateur** = user-selectable ou user-definable; **attributs programmables par l'utilisateur** = user-selectable attributes; **calculatrice programmable** = programmable calculator; **circuit logique programmable** = programmable logic array (PLA); **contrôleur d'interruptions programmable** = programmable interrupt controller; **dispositif à champ programmable** = field programmable device; **horloge programmable** = programmable clock; **logique câblée programmable** = programmable logic device (PLD); **mémoire morte programmable** = programmable memory ou programmable read only memory (PROM); **mémoire morte programmable (PROM) effaçable par ultraviolet** = ultraviolet erasable PROM; **mémoire ROM programmable et effaçable** = erasable programmable read-only memory (EPROM); **mémoire ROM programmable et effaçable**

électriquement = electrically erasable programmable read-only memory (EEPROM); **touche (de fonction) programmable** = programmable key *ou* soft key; **la feuille de style comporte 125 symboles programmables (selon les besoins de l'utilisateur)** = the style sheet contains 125 user-definable symbols

◊ **programmateur** *nm* **programmateur de PROM** = PROM burner *ou* programmer

◊ **programmathèque** *nf* program library

◊ **programmation** *nf* programming; **programmation automatique** = automatic programming; **programmation de champ** = field programming; **programmation défensive** = defensive computing; **programmation élégante** *ou* **bien conçue** = elegant programming; **programmation en langage machine** = machine language programming; **programmation linéaire** = linear programming; **programmation modulaire** = modular programming *ou* modularization; **programmation visuelle** = visual programming; **aides à la programmation (dans un langage déterminé)** = language support environment; **feuille** *ou* **formulaire de programmation** = program coding sheet *ou* form; **langage de programmation** = programming language; **langage de programmation évolué** *ou* **de haut niveau** = high-level (programming) language (HLL); **langage de programmation PL/1** = programming langage/1 *ou* PL/1; **normes** *ou* **standards de programmation** = programming standards; **ordinogramme de programmation** = program flowchart; **outil de programmation** = software tool; **pas** *ou* **étape de programmation** = program step

programme *nm* **(a)** *(d'ordinateur)* (computer) program; **j'ai omis une instruction importante ce qui a produit le crash du programme et détruit tous les fichiers contenus sur le disque** = I forgot to insert an important instruction which caused a program to crash, erasing all the files on the disk; **programme activé par commande** = command-driven program; **programme agenda** = diary management; **programme d'application** = applications program; **programme d'amorçage** = bootstrap loader; **programme d'assemblage** = assembly (language) program; **programme de**

bibliothèque = library program *ou* library routine; **programme canon** = *(qui tourne sans erreur du premier coup)* blue-ribbon program; **programme sur cartes perforées** = program cards; **programme de commande** = master control program (MCP); **programme compilateur** = translator program; **programme de contrôle** = checking program *ou* monitor program; **programme de contrôle d'entrée/sortie** = input/output control program; **programme de contrôle de tâche** = job control program; **programme convertisseur** *ou* **programme de conversion** = conversion program; **programme débogué** *ou* **déverminé** = debugged program; **programme de diagnostic** = maintenance routine; **programme du domaine public** *ou* **qui n'est plus protégé par un copyright** = program which is in the public domain; **programme éditeur** = editor program; **programme d'édition de texte** = text editor; **exécution d'un programme d'édition** = editing run; **programme extensible** *ou* **ouvert** = open-ended program; **programme de fusionnement de données** = collator; **programme d'insertion directe** = direct-insert routine *ou* subroutine; **programme intégré** = integrated program *ou* integrated software; **programme interpréteur** = interpreter; **programme interprétatif** = interpretative program; **programme itératif** = loop program *ou* looping program; **programme de lancement (d'un système)** = bootstrap; **programme linéaire** = in-line program *ou* linear program; **programme de localisation de panne** = fault location program; **programme en logique câblée** = hardwired program; **programme de maintenance** = housekeeping routine *ou* maintenance program; **programme en mémoire centrale** = core program; **programme (élémentaire) de mise en route** = bootstrap (loader); **programme multiphase** = multiphase program; **programme objet** = object program; **programme portable** *ou* **transportable (d'une machine à l'autre)** *ou* **programme d'une grande portabilité** = portable program *ou* canned program; **programme prêt à être exécuté** = executable form; **programme prioritaire** = high priority program *ou* foreground program; **programme non prioritaire** = background program; **programme résident** = internally stored program; **programme de retraitement** =

postprocessor; **programme source** *ou* **d'origine** = source program; **programme superviseur** = executive program *ou* supervisor program; **programme système** = systems program; **programme de test** = exerciser; **programme de traduction** *ou* **d'interprétation** *ou* **programme traducteur** = translator (program); **programme (d')** **utilisateur** = user program; **programme à** **usage multiple** *ou* **multi-fonction** = general purpose program; **programme utilitaire** = utility (program); **appeler un** **programme** = to call a program; **bibliothèque de programmes** = program library; **bibliothèque de programmes** **d'entrée/sortie** = input/output library; **boucle de programme** *ou* **looping** program; **branche d'un** **programme** = program branch; **chargeur de programme de lancement** = initial program loader (IPL); **commande** *ou* **instruction d'un programme** = program instruction; **compilation de programme** = program compilation; **contrôle d'un** **programme sur papier** = desk check; **crash** *ou* **défaillance d'un programme** = program crash; **création d'un programme** = program generation; **développement** **d'un programme** = program development; **documentation relative à** **l'utilisation d'un programme** = program documentation; **écrire un programme** = to program *ou* to write a program; **l'utilisateur ne peut pas écrire de** **programme avec ce système** = the user cannot write a computer program with this system; **éditeur de programme** = program editor; **édition listée d'un** **programme sur imprimante** *ou* **listage** **d'un programme** = program listing; **environnement de développement de** **programmes** = program development system; **essai d'un programme** = program testing; **exécution d'un** **programme** = computer run *ou* program execution *ou* program run; **fichier** **programme** = program file; **générateur** **de programme** = program generator; **lanceur de programme de chargement** = initial program header; **langage de** **conception de programme** = program design language (PDL); **ligne** **(d'instruction) d'un programme** = program line; **numéro de référence d'une** **ligne d'un programme** = program line number; **maintenance d'un programme** = program maintenance; **mémoire (de)** **programme** = program storage; **mise en** **place d'un programme concurrent** = counterprogramming; **nom d'un**

programme = program name; **pile** **d'instructions d'un programme** = program stack; **segment de programme** = overlay *ou* program segment; **spécifications d'un programme** = program specifications; **structure d'un** **programme** = program structure; **technique d'évaluation et de révision de** **programme** = program evaluation and review technique (PERT); **test de** **programme** = program testing; **transfert** **d'un programme (dans une autre partie de** **la mémoire)** = program relocation; **vérification (du bon fonctionnement) d'un** **programme** = program verification **(b)** *(de radio ou de télévision)* programme; *US* program; **les programmes destinés** **aux enfants sont présentés tôt dans la** **soirée** = children's programmes are scheduled for early evening viewing; **ils** **tournaient un programme sur les** **animaux sauvages** = they were filming a wild life programme; **programme de** **télévision (de caractère) éducatif** = educational TV (ETV) programme; **programme filmé** *ou* **en différé** = canned programme

◊ **programmé, -ée** *adj* programmed *ou* set; **arrêt programmé** = programmed halt; **saut de page programmé** = forced page break; **signalisation à contrôle** **programmé (en mémoire)** = stored program signalling; **programmé d'avance** = preprogrammed *ou* preset

◊ **programmer** *vtr* to code *ou* to program *ou* to set; *(une PROM)* to blast; **nous avons programmé la marge de droite** **à 80 caractères** = we set the right-hand margin at 80 characters; **qui peut être** **programmé suivant les besoins de** **l'utilisateur** = user-selectable; **programmer d'avance** = to preprogram *ou* to preset; **on avait programmé d'avance** **les nouveaux paramètres de page de** **l'imprimante** = the printer was preset with new page parameters; **programmer** **de nouveau** = to reprogram *ou* to reset; **programmer les points d'arrêt** = to set breakpoints

◊ **programmeur, -euse** *n* (computer) programmer; **le programmeur n'a pas** **encore terminé le nouveau logiciel** = the programmer is still working on the new software; **programmeur d'application** = applications programmer; **programmeur** **de ROM** *ou* **de mémoire morte** = burner; **programmeur (de) système** = systems programmer; **ingénieur programmeur** = software engineer

progressif, -ive *adj* progressive; **changement progressif** = phased change-over; **dégradation progressive** = graceful degradation; **système disjoncteur progressif** = fail soft system

projecteur *nm* projector; **projecteur de diapositives** = slide projector *ou* diascope; **magnétophone avec interface synchro pour projecteur de diapos** = slide/sync recorder; **projecteur de documents opaques** = episcope *ou* epidiascope; **projecteur de cinéma** *ou* **de films** = film projector; **projecteur synchronisé** = interlock projector; **projecteur (de) télévision** = television projector
◊ **projection** *nf* projection; **la projection du film est commencée** = the film is now being screened; **salle de projection** = projection room

projet *nm* plan *ou* project
◊ **projeter** *vtr* (a) *(un film)* to screen *ou* to replay; **nous avons projeté le film image par image** = we played *ou* stepped forward the film one frame at a time (b) to plan; **il projette maintenant d'informatiser le service des ventes** = his latest project is computerizing the sales team *ou* now he's planning to computerize the sales team
◊ **projeteur** *nm* designer

PROLOG = PROGRAMMING IN LOGIC; **langage PROLOG** = PROLOG

PROM = PROGRAMMABLE READ ONLY MEMORY; **charger une PROM** = to blow a PROM; **effacer une PROM** = to wash PROM; **mémoire PROM** = programmable memory (PROM); **PROM effaçable par ultraviolet** = ultraviolet erasable PROM; **programmateur de PROM** = PROM burner *ou* programmer; *voir aussi* MEMOIRE

promouvoir *vtr (par publicité)* to plug *ou* to promote

propagation *nf* (a) propagation; **propagation d'erreurs** = error propagation (b) **délai** *ou* **temps de propagation** = gate delay *ou* propagation time; **le délai de propagation dans une voie de communication crée une** distorsion du signal = propagation delay in the transmission path causes signal distortion; **temps de propagation aller (et) retour** = up and down propagation time
◊ **propagé, -ée** *adj* **erreur propagée** = propagated error
◊ **propager** *vtr* to propagate
◊ **se propager** *vpr* to propagate; **erreur qui se propage** = propagating error

proportion *nf* proportion
◊ **proportionnel, -elle** *adj* **espacement proportionnel** = proportional spacing
◊ **proportionnellement** *adv* proportionally *ou* in proportion

propriété *nf* **propriété littéraire** = copyright

prospectus *nm* booklet; **prospectus publicitaire** = brochure; *US* broadside; **envoi de prospectus publicitaires** = mailing shot; **prospectus envoyé par la poste** = mailing piece; **prospectus publicitaires sans intérêt** = junk mail

protecteur, -trice *adj* protective
◊ **protection** *nf* (a) *(de logiciel ou de mémoire)* protection; **protection des accès mémoire** = fetch protect; **(dispositif de) protection anticopie** *ou* **contre la copie** = copy protect *ou* copy protection (device); **il arrive qu'une protection anticopie défectueuse entraîne la détérioration du disque dur** = a hard disk may crash because of faulty copy protection; **protection des données** = data protection; **(logiciel** *ou* **dispositif de) protection de fichier** = file protection *ou* file security; **protection des limites (de mémoire)** = boundary protection; **(dispositif de) protection de la mémoire** = memory protect (device); **(dispositif de) protection par mot de passe** = interlock; **protection de page** = page protection; **anneau** *ou* **bague de protection d'écriture** = write-permit ring; **bande de protection** = guard band; **bit de protection** = guard bit; **les disquettes sont rangées dans des boîtiers de protection rigides** = the disks are housed in hard protective cases; **clé de protection** = protection key; **encoche** *ou* **volet de protection d'écriture** = write-protect tab; **dispositif de protection d'écriture (de fichier)** = file protect tab (b) *(d'un fil)* **mise à nu de protection** =

demarcation strip; *(électrique)* **transformateur de protection** = isolation transformer

◊ **protégé, -ée** *adj* **(a)** protected; **protégé contre toute détérioration** *ou* **destruction (accidentelle)** = crash-protected; **si vous vous servez d'un disque protégé contre la destruction accidentelle, vous ne perdrez jamais vos données** = if the disk is crash-protected, you will never lose your data; **champ protégé** = protected field; **non protégé** = unprotected; **champ non protégé** = unprotected field; **emplacement protégé** = protected location; **mémoire protégée** = protected storage; **routage adaptatif protégé** = isolated adaptive routing; **zone protégée** = isolated location **(b)** *(par un copyright)* copyright *ou* copyrighted; **oeuvre protégée par un copyright** = work which is copyrighted *ou* copyright work *ou* work still in copyright; **programme qui n'est plus protégé par un copyright** = program which is out of copyright *ou* which is in the public domain

◊ **protéger** *vtr* **(a)** to protect; **tous les disques sont protégés contre la copie** = all disks are copy protected; **le programme n'est pas protégé contre la copie** = the program is not copy protected; **le nouveau programme ne sera pas protégé contre la copie** = the new program will come without copy protection; **protéger (une disquette) contre l'écriture indésirée** = to write protect (a disk); **le mot de passe est censé protéger la base de données contre le piratage** = the password is supposed to exclude hackers from the database; **il est protégé par un relais à 5A** = it is relay-rated at 5 Amps **(b)** *(à l'aide d'un écran)* to screen *ou* to shield

protocole *nm* protocol; **protocole de communication** = line control *ou* link control procedure (LCP); *(entre deux postes)* **protocole de mise en communication** = full handshaking; *(entre CPU et périphérique)* **protocole d'échange d'informations** = CPU handshaking; **protocoles (de communication) normalisés** = protocol standards; *(entre deux postes)* **protocole d'interfaçage HDLC** = high-level data link control (HDLC); *(de message)* **protocole de routage** = routing overheads; **protocole standard de contrôle de liaisons** = basic mode link

control; *(d'un système)* **protocole de traçage** *ou* **de contrôle** *ou* **de vérification** = audit trail; **protocole de validation de transfert (de données)** = handshake *ou* handshaking

prototypage *nm* prototyping

◊ **prototype** *nm* prototype; **fabrication de prototype(s)** = prototyping

provenant *adj* coming from *ou* generated by; **interruption provenant d'une machine** = hardware interrupt

◊ **provenir (de)** *vi* to derive (from)

provisoire *adj* temporary; **correction** *ou* **modification provisoire** = patch

Ps = PICOSECONDE

pseudo- *préfixe* pseudo-

◊ **pseudo-aléatoire** *adj* pseudo-random; **générateur de nombres pseudo-aléatoires** = pseudo-random number generator

◊ **pseudocode** *nm* P-code *ou* pseudo-code

◊ **pseudo-instruction** *nf* pseudo-instruction *ou* quasi-instruction *ou* P-code

pub *nf (familier)* commercial; **ils ont fait un véritable matraquage publicitaire avec leurs six pubs sur les séjours en Espagne** = they ran six commercials plugging holidays in Spain

public *nm* **entreprise de diffusion d'informations grand public** = common carrier; **revue grand public** = mass market magazine

◊ **public, publique** *adj* public; **code chiffré** *ou* **cryptage à clé publique** = public key cipher (system); **domaine public** = public domain (PD); **progiciel du domaine public** = program in the public domain *ou* program which is out of copyright; **réseau public de transmission de données** = public data network; **réseau téléphonique public commuté** = public switched telephone network (PSTN); **connexion au réseau public commuté** = public dial port; **satellite de transmission publique** = domestic satellite

publication *nf* (a) *(action)* publication *ou* publishing; **la publication du rapport sur la confidentialité de l'information =** the publication of the report on data protection; **publication assistée par ordinateur (PAO) =** desktop publishing (DTP) *ou* electronic publishing (b) *(écrit)* publication

publicitaire *adj* (a) imprimé *ou* **matériel publicitaire =** publicity matter *ou* display material; **prospectus publicitaire =** leaflet *ou* mailing piece; **envoi de prospectus publicitaires =** mailing shot; **support publicitaire =** advertising medium

◊ **publicité** *nf* (a) publicity; **la publicité pour la nouvelle voiture a été faite dans la presse nationale =** the new car has been advertised in the national press; **publicité directe =** direct mailing; **publicité lieu de vente (PLV) =** point-of-sale material (b) *(à la télévision)* **la publicité =** commercials

publier *vtr* to publish; **la maison d'édition publie principalement des livres de référence =** the company specializes in publishing reference books; **la maison publie des revues destinées aux hommes/femmes d'affaires =** the company specializes in publications for the business reader; **la société a publié un communiqué de presse au sujet du lancement du nouveau scanner =** the company sent out a press release about the launch of the new scanner

publipostage *nm* direct mailing

puce *nf* (a) chip *ou* microchip; **nombre de puces (sur une carte, etc.) =** chip count; **le nombre de puces est malheureusement encore trop élevé =** it's no good, the chip count is still too high; **puce de diagnostic =** diagnostic chip; **ils font des recherches sur les puces de diagnostic destinées au contrôle des ordinateurs équipés de processeurs =** they are carrying out research on diagnostic chips to test computers that contain processors; **puce géante =** jumbo chip; **puce mémoire =** memory chip; **puce microprocesseur =** microprocessor chip; **puce musicale =** music chip *ou* sound chip; **puce RAM =** RAM chip;

puce de silicium = silicon chip; **puce de synthèse vocale =** speech chip; **carte à puce =** chip card *ou* smart card; **les cartes à puce aident à réduire le nombre de fraudes =** smart cards reduce fraud; **micro-ordinateur de contrôle à puce unique =** single chip microcontroller; **ordinateur à puce unique =** single chip computer (b) *(imprimerie)* bullet

> bourrer les armes de puces électroniques ne suffit pas; il faut aussi des programmes pour les faire fonctionner
>
> *L'Express*
>
> la puce avec la plus grande capacité disponible actuellement sur le marché peut contenir 4 millions de bits d'information
>
> *Electronique (Suisse)*

puissance *nf* (a) power; **puissance de calcul =** computing power; **puissance maximale** *ou* **réelle disponible =** available power; **puissance d'un ordinateur =** computer power; **puissance d'ouverture effective =** effective aperture; **ordinateur de grande puissance =** supercomputer; **unité de puissance vocale =** voice unit (b) *(math)* **5 à la puissance deux égale 25 =** 5 to the power 2 is equal to 25; **élévation (d'un nombre) à la puissance x =** exponentiation; **puissance fractionnaire =** root

puits *nm* (data) sink; **arborescence en puits =** sink tree

pupitre *nm* console; **pupitre de commande d'un opérateur =** operator's console

◊ **pupitreur, -euse** *n* keyboarder

pur, -e *adj* pure; **code pur =** pure code; **son pur =** pure tone

purée *nf (familier)* mush; **zone de purée =** mush area

purger *vtr* to purge

pylône *nm (de radio ou de télévision)* radio mast *ou* TV mast

pyramidal, -e *adj* **facteur pyramidal d'entrée =** fan-in; **facteur pyramidal de sortie =** fan-out

Qq

QD = QUADRUPLE DENSITE *voir aussi* QUADRUPLE

quadr- *préf* quadr-

quadrat *nm (papier)* quad

quadrature *nf (vidéo)* **(erreur de) quadrature** = quadrature

quadrillé, -ée *adj* **papier quadrillé** = graph paper

quadriphonique *adj* quadrophonic

quadruple **1** *nm* quadruple **2** *adj* quadruple *ou* quad; **quadruple densité** = quad density; **disquette quadruple densité (QD)** = quad density disk (QD)
◊ **quadruplex** *nm (signaux)* quadruplex

qualité *nf* **(a)** grade *ou* quality; **nous vérifions chaque lot pour nous assurer de la qualité** = we check each batch to make sure it is perfect; **qualité d'un circuit** = circuit grade; **qualité des données** = data reliability; **qualité du matériel** = hardware reliability; **de qualité supérieure** = high quality *ou* top quality; **assurance de qualité** = quality assurance; **bonne qualité** = good quality; **il existe un marché pour les ordinateurs d'occasion de bonne qualité** = there is a market for good quality secondhand computers; **contrôle de (la) qualité** = quality control; **responsable du contrôle de (la) qualité** = quality controller; **label de qualité** = quality label **(b)** *(sortie d'imprimante)* **qualité brouillon** *ou* **qualité listing** = draft printing; **qualité courrier** = near-letter-quality (NLQ); **qualité d'impression d'une imprimante** = printer quality

> doté d'une tête à 18 aiguilles, cette imprimante matricielle atteint la vitesse de 600cps (caractères par seconde) en qualité brouillon, et 150cps en qualité courrier
> *Action PC*

quantifiable *adj* quantifiable
◊ **quantificateur** *nm* **(a)** *(d'une quantité)* quantifier **(b)** *(d'une grandeur physique)* quantizer

◊ **quantification** *nf* **(a)** *(attribution d'une quantité)* quantification **(b)** *(d'une grandeur physique)* quantization; **erreur de quantification** = quantization error; **quantification d'amplitude** = amplitude quantization; **quantification de niveau quatre** = quaternary level quantization; **bruits de quantification** = quantizing noise

◊ **quantifier** *vtr* **(a)** *(attribuer une quantité)* to quantify; **il est impossible de quantifier l'effet du nouveau système informatique sur notre production** = it is impossible to quantify the effect of the new computer system on our production **(b)** *(une grandeur physique)* to quantize

quantité *nf* amount *ou* quantity; **grande quantité** = large quantity; **il a acheté une grande quantité de pièces détachées** = he bought a large quantity of spare parts; **quelle est la quantité maximale de données qu'on puisse traiter en une heure?** = what is the largest amount of data which can be processed in one hour?; **en grande quantité** = in bulk

quantum *nm* quantum

quarante *adj num* **disquette (de) quarante pistes** = forty-track disk

quartile *nm* quartile

quartz *nm* quartz; **horloge à quartz** = quartz (crystal) clock; **microphone à quartz** = crystal microphone; **oscillateur à quartz** = crystal oscillator

quasi- *préf* quasi-

quaternaire *adj* quaternary; *(voies de communication)* **groupe quaternaire** = super mastergroup

quatre 1 *nm* **quantification de niveau quatre** = quaternary level quantization 2 *adj num* **instruction à quatre adresses** = four-address instruction; **instruction quatre adresses plus une** = four-plus-one address instruction; **en quatre exemplaires** = in quadruplicate; **les relevés sont imprimés en quatre exemplaires** = the statements are printed in quadruplicate; **magnétophone à quatre pistes** = four-track recorder

◇ **quatrième** *nm&adj* fourth; **langages de quatrième génération** = fourth generation languages; **ordinateurs de quatrième génération** = fourth generation computers

◇ **quatre-vingts** *adj num* **disque de quatre-vingts pistes** = eighty-track disk; **écran (de) quatre-vingts colonnes** = eighty-column screen

question *nf* query *ou* question; **poser une question** = to query (something) *ou* to ask a question; **poser une question à quelqu'un** = to ask someone a question; **répondre à une question** = to answer a question; **elle a refusé de répondre aux questions concernant les claviers défectueux** = she refused to answer questions about faulty keyboards

◇ **questionnaire** *nm* questionnaire; **remplir** *ou* **compléter un questionnaire** = to answer *ou* to fill in a questionnaire; **envoyer un questionnaire concernant le système pour faire un sondage d'opinion auprès des utilisateurs** = to send out a questionnaire to test the opinions of users of the system

quintet *nm* quintet

quitter *vtr* to quit; **n'oubliez pas de sauvegarder votre texte avant de quitter le système** = do not forget to save your text before you quit the system; **pour mettre des en-têtes, il faut quitter ce programme et entrer dans un autre** = you have to exit to another editing system to add headlines

quotidien *nm (journal qui paraît tous les jours)* daily (newspaper); **les grands quotidiens** = the main dailies *ou* the national press

quotient *nm* quotient

QWERTY *(utilisé surtout dans les pays anglo-saxons)* **clavier QWERTY** = QWERTY keyboard; **l'ordinateur possède un clavier QWERTY ordinaire** = the computer has a normal QWERTY keyboard

Rr

R et D = RECHERCHE ET DEVELOPPEMENT; **service R et D =** R & D department; *voir aussi* RECHERCHE

raccord *nm (de bande ou de film)* **faire un raccord =** to splice; **ruban de raccord =** splicing tape

◊ **raccordement** *nm (câble de télévision)* drop line; *(au réseau téléphonique)* interconnection; **boîte de raccordement =** junction box; **cordon de raccordement d'un tableau de distribution =** patchcord; *(de téléphone)* **ligne de raccordement =** recording trunk; **panneau de raccordement =** plugboard *ou* patchboard; **point de raccordement =** terminal

◊ **raccorder** *vtr* to join; *(film)* to splice; **utilisez de la colle ou du ruban gommé pour raccorder les extrémités du film =** you can use glue or splicing tape to splice the ends of the film

raccourcir *vtr* to shorten; **nous avons dû raccourcir le fichier pour réussir à le sauvegarder sur une seule disquette =** we had to shorten the file to be able to save it on one floppy

raccroché, -ée *adj (combiné)* on hook; **coupure au premier raccroché =** first party release

◊ **raccrocher** *vtr&i* to hang up; **à la fin de la conversation téléphonique, elle a raccroché =** after she had finished talking (on the telephone) she hung up

racine *nf* root; **racine carrée =** square root; **la racine carrée de 25 est 5 =** the square root of 25 is 5

rack *nm* rack; **(cartes) montées en rack =** rack mounted (boards)

radar *nm* = RADIO DETECTING AND RANGING radar

radial *adj* radial; *(données ou programmes)* **transfert radial =** radial transfer

radiateur *nm* radiator

radiation *nf* radiation

radier *vtr* to remove *ou* to delete; **le fichier a été radié du répertoire de la disquette =** the file entry was removed from the floppy disk directory

radio *nf* **(a)** *(radiodiffusion)* radio; **j'ai entendu la nouvelle à la radio =** I heard the news on the radio; **il a diffusé les dernières informations à la radio =** he broadcast the latest news over the radio; **radio à large bande =** broadband radio; **radio CB** *ou* **radio à bande CB =** citizens band radio (CB); **le signal de cet émetteur radio est très faible =** the signal from this radio station is very weak; **émetteur/récepteur radio =** radio transceiver; **fréquence radio =** radio frequency (RF); **micro radio =** radio microphone; **poste (de) radio =** radio; **récepteur radio =** radio receiver; **spectre de fréquences radio =** radio spectrum; **station de radio =** broadcasting station *ou* radio station; **transmission de données par radio =** radio transmission of data **(b)** = RADIOGRAPHIE X-ray

◊ **radio-amateur** *nm* radio ham

◊ **radiocommunication** *nf* radiocommunications

◊ **radiodiffusion** *nf* broadcast *ou* broadcasting; **radiodiffusion par satellite =** satellite broadcasting; **réseau de radiodiffusion =** broadcast network

◊ **radioélectrique** *adj* **ondes radioélectriques =** radio waves

◊ **radiofréquence** *nf* radio frequency (RF); **la gamme des radiofréquences s'étend de seulement quelques hertz à des centaines de gigahertz =** the radio frequency range extends from a few hertz to hundreds of gigahertz

radiographie *nf* X-ray
◊ **radiographier** *vtr* to X-ray

radiophonique *adj* **diffusion radiophonique** = broadcast; **le récepteur a capté l'émission radiophonique** = the receiver picked up the broacast; **réseau radiophonique** = radio network

radiorecherche *nf* **(système de) radiorecherche de personne** = radio paging

radioscopie *nf* X-ray imaging

radiotélégraphie *nf* radio telegraphy *ou* carrier telegraphy

radiotéléphone *ou* **radio-téléphone** *nm* radio phone *ou* radio telephone *ou* private mobile radio (PMR); **radiotéléphone (de type) cellulaire** = cellular radio; **radiotéléphone mobile** = mobile radiophone; **radiotéléphone portatif** = hand portable set
◊ **radiotéléphonique** *adj* **réseau radiotéléphonique** = cellular service

radiotransmission *nf* radio transmission of data

rafale *nf* burst; **rafale d'erreurs** = error burst; **rafale de signaux couleur** = colour burst

rafraîchir *vtr* to refresh; **(instruction de) rafraîchir l'écran** = screen refresh; **mémoire qui demande à être rafraîchie** = regenerative memory; **une RAM dynamique a besoin d'être rafraîchie toutes les 250ns** = dynamic RAM is regenerative memory - it needs to be refreshed every 250ns; **l'écran peut être comparé à une mémoire qui demande à être rafraîchie; il doit être balayé régulièrement pour éviter de présenter des images instables** = the CRT display can be thought of as regenerative memory, it requires regular refresh picture scans to prevent flicker
◊ **rafraîchissement** *nm (de l'écran ou de la mémoire)* **fréquence de rafraîchissement** = refresh rate;

fréquence de rafraîchissement de la mémoire RAM *ou* **de la mémoire vive** = RAM refresh rate; **signal de rafraîchissement de la mémoire** = memory refresh signal; **(signal de) rafraîchissement de la mémoire RAM** = RAM refresh (signal)

raie *nf* stripe; **raie de couleur** = colour stripe

ralenti *nm* slow motion; **repassez ce film au ralenti** = play the film again in slow motion; **le film enchaîne sur un ralenti** = the film switched to slow motion

RAM *nf* = RANDOM ACCESS MEMORY; **RAM autorafraîchie** *ou* **auto-entretenue** *ou* **autorégénérable** = self-refreshing RAM; **RAM dynamique** = dynamic RAM *ou* dynamic random access memory (DRAM); **RAM partielle** = partial RAM; **(mémoire) RAM statique** = static RAM; **RAM vidéo** = video memory *ou* video RAM (VRAM); **disque RAM** = silicon disk *ou* RAM disk; **mémoire RAM** = random access memory (RAM); **puce RAM** = RAM chip; *voir aussi* MÉMOIRE

rang *nm* row; **système à double rang de broches (parallèles)** = dual-in-line package (DIL *ou* DIP)

rangement *nm* storing; *(en mémoire)* **emplacement de rangement** = bucket
◊ **ranger** *vtr (en mémoire)* to plant *ou* to store *ou* to write; **le temps d'accès est le temps requis pour lire ou pour ranger une donnée en mémoire** = access time is the time taken to read from or write to a location in memory

rapide *adj* fast *ou* quick *ou* rapid; **c'est un disque dur très rapide avec un temps d'accès de 28ms** = this hard disk is fast, it has an access time of 28ms; **accès rapide** = rapid access; **mémoire à accès rapide** = fast access memory (FAM); **clavier rapide** = key rollover *ou* N-key rollover; **exécution rapide d'un programme** = fast program execution; **ligne de transmission rapide** = fast line; **mémoire centrale rapide** = fast core; **dans ce système, la mémoire centrale rapide sert de bloc-notes pour tous les**

calculs = the fast core is used as a scratchpad for all calculations in this system; **périphérique rapide =** fast peripheral; **report rapide =** high speed carry *ou* ripple-through carry; **saut rapide =** high-speed skip; **terminal de mise à jour rapide =** bulk update terminal; **tri rapide =** quicksort

◇ **rapidement** *adv* quickly

◇ **rapidité** *nf* speed

rappel *nm* **(a)** *(de données en mémoire)* recall **(b)** *(téléphone)* redial; **système de rappel automatique =** ring back system; **modem** *ou* **téléphone avec système de rappel automatique =** auto-redial modem *ou* telephone **(c)** *(machine à écrire ou traitement de texte)* backspace; **caractère de rappel (du curseur) =** backspace character

◇ **rappeler** *vtr* **(a)** *(de la mémoire)* to recall; **rappeler de mémoire centrale en mémoire auxiliaire =** to roll out; **rappelez le fichier précédent à l'écran =** call up the previous file **(b)** *(au téléphone)* to phone back; **M. Dubois a téléphoné en votre absence et a demandé que vous le rappeliez =** Mr Dubois called while you were out and asked if you would phone him back; **le président est en conférence, pourriez-vous rappeler dans une demi-heure environ? =** the chairman is in a meeting, can you phone back in about half an hour? **(c)** to quote; **veuillez rappeler ce numéro de référence dans votre réponse =** in your reply please quote this number

rapport *nm* **(a)** ratio; **le rapport 10 sur 5 est égal à 2:1 =** the ratio of 10 to 5 is 2:1; **code à rapport (de bits) constant** *ou* **fixe =** constant ratio code; **rapport de contraste d'un imprimé =** print contrast ratio; **rapport de discrimination** *ou* **rapport un à zéro =** one to zero ratio; **rapport longueur/largeur (d'un pixel) =** aspect ratio; **rapport signal/bruit =** signal to noise ratio *ou* s/n ratio (of a pixel) **(b)** relationship; **(données) qui n'ont aucun rapport (entre elles) =** disjointed (data) **(c)** report; **rapport d'exceptions** *ou* **d'anomalies =** exception report

le laboratoire de la FNAC a réalisé des mesures et obtenu un rapport signal/bruit de 76 à 83dB, selon les appareils
Science et Vie

rapprocher *vtr (lignes ou caractères)* to close up

rassembler *vtr* to accumulate *ou* to collect *ou* to gather; **nous avons rassemblé progressivement un impressionnant fichier d'adresses =** we have gradually accumulated a large databank of names and addresses

raster *nm* raster

ratelier *nm* **un ratelier pour** *ou* **à bandes magnétiques =** a rack for holding mag tapes

ratio *nm* ratio; **ratio d'activité d'un fichier =** file activity ratio

rationnel, -elle *adj* rational; **nombre rationnel =** rational number; **24/7 est un nombre rationnel =** 24 over 7 is a rational number; **on peut écrire 0,333 sous la forme du nombre rationnel 1/3 =** 0.333 can be written as the rational number 1/3

rayer *vtr* to delete

rayon *nm* beam *ou* ray; **tube à rayons cathodiques =** cathode ray tube (CRT); **les rayons lumineux se propagent dans la fibre optique =** rays of light pass down the optical fibre; **déflexion d'un rayon lumineux =** beam deflection; **le laser émet un mince rayon lumineux =** a laser produces a thin beam of light; **rayons X =** X-rays

◇ **rayonnant, -e** *adj* radiant; **élément rayonnant =** radiating element; *(d'une antenne)* radiator; **énergie rayonnante =** radiant energy

◇ **rayonnement** *nm* radiation *ou* ray *ou* light; **rayonnement électromagnétique =** electromagnetic radiation; **rayonnement indirect =** indirect ray; **rayonnement infrarouge =** infrared light (IR light); **rayonnement ultraviolet =** ultra-violet light (UV light); **de rayonnement =** radiant; **énergie de rayonnement =** radiant energy

◇ **rayonner** *vi* to radiate

rayures *nfpl (sur image)* streaking

réacheminement *nm* redirection *ou* re-routing; *(téléphone)* **dispositif de réacheminement d'appel** = call diverter

◊ **réacheminer** *vtr* to redirect *ou* to reroute; **le dispositif de transfert d'appel sert à réacheminer les appels** = the call diverter will re-route calls

réactance *nf* reactance

◊ **réactif, -ive** *adj* **mode réactif** = reactive mode

◊ **réaction** *nf* **(a)** reaction *ou* response; **réaction chimique** = chemical reaction; **la réaction des films photosensibles varie suivant l'intensité de la lumière** = light-sensitive films register light intensity; **entrer en réaction avec une autre substance** = to react with something **(b)** *(information)* feedback; **nous commençons à connaître les réactions des clients face au nouveau système** = we are getting customer feedback on the new system; **boucle de réaction** = feedback loop **(c)** *(d'un circuit)* **boucle de réaction** = feedback loop

réadressable *adj* relocatable; **programme réadressable** = relocatable program

◊ **réadressage** *nm* relocation

réagir *vi* to react; **réagir à quelque chose** = to react to something

réaligner *vtr* **réaligner à gauche** = range left

réalisateur, -trice *n* *(d'un film)* director

◊ **réalisation** *nf* **(a)** *(d'un projet)* implementation **(b)** *(d'un film)* direction

◊ **réaliser** *vtr* **(a)** *(un projet)* to implement **(b)** *(un film)* to direct **(c)** *(dessiner)* **c'est elle qui a réalisé le nouvel ordinateur** = she is the designer of the new computer

réapprovisionnement *nm* **système de réapprovisionnement informatisé** *ou* **géré par ordinateur** = computerized stock control

réassemblage *nm* *(hashing)* folding

rebond *nm* bounce; **rebond de contact** = contact bounce; **rebond d'une touche de clavier** = keyboard contact bounce

rebours *nm* **à rebours** = backward *ou* backwards; **aller à rebours** = to backtrack

rebut *nm* junk; **informations de rebut** = garbage

◊ **rebuter** *vtr* to discard

recadrage *nm* *(d'une image sur l'écran)* elastic banding *ou* rubber banding; **le recadrage d'une image est plus facile à réaliser avec la souris** = elastic banding is much easier to control with a mouse

récemment *adv* recently; **algorithme utilisé le moins récemment** = least recently used algorithm

◊ **récent, -e** *adj* recent *ou* new *ou* up to date; **un système informatique de modèle récent** = an up-to-date computer system

récepteur *nm* receiver; *(pour système d'appel de personne)* **récepteur de poche** = pager *ou* radio pager *ou* radio paging device; **vous pourriez contacter votre vendeur s'il était équipé d'un récepteur de poche** = you could contact your salesman if he had a radio pager; **récepteur portatif** = hand receiver; **récepteur radio** = radio receiver; **votre signal a été capté très clairement par le récepteur radio** = the radio receiver picked up your signal very strongly; **contrôle par le récepteur** = backwards supervision

◊ **récepteur, -trice** *adj* **bobine réceptrice** = pickup reel; **terminal récepteur (de données)** = data sink

◊ **réception** *nf* **(a)** *(d'un signal)* reception; **cette antenne ne donne pas un bonne réception** = signal reception is bad with that aerial; **accusé de réception** = acknowledgement; *(d'un message)* acknowledge; **caractère d'accusé de réception** = acknowledge character; **envoyer un accusé de réception** = to acknowledge; **accusé de réception négatif** = negative acknowledge (NAK *ou* NACK); **accusé de réception positif** = affirmative acknowledge (ACK *ou* ACKNLG); **accuser réception** = to acknowledge; **point de réception** = far end *ou* receiving end; **terminal de réception** = receive only terminal **(b) angle de réception** = acceptance angle; **un rayon lumineux d'incidence supérieure à l'angle de réception ne sera pas transmis** = a light beam at an angle greater than the acceptance angle of the lens will not be transmitted **(c) bobine de réception** = take-up reel; **placez la bobine pleine sur cet axe-ci et la bobine de réception sur celui-là** = put the full reel on this spindle, and feed the tape into the take-up reel on the other spindle

◊ **réceptrice** *voir aussi* RECEPTEUR

recevoir *vtr (signal)* to receive; **un multiplexeur 4/1 reçoit sur 4 canaux et émet sur un seul** = a 4 to 1 multiplexor combines four inputs into a single output; **le signal reçu devrait être amplifié** = the received *ou* RXed signal needs to be amplified; **(signal de) prêt à transmettre/recevoir** = data set ready (DSR)

rechargeable *adj* rechargeable; **batterie** *ou* **pile rechargeable** = rechargeable battery; **on utilise une pile rechargeable comme alimentation auxiliaire pour la mémoire RAM quand le système est éteint** = a rechargeable battery is used for RAM back-up when the system is switched off

◊ **rechargement** *nm* **(a)** *(d'une pile)* recharging **(b)** *(d'un programme, après incident)* reloading *ou* rollback

◊ **recharger** *vtr* **(a)** *(une batterie d'accumulateurs)* to replenish; *(une pile)* to recharge **(b)** *(un programme)* to reload; **nous avons rechargé le programme après la panne** = we reloaded the program after the crash

recherche *nf* **(a)** search retrieval; **recherche associative** = chaining search; **recherche (par coupe) binaire** = binary search *ou* binary chop *ou* binary look-up; **recherche de bloc** = block retrieval; **recherche en chaîne** = chaining search; **système de recherche par descripteurs** = aspect system; **(méthode de) recherche dichotomique** *ou* **par dichotomie** = dichotomizing search *ou* binary chop; **recherche documentaire** = data retrieval *ou* information retrieval (IR) *ou* text retrieval; **recherche documentaire en ligne** = on-line information retrieval; **centre de recherche documentaire** =

information retrieval centre; **système de recherche documentaire** *ou* **de documents** = document retrieval system; **recherche effective** = effective search; **vitesse de recherche effective** = effective search speed; **recherche exhaustive** *ou* **très poussée** = exhaustive search; **recherche par mots-clés** = disjunctive search; **clé de recherche** = (search) key; **nous avons sélectionné les enregistrements en utilisant le mot DISK comme clé de recherche** = we selected all the records with the word DISK in their keys; **recherche rétrospective** = retrospective search; **recherche séquentielle** = sequential search *ou* linear search; **recherche (et extraction) de texte** = text retrieval; **recherche de zone** = area search; **faire une recherche** = to search; **zone de recherche** = seek area **(b)** *(traitement de texte) (instruction)* **recherche et remplace** = search and replace *ou* find and replace; **recherche globale et remplace** = global search and replace **(c)** *(imprimante à)* **recherche logique** = logic-seeking (printer); **récepteur à recherche de signal** = scanning radio receiver **(d)** research; **recherche et développement (R et D)** = research and development (R & D); **service de Recherche et Développement** *ou* **service R et D** = R & D department; **la société a dépensé des millions de dollars pour la recherche et le développement** = the company has spent millions of dollars on R & D

réciproque *adj (fonction logique)* **exclusion réciproque** = inequivalence *ou* symmetric difference

réclame *nf* publicity

recommencer *vtr* to start again; **recommencer l'exécution** = to rerun (a program)

reconfiguration *nf* reconfiguration

◊ **reconfigurer** *vtr* to reconfigure; **avec ce programme, il est possible de reconfigurer le système selon nos besoins** = this program allows us to reconfigure the system to our own requirements; **j'ai reconfiguré la structure des champs du fichier** = I reconfigured the field structure in the file

reconnaissable *adj* recognizable; **police de caractères reconnaissable par lecture optique** = optical font *ou* OCR font

reconnaissance *nf* **(a)** recognition *ou* sense; **reconnaissance automatique de débit d'une ligne (en bauds)** = auto-baud scanning *ou* auto-baud sensing; **reconnaissance de caractères magnétiques** = magnetic ink character recognition (MICR); **système de reconnaissance de caractères CSM (par identification des caractéristiques combinées)** = combined symbol matching (CSM); **reconnaissance de formes** = pattern recognition; **reconnaissance optique de caractères** = character recognition *ou* optical character recognition (OCR); **reconnaissance optique de marques** *ou* de **signes** *ou* de **symboles** = optical mark recognition (OMR); **reconnaissance de la parole** *ou* **reconnaissance vocale** = speech recognition *ou* voice recognition; **activé par reconnaissance des données** = data-driven; **logique de reconnaissance** = recognition logic **(b)** **label de reconnaisance de bande** = header label

◊ **reconnaître** *vtr* to recognize *ou* to distinguish; **le lecteur optique reconnaît difficilement certains caractères** = an OCR has difficulty in distinguishing certain characters; **le scanner reconnaît la plupart des polices de caractères** = the scanner will recognize most character fonts; **ne pas reconnaître** = to ignore

reconnecter *vtr* to reconnect

reconstituer *vtr (un message crypté)* to de-scramble; *(des données)* to reconstitute

◊ **reconstitution** *nf* **(a)** *(d'un message)* descrambling **(b)** *(de données)* reconstitution; **reconstitution de procédure** = backward recovery

recopier *vtr* to copy

record *nm* record; **production record** = peak output

recouvrement *nm* overlap; *(de segments de programme)* overlay; **segment de recouvrement** = overlay segment; **gestionnaire de segment de recouvrement** = overlay manager; **zone de segment de recouvrement** = overlay region; **utilisation d'une technique de recouvrement** = overlaying; **réseau à zone de recouvrement** = overlay network

recouvrir *vtr* **(a)** to overlap **(b)** *(d'une mince couche)* to coat with a thin layer *ou* to deposit a thin layer (of something)

◊ **se recouvrir** = *vpr* to overlap

recréer *vtr* to regenerate

rectangulaire *adj* rectangular; **coordonnées rectangulaires** = rectangular coordinates; **guide d'ondes rectangulaire** = rectangular waveguide

recto *nm (d'une feuille)* recto *ou* right-hand page; **presse qui imprime recto/verso** = perfector

reçu *nm* receipt; **reçu en double exemplaire** = receipt in duplicate

◊ **reçu, -e** *adj* **message reçu** = incoming message; **(nombre de) messages reçus** *ou* **données reçues** = incoming traffic

récupérable *adj* recoverable; **les données sont récupérables mais il faudra beaucoup de temps pour y arriver** = it is possible to recover the data but it can take a long time; **erreur récupérable** = recoverable error

◊ **récupération** *nf* recovery; **récupération de document** = document recovery; **récupération de fichier** = file recovery; *(à rebours)* backward recovery; **programme de récupération de fichier(s)** = file-recovery program *ou* utility; **la récupération des fichiers perdus peut se faire par une procédure de restauration** = the recovery of lost files can be carried out using a recovery procedure; **logiciel de récupération de fichiers (après incident)** = file-recovery utility

◊ **récupérer** *vtr* to recover *ou* to restore *ou* to retrieve; **il est impossible de récupérer un fichier perdu sans l'aide d'un programme de récupération de fichier** = a lost file cannot be found without a file-recovery utility; **(instruction de) récupérer des données et les transférer dans un registre** = collect transfer

récurrence *nf* boucle de récurrence = daisy-chain recursion

◊ **récurrent, -e** *adj* balayage récurrent = raster scanning

récursif, -ive *adj* recursive; **appel récursif** *ou* **procédure récursive** = recursive call; **routine récursive** = recursion *ou* recursive routine

rédaction *nf* editing; *(le bureau)* **la rédaction** = (i) editorial office; (ii) editorial board; **il travaille à la rédaction d'une revue de micro-informatique** = he edits a computer magazine

redéfinir *vtr* to redefine; **redéfinir la fonction d'une touche** = to redefine a key; **j'ai redéfini cette touche pour obtenir un 5** = I have redefined this key to display the figure five when pressed; **touche qui peut être redéfinie** = redefinable key

redémarrage *nm* restart; **redémarrage automatique** = auto restart

◊ **redémarrer** *vtr* to restart

redessiner *vtr* to redraw

rédiger *vtr* to write *ou* to put in writing; **rédiger un accord** = to put the agreement in writing

redistribution *nf* routage par redistribution = flooding

redondance *nf* redundancy; **contrôle par redondance** = redundancy checking; **contrôle par redondance cyclique** = cyclic redundancy check (CRC)

◊ **redondant, -e** *adj* redundant; **code redondant** = redundant code; **équipement redondant** = redundant equipment; **liaisons redondantes d'un réseau** = network redundancy

redonner *vtr* to give back *ou* to send back; **l'instruction RETOUR à la fin d'une routine permet de redonner la main au programme principal** = the RETURN instruction at the end of the routine sends control back to the main program

redressé, -ée *adj* rectified; **erreur qui peut être redressée** = recoverable error

◊ **redresser** *vtr* to rectify

◊ **redresseur** *nm&adj* **redresseur (de) simple alternance** = half wave rectifier; **circuit redresseur** = rectifier

réducteur *nm (de bruit)* muting device; **réducteur de fréquence** = frequency divider; **réducteur de signal audio** = audio compressor; **réducteur (de largeur de bande) vidéo** = video compressor

◊ **réduction** *nf* reduction; **réduction de bruit** = muting; **réduction du bruit d'interférence interstation** = interstation muting; **réduction de données** = data reduction; **réduction des performances** = (efficiency) degradation; **forte réduction** = high reduction

◊ **réduire** *vtr* to cut *ou* to minimize *ou* to reduce *ou* to shorten *ou* to shrink; **il nous faut réduire la reproduction en simili de 25% pour pouvoir l'insérer dans l'espace fixé** = we need a 25% reduction to fit the halftone in the space; **nous avons réduit les frais en diminuant le nombre des composants** = we minimized costs by cutting down the number of components; **les éditeurs ont demandé de réduire le premier chapitre** = the editors have asked for cuts in the first chapter; **on a demandé à l'auteur de réduire son manuscrit à 250 pages** = the author was asked to cut his manuscript to 250 pages; **on a réduit le dessin pour le faire entrer dans l'emplacement prévu** = the drawing was shrunk to fit the space; **réduire en proportion** = to scale down

◊ **réduit, -e** *adj* **affichage réduit** = part page display; **base de temps réduite** = fast time-scale; **carte (de taille) réduite** = short card; **processeur à jeu d'instructions réduit** = reduced instruction set computer (RISC); **matrice réduite** *ou* **tableau réduit** = sparse array; *(d'un livre)* **tirage réduit** = short run; **livre à tirage réduit** = short-run book

réécrire *vtr* to rewrite

réel, -elle *adj* real; **adresse réelle** = first-level address; **mémoire réelle** = real memory; **nombre réel** = real number; **temps réel** = real time; **entrée en temps réel** = real-time input; **exécution (d'un programme) en temps réel** = real time execution; **horloge en temps réel** = real-time clock; **multitâche en temps réel** = real-time multitasking; **système en temps réel** = real-time system; **dans un système en temps réel, le déplacement de l'image vers la gauche est parfaitement synchronisé au mouvement du manche à balai vers la gauche; s'il se produit un délai entre l'action et le résultat, il ne s'agit pas d'un véritable système en temps réel** = in a real-time system, as you move the joystick left, the image on the screen moves left; if there is a pause for processing it is not a true real-time system; **traitement en temps réel** = real-time processing

ré-entrant *adj* re-entrant; **programme ré-entrant** = re-entrant program *ou* code *ou* routine; **sous-programme ré-entrant** = closed *ou* linked subroutine

◊ **ré-entrée** *nf* re-entry; **point de ré-entrée** = re-entry point

refaire *vtr* to redo; **refaire à partir du début** = to redo from start; **est-ce que l'ordinateur peut refaire le graphique du produit de façon à en présenter une vue plongeante?** = can the computer redraw the graphics showing the product from the top view?

référençage *nm* referencing; **référençage d'entrée/sortie** = input/output referencing

◊ **référence** *nf* (a) reference *ou* cross reference; **référence par anticipation** = forward reference; **référence croisée** = cross reference; **adresse de référence** = reference address; **adresse de référence directe** = direct reference address; **faire référence (à)** = to refer (to); **fichier** *ou* **liste de référence** = authority file *ou* reference file *ou* list; **liste de référence** = reference list; **niveau de référence** = reference level; **période de référence** = reference time; **piste de référence** = library track; **système de référence** = reference retrieval system; **table** *ou* **tableau de référence** = reference table *ou* look-up table (LUT) *ou* translation table *ou* conversion table; **variable de référence d'une cellule** = cell reference variable (b) *(lignes guides)* **bord de référence** = aligning edge; **lignes de référence** = guide bars

◊ **référencer** *vtr* to reference

référentiel *adj* ensemble référentiel = universal set; **l'ensemble référentiel des nombres premiers inférieurs à dix et plus grands que deux est 3,5,7** = the universal set of prime numbers less than ten and greater than two is 3,5,7

référer *vtr (à une autre section d'un document)* to cross-reference
◊ **se référer (à)** *vpr* to refer (to)

refermer *vtr* to close up

réfléchi, -ie *adj* **code réfléchi** = reflected code; **code binaire réfléchi** = cyclic code; **code décimal réfléchi** = cyclic decimal code; **onde (radio) réfléchie** = backscatter; **signal réfléchi** = signal reflection
◊ **réfléchir** *vtr* to reflect; **dans un appareil reflex, l'image est refléchie par un miroir interne** = in a reflex camera, the image is reflected by an inbuilt mirror
◊ **réfléchissant, -e** *adj* reflective; **disque laser à surface réfléchissante** = reflective disk
◊ **réflectance** *nf* reflectance

reflet *nm (sur un film)* flare; **marqué d'un reflet** = flared
◊ **refléter** *vtr (une image)* to mirror

reflex *nm* **appareil (photo) reflex** = reflex (camera); **dans un appareil reflex, l'image est refléchie par un miroir interne** = in a reflex camera, the image is reflected by an inbuilt mirror

réflexion *nf* (a) glare *ou* reflection; **disque laser à réflexion** = reflective disk; **la réflexion sur l'écran me fait mal aux yeux** = the glare from the screen makes my eyes hurt (b) **coefficient de réflexion d'un signal** = signal reflection

reformatage *nm* reformatting; **toutes les données contenues sur un disque sont détruites par le reformatage** = reformatting destroys all the data on a disk
◊ **reformater** *vtr* to reformat; **si vous reformatez, vous détruirez toutes les données du disque** *ou* **vous blanchirez le disque** = by reformatting you will wipe the disk clean; **évitez de reformater votre**

disque dur à moins qu'il n'y ait aucune autre solution = do not reformat your hard disk unless you can't do anything else

réfracter *vtr* to refract
◊ **réfraction** *nf* refraction; **indice de réfraction** = refractive index

refus *nm* refusal; **erreur de refus** = rejection error

régénérateur, -trice *adj* lecture régénératrice (de données) = regenerative reading
◊ **régénération** *nf* regeneration *ou* recovery; **régénération de document** = document recovery; **régénération de l'image de l'écran** = screen refresh; **fréquence de régénération (de l'image)** = (image) refresh rate; **fréquence de régénération de la mémoire RAM** *ou* **de la mémoire vive** = RAM refresh rate; **signal de régénération de la mémoire RAM** = RAM refresh signal; **régénération de signal** = signal regeneration
◊ **régénérer** *vtr* to regenerate *ou* to refresh; **(signal de) régénérer l'image de l'écran** = screen refresh (signal)

régime *nm* **travailler à plein régime** = to work at full capacity

région *nf* region; *(ionosphère)* **région D** = D-region; **la région D est la principale cause d'affaiblissement des ondes radioélectriques** = the D-region is the main cause of attenuation in transmitted radio signals; **région F** = F-region
◊ **régional, -e** *adj* **antenne de relais régional** = master antenna television system (MATV); *(du téléphone)* **indicatif régional** = area code; **les journaux régionaux** = the regional papers *ou* the local press

registre *nm* register; **registre d'addition** = add register; **registre d'adresse** = address register; **registre d'adresse courante** = current address register (CAR); **registre d'adresse indexé** = B register; **registre d'adresse d'instruction** = instruction address register (IAR) *ou* instruction counter; **registre (d'adresse) de limites** = boundary register; **registre d'adresse en**

mémoire = memory address register (MAR); **pour obtenir un registre d'adresse de 16 bits avec un processeur de 8 bits, on lui associe un deuxième registre (de 8 bits)** = the 8-bit CPU uses a paired register to provide a 16-bit address register; **registre d'affichage** = display register; **registre auxiliaire de routage d'adresse** = B-line counter; **registre des balises** = flag register; **registre banalisé** *ou* **général** *ou* **polyvalent** = general register *ou* general purpose register (gpr); **registre de base** = base register; **registre à bits circulants** = circulating register; **registre de commande** = command register; **registre compteur** = instruction *ou* program counter (PC) *ou* instruction address register (IAR); **registre de contrôle** = *(commande)* control register; *(vérification)* check register; **registre de cumul** = accumulator *ou* ACC (register); **registre à** *ou* **de décalage** = circulating register *ou* shift register; **registre de données** = data register; **registre des données en mémoire** = memory data register (MDR); **vider le registre de données** = to clear the data register; **registre d'entrée** = input register *ou* receiver register; **registre d'entrée/sortie** = input/output register; **registre externe** = external register; **registre d'index** = index register (IR); **registre d'instruction** = instruction register (IR) *ou* program register; **registre d'instruction courante** = current instruction register (CIR); **registre d'instruction à exécuter** *ou* **registre de la prochaine instruction** = next instruction register; **registre de masque** = mask register; **registre de mémoire associative** = associative storage register; **registre de mémoire tampon** = memory buffer register (MBR); **registre des mots d'état** = program status word register (PSW register); **registre d'opération** *ou* **de code d'opération** = operation register *ou* op register; **registre de pagination à accès direct** = direct page register; **registre secondaire** = B box; **registre (de) sortie** = output register; **registre tampon** = buffer register; **registre tampon des entrées** = input buffer register; **registre tampon de sortie** = output buffer register; **registre des témoins** = flag register; **registre temporaire** = temporary register; **registre de texte** = text register; **adressage de registre** = register addressing; **fichier de registres** = register file; **instruction de décalage dans le registre** = accumulator shift instruction;

mettre en registre = to deposit in the register; **taille d'un registre** = register length

réglable *adj* **(a)** *(son, densité, contraste)* adjustable **(b)** *(vitesse, etc.)* selectable *ou* programmable; **réglable (par l'utilisateur)** = user-selectable; **les vitesses (de réception et de transmission) de ce modem sont réglables par l'utilisateur** = this modem has user-selectable baud rates

◊ **réglage** *nm* **(a)** *(action)* adjustment *ou* setting; **réglage des contrastes** = contrast setting; **réglage de densité d'impression** = density dial; **réglage de la luminosité** = brightness setting; **la luminosité a besoin d'un réglage** = the brightness needs adjustment **(b)** *(touche ou bouton)* dial *ou* control; **réglage du volume** = volume control

règle *nf* **(a)** *(dispositif de mesure)* **règle graduée** = ruler; **règle de tabulation** = tab rack *ou* ruler line; **la règle de tabulation indique les marges de gauche et de droite** = a tab rack shows you the left and right margins **(b)** *(lignes directrices)* **en règle générale, vous devez attendre le signal CTS avant de commencer à transmettre** = the rule states that you wait for the clear signal before transmitting; **règles propres à un langage** = language rules; **agir contre les règles** = to act illegally; **qui va contre les règles de la syntaxe** = illegal; **système à base de règles** = rule-based system

◊ **règlement** *nm* rule *ou* regulation; **règlements écrits** = printed regulations

réglé, -ée *adj* *(son, densité, contraste)* adjusted; *(paramètres de vitesse, etc.)* selected *ou* programmed

◊ **régler** *vtr* *(un appareil)* to set *ou* to tune; *(courant)* to regulate; *(son, densité, contraste)* to adjust; *(paramètres)* to program *ou* to select; **vous n'avez qu'à tourner un bouton pour régler la luminosité et le contraste** = you can adjust the brightness and contrast by turning a knob; **régler (un appareil) avec grande précision** = to fine tune (a machine); **la camera est réglée pour le premier plan** = the camera is focused on the foreground; **qui peut être réglé suivant les besoins de l'utilisateur** = user-selectable

réglure *nf (ligne mince)* rule

regroupé, -ée *adj* grouped; *(en série)* ganged

◊ **regroupement** *nm* group; **regroupement de commutateurs (en série)** = ganged switch

◊ **regrouper** *vtr* to group *ou* to batch *ou* to bracket together *ou* to gather

régulateur *nm* regulator; **régulateur de tension** = voltage regulator

◊ **régulation** *nf* **bus de régulation** = contention bus

◊ **régulé, -ée** *adj* regulated; **courant régulé** = regulated power supply

◊ **réguler** *vtr* to regulate

régulier, -ière *adj* regular; **l'horloge émet un signal à intervalles réguliers** = the clock signal is periodic

réimpression *nf* reprint; **faire une réimpression** = to reprint

◊ **réimprimer** *vtr* to reprint; **nous réimprimons 10 000 exemplaires** = we have ordered a 10,000 copy reprint

ré-initialisation *ou* **réinitialisation** *nf* reset; **ré-initialisation automatique à la mise sous tension** = power-on reset; **ré-initialisation (du système) par commande** = soft reset; **ré-initialisation (du système en) utilisant le contacteur** = hard reset; **bouton de ré-initialisation** = reset button *ou* key; **signal de ré-initialisation** = return to zero signal

◊ **ré-initialiser** *vtr* to reset

rejet *nm* rejection; **caractère de rejet d'un bloc (dont les données sont mauvaises)** = block ignore character; **erreur de rejet** = rejection error

◊ **rejeter** *vtr* to reject *ou* to ignore; **l'ordinateur rejette toute donnée venant de sources non compatibles** = the computer rejects all incoming data from incompatible sources

rejouer *vtr* to play back; **rejouer une bande** = to replay a tape *ou* to re-run a tape

relais *nm* relay; **ce circuit comporte un relais** = there is a relay in the circuit; **il est protégé par un relais à 5A** = it is relay-rated at 5 Amps; **relais hertzien** = microwave relay; **relais d'hyperfréquence** = microwave relay; **relais de télévision câblée** = cable TV relay station; **disque relais** = milk disk; **station relais** = local distribution service (LDS)

relance *nf* restart; **relance automatique** = auto restart; **horloge à relance automatique** = delta clock

◇ **relancer** *vtr* to restart *ou* to reboot *ou* to reload; **essayez d'abord de relancer (votre système)** = first try to restart your system; **nous avons relancé le système et les fichiers ont réapparu sur l'écran** = we rebooted and the files reappeared on the screen

> le système est tel que l'utilisateur peut lui-même identifier la panne, autorisant ainsi la relance automatique ou la reconfiguration à distance de l'élément déficient
> *Le Monde informatique*

relatif, -ive *adj* relative; **adressage relatif** = base addressing; **adresse relative** = floating address *ou* floating symbolic address *ou* relative address; **codage relatif** = relative coding; **coordonnées relatives** = relative coordinates; **données relatives** = relative data; **erreur relative** = relative error; **horloge relative** = relative-time clock; **valeur (adresse) relative** = offset value *ou* offset word

relation *nf* relationship; **(données) qui n'ont aucune relation** = disjointed (data); **relation booléenne** = Boolean connective; **graphe de relation** = derivation graph

◇ **relationnel, -elle** *adj* base de données **relationnelle** = plex database *ou* relational database; **opérateur relationnel** = relational operator *ou* logical operator; **requête relationnelle** = relational query

> il faut prévoir le nombre et les types de rubriques et la séparation de celles-ci en fichiers pour bénéficier des structures relationnelles construites visuellement à l'aide de la souris
> *L'Ordinateur Individuel*

relecture *nf* **(a)** *(d'épreuves d'imprimerie)* proofreading; **la relecture des épreuves est-elle terminée?** = has all

the text been proofread yet? **(b)** *(disque ou bande)* read back *ou* replay; **relecture immédiate** *ou* **instantanée** = instant replay; **contrôle par relecture** = read back check

relève *nf* **prendre la relève** = to take over (from); **en cas de panne d'électricité, nous avons un onduleur qui peut prendre la relève** = if there is a power failure, we have a safety net in the form of a UPS

relever *vtr* to enhance

relié, -ée *adj* **(a)** linked *ou* joined; **procédé relié aux résultats d'un autre procédé** = a process which is dependent on the result of another process **(b)** connected *ou* linked *ou* joined; *(en ligne)* on-line; **les deux ordinateurs sont reliés** = the two computers are linked; **processeur auxiliaire relié au processeur central** = attached processor; **une série de postes reliés les uns aux autres** = a series of interconnected terminals **(c)** *(livre)* bound; **relié sans couture** = perfect bound; **édition reliée** = hardcover edition *ou* hardback

relief *nm* relief; **impression en relief** = relief printing

relier *vtr* **(a)** to join *ou* to link *ou* to connect (to); *(utilisant une interface)* to interface with; **relier les un(e)s aux autres** = to interconnect; **relier en chaîne** *ou* **en cascade** *ou* **en série** = to daisy-chain; **relier en réseau** = to network; **les postes ont été reliés en réseau plutôt que d'être utilisés comme postes autonomes** *ou* **comme postes individuels** = the workstations have been networked together rather than used as stand-alone systems **(b)** *(livre)* **relier avec couverture cartonnée** = to case (a book)

◇ **relieur, -euse** *n (personne)* binder

◇ **reliure** *nf* **(a)** binding; **reliure sans couture** = perfect binding **(b)** **(l'art de) la reliure** = binding; **atelier de reliure** = bindery; **les feuilles ont été envoyées à la reliure** = the sheets have been sent to the bindery for binding; **imprimerie et reliure** = bookwork

REM = REMARK *(pour introduction de commentaire)* **instruction REM** = REM

rémanence *nf* lag; **rémanence cathodique** = cathode ray tube storage; **rémanence de l'image** = image retention *ou* hangover

rembobiner *vtr (un film, etc., sur bobine)* to rewind

remerciement *nm (dans un livre)* **remerciements** = acknowledgements

remettre *vtr* to put back; **il a remis la bande** = he replayed the tape; **remettre en bon état** = to restore; **remettre en marche** = to restart; **essayez d'abord de remettre votre système en marche** = first try to restart your system; **remettre à zéro** = to reset *ou* to zero; **remettre à zéro un dispositif programmable** = to zero a device

◊ **remise** *nf* **remise en état** = *(machine)* repair; *(fichier)* recovery; **programme de remise en état automatique** = automatic recovery program; **remise à l'état initial commandée par l'émetteur** = forward clearing; **remise en marche** = restart; *(après une panne)* **remise en marche** *ou* **remise en route au point de reprise** *ou* **au point d'arrêt** = failure recovery *ou* fall back recovery

remplacement *nm* **instruction de remplacement** = replace instruction; **mode remplacement** = replace mode; **fonction** *ou* **instruction de recherche et remplacement** = search and replace *ou* find and replace **fonction** *ou* **instruction**

◊ **remplacer** *vtr* to replace *ou* to supersede; **le nouveau programme, qui remplace le précédent, est beaucoup plus rapide** = the new program supersedes the earlier one, and is much faster; **les nouvelles données ont remplacé les données anciennes (par superposition d'écriture)** = the latest data input has overwritten the old information; **remplacer des données par superposition d'écriture** = to overwrite (data); *(instruction)* **(re)cherche et remplace** = search and replace

remplir *vtr* to fill (up) *ou* to pad

◊ **remplissage** *nm* filling *ou* padding; **remplissage de bits** = bit stuffing; **remplissage avec caractères blancs** = character fill *ou* character stuffing; **caractère de remplissage** = (i) fill character *ou* pad character; (ii) null character *ou* redundant character *ou* ignore character *ou* gap character; **insertion (en mémoire) de caractères de remplissage** = character fill; **chiffre de remplissage** = gap digit; **instruction de remplissage** = (i) dummy instruction *ou* waste instruction; (ii) blank instruction *ou* null instruction *ou* no-operation *ou* no-op instruction *ou* pseudo-instruction

rendement *nm* throughput; **rendement effectif** = effective throughput; **rendement estimé** = rated throughput; **rendement de phosphorescence** = phosphor efficiency; **capacité de rendement** = industrial *ou* manufacturing *ou* production capacity; **travailler à plein rendement** = to work at full capacity

rentrée *nf* re-entry; **point de rentrée** = re-entry point

renvoi *nm (note dans un document)* cross-reference; *(signe de la note)* reference mark; **renvoi en bas de page** = footnote; **faire un renvoi** = to cross-reference *ou* to cross-refer; **les unités SI font l'objet d'un renvoi à l'appendice** = the SI units are cross-referenced to the appendix; **générateur de renvois** = cross-reference generator

réorganiser *vtr* to reorganize; **il faut attendre que la base de données du correcteur orthographique soit réorganisée** = wait while the spelling checker database is being reorganized

repaginer *vtr* to renumber the pages *ou* to repaginate; **le système de PAO permet de repaginer** = the dtp package allows simple repagination; **le texte a été repaginé après modification de la longueur des lignes** = the text was repaginated with a new line width

réparable *adj (machine)* repairable; **erreur réparable** = recoverable error

◊ **réparation** *nf* repair *ou* corrective maintenance; **moyenne de temps requis pour réparation** = mean time to repair

◊ **réparer** *vtr* to repair *ou* to fix *ou* to service; **l'ordinateur ne peut être réparé** = the computer has a terminal fault; **pouvez-vous réparer le photocopieur?** =

can you fix the photocopier?; **les techniciens essayent de réparer le standard téléphonique** = the technicians are trying to repair the switchboard; **nous avons fait réparer les lecteurs de disquettes hier et tout fonctionne très bien** = the disk drives were serviced yesterday and are working well; **déceler et réparer une panne** = to troubleshoot

réparti, -e *adj* distributed; **informatique répartie** = distributed data processing (DDP); **intelligence répartie** = distributed intelligence; **système réparti** = distributed system; **système de base de données réparti** = distributed database system; **système à fichiers répartis** = distributed file system

◊ **répartir** *vtr* to allocate *ou* to distribute

repartir *vi* to resume

répartiteur *nm (d'une ligne)* splitter

◊ **répartition** *nf* **(a)** allocation; **répartition des tâches** = job scheduling **(b) multiplexage par répartition en fréquence** = frequency division multiplexing (FDM); **multiplexage par répartition dans le temps (MRT)** = time division multiplexing (TDM)

repasser *vtr (un film ou une bande)* to play again *ou* to replay; **il a repassé la bande** = he replayed the tape; **repassez ce film au ralenti** = play the film again in slow motion

repérage *nm* register; **les deux couleurs ne sont pas en repérage** = the two colours are out of register

◊ **repère** *nf* mark *ou* indicator; *(d'alignement)* register marks; **repère de positionnement (sur microfilm)** = editing symbol; **repères de tabulation** = tabulation markers; **positionnement sur repères** = register

◊ **repérer** *vtr* to find *ou* to locate; **ils ont repéré le composant défectueux** = they established which component was faulty; **le débogueur a repéré la faute très rapidement** = the debugger found the error very quickly; **les ingénieurs de maintenance ont repéré la source de la panne du système** = the maintenance engineers have identified the cause of the system failure

reperforatrice *nf* reperforator

répertoire *nm* **(a)** disk directory; **on trouve les titres des fichiers, la date et l'heure de leur création dans le répertoire** = the disk directory shows the file names, date and time of creation; **le nom d'un fichier qui est effacé disparaît aussi du répertoire du disque** = the entry in the disk catalogue is removed when the file is deleted; **répertoire d'adresses** = address list *ou* directory; **répertoire de caractères** *ou* **répertoire typographique** = character repertoire; **répertoire d'exceptions** = exception dictionary; **répertoire de fichiers** = file directory; **répertoire des fichiers d'un disque** *ou* **d'une disquette** = disk catalogue; **répertoire hiérarchique** = hierarchical directory; **répertoire d'instructions** = instruction repertoire; **routage par répertoire** = directory routing **(b)** contents *ou* index *ou* repertoire; **le répertoire entier est inclus dans le manuel** = the manual describes the full repertoire **(c) répertoire d'adresses par rues** = street directory; **répertoire d'entreprises** = commercial directory *ou* trade directory **(d)** *(films ou pièces à l'affiche)* listings

◊ **répertorier** *vtr* to catalogue; **tous les terminaux ont été répertoriés avec indication de leur emplacement, de leur code d'appel et de leur table d'attributs** = all the terminals were catalogued, with their location, call sign and attribute table

répéter *vtr* to repeat; **groupe (de données) qui se répètent de façon périodique** = repeating group

◊ **répéteur** *nm* repeater; **ce répéteur bon marché ne régénère pas les signaux** = this cheap repeater does not regenerate signals

◊ **répétition** *nf* **(a)** repeat; **répétition automatique** = automatic repeat *ou* auto repeat; **compteur de répétitions** = repeat counter; **groupe (de données) à répétition** = repeating group; **touche répétition** = repeat key **(b)** *(d'une séquence de film, au ralenti)* replay

repiquage *nm* **repiquage vidéo d'un film** = film pickup

replacer *vtr* to relocate

replâtrage *nm (d'un programme)* bug patches

replier *vtr* to fold

répondeur *nm* répondeur téléphonique = (telephone) answering machine *ou* answerphone; **répondeur avec message vocal de synthèse** = voice answer back; **répondeur vocal** = audio response unit
◊ **répondre** *vi* **(a)** répondre (à) = to respond (to); *(à quelqu'un ou à une lettre ou au téléphone)* to answer (someone *ou* a letter *ou* the telephone); **répondre à un appel** *ou* **répondre au téléphone** = to answer the phone *ou* to take a (phone) call; **le premier modem transmet l'appel tandis que le second y répond** = the first modem originates the call and the second answers it **(b)** *(satisfaire)* **ce lot de disquettes ne répond pas aux normes de qualité** = this batch of disks is not up to standard; **le logiciel ne fonctionnera pas s'il ne répond pas aux normes du système d'exploitation** = the software will not run if it does not conform to the operating system standards; **le travail ne répond pas aux spécifications du client** *ou* **au cahier des charges** = the work is not up to specification *ou* does not meet the customer's specifications
◊ **réponse** *nf* **(a)** *(téléphone ou modem)* answer; **réponse automatique** = auto-answer **(b)** response *ou* answer; *(signal)* **réponse affirmative** *ou* **positive** = positive response; **réponse aux basses fréquences** = bass response; **réponse en fréquence** = frequency response; **réponse intrinsèque** *ou* **par défaut** = default response; **délai de réponse** = gate delay; **signal de réponse** = answer back; **temps de réponse** = answer time *ou* access time *ou* response time; **le temps de réponse de ce simulateur de vol est excellent** = the response time of this flight simulator is very good **(c)** **emplacement** *ou* **case réservé(e) à la réponse** = response position; **(fonction) interrogation/réponse** *ou* **demande/réponse** = inquiry/response (function)

report *nm (math)* carry; **report en cascade** = cascade carry *ou* high speed carry; **report circulaire** *ou* **en boucle** = end-around carry; **report partiel** = partial carry; **report rapide** *ou* **simultané** = ripple-through carry; **bit de report** = carry bit *ou* flag; **signal de fin de report** = carry complete signal; **signe de report** = carry bit *ou* flag; **temps de report** = carry time

reportage *nm* press coverage *ou* media coverage; **reportage électronique** = electronic news gathering (ENG)

reporter *vtr* to transfer

repos *nm* **au repos** = *(machine)* idle *ou* inactive; *(circuit ou dispositif)* quiescent

reprendre *vtr* to repeat *ou* to resume; **le travail reprend normalement après la panne de l'imprimante** = work is flowing normally again after the breakdown of the printer; **nous avons repris le fichier, entrée par entrée** = we stepped forward through the file one record at a time; **reprendre l'exécution d'un programme** = to rerun a program

représentatif, -ive *adj* representative
◊ **représentation** *nf* representation; **vous pouvez voir le nouveau modèle sur cette représentation** = this picture shows the new design; **représentation graphique** = graphics *ou* graphic display; **les représentations graphiques telles que histogrammes, camemberts, etc** = graphics output such as bar charts, pie charts, etc.; **représentations graphiques sur ordinateur** = computer graphics *ou* computer-generated graphics; **représentation numérique** = digital representation
◊ **représenter** *vtr* to represent; **l'architecture** *ou* **la structure de l'ordinateur était représentée graphiquement** = the computer structure was expressed graphically

reprise *nf* **(a)** restart; *(sans repartir à zéro)* **reprise sur incident** *ou* **remise en marche au point de reprise** = fall back recovery *ou* error recovery *ou* failure recovery; **reprise sur l'instruction d'arrêt** *ou* **reprise au point d'arrêt** = warm start; **reprise totale** = cold start; **point de reprise** = check point *ou* rerun point; **(instruction de) vidage et reprise** = dump and restart **(b)** *(d'un article)* part exchange

repro *nf* = REPROGRAPHIE

reproduction *nf (d'un document)* duplication *ou* reproduction; **reproduction illégale d'une oeuvre protégée** = infringement of copyright *ou* copyright infringement; **oeuvre dont les droits de reproduction sont réservés** work (still) in copyright
◊ **reproduire** *vtr (un document)* to reproduce *ou* to duplicate; *(imprimerie)* **copie prête à reproduire** = camera-ready copy (crc)

reprogrammer *vtr* to reprogram

reprographie *ou* **repro** *nf* repro

requête *nf* query *ou* request *ou* enquiry *ou* inquiry; **requête d'entrée/sortie** = input/output request (IORQ); **requête (définie) par l'exemple** = query by example (QBE); **requête relationnelle** = relational query; **la requête relationnelle 'trouver tous les individus mâles de moins de 35 ans' ne peut pas être traitée par ce système** = the relational query 'find all men under 35 years old' will not work on this system; **caractère de requête** = inquiry character (ENQ); **langage de requête** = query language (QL); **traitement de requête** = query processing; **utilitaire de requête** = query facility

requis, -e *adj* wanted; **non requis** = unwanted

réseau *nm* **(a)** *(d'ordinateurs)* network *ou* networking; **cette société informatique est une société britannique spécialisée en réseaux** = this computer firm is a UK networking specialist; **réseau en anneau** = ring (data) network *ou* loop network; **réseau de type bus** = bus network; **réseau décentralisé** = decentralized computer network; **réseau démocratique** = democratic network; **réseau (avec synchronisation) despotique** = despotic network; **réseau à distance** = wide area network (WAN); **réseau à grande distance** = long haul network; **réseau de distribution** = distribution network; **réseau étendu** = wide area network (WAN); **réseau très étendu** = long haul network; **il a diffusé les dernières informations via le réseau étendu** = he broadcast the latest news over the WAN; **réseau informatique** *ou* **d'information** = information network; **expert** *ou*

spécialiste en réseaux informatiques = networking specialist; **réseau informatique centralisé** = centralized computer network; **réseau informatique hétérogène** = heterogeneous network; **réseau informatique homogène** = homogeneous computer network; **réseau intégralement interconnecté** = plex structure; **réseau local d'entreprise** = local area network (LAN); **réseau local en bande de base** = base band local area network; **modem pour réseau local d'entreprise** = limited distance modem; **serveur de réseau local d'entreprise** = local area network server *ou* LAN server; **réseau maillé** = mesh network; **réseau totalement maillé** = fully connected network; **ils exploitent un réseau de micros** = they run a system of networked micros; **réseau d'ordinateurs** *ou* **réseau informatique** = computer network; **réseau d'ordinateurs hiérarchisé** = hierarchical computer network; **architecture** *ou* **configuration de réseau** = network architecture *ou* systems network architecture (SNA); **base de données en réseau** = network database; **système de base de données en réseau** = distributed database system; **configurer en réseau** = to network; **contrôleur de réseau** = network controller; **couche réseau** = network layer; **diagramme (de configuration** *ou* **de topologie) de réseau** = network diagram; **disposer en réseau** = to network; **gestion de réseau** = network management; **liaisons redondantes** *ou* **auxiliaires d'un réseau** = network redundancy; **logiciel de** *ou* **pour réseau** = networking software *ou* network software *ou* common software; **matériel** *ou* **équipements de réseau (informatique)** = network hardware *ou* networking hardware; **mise en réseau (d'ordinateurs)** = networking; **les postes de travail ont été reliés en réseau plutôt que d'être utilisés indépendamment** = the workstations have been networked together rather than used as standalone systems; **processeur de réseau** = network processor; **processeur de réseau de communication** = communications network processor; **programme de contrôle de réseau** = network control program; **structure en réseau** = network structure; **synchronisation de réseau** = network timing; **tête de réseau** = head end **(b)** *(téléphonique* *ou* *télécommunication* *ou* *radio* *ou* *télévision)* network; **réseau de communication** *ou* **de télécommunications** = communications network; **réseau commuté** = circuit switched network; **réseau numérique à intégration de services (RNIS)** = integrated services digital network (ISDN); **réseau numérique intégré (RNI)** = integrated digital network (IDN); **accès au réseau numérique intégré** = integrated digital access (IDA); **réseau public (de transmission de données)** = public data network; **réseau radiophonique** *ou* **de radiodiffusion** = broadcast network *ou* radio network; **réseau radiotéléphonique** = cellular service; **réseau téléinformatique** *ou* **de transmission de données** = data communications network *ou* data network; **réseau téléphonique** = telephone network; **accès direct au réseau (téléphonique)** = direct outward dialling; **réseau téléphonique (public) commuté** = public switched telephone network (PSTN); **réseau de télévision** = television network; **programme transmis sur (tout) un réseau de télévision** = networked TV programme; **transmission** *ou* **diffusion sur (tout) un réseau** = networking; **réseau à valeur ajoutée** = value added network (VAN); **réseau à zone de recouvrement** = overlay network **(c)** array; **réseau logique** = logic array; **circuit logique en réseau** = gate array; **antenne en réseau** = array antenna **(d)** *(ensemble)* **réseau câblé** = cabling; **réseau de lignes (parallèles)** = raster

réserve *nf* **(a) avec réserve** = (i) conditional; (ii) conditionally; **sans réserve** = (i) unconditional; (ii) unconditionally **(b) (appareil** *ou* **dispositif) de réserve** = standby (device) ◊ **réservé, -ée** *adj* reserved; **espace mémoire réservé (à l'usage d'un utilisateur)** = private address space; **ligne réservée** = private line; **mot réservé** = reserved word; **port réservé** = private dial port; **il n'y a qu'un seul poste réservé aux graphiques sur ce réseau** = there's only one dedicated graphics workstation in this network; **secteur réservé** = reserved sector

résident, -e *adj* resident *ou* memory-resident; **logiciel résident** = resident software *ou* memory-resident software; **police résidente** = resident font; **programme résident** = memory-resident program *ou* internally stored program; **le système peut planter si vous introduisez un trop grand nombre de programmes**

résidents = the system can bomb if you set up too many memory-resident programs at the same time; **zone (de mémoire) des programmes non résidents** = transient area

ces produits sont constitués de programmes de communication résidents, qui possèdent toutes les caractéristiques des réseaux, mais sont limités à deux PC

Action PC

résiduel, -elle *adj* residual; **bande latérale résiduelle** = vestigial sideband; **oscillations résiduelles (sur un courant)** = ripple; **taux d'erreur résiduel** = residual error rate

résine *nf* resin; **résine photosensible** = photoresist; **(méthode de la) résine photosensible en positif** = positive photoresist; **pour faire un circuit imprimé il faut d'abord recouvrir la carte d'une résine photosensible** = to make the PCB, first coat the board with photoresist

résistance *nf* **(a)** resistance **(b)** *(device)* resistor; **résistance variable** = variable resistor; **logique (à) transistors (et) résistances (LTR)** = resistor transistor logic (RTL) ◊ **résister (à)** *vi* to resist

résolution *nf* **résolution d'un nombre binaire** = digital resolution; **langage de résolution de problème** = problem-orientated language (POL); **pouvoir de résolution** = resolving power

la plupart ont une résolution de 300 x 300 points avec un débit de l'ordre de 6 pages/minute, la résolution des meilleurs modèles atteignant les 400 points par pouce

L'Ordinateur Individuel

résonance *ou* **résonnance** *nf* resonance; **sonnerie à résonance de fréquence** = decimonic ringing; **imagerie par résonance magnétique (IRM)** = magnetic resonance imaging

résoudre *vtr* to solve; **résoudre un problème** = to solve a problem; **problèmes de traitement qui peuvent être résolus** = processing problems which are still manageable

respecter *vtr* to respect; **respecter un délai** = to meet a deadline

responsable *adj (de département)* (department) director *ou* manager *ou* head *ou* chief; **responsable de base de données** = database administrator (DBA); **responsable du contrôle de (la) qualité** = quality controller; **responsable du service informatique** = data processing manager (DPM); *(d'un film)* **responsable de la distribution** = casting director

resserrer *vtr* to close up; **en resserrant les lignes, nous gagnerons une page** = if we close up the lines, we should save a page

ressortir *vi* **(a)** *(une ligne de paragraphe)* **faire ressortir** = to outdent **(b)** *(par surbrillance)* **faire ressortir** = to highlight; **les titres sont en caractères gras pour les faire ressortir** = the headings are highlighted in bold

ressource *nf* resource; **ressource critique** = critical resource; **allocation de ressources** = resource allocation; **partage de ressources** = resource sharing

restauration *nf* recovery; **procédure de restauration** = recovery procedure; **programme de restauration automatique** = automatic recovery program
◊ **restaurer** *vtr* to restore; **restaurer (des données)** = to reconstitute (data)

reste *nm* remainder *ou* residue; **contrôle sur reste** = residue check
◊ **rester** *vi* to remain; **7 divisé par 3 égale 2 reste 1** = 7 divided by 3 is equal to 2 remainder 1

restituer *vtr (donnée ou fichier)* to retrieve; **il est impossible restituer les fichiers depuis la panne** = the files are irretrievable since the computer crashed; **(fichier) qui ne peut être restitué** = irretrievable (file)
◊ **restitution** *nf* **restitution de données** = information retrieval (IR); **stockage et restitution de données** = information storage and retrieval (ISR)

restreint, -e *adj* restricted; **ce document de diffusion restreinte ne doit pas être rendu public** = the document is restricted, and cannot be placed on open access; **complément restreint** =

diminished radix complement; **test sélectif restreint** = crippled leapfrog test
◊ **restriction** *nf* restriction

résultat *nm* result; **procédé dépendant des résultats** *ou* **relié aux résultats d'un autre procédé** = a process which is dependent on the result of another process; **le résultat de sortie est fonction de l'état (physique) des liaisons** = the output is dependent on the physical state of the link; **à données erronées, résultats erronés** *ou* **des données douteuses produisent des résultats douteux** = garbage in garbage out (GIGO)

résumé *nm* abstract; **dans notre bibliothèque, les résumés sont réunis en volumes distincts ce qui assure la facilité et la rapidité des recherches sur un sujet particulier** = in our library, abstracts are gathered together in separate volumes allowing an easy and rapid search for a particular subject; **résumé critique** = evaluative abstract; **résumé et indexation** = abstracting & indexing (A&I)
◊ **résumer** *vtr (un article)* to make an abstract (of an article)

rétablir *vtr* **rétablir une liaison** = to reconnect; **les techniciens du téléphone essayent de rétablir la liaison téléphonique** = the telephone engineers are trying to reconnect the telephone

retaper *vtr* **programme** *ou* **système qui a été retapé** = kludge

retard *nm* **(a)** delay *ou* lag; **retard de contention** *ou* **de maintien** = contention delay; **retard d'effacement** = lag; **distorsion due au retard du signal** = delay distortion; **ligne à** *ou* **de retard** = delay line; **ligne à** *ou* **de retard au mercure** = mercury delay line; **mémoire à ligne de retard** = delay line store; **vecteur de retard** = delay vector **(b)** delay; **en retard** = late; **travail en retard** = backlog; **les programmeurs ne réussissent pas à venir à bout de toute la programmation en retard** = the programmers can't deal with the backlog of programming work
◊ **retarder** *vtr* to delay

retenir *vtr (math)* **lorsqu'on additionne 5 et 7, on abaisse 2 et on retient 1 sur la**

colonne des dizaines, ce qui fait 12 = when 5 and 7 are added, there is an answer of 2 and a carry which is put in the next column, giving 12

rétention *nf* retention

retenue *nf (math)* carry; **retenue anticipée** = carry look ahead; **addition sans retenue** = addition without carry; **additionneur à retenue automatique (très rapide)** = carry look ahead; **indicateur** *ou* **témoin de retenue** = carry flag

retouche *nf* touching (up) *ou* retouching; **il y a quelques retouches à faire au dessin** = the artwork for the line drawings needs retouching in places

◇ **retoucher** *vtr* to retouch *ou* to touch up

retour *nm* **(a)** *(instruction)* return; **(code** *ou* **touche de) retour (du) chariot** *ou* **retour à la ligne** = carriage return (CR); **les clavistes trouvent que la touche de retour est mal placée** = the carriage return key is badly placed for touch-typists; **retour (du) chariot/retour à la ligne** = carriage return/line feed (CR/LF); **retour à la ligne (en limite d'écran)** = horizontal wraparound *ou* word wrap *ou* wraparound; **retour à la ligne automatique** = automatic carriage return *ou* word wrap *ou* wraparound **(b)** *(du curseur)* **retour arrière** = backspace; **caractère de retour arrière** = backspace character; **touche de retour arrière** = backspace key; **pour corriger une erreur de saisie de texte, utilisez la touche de retour arrière** = if you make a mistake entering data, use the backspace key to correct it; **retour à la source** *ou* **à l'origine** = homing **(c)** *(d'un balayage)* flyback; **retour de ligne** = line flyback; **délai de retour de ligne** = line blanking interval; **retour de trame** = field flyback **(d)** *(transmission)* **canal** *ou* **voie de retour** = reverse channel *ou* backward channel; **contrôle par retour** = feedback control; **transmission sans contrôle de retour** = free wheeling **(e)** *(rétroaction)* feedback; **ne placez pas le micro trop près du haut-parleur sinon le retour va saturer l'ampli** = make sure the microphone is not too close to the loudspeaker or positive feedback will occur and you will overload the amplifier; **retour acoustique** = acoustical feedback **(f)** **commande de retour au texte original** = revert command

◇ **retournement** *nm* turnaround; **délai de retournement** = turnaround time (TAT) *ou* sense recovery time

retrait *nm* withdrawal; **carte de retrait bancaire** = cash card

retraitement *nm* postprocessing; **programme de retraitement** = postprocessor

retransmettre *vtr* to relay *ou* to retransmit; **tous les messages sont retransmis par l'intermédiaire de ce petit micro** = all messages are relayed through this small micro

◇ **retransmission** *nf* retransmission; **correction d'erreurs par retransmission** = backward error correction; **(système avec facilité de) stockage et retransmission** = store and forward (system)

rétro- *préf* retro-

◇ **rétroaction** *nf* feedback; **rétroaction négative** = negative feedback; **rétroaction positive** = positive feedback; **boucle de rétroaction** = feedback loop

◇ **rétroéclairé, -ée** *adj (écran)* backlit (display)

◇ **rétroprojecteur** *nm* overhead projector

◇ **rétroprojection** *nf* front projection

◇ **rétrospectif, -ive** *adj* retrospective; **recherche rétrospective** = retrospective search; **test rétrospectif en parallèle** = retrospective parallel running

retrouver *vtr* to find *ou* to recover

réunion *nf* conference; *(opération logique)* **opération de réunion** *ou* **d'union** = disjunction *ou* either-or operation

réussir *vtr&i* to achieve (something) *ou* to master (something) *ou* to manage to do (something); **ne pas réussir quelque chose** = to fail (to do something); **l'imprimante ne réussit pas très bien à imprimer les lignes trop fines** = the printer has difficulty in reproducing very fine lines

réutilisable *ou* **ré-utilisable** *adj* reusable; **ruban non ré-utilisable** = singlestrike ribbon; **support (magnétique) réutilisable** = erasable storage *ou* erasable memory

révélateur *nm (photographique)* developer
◊ **révéler** *vtr* to reveal

revendeur, -euse *n* dealer; **n'achetez votre matériel informatique que chez un revendeur agréé** = always buy hardware from a recognized dealer; **revendeur d'équipements informatiques** = computer equipment supplier; **revendeur de systèmes à valeur ajoutée** = value added reseller (VAR)

réversible *adj* **disquette réversible** = flippy

revêtir *vtr (d'une substance)* to coat

réviser *vtr* to review *ou* to revise; *(un texte avant l'impression)* to edit *ou* to sub-edit *ou* to sub; *(une machine ou une voiture)* to service; **nous avons fait réviser les lecteurs de disquettes hier et tout fonctionne très bien** = the disk drives were serviced yesterday and are working well
◊ **révision** *nf (d'un article ou d'un manuscrit)* editing *ou* sub-editing *ou* subbing; *(d'une machine)* service

revoir *vtr* to revise; **la version revue et corrigée ne contient aucune erreur** = the revised version has no mistakes

révolution *nf* revolution; **la révolution technologique** = the technological revolution

revue *nf* magazine; **la maison publie des revues detinées aux hommes/femmes d'affaires** = the company specializes in publications for the business reader; **il travaille à la rédaction d'une revue de micro-informatique** = he edits a computer magazine; **une revue hebdomadaire** = a weekly magazine; **les revues de luxe** = *(familier)* the glossies; **revue spécialisée** *ou* **revue savante** = learned journal

rhéostat *nm* rheostat

rigide *adj* rigid; **les disquettes sont rangées dans des boîtiers de protection rigides** = the disks are housed in hard protective cases

RISC = REDUCED INSTRUCTION SET COMPUTER *voir aussi* INSTRUCTION

RNI = RESEAU NUMERIQUE INTEGRE
◊ **RNIS** = RESEAU NUMERIQUE A INTEGRATION DE SERVICES

robot *nm* robot
◊ **robotique** *nf* **la robotique** = robotics

roder *vtr* to run in

rogné, -ée *adj (pages)* trimmed; **non rogné** = ragged; **bord non rogné** = deckle edge; **livre dont les pages ne sont pas rognées** = uncut book
◊ **rogner** *vtr (pages)* to trim; **après l'impression, on rogne pour obtenir des pages de 198 x 129mm** = the printed pages are trimmed to 198 x 129mm

ROM *nf* = READ ONLY MEMORY; **ROM auxiliaire** = sideways ROM; **ROM enfichable** *ou* **ROM amovible** *ou* **cartouche ROM** = ROM cartridge; **cet ordinateur portatif n'est pas équipé d'un lecteur de disquettes mais possède un connecteur pour cartouches ROM** = the portable computer has no disk drives, but has a slot for ROM cartridges; **le constructeur a fourni le programme de commande du moniteur sur deux circuits ROM** = the manufacturer provided the monitor program in two ROM chips; **mémoire ROM** = read only memory (ROM); **ROM fantôme** = phantom ROM; **ROM effaçable électriquement** = electrically erasable read-only memory (EEROM); **ROM modifiable électriquement** = electrically alterable read-only memory (EAROM); **ROM programmable et effaçable** = erasable programmable read-only memory (EPROM); **ROM programmable et effaçable électriquement** = electrically erasable programmable read-only memory (EEPROM); **ROM programmable, modifiable électriquement** = electrically alterable, programmable read-only memory

(EAPROM); **ROM personnalisée =** custom ROM (PROM); **programmes sur ROM =** romware; **programmeur de ROM =** burner; *voir ausi* MEMOIRE

romain, -e *adj* **(a)** roman; **chiffres romains =** Roman numerals **(b) le texte est (composé) en Times Romain =** the text is set in Times Roman

rond, -e *adj* round; **en chiffres ronds =** in round figures

rotatif, -ive *adj* rotary; **caméra rotative =** rotary camera; **presse rotative =** rotary press
◊ **rotation** *nf* rotation; **rotation de matrice =** matrix rotation; *(transmis manuellement)* **mouvement de rotation =** spindling

roue *nf* wheel; **roue à picots =** sprocket wheel

rouge *nm* red; *(couleurs utilisées pour la télévision)* **rouge, vert, bleu =** red, green, blue (RGB)

rouleau *nm* **(a)** *(de papier, etc.)* roll; **rouleau de papier pour télécopieur =** roll of fax paper **(b)** *(de machine à écrire ou d'imprimante)* platen; **entraînement par rouleaux =** friction feed

routage *nm* routing; **routage adaptatif** *ou* **flexible =** distributed adaptive routing; **routage adaptatif protégé =** isolated adaptive routing; **routage par dispersion** *ou* **par redistribution =** flooding; **routage des données =** data routing; **routage dynamique =** adaptive routing; **routage optimisé =** minimum weight routing; **routage par répertoire =** directory routing; **page de routage =** routing page; **protocole de routage (d'un message) =** routing overheads; **la vitesse de transmission d'informations est beaucoup moins grande une fois qu'on tient compte du protocole de routage =** the information transfer rate is very much less once all routing overheads have been accommodated; **registre auxilliare de routage d'adresse =** B-line counter; **table de routage =** routing table
◊ **route** *nf* route *ou* path; **mettre en route =** to start; **mise en route =** start; **chargeur** *ou* **programme (élémentaire) de**

mise en route = bootstrap (loader); **n'arrêtez pas la vérification de l'orthographe en cours de route =** do not interrupt the spelling checker while it is running

routine *nf* routine; **la routine permet d'imprimer le contenu de l'écran =** the routine copies the screen display onto a printer; **l'instruction RETOUR à la fin d'une routine permet de redonner la main au programme principal =** the RETURN instruction at the end of the routine sends control back to the main program; **routine auxiliaire =** open routine; **routines de clôture (d'exécution) =** end of run routines; **routine de compression =** packing routine; **routine de diagnostic =** diagnostic routine; **routine d'entrée** *ou* **d'introduction de données =** input routine; **routine de gestion de périphérique =** peripheral software driver; **routine interactive =** interactive routine; **routines d'interface =** interface routines; **routine itérative =** iterate *ou* iterative routine; **routine de manipulation de fichier =** file handling routine; **routine de normalisation =** normalization routine; **routine ouverte =** open routine; **routine principale =** main routine; *(en cas de panne)* **routines de secours =** fall back routines; **routine de traitement d'erreur =** error routine; **routines de traitement de la virgule flottante =** floating-point routines; **appeler une routine =** to call a routine

RS-232C *(pour interface série)* **norme RS-232C =** RS-232C (standard)

RSA = RIVEST, SHAMIR AND ADLEMAN; **code de cryptage RSA =** RSA cipher system

RTL = RESISTOR TRANSISTOR LOGIC; **logique RTL =** RTL

ruban *nm* **(a) mètre à ruban =** tape measure **(b)** *(pour machine à écrire ou imprimante)* ribbon; **ruban (en) tissu =** fibre ribbon; **ruban carbone =** carbon ribbon; **ruban en cartouche =** cartridge ribbon; **ruban d'imprimante =** printer ribbon; **ruban multifrappe =** multi-strike printer ribbon; **ruban à un seul passage** *ou* **non réutilisable =** single strike ribbon; **cartouche de ruban =** ribbon cartridge **(c)** *(pour film)* **ruban de raccord =** splicing tape **(d)** *(bande papier)* **ruban perforé =** perforated tape

rubrique *nf* heading *ou* rubric; **rubrique de déclaration des données =** data division

ruiner *vtr (des données ou un fichier)* to mung up

rupteur *nm (de papier listing)* burster

◊ **rupture** *nf* break; **système de sécurité en cas de rupture de courant =** fail safe system

rustine *nf* bug patches

rythme *nm* clock pulse

Ss

S-100 bus (de type) S-100 = S-100 bus

SAFE technique de validation de signature SAFE = safe signature analysis using functional analysis (SAFE)

saisie *nf (données)* (data) input (i/p *ou* I/P); *(action)* data capture *ou* data entry; **la saisie commence dès réception du signal d'interruption** = data capture starts when an interrupt is received; **saisie automatique de données** = automatic data capture; **saisie par balayage** = scanning; **logiciel de saisie par balayage** = scanning software; **saisie au** *ou* **sur** *ou* **par clavier** = keyboarding *ou* keying *ou* manual entry *ou* manual input; **le coût de saisie est calculé sur une base de frappes/heure** = the cost of keyboarding is calculated in keystrokes per hour; **saisie au clavier contrôlée par ordinateur** = processor-controlled keying; **saisie directe de données au clavier** = direct data entry (DDE); **saisie directe sur disque(tte), par clavier** = keyboard to disk entry *ou* key-to-disk; **saisie vocale** = voice data entry *ou* input; **masque de saisie** = form
◊ **saisi, -e** *adj* input *ou* captured; **données saisies** = input (data)
◊ **saisir** *vtr* **(a)** *(mécaniquement)* grab *ou* grip; **dans l'entraînement par friction le papier est saisi par les rouleaux** = in friction feed, the paper is gripped by the rollers **(b)** *(données)* to input *ou* to enter *ou* to capture; **les données ont été saisies** = the data has been entered; **saisir (des données) au clavier** *ou* **sur clavier** = to keyboard *ou* to key in (data); **il était plus économique de faire saisir le manuscrit par une société de services informatiques** = it was cheaper to have the manuscript keyboarded by another company; **ils ont saisi les toutes dernières données (sur clavier)** = they keyed in the latest data; **utilisez le pavé numérique pour saisir les chiffres** = you can use the numeric keypad to enter the figures

salle *nf* room; **salle de conférence(s)** = conference room; **salle de montage** = cutting room; **salle de projection** = projection room

salon *nm* exhibition; **salon de la bureautique** = business efficiency exhibition

saphir *nm* sapphire

satellite *nm* **(a)** satellite; **satellite de diffusion directe** = direct broadcast satellite (DBS); **satellite domestique** *ou* **national** = domestic satellite; **satellite géostationnaire** = geostationary satellite; **satellite météorologique** = weather satellite; **satellite de télécommunication** = communications satellite; **liaison par satellite** = satellite link; **radiodiffusion par satellite** = satellite broadcasting; **technique de diffusion par satellite** = broadcast satellite technique; **(re)transmission par satellite** = satellite transmission **(b)** *(système dépendant)* ordinateur satellite = satellite computer; **réseau satellite** = satellite network; **système satellite** = satellite (system); **terminal satellite** = satellite terminal

un PC 'satellite' communique avec un PC 'serveur', soit par le port série à une vitesse maximale de 115 200bps, soit par le port parallèle à 50 000bps
Action PC

satiné, -ée *adj* papier couché satiné = glossy paper

satisfaction *nf* satisfaction; **qui donne satisfaction** = satisfactory *ou* reliable; **les premières versions du logiciel ne donnaient pas complète satisfaction** = the early versions of the software were not completely reliable

saturation *nf* saturation; **saturation d'un canal** *ou* **d'une voie** = channel overload; **saturation de couleur** = colour saturation; **bruit de saturation (magnétique)** = saturation noise; **tests de saturation** = saturation testing

◊ **saturer** *vtr* to saturate *ou* to overload; **ne placez pas le micro trop près du haut-parleur sinon le retour va saturer l'ampli** = make sure the microphone is not too close to the loudspeaker or positive feedback will occur and you will overload the amplifier; **chaque fois que vous prononcez un 'p' vous saturez l'enregistrement, placez donc ce filtre pour que cela cesse** = every time you say a 'p' you overload the tape recorder, so put this pop filter in to stop it

saut *nm* **(a)** *(movement)* jump *ou* skip; **saut du papier** = paper throw; *(de l'imprimante)* **saut rapide** = high-speed skip **(b) saut d'image** = frame flyback; **saut de ligne** = line feed (LF); **saut de ligne automatique (en limite d'écran)** = horizontal wraparound; **(instruction de) saut de page** = form feed; **saut de page obligatoire** *ou* **programmé** = forced page break; *(traitement de texte)* **capacité de saut** = skip capability **(c)** *(branchement)* jump *ou* transfer; **saut conditionnel** = conditional jump *ou* branch *ou* transfer; **instruction de saut** = jump instruction *ou* branch instruction *ou* skip instruction; **GOTO est une instruction de saut** = GOTO is a jump instruction

◊ **saute** *nf (de courant)* fluctuation; **les sautes de courant peuvent nuire au bon fonctionnement de l'ordinateur** = voltage fluctuations can affect the functioning of the computer system

◊ **sauter** *vi* **(a)** to jump *ou* to skip; **le claviste a sauté plusieurs lignes du manuscrit** = several lines of manuscript have been missed by the keyboarder; **l'imprimante a sauté les trois lignes suivantes** = the printer skipped the next three lines of text; **le système de pagination a sauté deux numéros de pages** = the paging system has jumped two folio numbers **(b)** *(exploser)* to blow; *(système)* to bomb; **faire sauter un plomb** *ou* **un fusible** = to blow a fuse; **on a fait sauter les plombs en branchant le climatiseur** = when the air-conditioning was switched on, it fused the whole system; **vous pouvez faire sauter le système si vous installez en même temps des accessoires de bureau ou plusieurs**

programmes résidents = the system can bomb if you set up several desk accessories or memory-resident programs at the same time

◊ **sautillement** *nm (de l'image d'écran)* jitter *ou* flicker

sauvegarde *nf* backup; **nous mettons toujours la plus récente (copie de) sauvegarde dans le coffre fort** = the most recent backup copy is kept in the safe; **sauvegarde sur bande** = tape backup; **copie de sauvegarde** = security backup *ou* backup copy; **cycle de rotation des fichiers de sauvegarde** = grandfather cycle; **disquette de sauvegarde** = backup disk; **faire une sauvegarde** = to do a backup *ou* to back up *ou* to save (a text *ou* a file); **ce système de traitement de texte fait une sauvegarde toutes les 15 minutes pour prévenir une défaillance** = this WP system saves the text every 15 minutes in case of a fault; **faire une sauvegarde sur deux disques** = to mirror (text *ou* file); **fichier de sauvegarde** = backup file; **procédure de sauvegarde** = backup procedure; **la procédure normale préconise une sauvegarde de tout le travail en fin de journée** = the normal procedure is for backup copies to be made at the end of each day's work; **unité de sauvegarde rapide sur bande magnétique** = tape streamer *ou* streaming tape drive *ou* stringy floppy; **vidage de sauvegarde** = rescue dump; **zone de sauvegarde** = save area

◊ **sauvegardé, -ée** *adj* saved; **original sauvegardé** = protection master

◊ **sauvegarder** *vtr* to save *ou* to back up (text *ou* file); **sauvegardez toujours vos données sur disquettes pour le cas où le fichier principal serait endommagé** = always keep backup copies in case of accidental damage to the master file; **ce programme permet de sauvegarder un fichier sur disque dur au moyen d'une seule commande** = the program enables users to back up hard disk files with a single command; **la comptabilité de la société avait été sauvegardée sur une disquette en cas d'incendie** = the company accounts were backed up on disk as a protection against fire damage; **n'oubliez pas de sauvegarder le fichier avant d'éteindre votre appareil** = don't forget to save the file before switching off; **sauvegarder de nouveau** = to resave; **cela permet de sauvegarder** automatiquement le texte de nouveau = it automatically resaves the text

> lorsque vous ne désirez plus travailler sur un fichier donné, sauvegardez-le grâce à la commande 'Enregistrer', du même fichier
> *L'Ordinateur Individuel*

savant, -e *adj* learned; **revue savante =** learned journal

scalaire *adj* **grandeur scalaire =** scalar; **une grandeur scalaire n'a qu'une dimension, un vecteur en possède au moins deux =** a scalar has a single magnitude value, a vector has two or more positional values

scan *nm* scan

◊ **scannage** *nm* scan *ou* scanning; **faire un scannage =** to scan; **cet appareil peut faire un scannage avec définition allant jusqu'à 300 points par pouce =** the machine scans at up to 300 dpi resolution

◊ **scanner** *nm* (optical) scanner *ou* scanning device; **l'examen au scanner a très vite repéré le composant qui surchauffait =** the heat scan of the computer quickly showed which component was overheating; **les scanners sont de type 'flatbed', ou possèdent un système d'entraînement du papier par rouleau =** scanners are either flatbed models or platen type, paper-fed models; **scanner de contrôle d'appel** *ou* **de demande de communication =** communications scanner; **scanner d'images =** image scanner; **scanner d'images vidéo =** video scanner; **les nouveaux scanners d'image vidéo ont été conçus pour la saisie (par balayage) d'objets à trois dimensions =** new video scanners are designed to scan three-dimensional objects; **scanner multifonction =** a multifunctional scanner

◊ **scanneur** *nm* scanner *ou* scanning device; **le scanneur peut lire les codes barres sur les étiquettes des produits grâce à un rayon laser et une photodiode =** a scanner reads the bar-code on the product label using a laser beam and photodiode; *voir aussi* SCANNER

◊ **scanning** *nm* scan *ou* scanning; **faire un scanning =** to scan

sceller *vtr* to seal; **le disque dur est contenu dans un boîtier scellé =** the hard disk is in a sealed case

scénario *nm* script

◊ **scénariste** *nm&f* scriptwriter

schéma *nm* schema *ou* diagram; *(du point de vue de l'utilisateur)* external schema; **schéma de base de données =** database schema; **schéma directeur =** outline flowchart; **schéma fonctionnel =** functional diagram; **schéma de procédure =** process chart; **sous forme de schéma =** schematic *ou* in diagrammatic form *ou* diagrammatically

◊ **schématique** *adj* schematic; **plan schématique =** schema *ou* schematic *ou* schematic plan

schmilblic *nm (familier)* gremlin; **schmilblic sur la ligne =** line gremlin

scie *nf* saw; **onde en dents de scie =** sawtooth waveform

scientifique *adj* scientific; **calculatrice avec fonctions scientifiques =** scientific calculator

scintillement *nm (d'enregistrement)* flutter; *(de l'image)* flicker; **le pleurage et le scintillement sont des défauts courants des magnétophones bon marché =** wow and flutter are common faults on cheap tape recorders

scrutation *nf* scanning; *(par appel)* polling

SCSI = SMALL COMPUTER SYSTEM INTERFACE *voir aussi* INTERFACE

> ainsi le protocole SCSI (Small Computer System Interface) a-t-il été systématiquement choisi en haut de gamme pour ses performances en terme de débit (5Mo/s) et pour ses capacités de connexion de périphériques (256 par contrôleur contre 2 floppies et 2 disques durs par contrôleur ESDI)
> *L'Ordinateur Individuel*

SDLC = SYNCHRONOUS DATA LINK CONTROL; **procédure SDLC =** SDLC

sec, sèche *adj* dry; **connexion sèche =** dry joint; **contact sec =** dry contact; **pile sèche =** dry cell

SECAM *(standard de télévision) =* SEQUENTIEL A MEMOIRE

second, -e 1 *adj (deuxième)* second; **la seconde partie du programme contient des erreurs =** the second half of the program contains some errors; **utilisation d'une seconde source de composants =** second-sourcing **2** *nf (imprimerie)* **épreuves en seconde =** galley proofs

◊ **secondaire** *adj* secondary *ou* sub-; **adresse secondaire =** subaddress; **canal** *ou* **voie secondaire =** secondary channel; **couleur secondaire =** secondary colour; **curseur secondaire =** ghost cursor; **entrée secondaire =** added entry; *(de voies de transmission à fréquence vocale)* **groupe secondaire =** supergroup; **mémoire secondaire =** secondary storage; **registre secondaire =** B box; **station secondaire =** tributary station; *(qui reçoit des données)* secondary station

seconde *nf (unité de temps)* second; **(nombre de) bits par seconde (bps) =** bits per second (bps); **(nombre de) caractères par seconde (cps) =** characters per second (cps); **(nombre d') images par seconde** *ou* **images/seconde =** frames per second (fps); **(nombre d') inférences logiques par seconde =** logical inference per second (LIPS); **(nombre de) mégabits par seconde =** megabits per second (Mbps); **(nombre de) pouces par seconde** *ou* **pouces/seconde =** inches per second (ips); **million(s) d'opérations en virgule flottante par seconde =** megaflops (MFLOPS)

secours *nm* help; **alimentation** *ou* **pile de secours =** battery backup *ou* auxiliary battery; **la salle des ordinateurs est équipée d'un bloc d'alimentation de secours en cas de panne de secteur =** the computer room has an auxiliary power supply in case there is a mains failure; **alimentation de secours de la mémoire =** memory backup capacitor; **dispositif de secours =** auxiliary *ou* standby (device); **temps de débit d'un dispositif de secours =** holdup; **équipement** *ou* **matériel** *ou* **système de secours =** standby equipment *ou* auxiliary equipment;

installation de secours prête à fonctionner = hot standby; **procédure de secours =** fall back procedure; **routines de secours =** fall back routines; **système de secours lancé manuellement =** cold standby; **système de secours prêt à fonctionner =** hot standby; **système de secours à démarrage semi-automatique =** warm standby

secousse *nf* **les disques durs sont très sensibles aux secousses =** hard disks are very sensitive to jarring

secteur *nm* **(a)** *(d'électricité)* **le secteur =** mains electricity; **fiche secteur à deux broches =** two-pin mains plug; **fiche secteur à trois broches =** three-pin mains plug; **panne de secteur =** power failure *ou* blackout *ou* black out; **il y a eu une panne de secteur =** the electricity supply was cut off **(b)** *(de disque)* disk sector; *(de disquette)* floppy disk sector; **secteur défectueux =** bad sector *ou* faulty sector; **secteur réservé =** reserved sector; **formatage de secteurs (d'un disque) =** (disk) sector formatting; **formatage de secteurs permanents =** hard-sectoring **(c)** **diagramme à secteurs =** pie chart **(d)** *(d'une ville)* zone

section *nf* section *ou* part; **section élémentaire de câble =** elementary cable section; **section d'entrée =** input section

sectoriser *vtr* to sector; **(disque) sectorisé par logiciel =** soft-sectored (disk)

sécurisation *nf* **(logiciel** *ou* **dispositif de) sécurisation de fichier =** file security *ou* file protection (software *ou* device); **sécurisation d'un système =** system security

◊ **sécurisé, -ée** *adj* secured *ou* protected; **système sécurisé =** secure system

◊ **sécuriser** *vtr* to secure *ou* to make secure *ou* to protect

◊ **sécurité** *nf* security *ou* protection; **la conception du système assure la sécurité des données en mémoire =** the system has been designed to assure the security of the stored data; **sécurité des données** *ou* **de l'information =** data security *ou* data protection; **sécurité du matériel =** hardware security; **contrôle de sécurité =**

security check; **marge de sécurité =** safety margin; *(en cas de défaillance ou de rupture de courant)* **système de sécurité =** fail safe system

segment *nm* segment; *(exécutable)* (program) section *ou* segment; **segment de format superposable =** form overlay; **segment de recouvrement =** overlay segment; **gestionnaire de segment de recouvrement =** overlay manager; **zone de segment de recouvrement =** overlay region

◊ **segmentation** *nf* segmentation de la mémoire = granularity

◊ **segmenter** *vtr* to segment

seize *adj num & nm* sixteen; **(système à) seize bits =** sixteen-bit *ou* 16-bit; **in seize** *ou* **in-16 =** sixteenmo *ou* 16mo

sélecteur *nm* selector; **tournez le sélecteur =** turn the selector control; **c'est là que se trouve le sélecteur d'amplitude =** the selector knob for the amplification is located there; **sélecteur de port =** port selector

◊ **sélecteur, -trice** *adj* selector; **canal sélecteur =** selector channel

◊ **sélectif, -ive** *adj* selective; **accès sélectif =** random access; **fichiers à accès sélectif =** random access files; **mémoire à accès sélectif =** random access storage; **appel sélectif =** polling *ou* selective calling; **appel sélectif de groupe =** group poll; **temps d'appels sélectifs =** polling overhead; **faire une lecture sélective =** scatter read; **recherche sélective =** area search; *(de mémoire)* **test sélectif =** leapfrog test; **test sélectif limité** *ou* **restreint =** crippled leapfrog test; **tri sélectif =** selective sort; **vidage sélectif =** selective dump

◊ **sélection** *nf* sélection; **la sélection des informations contenues dans une vaste base de données peut demander beaucoup de temps =** selection of information from a large database may take some time; **sélection automatique de vitesse de transmission** *ou* **de débit d'une ligne (en bauds) =** auto-baud scanning *ou* auto-baud sensing; **sélection des couleurs =** colour separation; **sélection par menu =** menu selection; **canal de sélection =** selector channel; **filtre de sélection du signal maximal** *ou* **minimal =** auctioneering device; **ligne de sélection d'un circuit intégré =** chip select line; **la**

ligne de validation de données est reliée à la ligne de sélection de la bascule = the data strobe line is connected to the latch chip select line; **marque de sélection d'un bloc =** block mark; **signal de sélection =** enabling signal

◊ **sélectionner** *vtr* to select *ou* to screen; *(activer)* to enable; *(par filtre)* to filter; **qui peut être sélectionné =** selectable; **(circuit** *ou* **dispositif) qui peut être sélectionné par cavalier =** jumper-selectable; **(paramètre) qui peut être sélectionné suivant les besoins de l'utilisateur =** user-selectable

◊ **sélectivité** *nf* selectivity

selon *prép* as per; **selon échantillon =** as per sample; **selon les spécifications =** as per specification

sémantique *nf&adj* la sémantique = semantics; **erreur de sémantique =** semantic error

sémaphore *nm (fonction ou technique)* semaphore

semblable *adj* identical

semi- *préfixe* semi-

◊ **semi-automatique** *adj* équipement de secours à démarrage semi-automatique = warm standby

◊ **semi-circulaire** *adj* antenne semi-circulaire = fan antenna

◊ **semi-compilé, -ée** *adj (programme)* semicompiled

◊ **semi-conducteur** *nm (composant)* semiconductor (device); **semi-conducteur CMOS =** complementary metal oxide semiconductor (CMOS); **semi-conducteur MOS =** metal oxide semiconductor (MOS); **semi-conducteur MOS à canal (de type) P =** p-channel MOS; **semi-conducteur à effet de champ MOSFET =** metal oxide semiconductor field effect transistor (MOSFET); **semi-conducteur de type P =** p-type semiconductor; **semi-conducteur au silicium =** silicon gate; **semi-conducteur simple =** pure semiconductor; **à base de semi-conducteurs =** solid-state; **dispositif à semi-conducteurs =** solid-state device; **mémoire à semi-conducteur =** semiconductor memory

◊ **semi-conducteur, -trice** *adj* semiconductor; **matériau semi-**

conducteur de type N = n-type material *ou* N-type material *ou* n-type semiconductor

semi-duplex *adj* half-duplex; **modem semi-duplex** = half-duplex modem; **certains modems peuvent fonctionner en mode semi-duplex si nécessaire** = some modems can operate in half-duplex mode if required

semi-perforé, -ée *adj* **bande semi-perforée** = chadded *ou* chadless tape

sensibilité *nf* sensitivity; **la sensibilité du scanner aux petits objets** = the scanner's sensitivity to small objects

◊ **sensible** sensitive; **cet ordinateur est sensible aux moindres variations du courant** = the computer is sensitive even to very slight changes in current; **les disques durs sont très sensibles aux secousses** *ou* **aux chocs** = hard disks are very sensitive to jarring; **sensible à la lumière** = light-sensitive; **(système) peu sensible aux dérangements** = fault-tolerant (system); **ils ont commercialisé, avec beaucoup de succès, une gamme de minis très peu sensibles aux dérangements** = they market a highly successful range of fault-tolerant minis

◊ **sensitif, -ive** *adj* **clavier sensitif** = touch-sensitive keyboard *ou* tactile keyboard

séparateur *nm* **(a)** *(symbole ou code)* delimiter; **séparateur de champs** = field marker *ou* separator **(b)** *(de papier listing)* burster

◊ **séparation** *nf* separation; **séparation chromatique** *ou* **séparation des couleurs** = colour separation; **masque de séparation** = aperture mask; **négatifs de séparation des couleurs** = colour separations

◊ **séparé, -ée** *adj* separated; **caractères graphiques séparés** = separated graphics

◊ **séparément** *adv* separately *ou* independently; **ces articles sont indexés séparément** = each item is indexed independently

◊ **séparer** *vtr* to separate; *(par filtre)* to filter

sept *adj num & nm* seven

◊ **septet** *nm (mot de sept bits)* septet

séquence *nf* sequence *ou* set; *(de mots ou caractères)* string; **séquence d'appel** = calling sequence; **séquence binaire** = binary sequence; **séquence de commande (d'exécution)** = control sequence; **planification de la séquence d'exécution des tâches** = job scheduling; **séquence de fusionnement** *ou* **de classement** = collating sequence; **séquence de marqueurs** *ou* **d'indicateurs** = flag sequence; **séquence d'ouverture de session** *ou* **d'identification** = logon sequence; *(en bits)* **séquence d'identification** = identity burst; **contrôle de séquence** = sequence check; **registre de contrôle de séquence** = sequence control register (SCR) *ou* sequence counter *ou* sequence register

◊ **séquenceur** *nm* sequencer

séquentiel, -ielle *adj* sequential *ou* serial *ou* linear; **accès séquentiel** = sequential access *ou* serial access; **fichier à accès séquentiel** = sequential file *ou* serial file; **mémoire à accès séquentiel** = sequential access storage *ou* serial access memory (SAM); **méthode d'accès séquentiel par clé** = keyed sequential access method (KSAM); **méthode d'accès séquentiel en file (d'attente)** = queued sequential access method (QSAM); **méthode d'accès séquentiel indexé (ISAM)** = indexed sequential access method (ISAM); **méthode d'accès séquentiel indexé en file (d'attente)** = queued indexed sequential access method (QISAM); **additionneur séquentiel** = serial adder; **si l'entrée dans le circuit séquentiel logique est 1101, la sortie sera toujours zéro (0)** = if the input sequence to the sequential logic circuit is 1101 the output will always be zero (0); **liste séquentielle** = linear list; **logique séquentielle** = sequential logic; **mémoire séquentielle** = serial memory *ou* serial storage; **la bande magnétique constitue une mémoire séquentielle d'une grande capacité** = magnetic tape is a high capacity serial memory; **mémoire séquentielle indexée** = indexed sequential storage; **mode séquentiel** = sequential mode; **traitement par lots en mode séquentiel** = sequential batch processing; **opération séquentielle** = sequential operation *ou* serial operation; **suivant un ordre séquentiel** = sequentially; **recherche séquentielle** = linear search *ou* sequential search; **stockage séquentiel** = serial storage;

traitement séquentiel = serial processing *ou* sequential processing

série *nf* **(a)** series *ou* suite *ou* set; *(de produits)* = family; **série de commutateurs** = switch train; **série d'erreurs consécutives** = error burst; *(math)* **série de Fourier** = Fourier series; **série de mots** = word serial; **série de programmes (l'un à la suite de l'autre)** = suite of programs; **le système de traitement de texte utilise une série de trois programmes reliés: un éditeur de texte, un correcteur d'orthographe et un contrôleur d'impression** = the word-processing system uses a suite of three programs: editor, spelling checker and printing controller **(b) en série** = serial; *(disposé ou monté)* serially; *(exécuté)* sequentially; **accès série** = serial access; **additionneur (en) série** = serial adder; **bus série** = daisy chain bus; **circuit (disposé en) série** = series circuit; **commutateurs en série** = switch train; **leur vitesse de transmission est de 64 000 bits par seconde avec connexion parallèle ou 19 200 avec connexion série** = their transmission rate is 64,000 bits per second through a parallel connection or 19,200 serially; **convertisseur série/parallèle** = serial to parallel converter; **entrée/sortie en série** = serial input/output (SIO); **entrée série/sortie parallèle** = serial input/parallel output (SIPO); **entrée parallèle/sortie série** = parallel input/serial output (PISO); **entrée série/sortie série** = serial input/serial output (SISO); **fichier série extensible** = extending serial file; **imprimante série** = serial printer; **interface série** = serial interface; **de façon générale, les connexions parallèles sont moins difficiles à mettre en place et à utiliser que les interfaces série, mais leur longueur est limitée à environ 6 mètres** = parallel connections are usually less trouble to set up and use than serial interfaces, but are usually limited to 20 feet in length; **interruption en série** = daisy chain interrupt; **ordinateur série** = sequential computer *ou* serial computer; **port série** = serial port; **relier en série** = to daisy-chain; **traitement en série** = serial processing; **transmission (en) série** = serial transmission; **transmission de données en série** = serial data transmission; **transmission d'octets en série** = byte serial transmission *ou* mode **(c) logiciel de série** = canned software

sérieux, -ieuse *adj* serious; *(d'équipement)* **panne sérieuse** = hard failure

serrage *nm* **molette de serrage** = pinchwheel

◊ **serré, -ée** *adj* compact

serveur *nm* server; *(ordinateur)* server; **serveur de fichier** = file server; **serveur de message** = interface message processor; **serveur de réseau local** = local area network server *ou* LAN server; **centre serveur** = information retrieval centre

service *nm* **(a)** service *ou* facility; **service de coupures de presse** = press-cutting service *ou* clipping service; **la société offre, entre autres, des services d'imprimerie et de saisie de données** = the company offers a number of bureau services, such as printing and data capture; **service (fournisseur) d'informations** *ou* **service de base de données spécialisée (pour vidéotex)** = information provider (IP); **services informatiques** = computer services; **nous offrons à nos clients un service de traitement de leurs propres disquettes** = we offer facilities for processing a customer's own disks; **service de maintenance** = maintenance (service); **service de téléinformatique** *ou* **de transmission de données** = data services; **réseau numérique à intégration de services (RNIS)** = integrated services digital network (ISDN); **société de services** = bureau; **nous faisons faire la manipulation de données par une société de services informatiques** = our data manipulation is handled by a bureau; **société de services et d'ingénierie informatique (SSII)** = computer bureau **(b)** *(section)* department; **service après-vente** *ou* **service clients** = customer service department; **service informatique** = computer department; **responsable** *ou* **chef du service informatique** = data processing manager **(c)** *(appareil)* **en service** = in use *ou* busy; **hors service** = out of use

se servir de *vpr* to use; **je regrette, mais il y a déjà quelqu'un qui se sert de l'imprimante** = sorry, the printer is already in use *ou* is already being used

servomécanisme   *nm* servo *ou* servomechanism

session *nf* session; **couche session =** session layer; **clore une session =** to log off *ou* log out; **clôture de session =** logging off *ou* logging out; **ouverture de session =** logging in *ou* logging on; **clé d'ouverture d'une session =** session key; **ouverture automatique d'une session =** automatic log on *ou* auto-login *ou* auto-logon; **ouvrir** *ou* **débuter une session =** to log in *ou* to log on; *(en s'identifiant)* to sign on; **sortie de session =** timeout; **terminer une session =** to log off *ou* to log out; *(en s'identifiant)* to sign off

seuil *nm* threshold; **circuit à seuil =** threshold gate; **jonction pn à seuil =** step pn-junction; **valeur de seuil =** threshold value; **zone interface pn à seuil =** step pn-junction

sextet *nm (mot de six bits)* sextet

Shannon *npr* **loi de Shannon =** Shannon's Law

◊ **shannon** *nm (unité d'information)* shannon

SI = SYSTEME INTERNATIONAL; **unités SI =** SI units

sibilance *nf* sibilance

sifflement *nm* hiss *ou* sibilance

sigle *nm* initials; **que signifie le sigle IBM? =** what do the initials IBM stand for?

signal *nm* signal; **le signal s'est affaibli** *ou* **s'est éteint rapidement =** the signal decayed rapidly; **signal d'appel =** call signal *ou* calling signal; **signal d'appel accepté** *ou* **d'acceptation d'appel =** call accepted signal; *(émis par un périphérique)* **signal d'appel externe =** external interrupt; **signal de basse fréquence =** bass signal; **signal bipolaire =** bipolar signal; **signal blanc =** white flag; **signal de chrominance =** chrominance signal; **signal continu =** continuous signal; **signal de contrôle** *ou* **de commande =** control signal; **signal de contrôle d'appel =** call control signal;

signal de détection de porteuse = data carrier detect signal *ou* DCD signal; **l'appel est bloqué si le logiciel ne reçoit pas de signal de détection de porteuse =** the call is stopped if the software does not receive a DCD signal from the modem; **les signaux élémentaires de ce système de radiotransmission sont 10ms à 40kHz pour le bit nul et 10 ms à 60 kHz pour le bit chargé =** the signal elements for the radio transmission system are 10ms of 40KHz and 10ms of 60KHz for binary 0 and 1 respectively; **signal d'entrée =** input signal; **signal d'exécution =** execute signal; **signal de fin de page =** end of page indicator; **signal de fin de report =** carry complete signal; *(d'un système stéréophonique)* **signal groupé =** M signal; **signal importé =** imported signal; **signal (d') interruption =** interrupt signal; **signal d'invalidation** *ou* **d'interdiction de transmission =** inhibiting input; **signal de lecture d'instruction =** fetch signal; **signal de luminance =** luminance signal; **signal numérique =** digital signal; **transmission de signaux numériques =** digital signalling; **signaux parasites =** garbage; **signal polarisé =** polar signal; **le message a été récupéré en traitant** *ou* **analysant le signal porteur =** the message was recovered by carrier signal processing; **signal de sélection =** enabling signal; **signal sonore =** alarm *ou* bleep; **un signal sonore prévient qu'il ne reste plus de papier dans l'imprimante =** an alarm rings when the printer has run out of paper; **caractère (de déclenchement) de signal sonore =** bell character; **signaux synchrones aux impulsions d'horloge =** clocked signals; *(télévision)* **signal de synchronisation =** hold (signal); **signaux de transmission de données =** data signals; **signal unipolaire =** unipolar signal; **signal de validation =** enabling signal; **signal vidéo =** video signal; **porteuse de signal vidéo =** image carrier; **signal vidéo composite =** composite video signal; **amplificateur de signal =** launch amplifier *ou* line driver; **conversion de signaux =** signal conversion; **convertisseur de signaux =** signal converter; **coupure** *ou* **perte** *ou* **distorsion d'un signal =** signal breakup; **distance entre signaux =** signal distance *ou* Hamming distance; **écoute de signal à accès multiple avec détection de collision** *ou* **protocole de transmission CSMA-CD =** carrier sense multiple access - collision detection (CSMA-CD); **élément (d'un)**

signal = signal element; **l'élément signal de ce système est une courte impulsion de tension qui représente un 1 binaire** = the signal element in this system is a short voltage pulse, indicating a binary one; **émettre un signal** = to signal; *(d'échantillonnage ou de validation)* to strobe; **le signal émis par l'ordinateur contenait la réponse** = the signal received from the computer contained the answer; **envoie un signal au réseau pour prévenir que nous sommes occupés** = signal to the network that we are busy; **générateur de signaux** = signal generator; **inhibition du signal** = signal blanking; **limiteur** ou **réducteur de signal audio** = audio compressor; **impulsion d'inhibition du signal** = blanking pulse; **mise en forme** ou **conversion de signaux** = signal conditioning; **niveau d'un signal** = signal level; **rapport signal/bruit** = signal to noise ratio ou S/N ou s/n ratio; **suppression du signal** = signal blanking; **traitement du signal** = signal processing; **ce système est à la disposition des étudiants qui se spécialisent dans la recherche sur les techniques de traitement du signal** = the system is used by students doing research on signal processing techniques; **transmettre un signal** = to signal; **transmission de signaux** = signalling; **transmission de signaux sur la bande vocale** = in band signalling; **transmission directe de signaux** = DC signalling

◊ **signaler** *vtr&i* to signal ou to send a signal; **signale au réseau que nous sommes occupés** = signal to the network that we are busy

◊ **signaleur** *nm (pour système d'appel de personne)* **signaleur d'appel** = pager ou radio pager ou radio paging device; **appeler** ou **chercher à joindre quelqu'un par signaleur d'appel** = to page someone ou to bleep someone

◊ **signalisation** *nf* signalling; **signalisation par canal banal** ou **par voie commune** = common channel signalling; **signalisation hors bande (vocale)** = out of band signalling; **signalisation multifréquence DTMF** = dual tone, multifrequency (DTMF); **signalisation tonale** = tone signalling

le signal de sortie de ces électrodes peut être décodé, donnant la position spatiale
Opto Electronique

signature *nf* signature; **reconnaissez-vous la signature sur le chèque?** = do you recognize the signature on the cheque?; **signature électronique** = electronic signature; **signature numérique** = digital signature

signe *nm* sign ou mark; **signe de l'addition (+)** = plus (sign); **signes de correction (d'épreuves d'imprimerie)** = proof correction marks; **signe diacritique** = diacritic; **signe de la division (÷)** = division sign; **signe du dollar ($)** = dollar sign; **signe et modulo** = sign and modulus; **signe de la multiplication (×)** = multiplication sign; **signe de polarité** = polarity sign; **signe de ponctuation** = punctuation mark; **signe de la soustraction (−)** = minus (sign); **binaire de signe** ou **bit de signe** ou **chiffre (indicateur) de signe** = sign digit ou sign bit ou sign indicator; **champ (de) signe** = signed field; **chiffre (de) signe** = sign and magnitude ou signed magnitude; **position du signe** = sign position; **reconnaissance optique de signes** = optical mark recognition (OMR); **sans signe** = unsigned

significatif, -ive *adj* significant; **bit significatif** ou **le plus significatif** = most significant bit (MSB); **le bit le plus significatif dans un mot de huit bits représente 128 en notation décimale** = the most significant bit in an eight bit binary word represents 128 in decimal notation; **bit le moins significatif** = least significant bit (LSB); **chiffre le moins significatif** = least significant digit (LSD) ou low-order digit; **6 est le chiffre le moins significatif du nombre 234156** = the number 234156 has a low-order digit of 6; **le chiffre le plus significatif** = most significant character ou most significant digit (MSD); **codes significatifs** = significant digit codes ou faceted codes

◊ **signification** *nf* significance

◊ **signifier** *vtr* to signify ou to represent ou to mean; **l'envoi d'un code CR signifie que la ligne saisie est terminée** = a carriage return code signifies the end of an input line; **le message DISK FULL signifie que le disque n'a plus l'espace voulu pour enregistrer de nouvelles données** = the message DISK FULL means that there is no more room on the disk for further data; **sauvegarder signifie faire la copie du fichier de travail actuel sur une deuxième disquette** = backing up involves copying current working files onto a separate storage disk

silence *nm* silence; **facteur de silence =** omission factor

◊ **silencieux, -ieuse** *adj* quiet; **les imprimantes laser sont beaucoup plus silencieuses que les imprimantes matricielles =** laser printers are much quieter than dot-matrix

silicium *nm* silicon; **silicium sur saphir =** silicon on sapphire (SOS); **fonderie de silicium =** silicon foundry; **pastille** *ou* **puce de silicium =** silicon chip; **tranche de silicium =** silicon wafer; **intégration sur tranche de silicium =** wafer scale integration; **transistor silicium =** silicon transistor

simili *nm* = SIMILIGRAVURE

◊ **similigravure** *nf (planche)* halftone; *(procédé)* halftone process *ou* halftoning; **on utilise du papier glacé pour l'impression de similigravures =** glossy paper is used for printing halftones

simple *adj* simple *ou* single; *(math)* **simple précision =** single precision; **disquette à simple densité =** single density disk (SD); **disquette simple face =** single-sided disk (SSD); **guillemets simples =** single quotes; **semi-conducteur simple =** pure semiconductor

◊ **simplex** *nm* simplex *ou* single operation

◊ **simplifié, -ée** *adj* **(a)** simplified **(b)** abbreviated; **adressage simplifié =** abbreviated addressing *ou* abb. add.

◊ **simplifier** *vtr* **(a)** to simplify; **les touches de fonction simplifient l'exploitation d'un programme =** function keys simplify program operation **(b)** to abbreviate

simulateur *nm* simulator; **simulateur (de) Turing =** Turing machine; **simulateur de vol =** flight simulator

◊ **simulation** *nf* simulation; **simulation en temps réel =** real-time simulation; **les techniques de simulation sont devenues très sophistiquées =** simulation techniques have reached a high degree of sophistication; **logiciel de simulation =** simulation software

◊ **simuler** *vtr* to simulate; **ce logiciel simule les manoeuvres aériennes** *ou* **est un simulateur de vol =** this software simulates the action of an aeroplane

> d'un côté, l'électronique rend la bataille de plus en plus abstraite - comme dans les simulateurs, le conducteur de char voit sa cible non plus à l'oeil nu, mais sur l'écran
> *L'Express*

simultané, -ée *adj* **(a)** simultaneous *ou* concurrent; **de façon simultanée =** simultaneously; **traitement simultané =** simultaneous processing; **transmission simultanée =** simultaneous transmission **(b)** **report simultané =** ripple-through carry

◊ **simultanéité** *nf* simultaneity

◊ **simultanément** *adv* simultaneously *ou* concurrently; **chacune des applications exécutées simultanément possède sa propre fenêtre =** each concurrent process has its own window

singulièrement *adv (étrangement)* abnormally; **le taux d'erreur de cette disquette est singulièrement élevé =** the error rate with this disk is abnormally high

sinon *voir aussi* ELSE

sinus *nm* sin *ou* sine

◊ **sinusoïdal, -e** *adj* sinusoidal; **onde sinusoïdale =** sine wave *ou* sinusoidal waveform

◊ **sinusoïde** **1** *nf* sine wave *ou* sinusoidal waveform; **le signal porteur est une sinusoïde =** the carrier has a sinusoidal waveform **2** *adj* sinusoidal

siphonage *nm* siphoning

site *nm* site; **les trois modèles offrent des possibilités d'extension sur site =** all three models have an on-site upgrade facility; **appel (à émettre) à tous les terminaux d'un site =** site poll; **licence de site =** software licence

situer *vtr* to locate

six *adj num & nm* six

SNOBOL = STRING ORIENTATED SYMBOLIC LANGUAGE *voir aussi* LANGAGE

société *nf* company *ou* firm; **société d'assistance technique** = a consultancy firm; **société de services** = bureau; **société de services et d'ingénierie informatique (SSII)** = computer bureau; **société de traitement de texte** = word-processing bureau

sodium *nm* **hyposulfite** *ou* **thiosulfate de sodium** = sodium thiosulfate; *(familier)* hypo

sol *nm* ground; **station au sol** = ground station

solaire *adj* solar; **énergie solaire** = solar power; **pile solaire** = solar cell; **calculatrice à pile(s) solaire(s)** = solar-powered calculator

solénoïde *nm* solenoid

solide *nm* **(a)** solid *ou* robust; **ce disque dur n'est pas très solide** = this hard disk is not very robust **(b) laser à composant solide** = solid-state laser
◊ **solidité** *nf* robustness

solution *nf* **(a)** *(liquid)* solution **(b)** *(réponse à un problème)* solution

sommaire *nm* summary; *(page vidéotex)* lead-in page

somme *nf* sum

son *nm* sound; **son dérivé** = derived sound; **son pur** = pure tone; **circuit intégré générateur de son** = sound chip *ou* music chip; **décalage en avance de la bande son** = sound advance; **synthétiseur de son** = music synthesizer *ou* sound synthesizer

sonar *nm* = SOUND NAVIGATION AND RANGING sonar

sonde *nf* biosensor

sonique *adj* sonic

sonner *vi* to ring; *(vibreur)* to buzz
◊ **sonnerie** *nf* **(a)** *(dispositif)* bell; *(vibreur)* buzzer; **sonnerie d'appel à harmonique** = harmonic telephone ringer **(b)** *(action)* ringing; **sonnerie décimonique** *ou* **sonnerie à résonnance de fréquence** = decimonic ringing
◊ **sonore** *adj* sound; **effets sonores** = sound effects; **tous les effets sonores du film sont produits électroniquement** = all the sound effects for the film are produced electronically; **effets sonores postsynchronisés** = dubbed sound; **onde sonore** = sound wave; **piste sonore** = sound track; **signal sonore** = bleep *ou* buzz *ou* alarm; **un signal sonore prévient qu'il ne reste plus de papier dans l'imprimante** = an alarm rings when the printer has run out of paper; **vibration sonore** = buzz; **émettre une vibration sonore** = to buzz
◊ **sonorisation** *nf* sound; *(système)* public address system (PA); **le studio est câblé pour la sonorisation** = the studio is wired for sound

sophistication *nf* sophistication
◊ **sophistiqué, -ée** *adj* sophisticated; **le nouveau progiciel est tout à fait sophistiqué** = the sophistication of the new package is remarkable; **les techniques de simulation sont devenues très sophistiquées** = simulation techniques have reached a high degree of sophistication

sortance *nf (d'un circuit)* fan-out

sorti, -e *adj* dernier entré premier sorti = last in first out (LIFO); **cet ordinateur gère la pile suivant la méthode du dernier entré premier sorti** = this computer stack uses a last in first out data retrieval method; **premier entré premier sorti** = first in first out (FIFO); **mémoire qui fonctionne sur le principe du premier entré premier sorti** = FIFO memory
◊ **sortie** *nf* **(a)** *(point)* outlet **(b) sortie de session** = timeout **(c)** *(de données)* output (o/p *ou* O/P); **sortie d'imprimante** = computer printout *ou* computer listing *ou* hard copy *ou* information output; **sortie (sur) microfilm** = computer output on microfilm (COM); **sortie numérique** = digital output; **sortie d'ordinateur** = computer output; **sortie vocale** = voice output; **appareil** *ou* **périphérique** *ou* **dispositif de sortie** =

output device; **commutateur à deux sorties** = D-type flip-flop; **données de sortie** = computer output *ou* output data; **facteur pyramidal de sortie** = fan-out; **fichier de sortie** = output file; **flux (de données) de sortie** = output stream; **formateur de données de sortie** = output formatter; **mode sortie** = output mode; **point de sortie** = exit point; **port (de) sortie** = output port; **registre (de) sortie** = output register; **registre tampon de sortie** = output buffer register; **vitesse de sortie de l'information** = information rate; **zone sortie (de la mémoire)** = output area *ou* block; *voir aussi* ENTREE/SORTIE

◊ **sortir** *vi* **(a)** to leave *ou* to quit **(b)** to originate from; **les données sortent du nouvel ordinateur** = the data originated from the new computer

il possède également une sortie vidéo et une sortie audio pour se connecter à un téléviseur
Hi-fi Vidéo

souder *vtr* to solder

◊ **soudure** *nf* solder; **sans soudure** = solderless; *voir aussi* DESSOUDER

soulignage *nm* underlining *ou* underscoring

◊ **soulignement** *nm* underlining *ou* underscoring

◊ **souligner** *vtr* to underline *ou* to underscore; **on souligne deux fois l'entête d'un chapitre et une seule fois celui d'un paragraphe** = the chapter headings are given a double underline and the paragraphs a single underline

souple *adj* flexible; **disque souple** = flexible disk *ou* floppy disk *ou* floppy *ou* FD *ou* fd

◊ **souplesse** *nf* flexibility

source *nf* **(a)** source; **source de données** = data source; *(société)* **source d'informations** = information provider (IP); **code source** = source code; **éditeur de (programme) source** = source editor; **fichier source** = source file; **langage source** = source language; **listing de (programme) source** = source listing; **ordinateur de source** = source machine; **processeur de programme source** = source machine; **programme source** = source program; *(du curseur)* **retour à la source** = homing **(b)** *(électricité)* **source**

d'alimentation = power supply; **brancher une ligne sur une source d'alimentation** = to pull up a line **(c)** **utilisation d'une seconde source de composants** = second-sourcing

sourd, -e *adj (personne)* deaf; *(chambre)* anechoic (chamber)

souris *nf* mouse; **(logiciel) contrôlé** *ou* **piloté par une souris** = mouse-driven (software); **(programme) pilote de souris** = mouse driver

pour activer une commande, il suffit de cliquer Gauche sur le nom de la commande. De même, pour visualiser les options à l'intérieur d'un champ, vous cliquez sur le bouton droit de la souris
L'Ordinateur Individuel

sous- *préfixe* sub-

◊ **sous-classe** *nf* subclass

◊ **sous-ensemble** *nm* subset; *(d'un programme)* bead

◊ **sous-exposé, -ée** *adj (film)* underexposed

◊ **sous-programme** *nm* subroutine *ou* subprogram; **appel d'un sous-programme** = subroutine call; **sous-programme additionnel** = inserted subroutine; **sous-programme de bibliothèque** = library subroutine; **sous-programme chaîné** = linked subroutine; **sous-programme à deux niveaux** = two-level subroutine; **sous-programme direct** = one-level subroutine; **sous-programme fermé** *ou* **réentrant** = closed subroutine *ou* linked subroutine; **sous-programme d'insertion directe** = direct-insert subroutine; **sous-programme mathématique** = mathematical subroutine; **sous-programme ouvert** = open subroutine; **sous-programme paramétrable** = dynamic subroutine; **sous-programme statique** = static subroutine

◊ **sous-répertoire** *nm* subdirectory

les fichiers MS-DOS d'un utilisateur sont stockés dans un sous-répertoire
L'Information professionnelle

sous-segment *nm* subsegment

◊ **sous-système** *nm* subsystem

◊ **sous-total** *nm* subtotal

soustracteur *nm* subtractor; **soustracteur complet** *ou* **à trois entrées** = full subtractor

◊ **soustraction** *nf* subtraction; **signe de la soustraction (-)** = minus *ou* minus sign
◊ **soustraire** *vtr* to subtract *ou* to deduct; **nombre à soustraire d'un autre** = subtrahend; **nombre duquel on soustrait** = minuend

soutenir *vtr* to back

spatial, -e *adj* space; **station spatiale** = space station; **véhicule** *ou* **engin spatial** = space craft

spécial, -e *adj* special; **caractère spécial** = special character; **effets spéciaux** = special effects; **fonte spéciale** = special sort; **système spécial** = special purpose system
◊ **spécialisé, -ée** *adj* **(a)** dedicated; **appareil de traitement de texte spécialisé** = dedicated word processor; **canal spécialisé** = dedicated channel; **fonction logique spécialisée** = dedicated logic; **ligne téléphonique spécialisée** = dedicated line; **logiciel d'application spécialisée** = single function software; **logiciel non spécialisé** = device-independent software; **ordinateur spécialisé** = applications terminal; **ordinateur non spécialisé** = general purpose computer; **terminal spécialisé** = applications terminal *ou* job-orientated terminal; **voie spécialisée** = dedicated channel **(b) revue spécialisée** = learned journal; **service de base de données spécialisées (pour vidéotex)** = information provider (IP)
◊ **se spécialiser (en)** *vpr* to specialize (in)
◊ **spécialiste** **1** *nm&f* expert *ou* specialist *ou* consultant; **c'est un spécialiste en informatique** = he is a computer expert; **c'est une spécialiste des langages de programmation** = she is an expert in programming languages; **c'est un spécialiste des systèmes CAO** = he specializes in the design of CAD systems **2** *adj* specialist

spécification *nf* **(a)** specification; *(copie d'un dessin)* blueprint; **le travail ne répond pas aux spécifications du client** = the work does not meet the customer's specifications; **spécifications de conception** *ou* **de création** = design parameters; **spécification fonctionnelle** = functional specification; **spécifications du système** = system specifications;

selon les spécifications = as per specification **(b)** *(d'un programme)* **spécifications de présentation des données** = layout specifications; **spécifications d'un programme** *ou* **relatives à un programme** = program specifications **(c) spécification (du nom) du fichier** = filename extension
◊ **spécificité** *nf* specificity
◊ **spécifier** *vtr* to specify
◊ **spécifique** *adj* **adresse spécifique** = specific address; **codage spécifique** = specific coding; **code spécifique** = direct *ou* one-level *ou* specific code

spectre *nm* spectrum; **spectre de fréquences électromagnétiques** = electromagnetic spectrum; **spectre de fréquences radio** = radio spectrum; **analyseur de spectre** = spectrum analyzer

sphérique *adj* spherical; **aberration sphérique** = spherical aberration

spooling = SPOULE

sporadique *adj* sporadic; **erreur sporadique** = sporadic fault

spot *nm* **spot de balayage** = picture beam *ou* scanning spot

spoule *nm* spooling; **faire un spoule** = to spool; **impression par spoule** = print spooling; **mémoire auxiliaire pour spoule** = spooler *ou* spooling device; **unité de bande magnétique pour spoule** = spooler *ou* spooling device

sprite *nm* sprite

SSII = SOCIETE DE SERVICES ET D'INGENIERIE INFORMATIQUE

stabilisation *nf* *(après échantillonnage)* **commande de stabilisation du signal** = hold
◊ **stabilité** *nf* stability; **stabilité de l'image** = image stability
◊ **stable** *adj* stable; **la bande magnétique est stable entre 0° et 40 °C** = magnetic tape is stable within a temperature range of 0° to 40°C; **état stable** = stable state

stade *nm* stage; **le texte en est au stade de l'impression** = the text is ready for printing

standard 1 *nm* **(a)** *(norme)* **standard de cryptage de données** = data encryption standard (DES); **standards de fabrication** = production standards; **standards de programmation** = programming standards; **standards vidéo** = video standards **(b) standard téléphonique** = (telephone) switchboard **2** *adj inv* standard *ou* universal; *(document ou formulaire ou paragraphe ou texte)* standard (document *ou* form *ou* paragraph *ou* text); **fonction standard** = standard function; **format standard** = normal format; **interface standard** = standard interface; **langage standard** = machine-independent language; **lettre standard** = form letter *ou* repetitive letter *ou* standard letter; **logiciel non standard** = machine-dependent software; **objectif standard** = medium lens; **protocole standard de contrôle de liaisons** = basic mode link control; **schéma (de base de données) standard** = canonical schema; **sous-programme standard** = standard subroutine
◊ **standardisé, -ée** *adj* **le contrôle standardisé des voies de transmission** = the standardized control of transmission links
◊ **standardiser** *vtr* to standardize

standardiste *nm&f* (telephone) operator *ou* switchboard operator *ou* telephonist; **appeler la standardiste** = to dial the operator

station *nf* **(a)** *(ordinateur)* station; **station auxiliaire** = secondary station; **station primaire** = primary station; **station secondaire** = tributary station; **station de travail** = operating console *ou* workstation; **la mémoire d'archivage a une capacité de 1200 Mo pour sept stations de travail (CAO)** = the archive storage has a total capacity of 1200 Mb between seven workstations **(b)** *(de radio ou télévision)* station; **le signal de cette station émettrice est très faible** = the signal from this radio station is very weak; **nous essayons de brouiller les signaux émis par cette station** = we are trying to jam the signals from that station; **station de radio** = broadcasting station *ou* radio station; **station relais** =

local distribution service (LDS); **station au sol** = ground station; **station terrestre** = earth station; **station terrestre mobile** = mobile earth terminal

stationnaire *adj* stationary; **état stationnaire** = steady state

statique *adj* static; **alimentation statique sans coupure** = uninterruptable power supply (UPS); **électricité statique** = static electricity; **mémoire statique** = static memory *ou* static storage; **mémoire vive** *ou* **mémoire RAM statique** = static RAM; **sous-programme statique** = static subroutine; **translation statique** = static relocation; **vidage statique** = static dump

statisticien, -ienne *n* statistician
◊ **statistique 1** *nf* **la statistique** = statistics **2** *adj* statistical; **multiplexage temporel statistique** = statistical time division multiplexing (STDM)

statut *nm* status

stencil *nnm* stencil; **on se sert d'un masque ou d'un stencil pour reproduire le tracé du circuit du transistor sur le silicium** = a mask or stencil is used to transfer the transistor design onto silicon

stéradian *nm* steradian

stéréo *adj inv* = STEREOPHONIQUE

stéréophonique *ou* **stéréo** *adj* stereophonic *ou* stereo; **disque stéréo** = stereo record; **magnétophone stéréophonique** = stereophonic recorder; **microphone stéréophonique** = stereophonic microphone

stochastique *adj* stochastic; **modèle stochastique** = stochastic model

stock *nm* stock; **numéro de stock** = stock code *ou* stock number
◊ **stockage** *nm* storage; **stockage de données** *ou* **de l'information** = data storage *ou* information storage; **stockage de données sur disque** *ou* **disquette** = disk storage; **stockage de données sur support optique** = optical storage; **stockage de**

fichier = file storage; **stockage holographique** *ou* **d'hologramme** = holographic storage; **stockage d'instruction** = instruction storage; **stockage et restitution de données** = information storage and retrieval (ISR); **(système avec facilité de) stockage et retransmission** = store and forward (system); **stockage temporaire** = temporary storage; **système de stockage par descripteurs** = aspect system; **zone de stockage de l'image** = image storage space; **zone de stockage des variables** = string area

◊ **stocker** *vtr (en mémoire)* to store; **stocker (des données) avant traitement** = to prestore; **stocker dans la mémoire cache** = to cache; **ce programme peut stocker une police de caractères, quelle qu'en soit la taille, dans la mémoire cache** = this program can cache any size font

> sa capacité énorme permet de stocker sur l'une de ses faces une très grande quantité de données
> *Micro Systèmes*

stopper *vtr* to inhibit *ou* to interrupt

streamer *nm* floppy tape *ou* tape streamer *ou* streaming tape drive *ou* stringy floppy; **notre nouveau modèle est équipé d'un streamer de 96 Mo** = our new product has a 96Mb streaming tape drive; *voir aussi* DEVIDEUR

stroboscope *nm* stroboscope *ou* strobe

Strowger *npr* **central Strowger** = strowger exchange

structure *nf* structure *ou* framework; **structure d'un bus** = bus structure; **structure cartésienne** = cartesian structure; **structure de données** = data structure *ou* information structure; **structure dynamique de données** = dynamic data structure; **structure hiérarchique de données** = data hierarchy; **structure d'un fichier** = file layout *ou* file structure; *(d'un réseau)* **structure à maillage intégral** = plex structure; **structure d'un programme** = program structure; **on a d'abord établi la structure du programme** = the program framework was designed first; **structure en réseau** = network structure; **code** *ou* **élément de structure** = overhead; **les**

numéros de lignes sont des éléments de structure en BASIC = the line numbers in a BASIC program are an overhead

◊ **structuré, -ée** *adj* structured; **données structurées** = data aggregate; **modèle structuré** = structured design; **programmation structurée** = structured programming

◊ **structurer** *vtr* to structure

studio *nm (de création* *ou* *d'enregistrement* *ou* *de prise de vues)* studio; **studio de création** *ou* **de design** = design studio; **studio de mixage** = mixing studio

STX = START OF TEXT *voir aussi* DEBUT

style *nm* style; **style d'impression** = print style; **style (de la) maison** = house style; **feuille de style** = image master *ou* style sheet; **la feuille de style comporte 125 symboles programmables (selon les besoins de l'utilisateur)** = the style sheet contains 125 user-definable symbols

stylet *nm (de traceur)* plotter pen

stylo *nm* pen; **stylo électronique** = electronic pen *ou* stylus *ou* wand; **stylo optique** = light pen *ou* optical bar reader *ou* bar code reader *ou* optical wand; **stylo optique graphique** = graphics light pen

subdivisé, -ée *adj* subdivided *ou* partitioned; **fichier subdivisé** = partitioned file

◊ **subdiviser** *vtr* to subdivide *ou* to partition

substance *nf* substance

substituer *vtr* to substitute

◊ **substitution** *nf* substitution; **caractère de substitution** = substitute character; **erreur de substitution** = substitution error; **table de substitution** = substitution table

substrat *nm* substrate

subvocal, -e *adj* **canal de fréquences subvocales** = subvoice grade channel

successif, -ive *adj* successive; **chacune des opérations successives ajoute de nouveaux caractères à la chaîne** = each successive operation adds further characters to the string

suffixe *nm* suffix *ou* postfix

◊ **suffixé, -ée** *adj* **notation suffixée** = postfix notation *ou* suffix notation; **en notation normale on écrit: (x-y) + z, en notation suffixée on écrit: xy- z+** = normal notation: (x-y) + z, but using postfix notation: xy - z +

suite *nf* (a) suite *ou* sequence; **suite de programmes** suite of programs; **suite de tâches** = job stream; **l'un(e) à la suite de l'autre** = consecutively; **les différentes sections du programme s'éxécutent l'une à la suite de l'autre** = the sections of the program run consecutively (b) *(d'une page)* continuation page

suivre *vtr* (a) to follow; **marche à suivre** = procedure (b) *(un appel ou une lettre)* **faire suivre** = to forward; **faire suivre un appel veut dire le réacheminer automatiquement** = call forwarding is automatic redirection of calls (c) *(surveiller)* to monitor; **il suit le progrès des programmeurs débutants** = he is monitoring the progress of the trainee programmers

super- *préfixe* super-; **intégration à super grande échelle** = super large scale integration (SLSI)

superflu, -e *adj* redundant; **les bits de parité des données reçues sont superflus et peuvent être supprimés** = the parity bits on the received data are redundant and can be removed

superhétérodyne *adj* superheterodyne; **radio superhétérodyne** = superheterodyne radio

supérieur, -e *adj* (a) upper *ou* top; **bac supérieur** = upper bin; **coin gauche supérieur de l'écran** = top left corner of a screen *ou* cursor home; **marge supérieure** = top margin *ou* top space; **partie supérieure** = top part (b) **de qualité supérieure** = high quality *ou* top quality

superposer *vtr* (a) to overlap; *(pour créer un nouveau caractère)* **superposer des caractères** = to overstrike; *(en détruisant les données en mémoire)* **superposer des données** = to overwrite data (b) *(deux circuits)* to piggyback; **superposez ces deux puces pour augmenter la capacité de la mémoire** = piggyback those two memory chips to boost the memory capacity

◊ **superposition** *nf* (a) overlap; **remplacer** *ou* **effacer** *ou* **détruire des données par superposition d'écriture** = to overwrite data; **les nouvelles données ont remplacé les anciennes par superposition d'écriture** = the latest data input has overwritten the old information (b) **superposition d'un accusé de réception au message suivant** = piggybacking

superstation *nf US* superstation

superviser *vtr* to supervise

◊ **superviseur** *nm&adj* supervisor; **(programme) superviseur** = supervisor (program) *ou* executive program *ou* supervisory program *ou* run-time system; *(pour multiprogrammation)* scheduler; **superviseur d'entrée/sortie** = input/output executive; **instruction de superviseur** = executive instruction; **terminal superviseur** = executive terminal

◊ **supervision** *nf* supervision; **de supervision** = supervisory; **signal de supervision** = supervisory signal

supplémentaire *adj* additional *ou* extra; *(dispositif)* add-on *ou* add-in (device); **peut-on ajouter trois postes** *ou* **stations de travail supplémentaires au réseau?** = can we add three additional workstations to the network?; **bit supplémentaire** = overhead bit

support *nm* (a) *(physique)* support *ou* carrier; **support de cartes** = card cage *ou* card frame *ou* card chassis; **support de carte d'extension** = card extender; **cartes montées sur supports** = rack mounted cards (b) medium *ou* support *ou* carrier; **support à accès direct** = direct access storage device (DASD); **support de données** *ou* **d'information** = data medium; **(code de) fin de support de données** = end of medium (EM); **tri sur support externe** = external sort; **support de données d'un fichier** = file storage;

support de polices de caractères = image carrier; **support intermédiaire** = intermediate materials; **ces diapositives et photos sont les supports intermédiaires qui doivent être recopiés sur le vidéodisque** = those slides and photographs are the intermediate materials to be mastered onto the video disk; **support magnétique** = magnetic material *ou* magnetic medium; **enregistrement sur support magnétique** = magnetic recording; **vidage de transfert sur support magnétique** = dump; **support magnétique effaçable** *ou* **réutilisable** = erasable storage *ou* erasable memory; **support magnétique haute densité** = high density storage; **un disque dur est un support de haute densité par rapport à une bande perforée** = a hard disk is a high density storage medium compared to paper tape; **support magnétique original** = magnetic master; **support magnétique vierge** = empty medium; **support de stockage** = storage medium; **il existe différents types de supports de stockage dont les bandes papier, les disques et bandes magnétiques, les cartes et microfiches** = data storage mediums such as paper tape, magnetic disk, magnetic tape, card and microfiche are available; **support de stockage de grande capacité** = bulk storage medium *ou* mass storage device; **un disque dur constitue un véritable support de stockage de grande capacité** = a hard disk is definitely a mass storage device; **la bande magnétique constitue un support de stockage de grande capacité très sûr** = magnetic tape is a reliable bulk storage medium; **support publicitaire** = advertising medium; **support de transmission** = transmission medium; **support vierge** = empty medium; **code support** = skeletal code

◇ **supporter** *vtr* to back *ou* to support

suppresseur *nm* suppressor; **suppresseur de diaphonie** = de-bounce

◇ **suppression** *nf* suppression *ou* deletion *ou* removal; **suppression du signal** = blanking; **(bouton de) suppression de signal d'appel parasite** = anti-tinkle suppression; **suppression horizontale (du signal)** = horizontal blanking; **suppression verticale (du signal)** = field blanking (interval); **caractère de suppression** = delete character

◇ **supprimer** *vtr* to suppress *ou* to delete *ou* to remove; *(d'un disque ou d'une mémoire)* to delete *ou* to scrub *ou* to scratch; **le traitement de texte permet de supprimer un fichier complet en appuyant sur cette touche** = the word-processor allows us to delete a whole file by pressing this key; **lorsqu'il s'agit de supprimer un texte assez long, servez-vous de la commande qui permet d'effacer en bloc** = use the global delete command to remove large areas of unwanted text; **ce filtre sert à supprimer les bruits parasites** = the filter is used to suppress the noise due to static interference

supravocal, -e *adj* above voice; *(transmission)* **données supravocales** = data above voice (DAV)

sûr, -e *adj* safe *ou* secure; **ce code chiffré est très sûr puisqu'il comporte une clé avec un très grand nombre de permutations possibles** = this cipher system is very secure since there are so many possible permutations for the key

sur- *préfixe* super-

◇ **surbrillance** *nf* mettre en surbrillance = to highlight; **mot** *ou* **caractères en surbrillance** = (display) highlights

◇ **surcharge** *nf* **(a)** overload; **surcharge d'une voie** *ou* **d'un canal** = channel overload **(b)** *(pour créer un nouveau caractère)* **faire une surcharge** = to overstrike

◇ **surcharger** *(canal ou voie ou système)* to overload; **l'ordinateur est vraiment surchargé par tout ce travail** = the computer is overloaded with that amount of processing

◇ **surchauffer** *vi* to overheat

◇ **suréquipement** *nm* **suréquipement de sécurité** = redundant equipment

surface *nf* **(a)** *(dessus)* surface; **monter en surface** = to piggyback **(b)** *(mesure)* area; **mesure de surface** = square measure

surimposer *vtr* to superimpose

◇ **surimpression** *nf* multipass overlap; *(pour créer un nouveau caractère)* **faire une surimpression** = to overstrike

surintensité *nf (de courant)* surge

surligneur *nm* marker pen

surmodulation *nf* overmodulation

surperforation *nf* overpunching

surtension *nf* surge *ou* over-voltage; **(dispositif de) protection contre la surtension** = over-voltage protection (device)

surveillance *nf* supervision *ou* control; **de surveillance** = supervisory; **instruction de surveillance** = supervisory instruction; *(micro espion)* **dispositif de surveillance** = bug
◊ **surveillant, -e** *n* supervisor
◊ **surveillé, -ée** *adj* supervised *ou* monitored *ou* attended *ou* controlled; **opération surveillée** = attended operation
◊ **surveiller** *vtr* to supervise *ou* to monitor *ou* to control; **la confection des cartes de circuits imprimés est très soigneusement surveillée** = the manufacture of circuit boards is very carefully supervised; **surveiller par micro-espion** = to bug

survenir *vi* to occur

survoltage *nm* surge *ou* over-voltage; **(dispositif de) protection contre le survoltage** = over-voltage protection (device)

symbole *nm* **(a)** symbol; **ce langage utilise le symbole ? pour la commande d'impression** = this language uses the symbol ? to represent the print command; **symbole d'arrêt (dynamique)** = breakpoint symbol; **symbole de décision** = decision box; **symboles ECMA** = ECMA symbols; **symbole graphique** = graphic symbol; **symbole logique** = logic symbol; **symboles d'un ordinogramme** = flowchart symbols; **symbole de positionnement (sur microfilm)** = editing symbol; **bibliothèque de symboles** = symbol library; **ligne de jonction des symboles d'un ordinogramme** = flowline; **reconnaissance optique de symboles** = optical mark recognition (OMR); **table de symboles** = symbol table **(b)** **symbole (d'une opération) arithmétique** = arithmetic operator

◊ **symbolique** *adj* symbolic; **adresse symbolique** = symbolic address *ou* floating symbolic address; **code** *ou* **instruction symbolique** = symbolic code *ou* instruction; **(programme de) débogage symbolique** = symbolic debugging; **langage symbolique** = symbolic language; **format de langage symbolique** = symbolic-coding format; **logique symbolique** = symbolic logic; **nom symbolique** = symbolic name; **programmation symbolique** = symbolic programming

symétrie *nf* balance

synchro = SYNCHRONISATION sync; **bit de synchro** = sync bit; **caractère de synchro** = sync character; **impulsions de synchro** = sync pulses; **magnétophone avec interface synchro pour projecteur de diapos** = slide/sync recorder
◊ **synchrone** *adj* synchronous; **communication synchrone binaire** = binary synchronous communications (BSC); **mode synchrone** = synchronous mode; **ordinateur synchrone** = synchronous computer; **repérage synchrone** = synchronous detection; **réseau synchrone** = synchronous network; **réseau de données synchrone** = synchronous data network; **système synchrone** = synchronous system; **transmission synchrone** = synchronous transmission
◊ **synchronisation** *ou* **synchro** *nf* synchronization; *(de bandes audio et vidéo)* interlock; *(de bande vidéo)* pix lock; **synchronisation de réseau** = network timing; **bit de synchronisation de trame** = framing bit; **boucle de synchronisation** = timing loop; **caractère de synchronisation** = synchronous idle character; **code de synchronisation de trame** = framing code; **impulsions de synchronisation** = synchronization pulses; **impulsion de synchronisation du balayage vertical** = field sync pulse; **impulsion de synchronisation horizontale** = horizontal synchronization pulse; **unité de synchronisation** = synchronizer
◊ **synchronisé, -ée** *adj* synchronized *ou* in phase *ou* in sync; **ces deux dispositifs ne sont pas parfaitement synchronisés** = the two devices are out of sync; **opération synchronisée** = fixed cycle operation; *(image/son)* **projecteur synchronisé** = interlock projector

◊ **synchroniser** *vtr* to synchronize *ou* to clock; *(signal avec horloge interne)* to lock onto; *(film avec piste sonore)* to lay in

◊ **synchroniseur** *nm* synchronizer; **synchroniseur de canaux** *ou* **de voies** = channel synchronizer

◊ **synchronisme** *nm* **en synchronisme** = in sync

> dès lors, le rôle du programme de gestion de données consiste aussi à synchroniser la lecture des différents blocs texte/image et son
>
> *Micro Systèmes*

syndicat *nm* trade union *ou* trade association; **syndicat européen des constructeurs d'ordinateurs** = European Computer Manufacturers Association (ECMA)

synonyme 1 *nm* synonym; **'erreur' et 'faute' sont des synonymes** = the words 'error' and 'mistake' are synonymous 2 *adj* synonymous

syntactique *adj* syntax; **analyse syntactique** = parsing *ou* syntax analysis *ou* syntactical analysis

◊ **syntaxe** *nf* **(a)** syntax; **faute de syntaxe** = grammatical error *ou* syntactic error *ou* syntax error **(b)** *(en informatique)* language rules; **qui va contre les règles de la syntaxe** = illegal

◊ **syntaxique** *adj* **analyse syntaxique** = parsing *ou* syntax analysis *ou* syntactical analysis

synthèse *nf* synthesis; **synthèse additive (de couleurs)** = additive colour mixing; **synthèse vocale** *ou* **de la parole** = voice synthesis *ou* speech synthesis; **langage de synthèse** = synthetic language; **puce de synthèse vocale** = speech chip; **voix de synthèse** = digital speech

◊ **synthétique** *adj* synthetic; **matériaux synthétiques** = synthetic materials

◊ **synthétiser** *vtr* to synthesize

◊ **synthétiseur** *nm* **synthétiseur de son** = music synthesizer *ou* sound synthesizer; **synthétiseur vocal** *ou* **de la parole** = voice synthesizer *ou* speech synthesizer

systématique *adj* systematic *ou* unconditional; **transfert systématique** = unconditional transfer

système *nm* **(a)** *(informatique)* system; **les ingénieurs n'ont pas terminé l'essai du nouveau système** = the engineers are still testing the new installation; **système d'aide à la décision (SAID)** = decision support system (DSS); **système à base de connaissances** *ou* **système expert** = (intelligent) knowledge-based system (IKBS) *ou* expert system; **système de base de données** = database system; **système de gestion de base de données** = database management system (DBMS) *ou* database manager; **système de base de données réparti** *ou* **en réseau** = distributed database system; **système binaire** = binary system; **système bureautique** *ou* **système informatique pour bureau** = computer office system; **système à bus auxiliaire** *ou* **à bus double** = dual bus system; **système de débogage interactif** *ou* **de déverminage interactif** = interactive debugging system; **système disjoncteur progressif** = fail soft system; **système double** = dual system; **système duplex** = duplex computer; **système évalué en cycles possibles par unité de temps** = duty-rated system; **système expert** = expert system; **système d'exploitation** = operating system (OS); **système d'exploitation de base** = basic operating system (BOS); **système d'exploitation CP** = control program/monitor *ou* control program for microcomputers (CP/M); **système d'exploitation de disque** *ou* **système d'exploitation DOS** *ou* **système DOS** = disk operating system (DOS); **système d'exploitation MS-DOS®** = MS disk operating system *ou* Microsoft DOS® (MS-DOS); **système extensible** = expandable system; **système à fichiers répartis** *ou* **partagés** = distributed file system; **système frontal** = front-end system; **système de gestion de l'information** = information management system; **système de hash code** = hash-code system; **système hybride** = hybrid system; **système imbriqué (dans un autre)** = embedded computer *ou* system; **système indéterminé** = indeterminate system; **système informatique** = computer system *ou* information system; **système informatique intégré** = computer-integrated system; **cette entreprise est un fournisseur réputé de systèmes informatiques intégrés qui permettent à la fois la pagination de très longs documents et le traitement personnalisé de chaque page** = this firm is a very well-known supplier of computer-integrated systems which allow both batch pagination of very long documents with alteration of individual pages; **système interactif** = interactive system; **système avec intégration de données** = firmware; **système ISO/OSI** = International Standards Organization Open System Interconnection (ISO/OSI); **système multiposte** = multi-terminal system; **système numérique** = digital system; **système ouvert** = open system; **système pilote** = pilot system; **système de recherche documentaire** *ou* **de documents** = document retrieval system; **système de reconnaissance de caractères CSM (par identification des caractéristiques combinées)** = combined symbol matching (CSM); **système sécurisé** = secure system; **système de sécurité** = fail safe system; **système en temps réel** = real-time system; **système de traitement de l'image** = image processor; **système de traitement par lots** *ou* **par paquets** = batch system; **système de traitement de texte** = word processing system *ou* word processor **(b) analyse de systèmes** = systems analysis; **analyste (de) système** = systems analyst; **architecture d'un système** = computer architecture; **bibliothèque du système** = system library; **conception** *ou* **design d'un système** = system design; **diagnostic de système** = system check; **disquette (de) programme système** = system disk; **durée de vie d'un système** = system life cycle; **formation assistée par système expert** = intelligent tutoring system;

génération d'un système *ou* **à laquelle appartient un système** = system generation *ou* sysgen; **ingénieur système** = systems engineer; **interface système/utilisateur** = user interface; **journal d'un système** = system log; **logiciel (de) système** = system software *ou* system firmware; **ordinogramme d'un système** = system flowchart; **panne de système** = system crash; **panneau de commandes d'un système** = system control panel; **programme système** = systems program; **programmeur système** = systems programmer; **sécurisation d'un système** = system security; **spécifications du système** = system specifications **(c)** *(autres systèmes)* **système d'alimentation** *ou* **d'entraînement (du papier)** = (paper) feeder; **système d'appel** = calling unit; **système d'appel automatique (d'un correspondant)** *ou* **système de numérotation automatique** = auto-dial system; **système auto-adaptable** *ou* **dynamique** = adaptive system; **système de communication** = communications system; **système de communication hiérarchisé** = hierarchical communications system; **système de commutation électronique** = electronic switching system; **systèmes de contrôle** = control systems; *(analogique)* **système à courants porteurs** = carrier system; **système haute-fidélité** *ou* **hi-fi** = high fidelity system (hi fi); **système multiplex** = carrier system; **système téléphonique automatique international** = international direct dialling (IDD); **système de transmission numérique** = digital transmission system; **système vidéo haute définition** = high definition video system (HDVS) **(d)** *(math)* **système décimal** *ou* **à base dix** = decimal system; **système duodécimal** = duodecimal number system

Tt

T jonction en T = T junction; **réseau en T** = T network

table *nf* **(a)** *(meuble)* table; **ordinateur de table** = desktop computer (system) **(b) table d'écoute** = wiretap; **brancher une ligne sur une table d'écoute** = to tap (a phone line) **(c)** *(format)* table; **disposé en table** = in tabular form; **disposer en table** = to tab *ou* to tabulate **(d)** *(liste)* **définir une table d'adressage binaire** = to bit-map; **table des adresses hash codées** = hash table; **table d'attributs** = image table; **table de Boole** = Boolean operation table; **tables de conversion** = translation tables *ou* conversion tables; **table de décision** = decision table; **table (de classement des fichiers) du disque** = disk map; **table d'équivalence** = look-up table (LUT) *ou* translation table *ou* conversion table; **voici la fonction de cette touche, pour la traduire en ASCII consultez la table d'équivalence** = this is the value of the key pressed, use a lookup table to find its ASCII value; **les tables d'équivalence sont préprogrammées et permettent de gagner du temps de traitement en évitant de recalculer les mêmes valeurs** = lookup tables are preprogrammed then used in processing to save calculating each result required; **on peut établir des tables d'équivalence qui serviront à convertir les données clients aux codes utilisés par notre système** = conversion tables may be created and used in conjunction with the customer's data to convert it to our systems codes; **table de fonctions** = function table; **table de Karnaugh** = Karnaugh map; **table des matières** = table of contents; **table de noms** *ou* **de symboles** = name table; **table de pages** = page table; **table des priorités d'interruption** = priority interrupt table; **table de référence** = reference table *ou* look-up table (LUT) *ou* translation table *ou* conversion table; **table de référence des programmes** = reference program table; **consultation d'une table de référence** = table lookup; **table de routage** = routing table; **table de substitution** = substitution table; **table de symboles** = symbol table; **table de vérité** = truth table **(e) table traçante** = flatbed plotter

tableau *nm* **(a)** table; *(sortie d'imprimante d'un tableur)* spreadsheet; **tableau de référence** = reference table; **disposé en tableau** = in tabular form; **disposer en tableau** = to tab *ou* to tabulate **(b)** *(structures pour données)* array; **tableau alphanumérique** = alphanumeric array; **tableau de chaînes de caractères** = string array; **tableau de chiffres** = numeric array; **tableau à deux dimensions** *ou* **bidimensionnel** = two-dimensional array; **tableau à trois dimensions** = three-dimensional array; **tableau à dimensions variables** = flexible array; **tableau multidimensionnel** = multidimensional array; **tableau numérique** = numeric array; **tableau réduit** = sparse array; **bornes d'un tableau** = array bounds; **dimension d'un tableau** = array dimension; **élément d'un tableau** = array element; **limites de tableau** = array bounds; **valeur dans un tableau** = array element **(c)** *(panneau)* **tableau d'affichage** = notice board; **tableau d'affichage électronique** = bulletin board system (BBS); **tableau de commande** = control panel *(téléphone)* **tableau de distribution** = plugboard *ou* patchboard; **tableau de distribution principal** = main distributing frame; **tableau noir** = blackboard; **tableau noir électronique** = electronic blackboard

tablette *nf* pad; **tablette graphique** = graphics pad *ou* tablet; **tablette à numériser** = digitizing pad; *(pour saisie de l'écriture manuelle)* writing pad *ou* data tablet; **un dessin précis s'obtient beaucoup plus facilement avec une tablette à numériser qu'avec une souris** = it is much easier to draw accurately with a tablet than with a mouse

tableur *nm (programme)* spreadsheet

tabulaire *adj* in tabular form; **disposition tabulaire** = layout in tabular form

◊ **tabulateur** *nm* tabulator

◊ **tabulation** *nf* tabbing *ou* tabulation; **la tabulation peut être incorporée au programme** = tabbing can be done from inside the program; **tabulation décimale** *ou* **sur la virgule** = decimal tabbing; **touche de tabulation décimale** = decimal tab key; **tabulation verticale** = vertical tab; **arrêt de tabulation** = tabulation stop *ou* tab stop; **mémoire de tabulation** = tab memory; **règle de tabulation** = tab rack *ou* ruler line; **la règle de tabulation indique les marges de gauche et de droite** = a tab rack shows you the left and right margins; **repères de tabulation** = tabulation markers; **touche de tabulation** = tab key; **en appuyant sur la touche de tabulation en début de ligne, pour se placer à la colonne 10, la liste avait été parfaitement alignée** = the list was neatly lined up by tabbing to column 10 at the start of each new line

◊ **tabulatrice** *nf (pour cartes perforées)* tabulator *ou* tabulating machine; **traitement de données par tabulatrice** = data tabulating

◊ **tabuler** *vtr* to tabulate *ou* to tab

tache *nf* tache lumineuse = *(sur film)* flare; *(sur l'écran)* bloom

◊ **taché, -ée** *adj (film)* taché d'un reflet lumineux = flared

tâche *nf* job *ou* load *ou* task; *(l'ensemble des tâches d'un ordinateur)* activities *ou* work load; **la tâche suivante consistera à trier tous les enregistrements** = the next job to be processed is to sort all the records; **tâche de premier plan** *ou* **prioritaire** = foreground task; **tâche non prioritaire** *ou* **d'arrière-plan** = low-priority work *ou* background task; **(instruction d') arrêter** *ou* **(de) virer une tâche** = kill job; **contrôle d'exécution des tâches** = job statement control; **fichier de contrôle de tâche** = job control file; **programme de contrôle de tâche** = job control program; **ensemble des tâches en cours d'exécution** = job mix; **fichier de tâches (à exécuter)** = job file; **(code de) fin de tâche** = end of job (EOJ); **flux des tâches** = job stream; **gestion de tâches** = job scheduling *ou* task management;

lancement *ou* **commande de tâches à distance** = remote job entry (RJE); **langage de commande de tâche** = job control language (JCL); **numéro de suite d'une tâche dans la file d'attente** = job number; **partage des tâches** = load sharing; **priorité d'une tâche** = job priority; **traitement de tâche** = job processing; **planification de la séquence d'exécution des tâches** *ou* **répartition des tâches** = job scheduling; **temps d'exécution d'une tâche** = elapsed time

TACS = TOTAL ACCESS COMMUNICATION SYSTEM *(pour système de radio-téléphone cellulaire)* **norme TACS** = TACS

tactile *adj* tactile; **clavier tactile** = tactile keyboard *ou* touch pad *ou* touch-sensitive keyboard; **écran tactile** = touch screen; **information tactile** = tactile feedback; **pavé tactile** = touch pad

taille *nf* **(a)** size *ou* length; **taille d'un bloc** = block length; **taille d'un caractère (en points)** = set size *ou* typesize; **taille des caractères utilisés dans la composition** = composition size; **taille d'une chaîne** = string length; **taille d'un champ** = field length; **taille d'un enregistrement** = record length; **taille d'un fichier** = file extent; **la taille d'impression a été augmentée pour la rendre plus lisible** = the size of the print has been increased to make it easier to read; **taille (de la) mémoire** = storage capacity; **taille de la mémoire tampon** = buffer length *ou* buffer size; **taille de la page** = page size; **taille d'un registre** = register length; **champ de taille constante** *ou* **fixe** = fixed field; **un système informatique de taille moyenne** = a medium-sized computer system; **champ de taille constante** *ou* **fixe** = fixed field; *(d'une illustration ou photo)* **mise à la taille** = sizing **(b)** *(gravure)* **impression en taille douce** = copperplate printing

talon *nf* talon de caractère = beard

tambour *nm* drum *ou* cylinder; **tambour d'impression** = impression cylinder; **tambour magnétique** = magnetic drum; **imprimante à tambour** = barrel printer; **traceur** *ou* **enregistreur à tambour** = drum plotter

tampon *nm (circuit ou mémoire)* buffer; **tampon à capacité variable** = elastic buffer; **tampon circulaire** = circular buffer; **tampon de clavier** = key rollover; **tampon de données** = data buffer; **tampon de transmission de données** = communications buffer *ou* data communications buffer; **tampon dynamique** *ou* **variable** = dynamic buffer *ou* elastic buffer; **tampon (d')** **entrée/sortie** = input/output buffer *ou* I/O buffer; **tampon d'imprimante** = printer buffer; **entrée/sortie utilisant une mémoire tampon** = buffered input/output; **mémoire avec tampon** = buffered memory; **taille de (la mémoire) tampon** = buffer length *ou* buffer size; **registre tampon** = buffer register; **registre de mémoire tampon** = memory buffer register (MBR); **registre tampon des entrées** = input buffer register; **registre tampon de sortie** = output buffer register; **utilisation de mémoire tampon** = buffering; *(entre périphérique lent et processeur rapide)* **utilisation de mémoire tampon auxiliaire** = spooling; **utilisation de double mémoire tampon** = double buffering; **utiliser une mémoire tampon** = to buffer; **vider la mémoire tampon** = to flush buffers

tandem *nm* tandem; **commutation (en) tandem** = tandem switching; **fonctionnement en tandem** = working in tandem

tangage *nm (mouvement autour d'un axe)* pitch

TAO = TEST ASSISTE PAR ORDINATEUR

taper *vtr* **(a)** to type; **tous ses rapports sont tapés sur sa petite (machine) portative** = all his reports are typed on his portable typewriter; **tapez la clé et vous pourrez décoder le dernier message** = type this key into the machine, that will decode the last message **(b)** to hit *ou* to press (a key); **taper une commande** = to key in a command; **taper un code** = to enter a code; **il a tapé CONTROL Z pour vider l'écran** = he pressed CONTROL Z and zapped all the text
◊ **tapuscrit** *nm* typescript

taquer *vtr (cartes perforées)* to joggle

taux *nm* **(a)** ratio; **taux d'activité** = activity ratio; **taux d'activité d'un fichier** = file activity ratio **(b)** rate; **taux de défaillance** = failure rate; **taux d'écoute** = ratings; **guerre de taux d'écoute** = ratings battle *ou* war; **taux d'erreur** = error rate; **taux d'erreur par bloc** = block error rate; **le taux d'erreur est inférieur à 1%** = the error rate is less than 1%; **taux par minute** *ou* **taux/minute** = rate per minute; **il existe un tarif forfaitaire d'utilisation plus un taux/minute de temps d'ordinateur** = there is a set tariff for logging on, then a rate for every minute of computer time used

TEC = TRANSISTOR A EFFET DE CHAMP

technicien, -ienne *n* technician; **le nouveau système a été mis en place par les techniciens** = the computer technicians installed the new system; **technicien de laboratoire** = laboratory technician; **technicien/réparateur informatique** = troubleshooter

technique 1 *nf* **(a)** technique *ou* method; **le société a mis au point une nouvelle technique de traitement des disquettes clients** = the company has developed a new technique for processing customers' disks **(b)** **techniques** = technology; **techniques de l'information** = information technology (IT); **techniques de pointe** *ou* **techniques nouvelles** = new technology; **l'introduction de techniques nouvelles** = the introduction of new technology **2** *adj* technical *ou* technological; **il offre une assistance technique** = he offers a consultancy service; **société d'assistance technique** = consultancy firm; **manuel technique** = installation manual *ou* technical manual; **ce document contient tous les renseignements d'ordre technique concernant le nouvel ordinateur** = the document gives all the technical details on the new computer

technologie *nf* technology; **technologie de la fibre optique** *ou* **de la transmission par fibre optique** = fibre optics; **(de) haute technologie** *ou* **(de) technologie avancée** = high specification *ou* high spec; **les câbles (de) haute technologie doivent être manipulés avec soin** = high spec cabling needs to be very carefully handled; **nouvelle technologie =** new technology

◇ **technologique** *adj* technological; **la révolution technologique =** the technological revolution

télé- *préfixe* tele-

◇ **télébanque** *nf* home banking

◇ **Télécarte**® *nf* phonecard

◇ **téléchargeable** *adj* downloadable; **polices de caractères téléchargeable =** downloadable fonts

◇ **téléchargement** *nm (vers un micro)* downloading; *(vers un gros ordinateur)* uploading; **le téléchargement des données dans l'unité centrale peut se faire par l'intermédiaire d'un modem =** you can download the data to the CPU via a modem; **on peut manipuler l'image avant son téléchargement sur l'ordinateur hôte =** the image can be manipulated before uploading to the host computer

◇ **télécharger** *vtr (vers un micro)* to download; *(vers un gros ordinateur)* to upload; **on a téléchargé le logiciel hier =** the telesoftware was downloaded yesterday; **il n'en coûte rien de télécharger, depuis le tableau d'affichage, un logiciel qui n'est pas protégé par un copyright =** there is no charge for downloading public domain software from the BBS; **logiciel téléchargé =** telesoftware (TSW)

> pour pallier ces limites, certaines machines autorisent le téléchargement de fontes dans leur mémoire interne
> *L'Ordinateur Individuel*

◇ **télécinéma** *nm* telecine

TELECOM *(pour modem)* **prise TELECOM =** data jack

télécommande *nf* remote control *ou* telecontrol; **ce magnétoscope est équipé d'une télécommande =** the video recorder has a remote control facility

télécommunication(s) *nf(pl)* telecommunications *ou* communications; **gestionnaire de télécommunication =** communications executive; **réseau de télécommunications =** communications network; **satellite de télécommunications =** communications satellite

télécomposition *nf* teletypesetting

téléconférence *nf* teleconference *ou* teleconferencing *ou* conference call; **téléconférence par sélection** *ou* **par composition =** dial conference; **téléconférence sur réseau informatique =** computer conferencing

télécopie *nf* facsimile transmission *ou* fax *ou* FAX; **envoyer par télécopie =** to fax; **nous enverrons les plans par télécopie =** we will send a fax of the design plan; **j'ai envoyé les documents par télécopie à notre bureau de New York =** I've faxed the documents to our New York office

◇ **télécopieur** *nm* fax (machine *ou* system); **rouleau de papier pour télécopieur =** roll of fax paper

> la télécopie se caractérise par sa capacité à transmettre des objets graphiques. Aucune valeur juridique n'est à attendre. Les vitesses utilisées classiquement, 4800 ou 9600 bits/seconde, sont élevées mais la lourdeur du procédé de transmission d'images ne saurait s'accommoder de débits plus faibles
> *Temps Micro*

télégramme *nm* telegram; *also GB* telemessage; **envoyer un télégramme =** to cable *ou* to telegraph *ou* to send a telegram; **il a envoyé un télégramme au bureau pour redemander de l'argent =** he sent a cable to his office asking for more money; **ils ont envoyé un télégramme confirmant leur accord =** they telegraphed their agreement

◇ **télégraphe** *nm* telegraph

◇ **télégraphie** *nf* telegraphy; **télégraphie par onde porteuse =** carrier telegraphy

◇ **télégraphier** *vtr* to cable *ou* to telegraph *ou* to send a telegram; **on a télégraphié les photos à New York =** the photographs were telegraphed to New York; **message télégraphié =** *GB* telemessage

◇ **télégraphique** *adj* telegraphic; **adresse télégraphique =** cable address *ou* telegraphic address; **chiffres et signes en code télégraphique =** figures case; **le bureau lui a envoyé un mandat télégraphique de 1000 francs pour couvrir ses frais =** the office cabled him 1,000 francs to cover his expenses

téléimprimeur *nm* teleprinter *ou* teletypewriter; **vous pouvez connecter un téléimprimeur sur ce port série modifié =**

you can drive a teleprinter from this modified serial port; **interface (pour) téléimprimeur =** teleprinter interface; **opérateur, -trice de téléimprimeur =** teleprinter operator; **rouleau de papier de** *ou* **pour téléimprimeur =** teleprinter roll

téléinformatique *nf* data communications; **appareils** *ou* **matériel téléinformatique =** data communications equipment (DCE); **réseau téléinformatique =** data communications network *ou* data network; **service (de) téléinformatique =** teleinformatic services *ou* data services

télémaintenance *nf* remote maintenance

télématique *nf* data communications *ou* telematics

télémétrie *nf* telemetry

téléphone *nm* **(a)** telephone *ou* phone; **téléphone à carte =** card phone; **téléphone cellulaire =** cellular telephone *ou* cell phone *ou* mobile radiophone; **téléphone à clavier =** pushbutton telephone; **téléphone de** *ou* **pour conférence =** conference telephone; **téléphone à impulsion numérique (de marque) Digipulse® =** Digipulse telephone; **téléphone interne =** house phone *ou* internal phone; **téléphone mobile =** private mobile radio (PMR); **téléphone sans cordon** *ou* **sans fil =** cordless telephone; **les abonnés du téléphone =** telephone subscribers; **amplificateur de téléphone =** telephone repeater; **annuaire du téléphone =** telephone directory *ou* telephone book; **numéro de téléphone =** telephone number *ou* phone number; **pouvez-vous me donner votre numéro de téléphone? =** can you give me your telephone number?; **le numéro de téléphone figure sur le papier à en-tête de la société =** the phone number is on the company notepaper; **il a une liste de numéros de téléphone dans un petit carnet noir =** he keeps a list of phone numbers in a little black book; **parler au téléphone =** to be on the phone; **elle a passé la matinée (à parler) au téléphone =** she has been on the phone all morning; **il a parlé au directeur** *ou* **il a eu le directeur au téléphone =** he spoke to the manager on

the phone; **répondre au téléphone =** to answer the phone *ou* to take a (phone) call; **l'utilisation du téléphone pour la transmission de données =** telephone as a data carrier **(b) par téléphone =** by telephone *ou* by phone; **achats par téléphone =** teleshopping; **contacter quelqu'un par téléphone =** to call someone *ou* to contact someone by phone; **contacter son bureau par téléphone =** to call in; **demander quelque chose par téléphone =** to phone for something; **faire une commmande par téléphone =** to place an order by telephone; **il a passé la commande directement à l'entrepôt par téléphone =** he phoned the order through to the warehouse; **ventes par téléphone =** telesales

◊ **téléphoner** *vtr* to make a phone call *ou* to make a telephone call *ou* to ring; **elle est en train de téléphoner à Hong Kong =** she is on the telephone to Hong Kong; **M. Dubois a téléphoné en votre absence et a demandé que vous le rappeliez =** Mr Dubois called while you were out and asked if you would phone him back; **sa secrétaire a téléphoné pour prévenir de son retard =** his secretary phoned to say he would be late; **téléphoner (à quelqu'un) =** to telephone (someone) *ou* to make a call (to someone) *ou* to call (someone) *ou* to phone (someone); **ne me téléphonez pas, c'est moi qui vous appellerai =** don't phone me, I'll phone you; **téléphoner au sujet de quelque chose =** to phone about something; **il a téléphoné au sujet de la commande de papier listing =** he telephoned about the order for computer stationery; **téléphoner en direct =** to dial direct

◊ **téléphonie** *nf* telephony

◊ **téléphonique** *adj* telephone *ou* phone; **nous avons une nouvelle installation téléphonique depuis la semaine dernière =** we had a new phone system installed last week; **annuaire téléphonique =** phone book *ou* telephone book *ou* telephone directory; **bande téléphonique =** voice band; **cabine téléphonique =** call box *ou* telephone booth; **central téléphonique =** telephone exchange; **indicatif téléphonique =** dialling code; **indicatif téléphonique international =** international dialling code; **indicatif téléphonique du pays =** country code *ou* international number; **indicatif téléphonique de zone =** area code; **ligne téléphonique spécialisée** *ou* **dédiée =**

dedicated line; **répondeur téléphonique =** telephone answering machine *ou* voice messaging (system); **réseau téléphonique (public) commuté =** public switched telephone network (PSTN); **standard téléphonique =** (telephone) switchboard; **système téléphonique automatique international =** international direct dialling (IDD)

◊ **téléphoniste** *nm&f* telephonist

téléscripteur *nm* teleprinter *ou* teletype (TTY); **clavier de téléscripteur =** ASR keyboard

téléspectateur, -trice *n* viewer

Télétex® *nm* Teletext

> mal connu et, de ce fait, peu aimé, le mode télétex combine cependant des avantages. Il fonctionne à 2400 bits/seconde, une vitesse tout à fait correcte pour transmettre de l'information codée. Les 309 symboles permettent la transmission de documents bien préparés avec un minimum de graphisme
> *Temps Micro*

télétraitement *nm* teleprocessing (TP)

télétransmission *nf* **poste informatique de télétransmission =** data station

télétype *nm* teleprinter
◊ **télétypiste** *nm&f* teleprinter operator

téléviseur *nm* television (receiver) *ou* television set *ou* TV set *ou* TV
◊ **télévision** *nf* **la télévision =** television *ou* TV; **télévision câblée =** cable télévision *ou* cable TV; **télévision câblée interactive =** interactive cable television; **télévision câblée payante =** pay TV; *US* paycable; *(familier)* feevee; **antenne collective de télévision câblée** *ou* **système de télévision câblée CATV =** community antenna television (CATV); **relai de télévision câblée =** cable TV relay station; **télévision en circuit fermé =** closed circuit television (CCTV); **câble de télévision =** CATV cable; **caméra de télévision =** television camera *ou* TV camera; **Comité National de Normalisation de la Télévision (NTSC)**

= National Television Standards Committee (NTSC); **moniteur (de) télévision =** television monitor; **poste (de) télévision =** television (receiver) *ou* TV set *ou* TV; **projecteur (de) télévision =** television projector; **programme de télévision =** television programme *ou* TV programme; **programme de télévision de caractère éducatif =** educational TV (ETV) programme; **réseau de télévision =** television network

télex *nm* **(a)** *(machine ou système)* telex; **nous n'avons pas le télex =** we don't have a telex; **il nous est impossible de joindre nos bureaux au Nigéria parce que le télex est en panne =** we cannot communicate with our Nigerian office because of the breakdown of the telex lines; **abonné du télex =** telex subscriber; **envoyer des renseignements par télex =** to send information by telex; **ligne (de) télex =** telex line; **opérateur de télex =** telex operator **(b)** *(message)* **un télex =** a telex; **envoyer un télex =** to telex; **il a envoyé un télex à son bureau =** he sent a telex to his office; **pouvez-vous envoyer un télex au bureau canadien avant son ouverture? =** can you telex the Canadian office before they open ?; **nous avons reçu son télex ce matin =** we received his telex this morning

◊ **télexer** *vtr* to telex; **télexer des renseignements =** to send information by telex; **la commande nous a été télexée =** the order came by telex

◊ **télexiste** *nm&f* telex operator

> le télex est lent (50 bits/seconde) et ses capacités de représentation de l'information sont limitées (48 symboles seulement). Son atout principal est sa valeur juridique
> *Temps Micro*

témoin *nm* **(a)** *(symbole)* flag *ou* indicator flag; **témoin de retenue =** carry flag; *(d'un appareil)* **témoin d'utilisation =** device flag; **clic témoin (de fonctionnement) de touche =** key click; **mise en place d'un témoin =** flag event; **registre des témoins =** flag register **(b)** *(voyant lumineux)* **témoin** *ou* **lampe témoin =** indicator light *ou* light emitting diode **(c)** **groupe témoin =** control group

température *nf* **(a)** temperature; **le marqueur du thermomètre indique la température maximum d'aujourd'hui =** the marker on the thermometer shows the peak temperature for today **(b)** **température de bruit** = noise temperature; **température chromatique** = colour temperature

temporaire *adj* temporary; **interrupteur temporaire** = momentary switch; **mémoire temporaire** = erasable storage *ou* erasable memory *ou* temporary storage *ou* working store *ou* scratchpad; **registre temporaire** = temporary register; **stockage temporaire** = temporary storage

◊ **temporairement** *adv* temporarily

temporel, -elle *adj* **accès temporel multiplexé** = time division multiple access; **commutation temporelle** = time division switching; **multiplexage temporel** = time division multiplexing (TDM)

temporisation *nf* **boucle de temporisation** = timing loop

temps *nm* **(a)** time; **de temps en temps** = periodic *ou* periodical *ou* periodically; **pendant quelque temps** *ou* **pendant un certain temps** = for a period of time **(b)** **temps d'accélération** = acceleration time; **temps d'accès moyen** = average access time; **temps d'addition** = add time *ou* addition time; **temps d'adressage** = address access time; **temps d'arrêt** *ou* **d'immobilisation** = stop time; **temps d'assemblage** = assembly time; **temps d'association (d'une adresse)** = binding time; **temps d'attente** = queuing time; **temps de compilation** = compilation time; **temps de connexion** = connect time; **temps de cycle** = cycle time; **temps de cycle d'instruction** = instruction cycle time; **vol de temps de cycle de la mémoire à accès directe** *ou* **de mémoire DMA** = DMA cycle stealing; *(d'un onduleur ou d'un dispositif de secours)* **temps de débit** = holdup; **temps de développement** *ou* **de mise au point d'un nouveau produit** = development time; **temps disponible** *ou* **de disponibilité** = available time; **temps d'exécution** = execution time *ou* execute time; **temps d'exécution d'une instruction** *ou* **temps d'instruction** = instruction execution time *ou* instruction time; **temps d'exécution d'un programme** = run-time *ou* run-duration; **temps d'exécution d'une tâche** *ou* **temps passé à une tâche** = operating time *ou* elapsed

time; **temps d'extinction d'un signal** = decay time; **temps de latence** = latency; **temps de mise en place** = positioning time; **temps de montée** *ou* **temps d'accélération** = rise time; **temps mort** = dead time *ou* down time *ou* idle time; **temps d'occupation de la ligne** = holding time; **temps d'ordinateur** = computer time; **tous ces rapports de vente coûtent cher en temps d'ordinateur** = running all those sales reports costs a lot in computer time; **temps de préparation** = make-ready time; **temps productif** *ou* **de bon fonctionnement** = up time *ou* uptime; **temps réel** = real time; **un système de navigation doit pouvoir faire le point en temps réel et prendre les mesures nécessaires pour éviter de heurter un écueil** = a navigation system needs to be able to process the position of a ship in real time and take suitable action before it hits a rock; **entrée en temps réel** = real-time input; **exécution (d'un programme) en temps réel** = real-time execution; **horloge en temps réel** = real-time clock; **multitâche en temps réel** = real-time multitasking; **traitement multitâche en temps réel** = real-time multi-tasking; **simulation en temps réel** = real-time simulation; **système en temps réel** = real-time system; **traitement en temps réel** = real-time processing; **temps de réponse** = response time; **temps de report** = carry time; **temps d'utilisation de l'unité centrale** *ou* **du processeur** *ou* **temps CPU** = CPU time **(c)** **accès multiple par division dans le temps** = time division multiple access; **analyse du signal dans le temps** = time domain analysis; **base de temps** = time base; **base de temps réduite** = fast time-scale; **créneau de temps** = time slot; **moyenne de temps de bon fonctionnement (entre les défaillances) (MTBF)** = mean time between failures (MTBF); **multiplexage par répartition dans le temps (MRT)** = time division multiplexing (TDM); **partage de temps** *ou* **(système) en temps partagé** = time-sharing; **signal de contrôle du temps écoulé** = time address code; **tranche de temps** = time slice; **visualisation en temps différé** = time shift viewing; **voie dérivée en temps** = time derived channel

tension *nf* voltage; **veillez à ce que la tension de crête ne dépasse pas 60 watts sinon l'amplificateur surchauffera** = keep the peak power below 60 watts or the amplifier will overheat; **chute** *ou*

baisse de tension = voltage dip *ou* dip in voltage *ou* power loss; **'hors tension'** = 'power off' *ou* 'off'; **mise hors tension automatique** = automatic power off; **niveau de tension d'une pile** = battery voltage level; **régulateur de tension** = voltage regulator; **'sous tension'** = 'power on' *ou* 'on'; **cadre sous tension** = hot frame; **chassis sous tension** = hot chassis; **mettre sous tension** = to power up *ou* to switch on *ou* to turn on; **ré-initialisation automatique à la mise sous tension** = power-on reset

> cette fonction permet de mesurer la chute de tension d'une fonction de semi-conducteur traversée par une intensité d'environ un milliampère
>
> *Electronique pratique*

téra- *préfixe* tera-

◊ **térahertz** *nm* terahertz

terminaison *nf* termination

terminal *nm* station *ou* terminal; **terminal à adressage protégé** = addressable terminal; **tous les messages sont transmis à tous les terminaux puisqu'aucun d'eux ne possède un adressage protégé** = all the messages go to all the terminals since none are addressable terminals; **terminal d'application** *ou* **terminal spécialisé** = job orientated terminal; **terminal asservi** = slave terminal; **terminal de CAO** = graphics terminal; **terminal central** = central terminal; **terminal conversationnel** = interactive terminal *ou* conversational terminal; **terminal dédié** *ou* **spécialisé** = applications terminal; **terminal directeur** = executive terminal; **terminal à distance** *ou* **éloigné** = remote terminal; **terminal d'entrée (de données)** = input *ou* i/p terminal; **terminal entrée/sortie** = input/output terminal *ou* keyboard send/receive (KSR); **terminal exécutif** = executive terminal; **terminal de gestion** *ou* **à usage professionnel** = executive unit *ou* terminal; **terminal graphique** *ou* **avec écran (à affichage) graphique** = graphics terminal *ou* graphics art terminal; **terminal informatique** = data terminal; **terminal intelligent** = intelligent terminal; **le nouveau terminal intelligent comporte un éditeur de texte** = the new intelligent terminal has a built-in text editor; **terminal non intelligent** = dumb terminal; **terminal interactif** = interactive terminal; **terminal maître** = master terminal; **terminal de mise à jour rapide** = bulk update terminal; **terminal d'ordinateur** = data terminal equipment (DTE); **terminal de point de vente** = point-of-sale terminal *ou* POS terminal; **terminal principal** = key terminal *ou* central terminal *ou* master terminal; **le gestionnaire de système utilise le terminal principal pour relancer le système** = the system manager uses the master terminal to restart the system; **terminal public** = public access terminal; **terminal récepteur (de données)** = data sink; **terminal de réception** = receive only terminal; **l'imprimante est un terminal de sortie d'ordinateur** = a printer is a data terminal for computer output; **terminal superviseur** = executive terminal; **terminal de transfert électronique de fonds** = electronic funds transfer point of sale (EFTPOS); **terminal vidéo** = video terminal; **terminal virtuel** = virtual terminal; **contrôleur de terminal** = terminal controller; **(code d') identification d'un terminal** = terminal identity; **interface de** *ou* **pour terminal** = terminal interface; **le contrôleur de réseau possède 16 interfaces pour terminaux** = the network controller has 16 terminal interfaces; **police de caractères utilisable par un terminal** = terminal character set; **système à plusieurs terminaux** = multi-terminal system

terminé, -ée *adj* complete *ou* finished *ou* closed

◊ **terminer** *vtr* to complete *ou* to close *ou* to finish *ou* to terminate; **la vérification orthographique est terminée** = the spelling check is complete; **une fois la saisie du texte terminée, servez-vous du correcteur orthographique pour corriger les fautes** = when you have completed the keyboarding, pass the text through the spelling checker; **elle a terminé la saisie avant le déjeuner** = she finished all the keyboarding before lunch; **la programmation ne sera pas terminée avant la semaine prochaine** = the programming will not be ready until next week; **terminer une session** = to log off *ou* log out

◊ **se terminer** *vpr* to finish *ou* to end

ternaire *adj* ternary

terre *nf* earth; **fil de terre** = earth (wire); **mettre à la terre** = to earth; *US* to ground; **tous les appareils doivent être mis à la terre** = all appliances must be earthed; **tous les fils non rattachés doivent être mis à la terre** = all loose wires should be tied to earth; **perte de terre** = ground absorption; **prise de terre** = earth; *US* ground

◊ **terrestre** *adj* **station terrestre** = earth station; **station terrestre mobile** = mobile earth terminal; *(de transmission par satellite)* **zone terrestre de couverture** = earth coverage

tertiaire *adj (voies de transmission)* **groupe tertiaire** = mastergroup

test *nm* test *ou* trial *ou* check; **faire un test** = to test; **l'ingénieur possède un équipement spécialisé pour effectuer les tests sur ce modèle** = the engineer has special test equipment for this model; **test à chaud** = burn-in; **test assisté par ordinateur (TAO)** = computer-aided *ou* assisted testing (CAT); **tests de contrôle de liens** = link trials; **test de diagnostic** = diagnostic test; **test d'étalonnage** = benchmark problem; **test d'évaluation de performance** = test run; **test de la fumée** = smoke test; **test opérationnel** = operation trial; **test de polarité** = polarity test; **tests de saturation** = saturation testing; **test sélectif** = leapfrog test; **test sélectif limité** *ou* **restreint** = crippled leapfrog test; **test de Turing** = Turing test; **équipement pour tests** = test equipment; **programme de test** = exerciser

◊ **tester** *vtr* to test *ou* to check; **tester en continu sur une longue période** = to soak; **l'appareil a été testé sous tous les angles avant la livraison** = the device was soak-tested prior to delivery; **tester un système** = to test a system

◊ **testeur** *nm* exerciser *ou* test equipment

tête *nf* **(a)** *(partie supérieure)* head; *(commencement)* **tête de chapitre** = chapter heading; **les têtes de chapitres sont en caractères gras de 12 points** = chapter headings are in 12 point bold; *(de papier listing)* **tête d'une page** = head of form (HOF); *(marge supérieure)* **blanc de tête** = top margin *ou* top space **(b)** *(de film ou de bande)* **tête de bobine** = head (of reel); *(titre, etc.)* **enregistrement de**

tête = leader record; *(de données en mémoire)* **zéro de tête** = leading zero **(c)** *(de connection)* **tête de réseau** = head end **(d)** **être à la tête de** *ou* **être en tête de** = to head (something); **c'est lui qui est maintenant à la tête du groupe de diffusion de logiciels** = he took over the direction of a software distribution group; **mon fichier était en tête de la file d'attente** = the queue was headed by my file **(e)** *(dispositif de lecture)* head; **tête d'écriture** *ou* **d'enregistrement** = write head *ou* record head; **tête d'effacement** = erase head; **tête flottante** = floating head *ou* flying head; **tête d'impression** = printhead; **la tête d'impression peut imprimer plus de 400 millions de caractères** = the printhead has a print life of over 400 million characters; **tête de lecture** = playback head *ou* read head *ou* sound head; *(de bandes magnétiques)* tape head *ou* tape playback head; *(de disque ou disquettes)* disk head *ou* disk playback head; **tête de lecture/écriture** = combined head *ou* read/write head; **(lecteur à) tête de lecture fixe** = fixed head (disk drive); **crash causé par la tête de lecture** = head crash; **tête magnétique** = magnetic head; **l'alignement des têtes va peut être demander un réglage différent lorsqu'il s'agit de bandes enregistrées sur d'autres machines** = azimuth alignment might not be correct for tape recorded on a different machine; **réglage d'alignement des têtes** = azimuth alignment; **démagnétiseur de tête** = head demagnetizer; **durée de vie de la tête** = headlife; **mise en position transport de la tête** = head park

tétra- *préfixe* quadr-

◊ **tétraphonique** *adj* quadrophonic

texte *nm* text *ou* copy; **les éditeurs ont généreusement annoté le texte avant le renvoi des épreuves pour correction** = the editors made many textual changes before the proofs were sent back for correction; **texte en clair** *ou* **non chiffré** = plaintext; **texte dactylographié** = typescript; **texte définitif** = fair copy *ou* final copy; **texte imprimé** = hard copy; **texte non justifié (à droite)** = ragged text; **texte au kilomètre avec changement de page automatique** = automatic text flow across pages; **texte d'un message** = message text; **texte préétabli** = form overlay; **texte publicitaire** = publicity copy; **le texte publicitaire doit nous**

arriver mardi, dernier délai = Tuesday is the last date for copy for the advertisement; **texte sans erreur** *ou* **sans modification =** clean copy; **affichage de texte =** character display; **zone d'affichage de texte** *ou* **écran texte =** text screen; *(pour une fonte donnée)* **calibrage d'un texte =** cast off *ou* casting off; **faire le calibrage d'un texte =** to cast off; **compression de texte =** text compression; **convertisseur texte/signal vocal =** text-to-speech converter; **(code de) début de texte =** start of text (SOT *ou* STX); **écran texte =** text screen; **éditer** *ou* **traiter texte sur ordinateur =** to word-process; **éditeur de texte** *ou* **programme d'édition de texte =** text editor; **cet éditeur de texte ne peut lire que les fichiers de moins de 64Ko =** the text editor will only read files smaller than 64Kbytes long; **fenêtre de texte =** text window; **fichier texte =** text file; **(code de) fin de texte =** end of text (EOT *ou* ETX); **logiciel** *ou* **programme de formatage de texte =** text formatter; **on utilise le formatage de texte comme programme de base de PAO =** people use the text formatter as a basic desk-top publishing program; **gestion de texte =** text management; **gestionnaire de texte =** text manager; **manipulation de texte =** text manipulation; **recherche (et extraction) de texte =** text retrieval; **registre de texte =** text register; **traitement de texte =** document processing *ou* text processing *ou* word-processing (WP); **appareil de traitement de texte spécialisé =** dedicated word processor; **bureau de traitement de texte =** word-processing bureau; **centre de traitement de texte =** editorial processing centre; **fonction (de) traitement de texte =** text-editing function; **une fonction traitement de texte est intégrée au programme =** the program includes a built-in text-editing function; **logiciel** *ou* **programme de traitement de texte =** word-processing program; **chargez le programme de traitement de texte avant de commencer à saisir le texte =** load the word-processing program before you start keyboarding; **machine de traitement de texte =** word-processor; **système de traitement de texte =** text-editing facilities

◇ **textuel, -elle** *adj* textual

théorie *nf* theory; **théorie des ensembles =** set theory; **théorie de l'information =** information theory

◇ **théorique** *adj* theoretical; **débit théorique =** rated throughput; **formation théorique =** hands off training

thermique *adj* thermal; **bruit thermique =** thermal noise; **dissipateur thermique =** heat sink; **impression thermique =** electrosensitive printing; **imprimante thermique =** thermal *ou* electrothermal printer; **imprimante thermique à étincelle =** spark printer; **papier thermique =** heat sensitive paper *ou* thermal paper; **transfert thermique =** thermal transfer; **imprimante à transfert thermique =** thermal transfer printer; **les techniques du jet d'encre et du transfert thermique se font concurrence =** colour ink-jet technology and thermal transfer technology compete with each other; **papier à transfert thermique =** electrosensitive paper

thermistor *nm* thermistor

thermosensible *adj* thermo-sensitive

thésaurus *nm* thesaurus

thiosulfate *nm (pour fixage en photographie)* **thiosulfate de sodium =** sodium thiosulfate; *(familier)* hypo

thyristor *nm* thyristor

tierce *nf (troisième épreuve d'imprimerie)* page proof

tiers *nm* third party

tilde *nm* tilde

tirage *nm* **(a)** *(imprimerie)* impression *ou* print *ou* printrun; **tirage d'épreuves =** proofing; **tirage réduit** *ou* **limité =** short-run; **un imprimeur qui se spécialise dans les petits tirages =** a printer specializing in short-run printing; **tirage à la suite =** run-on; **faire un tirage à la suite =** to run on; **nous avons décidé de faire un tirage à la suite de 3000 exemplaires =** we decided to run on 3,000 copies to the first printing; **prix du tirage à la suite =** run-on price **(b)** circulation; **quel est le**

tirage de cette revue d'informatique? *ou* à combien d'exemplaires tire cette revue d'informatique? = what is the circulation of this computer magazine?; **les journaux à gros tirage** = the national press

◊ **tiré** *nm* tiré à part = offprint

◊ **tirer** *vtr* **(a)** to drag **(b)** *(imprimerie)* **tirer les épreuves (d'un texte)** = to proof *ou* to print; **un journal spécialisé qui tire à plus de 10 000 exemplaires** = a specialized magazine with a circulation of over 10,000; **tirer à la suite** = to run on

tiret *nm* dash; **tiret de césure** *ou* **tiret court** *ou* **tiret demi-cadratin (dont la longueur équivaut à un 'n')** = en dash *ou* en rule; **tiret long** *ou* **tiret cadratin (dont la longueur équivaut à un 'm')** = em dash *ou* em rule

tissu *nm (pour machine à écrire)* **ruban (en) tissu** = fibre ribbon

titre *nm* **(a)** title; **c'est la dernière image du film, faites apparaître les titres** = this is the last frame of the film so pop on the titles; **titre d'une disquette** = title of disk **(b)** *(d'un livre)* title; **faux-titre** = half title; **page de titre** = title page **(c)** *(d'une page* ou *d'un chapitre)* heading; **titre courant** = running heading *ou* headline; *(d'un journal)* **gros titres à la une** = banner headlines **(d)** *(nouveaux livres d'une bibliothèque)* **nouveaux titres** = accessions

titulaire *nm* owner; **titulaire d'un droit d'auteur** *ou* **d'un copyright** = copyright owner

token *nm* **réseau token ring** = token ring network

tolérance *nf* tolerance *ou* robustness; **tolérance au bruit** = noise immunity; **limite de tolérance au bruit** = noise margin; **tolérance aux dérangements** *ou* **tolérance de pannes** = fault tolerance; **tolérance aux interférences** = interference immunity

◊ **tolérant, -e** *adj* ils ont commercialisé, avec beaucoup de succès, une gamme de minis très tolérants aux dérangements = they market a highly successful range of fault-tolerant minis; **(système) tolérant**

aux dérangements = fault-tolerant (system)

tombée *nf* off-cut

◊ **tomber** *vi* l'ordinateur est tombé en panne deux fois cet après-midi = the computer system went down twice during the afternoon

tomo- *préfixe* tomo-

◊ **tomodensitométrie** *nf* computerized axial tomography (CAT)

◊ **tomographie** *nf* tomography

◊ **tomographique** *adj* **image tomographique** = tomogram

ton *nm* **(a)** *(son)* tone **(b)** *(couleur)* tone *ou* shade

◊ **tonal, -e** *adj* **numérotation sur clavier tonal** = tone dialling; **enveloppe tonale** = pitch envelope; **signalisation tonale** = tone signalling

◊ **tonalité** *nf* tone; **tonalité d'appel** = dial tone *ou* dialling tone; **tonalité 'occupé'** = line busy tone *ou* engaged tone

◊ **toner** *nm* *(pour photocopieur, imprimante laser, etc.)* toner; **cartouche de toner** = toner cartridge

topage *nm (de signal vidéo)* pix lock

topologie *nf* topology; **topologie d'une base de données** = database mapping; **topologie de réseau** = network topology

tore *nf* **tore magnétique** = magnetic core

torsadé, -ée *adj* twisted; **câble à paire torsadée** = twisted pair cable

tortue *nf* turtle; **graphisme généré avec une tortue** = turtle graphics; **la présentation graphique a été préparée à l'aide d'une tortue** = the charts were prepared using turtle graphics

total *nm* total; **le total des caractères saisis est de dix millions** = the total keyboarded characters amount to ten million; **en ajoutant l'appendice, nous ferons 256 pages au total** = by adding the appendix, we will increase the page extent to 256; **total de contrôle** = control total *ou* checksum *ou* check total; **les**

données sont sûrement corrompues si le total de contrôle est faux = the data must be corrupted if the checksum is different; **total par groupe** *ou* **par lot** = batch total; **total de vérification** = checksum *ou* check total *ou* control total; **total de vérification pour hash code** = hash total

◇ **total, -e** *adj* total *ou* global; **arrêt total** = dead halt *ou* drop dead halt; **le manuel n'explique pas la marche à suivre en cas d'arrêt total de la machine** = the manual does not say what to do if a dead halt occurs; **nombre total de pages (d'un document)** = extent (of a document)

◇ **totalement** *adv* totally *ou* fully; **réseau totalement maillé** = fully connected network

◇ **totalisation** *nf* adding up *ou* addition (to make a total); **contrôle par totalisation** = summation check

touche *nf* key *ou* pushbutton; **le clavier comporte 84 touches** = there are 84 keys on the keyboard; **touche alphanumérique** = alphanumeric key; **touche des capitales** = shift key; *(de verrouillage)* caps lock; **le témoin s'allume quand la touche (des) capitales est verrouillée** = the LED lights up when caps lock is pressed; **touche de caractère** = character key; **touches qui ne produisent pas de caractères** = dead keys; **touche (du) chariot** = carriage return (CR); **touche de commande** = control (key) *ou* CTRL; **touche (de) contraste** = contrast key *ou* button; **touche de contrôle** = control (key) *ou* CTRL; **touches de contrôle du curseur** = cursor pad *ou* cursor control keys; **touche d'échappement** *ou* **touche ESC** = escape key *ou* ESC; **appuyez sur la touche ECHAPPEMENT pour arrêter le programme** = to end the program, press ESCAPE; **touche d'édition** = edit key; **il y a plusieurs touches d'édition - celle-ci permet de reformater le texte** = there are several special edit keys - this one will reformat the text; **touche d'enregistrement** = record button; **touches fléchées** = cursor pad *ou* arrow keys; **touche de fonction** = function key; **en appuyant sur la touche de fonction F5 on se met en mode entrée** = hitting F5 will put you into insert mode; **on peut allouer des étiquettes aux touches de fonction** = tags can be allocated to function keys; **touche de fonction programmable** = programmable key; **touche d'intervention** = attention key; **touche**

des **majuscules** = shift key; *(de verrouillage)* caps lock; **touches programmables** = soft keys; **touche répétition** = repeat key; **touche de retour arrière (du curseur)** = backspace key; **pour corriger une erreur de saisie de texte, utilisez la touche de retour arrière** = if you make a mistake entering data, use the backspace key to correct it; **touche de retour du chariot** = carriage return key *ou* carriage return (CR); **les clavistes trouvent que la touche de retour est mal placée** = the carriage return key is badly placed for touch-typists; **touche de tabulation décimale** = decimal tab key; **touche de validation d'entrée** = enter key; **touche de verrouillage des majuscules** = caps lock; **action sur deux touches en même temps** = chord keying; **actionner une touche** = to key; **pression nécessaire pour actionner une touche** = key force; **(logiciel) activé par une seule touche** = single key response; **clic témoin (de fonctionnement) de touche** = key click; **code numérique d'une touche** = key number; **contrôle des touches** = keystroke verification; **contrôle (par balayage)** *ou* **reconnaissance d'utilisation de touches** = keyboard scan; **course d'une touche** = key travel; **encodeur des touches** = keyboard encoder; **implantation** *ou* **disposition des touches d'un clavier** = keyboard layout; **jeu vertical d'une touche** = key travel; **matrice des touches sur un clavier** = key matrix; **mémento de fonction des touches** = key overlay; **rebond d'une touche de clavier** = keyboard contact bounce

◇ **toucher** *vtr* to touch

> vous vous déplacez principalement à l'aide des touches de direction
> *L'Ordinateur Individuel*

tour *nm* **(a)** turn; **(utilisation d'un appareil) à tour de rôle** = round robin; **tour à tour** = alternately **(b)** *(d'enroulement)* loop

tournage *nm* filming *ou* shooting; **tournage d'une scène** = action shot; **le tournage commencera la semaine prochaine s'il fait beau** = filming will start next week if the weather is fine

◇ **tourner** *vi* **(a)** to spin *ou* to roll; *(autour d'un axe)* to rotate; **le lecteur faisait tourner la disquette** = the disk was spun by the drive; **le moteur du lecteur de disquettes tourne à vitesse constante** =

the disk drive motor spins at a constant velocity **(b)** *(un film)* to film *ou* to shoot a film; **ils tournaient un programme sur les animaux sauvages** = they were filming a wild life programme; **les extérieurs pour ce programme ont été tournés en Espagne** = the programme was shot on location in Spain

traçage *nm* **(a)** outlining *ou* drawing; **gabarit de traçage** = template; **pochoir de traçage** = stencil **(b)** *(d'un programme ou d'un procédé)* **traçage de panne** = fault trace; **point de contrôle (du registre) dans un programme de traçage** = trace trap; **programme de traçage** = trace program; **protocole de traçage** = audit trail

◊ **traçant, -e** *adj* **table traçante** = flatbed plotter

◊ **tracé** *nm* line *ou* design; *(graphique)* plot; **tracé d'un circuit** = circuit design

◊ **tracer** *vtr* **tracer une courbe** *ou* **un graphe (par points numérisés)** = to plot a curve

◊ **traceur** *nm* graph plotter; **traceur de courbes** *ou* **de graphiques** = X-Y plotter *ou* graph plotter; **pilote de traceur de courbes** = plotter driver; **traceur graphique** = pen recorder; **traceur incrémentiel** *ou* **à incrémentation** = incremental plotter; **traceur numérique** = digital plotter; **traceur à tambour** = drum plotter

traducteur *nm* **(a)** *(personne)* translator **(b)** *(programme)* **traducteur de langage** = language translator *ou* translator program

◊ **traduction** *nf* **(a)** *(en langue étrangère)* translation; **traduction assistée par ordinateur** = machine translation **(b)** *(informatique)* **traduction de données** = data translation; **traduction d'un langage (informatique)** = language translation; **programme de traduction** = translator (program)

◊ **traduire** *vtr* **(a)** *(en langue étrangère)* to translate **(b)** *(langage informatique)* to translate; *(à l'exécution)* to interpret

trafic *nm* *(sur une ligne)* traffic; **trafic d'entrée** *ou* **d'arrivée** = incoming traffic; **trafic d'une ligne** = line load; **analyse du trafic** = traffic analysis; **densité du trafic** = traffic density

train *nm* train *ou* stream; **train de bits** = bit stream; **train d'impulsions** = pulse stream

traînage *nm* *(distorsion d'image)* streaking

◊ **traînée** *nf* **traînée d'image** = hangover *ou* extra

trait *nm* **(a)** bar *ou* line; *(sous un mot ou une ligne de texte)* underline *ou* underscore; **trait oblique** = slash *ou* oblique stroke; **dessin au trait** = line drawing **(b)** **trait d'union** = hyphen *ou* dash; **mot qui s'écrit avec un trait d'union** = hyphenated word; **le mot 'porte-clés' s'écrit toujours avec un trait d'union** = the word 'porte-clés' is always hyphenated; **trait d'union obligatoire** = hard hyphen

traité, -ée *adj* processed; **données non traitées** = raw data

◊ **traitement** *nm* process *ou* processing; **effectuer un traitement** = to process (data, etc.); **traitement d'arrière-plan** *ou* **traitement de fond** = background processing; **traitement de bases de données** = database processing; **machine dédiée au traitement de bases de données** = database machine; **traitement de contrôle de bloc à l'entrée** = block input processing; **traitement (en) différé** *ou* **hors ligne** *ou* **off-line** = off-line processing; **traitement de données** = data processing (DP *ou* dp) *ou* information processing; **le traitement des données sera assez long** = processing all the information will take a long time; **traitement de données sur demande** *ou* **immédiat** = demand processing; **traitement aléatoire** *ou* **direct des données** = random processing; **traitement automatique de données** = automatic data processing (ADP); **traitement centralisé des données** *ou* **de l'information** = centralized data processing; **traitement décentralisé des données** = decentralized data processing; **traitement électronique de données** = electronic data processing (EDP); **capacité de traitement électronique de données** = electronic data processing capability *ou* EDP capability; **système de traitement de données intégré** = integrated data processing (IDP); **vitesse de traitement de données** = data rate; **(procédure de) traitement des erreurs** = error handling *ou* management; **traitement de fichier =** file processing; **traitement instantané d'un film =** in camera process; **traitement frontal =** foreground processing *ou* foregrounding; **traitement de l'image =** image processing *ou* picture processing; **traitement informatique de l'image =** computer image processing; **caméra de traitement de l'image =** process camera; **système de traitement de l'image =** image processor; **traitement immédiat** *ou* **sur demande =** immediate processing; **traitement de l'information =** data processing (DP *ou* dp) *ou* information processing; **traitement en ligne** *ou* **on-line =** in-line processing *ou* on-line processing; **traitement hors ligne** *ou* **off-line =** off-line processing; **traitement de liste =** list processing; **traitement par lots** *ou* **par paquets =** batch processing; **mode de traitement par paquets =** (processing data in) batch mode; **partition** *ou* **zone de traitement par lots =** batch region; **processeur de traitement par lots** *ou* **par paquets =** batch processor; **système de traitement par lots** *ou* **par paquets =** batch system; **traitement multitâche en temps réel =** real-time multi-tasking; **traitement non prioritaire =** background processing; **traitement de requête =** query processing; **traitement en série =** serial processing; **traitement de tâche =** job processing; **traitement en temps réel =** real-time processing; **traitement de texte =** *(logiciel)* word-processor *ou* text-processor; *(action)* text processing *ou* word-processing (WP) *ou* document processing; **le temps d'ordinateur requis pour le traitement d'une page de texte varie en fonction de la complexité du document =** page processing time depends on the complexity of a given page; **machine de traitement de texte =** word-processor *ou* text-processor; **machine de traitement de texte spécialisé =** dedicated word-processor; **bureau de traitement de texte =** word-processing bureau; **centre de traitement de texte =** editorial processing centre; **fonction (de) traitement de texte =** text-editing function; **une fonction traitement de texte est intégrée au programme =** the program includes a built-in text-editing function; **logiciel de traitement de texte =** word-processing program *ou* word-processing software *ou* word-processor; **machine de traitement de texte =** word-processor; **programme de traitement de texte =** word-processing program;

chargez le programme de traitement de texte avant de commencer à saisir le texte = load the word-processing program before you start keyboarding; **(programme) limité par le traitement** *ou* **avec contrainte de traitement =** process-bound (program); **système de traitement de texte =** word-processing system *ou* system with text-editing facilities

◊ **traiter** *vtr (des données, etc.)* to process (data, etc.); **nous avons traité les nouvelles données =** we processed the new data; **traiter un texte sur ordinateur =** to word-process a text *ou* to process a text; **disque à traiter =** milk disk

trajectoire *nm* trajectory; **trajectoire elliptique =** elliptical orbit

trajet *nm (de données)* data path

trame *nm* **(a)** *(télévision)* trame d'image = field; **balayage (vertical) de trame =** raster scanning; **impulsion de contrôle du balayage vertical de la trame =** field sync pulse; **fréquence de trame =** field frequency; **retour de trame =** field flyback; **intervalle de trame** *ou* **suppression verticale de la trame =** field blanking (interval) **(b)** *(de transmission)* message slot **(c)** *(de données sur bande)* **erreur de trame =** frame error; **synchronisation de trame =** framing

tranche *nf* **(a)** slice; **tranche (de silicium) =** silicon wafer; **intégration sur tranche de silicium =** wafer scale integration **(b)** **architecture de (processeur) en tranches =** bit-slice architecture; **microprocesseur en tranches =** bit-slice microprocessor; **processeur en tranches =** bit-slice processor; **le processeur en tranches utilise quatre processeurs à 4 bits pour réaliser un processeur à 16 bits =** the bit slice design uses four 4-bit word processors to construct a 16-bit processor **(c)** **tranche de temps** *ou* **tranche horaire =** time slice

transaction *nf* transaction; **transaction de données =** data transaction; **enregistrement de transactions =** transaction record; **fichier de transactions =** transaction file

◊ **transactionnel, -elle** *adj* **système transactionnel =** transaction-driven system (TDS); **traitement transactionnel en ligne** = on-line transaction processing

transcodeur *nm* transcoder; **utilisez le transcodeur pour la conversion de PAL en SECAM** = use the transcoder to convert PAL to SECAM

transcription *nf* transcription
◊ **transcrire** *vtr* to transcribe

transducteur *nm* transducer; **un transducteur de pression transforme un signal physique de pression en signal électrique** = a pressure transducer converts physical pressure signals into electrical signals

transférer *vtr* to transfer *ou* to output; *(d'un gros processeur à un plus petit)* to download; *(d'un petit ordinateur à un plus gros)* to upload; *(entre périphérique lent et processeur rapide)* to spool; *(vider sur disque ou sur imprimante)* to dump; **toutes les opérations de traitement ont été transférées sur l'ordinateur principal** = all processing activities have been transferred to the mainframe; **avec cette machine, on peut transférer des documents d'une machine à l'autre sans qu'il soit nécessaire de reformater** = the machine allows document interchange between it and other machines without reformatting; **l'utilisateur peut transférer les données d'un micro sur un gros ordinateur, pour mettre les applications à jour** = the user can upload PC data to update mainframe applications; **les résultats comptables ont été transférés sur le disque de sauvegarde** = the account results were dumped to the backup disk; **récupérer des données et les transférer dans un registre** = to collect transfer
◊ **transfert** *nm* **(a)** *(de données)* transfer; *(échange)* interchange *ou* change-over; **transfert d'un bloc** *ou* **d'un paragraphe** = block transfer; **transfert conditionnel** = conditional transfer; **transfert de contrôle à l'unité centrale** = control transfer to the CPU; **transfert direct** = direct change-over *ou* direct transfer; *(sur dispositif hors ligne)* **transfert de données** = data migration; **transfert des données par accès direct (à la mémoire) entre la mémoire principale et le second processeur** = direct memory access transfer between the main

memory and the second processor; **bus de transfert des données** = data highway; **transfert de fichier** = file transfer; **transfert de fichier bidirectionnel** = bi-directional file transfer; **transfert électronique de fonds** = electronic funds transfer (system) (EFT); **terminal de transfert électronique de fonds** = electronic funds transfer point of sale (EFTPOS); **transfert intercouche** = radial transfer; *(de signaux)* **mode de transfert par paquets** = burst mode; *(dans la mémoire)* **transfert d'un programme** = program relocation; **transfert radial** = radial transfer; *(de mots binaires)* **transfert en série** = word serial; **transfert d'un support magnétique à un autre** *ou* **transfert magnétique** = magnetic transfer; **transfert systématique** *ou* **automatique** = unconditional transfer; **dispositif de transfert** = diverter; **instruction de transfert** = transfer command; **temps de transfert** = transfer time; **protocole de validation de transfert (de données)** = handshake *ou* handshaking; **système à transfert de mémoire** = memory switching system; **vidage de transfert sur disque** *ou* **sur support magnétique** = dump; **vitesse de transfert** = transfer rate; **vitesse de transfert de données** **(b)** *(téléphonique)* **transfert d'appel (automatique)** = call forwarding; **nous avons demandé le transfert à la maison des appels que nous recevons au bureau** = we are having all calls forwarded from the office to home; **dispositif de transfert d'appel** = call diverter **(c)** *(d'imprimante)* **film de transfert** = carbon tissue; **transfert thermique** = thermal transfer; **les techniques du jet d'encre et du transfert thermique se font concurrence** = colour ink-jet technology and thermal transfer technology compete with each other; **papier à transfert thermique** = thermal *ou* electrosensitive paper **(d)** **transfert photomécanique** = photomechanical transfer (PMT)

transformateur *nm* transformer; **transformateur de couplage** = matching transformer; **transformateur d'isolement** *ou* **de protection** = isolation transformer

transformation *nf* transformation; **règles de transformation** = transformational rules
◊ **transformer** *vtr* to transform

transfrontière *adj* **flux de données transfrontière** = transborder data flow

transgression *nf* infringement

transistor *nm* transistor; **transistor bipolaire** = bipolar transistor; **transistor à effet de champ (TEC)** = field effect transistor (FET); **transistor à jonction bipolaire** = bipolar junction transistor (BJT); **transistor à jonction pnp** *ou* **npn** = bipolar junction transistor (BJT); **transistor (de type) npn** = npn transistor; **transistor (de type) pnp** = pnp transistor; **transistor silicium** = silicon transistor; **transistor unipolaire** = unipolar transistor; **logique transistor résistance (LTR)** = transistor-resistor logic (TRL); **logique transistor transistor (LTT)** = transistor-transistor logic (TTL)

◊ **transistorisé, -ée** *adj* **dispositif transistorisé** = solid-state device; **laser transistorisé** = semiconductor laser; **mémoire transistorisée** = solid-state memory device

transit *nm* **de transit** = transient; **courant de transit** = line transient *ou* voltage transient

transitif *adj* **disque optique transitif** = transmissive disk

transition *nf* transition; **équipement** *ou* **logiciel de transition** = bridge *ou* bridging product *ou* bridgeware; **point de transition** = transition point

transitoire *adj* transient; **courant transitoire** = line transient *ou* voltage transient; **limiteur** *ou* **éliminateur de courant transitoire** = transient suppressor

translatable *adj* relocatable; **programme translatable** = relocatable program; **ce système d'exploitation peut charger et exécuter un programme translatable sans distinction de la zone d'origine** = the operating system can load and run a relocatable program from any area of memory

◊ **translater** *vtr* to relocate

◊ **translation** *nf* relocation; **translation dynamique** = dynamic relocation; **translation statique** = static relocation;

constante de translation = relocation constant

transmetteur *nm* transmitter (TX)
◊ **transmetteur/répondeur** *nm* transponder

transmettre *vtr* **(a)** to transmit *ou* to carry *ou* to channel; **transmettre de nouveau** = to retransmit; **transmettre un signal** = to send a signal *ou* to signal; **toutes les données ont été transmises par fibres optiques** = the fibre optic link carried all the data; **les données ont été transmises à l'ordinateur par l'intermédiaire de la ligne téléphonique** = the computer received data via the telephone line; **les signaux nous ont été transmis par satellite** = the signals have reached us via satellite; **(signal d')invitation à transmettre** = go ahead; **(signal de) prêt à transmettre** = clear to send (CTS); *(de modem)* **prêt à transmettre/recevoir** = dataset ready (DSR) *ou* data terminal ready (DTR) **(b)** *(à un périphérique)* to output; **les documents qui sont prêts peuvent être transmis à l'imprimante laser** = finished documents can be output to the laser printer

◊ **transmis, -e** *adj* **erreur transmise** = inherited error

◊ **transmission** *nf* transmission *ou* communications; **transmission asynchrone** = asynchronous transmission; *(téléphonique)* **transmission en aveugle** *ou* **sans décrochage** = blind dialling; **transmission bidirectionnelle à l'alternat** = either-way operation; **transmission sans contrôle de retour** = free wheeling; **transmission de données** = data communications *ou* data transmission; **transmission de données en parallèle** = parallel data transmission; **transmission de données subvocales** = data under voice (DUV); **transmission de données vocales** = data in voice (DIV); **arrêt de transmission de données** = data break; **canal de transmission de données** = data channel; **circuit de transmission de données** = data circuit; *(causée par un défaut du support magnétique)* **brève interruption de transmission de données** = data check; **lignes de transmission de données** = bus data lines; **mémoire tampon de transmission de données** = data communications buffer; **mode de transmission de données par paquets** *ou*

burst = burst mode; **réseau de transmission de données** = data communications network; **service de transmission de données** = data services; **signaux de transmission de données** = data signals; **(mémoire) tampon de transmission de données** = (data) communications buffer; **vitesse de transmission de données** = data rate *ou* data signalling rate; *(en bauds)* baud rate; **voie de transmission de données** = data path; **transmission électronique** = electronic traffic; **transmission de fac-similé** = fax transmission; **(technologie de la) transmission par fibre optique** = fibre optics; **transmission hertzienne** *ou* **par hyperfréquence** = microwave transmission; **transmission d'images** = picture transmission; **transmission de l'information** = data communications; **canal** *ou* **voie de transmission de l'information** = information transfer channel *ou* information bearer channel; **transmission multicible** = multicasting; **transmission neutre** = neutral transmission; **(système de) transmission numérique** = digital transmission (system); **transmission par onde porteuse** = carrier signalling; **transmission (en) parallèle** = parallel transmission; **transmission par satellite** = satellite transmission; **transmission (en) série** = serial transmission; **transmission d'octets en série** = byte serial transmission *ou* mode; **transmission de signaux sur la bande vocale** = in-band signalling; **transmission de signaux en binaire** = binary signalling; **transmission de signaux numériques** = digital signalling; **transmission directe de signaux** = DC signalling; **voie de transmission de signaux** = feeder; **transmission simultanée** = simultaneous transmission; **transmission synchrone** = synchronous transmission; **transmission de télécopie** = fax transmission; **transmission unidirectionnelle** = simplex *ou* unidirectional transmission; **transmission vidéo** = video transmission; **déconcentrateur pour transmission vidéo** = video expander; **(code** *ou* **signal de) fin de la transmission** = end of transmission (EOT); **canal de transmission** = communications channel; **la capacité de transmission de cette liaison est excellente** = the information-carrying abilities of this link are very good; **commandes** *ou* **protocole de transmission** = line control; **contrôle de ligne de transmission** = communications link

control; **ordinateur de contrôle des transmission** = communications computer; **contrôleur de transmission** = communications control unit (CCU); **débit maximal de transmission** = maximum transmission rate; **erreur de transmission** = transmission error; **correction d'erreur en cours de transmission** = forward error correction; **fenêtre de transmission** = transmission window; **ligne de transmission** = communications link; **moyens** *ou* **supports de transmission** = transmission media; **perte de transmission** = link loss; **protocole de transmission** = link control procedure (LCP); **système avec facilité de transmission en différé** = store and forward system; **vitesse de transmission** = transmission rate; *(en bauds)* baud rate; **vitesse maximale de transmission** = maximum transmission rate; **adaptateur de vitesse de transmission** = baud rate generator; **la vitesse moyenne de transmission est de 64 000 bits par seconde en connexion parallèle et 19 200 bits par seconde en connexion série** = the average transmission is 64,000 bits per second (bps) through a parallel connection or 19,200 bps through a serial connection; **la vitesse de transmission (en bauds) du signal binaire était de 300 bits par seconde** = the baud rate of the binary signal was 300 bits per second; **voie** *ou* **canal de transmission** = transmission channel

le produit possède jusqu'à 4Mo de mémoire avec une vitesse de transmission de 115 200 bauds et un débit de 12 500 caractères par seconde
Le Monde informatique

transmittance *nf* transmittance

transordinateur *nm* transputer

transparence *nf* **(a)** show-through **(b)** *(de film)* **(procédé de) transparence** = back projection; **(procédé de) transparence non prioritaire** *ou* **d'arrière-plan** = background projection

◊ **transparent** *nm (pour rétroprojecteur)* transparency *ou* acetate; **les graphiques avaient été dessinés sur des transparents pour être montrés au rétroprojecteur** = the graphs were plotted on acetate, for use on an overhead projector

◇ **transparent, -e** *adj* **(a)** transparent; **le papier de mauvaise qualité est beaucoup trop transparent =** bad quality paper gives too much show-through **(b)** *(informatique)* **interruption transparente =** transparent interrupt; **pagination transparente =** transparent paging

transphaseur *nm* transphasor

transpondeur *nm* transponder

transport *nm* transport; **couche transport =** transport layer
◇ **transportable** *adj* **programme transportable d'une machine à une autre =** canned program
◇ **transporter** *vtr* to carry *ou* to transport *ou* to convey
◇ **transporteur, -euse** *adj* **bande transporteuse =** conveyor

transposition *nf* transposition

Transputer® *nm* transputer

transversal, -e *adj* **(a)** transverse; **balayage transversal** *ou* **lecture transversale =** transverse scan **(b) clé transversale =** vertical redundancy check (VRC); **clé de parité transversale =** vertical parity check

trappe *nf* trap

travail *nm* **(a)** work; **bande de travail =** scratch tape; **charge de travail =** workload *ou* work load; **disque de travail =** work disk; **espace de travail =** workspace *ou* work area; **fichier de travail =** scratch file *ou* work file; **poste de travail =** workstation *ou* operating console *ou* terminal; **poste de travail multifonction =** multifunction workstation; **poste de travail d'un opérateur =** operator's console; **le système comprend cinq postes de travail reliés en anneau =** the system includes five workstations linked together in a ring network; **station de travail =** workstation; **la mémoire d'archivage a une capacité de 1200 Mo pour sept stations de travail =** the archive storage has a total capacity of 1200 Mb between seven workstations; **zone de travail =** *(en mémoire)* work area *ou* memory

workspace **(b)** *(tâche)* job *ou* task; **contrôle de travaux groupés (en pile) =** stacked job control; **ensemble des travaux en cours d'exécution =** job mix; **fichier de travaux à exécuter =** job file; **file d'attente des travaux à exécuter =** task queue; **ordonnancement des travaux =** job scheduling

◇ **travailler** *vi* to work; **travailler à plein régime** *ou* **à plein rendement =** to work at full capacity

tréma *nm* umlaut

tremblement *nm* *(de la lumière)* flicker; *(de l'image)* jitter
◇ **trembler** *vi* *(lumière)* to flicker
◇ **tremblotter** *vi* *(image)* to jitter; **j'ai mal à la tête à force de regarder cet écran qui tremblotte =** looking at this screen jitter is giving me a headache

trente-deux *adj num* thirty-two; **système (informatique) de 32 bits =** thirty-two bit system

tresse *nf* **tresse de mise à la masse =** fanning strip

tri *nm* sort; *(action)* sorting; **tri par arborescence =** tree selection sort; **tri bulle =** bubble sort; **effectuer un tri bulle** *ou* **un tri par permutation de bulles =** to bubble sort; **tri sur disque =** external sort; **tri par échange =** exchange selection; **tri enveloppe =** shell sort; **effectuer un tri enveloppe** *ou* **un tri bloc par bloc =** to shell sort; **tri de fichiers =** file sort; **(application de) tri et fusion =** merge sort; **tri en mémoire interne =** internal sort; **tri par ordre croissant =** forward sort; **tri par ordre décroissant =** backward sort; **tri par permutation de paires =** bubble sort; **tri rapide =** quicksort; **tri sélectif =** selective sort; **tri sur support externe =** external sort; **clé** *ou* **champ de tri =** sortkey *ou* sort field; **passage de tri =** sorting pass

entrez le nom du champ sur lequel doit porter le tri; définissez ensuite l'ordre du tri, croissant (A à Z) ou décroissant (Z à A). Validez la définition
L'Ordinateur Individuel

triade *nf* triad

triangle *nm* triangle; **connection (en) triangle** *ou* **(en) delta** = delta (connexion)

tributaire *adj* dependent; **(programme) non tributaire** = device-independent (software)

tridimensionnel, -elle *adj* three-dimensional *ou* 3D

trier *vtr* to order *ou* to sort; **non trié** = unsorted; **les commandes ont été triées sur le champ date** = the orders were sorted according to dates *ou* by assigning the date field as the sortkey; **liste triée en ordre (alphabétique, etc.)** = ordered list; **(instruction** *ou* **fonction de) trier/fusionner** = sort/merge (instruction *ou* function)

Troie *npr* **cheval de Troie** = Trojan Horse

trois *adj num & nm* **instruction à trois adresses** = three-address instruction; **à trois dimensions** = three-dimensional *ou* 3D; **circuit logique à trois états** = three state logic

◊ **troisième** *adj* third; **ordinateur de troisième génération** = third generation computer

troncature *nf* rounding *ou* truncation; **erreur de troncature** = truncation error *ou* rounding error

◊ **tronquer** *vtr* to truncate; **3,5678 tronqué à 3,56** = 3.5678 truncated to 3.56

trop *adv&n* **en trop** = redundant

troposphère *nm* troposphere

trou *nm* hole

trousse *nf (d'outils ou de nettoyage, etc.)* pack *ou* kit

trouvaille *nf* hit

◊ **trouver** *vtr* to find *ou* to detect *ou* to diagnose *ou* to locate; **il a fallu beaucoup de temps pour trouver la puce défectueuse**

= it took a lot of time to find the faulty chip; **il est difficile de trouver la source du problème** = the detection of the cause of the fault is proving difficult; **on a trouvé au bout de quelques secondes à peine** = there was a hit after just a few seconds; **on trouve le nouveau progiciel dans presque tous les magasins** = you can find the new software package in any shop *ou* the availability of the latest software package is very good

◊ **se trouver** *vpr* to be located; **l'ordinateur se trouve dans l'édifice principal** = the computer is located in the main office building

T.S.F. = TELEGRAPHIE SANS FIL; **poste de T.S.F.** *ou* **une T.S.F.** = radio *ou* wireless

TTL = TRANSISTOR-TRANSISTOR LOGIC; **compatible (avec) TTL** = TTL compatible; **logique TTL** = TTL logic *ou* transistor-transistor logic; *voir aussi* TRANSISTOR

tube *nm* tube; **tube à rayons cathodiques** *ou* **tube cathodique** = cathode ray tube (CRT); *(pour télévision)* television tube; **tube ombré** = dark trace tube; **tube à vide** = vacuum tube *ou* valve

tulipe *nf* **imprimante à tulipe** = thimble printer

Turing *npr* **machine de Turing** *ou* **simulateur (de) Turing** = Turing machine; **test de Turing** = Turing test

tutoriel *nm* tutorial

tuyau *nm* conduit

type *nm* **(a)** *nm* type; **type de données** = data type **(b) lettre type** = form letter *ou* standard letter

typographe *ou* **typo** *nm* typographer *ou* typesetter

◊ **typographie** *nf* typography; **ce travail ne demande aucune expérience en typographie** = no typographical skills are required for this job

◇ **typographique** *adj* typographic *ou* typographical; **annotation typographique** = marking up; **une erreur typographique à la composition donne ce qu'on appelle une 'coquille'** = a typographical error made while typesetting is called a 'typo'; **point typographique (0.324 mm) =** point; **répertoire typographique =** character repertoire

Uu

UV = ULTRAVIOLET

UAL = UNITE ARITHMETIQUE ET LOGIQUE

ultra *préfixe* ultra-; **ultra-haute fréquence** = super high frequency (SHF) *ou* ultra high frequency (UHF); **ultra-rapide** = high-speed; **un gestionnaire de base de données ultra-rapide permet la manipulation d'une très grande quantité de données** = a high-speed database management program allows the manipulation of very large amounts of data

◊ **ultracourt, -e** *ou* **ultra-court, -e** *adj* **ondes ultracourtes** = ultra high frequency (UHF)

◊ **ultrasensible** *ou* **ultra-sensible** *adj* *(film)* high-speed (film)

◊ **ultrason** *ou* **ultra-son** *nm* ultrasound

◊ **ultrasonique** *adj* ultrasonic

◊ **ultrasonore** *adj* ultrasonic

les premières applications médicales des ultra-sons à des fins thérapeutiques datant de 1941, il faut attendre 1945 pour que les applications à des fins diagnostiques apparaissent pour la première fois
Techniques hospitalières

ultraviolet *ou* **ultra-violet** *nm* **(l')** **ultraviolet** = ultraviolet (light); **mémoire morte programmable (PROM) effaçable par ultraviolet** = ultraviolet erasable PROM

◊ **ultraviolet, -ette** *ou* **ultra-violet, -ette** *adj* ultraviolet *ou* UV (light); **lumière ultraviolette** *ou* **rayonnement ultraviolet** = ultraviolet light *ou* UV light

un *nm* one; **complément à 1** = one's complement; **le complément à 1 de 10011 est 01100** = the one's complement of 10011 is 01100

◊ **un, -e** *adj num* **une adresse plus une** = one-plus-one address; *(langage de programmation)* **un pour un** = one for one

uni- *préf* uni-

◊ **unidirectionnel, -elle** *adj* unidirectional; **antenne unidirectionnelle** = directional antenna; **microphone unidirectionnel** = unidirectional microphone; **transmission unidirectionnelle** = simplex *ou* single operation transmission

uniforme *adj* uniform; *(imprimerie)* **espacement uniforme** = monospacing

◊ **uniformiser** *verb* to make uniform; *(traitement de texte)* **uniformiser (en majuscules** *ou* **en minuscules)** = to normalize

union *nf* union; **fonction logique d'union** = join; **opération d'union** = disjunction *ou* either-or operation *ou* OR operation

◊ **trait d'union** *nm* hyphen; **trait d'union d'écran** = soft hyphen; **trait d'union obligatoire** = hard hyphen

unipolaire *adj* unipolar; **commutateur unipolaire** = single pole switch; **signal unipolaire** = unipolar signal; **transistor unipolaire** = unipolar transistor

unique *adj* **(a)** single *ou* unique; **adresse unique** = single *ou* unique address; **chaque octet de mémoire a une adresse unique** = each separate memory byte has its own unique address; **instruction à adresse unique** = one address instruction *ou* single address instruction; **code d'instruction à adresse unique** = single address code; **ordinateur à adresse unique** = one address computer; **bande latérale unique** = single sideband; **micro-ordinateur à carte unique** = single board microcomputer; **ordinateur à carte unique** = single board computer (SBC); **enregistrement unique** = unit record;

micro-ordinateur de contrôle à puce unique = single chip microcontroller; **ordinateur à puce unique** = single chip computer; **code à usage unique** = one-time pad **(b) tarif unique** = flat rate

unitaire *adj (d'une rame de papier)* **poids unitaire** = basic weight

unité *nf* **(a)** *(appareil ou système)* unit; **unité centrale (de traitement)** = central processing unit (CPU) *ou* central processor; **éléments de l'unité centrale** = CPU elements; **(temps de) cycle de l'unité centrale** = CPU cycle; **temps d'utilisation de l'unité centrale** = CPU time; *(processeur en tranches)* **unité centrale de calcul** = central processing element (CPE); **unité de commande** *ou* **unité de contrôle de périphérique** = peripheral control unit (PCU); **unité de contrôle (de processus)** = control unit (CU); **unité de disque** *ou* **de disquettes** = (magnetic) disk unit; **unité de disquettes demi-hauteur** = half-height drive; **unité de disque dur** = hard disk drive; **unité d'extension d'une ligne** = line extender; *(d'appareils pour télévision)* **unité mobile** = mobile unit; **unité multinorme** *ou* **unité multistandard** = a multistandard unit; **unité de visualisation** *ou* **de visu** = visual display unit **(b)** *(le plus petit élément)* unit *ou* item; **unité d'appel** = calling unit; **unité arithmétique et logique** = arithmetic and logic unit (ALU); **unité d'information** = computer word; **dimension d'une unité d'information** = item size; **une unité d'information peut être soit un mot, une série de chiffres ou une entrée dans un fichier** = a data item can be a word or a series of figures or a record in a file; **unité physique** = physical record; **unité de puissance vocale** = voice unit; **système évalué en cycles possibles par unité de temps** = duty-rated system

universel, -elle *adj* universal; **bus universel GPIB** *ou* **bus d'interface universel** = general purpose interface bus (GPIB); **canal universel de transmission par blocs** = universal block channel (UBC); **dispositif universel** = universal device (UART, USRT, USART); **émetteur/récepteur asynchrone universel** = universal asynchronous receiver/transmitter (UART); **contrôleur d'émetteur/récepteur asynchrone universel** = UART controller;

émetteur/récepteur synchrone asynchrone universel = universal synchronous asynchronous receiver/transmitter (USART); **émetteur/récepteur synchrone universel** = universal synchronous receiver/transmitter (USRT); **interface universelle** = standard interface; **interface universelle GPIA** = general purpose interface adapter (GPIA); **langage universel** = machine-independent language; **programmation en langage universel** = universal programming

UNIX® *n* système d'exploitation UNIX = Unix system

urbain , -e *adj* **communication (téléphonique) urbaine** = local call

urgence *nf* emergency; **plan d'urgence** = contingency plan

usage *nm* use; **faire usage de quelque chose** = to make use of something; **terminal à usage professionnel** = executive terminal

usinage *nm* machining
◇ **usine** *nf* factory; **ils ont ouvert une nouvelle usine de composants électroniques** = they have opened a new components factory; **usine de construction d'ordinateurs** = computer factory

utile *adj* **(a)** helpful *ou* useful; **document utile se rapportant à un logiciel** = software documentation; **il trouve la machine de traitement de texte très utile pour le travail de bureau** = he finds his word-processor a great help in the office **(b)** *(efficace)* **ouverture utile** = effective aperture

utilisable *adj* usable; **maximum de fréquence utilisable** = maximum usable frequency; **cet ordinateur individuel possède 512K de mémoire utilisable** = the PC has 512K of usable memory

utilisateur, -trice *n* **(a)** user *ou* end user; **utilisateur intermédiaire** = mid-user; **la société cherche à créer un ordinateur adapté aux besoins de l'utilisateur** = the company is creating a computer with a specific end user in mind; **code personnel** *ou* **mot de passe d'un utilisateur =** user ID; **groupe d'utilisateurs =** user group; **j'ai trouvé la solution au problème en me renseignant auprès des autres utilisateurs rencontrés à la réunion =** I found how to solve the problem by asking people at the user group meeting; **groupe fermé d'utilisateurs =** closed user group (CUG); **langage (d') utilisateur =** user language *ou* user-operated language; **interface utilisateur/machine =** man/machine interface (MMI); **nombre maximum d'utilisateurs =** maximum users; **notice d'utilisation destinée à l'utilisateur =** user documentation; **programmable** *ou* **modifiable** *ou* **réglable par l'utilisateur =** user-selectable *ou* user-definable; **qui peut être programmé** *ou* **modifié** *ou* **réglé** *ou* **sélectionné** *ou* **validé suivant les besoins de l'utilisateur =** user-selectable *ou* user-definable; **le vidéo offre un choix de 640 x 300, 240 ou 200 pixels que l'utilisateur peut programmer lui-même =** the video resolution of 640 by 300, 240 or 200 pixels is user-selectable; **caractères programmés par l'utilisateur =** user-defined characters; **programme (d') utilisateur** *ou* **programme écrit par l'utilisateur =** user's program *ou* user program; **zone pour programme utilisateur** *ou* **zone utilisateur =** user area; **schéma de l'utilisateur =** external schema

◊ **utilisation** *nf* use; *(machine ou logiciel)* **d'utilisation facile =** user-friendly *ou* simple to use; **logiciel d'utilisation facile =** user-friendly software; **utilisation de mémoire tampon =** buffering; **utilisation de double mémoire tampon =** double buffering; **(mode de) chargement en fonction de la fréquence d'utilisation =** activity loading; **contrôle d'utilisation de touches =** keyboard scan; **(bit) indicateur** *ou* **marqueur** *ou* **témoin d'utilisation =** device flag; **manuel d'utilisation =** user guide *ou* instruction manual *ou* user's manual *ou* operations manual; **manuel**

d'utilisation élémentaire = primer; **notice d'utilisation =** operational information; **notice d'utilisation destinée à l'utilisateur =** user documentation; **notice d'utilisation d'un logiciel =** software documentation; **l'excellente notice d'utilisation facilitait l'emploi du progiciel =** using the package was easy with the excellent user documentation; **temps d'utilisation de l'unité centrale** *ou* **du processeur =** CPU time

> l'utilisateur moyen risque de ne pas exploiter toute la capacité de son ordinateur
>
> *Temps Micro*

utilisé, -ée *adj* used *ou* in use

◊ **utiliser** *vtr* to use; **utiliser quelque chose =** to make use of something; **utiliser une mémoire tampon =** to buffer; **utilisez le pavé numérique pour saisir les chiffres =** you can use the numeric keypad to enter the figures; **les commerciaux utilisent l'ordinateur trop souvent =** the computer is used too often by the sales staff; **le nouveau progiciel peut être utilisé sur notre PC =** the new package runs on our PC; **facile à utiliser =** user-friendly *ou* easy-to-use; **c'est un appareil extrêmement facile à utiliser =** it's such a user-friendly machine; **les données devraient être réparties en fichiers plus courts et plus faciles à utiliser =** data should be split into manageable files

utilitaire *nm&adj* **(programme) utilitaire =** utility (program) *ou* housekeeping routine *ou* service program; **(programmes) utilitaires =** toolkit; **il est impossible de récupérer un fichier perdu sans l'aide d'un (programme) utilitaire =** a lost file cannot be found without a file-recovery utility; **la disquette comporte un utilitaire qui permet la sauvegarde de fichiers sur disque dur =** on the disk is a utility for backing up a hard disk; **utilitaire de requête** *ou* **d'interrogation =** query facility

Vv

V = VOLTAGE

V *(pour modems)* **normes** *ou* **protocoles de transmission série V** = V series

V & V = VERIFICATION AND VALIDATION

vacillement *nm* flicker; **(image** *ou* **affichage) sans vacillement** = flicker-free (screen *ou* display)
◊ **vaciller** *vi* to flicker; **l'image sur l'écran vacille à la mise sous tension de l'imprimante** = the image flickers when the printer is switched on

vacuum *nm* vacuum

valeur *nf* **(a)** value; **la variable a pris la valeur de la donnée saisie** = the variable was equated to the input data; **valeur absolue** = absolute value; **la valeur absolue de -62,34 est 62,34** = the absolute value of -62.34 is 62.34; **valeur binaire** *ou* **booléenne** = truth value *ou* Boolean value; **valeur complémentaire (d'un nombre)** = offset; **valeur par défaut** *ou* **intrinsèque** *ou* **pré-programmée** = default value; *(d'amplitude* *ou* *d'intensité, etc.)* **valeur efficace** = root mean square (RMS); **la valeur efficace d'une sinusoïde parfaite équivaut à 0,7071 de son amplitude** = the root mean square of the pure sinusoidal signal is 0.7071 of its amplitude; *(en début de programme)* **valeur initiale** = initial value; *(d'une adresse)* **valeur relative** = offset value *ou* offset word; **valeur de vérification pour hash code** = hash value; **erreur à valeur moyenne nulle** = balanced error; **gamme de valeurs** = number range; **ordinateur à valeurs variables** = incremental computer **(b) valeur dans un tableau** = array element **(c) réseau à valeur ajoutée** = value added network (VAN); **revendeur de systèmes à valeur ajoutée** = value added reseller (VAR)

validation *nf* validation; **validation de données** = data validation *ou* data vetting; **validation de fichier** = file validation; *(ligne de caractères)* **(commande de) validation de ligne** = line input; **protocole de validation de transfert de données** = handshake *ou* handshaking; **vérification et validation** = verification and validation (V & V); **ligne de validation d'un circuit intégré** = chip select line; **signal de validation** = enabling signal; **signal de validation d'adresse** = address strobe; **signal de validation de données (transmises)** = data strobe; **touche de validation d'entrée** = enter key
◊ **valide** *adj* valid; **il a tenté d'utiliser un mot de passe qui n'était pas valide** = he tried to use an invalid password; **adresse valide** = valid memory address
◊ **validé, -ée** *adj (activé)* armed *ou* selected *ou* enabled *ou* activated; **configuration validée** = configured-in; **interruption validée** = armed interrupt
◊ **valider** *vtr* **(a)** *(données, etc.)* to validate **(b)** *(activer)* to select *ou* to arm *ou* to enable *ou* to activate; **valider un circuit intégré** = to chip select (CS); **(circuit** *ou* **dispositif) qui peut être validé par cavalier** = jumper-selectable; **qui peut être validé suivant les besoins de l'utilisateur** = user-selectable (device); **valider une interruption** = to interrupt enable **(c)** *(par une impulsion)* to strobe
◊ **validité** *nf* **(a)** validity; **(test de) vérification de validité des données** = validity check **(b) signal de validité d'adresse** = address strobe

valve *nf* valve

variable 1 *nf* variable; **nom de variable** = variable name; **variable binaire** = binary variable; **variable booléenne** = Boolean variable; **variable de chaîne** *ou* string variable; **variable chaînée** *ou* **de type chaîne de caractères** = string type variable; **variable factice** = dummy variable; **variable globale** *ou* **commune** *ou* **générale** = global variable; **variable indicée** *ou* **caractérisée par un indice** = subscripted variable; **variable locale** = local variable; **variable de location** *ou* **de référence d'une cellule** = cell reference variable; **variable de type non précisé** = variable data type **2** *adj* variable *ou* fluctuating; **condensateur variable** = variable capacitor; **donnée(s) variable(s)** = variable data; **format variable** = V format *ou* variable format; **enregistrement à longueur variable** = variable length record; **ordinateur à mots de longueur variable** = variable word length computer; **résistance variable** = variable resistor; **objectif à focale variable** = zoom lens; **tableau à dimensions variables** = flexible array; **intensité variable du signal** = signal strength; **processeur à mots variables** = byte machine; *(d'un programme)* **point d'arrêt variable** = regional breakpoint; **tampon (de capacité) variable** = dynamic *ou* elastic buffer; **ordinateur à valeurs variables** = incremental computer

> pendant longtemps le traitement du signal s'est essentiellement intéressé aux signaux dépendant d'une seule variable (le temps)
> *Traitement du signal*

variateur *nm (d'un potentiomètre)* wiper

◊ **variation** *nf* variation *ou* fluctuation; *(non voulue)* **variation chromatique** = colour shift; **variation de fréquence** = frequency variation; *(d'un magnétophone)* **variation de vitesse** = flutter; **le pleurage et les variations de vitesse sont des défauts courants des magnétophones bon marché** = wow and flutter are common faults on cheap tape recorders

◊ **varier** *vi* **(a)** to vary *ou* to fluctuate; **la clarté du signal peut varier avec la tension du courant d'alimentation** = the clarity of the signal can vary with the power supply; **qui varie** = fluctuating **(b) varier (de ... à)** = to range (from ... to)

vecteur *nm* vector; **vecteur de retard** = delay vector

◊ **vectoriel, -ielle** *adj* vector; **image** *ou* **infographie vectorielle** = vector graphics *ou* vector image *ou* vector scan; **police de caractères vectorielle** = dynamically redefinable character set; **processeur vectoriel** = vector processor *ou* array

processor; **le processeur vectoriel permet de faire pivoter le tableau qui contient l'image écran, à l'aide d'une seule commande** = the array processor allows the array that contains the screen image to be rotated with one simple command

◊ **vectorisé, -ée** *adj* vectored; **interruption vectorisée** = vectored interrupt

vedette *nf* star; **programme vedette** = star program

véhiculer *vtr (données ou signaux)* to channel *ou* to carry

veille *nf* **courant de veille** = hold current

Veitch *npr* **diagramme de Veitch** = Veitch diagram

vendre *vtr* to sell; *(livres)* **vendre à bas prix** = to remainder; **articles vendus sur commande uniquement** = available to order only

venir de *vi* **(a)** to originate from; **les données viennent du nouvel ordinateur** = the data originated from the new computer **(b) qui vient de l'extérieur** = incoming (message *ou* data)

Venn *npr* **diagramme de Venn** = Venn diagram

vente *nf* sale; **vente(s) par téléphone** = telesales; **publicité lieu de vente (PLV)** = point-of-sale material; **point de vente** = point-of-sale (POS); **point de vente électronique** = electronic point-of-sale (EPOS); **terminal de point de vente** = point-of-sale terminal *ou* POS terminal

ventilateur *nm* fan; **si le ventilateur tombe en panne, le système va rapidement (sur)chauffer** = if the fan fails, the system will rapidly overheat

ventiler *vtr* to fan

vérificateur, -trice *n&adj* **vérificateur d'orthographe** = spellchecker *ou* spelling checker

◊ **vérificatrice** *nf* verifier

◊ **vérification** *nf* **(a)** control *ou* check *ou* verification *ou* test; **vérification automatique** = auto verify; **équipement de vérification automatique (EVA)** = automatic test equipment (ATE); **vérification de boucle** = loop check; **vérification de caractère** = character check; **vérification de données** = data vetting; **code de vérification et correction d'erreurs** = error checking and correcting code (ECCC); **faire une vérification orthographique** = to spellcheck; **programme de vérification orthographique** = spellchecker *ou* spelling checker; **vérification d'un programme** = program verification; **vérification et validation** = verification and validation (V & V); **protocole de vérification (d'utilisation)** = audit trail; **total de vérification** = checksum *ou* check total **(b)** *(relecture)* **vérification (d'un article** *ou* **d'un manuscrit)** = subbing *ou* sub-editing

◊ **vérifier (a)** *vtr* to verify *ou* to check *ou* to control *ou* to monitor; *(pression ou niveau)* to gauge; **le programme permet de vérifier l'orthographe** = the program allows the user to review all wrongly spelled words; **les éditeurs ont vérifié toutes les références à la bibliothèque locale** = the editors have checked all the references in the local library; **nous vérifions chaque lot pour nous assurer de la qualité** = we check each batch to make sure it is perfect; **il a vérifié la sortie d'imprimante avec les factures** = he checked the computer printout against the invoices; **il faudrait vérifier la manette de commande qui reste parfois coincée** = I think the joystick needs adjustment as it sometimes gets stuck **(b)** *(un texte)* to sub-edit *ou* to sub (a text)

◊ **vérin** *nm* actuator

◊ **véritable** *adj* genuine

◊ **vérité** *nf* truth; **table de vérité** = Boolean operation table *ou* truth table

◊ **véroler** *vtr (familier)* to corrupt; **un problème de tension pendant l'accès au disque peut véroler les données** = power loss during disk access can corrupt the data

verrou *nm* **(a)** lock; **verrou électronique** = electronic lock **(b)** *(du niveau de sortie)* latch

◊ **verrouillage** *nm,* **(a)** locking; **verrouillage d'un fichier** = locking a file **(b)** *(du niveau de sortie)* **dispositif de verrouillage** = latch **(c)** *(par logiciel)* interlock

◊ **verrouillé, -ée** *adj* locked; **entrée sur un système** *ou* **sur un terminal mal verrouillé** = piggyback entry; **système verrouillé** = secure system

◊ **verrouiller** *vtr* **(a)** to lock; **verrouiller (l'accès d')un fichier** = to lock a file **(b)** *(par logiciel)* to interlock **(c)** *(un niveau de sortie)* to latch **(d)** *(le voltage d'un signal)* to clamp

version *nf (d'un programme)* version *ou* implementation *ou* release; **version avancée** *ou* **évoluée** = advanced version; **dernière** *ou* **nouvelle version** = rewrite *ou* update (of a program); **le programme en est à sa deuxième version** = the program is in its second rewrite; **cette version du BASIC offerte par le fabricant est un peu différente de celle que j'utilise** = this manufacturer's dialect of BASIC is a little different to the one I'm used to; **comparée à la version précédente, celle-ci est très conviviale** = compared with the previous version this one is very user-friendly; **la dernière version du logiciel comprend une routine graphique améliorée** = the latest version of the software includes an improved graphics routine; **la dernière version du logiciel porte le numéro 5** = the latest software is release 5; **la dernière version du logiciel est beaucoup plus rapide** = the latest implementation of the software runs much faster

verso *nm* verso

vert , -e *adj* green; **phosphore vert** = green phosphor

vertical, -e *adj* vertical; **balayage vertical** = field sweep; **impulsion de contrôle** *ou* **de synchronisation du balayage vertical** = field sync pulse; **coordonnée verticale** = Y-coordinate; **défilement vertical** = vertical scrolling; **délai de retour vertical** = vertical blanking interval; **jeu vertical d'une touche** = key travel; **justification verticale** = vertical justification; **on a fait**

une justification verticale de la page = the page has been justified vertically; **(antenne, etc) à polarisation verticale =** vertically polarized (antenna); **signal avec polarisation verticale =** vertically polarized signal; **suppression verticale =** field blanking (interval); **tabulation verticale =** vertical tab; **unité de formatage vertical =** vertical format unit (VFU)

◊ **verticale** *nf (coordonnée)* Y-direction

◊ **verticalement** *adv* vertically; **signal polarisé verticalement =** vertically polarized signal

via *prép* via

vibration *nf* **(a)** judder **(b)** vibration sonore = buzz; **émettre une vibration sonore =** to buzz

◊ **vibreur** *nm* vibreur sonore = buzzer

vice *nm* defect; *(dans un programme)* **vice caché =** hidden defect (in a program)

vidage *nm (sur imprimante ou sur support magnétique)* dump; **vidage par autopsie =** post mortem (dump); **vidage binaire =** binary dump; **vidage de contrôle (sur imprimante) =** check point dump; **vidage dynamique =** dynamic dump; **vidage d'écran (sur imprimante) =** screen dump; **vidage de fichier =** file cleanup *ou* file purge; **vidage au format =** formatted dump; **vidage hexadécimal =** hex dump; **vidage sur imprimante =** dump; **vidage irréversible =** disaster dump; **vidage de mémoire (sur imprimante) =** storage dump *ou* memory dump; **vidage (sur imprimante) après mouvements =** change dump; **point de vidage =** dump point; **(instruction de) vidage et reprise =** dump and restart; **vidage de sauvegarde =** rescue dump; **vidage sélectif =** selective dump; **vidage statique =** static dump

◊ **vide 1** *nm* vacuum; **on a fait le vide dans le tube cathodique scellé =** there is a vacuum in the sealed CRT; **tube à vide =** vacuum tube **2** *adj* **(a)** empty; **case vide =** *(d'un formulaire)* blank; *(pour carte d'extension)* empty slot **(b)** **chaîne vide =** empty *ou* null *ou* blank string; **instruction vide =** no-operation instruction *ou* no-op instruction; **liste vide =** empty *ou* null list

vidéo *nf* video; **vidéo interactive =** interactive video; **vidéo inversée =** inverse video *ou* reverse video; **bande vidéo =** video cassette tape *ou* videotape; **films d'épouvante** *ou* **d'horreur sur bandes vidéo =** video nasties; **largeur de bande vidéo =** video bandwidth; **concentrateur** *ou* **réducteur (de largeur de bande) vidéo =** video compressor; **circuit intégré de carte vidéo =** video interface chip; **disque vidéo =** videodisk; **écran** *ou* **moniteur vidéo =** video monitor *ou* video display; **écran vidéo avec clavier =** video terminal; **image vidéo =** video image *ou* video frame; **une image vidéo imprimable peut être envoyée sur une imprimante laser classique par le port vidéo =** a printer-readable video image can be sent to a basic laserprinter through a video port; **capteur d'image vidéo =** frame grabber; **scanner d'images vidéo =** video scanner; **jeu vidéo =** video game; **lecteur vidéo =** video player; **mémoire vidéo =** video memory; **mémoire vidéo à accès aléatoire =** video random access memory (VRAM); **moniteur** *ou* **écran vidéo =** video monitor *ou* video display; **normes vidéo =** video standards; **port vidéo =** video port; **déconcentrateur pour transmission vidéo =** video expander; **RAM vidéo =** video RAM (VRAM); **repiquage vidéo d'un film =** film pickup; **signal vidéo =** video signal; **porteuse de signal vidéo =** image carrier; **signal vidéo composite =** composite video signal; **standards vidéo =** video standards; **système vidéo haute définition =** high definition video system (HDVS); **terminal vidéo =** video terminal

◊ **vidéocaméra** *nf* video camera; **vidéocamera à infrarouge =** infrared video camera; **certains instructeurs utilisent une vidéocaméra à infrarouge pour suivre leurs élèves =** some instructors monitor their trainees with an infrared video camera

◊ **vidéocassette** *nf* video cassette

◊ **vidéoconférence** *nf* video conference

◊ **vidéodisque** *nm* videodisk

---

il assure l'acquisition, le traitement et le stockage sur vidéodisque

01 Informatique

◊ **vidéographie** *nf* *(vidéotex)* **vidéographie interactive =** interactive videography *ou* videotext

◊ **vidéophone** *nm* videophone *ou* video phone

◇ **vidéoscanner** *nm* video scanner; **les nouveaux vidéoscanners ont été conçus pour le balayage d'objets à trois dimensions** = new video scanners are designed to scan three-dimensional objects

◇ **vidéotex** *nm* videotext; **dialogue vidéotex** = interactive videotext

◇ **vidéothèque** *nf* video library

vider *vtr* (a) to clear; **vider le registre de données** = to clear the data register; **vider l'écran** = to clear *ou* to zap (the screen); **il a tapé CONTROL Z pour vider l'écran** = he pressed CONTROL Z and zapped all the text; **tous les tableaux sont vidés chaque fois que le programme est lancé** = all arrays are cleared each time the program is run; **vider une zone de mémoire** = to clear an area of memory (b) *(sur imprimante)* to dump; *(le contenu d'une mémoire)* = to deposit (c) to flush *ou* to purge; **vider la mémoire tampon** = to flush buffers

vie *nf* life; **durée de vie d'un produit en magasin** = shelf life of a product; **durée de vie d'une imprimante** = print life; **durée de vie de la tête de lecture** = headlife

vierge *adj (disquette ou bande)* virgin *ou* clean *ou* blank (disk *ou* tape); **support magnétique vierge** = empty medium

vieux, vieille *adj (journal ou revue)* **vieux numéro** = back number

vif, vive *adj* (a) fast *ou* rapid (b) **mémoire vive** = random access memory *ou* RAM; **mémoire vive dynamique** = dynamic RAM *ou* dynamic random access memory (DRAM)

vigueur *nf* **entrer en vigueur** = to come into force; **les nouveaux règlements entreront en vigueur le 10 janvier** = the new regulations will come into force on January 10th

violation *nf* infringement; **violation du droit d'auteur** = infringement of copyright *ou* copyright infringement

virer *vtr (familier)* **virer un fichier** = to junk a file; **(instruction de) virer une tâche** = kill job

virgule (,) *nf* (a) comma; **point-virgule (;)** = semi-colon (b) **virgule (décimale)** = decimal point; **alignement automatique des virgules** = automatic decimal adjustment; **emplacement de la virgule** = radix point; **tabulation sur la virgule** = decimal tabbing; **virgule binaire** = binary point (c) **arithmétique à virgule fixe** = fixed-point arithmetic; **notation à virgule fixe** = fixed-point notation; **la mise en mémoire de nombres à virgule fixe utilise deux octets pour le nombre entier et un octet pour la partie décimale** = storage of fixed point numbers has two bytes allocated for the whole number and one byte for the fraction part; **arithmétique en virgule flottante** = floating point arithmetic; **notation en virgule flottante** = floating point notation; **en virgule flottante, le nombre 56,47 serait écrit 0,5647 puissance 2** = the fixed number 56.47 in floating-point arithmetic would be 0.5647 and a power of 2; **nombre en virgule flottante** = floating point number; **opération en virgule flottante** = floating point operation (FLOP); **(nombre d') opérations en virgule flottante par seconde** = FLOPs per second; **million(s) d'opérations en virgule flottante par seconde** = mega floating point operations per second *ou* megaflops *ou* MFLOPS; **processeur en virgule flottante** = floating point processor; **ce modèle est équipé d'un processeur en virgule flottante** = this model includes a built-in floating point processor; **le processeur en virgule flottante accélère la vitesse de traitement de ce logiciel graphique** = the floating point processor speeds up the processing of the graphics software; **routines de traitement de la virgule flottante** = floating-point routines

virtuel, -elle *adj* virtual; **adresse virtuelle** = virtual address; **appareil virtuel** = virtual terminal; **circuit virtuel** = virtual circuit; **communication virtuelle commutée** = switched virtual call; **disque virtuel** = silicon disk *ou* RAM disk *ou* virtual disk; **machine virtuelle** = virtual machine; **mémoire virtuelle** = virtual memory *ou* virtual storage (VS); **terminal virtuel** = virtual terminal

virus *nm (dans un programme)* virus

viseur *nm (d'une caméra)* eyepiece *ou* viewfinder; **viseur électronique** = electronic viewfinder

visible *adj* visible; **lumière visible** = visible light

visioconférence *nf* video conference

vision *nf* sight; **instruments de vision aux infrarouges** *ou* **caméra de vision nocturne** = infrared sights

visionnage *nm (d'un film)* viewing *ou* replay; *(d'une séquence de TV ou vidéo)* action replay; **visionnage immédiat** *ou* **instantané** = instant replay; **ce magnétoscope posséde une fonction 'visionnage'** = this video recorder has a replay feature; **visionnage (d'une séquence de film) au ralenti** = slow-action replay; **le visionnage du ralenti ne laisse aucun doute sur le vainqueur** = the action replay clearly showed the winner; **visionnage en temps différé** = time shift viewing
◊ **visionner** *vtr (film)* to view *ou* to replay; **elle a enregistré le programme de télévision sur une bande vidéo et l'a visionné le lendemain soir** = she recorded the TV programme on a videotape and replayed it the next evening
◊ **visionneuse** *nf* viewer; *(qu'on tient à la main)* hand viewer

visiophone *nm* picture phone *ou* video phone *ou* videophone

visu *nf* = VISUEL *(familier)* visual display unit *ou* VDU

visualisation *nf* display; **visualisation de contrôle d'entrée** = marching display; **attributs de visualisation** = screen attributes; **console de visualisation** = visual display unit *ou* VDU; **mode visualisation** = display mode; **unité de visualisation** *ou* **écran de visualisation** = visual display unit (VDU) *ou* visual display terminal (VDT) *ou* display screen
◊ **visualiser** *vtr* **(a)** to display *ou* to view; **l'utilisateur paie un droit pour visualiser le tableau d'affichage** = the user has to pay a charge for viewing pages on a bulletin board **(b)** *(imaginer)* to picture *ou* to visualize; **essayer de visualiser l'implantation avant de commencer à dessiner** = try to picture the layout before starting to draw it in
◊ **visuel** *nm* visual display unit *ou* VDU
◊ **visuel, -elle** *adj* visual; **programmation visuelle** = visual programming

vitesse *nf* **(a)** speed; **vitesse de balayage** = scanning speed; **vitesse de calcul (par ordinateur)** = computing speed; *(d'une bande magnétique)* **vitesse de défilement** = playback speed; **vitesse moyenne** = medium speed; **vitesse d'ouverture d'un objectif** = lens speed; **vitesse de recherche effective** = effective search speed; **vitesse en sténographie** = dictation speed; **grande vitesse** = high-speed; **duplicateur grande vitesse** = high-speed duplicator; *(de bande)* **variation de vitesse** = flutter; **le pleurage et les variations de vitesse sont des défauts courants des magnétophones bon marché** = wow and flutter are common faults on cheap tape recorders **(b)** rate; **modem à deux vitesses** = split baud rate modem; **vitesse d'entrée** = input rate; **(programme) limité par la vitesse d'entrée** *ou* **avec contrainte de vitesse d'entrée** = input-bound *ou* input-limited (program); **(programme) limité par la vitesse d'entrée/sortie** = I/O bound (program); **vitesse d'exécution** = execution rate; **la vitesse d'exécution des commandes de ce processeur est plus rapide qu'avec l'ancienne version** = the processor's instruction execution rate is better than the older version; **vitesse de frappe** = keystroke rate; **vitesse d'horloge** = clock rate; **vitesse de lecture** = read rate; **avec contrainte de vitesse de périphérique** = peripheral-limited; **vitesse de sortie de l'information** = information rate; **vitesse de traitement de données** = data rate; **vitesse de transfert** = transfer rate; **vitesse de transfert (de données)** = data transfer rate; **vitesse de transmission** = transmission rate; **vitesse maximale de transmission** = maximum transmission rate; **vitesse de transmission (en bauds)** = baud rate; **la vitesse de transmission (en bauds) du signal binaire était de 300 bits par seconde** = the baud rate of the binary signal was 300 bits per second; **la vitesse moyenne de transmission est de 64 000 bits par seconde en connexion parallèle et**

19 200 bits par seconde en connexion série = the average transmission is 64,000 bits per second (bps) through a parallel connection or 19,200 bps through a serial connection; **adaptateur de vitesse de transmission** = baud rate generator; **reconnaissance automatique de vitesse de transmission** = auto-baud scanning *ou* auto-baud sensing; **vitesse de transmission de données** = data signalling rate (c) velocity; **le moteur du lecteur de disquettes tourne à vitesse constante** = the disk drive motor spins at a constant velocity

vocabulaire *nm* vocabulary; **vocabulaire contrôlé** = controlled vocabulary

vocal, -e *adj* (of) speech *ou* (of) voice; **bande (de fréquence) vocale** = voice band; **interpolation de signaux sur bande vocale** = time assigned speech interpolation (TASI); **transmission de signaux sur la bande vocale** = in-band signalling; **circuit vocal** = dry circuit; **empreinte vocale** = voice print; **reconnaissance vocale** = voice recognition *ou* speech recognition; **répondeur vocal** *ou* **répondeur avec message vocal de synthèse** = voice answer back *ou* audio response unit; **saisie vocale** = voice data entry *ou* input; **signal vocal** = speech signal; **processeur du signal vocal** = speech processor; **sortie vocale** = voice output; **synthèse vocale** = voice synthesis *ou* speech synthesis; **puce de synthèse vocale** = speech chip; **synthétiseur vocal** = voice synthesizer; **transmission vocale étendue** = speech plus; **unité de puissance vocale** = voice unit

voie *nf* **(a)** *(de communication)* channel *ou* path *ou* line; **voie d'accès** = facility; **voie d'accès direct à la mémoire** = direct memory access channel; **voie d'acheminement de signaux** = feeder; **signalisation par voie commune** = common channel signalling; **voie double** = dual channel; **voie (d') entrée/sortie** = I/O channel; **voie de lecture/écriture** = read/write channel; **voies de liaison d'un bus d'adresses** = bus address lines; **voie logique** = logical channel; **voie de retour** = backward channel; **voie spécialisée** = dedicated channel; **voie de transmission** = transmission channel; **capacité** *ou* **débit d'une voie de transmission** =

channel capacity; **voie de transmission de données** = data path; **voie de transmission de l'information** = information transfer channel; **voie de transmission de signaux** = feeder; **groupement de voies** = channel group; **saturation** *ou* **surcharge d'une voie** = channel overload; **synchroniseur de voies** = channel synchronizer **(b)** means; **la publicité pour le produit s'est faite par voie de presse spécialisée** = the product was advertised through the medium of the trade press

voile *nm (photographie)* fog

voir *vtr* to see; **ce que vous voyez est ce que vous obtenez** = What-You-See-Is-What-You-Get (WYSIWYG); **ce que vous voyez est tout ce que vous obtenez** = What-You-See-Is-All-You-Get (WYSIAYG)

voix *nf* voice; *(parole)* speech; **voix hors champ** *ou* **voix off** = voice-over; **voix numérisée** *ou* **de synthèse** = digital speech

vol *nm* **(exploitation par) vol de cycle** = cycle stealing; **vol de temps de cycle de la mémoire à accès direct** = DMA cycle stealing; *voir aussi* ACCES

volatile *adj* volatile; **mémoire volatile** = volatile memory *ou* volatile (dynamic) storage
◊ **volatilité** *nf* volatility

volée *nf (vérification de données)* **à la volée** = on the fly
◊ **voler 1** *vtr (dérober)* to steal **2** *vi (se mouvoir dans l'air)* to fly

volet *nm (d'une disquette)* **volet de protection d'écriture** = write-protect tab

volt *nm* volt
◊ **voltage** *nm* voltage; **verrouiller le voltage (d'un signal)** = to clamp a voltage

volume *nm (du son)* volume *ou* loudness *ou* level; **baissez le volume (du son) qui est vraiment trop fort** = turn the sound level down, it's far too loud; **bouton** *ou* **contrôle** *ou* **réglage du volume** = volume control

voyant *nm* **voyant (lumineux) =** (i) indicator light; (ii) light emitting diode; **voyant d'alarme =** warning light; **lorsque le voyant placé sur le panneau avant s'allume, il faut éteindre le système =** when the warning light on the front panel comes on, switch off the system

vrac (en) *loc adv* in bulk; **épreuves en vrac =** scatter proofs

vrai, -e *adj* genuine *ou* real; *(logique)* true

VRAM = VIDEO RANDOM ACCESS MEMORY *voir aussi* VIDEO

vue *nf* view; **vue plongeante** *ou* **aérienne** = aerial image; **prise de vue =** shot; **prise de vue d'une scène =** action shot; **prise de vue à cadence lente =** memomotion; **prise de vue en extérieur =** shot on location *ou* location shot

Ww

watt (W) *nm* Watt (W)

WHILE *(alors que)* **boucle conditionnelle 'WHILE' =** while-loop

Winchester *npr (disque dur)* **disque (de type) Winchester =** Winchester disk; **disque Winchester amovible =** removable Winchester; **lecteur de disque Winchester =** Winchester drive; **minidisque (de type) Winchester =** miniwinny

WISC = WRITABLE INSTRUCTION SET COMPUTER *voir aussi* MODIFIABLE

WORM = WRITE ONCE, READ MANY TIMES MEMORY *(permettant une seule écriture et des lectures multiples)* **disque optique WORM =** WORM

WYSIAYG = WHAT YOU SEE IS ALL YOU GET *voir aussi* VOIR

WYSIWYG = WHAT YOU SEE IS WHAT YOU GET *voir aussi* VOIR

Xx

X = EXTENSION

X (a) *(coordonnée)* **axe des X =** X-axis; **distance sur l'axe des X =** X distance **(b)** *(de carte perforée)* **perforation X =** x punch **(c)** *(communication)* **protocoles de télétransmission de la série X =** X-series **(d) rayon X =** X-ray

xérographie *nf* xerography

◊ **xérographique** *adj* **imprimante xérographique =** xerographic printer

◊ **Xerox**® **photocopieur Xerox =** Xerox; **photocopie faite avec une machine Xerox = xerox; photocopier une lettre avec une machine Xerox =** to make a xerox copy of a letter; **il faut commander de nouveau du papier Xerox pour le photocopieur =** we must order some more xerox paper for the copier; **on nous installera une nouvelle machine** *ou* **un nouveau photocopieur Xerox demain =** we are having a new Xerox machine installed tomorrow

Nintendo est maintenant synonyme de jeu vidéo, de même que Kleenex veut dire mouchoir et Xerox photocopie

L'Express

Yy

Y (a) *(coordonnée)* **axe des** Y = Y-axis; **distance sur l'axe des** Y = Y-distance **(b)** *(de carte perforée)* **perforation** Y = y punch

Zz

Z *(coordonnée)* **axe des Z =** Z-axis

zébrure *nf* streaking

zéro *nm* zero; **le compteur revient automatiquement à zéro dès qu'il atteint 999 =** when it reaches 999 this counter resets to zero; **(en Grande-Bretagne) le code téléphonique international est zéro un zéro (010) =** (from Great Britain) the code for international calls is zero one zero (010); **effectuer un branchement (conditionnel) à zéro =** to jump on zero; **(instruction de) branchement conditionnel à l'indicateur zéro =** jump on zero; **l'instruction de branchement conditionnel à zéro teste l'indicateur zéro =** the jump on zero instruction tests the zero flag; **élimination des zéros (non significatifs) =** zero compression *ou* zero suppression; **garnir de zéros =** to zero fill; **(connecteur) à force d'insertion zéro =** zero insertion force (ZIF); **indicateur (binaire) zéro =** zero flag; **remettre à zéro =** *(un dispositif)* to reset *ou* to zero; *(un fichier)* to erase *ou* to rub out; **remettre à zéro un dispositif (programmable) =** to zero a device; **signal de remise** *ou* **de retour à zéro =** return to zero signal; **boucle avec retour automatique à zéro =** self-resetting *ou* self-restoring loop; **non-retour** *ou* **non-remise à zéro =** non return to zero (NRZ); **zéro de tête =** leading zero

zonage *nm* fielding

◊ **zone** *nf* **(a)** *(de mémoire)* area *ou* region *ou* zone; **zone de code =** code area; **zone commune de la mémoire =** common storage area; **zone de données =** data area *ou* data field; **zone d'entrée de données =** input area; **zone d'image =** image area; **zone d'image reçue =** safe area; *(dans une mémoire)* **zone d'instruction =** instruction area; **zone de recherche =** seek area; **zone de segment de recouvrement =** overlay region; **zone sortie de la mémoire =** output area *ou* output block; **zone de stockage de l'image =** image storage space; **zone de traitement par lots =** batch region; **zone de travail (en mémoire) =** memory workspace *ou* work area; **recherche de zone =** area search **(b)** *(d'écran)* **zone d'affichage =** image area; **zone de brouillage** *ou* **de purée =** mush area **(c)** *(transmission)* **zone terrestre de couverture =** earth coverage; *(téléphonique)* **indicatif (téléphonique) de zone =** area code **(d)** **zone de connexions =** terminal area; *(de matériel)* **zone protégée =** (hardware) isolated location; **réseau à zone de recouvrement =** overlay network **(e)** *(entre deux marges)* **zone de texte =** hot zone *ou* soft zone

zoom *nm* **(a)** *(action)* zooming; **faire un zoom =** to zoom **(b)** *(lentille)* zoom lens